The Rough Guide to

Central
America
ON A BUDGET

this edition written and researched by
Jamey Bergman, Flo Chick, Sarah Cummins, Kiki Deere,
Amber Dobrzensky, Donald Eastwood, Ingrid Gustafson, Neil McQuillan,
Charlotte Melville, Alex Trillo

**ROUGH
GUIDES**

LONDON • DELHI
www.roughguides.com

Contents

Chetumal

Banco Chinchorro

Corozal

Orange Walk

Ambergris Caye

MEXICO

Río Azul

Caye Caulker

BELIZE

Belize City

Tikal

BELMOPAN

Lighthouse Reef

Lago Petén Itzá

San
Ignacio

Río Usumacinta

Flores

Dangriga

Golfo de
Honduras

Bay Islands

Punta Gorda

Puerto
Barrios

Puerto
Cortés

La
Ceiba

Trujillo

GUATEMALA

Tela

Cobán

San Pedro Sula

HONDURAS

Tapachula

Copán

Quetzaltenango

GUATEMALA CITY

Comayagua

Antigua

TEGUCIGALPA

Lago de
Atitlán

Santa Ana

Puerto San José

SAN SALVADOR

San Miguel

NICARAGU

EL SALVADOR

Choluteca

Matagalpa

Golfo de Fonseca

Estelí

Chinandega

León

MANAGUA

Granada

Lago de
Nicaragua

S
Ca

Liberia

Nicoya Peninsula

Puntarenas

PACIFIC OCEAN

0   100 km

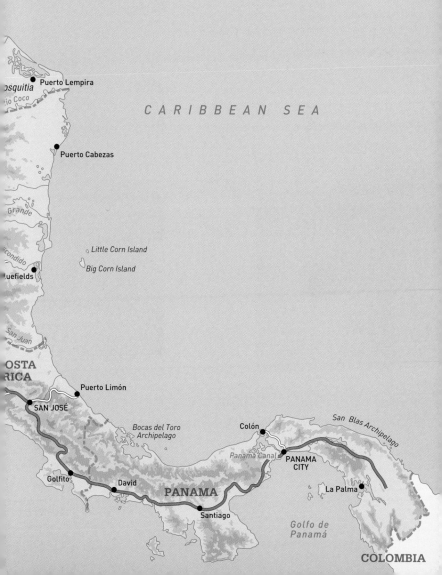

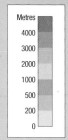

Metres
4000
3000
2000
1000
500
200
0

N

osquitia ● Puerto Lempira

io Coco

C A R I B B E A N   S E A

● Puerto Cabezas

Grande

○ Little Corn Island

condido

uefields ● Big Corn Island

San Juan

OSTA
RICA

● Puerto Limón

● SAN JOSÉ

Bocas del Toro
Archipelago

● Colón

San Blas Archipelago

Panamá Canal

● PANAMA
CITY

Golfito ● David

PANAMA

● La Palma

● Santiago

Golfo de
Panamá

COLOMBIA

Introduction to
Central America

Serving as both a link and a barrier between oceans and continents, Central America's small area belies an astounding diversity of culture, wildlife, history and terrain. Travellers here have access to a perfectly-sized package tour that's unique for every visitor. One day's itinerary could have you on a water-taxi ride to a surf break, an afternoon trek through pristine jungle and a night out clubbing. The next day, you could be whitewater rafting on world-class rapids, taking a spa in geothermal pools, and then cosying up for a pleasantly cool dinner under the highland stars.

Central America falls from Mexico's southern edges in a tapering southeasterly slide from Belize and Guatemala to Panama. From its widest point on the Honduran/Nicaraguan border, the isthmus is squeezed until a mere 40 miles of land keeps the Atlantic and Pacific Oceans at bay. Crammed onto the land bridge, coral-fringed beaches give way to jungle that, in turn, yields to shrouded volcanic highlands. Modern cities jut skyward metres from where the cobbled streets of Maya ruins still linger. Wealth and poverty, ancient religion and a colonial legacy mingle together to make a fascinating mix for veteran and uninitiated travellers alike.

With its proximity to North America, there is no question that a reciprocal exchange of people and ideas has had an impact on both sides of the Rio Grande. Much of the isthmus has certainly adopted the consumption habits of its North American neighbours: shopping malls, fast-food outlets and multiplex cinemas are de rigeur for many citizens here. However, the majority of this commercialization is restricted to the region's main metropolitan centres, and it is easy to find authenticity in culture, custom or cuisine no matter where you go.

Chicken Buses

One authentic piece of Latin American culture that you'll soon become familiar with is the "Chicken Bus". Called "camionetas", "collectivos" or simply "buses" (pronounced "boo-ses") in Spanish, these contraptions are colourfully repainted and repurposed US school buses. In pastel or primary colours, with decorations both religous and profane dangling and jangling from every corner and destinations hand-lettered on the front windscreen, travelling by chicken bus is an economical and unforgettable experience. Passengers, goods and livestock jostle along bumpy roads, embarking and departing with great frequency in a boistrous and generally well-timed dance of old tires, children, overstuffed luggage and boxes of peeping chicks (the buses namesake). Though Guatemala is particularly known for its chicken buses, versions of this mode of transportation can be found virtually anywhere in Latin America.

The North American economy has also had an effect on overall regional prices, and depending on which country you're travelling in, the daily cost of living can be higher than you might expect. Despite this, Central America is a premiere destination for budget travel: a growing tourist infrastructure combined with a spectacular diversity of natural and cultural landscapes make it a budget traveller's dream. This guide is packed with information tailored to inspire travellers on a shoestring. From our budget-friendly Author's Picks to suggestions for where to splurge and treat yourself, we will help you to find the very best Central America has to offer.

Ecotourism

Ecotourism is widespread in all its forms in Central America. But, whether you're zip-lining down a jungled hillside in the cloudforest, birdwatching in a national park, or volunteering to protect an endangered species of sea turtle, try to be sure that what you're doing truly is environmentally ethical. While imitators misrepresenting themselves as environmentally friendly operators are common, Central America is widely recognized to be at the cutting edge of ecotourism. Tourists are encouraged to travel responsibly with the intent of experiencing nature while engaging in environmental conservation and seeking to improve the well-being of the local community. Belize and Costa Rica in particular have paved the way with conservation strategies that support sustainable tourism.

Whether your tastes are expensive or thrifty, our itineraries section (see p.17) gives a selection of the greatest journeys across the region. In Belize, you can dive the longest barrier reef in the Americas or spend a few nights on the lookout for big cats in the world's only Jaguar reserve. Discover Maya ruins struggling to free themselves from the ever encroaching bonds of the jungle in Belize, Guatemala, El Salvador and Honduras. For a glimpse of the area's colonial history and architecture, Antigua in Guatemala and Granada in Nicaragua are top destinations. The cloudforests of Honduras and Costa Rica, crater lakes in Guatemala, and geothermal hot springs in Panama are sights unique to the highlands. On the coast, Costa Rica and Panama are both widely known as top international surfing scenes, but inland, both also offer world-class whitewater rafting experiences.

When to go

From its position along a major fault line, a backbone of volcanic terrain rises and runs the length of the region's seven countries. Thick jungles adress coral reefs across golden slivers of shoreline. The sub-tropical climate of Central America overflows with verdant landscapes, nourished by the semi-annual rhythms of the wet and dry seasons.

TODOS SANTOS CUCHUMATÁN, GUATEMALA

Peak tourist times occur during the dry season – or "summer" (*verano*) – that runs from November to April. The rainy season, often called "winter" (*invierno*), lasts from May until October. The different seasons are more distinctly felt on the Pacific side of the isthmus than they are on the Caribbean, and the major determining factor of climate here is altitude. Coming from sea level or the lowland plains to the interior highlands can grant welcome relief from high heat and humidity. Average temperatures here are 15 to 20 degrees cooler than in low-lying areas, where humidity levels can be uncomfortable and temperatures hover in the nineties for much of the year.

Coming to Central America to escape the dreary winter days of more temperate climate zones is always a welcome escape, but great deals can be found during the wet season when tourism lulls. Extra care should be taken when making preparations this time of year, as road conditions can deteriorate significantly with heavy rains, making travel more difficult. However, rain showers are short-lived afternoon downpours, more often than not, and there's a good chance that changes in the weather will hardly interfere with your trip.

MURAL IN JUAYÚA, EL SALVADOR

Ideas Festivals and events

TODOS SANTOS CUCHUMATÁN, GUATEMALA A massive stampede and inebriated riders characterize this outrageous all-day horse race. See p.189

CARNAVAL, PANAMA CITY Four days of raucous and vibrant celebrations. See p.597

GARÍFUNA SETTLEMENT DAY, BELIZE Enthusiastic celebrations to mark the arrival of the Garífuna people in Belize. **See p.64**

DAY OF THE DEAD, SANTIAGO SACATEPÉQUEZ, GUATEMALA Massive, beautiful kites are flown in the cemetery to commemorate the dead. **See p.152**

SEMANA SANTA, ANTIGUA, GUATEMALA Spectacular street processions to mark Holy Week. **See p.143**

Ideas History and culture

COPÁN, HONDURAS
Magnificent Maya site displaying impressive craftsmanship. **See p.361**

KUNA CULTURE, KUNA YALA, PANAMA
Experience the fascinating island life of the San Blas Archipelago. **See p.637**

WAR MEMORIAL, MOZOTE, EL SALVADOR
A moving monument to the country's worst wartime massacre. **See p.294**

TIKAL, GUATEMALA Five awe-inspiring pyramids tower above the rainforest.
See p.234

**COWBOY CULTURE,
GUANACASTE, COSTA RICA**
A distinct region known for its
sabanero (cowboy) culture.
See p.564

**COLONIAL
ARCHITECTURE, LEÓN,
NICARAGUA** The energetic old
capital is home to some beautiful
colonial buildings. See p.429

Ideas Outdoor activities

VOLCANO HOPPING, COSTA RICA Activities abound in this spectacular volcanic landscape. **See p.491**

RAFTING, PANAMA Exhilarating white-water trips on the Chiriquí River. **See p.661**

HIKING, NICARAGUA The forested mountains surrounding Matagalpa provide fantastic hiking opportunities. **See p.441**

JAGUAR SPOTTING, BELIZE
Explore the stunning Belizean rainforest in search of these beautiful creatures. **See p.107**

DIVING IN THE BAY ISLANDS, HONDURAS
Abundant marine life, clear waters and a stunning coral reef. **See p.392**

SURFING, EL SAVADOR The Pacific coast boasts some of Central America's best surfing beaches. **See p.251**

ITINERARIES

ITINERARIES

Central America itineraries

You can't expect to fit everything Central America has to offer into one trip and we don't suggest you try. On the following pages are a selection of itineraries that guide you through the different countries, picking out a few of the best places and major attractions along the way. Enjoy the region's startling natural beauty, from the cloudforests of Costa Rica to the sand-fringed islands of Panama's San Blas archipelago; explore the unique indigenous culture of the Maya; and discover remote beaches and world-class diving on the Caribbean coast.

INDIGENOUS CULTURES

❶ HOPKINS, BELIZE Stretching along a bay, this small Garífuna village comes alive with the enthusiastic celebrations of Settlement Day, and is a great place to sample the local cuisine. See p.106

❷ IXIL TRIANGLE, GUATEMALA Though remote, the three towns of the Ixil triangle are worth the effort for a glimpse of the traditional Ixil way of life, and for spectacular hikes into the surrounding hills. See p.174

❸ TODOS SANTOS CUCHUMATÁN, GUATEMALA The unique culture of the indigenous Maya, combined with the beautiful alpine scenery, makes this a favourite with travellers – especially for the experience of the Día de Todos Santos. See p.189

❹ LA ESPERANZA, HONDURAS Best visited for its colourful weekend market, when Lenca farmers from the

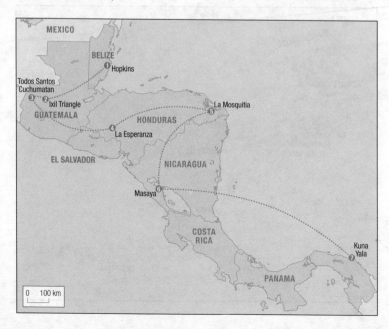

surrounding villages come into town. In nearby San Juan Intibucá you can watch traditional handicrafts being made. **See p.352**

⑤ LA MOSQUITIA, HONDURAS
Indulge your spirit of adventure by getting right off the beaten track to explore the indigenous villages of the Caribbean Coast in this southeastern corner of the country. **See p.389**

⑥ MASAYA, NICARAGUA The centre of Nicaragua's *artensania* production, the attractive town of Masaya is home to two craft markets and is a great place to pick up hammocks, traditional clothing and other handicrafts. **See p.443**

⑦ KUNA YALA, PANAMA
Encompassing the tropical islands of the San Blas archipelago, the autonomous territory of the Kula people offers a unique opportunity to learn about community life, while enjoying the beautiful beaches. **See p.637**

ALONG CA-1

From Guatemala to Panama, Central America Highway 1 (part of the Pan-American Highway) runs for over a thousand kilometres past beaches, cities and jungles. The following sites are all en – or just off – route.

① TOTONICAPÁN, GUATEMALA
Quiet, handsome Guatemalan town distinguished by its traditional weaving, with twice-weekly markets, artisan tours and classes. **See p.184**

② SAN SALVADOR, EL SALVADOR
El Salvador's buzzing capital is occasionally intimidating and rarely peaceful. But with its slowly smartening Centro Histórico, surprisingly green outskirts and politicized museums, it repays a visit. **See p.256**

③ SAN VICENTE, EL SALVADOR
Climb El Salvador's second highest volcano, eye the famous clock tower and relish the stunning drive to this relaxed city. **See p.286**

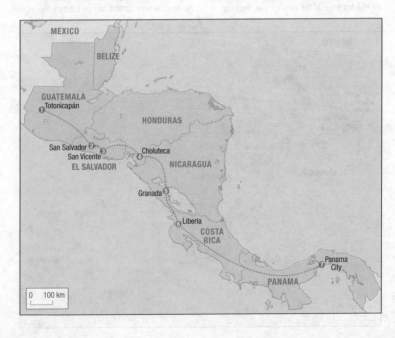

❹ CHOLUTECA, HONDURAS
Steamy, substantial city containing one of Honduras' finest old colonial quarters – the tranquil park and imposing cathedral are among the highlights. **See p.345**

❺ GRANADA, NICARAGUA
Take a detour off CA-1 for Granada, home to some of Central America's most inspiring architecture. There are attractions aplenty, but an idle wander through its centre is, perhaps, most rewarding. **See p.447**

❻ LIBERIA, COSTA RICA
This beautiful "White City" is home to a number of festivals and the sleepy colonial Calle Real district. **See p.564**

❼ PANAMA CITY, PANAMA
Both a base for visiting the nearby wildlife and famous canal and a sparkling, cosmopolitan city, this is one of the continent's must-visits. **See p.598**

THE CARIBBEAN COAST

❶ PLACENCIA, BELIZE
Away from the tourist hustle of the north, this relaxed fishing village has Belize's best beaches, inexpensive accommodation and a growing arts scene. **See p.108**

❷ LÍVINGSTON, GUATEMALA
Carib cuisine, punta rock and reggae make Lívingston a great place to party and an intriguing contrast to Guatemala's latino interior. **See p.203**

❸ BAY ISLANDS, HONDURAS
This 125-kilometre chain of islands off Honduras's Caribbean coast is a perfect destination for world-class (and affordable) diving, sailing and fishing. **See p.392**

❹ RÍO PLÁTANO BIOSPHERE RESERVE, HONDURAS
This World Heritage Centre on the remote Mosquito Coast preserves one of the finest remaining stretches of Central American rainforest. **See p.391**

❺ THE CORN ISLANDS, NICARAGUA
Once a haven for pirates, these unspoilt islands offer swaying palm trees, white-sand beaches and warm clear water – a perfect place to recharge. **See p.475**

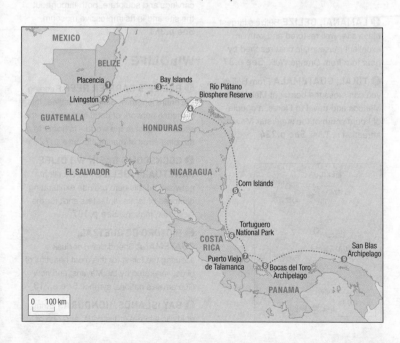

6 TORTUGUERO NATIONAL PARK, COSTA RICA While turtle-watching is the big draw at this coastal national park, a trip along the Tortuguero Canal in a dugout canoe comes a close second. See p.521

7 PUERTO VIEJO DE TALAMANCA, COSTA RICA Perhaps the liveliest backpacker town in Central America, Puerto Viejo also boasts one of the best surf breaks on the Caribbean coast. See p.528

8 BOCAS DEL TORO ARCHIPELAGO, PANAMA Described as "the Galapagos of the twenty-first century", this once-isolated region is growing in popularity as an ecotourism destination. See p.662

9 SAN BLAS ARCHIPELAGO, PANAMA Part of the autonomous Kuna region, these idyllic offshore islands offer a mix of beach holiday and the chance to sample a unique culture. See p.637

MAYA RUINS

1 LAMANAI, BELIZE Belize's largest Maya site, well restored and with an excellent museum, is best reached by boat tour from Orange Walk. See p.87

2 TIKAL, GUATEMALA From Belize you can cross the border at Melchor de Mencos and travel to Flores, a couple of hours south of the superstar Mayan attraction at Tikal. See p.234

3 EL MIRADOR, GUATEMALA Reaching it requires time and stamina – it's only accessible by foot and mule, and most opt for a five-day trip from Flores, including up to eight hours' jungle trekking a day – but the reward is spectacular. Remote and mysterious El Mirador is a vast preclassical Mayan city much of it still enveloped in jungle. See p.239

4 CANCUÉN, GUATEMALA An affluent Mayan trading town, and one of the attractions of the Puerta al Mundo Maya organization, which supports community-run, sustainable tourism. Spend a couple of days on the road from Flores to Cóban visiting their various sights. See p.224

5 TAZUMAL, EL SALVADOR Smaller than its Guatemalan counterparts, but with a certain charm, the site features both Maya and Pipil constructions. See p.315

6 COPÁN, HONDURAS One of the country's main tourist destinations, Copán is smaller than Tikal but features exquisite carvings and sculpture, both throughout the site and in its impressive museum. See p.361

WILDLIFE

1 BELIZE'S BARRIER REEF Running the entire length of Belize's coastline, this immense network of coral and cayes – the second largest in the world – is home to a dazzling array of marine life. See p.72

2 COCKSCOMB BASIN WILDLIFE SANCTUARY, BELIZE The excellent network of trails here provide exhilarating glimpses of tapirs, anteaters and, for the lucky few, jaguars. See p.107

3 BIOTOPO DE QUETZAL, GUATEMALA Spend dawn or dusk scouring the forest for this most beautiful of birds, venerated by the Mayans, and now Guatemala's national symbol. See p.213

4 BAY ISLANDS, HONDURAS String of idyllic white-sand islands, and one of

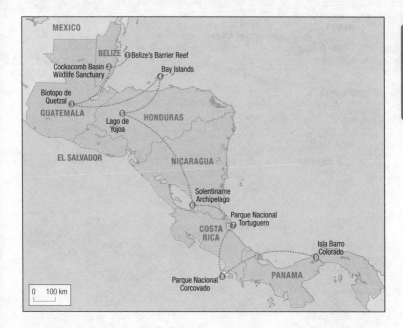

the few places on earth where you can go diving with whale sharks. **See p.392**

⑤ LAGO DE YOJOA, HONDURAS
Take an early morning paddle on this picturesque lake, surrounded by mountains and home to over four hundred species of birds. **See p.349**

⑥ SOLENTINAME ARCHIPELAGO, NICARAGUA Isolated scattering of islands, marooned in the middle of mighty Lago Nicaragua. Spot sloths, howler monkeys, parrots and macaws. **See p.467**

⑦ PARQUE NACIONAL TORTUGUERO, COSTA RICA The fantastic journey here – drifting through verdant jungle, past wooden houses on stilts – is only a sideshow to the main event: the *desove*, where hundreds of green, hawksbill and leatherback turtles haul themselves ashore each night to lay their eggs. **See p.521**

⑧ PARQUE NACIONAL CORCOVADO, COSTA RICA The most biologically diverse area in Central America – akin to the Amazon in the eyes of some

experts – Corovado harbours everything from tapirs to tayras; you'll most likely stumble across them on one of the park's mammoth jungle treks. **See p.582**

⑨ ISLA BARRO COLORADO, PANAMA Sitting plum in the middle of the Panama Canal, Barro Colorado is a living laboratory, six square miles of biodiversity. Hike through its rainforest with specialist guides from the Smithsonian Institute. **See p.620**

THE GRAND TOUR

① BELIZEAN CAYES & ATOLLS
Snorkel, scuba dive or fish off the hundreds of cayes which form part of Belize's spectacular Great Barrier Reef, and don't miss the Great Blue Hole, a collapsed cave. **See p.72**

② TIKAL, GUATEMALA Arguably the most impressive Maya ruin in Central America, this ancient city is dominated by five temples and surrounded by thousands of other structures, all surrounded by jungle. **See p.234**

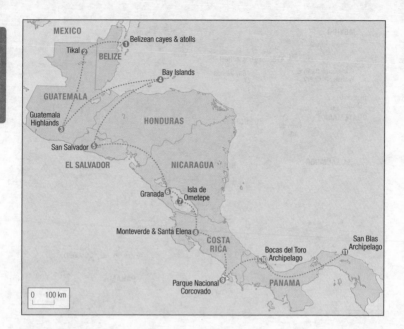

③ GUATEMALA HIGHLANDS With its volcanoes, mountain ranges, lakes and valleys, this is one of Guatemala's most beautiful areas. See p.166

④ BAY ISLANDS, HONDURAS To catch a glimpse of the elusive whale shark, head to this string of islands in October or November – or simply spend days sailing or fishing on a remote island. See p.392

⑤ SAN SALVADOR, EL SALVADOR Nestled at the foot of a volcano, El Salvador's buzzing capital is a heady mix of galleries, museums and nightclubs. See p.256

⑥ GRANADA, NICARAGUA With its pastel colonial buildings, Granada is the most architecturally interesting town in Nicaragua, and makes an ideal base for exploring nearby lakes and volcanoes. See p.447

⑦ ISLA DE OMETEPE, NICARAGUA This magical island, formed by two volcanoes, sits in the middle of a freshwater lake. There's jungle rainforest

teeming with monkeys as well as beaches and mountains to explore. See p.460

⑧ MONTEVERDE & SANTA ELENA, COSTA RICA These nature reserves are known as cloudforests because of their high altitude. Take a canopy tour to see lush vegetation and hundreds of wildlife species. See p.534

⑨ PARQUE NACIONAL CORCOVADO, COSTA RICA Most people come to the park in search of rare animals like ocelot and tapir, and there are also deserted beaches, waterfalls and rain forests to explore. See p.582

⑩ BOCAS DEL TORO ARCHIPELAGO, PANAMA One of the most remote and beautiful provinces in Panama, this diverse archipelago boasts tropical rainforests, beaches and mangroves. See p.662

⑪ SAN BLAS ARCHIPELAGO, PANAMA Strung out along the Caribbean coast, the vast majority of these islands are uninhabited. Come here to get away from it all. See p.637

BASICS

Basics

Getting there

While you can get to Central America overland from Mexico or by sea from Colombia, your most likely point of entry to Central America is through one of the region's international airports. Of these, the most popular gateways are Guatemala City, San José and Panama City.

Prices for flights to the region with established carriers can vary hugely. For the best fares on scheduled flights, book well in advance of travel, as airlines only have a fixed number of seats at their lowest prices. Fully check conditions before making a booking, however, as these cheap fares are almost always heavily restricted; the one provision nearly all carriers attach to tickets is the required duration of trip – generally the best prices allow a maximum stay of one to three months, with prices rising for a six-month duration, and again for a year's validity. It is not always cheapest to book direct with the airline; some **travel agents** (see p.31) can negotiate discounted fares, in particular for students or those under 26. It may be worth considering a **one-way ticket** if you are planning a long trip (although you may have difficulties passing through immigration without an onward ticket – see "Entry requirements", p.48).

Another option for bargain hunters is to look into routes operated by **charter airlines** to package holiday destinations. For the most part these are available from the US to Belize, Costa Rica and Panama, although it is also possible to reach Cancún in Mexico's Yucatán Peninsula from the UK. These charter flights allow limited flexibility, usually for a fixed period of one or two weeks, but can be picked up last minute at very reasonable prices.

If planning a substantial amount of overland travel in Central America consider purchasing an **open-jaw ticket** (for example, arriving in Guatemala City and returning from Panama City). Prices for open-jaw tickets are usually comparable to a straightforward return. Alternatively, **round-the-world (RTW)** itineraries can incorporate Central American destinations if you travel via the US and onward to Auckland, Sydney, etc. British Airways/Qantas and United/Air New Zealand Star Alliance fares from London start at around £1000 (plus a probable £500 in taxes), and allow multiple stops in several continents within a certain mileage.

FROM THE US AND CANADA

Several US carriers operate **direct flights** to all Central American capitals. The main US hubs, offering good connections with other North American cities, are Houston (Continental Airlines), Miami, Dallas (American and United Airlines) and Atlanta (Delta), but there are also direct routes from New York and Los Angeles to Guatemala City, San Salvador, San José and Panama City. Flights are frequent and can take as little as two hours (Miami to Belize City, for example). Prices vary – advance purchase fares start from as little as US$130 (plus taxes), though a more realistic estimate would be in the region of US$300–500. Taxes should be estimated at a minimum of US$100.

From **Canada** you can fly direct from Toronto to San José (5hr 15min) with Air Canada, and also to San José via San Salvador, with Lineas Aereas Costarricenses (LACSA). Alternatively, there are many connections to all Central American capitals through the US. For direct flights from Toronto fares start at CAN$610, plus taxes of approximately CAN$200.

FLY LESS – STAY LONGER! TRAVEL AND CLIMATE CHANGE

Climate change is the single biggest issue facing our planet. It is caused by a build-up in the atmosphere of carbon dioxide and other greenhouse gases, which are emitted by many sources – including planes. Already, flights account for around three to four percent of human-induced global warming: that figure may sound small, but it is rising year on year and threatens to counteract the progress made by reducing greenhouse emissions in other areas.

Rough Guides regard travel, overall, as a global benefit, and feel strongly that the advantages to developing economies are important, as are the opportunities for greater contact and awareness among peoples. But we all have a responsibility to limit our personal "carbon footprint". That means giving thought to how often we fly and what we can do to redress the harm that our trips create.

Flying and climate change

Pretty much every form of motorized travel generates CO_2, but planes are particularly bad offenders, releasing large volumes of greenhouse gases at altitudes where their impact is far more harmful. Flying also allows us to travel much further than we would contemplate doing by road or rail, so the emissions attributable to each passenger become truly shocking. For example, one person taking a return flight between Europe and California produces the equivalent impact of 2.5 tonnes of CO_2 – similar to the yearly output of the average UK car.

Less harmful planes may evolve but it will be decades before they replace the current fleet – which could be too late for avoiding climate chaos. In the meantime, there are limited options for concerned travellers: to reduce the amount we travel by air (take fewer trips, stay longer!), to avoid night flights (when plane contrails trap heat from Earth but can't reflect sunlight back to space), and to make the trips we do take "climate neutral" via a carbon-offset scheme.

Carbon-offset schemes

Offset schemes run by Ⓦ www.climatecare.org, Ⓦ www.carbonneutral.com and others allow you to "neutralize" the greenhouse gases that you are responsible for releasing. Their websites have simple calculators that let you work out the impact of any flight. Once that's done, you can pay to fund projects that will reduce future carbon emissions by an equivalent amount (such as the distribution of low-energy light bulbs and cooking stoves in developing countries). Please take the time to visit our website and make your trip climate neutral.

Ⓦ www.roughguides.com/climatechange

FROM THE UK AND IRELAND

There are **no direct flights** from the UK or Ireland to Central America. The majority of routes available are offered by the US carriers (namely, American, United, Continental and Delta), all of which involve connections in the States. Onward flights to Central America may be operated by regional airlines such as Copa, TACA and Lineas Aereas Costarricanes (LACSA). A few European airlines also offer flights through their hub cities to Guatemala City, San José or Panama City – these include Iberia, Air Comet or Air Europa (via Madrid) and KLM or Martinair (via Amsterdam). As clearing US immigration and customs can be a lengthy process, these European flights can frequently be faster. Alternatively – and less expensively – a wide network of carriers flies from Europe direct to Mexico, from where you can travel to Central America (see opposite).

Journey times from the UK and Ireland vary according to connection times, but it is possible to get door-to-door in a day. Published **fares** from London to Central American capitals start at around £350 (plus taxes of at least £150).

FROM AUSTRALIA, NEW ZEALAND AND SOUTH AFRICA

There are **no direct flights** from Australasia or South Africa to Central America, but it's easy enough to connect with flights in the US or Europe. From **Australia** and **New Zealand**, the quickest route is through Los Angeles and then Dallas or Houston (approximately 20hr; AUS$2750/NZ$3300). From Johannesburg, the options include Iberia via Madrid (from ZAR12,000) and Delta via Dakar and Atlanta (from ZAR14,700). Connections are not great and the journey will take at least 24 hours.

Round-the-world (RTW) flights

Round-the-world flight tickets connect Sydney, Perth, Auckland and Johannesburg to Mexico City, Guatemala City, San José and Panama City, usually via Los Angeles or London using American Airlines or code-share partners. It is also possible to reach Australasia from both Santiago (Chile) and Buenos Aires (Argentina) as part of the same RTW tickets with BA/Qantas's Oneworld.

FROM MEXICO

It is fairly straightforward to travel overland **by bus** from Mexico to Guatemala and Mexico to Belize. Several companies offer services with varying degrees of comfort (worth taking into consideration, given the length of most trips – Palenque to Flores is ten hours, Tulum to Belize City is nine). Popular routes include: Cancún/Tulum (via Chetumal/Corozal) to Belize City; Palenque (via Frontera Corozal/Bethel) to Flores, Guatemala; San Cristóbal de las Casas (via Ciudad Cuauhtémoc/La Mesilla) to Huehuetenango; and the Mexican Pacific coast (via Ciudad Hidalgo/Ciudad Tecún Umán) to Quetzaltenango.

Unfortunately, one annoyance experienced by many travellers (particularly crossing into Guatemala) is the demand for unofficial "fees" at immigration; it's often easier to go with local services than one of the long-distance carriers – travelling with a busload of gringos can prove expensive. It is worth changing pesos at the border with moneychangers, as an opportunity may not arise later. Be sure to do your sums prior to agreeing to a transaction and check what you're given before handing over your cash.

It's possible, too, to **fly** from many of Mexico's airports onward to Central America's main cities with airlines such as TACA and Copa; tickets start around US$200.

Regional bus contacts

Tica Bus ⓦ www.ticabus.com. Departs from Tapachula (Mexico) for Guatemala City and beyond.
Transportes Galgos ⓦ transgalgosinter.com.gt. Departs Tapachula (Mexico) for Quetzaltenango and Guatemala City.

FROM SOUTH AMERICA

There is currently **no overland passage** between Central and South America due to lack of infrastructure and a guerrilla presence in the Darién jungle bordering Colombia and Panama. Known as the "Darién Gap", this break in the Interamericana Highway means

that inter-continental travellers will need to move on either **by air** or **by sea**.

Unless part of an airpass or RTW ticket, **flights** from South to Central America are typically cheaper bought in the country of departure (agents there will have access to discounted fares). However, as always, booking at the last minute can mean settling for the highest prices, so ideally you should plan at least a few weeks in advance. One-way fares from Quito/Bogota to Panama are in the region of US$500 (considerably cheaper with a student card).

There's a steady flow of **sea traffic** between Panama and Colombia via the Caribbean, and private sailboats often offer passage as crew for the two- or three-day journey between Colón and Cartagena. Boats do not run to regular schedules, but rather at the whim of the captain and depending on demand. Latest departures are posted on notice boards in Cartagena, Colón and Panama City hostels and budget hotels. Sailing vessels vary greatly in size and facilities, so it's worth asking other travellers for recommendations. It should be noted that arranging onward transportation by boat might take several days, so plan to be hanging around at your departure point for some time. Expect to pay US$250–300 for passage, full board and administration of documents at *migración*. Many boats incorporate the voyage with a visit to Panama's enchanting San Blas Archipelago (see p.637), making the journey an inclusive tour and well worth any extra paid above the cheapest flight price. See the Panama chapter for more information.

AIRLINES, AGENTS AND OPERATORS

Online booking

ⓦ www.expedia.co.uk (in UK), ⓦ www
.expedia.com (in US), ⓦ www.expedia.ca
(in Canada)
ⓦ www.lastminute.com (in UK)
ⓦ www.opodo.co.uk (in UK)
ⓦ www.orbitz.com (in US)
ⓦ www.travelocity.co.uk (in UK), ⓦ www
.travelocity.com (in US), ⓦ www.travelocity
.ca (in Canada)
ⓦ www.travelonline.co.za (in South Africa)
ⓦ www.zuji.com.au (in Australia), ⓦ www
.zuji.co.nz (in New Zealand)

Airlines

Aeromexico US ℡1-800/237-6639, ⓦwww
.aeromexico.com.

Air Canada US & Canada ℡1-888/247-2262, UK
℡0871/220 1111, Republic of Ireland ℡01/679
3958, Australia ℡1300/655 767, New Zealand
℡0508/747 767; ⓦwww.aircanada.com.

Air Comet UK ℡0808 2345186 ⓦwww
.aircomet.com

Air Europa US ℡1-800/238-7672, UK
℡0870/777 7709; ⓦwww.aireuropa.com.

Air New Zealand New Zealand ℡0800/737000,
Australia ℡0800/132 476, UK ℡0800/028 4149,
US ℡1800-262/1234, Canada ℡1800-663/5494;
ⓦwww.airnz.co.nz.

American Airlines US ℡1-800/433-7300, UK
℡0845/7789 789, Republic of Ireland ℡01/602
0550, Australia ℡1800/673 486, New Zealand
℡0800/445 442;ⓦwww.aa.com.

British Airways US & Canada ℡1-800/AIR-WAYS,
UK ℡0870/850 9850, New Zealand ℡09/966
9777, South Africa ℡114/418 600; ⓦwww
.ba.com.

Continental Airlines US & Canada ℡1-800/523-
3273, UK ℡0845/607 6760, Republic of Ireland
℡1890/925 252, Australia ℡02/9244 2242, New
Zealand ℡09/308 3350, International ℡1800/231
0856; ⓦwww.continental.com.

Copa Airlines US ℡1-800/FLY-COPA, ⓦwww
.copaair.com.

Delta US & Canada ℡1-800/221-1212, UK
℡0845/600 0950, Republic of Ireland ℡1850/882
031 or 01/407 3165, Australia ℡1300/302 849,
New Zealand ℡09/9772232; ⓦwww.delta.com.

Iberia US ℡1-800/772-4642, UK ℡0870/609
0500, Republic of Ireland ℡0818/462 000, South
Africa ℡011/884 5909; ⓦwww.iberia.com.

KLM (Royal Dutch Airlines) US & Canada
℡1-800/225-2525, UK ℡0870/507 4074,
Republic of Ireland ℡1850/747 400, Australia
℡1300/392 192, New Zealand ℡09/921 6040,
South Africa ℡11/961 6727; ⓦwww.klm.com.

Martinair US ℡1-800/627-8462, Canada
℡1-416/364-3672; ⓦwww.martinair.com

Mexicana US ℡1-800/531-7921, Canada ℡1-
866/281-3049, UK ℡020/8492 0000, Australia
℡03/9699 9355, New Zealand ℡09/9772 213,
South Africa ℡11/781 2111; ⓦwww.mexicana.com.

Qantas Airways US & Canada ℡1-800/227-
4500, UK ℡0845/774 7767, Republic of Ireland
℡01/407 3278, Australia ℡13 13 13, New Zealand
℡0800/808 767 or 09/357 8900, South Africa
℡11/441 8550; ⓦwww.qantas.com.

South African Airways South Africa ℡11/978
1111, US & Canada ℡1-800/722-9675, UK
℡0870/747 1111, Australia ℡1800/221 699, New
Zealand ℡09/977 2237; ⓦwww.flysaa.com.

Grupo TACA US ℡1-800/400-TACA, Canada
℡1-800/722-TACA, UK ℡0870/2410 340,
Australia ℡02/8248 0020; ⓦwww.taca.com.

United Airlines US ℡1-800/UNITED-1, UK
℡0845/844 4777, Australia ℡13 17 77; ⓦwww
.united.com.

Agents and operators

ebookers UK ℡0800/082 3000, ⓦwww.ebookers
.com; Republic of Ireland ℡01/488 3507, ⓦwww
.ebookers.ie. Low fares on an extensive selection of
scheduled flights and package deals.

Journey Latin America UK ℡020/8622 8469,
ⓦwww.journeylatinamerica.co.uk. Long established UK-based tour operator offering tailormade
itineraries as well as sound advice on travel in
the region.

North South Travel UK ℡01245/608 291,
ⓦwww.northsouthtravel.co.uk. Friendly,
competitive travel agency, offering discounted fares
worldwide. Profits are used to support projects in
the developing world, especially the promotion of
sustainable tourism.

South American Experience UK ℡0845/277
3366, ⓦsouthamericanexperience.co.uk. Tour
operator with some coverage and general
information for Central America.

STA Travel US ℡1-800/781-4040, UK
℡0871/230 0040, Australia ℡134 STA, New
Zealand ℡0800/474 400, South Africa ℡0861/781
781; ⓦwww.statravel.com. Worldwide specialists in
independent travel; also student IDs, travel insurance,
car rental, rail passes, and more. Good discounts for
students and under-26s.

Trailfinders UK ℡0845/058 5858, Republic of
Ireland ℡01/677 7888, Australia ℡1300/780
212; ⓦwww.trailfinders.com. One of the best-
informed and most efficient agents for independent
travellers.

Getting around

If you're not in a hurry and are willing to travel on public transport, you can get around most of Central America on US$1 an hour (probably slightly more in Belize, Costa Rica and Panama). While public transport systems are sometimes slow – and almost always crowded and sweaty – they can often also be extremely efficient: in most places you will rarely have to wait long for onward transportation, making it ideal territory for exploration. On major roads especially, buses run with high frequency and can be a great insight into the day-to-day life of the country. Flights are relatively expensive but shuttle long-distance between major cites and can help access remote areas, such as the region's many wonderful islands. All things considered, getting around Central America can be fun and easy, despite the inevitable complications along the way.

The following is a general guide to Central American transport. More specific information on each country's infrastructure can be found in the "Getting around" section of each country's introductory chapter.

BY BUS

Travelling **by bus** in Central America is by far the most convenient and comprehensive way to get around the region. The **cost** of travel depends mainly on the quality of the transport – you can look forward to paying anywhere from approximately US$1 per hour for one of the region's infamous "chicken buses" (see box, p.123) to US$3 for a guaranteed seat on a more comfortable "Pullman"-style coach.

Chicken buses generally serve as second-class, or local, services. They stop on demand, wherever passengers request

to get off or people flag down passing services. Sometimes it can seem like you're stopping every thirty metres, but these buses are handy for impromptu itineraries and each country's extensive network of routes allows you to get off the beaten path with relative ease. In most places chicken buses tend to run **on demand** rather than to schedules, departing when full, though in Costa Rica and Panama schedules are a bit more regular – in those countries it is wise to check at bus terminals in advance of travel for current timetable information. **Tickets** are usually bought onboard, once the journey is underway, either from the conductor or from his assistant. It is always worth checking the price before boarding to avoid rip-offs, which are not unknown. **Luggage** usually goes on the roof; always keep valuables on your person and an eye on your stuff as best you can, as theft on

---

NAVIGATING CENTRAL AMERICAN CITIES

The majority of Central American cities are laid out on a **grid system**, making navigation fairly straightforward: usually numbered *calles* (streets) run east–west and numbered *avenidas* (avenues) run north–south, with a parque or plaza as the point zero. For more information on specific city addresses, see the relevant chapter in the main guide.

buses is unfortunately all too common – interior overheard luggage racks are particularly risky.

Pullman buses generally cover long-distance routes and operate to a schedule, making much quicker progress and so remaining economical when you wish to cover ground more rapidly. Seats should be reserved at the appropriate ticket office in advance. Several bus companies run services from one country to another as well as within individual countries (see below for some listings).

Travelling by bus **at night**, regardless of service type, is not recommended due to the high rate of highway robbery and traffic accidents.

Regional bus contacts

Hedman Alas Ⓦ www.hedmanalas.com. Connecting major cities in Honduras to Guatemala City and Antigua.

Tica Bus Ⓦ www.ticabus.com/ingles. Routes span the region from Panama City through to Chiapas, Mexico, covering most major cities.

Transnica Ⓦ www.transnica.com. Routes from Managua to San Salvador, San José and Tegucigalpa.

BY AIR

Although Central America has a good **international flight network**, connecting the region's key points of interest with its capital cities, unless you are severely pushed for time few flights are worth the money you will have to spend on them, since distances are usually short and accessible by bus and prices aren't particularly cheap (eg, Guatemala City–San José is US$200/US$400 student/standard fare). Regional carriers Grupo TACA and Copa both offer youth fares; to be eligible you will need to have an ISIC card (see p.46). If you do plan to do a bit of flying, airpasses (allowing short hops within Central America, as well as routes to Mexico, the US and some South American destinations) can be bought in conjunction with your international ticket in your country of origin. However, these usually force you to specify your route in advance and rarely allow for trips to your preferred destinations (most travellers are not necessarily interested in visiting the region's chaotic capital cities).

Of greater interest to budget travellers are the **domestic flights** that connect isolated tourist destinations – such as Nicaragua's

Corn Islands, Panama's Bocas del Toro and Honduras' Bay Islands, all of which are more than a day's travel by bus from their respective capital cities – to the region's more populous areas. Internal flights can be reasonably priced, especially if bought in advance, although in general you will have to purchase them locally.

BY BOAT

You're likely to travel **by boat** at some point if you spend any time in Central America – in some places watercraft are the only way to get around, in others they can provide a welcome break from the monotony of bumpy bus rides. Vessels range from the canoe-like "lanchas" with outboard motor to chugging ferries to speedy catamarans. Watery journeys of note include: Placencia (Belize) to Livingston (Guatemala) and onward to the Río Dulce area (see p.206); across Lago de Nicaragua to Isla de Ometepe (see p.460); down the Río San Juan to the Caribbean (see p.456); and through the banana plantations around Changuiola to the Caribbean cayes of Bocas del Toro (Panama; see p.662). Passage through the world-famous Panama Canal costs vessels from US$170,000 cash – perhaps not quite feasible for the budget traveller.

BY CAR

Considering the prevalence of public transport and the relative expense of renting **a car**, hiring a vehicle is unlikely to have much appeal. If, however, you want to reach isolated spots, and can form a trusted group to share the costs and/or risks, renting a car (or 4WD) does give you some flexibility. **Prices** for car hire vary throughout the region (see individual chapters for details). Always familiarize yourself with the conditions of hire before signing a contract. Beware that in the event of an accident, insurance excess levels are usually huge. If you do decide to rent a vehicle you will need a full driving licence and credit card and passport. Some agencies do not rent to under-25s, although others may have an age limit of 21. Always park securely, preferably in a parking lot with attendant, especially in cities. There are no breakdown services available, but petrol stations are plentiful; the price of fuel is slightly higher than in the US and considerably cheaper than in Europe.

Taxis

Travelling by **taxi** in Central America is something of a gamble, but a necessary one: drivers are either some of the friendliest, helpful folk you'll encounter or some of the biggest swindlers, but at night, especially in large cities, they provide the only safe mode of transport. Always settle on a price before getting in (even if there is a meter, try to get an estimate), clarifying that the price is for the journey, regardless of the number of passengers or amount of luggage; throughout the region most journeys are a minimum of US$2. In terms of safety, always use registered taxis (we've indicated how to recognize these throughout the guide) and ask the staff at your accommodation for recommendations and price estimates. It also pays to keep an eye on the map as your journey progresses – a possible deterrent to drivers quite literally taking you for a ride.

BY BIKE

Despite the prevalence of **bicycle** use among locals, bike rental is not widely available in Central America. However, some countries, like Belize, are seeing increased bicycle tourism, and a number of travellers are also touring the region with their own bikes. Notwithstanding the dangers of Central America's anarchic road customs, cycling in the region is facilitated by the mostly flat terrain, relatively short distances between settlements and ease of transporting bicycles aboard buses.

Accommodation

Budget accommodation in Central America is plentiful, and often of excellent quality. As anywhere, some of the region's places to stay are truly memorable for their warm atmosphere, great facilities and stunning location. Others, however, can promise cockroaches, poor sanitation and noisy neighbours. Never be afraid to shop around for a place you are comfortable with.

HOTELS AND GUESTHOUSES

The mainstays of travellers' accommodation in Central America are **hotels** and **guesthouses** (and their regional equivalents: *posadas*, *pensiones*, *cabinas* and *hospedajes*). A basic double room (around US$10–15) will have a bed, a light and probably a fan (*ventilador*). Most places offer the choice of private or shared **bathroom**; a private bath (*baño privado*) will cost a few dollars more than a shared one (*baño compartido*). Hot water is a rarity unless splurging on a swankier room; keep an eye out for gas-fired hot water systems – the standard (and decidedly dodgy) electrical showerheads tend to produce tepid water at best and can also deliver electric shocks. Some hotels will provide you with towels and soap and most with toilet paper. By paying a few extra dollars you can also find rooms including cable TV, fridge, air-conditioning,

mosquito nets and/or balcony. Double rooms are often equivalent in price to two dorm beds (good news for couples and something for friends to consider). Private single rooms, on the other hand, are often only marginally discounted (if at all) from the standard price for a double.

As a rule, you should ask to view rooms before agreeing to stay. Do not be afraid to walk away and look at alternatives – this may even precipitate a drop in prices. Booking ahead is generally not necessary (and often not possible). However, during holiday periods in busy tourist centres, plan on arriving early or calling in advance.

HOSTELS

Hostels, while not particularly widespread, are increasingly common in Central America, often run by foreigners with a keen eye for backpackers' needs. These establishments offer some of the most sociable and comfortable lodgings in the region. A dorm bed

---

ACCOMMODATION PRICE CODES

Throughout the guide all **accommodation** is coded on a scale of ❶ to ❾, which is outlined below. For places with dorms the code indicates the cost of a bed, for hotels and guesthouses the cheapest private single or double room and for campsites the cost of a night's stay per person. All codes represent high-season prices; when a price range is indicated, it means that the establishment offers a variety of services – as indicated in the listing. Note that many, but not all, establishments in Central America quote prices per person rather than per room – always check this.

❶ up to US$5
❷ US$6–10
❸ US$11–15
❹ US$16–25
❺ US$26–35
❻ US$36–45
❼ US$46–60
❽ US$61–80
❾ over $81

JUNGLE LODGES

Throughout Central America you will find an array of rural **jungle lodges** in some truly magical locations. And while many lodges charge fairly exorbitant prices, not all are beyond a budget traveller's means. If you have the opportunity, staying at a lodge is usually well worth the splurge and/or detour. However, as lodges are usually isolated, you will be captive to spending all your cash in one place. Lodge owners are of course wise to this and lay on all sorts of tempting treats to help relieve you of your *dinero*.

should cost around US$5–10, but in capital cities expect to pay at least double (more still in San José). Most hostels have a few private rooms as well as dormitories.

The best hostels may provide kitchen facilities, internet service, lockers, bar and restaurant areas, TV and movies, as well as tours and activities. The lockers are a definite plus – theft does occur, so do not leave valuables lying around; you might consider travelling with your own padlock. Some hostels will even offer free board and lodging if you want to stay put and work for a period (see "Work and study", p.39, for more details).

Hostelling International cards are little or no use in Central America.

CAMPING

Organized **campsites** are a rarity in Central America. However, some **national parks** do allow camping and have limited facilities such as drinking water, toilets and campfire provisions. Expect to pay around US$3–5 per person to pitch a tent (more in Costa Rica). Camping doesn't hold much appeal for locals, so don't expect to find gear on sale or for rent – you will need to carry what you need. It is also possible to pay to hang a hammock (your own or hired) in some areas. This may seem more appealing than an airless room, but the mosquitoes can be fierce – make sure you have a net.

 # Culture and etiquette

Despite a pervasive media image portraying Latin America as a scantily clad world of steamy salsa and sizzling hot spirit, the reality is much more conservative. Throughout Central America the church (both Catholic and Evangelical Protestant) retains a powerful influence on everyday life. Information about social customs specific to each country is found in the relevant chapter.

Traditional **family values** are prevalent throughout Central America: children are commonly considered to be a blessing – a sign of virility and in many cases an economic asset – and consequently families are often large in size. Travellers without children of their own may be regarded somewhat suspiciously by locals, especially in areas like the Guatemalan highlands. **Homosexual** relationships are publicly frowned upon if not actively condemned; gay and lesbian travellers should be discreet.

Whilst undeniably friendly, local people can seem shy and unsure about gringos squeezed into their regular chicken bus. You will seldom experience hostility, but it pays to greet fellow passengers with a simple "Buenas" and a smile to break the ice.

Politeness is valued highly, so even if your Spanish is poor, take the trouble to learn key pleasantries and they'll serve you well. Public **drunkenness** occurs rarely; try to follow this lead, even in backpacker-heavy areas.

DRESS

Most locals **dress modestly** but smartly and visitors not wishing to draw unwelcome attention should do the same. You will make a better impression if you do – especially worthwhile with officials. Flashy exhibitions of wealth are not recommended (jewellery should be left at home). Shorts (for men and women) are not generally worn away from beaches, but low-cut tops for women are becoming more usual, especially among the young. If visiting places of worship, especially, please dress accordingly – skimpy shorts and flesh-revealing tops are not appropriate. Women will probably also want something to cover their heads.

MACHISMO

Machismo is an ingrained part of Central American culture – **female travellers** will frequently experience whistling, tssking and even blatant catcalls, though probably not anything more sinister than guys showing off to their friends. It can be worth trying to form alliances with local women (simply making eye contact is enough), who do not tolerate public heckling. If they do not scare your unwanted suitors off, a handy phrase to try is "déjame en paz!" – literally, "leave me in peace!". No matter how modestly you behave, though, you will probably not counteract the view that foreign women are not only desirable, but also easily attainable.

MONEY MATTERS

Travellers to Central America, especially Westerners, are likely to experience the uncomfortable assumption by locals that you are in fact a multi-millionaire (even if you are looking extremely scruffy). Although you may be on a strict budget, the very fact that you have been able to travel abroad, coupled with your potential earning power back home, means you have an economic freedom unobtainable to many you will encounter. As a rule, however, you will ultimately be judged on your conduct and not your wealth: it isn't helpful, therefore to be too liberal or too mean with your cash. Instead, show appreciation for good service by **tipping** (as part of your budget), pay what will satisfy both parties when haggling and exchange friendship and hospitality for free. **Haggling** is accepted in markets (both tourist and local). You can also haggle – gently – over room prices, tour prices and taxi fares. Prices in shops are generally fixed, although it's usually worth asking if there are discounts ilf you buy more than one item.

Work and study

A high unemployment rate and innumerable bureaucratic hurdles make the possibility of finding paid work in Central America very unlikely, although there are limited opportunities to teach English, especially in wealthier countries like Costa Rica. It's far easier to work as a volunteer – many NGOs operate in the region, relying mainly on volunteer staff. Opportunities for studying Spanish are plentiful and often fairly cheap, with a number of congenial Central American locations drawing students from all over the world.

TEACHING ENGLISH

There are two options for **teaching English** in Central America: find work before you go, or just wing it and see what you come up with after arriving; the latter is slightly less risky if you already have a degree and/or teaching experience. You can get a **CELTA** (Certificate in English Language Teaching to Adults), a **TEFL** (Teaching English as a Foreign Language) or a **TESOL** (Teaching English to Speakers of Other Languages) qualification before you leave home or even while you're abroad. Courses are not cheap (about £1025/US$2250–2500/AUS$2550 for the month's full-time tuition) and you are unlikely to make this investment back very quickly on Central American wages. Once you have the necessary qualifications, the **British Council's** website (🌐www.britishcouncil.org/work/job) and the **TEFL** website (🌐www.tefl.com), both have a list of English-teaching vacancies.

Places like Guatemala City and San José in Costa Rica are your best bet for teaching in Central America, although colonial, tourist-oriented towns like Antigua in Guatemala and Granada in Nicaragua are also likely spots.

VOLUNTEERING

There are **voluntary positions** available in Central America for everything from conservation work in Costa Rica to human-rights work in Guatemala. If you have a useful skill or specialization, you might have your room and board paid for and perhaps even earn a little pocket money, although more often than not you'll have to fund yourself. If you don't have any particular skills, you'll almost definitely have to pay for the privilege of volunteering and in many cases – particularly in conservation work – this doesn't come cheap. While many positions are organized prior to arrival, it's also possible to fix something up on the ground through word of mouth. Notice boards in the more popular backpacker hostels are always good sources of info.

STUDYING SPANISH

Some people travel to Central America solely to **learn Spanish** and there are many cities and towns with highly respected schools. Antigua and Quetzaltenango in Guatemala, San José in Costa Rica and to a lesser extent, Granada and San Juan del Sur in Nicaragua are all noted centres for language instruction. Prices vary, but you can expect to pay around US$200 per week, to include room and board with a local family, a standard feature of many Spanish courses and great for full cultural immersion. Some schools will also include activities, allowing you to take your learning out of the classroom and providing an insight into the local area. Courses usually run Monday to Friday, but should include seven nights' homestay to take in the weekend. Cheaper courses are available if you are simply interested in lessons without lodging or activities, although your learning curve is unlikely to be as steep. See individual city Directories for language-school recommendations.

USEFUL CONTACTS

In the US and Canada

AFS Intercultural Programs US ☎ 1-800/AFS-INFO, Canada ☎ 1-800/361-7248 or 514-288-3282, ⓦ www.afs.org. Cultural immersion programmes for high-school students and graduates in Costa Rica, Guatemala, Honduras and Panama.

Alliances Abroad ☎ 1-888/6-ABROAD or 512/457-8062, ⓦ www.alliancesabroad.com. Combined language- and conservation-themed voluntary placements in Costa Rica lasting two weeks to one year. Intermediate Spanish ability required.

American Institute for Foreign Study US ☎ 1-866/906-2437, ⓦ www.aifs.com. Language study and cultural immersion in Costa Rica.

AmeriSpan ☎ 1-800/879-6640, ⓦ www.amerispan.com. Language programmes, volunteer/internship placements (English teaching, healthcare, environment, social work, etc) and academic study-abroad courses throughout Central America.

Amigos de las Américas ☎ 1-800/231-7796 or 713/782-5290, ⓦ www.amigoslink.org. Veteran nonprofit organization placing high school- and college-age students in child health promotion and other community projects in Costa Rica, Honduras, Nicaragua and Panama.

Council on International Educational Exchange (CIEE) ☎ 1-800/2COUNCIL, ⓦ www.ciee.org. Semester and summer study programmes in Costa Rica, with subjects ranging from agriculture and agroecology to Spanish language.

Earthwatch Institute ☎ 1-800/776-0188, ⓦ www.earthwatch.org. Voluntary positions in Costa Rica, Nicaragua and Panama assisting scientists in the field.

Peace Corps ☎ 1-800/424-8580, ⓦ www.peacecorps.gov. US institution which recruits volunteers of all ages (minimum 18) and from all walks of professional life for two-year postings throughout Central America. All applicants must be US citizens.

World Learning ☎ 1-800/336-1616, ⓦ www.sit.edu. Accredited college semesters abroad. The large Latin American studies programme includes an ecology/conservation course in Belize and a politically themed course in Nicaragua.

In the UK and Ireland

AFS UK ☎ 0113/242 6136, ⓦ www.afsuk.org. Six-month community volunteer placements for young people aged 18 to 34 in Costa Rica, Guatemala, Honduras and Panama.

British Council ☎ 020/7930 8466. The Council's Central Management of Direct Teaching (☎ 020/7389 4931) recruits TEFL teachers for posts worldwide (check ⓦ www.britishcouncil.org/work/jobs for a current list of vacancies). It also publishes a book, *Year Between*, aimed principally at gap-year students detailing volunteer programmes and schemes abroad.

BUNAC US ☎ 1-800/GO-BUNAC, UK ☎ 020/7251 3472, Republic of Ireland ☎ 1/477 3027, ⓦ www.bunac.org. Organizes working holidays in Costa Rica for students.

Cactus Languages ☎ 0845/130 4775, ⓦ www.cactuslanguage.co.uk. Brighton-based language-holiday specialist with wide range of courses in Costa Rica, Guatemala, Honduras, Nicaragua and Panama. Prices often lower than applying directly to the schools.

Camp America UK ☎ 020/7581 7373, Canada ☎ 902/ 422 1455, Australia ☎ 03/9826 0111, NZ ☎ 9416 5337, South Africa ☎ 021/419 5740, ⓦ www.campamerica.co.uk. Organizes cultural exchange programs all over the world.

Earthwatch Institute ☎ 01865/318 838, ⓦ www.uk.earthwatch.org/europe. International nonprofit organization dedicated to environmental sustainability. Voluntary positions assisting archeologists, biologists and even ethnomusicologists in the field in Costa Rica, Nicaragua and Belize.

Gapyear.com ⓦ www.gapyear.com. Comprehensive resource with search engine providing links to volunteer and language teaching/learning options worldwide.

Peace Brigades International ☎ 020/7561 9141, ⓦ www.peacebrigades.org. NGO dedicated to protecting human rights with placements accompanying human-rights workers in Guatemala. Costs (including a small monthly stipend) are covered although fundraising is encouraged and applicants need to be 25 or older and fluent in Spanish.

Raleigh International ☎ 020/7371 8585, ⓦ www.raleigh.org.uk. Long-established youth-development charity working on community and environmental projects worldwide. Opportunities for both young volunteers (17–25) and older skilled staff (25+). Central American projects in Costa Rica and Nicaragua.

In Australia, New Zealand and South Africa

AFS Australia ☏ 1300/131 736 or 02/9215 0077, NZ ☏ 0800/600 300 or 04/494 6020, South Africa ☏ 11/447 2673. international enquiries ☏ 1-212-807-8686,
Australian Volunteers International ☏ 03/9279 1788, ⓦ www.ozvol.org.au. Postings of up to two years in Costa Rica, Guatemala, El Salvador and Nicaragua with shorter-term, team-based assignments for younger volunteers.
Council on International Educational Exchange (CIEE) US ☏ 1-800/40-STUDY or 1-207/533-7600,

UK ☏ 020/8939 9057, ⓦ www.ciee.org. Leading NGO offering study programs and volunteer projects around the world.
Earthwatch Australia ☏ 03/9682 6828, ⓦ www .earthwatch.org/australia. Australian branch of this nonprofit organization that places prospective volunteers with an array of scientists from various fields in locations throughout Central America.
Global Volunteer Network ☏ 04/569 9080, ⓦ www.volunteer.org.nz. Voluntary placements on community projects worldwide. No Central American destinations at the time of writing, although new programmes are being researched all the time and it's worth having a check on the website.

Health

It's always easier to get sick in a country with a different climate, food and germs, and certainly still more so in a poor country with lower standards of sanitation than you might be accustomed to. Most visitors, however, get through Central America without catching anything more serious than a dose of "traveller's diarrhoea", as long as they observe basic precautions about hygiene, untreated water and insect bites.

Above all, it's important to get the best health advice you can before you depart: visit your doctor or a travel clinic. You should also invest in medical insurance (see p.50).

GENERAL PRECAUTIONS

There's no need to freak out and go overboard, but as you are packing consider putting together a **travel medical kit**. Components to include might be: painkillers and anti-inflammatory drugs, antiseptic cream, band-aids and gauze bandages, surgical tape, anti-diarrhoeal medicine (Imodium or Lomotil) and rehydration salts, diarrhoeal remedies (Pepto Bismol or similar), insect repellent, sun block, anti-fungal cream and sterile scissors and tweezers.

Once in Central America, basic hygienic practices will go a long way towards keeping you healthy. **Bathe** frequently, **wash your hands** before eating and avoid sharing water bottles or utensils. Make sure to eat a **balanced diet** – eating peeled fresh fruit helps keep up your vitamin and mineral intake (see p.42 for information about avoiding intestinal troubles); malnutrition can lower your resistance to germs and bacteria. Hepatitis B, HIV and AIDS – all transmitted through blood or sexual contact – are common in Central America. You should take all the usual, well-publicized precautions to avoid them. Two other causes of frequent problems in the region are **altitude** and the **sun**. The answer in both cases is to take it easy; allow yourself time to acclimatize and build up exposure to the sun gradually. Avoid dehydration by drinking enough – water or fruit juice rather than beer or coffee (see below for information about water safety). Overheating can cause heatstroke, which is potentially fatal. Lowering body temperature (by taking a tepid shower, for example) is the first step in treatment.

INOCULATIONS

If possible, all **inoculations** should be sorted out at least ten weeks before departure with your local health clinic. The only obligatory jab required to enter Central America is a **yellow fever** vaccination; however, this is only needed if you're arriving from a "high-risk" area – northern South America and much of central Africa – in which case you need to carry your vaccination certificate. A yellow fever shot is also highly recommended if travelling in Panama east of the canal. Long-term travellers should consider the combined hepatitis A and B and the rabies vaccines. And all travellers should check that they are up to date with the usual polio, diphtheria, tetanus, typhoid and hepatitis A jabs.

FOOD AND WATER SAFETY

People differ in their sensitivity to food. If you are worried or prone to digestive upsets then there are a few simple things to keep in mind: steer clear of raw shellfish and seafood when inland; only eat raw fruits and vegetables if they can be peeled; avoid salads unless rinsed in purified water.

Contaminated water is a major cause of sickness in Central America, and even if it looks clean, all drinking water should be regarded with caution (even when cleaning teeth and showering). That said, however, it's also essential to increase fluid intake to prevent dehydration. Bottled water is widely available, but always check that the seal is intact, since refilling empties with tap water for resale is not unknown. Many restaurants use purified water (*agua purificada*), but always ask.

There are various methods of **treating water** while you are travelling: boiling for a minimum of five minutes is the most effective method of sterilization, but it is not always practical, and will not remove unpleasant

tastes. Water filters remove visible impurities and larger pathogenic organisms (most bacteria and parasites). To be really sure your filtered water is also purified, however, chemical sterilization – using either chlorine or iodine tablets, or a tincture of iodine liquid – is advisable; iodine is more effective in destroying amoebic cysts. Both chlorine and iodine unfortunately leave a nasty aftertaste (which can be masked with lime juice). Pregnant women or people with thyroid problems should consult their doctor before using iodine tablets or purifiers. Inexpensive iodine removal filters are recommended if treated water is being used continuously for more than a month.

Any good outdoor equipment shop will stock a range of water treatment products; their staff will give you the best advice for your particular needs.

INTESTINAL TROUBLES

Diarrhoea is the stomach ailment you're most likely to encounter. Its main cause is simply the change in your diet: the food in Central America contains a whole new set of bacteria, as well as perhaps rather more of them than you're used to. Don't try anything too exotic in the first few days, but do try to find some local natural yogurt, which is a good way to introduce friendly bacteria to your system. Powdered milk, however, can be troublesome, due to being an unfamiliar form of lactose.

If you're afflicted with a bout of diarrhoea, the best cure is the simplest one: take it easy for a day or two and make sure you rehydrate. It's a good idea to carry sachets of rehydration salts, although you can make up your own solution by dissolving five teaspoons of sugar or honey and half a teaspoon of salt in a litre of water. Reintroduce only bland foods at first (rice, dry toast, etc) – papaya and coconut are also good. Diarrhoea remedies like Imodium and Lomotil should be saved for emergencies, like if you need to travel immediately. Only if the symptoms last more than four or five days do you need to worry. If you can't get to a doctor for an exact diagnosis, a last resort would be a course of Ciproxin (ciprofloxacin), which you may want to consider carrying in your medical kit.

Cholera, an acute bacterial infection, is recognizable by watery diarrhoea and vomiting, though many victims may have only mild or even no symptoms. However, risk of infection is considered low, as Central America was recently declared a cholera-free zone by the Pan American Health Organisation.

If you're spending any time in rural areas you also run the risk of picking up various parasitic infections: protozoa – amoeba and giardia – and intestinal worms. These sound hideous, but they're easily treated once detected. If you suspect you have an infestation take a stool sample to a good pathology lab and go to a doctor or pharmacist with the test results (see "Getting medical help", p.44). More serious is amoebic dysentery, which is endemic in many parts of the region. The symptoms are more or less the same as a bad case of diarrhoea, but include bleeding. On the whole, a course of Flagyl (metronidazole or tinidozole) will cure it; if you plan to visit the isolated rural reaches of Central America then it's worth carrying these, just in case. If possible get some, and some advice on their usage, from a doctor before you go. To avoid contracting such parasites think carefully about swimming in rivers and lakes during or just after the rainy season, when trash washes down hillsides into the water.

MALARIA

Malaria, caused by the transmission of a parasite in the saliva of an infected anopheles mosquito (active at night), is endemic in many parts of Central America, especially in the rural Caribbean lowlands. There are several different anti-malarial **prophylactics** available, all of which must be started in advance of travel, so make sure you leave plenty of time to visit your doctor. The recommended prophylactic for all of Central America, except for the area east of the Panama Canal, is chloroquine; east of the canal, including the San Blas Islands, it's mefloquine. Mefloquine (also known as Lariam), however, can have upsetting side effects; Malarone™ is a less controversial alternative, with minimal side effects, although its cost (around

£20 per week) can be prohibitive. Another alternative to mefloquine is doxycycline, which is cheaper but can cause increased sensitivity to sunlight. Consult your doctor about which drug will be best for you. It's extremely important to finish your course of anti-malarials, as there is a time lag between bite and infection. If you do become ill after returning home, consult your doctor and be sure to inform him or her that you've been in a malarial risk area.

OTHER BITES AND STINGS

Taking steps to avoid getting bitten by insects, particularly **mosquitoes**, is essential. In addition to malaria, mosquitoes can transmit dengue fever, a viral infection that is prevalent – and on the increase – throughout Central America (usually occurring in epidemic outbreaks). Unlike malaria, the mosquitoes that pass dengue fever are active during the day, and there's no vaccine or specific treatment, so you need to pay attention to avoiding bites. In general, sleep in screened rooms or under nets, burn mosquito coils containing permethrin (available everywhere), cover up arms and legs (though note that mosquitoes are attracted to dark-coloured clothing), especially around dawn and dusk when mosquitoes are most active, and use insect repellent containing over 35 percent DEET.

Sand flies, often present on beaches, are tiny and very difficult to see, and hence avoid – you will be made aware of their presence only when they bite, and by then it can be too late. The bites, usually found around the ankles, itch like hell and last for days. Don't give in to the temptation to scratch, as this causes the bites to get worse and last longer. Sandflies can spread cutaneous leishmaniasis, an extremely unpleasant disease characterized by skin lesions that can take months and even years to heal if left untreated. Chiggers (*coloradillas*) are also a nuisance, small red mites which bite around the waistband.

Scorpions are common: mostly nocturnal, they hide during the heat of the day under rocks and in crevices. Their sting is painful (occasionally fatal) and can become infected, so you should seek medical treatment. You're less likely to be bitten by a spider, but the advice is the same as for scorpions and venomous insects – seek medical treatment if the pain persists or increases.

You're unlikely to see a snake, but wearing boots and long trousers will go a long way towards preventing a bite in the event you do – walk heavily and they will usually slither away. Most snakes are harmless – exceptions are the fer-de-lance (which lives in both wet and dry environments, in both forest and open country, but rarely emerges during the day) and the bushmaster (found in places with heavy rainfall, or near streams and rivers), both of which can be aggressive, and whose venom fatal. If you do get bitten remember what the snake looked like (kill it if it's safe to do so), wrap a lightly restrictive bandage above and below the bite area, but don't apply enough pressure to restrict blood flow and never use a tourniquet. Disinfect the bite area and apply hard pressure with a gauze pad, taped in place; then immobilize the bitten limb as far as possible. Seek medical help immediately.

Swimming and snorkelling might bring you into contact with potentially dangerous sea creatures. It's extremely unlikely you'll be a victim of shark attack, but jellyfish are common and all corals will sting. Some jellyfish, like the Portuguese man-o'-war, with its distinctive purple, bag-like sail, have very long tentacles with stinging cells, and an encounter will result in raw, red welts. Equally painful is a brush against fire coral: in each case clean the wound with vinegar or iodine and seek medical help if the pain persists or infection develops.

Rabies does exist in Central America. You'll see stray dogs everywhere; the best advice is to give them a wide berth. Many strays are accustomed to having rocks hurled at them, so often simply bending over with a look of intent is enough to scare them. If you are bitten or scratched wash the wound immediately with soap and running water for five minutes and apply alcohol or iodine. Seek treatment immediately – rabies is fatal once symptoms appear. If you're going to be working with animals, or planning a long stay, especially in rural areas far from medical help,

you may well want to consider a pre-exposure vaccination, despite the hefty cost. Although this won't give you complete immunity, it will give you a window of 24–48 hours to seek treatment and reduce the amount of post-exposure vaccine you'll need if bitten. Bats can also carry the rabies virus; keep an eye out for them when entering carves.

GETTING MEDICAL HELP

For minor medical problems, head for the local *farmacia* (pharmacy) – look for a green cross. Pharmacists are knowledgeable and helpful, and many speak some English. They can also sell drugs over the counter (if necessary) that are only available by prescription at home. Most large cities have doctors and dentists, many trained in the US, who are experienced in treating visitors and speak good English. Your embassy will always have a list of recommended doctors and hospitals, and we've included some in our "Listings" for the main towns. Medical insurance (see p.50) is essential. If you suspect something is amiss with your insides, it might be worth heading straight for a pathology lab (*laboratorio médico*), found in all main towns, before seeing a doctor, as the doctor will probably send you there anyway. Many rural communities have a health centre (*centro de salud* or *puesto de salud*), where healthcare is free, although there may be only a nurse or health-worker available and you can't rely on finding an English-speaker. Should you need an injection or transfusion, make sure that the equipment is sterile (it might be worth bringing a sterile kit from home) and ensure any blood you receive is screened.

Medical resources for travellers

In the US and Canada
CDC ☎1-877/394-8747, ⊛www.cdc.gov/travel. Official US government travel health site.
International Society for Travel Medicine ☎1-770/736-7060, ⊛www.istm.org. Has a full list of travel health clinics.
Canadian Society for International Health ⊛www.csih.org. Extensive list of travel health centres.

In the UK and Ireland
British Airways Travel Clinics ☎ 0845/600 2236, ⓦ ww.britishairways.com/travel/healthclinintro/public/en_gb for nearest clinic.
Hospital for Tropical Diseases Travel Clinic ☎ 0845/155 5000 or 020/7387 4411, ⓦ www.thehtd.org.
MASTA (Medical Advisory Service for Travellers Abroad) ☎ 0870/606 2782 or ⓦ www.masta.org for the nearest clinic.

Travel Medicine Services ☎ 028/9031 5220.
Tropical Medical Bureau Republic of Ireland ☎ 1850/487 674, ⓦ www.tmb.ie.

In Australia, New Zealand and South Africa
Travellers' Medical and Vaccination Centre ☎ 1300/658 844, ⓦ www.tmvc.com.au. Lists travel clinics in Australia, New Zealand and South Africa.

Travel essentials

COSTS

Your **daily expenses** are likely to include accommodation, food and drink and transport. You may wish to budget separately for activities, as one-off costs (for example, a day's snorkelling or diving) can be high and would blow a daily budget. In general, the cheapest countries in the region are Guatemala, El Salvador, Honduras and

---

BUDGET TIPS

- Slow down. Racing from place to place eats into your budget, as you'll be forking out for transport and tours every day.
- Eat and drink what the locals do. Local staples can be half the price of even the most reasonable tourist menu. Set lunches in traditional *comedores* are great value.
- Cut down your beer bill. When buying booze it's cheapest to get it from the small *tiendas* (shops) and take back the bottles to claim the deposit. Litre bottles are more economical than the small 330ml ones.
- Refill your water bottle. Many hostels/hotels offer water refills for free or a small fee. Alternatively, in some countries you can buy 500ml bags (*bolsitas*) of water. If staying still, invest in larger gallon bottles.
- Use local transport. Tourist shuttles should be the exception, not the norm.
- Let your money work for you. Try to get a bank account that allows free withdrawals at ATMs. This also allows you to carry small amounts of cash, as ATMs are plentiful.
- Share costs with other travellers. The price of a private room for two is often cheaper than two dorm beds; a triple is even better value.
- Walk as much as possible. Taxis are often a disproportionately expensive method of transport.
- Shop in markets, bakeries and supermarkets. Self-catering is worthwhile if you're staying in one place and can eat your leftovers for breakfast.
- Learn to haggle. Bargaining can be fun. Don't be afraid to confront taxi drivers or chancers who you suspect are trying to rip you off. However, don't be too ruthless – bargaining over a few cents is not cool.
- Remember that everyone has their own budget and economizing is not a competition or an indicator of your backpacking credentials.

YOUTH AND STUDENT DISCOUNTS

There are few youth or student discounts in the region. Indeed, often you will find yourself charged more than employed locals simply because you are a foreigner. It is always worth enquiring if discounts are available, however, as on occasion entrance fees may be tiered (and applicable to foreigners as well as nationals). If a discount is applicable you will need to show ID. Most useful is the International Student Identity Card (ISIC), which can also be used to obtain discounts on flight bookings. You can get these from STA Travel (see p.31) and affiliated agencies with current official ID issued by your school/university (note: enrolling at a Spanish language school is generally not sufficient to obtain official student ID).

Nicaragua, with Belize, Costa Rica and Panama more expensive. However, even in these countries it is still possible to travel on a budget of around US$30 per day, with the most significant difference being the cost of public transport and accommodation. By following the cost-saving tips on p.45, it is possible to travel in Guatemala, for example, for as little as US$15 per day.

Generally speaking, the price quoted in restaurants and hotels is the price you pay. However, in some more upmarket establishments an additional tax will appear on your bill; it's worth checking if tax is included from the outset. Service is almost never included, and while not expected, tipping for good service can make a huge impact to the basic wage. Prices for accommodation (as well as some airfares and organized tours) can be considerably cheaper in low season (Sept–Dec), when it's always worth negotiating to obtain the best price (prices

quoted in this guide are based on high season rates).

Tiered pricing (charging foreigners more than nationals) is becoming more common, in particular for entrance fees. This is based on the premise that tourists can afford considerably more to enjoy visiting attractions than those on local salaries. There's nothing you can do about it.

CRIME AND PERSONAL SAFETY

While political violence has decreased over recent years, **crime rates** in Central America continue to rise, and tourists make handy targets. Though the majority of crime is **opportunistic theft** – bag snatching or pick-pocketing – some criminals do operate in gangs and are prepared to use extreme violence. It is commonly accepted that Guatemala tops the list for crimes committed against tourists, but it is possible to be the victim of crime anywhere in the region, especially if you let your guard down.

General precautions

As you're packing, keep the sentimental value of what you take with you to a minimum. Do not wear jewellery, and carry only a small amount of cash in your wallet, with dummy credit cards (past their expiry date) to offer muggers as a decoy. Larger volumes of cash and credit cards should be kept close to your body – in a money belt, hidden pocket or even in your shoes. Scan photocopies of any important documents (passport, insurance, etc) into a computer and email them to yourself, so you can access them even if you lose everything.

PRICES

At the beginning of each chapter you'll find a guide to "rough costs", including food, accommodation and travel. Prices are quoted in US dollars for ease of comparison. Within the chapter itself prices are quoted mainly in local currency, though as US dollars are widely accepted prices are occasionally quoted in that currency as well. Note that prices change all the time; we have done our best to make sure that all prices are accurate, but as tourism increases in popularity throughout the region it's likely that prices will rise incrementally.

GOVERNMENT TRAVEL ADVICE SITES

Australian Department of Foreign Affairs Ⓦ www.dfat.gov.au, Ⓦ www
.smartraveller.gov.au.
British Foreign & Commonwealth Office Ⓦ www.fco.gov.uk.
Canadian Department of Foreign Affairs Ⓦ www.dfait-maeci.gc.ca.
Irish Department of Foreign Affairs Ⓦ www.foreignaffairs.gov.ie.
New Zealand Ministry of Foreign Affairs Ⓦ www.mft.govt.nz.
US State Department Ⓦ www.travel.state.gov.

It's worth carrying a paper copy too, so that you can leave the originals in a hotel safe. There is always a dilemma about whether to carry electronic devices (such as a camera or MP3 player) on your person or leave them in your hotel. If you choose to leave them, make sure they're not accessible – it's worth packing a small padlock and short length of chain (or cable lock), so that you can create a DIY safe in a wardrobe or under a bed.

It's very important in Central America to keep an eye on your belongings at all times. Never put anything down or let your possessions out of your sight unless you're confident they are in a safe place. The highest-risk areas for opportunistic theft are large urban centres, bus stations, at ATMs and at border crossings. Buses are also a focus for petty thievery. When travelling by bus you'll often be separated from your main bag – it will usually end up on the roof. This is generally safe enough (and you'll probably have little option in any case). Theft of the bag itself is unlikely, but opportunist thieves may dip into zippers and outer pockets, so don't leave anything you'd miss accessible. Some travellers choose to put their pack into a sack to disguise it, prevent pilfering and also keep it clean and dry – not a bad idea. If you carry a day-pack, fill it wisely and keep it on your person (preferably strapped to you). Do not use overhead racks on buses. Needless to say, there is a greater risk of crime after dark, so try to arrive in new towns in daylight so that you're not wandering unlit streets with all your gear. Bear in mind, too, that the threat of petty crime does not exclusively come from the local population – unscrupulous fellow travellers have been known to help themselves to anything of value.

Violent crime does occur in Central America. Muggings at knifepoint, armed robbery (particularly of buses) and rape are all dangers to be aware of. If threatened with a weapon, do not resist. You can reduce your chances of falling victim to these crimes by staying in populated areas or around other travellers. However, it should be noted that tourist shuttles are actually more likely to be a target for hijackers, especially at night.

Drugs

Drugs of all kinds are available everywhere. Buying or using really isn't worth the risk: penalties are very strict. If you are arrested with drugs your embassy will probably send someone to visit you, and maybe find an English-speaking lawyer, but otherwise you're on your own. Practically every capital city has foreigners incarcerated for drug offences who'd never do it again if they knew what the punishment was like.

Reporting a crime

If you are unfortunate enough to suffer a crime, report the incident immediately to the police – if there is a tourist police force, try them first – if only to get a copy of the report (*denuncia*) which you'll need for insurance purposes. The police in Central America are poorly paid and, in the case of petty crime, you can't expect them to do much more than make out the report. If you can, also report the crime to your embassy – it helps the consular staff to build up a higher-level case for the better protection of tourists.

ELECTRICITY

All countries in the region use sockets accepting the flat two-pronged plug common to the majority of the Americas; ⓦwww.kropla.com is a useful website with information about adapters and converters. Standard **voltage** is 110–120v. Be wary of electric showerheads, often with protruding wires, in budget accommodation. If it isn't working (more than likely), do not touch the fitting. You may want to consider using a towel to turn off the conductive taps, too.

ENTRY REQUIREMENTS

Nationals of the UK, Ireland, Canada, the US, Australia and New Zealand do not need **visas** to visit any of the seven Central American countries. Visitors are eligible for stays of either thirty days (Belize, Panama) or ninety days (Costa Rica and the CA-4 countries – see box below). You should have a valid passport with at least six months remaining and, officially, an onward ticket and proof of funds (these are seldom checked but may be a sticking point at border crossings or customs, especially entering Costa Rica). For more information about specific countries and border crossings in Central America, see the relevant guide chapter. You should also always check with your embassy before travelling. A useful website for specific details of embassy locations worldwide is ⓦwww .embassiesabroad.com

Embassies in Central America

Belize UK, PO Box 91, Belmopan ☎(501) 822-2146, ⓔbrithicom@btl.net; US, Floral Park Rd, Belmopan ☎(501)822-4011, ⓔembbelize @state.gov.
Costa Rica Canada, Apartado 351–1007, Edificio Centro Colón, San José ☎(506) 2242-4400,

ⓦwww.dfait-maeci.gc.ca/sanjose; UK, Apartado 815-1007, Edificio Centro Colón (piso/floor 11), San José ☎(506) 2258-2025, ⓔbritemb@racsa.co.cr; US, C 120/Av 0, Pavas, San José ☎(506) 2519-2000, ⓕ(506) 2519-2305.
El Salvador US, Final Blvd Santa Elena, Antiguo Cuscatlán, La Libertad, San Salvador ☎(503) 2501-2600, ⓕ(503) 2278-5522; Canada, Centro Financiero Gigante, 63 Av Sur y Alameda Roosevelt, Local 6, Nivel Lobby II, San Salvador, ☎(503) 2279-4655, ⓦwww.dfait-maeci.gc.ca/elsalvador; UK (Honorary Consul), PO Box 242, San Salvador ☎(503) 2281-555, ⓔclaims@gibson .com.sv.
Guatemala Canada, 13 Calle 8-44, Zone 10, Edificio Edyma Plaza, Guatemala City ☎(502) 2363 4348, ⓦwww.dfait-maeci.gc.ca/guatemala /menu-en.asp; UK, Edificio Torre Internacional, Nivel 11, 16 Calle 0-55, Zona 10, Guatemala City ☎(502) 2367 5425, ⓕ(502) 2367 5430, ⓔconsular .guatemala@fco.gov.uk; US, Av Reforma 7-01, Zona 10, Guatemala City, ☎(502) 2326 4000, ⓔAmCitsGuatemala@state.gov.
Honduras Canada, Centro Financiero Banexpo Tercer Piso, Blvd San Juan Bosco, Colonia Payaqua, Tegucigalpa ☎(504) 232 4551, ⓦwww .dfait-maeci.gc.ca/sanjose/tglpa-en.asp; US, Av La Paz, Tegucigalpa ☎(504) 236 9320/238 5114, ⓕ(504) 236 9037.
Nicaragua Canada, Costado Oriental de la Casa Nasareth, Una cuadra arriba, Calle El Noval, Managua ☎(505) 268-0433/3323, ⓦwww .dfait-maeci.gc.ca/sanjose/mngua-en.asp; US, Km5 1/2 (5.5) Carretera Sur, Managua ☎(505) 252-7100, ⓔconsularmanagua@state.gov.
Panama Canada, World Trade Center First Floor, Commercial Gallery, Calle 53E, Marbella, Panama City ☎ (507) 264 9731, ⓦwww.dfait-maeci.gc.ca /panama/menu-en.asp; UK, MMG Tower, Calle 53, Panama City ☎(507) 269 0866, ⓔbritemb @cwpanama.net; US, PAS Building 783, Demetrio Basilio Lakas Avenue Clayton, Panama City ☎(507) 207 7000, ⓔpanamaweb@state.gov.

CENTRAL AMERICA BORDER CONTROL AGREEMENT

Guatemala, El Salvador, Honduras and Nicaragua are party to the **Central America Border Control Agreement (CA-4)**. Under the terms of this agreement, tourists may travel within any of these four countries for a period of up to ninety days without completing entry and exit formalities at border and immigration checkpoints. The ninety-day period begins at the first point of entry to any of the CA-4 countries. Fines are applied for travellers who exceed the ninety-day limit, although a request for an extension can be made for up to thirty additional days by paying a fee before the limit expires. If you are expelled from any of the four countries you are also excluded from the entire CA-4 region.

Central American embassies abroad

Belize Canada, c/o McMillan Binch, Suite 3800, South Tower, Royal Bank Plaza, Toronto, Ontario ☎(416) 865-7000; El Salvador, C El Bosque Norte, Col La Lima IV, San Salvador ☎(503) 2248 1423; Guatemala, 5 Av 5-55, Zona 14, Europlaza, Torre II, Oficina 1502, Guatemala City ☎(502) 2367 3883, ✉embelguat@yahoo.com; Honduras, Hotel de Honduras, R/do Hotel Honduras Maya, Tegucigalpa ☎(504) 238 4614, ✉consuladobelize@yahoo .com; Panama, PO Box 0819-12297, El Dorado, ☎(507) 236 4132; UK, Belize High Commission, 3rd Floor, 45 Crawford Place, London, W1H 4LP ☎0207723 3603, ✉bzhc-lon@btconnect .com; US, 2535 Massachusetts Ave NW, Washington DC, 20008 ☎(202) 332-9636, ⊛www.embassyofbelize.org.

Costa Rica Australia, De la Sala House, Piso 11, 30 Clarence St, NSW, 2000, Sydney ☎(02) 9261 1177; Canada, 208-135 York St, Ottawa, ON K1N 5T4 ☎(613) 562-2855; Panama, Avenida Samuel Lewis, Edificio Omega Piso 3ro, a un costado del Santuario Nacional, Panama City ☎(507) 264 2980; UK, Flat 1, 14 Lancaster Gate, London, W2 3LH, ☎(020) 7706 8844; US, 2114 S Street, N.W., 20008, Washington DC ☎(202) 234-2945, ⊛http://costarica-embassy.org.

El Salvador Belize, 49 Nanche St, Belmopan ☎(501) 235-162; Canada, 209 Kent St, Ottawa, K2P 1Z8 ☎(613) 238-2939; Costa Rica, Paseo Colon, Av 1a C 30 No.53 "N", San José ☎(506) 2256-0043; Guatemala, 5a Av 8-15, Zona 9, Guatemala City ☎(502) 2360 7660; Honduras, Colonia Ruben Dario, 2a Av y 5a C No.620, apartado Postal 1936, Tegucigalpa ☎(504) 239 0901, ✉embasalva@cablecolor.hn; Nicaragua, Km 9 1/2 Carretera a Masaya, Residential Las Colinas, Pasaje Los Cerros 142, Managua ☎(505) 276-0712, ✉embelsa@cablenet.com.ni; Panama, Edificio Metropolis, C Manuel Espinoza Batista, Piso 4, Apt 4-A, Postal 8016, Zona 7, Panama City ☎(507) 223 6385, ✉embasalva@cwpanama.net.

Guatemala Australia (Consulate), 41 Blarney Ave, Killarney Heights, NSW 2087 ☎(02) 9551 3018; Belize, 8 A St, Belize City, ☎(501) 33314; Canada, 130 Albert St, Suite 1010, Ottawa, Ontario, K1P 5G4 ☎(613) 233-7237, ✉embguate@ottawa.net; Costa Rica, De Pops de Curridabat, 500Sur, 30 Oeste, 2da Casa Izquierda, San José ☎(506) 283-2555, ✉embguat@sol.racsa.co.cr; El Salvador, 15 Av Nte, No.135, San Salvador ☎(503) 271225, Honduras, C Principal, Col Loma Linda Norte, Tegucigalpa ☎(504) 311596, ✉embguat@david.intertel.

hn; Nicaragua, KM.11, 1/2 Carretera a Masaya, Managua, ☎(505) 799609; Panama, C Abel Bravo y Calle 57, Barrio Bella Vista, Edif. Torre Cancun, Apto 14-A, Panama City ☎(507) 269 3475; UK, 13 Fawcett St, London SW10 9HN ☎(020) 73513042, ✉embaguatelondon@btinternet.com; US, 2220 R Street NW 20008, Washington DC ☎(202) 745-4952, ⊛www.guatemala-embassy.org.

Honduras Belize, 22 Gabourel Lane, PO Box 285, Belize City ☎(501) 224-5889, ✉embhonbe@btl.net; Canada, 151 Slater St, Suite 805-A, Ottawa, Ontario, KIP 5-H3 ☎(1-613) 233-8900, ⊛www .embassyhonduras.ca; Costa Rica, Urbanizacion Trejos Montealegre, De Banca Promerica 100 al Oeste, 100 Sur y 350 al Oeste, San Rafael de Escazu, San José ☎(506) 2915147, ✉emhondcr @sol.racsa.co.cr; El Salvador, 89 Av Nte entre 7 y 9 C Pte, No.561 Colonia Escalón, San Salvador ☎(503)263-2808; Guatemala, 19 Av "A", 20-19 Zona 10, Guatemala City 0101 ☎(502) 366 5640, ✉embhond@intelnet.net.gt; Nicaragua, Reparto San Juan, del Gimnasio Hércules 1 cuadra al Sur, 1 cuadra al Este, C San Juan, no. 312, Apartado Postal No.321 ☎(505) 270-4133, ✉embhonduras @cablenet.com.ni; Panama, C 31, Av Justo Arosemena, Apdo. Postal 8704, Zona 5, Panamá City ☎(507) 264 5513, ✉ehpam@cableonda .net; UK, 115 Gloucester Place, London W1U 6JT ☎(020)74864880; US, 3007 Tilden St NW, Suite 4M, Washington DC 20008 ☎(202)966-7702, ✉embassy@hondurasemb.org.

Nicaragua Costa Rica, Avenida Central # 2540, Barrio La California, Frente al Pizza Hut, San José, ☎(506) 223-1489, ✉embanic@racsa.co.cr; UK, Vicarage House, Suite 12, 58-60 Kensington Church St, London W8 4DB, ☎(020) 793 82373, ✉emb .ofnicaragua@virgin.net; US, 1627 New Hampshire Ave NW, Washington DC, 20009, ☎(202) 939-6570, ✉agnesalvarado@embanic.org.

Panama Canada, 130 Albert St., Suite 300 Ottawa, Ontario K1P 5G4 ☎(613) 236-7177, ✉embassyofpanama@gmail.com; Costa Rica, Barrio La Granja, del Antiguo Higueron de San Pedro 200 sur y 25 este, San Pedro, Apartado 103-2050 San Pedro de Montes de Oca, San José ☎(506) 280-1570, ✉panaembacr@racsa.co.cr; El Salvador, Av Bungamilias #21 Colonia San Francisco, San Salvador ☎(503) 2298-0773; Guatemala, 12 C 2-65, Zona 14, Guatemala City ☎(502) 2366 3338, ✉panaguate@hotmail.com; Honduras, Colonia Palmira, Edificio Palmira Piso 2, Frente al Hotel Honduras, Maya Tegucigalpa, ☎(504) 239 5508; Nicaragua, Reparto Mantica, del Cuartel General de Bomberos, 1c. abajo, Casa no. 93, Esquina Opuesta al Restaurante, Managua ☎(505)266-8633; UK, Panama House, 40 Hertford

BORDER CROSSINGS

Most travellers in Central America take advantage of the close proximity of the region's many distinct nations, crossing international borders regularly. While for the most part this is straightforward, "border days" can also be some of the most exhausting of your trip – hopefully these tips will help ease the strain.

- Always check specific entry requirements before heading for the border.
- Ensure that your passport is stamped on both entry and exit. (See box, p.48, for information on getting stamped in the CA-4 countries.)
- Try to cross in the morning, when public transport links are more frequent and queues lighter.
- Research current exchange rates online at ⓦ www.oanda.com or www.xe.com and be savvy when dealing with moneychangers.
- If asked for "processing fees" request a receipt (such as the stamp given by Panama). Without one, said fees are not legal.
- Do not engage in discussion of your business with strangers. Borders are notorious hang-outs for petty criminals and con men. If you are confused about how to proceed, ask a uniformed official.
- At popular crossings avoid group transportation, which will slow your progress considerably. Chicken buses operate these routes as frequently as any other (although not at night).
- If given a stamped entry document do not lose it – you will require it later for departure.

St, London W1Y 7TG ☎ (020) 7409 2255, ⓦ www .panaconsul.com; US, 2862 McGill Terrace NW, Washington DC, 20008 ☎ (202) 483-1407, ⓦ www.embassyofpanama.org.

Customs

All Central American countries allow the import and export of a small amount of tobacco and alcohol. The exact amounts vary, but at their minimum levels 80 cigarettes and 1.5 litres of alcohol are allowed. Belize and Panama do not allow the import or export of plants, fruit, vegetables, meat or animal products. In Belize you are restricted to bringing in and taking out up to 100 Belizean dollars of local currency, while in Guatemala the import/export of local currency (quetzales) is completely prohibited. At some border crossings (especially on the Interamericana Highway) you should expect to have your bags searched, often a lengthy process when travelling by long-distance bus.

GAY AND LESBIAN TRAVELLERS

While there are no laws forbidding the practice of consensual homosexual acts, homosexuality is widely condemned by conservative Central American society, and harassment of, particularly, gay men by police and officials does exist. Gay and lesbian travellers are unlikely to experience problems, however, if they remain discreet. Unsurprisingly, there is little in the way of an open gay community or scene. In the more cosmopolitan capital cities a few gay nightspots exist, although these are almost entirely geared towards men.

INSURANCE

You'd do well to take out an **insurance policy** before travelling to cover against theft, loss, illness or injury. Before paying for a new policy, however, it's worth checking whether you are already covered on any existing home or medical insurance policies that you may hold. A typical travel insurance policy usually provides cover for the loss of baggage, tickets and – up to a certain limit – cash or cheques, as well as cancellation or curtailment of your journey. Most of them exclude so-called dangerous sports unless an extra premium is paid: in Central America this can mean scuba-diving, white-water rafting, surfing and trekking. If you have a choice of medical coverage options, the lower value should be sufficient for Central America. It is also useful to have a policy providing a 24-hour medical emergency number. When securing baggage cover, make sure that the per-article limit – typically under £500/$1000 – will cover your most valuable possession. If you need to make a claim, you should keep receipts for medicines and medical treatment as well as any high-value items that are being insured. In the event that you have anything stolen, you must obtain a *denuncia* from the police.

Several companies now offer tailored "backpacker" insurance, which provides low-cost coverage for extended durations (beyond the standard 30-day holiday policies). These include Rough Guides own recommended insurance (see box above).

INTERNET

Central America is increasingly well connected to the internet and you should have little difficulty getting online. Even smaller towns usually have at least one cybercafé, often populated by noisy gaming school kids. Many cybercafés are well equipped with webcams and headphones as well as the facility to download digital photos onto CD. On average expect to pay US$1 per hour. Many hostels also provide internet access, although they may be more restrictive on usage and marginally more expensive. Check Ⓦwww.kropla.com for details of how to plug your laptop in when abroad.

MAIL

With the prevalence of email, the need to negotiate the idiosyncrasies of foreign mail systems is thankfully becoming less frequent. Should you wish to investigate, however, you will find that stamps are rarely available outside the post office/*correo* (although it can

be worth asking if you are buying a postcard, for example, as occasionally souvenir shops and stationers do stock them). Sending mail from the main post office in any capital city is probably the best way to ensure speedy and efficient delivery of your mail. The cost and speed of mailing items varies from country to country, but is by far cheapest and quickest from Panama. To receive mail by *poste restante* you should address it to yourself at "Lista de Correos" at the "Correo Central" in the capital city of the appropriate country. See the relevant guide chapter for information specific to each country.

MAPS

The best overall map of Central America, covering the region at a scale of 1:1100000, is produced by Canada's International Travel Maps and Books (Ⓦwww.itmb.com). They also publish individual country maps at various scales. Unless you are lucky, maps are hard to find once you get to Central America, so it's wise to bring them with you when possible.

MONEY

Cash payments are the norm in Central America, with the most convenient way to access money being via an **ATM** (*cajero automático*). Most machines accept Visa and MasterCard credit cards, as well as Visa debit cards, and are increasingly widespread throughout the region. However, it is always advisable to check specific destination listings in this guide in advance of travel to confirm that smaller settlements have an ATM, as not all do. If you do rely on ATMs, it's worth having a back-up card in case the first is lost or stolen. If you plan to be abroad for a significant period, it is worth thoroughly researching your bank's terms for cash withdrawals abroad – some make no charge at all, allowing you to make frequent withdrawals and carry only small amounts of cash around urban areas. As a possible alternative some banks will give **cash advances** over the counter (sometimes at a small fee). Try to hoard notes of small denominations; you will constantly encounter problems obtaining change from local businesses, often stalling transactions as no one has anything smaller than a US$1 bill (or its equivalent). In general, budget-friendly hotels and restaurants do not take **credit cards**, though a few mid-range establishments and tourist handicraft shops may accept them. **Traveller's cheques** can be difficult to change for the same reason, but are good to carry as a back-up, as they are a secure way to hold money.

Belize, Guatemala, Honduras, Nicaragua and Costa Rica each have their own **national currency** (see box above), while El Salvador and Panama both use the US dollar (in Panama the dollar is divided into 100 balboas – although US cents are also legal tender). However, **US dollars** are accepted throughout Central America and in many places prices for tourist services (eg, language school fees, plane tickets, tour fees) are quoted exclusively in them. Indeed, some ATMs (particularly those in Nicaragua) will actually dispense dollars on request. Local currency is always accepted at the current exchange rate, though, so there is no need to carry huge amounts of dollars in cash, though it is certainly useful to carry some to exchange at border crossings. Generally speaking, you should also get rid of any remaining unwanted local currency at border crossings, as it will be more difficult to exchange the further away from the border you are. Try to research the current exchange rates before dealing with moneychangers (ⓦwww.oanda .com, ⓦwww.xe.com or similar).

It is possible to **wire money** to Central America using services such as Western Union (who charge a percentage) or Moneygram (who charge a flat fee of approximately US$10). Western Union have branches in major towns, while Moneygram are an agency represented in many banks throughout the region.

PHONES

It's easy enough to phone home from most cities and towns in Central America. Each country in the region has a national telecommunications company with offices throughout the countryside. It's also worth keeping an eye out for internet cafés that offer Skype, for excellent-value international calls. Mobile phones are as prolific as they are in the developed world; despite living in relative poverty, the rural population can often be spotted checking their SMS messages. You may find that taking your own phone comes in useful in emergencies, but on the other hand, it does become one more item to keep secure. Also remember that rates to receive calls and messages while abroad are often extortionate. Alternatively, you may consider purchasing a phone locally, as packages that include call-time are reasonable. However, practically speaking, if you only anticipate making

CALLING FROM ABROAD

To phone abroad from the following countries, you must first dial the international access code of the country you are calling from, then the country code of the country you are calling to, then the area code (usually without the first zero) and then the phone number.

International access codes when dialing from:

Australia ☏ 0011
Belize ☏ 00
Canada ☏ 011
Costa Rica ☏ 00
El Salvador ☏ 00 (144+00 with Telefonica)
Guatemala ☏ 00 (130+00 with Telefonica; ☏ 147+00 with Telgua)
Honduras ☏ 00
Ireland ☏ 00
Nicaragua ☏ 00
New Zealand ☏ 00
Panama ☏ 00 (088+00 with Telecarrier; 055+00 with Clarocom)
South Africa ☏ 00

UK ☏ 00
US ☏ 011

Country codes when dialling to:

Australia ☏ 61
Belize ☏ 501
Canada ☏ 1
Costa Rica ☏ 506
El Salvador ☏ 503
Guatemala ☏ 502
Honduras ☏ 504
Ireland ☏ 353
Nicaragua ☏ 505
New Zealand ☏ 64
Panama ☏ 507
South Africa ☏ 27
UK ☏ 44
US ☏ 1

the odd call, forget mobile and simply use local payphones, which are usually easy to come by.

SHOPPING

Shopping sprees in Central America are basically limited to locations where what's on offer is either significantly cheaper or significantly different to what's available back home – places like the Guatemalan highlands, where indigenous handicraft markets abound, and Panama City, where glitzy shopping malls offer cut-price designer clothing and shoes. Throughout the region you can also buy locally sourced coffee, thereby supporting local farmers.

In handicraft and local markets haggling is standard practice. Try not to get cornered by stall-holders, who will try to pressure you into buying on the spot. It is always wise to research various sellers' best prices before agreeing to a sale. It is also worth scouting out official tourist shops (where prices are fixed) to get a ballpark figure to try and beat in markets. If you plan to buy several items you will get the best prices if you buy in bulk from the same seller. Haggling is not commonplace in shops. However, if you are unsure about whether or not prices are

fixed, simply ask if discounts apply: "Hay descuentos?".

TIME

Panama is GMT-6, all the other countries are seven hours behind GMT In recent years Central American governments have gone back and forth on the issue of whether or not to apply daylight savings as an energy–saving measure, and will no doubt continue to so in the future.

TOURIST INFORMATION

Official sources of tourist information in Central America are spotty at best. For the budget traveller, often the best way to obtain the latest advice is to talk to other backpackers about their experiences. Similarly, popular hostels usually have notice-boards and the best have clued-up staff with local knowledge. All Central American countries do have their own official tourist information offices, but the prevalence of these on the ground is not great. However, the following tourist office websites provide a useful reference, especially for pre-trip planning. See too the "On the net" boxes in the individual chapters for further suggestions.

Central American tourist office websites

Belize Ⓦ www.travelbelize.org
Costa Rica Ⓦ www.tourism-costarica.com
El Salvador Ⓦ www.elsalvadorturismo.gob.sv
Guatemala Ⓦ www.visitguatemala.com
Honduras Ⓦ www.hondurasinfo.hn
Nicaragua Ⓦ www.intur.gob.ni
Panama Ⓦ www.panamatravel.com

TRAVELLERS WITH DISABILITIES

Central America is not the most accessible part of the world for travellers with disabilities. On the whole, it's the top-end hotels and services that may offer equipped facilities – out of the price range for most budget travellers. However, for the most part, Central American society is community-orientated and strangers take pleasure in helping and facilitating the passage of others. Costa Rica (where tourist facilities are well developed) and Panama (where there is a large ex-pat community) have the best infrastructure, relative to the rest of the region.

The best course of action is to plan thoroughly in advance of travel. There are many specialist websites advising travellers with disabilities, including Ⓦ www.able-travel.com, Ⓦ www.globalaccessnews.com and Ⓦ www.dptac.gov.uk/door-to-door.

WOMEN TRAVELLERS

Despite the blatant machismo of Latino culture, most female travellers report positive experiences in the region. Indeed, several will testify that they feel better treated by locals than their fellow male travellers. There are, however, still precautions to be taken. Women will encounter attention wherever they go – this can range from mildly irritating whistles to persistent and even forceful sexual advances. Golden rules when dealing with hopeful suitors include staying sober, stating your intent clearly and loudly and involving outside parties if you feel uncomfortable. Remember that local women are firm and direct with guys and do not tolerate disrespect – you should follow their lead. At night, female travellers should try to move in groups.

Women travelling as part of a straight couple should be prepared to be invisible in many social interactions. Even if the woman is the only one to speak Spanish, for example, locals will often automatically address their reply to the man's perceived authority.

Belize

CAYE CAULKER:
admire the colourful coral and dazzling array of fish ✪

SAN IGNACIO:
excellent accommodation and a fantastic choice of adventure trips

BLUE HOLE:
dive deep into the inky waters of this coral-encrusted cavern ✪

COCKSCOMB BASIN WILDLIFE SANCTUARY:
hike the winding jungle paths of the world's first jaguar reserve ✪

CARACOL:
explore Belize's greatest and most extensive Maya site ✪

PLACENCIA:
relax on Belize's most beautiful, white-sand beaches ✪

ROUGH COSTS

DAILY BUDGET Basic US$30/ occasional treat US$60

DRINK Rum (1L) US$9

FOOD Jerk chicken US$4

CAMPING/HOSTEL/BUDGET HOTEL US$5/US$10–15/US$15–25

TRAVEL Belize City–Caye Caulker (35km) by ferry: 45min, US$8; Belize City–San Ignacio (120km) by bus: 2hr 30min, US$4

FACT FILE

POPULATION 294,000

AREA 22,966 sq km

LANGUAGE English

CURRENCY Belize Dollar (Bz$)

CAPITAL Belmopan (population: 15,000)

INTERNATIONAL PHONE CODE ☎501

TIME ZONE GMT –6hr

Introduction

With far less of a language barrier to overcome than elsewhere in Central America, Belize, perched on the isthmus' northeast corner, is the ideal first stop on a tour of the region. And, although it is the most expensive country in Central America, its reliable public transport and numerous hotels and restaurants make it an ideal place to travel independently.

Belize offers some of the most **breath-taking scenery** anywhere in the region: thick tropical forests envelop much of the country's southern and western regions, stretching up towards the misty heights of the sparsely populated Maya Mountains, while just offshore dazzling turquoise shallows and cobalt depths surround the **Mesoamerican Barrier Reef**, the longest such reef in the Americas, as well as the crown jewels in Belize's natural crown: three of the four **coral atolls** in the Caribbean.

Scattered along the barrier reef, a chain of islands – known as **cayes** – protect the mainland from the ocean swell, and make wonderful bases for snorkelling and diving; the cayes are most travellers' top destination in the country. **Ambergris Caye** and **Caye Caulker** are the best known, though many of the less developed islands, including picture-perfect Tobacco Caye, are gaining in popularity. The **interior** has remained relatively untouched, thanks to a national emphasis on conservation: in the west, the dramatic landscape – especially the tropical forests and cave systems – of the **Cayo District** provides numerous opportunities for adventure-seekers. Inexpensive **San Ignacio**, the region's transportation hub, gives access to the heights of the **Mountain Pine Ridge Forest Reserve** and the rapids of the **Macal** and **Mopan rivers**. For those with an adventurous spirit of a different sort, hectic **Belize City** offers a fascinating – if nerve-wracking – opportunity to explore the country's energetic multicultural spirit. **Dangriga**, the main town of the south-central region, serves as a jumping-off point for the **Cockscomb Basin Wildlife Sanctuary**, while the **Placencia Peninsula** has some of the country's best **beaches**. In the far south, Belize's most isolated region, the **Maya Mountains** rise to over 1100m and border some of the country's only **rainforest**. Throughout the country, the archeological treasures of the **ancient Maya** dot the landscape.

WHEN TO VISIT

The country's climate is subtropical, with temperatures warm throughout the year, generally 20–27°C from January to May (the dry season) and 22–32°C from June to December (the wet season). The best time to visit the country, therefore, is usually between January and March, when it's not (quite) as hot or humid. That said, these months are also Belize's peak tourist season, and prices tend to be higher.

CHRONOLOGY

200–800 AD Classic period: Maya culture flourishes throughout Belize.

800–900 AD Maya cities across central and southern Belize decline, though Lamanai and other northern cities continue to thrive throughout the Postclassic period (900–1540 AD).

1530s The Spanish, led by Francisco de Montejo, engage in the first of numerous unsuccessful attempts to conquer the Maya of Belize.

1544 Gaspar Pacheco subdues Maya resistance and founds a town on Lake Balcar.

1570 Spanish mission is established at Lamanai.

1638 The Maya rebel, forcing the Spanish to abandon the areas they have settled.

1630–1670 British buccaneers, later known as Baymen, plunder Spanish treasure ships along the Belizean coast, then begin to settle the coastline and harvest logwood, used for textile dyes in Europe. They rely heavily on slave labour from Africa.

1700s Spain and Britain clash over control of Belize. In 1763, Spain officially grants British settlers logging rights, but does not abandon territorial claims on the region.

1798 The British defeat the Spanish in the Battle of St George's Caye, gaining control of the region.

1838 Slavery is abolished.

1839 Citing Spanish territorial claims, newly independent Guatemala first asserts sovereign authority over Belize.

1847 Mexican refugees fleeing the Caste Wars in the Yucatán arrive in Belize.

1859 Britain and Guatemala sign a treaty the acknowledges British sovereignty over Belize.

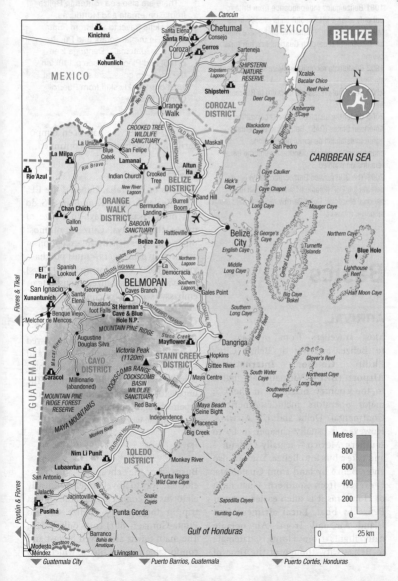

1862 Belize officially becomes a British colony, and part of the Commonwealth, called British Honduras.
1931 Hurricane floods Belize City and kills several thousand.
1961 A second hurricane (Hurricane Hattie) devastates Belize City and kills 262, after which plans are made to move the country's capital to Belmopan.
1964 British Honduras becomes an internally self-governing colony.
1973 British Honduras is renamed Belize
1981 Belize gains independence from Britain, but only after a UN Resolution is passed in its favour, and Britain, Guatemala and Belize reach an agreement regarding Guatemala's territorial claims.
1992 Guatemala recognizes Belize's independent status.
2000 Guatemala reasserts its claim to Belizean territory.
2005 Under the auspices of the Organization of American States (OAS), Belize and Guatemala agree to establish peaceful negotiations concerning the border dispute, though the issue remains unresolved.
2008 The UDP (United Democratic Party) easily defeats the PUP (People's United Party) in the national elections; Dean Barrow replaces Said Musa as prime minister.

Basics

ARRIVAL

Most travellers from overseas **fly** to Belize, arriving at Belize City's **Philip Goldson International Airport (BZE)**. Virtually all flights to the country originate in the US; major operators include American, Continental, Delta and US Airways. However, it usually cheaper to fly to southern Mexico – usually Cancún – and take a **bus** into Belize. You can also enter Belize by land from Guatemala. However, from southern Guatemala or Honduras it is often easier to enter Belize by **boat**. **Local airlines** Maya Island Air and Tropic Air operate daily flights from Flores, Guatemala to Belize City, though at the time of

LAND AND SEA ROUTES TO BELIZE

Belize has **two land border crossings**: one from Santa Elena to Chetumal, Mexico (see box, p.90), and one from Benque Viejo del Carmen to Melchor de Mencos, Guatemala (see box, p.101).

There are also **sea routes** to Belize from Guatemala and Honduras. Daily skiffs travel to and from Punta Gorda, in the far south, and Puerto Barrios, Guatemala. Dangriga (see p.105) and Placencia (see p.110), on the southern coast, are served by at least one weekly skiff from Puerto Cortés, Honduras.

writing, this service had been temporarily, but indefinitely, discontinued.

VISAS

Citizens of Australia, Canada, the EU, New Zealand, the UK and the US do not need **visas** for stays in Belize of up to **thirty days**. Citizens of most other countries – with the exception of cruise-ship passengers – must purchase visas (US$50; valid for up to 90 days) in advance from a Belizean consulate or embassy (see p.49 for contact details).

GETTING AROUND

Belize only has three major paved highways (the Northern, Western and Southern), but the majority of the country is well served by **public transport**. The unpaved side roads are sometimes in poor repair, though they are usually passable except in the worst rainstorms.

By bus

Buses are the cheapest, and most efficient, way to travel in Belize – nearly all towns are connected, and the longest trip in the country (Belize City to Punta Gorda; 5–8hr) costs only Bz$25. The main towns are served by fast and comfortable **express buses**, which stop only at the towns' terminals. For villages off the main highways, however, you'll have to rely on slower **local services**, often with just one bus a day running Monday to Saturday only. These buses are brightly painted, recycled North American school buses, which will pick up and drop off anywhere along the roadside. The most frequent services operate along the Western and Northern highways, usually from very early in the morning to mid-evening. The Hummingbird and Southern highways, to Dangriga, Placencia and Punta Gorda, are not quite so well provided for, though services are improving. **Tickets** are purchased from the conductor.

By car

In the most remote parts of Belize bus services will probably only operate once a day, if at all, and unless you have your own transport (expensive), **hitching** is the only option. Though common among locals, it is important to remember that this practice is never completely safe. Otherwise, the main drawback is the shortage of traffic; if cars do pass they'll usually offer you a lift, though you may be expected to offer the driver some money in return.

All **taxis** in Belize are licensed, and can be identified by their green plates. They operate from special ranks in the centre of all mainland towns. There are no meters, so establish your fare in advance; within towns a Bz$6–7 **fixed rate** should apply. It is also possible to negotiate taxi rides between cities, though this option can be quite expensive: usually at least US$60–90 per person for a three-hour ride.

By bike

Cycling can be a great way to reach Belize's more isolated ruins and towns. **Bikes** are increasingly available for rent (usually Bz$15–25 per day), especially in San Ignacio and Placencia. Though biking along major highways is certainly possible, it is very uncommon, and drivers will not be watching for cyclists; it is therefore important to remain exceptionally alert during the day and to avoid cycling at night. You'll find repair shops in all towns. One thing to note, however, is that Belizean buses don't have roof racks, as they do in Guatemala; if there's room, the driver might let you take your bike onto the bus.

By boat

If you plan on visiting the cayes, you'll have to travel by **boat**, which will likely be a fast **skiff**, usually partially covered, though sometimes open to the elements (bring a raincoat). **Tickets** (usually Bz$25–45) cannot be purchased in advance for domestic routes, so it's worth showing up a half-hour before your departure time, though there's usually plenty of room. Numerous skiffs run daily between Belize City, Caye Caulker and Ambergris Caye, and also connect Ambergris Caye with Corozal.

By air

Though quite expensive, some budget travellers do choose to travel by **air**, as flights are not only much faster than buses, but also connect destinations unreachable by road. Maya Island Air (☎223-1140, ⍟www.mayaairways .com) and Tropic Air (☎226-2012, ⍟www.tropicair.com) each operate numerous daily flights from the Belize City Municipal Airport to San Pedro, Ambergris Caye (20min; US$32) and Caye Caulker (8min; US$32). Together, they operate at least ten daily flights from Belize City to Dangriga (15min; US$38), Placencia (35min; US$72), and Punta Gorda (1hr; US$93) and at least five daily flights between San Pedro and Corozal (25min; US$41).

ACCOMMODATION

Belizean **accommodation** is expensive by Central American standards, but there are nonetheless plenty of budget hotels in all towns, and the most popular tourist destinations – Caye Caulker, San Ignacio, Placencia – have a great deal of choice and are often less expensive than the rest of the country. **Finding a room** is usually no problem, though at Christmas, New Year and Easter booking ahead is advisable.

Hostels are uncommon in Belize, though some dormitory accommodation (usually US$10–15; ❷–❸) is available in Belize City, Caye Caulker, Dangriga, Placencia, San Ignacio and San Pedro. Most budget travellers rely instead on **budget hotels**, which usually charge US$15–30 (❸–❺) for a double, depending on the city. Check out Toucan Trail (ⓦwww.toucantrail.com), which lists over 130 good-value places to stay for under US$60, for ideas.

There are also few proper **campsites** in the country, and those that do exist have only the most basic services. Some mid-priced hotels in smaller villages and on the coast will allow you to pitch a tent on their grounds, but this can be shockingly expensive, and is impossible in San Pedro. In order to camp in any protected area, you'll have to get permission from park authorities – except at the entrances to the Mountain Pine Ridge Forest Reserve and the Jaguar Reserve, where reservations usually are not necessary. In the south, a tent is handy if you plan on spending time wandering inland around the Maya villages and ancient sites.

See p.35 for an explanation of the accommodation price codes used in this guide.

FOOD AND DRINK

Belizean food is a mix of Latin American and Caribbean, with Creole flavours dominating the scene in local restaurants, but with a number of international options as well – Indian and Chinese are the most prevalent. The basis of any Creole main meal is **rice and beans**, and this features heavily in smaller restaurants, where most meals run Bz$6–10. The white rice and red beans are cooked together in coconut oil and usually served with stewed chicken or beef, or fried fish; there's always a bottle of hot sauce on the table for extra spice. **Seafood** is almost always excellent. Red snapper or grouper is invariably fantastic, and you might also try a barracuda steak, conch fritters or a plate of fresh shrimp. In San Pedro, Caye Caulker, San Ignacio and Placencia the food can be exceptional, and the only concern is that you might get bored with **lobster**, which is served in a vast array of dishes. The **closed season** for lobster (when it should not be served) is from mid-February to mid-June.

Breakfast (Bz$4–8) is usually served from 7am to 10am and will likely include eggs and flour tortillas. The **lunch hour** (noon–1pm) is observed with almost religious devotion – you will not be able to get anything else done. **Dinner** is usually eaten quite early, between 6 and 8pm; few restaurants stay open much later.

Vegetables are scarce in Creole food, but there's often a side dish of potato or coleslaw. There are few specifically **vegetarian** restaurants, but in well-touristed areas many places offer a couple of vegetarian dishes. Otherwise, you're likely to be offered chicken or ham even if you say you don't eat meat. Your best bet for a vegetarian meal outside the main tourist areas may well be one of Belize's many Chinese restaurants.

Drink

The most basic drinks to accompany food are water, beer and the usual soft drinks. Tap **water**, in the towns at least, is safe but highly chlorinated, and many villages (though not Caye Caulker) have a potable water system. Many travellers nonetheless choose to purchase filtered bottled water, which is sold everywhere for around Bz$2 per bottle. Belikin, Belize's main **beer**, comes in several varieties: regular, a lager-type bottled and draught beer; bottled stout; and Lighthouse and Premium, more expensive bottled brews. Cashew-nut and berry **wines** are bottled and sold in some villages, and you can also get hold of imported wine, though it's not cheap. Local **rum**, in both dark and clear varieties, is the best deal in Belizean alcohol. The legal drinking age for alcohol in Belize is 18.

Despite the number of citrus plantations, **fruit juices** are rarely available, though you can usually get very good fresh orange juice and sometimes pineapple. **Coffee**, except in the best establishments, will almost certainly be instant, though decent **tea** is quite prevalent. One last drink that deserves a mention is **seaweed**, a strange blend of seaweed, milk, cinnamon, sugar and cream.

CULTURE AND ETIQUETTE

Belizeans are generally welcoming and accustomed to tourists, though it's important to remember that the country is, on the whole, quite **conservative**. Dress, except among professionals, is usually casual, though tourists – especially women – who wear revealing clothing will probably be looked down upon, particularly in the country's many churches.

The country's laid-back attitude usually carries over into conversation; when approaching Belizeans, it's best to be friendly, relaxed and patient. **Women travellers** may receive advances from local men. Ignoring such attentions completely will sometimes only be met by greater persistence; walking away

KRIOL WORDS AND PHRASES

Good morning Gud maanin
What's up? Weh di go aan?
What's your name? Weh yu naym?
My name is … Mee naym …
How are you? Da how yu di du?
Fine Aarait.
What time is it? Weh taim yu gat?
How much does this cost? Humoch dis kaas?
I don't understand Mee noh andastan.
I don't know Mee noh know.
Where am I? Weh I deh?
It doesn't matter Ih noh mata.

while flashing a quick smile and wave usually gets the message across, while remaining polite.

Belizeans are not particularly accepting of **homosexuality** and rarely open about sexual orientation. Though it is unlikely that locals will express disapproval, it is a good idea to avoid public displays of affection. There are no gay venues in the country.

Belizeans rarely **tip**, though foreigners are usually expected to give around ten percent in taxis and in restaurants. **Haggling** is also uncommon in Belize and will likely be considered rude, except at street markets.

SPORTS AND OUTDOOR ACTIVITIES

Football (soccer) and **basketball** are very popular in Belize, though the country's size and resources limit teams to the semi-professional level, and visitors will find few spectator events.

However, Belize is a haven for a wide range of **outdoor activities**. Many travellers will participate in some form of **water sports**, including snorkelling, diving, windsurfing, kayaking and sailing. Companies in San Pedro, Caye Caulker, and Placencia offer diving courses and lead multi-day kayaking and sailing trips to the cayes. See p.78, p.74 and p.108, respectively, for information about local operators. Inland, canoeing and rafting are popular, particularly out west in the Cayo district. Also in this region, operators organize hiking trips through the local jungle and Mountain Pine Ridge Forest, as well as horseriding to Maya ruins and natural sights. Stunning cave systems dot the south and west and spelunking tours are becoming more widespread and popular. See p.95 for operator listings in San Ignacio.

COMMUNICATIONS

Though more efficient (and expensive) than the rest of Central America, Belize postal services can still be unreliable. Most towns have post offices, usually open Monday to Thursday 8am to 4pm and Friday 8am to 5pm. Sending letters, cards and parcels home is straightforward: a normal airmail letter takes around four days to reach the US (Bz$0.60), eight to Europe (Bz$0.80) and two weeks to Australia (Bz$1).

Belize has a modern phone system, with payphones plentiful throughout the country. Payphones can only be used with phonecards, which are widely available from BTL (Belize Telecommunications Limited) offices, as well as hotels, shops and gas stations. There are no area codes in Belize; so you need to dial all seven digits. Calling home collect is easy using the Home Country Direct

service, available at BTL offices, most payphones and larger hotels – simply dial the access code (printed on some payphones and in the phone book) to connect with an operator in your home country. Mobile phones are becoming quite common in Belize, and almost all of the country receives excellent service. North Americans can usually connect to local systems with their regular service, albeit at very high roaming charges. Alternatively, BTL sells SIM cards to visitors with compatible international phones and can usually help find rental mobile phones for around Bz$20 a day.

Belizeans are also avid users of the internet, and web access is readily available in all the main towns and for guests at many hotels, though it can be quite expensive in touristed areas – up to Bz$12 an hour.

CRIME AND SAFETY

Though Belize does have a relatively high crime rate, general crime against tourists is rare, especially in comparison to other Central American countries, and violent crime against tourists is seldom experienced, even in Belize City. It is important to note, however, that several attacks on tourist groups have occurred in recent years near the Guatemalan border, though most tour operators now take precautions to prevent this. Elsewhere in the country, theft does occur, the majority of cases involving break-ins at hotels: bear this in mind when you're searching for a room. Out and about there's always

BELIZE ON THE NET

ⓦ www.belizeaudubon.org The latest information on Belize's growing number of reserves, national parks and associated visitor centres.

ⓦ www.belizefirst.com Online magazine dedicated to Belize, featuring accurate reviews and articles about hotels, restaurants and destinations.

ⓦ www.belizenet.com Excellent website with numerous links to tourism-related websites.

ⓦ www.spear.org.bz In-depth information on social, cultural, political and economic matters concerning Belize.

ⓦ www.travelbelize.org Belize's official tourism website offers excellent advice on travelling in Belize and can even help book accommodation and tours.

a slight danger of **pickpockets**, but with a bit of common sense you've nothing to fear. **Verbal abuse** is not uncommon, especially in Belize City. The vast majority of this harassment is harmless, though the situation can be more threatening for **women travelling alone**; most hecklers, however, will be satisfied with a smile and wave as you move quickly onwards. When making new acquaintances, women travellers should also keep in mind that there have been reports of incidences involving date-rape drugs in Belize, and should not accept food or drink from strangers. If you do need to **report a crime**, your first stop should be the newly appointed tourism police, ubiquitous in Belize City and becoming more common in many tourist hotspots, including Caye Caulker, Ambergris Caye and Placencia.

Many of the country's violent crimes are related to the **drug trade**, of which Belize is an important link in the chain between South and North America. Marijuana, cocaine and crack are all readily available, and whether you like it or not you'll receive regular offers. All such substances are **illegal**, and despite the fact that dope is smoked openly in the streets, the police do arrest people for possession of marijuana – they particularly enjoy catching tourists. If you are arrested you'll probably spend a couple of days in jail and pay a fine of several hundred US dollars: expect no sympathy from your embassy.

MEDICAL CARE AND EMERGENCIES

Health standards in Belize are quite high for the region, and Belize City has **hospitals** as well as a number of

EMERGENCY NUMBERS

Emergency ☎90 or 911
Tourist police (in Belize City)
☎227-2222

private physicians (see p.74). All other large towns have well-stocked **pharmacies** and **clinics**, which are usually free, though many will expect a donation for their services.

INFORMATION AND MAPS

Information on travelling in Belize is abundant, though often only available online, as even some major towns (except Belize City, Punta Gorda, Placencia and San Pedro) don't have a local tourist information centre. The office of the country's official source of tourist information, the **Belize Tourism Board** (BTB; ☎227-2420, ⓦwww.travelbelize.org), is in Belize City and is not particularly helpful, though the Board's website is excellent. The **Belize Tourism Industry Association** (BTIA; ⓦwww.btia.org), which regulates many of the country's tourism businesses, has helpful representatives in touristed areas.

Local **maps** can be difficult to find and are often non-existent in smaller towns and villages (where most streets won't have names), though the better hotels will usually be able to provide them to guests.

MONEY AND BANKS

The national currency is the **Belize dollar**, which is divided into 100 cents and fixed at two to one with the US dollar (US$1=Bz$2); US dollars are also widely accepted (sometimes preferred), either in cash or traveller's cheques. On account of this dual-currency system, always check whether the price you are quoted is in Belizean or US dollars; we have noted prices in local currency unless an operation has specifically quoted their fees in US dollars.

Credit and debit cards are widely used in Belize and are increasingly accepted, even in smaller hotels and restaurants. Visa is the best option, though many establishments also accept MasterCard. Before you pay, check if there's a charge for using plastic, as you might have to pay an extra five or seven percent for the privilege. Any bank can give you a Visa/MasterCard **cash advance**, but Atlantic Bank, Belize Bank and First Caribbean Bank are the only banks with **ATMs** that accept foreign-issued cards.

Taxes in Belize are quite high; both the sales tax and hotel tax are 9 percent. Leaving Belize, you'll have to pay a US$15 **exit tax**, plus a PACT conservation fee of US$3.75; add US$15 if you are flying out of the country.

You'll find at least one **bank** in every town. Although the exchange rate is fixed, banks in Belize will give slightly less than Bz$2 for US$1 for both cash and traveller's cheques, so it can be a good idea simply to pay in US dollars if they are accepted and if you have them. Other than banks, only licensed *casas de cambio*, which can be difficult to find, are allowed to **exchange currency**, though there's usually a shop where locals go. To buy US dollars, you'll have to show an onward ticket.

OPENING HOURS AND HOLIDAYS

It's difficult to be specific about **opening hours** in Belize but in general most **shops** are open 8am to noon and 1pm to 5pm. The **lunch hour** (noon–1pm) is almost universally observed. Some shops and businesses work a half-day on Saturday, and everything is liable to close early on Friday. **Banks** (generally Mon–Thurs 8am–2pm, Fri 8am–4pm) and government offices are only open Monday to Friday. Watch out for **Sundays**, too, when shops and restaurants outside tourist areas are likely to be closed, and fewer bus services and internal flights operate. Archeological sites, however, are open every day. The main **public holidays**, when virtually everything will be closed, are listed in the box

> ## PUBLIC HOLIDAYS
>
> **January 1** New Year's Day
> **March 9** Baron Bliss Day
> **March/April (variable)** Good Friday, Holy Saturday, Easter Monday
> **May 1** Labour Day
> **May 24** Commonwealth Day
> **September 10** St George's Caye Day/National Day
> **September 21** Independence Day
> **October 12** Columbus Day (Pan America Day)
> **November 19** Garífuna Settlement Day
> **December 25** Christmas Day
> **December 26** Boxing Day

above, though note that if the holiday falls mid-week, it is observed on the following Monday.

FESTIVALS

Belize's calendar is full of **festivals**, ranging from the local to the national. The calendar below only includes a few highlights – you'll find plenty of entertainment at any given time.

February Carnival is celebrated with dancing, parades, costumes and drinking.
March Celebrations throughout the country in honour of Baron Bliss Day (March 9); La Ruta Maya River Challenge in San Ignacio.
April Fiesta in San Jose Succotz honouring the village's patron saint.
May Cashew Festival in Crooked Tree; Toledo Cacao-Fest in Punta Gorda; National Agriculture and Trade Show in Belmopan.
June Coconut Festival in Caye Caulker; three-day Día de San Pedro festival in San Pedro; Placencia Lobster Festival.
July Caye Caulker Lobster Fest.
August Week-long Deer Dance Festival in San Antonio; Costa Maya festival in San Pedro.
September Celebrations commemorating St George's Caye Day and Independence Day.
November Garífuna Settlement Day (Nov 19) is the most important day on the Garífuna calendar (see box, p.103).

Belize City

Even to the most jaded cosmopolite **BELIZE CITY** – the country's largest city, though not the capital – can be a daunting place. Dilapidated wooden buildings stand right on the edge of the road, offering pedestrians little refuge from the ever-increasing traffic, and local attention ranges from simple curiosity and good-natured joking to outright heckling. Still, travellers who approach the city with an open mind – and those who are willing to spend more than a few hours here – may actually enjoy themselves. The streets, which certainly are chaotic, buzz with energy, the result of the diversity of the city's 75,000 citizens. And the city is, without a doubt, an experience; those who manage to feel comfortable here should have no problems anywhere else in the country.

What to see and do

Belize City is divided into northern and southern halves by **Haulover Creek**, a branch of the Belize River. The pivotal (literally) point of the city centre is the manually operated **Swing Bridge**, always crawling with traffic and opened twice a day (5.30am & 5.30pm) to allow larger vessels up and down the river. **North** of the bridge is the slightly more upmarket part of town, home to the most expensive hotels. **South** of the Swing Bridge is the market and commercial zone, home to the city's banks and a couple of supermarkets. It's all compact enough that **walking** is the easiest way to get around.

Image Factory

The **Image Factory**, north of the Swing Bridge at 91 N Front St (Mon–Fri 9am–5pm; free, but donations welcome; ☎223-4093, ⓦwww.imagefactory.bz), hosts displays by Belize's hottest contemporary artists. The gallery holds outstanding, frequently provocative exhibitions, and you often get a chance to chat with the artists themselves.

Tourism Village

Continuing east along North Front Street, you'll encounter an advance guard of trinket sellers, street musicians, hustlers and hair-braiders, announcing you're near **Tourism Village**, Belize's **cruise ship terminal**. The Village itself is little more than a dock for the boats to disembark their passengers, and an attached shopping mall. Across the street, the **Fort Street Plaza** serves as an extension of the Village and includes a restaurant, bar and additional shops. A number of temporary vendors line the streets in this area, though the items tend to be overpriced; you're better off buying souvenirs in town or at the National Handicraft Center (see p.71).

SAFETY IN BELIZE CITY

Walking in Belize City in daylight is perfectly safe if you use common sense: be civil, don't provoke trouble by arguing too forcefully and never show large sums of money on the street. Women should dress conservatively: female travellers, especially those wearing short shorts or skirts, will likely attract mild verbal harassment from local men. However, the presence of a specially trained tourism police (☎227-2222), together with the legal requirement that all tour guides be licensed, generally prevent serious crime.

The chances of being mugged do increase after dark, but you'll find that you can walk – with others – around the centre in relative safety; you'll certainly encounter tourism police in this area. If you're venturing further afield, or if you've just arrived by bus at night, travel by taxi.

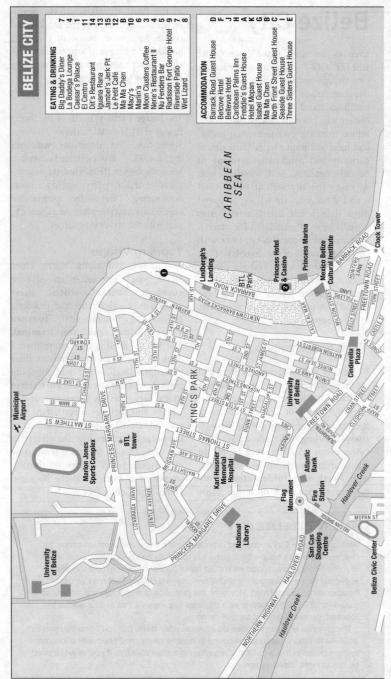

BELIZE CITY

EATING & DRINKING
Big Daddy's Diner	7
La Bodega Lounge	4
Caesar's Palace	1
El Centro	11
Dit's Restaurant	14
Iguana Rana	13
Jambel's Jerk Pit	15
Le Petit Café	12
Ma Ma Chen	B
Macy's	10
Marlin's	6
Moon Clusters Coffee	3
Nerie's Restaurant II	4
Nu Fenders Bar	5
Radisson Fort George Hotel	9
Riverside Patio	7
Wet Lizard	8

ACCOMMODATION
Barrack Road Guest House	D
Belcove Hotel	F
Bellevue Hotel	J
Caribbean Palms Inn	H
Freddie's Guest House	A
Hotel Mopan	K
Isabel Guest House	G
Ma Ma Chen	B
North Front Street Guest House	C
Seaside Guest House	I
Three Sisters Guest House	E

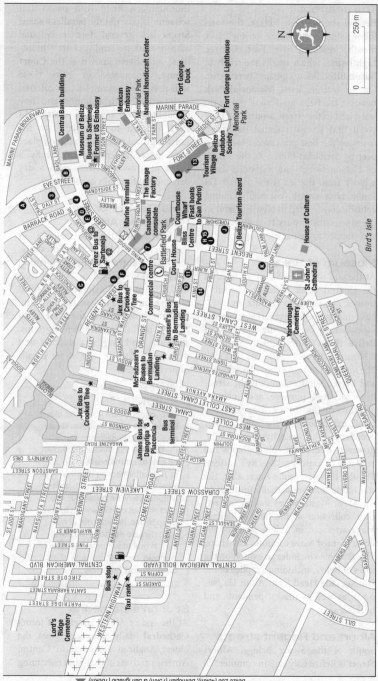

BELIZE

BELIZE CITY

N

0   250 m

MARINE PARADE BOULEVARD

Central Bank building

Museum of Belize
Buses to Sarteneja
Former US Embassy

Mexican
Embassy

Memorial Park
National Handicraft Center

MARINE PARADE

Fort George Dock

Fort George Lighthouse
Memorial Park

EVE STREET

CORK   STREET

DREDGE ST

9

12

FORT STREET

Tourism
Village

Belize
Audubon
Society

13

8

BARRACK ROAD

HANDYSIDE ST

BRIDES ALLEY

The Image
Factory

Marine Terminal

NORTH FRONT STREET

Canadian
consulate

7

Courthouse
Wharf
(Fast boats
to San Pedro)

FORESHORE

Belize Tourism Board

Battlefield Park

Perez Bus to Sarteneja

SWING BRIDGE

Commercial centre

Court House

Bliss
Centre

H 15

REGENT STREET

Jex Bus to Crooked Tree

Bagdad St

ORANGE ST

CHURCH ST

BISHOP ST

PRINCE ST

SOUTH ST

House of Culture

McFadzean's Buses to Bermudian Landing

Russell's Bus to Bermudian Landing

10 11

KING ST

14

ALBERT STREET

DEAN ST

St John's
Cathedral

K

Bird's Isle

Jex Bus to Crooked Tree

WOODS ST

JOHNSON ST

MAGAZINE ROAD

WEST CANAL STREET

Yarborough
Cemetery

James Bus for Dangriga & Placencia

Bus terminal

WELCH ST

CANAL STREET

EAST COLLET CANAL STREET

AMARA AVENUE

EUPHRATES AVENUE

CURASSOW STREET

WEST COLLET

Collet Canal

VERNON STREET

LAKEVIEW STREET

CEMETERY ROAD

BANAK STREET

CENTRAL AMERICAN BOULEVARD

FAIRWEATHER ST

Lord's
Ridge
Cemetery

WESTERN HIGHWAY

Bus stop

Taxi rank

GILL STREET

▼ Belize Zoo (46km), Belmopan (75km) & San Ignacio (106km)

67

The seafront

Beyond the Tourism Village, the road follows the north shore of the river mouth, reaching the **Fort George Lighthouse**, which marks the tomb of **Baron Bliss**, Belize's greatest benefactor. On the seafront itself, **Memorial Park** honours the Belizean dead of the world wars, and in the streets around the park you'll find several colonial mansions, many of the best preserved now taken over by upmarket hotels. At the corner of Hutson Street and Gabourel Lane a block from the sea is the former **US Embassy**: a superb "colonial" building actually constructed in New England in the nineteenth century then dismantled and shipped to Belize.

Museum of Belize

At the end of Queen Street, in front of the Central Bank building, the city's former colonial prison, built in 1857, has undergone a remarkable transformation to become the **Museum of Belize** (Mon–Thurs 8.30am–5pm, Fri 8.30am–4.30pm; Bz$10; ☎223-4524). The lower floor, with exposed brickwork and barred windows, recalls the structure's original purpose and includes a reconstruction of a cell as well as a small exhibition on the jail's former occupants. The majority of the floor, however, is devoted to photographs and artefacts chronicling the city's history. Though these are quite interesting, the star attractions are actually upstairs, in the Maya Masterpieces gallery: a first-class collection of the best of Belize's Maya artefacts, including some of the finest painted Maya ceramics anywhere. This floor also includes an exhibit on the jades of Belize, including a replica of the famous **Jade Head** from Altun Ha (see p.83), as well as masks, pendants and necklaces.

Albert and Regent streets

South of the Swing Bridge, **Albert Street** is Belize City's main commercial thoroughfare, lined with banks and souvenir shops. On the parallel **Regent Street** are several former colonial administration and court buildings, collectively known as the **Court House**. Completed in 1926, these well-preserved examples of colonial architecture, with columns and fine wrought iron, overlook **Battlefield Park** (named to commemorate the noisy political meetings that took place here before independence), really a patch of grass and trees with a dry ornamental fountain in the centre.

Bliss Centre for the Performing Arts

A block behind the Court House, on the waterfront at 2 Southern Foreshore, the **Bliss Centre for the Performing Arts** (Mon–Fri 8am–5pm; free; ☎227-2110) hosts exhibitions of local artwork and has a 600-seat auditorium. Performances usually showcase local talent, including children's groups, solo acts and Garífuna dancers and drummers. Call or stop by for details of performances.

> **BARON BLISS**
> Throughout Belize you'll find places bearing the name of Baron Bliss, an eccentric Englishman with a Portuguese title. A keen fisherman, he arrived off the coast of Belize in 1926 after hearing that the local waters were rich with game. Unfortunately, he became ill and died without ever making it ashore. Despite this, he left most of his considerable estate to the colony and, in gratitude, the authorities declared March 9, the date of his death, Baron Bliss Day.

St John's Cathedral

At the end of Albert Street is **St John's Cathedral** (daily 6am–6pm; free), the oldest Anglican cathedral in Central America and one of the oldest remaining buildings in Belize. Begun in 1812, its red bricks were brought over as ballast in British ships – it does look more like a large English parish church than most of the other buildings here.

House of Culture

East of the cathedral, on the seafront, the renovated former Government House, now renamed the **House of Culture** (Mon–Sat 8.30am–4.30pm; Bz$10), is one of the most beautiful spots in Belize City, with its manicured lawns and sea views. Built in 1814, the structure served as the British governor's residence until Belizean independence in 1981. The main room downstairs exhibits the possessions of former governors as well as colonial silverware, glasses and furniture; temporary historical and cultural exhibitions are also on this floor. Upstairs are rooms for painting, dance and drumming workshops, art exhibits and musical performances.

Arrival and information

By air International flights land at Phillip Goldson International Airport, 17km northwest of the city. Taxis are the only way to get into town (with the exception of hitchhiking); they cost Bz$50. There's a branch of the Belize Bank (with ATM) in the terminal. Domestic flights come and go from the municipal airport, a few kilometres north of town on the edge of the sea; taxis from here to the city centre charge Bz$8.
By boat Boats to and from the cayes pull in at either the Marine Terminal on the north side of the Swing Bridge or at Courthouse Wharf on the south side.
By bus Bus services terminate at various points throughout the city centre, but all buses will stop – at least briefly – at the main bus terminal at 19 West Collet Canal (☎227-2255), which is in a fairly derelict area on the western side of the city. It's only 1km or so from the centre, so you can walk to any of the recommended hotels, but take a taxi at night.
Tourist information The Belize Tourism Board (BTB; Mon–Fri 8am–5pm; ☎223-1913) is on the corner of Regent and South streets. Visiting here is not particularly helpful, but the office does hand out city maps, hotel guides and brochures;

they can also recommend tour guides for nearby sights. Inside the Marine Terminal, the Kaisa International shop has reliable information on bus and boat schedules, and sells tickets for the express buses to Chetumal, Flores and Guatemala City.

City transport

Walking The best way to get around Belize City's compact centre is on foot; even going from one side to the other should only take around 15min. Buses do not operate within the centre, running only to the city's outskirts, and are, therefore, unnecessary for most visitors.
Taxis Identified by green licence plates, taxis charge Bz$5–7 for one or two passengers within the city limits.

Accommodation

Accommodation in Belize City is generally more expensive than elsewhere in the country, so prices for even budget rooms can come as quite a shock. There's usually no need to book in advance unless you're eager to stay in a particular hotel – you'll always be able to get something in the price range you're looking for. Keep in mind, however, that the further south and west you go, the more dangerous the area becomes; if you are travelling alone you may want to stay north of the river near Queen Street, the city's most populated area.

North of the river

Barrack Road Guest House 8 Barrack Rd ☎624-8786. Set back from the road down a winding alley, this basic guesthouse offers decent, if somewhat shabby, rooms with private baths and fans. ❷ .
Freddie's Guest House 86 Eve St, on the city's edge near the waterfront ☎233-3851. Three clean and comfortable fan-cooled rooms, one with private bath. ❹
Ma Ma Chen 7 Eve St, near the end of Queen St ☎223-1913. A Taiwanese couple runs this quiet, simple guesthouse/restaurant. Very basic rooms (some with a/c and private bath) line a hallway in the family home. ❺
North Front Street Guest House 124 North Front St, two blocks from Marine Terminal ☎227-7595, ✉thoth@btl.net. Rooms in this budget travellers' favourite are small and basic but clean; all share cold-water showers. ❸
Three Sisters Guest House 36 Queen St ☎203-5729. Large, clean rooms (one with private bath) in a wooden building run by a friendly, mainly Spanish-speaking family. Single ❸ , doubles ❺

South of the river

Belcove Hotel 9 Regent St West ☎227-3054, ⓦwww.belcove.com. Basic, very clean rooms, some with a/c and private bath. Although it's on the edge of the dangerous part of town, the hotel itself is quite safe. Singles ④, doubles ⑤–⑦

Bellevue Hotel 5 Southern Foreshore ☎227-7051, ⓔbellevue@btl.net. Large hotel directly on the seafront with both renovated and unrenovated rooms, all with private baths and some with a/c. The courtyard contains a pool and bar, and there's a bar and disco that open sporadically on weekends. ⑥–⑦

Caribbean Palms Inn 26 Regent St, at the corner with King St ☎227-0472, ⓔcpalms@hotmail.com. Somewhat large hotel where a/c rooms all have private baths and some have TVs. Meals can be arranged, and there's internet access and laundry service. One shared budget room (Bz$36 per person). ⑥–⑧

Hotel Mopan 55 Regent St ☎227-7351, ⓦwww.hotelmopan.com. Wood-fronted building with recently renovated rooms, all with private bath and some with a/c, TV and balcony. Restaurant serves good-value breakfasts (other meals can be ordered) and internet access for guests is Bz$8/hr. ⑤–⑥

Isabel Guest House 3 Albert St, 2nd floor ☎207-3139. Follow the signs from the Swing Bridge to this small guesthouse offering large rooms with private baths and small refrigerators. Singles ⑤, doubles ⑥

Seaside Guest House 3 Prince St, half a block from the Southern Foreshore ☎227-8339, ⓔseasidebelize@btl.net. Clean, social, very safe hotel. Rooms, including dorm beds (Bz$40 per person), are expensive but worth it for the services: internet access for Bz$10/hr, good tourist information and a balcony facing the sea. Breakfast is available, and other meals can be arranged. Dorms ④, singles ④, doubles ⑥

Eating

Belize City's selection of restaurants is quite varied, though simple Creole fare (rice and beans) still predominates at the lower end of the price scale. Be warned that many restaurants close early in the evening and on Sundays. The city's largest supermarkets, Romac's and Brodie's, are on Albert Street, and are quite expensive, as most of the selection is imported.

North of the river

Le Petit Café Cork St, at the *Radisson Hotel*. Outdoor tables make *Le Petit* a great place to enjoy a genuine café atmosphere. Good coffee and baked treats, including croissants, for Bz$2–6.

Ma Ma Chen 7 Eve St ☎223-4568. Simple restaurant with tasty Taiwanese fare, including spring rolls for Bz$6 and other vegetarian dishes for Bz$8. See p.69 for the adjoining guesthouse.

Moon Clusters Coffee 36 Daly St. One of the only true coffee shops in Belize City. Relax in the bright and quirky interior with an excellent cup for Bz$5 or a coffee drink for Bz$8.

Nerie's Restaurant II At the corner of Queen and Daly sts ☎223-4028. Great Belizean food at reasonable prices: main dishes run from Bz$5 for rice and beans to Bz$12 for fish. The conch soup is a meal in itself.

Wet Lizard Fort St, next to the Tourism Village ☎203-0400. Great views overlooking the sea make for a tourist-dominated clientele. The diverse menu includes tangy spring rolls, Thai and Mexican specialities and seafood. Main dishes Bz$10–20. Open only when cruise ships are in.

South of the river

Big Daddy's Diner Upstairs in the market building; follow the signs. Excellent breakfasts and Belizean dishes, with a daily lunch special (usually fish) for Bz$12, served cafeteria-style.

El Centro 4 Bishop St ☎227-2013. For those who need a break from rice and beans, this large restaurant serves a variety of fried foods and burgers at lunch (Bz$5–10) and chicken and steak dishes at dinner (Bz$12–20).

Dit's Restaurant 50 King St. A variety of Belizean and Mexican snacks (Bz$3–10) in a no-frills atmosphere. A great place for dessert, as well as a filling breakfast.

Jambel's Jerk Pit 2B King St ☎227-6080. Very tasty Jamaican-influenced and Belizean dishes. Specialities include the obvious jerk chicken, but also delicious, spicy seafood dishes such as jerk lobster. Main dishes Bz$10–24.

Macy's 18 Bishop St ☎207-3410. Long-established, reasonably priced Creole restaurant popular with locals and busy at lunchtime. The menu includes a variety of fish, including whole sea bass, and game dishes for Bz$8–18.

Marlin's 11 Regent St West, next to the *Belcove Hotel*. Great, inexpensive local food served in large portions on a veranda overlooking the river. Traditional rice and beans, soups or breakfasts Bz$5–8.

Drinking and nightlife

Belize City's nightlife really comes into its own on Fridays and Saturdays; any other night of the week, you'll likely find the city deserted after 9pm, with only a few hard-drinking (and often rowdy) locals frequenting the bars that are open. On weekends, however, there are plenty of venues around, playing everything from techno to Latin grooves to punta, soca and reggae, though even then don't arrive much before midnight, or you'll find many places empty. A relatively safe area of town with a variety of bars/clubs is the strip of Barracks Newtown Road from the *Princess Hotel* (T 223-0638, w www .princessbelize.com) to *Caesar's Palace* bar.

Bars

La Bodega Lounge Upstairs from *Nerie's Restaurant*, at the corner of Queen and Daly sts. Hosts a popular karaoke night on Fri and Caribbean music on Sat.
Iguana Rana In the Tourism Village. Most of the time a relaxed bar frequented by tourists, but on Fri nights locals take over to dance and sip cocktails next to the sea.
Nu Fenders Bar At the corner of Queen and Daly sts, opposite *Nerie's*. A relatively tame place to catch a drink with the locals almost any night of the week, though it's packed and rowdy on weekends.
Riverside Patio Regent St, next to the market building. Come here to have a beer with hard-drinking locals and watch the sun go down. Closes at 7pm.

Clubs

Caesar's Palace Newtown Barracks Rd, across from BTL Park. An energetic crowd comes here to dance to Latin, techno and reggae beats here after 10pm on Fri and Sat.
Club Next In the *Princess Hotel*. A lively local favourite. DJs play a variety of music and the dancefloor is packed late on Fri and Sat nights. Bz$15 cover.

Entertainment

Bowling The *Princess Hotel*, on Newtown Barracks Rd, has a few lanes. There's also pool tables and an arcade.
Casino At the *Princess Hotel*, on Newtown Barracks Rd. Open daily noon–4pm, with a Bz$50 minimum.
Cinema At the *Princess Hotel*, on Newtown Barracks Rd. The only cinema in the city, it has one showing nightly of a recent Hollywood blockbuster. It is also the venue for Belize's Film Festival, held annually in March.
Performing arts The cultural centre of Belize is the Bliss Centre for the Performing Arts (see p.68), which stages a variety of events – everything from plays to concerts – in a 600-seat auditorium. The House of Culture (see p.69) also hosts exhibitions and events,

including classical concerts, in its intimate upstairs rooms. Both venues are affordable (shows range from free to Bz$30), but shows can be sporadic.

Shopping

Books Book Center, 2 Church St (Mon–Sat 8.30am–noon & 1.30–5.30pm; T 227-7457), and Angelus Press, 10 Queen St (Mon–Fri 7.30am– 5.30pm, Sat 8am–noon; T 223-5777), have a wide range of Belize-related books and maps.
Crafts and souvenirs For items like T-shirts, shells, wooden carvings and beaded jewellery, head to the Tourism Village (see p.65); Sing's, 35 Albert St; or the National Handicraft Center, 2 South Park St (Mon–Fri 8am–5pm, Sat 8am–4pm), which sells high-quality Belizean arts and crafts at fair prices. The shop at the Image Factory (see p.65) also offers good souvenirs, books and local art.
Pharmacies and supermarkets Albert St, south of the Swing Bridge, is the city's central commercial district. A number of pharmacies and supermarkets line the street, as well as a department store, Brodie's.

Directory

Consulates Current addresses and phone numbers can be found under "Diplomatic Listings" in the green pages of the telephone directory: Canada T 223-1060; Guatemala T 223-3150; Honduras T 224-5889; Mexico T 223-0193. Most are normally open Mon–Fri mornings. The US embassy (T 822-4011) and British High Commission (T 822-2146) are in Belmopan (see p.92).
Exchange The main banks have branches on Albert St (usually Mon–Thurs 8am–2pm, Fri 8am– 4.30pm). Only the Belize and First Caribbean banks have ATMs that accept foreign-issued cards; others will process cash advances over the counter. For Guatemalan quetzales and Mexican pesos try Kaisa International in the Marine Terminal.
Immigration In the Government Complex on Mahogany St, near the junction of Central American Blvd and the Western Highway (Mon–Thurs 8.30am–4pm, Fri 8.30am–3.30pm; T 222-4620). Thirty-day extensions of stay (the maximum allowed) cost US$12.50.
Internet Two centrally located establishments are Angelus Press (see above; Bz$3/hr) and Belize Photo Lab (see p.000; Bz$4/hr). Many hotels now offer internet access to guests as well.
Laundry G's Laundromat, 22 Dean St (daily 7.30am–6.30pm). Bz$5 wash, Bz$5 dry.
Medical care Dr Gamero, Myo-On Clinic, 40 Eve St (T 224-5616); Karl Huesner Memorial Hospital,

Princess Margaret Drive, near the junction with the Northern Highway (☎ 223-1548).

Police The main police station is on Queen St, a block north of the Swing Bridge (☎ 227-2210). Alternatively, contact the Tourism Police (see box, p.65).

Post office North Front St, opposite the Marine Terminal (Mon–Thur 8am–4.30pm, Fri 8am-5pm).

Telephones There are payphones (operated using pre-paid cards) dotted all around the city, or visit the main BTL office, 1 Church St (Mon–Sat 8am–6pm), which also has fax and email services.

Moving on

Some travellers do leave Belize City via boat or plane, but buses are by far the most common and cheapest way to move around the country.

By bus

Belize's main bus company is **National Transport Services Limited (NTSL)**, although the company's original name – Novelo's – still appears on some signs. Other, smaller companies also serve specific destinations. Most buses depart from the terminal at 19 West Collet Canal (☎ 227-2255), but many companies maintain independent stops in the streets nearby. Services operate seven days a week, though departure times may be erratic on Sun.

Bus companies and stops

James Bus (JA) Departs for Dangriga and Punta Gorda (via Belmopan) from the Shell station, Cemetery Rd, near the bus terminal. Information on ☎ 702-2049.

Jex Bus (JX) Departs for Crooked Tree from Regent St West (Mon–Sat 10.55am) and Pound Yard, Collet Canal (Mon–Fri 4.30pm). Information on ☎ 225-7017.

McFadzean's Bus (MF) Departs for Bermudian Landing (via Burrell Boom) from Euphrates Ave, off Orange St, near the main bus depot.

NTSL All services depart from the terminal. Information on ☎ 227-6372.

Perez Bus (PE) Departs for Sarteneja from North Front St (5pm).

Russell's Bus (RU) Departs for Bermudian Landing from Cairo St, near the corner of Cemetery Rd and Euphrates Ave.

Sarteneja Bus Company (SC) Departs for Sarteneja from the south side of the Swing Bridge.

Southern Transport (ST) Departs for the Hummingbird and Southern highways from the terminal. Information on ☎ 502-2160.

Western Transport (WT) Departs for the Western Highway from the terminal. Information on ☎ 227-1160.

Bus destinations

Belmopan With NTSL, JA, WT, ST. Departures hourly 5am–9pm (express); 1hr 15min.

Benque Viejo del Carmen With NTSL. Departures hourly 5am–9pm (express); 3hr 30min (for the Guatemalan border).

Bermudian Landing With MF, RU. Departures Mon–Sat noon, 4.30pm & 5.30pm; 1hr 15min.

Chetumal, Mexico With NTSL. Departures hourly 5am–7pm (express); 3hr 30min.

Corozal With NTSL. Departures hourly 5am–7pm (express); 2hr 30min.

Crooked Tree With JX. Departures Mon–Sat 10.55am & 4.30pm; 1hr 30min.

Dangriga With JA, NTSL. Twelve departures daily 6am–5pm (express); 2hr via Coastal Rd, 3hr 30min via Belmopan.

Gales Point With NTSL. Two departures weekly; 1hr 40min.

Orange Walk With NTSL. Departures hourly 5am–7pm (express); 1hr 30min.

Placencia With JA, NTSL. Four departures daily, via Belmopan and Dangriga; 5–7hr.

Punta Gorda With JA, ST. Twelve departures daily, all via Belmopan and Dangriga (express); 5–8hr.

San Ignacio With NTSL. Departures hourly 5am–9pm, via Belmopan; 2hr 30min.

Sarteneja With PE, SC. Three departures daily (10:30am, noon, 5pm), Mon–Sat only. The 10:30am and noon are with SC, the 5pm with PE.

Other transport

By air Domestic flights (see p.59) to all main towns leave from the Municipal Airport.

By boat Skiffs to Caye Caulker (45min) and Ambergris Caye (75min) are operated by the Caye Caulker Water Taxi Association (☎ 223-5752, ⓦ www.cayecaulkerwatertaxi.com) and depart from the Marine Terminal at least every 90min from 8am to 4pm daily. Triple J's runs slightly cheaper boats to Caye Caulker from Courthouse Wharf, on the south side of the Swing Bridge.

The cayes and atolls

Belize's spectacular **Barrier Reef**, with its dazzling variety of underwater life, string of exquisite **cayes** (pronounced "keys") and extensive opportunities for all kinds

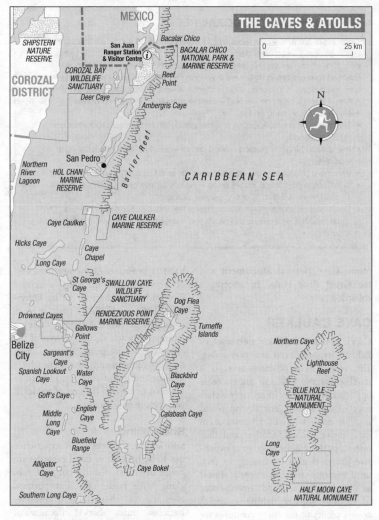

THE CAYES & ATOLLS

0   25 km

SHIPSTERN
NATURE
RESERVE

MEXICO

Bacalar Chico

San Juan
Ranger Station (i)
& Visitor Centre

BACALAR CHICO
NATIONAL PARK &
MARINE RESERVE

COROZAL BAY
WILDLIFE
SANCTUARY

COROZAL
DISTRICT

Reef
Point

Deer Caye

Ambergris Caye

N

Barrier Reef

San Pedro

Northern
River
Lagoon

HOL CHAN
MARINE
RESERVE

CARIBBEAN SEA

Barrier Reef

Caye Caulker

CAYE CAULKER
MARINE RESERVE

Hicks Caye

Long Caye

Caye
Chapel

St George's
Caye

SWALLOW CAYE
WILDLIFE
SANCTUARY

Dog Flea
Caye

Drowned Cayes

RENDEZVOUS POINT
MARINE RESERVE

Turneffe
Islands

Gallows
Point

Northern Caye

Belize
City

Sargeant's
Caye

Lighthouse
Reef

Spanish Lookout
Caye

Water
Caye

Blackbird
Caye

BLUE HOLE
NATURAL
MONUMENT

Goff's Caye

Middle
Long
Caye

English
Caye

Calabash Caye

Bluefield
Range

Long
Caye

Alligator
Caye

Caye Bokel

Southern Long Caye

HALF MOON CAYE
NATURAL MONUMENT

of water sports, is the country's main attraction for most first-time visitors. The longest barrier reef in the western hemisphere, it runs the entire length of the coastline, usually 15 to 40km from the mainland, with most of the cayes lying in shallow water behind the shelter of the reef. **Caye Caulker** is the most popular destination for budget travellers. The town of **San Pedro** on **Ambergris Caye**, meanwhile, has transformed from a predominantly fishing community to

one dominated by tourism. There are still some beautiful spots though, notably the protected sections of reef at either end of the caye: **Bacalar Chico National Park** and **Hol Chan Marine Reserve**.

Beyond the barrier reef are two of Belize's three **atolls**, the **Turneffe Islands** and **Lighthouse Reef**, regularly visited on day-trips from San Pedro and Caye Caulker. Lighthouse Reef encompasses two of the most spectacular diving and snorkelling sites in the country – **Half**

Moon Caye Natural Monument and the **Great Blue Hole**, an enormous collapsed cave.

CAYE CAULKER

CAYE CAULKER, 35km northeast of Belize City, is relaxed and easy-going. The **reef**, 1.5km offshore here, is a **marine reserve**, offering unbelievable opportunities for any imaginable watersport. Even so, in general, the island is affordable, with an abundance of inexpensive accommodation and tour operators, though the number of expensive places is also increasing. In fact, until recently, tourism existed almost as a sideline to the island's main source of income, **lobster fishing** – there's always plenty of the spiny creatures for the annual **Lobster Fest**, held in the third weekend of June to celebrate the opening of the season.

What to see and do

Caye Caulker is a little over 8km long. The settlement is at the southern end, which curves west like a hook; the northern tip, meanwhile, forms the **Caye Caulker Forest Reserve**, designated to protect the caye litoral forest, one of the rarest habitats in Belize. At the northern end of the village lies "**the Split**", a narrow (but widening) channel cut by Hurricane Hattie in 1961; it's a popular place to relax and swim. Although there's a reasonable beach along the front of the caye (created by pumping sand from the back of the island), the sea nearby is shallow and full of seagrass, so head to the Split or hop off the end of a dock if you want to go for a dip.

Snorkelling

Snorkelling the reef is an experience not to be missed; its coral canyons are home to an astonishing range of fish, along with eagle rays and perhaps even the odd shark (almost certainly harmless nurse sharks). Because of the reef's fragility, visits to the marine reserves and the reef itself must be accompanied by a licensed guide. **Trips** are easily arranged by the island's snorkel and dive shops – expect to pay US$20–25 per person for a half-day and US$40–50 for a full-day. Most day-trips stop at the reef as well as **Hol Chan Marine Reserve** (see p.79) and **Shark-Ray Alley**. See p.76 for listings of operators. It is possible to rent **sea kayaks** from several places on Front Street for

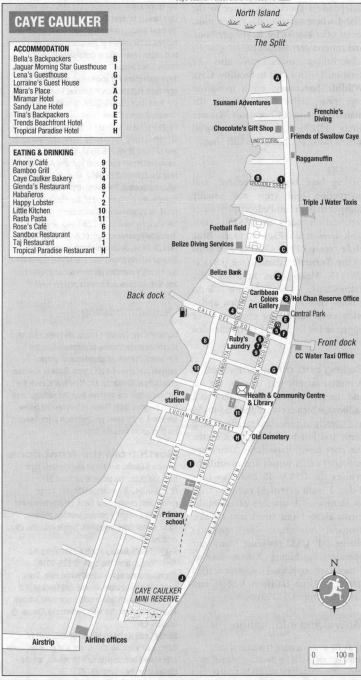

Caye Caulker Forest & Marine Reserve ▲

North Island

The Split

CAYE CAULKER

ACCOMMODATION
Bella's Backpackers	B
Jaguar Morning Star Guesthouse	I
Lena's Guesthouse	G
Lorraine's Guest House	J
Mara's Place	A
Miramar Hotel	C
Sandy Lane Hotel	D
Tina's Backpackers	E
Trends Beachfront Hotel	F
Tropical Paradise Hotel	H

EATING & DRINKING
Amor y Café	9
Bamboo Grill	3
Caye Caulker Bakery	4
Glenda's Restaurant	8
Habañeros	7
Happy Lobster	2
Little Kitchen	10
Rasta Pasta	11
Rose's Café	6
Sandbox Restaurant	5
Taj Restaurant	1
Tropical Paradise Restaurant	H

A

Tsunami Adventures

Frenchie's Diving

Chocolate's Gift Shop

Friends of Swallow Caye

LIND'S CORAL

Raggamuffin

B 1
CROCODILE STREET

Triple J Water Taxis

Football field

Belize Diving Services

D C 2

Belize Bank

Caribbean Colors Art Gallery

3 Hol Chan Reserve Office

Central Park

Back dock

CALLE DEL SOL

E
4
6 7
5 F

Front dock

Ruby's Laundry

9

CC Water Taxi Office

8

10

G

Fire station

Health & Community Centre & Library

11

LUCIANO REYES STREET

AVENIDA LANGOSTA

AVENIDA HICACO (FRONT STREET)

MIDDLE STREET

H Old Cemetery

I

Primary school

AVENIDA MANGLE (BACK STREET)

AVENIDA PUEBLO NUEVO

PLAYA ASUNCION

J

N

CAYE CAULKER MINI RESERVE

Airstrip   Airline offices

0   100 m

BELIZE

THE CAYES AND ATOLLS

independent snorkelling closer to the island, where some coral is visible; most shops offer kayaks for Bz$12 per hour, and snorkel gear for Bz$10.

Snorkelling tours can also be combined with a visit to **Swallow Caye Wildlife Sanctuary**, on a mangrove caye near Belize City, to view the **manatees**; contact Chocolate's Manatee Tours (☎226-0151, ⓔchocolate@btl .net; US$40), at Chocolate's Gift Shop.

Diving

Diving here is also excellent, and instruction and trips are usually cheaper than in San Pedro: open-water certification starts at US$250, two-tank dives at US$75, trips to the **Blue Hole** (see p.82) at US$175 and trips to the **Turneffe Islands** (see p.81) at US$115. Most places in town offer enthusiastic, knowledgeable local guides, regular fast boat trips and a wide range of diving courses – see opposite for listings of recommended operators.

Sailing and other activities

A more romantic way to enjoy the sea and the reef is to spend the day on a **sailboat**, which costs around US$40–50 and usually includes several snorkelling stops and lunch, arriving back as the sun goes down. Ragamuffin Tours (see opposite) offers **sunset** and **moonlight cruises** for US$20–40 and also runs 3-day, 2-night overnight camping trips to Placencia. A number of establishments along Front Street rent **kayaks**: Tsunami Adventures (see opposite) charge only US$8 per hour. Many tour operators, including Anwar Snorkel Tours (see opposite), organize trips inland to Altun Ha (from US$80) and Lamanai (from US$125).

Arrival and information

By air The airstrip is about 1km south of the centre and within walking distance (15min) of the town centre. Alternatively, you can take one of the island's numerous golf carts (Bz$5–6), which usually wait to meet flights.

By boat Boats pull into the Front Dock, which is located in the middle of the island's eastern edge and within easy walking distance of the any of the hotels listed below.

Tour operators For snorkelling, recommended operators include: Anwar Snorkel Tours, north of the front dock (☎226-0327, ⓔjavi66_novelo @hotmail.com); Carlos Tours, near the *Sandbox* (☎226-0058 or 600-1654, ⓔcarlosayala10 @hotmail.com); Ragamuffin Tours, near the north end of Front St (☎226-0348, ⓦwww .ragamuffintours.com); and Tsunami Adventures, near the Split (☎226-0462, ⓦwww.tsunami adventures.com). For diving, try: Frenchie's, towards the northern end of the village (☎226-0234, ⓦfrenchiesdivingbelize.com); Belize Diving Services, on Back St (☎226-0143, ⓦwww .belizedivingservice.com); or Big Fish, on Front St (☎226-0450, ⓦwww.bigfishdivebelize.com).

Tourist information There's no official tourist office, but the city's websites (ⓦwww.gocayecaulker.com and ⓦwww.cayecaulkerbelize.net) are helpful.

Accommodation

Some of Caye Caulker's hotels are being renovated to provide more upscale accommodation, but the island still has an abundance of simple, inexpensive, shared-bath rooms. Book in advance, especially at Christmas and New Year's. Even the farthest hotels are no more than ten minutes' walk from the front dock. Those recommended below are listed in the order you approach them, heading north or south from the dock.

North from the front dock

Trends Beachfront Hotel Immediately right from the dock; the office is on Front St ☎226-0094, ⓔtrendsbze@btl.net. Large rooms with comfortable beds, private baths and fridges in a brightly painted wooden building; some rooms have balconies. Single cabañas ④, doubles ⑤

Tina's Backpackers 75m along the beach from the dock ☎226-0019, ⓔtinasbackpackershostel@yahoo.com. Dorm beds and comfortable, shared-bath rooms in a very social beach house with communal kitchen. There's also a garden with hammocks. Dorms ②, doubles ④

Sandy Lane Hotel On Middle St ☎226-0117. Basic, well-worn wooden rooms and cabañas, some with shared bath and some with private, are the cheapest on the island. ②–③

Miramar Hotel On Front St ☎ 206-0357. Basic rooms, some with private bath, in a wooden building with a large balcony overlooking the sea; there's one hot shower on the second floor. Singles ③, doubles ③—④

Bella's Backpackers On Crocodile St ☎ 226-0360, ✉ monkeybite@btl.net. Dorm beds and private rooms, all with shared bath, in a clean, wooden building at the back of the island. There's a communal kitchen and common room, as well as canoes for guest use. You can also camp (Bz$15 per person) in the yard. Dorms ②, doubles ④

Mara's Place Near the Split ☎ 600-0080, ✉ maras_place@hotmail.com. Comfortable, clean, quiet cabins with private bath, TV and porch. There's also a communal kitchen and private sundeck. Doubles ⑥

South from the front dock

Lena's Guesthouse 250m south of the front dock ☎ 226-0106, ✉ lenas@btl.net. Basic wooden rooms with private bath, just steps from the sea. Two-night minimum stay. ⑤—⑦

Tropical Paradise Hotel At the southern end of Front St ☎ 226-0124, 🌐 www.tropicalparadise -cayecaulker.com. A wide range of rooms, all with hot showers, private baths and fans, and some with a/c, in a series of brightly painted wooden buildings. The adjoining restaurant serves inexpensive meals. Doubles ⑥

Jaguar Morning Star Guest House Across from the island's only school ☎ 226-0347, ✉ joanne @btl.net. Two large rooms in a house overlooking a beautiful garden and a cabana. Rooms have private bath, coffee pot, fridge, cable TV and fan. wi-fi Bz$15 per day. ⑥

Lorraine's Guest House At the southern end of the island, on the beach ☎ 206-0162. Wooden cabins with private baths are a bit shabby but inexpensive. ④

Eating and drinking

Restaurant prices in Caye Caulker are quite high compared to the rest of the country, and it can be difficult to find a meal for less than Bz$15. Still, lobster (in season) and seafood are generally good value. You can self-cater from several shops and supermarkets on the island, and children sell home-baked banana bread, coconut cakes and other goodies. Some bars have live music; otherwise, evening entertainment mostly consists of relaxing in a restaurant over dinner or a drink, or gazing at the tropical night sky. Note that the tap water is unfit to drink; rainwater and bottled water are widely available.

North from the front dock

Sandbox Restaurant Immediately north of the dock ☎ 226-0200. One of the most inexpensive restaurants on the island, with great breakfasts, Belizean cuisine and seafood both indoors and outside on the beach. The daily soup (Bz$6) is a great deal. Mains Bz$3—27.

Caye Caulker Bakery On Middle St. Delicious baked goods and desserts for Bz$1—4.

Bamboo Grill On the beach. Good Belizean cuisine and seafood (Bz$14—40) served at high tables with wooden swings. The bar stays open late.

Happy Lobster On Front St. Great seafood and Creole cuisine in a large, popular restaurant at inexpensive prices; most mains are Bz$12—30.

Taj Restaurant at the northern end of Front St. Very traditional, authentic Indian cuisine (from Bz$10) in an open restaurant facing the beach.

> **TREAT YOURSELF**
>
> Habaneros On Front St. The island's best restaurant: attentive staff pairs up superb seafood and Latin-inspired dishes – such as seafood satay (Bz$36) and "Brazilian Beef" ($40) – with fine wines on a romantic, open-air veranda. Reservations recommended.

South from the front dock

Rose's Café On Calle del Sol at Front St. Popular place for breakfast and simple Belizean and Mexican dishes. Mains Bz$7—20.

Amor y Café On Front St. Very popular restaurant serves excellent coffee, breakfasts and sandwiches (Bz$5—9) on a veranda overlooking the street. Only open 6.30am—noon.

Glenda's Restaurant On Back St. Known for its cinnamon rolls, *Glenda's* dishes up breakfast and lunch for Bz$7—10.

Little Kitchen On Back St. This tiny, out-of-the-way shack offers some of the cheapest and best food on Caye Caulker. Excellent seafood for Bz$10—25, and lobster starts at only Bz$20.

Rasta Pasta On Front St. Very popular restaurant features pasta and seafood, as well as enormous, delicious burritos, for Bz$15—25.

Tropical Paradise Restaurant At the southern end of Front St. The friendly staff here serves Belizean cuisine and seafood in an open-air setting. Daily specials, usually Bz$20, are a great deal and include a free mixed drink.

Directory

Exchange Atlantic Bank, just south of the centre, gives Visa cash advances (US$5 fee) and has a 24hr ATM.

Internet Cyber Café, just north of the *Sandbox Restaurant*, serves drinks, has a book exchange and gift shop and offers international calling as well as internet access.

Laundry Drop-off services at Ruby's, on Calle del Sol.

Post office On Front St. The BTL office is on Back St.

Moving on

By boat Boats operated by the Caye Caulker Water Taxi Association (☎ 223-5752, ⓦ www .cayecaulkerwatertaxi.com) depart for Belize City (Bz$15) at least every 90min from 6.30am to 4pm (5pm on weekends and holidays), and for San Pedro (Bz$15) at least every 2hr from 7am to 3.50pm.

AMBERGRIS CAYE AND SAN PEDRO

The most northerly and, at almost forty kilometres long, by far the largest of

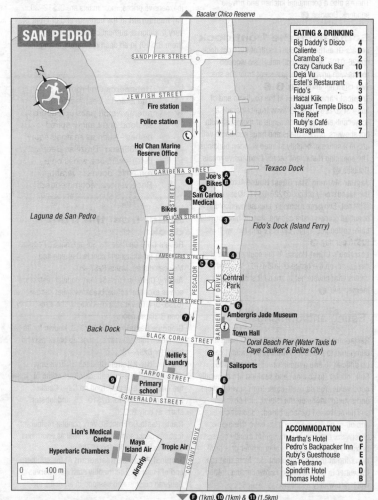

▲ Bacalar Chico Reserve

SAN PEDRO

EATING & DRINKING

Big Daddy's Disco	4
Caliente	D
Caramba's	2
Crazy Canuck Bar	10
Deja Vu	11
Estel's Restaurant	6
Fido's	3
Hacal Kiik	9
Jaguar Temple Disco	5
The Reef	1
Ruby's Café	8
Waraguma	7

SANDPIPER STREET

JEWFISH STREET

Fire station

Police station

Hol Chan Marine Reserve Office

CARIBENA STREET

Texaco Dock

Joe's Bikes

San Carlos Medical

Bikes

PELICAN STREET

Fido's Dock (Island Ferry)

Laguna de San Pedro

AMBERGRIS STREET

Central Park

BUCCANEER STREET

Ambergris Jade Museum

Town Hall

Coral Beach Pier (Water Taxis to Caye Caulker & Belize City)

BLACK CORAL STREET

Back Dock

Nellie's Laundry

Sailsports

TARPON STREET

Primary school

ESMERALDA STREET

Lion's Medical Centre

Maya Island Air

Tropic Air

Hyperbaric Chambers

Airstrip

COCONUT DRIVE

0   100 m

ACCOMMODATION

Martha's Hotel	C
Pedro's Backpacker Inn	F
Ruby's Guesthouse	E
San Pedrano	A
Spindrift Hotel	D
Thomas Hotel	B

▼ **F** (1km), **10** (1km) & **11** (1.5km)

the cayes, is **AMBERGRIS CAYE**. The island's main attraction is the former fishing village of **SAN PEDRO**, facing the reef just a few kilometres from the caye's southern tip. San Pedro is a small town, but its population of over nine thousand makes it the biggest of any of the cayes. As the result of massive recent development, it has lost most, though certainly not all, of its Caribbean charm: it still retains a wonderfully relaxed atmosphere, despite the fact that some of the most exclusive hotels, restaurants and bars in Belize have been built here. The island's only budget places are in the original village of San Pedro, though even these are extremely expensive. To save money and still visit Ambergris, consider staying on Caye Caulker (see p.74) and doing a day-trip.

What to see and do

San Pedro's main streets are only half a dozen blocks long and the town does not boast any particular sights. The main focus of daytime entertainment is the **sea** and the **reef**, with activities from sunbathing to windsurfing, sailing, fishing, diving, snorkelling and glass-bottomed boat rides. **Beaches** on the caye are narrow and the sea immediately offshore is shallow, with a lot of seagrass, so in town you'll usually need to walk to the end of a dock if you want to **swim**. Be careful, though: there have been accidents in San Pedro in which speeding boats have hit people swimming off docks. A line of buoys indicates the "safe area", but speedboat drivers can be a bit macho, so watch where you swim.

Diving and snorkelling

The most central snorkelling and diving spot on Ambergris is the **reef** opposite San Pedro, but it's also heavily used. You're better off heading north, to **Mexico Rocks**, or south, to Hol Chan (see opposite). For qualified divers, a two-tank local dive from

Ambergris Caye costs around US$75. Open-water certification courses run around US$425, while a more basic, single-dive resort course ranges from US$140; both include equipment. All the dive shops in San Pedro also offer snorkelling trips, costing around US$25–35 for two to three hours and US$40–55 for four to five, and many will rent diving and snorkelling supplies; trips to the Blue Hole (see p.82) run around US$250 and trips to the Turneffe Islands (see p.81) US$185. See p.76 for recommended dive shops.

Hol Chan Marine Reserve

The **Hol Chan Marine Reserve** (Bz$20), 8km south of San Pedro, at the southern tip of the caye, takes its name from the Maya for "little channel" – it is this break in the reef that forms the focus of the reserve. Its three zones preserve a comprehensive cross-section of the marine environment, from the open sea through seagrass beds and mangroves. Tours to Hol Chan must be led by a licensed guide, and also stop at **Shark-Ray Alley**, another part of the reserve, where you can swim with three-metre **nurse sharks** and enormous **stingrays** – an extremely popular attraction. It's also somewhat controversial: while swimming here poses almost no danger to snorkellers, as humans are not part of their normal diet, biologists claim that the practice of feeding the fish to attract them alters their natural behaviour.

Other watersports

While most travellers come to the cayes to snorkel or dive, **windsurfing** and **sailing** are popular as well, though learning either sport can be quite expensive. The best rental and instruction for both is offered by SailSports Belize (☎226-4488, ⓦwww.sailsportsbelize .com), on the beach in front of the *Holiday Hotel*. Sailboard rentals cost US$22–27 an hour, or US$72–82 for a seven-hour day; sailboat rental is US$22–49 an hour, with discounts for multiple hours. They also offer **kite-surfing** lessons (US$250 for a two-day, 8hr course; in a group US$195 per person) and sailing lessons (US$66 per hr).

Guided day-trips

Day-trips from San Pedro to the ruins of **Altun Ha** (US$75–90; see p.83) or **Lamanai** (US$135–160; see p.87) are becoming increasingly popular, but can be done more cheaply from other parts of the country. However, with a good guide this is an excellent way to spot wildlife, including crocodiles and manatees, and the riverbank trees are often adorned with orchids. See opposite for recommended guides.

It is also possible to visit some of the local ancient Maya sites on the northwest coast of Ambergris, many of which are just in the process of being excavated. On **San Juan** beach you'll be scrunching over literally thousands of pieces of Maya pottery, but perhaps the most appealing site is **Chac Balam**, a ceremonial and administrative centre with deep burial chambers.

Arrival and information

By air The airport is just south of the city centre, within easy walking distance of any of the recommended hotels, though golf buggies and taxis also line up to give you a ride for around Bz$6–8 should you choose.

By boat Boats arriving from Belize City and/or Caye Caulker usually dock at the Coral Beach pier on the front (reef) side of the island at the eastern end of Black Coral St, though the *Thunderbolt* from Corozal (see p.88) pulls in at the back of the island at the western end of Black Coral St. Arriving at either dock, you're pretty much in the centre and within walking distance of most of the hotels listed below.

Tour operators For diving trips and courses, try: Belize Academy of Diving, based at Mexico Rocks, 7km north of San Pedro (☎226-2873, ⓦwww .belize-academy-of-diving.com); Belize Diving Adventures (☎226-3082, ⓦwww.belizediving adventures.net); Ecologic Divers (☎226-4118, ⓦwww.ecologicdivers.com); Protech Belize, in

front of the *Spindrift Hotel* (☎226-3008, ⓦwww .protechdive.com); and Seaduced by Belize (☎226-2254, ⓦwww.seaducedbybelize.com). Several of these operators also do inland tours to Maya ruins, manatee tours and fishing trips.

Tourist information The official tourist information office is on Barrier Reef Drive at Black Coral St. Ambergris Caye also has a good website (ⓦwww.ambergriscaye.com) with links to most of the businesses on the island. For listings, pick up a copy of *The San Pedro Sun* or *Ambergris Today*, the island's tourist newspapers (Bz$1), available from the tourist office and at most hotels and restaurants.

Accommodation

Accommodation in San Pedro is some of the most expensive in the country – all but a few places cost at least US$70. Most of the year reservations are not necessary, though it's risky to turn up at Christmas, New Year or Easter unless you've booked a room.

Martha's Hotel Pescador Drive, across from *Elvi's Kitchen* ☎226-2053, ⓔmarthashotel@yahoo.com. Simple but clean rooms with private baths and fans in a concrete building in the centre of town. A great bargain. Singles ❷, doubles ❺

Pedro's Backpacker Inn Coconut Drive, 1km south of town ☎226-3825, ⓦwww.backpackersbelize .com. A bit of walk from town, but the basic budget rooms (two single beds, lockers and shared showers) come at the cheapest rate on the island. There's also a very social bar on-site. ❹

Ruby's Guesthouse Barrier Reef Drive, just north of the airstrip ☎226-2063, ⓔrubys@btl.net. Family-run hotel on the seafront; rooms with a/c, rooms with private baths and rooms on the higher floors cost more, but all are good value, especially those in the annex on the lagoon. ❻–❼

San Pedrano Corner of Barrier Reef Drive and Caribeña St ☎226-2054, ⓔsanpedrano@btl.net. Family-run hotel in a wooden building set back slightly from the sea, with comfortable, private-bath rooms (some with a/c and all with TVs) and breezy verandas. ❻

Spindrift Hotel Barrier Reef Drive ☎226-2174, ⓔspinhotel@btl.net. Centrally located and well-decorated hotel with large garden and adjoining restaurant. All rooms have private bath and fans; more expensive rooms have a/c and balconies. ❼–❾

Thomas Hotel Barrier Reef Drive, north of the centre ☎226-2061. Rooms here (some with a/c) are a great deal, with private baths, fridges and TVs. ❺–❻

Eating

Eating prices in San Pedro are also generally higher than elsewhere in Belize. Seafood is prominent at most restaurants, and you can also rely on plenty of steak, shrimp, chicken, pizza and salads. There are several Chinese restaurants too, and in the evening several inexpensive fast-food stands open for business along the front of Central Park. Self-catering isn't much of a bargain: there's no market and the supermarkets are stocked with expensive imported canned goods.

Restaurants

Caliente On the beach at *Spindrift Hotel* ☎ 226-2170. Enjoy Mexican and Latin cuisine on a patio overlooking the sea.

Caramba's Near the north end of Pescador Drive ☎ 226-4321. A lively crowd comes to this large restaurant for a variety of dishes, including Mexican and Caribbean cuisine as well as seafood. Mains Bz$11–50.

Estel's Restaurant On the beach just south of the park ☎ 226-2019. Locally owned restaurant serves breakfast all day and Belizean and Mexican food at lunch for Bz$5–22.

Fido's On Barrier Reef Drive. A favourite of tourists and expats, who come to eat seafood and international cuisine and sip cocktails. There's a terrace overlooking the sea. Mains Bz$18–28.

Hacal Kiik Just north of the airstrip on Esmerelda St ☎ 226-3115. Great baked goods and coffee for Bz$1 and up.

The Reef Near the north end of Pescador Drive ☎ 226-4145. Good Belizean food, including delicious seafood, at relatively inexpensive prices for the island; most mains are Bz$10–22.

Ruby's Café Barrier Reef Drive, next to *Ruby's Guesthouse*. Delicious home-made cakes, pies and sandwiches, and freshly brewed coffee. Opens at 6am.

Waraguma Towards the south end of Pescador Drive. A tiny, very inexpensive restaurant featuring Creole, Garífuna and Mexican cuisine starting at Bz$2.

Drinking and nightlife

San Pedro is the tourist entertainment capital of Belize, and if you check locally, you'll find live music on somewhere every night of the week. Most of the hotels have bars, several of which offer happy hours, while back from the main street are a couple of small cantinas that serve both locals and tourists.

Bars and clubs

Big Daddy's Disco On the beach just south of the park. Locals flock to this beach bar and club for reggae and Latin beats on weekend nights. Cover Bz$10.

Crazy Canuck Bar south of town at *Exotic Caye Beach Resort*. A slightly more mature crowd sip cocktails and dance to live bands on Mon nights. Open until midnight.

Deja Vu 1.5km south of town. Large, loud club and bar (formerly known as the *Barefoot Iguana*) with a live band or DJ most nights of the week.

Fido's On Barrier Reef Drive. A restaurant by day, by night *Fido's* becomes one of the most popular evening spots in San Pedro, hosting a live band most evenings.

Jaguar Temple On Barrier Reef Drive opposite the park. Tourists and locals pack this large, colourfully painted club on most nights.

Directory

Exchange Belize Bank on Barrier Reef Drive has an ATM, and the other banks will give cash advances, but traveller's cheques and US dollars are accepted – even preferred – everywhere.

Internet Caribbean Connection, on Barrier Reef Drive, offers internet access for Bz$10/hr and cheap international phone calls.

Laundry There are two laundries on Pescador Drive.

Post office In the Alijua building, opposite the Atlantic Bank on Barrier Reef Drive (Mon–Thurs 8am–noon and 1–4pm, Fri until 3.30pm).

Moving on

By boat Boats from San Pedro to Caye Caulker (Bz$15) and Belize City (Bz$20) are operated by the Caye Caulker Water Taxi Association (☎ 226-0992, ⓦ www.cayecaulkerwatertaxi.com) and leave from the front dock at least every 90min 7am–3.30pm (4.30pm on weekends and holidays). The Thunderbolt (☎ 610-4475 or 601-7759) also operates from the back dock in San Pedro to Corozal (daily 7am and 3pm; 1hr 30min).

TURNEFFE ISLANDS

Although Caye Caulker and San Pedro are the only villages on the reef, there are a couple of dozen other inhabited islands, as well as some excellent diving spots. The virtually uninhabited **TURNEFFE ISLANDS**, 40km from Belize City and south of cayes Caulker and Ambergris, comprise an oval archipelago of low-lying mangrove islands around a shallow lagoon 60km long. These are enclosed by a beautiful coral reef, which offers some of the best diving and snorkelling in Belize. The island boasts several resorts, all of which are out of the reach of the typical budget traveller, but you can still visit this incredible spot on a day-trip from San Pedro and Caye Caulker. See p.80 and p.76 for tour operators.

LIGHTHOUSE REEF

About 80km east of Belize City is Belize's outermost atoll, **LIGHTHOUSE REEF** is home to the popular underwater attractions of the Great Blue Hole and Half Moon Caye Natural Monument.

The Blue Hole

The **Blue Hole**, technically a karst-eroded sinkhole, is over 300m in diameter and 135m deep, dropping through the bottom of the lagoon and opening out into a complex network of caves and crevices; its depth gives it an astonishing deep blue colour that is, unfortunately, best appreciated from the air. Though visibility is generally limited, many divers still find the trip worthwhile for the drop-offs and underwater caves, which include stalactites and stalagmites. Unfortunately for budget travellers, trips to the Blue Hole – which must be led by a licensed guide or company – usually cost at least US$250.

Half Moon Caye Natural Monument

The **Half Moon Caye Natural Monument**, the first marine conservation area in Belize, was declared a national park in 1982 and became one of Belize's first World Heritage Sites in 1996. The 180,000-square-metre caye is divided into two distinct ecosystems. In the west, guano from seabirds fertilizes the soil, enabling the growth of dense vegetation, while the eastern half has mostly coconut palms. A total of 98 bird species has been recorded here, including frigate birds, ospreys, and a resident population of four thousand red-footed boobies, one of only two such nesting colonies in the Caribbean. Upon arrival (most people come as part of a tour), visitors must pay the Bz$20 entrance fee at the visitors' centre; you can **camp** here (☎223-5004; ❹), but you need to call ahead for permission.

The north

The level expanses of northern Belize are a mixture of farmland and rainforest, dotted with swamps, savannas and lagoons. Most visitors come to the region for its **Maya ruins** and **wildlife reserves**. The largest Maya site, **Lamanai**, served by regular boat tours along the New River Lagoon, features some of the most impressive pyramids and beautiful scenery in the country. The site of **Altun Ha**, meanwhile, is usually visited on a day-trip from Belize City. The northern reserves also host an astonishingly diverse array of wildlife. At the **Community Baboon Sanctuary**, a group of farmers have combined agriculture with conservation to the benefit of the black howler monkey, and at the stunning **Crooked Tree Wildlife Sanctuary**, rivers and lagoons offer protection to a range of migratory birds.

Many of the original residents in this region were refugees from the nineteenth-century Caste Wars in Yucatán, and some of the northernmost towns are mainly Spanish-speaking. The largest settlement today is **Orange Walk**, the country's main centre for sugar production. Further north, near the border with Mexico, **Corozal** is a small Caribbean town, strongly influenced by Maya and mestizo culture.

COMMUNITY BABOON SANCTUARY

Heading north from Belize City, the **COMMUNITY BABOON SANCTUARY** (Bz$10; ⓦwww.howler monkeys.org), to the west off the Northern Highway, is one of the most interesting conservation projects in Belize. It was established in 1985 by Dr Rob Horwich and a group of local farmers (with help from the World Wide Fund for Nature), who developed a code of conduct of sustainable living and farming practices. A mixture of farmland and broad-leaved forest along the banks of the Belize River, the sanctuary coordinates seven villages, of which **Bermudian Landing** is the most convenient, and more than a hundred landowners, in a project of conservation, education and tourism.

The main focus of attention is the **black howler monkey** (known locally as a "baboon"). These primates generally live in groups of between four and eight, and spend the day wandering through the canopy, feasting on leaves, flowers and fruits. At dawn and dusk they let rip with their famous howl: a deep and rasping roar that carries for miles. The sanctuary is also home to over two hundred bird species, as well as iguanas, peccaries and coatis. You can find exhibits and information on the riverside habitats and animals you are likely to see in the natural history museum – actually Belize's first – at the reserve's visitors' centre in Bermudian Landing.

Arrival and information

By bus Buses arriving from Belize City circle the village of Bermudian Landing, and stop at the sanctuary's visitors' centre only a few minutes' walk from all recommended accommodation.
Visitor information The reserve's visitors' centre (daily 8am–5pm; ☎220-2181) is at the west end of Bermudian Landing. In addition to the natural history museum, there is a payphone and internet access.

Accommodation

If you have your own tent, you can camp at the visitors' centre (❷). Alternatively, a number of local families offer rooms in B&Bs (❹); enquire at the visitors' centre. Howler Monkey Lodge (☎220-2158, ⓦwww.howlermonkeylodge.com; ❷–❺), on the river near the visitors' centre, has cabins with private baths and fans (some with a/c) and three rooms with shared bath.

Eating

Community Restaurant Behind the visitors' centre in Bermudian Landing. Run by the village's women's group, this basic restaurant offers traditional Creole fare.
Russell's Restaurant In the centre of Bermudian Landing (where one of the buses parks for the night). Simple Belizean cuisine is served on tables overlooking the river.

Moving on

By bus Buses circle the village and return to Belize City between 5.30am and 6.30am Mon–Sat.

ALTUN HA

Fifty-five kilometres north of Belize City and just 9km from the sea is the remarkable Maya site of **ALTUN HA** (daily 8am–5pm; Bz$10), which was occupied for twelve hundred years, until it was abandoned around 900 AD. Its position close to the Caribbean suggests that it was sustained as much by trade as by agriculture – a theory upheld by the discovery here of obsidian and jade, neither of which occurs naturally in Belize.

Altun Ha clusters around two Classic period plazas. Entering from the road, you come first to **Plaza A**, enclosed by large temples on all sides. A magnificent tomb was discovered beneath Temple A-1, the **Temple of the Green Tomb**. Dating from 550 AD, this yielded jades, jewellery, stingray spines, skin, flints and the remains of a Maya book. The adjacent Plaza B is dominated by the site's largest temple, the **Temple of the Masonry Altars**. Several tombs have been uncovered within the main structure; in one, archeologists discovered a carved jade head of Kinich Ahau, the Maya sun god. Just under 15cm high, it is the largest carved jade found in the Maya world; a replica is on display in the Museum of Belize (see p.68).

Outside these two main plazas are several other areas of interest, though little else has yet been restored. A short trail leads south to **Rockstone Pond**, a reservoir in Maya times, at the eastern edge of which stands another mid-sized temple. Built in the second century AD, this contained offerings from the great city of Teotihuacán in the Valley of Mexico.

Arrival and information

By bus Altun Ha is difficult to reach independently. In theory there are buses from the Belize City terminal to the village of Maskall (call the community phone – ☏ 209-1058 – to check times), passing the turn-off to the site at the village of Lucky Strike, but service is erratic.
Tours Travel agents in Belize City can arrange tours (US$80–150 per group) and increasing numbers of people visit on a day-trip from San Pedro and Caye Caulker (US$75–85 per person). Your best bet to save money is to find a group in Belize City and split the cost.

CROOKED TREE WILDLIFE SANCTUARY

Midway between Belize City and Orange Walk, a branch road heads west to **CROOKED TREE WILDLIFE SANCTUARY** (Bz$8), a reserve that encompasses swamps, wetlands and four separate lagoons. Designated Belize's first Ramsar site (to protect wetlands of international importance), the sanctuary provides a resting place for thousands of migrating and resident birds, such as snail kites, tiger herons, snowy egrets, ospreys and black-collared hawks. The reserve's most famous visitor is the **jabiru stork**, the largest flying bird in the New World, with a wingspan of 2.5m. The **best months** for bird watching are late February to June, when the lagoons shrink to a string of pools, forcing wildlife to congregate for food and water.

In the middle of the reserve, straggling around the shores of a lagoon, is the village of **Crooked Tree**, which is linked to the mainland by a **causeway**. One of the oldest inland villages in the country, Crooked Tree is also one of Belize's loveliest, with well-kept houses and lawns dotted along tree-lined lanes. Though guided tours to the lagoon are quite expensive (at least US$40–80), numerous trails, signposted from the roads, wind around the island and along the shoreline, where you'll see plenty of birds and wildlife even without a guide.

Arrival and information

By bus Buses from Belize City make a loop around the village of Crooked Tree before heading to the causeway. Hitching is a viable (and common) option; any non-express bus can drop you at the junction with the Northern Highway.
Visitor information The wildlife sanctuary visitors' centre (8am–4.30pm) is at the end of the causeway in Crooked Tree. Pay the reserve's Bz$8 entrance fee here.

Accommodation

Most of the accommodation in Crooked Tree is in mid-priced hotels, though some of these also have camping space.

TREAT YOURSELF

Bird's Eye View Lodge On the lakeshore, clearly signposted through the village ☏ 225-7027, ⓦ www.birdseyeviewbelize .com. Worth the splurge for its idyllic, isolated location right on the lagoon. Comfortable rooms have private baths and a/c, and some have balconies. There's a restaurant downstairs, and tours of the sanctuary, as well as nearby Maya sites, can be arranged. ❼–❾

Rhaburn's Rooms ☎ 225-7035. Turn left at the large Crooked Tree sign, then right through the field after the Church of the Nazarene. A friendly couple manages four small, simple rooms with fans and a clean shared bath. Singles ②, doubles ③

Sam Tillet's Hotel In the centre of the village along the bus route ☎ 220-7026, ⓔ samhotel@btl.net. Good-value hotel set amid lovely gardens. Rooms have private baths and fans; most share a balcony. You can camp on the grounds (②), the restaurant serves delicious breakfasts and dinners and tours can be arranged. ⑤–⑦

Eating

3-J's In the centre, in a green building on the bus route. Friendly place serving Creole meals and international fare.

Bird's Eye View Restaurant On the hotel grounds. Worth the one-mile walk from the centre, with a patio overlooking the lagoon. Serves large breakfasts and light, fresh lunches for around Bz$10. Dinner (Bz$25) is usually a three-course affair, though you can also ask solely for the main course.

Moving on

By bus to: Belize City (Mon–Sat 6.30am & 7am).

ORANGE WALK

Like many of Belize's northern cities, **ORANGE WALK**, the largest town in the region, was founded by mestizo refugees fleeing the Caste Wars in the Yucatán.

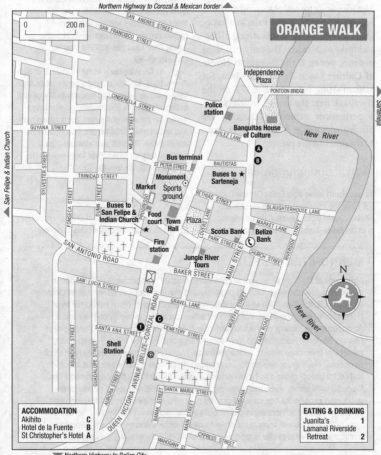

Northern Highway to Corozal & Mexican border ▲

ORANGE WALK

0   200 m

SAN ANDRES STREET

SAN FRANCISCO STREET

Independence
Plaza

PONTOON BRIDGE

CINDERELLA STREET

**Police
station**

**Banquitas House
of Culture**

New River

Sarteneja ▶

GUYANA STREET

AVILEZ LANE

MEJIBA STREET

SYLVESTER STREET

TRINIDAD STREET

Bus terminal

ST PETER STREET

BAUTISTAS

Ⓐ
Ⓑ

Monument

**Buses to ★
Sarteneja**

Market

**Sports
ground**

BETHIAS STREET

FONSECA STREET

DUNN STREET

PROGRESSO ST

SLAUGHTERHOUSE LANE

LOVERS LANE

MARKET LANE

**Buses to
San Felipe &
Indian Church**

**Food
court**

**Town
Hall**

Plaza

Scotia Bank

**Belize
Bank** Ⓒ

RIVERSIDE STREET

◀ San Felipe & Indian Church

SAN ANTONIO ROAD

**Fire
station**

PARK STREET

CHURCH STREET

MAIN STREET

**Jungle River
Tours**

BAKER STREET

MUEFFEL STREET

SAN LUCIA STREET

✉
@

GRAVEL LANE

N

CEMETERY STREET

FARM ROAD

SANTA ANA STREET

❶

GUADALUPE STREET

ASUNCION STREET

AURORA STREET

**Shell
Station** ⛽

QUEEN VICTORIA AVENUE (BELIZE–COROZAL ROAD)

SANTA MARIA STREET

BANAK STREET

SANTA MARIA STREET

MAIN STREET

LOUISIANA

CYPRESS STREET

MAHOGANY ST

New River

❷

ACCOMMODATION	
Akihito	C
Hotel de la Fuente	B
St Christopher's Hotel	A

EATING & DRINKING	
Juanita's	1
Lamanai Riverside
Retreat	2

Long before their arrival, however, the area around Orange Walk had been worked as some of the most productive arable farmland in Belize – aerial surveys have revealed evidence of raised fields and a network of irrigation canals dating from ancient Maya times. Today, Orange Walk is a thriving community by Belizean standards, and though there aren't many attractions in the town itself, it's a great, low-key base for those looking to explore one of the region's highlights: the nearby ruins at Lamanai.

What to see and do

The town centres around a distinctly Mexican-style formal plaza, and the town hall is referred to as the Palacio Municipal, reinforcing the town's strong historical links to Mexico. The only real sight in town, per se, is the **Banquitas House of Culture** (Mon–Fri 8.30am–4pm, Sat 8.30am–1pm; free; ☎322-0517), on the riverbank near the bridge, which houses a permanent exhibition charting the history of Orange Walk District from Maya times to the present.

Arrival and information

By bus Hourly buses from Belize City and Corozal pull up on the main road in the centre of town, officially Queen Victoria Ave but always referred to as the Belize–Corozal Rd. Services to and from Sarteneja stop at Zeta's Store on Main St, two blocks east.

Internet Access is cheap and plentiful; K & N Printshop, on the Belize–Corozal Rd a block south of the post office, is the most convenient.

Post office Right in the centre of town, on Queen Victoria Ave.

Accommodation

Akihito 22 Queen Victoria Ave ☎302-0185. Provides mainly basic accommodation – dorm beds, and some rooms with private baths and a/c – in a concrete building a few blocks from the centre. There's also one "deluxe" room with Jacuzzi. There's a Japanese restaurant downstairs and internet access for Bz$4/hr. Dorms ➋, doubles ➌–➎

Hotel de la Fuente 14 Main St ☎322-2290, Ⓦwww.hoteldelafuente.com. Bright rooms in a good-value hotel include private baths, refrigerators, coffee makers and wireless internet. The owners can arrange to have guests picked up by Jungle River Tours (see p.87) for trips to Lamanai. ➎–➐

St Christopher's Hotel 10 Main St ☎302-1064, Ⓦhttp://stchristophershotelbze.com. Very clean, well-decorated rooms with TVs, private baths, refrigerators and balconies overlooking a garden on the edge of the river. Some rooms have a/c, and internet (Bz$4/hr) and laundry services are available. The staff also arranges trips to Lamanai through Reyes River Tours (see p.87). Singles ➎–➏, doubles ➎–➏

Eating

Orange Walk has a plethora of Chinese restaurants as well as establishments serving traditional

---

MENNONITES IN BELIZE

Members of Belize's Mennonite community, easily recognizable in their denim dungarees, can be seen trading produce and buying supplies every day in Orange Walk and Belize City. The Mennonites, a Protestant group often noted for their pacifist beliefs and rejection of modern advancements, arose from the radical Anabaptist movement of the sixteenth century and are named after Dutch priest Menno Simons. Recurring government restrictions on their lifestyle, especially regarding their objection to military service, have forced them to move repeatedly over time. Having emigrated to Switzerland, they then travelled to Prussia, and in 1663 a group moved to North America. After World War I they migrated from Canada to Mexico, eventually arriving in Belize in 1958. In recent years, farm-produced prosperity has caused drastic changes in their lives: the Mennonite Church in Belize is increasingly split between a modernist section – who use electricity and power tools, and drive trucks, tractors and even cars – and the traditionalists, who prefer a stricter interpretation of beliefs.

Creole and Mexican-influenced fare. The food court behind the town hall, near the market, has a line of cafés and vendors offering cheap eats, including Mexican snacks for Bz$1–2 and good-sized breakfasts for Bz$5–8. It's usually open until early afternoon.

Restaurants
Juanita's 8 Santa Ana St, across from the Shell station. This small, simple restaurant is popular with locals and serves good breakfasts and traditional Creole fare. Closed Sun.
Lamanai Riverside Retreat Lamanai Alley, on the bank of the New River ☎ 302-3955. Enjoy breakfast, dinner or just a beer on an outdoor patio right on the riverbank. The restaurant offers a wide variety of Mexican-influenced and traditional Creole dishes as well as burgers and fries for Bz$8–25. One of the few places in town open on Sun.

Moving on

By bus to: Belize City (hourly; 1hr 30min); Chetumal (hourly; 2hr); Corozal (hourly; 1hr); Sarteneja (3 daily Mon–Sat; 2hr). Local buses to the surrounding villages leave from the market area, behind the town hall and fire station.

LAMANAI

Extensive restoration, a spacious new museum and a stunning jungle setting make **LAMANAI** (Mon–Fri 8am–5pm, Sat, Sun & holidays 8am–4pm; Bz$10) the most impressive Maya site in northern Belize. It is also one of the few sites whose original Maya name – *Lama'an ayin* ("Submerged Croco-dile") – is known, hence the numerous representations of crocodiles on stucco carvings and artefacts found here. *Lamanai*, however, is a seventeenth-century mis-transliteration, which actually means "Drowned Insect." The site was continually occupied from around 1500 BC up until the sixteenth century, when Spanish missionaries built a church alongside to lure the Indians from their "heathen" ways.

Today the site is perched on a bank of the New River Lagoon inside a 950-acre Archeological Reserve, where the jungle surroundings give the site a feeling of tranquillity. Before heading to the ruins, visit the spacious new **archeological museum**, which houses an impressive collection of artefacts, eccentric flints and original stelae. Within the site itself, the most remarkable structure is the prosaically named N10-43 (informally the "High Temple"), a massive **Late Preclassic temple** over 37m tall and the largest from the period in the Maya region. The view across the surrounding forest and along the lagoon from the top of the temple is magnificent, and well worth the daunting climb. North from here is N9-56, a small **sixth-century pyramid** (often called the "Mask Temple", for its exceptionally well-preserved four-metre-high stucco mask of a ruler represented as a deity, probably Kinich Ahau, the sun god). At the southern end of the site, on a grand plaza, is another sixth-century pyramid, structure N10-9, known as the **Jaguar Temple** for the two large, stylized jaguar masks adorning its lowest level.

Arrival and information

By boat The easiest, most pleasant way to get to Lamanai is by river; the cheapest and most informative way to do this is as part of an organized tour (see below).
By bus It is theoretically possible to reach Lamanai independently via the local bus from Orange Walk to the nearby village of Indian Church, but buses run only sporadically, and transportation and accommodation hassles make it much more practical to go as part of an organized day-trip (see below).
Tour operators A number of operators organize day-trips from Orange Walk, departing around 9am; the price (US$40–50) will usually include lunch. The most informative are ⚵ Jungle River Tours, 20 Lover's Lane (☎ 302-2293, ✉ lamanaimayatour @btl.net), run by the Novelos. Another good operator is Reyes River Tours (☎ 322-3327), whose trips depart from the Tower Hill Toll Bridge, 11km south of Orange Walk. To get to the bridge independently from Belize City, take the Northern Transport bus that leaves Belize City at 7am for Chetumal (the driver will drop you at the right place in good time for the 9am start).

SARTENEJA AND SHIPSTERN NATURE RESERVE

Across Chetumal Bay from Corozal, the largely uninhabited **Sarteneja peninsula** is covered with dense forests and swamps that support an amazing array of wildlife. **SARTENEJA**, the peninsula's only settlement, is a quiet, Spanish-speaking lobster-fishing centre that boasts several hotels and restaurants.

All buses to Sarteneja pass the entrance to **SHIPSTERN NATURE RESERVE** (daily 9am–4pm; Bz$12.50, including guided tour; ⓦwww.shipstern.org), 5km before the village, though you can also get here by renting a bike from *Fernando's* or *Backpackers Paradise* in Sarteneja (see opposite). The reserve encompasses an area of eighty square kilometres, including large areas of tropical moist forest, some wide belts of savanna, and most of the shallow Shipstern Lagoon, dotted with mangrove islands. The **visitors' centre** offers a variety of guided walks, though even if you choose the shortest, you'll encounter more named plant species here than on any other trail in Belize. Shipstern is also a birdwatcher's paradise: the lagoon system supports blue-winged teal, American coot and huge flocks of lesser scaup, while the forest is home to keel-billed toucans and at least five species of parrot. Other wildlife in the reserve includes crocodiles, jaguars, peccaries and an abundance of wonderful butterflies.

Arrival

By boat The *Thunderbolt* skiff, running between Corozal and Ambergris Caye, can call at Sarteneja if there's sufficient demand (☎610-4475/7759), pulling into the main dock on North Front St.
By bus Buses pull into Sarteneja at its southern end and make a loop around town; if you talk to the driver beforehand, he or she will usually drop you off wherever you like.

Accommodation

Backpackers Paradise La Bandera Rd ☎403-2051, ⓦwww.cabanasbelize.com. Super-cheap cabañas and camping just 5min out of town; ask the bus driver to drop you off at the Sarteneja Monument. There's also a restaurant (meals Bz$2–8), bike rental (Bz$10/day) and laundry service (Bz$8). The staff can arrange horseriding excursions and pick-up from the pier. Camping ❶, cabañas ❷
Fernando's Guesthouse On North Front St, 100m along the shoreline from the main dock ☎423-2085, ⓦwww.cybercayecaulker.com/sarteneja .html. Three large, tiled rooms and a "cabana" room with thatched roof have private baths and share a veranda overlooking the sea. Meals and snorkelling and nature tours can be arranged. Bike rental available (Bz$20/day). ❺–❻
Oasis Guesthouse One block south of North Front St, west of the main dock ☎423-2121, ⓔoasis @corozal.bz. Wooden building with four large rooms with private bath. ❺

Eating

88 Chinese Restaurant On La Bandera Rd, one block west of the main dock. Serves international cuisine and Chinese staples for Bz$4–18. Open late.
Brisi's Mini-Shop and Restaurant Across from *88 Chinese Restaurant*. Tiny restaurant offering Mexican snacks, burgers and sandwiches, most Bz$4–12.
Lily's At the eastern end of the village. Come here for traditional Belizean fare (Bz$6–12). Closed Sun.

Moving on

By boat The *Thunderbolt* skiff (☎610-4475/7759) departs for Corozal (8.20am & 4.20pm) and San Pedro (7.30am & 3.30pm) if there's sufficient demand.
By bus to: Belize City (5–6 daily, 4–6.30am; 3hr 30min); Chetumal (daily, usually at 5.30am; 3hr 30min). All buses to and from Sarteneja operate Mon–Sat only, and all pass through Orange Walk.

COROZAL

South from the Mexican border, the road meets the sea at **COROZAL**, near the mouth of the New River. The **ancient Maya** prospered here by controlling river and seaborne trade, and the impressive site of **Cerros** is nearby, if complicated to

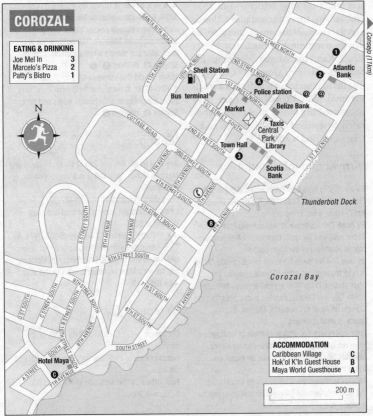

COROZAL

EATING & DRINKING
Joe Mel In	3
Marcelo's Pizza	2
Patty's Bistro	1

SANTA RITA ROAD
3RD STREET NORTH
2ND STREET NORTH
10TH AVENUE
11TH AVENUE
1ST STREET NORTH
Shell Station
Police station
Bus terminal
1ST STREET SOUTH
Market
Belize Bank
2ND STREET SOUTH
COTTAGE ROAD
Taxis
Central
Park
Town Hall
Library
2ND STREET SOUTH
Scotia
Bank
3RD STREET SOUTH
7TH AVENUE
8TH AVENUE
9TH AVENUE
4TH STREET SOUTH
5TH STREET SOUTH
6TH STREET SOUTH
G STREET SOUTH
7TH STREET SOUTH
8TH ST SOUTH
7TH ST SOUTH
9TH AVENUE
7TH AVENUE
8TH STREET SOUTH
C STREET SOUTH
D STREET SOUTH
A STREET
SOUTH STREET
7TH AVENUE
Hotel Maya

Consejo (11km)

Atlantic
Bank

Thunderbolt Dock

Corozal Bay

ACCOMMODATION
Caribbean Village	C
Hok'ol K'In Guest House	B
Maya World Guesthouse	A

0   200 m

reach. Present-day Corozal was founded in 1849 by refugees from Mexico's Caste Wars, although today's grid-pattern town, a neat mix of Mexican and Caribbean, is largely due to reconstruction in the wake of Hurricane Janet in 1955.

What to see and do

There's little reason to spend time in Corozal unless you are trying to get to Cerros. If you do have some extra time, however, the breezy shoreline **park** is good for a stroll, while on the tree-shaded main plaza, the **town hall** is worth a look inside for a mural by Manuel Villamar Reyes, which vividly describes local history. In the block west of the plaza you can see the remains of **Fort Barlee**, built to ward off Maya attacks in the 1870s.

Santa Rita

The small Maya site of **Santa Rita** (open 24hr; free) is within walking distance of the centre, about 15 minutes' north-west of town; follow the main road towards the border, bear right at the fork and turn left at the Super Santa Rita store. Though it is a pleasant spot if you have time to kill, the site is no longer maintained and does not justify extending your stay in Corozal. Founded around 1500 BC, Santa Rita was in all probability the powerful Maya city later known as Chactemal. It was still a thriving settlement in 1531 AD, when the conquistador Alonso Davila entered the town, only to be driven out almost immediately by Na Chan Kan, the Maya chief, and his Spanish adviser Gonzalo Guerrero. The main remaining building is a small pyramid, and excavations here have uncovered the burial sites of an elaborately bejewelled elderly woman and a Classic-period warlord.

Arrival and information

By air Flights from San Pedro arrive at the airstrip 2km south of town. Taxis meet flights and charge Bz$7–10 for a trip to the centre.
By boat The *Thunderbolt* skiff arriving from San Pedro pulls into the main dock on 1st Ave, just two blocks southeast of the town centre.
By bus The Northern Transport depot (☏ 402-3034) is near the northern edge of town, opposite the Shell station. In addition to local services between Belize City and Corozal, express buses pass through Corozal on route to Chetumal, Mexico, roughly hourly in each direction.
Tour operators For organized tours to local nature reserves and archeological sites, contact Henry Menzies (☏ 422-2725); he's also an expert on travel to Mexico.
Tourist information Corozal has no tourist office, but the city's website (🌐 www.corozal.com) can be a good place to find information.

Accommodation

Caribbean Village On 7th Ave, 2.5km south of the centre ☏ 422-2725. A campsite and RV park on the water's edge. The owners can arrange transport to anywhere in Belize, as well as Flores, Guatemala. Office open daily 8am–6pm. Tent space ❶, RV sites ❹

Hok'ol K'In Guest House 89 4th Ave ☏ 422-3329. Great-value hotel on the seafront. Large, clean rooms include private baths, fans and balconies; some have a/c. The outdoor bar is open 24hr and there's a restaurant downstairs. Singles ❹, doubles ❺–❼
Maya World Guesthouse 16 2nd St North ☏ 624-4790, ✉ byronchuster@gmail.com. Very basic budget hotel with private baths and fans. Singles ❸, doubles ❹

Eating

Joe Mel In 5th Ave and 2nd St South. Belizean and Mexican dishes (from Bz$5) in a large, open-air restaurant.
Marcelo's Pizza 25 4th Ave ☏ 422-3275. Small, friendly restaurant serving fast food and pizza starting at Bz$8.
Patty's Bistro 13 4th Ave ☏ 402-0174. A brightly decorated, small place that draws both locals and tourists. Great Belizean, Mexican and American fare – cheeseburgers to fish soups – for Bz$5–15.

Directory

Exchange Belize Bank (with 24hr ATM), on the north side of the plaza.
Internet Easy to find; look for signs along 4th and 5th aves.
Post office On the west side of the plaza (Mon–Fri 8.30am–4.30pm).

Moving on

By boat The *Thunderbolt* (☏ 610-4475 or 601-7759) runs to San Pedro, on Ambergris Caye, from the dock southeast of the centre (daily 7am & 3pm; 1hr 30min; Bz$45).
By bus to: Belize City (hourly 4am–6pm; 2hr 30min); Chetumal (hourly 6am–9pm; 1hr); Orange Walk (hourly; 1hr). Buses for surrounding villages (including

INTO MEXICO: SANTA ELENA

It's less than four hours by bus along the Northern Highway from Belize City to Chetumal, Mexico via the border crossing at Santa Elena. Entering Belize, Mexican immigration and customs posts are on the northern bank of the Río Hondo, 12km from Chetumal; when you're finished there, the bus will pick you up again to take you to Belizean immigration. Leaving Belize, you'll have to pay an exit tax of Bz$30 and the PACT conservation fee of Bz$7.50. Moneychangers wait on the Belize side of the border; make sure to get rid of your Belize dollars before crossing into Mexico.

Copper Bank, see below) leave from the market area. If booked in advance, the Linea Dorada express bus to Flores, Guatemala can pick you up from *Hotel Maya*, on 7th Ave, 2km south of the centre.

CERROS

Built in a strategic position at the mouth of the New River, the late Preclassic centre of **CERROS** (daily 8am–5pm; Bz$10) was one of the first places in the Maya world to adopt the rule of kings. Despite this initial success, however, Cerros was abandoned by the Classic period. The ruins of the site now include three large acropolis structures, ball courts and plazas flanked by pyramids. The largest building is a 22-metre-high temple, whose intricate stucco masks represent the rising and setting sun.

Until recently, Cerros could be reached quite easily from Corozal via a bus to the nearby village of **Copper Bank**. However, in 2007 Hurricane Dean seriously damaged the access road, and now the best way to reach the ruins is via a boat – which you'll have to charter – with a guide; boats leave from the dock in Corozal just south of the *Thunderbolt*'s point of departure (see p.90). Although it is possible to approach boat-owners independently, hotels in Corozal can give advice on arranging a tour, though either way this option is quite expensive, usually at least US$100. Alternatively, buses still run sporadically to Copper Bank, usually leaving late in the evening from the market in Corozal and returning at 6.30am; you can then rent a bike in Copper Bank to access the ruins (20min). If you do venture to Copper Bank on your own, you'll most likely have to spend a night or two; *Copperbank Inn* (☏608-0838, ⓦwww .copperbankinn.com; ❺–❻) offers large, tiled rooms (some with a/c) with private bath, TVs and verandas, and also has a restaurant. Lastly, visitors should note that mosquitoes around the site are particularly pesky – prepare accordingly.

The west

Heading west from Belize City towards the Guatemalan border, you'll traverse varied landscapes, from open grassland to dense tropical forest. A fast, paved road, the **Western Highway**, runs the entire way, moving from the heat and humidity of the coast to the cooler, lush foothills of the Maya Mountains.

Before reaching Belize's tiny capital, **Belmopan**, the road passes two excellent attractions: the **Belize Zoo** and the **Monkey Bay Wildlife Sanctuary**. West of Belmopan, following the Belize River valley, the road skirts the **Maya Mountains**. You're now in **Cayo District**, the largest of Belize's six districts and arguably the most beautiful. South of the road, the **Mountain Pine Ridge** is a pleasantly cool region of hills and pine woods. **San Ignacio**, on the Macal River, makes an ideal base for exploring the forests, rivers and ruins of western Belize, including **Caracol**, the largest Maya site in Belize, and the region's many dramatic **caves**, often filled with Maya artefacts.

BELIZE ZOO

The **BELIZE ZOO**, at Mile 29 on the Western Highway (daily 8.30am–5pm; Bz$16; ⓦwww.belizezoo.org), is easily visited on a half-day trip from Belize City or as a stop on the way west. Probably the finest zoo south of the US, and long recognized as a phenomenal conservation achievement, the zoo originally opened in 1983. Now organized around the theme of "a walk through Belize", the zoo offers the chance to see the country's native animals at close quarters. Residents include tapirs, a wide variety of birds and all the Belizean cats. To **get to the zoo** take any bus between Belize City and Belmopan and ask the driver to drop you at the signed turn-off, a 200-metre walk from the entrance; you can leave your luggage at the visitors' centre. If you'd like to stay overnight in the area, the **Tropical Education Centre** (T220-8003, Etec @belizezoo.org), on the opposite side of the highway about 300m back towards Belize City, offers three wooden dorms (5) with shared baths and hot showers. Guests can take a nocturnal tour of the zoo for Bz$30.

One kilometre past the zoo, the **Coastal Road** (served by only two weekly buses in each direction) provides an unpaved short cut to Gales Point (see p.105) and Dangriga. A kilometre or so past the junction is *Cheers*, a friendly **restaurant** with good food at reasonable prices, and reliable information.

MONKEY BAY WILDLIFE SANCTUARY

Half a kilometre past *Cheers* and 300m off the Western Highway, **MONKEY BAY WILDLIFE SANCTUARY** (T820-3032, Wwww.monkeybaybelize .org), a 44-square-kilometre protected area extending to the Sibun River, offers birding and nature trails through five distinct types of vegetation and habitat. Adjoining the sanctuary is the **Monkey Bay National Park**, enclosing a biological corridor that runs south through karst limestone hills to connect with the Manatee Forest Reserve. Apart from being a relaxing place **to stay** in a private room (4) or to camp under thatched shelters (2), Monkey Bay is a viable experiment in sustainable living, using solar power, rainwater catchment and biogas fuel for cooking; the food (some of it grown in the station's organic gardens) is plentiful and delicious, and the staff arranges excursions. *Amigos Bar* next to Monkey Bay has great food, a daily happy hour and internet access.

GUANACASTE NATIONAL PARK

Just off the highway at the turnoff towards Belmopan is tiny **GUANACASTE**

NATIONAL PARK (daily 8am–4pm; Bz$5), a 52-acre area of beautiful tropical forest. Several short, circular trails leave from the **visitors' centre**, winding through the forest and passing the Belize and Roaring rivers; there's even a spot for swimming. Although a visit here isn't necessary if you're planning on spending time in Belize's other forested areas, Guanacaste provides an excellent introduction to the country's flora and fauna and is exceptionally accessible; any bus heading west can drop you off at the visitors' centre, where you can leave your belongings while you explore.

BELMOPAN

At Guanacaste, the Hummingbird Highway (see p.102) splits from the Western Highway and heads south to **BELMOPAN** (and eventually, Dangriga). The city was founded in 1970, after Hurricane Hattie swept much of Belize City into the sea. The government decided to use the disaster as a chance to move to higher ground and, in a bid to focus development on the interior, chose a site at the geographical heart of the country. The name of the city combines the words "Belize" and "Mopan", the language spoken by the Maya of Cayo, and the layout of the main government buildings is modelled loosely on a Maya city, with buildings grouped around a central plaza. When built, Belmopan was meant to symbolize a new era, with tree-lined avenues, banks, embassies and communications worthy of a world centre. Few people, however, chose to move here, and Belmopan remains the smallest capital city in the world. And although the population is growing slowly, there's little reason to stay any longer than it takes your bus to leave.

Arrival and information

By bus Buses from Belize City to San Ignacio, Benque Viejo, Dangriga and Punta Gorda all pass through Belmopan, so there's at least one service in either direction every 30min. All buses stop at

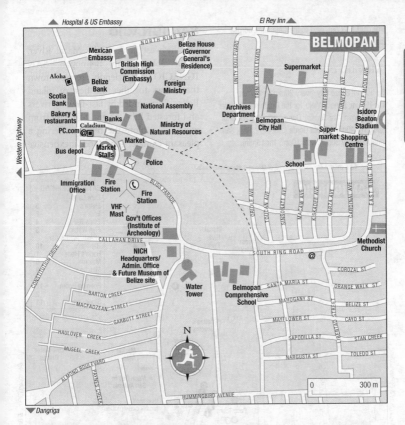

the terminal, which is located in the city centre and within walking distance of most of the city's hotels.

Accommodation

Most of Belmopan's **accommodation** is expensive and aimed at visiting dignitaries and professionals. If you do have to stay here, El Rey Inn, 23 Moho St (☏822-3438, ✉hibiscus@btl.net; doubles ❺, triples ❻) has the cheapest rooms in town, all with private bath. It is, however, quite a long walk from the bus station (20–30min), so consider taking a taxi (Bz$3–4).

Eating and drinking

Many restaurants in Belmopan are closed on Sunday, so snacks from the bus terminal may be your only option if you're passing through then, unless you are willing to wander quite a bit farther afield.

Aloha A few blocks north of the bus terminal. Belizean cuisine, as well as Taiwanese dishes and burgers.

Caladium Beside the bus terminal. Good Belizean food, with an inexpensive daily special.

Directory

Exchange Banks (with ATMs) are close to the bus terminal.

Immigration The office is in the main government building by the fire station.

Internet PC.Com, next to the Caladium, across from the bus station.

Moving on

By bus to: Belize City (every 20min, until 7pm; 1hr 15min); Benque Viejo, for the Guatemalan border (every 30min; 1hr 30min); Dangriga (every 2hr, until 6pm; 1hr 40min); Punta Gorda (every 2hr; 6hr); San Ignacio (every 30min, until 10pm; 1hr 15min).

SAN IGNACIO

On the west bank of the Macal River, about 35km from Belmopan, **SAN IGNACIO** is a friendly, relaxed town that draws together the best of inland Belize. Surrounded by fast-flowing rivers and forested hills, it's an ideal base from which to explore the region, offering a pleasant climate, good food, inexpensive

SAN IGNACIO

A & Branch Mouth (confluence of Mopan & Macal Rivers)

EATING & DRINKING

Café Cayo	8
Elvira's	5
Erva's	E
Eva's Bar	4
Fiya Water Restaurant & Bar	3
Hannah's	10
Hode's Place	1
Maxim's	6
Mincho's	9
Pop's	7
Roomba Room	12
Serendib	2
Stork Club	11

ACCOMMODATION

Casa Blanca Guest House	H
Central O'tel	F
Cosmos Campground	A
Hi-Et Hotel	G
Mana Kai Campground	B
Pacz Hotel	E
Tropicool Hotel	D
Venus Hotel	C

Cahal Pech Maya Site, Benque Viejo & Guatemala Border (15km)

Bullet Tree Village (5km) & El Pilar (20km)

Belmopan (36km) & Belize City (115km)

0   100 m

hotels and frequent bus connections. The town is usually referred to as **Cayo** by locals, the same word that the Spanish use to describe the offshore islands – an apt description of the area, which is set in a peninsula between two converging rivers. The early Spanish Conquest in 1544 made little impact here, and the area was a centre of rebellion in the following decades. **Spanish friars** arrived in 1618, but the population continued to practice "idolatry", and in 1641 Maya priests threw out some Spanish clerics. Tipu, the region's capital, retained a measure of independence until 1707, when the population was forcibly removed to Guatemala.

What to see and do

There's little to do in San Ignacio proper, though relative to other Belizean towns, one can spend many pleasant days here, as it's both relaxed and low-hassle and the streets of the centre are lined with bars and restaurants. Numerous independent local operators – see the box below for listings – offer superb guided trips to attractions around San Ignacio, including Actun Tunichil Muknal (see p.98) and Caracol (see p.100). There's some turnover among tour operators, so it's always worth asking at your hotel or at *Eva's Bar* (see p.96) about what's currently being offered.

Arrival and information

By bus Services from Belize City stop in the centre of town just south of Coronation Park, within easy walking distance of all of the recommended hotels.
Tourist information There is no official tourist office in San Ignacio. The best stop for local advice is the long-established *Eva's Bar* on Burns Ave (see p.96) – the owner knows almost everything about Cayo.
Travel agent For domestic and international air tickets head to Exodus Travel, 2 Burns Ave (☎ 824-4400).

Accommodation

San Ignacio has some of the best-value budget accommodation in the country, and you'll almost always find space. For camping, try Cosmos or Mana Kai.
Casa Blanca Guest House 10 Burns Ave ☎ 824-2080, ⓦ www.casablancaguesthouse.com. Very popular hotel with immaculate rooms, all with private bath and cable TV (some with a/c) and a comfortable sitting area with fridge, coffee and tea. Booking is advisable. Singles ❹, doubles ❺–❻
Central O'tel 24 Burns Ave ☎ 824-3734, ⓔ easyrider@btl.net. Simple, somewhat shabby rooms with shared baths at the cheapest rates in town; the balcony with hammocks is a great place from which to watch the street below. Singles ❷, doubles ❸
Cosmos Campground 1km along the Branch Mouth Rd ☎ 824-2116, ⓔ cosmoscamping@btl .net. Campsite with showers, flush toilets and a kitchen (❶) and a simple cabin (❹) with shared hot-water showers.

TOUR OPERATORS IN SAN IGNACIO

Easy Rider In the Arts and Crafts store on Burns Ave just past *Eva's Bar* ☎ 824-3734, ⓔ easyrider@btl.net. Charlie Collins organizes the best-value horseriding packages in San Ignacio (US$30 for a half-day, US$46 for a full day).
Mayawalk Adventures 19 Burns Ave ☎ 824-3070, ⓦ www.mayawalk.com. A wide variety of tours, including trips to Actun Tunichil Muknal (US$80), the ruins at Caracol (US$75), Tikal, in Guatemala (US$85) and Mountain Pine Ridge (US$40).
Pacz Tours On Burns Ave, just after *Eva's Bar* ☎ 824-2477, ⓔ pacztours@btl.net. A number of tours, including the least expensive trip to Actun Tunichil Muknal (US$75) and one to Caracol (US$80).

Toni's River Adventures At *Eva's Bar* ☎ 824-3292, ⓔ evas@btl.net. Toni Santiago runs the best-value guided canoe trip on the Macal River; it's US$25, including lunch, for a paddle upriver to the Rainforest Medicine Trail (see p.98). He also organizes fantastic overnight camping trips along the river.

Hi-Et Hotel 12 West St ☎ 824-2828, ✉ thehiet@yahoo.com. Popular, comfortable hotel with shared-bath rooms in a beautiful old wooden building, each with a tiny balcony, and larger rooms with private bath in a new concrete building. Book ahead. Singles ❸–❹, doubles ❹

Mana Kai Campground On Branch Mouth Rd ☎ 824-2317. Centrally located campsite with hammocks and showers. ❶

Pacz Hotel 4 Far West St, two blocks behind *Eva's Bar* ☎ 604-4526, ✉ paczghouse @btl.net. Five clean, comfortable rooms (some with private baths) at bargain rates. One room functions as a dorm (❷). The sitting room has a fridge and cable TV. Good for information. Singles ❸–❹, doubles ❹

Tropicool Hotel On Burns Ave, 75m past *Eva's* ☎ 824-3052, ✉ tropicool@btl.net. Bright, clean rooms with shared hot-water baths, and wooden cabins with private showers and cable TV. The sitting room has a TV and a laundry area. Singles ❸, doubles ❸–❹, cabins ❺

Venus Hotel 29 Burns Ave ☎ 824-3203, ✉ midas@btl.net. Two-storey hotel with a variety of accommodation, including shared-bath economy rooms as well as rooms with private baths, a/c and cable TV. Singles ❸–❹, doubles ❹–❻

Eating

San Ignacio has an abundance of good, inexpensive restaurants. The Saturday market is also one of the best in Belize, with local farmers bringing in fresh produce.

Restaurants

Café Cayo 12 Burns Ave. Large, open restaurant with patio offers pasta (from Bz$18), as well as pizza, salads and fried foods. Also offers internet access.

Elvira's 6 Far West St. Delicious Belizean cuisine at some of the cheapest prices in town – most dishes are Bz$10 or under.

Erva's 4 Far West St, under *Pacz Hotel*. Traditional Belizean dishes for under Bz$10, as well as seafood and filling, topping-laden pizzas from Bz$16 served on a pleasant patio. Popular with both tourists and locals.

Hannah's 5 Burns Ave. Small restaurant with some of the most delicious food in the country – everything from Belizean to Burmese, accompanied by fresh salads – at great prices; get here early or you'll have to wait. Mains Bz$8–20.

Maxim's Far West St. The best of San Ignacio's numerous Chinese restaurants. Most dishes come in either small (typically large enough for a meal) or large portions for Bz$6–25.

Mincho's Burns Ave, next to *Hannah's*. Locals crowd around this tiny food stand for Mexican snacks, including tacos and burritos, for Bz$3–5.

Pop's Far West St. Huge, inexpensive breakfasts and bottomless cups of coffee for Bz$10, as well as traditional Belizean dishes.

Serendib 27 Burns Ave. Inexpensive Sri Lankan cuisine for Bz$10–15. Closed Sun.

Drinking and nightlife

As tourism to San Ignacio increases, so does the number of bars, some of which can get quite rowdy later at night. The town is also a popular weekend spot for many Belizeans, so there's also live music and dancing on Friday and Saturday nights.

Eva's Bar Burns Ave. This long-established bar is a great place to relax and meet other travellers over a drink, and to find answers to any questions you might have about Cayo.

Fiya Water Restaurant & Bar Burns Ave, across from *Eva's*. Laid-back restaurant by day, *Fiya* becomes a popular bar at night, open until late, with pool tables and dartboards.

Hode's Place on Bullet Tree Rd. Popular with locals and travellers, this bar and grill has a patio and pool tables.

Roomba Room on the way to Cahal Pech, on Old Benque Rd at Buena Vista. Young locals come here to dance to reggae on Fri and Sat nights.

Stork Club 18 Buena Vista St, in *San Ignacio Resort Hotel*. Relaxed and somewhat upscale bar most nights, with karaoke on Thurs and a DJ or band on Fri.

Directory

Exchange Belize, Scotia, and Atlantic banks are on Burns Ave; all have 24hr ATMs. Moneychangers will approach anyone they think is heading west to exchange for Guatemalan quetzales; they also board buses bound for Benque before departure.

Internet Tradewinds, on West St at Waight's Ave, offers internet access for Bz$5/hr.

Laundry Drop-off laundry at *Martha's Guest House*, on West St.

Post office Next to Courts furniture store in the centre of town.

Moving on

By bus to: Belize City via Belmopan (every 30min from 4am–6pm; 3hr); Benque Viejo, for the Guatemalan border (every 30min; 15min). It's more comfortable to get a shared taxi from San Ignacio to the border for Bz$5 than taking the bus, though.

AROUND SAN IGNACIO

San Ignacio makes a great base from which to explore the **Cayo District**'s impressive **Maya ruins** and stunning natural scenery. You'll be required to hire a local guide in order to visit several of the region's highlights, though this is often a good idea anyway, to get the best experience; see the box on p.95 for recommended tour operators.

Cahal Pech

The hilltop Maya site of **Cahal Pech** (daily 6am–6pm; Bz$10), twenty minutes west of San Ignacio along the road to Benque Viejo, is well worth a visit. There's

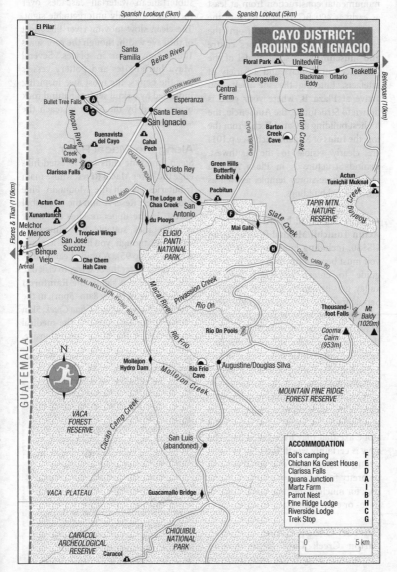

Spanish Lookout (5km) ▲   ▲ Spanish Lookout (5km)

CAYO DISTRICT: AROUND SAN IGNACIO

El Pilar
Santa Familia
Belize River
Floral Park ⚑ Unitedville
Georgeville
Blackman Eddy Ontario Teakettle
Belmopan (10km)
WESTERN HIGHWAY
Central Farm
Esperanza
Bullet Tree Falls Ⓐ Ⓑ Ⓒ
Santa Elena
San Ignacio
Mopan River
Buenavista del Cayo
Cahal Pech
CASA MAYA ROAD
CHIQUIBUL ROAD
Barton Creek Cave
Barton Creek
Callar Creek Village Ⓓ
Clarissa Falls
Cristo Rey
Green Hills Butterfly Exhibit ♦
Pacbitun ⚑
Actun Tunichil Muknal ⚑
Roaring Creek
TAPIR MTN. NATURE RESERVE
CHIAL ROAD
The Lodge at Chaa Creek
San Antonio Ⓔ ⚑
Slate Creek
Actun Can ⚑
Xunantunich ⚑
du Plooys
Ⓕ
Mai Gate
Ⓗ
COOMA CAIRN RD
Melchor de Mencos
Flores & Tikal (110km)
Ⓖ Tropical Wings
San José Succotz
ELIGIO PANTI NATIONAL PARK
Benque Viejo
Che Chem Hah Cave
Ⓘ
ARENAL/MOLLEJON HYDRO ROAD
Arenal
Macal River
Privassion Creek
Thousand-foot Falls
Mt Baldy (1020m)
Río On
Cooma Cairn (953m)
Río Frio
Rio On Pools ⌇
GUATEMALA
N
Mollejon Hydro Dam
Mollejon Creek
Rio Frio Cave
Augustine/Douglas Silva
MOUNTAIN PINE RIDGE FOREST RESERVE
Cacao Camp Creek
VACA FOREST RESERVE
San Luis (abandoned)
VACA PLATEAU
Guacamallo Bridge ♦
CHIQUIBUL NATIONAL PARK
CARACOL ARCHEOLOGICAL RESERVE
Caracol ⚑

ACCOMMODATION

Bol's camping	F
Chichan Ka Guest House	E
Clarissa Falls	D
Iguana Junction	A
Martz Farm	I
Parrot Nest	B
Pine Ridge Lodge	H
Riverside Lodge	C
Trek Stop	G

0   5 km

a good chance you'll have the forested ruins all to yourself, and although the structures are not particularly tall, the maze of restored corridors, stairways, plazas and temples is enchanting. Cahal Pech was the royal acropolis-palace of an elite Maya family during the Classic period, and there's evidence of monumental construction from at least as early as 400 BC, though most of the remaining structures date from the eighth century AD. The **visitors' centre and museum** has a scale model of the site, excellent displays and a variety of artefacts. Entering the site itself, you arrive at **Plaza B**, where your gaze is drawn to Structure 1, the **Audiencia**, the highest building at Cahal Pech. From the top, the ruins of Xunantunich (see p.101) are clearly visible to the southwest. Behind Structure 1, in **Plaza A**, is a restored three-storey temple, as well as other sacred buildings.

Actun Tunichil Muknal

Actun Tunichil Muknal (tours around US$80, including lunch and entry fee; you must be accompanied by a licensed guide to enter), in Roaring Creek valley, gets its name ("Cave of the Stone Sepulchre") for the astonishingly well-preserved skeletons, fourteen in total, of Maya human sacrifices found here. As the cave has historically been inaccessible to looters, little has been touched since the Maya stopped using it over a millennium ago, and the artefacts are spellbinding. Perhaps the most dramatic sight is the skeleton of a young woman lying below a rock wall – and nearby the stone axe that may have killed her. The cave is certainly worth the high price of a tour; note, though, that you'll need to be pretty fit and able to swim to do the trip; for much of the time you're wading knee- or even chest-deep in water.

Barton Creek Cave

Barton Creek Cave (tours around US$40, including Bz$20 entry fee; you must be accompanied by a licensed guide to enter) is also accessible only by river, though this time by canoe. Framed by jungle, the cave's entrance is at the far side of a pool, and inside the river is navigable for about 1600m before ending in a gallery blocked by a huge rockfall. If it's been raining, a subterranean waterfall cascades over the rocks – a truly unforgettable sight. The clear, slow-moving river fills most of the cave width, though the roof soars 100m above you in places. Several **Maya burial sites** and pottery vessels line the banks, the most awe-inspiring indicated by a skull set in a natural rock bridge used by the Maya to reach the sacred site.

Along the Macal River

Steep limestone cliffs and forested hills edge the lower **Macal River**, whose main tributaries rise in the Mountain Pine Ridge Forest Reserve and the Chiquibul Forest. In the upper reaches the water is sometimes suitable for whitewater kayaking, though you'll need a guide for this (see p.95). A guided canoe trip, however, is by far the best way to visit one of the river's top sights, the **Rainforest Medicine Trail** (daily 8am–5pm), in the grounds of *The Lodge at Chaa Creek*, 5km upriver from San Ignacio. The medical knowledge of the Maya was extensive, and the trail, dedicated to a Maya bush doctor (*curandero*), is fascinating: among the plants here you'll see the negrito tree, whose bark was once sold in Europe for its weight in gold as a cure for dysentery. The **Chaa Creek Natural History Centre**, next to the Medicine Trail (daily 8am–5pm), offers a marvellous introduction to Cayo's history, geography and wildlife. A combined ticket for both the above is Bz$18. At *du Plooy's* resort, a few kilometres upstream from *Chaa Creek*, the ambitious **Belize Botanic Gardens** (daily 7am–5pm; Bz$10, guided tour Bz$20) aim to conserve many of Belize's native plant species in small areas representative of their habitats.

Most **accommodation** on the Macal River is in high-end resorts, though there is one less expensive option (see box, p.101).

Along the Mopan River

Rushing down from the Guatemalan border, the **Mopan River** offers some attractive and not too serious **white-water rapids**. Though there's less **accommodation** along the Mopan branch of the Belize River than there is along the Macal, what's available is more within reach of the budget traveller. The places listed below are in order of distance from San Ignacio. All of them can arrange river trips, as well as trips throughout Cayo.

Accommodation

Iguana Junction Bullet Tree Falls village centre, 5km west of San Ignacio ☎824-2249, ⓦwww .iguanajunction.com. Four wooden cabins with private bath and four simple rooms with shared showers in a riverside setting. Excellent home-cooked meals. Doubles ⑤, cabins ⑥

Parrot Nest Bullet Tree Falls, at the end of the track just before the bridge ☎820-4058, ⓦparrot-nest .com. Six cabins (two up a tree and one with private bath) set in beautiful gardens on the riverbank, with shared, hot-water baths. Filling meals are available, and there's a free shuttle to *Eva's* in San Ignacio. ⑦

Riverside Lodge Bullet Tree Falls ☎820-4007, ⓦriversidelodgebelize.com. Simple cabins with private bath and fan are some of the cheapest in

the area, and there's a restaurant serving good, home-made meals. Singles ⑤, doubles ⑥

Clarissa Falls 2km along a signed track, to the right off the Western Highway ☎824-3916, ⓦwww.clarissafalls.com. Restful place on the river with simple, clean cabins (⑥) with private bathrooms, plus camping (②) with shared hot-water showers. There's also a restaurant, and the staff can arrange a variety of tours.

MOUNTAIN PINE RIDGE FOREST RESERVE

South of San Ignacio, the **MOUNTAIN PINE RIDGE FOREST RESERVE** comprises a spectacular range of rolling hills, jagged peaks and gorges interspersed with areas of grassland and pine forest. In the warm river valleys the vegetation is gallery forest, giving way to rainforest south of the Guacamallo Bridge, which crosses the upper Macal River. One of the most scenic of the many small rivers in the Pine Ridge is the **Río On**, rushing over cataracts and into a gorge. On the northern side of the ridge are the **Thousand-Foot Falls**, actually over 1600ft (488m) and the highest in Central America. The reserve also includes limestone areas riddled with caves, the most accessible being the **Río Frio**. The area is virtually uninhabited but for a few tourist lodges and one small settlement, **Augustine/Douglas Silva**, site of the reserve headquarters.

What to see and do

It can be very difficult to get around the reserve, as there are not many roads. A mountain bike can be very helpful in this respect – the whole area is perfect for **hiking** and **mountain biking**; hitching is another option.

San Antonio

Nestled in the Macal River valley, San **Antonio** is the southernmost settlement outside the reserve. It's a good place to learn about traditional Maya practices: the village was the home of famous Maya healer Don Eligio Panti, and there's a small, informal museum in the village, dedicated to his life and work. The Garcia sisters, Don Eligio's nieces, run the inexpensive *Chichan Ka Guest House* (☎660-4023, ✉tanah _info@awrem.com; ③–⑤) on the road approaching the village; buses from San Ignacio stop outside. The sisters also serve traditional meals, offer courses in the gathering and use of medicinal plants and are also renowned for their slate carvings – their **gift shop** has become a favourite tour-group stop. Nearby, the **Tanah Museum** has exhibits on village life.

The reserve

Not far beyond San Antonio, the two entrance roads meet and begin a steady climb to the **reserve**. One kilometre beyond the junction is a **campsite** (①) run by Fidencio and Petronila Bol, who operate Bol's Nature Tours; Fidencio can guide you to several nearby caves. About 5km uphill from the campsite is the **Mai Gate**, a checkpoint with information about the reserve, toilets and drinking water. There are plans to levy an **entrance fee**, but for the moment all the guards do is write your name in the visitors' book (to ensure against illegal camping).

Once in the reserve, pine trees replace the dense, leafy forest. After 3km a road heads off to the left, running for 16km to a point overlooking the **Thousand-Foot Falls** (Bz$2). The setting is spectacular, with thickly forested slopes across the steep valley. The waterfall is about 1km from the viewpoint, but try to resist the temptation to climb around for a closer look, as the slope is a lot steeper than it first appears.

Around 11km farther on from the junction to the falls lies one of the reserve's main attractions, the **Río On Pools** – a gorgeous spot for a swim. Another 8km from here and you reach the reserve headquarters at **Augustine/Douglas Silva**. You can

camp here and the village store has a few basic supplies. The huge **Río Frio Caves** are a twenty-minute walk from Augustine/Douglas Silva, following the signposted track from the parking area through the forest to the main cave. Sandy beaches and rocky cliffs line the Río Frio on both sides as it flows through the cave.

Caracol

Beyond Augustine/Douglas Silva, the Maya Mountains rise up to the south, while to the west is the wild Vaca plateau. Here the ruins of **Caracol** (daily 8am–4pm; Bz$15), the most magnificent Maya site in Belize, and one of the largest in the Maya world, were lost for over a thousand years until their rediscovery in 1936. Two years later they were explored by A.H. Anderson, who named the site Caracol – Spanish for "snail" – because of the large numbers of snail shells found there. The first detailed, full-scale excavation of the site began in 1985, and research and restoration continues today.

Most arrive with a guided tour from San Ignacio (see p.94), as there is no public transportation to, or even near, the site. If you manage to make it here on your own, you'll be guided around by one of the guards. The **visitors' centre** is one of the best at any Maya site in Belize and an essential first stop. Of the site itself, only the core of the city, comprising thirty-two large structures and twelve smaller ones grouped round five main plazas, is open to visitors – though even this is far more than you can effectively see in a day. The most massive structure, **Caana** ("Sky Place") is 42m high and still one of the tallest buildings in Belize. Hieroglyphic inscriptions here have enabled epigraphers to piece together a virtually complete dynastic record of Caracol's rulers from 599 AD. One altar records a victory over Tikal in 562 AD – a triumph that sealed the city's rise to power.

INTO GUATEMALA: BENQUE VIEJO DEL CARMEN

The westernmost town in Belize, 2km before the Guatemalan border, is Benque Viejo del Carmen. This quiet town is served by constant buses (which terminate here); to get to the border itself you'll need to take a shared taxi (Bz$2).

Leaving Belize you pay an exit tax of Bz$30, plus the PACT Conservation fee of Bz$7.50. There's no charge to enter Guatemala for North Americans or citizens of the EU, Australia and New Zealand; if you do require a visa (up to US$10), they can sometimes be issued here, though it's a good idea to check if you need one in advance. The Guatemalan border town of Melchor de Mencos has little to recommend it, so it is best to continue as soon as you're ready. Moneychangers will be waiting on either side of the border, though you might want to bargain with them to get the best rate.

Minibuses (US$10–15) to Flores or Tikal will likely be waiting just over the border, and colectivo minibuses to Flores will be waiting just over the bridge at the border; regular second-class buses pass the junction just beyond the bridge.

Arrival and information

Arrival There are two entrance roads to the Mountain Pine Ridge Reserve, one from the village of Georgeville, on the Western Highway, and the other from Santa Elena, along the Cristo Rey road and through the village of San Antonio. If you're fit, a good way to get around is to rent a mountain bike in San Ignacio; you can take it on the bus to San Antonio. There are also four Mesh buses a day (Mon–Sat) from San Ignacio to San Antonio via Cristo Rey.
Tours Tours can be arranged from San Ignacio (see box, p.95).

Accommodation

The resorts in Mountain Pine Ridge include some of the most luxurious and expensive accommodation

in the interior of Belize. There is no budget accommodation, and none of the resorts allow camping – the only options are Bol's Nature Tours (see p.100) and in Augustine/Douglas Silva (see p.100).

XUNANTUNICH

On the Western Highway, around 12km west of San Ignacio, the quiet village of **San José Succotz** is home to the ruins of **XUNANTUNICH** (pronounced Shun-an-tun-ich), "the Stone Maiden" (daily 8am–5pm; Bz$10). This impressive Maya site is also one of the most accessible in Belize; any bus heading west from San Ignacio can drop you at the old cable-winched ferry that crosses the river (daily 8am–5pm; free). From the other side, a steep road leads through the forest for about two kilometres to the site.

Your first stop should be the **visitors' centre**, with a scale model of the ruins. The site itself, on an artificially flattened hilltop, includes five plazas, although the surviving structures are grouped around just three. Recent investigations have found evidence of Xunantunich's role in the power politics of the Classic period, during which it probably joined Caracol and Calakmul in an alliance against Tikal. By the Terminal Classic period, Xunantunich was already in decline, though still apparently inhabited until around 1000 AD.

The track from the entrance brings you out into Plaza A-2, with large structures on three sides. Plaza A-1, to the left, is dominated by **El Castillo**, at 40m the city's tallest structure. The climb up can be daunting, but the views from the top are superb, with the forest stretching out all around and the rest of the ancient city beneath you.

Accommodation

🏃 **The Trek Stop** Signed on the left just before San José Succotz ☎823-2265, ⓦwww .thetrekstop.com. A wonderful budget place to stay, with clean cabins (one with private bath) and a campsite. The restaurant serves large portions and has good vegetarian choices, and there's a shared kitchen, free wi-fi, and bikes, kayaks and tubes available for rent. Next door is the well-designed Tropical Wings Nature Center (daily 8am–5pm; Bz$5). Camping ❶, singles ❸, doubles ❹–❻

The south

South of Belmopan lies Belize's most rugged terrain. Population density in this part of Belize is low, with most of the towns and villages located on the water. **Dangriga**, the largest settlement, is home to the **Garífuna** people and is the transportation hub for much of the region. Farther south, the **Placencia peninsula** is the area's focus for coastal tourism, boasting some of Belize's only true beaches, and is also the departure point for the south's idyllic cayes. The Southern Highway comes to an end in **Punta Gorda**, from where you can head to Guatemala or visit **ancient Maya sites** and present-day **Maya villages**.

Inland, the **Maya Mountains** form a solid barrier to land travel except on foot or horseback. The Belizean government, showing supreme foresight, has placed practically the whole massif under some form of protection. The most accessible area of rainforest is the **Cockscomb Basin Wildlife Sanctuary**, a reserve designed to protect the area's sizeable jaguar population.

THE HUMMINGBIRD HIGHWAY

Southeast from Belmopan, the **Hummingbird Highway** heads towards Dangriga, passing through magnificent scenery. On the right the eastern slopes of the **Maya Mountains** become visible, forming part of a ridge of limestone mountains riddled with underground rivers and **caves**, several of which are accessible.

St Herman's Cave

About 19km out of Belmopan the road crosses the **Caves Branch River**, a tributary of the Sibun River. Just beyond, by the roadside on the right, is **St Herman's Cave** (daily 8am–4.30pm; Bz$8; includes entrance to the Blue Hole National Park, see p.103). After paying the entrance fee at the visitors' centre, a ten-minute walk on a marked trail leads to the cave entrance, located beneath a dripping rock face; you'll need a flashlight to enter, heading down steps that were originally cut by the Maya. Inside, clamber over the rocks and splash through the river for about 300m, admiring the stunning natural formations, before the section of the cave accessible without a guide ends. To go further, consider hiring a guide (see p.103). Behind the visitors' centre and

> **TREAT YOURSELF**
>
> **Caves Branch Jungle Lodge** Between St Herman's Cave and the Blue Hole, about 1km from the highway ☎822-2800, ⓦwww.cavesbranch.com. To fully appreciate caving in Belize, consider staying here – there's a variety of excellent accommodation, but it's the tours on offer that really make it worth the splurge. Camping ❶, bunkhouse ❸, cabañas ❾

cave, trails lead through the surrounding forest and, after 4km, to a **campsite**. All buses between Belmopan and Dangriga can drop you at St Herman's Cave or the Blue Hole.

Blue Hole National Park

Two kilometres past St Herman's Cave, accessible from the highway or via a marked trail from the visitors' centre, is **Blue Hole National Park**, centred on a beautiful pool whose cool turquoise waters are perfect for a refreshing dip. The "Hole" is actually a short stretch of underground river, whose course is revealed by a collapsed cavern. Other trails depart from here, including the Hummingbird Loop.

The **guided cave and rappelling trips** run by *Caves Branch Jungle Lodge* (see p.102) aren't cheap (from US$85 per person), but well worth it for the experience. Many of the caves contain Maya artefacts – burials, ceramics and carvings. The best independent guide to the area is Marcos Cucul, based in Belmopan (℡600-3116, ⓦwww .mayaguide.bz).

DANGRIGA

From the junction of the Hummingbird and Southern highways, it's 10km to **DANGRIGA** (formerly known as Stann Creek), the district capital and the largest town in southern Belize. Dangriga is the cultural centre of the **Garífuna**, a people of mixed indigenous Caribbean and African descent, who overall make up about eleven percent of the country's population. The town is also home to some of the country's most popular artists, including painters and drum-makers, and you may catch an exhibition or performance. Still, for most travellers the town is of little interest unless you're here during a festival, though it makes a very useful base for visiting **Tobacco Caye** offshore and the **Jaguar Reserve** near Hopkins (see p.106).

Arrival and information

By air Dangriga's airstrip, served by at least eight daily flights on the run from Belize City to Punta Gorda, is on the shore just north of the *Pelican*

THE GARÍFUNA

The Garífuna trace their history to the island of St Vincent, in the eastern Caribbean, where two Spanish ships carrying slaves from Nigeria to America were wrecked off the coast in 1635. The survivors took refuge on the island, which was inhabited by Caribs, themselves recent arrivals from South America. At first the Caribs and Africans fought, but the Caribs had been weakened by disease and wars against the native Kalipuna, and eventually the predominant race became black with some indigenous blood, known by the English as the Black Caribs, or Garífuna.

For most of the seventeenth and eighteenth centuries St Vincent fell nominally under British control, though in practice it belonged to the Garífuna, who fended off British attempts to gain full control until 1796. The British colonial authorities, however, would not allow a free black society, so the Carib population was hunted down and transported to Roatán, off the coast of Honduras (see p.399). The Spanish Commandante of Trujillo, on the Honduran mainland, took the surviving Black Caribs to Trujillo, where they became in demand as free labourers, fishermen and soldiers.

In the early nineteenth century small numbers of Garífuna moved up the coast to Belize. The largest single migration took place in 1832, when thousands fled from Honduras after they supported the wrong side in a failed revolution to overthrow the government. It is this arrival that is today celebrated as Garífuna Settlement Day (see p.64).

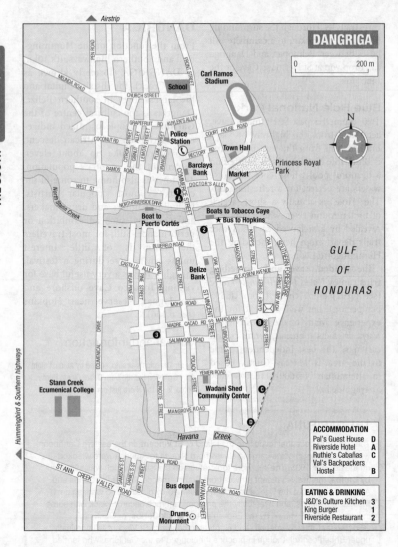

DANGRIGA

0   200 m

Airstrip

PEN ROAD

MELINDA ROAD

FRONT STREET

Carl Ramos
Stadium

CHURCH STREET

School

COURT HOUSE ROAD

GRAPEFRUIT RD

KUMLEN'S ALLEY

COCONUT RD

GRNUT STREET

CITRUST STREET

LEMON STREET

PLUM STREET

ORANGE ST

Police
Station

RECTORY RD

Town Hall

RAMOS ROAD

Barclays
Bank

COMMERCE STREET

Market

Princess Royal
Park

WEST ST

North Stann Creek

DOCTOR'S ALLEY

❶
Ⓐ

NORTHRIVERSIDE DRIVE

Boat to
Puerto Cortés

Boats to Tobacco Caye
★ Bus to Hopkins

❷

BLUEFIELD ROAD

GULF

CASTILLO ALLEY

CANAL STREET

CEDAR STREET

Belize
Bank

OAK STREET

MAGOON STREET

ALEJO BENI AVENUE

ST VINCENT STREET

KNAPP'S STREET

CHATUYE STREET

SOUTHERN FORESHORE

OF

REAR PINE ST

PINE STREET

MOHO ROAD

HONDURAS

DRIVE

MADRE CACAO RD

MAHOGANY ST

GANEY STREET

HOWE STREET

❸

SALMWOOD ROAD

TUBROOSE STREET

Ⓑ

SHARP STREET

ECUMENICAL

ZIRICOTE STREET

POLACK STREET

YEMERI ROAD

Stann Creek
Ecumenical College

MANGROVE ROAD

Wadani Shed
Community Center

Ⓒ

Ⓓ

Hummingbird & Southern highways

Havana   *Creek*

ST ANN CREEK VALLEY ROAD

ISLA ROAD

Bus depot

SAMSON'S ST

DANIEL'S ST

UNITY STREET

HAVANA STREET

CABBAGE ROAD

Drums
Monument

ACCOMMODATION
Pal's Guest House   **D**
Riverside Hotel   **A**
Ruthie's Cabañas   **C**
Val's Backpackers
   Hostel   **B**

EATING & DRINKING
J&D's Culture Kitchen   **3**
King Burger   **1**
Riverside Restaurant   **2**

Beach Hotel, 2km north of town; taxis into town cost Bz$5–8.

By bus NTSL and James buses pull up at the terminal 1km south of the centre. Though taxis are usually available for Bz$3–5, all of the hotels we recommend are an easy 10–15min walk from the terminal.

Tour operators Island Expeditions, on the Southern Foreshore, rents sea kayaks (singles Bz$70/day, doubles Bz$110/day), and also will shuttle you and your boat out to the nearby cayes.

Tourist information There's no tourist office in Dangriga, but the *Riverside Restaurant* (see p.105) can answer questions on transport and local information. The town's website (ⓦ www.dangrigalive.bz) is also very helpful and has a downloadable map.

Accommodation

Pal's Guest House 868 Magoon St ☎ 522-2095, ⓔ palbze@btl.net. Quiet hotel set right on the beach north of the creek. Basic, tiled rooms have private baths and TVs. ❹–❺

Riverside Hotel Commerce St, beside the bridge ☎ 522-2168. Very central hotel has clean rooms with shared bath and views over the river. ❸

Ruthie's Cabañas 31 Southern Foreshore ☎ 502-3184. Two bargain, thatched cabañas on the beach with private bath and porch. Ruthie will cook meals by arrangement. ❺

🏃 **Val's Backpackers Hostel** 1 Sharp St, near the beach ☎ 502-3324, ℰ valsbelize@yahoo.com. Though the dorms and private rooms in this concrete building are not the most attractive, they are clean, and the hostel offers same-day laundry service, an internet café, a book exchange, ice cream and lovely views of the sea from its veranda. Dorms ❷, doubles ❹

Eating and drinking

Despite Dangriga's central position in Garífuna culture, few restaurants specialize in Garífuna cuisine, though some serve a few dishes – you'll find it's generally more readily available in Hopkins (see p.106).

Restaurants

J&D's Culture Kitchen On Canal St. Small, local restaurant serving Creole and Garífuna dishes, usually for Bz$8–12.

King Burger On Commerce St. Take-out and sit-down restaurant popular with locals. Serves fast food, Belizean cuisine and seafood for Bz$4–10.

Riverside Restaurant On the south bank of the river by the bridge. Serves tasty Creole cuisine, including great breakfasts and a daily special, for Bz$8–25. Also a great place to find tourist information.

Directory

Exchange Banks are on St Vincent St. Approaching the river from the south, the Atlantic Bank is on your right, and the Belize Bank is on your left; both have 24hr ATMs.

Internet The internet café in *Val's Backpackers* charges Bz$4/hr.

Laundry *Val's Backpackers* has a same-day drop-off laundry service.

Post office On Mahogany St at Ganey St.

Moving on

By boat Boats to Tobacco Caye (40min; Bz$35) leave from the bridge near the *Riverside Restaurant*, though there are no scheduled departures; ask in the restaurant for Captain Buck.

> ### INTO HONDURAS: DANGRIGA
>
> A fast skiff (☎ 522-3227) leaves Dangriga for Puerto Cortés, Honduras, each Saturday at 9am (US$50; 3hr) from the north bank of the river. Get there an hour before departure to deal with formalities.

By bus to: Belize City, mostly via Belmopan with two weekly services via Gales Point (at least every 2hr; 2–3hr); Placencia (4 daily; 2hr); Punta Gorda (6–8 daily; 3hr). The 10.30am and 4pm Placencia buses also pass through Hopkins (30min) and continue south via the Sittee River.

AROUND DANGRIGA

Dangriga serves as the jumping-off point for two of the coast's most intriguing and least-visited sights, including the small village of **Gales Point**, where visitors can learn the art of traditional drumming, and **Tobacco Caye**, a tiny, stunning island located right on the reef.

Gales Point

Fourteen kilometres along the Hummingbird Highway back towards Belmopan from Dangriga, a coastal road heads north to the small Creole village of **Gales Point**. The village straggles along a narrow peninsula that juts into the **Southern Lagoon**, a large, shallow body of water which – along with **Northern Lagoon**, to which it's connected – comprises **Gales Point Wildlife Sanctuary**, a breeding ground for rare wildlife, including jabiru storks, turtles, manatee and crocodiles. The area is bounded to the west by limestone hills, riddled with caves and cloaked with mangroves. Gales Point is also a centre of **traditional drum-making**; you can learn to make and play drums at the Maroon Creole Drum School (☎ 603-6051, ℰ methos_drums@hotmail.com).

Several houses in Gales Point offer simple **rooms**, including *Ionie's* (☎ 220-8066; ❸), which has five simple rooms with shared bath and fans, and where you can arrange meals; it's in the first shop as you enter the village. *Metho's Coconut Camping* (❶) has space in a sandy spot in the northern part of the village.

Gales Point is served by two weekly **buses** in each direction on the Coastal Road, usually leaving Belize City and Dangriga on Mondays and Fridays; other traffic passes the junction, 4km from the village, and hitching is relatively easy.

Tobacco Caye

About 20km offshore from Dangriga is **Columbus Reef**, a superb section of the Barrier Reef. **Tobacco Caye**, idyllically perched on its southern tip, is the easiest of the cayes in the area to visit and has a number of places to stay. The island is tiny: stand in the centre and you're only a couple of minutes from the shore in any direction, with the unbroken reef stretching north for miles. The reef is so close to shore that you won't need a boat to go **snorkelling** or **diving**, and several of the resorts, including *Reef's End Lodge*, have dive shops that rent gear even to those who are not guests; snorkelling gear costs US$7.50 and diving gear US$25.

Boats (40min; Bz$35) leave daily from near the bridge in Dangriga, though there are no scheduled departures; ask at the *Riverside Restaurant* for Captain Buck. Though accommodation on the caye is simple, it remains quite expensive; however, all places to stay include three meals. The best-value choices are *Gaviota Coral Reef Resort* (☎509-5032; ❺), which offers cabins on the sand and less expensive rooms in the main building, all with shared bath, and *Tobacco Caye Paradise* (☎520-5101, ✉bluefield@btl.net; doubles ❹, cabañas ❺), with simple, shared-bath rooms in a wooden house and cabañas overlooking the sea.

HOPKINS

The small village of **HOPKINS**, south of Dangriga and stretching along a

bay, is home to upwards of a thousand Garífuna. Garífuna Settlement Day, on November 19, is celebrated enthusiastically here, but at other times it's a very quiet, pleasant place to spend a few days relaxing. Hotels, cabañas and resorts line the beach, though you will rarely see other tourists in town. You can rent **kayaks** at *Kismet Inn* (Bz$30) – the lagoon just north of the village is a great place for kayaking; windsurfing equipment at *Windschief*; and **bicycles** (Bz$20/day) from Tina's Bike Rental, on the road toward the village's south end. Many hotels can also arrange **snorkelling** or **diving** trips to the reef and cayes farther out.

Arrival

By bus The 10.30am and 4pm buses from Dangriga make a loop around town before heading south to the Sittee River; let the bus driver know beforehand where you want to get off. Alternatively, any bus on the Southern Highway can drop you at the turn-off to the village, from where it's quite easy and common to hitch a ride into town. There are no street names in Hopkins; the main point of reference is where the road from the Southern Highway enters the village – dividing Hopkins into north and south – and signs point the way to the many hotels and restaurants.

Accommodation

Kismet Inn On the beach, just past the north end of the village ☎523-7280, ✖www.kismetinn.com. A quirky, social hotel with several thatched cabañas with private bathrooms, as well as budget rooms with shared bath in a wooden house designed to resemble a ship. Breakfast (Bz$7) includes home-made bread, coffee and fresh fruit; lunch and dinner can be arranged. There's also free bike use and kayak rental. Camping ❶, singles ❸, doubles ❹
Tania's Guest House South of the centre, just past the basketball court ☎523-7058, ✉taniaprim @yahoo.com. Exceptionally friendly staff offers clean, basic rooms with private bath in wooden building. Singles ❸, doubles ❹
Windschief On the beach, south of the centre ☎523-7249, ✖www.windschief.com. Two simple cabins, one with a double bed (❹) and the other with two double beds and a fridge (❻). Both have

private bath with cold-water showers and coffee-makers. There's also a shared hot-water shower and free wi-fi. Windsurfing lessons Bz$60/hr, rental Bz$60/day.

Eating

Though your choice may be limited out of the tourist season, the village has enough restaurants and bars that you'll always find good, simple Garifuna and Creole meals, though in many establishments you'll simply get a serving of whatever has been made for that meal, as opposed to choosing from a menu.

Iris Restaurant at the southern end of the village. Good Belizean cuisine and fast food, as well as large breakfasts, for Bz$4–10.

Laruni Hatie Beyabu Restaurant north of the centre, on the beach. Popular, thatched restaurant with a beautiful view of the sea serves large portions of Belizean and Garifuna cuisine, usually for around Bz$7.

Watering Hole at the southern end of the village, next to *Iris Restaurant*. One of the best restaurants in the village, dishes up great seafood and Belizean cuisine for Bz$8–12.

Drinking and entertainment

For a **drink** with the locals, head to *King Cassava*, which often has **live music** on the weekends. On most nights, the Lebeha Drumming Center (🌐www.lebeha.com), at the northern end of the village, hosts a performance of Garifuna drumming; stop by in advance to check the schedule.

GLOVER'S REEF

GLOVER'S REEF, the southernmost of Belize's three coral atolls, lies around 40km off the coast from Hopkins. Roughly oval in shape, it stretches 35km north to south, with a number of cayes in its southeastern section. Famous for its wall diving, which is thought to be among the best in the world, the atoll also hosts a stunning lagoon, which offers spectacular snorkelling and diving, as well as a staggering diversity of wildlife. The entire atoll is a **marine reserve** (Bz$20 entry fee, usually payable to your accommodation or tour guide), with a research station on Middle Caye.

Glover's is something of an anomaly among the remote atolls: it offers **accommodation** within the reach of budget travellers at *Glover's Atoll Resort* (☎520-5016, 🌐www.glovers.com.bz), on **Northeast Caye**. Thatched cabins over the water or on the beach (❾) overlook the reef, or there are dorm beds (❻) in a wooden house and camping space (❾); all rates are weekly, and include transport from Sittee River in the resort's boat (leaves Sun 9am, returns following Sat; 3hr). Meals are not included, so you can either bring your own food or eat at the restaurant. The staff pretty much leaves you to your own devices – you can choose to enjoy the simple desert-island experience or take part in activities (paid for separately), including sailing, sea kayaking, fishing, snorkelling and diving (including dive training), which is spectacular, thanks to a huge underwater cliff and some tremendous wall-diving.

COCKSCOMB BASIN WILDLIFE SANCTUARY

Back on the mainland, the jagged peaks of the **Maya Mountains** rise to the west of the Southern Highway. The tallest summits are those of the Cockscomb range, which includes **Victoria Peak** (1120m), the second highest mountain in Belize. Beneath the ridges is a vast bowl of stunning rainforest, over four hundred square kilometres of which is protected by the **COCKSCOMB BASIN WILDLIFE SANCTUARY** – better known as the **Jaguar Reserve** (daily 7.30am–4.30pm; Bz$10). The basin could be home to as many as sixty of Belize's 800-strong **jaguar population**, and though you'll almost certainly come across their tracks, your chances of actually seeing one are very slim, as they are mainly active at night and avoid humans. Over 290 species of **birds** have also been recorded here, including the endangered scarlet macaw, the great curassow and the king vulture.

The sanctuary is at the end of a rough ten-kilometre road that branches off the main highway at the village of **Maya Centre**, runs through towering forest and fords a couple of streams before crossing the Cabbage Hall Gap and entering the Cockscomb Basin. Here, you'll find the sanctuary headquarters, where you can pick up maps of the reserve. Beyond the headquarters, a system of very well-maintained trails of varying lengths winds through tropical moist forest, crossing streams and leading to a number of picturesque waterfalls and ridges. For those who have the time – and have made the necessary preparations – it is also possible to take the four- or five-day hike and climb to the summit of Victoria Peak. If you're looking for a more relaxing experience, however, you can float down South Stann Creek in an inner tube, available for rent (Bz$5 per day) at the headquarters.

Arrival and information

By bus All between Dangriga and Punta Gorda pass Maya Centre. If visiting the reserve, you need to sign in and pay the entrance fee at the craft centre at the junction of the road leading up to the Cockscomb. From the craft centre in Maya Centre, you can catch a ride with a taxi or truck to the reserve headquarters; this usually costs about Bz$35–40 for up to 5 people. The 10km walk to the reserve from this point, however, is relatively easy and should only take several hours.

Internet Julio's Store, just beyond the intersection, sells basic supplies and cold drinks (there's no shop in the reserve), and it's also a bar with internet access. The owner runs Cockscomb Maya Tours (☎520-3042, ✉julio_saqui@hotmail.com) and can arrange guides and transport into the reserve.

Accommodation

The reserve headquarters offers a variety of accommodation, including private furnished cabins for four or six people (**7**), wooden dorm rooms with showers (**4**) and a more "rustic" cabin with dorm beds (**2**). Camping space (**1**) is available, though you can also camp (**1**) at two other designated sites along the trails, for which you'll need to get a permit at the reserve headquarters. Maya Centre also has several inexpensive places to stay, all of which can arrange meals, tours, guides and transport.

In Maya Centre

Nu'uk Che'il Cottages 500m up the track to the reserve ☎520-3033, ✉nuukcheil @btl.net. Delightful rooms with private bath and a large wooden cabin with shared showers and dorm beds (**2**), as well as double beds (**4**). The restaurant serves excellent Maya cuisine (Bz$5–15), and the owner has developed a medicinal plant trail out back. **5**

Tutzil Nah Cottages On the highway just before the junction ☎520-3044, ✉www.mayacenter .com. Two clean cabins, one wood and one concrete, house four rooms with shared bath. Run by the Chun brothers, excellent guides to the reserve. Out front, the family also runs a small grocery store. Singles **3**, doubles **4**

PLACENCIA

Sixteen kilometres south of Maya Centre, a dirt road cuts east from the Southern Highway, heading through pine forest and banana plantations before reaching the sea and snaking south down the narrow **Placencia Peninsula**, immensely popular for its sandy beaches, which are among the best in Belize. Though accommodation throughout most of the peninsula, including the villages of Maya Beach and Seine Bight, is limited to upscale resorts and hotels, **PLACENCIA** village itself has an abundance of budget options. Shaded by palm trees and cooled by the sea breeze, it's a great place to relax.

What to see and do

Apart from simply hanging out on the beach, Placencia is a good, if expensive, base for snorkelling and diving trips to the southern cayes and reef or a day-trip to the **Monkey River**.

Diving and snorkelling

Diving options from Placencia are excellent, but the distance to most dive sites (at least 30km) means that trips here can be more expensive than

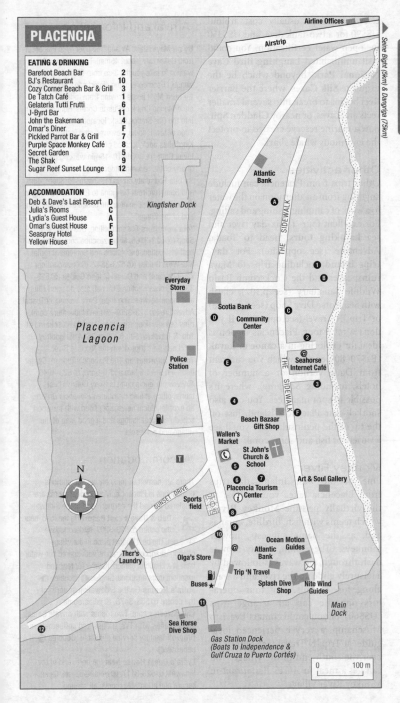

PLACENCIA

EATING & DRINKING

Barefoot Beach Bar	2
BJ's Restaurant	10
Cozy Corner Beach Bar & Grill	3
De Tatch Café	1
Gelateria Tutti Frutti	6
J-Byrd Bar	11
John the Bakerman	4
Omar's Diner	F
Pickled Parrot Bar & Grill	7
Purple Space Monkey Café	8
Secret Garden	5
The Shak	9
Sugar Reef Sunset Lounge	12

ACCOMMODATION

Deb & Dave's Last Resort	D
Julia's Rooms	C
Lydia's Guest House	A
Omar's Guest House	F
Seaspray Hotel	B
Yellow House	E

Airline Offices

Airstrip

Seine Bight (5km) & Dangriga (75km)

BELIZE

THE SOUTH

Atlantic Bank

THE SIDEWALK

Kingfisher Dock

A

Everyday Store

Scotia Bank

Community Center

Placencia Lagoon

Police Station

Seahorse Internet Café

THE SIDEWALK

Beach Bazaar Gift Shop

Wallen's Market

St John's Church & School

Art & Soul Gallery

N

SUNSET DRIVE

Sports field

Placencia Tourism Center

Ocean Motion Guides

Ther's Laundry

Olga's Store

Atlantic Bank

Trip 'N Travel

Buses

Splash Dive Shop

Nite Wind Guides

Main Dock

Sea Horse Dive Shop

Gas Station Dock
(Boats to Independence &
Gulf Cruza to Puerto Cortés)

0   100 m

elsewhere. Trips usually cost around US$90 for a two-tank dive, and US$350 for open-water certification. You could visit uninhabited **Laughing Bird Caye National Park**, beyond which lie the exquisite **Silk Cayes**, where the Barrier Reef begins to break into several smaller reefs and cayes, or nearby **Gladden Spit**, now a marine reserve created to protect the enormous **whale shark**.

Other activities

Other trips from Placencia can include anything from an afternoon on the water to a week of camping, fishing and sailing. For excellent four- to six-day river and sea **kayaking tours**, head to Toadal Adventure (see opposite). For **day-trips inland**, including trips to Maya ruins, caves and the Cockscomb Basin Wildlife Sanctuary (see p.107), check with Sea Horse Dive Shop (see opposite) or Trip 'N Travel (see opposite). If you don't want a tour, Placencia's lagoon is ideal for exploring in a **canoe** or **kayak** (Bz$70–80 per day, which you can rent from Dave Vernon or a number of hotels, including *Seaspray*), where it's possible to spot manatees. You can also snorkel near Placencia Island, just off the tip of the peninsula; here you'll see a variety of fish and some coral.

Monkey River

One of the best inland day-trips from Placencia takes you by boat to the virtually pristine **Monkey River**, which teems with fish, birdlife, iguanas and, as the name suggests, howler monkeys. The 20km, thirty-minute dash through the waves is followed by a leisurely glide up the river and a walk along forest trails. The tour operators opposite can all arrange trips (US$60), or you could contact Evaristo Muschamp, a very experienced local guide, at Trip 'N Travel (see opposite), near the south end of the village. You can get a meal in *Alice's Restaurant* in Monkey River village.

Arrival and information

By air Maya Island Air and Tropic Air fly to Placencia from Belize City (about 45min). Taxis are usually waiting to take you the 3km from the airstrip to the village, or someone in the airport can call one for you.
By boat Most boats arriving from Independence/Mango Creek or Puerto Cortés, Honduras pull into the Gas Station Dock, located at the southern edge of town; some, however, stop instead at the Kingfishes dock, located on the northwest edge of town. Both are within 10–15min walking distance of any of the recommended hotels.
By bus Four daily buses (10.30am, 11.30am, 4pm, and 5pm) run from Dangriga to Placencia, pulling in at the petrol station near the beach at the southern end of the village.
Tour operators For snorkelling, Sea Horse Dive Shop (℡523-3166, ⓦbelizescuba.com) offers the best instruction, excursions and equipment rental. Nite Wind Guides (℡523-3847, ⓔdoylegardiner@yahoo.com) and Ocean Motion Guides (℡523-3363, ⓔoceanmotion@btl.net) also do snorkelling and manatee-watching trips. Dave Vernon, of Toadal Adventure (℡523-3207, ⓦtoadaladventure.com), runs sea kayaking trips, and Evaristo Muschamp at Trip 'N Travel (℡523-3205 or 3614. ⓔlgodfrey@btl.net) runs trips down the Monkey River.
Tourist information The Placencia Tourism Center (Mon–Fri 9–11.30am and 1–5pm; ℡523-4045, ⓦwww.placencia.com) is likely Belize's best tourist office. It also distributes *Placencia Breeze*, an excellent local newspaper filled with transport schedules, local listings and a good map of the village and peninsula.

Accommodation

There are numerous inexpensive accommodation options in Placencia. Most budget rooms are clustered around the northern end of the Sidewalk.

Deb & Dave's Last Resort On the road, near the centre ℡523-3207, ⓔdebanddave@btl.net. The best budget place in the village, offering clean, colourful rooms with shared hot-water bath in a beautiful garden. Kayaks for rent and excellent tours arranged. Singles ➍, doubles ➍
Julia's Rooms On the Sidewalk just north of the centre ℡503-3478, ⓔjuliasrooms@juliasrooms.com. Two rooms with private baths, and cabañas with TVs, fridges and coffeemakers. Drop-off laundry service available. Doubles ➏, cabañas ➍
Lydia's Guest House Near the north end of the Sidewalk ℡523-3117, ⓔlydias@btl.net. Clean, secure and affordable rooms, all sharing

immaculate bathrooms, in a quiet location near the beach. Lydia cooks breakfast on request and rents kayaks. Singles ❹, doubles ❺

Omar's Guest House On the Sidewalk in the centre ☎600-8421. Very simple rooms with shared baths. Although beds in the dorm room (❸) are a bit expensive, you get a discount for multiple-night stays. There's a shared fridge and a restaurant downstairs. ❹

Seaspray Hotel On the beach, in the centre of the village ☎523-3148, ⓦwww.seasprayhotel.com. Popular, well-run hotel in a great location, with a variety of excellent accommodation, all with private bath and fridge and some with TV, kitchenette and balcony. There are hammocks on the beach and kayaks for rent. ❺–❼

The Yellow House In the centre of the village, between the road and the Sidewalk ☎523-3047, ⓔlance@ctbelize.com. Bargain rooms, all with private bath and some with fridge, in a bright yellow wooden building with balcony and hammocks. Deals on multiple-night stays. ❺

Eating

There are plenty of good restaurants in Placencia, but establishments change management fast, so ask locally for the latest recommendations. Most places close early and you'll certainly have a better choice if you're at the table by 8pm. Fresh bread is available from *John The Bakerman* near the centre of the Sidewalk.

Restaurants

BJ's Restaurant On the road just past the sports field. Great Belizean cuisine at very inexpensive prices; most mains are Bz$8–12.

De Tatch Café On the beach, just past *Seaspray Hotel*. Excellent international and Belizean cuisine and seafood, served in a quiet, open-air restaurant right by the sea. There's a lunch special for Bz$10 and a dinner special for Bz$25, as well as internet access. Other mains Bz$10–30.

Gelateria Tutti Frutti Near the southern end of the road. Without a doubt the best ice cream in Belize, available in literally dozens of flavours for Bz$4 and up. Closed Wed.

Omar's Diner On the Sidewalk in the centre. Very inexpensive, small restaurant serving filling breakfasts, Mexican cuisine and seafood. Breakfast and lunch Bz$7–16, dinner Bz$16–40.

Pickled Parrot Bar & Grill Set back from the road near the centre. Popular, open-air restaurant and bar featuring fresh seafood, pizza, and international dishes, as well as fantastic blended cocktails. Mains Bz$14–40. Closed Sun.

Purple Space Monkey Café On the road opposite the sports field. Offers good coffee, breakfasts, burgers, sandwiches and seafood. Though dinner is quite expensive (Bz$27–40), breakfast and lunch are very reasonable (Bz$4–12). There's also an internet café and paperback exchange inside.

Secret Garden Opposite the sports field. Set back from the road in a quiet, secluded spot, this coffeehouse and spa serves great breakfasts and fresh seafood.

The Shak On the road south of the centre. Small, outdoor restaurant serving delicious smoothies made right in front of you, as well as healthy salads and breakfasts for Bz$6–12. Closed Sun.

Drinking and nightlife

Although most of the restaurants also serve drinks, there are a few places with live music and more of a bar atmosphere.

Bars

Barefoot Beach Bar Off the Sidewalk near the beach. Very popular bar serving great cocktails (happy hour 6–7pm). Open late most nights.

Cozy Corner Beach Bar & Grill On the beach. Lively bar and restaurant that is often packed and sometimes hosts live music on weekends.

J-Byrd Bar Near the south dock. A great place to meet local characters and sometimes catch live music.

Sugar Reef Sunset Lounge On Sunset Drive, at the southwest tip of the island. Features a daily happy hour, bar games, karaoke and either a DJ or a live band.

Directory

Exchange The Atlantic Bank (with 24hr ATM), near the petrol station, can give cash advances. They have a second ATM on the road near the tourist office.

Internet Many restaurants, including *De Tatch* and *Purple Space Monkey*, have small internet cafés. Placencia Office Supply, on the road south of the centre, has numerous computers and a reliable connection.

Laundry *Julia's Rooms* has a drop-off laundry service.

Post office On the end of the Sidewalk.

Moving on

By air Belize City (45min); Dangriga (20min).
By boat The *Hokey Pokey* ferry (6–7 daily; 20min) departs from either the Main Dock near the petrol station or the Kingfisher Dock on the lagoon for

Independence/Mango Creek, where buses on the Dangriga–Punta Gorda line are usually timed to meet the ferry. The fast skiff *Gulf Cruza* leaves Placencia for Puerto Cortés in Honduras (☎202-4506; US$50; 4hr) every Fri at 9.30am.

By bus to: Dangriga (4 daily, usually at 5am, 6am, 1.30pm and 2pm; 2hr).

THE FAR SOUTH

Beyond Independence, the Southern Highway leaves the banana plantations, first twisting through pine forests, crossing numerous creeks and rivers, and arriving in the sparsely populated **Toledo District**, Belize's least developed region. Here, the Mopan and Kekchi, the country's two main Maya groups, comprise almost half the population. About 73km from the Placencia junction lies **Nim Li Punit** (daily 9am–5pm; Bz$10), a Late Classic Maya site, possibly allied to nearby Lubaantun and to Quiriguá in Guatemala (see p.200). The ruins stand on top of a ridge, surrounded by the fields of the nearby Maya village of **Indian Creek**. The **visitors' centre** has a good map of the site and explanations of some of the carved texts found here, which include eight stelae, among them **Stela 15**, at over 9m the tallest yet found in Belize. The site is only 1km off the highway, making it an easy day-trip from Punta Gorda.

Accommodation

If you're looking to be isolated in Toledo's wilderness, there are several good places to stay along the southern highway, located along the final 22 kilometres to Punta Gorda.

Casa Bonita Apartments In Cattle Landing, 3km north of Punta Gorda ☎722-2270, ✉cba4cnn@btl .net. A good range of furnished, private apartments in a concrete building facing the sea. Discounts for students, and meals can be arranged. ❻–❽

Sun Creek Lodge In Sun Creek, 3km south of the Dump junction ☎614-2080, ✇www .suncreeklodge.com. Five beautiful thatched cabañas, all with electricity, but only one with private bath. One of the owners knows the area exceptionally well and can organize tours. Internet access available and breakfast included. Cabañas ❻–❼

Tranquility Lodge In Jacintoville, 10km south of the Dump junction ✇www.tranquility-lodge .com. Set in gardens on the bank of Jacinto Creek, the lodge offers a/c comfort in spacious en-suite rooms. The restaurant upstairs provides great views, and the creek is perfect for a dip. ❼

PUNTA GORDA

The Southern Highway comes to an end in **PUNTA GORDA**, the heart of the still isolated Toledo District. The town is populated by a mixture of six thousand Creoles, Garífuna and Maya – who make up more than half the population of the district – and is the focal point for a large number of villages and farming settlements. The busiest day in town is Saturday, when people from the surrounding villages come to trade. Though there's little to see at other times in Punta Gorda, the town is very laid-back and has a lovely shoreline; primarily, though, it makes an excellent base from which to explore the nearby Maya villages and ruins.

Arrival and information

By air Maya Island Air and Tropic Air both operate 4–5 daily flights from Belize City (via Dangriga and Placencia), landing at the airstrip five blocks west of the main dock and a 5–10min walk from any of the recommended hotels.

By boat Skiffs from Puerto Barrios and Lívingston, Guatemala use the main dock, near the centre of the seafront.

By bus Buses from Belize City (5–7hr) via Dangriga (3hr) circle the town, usually stopping at the petrol station at the northeast edge of the centre, which is within easy walking distance of all the recommended hotels – though you usually can convince the bus driver to drop you anywhere within the centre.

Tour operators The local TIDE (Toledo Institute for Development and the Environment; ☎722-2192, ✇www.tidetours.org) is involved with many conservation projects and also offers mountain-bike and kayak tours and camping trips to Payne's Creek National Park.

Tourist information The staff at the excellent tourist information office, on Front St and run by the Belize Tourism Industry Association (☎722-2531), can help with transportation schedules and assist in setting up tours of the outlying cayes and sites in Toledo District.

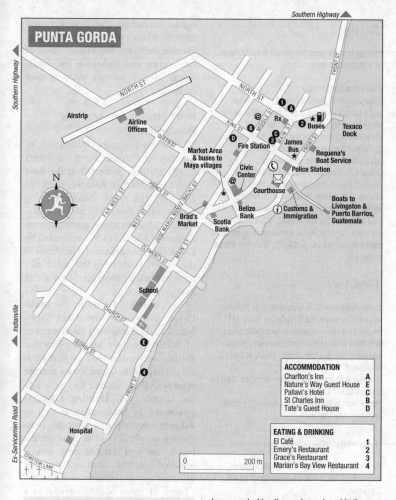

ACCOMMODATION

Charlton's Inn	A
Nature's Way Guest House	E
Pallavi's Hotel	C
St Charles Inn	B
Tate's Guest House	D

EATING & DRINKING

El Café	1
Emery's Restaurant	2
Grace's Restaurant	3
Marian's Bay View Restaurant	4

0   200 m

Accommodation

Accommodation in Punta Gorda is generally inexpensive. For an alternative to staying in town, contact *Nature's Way Guest House* which operates a programme of guesthouse accommodation in surrounding villages in conjunction with the Toledo Ecotourism Association (TEA).

Charlton's Inn 9 Main St ☏ 722-2197, ✆ wagnerdm@btl.net. Rooms with private, hot-water showers (most with a/c) in a two-storey concrete building. Singles ❹–❻, doubles ❺–❼

Nature's Way Guest House 65 Front St ☏ 702-2119. The best budget place in Punta Gorda and a good place to meet other travellers and get information. Clean rooms and dorms overlooking the sea have shared baths and cold showers. Serves breakfast and has a paperback exchange. ❹

Pallavi's Hotel 19 Main St ☏ 702-2414, ✆ gracemcp@hotmail.com. Clean, tiled rooms with private bath in the centre of town. Singles ❹, doubles ❺

St Charles Inn 23 King St ☏ 722-2149, ✆ stcharles@btl.net. One of Punta Gorda's smartest options, with very friendly staff. All rooms have private bath, and most have TV and a/c. ❹–❺

Tate's Guest House 34 José María Nuñez St, two blocks west of the town centre ☏ 722-0417, ✆ tatesguesthouse@yahoo.com. Quiet, friendly family-run hotel. All rooms have private bath and TV and some have a/c. Singles ❺, ❺–❻

Eating

It's easy to get a good, filling meal in Punta Gorda for a reasonable price.

Restaurants

El Café North St, behind *Charlton's Inn*. Small, bright restaurant serving good breakfasts, pastries, burgers and Belizean cuisine for Bz$3–12.

Emery's Restaurant At the northern end of Main St. Excellent, fresh seafood and international cuisine in a large, open-air restaurant.

Grace's Restaurant 19 Main St. Good, basic Belizean fare in clean, tiled surroundings.

Marian's Bay View Restaurant On Front St, across from *Nature's Way*. Large restaurant on the third floor of a concrete building with a beautiful view over the sea. Choose from a small menu of fresh Belizean cuisine (Bz$8–12). Breakfast served on request.

Directory

Exchange Belize Bank (with ATM) is on the main square across from the Civic Center. There will usually be a moneychanger outside the immigration office when international boats are coming and going, and you can change money in Grace's Restaurant.

Internet V-Comp (Mon–Sat 8am–8pm), on Main St, charges Bz$4/hr.

Post office In the government buildings a block back from the ferry dock.

Moving on

By air Maya Island Air and Tropic Air operate 4–5 daily flights to Belize City via Dangriga and Placencia.

By boat Departures daily to: Puerto Barrios, Guatemala (Bz$35; 1hr) at 9am, 2pm, and 4pm; Lívingston, Guatemala (Bz$40; 1hr) at 10am.

By bus to: Belize City via Dangriga and Belmopan (12 daily; 5–7hr); the express bus departs at 6am from the petrol station. Buses to the Maya villages leave from the market area, usually around noon: San Antonio (2 daily); San Pedro Columbia (for Labaantun; 4 per week); Jalacte and Pueblo Viejo (for Uxbenka; 4–8 per week).

AROUND PUNTA GORDA

As the only transportation hub in the far south, Punta Gorda serves as an important base for all of the region's sights, including the beautiful and tranquil islands of the **Port Honduras Marine Reserve**, the Mayan ruins of **Labaantun** and **Uxbenka**, and traditional Mayan villages such as **San Antonio**.

Port Honduras Marine Reserve

Six hundred square kilometres of the bay and coast north of Punta Gorda are now protected as the **Port Honduras Marine Reserve**, partly to safeguard the many **manatees** living and breeding there. The main reef has started to break up here, leaving several clusters of islands, each surrounded by a small independent reef. Hundreds of these tiny islands lie in the mouth of a large bay, whose shoreline is a maze of mangrove swamps.

North of Punta Gorda are the **Snake Cayes**, idyllic and uninhabited Caribbean islands that draw a small number of visitors for their stunning beaches. Farther out in the Gulf of Honduras are the **Sapodilla Cayes**, now a **marine reserve** (Bz$20 entrance fee), of which the largest caye, **Hunting Caye**, is frequented by Guatemalan as well as Belizean day-trippers; though most visitors simply choose to relax on the beach, the reef, located only several hundred metres offshore, provides excellent opportunities for snorkellers.

Some of these islands already have accommodation, and more resorts are planned, though at present the cayes and reserve receive relatively few foreign visitors and are fascinating to explore on a day-trip from Punta Gorda; contact TIDE (see tour operators, p.112) for more information on how to visit the reserve and cayes.

San Antonio

Perched on a small hilltop, the Mopan Maya village of **San Antonio** is one of the only towns served by daily buses from Punta Gorda (usually Mon–Sat only). The founders of San Antonio came from the village of San Luis, just across the border in Guatemala, and they maintain many age-old traditions, including their patron saint, San Luis Rey, whose beautiful church stands in the centre of the village.

The area around San Antonio is rich in wildlife, dominated by jungle-clad hills and swift-flowing rivers. Though most visitors come to town to relax and to learn about Maya village life, this stunning region also provides excellent hiking opportunities. In town, *Bol's Hill Top Hotel* (community phone ☎702-2144; ❸), offers basic **rooms** with shared bath and superb views, and is a good place to get information on local natural history and archeology.

Blue Creek

About 4km back towards Punta Gorda, and down a branch road heading southwest, lies the village of **Blue Creek**, whose main attraction is a beautiful stretch of water running through magnificent rainforest. To get to the best swimming spot, a lovely turquoise pool, walk ten minutes upriver along the right-hand bank. Near the pool is *Blue Creek Rainforest Lodge* (☎523-7076, ⦿www.ize2belize.com; ❼), which has bunk-bed accommodation in six wooden cabins with porches overlooking the creek. Though expensive, the price includes three daily meals and two daily activities, making the lodge a good deal. Alternatively, you could try to rent a room in the village. The creek's source, **Hokeb Ha** cave, is another fifteen minutes' walk upriver through the privately owned **Blue Creek Rainforest Reserve**. A guide can take you to Maya altars deep in the cave. To get to Blue Creek, take the village bus to San Benito Poite.

Uxbenka

Seven kilometres west from San Antonio, towards the village of **Santa Cruz**, which is served by four weekly buses, the ruins of **Uxbenka**, a small Maya site, are superbly positioned on an exposed hilltop with great views towards the coast. As you climb the hill before the village you'll be able to make out the shape of two tree-covered mounds and a plaza, and there are several stelae protected by thatched shelters.

If you do make it out here you can enjoy some wonderful **waterfalls** within easy reach of the road. Between Santa Cruz and Santa Elena, the **Rio Blanco Falls** tumble over a rocky ledge into a deep pool, and at **Pueblo Viejo**, 7km further on, an impressive series of cascades provides a spectacular sight. Trucks and buses continue 13km further west to **Jalacte**, at the Guatemalan border, used regularly as a crossing point by nationals of both countries, though it's not currently a legal entry or exit point for tourists.

Lubaantun

The Maya site of **Lubaantun** (daily 8am–5pm; Bz$10) is an easy visit from Punta Gorda via the bus to **San Pedro Columbia**. To get to the ruins, head through the village and cross the Columbia River; just beyond you'll see the track to the ruins, a few hundred metres away on the left. Some of the finds made at the site are displayed in glass cases at the **visitors' centre**, including astonishing, eccentric flints and ceramics.

Lubaantun ("Place of the Fallen Stones") was a major Late Classic Maya centre, though it was occupied only briefly, likely from around 750 to 890 AD. The ruins stand on a series of ridges which Maya architects shaped and filled, building retaining walls up to 10m high. The whole site is essentially a single acropolis, with five main plazas, eleven major structures, three ball courts and some impressive pyramids surrounded by forest.

Lubaantun's most enigmatic discovery came in 1926, when the famous **Crystal Skull** was found beneath an altar by Anna Mitchell-Hedges, the daughter of the British Museum expedition's leader. The skull was given to the local Maya, who in turn presented it to Anna's father as a token of their gratitude for the help he had given them. Carved from pure rock crystal, the skull's origin and age remain unclear, though much contested.

Guatemala

HIGHLIGHTS ✪

TIKAL:
once a great
Maya metropolis, now
an incomparable site

SEMUC CHAMPEY & LANQUÍN:
chill in idyllic turquoise waters,
then explore nearby caves

LAGO DE ATITLÁN:
a breathtaking,
steep-sided crater lake

ANTIGUA:
the former capital, boasting
restored buildings and
ruined churches

HIGHLIGHT VILLAGES:
for an insight into Maya life,
spend some time in a
traditional Highland village

MONTERRICO:
a sweeping, almost undeveloped
Pacific beach visited by sea turtles

ROUGH COSTS

DAILY BUDGET Basic US$15–20/
occasional treat US$30

DRINK Beer (330ml) US$2

FOOD Burrito US$1

CAMPING/HOSTEL/BUDGET HOTEL
US$3–5/US$5–6/US$10–20

TRAVEL Guatemala City–Antigua
(45km) by chicken bus: 1hr, US$1;
Antigua–Cobán (258km) by shuttle
minibus: 5hr, US$15

FACT FILE

POPULATION 13 million

AREA 109,000 sq km

LANGUAGES Spanish (official), plus
23 indigenous languages

CAPITAL Guatemala City
(population: 3 million)

CURRENCY Quetzal (Q)

INTERNATIONAL PHONE CODE
☏502

TIME ZONE GMT – 6hr

Introduction

Tourism is booming in Guatemala, and understandably so: the country simply overflows with natural, historical and cultural interest. In established destinations – Antigua, around Lago de Atitlán, Flores – you'll have your choice of home-like comforts and cheap, well-facilitated travel. Get off the beaten track, though, and opportunities for activities like jungle trekking, exploring ancient Maya ruins and modern Maya villages and cooling off in crystalline pools and waterfalls abound. Whatever preconceived notions you have, throw them away – you'll doubtless be surprised by the variety of experiences the country has to offer.

Guatemala's landscape, full of extremes, is undoubtedly one of the greatest attractions for visitors. Rising steeply from the Pacific coast, and contributing to the country's status as the most mountainous Central American nation, is a chain of volcanoes (some still smoking). In many **highland villages** these behemoths are just a part of life. Then there are the **lowlands** – on the flat, steamy Pacific side you'll find black-sand beaches, turtles and mangroves, while the Caribbean side remains unmistakably tropical. **El Petén**, the country's least populous yet largest department, fosters everything from savanna to rainforest, and is extraordinarily rich in both **Maya ruins** and wildlife. If cities are more your cup of tea, Guatemala has some nice ones: **Antigua** is home to irresistible colonial architecture, cobbled streets and a plethora of restaurants, cafés and Spanish schools. Even **Guatemala City**, avoided by many, possesses its own gritty charm.

The country's landscape has had an undeniable effect on the history and lifestyle of its people. **Indigenous groups** (mostly Maya) are in the majority here, especially in the highlands, where there have been communities since the eighth century (see p.167); villages such as Todos Santos, Chichicastenango and Nebaj display riotously coloured textiles, strikingly wizened Maya faces and some of the most sense-assaulting markets in the world. Throughout the country you'll find that Guatemalans

---

WHEN TO VISIT

When you go to Guatemala should depend on what you want to see and do; as with all mountainous countries, Guatemala's climate is largely governed by altitude. Many places of interest are between 1300 and 1600m (including Antigua, Lago de Atitlán and Cobán), where it can be downright cool at any time; in winter (Nov–March) especially, if the sun isn't out, it can feel distinctly damp and cold. Low-lying Petén is a different world, with steamy conditions most of the year. The Pacific and Caribbean coasts are equally hot and humid.

The summer, or rainy season, is roughly from May to October. Precipitation is usually confined to the late afternoon, and the rest of the day is often warm and pleasant. As a rule, it's only in remote areas that rain can affect travel plans. The busiest times for tourism are during July and August, and Easter, when Holy Week (Semana Santa) celebrations are quite a spectacle to behold.

(or Chapines, as they call themselves), while perhaps more reserved than some of their neighbours, are polite, helpful and welcoming at every turn.

CHRONOLOGY

1500 BC Nomads settle into agricultural communities and are regarded as the first Maya.

300 BC–300 AD Explosion of Maya culture. City-states such as Tikal boom.

300–900 AD Classic Period of Maya culture sees advances in architecture, astronomy and art, and the emergence of political alliances/rivalries.

750 AD Warring increases and Maya cities gradually decline. Highland villages begin to take shape, becoming the home of the last vestiges of Maya culture.

1200s Toltecs invading from Mexico institute a militaristic society that fosters highland tribal rivalries.

1523 Conquistador Pedro de Alvarado arrives, and takes advantage of tribal rivalries to bring the Maya under Spanish control.

1540 The last of the highland tribes are subdued.

1541 Guatemala's capital (present-day Antigua) presides over the provinces of modern-day Costa Rica, Nicaragua, El Salvador, Honduras and Chiapas.

1773 Antigua is destroyed by an earthquake, resulting in the relocation of the capital to its present-day site.

1821 The Captain-General of Central America signs the Act of Independence and Guatemala briefly becomes a member of the Central American Federation.

1847 Guatemala declares itself an independent republic.

1871 Rufino Barrios arrives from Mexico to start a liberal revolution, which heralds sweeping social change but crushes dissent and marginalizes the rural poor.

1901 The United Fruit Company begins to grow bananas in Guatemala. They monopolize railways and port facilities, and establish a pervasive political presence.

1930 Jorge Ubico becomes president, promising reform; he doesn't succeed, but does build a nice palace.

1944 Student violence leads to Ubico's resignation. Guatemala embarks on a 10-year experiment with "spiritual socialism".

1952 Law redistributing United Fruit Company land is passed, to the benefit of 100,000 peasant families.

1954 The CIA sets up an invasion of Guatemala to overthrow its "communist-leaning" government.

1955–1985 Military governments send the country into a spiral of violence, economic decline and corruption.

1976 Huge earthquake strikes, leaving 23,000 dead, 77,000 injured and a million homeless. Presence of guerrilla groups increases in the wake of the destruction.

1978 Lucas García takes over, escalating the civil war and massacring some 25,000 peasants, intellectuals, politicians, priests and protesters.

1982 Efraín Ríos Montt stages a successful coup. His Civil Defence Patrols polarize the country, trapping peasants between armed forces and guerrilla groups.

1985 The first legitimate elections in 30 years are won by Vinicio Cerezo, but the army is still clearly in control.

1992 Civil war rumbles on. Rigoberta Menchú is awarded the Nobel Peace Prize for campaigning on behalf of Guatemala's indigenous population.

1996 Peace accords are signed on December 29.

1998 Bishop Juan Gerardi is assassinated two days after publishing an investigation of wartime atrocities, exposing the military's continuing strength

1999 Alfonso Portillo takes office. Despite promises to tackle the military and criminal gangs, his reign is plagued by corruption, and he virtually bankrupts the country.

2004 Newcomer Oscar Berger is inaugurated president; he appoints Rigoberta Menchú as a goodwill ambassador to implement the peace accords. The faltering economy makes some teetering progress.

2007 Guatemala's first left-leaning president in 50 years, Alvaro Colom, is elected. His wife, Sandra de Colom, is set to become Guatemala's Evita, with a remit to front a committee for the alleviation of poverty.

Basics

ARRIVAL

The vast majority of Guatemala's visitors arrive at **La Aurora International Airport** (GUA), 6km south of Guatemala City. Most long-haul flights arrive from the US (with the main carriers Delta, Continental and American Airlines flying from Atlanta, Houston, Dallas Fort-Worth/Miami

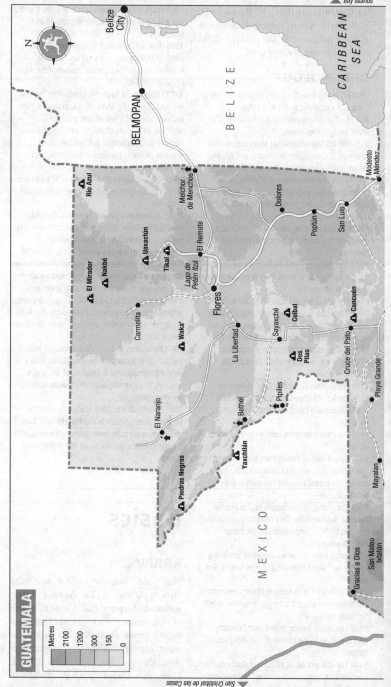

GUATEMALA

Metres
2100
1200
300
150
0

CARIBBEAN SEA

▲ Bay Islands

BELIZE

Belize City

BELMOPAN

Modesto Méndez

Río Azul

Melchor de Menchos

Dolores

Uaxactún

Tikal

El Remate

Poptún

San Luis

El Mirador

Nakbé

Lago de Petén Itzá

Flores

Carmelita

Waka'

Sayaxché

Ceibal

Cancuén

La Libertad

Dos Pilas

Cruce del Pato

Playa Grande

El Naranjo

Bethel

Pipiles

Piedras Negras

Yaxchilán

M E X I C O

Mayalan

Gracias a Dios

San Mateo Ixtatán

▼ San Cristóbal de las Casas

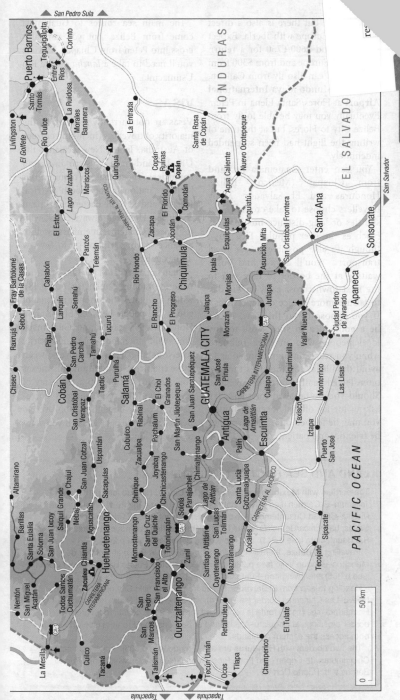

pectively), but there is also a direct flight from Europe with Iberia. Expect to pay around £600/€750 for a return ticket from Europe and from $300 from the US. You can also fly from Cancún, Mexico to **Mundo Maya International Airport** at Flores/Santa Elena in Petén. Eventually you may be able to fly from Belize City to Flores, but at the time of writing the flight had been suspended indefinitely.

You can enter Guatemala by **land** from Chiapas (Mexico), Belize, Honduras and El Salvador. Many travellers choose to take cross-border shuttles or long-distance **bus** services (such as the ever popular Tica Bus), though it's also possible to use local transport – you'll always find buses waiting at the border to take you to the next town (cross early in the day to ensure more choice of departures). If you choose to go this way, it can be a good idea to stick close to any local people who may be onboard when you reach immigration, so as to avoid the illegal entrance fees that are often levied against foreign travellers. Should you be targeted for these, try asking for an official receipt (though you may be fobbed off). Stay firm, but be friendly and patient.

The main **sea routes** to Guatemala come from Belize, but you can also cross into Petén from Chiapas, Mexico; you'll need to take a *lancha* on the Río Usumacinta.

VISAS

Visas are not currently required by the majority of travellers (including citizens of Australia, Israel, New Zealand, the UK, US and most Western European countries). Those that do require visas include nationals of South Africa, Iceland and several Eastern European countries. However, always check with the closest Guatemalan embassy well in advance of your trip, or go to ⓦwww .minex.gob.gt.

Guatemala is part of the CA-4 Central America trade agreement (see box, p.48), which facilitates the smooth passage of goods and people between El Salvador, Honduras, Nicaragua and Guatemala. You will, therefore, not necessarily receive a stamp when you move between these countries. In addition, this means you are only entitled to a total stay of ninety days in all four countries. Fortunately, it's easy enough to pop over to Belize and come back again if you want to stay for longer.

LAND AND SEA ROUTES TO GUATEMALA

The borders with Mexico are at: Tecún Umán–Ciudad Hidalgo (see p.191) and Talismán–El Carmen (see p.191), both close to the Mexican city of Tapachula; La Mesilla–Ciudad Cuauhtémoc (see p.190), convenient for San Cristóbal de Las Casas; LaTecnica/Bethel–Frontera Corozal, connecting Palenque to Flores via the Río Usumacinta (see p.241); and Pipiles, for Benemerito (see p.241).

Travelling to Belize, there's either the land crossing in Petén at Melchor de Menchos–Benque Viejo (see p.230) or two boat routes: Puerto Barrios–Punta Gorda (see p.206) and Lívingston–Punta Gorda (see p.206).

Heading to and from El Salvador, traffic from Guatemala City uses the Valle Nuevo–Las Chinamas border (see p.314), while the Ciudad Pedro de Alvarado–La Hachadura (see p.197) route is convenient for the Pacific coast. There are two border crossings at Anguiatú–Anjiatú and at San Cristóbal Frontera (see p.199); both access the eastern highlands.

The two borders with Honduras are at El Florido (see p.206), which connects Chiquimula with Copán, and Entre Ríos–Corinto (see p.203), which links Puerto Barrios with Puerto Cortés.

GUATEMALA'S CHICKEN BUSES

Guatemala's "chicken buses" are legendary. They'll probably look familiar at first glance – that's because they're old school buses from North America, just with a few important modifications to get them ready for the rigours of travel: most likely some Jesus stickers, elongated seats for extra bums and a speaker system for the reggaeton soundtrack. Once you find the bus you need, get on and wait for it to fill up around you; luggage (livestock, bicycles, chickens, the kitchen sink, your backpack) goes wherever it will fit. Just when you think the bus couldn't possibly get any fuller, twenty snack vendors will jump aboard, screaming at you to buy various tempting goodies. Journeys are never dull. But besides entertainment, all the madness does provide one of the best opportunities to chat to local people. Even if your Spanish is shaky, a smile and a simple "Buenas" goes a long way. Once the ice is broken, your fellow passengers will undoubtedly help you to reach your destination with ease.

GETTING AROUND

Expect to get what you pay for when it comes to Guatemalan **transport**: the methods available range from the country's "chicken buses" (see box above) to luxury shuttles with DVD players. If you're in a hurry, you can also expect to be frustrated – despite frequent services and an improved road network, delays are still common. Be aware, too, that safety remains a major issue when travelling in Guatemala; premium services are not necessarily more secure. Highway robberies do occur, and tourist vehicles are lucrative targets; keep your valuables close and your wits about you. Traffic accidents are also frighteningly common (you'll soon see why). If you're feeling uncomfortable with your driver, consider asking him to slow down (if a private shuttle), or if on public transport, getting off and waiting for the next bus.

By bus

Buses in Guatemala are incredibly crowded, but they're also cheap and the easiest way to get around. In urban and rural areas alike, **second-class buses** – known as *camionetas* to Guatemalans and "chicken buses" to foreigners – are by far the most numerous. Second-class buses generally start and stop at the local terminal (chaotically often in the same place as the local market), though you can get off or on at any point in-between. They don't generally have schedules (except on more remote routes), instead leaving every thirty minutes or when full. Pay your **fare** (expect it to be about US$1 per hour of travel) to the *Ayudante* (conductor) on the bus. It pays to be open to help from locals when trying to negotiate your passage – the *ayudantes* are invariably friendly, knowledgeable and for the most part honest.

In rural areas the transport often comes in the form of **microbuses** or *micros*. You can expect to pay in the region of US$2 per hour of travel, but don't expect a guaranteed seat. Microbuses sometimes depart from a central terminal, although in larger towns and cities each route may have their own individual terminal.

First-class, or **Pullman**, buses are more comfortable and make fewer stops. Each passenger has a seat to him or herself, and tickets can be bought in advance (but drivers will usually stop for you en-route if they have space). Pullmans usually leave from the bus company's office rather than a town's main bus terminal. Prices are reasonable (also around US$2 per hour of travel). All the main tourist routes are also served by **shuttle buses** that will whisk

ADDRESSES IN GUATEMALA

Like the majority of towns and cities in Central America, Guatemala's streets generally follow a grid system, with the occasional diagonal thrown in for variety. In most towns, avenidas run north–south and are numbered from 1 Avenida (on either the west or east of side of town), while calles run east–west (and will start at 1 Calle in the north). Even small towns will centre on a plaza (with the exception of waterside settlements such as Panajachel and Lívingston), usually intersected by the settlement's primary avenidas and calles. In the capital and a few other cities (Cobán and Quetzaltenango, for example) the ever-expanding street network is divided into zonas, each of which may have its own separate set of numbered calles and avenidas (ie, 1 Calle may exist in more than one zona). Addresses in Guatemala (and in this guide) are given listing first the calle or avenida that the property is on, followed by a number signifying the calle/avenida that intersects to the north/west. The final number given is the property number. For example "6 Av 9–14, Zona 1" is in Zona 1, on 6 Avenida south of 9 Calle, house number 14.

you around in a lot more comfort, for a price (Flores–Tikal return is around US$7). Tickets are booked (best the day before) through a travel agent or your hotel. You'll be picked up from your accommodation and dropped off where you want.

By car

Driving in Guatemala is pretty straightforward. **Parking** and **security** are the main problems; in the larger towns you should always get your car shut away in a guarded car park. The main routes are paved, but minor roads are often extremely rough. **Gas** costs around US$2 a gallon, **diesel** about US$1.50. **Renting a car** will run around US$45 a day (around US$230 a week) for a small vehicle by the time you've added the extras. However, excesses on any damage caused can be huge, so be sure to check your agreement fully. All major rental firms have an office at the airport in Guatemala City (see p.137).

If you plan to visit the more remote parts of the country, then it's almost inevitable that you will **hitch a ride** with a pick-up or truck from time to time. You'll usually have to pay for your lift – around the same as the bus fare. This said, hitching is never entirely safe, and carries obvious risks.

Taxis are available in all the main towns. Rates are fairly low (around US$3 for a 3km trip), but except in Guatemala City, meters are nonexistent, so it's essential to **fix a price** before you set off (clarify that the price is for the journey, not per person). Local taxi drivers will almost always be prepared to negotiate a price for a half-day or day's excursion to villages or sites.

By bike

Cycling is the most exhilarating way to see Guatemala, but the country's poor roads make it quite challenging. If you set out and it all gets too much, most buses will carry bikes on the roof. You can rent mountain bikes in Antigua and Panajachel (see p.151 & p.159), as well as several other cities. You should have no problem finding repair shops.

By boat

Small speedy motorized boats called **lanchas** are the main form of water transport, though there's still a slow ferry service between Puerto Barrios and Lívingston. The two definitive boat trips in Guatemala are through the Río Dulce gorge system, starting in either Lívingston or Río Dulce, and across Lago de Atitlán, usually beginning in Panajachel.

By air

The only internal **flight** most people are likely to take is from Guatemala City to Flores (from US$200 return), with two airlines, TACA and TAG, offering daily services. Virtually any travel agent in the country can book you a ticket.

ACCOMMODATION

Accommodation in Guatemala comes in different guises: *pensiones*, *posadas*, *hospedajes* and hotels. The names don't actually mean much, however, as they're approximately the same thing, although in general hotels are towards the top end of the price scale and most *hospedajes* and *pensiones* towards the bottom. Budget options are plentiful and even in tourist centres you can sleep for as little as US$2–3 if you're prepared to live with minimum comfort. **Hostels** and lodges tailored to backpackers are springing up across the country; most have dorms and camping facilities as well as private rooms. Wherever you stay, **room prices** are fixed by Inguat, the tourist board, and there should be a tariff posted by the door of your room. You should never pay more than the posted rate. See p.35 for an explanation of the accommodation price codes used in this guide.

Rates rarely include breakfast; however, many moderately priced rooms (US$10–20; ❷–❹) come with cable TV and the promise of hot-water showers. Actually getting a hot-water shower is a different story, as electric shower-head water heaters are notoriously ineffective (and dangerous). Keep your eyes open for gas-fired hot-water systems – much safer bets. Only on the coasts and in Petén will you need a **fan** or **air-conditioning**, while you'll need heavy-duty blankets in the highlands. A **mosquito net** is sometimes provided in lowland areas, but if you plan to spend time in Petén or on either coast it's probably worth investing in one. They're essential if you plan to do any jungle trekking or camping.

Camping facilities are becoming more common. Towns with formal provisions for camping include Panajachel, Semuc Champey, Lanquín, Laguna Lachua, Poptún, El Remate and Tikal. A tent is a good idea if you plan to set off into the wilds; it's possible to rent one, or a hammock, for use in many backpacker centres.

FOOD AND DRINK

You can be well fed in Guatemala for only a few dollars a day. **Lunch** is the main meal of the day, and cheap eats are abundant, from fresh produce at markets to street stalls selling tasty wraps and grilled meats, to *comedores* where you can get a two-course lunch, with drink, for US$3. These *menú del día* or *almuerzo* set menus are usually served noon–3pm. **Breakfast** is also good value, with traditional breakfasts including a combination of eggs, beans, tortillas, cheese, fried plantains and cream. Most places in tourist centres also offer Continental options for slightly more money. Alternatively, fresh fruit can be bought from street vendors and muffins and breads from bakeries, cutting your breakfast bill to a single dollar. **Evening meals** in restaurants are generally more expensive (from US$4).

Maya cuisine is at the heart of Guatemalan cooking. Maize is an essential ingredient, appearing most commonly as a **tortilla**. **Beans** (*frijoles*) are served as they are in the rest of Central America, either refried (*volteados*) or whole (*parados*). Chillis, usually in the form of a spicy sauce (*salsa picante*), are the final ingredient in a Maya meal. Popular **market snacks** include *pupusas* (thick stuffed tortillas topped with crunchy grated salad vegetables) and *tostadas* (corn crisps smeared with avocado, cheese and other toppings). On the Caribbean coast there is a distinct **Creole cuisine**, heavily based on fish, seafood, coconuts, plantains and banana. *Tapado* (a coconut-based fish or shellfish soup) is the signature dish in these parts. In small towns and rural areas across the country, you can expect your choice to be confined to rice, tortillas and beans, and fried chicken and hamburgers. Vegetarians receive a mixed bag; Guatemala City offers some gems (even for vegans) and gringo towns such as Flores and Antigua present interesting veggie menus too.

Drink

Guatemalan **coffee** is great – unfortunately, most of it is exported, so the stuff you get in country is pretty weak. During the day locals drink water or **refrescos**, water-based drinks with some fruit flavour. **Soft drinks** (all called *aguas* or *gaseosas*) are also common and popular. For a healthy treat, order a **licuado**: a thick, fruit-based drink with either water or milk (milk is safer). **Bottled water** (*agua mineral* or *agua pura*) is available almost everywhere and cheapest bought in 500ml bags (*bolsitas*).

The national **beer** (*cerveza*) is Gallo, a medium-strength, bland lager that comes in 330ml or litre bottles (around US$2 and US$4 respectively in a bar; much less in a supermarket). Also widely available, and often cheaper on special offer, is Brahma, a Brazilian import. Moza, a dark brew with a slight caramel flavour, is worth trying, too. Better still, and served in traditional bars, is a *mixta* – a mix of draft clear (*clara*) and dark (*oscura*) beers. **Rum** (*ron*) and **aguardiente**, a clear and lethal sugarcane spirit, are also popular and cheap; Ron Botran Añejo is an acceptable brand (around US$5 a bottle). Hard drinkers will soon get to know Quetzalteca, a local *aguardiente*. Guatemalan **wine** does exist but bears little resemblance to the real thing. Chilean wines are the best value, with bottles available from around US$8 in supermarkets and twice that in restaurants.

CULTURE AND ETIQUETTE

Perhaps more so than in other Central American countries, **religious doctrine** – Catholic, Evangelical Protestant, indigenous spiritual beliefs – continues to influence cultural behaviour in Guatemala. Consequently, Guatemalans are fairly modest, reserved folk. This is particularly true of the Maya, who can be suspicious of outsiders; tradition rules in indigenous communities. *Ladino* culture is generally less rigid, thanks to the more immediate effects of globalization. Women show more skin, and the Latin American **machismo** is more obvious. Even this, though, is pretty inoffensive – mostly whistles and catcalls from men trying to impress their friends – and can be ignored by female travellers. **Homosexuality** is not illegal, though it is generally frowned upon. There's a small gay community in Guatemala City, but few public meeting places.

It would be a mistake to take Guatemalan reserve for unfriendliness, however. You are likely to receive gracious hospitality from all levels of society, as Guatemalans regard hosting

GUATEMALAN LANGUAGE

Expressions

Baa "right" (often used at the start of sentences, or on its own as an affirmative)

Buena onda "cool"

Fijase "it's like this" (often used to preface why something hasn't gone according to plan)

Chapin/Guatemalteco/ Guatemayan Guatemalan/Ladino/ Maya

Gestures

Rubbing one's elbow signifies that somebody is cheap.

Pulling one's collar signifies that someone has clout/power.

guests as a great honour. **Politeness** is valued highly by Ladino and Maya society alike, and there is a pleasantry for nearly every occasion – you will endear yourself to locals by returning these. "Buen provecho", for example, is often exchanged among strangers in restaurants; it literally translates to "I hope your meal is of good benefit to you!". Be prepared, though, for the fact that **noise** and **personal space** are almost foreign concepts: it is quite usual to be woken by firecrackers at 5am, and even in rural areas Evangelical PA systems blare. In addition, since Guatemalans are used to fairly cramped quarters, expect a good deal of pushing and shoving (especially on buses).

Tipping in restaurants and *comedores* is not expected, but is certainly appreciated.

SPORTS AND OUTDOOR ACTIVITIES

Football is the country's top spectator sport, by a mile. The two big local teams, both from Guatemala City, are Municipal and Communications. Admission to games is inexpensive (starting at just US$3). Football also provides for easy cross-cultural conversation, as most Guatemalan men are well versed on the topic.

Guatemala is something of a paradise for outdoor activities. With a sturdy pair of shoes, you can **hike** volcanoes, jungles and national parks, and even "circumstroll" around Lago de Atitlán. **Caving** is another popular activity, especially in the area around Cobán (see p.218), where you can view stalagmites, squeeze through nooks and float down underground rivers. Other good caving trips can be found in Lanquín, Chisec, Candelaria and at Finca Ixobel (see p.226), near Poptún. Finca Ixobel also makes a good base for exploring the countryside on horseback; the trek to El Mirador in the far north of Petén also allows for **horseriding**.

Wildlife- and **birdwatching** are two of the country's more exotic outdoor options: Guatemala is home to ten percent of the world's registered species and encompasses 19 ecosystems and some 300 microclimates. Several national parks and reserves are good for animal-spotting, including Cerro Cahui (see p.232), Biotopo del Quetzal (see p.213) and Reserva Natural Atitlán (see p.155). Other, more eclectic activities on offer include **cycling** in the highlands, **whitewater rafting** on the Río Cahabón (see p.220), **altitude diving** in Lago de Atitlán's volcanic caldera (see p.155) and **surfing** on the Pacific coast. You can also **sail** from Río Dulce – one popular route takes you to Belize's more remote cayes.

COMMUNICATIONS

The cheapest way to make an **international phone call** is usually from a cybercafé or a privately owned communications business, both of which are common throughout the country. Prices start at around US$0.15 per minute to the US or US$0.25 to Europe via web-phone facilities; you generally agree on a rate and then pay cash at the end of the call. **Local calls** are very cheap, and can be made from either a communications office or a phone booth; Guatemalan numbers are always eight digits, generally formatted in two groups of four. If you plan to make a number of them, it pays to get a phonecard, which you can purchase in many shops; look for the Ladatel symbol – shops selling cards usually have a little sign with the symbol hanging outside. Alternatively, you can simply drop a few quetzals in the coin slot. Teluga maintains the country's phone booths, which display instructions for making domestic and international collect calls. However, this service only seems to be consistently effective when dialling the US and Canada. If you're staying in Guatemala for an extended period, consider purchasing a **mobile phone**. They're very popular, and the network is extensive. You can pick up a phone for as little as US$20 (including US$20 of calling credit). Keep an eye out for the "double" and "triple" offer days, when you can get two to three times the top-up credit you pay for.

Guatemalan **postal services** are fairly efficient by Latin American standards, and even the smallest of towns has a *correo* (post office); hours are generally Monday to Friday 8am to 5pm. Airmail letters generally take around a week to the US, and a couple of weeks or so to Europe. Post coming into Guatemala is fairly reliable too, though note that the **poste restante** (*Lista de Correos*) method of holding mail is no longer operational.

Guatemala is very well wired to the **internet**. Most small towns have at least two or three **cybercafés**, while they are found practically every other block in bigger settlements. Rates vary between US$0.80 and US$4 an hour. Many hotels also provide internet facilities (sometimes included in the price of your room).

CRIME AND SAFETY

Personal safety is a valid concern for visitors to Guatemala. Most worrying are the recorded incidents of gangs actively targeting tourists, including groups on shuttle buses. And though unlikely, tourists have also been attacked (and even killed) by mobs of villagers believing them to be stealing children (or their organs). **Muggings** and acts of **violent crime** occur most often in Guatemala City; there's not too much danger in the daylight hours, but use a taxi at night. There have also been a few cases of armed robbery in Antigua and around Lago de Atitlán.

All this said, relatively few tourists actually have trouble. However, it's essential that you minimize your chances of becoming a victim. **Petty theft** and **pickpocketing** are likely to be your biggest problems – as anywhere, theft is most common in bus stations and crowded markets. As a rule, ask for local advice on the safety of remote areas; if you do plan to be in a risky spot, don't take more than you can afford to lose – many travellers carry "decoy" wallets with just a small amount of cash to satisfy muggers. In indigenous communities show deference and always ask permission before taking photos.

If you are robbed you should file a report with the police – at the very least for insurance purposes – though Guatemala's civilian **police** force has a poor reputation. In Antigua, Panajachel and Tikal there are well-established **tourist police** forces. Also useful is the "Asistur" service, dedicated to assisting tourists. They have representatives in Antigua and Flores (see box, p.153, for contact details).

Drugs (particularly marijuana and cocaine) are quite widely available. Don't partake: **drug offences** are dealt

EMERGENCY NUMBERS

Ambulance ☎122/123/128
Asistur (tourist assistance) ☎1500 or
2421 2810
Fire ☎122/123
Police ☎110/120
Red Cross ☎125

with severely – even the possession of marijuana could land you in jail.

MEDICAL CARE AND EMERGENCIES

Guatemala's **pharmacies** can provide many over-the-counter medications, and some pharmacists can diagnose ailments and prescribe the appropriate pills. However, pharmacists are not qualified medics – so get your Spanish correct.

Even in remote communities there are basic **health centres**, although you may find only a nurse or health worker available. In case of serious illness, head for a city and a private **hospital**. Guatemala's doctors often speak English, and many were trained in the US. You must travel with medical insurance (see p.50), as without it you'll need to pay for any hospital treatment up front.

MONEY AND BANKS

The Guatemalan currency is the **quetzal**; the exchange rate at the time of writing was Q7.50 to US$1. US dollars are also accepted in many of the main tourist centres; prices for tours are often quoted in dollars, and some ATMs in Antigua will allow you to

withdraw dollars as well as quetzals. In general, ATMs dispense Q100 bills. You will soon learn that some Guatemalan businesses would, seemingly, rather lose a sale than have to find change for one of these, so keep a stash of *sencillo* (change) about you.

Credit or debit cards are the easiest and most convenient way to get money. Visa/Plus cards have the most machines, though MasterCard/Cirrus ATMs are becoming more widespread. The most common are the "5b" Cajeros (Cash Machines), recognizable by their yellow and blue signs. Most banks will also give cash advances with cards if there's no hole in the wall. **Traveller's cheques** are an alternative; US dollar cheques are accepted in most banks, but check before you queue up. **Bank hours** are extremely convenient, with many opening until 7pm (and some as late as 8pm) from Monday to Friday and until 12.30pm or 1pm on Saturdays. All currency exchange in the country is done at banks, or with moneychangers on the street if necessary.

INFORMATION AND MAPS

The national tourist board, **Inguat** (ⓦwww.visitguatemala.com), with offices in Guatemala City, Panajachel, Antigua, Flores and Quetzaltenango, gives out glossy brochures and will try to help you with your trip, but don't expect too much independent travel advice. The main office in Guatemala City (see p.148) has a library of information about tourism in the country (mostly in Spanish), and can also provide you with

YOUTH AND STUDENT DISCOUNTS

Many places in Guatemala will accept the International Student Identity Card (ISIC) as eligibility for a discount. You can obtain an ISIC card at any STA affiliated branch, or in Guatemala at several of Antigua's travel agencies. You will need official written confirmation from your school (on headed paper) or a valid student ID. Antigua agencies no longer issue cards for language school students. Student discounts are also offered by some airlines, as well as several museums. Unfortunately, there are no discounts available at Guatemala's Maya ruins.

PUBLIC HOLIDAYS

January 1 New Year's Day

Semana Santa Easter Week (variable Feb–April)

May 1 Labour Day

June 30 Army Day, anniversary of 1871 revolution

August 15 Guatemala City fiesta (capital only)

September 15 Independence Day

October 12 Discovery of America (only banks closed)

October 20 Revolution Day

November 1 All Saints' Day

December 25 Christmas Day

a free copy of the excellent *Mapa Vial Turístico de Guatemala*, which includes the capital, most towns and a decent road atlas.

OPENING HOURS AND HOLIDAYS

Most offices and shops are **open** between 8am and 5pm, though some take a break for lunch. **Archeological sites** are open every day, usually from 8am to 5pm, (Tikal maintains longer hours), while most museums open Tuesday through Sunday from 9am to 4pm. **Sundays** remain distinguishable – many businesses close and transport is less frequent, though tourist centres such as Antigua keep buzzing. On public holidays virtually the entire country shuts down, so don't expect to be travelling anywhere.

FESTIVALS

Traditional **fiestas** are one of the great excitements of a trip to Guatemala, and every town and village, however small, devotes at least one day a year to celebration. Many of the best fiestas include some specifically local element, such as the giant kites at **Santiago Sacatepéquez** (see p.152), the religious processions in Antigua and the horse race in **Todos Santos Cuchumatán** (see p.189). At certain times virtually the whole country erupts simultaneously. The following is only a selection of some of the most interesting regional and national festivals.

January The town fiesta in Rabinal, in Baja Verapaz, is renowned for pre-colonial dance (Jan 23–24).

March/April Semana Santa (Easter week) is celebrated nationwide. Particularly impressive processions take place in Antigua, Guatemala City, Santiago Atitlan & San Cristóbel Verapaz. Every Sunday of Lent sees massive street processions in Antigua, which culminate with the main event on Easter Sunday.

July Cubulco, Baja Verapaz, hosts the Palo Volador, a pole-spinning ritual (July 25); Cobán celebrates the national folklore festival (July 31–Aug 6).

August Guatemala City fiesta (Aug 15).

November The first of the month is All Saints' Day, with celebrations all over, but most dramatic in Todos Santos Cuchumatán and Santiago Sacatepéquez, where massive paper kites are flown.

December Bonfires (the Burning of the Devil) take place throughout the country on Dec 7; main fiesta in Chichicastenango (Dec 13 & 21). Christmas is celebrated country-wide (Dec 25).

Guatemala City

Spilling across a highland basin, surrounded on three sides by jagged hills and volcanic cones, **GUATEMALA CITY** is now the largest city in Central America, home to over three million people. Characterized by an intensity and a vibrancy that simultaneously fascinate and horrify, Guatemala's capital is a shapeless and swelling metropolitan mass, and the undisputed centre of the country's politics, power and wealth. Not even a wild imagination will be able to make it

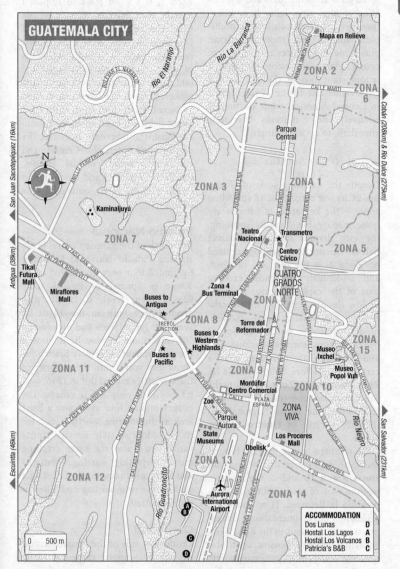

GUATEMALA CITY

San Juan Sacetepéquez (16km)

Antigua (38km)

Escuintla (46km)

Cobán (208km) & Río Dulce (275km)

San Salvador (231km)

Río La Barranca

Río El Naranjo

BOULEVAR EL NARANJO

AVENIDA SIMEÓN CAÑAS

Mapa en Relieve

ZONA 2

CALLE MARTÍ

ZONA 6

ANILLO PERIFÉRICO

Parque Central

ZONA 3

ZONA 1

AVENIDA ELENA

6A AVENIDA

7A AVENIDA

Kaminaljuyú

ZONA 7

Teatro Nacional

Transmetro

ZONA 5

AVENIDA BOLÍVAR

Centro Cívico

CALZADA SAN JUAN

CALZADA ROOSEVELT

Tikal Futura Mall

Miraflores Mall

CUATRO GRADOS NORTE

Buses to Antigua

CALZADA ATANASIO TZUL

Zona 4 Bus Terminal

ZONA 4

AVENIDA BARRANQUILLA

ZONA 8

TREBOL JUNCTION

Torre del Reformador

AVENIDA REFORMA

BOULEVAR VISTA HERMOSA

ZONA 15

Buses to Western Highlands

Museo Ixchel

Buses to Pacific

ZONA 11

6A AVENIDA

7A AVENIDA

ZONA 9

Museo Popol Vuh

CALZADA RAÚL AGUILAR BATRES

CALZADA REAL DE PETAPA

BOULEVAR LIBERACIÓN

12 CALLE

Montúfar Centro Comercial

PLAZA ESPAÑA

ZONA 10

C. REAL VILLA GUADALUPE

Zoo

ZONA VIVA

Río Negro

Parque Aurora

State Museums

Obelisk

Los Proceres Mall

ZONA 13

BULEVAR LOS PRÓCERES

C. 20

ZONA 12

Río Guadroncito

Aurora International Airport

AVENIDA HINCAPIÉ

AVENIDA LAS AMÉRICAS

ZONA 14

A
B

C

D

0   500 m

ACCOMMODATION	
Dos Lunas	D
Hostal Los Lagos	A
Hostal Los Volcanos	B
Patricia's B&B	C

out as a pleasant environment – indeed, for many travellers time spent in the capital is an exercise in damage limitation, struggling through bus exhaust and swirling crowds. However, once you get used to the pace, Guatemala City can offer some surprises, including a satisfying variety of restaurants, some great authentic bars and a sprinkling of interesting sights. In addition, there are the home comforts of multiplex cinemas and shopping plazas, plus some good places to stay and, of course, plenty of welcoming faces. It is important to note, though, that the city's crime rate is one of the highest in Central America; while daytime is relatively safe, conditions deteriorate after dark, so act accordingly.

What to see and do

Despite the daunting scale of Guatemala City – it consists of 18 sprawling zones – the key areas of interest are quite manageable. Broadly speaking, the city divides into two distinct halves. The northern section, centred on **Zona 1**, is the old part of town, and undeniably the most exciting part of the capital. A squalid world of low-slung, crumbling nineteenth-century townhouses and faceless, modern concrete blocks, all joined by broken pavements, parking lots and lined with street vendors, it has a certain brutal allure. South of Calle 18, Zona 1 merges into **Zona 4**, home to the Municipalidad, tourist and immigration offices, the Teatro Nacional and the arty enclave of **Quatro Grados Norte**.

The southern half of the city, beyond the Torre del Reformador, begins with **zonas 9 and 10** and is the modern, wealthy part of town, split in two by **Avenida la Reforma**. Here you'll find exclusive offices, international hotels, private museums and, in the **Zona Viva**, Guatemala's most expensive nightclubs, restaurants and cafés. Continuing south,

across Bulevar Liberación/Los Proceres **zonas 13 and 14** are rich leafy suburbs and home to the airport, zoo and the state museums.

Parque Central

The windswept expanse of the **Parque Central**, at the northern end of Zona 1, is a good place to stop and absorb the flavours of Guatemala City. The concrete "park" is full of life, especially on Sundays and public holidays; pigeons, shoe-shiners, herds of goats, raving Evangelicals and the odd gaggle of European package tourists make it of far more interest than the zoo in Zona 13 (see p.136). Most of the city's major sights – the cathedral, the Palacio Nacional, the Biblioteca Nacional, the underground Mercado Central and two semi-restored colonial arcades, the Pasaje Aycinena and Pasaje Rubio (leading off the park's south side) – lie nearby.

Palacio Nacional

Just north of the Parque Central is the striking **Palacio Nacional** (entrance by guided tour only, conducted every 30min in Spanish or English daily 9am–4.30pm; free), a lavish, pale green palace built in the 1940s by president Jorge Ubico and nicknamed "El Guacamole" by locals. It housed the government's executive branch for about fifty years, until the majority of the ministries moved out in 1996; now it's home to only a few offices. The twenty-minute tour gives you a brief look at the interior, worth a look for its two Moorish-style interior courtyards; you'll also see some cracking murals depicting warring Spaniards and Maya, plus a few items of nostalgia such as the original flag and rifles of the revolution.

Cathedral

On the east side of the Parque Central sits the blue-domed **cathedral** (daily

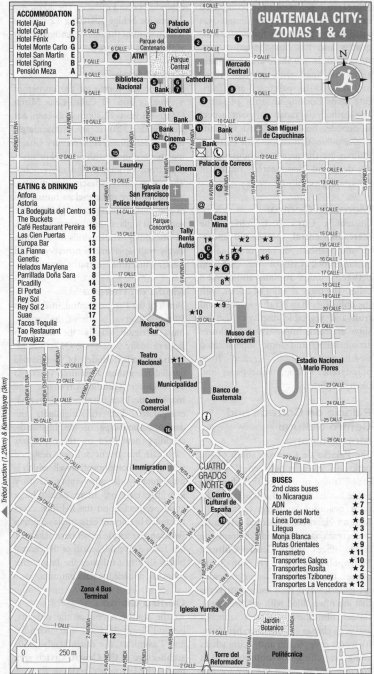

GUATEMALA CITY: ZONAS 1 & 4

N

ACCOMMODATION
Hotel Ajau	C
Hotel Capri	F
Hotel Fénix	D
Hotel Monte Carlo	G
Hotel San Martín	E
Hotel Spring	B
Pensión Meza	A

EATING & DRINKING
Anfora	4
Astoria	10
La Bodeguita del Centro	15
The Buckets	9
Café Restaurant Pereira	16
Las Cien Puertas	7
Europa Bar	13
La Fianna	11
Genetic	18
Helados Marylena	3
Parrillada Doña Sara	8
Picadilly	14
El Portal	6
Rey Sol	5
Rey Sol 2	12
Suae	17
Tacos Tequila	2
Tao Restaurant	1
Trovajazz	19

BUSES
2nd class buses to Nicaragua	★ 4
ADN	★ 7
Fuente del Norte	★ 8
Línea Dorada	★ 6
Litegua	★ 3
Monja Blanca	★ 1
Rutas Orientales	★ 9
Transmetro	★ 11
Transportes Galgos	★ 10
Transportes Rosita	★ 2
Transportes Tziboney	★ 5
Transportes La Vencedora	★ 12

Palacio Nacional

Parque del Centenario

ATM

Parque Central

Mercado Central

Biblioteca Nacional

Bank

Cathedral

Bank

Bank

Bank

Bank

Bank

Cinema

San Miguel de Capuchinas

Laundry

Cinema

Palacio de Correos

Iglesia de San Francisco

Police Headquarters

Parque Concordia

Casa Mima

Tally Renta Autos

Mercado Sur

Museo del Ferrocarril

Teatro Nacional

Estadio Nacional Mario Flores

Municipalidad

Banco de Guatemala

Centro Comercial

Immigration

CUATRO GRADOS NORTE

Centro Cultural de España

Zona 4 Bus Terminal

Iglesia Yurrita

Jardín Botánico

Torre del Reformador

Politécnica

GUATEMALA

GUATEMALA CITY

◀ Trebol junction (1.25km) & Kaminaljuyu (3km)

0   250 m

7am–1pm & 3–7pm), completed in 1868. Its solid, squat design was intended to resist the force of earthquakes and has, for the most part, succeeded. Inside there are three main aisles, all lined with arching pillars, austere colonial paintings and intricate altars housing an array of saints. The cathedral's most poignant aspect is outside, however: etched into the twelve pillars that support the entrance railings are the names of thousands of the dead and "disappeared" victims of the country's civil war.

Mercado Central

Guatemala City's best market, the **Mercado Central**, spreads out underground, beneath of one of Zona 1's parking lots, east of the cathedral between 8 and 9 avenidas and 6 and 8 calles. The place is a riot of colour, with the obligatory handicraft souvenirs and fruit and vegetable displays. Also on show are some impressive fresh flower arrangements and some sophisticated wedding decorations crafted from polystyrene, ribbon, tissue paper and plenty of glitter.

Palacio de Correos and Centro Cultural Metropolitano

The **Palacio de Correos**, south of the park on 7 Avenida between 11 and 12 calles, is one post office that shouldn't prove too hard to find – it's one of the most beautiful buildings in the city, with an elaborately restored terracotta and cream facade. Inside, behind the *correo* offices, is the **Centro Cultural Metropolitano** (Mon–Fri 9am–5pm), home to interesting contemporary art galleries and nice leafy courtyards that are often filled with art and music classes; film showings, book launches and yoga classes are also often held here. It's worth dropping in and seeing what's going on (check the noticeboards) if you're going to be in the city for any

extended period of time. The adjoining decorative bridge spanning 12 Calle is reminiscent of the one in Antigua – just without the backdrop.

Casa Mima

South of the *correo*, at the corner of 8 Avenida and 14 Calle, **Casa Mima** (Mon–Fri 9am–12.30pm & 2–6pm, Sat 9am–5pm; Q20) is an immaculately restored late nineteenth-century Guatemalan townhouse with original furnishings from various design movements. The decor offers a fascinating glimpse into a wealthy middle-class household of the past. Among the highlights are some scary, glassy-eyed porcelain dolls, a wondrously detailed dolls' house, some lovely wallpaper and a ninety-year-old "talking machine" (a gramophone).

Mapa en Relieve

North of the Parque Central, in Zona 2's Parque Minerva, is one of the capital's most intriguing sights, the **Mapa en Relieve** (daily 9am–5pm; Q25), a huge, open-air relief model of Guatemala created more than a hundred years ago by engineer Claudio Urrutiam. The map's vertical scale has been somewhat exaggerated, but still highlights the dramatic landscape of the highlands, shedding new light on those perilous mountain bus journeys. It was designed with a water component as well, which is unfortunately usually empty; if they kept the taps on, there would be a good perspective on the Belizean cayes (included because of Guatemala's claim to Belizean territory). To get here, take a #1 bus from 3 Avenida north of the central plaza; after five minutes the bus terminates just outside the park entrance.

Centro Cívico

At the southern end of the old city, beyond sleazy 18 Calle and around 6 and 7 avenidas, the distinctively 1960s architecture of the **Centro Cívico** area marks the boundary between zonas 1 and 4. It's more of a spaghetti junction of careening buses and taxis – the area is a huge transport hub – than a place for sight-seeing, but there are at least a couple of footbridges that give perspective on it all. Looming over 7 Avenida is the **Banco de Guatemala** building, bedecked with bold modern murals and stylized glyphs recounting the history of Guatemala and the conflict between Spanish and Maya. Just south of the bank is the main Inguat office (see p.137), and a short walk southeast of here are the artsy, pedestrianized (for two blocks) streets of boho **Cuatro Grados Norte**, which is fairly quiet midweek, but worth a look outside of office hours. On a small rise to the west of 6 Avenida is the futuristic **Teatro Nacional**, designed to resemble a ship (see p.141). The area is also home to another of the capital's markets, **El Mercado Sur**.

0   250 m

N

ZONA 5
ZONA 4
32 CALLE
Jardín Botánico
Politécnica
Torre del Reformador
ZONA 9
US Embassy
Hedman Alas ★
Laundry
STA Travel
ZONA VIVA
Pullmantur ★
Los Proceres Mall
Obelisk
ZONA 10
Museo Ixchel
Museo Popol Vuh
Hospital Centro Médico
Centro Gerencial Las Margaritas

EATING & DRINKING
La Chapinita   1
El Establo   5
Rattle & Hum   6
Sophos   3
Tacontento   4
El Tamal   2

GUATEMALA CITY: ZONAS 9 & 10

ACCOMMODATION
Xamanek Hostel   A

Jardín Botánico

The city's **Jardín Botánico**, or botanical garden (Mon–Fri 8am–3pm, Sat 9am–noon; Q10), on Avenida La Reforma at Calle 1, around the boundary between zones 4 and 10, is a part of the San Carlos University. It's a beautiful little space with quite a selection of species, all neatly labelled in Spanish or Latin. An anachronistic natural history museum, the **Museo de Historia Natural**, also sits within the grounds; the collection is pretty dull, mainly mangy stuffed animals.

Torre del Reformador

South of the Centro Cívico, at the junction of 7 Avenida and 2 Calle, in Zona 9, is the landmark **Torre del Reformador**, Guatemala's version of the Eiffel Tower. The steel structure was built in honour of President Barrios, whose liberal reforms transformed the country between 1871 and 1885. Unfortunately, you can only admire it from below. Just to the north, at the junction with Ruta 6, is the **Iglesia Yurrita** (Tues–Sun 8am–noon & 3–6pm), built in a weird neo-Gothic style reminiscent of a horror-movie set.

Museo Ixchel and Museo Popul Vuh

The campus of the University Francisco Marroquín, reached by following 6 Calle Final off Avenida la Reforma to the east, is home to two privately owned **museums** in their own purpose-built cultural centre. The **Museo Ixchel** (Mon–Fri 9am–5pm, Sat 9am–1pm;

Q35, students Q15) shouldn't be missed if you're a fan of textiles, or just can't get enough of Guatemalan traditional dress: its collection is dedicated to Maya culture, with particular emphasis on traditional weaving. There's a number of stunning hand-woven fabrics, including some impressive examples of ceremonial costumes, with explanations in English, plus information about techniques, dyes, fibres and weaving tools and the ways in which costumes have changed over time.

The excellent **Museo Popol Vuh** (Mon–Fri 9am–5pm, Sat 9am–1pm; Q35, students Q15), next door, is home to an outstanding collection of artefacts from archeological sites all over the country. The small museum is divided into Preclassic, Classic, Postclassic and Colonial rooms, and all the exhibits are top quality. Particularly interesting is a copy of the Dresden Codex, one of very few surviving written and illustrated records of Maya history.

Parque Aurora

Further south, in Zona 13 (reachable by bus #63 from 4 Av or #83 from 10 Av), **Parque Aurora** houses the city's **zoo** (Tues–Sun 9am–5pm; Q20). Here you can see African lions, Bengal tigers, crocodiles, giraffes, Indian elephants, hippos, monkeys and all the Central and South American big cats, including some jaguars. As zoos go, it's not bad, although some will no doubt find it depressing. The grounds are nice, though.

Museo Nacional de Arqueología y Etnología

Opposite the Parque Aurora is a complex of three state-run museums, of which the **Museo Nacional de Arqueología y Etnología** (Tues–Fri 9am–4pm, Sat & Sun 9am–noon & 1.30–4pm; Q30, students free) is the best. The collection includes a world-class selection of Maya treasures, though the layout and displays are somewhat

confused. Noteworthy pieces include some spectacular jade masks from Abaj Takalik, a stunning wooden temple-top lintel from Tikal and artefacts from Piedras Negras, one of the remotest sites in Petén. Stela 12, dating from 672 AD, depicts a cowering captive king begging for mercy, and there's an enormous carved stone throne from the same site, richly engraved with glyphs and decorated with a two-faced head.

Museo Nacional de Arte Moderno

Opposite the archeological museum, and part of the same complex, the city's **Museo Nacional de Arte Moderno** (Tues–Fri 9am–4pm, Sat & Sun 9am–noon & 1.30–4pm; Q15) also suffers from poor presentation, but does boast some imaginative geometric paintings by Dagoberto Vásquez, and a collection of startling exhibits by Efraín Recinos, including a colossal marimba-cum-tank sculpture. Both Vásquez and Recinos are twentieth-century Guatemalan artists particularly noted for their mural work, which can be seen on various public buildings throughout the city, including the Banco de Guatemala and the Biblioteca Nacional. There's also a permanent collection of Cubist art and massive murals by Carlos Mérida, Guatemala's most celebrated artist.

Museo Nacional de Historia Natural

The third museum in the complex, the **Museo Nacional de Historia Natural** (Tues–Fri 9am–4pm, Sat & Sun 9am–noon & 1.30–4pm; Q15), is pretty dismal, featuring a range of miserable stuffed animals from Guatemala and elsewhere and a few mineral samples. Close by on 11 Avenida is the touristy **Mercado de Artesanías** (see p.141).

Kaminaljuyú

Way out on the western edge of the city lies Zona 7, which wraps around the ruins of pre-colonial **Kaminaljuyú** (daily 9am–4pm; Q40). Archeological digs have uncovered more than three hundred mounds and thirteen ball-courts here, though unlike the massive temples of the lowlands, these structures were built of adobe, and most of them have been lost to erosion and urban sprawl. Today the site (incorporating only a tiny fraction of the original city) is little more than a series of earth-covered mounds, and it's virtually impossible to get any impression of Kaminaljuyú's former scale and splendour. To **get to** the ruins, take bus #35 from 4 Av in Zona 1. Alternatively, any bus from the Parque Central that has a small "Kaminaljuyú" sign in the windscreen passes within a block or two.

You can visit the **Museo Miraflores** (Tues–Sun 9am–7pm; Q40), a ten-minute walk south of the ruins on Calzada Roosevelt, to learn more about the ancient city; displays explain the history of Kaminaljuyú and its importance as a trading centre. To get there, take any bus headed to "Tikal Futura"; the museum is between the Miraflores shopping centre and the Tikal Futura Tower.

Arrival and information

By air Aurora International Airport is in Zona 13. There are a couple of banks (Mon–Fri 6am–8pm, Sat & Sun 8am–6pm) here, where you can change US dollars and traveller's cheques, plus 24hr ATMs. The easiest way to get from the airport is by taxi (US$5/Q40 to zonas 9 and 10, US$10/Q80 to Zona 1), though it is cheaper to take the bus (Q1): on exiting the arrivals hall, cross the road to the parking garage and take the elevator to Level 3; upstairs, walk to your left, towards the three flagpoles, to find the pedestrian ramp to the bus stops. Wait here for the #83 bus (note that the #83 takes two different routes – see box, p.138). Do not travel by bus after dark. There are regular shuttle-bus services from the airport to Antigua (US$10/Q80) until about 10pm, though they don't have a fixed schedule and only leave when they have at least three passengers. Alternatively, take the #83 bus via Trebol junction, and get off

before the Santa Cecilia Transmetro for local connections.

By bus First-class (Pullman) buses arrive at the private terminal of whichever company you're using – most are in Zona 1 (see p.142 for listings). Few international companies now use the Zona 4 terminal, but La Vencedora for San Salvador is close by at 3 Av and 1 C and some other operators (including Tica Bus, Hedman Aas and Pullmantur) have offices in Zona 10. From here to Zona 1, take any northbound bus from Av la Reforma marked Plaza/Parque Central, or a taxi should be $5. Be aware that around 18 Calle, where many companies are located, is particularly seedy at night. Second-class buses from the coast or highlands arrive in Zona 8 close to Trebol junction. The Transmetro runs from here north to Plaza Municipalidad; alternatively, take a taxi.

Tourist information The main Inguat office (Mon–Fri 8am–4pm; ☎ 2421 2800, ✉ info@inguat.gob .gt) is at 7 Av 1–17, Zona 4. The information desk on the ground floor has plenty of material (including an excellent free city/country map), and there's always someone who speaks English. There are also information desks (both daily 6am–9pm) on the upper (departures) and lower (arrivals) floors of the airport.

Travel agents There are a couple of agencies inside the Torre Estacionamiento, on the corner of 5 Av and 11 C in Zona 1, and many in Zona 10, including a branch of STA at Isyta 11 C 0–49 (☎ 2332 7629).

City transport

Buses Buses (6.30am–9.30pm; Q1) stop pretty much wherever you want them to; you'll often find people on a street corner waiting to flag one down. Windscreens carry signs to help you predict the route (see box, p.138, for the most useful). Have your fare ready – drivers will not wait. Don't use buses after dark.

#63 4 Av, Zone 1–Zone 13 museums.

#82 8 or 10 Av, Zone 1–Av la
Reforma

#83 Bolívar Airport–Trebol junction–
Av Bolívar–3 Av, Zone 1

#83 Terminal Airport–7 Av, Zone
9–Zone 4 bus terminal–9 Av, Zone 1

#101 8 or 10 Av Zone 1–Av la
Reforma–20 C Zone 10. This route
passes many of the embassies, the
Popol Vuh and Ixchel museums and
the Los Próceres mall.

Taxis There are currently both metered and non-
metered taxis. Metered taxis are comfortable and
cheap; Amarillo (☎2470 1515) is highly recommended and will pick you up from anywhere in the
city. The fare from Zona 1 to Zona 10 is about Q40,
or a short hop within zones will be around Q15.
With non-metered taxis, always set a price before
you get in. Always take taxis after dark.
Transmetro Operating like a tram, the Transmetro
(Q1, paid at the turnstile on entry) runs from the
Centro Cívico southwest on Av Bolivar, to Trebol
junction and beyond – particularly useful for
connecting chicken buses to/from the highlands
with zonas 1/4. The network runs until 11pm;
there's always a security guard onboard.

Accommodation

Zona 1 has a good range of decent accommodation;
the cluster of options around 16 Calle are very handy
for bus connections. However, be aware that this is
not a safe neighbourhood, so after dark either take
a taxi or stay in with take-away. Many travellers
choose to stay close to the airport, in Zona 13, where
there are some good hostels and easy bus links to
Zona 1, but few places to eat or drink. To have bars
and restaurants on your doorstep, you'll need to head
for Zona 10; however, most hotels here will involve a
considerable splurge.

Zona 1

Hotel Ajau 8 Av 15–62 ☎2232 0488,
ⓔhotelajau@hotmail.com. Atmospheric colonial
building with original floor tiles and wood banisters.
Basic rooms are small and dark but clean, and
come with safe and TV; front rooms have private
bath and large windows facing the street. There's a
café in the downstairs courtyard, plus internet and
parking. ❹

Hotel Capri 9 Av 15A–63 ☎2251 3737. In a rather
musty five-floor breeze-block building. If you can
handle the stairs, the top floor rooms are best, with
panoramic views; otherwise, rooms at the rear also
have views and are quieter. Free mineral water,
safes, internet and parking. ❹

Hotel Fénix 7 Av 15–81 ☎2251 6625. A crumbling
old place, but still one of the better bets in the
area. Rooms are light, airy and rickety, and there's
a quirky café downstairs, as well as a TV lounge,
book swap and internet access. ❸

Hotel Monte Carlo 9 Av 16–20 ☎2238 0735.
A reasonable option, with a cute courtyard and
part-time candle-lit fountain. Rooms are rather
dark and pieced together, but clean enough and all
with TV. ❹

Hotel San Martín 16 C 7–65 ☎2238 0319. Not
fancy, but cheap, safe and friendly. Rooms are
clean, and some have private bath. This is one
of the best deals at the lower end of the price
scale. ❷

🏃 **Hotel Spring** 8 Av 12–65 ☎2230 2858,
ⓦwww.hotelspring.com. Spacious rooms,
with or without private bath, come with cable TV
and are set around a pretty courtyard. Breakfast is
available, plus mineral water, safes and internet at a
charge. An excellent deal for the location, ambience
and facilities. Book ahead. ❹

Pensión Meza 10 C 10–17 ☎2232 3177. A
legendary travellers' hangout; even Che Guevara
stayed here back in the day. It's now fairly
ramshackle, though oozes character: the dorms
and private rooms are not too clean, but do boast
some interesting graffiti. There's a handy *comedor*
and bar next door, and a nice courtyard at the rear,
as well as a useful notice board, book exchange
and helpful, English-speaking owner. Dorms ❶,
rooms ❷–❸

Zona 10

Xamanek Hostel 13 C 3–57 ☎2360 8345,
ⓦwww.mayaworld.net. Currently the only budget
place in Zona 10. The owners are exceptionally
friendly, speak good English and can provide useful
advice. Free services include breakfast, internet,
book exchange and DVD library; for a small charge,
you can use the kitchen and laundry. The building is
bright and airy, and rooms spacious and spotlessly
clean. Dorms ❸, doubles ❼

Zona 13

🏃 **Dos Lunas** 21 C 10–92 ☎2261 4248,
ⓦwww.hoteldoslunas.com. Very well-run
guesthouse on a safe, quiet street near the airport
(free pick-up and drop-off). The super-friendly
owner speaks fluent English, offers reliable travel

advice and can arrange onward transport. There are lounge areas with cable TV and good DVD/reference book collections; free breakfast and internet also available. Very popular, so book well ahead. Dorms ❸, doubles ❺

Hostal Los Lagos 8 Av 15–85 ☎ 2261 2809, ⓦ www.loslagoshostal.com. Another option close to the airport with included transfers, breakfast, BBQ facilities, cable TV, internet and a lovely garden. Dorms ❹

Hostal Los Volcanes 16a C 8–00 ☎ 2261 3040, ⓦ www.hostallosvolcanes.com. A respectable B&B, close to the airport, with clean rooms (both dorms and private), a pleasant sitting area and garden. All rooms have cable TV and rates include breakfast, airport transfers and internet use, but not tax. Dorms ❸, doubles ❺–❻

Patricia's B&B 19 C 10–65 ☎ 5402 3256, ⓦ www.patriciashotel.com. A small, family-run establishment with five rooms and shared bath set around a pretty garden. Airport transfers and breakfast included. ❸

Eating

There are restaurants all over the city. Zona 1 has some great budget options, while in the smarter parts of town, notably Cuatro Grados Norte and the Zona Viva, the emphasis is more on refined dining, but even here there are some decent, less expensive places. Wherever you are, you are never far away from a market, street vendor or fast-food chain. For super-markets, head to one of the city's many shopping malls (see p.141). Note that most *comedores* and cafés tend to close fairly early – usually around 7pm.

Zona 1

Anfora 6 C 3–34. European–style café with alpine decor and tempting pastries. Breakfast with coffee and juice costs Q20, filled baguettes Q30. *Café de Imeri*, next door, is the take-away branch of the same business.

Astoria 7 Av & 10 C. Interesting deli with seating at rear and shop out front. There is a good range of sandwiches, burgers and wurst, including combos (with fries and drink), from Q20, as well as draft beer and take-away wine. Mon–Sat 8am–8pm, Sun 9am–5pm.

The Buckets 9 C 7–64. This bar/grill is conveniently located across the road from some of Zona 1's best bars. The building has a refined dining atmosphere, although prices remain moderate (Q25–50). A selection of daily combos (main meal of meat and two veg plus drink; Q15–35) are offered at lunch (noon–3pm). The friendly management speaks English. Closed Sun.

La Fianna 10 C 7–24. Pleasant courtyard restaurant serving economical buffet breakfasts and lunches (Q20), as well as dinner plates (Q18). Breakfasts are especially good value, with coffee/tea, juice, granola, yogurt, fresh fruit, eggs, sausages, plantain, hash browns, bread and, of course, beans, for less than Q20.

Helados Marylena 6 C 2–49. Come here for a choice of more than 150 flavours of ice cream, including such unusuals as yucca and chilli and fish (served with fresh lemon and a sprinkle of salt). Waffle cones start at Q10.

Parrillada Doña Sara 9 Av & 9 C. Recognizable for its Argentine owner, who stands aproned in the doorway grilling tasty steaks and stirring paella. There are rows of film and football memorabilia on the walls. Snacks Q8–20, mains Q25–40, beer Q10.

Picadilly 6 Av & 11 C. Canteen-style place with reasonable pastas (Q25–30), pizzas (Q40–50), burgers (Q20–25) and more. A mug of draught beer goes for Q17. It's clean and friendly, and worth the visit to watch the world of Zona 1 pass by the fishbowl windows.

🏃 **Rey Sol** On the south side of the Parque del Centenario, with a second branch at 11 C 5–51. Vegetarian café/restaurant with tasty, healthy and imaginative food. They do a hearty lunch buffet (noon–4pm) – try the cheesy stuffed peppers and fried yucca with a *refresco* for Q30. Closed Sun.

Tao Restaurant 5 C 9–70. There's no menu here – you just eat the meal of the day at tiny tables around a plant-filled courtyard. Three-course veggie lunch Q15. Open for lunch only, Mon–Fri noon–2.30pm.

Zona 4

Café Restaurant Pereira Inside the Centro Comercial mall (6 Av & 24 C), no. 138. This popular *comedor*-cum-restaurant just a couple of blocks west of Inguat makes a good lunch stop if you're in this part of town. The *menú del día* is served 1–4pm, and includes soup, main course, dessert and drink for Q25.

🏃 **Suae** Via 5, Cuatro Grados Norte. Known for its 70s-style leather couches and pink fluffy stools. There are great snacks served here for under Q20, including filled baguettes; try the vegetarian "Yoko Ono", or the marinated chicken "Chicken Bus". Closed Mon.

Zona 10

La Chapinita 1 Av 10–24. Eat lunch (noon–3pm) with suited and booted office workers in this bright and leafy *comedor*. Soup, main course and *refresco* for Q25.

The Zona Viva is home to a mouth-watering array of international restaurants good for a splurge. Among the offerings are steakhouses, sushi bars, tapas bars, crêperies and seafood buffets. Expect to pay US$10–20 for a main course and premium prices for drinks.

Sophos Av Reforma 13–89. Attached to a smart bookstore, this popular café has an extensive tea and coffee menu as well as pastas, sandwiches and pastries for under Q30.

Tacontento 2 Av & 14 C. One of the Zona Viva's more affordable restaurants, with tacos and wraps at Q20–40 and shared plates from Q46 per person. The pastel-coloured outdoor tables and chairs are a great place to watch the activity of the Zona Viva pass by.

El Tamal 13 C 2–35. Budget eateries are few and far between in the Zona Viva, but this one does the trick. Tamales start at Q25, or a *típico* plate with drink is Q40. There is also a small deli counter.

Drinking and nightlife

Guatemala City isn't going to win any prizes for its nightlife. The retro enclave of Cuatro Grados Norte is limited to a brief two pedestrianized blocks, and Zona 10's Zona Viva, largely the domain of wealthy Guatemaltecos, will put a sizeable dent in your wallet. (This said, watch for drinks promotions in this area – check posters and flyers to see what's on offer.) Zona 1 has a grungy appeal and a clutch of interesting old-time revolutionary hangouts where the educated elite still drink, but the area is quite unsafe after dark. Do not expect much nightlife anywhere between Sunday and Wednesday. Almost all bars listed below serve free tapas/snacks to evening drinkers. Guatemala City's small gay nightlife scene is mostly underground. The key venue is *Genetic* at Vía 3 and Ruta 3 in Zona 4. There are no specifically lesbian clubs or bars.

Zona 1

Las Cien Puertas Pasaje Aycinena, 9 C between 6 & 7 Av. Bohemian bar in a beautiful, shabby colonial arcade with graffiti-plastered walls. Popular with artists, students and political activists. Good Latin music and reasonable prices. Closed Sun.

Europa Bar 11 C 5–16. Long-running, popular expat hang-out set inauspiciously beneath a multi-storey car park. A good place to catch a football match or other sports, as well as grab cheap snacks. Closed Sun.

El Portal Pasaje Rubio, 9 C between 6 & 7 Av. *Chibolas* of *cerveza mixta* have been served across the long oak bar here since 1932, and past patrons have included Fidel Castro and Che Guevara. There is traditional music from a live marimba band on Fri afternoons and during lunch service Mon, Tues, Thurs & Sat. Closed Sun.

Tacos Tequila 7 Av 5–47. This two-storey bar is decorated with hanging skeletons, tequila bottles, flags and murals of Bob Marley and Che Guevara. You should find the place buzzing before sunset, making it a good spot for pre-dinner drinks. A huge bowl glass or *chibola* of beer goes for Q20. Closed Sun

Zona 4

Genetic Via 3 & Ruta 3. Recognizable by the gold-embossed relief of two strapping chaps on the exterior wall, Guatemala's most established gay club is relatively mixed and plays trance/house music on weekend nights. There is a pleasant rooftop patio. Open Fri & Sat 9pm–1am.

Suae Via 5, Cuatro Grados Norte. This funky place functions as a mellow café (see p.139) and retro clothing boutique by day, and glittery, urban-chic electro-disco by night. Occasional drinks promotions. Closed Mon.

Zona 10

El Establo 14 C 5–08. European-owned bar that attracts mostly a middle-aged crowd. There's a quiet, polished wood interior, good food and an extensive vinyl/CD collection in pride of place behind the bar. Reasonable prices for the Zona Viva, with beers at Q15.

Rattle & Hum 4 Av 16–11. Snug and stylish Australian-owned bar, popular with both expats and locals, with lively atmosphere and rock music on the stereo.

Entertainment

If you're fortunate in your travels around Zona 1, you'll happen across impromptu marimba recitals – especially at the weekend or during fiestas. Try *El Portal* (see above) at lunch time, or catch the official Police Marimba Band outside their fortress-like HQ (6 Av & 14 C) on Fridays and Saturdays from 11am to 2pm. For full listings of cultural events in the city, see the Municipalidad's website (Ⓦwww.cultura .muniguate.com or Ⓦwww.consultas.muniguat .com/consultas/cultura_c/), or alternatively consult supplements in the national press (best are *Prensa Libre* and *El Periódico*).

Cinema

There are plenty of cinemas in the city showing both Hollywood blockbusters and alternative art house films. For English audio with Spanish subtitles, head for the shopping-mall multiplexes, including: Los Proceres (Zona 10) and Miraflores and Tikal Futura (Zona 11). There are also screens in Zona 1 at 6 Av & 11 Calle and inside the Centro Capital on 6 Av. Check the listings at the Centro Cultural de España, Via 5 1–23, Zona 4 (ⓦwww .centroculturalespana.com.gt) and at the Centro Cultural Metropolitano (inside the post office, Zona 1) for art house movies – often with free admission.

Live music

La Bodeguita del Centro 12 C 3–55, Zona 1. Large venue with live music, comedy, poetry and all manner of arty events. Free entry during the week, with a cover around Q30 at weekends. Definitely worth a visit for the Che Guevara memorabilia alone. Tues–Sun 8pm.

Trovajazz Via 6 3–55, Zona 4 ⓦwww.trovajazz .com. Decent place in Cuatro Grados Norte district for jazz, blues and folk. Closed Mon.

Theatre

Teatro Nacional The city's main theatre stages productions most weekends.

Shopping

Books Sopho's, Av la Reforma 13–89, Zona 10, is the best bookshop for English-language fiction and travel guides.

Malls Probably most convenient is Los Proceres in Zona 10, which opens onto the southern end of the Zona Viva. There are also a couple of slightly dated places (Plaza Zona 4 and Centro Comercial) at the junction of 6 Av and Ruta 2 in Zona 4. Heading west out of the city on Calzada Roosevelt towards Antigua are the malls of Tikal Futura and Miraflores.

Markets In true Guatemalan fashion, most markets are centred on transport hubs. Best is the Mercado Central, in an underground warren between 8 & 9 Av and 6 & 8 C. There is one at Zona 4's increasingly disused bus terminal, and another, the Mercado Sur, just north of the Teatro Nacional in the Centro Cívico. The city's biggest market is at Centra Sur (the terminus of the Transmetro route). There is also the touristy Mercado de Artisanas opposite the zoo in Zona 13. However, traditional handicrafts will be cheaper, and the selection better, in local highland markets.

Directory

Car rental About a dozen companies have offices opposite the airport. Also in Zona 1 is Tally Renta Autos (7 Av 14–60; ☎5900 4488).

Embassies Most embassies are in the south-eastern quarter of the city, along Av Reforma and Av las Américas: Canada, 13 C 8–44, 8th floor, Edificio Edyma Plaza, Zona 10 ☎2333 6102; Germany, 20 C 6–20, Zona 10 ☎2364 6700; Israel, 13 Av 14–07, Zona 10 ☎2333 4624; UK, 16 C 0–55, 11th floor, Torre Internacional, Zona 10 ☎2367 5425; US, Av Reforma 7–01, Zona 10 ☎2326 4000.

Exchange The airport has two banks where you can exchange currency. Most of the major banks in Zona 1 will change traveller's cheques, give Visa/ MasterCard cash advances and exchange foreign currency. These include: Banco Industrial, 7 Av & 11 C, and Credomatic, 5 Av & 11 C. If you are stuck for cash on a Sunday, head for Banco Industrial 12 C 0–93, Zona 9, Centro Comercial Montúfar (daily 9am–8pm). There are several 24hr ATMs throughout the city.

Immigration The main immigration office (migración) is in a low-slung terra cotta building at 6 Av Ruta 3–11, Zona 4 (☎2411 2411).

Internet There are plenty of cybercafés throughout the city. Expect to pay around Q6/hr, although it's possible to sniff out places offering Q3; hotels seem to charge Q10.

Laundry Lavandería el Siglo 2 C 3–42 Zona 1 (Mon–Sat 8am–6pm). Q40 for wash and dry.

Medical care The Centro Médico, 6 Av 3–47, Zona 10 (☎2332 3555), is a private hospital with 24hr cover. Central Dentist de Especialistas, 20 C 11–17, Zona 10 (☎2337 1773), is the best dental clinic in the country.

Pharmacies Farmacia del Ejecutivo, 7 Av & 15 C.

Police The police headquarters are in the fortress building on 6 Av. However, if you actually need anything, go to the yellow and blue office on the corner of 11 Av and 4 C, Zona 1.

Post office The main post office is at 7 Av and 12 C, Zona 1 (Mon–Fri 8.30am–5.30pm, Sat 8.30am–noon).

Telephones There is a large Telgua office one block south of the post office (daily 7am–midnight).

Moving on

Travellers do leave Guatemala City via plane (mostly for international destinations), but buses are the most common way to other parts of the country.

By air

Flights depart Aurora Airport for other Central American cities, a variety of US hubs and Spain (with Iberia). For connections to South America you will probably have to change in Panama City. There are also three daily domestic flights to Flores (6am, 6.15am & 10am). There is a Q20/US$3 airport security tax payable by all passengers departing from Aurora Airport.

By bus

First-class buses depart from the offices of the relevant bus company (see listings, below). Chicken buses (second-class) now depart from points scattered around Trebol junction, leaving the old Zona 4 Terminal almost deserted (at the time of writing there were a few departures heading east from here, but authorities are attempting to move buses away from this overcrowded area). Chicken buses for Antigua leave from 6 Av of Zona 3; those for other highland destinations (including Xela, Panajachel and Chichicastenango) leave from 41 C in Zona 8, and those headed south towards the Pacific leave from 8 Av and 4 C in Zona 12. Note that buses listed as having regular departures (hourly or more frequent) run from 5am–6pm, unless otherwise stated.

Bus companies and stops

ADN Mayan World (ADN) Departs for Flores from 8 Av 16–41, Zona 1. Information on ☎2251 0610.

Fuente del Norte (FN) Departs for Copán (Honduras), Flores and La Ceiba (Honduras) from 17 C 8–46, Zona 1. Information on ☎2238 3894.

Hedman Alas (HA) Departs for Copán (Honduras), La Ceiba (Honduras) and San Pedro Sula (Honduras) from 2 Av 8–73, Zona 10. Information on ☎2362 5072.

Línea Dorada (LD) Departs for Flores, Huehuetenango, Poptún, Quetzaltenango and Río Dulce from 10 Av and 16 C, Zona 1. Information on ☎2415 8900.

Litegua (L) Departs for Puerto Barrios and Río Dulce from 15 C 10–40, Zona 1. Information on ☎2220 8840.

Monja Blanca (MB) Departs for Cobán from 8 Av 15–16, Zona 1. Information on ☎2238 1409.

Pulmantur (P) Departs for San Salvador (El Salvador) and Tegucigalpa (Honduras) from the *Holiday Inn*, 1 Av 13–22, Zona 10. Information on ☎2363 6240.

Rutas Orientales (RO) ☎79431366. For Chiquimula; leaves from 19 C 8–18, Zona 1.

Tica Bus (TB) Departs for San Salvador (El Salvador) and Tapachula (Mexico) from Blvd los Proceres, 26–55, Zona 10. Information on ☎2459 2848.

Transportes Galgos (TG) Departs for Quetzaltenango and Tapachula (Mexico) from 7 Av 19–44, Zona 1. Information on ☎2253 4868.

Transportes Margarita (TM) Departs for Managua (Nicaragua) from 9 Av 15–69, Zona 1.

Transporte Maria Jose (MJ) Departs for Managua (Nicaragua) from 9 Av 15–69, Zona 1.

Transportes Rosita (TR) Departs for Flores and Poptún from 15 C 9–58, Zona 1. Information on ☎2253 0609.

Transportes Tziboney (TT) Departs for Cobán from 16 C 8–83, Zona 1.

Transportes La Vencedora (V) Departs for San Salvador (El Salvador) from 3 Av 1–38, Zona 9.

Domestic bus destinations

Antigua With various second-class services (from 6 Av, Zona 3). Departures every 15min; 1hr.

Chichicastenango With various second-class services (from 41 C, Zona 8). Departures every 30min; 3hr 15min.

Chiquimula With RO. 1–2 departures hourly; 3hr 30min.

Cobán With MB: departures every hour; 4hr 30min. With TT: 1–2 departures hourly; 5hr.

Escuintla With various second-class services (from 8 Av & 4 C, Zona 12). Departures every 10min; 1hr 15min.

Flores With FN: 18 departures daily 1am–10pm; 8–9hr. With LD: 3 departures daily, 10am, 1pm, 9pm; 8hr. With ADN: 2 departures daily, 9pm & 10pm; 8hr. With TR: 2 departures daily, 5pm & 8pm; 8hr.

Huehuetenango With LD: 3 departures daily, 6.30am, 4pm, 10.30pm; 5hr.

Monterrico With various second-class services (from 8 Av & 4 C); change in Escuintla for Monterrico.

Panajachel With various second-class services (from 41 C, Zona 8). 1–2 departures hourly; 3hr.

Puerto Barrios With L: 18 departures daily; 5hr 30min.

Poptún With LD: 2 departures daily, 10am & 9pm; 6hr. With TR. 2 departures daily, 5pm & 8pm; 6hr.

Quetzaltenango With LD: 2 departures daily, 8am & 3pm; 5hr. With TG: 3 departures daily, 8.30am, 2.30pm, 5pm; 4hr.

Río Dulce With LD: 3 deparutres daily, 10am, 1pm, 9pm; 6hr. With L: 5 departures daily, 6am, 9am, 11.30am, 1pm, 4pm; 6hr.

Santa Cruz del Quiché With various second-class services (from 41 C, Zona 8). 1–2 departures hourly; 4hr.

International bus destinations

Copán (Honduras) With HA: 2 departures daily, 5am & 9am; 5hr. With FN: 1 departure daily, 6am; 5hr.

La Ceiba (Honduras) With HA: 2 departures daily, 5am & 9am; 12hr. With FN: 1 departure daily, 6am; 12hr.

Managua (Nicaragua) With MJ & TM: 2 departures weekly, Tues & Sat 8am; 18hr.

San Pedro Sula (Honduras) With HA: 2 departures daily, 5am & 9am; 8hr.

San Salvador (El Salvador) With V: departures hourly; 5hr. With TB: 1 departure daily, 1pm; 5hr. With P: 2 departures daily, 7am & 3pm; 5hr.

Tapachula (Mexico) With TG: 2 departures daily, 7.30am & 2pm; 7hr. With TB: 1 departure daily, noon; 6hr.

Tegucigalpa (Honduras) With P: 1 departure daily, 7am; 12hr.

Antigua

A visit to the colonial city of **ANTIGUA** is a must for any traveller in Guatemala. Nestled among the Agua, Acatenango and Fuego volcanoes, the city was founded at the beginning of the sixteenth century, built on a grand grid pattern inspired by the Italian renaissance. Named the capital of Guatemala in 1541, Antigua grew in importance over the next two hundred years, peaking in the mid-eighteenth century, before being largely destroyed by an earthquake in 1773. Since then, it's become something of an open-air architectural museum, with many of its major remaining structures and monuments preserved as ruins – the impressive churches and magnificent buildings on view today date back to the Spanish empire. Local conservation laws are strict, ensuring that the city will remain in its current atmospheric state, and continue to draw in thousands of visitors every year.

Long favoured by travellers as an antidote to hectic, nearby Guatemala City, in recent years Antigua has seen its population be joined by both large numbers of *guatemaltecos* from "la capital" and many expats attracted by the city's sophisticated and relaxed atmosphere. Tourists of every nationality continue to permeate the town, along with numerous foreign students attending the city's language schools. With smart restaurants and wine bars catering to this international, cosmopolitan crowd, Antigua's civilized world can at first seem a bit too comfortable, but like most travellers, you will probably end up staying a lot longer than planned.

What to see and do

Antigua is laid out as a grid, with avenidas running north–south, and calles east–west. Each street is numbered and has two halves, either a north (*norte/nte*) and south (*sur*) or an east (*oriente/ote*)

SEMANA SANTA IN ANTIGUA

Antigua's Semana Santa (Holy Week) celebrations are some of the most impressive and remarkable in all Latin America. The celebrations start on Palm Sunday with a procession representing Christ's entry into Jerusalem, and continue through to Good Friday, when processions re-enact the progress of Christ to the Cross. Setting out at about 8am from La Merced, Escuela de Cristo and the village of San Felipe, and accompanied by solemn dirges and clouds of incense, penitents carry images of Christ and the Cross on massive platforms. Intially garbed in either purple or white, after 3pm, the hour of the Crucifixion, the penitents change into black. Some of the images they carry date from the seventeenth century, and the procession itself is thought to have been introduced in the early years of the Conquest.

Check the exact details of events with the tourist office (see p.148). Remember that hotels fill up during Holy Week – reserve in advance if you want to stay in the city.

and west (*poniente/pte*). with the city's main plaza, the **Parque Central**, at their centre. Despite this apparent simplicity, most people get lost here at some stage. If you're confused, remember that Volcán Agua, the one closest to town, is almost directly south.

Parque Central

Antigua's focal point is its main plaza, the **Parque Central**. It's a popular local hangout, with couples, friends and families coming to the Parque to watch the world go by, seated on one of its many benches or around the **Fuente de Las Sirenas**, built in 1739. For travellers, the square is not only an easy rendezvous point, but is also a good place to begin exploring

the city, starting with the Cathedral and the Palacios de los Capitanes, both of which look onto the square. The Parque is perfectly safe during the day, but try not to walk around alone late at night – dodgy characters sometimes roam around the area.

Catedral de San José

Of the structures surrounding the plaza, the **Catedral de San José**, on the east side, is the most arresting. Built in 1670, the cathedral was quite elaborate for its time and location – it boasted an immense dome, five aisles, eighteen chapels and an altar inlaid with mother-of-pearl, ivory and silver – but the 1773 earthquake destroyed the building.

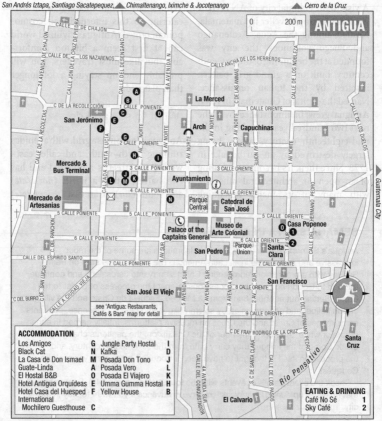

San Andrés Iztapa, Santiago Sacatepequez, ▲ Chimaltenango, Iximche & Jocotenango ▲ Cerro de la Cruz

ANTIGUA

0   200 m

▶ Guatemala City

ACCOMMODATION

Los Amigos	G	Jungle Party Hostal	I
Black Cat	N	Kafka	D
La Casa de Don Ismael	M	Posada Don Tono	J
Guate-Linda	A	Posada Vero	L
El Hostal B&B	O	Posada El Viajero	K
Hotel Antigua Orquídeas	E	Umma Gumma Hostal	H
Hotel Casa del Huesped	F	Yellow House	B
International			
Mochilero Guesthouse	C		

EATING & DRINKING

Café No Sé	1
Sky Café	2

San Juan del Obispo & Santa María de Jesús ▼

ANTIGUA: RESTAURANTS, CAFÉS & BARS

CAMPO SECO ❶

La Merced ✝

0   100 m

1 CALLE PONIENTE   1 CALLE ORIENTE

San Jerónimo ✝

❹ ❷ ❸
✝ ❺
❻
❼ ✝   Capuchinas ✝
Arch
❾ ❽

2 CALLE PONIENTE   2 CALLE ORIENTE

✝

❿

3 CALLE PONIENTE   3 CALLE ORIENTE

@ ⓫
✝
Ayuntamiento ⓬ ⓭ ⓮⓯⓰
ⓘ

4 CALLE ORIENTE

Taxis ★
Parque Central   Catedral de San José ✝

⓱
⓲   Museo de Arte Colonial
⓳

5 CALLE PONIENTE   5 CALLE ORIENTE

@⓴
㉑   Palace of the Captains General
㉓
㉒   ㉔

6 CALLE PONIENTE   6 CALLE ORIENTE

㉖   ㉕   San Pedro ✝   Parque Unión   Santa Clara ✝

7 CALLE ORIENTE

San José El Viejo ✝   8 CALLE ORIENTE

N

9 CALLE ORIENTE

EATING & DRINKING

The Bagel Barn	19	Mono Loco	20
Café Condesa	17	Portal Café	18
Café Rubi	15	Perú Café	13
La Casbah	6	Rainbow	
La Chimenea	9	Reading Room	22
Coco'S Art Café	26	Red's	3
Doña Luisa's	14	Reilly's	5
La Escudilla	12	Riki's Bar	12
Fernando's Kaffee	1	El Sabor del Tiempo	11
Fridas	7	La Sala	25
La Fuente	16	La Sin Ventura	21
Hector's	2	Travel Menu	23
Kafka	4	Viejo Café	10
Luna de Miel	8	Y Tu Piña También	24

Today only two of the original interior chapels have been rebuilt; take a peek inside and you will find a gold cloister, several colonial images and a crypt used by the Maya for religious purposes. To get some idea of the scale of the colonial cathedral, check out the ruins of the rest of the original structure (enter from 5 C Ote; daily 9am–5pm; Q5), which sit behind the church – here you'll find a mass of fallen masonry and rotting beams, broken arches and hefty pillars. Buried beneath the floor are some of the great names of the Conquest, including Pedro de Alvarado and his wife, Bishop Marroquín and the historian Bernal Díaz del Castillo. At the very rear of what was once the nave, steps lead down to a burial vault that's regularly used for Maya religious ceremonies – an example of the coexistence of pagan and Catholic beliefs that's so characteristic of Guatemala.

Palacio de los Capitanes

One of the oldest buildings in Antigua, the **Palacio de los Capitanes**, or the

145

Palace of the Captains-General, takes up the entire south side of the Parque Central. Dating to 1558, it's been rebuilt more than once, and been through several incarnations, serving as the mint for all of Latin America, the home of the colonial rulers, dragoon barracks, stables, law courts, ballrooms and more. Today it houses the local government offices, but you are free to roam around the ruins in the courtyard. Note the little fountain in the centre, which was brought here during Jorge Ubico's time as president of Guatemala – it's one of the few things in the yard left relatively intact.

Ayuntamiento

Directly across from the Palace of the Captains-General sits the **Ayuntamiento** (City Hall), which dates from 1740. It's so solidly built that even after three centuries of earthquakes not a lot of reconstruction has had to be undertaken: the walls, more than one metre thick, and the vaulted stone facade are good examples of anti-seismic building techniques. When the capital moved to Guatemala City following the 1773 earthquake the Ayuntamiento was abandoned, but was later restored in 1853. Today it houses two museums, the **Museo de Santiago** (Tues–Sun 9am–4pm; Q10), housed in the section of the building that was once the city jail and containing a collection of colonial artefacts, and the **Museo del Libro Antiguo** (same hours; Q10), in the rooms that held the first printing press in Central America. A replica of the press is on display, alongside some copies of the works produced on it. From the upper floor of the Ayuntamiento there's a wonderful **view** of the three volcanoes that surround the city – it's especially fine at sunset.

Museo de Arte Colonial

Across 5 Calle Oriente from the ruined cathedral is the **Museo de Arte Colonial** (Tues–Fri 9am–4pm, Sat & Sun 9am–noon & 2–4pm; Q25), located on the site of the former Universidad de San Carlos (now removed to Guatemala City). The museum building's ornate Moorish-style arcades make it one of the finest architectural survivors in the city, and the collection inside is good, too: mostly dark and brooding religious art, sculpture, furniture and murals depicting life on the colonial university campus.

Casa Popenoe

Further down 5 Calle Oriente, at the corner with 1 Avenida Sur, is the **Casa Popenoe** (Mon–Sat 2–4pm; Q15), a restored seventeenth-century mansion that offers an interesting glimpse into the domestic life of the colonial elites. It was painstakingly refurbished in the 1930s by United Fruit Company scientist Dr Wilson Popenoe, who furnished the house with antiques – you can see the bread ovens, herb garden and pigeon loft, whose occupants would have provided the mansion's owners with their mail. There are also some interesting paintings, including portraits of Bishop Marroquín and a menacing-looking Pedro de Alvarado.

Church of San Francisco

South on 1 Avenida Sur from the Casa Popenoe is the colossal **Church of San Francisco** (daily 6am–6pm). One of the oldest churches in Antigua, dating from 1579, during the colonial period it served as a vast religious and cultural centre that included a school, a hospital, music rooms, a printing press and a monastery. All of this was lost, though, in the 1773 earthquake. Restoration of the chapel started in 1960 and today very little remains of what was once the original monument. However, the **ruins** of the monastery (daily 8am–5pm; Q5) are still visible, and among the city's most striking, including a large bell tower. The fallen arches, pillars and pleasant grassy verges make a good background for a picnic. Inside the church, meanwhile, is the tomb of **Hermano Pedro de Betancourt**, a Franciscan from the Canary Islands who founded the Hospital of Belén in Antigua, and is credited with powers of miraculous intervention. Pope John Paul II made him Central America's first saint in 2002 and his tomb is regularly visited by religious pilgrims.

Parque Unión

One block west and one block north of San Francisco is **Parque Unión**, flanked on each end by a church (both daily 8am–4.30pm). The one on the western side is **San Pedro**, dating from 1680, and the one to the east is **Santa Clara**, a former convent with a fine ornate facade. In colonial times the latter was a popular place for aristocratic ladies to take the veil – the hardships were not too extreme, and the nuns gained a reputation for their fine cooking. In front of Santa Clara is a large *pila* (washhouse) where women today gather to scrub, rinse and gossip.

Las Capuchinas

At the junction of 2 Calle Oriente and 2 Avenida Norte are the remains of **Las Capuchinas** (daily 9am–5pm; Q30), dating from 1726, once the largest and most beautiful of the city's convents. These ruins are among Antigua's best preserved, and yet least documented: the Capuchin nuns who lived here were not allowed any contact with the outside world, and vice versa. Food was passed to them by means of a turntable, and they could only speak to visitors through a grille. You should wander through the ruins – they are beautiful, with fountains, courtyards, massive pillars and a unique tower, or "retreat", which has eighteen tiny cells set into the walls on the top floor and a cellar that probably functioned as a meat storage room. The exterior of the tower is also interesting, ringed with small stone recesses representing the Stations of the Cross. The convent was damaged following the 1751 earthquake, and in 1773 the sisters left the premises for a home in the adjoining Finca La Chacra. The building lay abandoned until 1813, when it was sold. Since 1972 it has been home to the National Council for the Protection of La Antigua Guatemala.

Santa Catalina and La Merced

A couple of blocks west of Las Capuchinas, spanning 5 Avenida Norte, the **arch of Santa Catalina** is all that remains of yet another convent, this one founded in 1609. The arch was built so that the nuns could walk between the two halves of the establishment without being exposed to the outside world. At the end of the street, just north, the church of **La Merced** boasts one of the most intricate facades in the entire city. Look closely and you'll see the outline of a corncob, a motif probably added by the original Maya labourers. The church is still in use, and the cloisters and gardens, including a monumental fountain, are open to the public (daily 8am–5pm; Q5).

Cerro de la Cruz

Northeast of Antigua, the **Cerro de la Cruz** has commanding views of the city and Volcán Agua. It is strongly advised you come here with a police escort (see p.153), as a number of muggings have been reported here in the past.

Arrival and information

By bus Antigua's main second-class bus terminal is beside the market; the street opposite (4 C Pte) leads directly to the Parque Central. Shuttle buses will drop you off at your hotel.

Tour operators Maya Mountain Bike Tours, 1 Av Sur 15 (☎7832 3383), have a wide range of trips, plus bike rental; Old Town Outfitters, 6 C Pte 7 (☎7832 4171 or 5399 0440, ⓦwww .bikeguatemala.com), run mountain-biking and rock-climbing trips, and offer tent, sleeping bag,

VOLCÁN PACAYA

Volcán Pacaya, one of Guatemala's many cones, is a spectacular Strombolian volcano (characterized by low-level, intermittent explosions). Though technically closer to Guatemala City than Antigua, it's nonetheless more commonly reached from the latter city – indeed, it is *the* trip to make in the area. Depending on Pacaya's activity level, you may be able to scale its slopes.

You can only visit the volcano with guided tours (prices start at about Q40), which are offered twice daily (6am & 2pm) by virtually all travel agents and tour operators in town. Tours entail a two-hour climb up the volcano where you can, quite literally, poke at the lava with a stick (make sure you wear good shoes, as thin soles can melt). The afternoon trip is highly recommended, as the views at sunset are breathtaking – remember to bring a torch, as it will be dark when you walk down. The volcano sits inside Pacaya National Park, for which entry is an additional Q40; make sure you find out if this is included in your ticket before you go. Note that sulphurous fumes and high winds can occasionally make the ascent impossible.

pack and bike rental; Adventure Travel Center Viareal, 5 Av Nte 25B (☎7832 0162, ⓦwww .adventravelguatemala.com), is good for adventure and sailing trips. Elizabeth Bell, 3 C Ote 28 (☎7832 2046, ⓦwww.antiguatours.com), offers excellent historical walking tours of the town.
Tourist information The tourist office (Mon–Fri 8am–1pm & 2–5pm, Sat & Sun 9am–1pm & 2–5pm; ☎&ⓕ7832 5682), on the east side of the plaza, is extremely helpful, providing reliable information. Otherwise, noticeboards in various tourist venues advertise everything from haircuts to private language lessons and apartments for let – probably the most informative are those at *Doña Luisa's* restaurant (see p.150) and the *Rainbow Reading Room* (see p.150).
Travel agents Of the dozens of travel agents in Antigua, Rainbow Travel Center, 7 Av Sur 8 (☎7832 4202, ⓦwww.rainbowtravelcenter.com), is very efficient, and Viajes Tivoli, 4 C Ote 10 (☎7832 4274/4287, ⓔantigua@tivoli.com.gt), is a good all-rounder. A number of tourists have reported bad experiences with the following agents: Centroamérica, Plus Travel, Sinfronteras and Universal.

City transport

Taxis Available taxis line up on the east side of the Parque Central close to the cathedral, or you can call ☎7832 0479.

Accommodation

There's a plentiful supply of excellent budget accommodation, including many good hostels, in Antigua. Be warned that rooms can get scarce (and prices increase) in July and August, and at Semana Santa.

Hotels and guesthouses

Los Amigos 2 C Pte 30 ☎5075 2679. Excellent cheap option with clean showers in communal bathrooms and good solid beds. The owners will cook you breakfast and lunch on request. ❸

Black Cat 6 Av Nte 1A ☎7832 1229, ⓔblackcatantigua@gmail.com. A great place to meet other travellers. Colourful, cosy private rooms and dorms are en suite, and there's a TV lounge and good restaurant. Rates include a massive, delicious breakfast and free internet. Dorms ❷, doubles ❹

La Casa de Don Ismael 3 C Pte 6 ☎7832 1932, ⓦwww.casadonismael.com. Down a quiet side street, this excellent option has seven rooms grouped around a lovely garden. The communal bathrooms are spotless, and rates include breakfast and internet use. ❹

Earth Lodge ☎5664 0713 or 5613 6934, ⓦwww.earthlodgeguatemala.com. 7km out of town, this Canadian/American-owned place is perfect for relaxation. You can stay in a treehouse, dorms or cabins, or you can camp. Excellent views, walking trails and good home-made meals. The owners will pick you up from town. ❸

Guate-Linda 7 Av Nte 80 ☎5252 5694, ⓦwww .guatelindacenter.com. Set around a pleasant courtyard, some rooms here have cable TV, and most have hot-water, en-suite baths. The friendly, multilingual owner will cook you meals on request, including great Italian food. Dorms (❷) and long-term rentals available. ❺

El Hostal B&B 1 Av Sur 8 ☎7832 0442, ⓔelhostal.antigua@gmail.com. Spotless rooms and dorms, all with lockers, and equally clean communal bathrooms with superb hot-water showers. Excellent service, and rates include breakfast. Dorms ❷, doubles ❹

Hotel Antigua Orquídeas Calzada Santa Lucía Nte 25D ☎5219 5406, ⓦwww.hotelantiguaorquideas .guat.ws. Clean dorms and private rooms with hot water and comfortable beds but a slightly musty smell. Ninfa plants, orchids and rustic wooden tables decorate the roof terrace. Rates include free laundry, breakfast and internet and use of the kitchen. Dorms ❷, doubles ❹

Hotel Casa del Huésped Calzada Santa Lucía Nte 16 ☎7832 3422. The kind owner at this place, locally known as *El Cafetín*, will make you feel right at home. Rooms are clean and spacious with very big beds. Home-made meals available on request, and special prices for language students. ❸

International Mochilero Guesthouse 1 C Pte 33 ☎7832 0520 or 2832 4791, ⓦwww .internacionalmochilero.com. One of the nicest places in town, this guesthouse is beautifully decorated with a number of old musical instruments in the hall. Clean dorms, private rooms and communal bathrooms. Dorms ❷, doubles ❸

Jungle Party Hostal 6 Av Nte 20 ☎4323 0663. *Jungle Party* has decent three- and five-bed dorms with solid wood bunk beds, and a chill-out area with hammocks and BBQ equipment. Keep an eye on your belongings, though, as there have been rumours of objects going missing. Dorms ❷

Kafka 6 Av Nte 40 ☎5270 6865. Very relaxed place with hammocks slung around the yard and terrace and a popular bar at the front. Sturdy beds with lockers and clean bathrooms. Excellent food served at the restaurant. ❹

Posada Don Tono 3 C Pte 4 ☎5777 3025. Family-run place with clean baths and rooms sleeping two, three, four or five. Not the best option for light sleepers – a vocal rooster roams the premises – but the chatty owner will cook you breakfast on request. ❹

Posada Vero 3 C Pte 4 ☎7832 0114. Fairly clean but quite small rooms with stuffy bathrooms. A number of colourful caged birds flutter around the courtyard. ❷

Posada El Viajero 7 Av Nte 18 ☎7882 4341. Rooms here are pleasant, clean and with semi-orthopedic beds, and there's a rooftop terrace from which you can enjoy incredible views of the nearby volcanoes. Rates include breakfast, internet and purified water, and laundry service is available. ❹

Umma Gumma Hostal 7 Av Nte 34 ☎7832 4413, Ⓔummagumma@itelgua.com. Despite the old-looking tiles, passable bathrooms and dark rooms downstairs, *Umma Gumma* has a nice roof terrace, free internet, hot water and a kitchen for self-caterers. Upstairs rooms are brighter. ❸

Yellow House 1 C Pte 24 ☎7832 6646. Environmentally friendly, this place has solar-powered

hot water and a nice roof terrace. Doubles are a lot better value than the dorms, and the clean communal bathrooms need a bit of ventilation. There is also a travel agency at the front. Dorms ❸, doubles ❹

Eating

Antigua boasts a terrific array of cafés and restaurants, with most types of global cuisine represented. The only thing that seems hard to come by is authentic Guatemalan *comedor* food – which will be quite a relief if you've been subsisting on eggs and beans. For extremely cheap and excellent burgers (Q6.25) head to a hole in the wall at the northern entrance of the Bodegona supermarket (see p.151). It's very popular with locals, who have a habit of queue jumping – be prepared to fight for your order. Restaurants in Antigua stay open till much later than in the rest of the country, making long (boozy) dinners possible.

Cafés

The Bagel Barn 5 C Pte 2. Well-liked place with a relaxed, cosy feel serving excellent bagels (Q15). Films (mainly Hollywood blockbusters) are also shown twice daily (4.15pm & 7.15pm).

Café Condesa On the west side of the Parque Central; enter through the Casa del Conde bookshop. Cosy place – some would liken aspects of it to a *Starbucks* – to enjoy an excellent breakfast (Q25), coffee and cake or lunch. The cobbled patio and period charm create a nice tone for the lazy Sunday brunches favoured by Antiguan society.

Coco's Art Café 7 Av Sur 8. Tuck into a huge wheat tortilla (Q23) in this little café while owner Carla reads your Maya horoscope. A mix of Guatemalan and international dishes are available, including some vegetarian dishes.

Fernando's Kaffee 7 Av Nte 43. Extremely fine coffee ground, roasted and served by a friendly, English-speaking Guatemalan. Chocolate-covered coffee beans (Q30 for 100g) available for purchase, too. Breakfasts (Q18) and light lunches, including empanadas (Q22) and salads (Q17), are available. Local women weave scarves and skirts in the courtyard at the back.

Portal Café On the west side of the Parque Central, next to *Café Condesa*. Favoured place among both expats and locals, serving very good coffee (Q8), bagels (Q10), sandwiches (Q20) and croissants (Q10).

Rainbow Reading Room 7 Av Sur 8. Long-standing popular café/restaurant with a bohemian atmosphere (live music most nights) and a great menu of imaginative salads and vegetarian choices. Also home to one of Antigua's best travel agents and a good secondhand bookshop.

Viejo Café 3 C & 6 Av Nte 12. The pleasant little courtyard here is decorated with antique knick-knacks. Baguettes, croissants and strudels all baked daily. All-day breakfast from Q16.50.

Y Tu Piña También 1 Av Sur 11. Colourful, hippyish little café. Try the "monkey's ass" juice (a blend of natural fruit juices – it's not as vile as it sounds; Q19), the Turkish sandwich (Q27) or one of the excellent soups (Q26). Free wi-fi.

Restaurants

Café Rubi 4 C Ote 14. If you're counting your quetzales and need a quick, cheap bite, come here and have a good *pupusa* (Q8) cooked in front of you. Closed Wed.

Doña Luisa's 4 C Ote 12. The menu at this two-storey converted colonial mansion is pretty basic – sandwiches, burgers (Q27.50) and salads (try the *ensalada taco guatelmalteco*) – but the in-house bakery really is the best in town. Pastries can be purchased from the adjoining shop.

La Escudilla 4 Av Nte 4. Agreeable, excellent-value courtyard restaurant offering a choice of European dishes and local cuisine (*plato típico* Q48). Always busy, but if you have to wait you can have a drink in *Riki's Bar*, also on the premises.

Fridas 5 Av Nte 29. Great Mexican food served up in lively surrounds festooned with 1950s Americana. Try the *enchilada de mole poblano* (Q59).

La Fuente 4 C Ote 14. Attractive courtyard restaurant with beautiful photographs and paintings of Guatemalan children available for purchase. You can eat relatively decent pastas (Q38) and fajitas (Q38) and sip a good coffee.

Luna de Miel 6 Av Nte 19. French-owned, this cosy crêperie has by far the best crêpes

(try the exquisite pesto one; Q30) in town and is also a good place to have a pastis.

Perú Café 4 Av Nte 7. Enjoyable, casual place with a dining room off a small patio. There's interesting fare including *causas* (Peruvian starters made of stuffed potatoes) from Q27. Closed Mon.

El Sabor del Tiempo 5 Av & 3 C. Relaxed, candle-lit restaurant with jazzy background tunes and well-dressed waiters. The menu includes Mediterranean-style dishes such as pizzas (Q57), paninis (Q33) and pastas (Q34); you can treat yourself to a bottle of Chilean Gato Negro Cabernet for Q85.

Travel Menu 6 C Pte 14. Popular with travellers, this candle-lit place has a boho feel and serves veggie food, including a delicious *plato típico* (Q32) and an equally good curry (Q25).

Drinking and nightlife

Antigua's main *zona viva* (lively zone) is centred around the arch on 5 Avenida Norte, though there's another clutch of good bars on 1 Avenida Norte. The city's club scene is fairly small but lively, even drawing a crowd from Guatemala City. All places (including clubs) officially close at 1am, but some of the bars also play music to which you can have a bit of a boogie. "After hours" parties (technically illegal), featuring local and visiting DJs, are held most weekends in private houses, publicized by flyers and word-of-mouth.

Bars

Café No Sé 1 Av Nte 11C. Atmospheric American-owned bar, where the owner's iPods provide eclectic background sounds and Tues–Sun there's an open mike and live music acts. Ask to be taken to the tequila bar at the back, where you can have a mezcal for Q22.

La Chimenea 7 Av Nte & 2 C Pte. Definitely a bit of a dive bar, but a good place to start a boozy evening with Q5 beers (9–10pm). Cocktail and spaghetti happy hours 5–9pm. Closed Sun.

Kafka 6 Av Nte 40. Cosy candle-lit bar with red tones attracting a relaxed crowd – ideal for a pre- or post-dinner drink before hitting the town. The restaurant also serves excellent food.

Mono Loco 2 Av Nte 6B. Gringo sports bar/Tex-Mex place, which, for some reason, is always packed. Tues' ladies' nights can be a bit of a meat market, but nonetheless the bar kitchen deserves some credit for its delicious, huge nachos (Q72).

Red's 1 C Pte 3. *The* place to watch English footie and have pub grub like fish & chips (Q40) or a good old curry (Q60). Pool table, darts and big patio at back.

Reilly's 5 Av Nte 31. By far the most happening place in town, this Irish bar is a popular meeting point and plays fun tunes to groove to while you drink. Always packed.

Riki's Bar 4 Av Nte 4. Very well-received due to its excellent location inside *La Escudilla*, eclectic funk and lounge music policy and an unrivalled happy hour (7–9pm). Crammed most nights.

La Sala 6 C Pte 9. Spacious, sociable bar, with a good drinks list and a mixed clientele of locals and foreigners. Concerts frequently take place.

Sky Café 1 Av Nte. Terrific views from the upper deck, great tunes and an infectious social vibe make this one of the top after-dark destinations in town.

Clubs

La Casbah 5 Av Nte 30. In a spectacular venue overlooking the floodlit ruins of a Baroque church, *La Casbah* attracts a well-heeled crowd. Commercial Latin house and electronica are the sounds of choice; drinks are expensive. Cover Q30; open bar on Tues for Q50.

La Sin Ventura 5 Av Sur. Head here for some Latin grooves on the little dance floor at the back. Gets pretty packed, as most patrons at *Mono Loco*, next door, eventually stumble over.

Entertainment

Art galleries Both La Antigua Galería de Arte, 4 C Ote 15 (☎7832 2124, ⓦwww.artintheamericas .com), and Art Gallery, 4 C and 1 Av Norte 10 (ⓔcaartgallery@intelnett.com), frequently host good art exhibitions.

Cinemas A number of small cinemas show a range of Western films daily, namely La Sin Ventura (see above); Cooperación Española, 6 Av Nte & 4 C; Café

2000, 6 Av Nte 2; and El Sitio, 5 C Pte 15, which has a good choice of Latin American and art house movies. Weekly listings are posted on noticeboards all over town.

Cultural institutes El Sitio, 5 C Pte 15 (☎7832 3037/1664), has an active theatre and art gallery and regularly hosts exhibitions and concerts. Mosaico Cultural, 3 C Ote 28 (☎7820 1220), organizes events year-round, including concerts and painting exhibitions, often in the park, in some of the ruins in town or at the Centro de Convenciones of the *Hotel Casa Santo Domingo*, where you can find out what's on.

Shopping

Books Available at Casa del Conde and Un Poco de Todo, both on the west side of the plaza; Librería Pensativo, 5 Av Nte 29; Hamley and White, 4 C Ote 12; and the *Rainbow Reading Room*, 7 Av Sur 8, which has by far the largest selection of second-hand books.

Markets The main shopping streets in town are 4 C from Pte to Ote and 5 Av Nte. The Mercado de Artesanías (daily 8am–6pm), west off 4 C Pte, and the Mercadito de Artesanías El Carmen on 3 Av (daily 8am–6pm), both sell handicrafts.

Supermarkets La Bodegona, 4 C Pte and Calzada Santa Lucía; La Despensa, Calzada Santa Lucía between 4 and 5 C.

Directory

Bike rental Maya Mountain Bike Tours and Old Town Outfitters (see p.147) rent mountain bikes from around Q125 a day, or Q700 weekly. La Ceiba, 6 C Pte 6 (☎7832 4168 or 5215 8269, ⓦwww .laceiba.centroamerica.com), rents out 250cc motorbikes for Q75/hr or Q340/day.

Car rental Tabarini, 6 Av Sur 22 (☎7832 8107, ⓦwww.tabarini.com), has cars from around Q290 a day and 4WD from Q865, including unlimited mileage and insurance.

Exchange Banco Industrial, on 4 C Pte 14 just south of the plaza, is one of the biggest banks in town. Banco Agromercantil, 4 C Pte 8, and Banco G&T Continental, Av Nte 2, both have ATMs and accept most cards.

Internet At dozens of cybercafés; rates are around Q8 an hour. Funky Monkey, 5 Av Sur 6 (next to *Mono Loco*), is open daily till 12.30am; Micronet, 3 C Pte (next to *Subway*), also has a fast connection with Skype.

Laundry Lavandería Detalles, 6 Av Nte 3B (Mon–Sat 7.30am–6.30pm, Sun 8am–4pm). A pound of washing costs Q5.

LANGUAGE SCHOOLS IN ANTIGUA

Antigua is an extremely popular place to attend language school. Listed here are only a few of the very many schools offering language courses.

APPE 1 C Ote 15 ℡7882 4284, ⓦwww.appeschool.com.

Centro America Spanish Academy Inside La Fuente, 4 C Ote 14 ℡7832 3297, ⓦwww.quik.guate.com/spanishacademy.

Centro Lingüístico Internacional Spanish School Av del Espíritu Santo 6 ℡7832 1039 ⓦwww.spanishcontact.com.

Centro Lingüístico Maya 5 C Pte 20 ℡7832 0656, ⓦwww.travellog.com /guatemala/antigua/clmaya/school.html.

Christian Spanish Academy 6 Av Nte 15 ℡7832 3922, ⓦwww.learncsa.com.

Guate Linda Language Center 7 Av Norte 80 ℡5252 5694, ⓦwww.guatelindacenter.com.

Ixchel Spanish School 7 C Pte 15 ℡7832 0364, ⓦwww.ixchelschool.com.

Probigua 6 Av Nte 41B ℡7832 2998, ⓦwww.probigua.org.

San José El Viejo 5 Av Sur 34 ℡832 3028, ⓦwww.sanjoseelviejo.com.

Spanish Academy Sevilla 1 Av Sur 17 C ℡7832 5101, ⓦwww.sevillantigua.com.

Tecún Umán Spanish School 6 C Pte 34 A ℡7832 2792 ⓦwww.tecunuman .centramerica.com.

Zamora Academia 9 C Pte 7 ℡7832 7670, ⓦwww.learnspanish-guatemala.com.

Medical care 24hr emergency service at the Hospital Privado Hermano Pedro (℡7832 1190). Dr Marco Antonio Bocaleti has a surgery on 3 Av Nte 1 (℡7832 4835) and speaks English and German.

Pharmacies Ivory Pharmacy, 6 Av Sur 11 (Mon–Fri & Sun 7am–10pm; ℡7832 5394); Farmacia Roca, 4 C Pte 11 (Mon–Sat 8am–7pm; ℡7832 0612).

Police The headquarters are outside town. In Antigua, go to Disetur (℡7882 4030), Rancho Nimajay, at the end of 6 C Pte, to report thefts, or Asistur, in the same building, which can put you in touch with your embassy. Alternatively, Inguat can also offer some help and put you in touch with the tourist police (see opposite).

Post office Alameda de Santa Lucía, opposite the bus terminal (Mon–Fri 8am–6pm).

Telephones The Telgua office is just south of the plaza on 5 Av Sur (8am–6pm), but rates are higher here than anywhere else and you'll have to queue. You can netcall on good lines at Funky Monkey (see p.151) for around Q1/min to North America and Q3 to Europe, Australia, New Zealand and the rest of the world.

Tourist police Behind the Mercado de Artesanías ℡4547 0791. Officers escort visitors to the colourful cemetery once a day or twice daily up to the Cerro de la Cruz, from where there's a panoramic view of Antigua and the surrounding volcanoes.

Moving on

By bus to: Chimaltenango (hourly 6am–4pm; 45min); Guatemala City (every 15 min 5.30am–6.30pm; 1hr); Monterrico, via Escuintla (11 daily 5.30am–4pm; 3hr); Panajachel (one direct service daily, 7am; 2hr 30min). For the following destinations you need to change in Chimaltenango: Chichicastenango, Panajachel (except for the one direct bus at 7am), Quetzaltenango, Tecpán and Todos Santos Cuchumatán.

AROUND ANTIGUA

The countryside **around Antigua** is extremely beautiful. The valley is dotted with small villages, ranging from the *ladino* coffee centre of Jocotenango to the *indígena* village of Santa María de Jesús. None of them is more than an hour or two from the city. For the more adventurous, the Agua, Acatenango and Fuego volcanoes offer strenuous but superb hiking, best done through a specialist agency (see p.147 for listings). Northwest of Antigua is **Santiago Sacatepéquez**, renowned for its annual Festival of the Day of the Dead, when beautiful, intricately decorated kites

– some with a diameter of up to seven metres – soar through the skies. Further west are the ruins of **Iximché**, the "Place of the Maize Tree", where you can visit what remains of a pre-Columbian archeological site.

Santa María de Jesús and Volcán Agua

Heading south from Antigua, a good paved road snakes through the coffee bushes and past the village of San Juan del Obispo before arriving in **Santa María de Jesús**. Perched on the shoulder of **Volcán Agua**, the village is some 500m above the city, with brilliant views over the Panchoy valley and east towards smoking Volcán Pacaya. Though the women wear beautiful purple *huipiles*, the village itself is of minimal interest – most people come through here on their way up Agua, the easiest and most popular of Guatemala's major cones to climb. The **trail** starts right in town: head straight across the plaza, between the two aging pillars, and up the street opposite the church doors. Turn right just before the end, then continue past the cemetery and out of the village. From here it's a fairly simple climb on a decent path. The ascent takes around six hours, and the peak, at 3766m, is always cold at night. There is shelter (though not always room) in a small chapel at the summit. If you're not up to the hike, you can rent horses at Ravenscroft Stables, 2 Av Sur 3, in the village of San Juan del Obispo (☎7830 6669). **Buses** run from Antigua to Santa María every 30 minutes or so from 6am to 6pm, and the trip takes thirty minutes.

Jocotenango

Despite being rather unattractive, the suburb of **Jocotenango**, just 2km north of Antigua, does boast a couple of interesting sights, both of which are grouped in the **Centro La Azotea** cultural centre (Mon–Fri 9am–4pm, Sat 8.30am–2pm; Q30, including tour in English). **Casa K'ojom**, which forms one half of the centre, is a purpose-built museum dedicated to Maya culture, especially music. Displays clearly present the history of indigenous musical traditions, beginning with its pre-Columbian origins and moving through sixteenth-century Spanish and African influences – which brought the marimba, bugles and drums – to today. Other rooms are dedicated to the village weavings of the Sacatepéquez department and the cult of Maximón (see overleaf). Next door, the 34-hectare **Museo de Café** plantation dates from 1883, and offers the chance to look around a working organic coffee farm. All the technicalities of husking, sieving and roasting are explained, and you can sample a cup of the home-grown brew after the tour. **Buses** from the Antigua terminal pass Jocotenango every thirty minutes on their way to Chimaltenango; the museums are about 500m west of plaza.

CRIME AROUND ANTIGUA

Visitors to the areas around Antigua should be aware that crime against tourists – including violent robbery and rape – is not common but does occur. Keep informed by taking local advice, and try to avoid walking alone, especially at night, or to isolated spots during the day. If you want to visit viewing spots like the Cerro de la Cruz, inform the tourist police (behind the Mercado de Artesanías; ☎4547 0791) and they will accompany you free of charge or even give you a ride there. If you are planning a longer trip you can either give the tourist police further details, such as destination and number plate, or you can request two police escorts to travel with you; to organize this get in touch with Nuri León at Inguat (☎2421 2800 ext 1305, ✉nleon@inguat.gob.gt).

San Andrés Itzapa

Past Jocotenango, the Antigua–Chimaltenango road ascends the Panchoy valley, past small farming villages, before a dirt track branches off to **San Andrés Itzapa**. San Andrés is known as the home of the cult of **San Simón** (or Maximón), the "evil saint" – a kind of combination of Judas Iscariot and Pedro de Alvarado – who is housed in his own pagan chapel. Despite being just 18km from Antigua, few tourists visit this shrine, and you may feel more welcome here than at his other places of abode, which include Zunil (see p.184) and Santiago Atitlán (see p.161). To reach the saint's "house" ("Casa de San Simón") – which is only open from sunrise to sunset, as the Maya believe he sleeps at other times – head for the central plaza, turn right when you reach the church, walk two blocks, then up a little hill, where you should spot street vendors selling charms, incense and candles. Once you've tracked down the shrine, you'll find that Maximón lives in a fairly strange world, his image surrounded by drunken men, cigar-smoking women and hundreds of burning candles, each symbolizing a request. You may be offered a *limpia*, or soul cleansing, which, for a small fee, involves being beaten by one of the resident women with a bushel of herbs. A bottle of *aguardiente* is also demolished: some is offered to San Simón, some of it you drink yourself and the rest is consumed by the attendant, who may spray you with alcohol (from her mouth) for your sins.

There are direct buses from the Antigua terminal to San Andrés at 2pm and 7pm. Alternatively, catch a bus to Chimaltenango (every 30min) and ask to be dropped off at the town.

Santiago Sacatepéquez

Santiago Sacatepéquez, almost directly east of Guatemala City on the Interamericana Highway, is notorious for its fiesta honouring the **Day of the Dead** (Nov 1). On this day, colourful, massive paper kites with bamboo frames – some take months to create – are flown in the town's cemetery, symbolizing the release of the souls of the dead from agony. Teams of young men struggle to get the kites aloft while the crowd looks on with bated breath, rushing for cover if a kite comes crashing to the ground. At other times of the year, there's little to see or do here – if you find yourself passing through on a Tuesday or a Sunday you might visit the town market, but that's about it.

To reach Santiago Sacatepéquez, catch a bus to San Lucas Sacatepéquez (buses running between Antigua and Guatemala City pass through), and then change there – many buses shuttle back and forth between the two.

Chimaltenango

Founded by Pedro de Portocarrero in 1526 on the site of the Kaqchikel Maya centre of Bokoh, **Chimaltenango** looks to have made few strides in development since then. It's a pretty dull place, with what employment there is being extracted from its position on the Carretera Interamericana – the roadside is littered with cheap *comedores*, mechanics' workshops and sleazy bars that become brothels at night. However, also thanks to this location, it is a transport hub: buses from Chimaltenango run to all points along the Interamericana. Most travellers to Guatemala find themselves passing through here at some point.

Frequent **buses** arrive in town from both Guatemala City and Antigua; you can change here for buses to points west into the highlands. Buses to Antigua leave every fifteen minutes between 6am and 6.30pm from the turn-off on the highway (the Cruce a los Aposentos).

Iximché

The ruins of **Iximché** (daily 8am–5pm; Q50) sit on a beautiful exposed hillside about 5km south of the small town of **Tecpán**, ninety minutes east of Guatemala City. These are the ruins of the pre-Conquest capital of the Kaqchikel Maya, who allied themselves with the conquistadors in the early days of the Conquest. As a result, the structures here suffered less than most at the hands of the Spanish. Time and weather have taken their toll, though, and the majority of the buildings – which once housed over ten thousand people – have disappeared, and only a few stone pyramids, plazas and ball-courts are left. Nevertheless, the site – protected on three sides by steep slopes and surrounded by pine forests – is quite peaceful; the grassy plazas make excellent picnic spots. You may have the place to yourself, but it's important to note that the ruins are still used as a Maya worship site: sacrifices and offerings take place down a small trail behind the final plaza.

Take any **bus** travelling along the Carretera Interamericana between Chimaltenango and Los Encuentros and ask to be dropped at Tecpán. Regular buses shuttle back and forth from Tecpán's plaza. Plan to be back on the Carretera Interamericana before 6pm to be sure of a bus. Tecpán itself is of no interest, but there are a number of restaurants and guesthouses, if you get stuck.

Lago de Atitlán

Lago de Atitlán, one of the most visited destinations in Guatemala's western highlands, was described by Aldous Huxley in 1934 as one of the most attractive lakes in the world – and it really is exceptionally beautiful. For travellers, Atitlán is of interest both for its majestic setting – it's hemmed in by three

LAGO DE ATITLÁN

volcanoes and steep hills – and for its cultural appeal – the highlands are home to the western hemisphere's largest groups of indigenous peoples, and the lake's shores are lined with thirteen diverse yet traditional Maya villages. With the exception of cosmopolitan **Panajachel** and **San Pedro La Laguna**, most of the villages are subsistence farming communities, and you can hike or take a boat between them; highlights include visits to **Santiago Atitlán**, where Maya men still wear traditional dress, and **Santa Cruz** and **San Marcos**, both of which give access to excellent hiking.

PANAJACHEL

Not too long ago **PANAJACHEL**, known locally as "Pana", was a quiet little village of Kaqchikel Maya, whose ancestors settled here centuries ago. These days, while no longer either quiet or little – the old village, northeast of town, has been enveloped by a building boom – somehow Panajachel manages to retain a traditional feel in spite of its cosmopolitan population: the river delta behind the town continues to be farmed, and the Sunday market, bustling with people from all around the lake, remains oblivious to the tourists who come in droves. For travellers, the town is something of an inevitable destination – with good travel connections and a lovely setting, it makes a comfortable base for exploring the area. No one ever owns up to actually liking Panajachel, but most people stay for a while.

What to see and do

There are two main daytime activities in Pana: **shopping** and simply **hanging out**, enjoying the town's

GETTING AROUND LAGO DE ATITLÁN

It is recommended that you take a boat – either a public boat or a *lancha* – to get around the lake, as it is much easier, quicker and safer than travelling by road (armed robberies can take place on some of the roads that connect the communities). *Lanchas* do not run to fixed schedules, but depart when the owner has enough passengers to cover fuel costs. Normally you won't have to wait too long – usually not more than thirty minutes or so.

Panajachel serves as a sort of hub for the lake, with two piers. The pier at the end of Calle del Embarcadero has departures for all villages on the north side of the lake: Santa Cruz (about 15min), Jaibalito (25min), Tzununá (30min) and San Marcos (40min). Direct (15min) and local (50min) boats also depart from here for San Pedro, from where you can easily get to San Juan and San Pablo. The second pier at the end of Calle Rancho Grande is for Santiago Atitlán (1hr by scheduled ferry at 8.35am, 10.30am, 1pm and 4.30pm, or 20min by unscheduled *lancha*). The last boats on all these routes leave around 5pm. A semi-official fare system operates: tourists pay Q10 for a short trip, Q20 for a longer journey (locals pay less).

Tours of the lake (Q100), visiting San Pedro, Santiago Atitlán, Santa Catarina, Panajachel and San Antonio Palopó, can be booked with travel agents in nearly every town; all leave around 9am and return by 4pm from the pier at Calle Rancho Grande.

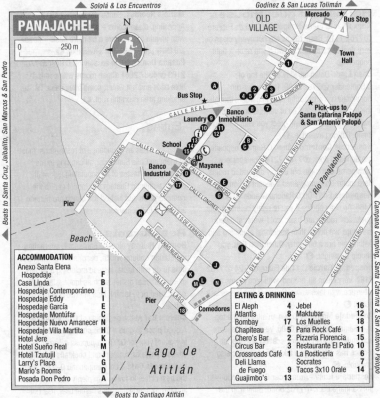

PANAJACHEL

0   250 m

N

Sololá & Los Encuentros

Godínez & San Lucas Tolimán

OLD VILLAGE

Mercado ★

Bus Stop

Town Hall

Boats to Santa Cruz, Jaibalito, San Marcos & San Pedro

CALLE DE LOS ÁRBOLES

CALLE PRINCIPAL

Bus Stop

CALLE REAL

Banco Inmobiliario

Laundry

★ Pick-ups to Santa Catarina Palopó & San Antonio Palopó

School

CALLE EL CHALI

Mayanet

Banco Industrial

CALLE SANTANDER

CALLE DEL EMBARCADERO

AVENIDA EL FRUTAL

Río Panajachel

CALLE 14 DE FEBRERO

CALLE RANCHO GRANDE

CALLE LONDRES

Pier

Beach

CALLE 15 DE FEBRERO

CALLE DEL RÍO

CALLE LOS SALPORES

CALLE DEL CEMENTERIO

CALLE BUENAS NUEVAS

Campana Camping, Santa Catarina & San Antonio Palopó

ACCOMMODATION

Anexo Santa Elena Hospedaje	F
Casa Linda	B
Hospedaje Contemporáneo	L
Hospedaje Eddy	I
Hospedaje García	E
Hospedaje Montúfar	C
Hospedaje Nuevo Amanecer	N
Hospedaje Villa Martita	H
Hotel Jere	K
Hotel Sueño Real	M
Hotel Tzutujil	J
Larry's Place	G
Mario's Rooms	D
Posada Don Pedro	A

CALLE DEL LAGO

Pier

Comedores

Lago de Atitlán

EATING & DRINKING

El Aleph	4	Jebel	16
Atlantis	8	Maktubar	12
Bombay	17	Los Muelles	18
Chapiteau	5	Pana Rock Café	11
Chero's Bar	2	Pizzeria Florencia	15
Circus Bar	3	Restaurante El Patio	10
Crossroads Café	1	La Rosticería	6
Deli Llama de Fuego	9	Socrates	7
Guajimbo's	13	Tacos 3x10 Orale	14

Boats to Santiago Atitlán

lakeside location. Weaving from all over Guatemala is sold here, mainly on Calle Santander. There is also a market at the top of Calle Principal, but it mainly deals with local produce. While the lake is inviting, it's probably best to swim elsewhere, as the lake water is not that clean close to town. You could rent a kayak (available on the lakeshore between the piers) for a few hours – mornings are usually much calmer.

Arrival and information

By boat See the box, opposite, for details of the two docks in Panajachel.

By bus Buses drop you beside the Banco Inmobiliario, very close to the main drag, Calle Santander, which runs down to the lakeshore. Straight ahead, up Calle Principal, is the old village.

Tourist information The tourist office, on C Santander (daily 9am–5pm; ☎ 7762 1106), has English-speaking staff, some hotel information and boat and bus schedules.

Travel agents Try Unión Travel, C Santander & C El Chali (☎ 7762 1156, ⓦ www.igoguate.com), or Servicios Turísticos Atitlán, C Santander near C 14 de Febrero (☎ 7762 2075, ⓦ www.turisticosatitlan .com).

Accommodation

There's no shortage of cheap accommodation in Pana, although most places take the form of *hospedajes* or hotels as opposed to hostels with dorm rooms. If you have a tent, your first choice is the *Campana* campsite (☎ 7762 2479; ❸), 1km east of the centre along the road to Santa Catarina, over the river bridge. Here you will find kitchen and storage facilities as well as sleeping bags and tents for rent. Don't camp at the public beach: more likely than not your stuff will be stolen.

Hotels and guesthouses

Anexo Santa Elena Hospedaje C 15 de Febrero ☎7762 1114. Basic rooms are not overly clean but very doable for a night or two if you're on a tight budget. ②

Casa Linda Down an alley off the top of C Santander ☎7762 0386. This family-run *hospedaje* has a beautiful central garden, though the rooms could use a bit of ventilation. The old owner and his family will greet you with a friendly smile. Parking available. ③

Hospedaje Contemporáneo C Ramos, opposite the Santiago dock ☎7762 2214. The spacious bathrooms and clean but simply decorated rooms here make *Contemporáneo* a decent option. ④

Hospedaje Eddy Off C Rancho Grande ☎7762 2466. An okay choice if you're really counting your quetzales: rooms are basic, cold-water showers are more like hoses than traditional plumbing and bathrooms are a bit grotty. Other than that, you should be alright. ②

Hospedaje García C 14 de Febrero 2–24 ☎7762 2187. Very clean all-around, with nice rooms and a terrace with lake views. However, the toilets lack seats. ③

Hospedaje Montúfar Down an alley off the top of C Santander ☎7762 0406. Very clean, secure accommodation in a quiet location; the rooftop terrace has volcano and lake views. Triples also available. ②

Hospedaje Nuevo Amanecer C Ramos, opposite the Santiago dock ☎7762 0636. Similar to the other places next door, this *hospedaje* has pleasant rooms, sparkling bathrooms with hot water and cable TV. Safe parking in the courtyard. ④

Hospedaje Villa Martita At the bottom of C Santander, towards the lake ☎no phone. Family-run *hospedaje* with three small but nice (and very cheap) rooms. ②

Hotel Jere C Rancho Grande ☎7762 2781, Ⓦwww.hoteljere.com. Local fabrics adorn the clean rooms (all with private bath and hot water), and knick-knacks decorate the staircases. Parking available. ④

🏃 **Hotel Sueño Real** C Ramos, opposite the Santiago dock ☎7762 0608/1097. Beautifully decorated rooms, most en suite and some with lake views and private terrace. All rooms have fans and rates include internet. ④

Hotel Tzutujil In a little alley off C Rancho Grande ☎7762 0102. Clean, simple rooms with cable TV and free drinking water. ③

Larry's Place C 14 de Febrero ☎7762 0767. Agreeably decorated rooms with wooden doors and furniture, all with private bath. Benches and hand-painted tables run along the hallway. ④

Mario's Rooms C Santander ☎7762 1313. Appealing, clean rooms – some are airy and light with private bath, others a bit more basic – but all are fairly pricey for what's available. ④

Posada Don Pedro In an alley off C Real ☎7762 2163 or 4387 2861. Clean rooms with comfortable beds and hot water; some have cable TV. The smoking area is on the roof. ④

Eating

Panajachel has an abundance of restaurants, most of them on Calle Santander, all catering to the cosmopolitan tastes of its population. For really cheap, authentic Guatemalan food, head to the *comedores* on and just off the beach promenade and close to the market.

Restaurants

Bombay Halfway along C Santander. Interesting vegetarian options which, despite the name, have little to do with India, instead including a variety of international dishes such as Indonesian *gado-gado*, fried rice, falafel, lasagna (Q61) and organic coffee.

Chero's Bar At the beginning of C de los Árboles. A good place to grab a fresh *pupusa* (made right in front of you) for Q7. Try a *pupusa mixta* (pork, cheese and beans). Beers and cocktails go for Q15.

Crossroads Café C del Campanario 0–27. Easily the best coffee in town, with plenty of combinations and flavours available, plus herbal teas, real hot chocolate and fresh-baked pastries. Closed Sun & Mon.

Deli Llama de Fuego At the top of C Santander. Little café with colourful chairs and lampshades made out of recycled glass. The menu includes burgers (Q30), breakfast (Q20) and even home-made English muffins (Q15). Closed Wed.

Guajimbo's Halfway up C Santander. A delight for meat lovers, this American-owned restaurant serves *churrasco uruguayo* (barbecued meat; Q58) and has live music in the evenings.

Jebel C Santander, opposite the school. Located on the first floor, this restaurant has nice views of town and good-value food. Try the *plato típico* for Q45.

Los Muelles By the Santiago Pier. Right above the water, with stunning views, this is one of the best of several lakeside choices. The menu features fish (including mojarra for Q50), *caldos* and sandwiches.

Pana Rock Café Towards the top of C Santander. A wanna-be *Hard Rock Café*, with "Pana Rock Café" T-shirts for sale and an old American school bus converted into a sitting area with tables. Very cheap breakfasts (Q10), but the size of the portion reflects the price.

Pizzeria Florencia C Santander, by the school. This no-frills place (think plastic chairs set by the street) is a good cheap option, serving empanadas (Q7), sandwiches (Q13) and pizzas (Q40).

Restaurante El Patio Towards the top of C Santander. Silver-painted chairs are set on exterior patio here, ideal to watch Pana life go by; the interior, on the other hand, is a bit motel-like. The burgers (Q20) are some of the best in town.

La Rosticeria At the beginning of C de los Árboles. American-owned, this place has six hammocks suspended from the window rim, and the window sill serves as a table. Cheap pizzas (Q23), suckling pig by order, alcohol shots (Q10) and beer (Q10).

Tacos 3x10 Orale Halfway up C Santander. This taco place, painted in bright yellow, offers three tacos for Q10 or fajitas for Q22.

Drinking and nightlife

Most bars and clubs are located around the southern end of Calle de los Árboles, which buzzes at weekends. Many have live music and some have great happy hours.

Bars

Atlantis At the beginning of C Principal. Atmospheric, candle-lit place with a number of Elvis posters and old-school ads decorating the walls. Also serves breakfast, lunch and dinner. Live music Fri & Sat evenings.

Circus Bar C de los Árboles. Eponymous memorabilia, such as clown masks, dangles from the ceiling, and there's a little puppet stage, an old piano and a number of fun black and white adverts covering the walls. Good pizzas (Q48) and live music every day at 8.30pm.

Maktubar Halfway up C Santander on the right. The bar is set under a straw roof, giving the place a pleasant, relaxed feel. Pizzas (Q55) are cooked in a clay oven. Happy hour 7–9pm, and there is live music on Fri & Sat.

Clubs

El Aleph On the northern end of C Santander. The musical flavour here is mainly reggae and reggaeton, with live acts some nights.

Chapiteau At the southern end of C de los Árboles. This nightclub is also known for its reggae, reggaeton and occasional live music, but its popularity is slowly waning.

Socrates On C Principal. Mainstream disco-club where a young local crowd gathers to dance to Latin pop and merengue.

Entertainment

Billiards You can play pool at Billares de León, on C Principal.

Cinema The best place to watch a movie is at *Solomon's Porch*, C Principal & C de Los Árboles. There's a selection of some 600 DVDs, a big screen and a surround system that you can book all for yourself while you munch on some buffalo wings. Q18 per person.

Directory

Bike rental Moto Servicio Queche, C de los Árboles & C Principal (℡ 7762 1192), rents mountain bikes for Q10/hr or Q60/day, and 200cc bikes for Q70/hr or Q350/day; Tono, in the alley opposite the school, also rents bikes for Q10/hr and Q60/day.

Books Librería Libros del Lago, C Santander 9, near the post office, has a good selection of books on Maya culture, maps and guidebooks; Get Guated Out sells guidebooks and secondhand English titles; Bus Stop Bookshop, C Principal 00–99, has 4000 used titles.

Exchange There's a Banco Inmobiliario, C Santander and C Principal (Mon–Fri 9am–5pm, Sat 9am–1pm); a 5B ATM, opposite, which takes MasterCard/Cirrus cards; and Banco Industrial, C Santander, which has a Visa/Plus ATM.

Internet There are a dozen or more cafés in Pana with very cheap rates (around Q8/hr). The best is probably Mayanet, midway along C Santander.

Language schools Try Escuela Jabel Tinamit, off C Santander (℡ 5786 0831, ⊕ www.jabeltinamit .com), or Jardín de América, C 14 de Febrero (℡ 7762 2637, ⊕ www.jardindeamerica.com).

Laundry Lavandería Santander, C Santander opposite *Pana Rock* (Mon–Sat 7am–8pm), charges Q4 for a pound of washing, drying and folding.

Medical care Dr Edgar Barreno speaks good English; his surgery is down the first street that branches to the right off C de los Árboles (℡ 7762 1008).

Pharmacy Farmacia La Unión, C Santander.

Police In the old village, behind the church and next to the town hall (℡ 7762 1120).

Post office C Santander & 15 de Febrero, or try Get Guated Out, C de los Árboles (℡ 7762 0595), for bigger shipments.

Telephones The businesses and cybercafés on C Santander offer good long-distance rates. Your best bet is Get Guated Out (see above), which charges Q1/min to all landlines worldwide and Q3.50 to all mobiles. Otherwise, Telgua (daily 8am–6pm) is near the junction of C Santander and C 15 de Febrero, with cheap rates to the US (Q1/min) but expensive to Europe (US$1/min).

Moving on

By boat See the box on p.156 for information on boat transport around Lago de Atitlán, including connections from Panajachel.

By bus The main bus stop is where Calle Santander and Calle Real meet. There are regular buses to Chichicastenango (1hr 30min), Guatemala City (3hr 30min) and Quetzaltenango (2hr 30min), and only one daily for Antigua (3hr). If there are no direct buses to your destination, catch a bus to Los Encuentros and change there. Shuttle buses serve most destinations, including Antigua and Chichicastenango, on market days, and can be organized with all travel agents.

AROUND PANAJACHEL

It's well worth taking the time to explore the area around Pana, the best connected of the lake towns. The landscape surrounding the different villages is so diverse that if you take the time to visit more than one or two it's easy to forget they all look over the same lake.

Sololá

Perched on a natural balcony overlooking Lago de Atitlán, **SOLOLÁ** is a fascinating town, largely ignored by the majority of travellers. It is probably the largest Maya town in the country, with the vast majority of the people still wearing traditional costume – the women covered in striped red cloth and the men in their outlandish "space cowboy" shirts, woollen aprons and wildly embroidered trousers. Although the town itself is nothing much to look at, its Friday **market** is one of Central America's finest, drawing traders from all over the highlands, as well as thousands of local Maya. There's also another smaller market on Tuesdays. Another interesting time to visit Sololá is on Sunday, when the *cofrades*, the elders of the Maya religious hierarchy, parade through the streets in ceremonial costume to attend the mid-morning Mass.

To **get to** Sololá, take one of the regular pick-ups or buses from Panajachel (every 30min 5am–7pm).

SANTIAGO ATITLÁN

SANTIAGO ATITLÁN, a microcosm of Guatemala's past, sits sheltered on the side of an inlet on the opposite side of the lake from Panajachel. The largest of the lakeside villages, it's one of the last bastions of traditional life here, serving as the main centre for the Tz'utujil-speaking Maya (most of the population don't speak Spanish). Though during the day the town is a fairly commercial place, by mid-afternoon, when the boats have left, the village is much quieter and becomes a lot friendlier and more accessible. It's worth taking a few hours to wander around town – and if you want to get away from the foreign crowds that pervade other parts of the lake, consider staying for a night or two.

What to see and do

There's not that much to do in Santiago other than stroll around and soak up the atmosphere. During the day the town's main street, which runs from the dock to the plaza, is lined with weaving shops and souvenir stands. **Market** day is Friday, with a smaller event on Sunday.

TRADITIONAL DRESS IN SANTIAGO ATITLÁN

You're likely to see Maya men and women in Santiago dressed in traditional costume, which here is both striking and unusual. The men wear long shorts, which, like the *huipiles* worn by the women, are striped white and purple and embroidered with birds and flowers. Some women also wear a *xk'ap*, a band of red cloth approximately 10m long, wrapped around their heads. Sadly, though, this head cloth is going out of use – you'll probably only see it at fiestas and on market days, and then mainly on older women.

FATHER ROTHER

Father Stanley Rother was an American priest who served in the parish from 1968 to 1981. Among his noted works were a translation of the New Testament into the Tz'utujil language and the establishment of a local hospital (sadly destroyed by a mudslide following Hurricane Stan in 2005, but now in the process of being rebuilt). A committed defender of his native parishioners in an era when, in his own words, "shaking hands with an Indian has become a political act", he was labelled a Communist by President García and assassinated by a paramilitary death squad in 1981. His body was returned to his native Oklahoma for burial but his heart was removed and buried in the church. Many Catholics in both Guatemala and Oklahoma consider Father Rother a martyr.

The one museum in town, the **Museo Cojolya** (Mon–Fri 9am–3pm, Sat 9am–1pm; free), about 100m up the main drag from the dock on the left, also takes weaving as its subject. Inside you'll find excellent displays (in English and Spanish) about the tradition of backstrap weaving in Santiago, and you can see some of the weavers in action at 11am and 1pm.

The old whitewashed Baroque Catholic **church** is also worth a look. The huge central altarpiece culminates in the shape of a mountain peak and a cross, which symbolizes the Maya world tree. On the right as you enter, there's also a stone memorial commemorating Father Stanley Rother (see box above).

Folk Catholicism plays an important role in the life of Santiago – the town is one of the few places where Maya still pay homage to **Maximón**, the "evil" saint (see p.154), known locally as Rilej Mam. Every May he changes residence – any child will take you to see him: just ask for the "Casa de Maximón". It costs Q2 to enter his current home and Q10 to take his picture.

Arrival and information

By boat The dock is 5–10min walk from the centre – when you get off the boat, walk up the hill, which will lead you into town.
Internet There are a number of internet cafés on C del Turista which have Skype.
Telephones You can make international calls from most of the internet cafés in town.

Tourist information Santiago does not have a tourist office. The website ⓦ www.santiagoatitlan.com has some good information in English on the town.

Accommodation

There are a few adequate budget hotels in town, all of which are no more than ten minutes' walk from the church in the centre of town.

Casa de las Buganvillas Opposite Salón Nico and Clínica Rxiin Tnamet in Cantón Chechiboy, about 5min east of the church ☎ 7820 7055. So new that at the time of writing owner Miguel hadn't settled on a name – it may be different from the one listed here. Nonetheless, definitely the best option in town with big, spotless rooms and wooden furniture, and a rooftop restaurant serving typical food. ❹
Hospedaje Colonial Rosita ☎ 5397 7187. Right by the church, this pleasant family-run *hospedaje* has basic rooms with hot water and fairly clean communal bathrooms. Lovely views of the San Pedro volcano and of the church. ❷
Hotel Chinim-Hotel Chinim-yá On C Chinim-yá ☎ 7721 7131. A decent enough option set on an interior courtyard, although the communal bathrooms don't have toilet seats and are not spick and span. The triple rooms are more spacious and have better light. ❸
Hotel Lago de Atitlán Uphill from the dock, on the left ☎ 7721 7174, ⓔ hotellagodeatitlan @hotmail.com. All rooms here have clean private bathrooms and cable TV, though contrary to what the management will tell you, there is not much of a lake view. ❹
Hotel Tzanjuyu In the Cantón Tzanjuyu, northwest of the church and facing the waterfront. Clean, bouncy beds, and hot water in the bathrooms, but no toilet seats. Rooms should have nice lake views but at the time of writing these were obstructed by construction. ❸

Eating

Comedor Brendy In the centre of town by the main square. Very simple *comedor* with good-value lunches for Q15.
Comedor Cayuco By the dock on the right. Cheap option, set between a number of little shops selling local fabrics and curios, serving fried chicken (Q20) and fish (Q25).
El Gran Sol One block up from the dock on the left. A family-run place with a palm roof, a little terrace and colourful *sutes de lana* (woollen tablecloths). Good for grilled meats (Q25) and soups (Q20).
Restaurante El Pescador Between the *Lago de Atitlán Hotel* and the *Tzanjuyu Hotel*. Enjoy dishes like black bass and churrascos (Q45) while watching Santiago street life from the patio, or the fluttering Christmas decoration atop the bar.

Moving on

By boat to: Panajachel (ferries at 6am, 11.45pm, 1.30pm, 3pm; 1hr); San Pedro La Laguna (9 daily 6am–5pm; 40min). The ferries are supplemented by *lanchas*.
By bus to: Guatemala City, via Cocales (7 daily 3am–3pm). The village is also well connected by bus with all lakeside destinations except Panajachel.

SAN PEDRO LA LAGUNA

Around to the west of Volcán San Pedro lies the village of **SAN PEDRO LA LAGUNA**, considered by most as *the* place to be. It's the party destination of the lake, with happening bars and clubs playing everything from electronica to trance till the early hours of the morning. As a town, it has everything you could possibly think of (including a pretty serious drug culture, although the town has clamped down a bit in the past few years). You may well love it and end up staying far longer than expected, although you may also hate it – come and have a look for yourself.

What to see and do

There's a decent little **beach** just south-east of town, below the road to San Juan (see p.164), and some **thermal pools** between the two boat docks offer another place to relax. **Volcán San Pedro**, which towers above the village at some 3020m, can be climbed in four to five hours. If you want to make the **hike**, hire a guide – the foliage is dense, the route very difficult to find and there have been occasional attacks on tourists on the slopes. Guides can be organized at Excursion Big Foot (see below). After the hike, unwind with a **massage** – see Ada at the *Hotel Villa Sol*, 100m from the Santiago dock, by the *Hospedaje Tikaaj*.

Arrival and information

By boat There are two docks in San Pedro. All boats from villages on the north side of the lake, including Panajachel, Santa Cruz and San Marcos, arrive and depart from the Panajachel dock on the north side of town, while boats from Santiago Atitlán use a separate dock to the southeast, a ten-minute walk away.
By bus Buses drop off in front of the church.
Tour operators Excursion Big Foot (☎7721 8203, ✉juansschool@yahoo.com), just left of the Panajachel dock, organizes hikes to a *mirador* nicknamed "Indian Nose", from where there's a great view of the lake. They also rent out horses for Q25/hr (guide included), bicycles for Q50/day and kayaks for Q10/hr.
Tourist information At the time of writing there was no Inguat office in town. Juan at Excursion Big Foot (see above) can give you all the information you need.

Accommodation

San Pedro has some of the cheapest accommodation around the lake, with a number of basic, clean guesthouses – many charge less than Q30 a person per night.
Hospedaje Casa Elena On the left after *Nick's Place* ☎ no phone. Not the very cheapest place in town, but the nine simple rooms are tidy and there's a dock for swimming. The management is honest about the functioning (or non-functioning) showers. ❸
Hotel Nahual Maya Turn left after *Nick's Place* ☎7721 8158. Well-run, friendly place with neat, clean rooms (with bathrooms) facing a lawn with hammocks. ❸
Hotel Tepepul Kaan Left off Pana dock ☎4301 2271, and then up the first path right up the hill.

Very colourful rooms (verging on the kitsch side) but spotless bathrooms, and there are hammocks dotted around each floor. ❸

Hotel Tolimán On the lakeside to the left of the dock. ☎7721 8114. A great cheap place with clean rooms and bathrooms and fantastic lakeside views. ❷

Hotel Villa del Lago Left off Pana dock and towards the end of the road ☎5628 6562. Good option with clean bathrooms and rooms, one of which has cable TV. ❷

Xocomil Left off Pana dock, and then up the first path right up the hill. Basic rooms, fairly clean bathrooms and a small but well-equipped kitchen for self-caterers. Excellent value, given the low price. ❷

Zoola Left off Pana dock, and right up the hill ☎5543 4111 or 5847 4857, ⓦwww .zoolapeople.com. By far the best option in town, and a great place to meet other travellers. Pleasant, clean dorms and rooms, a relaxed atmosphere created by hammocks, a chill-out room and a TV room with movies for rainy days. Book in advance. ❷

Eating

San Pedro's restaurants, most of which are excellent value for money, have a decidedly international flavour. Vegetarians are well catered for. There are also a few typical Guatemalan *comedores* in the centre of the village and by the Santiago dock.

Restaurants

Buddha Bar Left at the Pana dock. A good chill-out spot with a Buddha-shaped pizza oven on the roof overlooking the lake. On the second floor you'll find benches in the shape of an om. Good salads, Indian curries (Q35) and Thai food. There's a ten percent discount on food on Thurs. Mon is open-mic night, and films shown Tues, Thurs & Sun at 7.30pm.

Fata Morgana Left at Pana dock. Pizzeria and cafeteria that serves very good cheap pies (Q30).

Freedom Turn left at Pana dock. Popular at all times of day, this place has a selection of excellent international dishes (Q30–50) and great views of the lake from its terrace. Live music some nights.

Nick's Place By Pana dock. A great spot to relax and watch the day go by. Big breakfasts available for Q20, and an eclectic range of Guatemalan and international mains for Q30.

Restaurante Chile's Right by *Nick's Place*. Nicely decorated place with wooden tables serving international and Guatemalan cuisine. Good hangover breakfasts (Q25), coffee (Q6), spaghetti (Q35) and veggie options. Free salsa classes Tues & Fri, live music Sat & Sun.

Zoola At *Zoola* hotel. The food here – mainly Israeli – is very good and includes chicken toasties (Q30), meat and potatoes (Q22) and huge sandwiches. The service is extremely slow, unfortunately, but you can chill on the cushions and play backgammon as you wait.

Drinking and nightlife

In addition to having good food, *Buddha Bar* is also a popular evening spot. When the bars shut down for a night the "after parties" start up; these are in a different place every night, so you'll just have to see what's happening. Occasionally full-moon parties take place as well.

Alegre Pub Near Pana dock, on the left. English pub showing premiership football and serving traditional grub such as Sunday roast (Q38) and fish 'n' chips (Q38).

D'Noz By Pana dock. Great place to hear some electronic tunes; they also serve Asian food and show a film nightly at 7.30pm.

Freedom Right at Pana dock. Probably the most popular place in town, this combination restaurant, bar and club has a pool table, great lake views and plays electronic and trance beats till the early hours. Try a "Freedom" shot (Q50; made of six drinks) if you want freedom from your coordination.

Directory

Cinema *Buddha Bar* and *D'Noz* both show films daily at 7pm and 7.30pm, respectively.

Exchange Banrural (Mon–Fri 8am–5pm, Sat 8.30am–12.30pm) will change traveller's cheques. There is an ATM by the Pana dock.

Internet The best set-up is above *D'Noz* by the Pana dock; you can also burn photos to disk here.

Language schools Try the Co-operative of Guatemalan Spanish Teachers (☎5398 6448 ⓦwww .cooperativeschoolsanpedro.com); Casa Rosario, south of Santiago Atitlán dock (ⓦwww.casarosario .com); Corazón Maya, south of Santiago dock (☎7721 8160, ⓦwww.corazonmaya.com); or San Pedro Spanish School, between the piers (☎5715 4604, ⓦwww.sanpedrospanishschool.com).

Market In the centre of town, and mainly sells food.

Post office In the centre of town, but with erratic hours.

Moving on

By boat Boats leave every 30min for most villages around the lake (first boat 6am, last boat 5pm), supplemented by *lanchas* whenever there's enough interest.

By bus Buses depart from opposite the church to Guatemala City (hourly; 5hr) and Quetzaltenango (two daily, 6am & 8am; 3hr), although the former is not recommended as it is a dangeous route (traffic accidents are frighteningly frequent). Alternatively, speak to Excursion Big Foot (see p.162) about arranging shuttle buses to Chichicastenango, Quetzaltenango, Antigua, Cobán, Guatemala City and the Mexican border.

SAN JUAN LA LAGUNA

Two kilometres west of San Pedro, at the back of another inlet and surrounded by shallow beaches, is **SAN JUAN LA LAGUNA**. The village specializes in the weaving of *petates*, lake-reed mats, and there are two large co-ops, Las Artesanías de San Juan, signposted on the left from the dock, and the Asociación de Mujeres de Color, on the right, both of which have goods for sale. Next to the latter is the simple *Hospedaje Estrella del Lago*, with secure rooms and a kitchen open to guests. Uphill, in the centre of the village, is a quiet *comedor*, *Restaurant Chi'nimaya*, and almost next door, a shrine to **Maximón** (see p.154), the evil saint, dressed in local garb.

Regular **pick-ups** run between San Pedro and San Juan, or you can walk. Leaving the village by footpath, you'll pass below the Tz'utujil settlement of **San Pablo La Laguna**, perched high above the lake. It's a fifteen-minute walk away, and connected to the Carretera Interamericana by a steep road.

SAN MARCOS LA LAGUNA

SAN MARCOS LA LAGUNA has a decidedly tranquil feel, all the more so if you have just come from a few nights' partying in San Pedro. The little village is a perfect place to kick back and relax – read a book in your hammock, catch some rays by the lake after a nice swim, take a quiet walk or treat yourself to a massage at one of the holistic centres in town. The bulk of bohemian hotels and restaurants are on the land closer to the water, while the Maya village sits

on higher ground further away from the shore.

Arrival and information

By boat *Lanchas* from other lakeside villages, including San Pedro, Pana and Santiago, pull up at the dock, which is about 5min walk from the centre of town.

What to see and do

Apart from a huge stone **church**, built to replace the colonial original destroyed in the 1976 earthquake, there are no sights, as such. Instead, the main draws are of the spiritual variety. One of these is the *Las Pirámides* yoga and meditation retreat (see opposite), but there's a surplus of other practitioners and masseurs, plus the requisite organic bakery and a healing centre – **San Marcos Holistic Center** (Ⓦwww .sanmholisticcentre.com), which offers acupuncture, reflexology and natural remedies; for a massage (Q210) all you need to do is sign up on the white board at the entrance. It's located next to the *Unicornio* hotel. Close by, the recently opened **Jazmín Therapy Centre** has a geodesic dome where you can take further acupuncture and yoga classes and therapy courses; they too offer excellent massages (Q220) – ask for Nadia. There's excellent swimming from a number of wooden jetties by the lakeshore, and a mesmerizing view of Atitlán's three volcanoes, including double-coned Tolimán, plus glimpses of Acatenango's grey peak, over 50km east.

Accommodation

There are plenty of good accommodation options in town. To get to most of the places listed here, get off at the westernmost dock, where *Posada Schumann* and *Las Pirámides* have jetties (look out for the mini-pyramid): all accommodation is signposted from there.

Hospedaje Panabaj ☏no phone. Basic, locally owned accommodation in a nice garden setting. ❷

Hotel Quetzal ☎5306 5039, ⓦwww
.hotelquetzal-gt.com. Excellent-value accommodation with fairly hard but clean beds;
wooden floors are burnished, which adds a nice
touch. ❸

Hotel Silani Turn right off the dock and walk
till the end of the path ☎2425 8088. Tranquil
setting with superb lakeside views and a lovely
little treehouse to stay in, as well as some more
traditional doubles. ❸

Las Pirámides ☎5205 7302/7151, ⓦwww
.laspiramidesdelka.com. Meditation retreat set in
leafy grounds. Courses (available for daily, weekly
and monthly enrolment) include hatha yoga, healing
and meditation techniques, all in a tranquil garden
setting in the centre of town. Accommodation is
in comfortable, pyramid-shaped cabañas; rates
include courses but not food (which is delicious and
vegetarian). ❸

Posada del Bosque Encantado ☎5208 5334,
ⓦwww.hotelposadaencantado.com. Rooms here
are pleasantly decorated and with private bath.
Outside, chair hammocks are slung around a
garden of ornamental and native flora. ❹

Unicornio ☎no phone, ⓦwww.hotelunicornio
.com. Inexpensive, unique English-Guatemalan-
owned place with small A-frame huts and rooms
(none with bath) in a nice garden, with a kitchen
and sauna. Excellent rates for single travellers. ❸

Aaculaax ☎5729 6101, ⓦwww
.aaculaax.com. This fantastic,
ecologically minded boutique
hotel was built by a German
craftsman from thousands
of recycled bottles, wood
and stained glass – giant
glass butterflies double as
lampshades. Some of the
bathrooms are made of stone,
with windows of recycled glass and
papier-mâché. Dorms are available,
but pricier private rooms are set on
two floors and come with stereo,
fridge, kitchenette, living room,
terrace and showers carved in stone.
Two rooms have a Jacuzzi on their
private terrace. Dorms ❷, doubles ❽

Eating

Los Abrazos On the road leading west into the
centre. The only sculpted restaurant in Guatemala
– eagle, condor and Mother Earth figures are
made of cob, an earth-friendly mixture of sand,
clay and straw. The birds' wings serve as
benches, while their bodies are the restaurant's
pizza (Q50) ovens.

Il Forno Right in the centre of town. A little pathway
through a vegetable garden leads you to this simple
Italian restaurant serving pizzas (Q27), focaccia
(Q25) and salads.

Las Mañanitas At *Aaculaax*. Excellent place with
a nice chill-out area on the terrace. Delicious fresh
breads and scrumptious breakfasts (Q20).

🏃 **Moon Fish** One of the best places in town,
with great lakeside views and organic food,
all of which is grown in the little yard at the front.
Excellent *huevos rancheros* (Q25) and chicken
burritos (Q26).

Posada Schumann Fairly pricey, quaint outdoor
dining area with an Old World appeal. Try the *pepián*
(chicken or beef in a slightly spicy sauce; Q66) or
the *lacha* (meat with tomato sauce; Q66).

El Taller 2min up the road that heads out of town.
Built on the side of the cliff, so with unobstructed
volcano views, this pleasant restaurant serves good
breakfasts (Q25) and home-grown coffee, including
espresso drinks. Custom-made textiles are woven
on the top floor.

Moving on

By boat Boats leave every 30min from the dock,
serving most villages around the lake (first boat
6.15am, last boat 5.15pm).

JAIBALITO

JAIBALITO, an isolated lakeside
settlement nestling between soaring
milpa-clad slopes, remains resolutely
Kaqchikel – very little Spanish is
spoken, and few women have ever
journeyed much beyond Lago de
Atitlán – though the opening of two
new hotels means that outside influence is growing. Both the *Volcano
Lodge* (☎5410 2237 or 5744 0620,
ⓦwww.vulcanolodge.com, ❺) and *La
Casa del Mundo* (see box, p.166) have
their own individual charm. From
Jaibalito it's around an hour to Santa
Cruz along a glorious, easy-to-follow
path that parallels the steep hillside.

Lanchas to Jaibalito leave San Pedro
and Panajachel (25min) regularly;
the last ones are at 5pm and 7.30pm
respectively.

La Casa del Mundo ⓦwww
.lacasademundo.com. This
astounding place, perched
above the lake, is the
culmination of twelve years' work
by its owners, a warm American-
Guatemalan host family.
There's a range of atmospheric
accommodation, including
doubles (rooms 1, 3, 11, 12 and
13 have the best views), detached
stone cabins and a suite. There's also
a good restaurant with family-style
meals (dinner Q75 per person) and
guests can rent kayaks and use the
lakeside hot tub (Q275 for up to 10
people). Book ahead. ⑤–⑦

SANTA CRUZ LA LAGUNA

Set well back from the lake on a shelf
100m or so above the water, **SANTA
CRUZ LA LAGUNA** is the largest of
the lake's northwest villages, with a
population of around four thousand.
There isn't much to see here, apart
from a fine sixteenth-century church,
and most people spend their time by
the lake swimming or just chilling out
with a book. Alternatively, there's some
excellent **hiking**, including a walk to
a waterfall above the village football
pitch, and another to Sololá along a
spectacular path that takes around
three hours. It is highly recommended
you go with a guide – this can be organized at *La Iguana Perdida*.

On the shore, you'll find the ⚘ *Iguana
Perdida* (☎5706 4117, ⓦ*www.laigua
naperdida.com*), owned by an English-
American couple, with one of the most
convivial atmospheres in Lago de Atitlán.
There are basic dorms (①), singles (②)
and doubles (②; the "Jerry Garcia" room
has its own balcony), as well as more
luxurious rooms (doubles ⑤, triples ⑥).
It's the gorgeous, peaceful site overlooking
the lake that really makes this place.
Dinner (Q50) is a wholesome, three-
course communal affair. There are fancy
dress nights on Saturdays and the hotel
also offers yoga classes and has massage
therapists on site. The *Iguana* is also home
to a professional PADI **dive school**, ATI
Divers (in Panajachel; ☎7762 2646).

Lanchas leave Panajachel about every
30 minutes or when the boat is full,
from 6am to 7pm. The last one from San
Pedro leaves at 5pm.

The western highlands

Guatemala's **western highlands** are
home to some of the most dramatic
and breathtaking scenery in the entire
country. The area also has the highest
concentration of one of the Americas'
largest indigenous groups, the Maya.

MARKET DAYS

Make an effort to catch as many highland market days as possible – they're second
only to local fiestas in offering a glimpse of the traditional Guatemalan way of life.
Monday Chimaltenango; Zunil.
Tuesday Chajul; Totonicapán; Nebaj.
Wednesday Chimaltenango; Todos Santos Cuchumatán; Santiago Sacatepéquez.
Thursday Chichicastenango; Nebaj; Sacapulas; San Juan Atitán; San Lucas
Tolimán.
Friday Chajul; Chimaltenango; Nebaj; San Francisco El Alto; Santa María de Jesús.
Saturday Todos Santos Cuchumatán; Totonicapán.
Sunday Chichicastenango; Momostenango; Nebaj; San Juan Atitán; San Lucas
Tolimán; San Martín Sacatepéquez; Santa María de Jesús.

HIGHLAND HISTORY

The **Maya** have lived in the Guatemalan highlands for some two thousand years. The Spanish arrived in the area in 1523, making their first permanent settlement at **Iximché** (see p.153), the capital of their Kaqchikel Maya allies. Not long after, Conquistador **Pedro de Alvarado** moved his base to a site near modern-day Antigua, and gradually brought the highlands under a degree of Spanish control. Eventually, **Antigua** also served as the administrative centre for the whole of Central America and Chiapas (now in Mexico). In 1773, however, the city was destroyed by a massive earthquake and the capital was moved to its present site.

The arrival of the Spanish caused great hardship for the native Maya. Not only were their numbers decimated by Spanish weaponry, but waves of infectious diseases also swept through the population. Over time, indigenous labour became the backbone of the Spanish Empire, with its **indigo** and **cacao** plantations. The departure of the Spanish in 1821 and subsequent **independence** brought little change at village level. *Ladino* authority replaced that of the Spanish, but Maya were still required to work the coastal plantations and at times were press-ganged to work, often in horrific conditions.

In the late 1970s, **guerrilla movements** began to develop in opposition to Guatemala's military rule, seeking support from the highland population and establishing themselves in the area. The Maya became the victims in this process, caught between the guerrillas and the army. A total of 440 villages were destroyed; around 200,000 people died and thousands more fled the country, seeking refuge in Mexico. Despite the harsh conditions and terrific adversity the Maya lived through, traditional costume is still worn in many areas (particularly by women), a plethora of indigenous languages still spoken and some remote areas even still observe the 260-day Tzolkin calendar.

Languages and traditional costume still remain largely intact – probably the most striking dress of all is that worn in **Todos Santos Cuchumatán**. From the wild and ragged mountains surrounding **Nebaj** to the bustling colourful market of **Chichicastenango**, you are bound to be captivated by the numerous riches the region has to offer. The western highlands are also home to the country's second most populous city, **Quetzaltenango**, which draws numerous language students and voluntary workers. Do note that travelling in some parts of the highlands can be arduous, although in recent years the government has heavily invested in roads, many of which are now paved.

CHICHICASTENANGO

CHICHICASTENANGO, Guatemala's "mecca del turismo", is known best for its twice-weekly markets, which are some of the most colourful in the country. It also offers an insight into indigenous Maya society in the highlands. Over the years, Maya culture and folk Catholicism have syncretised here; the church overtly accepts this unconventional pagan worship, evident in the billowing clouds of incense that more often than not envelop the church building. You'll also see traditional weaving adhered to here as well, mostly by the women, who wear beautiful, heavily embroidered *huipiles*. For the town's fiesta (Dec 14–21), and on Sundays, though, a handful of *cofrades* (elders of the religious hierarchy) still wear traditional clothing and carry spectacular silver processional crosses and incense burners.

What to see and do

Although Chichi's main attraction is undoubtedly its vibrant markets, the town also offers other sights of cultural interest.

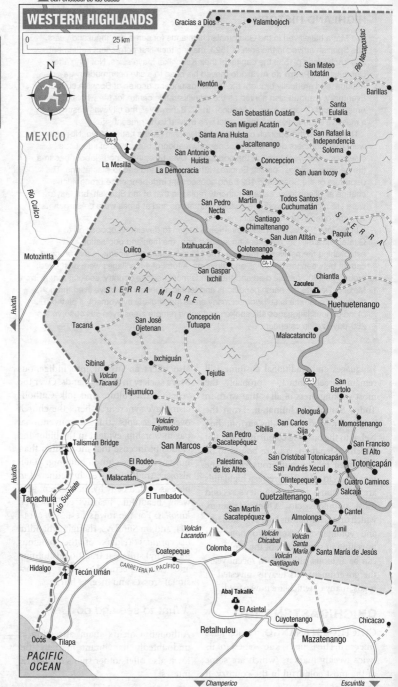

WESTERN HIGHLANDS

0   25 km

N

MEXICO

San Cristóbal de las Casas

Gracias a Dios   Yalambojoch

Río Mazapoxlac

San Mateo Ixtatán

Nentón   Barillas

San Sebastián Coatán   Santa Eulalia
San Miguel Acatán
Santa Ana Huista   San Rafael la Independencia
Jacaltenango   Soloma
San Antonio Huista   Concepcion
La Mesilla   San Juan Ixcoy
La Democracia

CA-1

Río Cuilco

San Martín   Todos Santos Cuchumatán
San Pedro Necta
Santiago Chimaltenango   Paquix
San Juan Atitán

SIERRA

Motozintla   Cuilco   Ixtahuacán   Colotenango

CA-1

San Gaspar Ixchil   Chiantla

SIERRA MADRE   Zaculeu   Huehuetenango

Huixta

Tacaná   San José Ojetenan   Concepción Tutuapa   Malacatancito

Sibinal   Ixchiguán
Volcán Tacaná
Tejutla
Tajumulco

CA-1

San Bartolo

Pologuá   Momostenango

Huixta

Volcán Tajumulco

San Pedro Sacatepéquez   Sibilia   San Carlos Sija   San Francisco El Alto

Talismán Bridge   San Marcos

El Rodeo   Palestina de los Altos   San Cristóbal Totonicapán   Totonicapán
San Andrés Xecul
Malacatán   Olintepeque   Cuatro Caminos
Salcajá

Tapachula   El Tumbador   Quetzaltenango   Cantel

Río Suchiate

San Martín Sacatepéquez   Almolonga
Volcán Lacandón   Volcán Chicabal   Zunil
Volcán Santa María   Santa María de Jesús
Coatepeque   Colomba   Volcán Santiaguito

Hidalgo   Tecún Umán

CARRETERA AL PACÍFICO

Abaj Takalik
El Asintal

Ocós   Tilapa   Cuyotenango   Chicacao
Retalhuleu   Mazatenango

PACIFIC OCEAN

Champerico   Escuintla

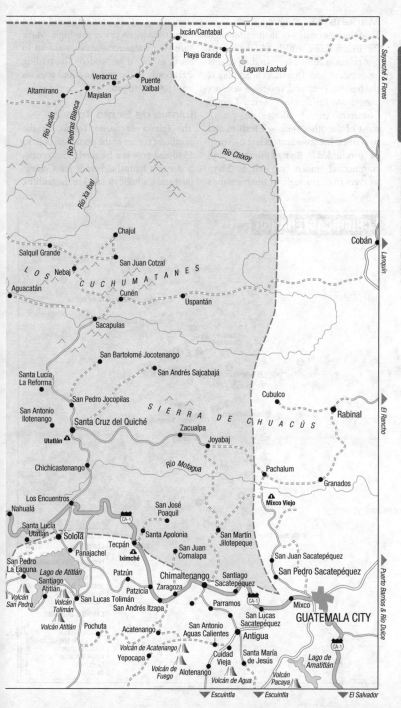

Ixcán/Cantabal

Playa Grande

Laguna Lachuá

Altamirano

Veracruz

Puente
Xalbal

Mayalan

Río Ixcán

Río Piedras Blancas

Río Chixoy

Río Xa Ibal

Chajul

Cobán

Salquil Grande

San Juan Cotzal

Nebaj

L O S

C U C H U M A T A N E S

Aguacatán

Cunén

Uspantán

Sacapulas

San Bartolomé Jocotenango

San Andrés Sajcabajá

Santa Lucía
La Reforma

San Pedro Jocopilas

S I E R R A   D E   C H U A C Ú S

Cubulco

San Antonio
Ilotenango

Santa Cruz del Quiché

Zacualpa

Rabinal

Utatlán

Joyabaj

Chichicastenango

Río Motagua

Pachalum

Granados

Mixco Viejo

Los Encuentros

San José
Poaquil

Nahualá

CA-1

Santa Lucía
Utatlán

Sololá

Santa Apolonia

San Martín
Jilotepeque

Panajachel

Tecpán

Iximché

San Juan
Comalapa

San Juan Sacatepéquez

San Pedro
La Laguna

San Pedro Sacatepéquez

Lago de Atitlán

Santiago
Atitlán

Patzún

Chimaltenango

Santiago
Sacatepéquez

*Volcán
San Pedro*

*Volcán
Tolimán*

San Lucas Tolimán

Patzicía

Zaragoza

Parramos

CA-1

Mixco

Volcán Atitlán

San Andrés Itzapa

San Lucas
Sacatepéquez

GUATEMALA CITY

Pochuta

Acatenango

San Antonio
Aguas Calientes

Antigua

Santa María
de Jesús

CA-1

Volcán de Acatenango

Yepocapa

Cuidad
Vieja

*Lago de
Amatitlán*

*Volcán de
Fuego*

Alotenango

Volcán de Agua

*Volcán
Pacaya*

Escuintla

Escuintla

El Salvador

Markets

Most visitors come to Chichicastenango for its **markets**, which fill the town's central plaza and all surrounding streets on Sundays and Thursdays – Sunday is the busiest. Fruit and vegetable vendors congregate inside the covered Centro Comercial (which adjoins the plaza); most of the other stalls sell textiles and souvenirs. The crowds are eclectic – you'll be surrounded by myriad foreigners and commercial traders, as well as Maya weavers from throughout the highlands – but many of the goods are geared to the tourist trade, so prices are high. Make sure your bargaining abilities are up to snuff, as they'll be needed. The trading starts early in the morning, and goes on until late afternoon.

Iglesia de Santo Tomás

The **Iglesia de Santo Tomás**, in the northeast corner of the plaza, was built in 1540 and now is a local religious centre, home to a faith that blends pre-Columbian and Catholic rituals. For the faithful,

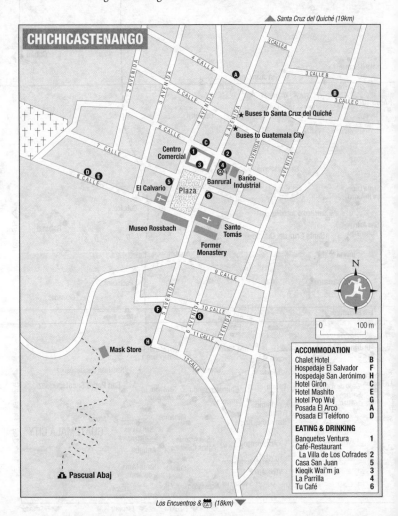

▲ *Santa Cruz del Quiché (19km)*

CHICHICASTENANGO

3 CALLE A
3 CALLE B
3 CALLE C

4 CALLE

2 AVENIDA
3 AVENIDA
5 CALLE
4 AVENIDA
5 AVENIDA
6 AVENIDA
7 AVENIDA

Ⓐ
Ⓑ

★ Buses to Santa Cruz del Quiché
★ Buses to Guatemala City

6 CALLE

7 CALLE

Centro Comercial
Ⓒ ❶
❷
Ⓓ Ⓔ ❸ ❹
8 CALLE @

El Calvario ❺
Plaza ❻
Banrural
Banco Industrial

Museo Rossbach
Santo Tomás
Former Monastery

9 CALLE

N

0   100 m

5 AVENIDA
6 AVENIDA
10 CALLE
4 AVENIDA
Ⓕ
Ⓖ
11 CALLE
Ⓗ
12 CALLE

Mask Store

⛰ Pascual Abaj

ACCOMMODATION	
Chalet Hotel	B
Hospedaje El Salvador	F
Hospedaje San Jerónimo	H
Hotel Girón	C
Hotel Mashito	E
Hotel Pop Wuj	G
Posada El Arco	A
Posada El Teléfono	D

EATING & DRINKING	
Banquetes Ventura	1
Café-Restaurant La Villa de Los Cofrades	2
Casa San Juan	5
Kieqik Wai'm ja	3
La Parrilla	4
Tu Café	6

the entire building is alive with the souls of the dead, each located in a specific part of the church. Before entering, it's customary to make offerings in a fire at the base of the steps or to burn incense in perforated cans. Don't enter the building by the front door, which is reserved for *cofrades* and senior church officials; use the side door instead and be warned that taking photographs inside the building is considered **deeply offensive** – don't even contemplate it. You are likely to find the devout here at all times of the day, in particular on Sundays, when the church is enveloped in incense and indigenous Maya swing censers and mutter prayers on the church steps. At the entrance there are candles scattered around the floor; these are put here by living Maya in honour of their ancestors, some of whom are buried beneath the church.

Beside the church is a former **monastery**, now used by the parish administration. It was here that a Spanish priest, Francisco Ximénez, became the first outsider to be shown the Popol Vuh, the Maya holy book; it is said that the Maya became interested in worshipping here after Ximénez began to read the book in the early eighteenth century. His copy of the manuscript is now housed in the Newberry Library in Chicago: the original was lost some time later in the eighteenth century. The text itself, a poem of over nine thousand lines that details the cosmology, mythology and traditional history of the K'iche', was written just to the north of here, in Utatlán, shortly after the arrival of the Spanish.

Rossbach Museum

On the south side of the plaza, often hidden by stalls on market day, the **Rossbach Museum** (Tues, Wed, Fri & Sat 8am–12.30pm & 2–4.30pm, Thurs 8am–4pm, Sun 8am–2pm; Q5) houses a broad collection of pre-Columbian artefacts, mostly small pieces of ceramics (including some demonic-looking incense burners), jade necklaces and earrings, and stone carvings (some two thousand years old). Also on show are some interesting old photographs of Chichi and local weavings, masks and carvings.

Pascual Abaj

The Iglesia de Santo Tomás is not the only religious site in the area: many of the hills that surround Chichicastenango are topped with shrines. The closest of these, **Pascual Abaj**, is less than a kilometre from the plaza and regularly visited by tourists. The shrine comprises small altars facing a stern pre-Columbian sculpture. Offerings are usually overseen by a shaman, and range from flowers to sacrificed chickens, always incorporating plenty of incense, alcohol and incantations. Remember that any ceremonies you may witness are deeply serious – keep your distance and be sensitive about taking photographs. To get to Pascual Abaj, walk down the hill beside Santo Tomás, take the first right, 9 Calle, and follow this as it winds its way out of town. You'll soon cross a stream and then a well-signposted route takes you past a mask workshop, continuing uphill for ten minutes through a pine forest.

Arrival and information

By bus There's no bus station in Chichi, but the corner of 5 C and 5 Av operates loosely as a terminal.

Tourist information There is no Inguat in town, but there is a tourist office (daily 8am–8pm; ☎7756 2022, ✉asochichi@itelgua.com) right by the theatre. However, this has very limited information and irregular hours that depend on the staff's eating and sleeping patterns. The Museo Rossbach is a lot better informed.

Travel agent Chichi Turkaj Tours (☎7742 1359 or 5927 9217, ✉chichiturkajtours@yahoo.com), in the *Hotel Chuguila*, 5 Av 5–24; they can come and pick you up from Guatemala City airport and take you straight to Chichi.

Accommodation

There are a few good budget hotels in town. These can be in short supply on Saturday nights before the Sunday market, but you shouldn't have a problem at any other time. Prices can also rise on market days, though at other times you can usually negotiate a good deal.

Chalet Hotel 3 C 7–44 ☎ 7756 1360. Welcoming hotel with little wooden carved animals and knick-knacks dotted around all the floors. Highland wool blankets and textiles add pleasing decorative touches to the comfortable beds. Free internet, and breakfast (Q20) is available. ⑤

Hospedaje El Salvador 5 Av 10–09 ☎ 7756 1329. Hotel with a warren of bare but fairly neat rooms, a bizarre colour scheme and low rates, although the communal bathrooms are not as spick and span as they might be. ②

Hospedaje San Jerónimo 5a Av & 12 C ☎ 7756 1838. This quiet, somewhat institutional *hospedaje* has clean, fairly bare rooms, all with en-suite, hot-water baths. Nice views of Chichi from the top-floor balcony. ②

Hotel Girón 6 C 4–52 ☎ 7756 1156. Spacious rooms with clean bathrooms and safe parking. Interesting plant pots made out of tree roots line the stairs. ②

Hotel Mashito 8 C 1–72 (on the road to the cemetery) ☎ 7756 1343. Painted bright green, this hotel has hot water and clean rooms, all with cable TV. ③

Hotel Pop Wuj 6 Av, between 10 & 11 C ☎ 7756 2014. Pleasantly decorated, spotless rooms, all en suite. The most expensive doubles have humungous beds. There is also a restaurant downstairs, although it's fairly dark. ④

Posada El Teléfono 8 C 1–64 ☎ 7756 1197. Friendly guesthouse with small, clean, bare rooms scattered up and down steep staircases. The communal bathroom is kept tidy. ②

TREAT YOURSELF

Posada El Arco 4 C 4–36 ☎ 7756 1255. Excellent guesthouse with eight large, attractive rooms with good wooden beds and reading lights. Each room is individually decorated with local fabrics and wooden statues; some also have fireplaces, and rooms 6 and 7 even have access to a pleasant terrace. There's also a beautiful garden and stunning countryside views. ⑤

Eating

There is plenty of good-value Guatemalan *comedor* food available in Chichicastenango, especially in the plaza on market day. Alternatively, there are a number of excellent cheap restaurants around the square.

Restaurants

Banquetes Ventura Inside the Centro Comercial, on the upper floor. Offers a terrific view of the vegetable market and good, simple local food – breakfasts start at Q21. Closed Mon.

Café-Restaurant La Villa de Los Cofrades 6 C & 5 Av, on the first floor. Observe local Chichi life from the first-floor balcony while you enjoy great *churrascos* and breakfasts (Q25). Real coffee and wine are available.

Casa San Juan Beside El Calvario church, at the southern end of the plaza. Restaurant/bar with a stylish interior, including plenty of artwork on display. The menu includes interesting sandwiches (Q12) as well as Guatemalan dishes such as *pepián de pollo*.

Kieqik Wai'm ja Inside the Centro Comercial, on the upper floor. The name may be unpro-nounceable, but the local food is tasty and reliable and the balcony views of the church of Santo Tomás are unrivalled. Try the delicious *chiles rellenos* (Q30).

La Parrilla 6 C & 5 Av. Set in a little courtyard, this is a good place to get away from the market crowds. Meat lovers must try the *especial la parrilla* (Q50).

Tu Café On the west side of plaza. Unpretentious place with plenty of choices for breakfast (Q22), as well as *antojitos*, sandwiches, *carne adobada* and good lunch-time mains (Q30).

Directory

Exchange Banrural, 6 C (Mon–Fri & Sun 9am–5pm, Sat 8am–noon) has a MasterCard/Cirrus ATM and changes US dollars. Banco Industrial, next door (Mon 10am–2pm, Wed & Fri 10am–5pm, Thurs & Sun 9am–5pm, Sat 10am–3pm) has a Visa/Plus ATM.

Internet C@fenet, 6C 5–37 has the fastest connec-tion in town for Q8/hr, although apparently the speed much depends on weather conditions.

Post office North of the square on 4 Av (Mon–Fri 8.30am–5.30pm, Sat 9am–1pm).

Moving on

By bus Buses heading between Guatemala City and Santa Cruz del Quiché pass through Chichicastenango about every 20min, stopping in town for a few minutes to load up with passengers.

SANTA CRUZ DEL QUICHÉ

SANTA CRUZ DEL QUICHÉ, known locally as "El Quiché", is capital of its eponymous department, and half an hour north of Chichicastenango. A good paved road connects the two towns, running through pine forests and ravines, and past the **Laguna Lemoa**, a lake which, according to local legend, was originally filled with tears wept by the wives of K'iche' kings after their husbands had been slaughtered by the Spanish. The town is best used as a base to explore the surrounding area, particularly Utatlán and some of the department's smaller towns; it's not home to any particular attractions of its own. In the central **plaza** there's a large colonial **church**, built by the Dominicans with stone from the ruins of Utatlán. In the middle of the plaza, a defiant **statue** of the K'iche' hero, Tecún Umán, stands prepared for battle. His position is undermined somewhat by the ugly urban tangle of hardware stores, bakeries and trash that surround the square, as well as the spectacularly ugly **market** building, home to the Thursday and Sunday produce markets.

Arrival and information

By bus Buses pull into the bus terminal, which is about four blocks south and a couple east of the central plaza. The street directly north of the terminal is 1 Av, which takes you into the heart of the town.

Exchange Several banks will change your traveller's cheques and US dollars, including Banrural (Mon–Fri 8am–5pm, Sat 8am–noon), which has a MasterCard and Visa ATM, and Banco Agromercantil (Mon–Fri 9am–7pm, Sat 9am–1pm), also with a Visa ATM; both are in the plaza.

Internet Try Internet Linus, just off the square inside the Comercial Linus (Q6/hr).

Accommodation

Hotel Leo 1 Av 9–02 ☎7755 0772/0530. Rooms here are pleasant, spacious and clean, and all have private bath, cable TV and hot water. ❹

Hotel Luisito 10 C 00–27 ☎7755 2547. Good-value place with simple rooms and spotless bathrooms. ❸

Hotel San Pascual 7 C & 1 Av ☎7755 1107. Run by a lovely old couple and set in a nice courtyard. The rooms – without private bath – are a bargain, but the communal bathrooms do not have hot water. Excellent rates for single travellers. ❷

Eating

Restaurante Frutilandia By the church. Breakfasts for Q18, sandwiches for Q9 and fresh juices from Q4.

Café San Miguel Opposite the Church. A clean restaurant with good-value food (empanadas for Q5 and sandwiches for Q11). Pastries also available at the front.

Moving on

Buses to: Guatemala City (every 20min 3.30am–5pm; 3hr 30min) via Chichicastenango (30min) and Los Encuentros (1hr); Nebaj (7 daily 8am–5pm; 2hr 45min); Quetzaltenango (10 daily; 3hr); Uspantán (7 daily 8am–4pm; 3hr 30min).

AROUND EL QUICHÉ

It's certainly worth taking the time to explore El Quiché's surrounding areas, home to some of the most breathtaking scenery in the entire country. Although not much remains of the ruins of Gumarkaaj, the history of the area is fascinating and serves to highlight the region's rich Maya heritage. The site is also still used for religious ceremonies.

Utatlán (Gumarkaaj)

Early in the fifteenth century, the K'iche' king Gucumatz (Feathered Serpent) founded a new capital, Gumarkaaj. A hundred years later, the Spanish arrived, renamed the city **Utatlán** and then destroyed it. Today you can visit the ruins, about 4km to the west of Santa Cruz del Quiché.

Once a substantial city, there has been little restoration at **the site** (8am–5pm; Q20), and only a few of the main structures are still recognizable, most buried beneath grassy mounds, but it is impressive nonetheless. The small **museum** has a scale model of what the original city may once have looked like. You should be able to make out the main plaza, three temple buildings, the foundations of a circular tower and the remains of a ball-court. Beneath the plaza is a long tunnel containing nine shrines. Perhaps the most interesting thing about the site today is that *costumbristas*, traditional Maya priests, still come to these shrines to perform **religious rituals**. If a ceremony is taking place you'll hear the murmurings of prayers and smell incense smoke as you enter the tunnel; don't disturb the proceedings by approaching too closely.

A **taxi** from Santa Cruz del Quiché's plaza with an hour at the ruins costs around Q100. To **walk**, head south from the plaza along 2 Avenida, and then turn right down 10 Calle, which will take you all the way out to the site – it's a pleasant forty-minute hike. You're welcome to **camp** close to the ruins, but there are no facilities or food.

SACAPULAS

Just over an hour from El Quiché, spectacularly situated on the Río Negro and beneath the foothills of the Cuchumatanes, lies the little town of **SACAPULAS**, with a small colonial church and a good market every Thursday and Sunday. The town is worth visiting for the journey itself, as the bus winds its way up and down the slopes of the ragged hills that form part of the dramatic Cuchumatanes mountain range. A two-minute walk outside of town takes you to some small **salt flats**; Luisa Aceituno, at the corner house opposite the *Tujaal* sign, will sell you a bag of black salt (Q5), which is said to have medicinal purposes.

Getting to Sacapulas is easy – catch any **bus** from Santa Cruz del Quiché heading to Uspantán or Nebaj. Leaving can be a bit trickier; in the late afternoon, buses south to Quiché are fewer, the last running around 4pm. There are seven daily buses to Nebaj (1hr 45min), two daily buses to Huehuetenango (4.30am & 5.30am; 2hr) and seven buses to Uspantán (2hr), plus regular pick-ups on all routes. If you get stuck here, there are two good, basic *hospedajes*: *Hospedaje y Restaurante Río Negro* (℡5385 7363, ❷) and *Comedor y Hospedaje Tujaal* (℡5983 5698, ❹); neither place has private bathrooms, but both serve good food.

NEBAJ

NEBAJ is the centre of Ixil country, and a rather harmonious mixture of old and new: white adobe walls and

THE IXIL TRIANGLE

The three small towns of Nebaj, Chajul and Cotzal, high in the Cuchumatanes, form the hub of the Ixil-speaking region, a massive area of over 100,000 inhabitants whose language is not spoken anywhere else. For all its charm and relaxed atmosphere today, the region's history is a bitter one. After many setbacks, the Spanish finally managed to take Nebaj in 1530, but by then they were so enraged that not only did they burn the town to the ground, but they condemned the survivors to slavery. Independence didn't improve conditions – the Ixil people continued to be regarded as a source of cheap labour, and were forced to work on the coastal plantations. Over a century later, in the late 1970s and early 1980s, the area was hit by horrific violence when it became the main theatre of operation for the EGP (the Guerrilla Army of the Poor). Caught up in the conflict, the civilians suffered terribly. Despite this bloody legacy, the region's fresh green hills are some of the most beautiful in the country, and the three towns are friendly and accommodating.

cobbled streets sit side-by-side new concrete structures. Though remote, it's well worth a visit, both for the glimpse it affords of the traditional Ixil way of life – the weaving, especially, spectacular, with the women's *huipiles* an artistic tangle of complex geometrical designs in superb greens, yellows, reds and oranges – but also for the spectacular hikes that can be done in the surrounding areas.

What to see and do

The **plaza** is the community's focal point, lined by its major shops, municipal buildings and police station. The small **market**, two blocks southeast, bears investigation. On Thursdays and Sundays the town explodes, as out-of-town traders visit with second-hand clothing from the US, stereos from Taiwan and Korea and chickens, eggs and produce from the highlands. The town **church**, a block west of the market, is also worth a look – inside its door on the left are dozens of crosses, forming a memorial to those killed in the civil war. If you're here for the second week in August, you'll witness the **Nebaj fiesta**, which includes processions, dances, drinking, fireworks and a marimba-playing marathon.

Hiking

There are several beautiful **hikes** in the hills around Nebaj, for which guides can be arranged at *El Descanso* (see p.176). One of the most interesting takes you to the village of **Acul**, two hours away. Starting from the church in Nebaj, cross the plaza and head along 5 C past *Hotel Turansa*. At the bottom of the dip, after *Tienda y Comedor El Oasis*, the road divides: take the right-hand fork and head out of town along a dirt track. This switchbacks up a steep hillside, and heads over a narrow pass into the next valley, where it drops down into Acul. The village was one of the country's original so-called "model villages" into which people were herded after their homes had been destroyed by the army during the civil war. If you walk on through the village and out the other side, you arrive at the alpine-lodge-like *Finca San Antonio* (℡ 5305 6240), run by an Italian family who have lived here for more than fifty years. They make some of the country's best cheese, which they sell at pretty reasonable prices, and they also rent out delightful **chalets** (④).

Arrival and information

By bus Buses from Santa Cruz del Quiché (7 daily) pull into the bus terminal, two blocks southeast of the plaza.

Tourist information The best place for information is *El Descanso* restaurant, two blocks north of the plaza on 3 C, where an excellent community tourism initiative has been established and numerous treks (from Q125/day) can be arranged.

Accommodation

Hospedaje Edmundo By the Quetzal petrol station ℡ 7755 8423. Family-run, this *hospedaje* appears to be a converted shack. Two people can share a single bed (you can just about fit in the S position) for a bargain price – no doubt an interesting experience if you really need to save those extra quetzales. ①

Hospedaje Ilebal Tenamsa 5min walk from the plaza on the road to Chajul/Cotzal ℡ 7755 8039. Well-run blue *hospedaje* with decent, very clean rooms, some with TV and private bathroom, reliably hot showers and safe parking. ②

Hostal Media Luna Medio Sol ℡ 5847 4747. The *Descanso* restaurant (see p.176) can show you the way here. Clean, simple rooms and dorm beds, as well as cooking facilities, a ping-pong table and TV room. Dorms ①, doubles ③

Popi's 5 C, two and a half blocks west of the square ℡ 7756 0159, ⓦ www.mayanhope.org. Run by an NGO with profits going to the local special-needs school, this hostel has excellent-value spacious dorms and private rooms. Also has a cheap restaurant, internet and book exchange. Dorms ①, doubles ②

Eating

Asados el Pasabien On the road to Sacapulas, this restaurant excels at its *churrascos* (Q35).

El Descanso Relaxed place with sofas, rocking chairs, arm chairs and a number of magazines to flick through as you wait for your food, which is well-prepared and inexpensive (burgers Q20, spaghetti Q22, burritos Q22 and meat *churrascos* Q28).

Popi's Restaurant Inside *Popi's* hostel. This little restaurant serves excellent-value food (burgers Q14, burritos Q15 and breakfasts from Q12). Run by an NGO; all profits go to the local special-needs school.

Directory

Exchange Banrural, in the shopping area underneath the plaza, has a 5B ATM for MasterCard/Cirrus/Visa cards.

Internet You can surf the net at *Popi's* or at *El Descanso* restaurant; the latter are behind the ⓦwww.nebaj.org website (Spanish only).

Language schools You will find the Nebaj Language School in the same building as *El Descanso* restaurant.

Moving on

By bus to: Guatemala City (11pm; 6hr); Santa Cruz del Quiché (2am, 3am, 4am, 5.30am, 8am, 11.30am; 2hr 30min). For Huehuetenango or Uspantán catch the bus to El Quiché and change in Sacapulas. Buses for Chajul and Cotzal leave regularly between 5.30am and 5pm.

By pick-up Pick-ups and trucks supplement the buses; the best place to hitch south is on the road out of town.

SAN JUAN COTZAL

SAN JUAN COTZAL, the second of the three Ixil towns, is about 30 to 45 minutes away from Nebaj. The town sits in a gentle dip in the valley, which is sheltered somewhat beneath the Cuchumatanes and often wrapped in a damp blanket of mist. Cotzal attracts very few Western travellers – there's really nothing to do, though there is some great hill-walking nearby – so you may find that many people assume you're an aid worker or attached to an Evangelical church. It's best to time your visit to coincide with **market days** (Wed & Sat), when there's more traffic around. Intricate turquoise *huipiles* are worn by the Maya women here, who also weave bags and rope from the fibres of the maguey plant.

Regular **buses** leave Cotzal for Nebaj between 5.30am and 5pm. It's possible to also visit Chajul the same day if you get an early start from Nebaj.

CHAJUL

CHAJUL, made up mainly of old adobe houses, with wooden beams and red-tiled roofs blackened by the smoke of cooking fires, is worth visiting as it is the most determinedly traditional and least bilingual of the Ixil towns. The women wear earrings made of old coins strung up on lengths of wool and dress in bright reds and blues, while boys still use blowpipes to hunt small birds, a skill that dates from the earliest of times. The colonial church is home to the **Christ of Golgotha** and the focus of a large pilgrimage on the second Friday of Lent, a particularly good time to be here. If you want to **stay**, local families rent out beds in their houses to the steady trickle of travellers who come to town; you won't have to look for them, they will find you.

On **market** days (Tues & Fri) there are regular morning **buses** from Nebaj between 5.30am and 5pm, returning at 11.30am and noon. You can also **walk** here from San Juan Cotzal, two to three hours away through the spectacular Ixil countryside. Follow the unpaved road that branches off to the main Nebaj–Cotzal road just before you enter Cotzal.

QUETZALTENANGO

QUETZALTENANGO, Guatemala's second city, sits in a beautiful mountain valley ringed by volcanoes. In pre-Columbian times the town belonged to the Mam Maya people, who named the town Xelajú, meaning "under the rule of the ten mountains" – hence the name, **Xela** (pronounced "Shay-La"), by which the city still goes; it was the Spaniards who dubbed the city Quetzal-tenango, roughly translated as "the land of the quetzal". Xela went on to flourish during colonial times, thanks in large part to the area's abundant coffee crops, but a massive earthquake in 1902 destroyed nearly the entire city. Subsequently almost completely rebuilt (all the Neoclassical buildings that you can see today date to this time), Xela is once again one of the country's major centres. Nonetheless, it manages to preserve an air of subdued, dignified calm, and remains popular among travellers, especially language students looking for more of an authentic Guatemalan experience than their counterparts in Antigua.

What to see and do

There aren't that many sights in the city itself, but if you have an hour or two to spare then it's worth wandering through the streets, soaking up the atmosphere and taking in the museum in the **Casa de la Cultura**. The city is divided into zones; you'll primarily be interested in zonas 1 and 3, home to the central plaza and the bus terminal, respectively. Most places are within walking distance, except the bus terminal.

Parque Centro América

The **Parque Centro América**, with a mass of mock-Greek columns and imposing bank facades, is at the centre of Xela. There's none of the buzz of business that you'd expect, though, except on the first Sunday of the month when the plaza hosts a good artisan market with blankets, baskets and piles of weavings for sale. On the west side of the plaza is the impressive **Pasaje Enríquez**; once planned as a sparkling arcade of upmarket shops, it was left derelict for many years, though it has now been partially revived.

Casa de la Cultura

At the southern end of the plaza, next to the tourist office, is the **Casa de la Cultura** (Mon–Fri 8am–noon & 2–6pm, Sat 9am–1pm; Q6), the city's blatant architectural homage to ancient Greece. On the ground floor you'll find a display of sports trophies and a room dedicated to the marimba, along with assorted documents, photographs and pistols from the liberal revolution and the state of Los Altos, which declared itself the sixth state of the Federal Republic of Central America in the 1830s, with Xela as capital. Upstairs there are some modest Maya artefacts, historic photographs and a bizarre natural history room. Among the dusty displays of stuffed bats, pickled snakes and animal skins are the macabre remains of assorted freaks of nature, including a sheep born with eight legs and a four-horned goat.

The rest of the city

Away from the plaza, the city spreads out, a mixture of the old and new. The commercial heart is **14 Avenida**, complete with blaring neon signs. At the top of 14 Avenida, at the junction with 1 Calle, stands the **Teatro Municipal**, another grandiose Neoclassical building (see p.182 for performance information). Further afield, Xela's role as a regional centre of trade is more in evidence. Out in Zona 3 is the **Mercado La Democracia**, a vast covered complex with stalls daily selling local produce. There's another Greek-style structure right out on the edge of town, the **Minerva Temple**, built to honour President Barrios's enthusiasm for education – it has no practical purpose. Below the temple are the sprawling daily produce **market**, and the **Minerva Bus Terminal**. It's here that you can really sense the city's role as the centre of the western highlands, with *indígena* traders from all over the area doing business. Just behind the market, **La Pradera** shopping plaza boasts over one hundred stores and a multiplex cinema.

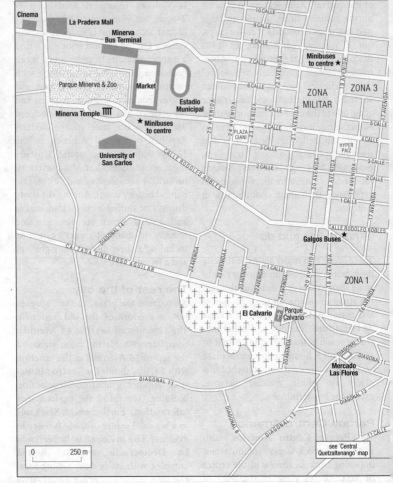

▲ San Pedro Sacatepéquez (51km) & San Marcos (53km)   Autopista (2km), Olintepeque (4km) & Cuatro Caminos (12km) ▲

Cinema

La Pradera Mall

Minerva
Bus Terminal

Minibuses
to centre ★

10 CALLE
9 CALLE
8 CALLE
7 CALLE
6 CALLE
5 CALLE
4 CALLE
3 CALLE
2 CALLE
1 CALLE

Parque Minerva & Zoo

Market

Estadio
Municipal

ZONA 3

ZONA
MILITAR

22 AVENIDA
21 AVENIDA
19 AVENIDA

5 CALLE
4 CALLE
3 CALLE

Minerva Temple 血

★ Minibuses
to centre

25 AVENIDA
24 AVENIDA
23 AVENIDA

PLAZA
CIANI

HYPER
PAÍZ

18 AVENIDA
17 AVENIDA

1 CALLE

University of
San Carlos

CALLE RODOLFO ROBLES

20 AVENIDA
19 AVENIDA

CALLE RODOLFO ROBLES

Galgos Buses ★

DIAGONAL 14

CALZADA SINFOROSO AGUILAR

24 AVENIDA
23 AVENIDA
22 AVENIDA

1 CALLE

20 AVENIDA
19 AVENIDA

ZONA 1

16 AVENIDA

DIAGONAL 11

El Calvario 血

Parque
Calvario

DIAGONAL 8

DIAGONAL 11

DIAGONAL 13

DIAGONAL 12

Mercado
Las Flores

21 CALLE

DIAGONAL 11

0   250 m

see 'Central
Quetzaltenango' map

Arrival and information

By bus Unfortunately, virtually all buses arrive
and depart from nowhere near the centre of town.
Second-class buses pull into the chaotic Minerva
Bus Terminal on the city's northwestern edge; to get
to the main plaza, walk 300m through the market
stalls to 4 C and catch a microbus marked "Parque".
There are three main companies operating first-
class buses to and from the capital, each with their
own private terminal: Líneas Américas, 7 Av 3–33,
Zona 2 (☎7761 2063); Alamo, 14 Av 5–15, Zona
3 (☎7767 7117); and Galgos, C Rodolfo Robles
17–43, Zona 1 (☎7761 2248).

Tour operators Adrenalina Tours, inside Pasaje
Enríquez, Plaza Central (☎7761 4509, ⓦwww
.adrenalinatours.com), offers various tours of
the region, including trips to Zunil and Fuentes
Georginas and San Andrés Xecul, shuttle buses,
volcano climbs (Volcán Santa María from US$15
per person) and sells airline tickets. Casa
Iximulew, 15 Av & 5 C, Zona 1 (☎761 5057,
ⓦwww.mayaexplor.com), runs organized trips
to most of the volcanoes and sights around Xela.
Quetzaltrekkers, inside *Casa Argentina* (see
opposite; ☎761 4520, ⓦwww.quetzalventures
.com) offers cultural tours and hiking trips to
volcanoes with all profits going to a charity for
street children.

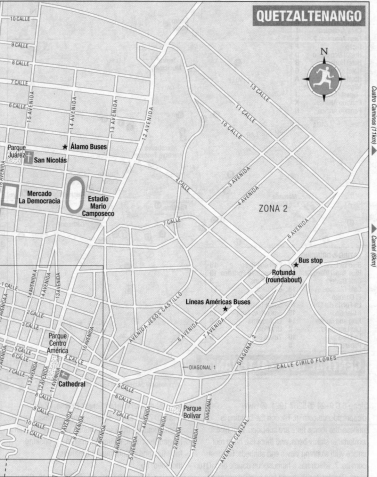

Salcajá (8km)

QUETZALTENANGO

N

Cuatro Caminos (11km)

Cantel (6km)

10 CALLE
9 CALLE
8 CALLE
7 CALLE
6 CALLE
5 AVENIDA
4 AVENIDA
3 AVENIDA
12 AVENIDA
13 CALLE
11 CALLE
10 CALLE

★ Álamo Buses
Parque Juárez
San Nicolás
16 AVENIDA

Mercado La Democracia
Estadio Mario Camposeco

4 CALLE
3 AVENIDA
4 AVENIDA
ZONA 2
6 AVENIDA
7 CALLE

Bus stop
Rotunda (roundabout)

★ Líneas Américas Buses
AVENIDA JESÚS CASTILLO
6 AVENIDA
7 AVENIDA
DIAGONAL 2

1 CALLE
15 AVENIDA
14 AVENIDA
13 AVENIDA
2 CALLE
3 CALLE
Parque Centro América
10 AVENIDA
4 CALLE
5 CALLE
6 CALLE
7 CALLE
12 AVENIDA
11 AVENIDA
★ Cathedral
8 CALLE
9 CALLE
10 CALLE
11 CALLE
9 AVENIDA
8 AVENIDA
7 AVENIDA
6 AVENIDA
5 AVENIDA
4 AVENIDA

DIAGONAL 1
CALLE CIRILO FLORES

Parque Bolívar
DIAGONAL 3
AVENIDA CENTRAL

Almolonga (4.5km) & Zunil (9km)

Tourist information The tourist office, on the main plaza (Mon–Fri 8am–1pm & 2–5pm, Sat 8am–1pm; ☎761 4931 ✉info-xela@inguat.gob .gt), has maps and local information. To find what's on in Xela, pick up a copy of *Xela Who (www .xelawho.com)*, available in many of the popular bars and cafés.

Accommodation

Once you've made it to the plaza, all the places listed here are within a ten-minute walk.

Black Cat Hostel 13 Av 3–33 ☎7761 2091, ⓦwww.blackcathostels.net. A good place to meet other travellers, this hostel has clean

spacious rooms and dorms with hot showers and an excellent restaurant that also serves alcohol. Rates include internet and a massive delicious breakfast. ❹

Casa Argentina 12 Diagonal 8–37 ☎7761 2470/0010, ✉casargentina.xela@gmail.com. Xela's definitive budget choice, with many single rooms, a large dorm (❶), a kitchen, a sun terrace and a café. Some of the water is heated with solar panels. It's also the home of Quetzaltrekkers (see opposite). ❷

Casa Argentina 2 6 C 15–37 ☎7761 2470/0010. Fairly scruffy rooms reflect the low rates, though kitchen facilities, hot water and purified water are included. Good prices for single travellers and long-term stays. ❷

179

▲ *Minerva (2km)*   ▲ *Mercado La Democracia (300m)*

ACCOMMODATION

Black Cat Hostel	C
Casa Argentina	I
Casa Argentina 2	E
Dicap	F
Hostal Don Diego	D
Hotel Horiani	B
Hotel Kiktem-já	G
Hotel Posada Real	A
Miguel de Cervantes Guest House	J
Pensión Altense	K
Pensión Andina	H

EATING & DRINKING

Bajo La Luna	10	Pool and Beer	19
Blue Angel Video Café	12	Restaurante Portofino	19
Café Baviera	7	Royal Paris	3
Café Clásicos	18	La Rumba	11
El Cuartito	17	Sabor de la India	1
La Fonda del Ché	16	Salón Tecún	8
Il Giardino	15	Smoothies Rum	13
King and Queen	14	La Taquería	9
Las Lagartijas	2	Ut'z Hua	4
La Luna	10	Zirkus Bar	6
Paparazzi	5		

CENTRAL QUETZALTENANGO

0 _____ 100 m

Almolongo (4.5km) & Zunil (9km) ▼

Dicap 6 C 9–24 ☎5287 1921, ⓦwww
.dicapresidence.com.gt. Though the building is
soulless, the rooms here are spacious, with nice
comfortable sturdy beds, and there is a huge roof
terrace with stunning views and sunbeds. Request
room no. 7, which has a humungous double bed (Q10
more). Cooking facilities and free purified water. ❹

🏃 **Hostal Don Diego** 6 C 15–20 ☎7763 1000
or 5511 3211, ⓔdondiegoxela@hotmail
.com. Excellent option with a pleasant courtyard,
guests' kitchen and basic rooms. Rates include
free purified water and breakfast. Very inexpensive
weekly and monthly deals. ❸

Hotel Horiani 12 Av 1–19 ☎5486 0164. Very
basic and fairly stuffy small rooms, but very good
value given the price. ❷

Hotel Kiktem-já 13 Av 7–18 ☎7761 4304. Simple
but nicely decorated rooms with wooden floors.
All have en-suite, hot-water baths and cable TV.
Secure parking. ❹

Hotel Posada Real 15 Av 3–08 ☎7761 4142. New
place with spotless rooms (one with a fireplace) and
a little interior courtyard. ❹

Miguel de Cervantes Guest House 12 Av
8–31 ☎7765 5554, ⓦwww.learn2speakspanish
.com. Pleasant little guesthouse within a Spanish
language school. Living room with TV, cooking
facilities and a Continental breakfast
included. ❸

Pensión Altense 9 C 10–41, ☎7765 4648. Clean,
simple rooms with cable TV are set on interior
courtyard with secure parking. A few sofas and
wooden chairs line the hallway. ❸

Pensión Andina 8 Av 6–07 ☎7761 4012. Set on
an interior courtyard, the rooms here are bare and
clean. There are also – rather bizarrely – a few soft
toy parrots hanging from a tree. ❸

Eating

Quetzaltenango has a fairly moderate choice of
cafés and restaurants, suiting its modest, unpretentious character. Almost nowhere opens before 8am,
so forget early breakfasts.

Cafés

Blue Angel Video Café 7 C 15–19. Popular, social hangout with a daily video programme. The menu is mostly vegetarian, with sandwiches for Q15 and pastas Q20; wine by the glass is also served, although the selection is limited. Try the delicious home-made chocolate or the excellent burritos. Free wi-fi.

Café Baviera 5 C 13–14. Anachronistic pine-panelled coffeehouse with old photos on the walls. This place is mainly about coffee (Q6), but the cakes, croissants (Q20) and sandwiches (Q30) are fine too.

El Cuartito 13 Av 7–09. Relaxed café with crooked bookshelves, funky lights (some made with glass jars and lots of bulbs, others just with blue bottles) and a hanging chair and door. The international food is all organic (bagels Q12.50, falafel pita Q26, coffee Q8) and free-trade. Live music on some nights. Free wi-fi.

La Luna 8 Av 4–11. Crammed with curios and antiques, *La Luna* has seven different varieties of wonderful drinking chocolate (Q6).

Smoothies Rum 7 C 15–23. A relaxed café with good bagels (Q12) and veggie and non-veggie curries (Q40). You can meditate or smoke a hookah pipe in the Indian room at the back, and once a month they have Guatemalan nights with dances or shows.

Restaurants

Il Giardino 19 Callejón 8–07. Set in an interior covered garden, this place serves pastas (Q50) and fairly good pizzas (Q30) with proper Italian prosciutto. For free delivery call ☎7765 8293. Closed Tues.

Las Lagartijas 15 Av A 3–05. Great food, though most ingredients are imported from Europe and the US: the menu includes veggie burgers (Q25), dates (Q20) and salmon sandwiches (Q25). Live trova music Fri at 8pm and poker night (Texas Hold'em) Wed at 8pm; it also hosts regular theatre performances, art expos and poetry readings. Try the excllent sangría (Q15). Closed Mon.

Restaurante Portofino 12 Av 10–21. At the same location as *Pool and Beer*, this Italian restaurant has a relaxed atmosphere and serves exquisite gnocchi – try the gnocchi with gorgonzola (Q40).

Royal Paris 14 Av A 3–06. Authentic, enjoyable French-owned restaurant with a diverse menu of really flavoursome dishes (meat dishes Q65), plus snacks like *croque-monsieur* (Q26). Prices are moderate, given the quality of the cuisine.

Sabor de la India 2 C 15 Av A 2–34 Callejón 15 (off 2 C, between 15 Av A & 16 Av). Excellent authentic Indian cuisine with vegetarian and non-vegetarian dishes (huge samosas Q15). Closed Mon.

La Taqueria 8 Av & 5 C. Enjoyable Mexican food with good-value tacos (Q9), enchiladas (Q28) and grilled meats (Q37).

Ut'z Hua 12 Av & 3 C. Excellent choice specializing in Guatemalan cuisine, including *jocon*, *quichom* (both Q30) and seven kinds of soup (Q20). Always a daily special, too.

Drinking and nightlife

There are a number of lively bars that fill up at the weekend; the main area for nightlife in central Xela is 14 Av A.

Bars and clubs

Bajo La Luna 8 Av 3–72. In an atmospheric cellar, this relaxed wine bar with background tunes is perfect for a quiet drink. You can nibble on a cheese platter (Q20–35) while you sip.

Café Clásicos Diagonal 13 8–02. Little café/bar with a comfy feel and a number of Indian wooden masks and Hawaiian posters adorning the walls. Veggie food served. Sat is karaoke night, and merengue, salsa, 80s music and hip-hop are also played. Closed Sun.

La Fonda del Ché 15 Av 7–43, in front of Paco Pérez Park. Candle-lit, intimate spot with warm tones and good live music most nights. Admission Q10. Closed Sun & Mon.

King and Queen 7 C 13–27. Popular place with fun murals painted on the walls. Hookah pipes are available, and they serve 2-for-1 tequilas at any time (Q15). They also have veggie food such as tofu burgers (Q20).

Paparazzi 14 Av A 3–32. The hippest place in town, playing eclectic tunes (reggaeton, electronica, salsa, merengue). Admission Q30. Open Wed–Sat.

Pool and Beer 12 Av 10–21. Pool tables and table football are available in this spacious bar with dim lights. A litre of beer will set you back Q25. 2-for-1 tequilas (Q15) at any time.

La Rumba 13 Av, across the road from *El Cuartito*. If you're into moving your pelvis to some merengue, this is the place to show off your moves. The music isn't too loud, so you can chat too. Open Tues–Sat.

Salón Tecún Inside the Pasaje Enríquez, on the west side of the plaza. This drinking den, a favourite of both locals and travellers, has good tunes and a raucous buzz most evenings. Food is also served.

Zirkus Bar 15 Av 3–51. Some circus and clown knick-knacks embellish this cosy joint. Friendly staff and very good food – try the delicious veggie tortillas (Q15). Q5 from every beer purchased goes towards a charity to stop domestic violence.

Entertainment

Cinema *Blue Angel* café has a daily video programme (Q10) at 8pm with a large selection of movies (mainly Hollywood blockbusters). *Zirkus Bar* shows movies daily at 4.30pm, while *Royal Paris* restaurant shows French and Italian movies on Tues at 7pm. There's a multi-screen cinema by La Pradera mall, near the Minerva terminal.

Cultural institutes The Teatro Municipal, 14 Av A & 1 C (℡ 7761 2218), hosts guitar and piano recitals, dances and theatre performances, concerts and exhibitions. Centro Cultural Casa Los Altos, 6 C 12–32 (℡ 7765 2226, ℮ casalosaltos@hotmail.com) hosts talks (in Spanish) on Guatemalan history, legends, anthropology and economics every week. *Las Lagartijas* restaurant, 15 Av A 3–05, hosts theatre performances, art expos and poetry reading evenings. it also has a library where you can read English titles.

Directory

Bike rental Vrisa bookstore (see below) has bikes for Q40 per day, Q100 per week and Q200 per month.

Books Vrisa, 15 Av 3–64, has over 5000 used titles. El Libro Abierto, 15 Av A 1–56, Zona 1, has political, social and anthropological books on Guatemala, as well as guidebooks and some used titles.

Consulate Mexico, 21 Av, Zona 1 (Mon–Fri 9am–noon & 2–3pm). Most nationalities do not need a visa or tourist card for Mexico, but if you do, hand in your paperwork in the morning and collect it in the afternoon.

Exchange Several banks on the main plaza will change traveller's cheques: Banrural (Mon–Fri 9am–7pm, Sat 9am–1pm) has a MasterCard/ Cirrus ATM; Banco Industrial (Mon–Fri 9.30am– 6.30pm, Sat 9.30am–1.30pm) has a Visa/Plus ATM.

Internet There are at least two dozen places in Xela where you can surf the net (most open until 9pm or later; around Q10/hr), including Alternativa's at 16 Av 3–35, Zona 3.

Laundry Lavandería Tikal, Diagonal 13 8–07 (daily 7.30am–1.30pm and 2–6.30pm); Q16 for a small load, washed and dried in two hours.

Medical care Hospital San Rafael, 9 C 10–41, Zona 1 ℡ 7761 4414/2956.

LANGUAGE SCHOOLS IN QUETZALTENANGO

Quetzaltenango is another popular place to come for language school, especially if you're looking for a more relaxed, more authentic atmosphere than you might find in, say, Antigua.

Casa de Español Xelajú Callejón 15, Diagonal 13–02, Zona 1 (℡ 7761 5954, ⓦ www.casaxelaju.com).

Celas Maya 6 C 14–55, Zona 1 (℡ 7761 4342, ⓦ www.celasmaya.com).

Centro Bilingüe Amerindía (CBA) 12 Av 10–27, Zona 1 (℡ 7761 8535, ⓦ www .xelapages.com/cba).

Centro Maya Xela 21 Av 5–69, Zona 3 (℡ 7767 0352 ⓦ www.centromayaxela.org). Also offers classes in Maya languages.

Educación para Todos Av El Cenizal 0–58, Zona 5 (℡ 5935 3815, ⓦ www .spanishschools.biz).

English Club International Language School Diagonal 4 9–46, Zona 9 (℡ 7767 3506). Also offers classes in K'iche' and Mam.

Escuela Juan Sisay 15 Av 8–38, Zona 1 (℡ 7765 1318 (week days) or 7761 1586 (weekends), ⓦ www.juansisay.com).

Guatemalensis 19 Av 2–14, Zona 1 (℡ 7765 1384, ⓦ www.geocities.com/spanland/).

Inepas 15A Av 4–59, Zona 1 (℡ 7765 1308, ⓦ www.inepas.org).

La Paz Diagonal 11 7–36, Zona 1 (℡ 7761 2159, ⓦ www.xelapages.com/lapaz).

Kie–Balam, Diagonal 12 4–46, Zona 1 (℡ 7761 1636, ⓦ www.kiebalam.com).

Centro de Estudios de Español Pop Wuj 1 C 17–72, Zona 1 (℡ 7761 8286, ℮ popwujxel@pronet.net.gt).

Proyecto Lingüístico Quetzalteco de Español 5 C 2–40, Zona 1 (℡ 7765 2140, ⓦ www.hermandad.com).

Sakribal 6 C 7–42, Zona 1 (℡ 7763 0717, ⓦ www.sakribal.com).

Post office 15 Av & 4 C (Mon–Fri 8.30am–5.30pm, Sat 9am–1pm).

Telephones You can make international calls from many internet cafés in town. Rates start at Q1 per min to the US, Canada and Europe.

Moving on

By bus There are regular chicken buses (though no fixed schedule – they usually leave when full, around every 30min) to most major destinations, including Antigua (4hr), Chichicastenango (3hr), Cuatro Caminos (30min), Guatemala City (4hr 30min), Huehutenango (2hr), Momostenango (1hr 30min), Panajachel (2hr 30min) and Retalhuleu (1hr). For the latest Pullman schedule to Guatemala City check out: ⊛ http://xelawho.com/bailing.htm.

AROUND QUETZALTENANGO

Based in Quetzaltenango, you could easily spend a week or two exploring the highlands. There are numerous smaller towns and villages nearby, mostly indigenous agricultural communities and weaving centres with colourful weekly markets, as well as some lovely hot springs. The area also offers excellent hiking. The most obvious climbs are Volcán Santa María, towering above Quetzaltenango itself, and up Volcán Chicabal to its sublime crater lake. Straddling the coast road to the south is Zunil and the hot springs of Fuentes Georginas, overshadowed by more breathtaking volcanic peaks, while to the north are Totonicapán, capital of the department of the same name, and San Francisco El Alto, a small town perched on an outcrop overlooking the valley. Beyond that lies Momostenango, the country's principal wool-producing centre and a centre of Maya culture. For organized tours to all these places, contact the agents in Quetzaltenango listed on p.178.

Volcán Santa María

Due south of Quetzaltenango rises Volcán Santa María (3772m). Though you can only see the peak from town,

in the rest of the valley the cone seems to preside over everything around it. The view from the top is, as you might expect, truly spectacular, with nine other volcanoes visible on clear days, including the smoking summit of Santiaguito directly below. You can climb the volcano as a day-trip, but to really see it at its best you need to be on top at dawn, either sleeping on the freezing peak, or camping at the site below and climbing the final section in the dark by torchlight. Either way you need to bring enough food and water for the entire trip; and make sure you're acclimatized to the altitude for a few days before attempting the climb. It is highly recommended you go with a guide; they can be organized at most of the tour operators in Quetzaltenango (see p.178).

Laguna Chicabal

Another spectacular excursion in the area of Xela is to Laguna Chicabal, a crater lake set in the cone of the Chicabal volcano, about 25km southeast of the city.

To visit the lake, either get a Coatepeque-bound bus (every 30min; 40min) from the Minerva terminal to the town of San Martín Sacatepéquez and then trek for two and a half hours to the reserve entrance, or get a microbus from Avenida 25 and 7 Calle to "La Laguna Seca" and from there walk for one hour to the entrance (Q15). Here you'll find a football field and some *palapas*, each with four bunk beds (❶), a *comedor* and a shop selling snacks, juice and water. The last bus from San Martín back to Xela leaves at 5pm.

Once you enter the reserve, a signposted route to the left shows you to a *mirador*, from where there are stunning views of the emerald lake, and the volcanoes of Santa María and Santiaguito, Tajamulco and Tacaná, or alternatively via precipitous steps straight down to the shore. Small sandy bays bear charred crosses and bunches of fresh-cut flowers mark the site of ritual sacrifice. On May 3 every year *costumbristas* gather here for ceremonies to mark the fiesta of the Holy Cross: never disturb any rituals that are taking place. You can camp at the shore, though you'll have to bring your own supplies.

Zunil

Ten kilometres south of Quetzaltenango is the village of **Zunil**, a vegetable-growing market town hemmed in by steep hills and a sleeping volcano. The main plaza is dominated by a beautiful white colonial church with a richly decorated facade; inside, an intricate silver altar is protected behind bars. The women of Zunil wear vivid purple *huipiles* and carry bright shawls – the plaza is awash with colour during the Monday market. Just below the plaza is a **textile co-operative**, where hundreds of women market these weavings. Zunil is also one of the few remaining places where **Maximón**, the evil saint (see p.154), is still worshipped. The Maya here are reluctant to display their Judas, who also goes by the name Alvarado, but his image is usually paraded through the streets during Holy Week, dressed in Western clothes and smoking a cigar. Virtually any child in town will take you to his current abode for a quetzal.

Buses to Zunil run from Quetzal-tenango's Minerva Bus Terminal every half-hour or so, though some also go from closer to the centre of town, stopping beside the Shell gas station at 10 Calle and 9 Avenida in Zona 1. The last bus back from Zunil leaves at around 6.30pm. Shuttle-bus trips organized by Adrenalina Tours (see p.178) leave Xela for Zunil daily.

Fuentes Georginas

High in the hills, 8km from Zunil, are the **Fuentes Georginas** (Q20), a set of luxuriant hot springs. Surrounded by fresh green ferns, thick moss and lush forest, the baths are sublime, and

to top it all there's a restaurant and a well-stocked bar (with decent wine) beside the main pool. It's easy to spend quite some time here soaking it all in (literally). Rustic stone **bungalows** are available for the night (☎no phone; ❸) complete with bathtub, two double beds, fireplace and barbecue.

Pick-up trucks from the plaza in Zunil are officially set at Q10 for the trip, no matter how many passengers there are – it's an exhilarating journey up a smooth paved road which switchbacks through magnificent volcanic scenery. The return trip is another Q10.

Totonicapán

A one-hour bus journey from Xela will take you to the town of **Totonicapán**, an intensely farmed little region surrounded by rolling hills and pine forests. The valley has always held out against outside influence, and it's still a quiet place, disturbed only by the Tuesday and Saturday **markets**, which fill the two plazas. Recently, it has become one of the highlands' chief centres of commercial weaving. To take a closer look at the work of local artisans, head for the town's visitor centre, the **Casa de la Cultura**, on 8 Av 2–17 (Mon–Sat 9.30am–5pm; ☎7766 1575), which organizes good, but slightly pricey tours (Q250; includes tour of the town, visiting weaving, ceramics and wood-carving centres where you can take classes, and a night's accom-modation); the fees funnel back into the community.

Totonicapán is best done as a day-trip from Xela, from which there are good connections from the Minerva Terminal; **buses** shuttle back and forth every quarter of an hour or so, via the Cuatro Caminos junction.

San Francisco El Alto

The small town of **San Francisco El Alto** overlooks the Quetzaltenango valley from a lovely hillside setting just north of Totonicapán. The view alone is worth a visit, with the great plateau stretching out below and Volcán Santa María on the horizon, but the main reason for a trip here is the **Friday market**, possibly the biggest in Central America and attended by traders from every corner of Guatemala – many arrive the night before, and some start selling by candlelight from as early as 4am. Throughout the morning a steady stream of buses and trucks fill the town to bursting; by noon the market is at its height, buzzing with activity, and things start to thin out in the early afternoon.

The market is separated into a few distinct areas. At the very top of the hill is an open field used as an **animal market**, full of everything from pigs to parrots. Buyers inspect the animals' teeth and tongues, and at times the scene degenerates into a chaotic wrestling match, with livestock and men rolling in the dirt. Below this is the town's plaza, dominated by **textiles**. On the lower level, the streets are filled with produce, pottery, furniture, cheap *comedores* and more. Many of the stalls deal in imported denim, but under the arches and in the covered area opposite the church is usually a nice selection of traditional cloth. For really good views of the market and the surrounding countryside, pay the church caretaker a quetzal and climb up to the church roof.

Buses go from Quetzaltenango to San Francisco, 16km away, leaving every twenty minutes or so from the Minerva terminal; the first is at 6am, and the last bus back leaves at about 5pm (45min).

Momostenango

Twenty-two kilometres from San Francisco is **Momostenango**, a small, isolated town and the centre of wool production in the highlands. The main reason for visiting is to take a walk to the *riscos*, a set of bizarre sandstone pillars, or beyond to the **hot springs** of Pala Chiquito, about 3km away to the north. The town's **Sunday market**, which fills the town's two plazas, is also interesting.

Momostecos travel throughout the country peddling their blankets, scarves and rugs – years of experience have made them experts in the hard sell and given them a sharp eye for tourists. The town is also famous for its unconventional folk-Catholicism, and it has been claimed that there are as many as three hundred Maya **shamans** working here.

Visits are best done as day-trips from Quetzaltenango, or you could also head on to Huehuetenango. **Buses** run from the Minerva terminal in Quetzaltenango, passing through Cuatro Caminos and (most) via San Francisco El Alto (every 30min 6am–5pm; 1hr 45min). Returning, they run from Momostenango between 6am and 4pm. There are additional services on Sundays, for the market.

HUEHUETENANGO

HUEHUETENANGO, capital of the department of the same name, lies at the foot of the Cuchumatanes mountain range. It's not a particularly exciting place, but it does have a real Guatemalan feel to it. The majority of the inhabitants are *ladino*, though there is also a sizeable *indígena* population as well. The attractive square at the centre of the *ladino* half of town is surrounded by shaded walkways and administrative offices, while a few blocks east around 1 Avenida the *indígena* part of town is always alive with activity, its streets packed with people and littered with rotting produce from the nearby market. Few travellers come out here to stay, but if you're coming or going from Mexico you'll probably find yourself in Huehue to change buses; the city also serves as a good starting point to explore the surrounding areas.

What to see and do

If you're in town, Huehue's main attraction is the *indígena* **market**, located in the hub of the Maya part of town,

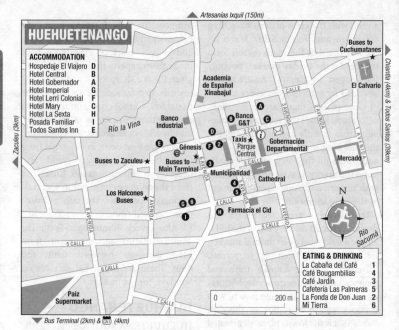

▲ *Artesanías Ixquil (150m)*

HUEHUETENANGO

ACCOMMODATION
Hospedaje El Viajero	D
Hotel Central	B
Hotel Gobernador	A
Hotel Imperial	G
Hotel Lerri Colonial	F
Hotel Mary	C
Hotel La Sexta	H
Posada Familiar	I
Todos Santos Inn	E

◄ *Zaculeu (3km)*

Río la Vina

Academia
de Español
Xinabajul

Banco
Industrial

Banco
G&T

Taxis ★

Génesis

Buses to Zaculeu ★

Buses to
Main Terminal

Los Halcones
Buses ★

Paiz
Supermarket

Parque
Central

Gobernación
Departamental

Municipalidad

Cathedral

Farmacia el Cid

Mercado

Chiantla (4km) & Todos Santos (39km) ►

El Calvario

Buses to
Cuchumatanes ►

Río Sacumá

N

EATING & DRINKING
La Cabaña del Café	1
Café Bougambilias	4
Café Jardín	3
Cafetería Las Palmeras	5
La Fonda de Don Juan	2
Mi Tierra	6

0   200 m

▼ *Bus Terminal (2km) & (CA1) (4km)*

where the streets are daily crowded with traders from the surrounding areas. This is also pretty much the only part of town where you will be able to see traditional dress, as most of the city's inhabitants wear western clothes.

Arrival and information

By bus The bus terminal is halfway between the Carretera Interamericana and town. Minibuses make constant trips between the town centre and the bus terminal at all hours of the day, though the frequency decreases after dark.

Tourist information There is no Inguat tourist office in town, but the Casa de la Cultura, 4 C & 2 Av (☏ 5259 5399), has limited tourist information.

Accommodation

There is not much in terms of good budget accommodation in Huehuetenango, but most places will pass muster for a night or two. Those listed below are all five to ten minutes' walk from the central plaza.

Hotel Central 5 Av 1–33 ☏ 7764 1202. This hotel is slightly worn around the edges, but rooms are

pretty large and there's a fantastic cheap *comedor*. Excellent rates for single travellers. ②

Hotel Gobernador 4 Av 1–45 ☏ 7764 1197. Bare rooms with clean bathrooms (some en suite) set on two inner courtyards. Excellent value given the price. Limited parking space available, so call ahead if you have a car. ②

Hotel Imperial 4 C 6–62 ☏ 5185 0926. Spacious, slightly dark rooms with hard beds, TVs and en-suite baths. ③

Hotel Lerri Colonial 2 C 5–49 ☏ 7764 1526. Dark and dingy rooms, all with cable TV. There is also a good-value *comedor* (lunches Q18). ②

Hotel Mary 2 C 3–52 ☏ 7764 1618. Centrally located hotel with fairly pleasant rooms with private, hot-water showers. ④

Hotel La Sexta 6 Av 1–49 ☏ 7764 6612. Fairly clean rooms, though some need ventilation. The private bathrooms are spick and span, the communal ones less so. ③

Posada Familiar 4 C 6–83 ☏ 7764 1189. The beds here sag dramatically, but both the rooms (28 of them en suite) and the bathrooms are clean and the management friendly. ②

Todos Santos Inn 2 C 6–74 ☏ 7764 1241. A friendly hotel, though the rooms (some with private bath) vary in quality – those upstairs are fairly bright and cheery, those downstairs much less so. The shared bathrooms are clean. Good rates for single travellers. ②

Eating

There are a few good budget options in town – the better restaurants are in the central area around the plaza. There is virtually nothing at all in terms of after-dark entertainment.

Restaurants

La Cabaña del Café 2 C 6–50. Café with an excellent range of coffees (Q6), including cappuccino, and sandwiches (there's even roast beef), plus great cakes.

Café Bougambilias Opposite the Church. Good place to grab some breakfast, all served with "mosh", which is actually a lot nicer than it sounds: hot milk with oats, cinnamon, wheat and sugar.

Café Jardín 3 C & 6 Av. Cheap, friendly place with a good Q22 set lunch, plus snacks and breakfasts.

Cafetería Las Palmeras Opposite the Church. Very clean and pleasant restaurant serving excellent *carne adobada* (Q25) and a number of other tasty Guatemalan dishes. Try the delicious *chuchitos* (similar to tamales, wrapped in maize husk and filled with cornmeal, pork and spices; Q5).

La Fonda de Don Juan 2 C 5–35. Large restaurant with gingham tablecloths. The menu includes good pizzas (Q30), pastas and burgers.

Mi Tierra 4 C 6–46. Great little café/restaurant, set in a covered patio with a welcoming atmosphere. There's plenty of choice on the menu, including *papas fritas* and fajitas, plus chicken and pork dishes. Proper coffee is served and the whole establishment is non-smoking. Also has a good noticeboard.

Directory

Exchange Banrural, 3 C and 6 Av (Mon–Fri 8.30am–7pm, Sat 8.30am–4pm), and G&T Continental on the main square (Mon–Fri 8am–8pm, Sat 8am–1pm), both have MasterCard/Cirrus/Visa/Plus ATMs and change traveller's cheques and US dollars.
Internet Try Génesis, 2 C 6–37 (Q5/hr).
Language school Xinabajul, 6 Av 0–69 (☎7764 1518, ℮academyxinabajul@hotmail.com).
Pharmacy Farmacia El Cid, 4 C & 5 Av (daily 8am–1pm & 2pm–7.30pm).
Post office At 2 C 3–51 (Mon–Fri 8.30am–5.30pm, Sat 9am–1pm).
Telephones The Telgua office (8am–6pm) is in the Centro Comercial el Triángulo, 10 Av & 6 C.

Moving on

By bus There are regular buses to Guatemala City (5hr), La Mesilla (2hr), Xela (2hr) and Todos Santos Cuchumatán (hourly between 11.30am & 4.30pm; 3hr) – get there early to mark your seat and buy a ticket. For Antigua get a Guatemala City bus and change at Chimaltenango. For Sacapulas there are two daily buses (2hr 30min) – check for the latest schedule. Depending on your destination, you may have to take the bus to Cuatro Caminos (any bus going to Guatemala City or Xela will drop you off here; 1hr 30min) and change.

AROUND HUEHUETENANGO

Huehuetenango serves as a good base to explore the nearby ruins of Zaculeu, the setting of one of the most legendary confrontations in the country's history – the Mam fought the Spanish here in a battle that lasted over a month.

Zaculeu

A few kilometres west of Huehuetenango are the ruins of **Zaculeu** (Tues–Sun

---

ZACULEU'S HISTORY

The site of Zaculeu, first occupied in the fifth century, is thought to have been a religious and administrative centre for the Mam, and the home of the elite; the bulk of the population most likely lived in small surrounding settlements or else scattered in the hills.

In 1525 Conquistador Pedro de Alvarado dispatched an army to conquer the area; the approaching Spanish were met by about five thousand Mam warriors, but the Mam leader, Caibal Balam, quickly saw that his troops were no match for the Spanish and withdrew them to the safety of Zaculeu, where they were protected on three sides by deep ravines and on the other by a series of walls and ditches. The Spanish army settled outside the city and besieged the citadel for six weeks until starvation forced Caibal Balam to surrender.

8am–5pm; Q50), once the capital of the **Mam**, who were one of the principal pre-Conquest highland Maya tribes. The site includes several large temples, plazas and a ball-court, all restored pretty unfaithfully by the United Fruit Company in 1946–47: the walls were recoated with white plaster, a technique seldom used for restoring pre-Columbian buildings, as it leaves them lacking the roof-combs, carvings and stucco mouldings that would have adorned the structures. Nonetheless, Zaculeu has a unique atmosphere – surrounded by pines, and with fantastic views of the mountains, its grassy plazas make excellent picnic spots. There's a small **museum** at the site (same hours as the grounds) with examples of some of the unusual burial techniques used and some ceramics found during excavation. To **get to Zaculeu** from Huehuetenango, take one of the **buses** that leave every thirty minutes from close to the school, at 7 Avenida between 2 and 3 calles – make sure it's heading for "Las Ruinas".

AGUACATÁN

It's 22km east from Huehue to **AGUACATÁN**, a small agricultural town strung out along a very long main street, and the only place in the country where the Akateko and Chalchitek languages are spoken. It is best done as a day-trip, preferably in time to see Aguacatán's huge Sunday **market**, which actually gets under way on Saturday afternoon, when traders arrive early to claim the best sites. On Sunday mornings, a steady stream of people pour into town, cramming into the market and plaza, and soon spilling out into the surrounding area. Around noon the tide turns as the crowds start to drift back to their villages, with donkeys leading their drunken drivers.

Aguacatán's other attraction is the source of the **Río San Juan**, which emerges fresh and cool from beneath a nearby hill, making a good place for a chilly dip. To get there, walk east along the main street out of the village for about a kilometre, until you see the sign. From the centre it takes about twenty minutes.

There are ten daily **buses** that run from Huehuetenango to Aguacatán between 6am and about 4pm (1hr). Beyond Aguacatán the road runs out along a ridge, with fantastic views stretching out below, eventually dropping down to the riverside town of **Sacapulas** an hour and a half away (see p.174); at present

THE CUCHUMATANES

The largest non-volcanic peaks in Central America, the Sierra de los Cuchumatanes rise from a limestone plateau close to the Mexican border, reaching their full height of over 3800m above Huehuetenango. This is magnificent mountain scenery, ranging from wild, exposed craggy outcrops to lush, tranquil river valleys. While the upper slopes are almost barren, scattered with boulders and shrivelled cypress trees, the lower levels are fertile, planted with corn, coffee and sugar. In the valleys are hundreds of tiny villages, simply isolated by the landscape. These communities are still some of the most traditional in Guatemala, and a visit, either for a market or fiesta, offers one of the best opportunities to see Maya life.

The most accessible of the villages in the vicinity, and the only one yet to receive a steady trickle of tourists, is Todos Santos Cuchumatán. Mountain trails from Todos Santos lead to other villages, including the equally anachronistic pueblo of San Juan Atitán.

Be wary of taking pictures of people in this region, particularly children. Rumours persist locally that some foreigners steal babies, and a tragic misunderstanding led to the death of a Japanese tourist here in 2000.

there's only one bus a day heading this way, though there are regular pick-ups.

TODOS SANTOS CUCHUMATÁN

TODOS SANTOS CUCHUMATÁN is many travellers' favourite place in Guatemala. Though the beauty of the alpine surroundings is one attraction, it's the unique culture that is most memorable: the majority of Todosanteros are indigenous Maya who speak Mam as their first language, and you'll see that most houses have a low mud-brick structure outside, called a *chuj*. This is similar to a sauna, with a wood fire lit under the rocks, and is used for family members to bathe. On the streets, Todosanteros still play a xylophone-like wooden marimba. But most striking of all is the local dress: the men wear straw hats, red-and-white striped trousers and pinstripe shirts decorated with pink and blue collars, while the women wear dark blue *cortes* and intricate purple *huipiles*. To really get immersed in Todosantero culture, try and make your stay coincide with the Día de Todos Santos (see box above).

What to see and do

The village itself is pretty – a modest main street with a few shops, a plaza and a church – but is totally overshadowed by the looming presence of the Cuchumatanes mountains. Though most of the fun of Todos Santos is in simply hanging out, it would be a shame not to indulge in a traditional **smoke sauna** while here. Most of the guesthouses will prepare one for you. If you want to take a shirt, pair of trousers or *huipil* home with you, you'll find an excellent co-op selling quality weavings next to the *Casa Familiar*. The **Museo Balam** (Q5), on the left after the Hispanomaya language school, is definitely worth a visit, with such eclectic local objects as old pottery and statues, a sheep's head, a deer's legs, old traditional hats made of beeswax, a drum and a hundred-year-old marimba.

Above the village – follow the track that goes up behind the *Comedor Katy* – is the small Maya site of **Qman Txun**, where you'll find a couple of mounds sprouting pine trees. The site is occasionally used by *costumbristas* for the ritual sacrifice of animals.

Arrival and information

By bus After a number of hair-raising bends through steep hills and dramatic spectacular mountain scenery dotted with corn and potato crops, buses will drop you off in town. Some carry on through the village, heading further down the valley to Jacaltenango.

Tourist information The Hispanomaya Spanish School (☏ 5163 9293, ⊛ www.hispanomaya.org) is a good source of tourist information. They have a book exchange here and can also organize guided walks. To get here walk from the main square, with the church on your left, and take the first left by the yellow house where there is also a sign for the Museo Balam. Román at *Casa*

Familiar can also take you on hikes to San Juan Atitlán and the surrounding areas.

Accommodation

Plenty of families rent out rooms very cheaply – ask at the Hispanomaya Spanish school. All hotels listed below are clustered close together just above the plaza past *Comedor Katy*. Note that *Hospedaje Casa Familiar* was being entirely rebuilt at the time of research.

Hotelito Todos Santos ☎7783 0603 or 5787 5907. Clean, functional tiled-floor rooms (some with bathroom), nice views from the top rooms and a restaurant (lunch Q20). ❸

Hotel Mam ☎5523 4148. Clean rooms with warmish showers. ❷

Hospedaje El Viajero ☎no phone. Fairly springy beds and a room that sleeps five. ❷

Eating

You'll find a number of *comedores* serving good local food scattered around town.

Comedor Katy One block from the square. There is always something bubbling on the hearth at this simple *comedor* with excellent food.

Hotelito Todos Santos A cheap restaurant (lunch Q20) with good local food.

Directory

Exchange On the square, Banrural (Mon–Fri 8.30am–5pm & Sat 7–11am) changes traveller's cheques and US dollars. Note that there are no ATM machines in town so make sure you have enough cash with you when you arrive.

Internet You can surf the net at Hispanomaya Spanish School (Q5/hr).

Language school Hispanomaya Spanish School (☎5163 9293, ⊛www.hispanomaya.org), by the Museo Balam.

Post office On the plaza there's a post office (Mon–Fri 8am–6pm, Sat 8am–noon).

Moving on

By bus Buses pass through Todos Santos on the way to Huehuetenango from Jacaltenango; ask around for the latest schedule.

AROUND TODOS SANTOS

It would be a real shame to miss out on one of the many hikes that can be done around Todos Santos – make sure you spend some time exploring the surrounding areas, home to some of the country's most breathtaking and dramatic scenery.

San Juan Atitán

The village of **San Juan Atitán** is around five hours on foot from Todos Santos across a beautiful isolated valley. It is strongly recommended you go with a guide: Hispanomaya Spanish School in Todos Santos organizes hikes, or you can look for Román at *Casa Familiar*. Follow the path that bears up behind the *Comedor Katy*, past the ruins and high above the village through endless muddy switchbacks until you get to the ridge overlooking the valley where, if the skies are clear, you'll be rewarded by an awesome view of the Tajumulco and Tacaná volcanoes. Take the easy-to-follow central track downhill from here past some ancient cloudforest to San Juan Atitán. There are two *hospedajes* (both ❶) if you want to stay, and morning **pick-ups** return to Huehue from 6am (1hr). Market days are Mondays and Thursdays.

Alternatively, you can continue west along the valley from Todos Santos to

---

INTO MEXICO: LA MESILLA

From Huehuetenango the Carretera Interamericana runs for 79km to the Mexican border at La Mesilla. There are buses every thirty minutes between 5am and 6pm (2hr). The two sets of customs and *migración* are 3km apart, connected by shared (*colectivo*) taxis. At Ciudad Cuauhtémoc on the Mexican side you can pick up buses to Comitán (1hr 15min) and even direct to San Cristóbal de Las Casas (2hr 30min). Heading into Guatemala, the last bus leaves La Mesilla for Huehuetenango at around 5.30pm.

San Martín and on to **Jacaltenango**, a route which also offers superb views. There's a basic *hospedaje* (❶) in Jacaltenango, so you could stay the night and then catch a bus back to Huehuetenango in the morning. Some buses from Huehue also continue down this route.

The Pacific coast

The **Pacific coast**, a strip of two hundred and fifty kilometres of black volcanic beaches, is known by Guatemalans as La Costa Sur. Once as rich in wildlife as the jungles of Petén, in recent years it's been ravaged by development, and is now the country's most intensely farmed region, with coffee grown on the volcanic slopes and entire villages effectively owned by vast cotton- and sugarcane-growing *fincas* (ranches or plantations). A few protected areas try to preserve some of the area's natural heritage; the **Monterrico Reserve** is the most accessible of these, a swampy refuge for sea turtles, iguanas, crocodiles and an abundance of birdlife. It also harbours a village with a long stretch of relatively clean sand. Compared to some other Central American beaches this one is nothing to get too excited about, but it remains the most popular destination on the coast, attracting swarms of people from Antigua and Guatemala City on the weekends.

You can glimpse the impressive art of the Pipil around the town of **Santa Lucía Cotzumalguapa**, and the Maya site of **Takalik Abaj** is worth a detour on your way to or from Mexico, or as a day-trip from Quetzaltenango. Otherwise, the region's pre-Columbian history isn't as visible as that in other parts of the country.

The main route along the coast is the **Carretera al Pacífico**, which runs from the Mexican border at Tecún Umán into El Salvador at Ciudad Pedro de Alvarado. It's the country's swiftest highway and you'll never have to wait long for a bus. Venture off this road, however, and things slow down considerably.

RETALHULEU

RETALHULEU, usually referred to as **Reu** (pronounced "Ray-oo"), may be one of the largest towns in the area, but that doesn't mean it's exciting. There is nothing much to do in the town itself – the main reason to visit is to see the ruins of Takalik Abaj, about 15km west (see p.192). However, it is something of a transportation hub, with virtually all **buses** running along the coastal highway stopping at the Retalhuleu terminal on 7 Avenida and 10 Calle, a ten-minute walk from the plaza. If

---

INTO MEXICO: EL CARMEN AND TECÚN UMÁN

There are two border crossings with Mexico in the coastal region. The northernmost is the Talismán Bridge (open 6am–9pm), also referred to as El Carmen. On the Mexican side, a constant stream of minibuses and buses leaves for Tapachula (30min). Coming from Mexico, there are regular buses to Guatemala City until about 7pm; if heading towards Quetzaltenango or the western highlands, take the first minibus to Malacatán and change there.

Further south and leading directly onto the Carretera al Pacífico, the Tecún Umán–Ciudad Hidalgo crossing (open 24hr) is favoured by most Guatemalan and virtually all commercial traffic. If you're Mexico-bound, there are very frequent bus services to Tapachula (40min) over the border. There's also a steady flow of buses to Guatemala City along the Carretera al Pacífico via Retalhuleu.

you find yourself waiting for a bus, the **Museo de Arqueología y Etnología**, in the plaza (Tues–Sat 8.30am–1pm & 2–5.30pm, Sun 9am–12.30pm; Q10), is home to an amazing collection of anthropomorphic figurines, mostly heads, and some photographs of the town dating back to the 1880s.

Also in the plaza are the **post office** (Mon–Fri 8.30am–5.30pm, Sat 9am–1pm) and a number of **banks**, including a Banco Agromercantíl with a MasterCard/Cirrus ATM and a Banco Industrial with a Visa/Plus ATM. Affordable **accommodation** is unfortunately in short supply; your best bet is the *Hospedaje San Francisco*, 6 C 8–30 (℡7771 0649; ❷), where the rooms are small but fairly clean and some have private bath. When it comes to **eating**, try the *Cafetería la Luna* on the plaza for good breakfasts (Q18) and lunches (Q24).

From Reu there are **buses** to Guatemala City, the Mexican border and Quetzaltenango about every thirty minutes, plus regular buses to Champerico and El Tulate until about 6.30pm.

TAKALIK ABAJ

TAKALIK ABAJ (daily 7am–5pm; Q50) – whose name was changed from "Abaj Takalik" to offer a better translation of its K'iche' name, meaning "standing stones" – is among the most important Mesoamerican sites of the country and one of the few that has both Olmec and Maya features. Though the remains of two large **temple platforms** have been cleared, it's the sculptures and stelae found carved around their base, including rare and unusual representations of frogs and toads (monument 68) and an alligator (monument 66), that make a trip here worthwhile. Among the finest carvings is stele 5, which features two standing figures separated by a hieroglyphic panel that has been dated to 126 AD. Look out for giant Olmec-style heads too, including one

with great chipmunk cheeks. In July 2002, archeologists unearthed a royal tomb, complete with jade necklace and mask belt, below the observatory structure 7A, confirming that following the Olmec, the site was later occupied by the Maya; Maya rituals occasionally still take place today. You will be able to get water at the entrance, and there is also a little restaurant.

To **get to Takalik Abaj**, take a local bus from Reu 15km west to the village of El Asintal, from where you can take a pick-up to the site 4km away.

CHAMPERICO

A fast highway runs the forty-odd kilometres south from Reu to the beach at **CHAMPERICO**, which, though it doesn't feel like it, is the country's third port, and best visited as a day-trip. The town enjoyed a brief period of prosperity many decades ago when it was connected to Quetzaltenango by rail, though there's little sign of this now apart from a rusting pier. The dark sand

TREAT YOURSELF

For a few days in an unspoilt natural habitat head to Reserva Los Tarrales (℡5136 3410 or 5919 8882, ⓦwww.tarrales .com) in Paulul Suchitepéquez, on the road between Cocales and San Lucas Tolimán. During the day you can birdwatch and do some spectacular hikes in the surrounding area, including the trek up Volcán Atitlán, as well as visit the *finca*'s own coffee museum. You are welcome to camp (❷) by the beautiful lagoon on the grounds or stay in one of the pleasantly decorated rooms (❹), all of which are built with natural materials. Meals (not included in rates) are all home-made and served in the finca's beautiful dining area.

To get here, catch a bus from Retalhuleu to Cocales and from there to San Lucas Tolimán – ask the driver to drop you off at the finca.

beach is impressive for its scale (though watch out for the dangerous undertow), but perhaps the best reason for visiting is the widely available and delicious fried seafood **meals**; for a treat, feast on paella (Q40) at the *Hotel Miramar*. Don't wander too far from the busiest part of the beach – muggings have occurred in isolated spots here. **Buses** run between Champerico and Quetzaltenango every hour or so, and there are services every 30 minutes from Retalhuleu. The last bus for Retalhuleu leaves Champerico at 7pm.

SANTA LUCÍA COTZUMALGUAPA

SANTA LUCÍA COTZUMALGUAPA, a rather nondescript coastal town, functions as a good base to explore three mysterious Pipil **archeological sites** that are scattered around the surrounding cane fields. Bear in mind, though, that getting to them all isn't easy unless you have your own transport or hire a taxi. If you're on a tight budget, the *Hospedaje Reforma* (❷), 4 Av 4–71, by the main square, has small, institutional rooms and unattractive bathrooms – only stay if you must. The most decent place nearest the plaza is *Hotel Internacional* (☎7882 5504; ❹), just south of the main highway, which has clean rooms with fans. For **food**, the *Comedor Miramar* by the *Pollo Campero* on 3 Avenida does reasonable Chinese meals (Q26), and *Taquería Palankiny*, one block north of the plaza on 4 Calle, has excellent tacos (Q6). **Banks** will change your traveller's cheques: Banco Industrial on 3 Avenida has a Visa/Plus ATM. Pullman **buses** passing along the highway will drop you at the entrance road to town, ten minutes' walk from the centre, while second-class buses go straight into the terminal, a few blocks from the plaza. Buses to the capital leave the terminal every thirty minutes until 4pm, or you can catch a bus from the highway.

AROUND SANTA LUCÍA COTZUMALGUAPA

Three **archeological sites** around Santa Lucía are all that remains of the Pipil civilization, an indigenous non-Maya culture with close links to the Nahuatl tribes of Central Mexico. To this day, it is unclear as to how these people, now known for their intricate stone carvings, came to live in this area (possibly as early as 400 AD), as it was largely inhabited by the Maya. It is possible, although not advisable, to visit the sites on foot passing through cane fields – beware that this can be dangerous, as muggers hide in the fields when the sugar cane is high (Nov–April). It is much safer to hire a taxi in the plaza in Santa Lucía – to visit all three sites in one day reckon on Q100.

Bilbao

Unearthed in 1860, the site of **Bilbao** has four sets of stones visible in situ, two of which perfectly illustrate the magnificent precision of the Pipil carving techniques, beautifully preserved in slabs of black volcanic rock hidden in sugar cane. To **get to** the site, walk uphill from the plaza, along 4 Avenida, until you reach the Convento Las Hermanas where you bear left, following a dirt track along the side of a cane field. About 200m further on is a fairly wide path leading left into the cane for about 20m. This brings you to two large stones carved with bird-like patterns, with strange circular glyphs arranged in groups of three: the majority of the glyphs are recognizable as the names for days once used by the people of southern Mexico. In the same cane field, further along the same path, is another badly eroded stone, and a final set with a superbly preserved set of figures and interwoven motifs. If you get lost at any stage, ask for "las piedras", as they tend to be known locally.

Finca El Baúl

The second site, in the grounds of the **Finca El Baúl**, is about 5km further afield and reached by following 3 Avenida north out of town. The hilltop site has two stones, one a massive half-buried stone head with wrinkled brow and patterned headdress. In front of the stones is a set of small altars on which local people make animal sacrifices, burn incense and leave offerings of flowers, usually around midday. The next stones of interest are at the **finca** itself, in the **Museo El Baúl** (admission free), a few kilometres further away from town, where the carvings include some superb heads, stone skulls, a massive jaguar, the emblem of Santa Lucía and an extremely well-preserved stele of two boxers (monument 27) dating from the Late Classic period. Alongside all this antiquity is the finca's old steam engine, a miniature machine that used to haul the cane along a system of private tracks.

To **get here**, catch one of the regular buses (every 30min) to Colonia Maya from either the bus terminal or the park in Santa Lucía.

Finca Las Ilusiones

The third site is on the other side of town, at **Finca Las Ilusiones**. Here another collection of artefacts and some stone carvings has been assembled in the **Museo Cultura Cotzumalguapa** (Mon–Fri 7am–4pm, Sat 7am–noon; Q10). Two of the most striking figures within are the pot-bellied statue (monument 58), probably from the middle Pre-classic era, and a copy of monument 21, which bears three figures, the central one depicting a ball player. There are several other original items, including a fantastic stele, plus some more replicas and thousands of small stone carvings and pottery fragments. To **get here**, walk out of town east along the highway for about 1km, and follow the signs on the left.

LA DEMOCRACIA

The next town east along the highway is Siquinalá, a run-down place from where

another branch road heads to the coast. Nine kilometres south along this road is **LA DEMOCRACIA**, worth visiting for its multiple collections of archeological relics taken from the site of **Monte Alto** to the east of town. Some of these are now displayed around the town plaza under a huge ceiba tree. Called "fat boys", these are massive stone heads with simple, almost childlike faces, carved in Olmec style and thought to date from the mid-Preclassic period, possibly from as far back as 500 BC. Some are attached to smaller rounded bodies and rolled over on their backs clutching their swollen stomachs like stricken Teletubbies. Also on the plaza, the town **museum** (Tues–Sat 9am–4pm; Q30) houses carvings, a wonderful jade mask, yokes worn by ball-game players, pottery, grinding stones and a few more carved heads.

There are regular **buses** here from both Santa Lucía and Escuintla. Buses leave from the plaza every thirty minutes heading to the capital, Escuintla and Santa Lucía.

ESCUINTLA

Sitting at the junction of the two main coastal roads from the capital, **ESCUINTLA** is the largest of the Pacific towns. Unfortunately, it's also the most dangerous, and the only reason you should find yourself in town is to change buses. It's not recommended, but if you do decide to hang around for a bit, you will get a sense of life on the coast – its heat, pace and energy, and the frenetic industrial and agricultural commerce that drives it. If you happen to miss your bus connection, your safest bet is probably the *Hotel Costa Sur*, 12 C 4–13 (☏5295 9528; ❹).

Buses to Guatemala City leave from 8 Calle and 2 Avenida. For other destinations, there are two terminals: for places en route to the Mexican border, buses run through the north of town and stop by the Esso station opposite the Banco

Uno (take a local bus up 3 Av); buses for the coast road and inland route to El Salvador are best caught at the main terminal on the south side of town, at the bottom of 4 Avenida (local bus down 4 Av). Buses leave every thirty minutes for the eastern border and hourly for Antigua.

MONTERRICO

MONTERRICO, further east and on the water, enjoys one of the finest settings on the Pacific coast. The scenery here is reduced to its basic elements: a strip of dead-straight sand, a line of powerful surf and an enormous curving horizon. The village is scruffy but friendly and relaxed, separated from the mainland by the waters of the Chiquimulilla canal, which weaves through a fantastic network of

mangrove swamps. Mosquitoes can be a problem during the wet season, but Monterrico is still certainly the best place on the coast to spend time by the sea, though take care in the waves as there's a vicious undertow.

What to see and do

Monterrico's long stretch of **beach** is perfect to kick back with a book and watch one of the many beautiful sunsets that tinge the sky pink.

Biotopo Monterrico-Hawaii nature reserve

Natural beauty aside, Monterrico's other attraction is the **Biotopo Monterrico-Hawaii nature reserve**, which embraces the village, the beach – an important **turtle** nesting ground – and

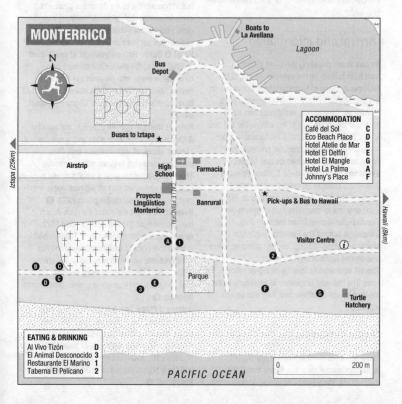

a large slice of the mangrove swamps behind. The reserve is actually home to four distinct types of mangrove, which act as a kind of marine nursery, offering small fish protection from their natural predators, while above the surface live hundreds of species of bird and a handful of mammals, including racoons and armadillos, plus iguanas, caimans and alligators. The best way to explore the reserve is in a small *cayuco* (kayak); these are best organized in a hotel. The reserve's **visitors' centre** (daily 8am–noon & 2–5pm; Q8), just off the beach between *Hotel Mangle* and the *Pez d'Oro*, has plenty of information about the environment (Spanish only) and an interesting **museum** featuring a number of marine species. The centre also acts as an important sea turtle hatchery; while caimans, iguanas and freshwater turtles are also bred here for release into the wild.

Arrival and information

By bus Buses run along the 17km of paved road from Taxisco, on the coastal highway, to La Avellana, a couple of kilometres from Monterrico on the opposite side of the mangrove swamp; boats (20min) shuttle passengers (Q5) and cars (Q75) back and forth from here to the village. The last bus leaves Taxisco at 6pm and La Avellana at 4.30pm – you'll find the latest schedules posted in the Proyecto Lingüístico Monterrico (see below).

Exchange Banrural (Mon–Fri 8.30am–5pm, Sat 9am–1pm) changes US dollars and traveller's cheques. The bank itself does not have an ATM – the only one in town (Visa/Plus only) is in the Tienda Super Monterrico on the main drag.

Language school The Proyecto Lingüístico Monterrico (☎5475 1265), on the main drag, offers one-on-one Spanish instruction.

Tourist information There is no inguat office in town. The Proyecto Lingüístico Monterrico is by far the best source of information; they also provide maps.

Accommodation

There is not too much in terms of real budget accommodation – there is only one hostel with dorm rooms. Many places increase prices by about 20 percent at weekends, when it's also best to book ahead. All places listed below are right on or just off the beach. Avoid the *Hotel Baule Beach*, as regular thefts have been reported.

Café del Sol Turn right at the beach, and walk for 250m ☎5810 0821, ⓦwww.cafe-del-sol.com. Friendly Swiss–Guatemalan-owned place with a variety of accommodation – some rooms are beachside, others not, and there is one "mirador" room with sea views as well as rooms for six and eight people – all with private bathroom. Tasty food and a small pool. ⑤

Eco Beach Place Turn right at the beach, and walk for 250m ☎5611 6637, ⓔecobeachplace @hotmail.com. Next to *Café del Sol*, this attractive but fairly pricey guesthouse has large, comfortable rooms (some sleep up to four), all with private bath. There's good food, a nice lounge/bar area, a small pool and stunning Pacific vistas from the veranda. Rates include breakfast. ⑦

🏃 **Hotel Atelie del Mar** On the road behind the beach, turning right at the sea front ☎5752 5528, ⓦwww.hotelateliedelmar.com. Multilingual owners Stig and Violeta will make you feel at home in the nicely decorated clean and colourful rooms, each of which overlooks a good-sized pool. Violeta's little art studio is in the attic; you can buy her fun paintings on silk. ⑤

Hotel El Delfin Fifty metres right at beach front ☎5702 6701, ⓔhoteldelfin@intelnett.com. Good-value place with pleasant but very small rooms. These can get stuffy in hot weather, but all have a fan and mosquito nets. Cheap restaurant, too. ③

Hotel El Mangle Turn left at beach, and walk for 300m ☎5514 6517. Nice place with a selection of small rooms, all with mosquito nets, fans, bathrooms and little terraces with hammocks. There's also a garden area, a small pool and a beachside restaurant that serves reasonable wood-oven pizzas at unreasonable prices (Q80). ④

Hotel La Palma At the end of the dock–beach road, on the right ☎5817 3911 or 7848 1622, ⓦwww.lapalmahotelmonterrico.it. The only B&B in town, this place is spotless all round and has a chill-out attic area with hammocks. The chatty Italian owners can rustle up some excellent Italian food and make you a proper espresso. Some rooms have a/c. ⑤

Johnny's Place Turn left at beach, and walk for 150m ☎5812 0409. Popular destination with single-sex dorms plus good-sized bungalows sleeping four. There are plenty of small bathing pools, a café/restaurant with ocean views and fairly priced tacos and pasta. Dorms ①, bungalows ⑦

INTO EL SALVADOR: CIUDAD PEDRO DE ALVARADO

Very regular buses run from Taxisco along the coastal highway to the border with El Salvador at Ciudad Pedro de Alvarado, just over an hour away, until 5pm. The border is a fairly quiet one, as most traffic uses the Valle Nuevo post to the north, but there are a few basic *hospedajes* and *comedores* on both sides of the border if you get stuck.

Eating and drinking

There are quite a few places to eat out in town, the cheapest being the *comedores* on the main drag.

Restaurants and bars

Al Vivo Tizón In the same premises as the *Eco Beach Place Hotel*. Steak and seafood restaurant right on the beach serving beef tenderloin (Q80), grilled fish (Q75) and burgers (Q35).

El Animal Desconocido By far the most lively bar (especially on weekends), this place blares an eclectic selection of rock and dance music and serves mean cocktails.

Restaurante El Marino Opposite *Hotel La Palma*. Cheap, colourful and clean restaurant on the main street. The good menu includes fried fish (Q50), seafood soup (Q60) and breakfasts (Q20).

Taberna El Pelícano Turn left at beach, and walk for 150m to behind *Johnny's Place*. Some of the best food in town, including pasta dishes (Q30) and *ragout de pescado* (Q65), is served at this Swiss-owned restaurant.

Moving on

By bus Several direct buses run between Taxisco and the Zona 4 bus terminal in Guatemala City (3hr). If you're travelling between Antigua and Monterrico there are several daily shuttle-bus services (US$10–15 each way) to La Avellena; tickets are bookable at any travel agency and most hotels.

The eastern highlands

The **eastern highlands**, southeast of the capital, are probably the least-visited part of Guatemala. The landscape lacks the appeal of its western counterpart – the peaks are lower and the volcanoes lie higgledy-piggledy – and the towns, whose residents are almost entirely Latinized, are nearly universely pretty dry and featureless. You're unlikely to want to hang around for long. **Esquipulas** is worth a visit, though, for its colossal church, home to the Cristo Negro Milagroso (Miraculous Black Christ) and the most important pilgrimage site in Central America. It's also positioned very close to the border with Honduras and El Salvador. However, if you're heading into Honduras, you're most likely to end up spending the night in **Chiquimula**, the gateway to the ruins of Copán, just over the border. Finally there's the idyllic crater lake on top of the **Volcán de Ipala** – its isolation adds to its appeal.

CHIQUIMULA

The town of **CHIQUIMULA**, sitting to one side of the San José river valley, is an unattractive, bustling *ladino* stronghold. Most travellers who come here are on their way to or from the Maya ruins of Copán, just over the border in Honduras (see p.361) – if you've just arrived, things only get better from here. Although the city centre itself is nothing to boast about, the little **Parque Calvario** square, a couple of blocks south of the main plaza, is a pleasant spot with a number of lovely cafés and restaurants; the square gives a good feel of what local life is like, especially in the evenings when the young come here to eat and drink and couples stroll around hand-in-hand.

Arrival and information

By bus The bus terminal is on 1 C between 10 & 11 Av, Zona 1.

Exchange There is a branch of the Banco G&T Continental at 7 Av 4–75 (Mon–Fri 9am–7pm, Sat 10am–1pm) that changes US dollars.

Internet Try Email Center at 6 Av 4–51 (daily 9am–9pm).

Telephones The Telgua office (daily 8am–6pm) is on the corner of the plaza.

Accommodation

Hotel Hernández 3 C 7–41 ☎7942 0708. An excellent selection with clean, simple rooms, all with fan and some with a/c and private bathrooms. ❸

Hotel Central 3 C 8–30 ☎7942 0118. Five pleasant rooms all with private bath and cable TV. ❹

Eating and drinking

When it comes to eating, the nicest places are on Parque Calvario, a trendy hangout among the young. All places listed below are around the square. There are inexpensive *comedores* in and around the market, centred on 3 C and 8 Av.

Jalisco on Parque Calvario square. Pleasant little café with a couple of tables set outside; try the exquisite burritos (Q20 as you sip on a great *licuado*.

Io Kaffé Crêpes (Q15) and paninis (Q25) are served in this little café with stylish leather sofas.

Peccato Café One of the most popular places in town to have a cocktail, with a selection of pastas (Q30) and a good *plato típico* (Q45). Closed Sun & Mon.

Moving on

By bus to: Guatemala City (every 30min 4am–5pm; 3hr 15min), Esquipulas (every 15min 5am–7pm; 1hr), Jalapa, via Ipala (7 daily 6am–4pm; 2hr 30min) and Puerto Barrios (hourly; 3hr).

INTO HONDURAS: EL FLORIDO

Buses leave Chiquimula's bus station frequently for the **El Florido**, and the **Honduran border** (every 30min 4.30am–5.30pm; 1hr 20min). Regular buses (every 30min 6.30am–6pm) then leave the border for Copán.

VOLCÁN DE IPALA

Reached down a side road off the main highway between Chiquimula and Esquipulas, the **VOLCÁN DE IPALA** (1650m) may at first seem a little disappointing – it looks more like a hill than a grand volcano. However, the cone is filled by a beautiful little **crater lake** ringed by dense tropical forest – you can walk round the entire lake in a couple of hours. The easiest route to the top is via a trail from the village of **El Chagüitón**; it's a 2km climb to the visitors' centre where you pay a Q15 entrance fee. It's well worth heading here if you're looking for some peace; chances are that if you visit on a weekday it should be pretty quiet.

The village of **Ipala** is connected by bus with Jutiapa to the south, Jalapa in the west and Chiquimula to the north. It's a pretty forlorn place with a few shops and few **places to stay**, the best of which is the *Hospedaje Pinal* (❷), which has good clean rooms with private bathroom. Buses and pick-ups run from Ipala towards the village of Agua Blanca hourly; get off at **El Sauce** at km 26.5, from where it's an hour and a half to the summit via El Chagüitón.

ESQUIPULAS

ESQUIPULAS is home to the most important Catholic shrine in Central America. For the past four hundred years pilgrims from all over Central America have flocked here to pay their respects to the **Cristo Negro Milagroso** (Miraculous Black Christ), whose image is found in the town's magnificent Basilica. The principal day of **pilgrimage** is January 15; if you're in town at this time make sure you book accommodation in advance. The rest of the town is a messy sprawl of cheap hotels, souvenir stalls and restaurants which have sprung up to serve the pilgrims.

THE BLACK CHRIST OF ESQUIPULAS

In 1595, following the indigenous population's conversion to Christianity, the town of Esquipulas commissioned famed colonial sculptor Quirio Cataño to carve an image of Christ. Sculpted in a dark wood, the image acquired the name Cristo Negro (Black Christ). Rumours of its miraculous capacities soon spread – according to the religious authorities, the first miracle took place in 1603, but it wasn't until 1737, when the archbishop Pardo de Figueroa was cured of an illness, that its healing properties were recognized. It has ever since been the object of the most important religious pilgrimage in Central America.

What to see and do

The **Black Christ** is the focus of the town, and is approached through the church's side entrance, past a little area full of candles which are lit upon exiting the building. The devout reverently stand in line, slowly making their way towards the image. The walls are plastered with anything and everything – golden plaques with engraved messages to Christ, passport-sized photos that the pious slip into large picture frames, interweaved gold and silver necklaces that viewed from a distance form the image of Christ. Pilgrims mutter prayers as they approach the image: some kneel, while others briefly pause in front of it, before getting moved on by the crowds behind. As they leave, they do so walking backwards so as to show their respects to Christ by not turning their back on Him.

Arrival and information

By bus Buses from Guatemala City will drop you off at the Rutas Orientales bus station on 11 C & 1 Av, just outside the town centre.

Exchange Banco Industrial has a branch with Visa ATM at 9 C & 3 Av, and there's also a Banco G&T Continental with a MasterCard ATM almost opposite.

Accommodation

Most budget options are clustered together in the streets off the main road, 11 Calle. Avoid staying on Saturday nights, when rooms cost double.

INTO EL SALVADOR: ANGUIATÚ, SAN CRISTÓBAL FRONTERA AND VALLE NUEVO

There are three border crossings with El Salvador in the region of Esquipulas.

Anguiatú

Buses go to the Anguiatú crossing from Chiquimula (every 30min 6am–6pm; 2hr) and Esquipulas (with Transportes Carlita, from 6 Av & 11 C, Zona 1; every 45min 6am–6pm; 1hr 30min). Note that if taking the bus from Esquipulas between 6am and 8am you will have to catch it one block up on Boulevard Quirio Cataño. From the Anguiatú border, buses go to Metapán (every 30min 6am–6pm; 20min), where you can get a connection to San Salvador and Santa Ana (buses leave for Santa Ana approximately every 45min, but only when full).

San Cristóbal Frontera

Buses connect El Progreso and Jutiapa with the San Cristóbal border crossing (1hr 30min), from where you can get a bus to Santa Ana (3hr). Regular buses travel between Guatemala City and El Progreso.

Valle Nuevo

Regular buses leave the bus station in Guatemala City, Zona 4, for Valle Nuevo, the name of the border crossing for Las Chinamas in El Salvador (every hour or so; 2hr 30min).

Hotel Villa Edelmira 3 Av 8–58 ☎ 7943 1431. Pleasant, family-run hotel with excellent rates for single travellers. ❸

Hospedaje San Antonio 2 Av 8–70 ☎ 5345 1191. The bathrooms aren't as tidy as you might like and the rooms are so bare they would give Sparta a bad name, but it is one of the cheapest options in town. ❸

La Favorita 2 Av 10–15 ☎ 7943 1175. Small but clean rooms, some en suite, 2min walk from the church. ❸

Eating and drinking

Many of the cheaper restaurants and *comedores* are on 11 Calle and the surrounding streets.

Pollo Campero On 11 C. For some cheap eats, head to this branch of Guatemala's most popular fast-food chain.

Restaurante La Frontera Opposite the park. Clean, fairly large place with a good range of fish and meat dishes.

Moving on

By bus There are regular minibuses to the borders with El Salvador (every 30min 6am–4pm; 1hr) and Honduras at Agua Caliente (every 30min 6am–5.30pm; 30min). Rutas Orientales (11 C & 1 Av) runs a half-hourly bus service between Esquipulas and Guatemala City (4hr). If you want to get to the ruins of Copán, you'll need to catch a bus to Chiquimula (every 15min or so; 45min) from the east side of 11 C, and change there for the El Florído border post (see p.198).

East to the Caribbean

Coming from Guatemala City, the Caribbean Highway passes through the upper Río Motagua valley before reaching the Río Hondo junction. Here the road divides, with one arm going south to Esquipulas and on to the border with Honduras and El Salvador and the main stretch heading towards the Caribbean. As you approach the coast, the landscape dramatically changes from dry, infertile terrain to lush, green vegetation. Although **Puerto Barrios** is nothing more than a port town, the relaxed town of **Lívingston**, home to the black Garífuna people, is a unique blend of Black Caribbean and Guatemalan cultures – you'd hardly think you were in Guatemala at all.

QUIRIGUÁ

Sitting in an isolated pocket of rainforest, surrounded by a forest of banana trees, the ruins of **QUIRIGUÁ** are home to some of the finest Maya carvings anywhere. Only Copán, across the border in Honduras (see p.361), offers any competition to the site's magnificent stelae, altars and so-called "zoomorphs", covered in well-preserved and superbly intricate glyphs and portraits.

What to see and do

Entering the site (daily 8am–4.30pm; Q80), you emerge at the northern end of the **Great Plaza**. By the ticket office is the **Museum of Quiriguá** (daily 7am–4pm; free), which explains the town's history (see box opposite) and discovery. The site is notorious for the **stelae** scattered across the Large Plaza, seven (A, C, D, E, F, H and J) of which were built during the reign of Cauac Sky and depict his image. The nine stelae are the tallest in the Mayan world - the largest of all is Stele E, elevated 8m above ground and weighing 65 tons. Note the vast headdresses, which dwarf the faces, as well as the beards, an uncommon feature in Maya life. As you make your way towards the **acrópolis**, you will be able to make out the remains of a **ball-court** on your right, before reaching six blocks of stone carved with images representing animal and human figures: the **zoomorphs**. Have a look at the turtle, frog and jaguar.

The **ruins** are some 70km beyond the junction at Río Hondo, and 4km down a turn-off from the main road. All **buses**

THE HISTORY OF QUIRIGUÁ

Quiriguá's early history is still relatively unknown, but during the Late Pre-classic period (250 BC–300 AD) migrants from the north established themselves as rulers here. In the Early Classic period (250–600 AD), the area was dominated by Copán, just 50km away, and doubtless valued for its position on the banks of the Río Motagua, an important trade route, and as a source of jade. It was during the rule of the great leader Cauac Sky that Quiriguá challenged Copán, capturing its leader 18-Rabbit in 737 AD, and was able to assert its independence and embark on a building boom: most of the great stelae date from this period. For a century Quiriguá dominated the lower Motagua valley. Under Jade Sky, who took the throne in 790, Quiriguá reached its peak, with fifty years of extensive building work, including a radical reconstruction of the acropolis. Towards the end of Jade Sky's rule, in the middle of the ninth century, the historical record fades out, as does the period of prosperity and power.

coming from Guatemala City on their way to Flores or Puerto Barrios, and going to Flores from Esquipulas and Chiquimula pass by. There's a fairly regular bus service from the highway to the site itself, plus assorted motor-bikes and pick-ups. You shouldn't have to wait too long to get a ride back to the highway, or you can walk there in around forty-five minutes.

PUERTO BARRIOS

Named after President Rufino Barrios in the 1880s, **PUERTO BARRIOS** soon fell into the hands of the American-owned United Fruit Company – the harbour was partly built by Theodore Roosevelt's Corps of Engineers in 1906–08 – and was used to ship its merchandise to New York and New Orleans. The Guatemalan government, dissatisfied that the port had been built to satisfy foreign interests, built a state-owned port, Santo Tomás de Castilla, six kilometres further south, and Puerto Barrios went into decline, from which it has never really recovered. Like most other port towns, the woebegone city has a seedy feel, with its potholed streets, numerous strip clubs and iffy characters wondering the streets. It's not somewhere you would want to hang around for too long – probably just enough time to hop on a boat to your next destination.

Arrival and information

By boat Boats from Livingston and Punta Gorda (Belize) arrive at the dock at the end of 12 C.
By bus There's no purpose-built bus station in Puerto Barrios. Litegua buses, which serve all destinations along the Caribbean Highway to Guatemala City, have their own terminal in the centre of town on 6 Av, between 9 & 10 C. All second-class buses, as well as services from Chiquimula and Esquipulas, arrive and depart from an unmarked stop directly opposite, beside the railway tracks.
Tourist information There's no Inguat office in town. You can get bus schedules at the Litegua terminal.

Accommodation

There is not much at all in terms of budget hotels in Puerto Barrios – for real cheap accommodation, your safest bet is *Hotel El Dorado*.
Hotel La Caribeña 4 Av between 10 & 11 calles ☎7948 0384. Large place with a variety of different-sized rooms (some with a/c), including doubles, triples and quads. The management is friendly and there's a good-quality seafood restaurant attached. ❸
Hotel El Dorado 7 Av & 13 C ☎7948 1581. Family-run place with basic but spacious good-value rooms, some with private bath. Owner Pedro says you can wash "libremente" in the courtyard, should you wish to get some fresh air. Ring the bell on 7 Av if you arrive late at night. ❷
Hotel Europa 2 3 Av & 12 C ☎7948 1292. Clean, safe and friendly place close to the dock. All the good-value rooms have fan and private shower, and there are good rates for single travellers. Sister hotel *Hotel Europa 1* is at 8 Av & 8 C (☎7948 0127). ❹

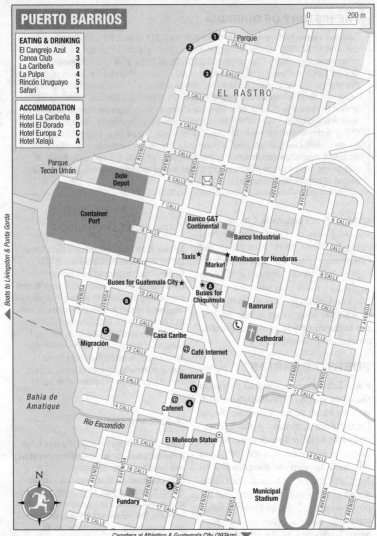

PUERTO BARRIOS

EATING & DRINKING
El Cangrejo Azul	2
Canoa Club	3
La Caribeña	B
La Pulpa	4
Rincón Uruguayo	5
Safari	1

ACCOMMODATION
Hotel La Caribeña	B
Hotel El Dorado	D
Hotel Europa 2	C
Hotel Xelajú	A

Parque

EL RASTRO

Parque Tecún Umán

Dole Depot

Container Port

Banco G&T Continental

Banco Industrial

Taxis ★

Market

★ Minibuses for Honduras

Buses for Guatemala City ★

★ Ⓐ Buses for Chiquimula

Banrural

Migración

Casa Caribe

Café Internet

Cathedral

Banrural

Bahía de Amatique

Cafenet

Río Escondido

El Muñecón Statue

Municipal Stadium

Fundary

N

Carretera al Atlántico & Guatemala City (293km) ▼

Hotel Xelajú ☎7948 0482. Right in the centre of town facing the market, this is another cheapie with simple rooms and private bath. ②

Eating

There's an abundance of *comedores* around the market. Most of the restaurants listed here serve fish and seafood but also have cheaper options such as burgers.

Restaurants

El Cangrejo Azul On the sea front. The menu here includes a *tapado especial* (seafood soup; Q45) and a number of other fish-based dishes.

La Caribeña 4 Av between 10 & 11 calles. Excellent local food, including meats and a delicious *sopa de mariscos* (Q90).

Rincón Uruguayo 10min walk south of the centre, at 7 Av & 16 C. A favourite for meat-eaters, this place excels at *parrilladas* (Q100 for two people). Closed Sun.

Safari 10min north of the centre on the seafront, at the end of 5 Av. Very popular restaurant with a big palm roof, serving huge portions of seafood platters (Q100), burgers (Q12) and *ceviches* (Q75).

Drinking and nightlife

Puerto Barrios has a few bars and nightclubs, offering the full range of late-night sleaze – a lot of the action is centred around 6 and 7 avenidas and 6 and 7 calles, by the Parque Tecún Umán.
Canoa Club 5 Av & 2 C. Reggae and punta rock are the main musical flavours here, especially on weekends.
La Pulpa 7 Av & 13 C. This bar and grill gets quite lively on some nights, and is a good place to have a drink.

Directory

Exchange At Banrural, 8 Av & 9 C (with MasterCard ATM), and 7 Av & 12 C; Banco Industrial, 7 Av & 7 C (with Visa ATM); and Banco G&T Continental, 7 C between 6 & 7 Av.
Immigration For Belize, clear *migración* before buying a ticket; the office is a block west of the dock on 12 C (7am–8pm).
Internet Available at Café Internet, 6 Av between 11 & 12 C (daily 7am–11pm), and Cafenet, 13 C & 6 Av (Mon–Sat 9am–9pm). Both charge Q5/hr.
Post office 6 C & 6 Av.
Taxis There are many taxis around town; available drivers honk for customers as they drive through the streets.
Telephones The Telgua office (daily 7am–6pm) is at the junction of 8 Av & 10 C.

Moving on

By boat *Lanchas* regularly go to Lívingston (Q35) but leave only when full, and to Punta Gorda in Belize (daily 10am, 1pm and 2pm; Q150).
By bus Transportes Litegua (6 Av & 9 C) has regular morning buses and one afternoon bus at 4pm to Guatemala City (5hr 30min), via Quiriguá. There

are also half-hourly buses for Chiquimula (4hr 30min), via Quiriguá, that leave from 6 Av & 9 C. For Río Dulce you will have to catch a bus heading to Chiquimula and change at La Ruidosa junction. There are also regular buses to the Honduran border that depart from 6 Av by the market (see box below).

LÍVINGSTON

Lying at the mouth of the Río Dulce and only accessible by boat, **LÍVINGSTON** is unlike anywhere else in Guatemala – it's largely inhabited by the displaced **Garífuna**, or black Carib people, whose communities are strung out along the Caribbean coast between southern Belize and northern Nicaragua (for a brief history of the Garífuna, see p.103). The town itself has a very laid-back feel – you're bound to see some Rastafarians soaking in the sun and chilling out in the company of some ganja. This unique fusion of Guatemalan and Caribbean cultures is manifest in all aspects of life, from the delicious *tapado* (spicy seafood soup) to the musical lilt of Garífuna patois.

What to see and do

Lívingston is a small place with not much to do other than kick back and relax. There is one interesting museum in town, the **Museo Garífuna** (take the first left from the dock; Q5) where you can learn more about the history and culture of the black Caribs.

If you want to catch some rays, you can use the **pool** at *Villa Caribe*, in town on the main drag on the right (Q50 per person). The local **beaches**, though safe for swimming, are not the stuff of Caribbean dreams, with dark sand and greyish water. The sole exception is

---

INTO HONDURAS: ENTRE RÍOS

Minibuses (every 30min; 6.30am–4.30pm; 1hr) for the border crossing to Honduras at **Entre Ríos** depart from the Puerto Barrios marketplace. Once there, you may be asked for an unofficial "exit tax" (US$1–2) on the Guatemalan side and an entry fee for a similar sum from the Hondurans. Pick-ups leave the border to the village of **Corinto**, 4km away, from where buses depart for Puerto Cortés (every 90min; 3hr) via Omoa.

LÍVINGSTON

0   100 m

ACCOMMODATION

Casa de la Iguana	D
Hotel California	B
Hotel Casa Rosada	F
Hotel Garífuna	A
Hotel Maya Quiriguá	E
Hotel Río Dulce	C
Hotel El Viajero	G

EATING & DRINKING

Antojitos Gaby	9
Bahía Azul	6
Bugamama	8
Happy Fish	7
Margoth	4
Tiburón Gato	5
Tilingo Lingo	3
Trópico La Playa	2
Ubafu	1

Bahía de Amatique

Misión Popular

Río Crique

Banco Reformador

Buganet

Banrrural

Immigration

Museo Garífuna

CALLE MARCOS SÁNCHEZ DÍAZ

Río Dulce

CALLE PRINCIPAL

Boats for Río Dulce Town, Puerto Barrios & Punta Gorda (Belize)

---

wonderful, white-sand **Playa Blanca**, though this is privately owned and can only be visited on a tour (see below). Don't walk alone on the beaches, as rapes and robberies have been reported.

The most popular trip around town is to **Las Siete Altares**, a group of waterfalls about 5km to the northwest, a good spot to take a few dips and have a picnic. There have been sporadic **attacks on tourists** walking out to the falls, but the police now supervise the area and it is now a relatively safe route, provided you walk in a group. The best option is to hire a local guide or visit as part of a tour (see below).

Arrival and information

By boat The only way to get to Lívingston is by boat, either from Puerto Barrios, the Río Dulce or Belize; they arrive at the main dock on the south side of town.

Travel agents Exotic Travel (☎7947 0049, ⓦwww.bluecaribbeanbay.com), in the same building as the *Bahía Azul* restaurant, and Happy Fish (☎7947 0661, ⓦwww.happyfishtravel.com), just down the road, are the best travel agents in town. They can arrange trips (minimum six people) around the area, including visits to lovely Playa Blanca and the Sapodilla Cayes off Belize for snorkelling (US$45). Several companies, including Exotic Travel, run morning boat trips up the Río Dulce (Q95 per person).

Accommodation

There is plenty of nice budget accommodation in town. Make sure you book ahead at the holidays; at other times you should easily be able to find a bed.

Casa de la Iguana Turn left at the dock and walk for 5min ☎7947 0064. A great place to meet other travellers, this fun hostel with dorms and rooms has a lively atmosphere, complete with family-style dinners every evening. The friendly English owner will keep you entertained. Doubles and triples are agreeable and cosy, and the bathroom tiles decorated with Rusty's handpainted motifs. You can also camp or sleep in hammocks for Q15. Satellite TV and 400 DVDs for rainy days. Dorms ❶, doubles ❹

Hotel California Turn left just before the *Bahía Azul* restaurant ☎ 7947 0176. This clean hotel offers reasonable, if sparse, rooms, most with private bath. Triples also available. ❸

🏃 **Hotel Casa Rosada** About 400m left of the dock ☎ 7947 0303, ⓦ www.hotelcasarosada .com. A delightful hotel with a harbourfront location and lush, spacious grounds. The small, cheery wooden cabins are a little overpriced but still charming. Excellent, healthful meals available as well. ❹

Hotel Garífuna Turn left off the main street towards the *Ubafu* bar and walk 250m ☎ 7947 0183, ⓔ quiqueboss@hotmail.com. Fairly clean, secure guesthouse with basic rooms, all with fan and private bath. ❷

Hotel Maya Quiriguá About 400m left of the dock ☎ 7947 0674. All in all, a good-value establishment. The downstairs rooms are cheaper (Q25/30 without/with private bath), but have spongy beds; those upstairs are more expensive, with springy beds. Downstairs ❶, upstairs ❷

Hotel Río Dulce About 3min walk up from the jetty ☎ 5143 0410. Recently refurbished, this hotel has very pleasant, spotless rooms with wooden floorboards. All rooms are en suite. ❸

Hotel El Viajero Turn left after the dock, and walk for 200m ☎ 5685 1635. Friendly, family-run place with excellent-value rooms, all with fan and private bath. Just know there's a brothel on one side and a fish market on the other, which may mean late nights and early mornings. ❷

Hotelito Perdido In the rainforest by the Río Lampara, 20min from town by boat ☎ 5725 1576 or 5785 5022, ⓦ www.hotelitoperdido.com. Relaxed and homely, this English–Polish-owned place has rustic bungalows in a jungle setting 12km from Lívingston, as well as a cosy little dorm room (❶) with only two beds. A perfect spot to kick back in a hammock or go kayaking. Call Chris or Aka and they will come and pick you up by boat. ❹

Eating

There are a number of excellent places to eat in Lívingston – make sure you try the *tapado* (seafood soup), the local speciality.

Restaurants

Antojitos Gaby Turn left at the dock, and walk for 250m. This family-run place offers one of the cheapest, biggest and tastiest *tapados* in town

(Q65). 20min of free internet use available when you order food.

Bahía Azul On the main street. A nonprofit restaurant whose proceeds go towards helping the local indigenous who have been displaced, this popular place has an inexpensive menu (*coco burguesa* Q20) and an excellent terrace for watching Lívingston streetlife.

Bugamama Just left of the jetty. Very good shrimp (Q75), pastas (Q35) and fish. Closed Mon.

🏃 **Happy Fish** On the main street. Top-notch food in a fun, friendly atmosphere and a very pleasant setting. There are a number of "Specialities Happy Fish" (try the grilled seafood) and meat dishes (Q45) available for non-fish lovers.

Margoth Turn left after *Tiburón Gato*. Another good place to try out some garífuna food – good fried fish dishes (Q95) and *ceviche*.

Tiburón Gato 2min from the jetty, on the main drag. Other than local specialities, this place also serves pasta (Q22), *ceviche* (Q38) and fried fish (Q45), all at very reasonable prices.

Tilingo Lingo At the end of the main drag heading north towards the beach. Serving an eclectic range of international dishes, including Indian food and pizzas, as well as a good *tapado*.

Drinking and nightlife

Lívingston has some groovy bars, most with African drum music and reggae beats playing in the background.

Trópico La Playa Here you'll hear an eclectic range of music – show off your moves on the dancefloor or chill in one of the hammocks and chairs on the beach. Closed Mon & Tues.

Ubafu Usually the liveliest place with some great African drum music, although it is very much hit-or-miss depending on the night.

Directory

Exchange Banco Reformador (Mon–Fri 9am–5pm, Sat 9am–1pm) has a Visa/Plus ATM; Banrural (Mon–Fri 8.30am–5pm, Sat 9am–1pm) has a Visa/Plus and MasterCard/Cirrus ATM. Both are on the main drag.

Internet Gaby's Internet, left at the dock, has the cheapest rates in town (Q6/hr). Alternatively, try *Happy Fish*, on the main drag (Q10/hr).

Immigration About 200m up the main drag (daily 8am–6pm). Get your visas for Belize here.

Post office Walk up the main street and take the first right (Mon–Fri 8.30am–12.30pm & 3.30–5.30pm, Sat 9am–1pm).

Taxis Can be grabbed from the dock. Rates are Q10 to anywhere in town.

Telephones The Telgua office (Mon–Fri 8am–6pm, Sat 9am–1pm) is on the right, up the main street from the docks, next door to the post office. You cannot make international calls, but you can buy phonecards.

Moving on

By boat to: Puerto Barrios (daily 5am & 2pm; 1hr 30min) and Punta Gorda, Belize (Tues & Fri 7am; 1hr). The Puerto Barrios ferries are supplemented by *lanchas* (Mon–Sat 6.30am, 7.30am, 9am, 11am and when full thereafter, Sun only when full).

Lago de Izabal and the Río Dulce

The largest lake in the country, **Lago de Izabal** remains largely unexplored and is well worth a visit if you're looking for some tranquillity. **El Estor** serves as a good base to explore the beautiful nature reserve to the west of the lake, which is home to numerous species of wildlife and secluded spots waiting to be discovered. The lake itself empties into the **Río Dulce**, which you can venture up (or down) to (and from) Lívingston, a breathtaking trip that takes two to three hours. The area is also home to one of the country's most curious natural phenomena, the Finca el Paraíso hot spring **waterfall**.

ALONG THE RÍO DULCE

From Lívingston the river leads into a system of **gorges** cut into sheer rock faces. Tropical vegetation and vines cling to the walls, and here and there you might see some varied birdlife. Six kilometres from Lívingston there's a nice river tributary, the **Río Tatín**, which most boatmen will venture up if you ask them. There's a good guesthouse up here, the *Finca Tatín* (☎5902 0831, ⓦ www.fincatatin.centramerica.com), which has rustic dorms (❶), rooms with private bath (❸) and bungalows (❹) set in dense jungle; it's reachable only by boat. Run by hospitable Argentines, there's also excellent healthful food, kayaks for hire, walking trails and Spanish classes available.

Continuing up the Río Dulce for another kilometre or so, you'll pass a spot where warm sulphurous waters emerge from the base of the cliff – this is a great place for a swim. Past here, the river opens up into the **Golfete** lake, the north shore of which has been designated the **Biotopo de Chocón Machacas** (daily 8am–5pm; Q30), designed to protect the **manatees** that live here. The reserve also protects the forest that still rings much of the lake; there are some specially cut trails where you might catch sight of a bird or two, or, if you've time and patience to spare, a tapir or jaguar. The river closes in again after the lake, passing the marina and bridge at the squalid town of **Río Dulce** (also known as Fronteras), where the boat trip comes to an end.

RÍO DULCE TOWN

Still commonly referred to as Fronteras, the town of **RÍO DULCE** is not somewhere you would want to stay for long. Once the stopover for ferries on their way to El Petén, it now attracts tourist traffic from yachters and travellers heading to or coming from Lívingston. The town is connected to the land on both sides of the river by a gargantuan concrete bridge, and buses travel in both directions.

Arrival and information

By boat A side road leads down to the dock from the north side of the bridge.

By bus If arriving by bus, ask to be dropped off on the north side of the bridge (unless you're planning on staying at *Hotel Backpackers* on the south side),

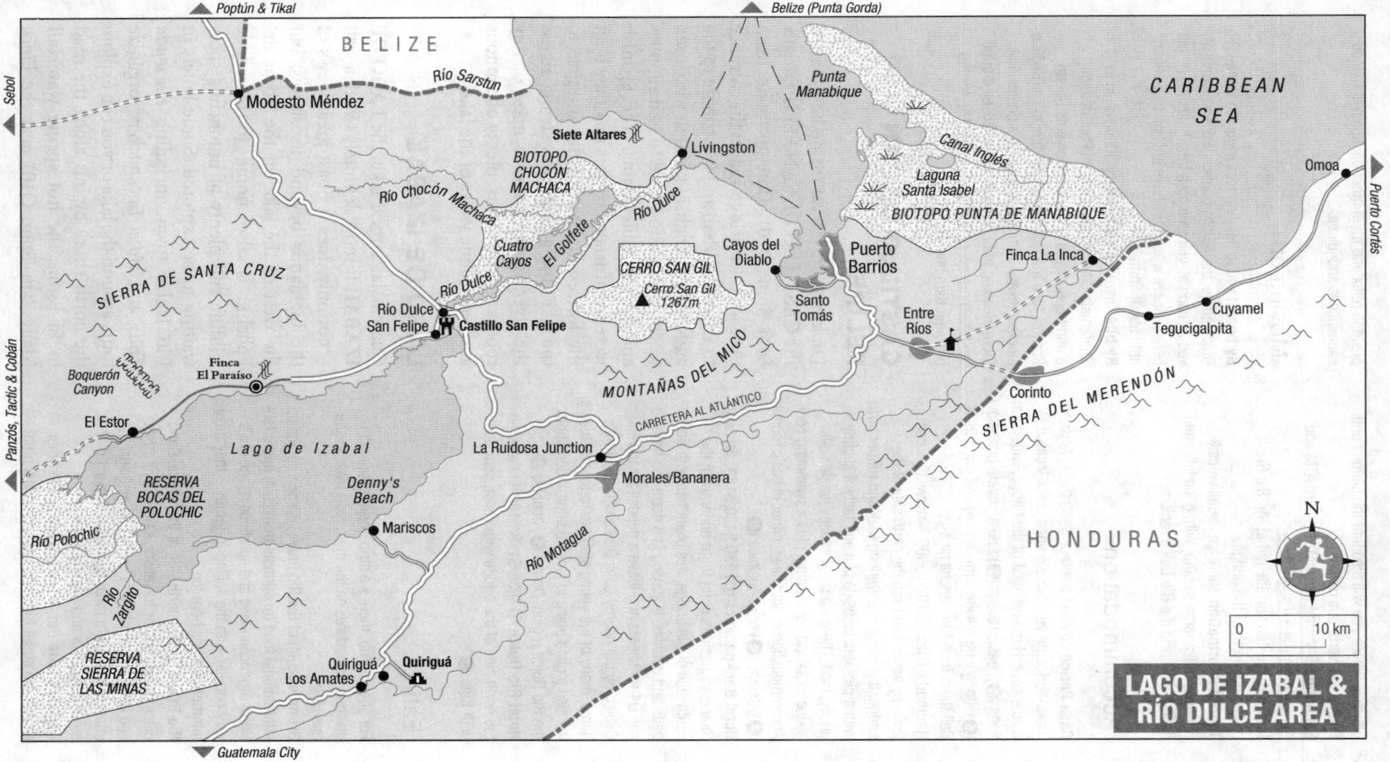

LAGO DE IZABAL & RÍO DULCE AREA

N

0   10 km

CARIBBEAN SEA

Puerto Cortés

Omoa

Cuyamel

Tegucigalpita

Corinto

HONDURAS

SIERRA DEL MERENDÓN

Finca La Inca

Punta Manabique

BIOTOPO PUNTA DE MANABIQUE

Laguna Santa Isabel

Canal Inglés

Entre Ríos

Puerto Barrios

Santo Tomás

Belize (Punta Gorda)

Livingston

Cayos del Diablo

CERRO SAN GIL

Cerro San Gil 1267m

MONTAÑAS DEL MICO

CARRETERA AL ATLÁNTICO

Morales/Bananera

Siete Altares

Río Dulce

BIOTOPO CHOCÓN MACHACA

El Golfete

Cuatro Cayos

Río Chocón Machaca

Castillo San Felipe

Río Dulce

San Felipe

Río Dulce

La Ruidosa Junction

Río Motagua

BELIZE

Río Sarstún

Modesto Méndez

SIERRA DE SANTA CRUZ

Boquerón Canyon

Finca El Paraíso

Lago de Izabal

El Estor

RESERVA BOCAS DEL POLOCHIC

Río Polochic

RESERVA SIERRA DE LAS MINAS

Río Túnico

Denny's Beach

Mariscos

Los Amates

Quiriguá

Quiriguá

Guatemala City

Poptún & Tikal

Sebol

Panzós, Tactic & Cobán

207

which is where you will also find the Litegua and Fuente del Norte bus offices.

Exchange Banrural has a MasterCard ATM and Banco Industrial a Visa ATM.

Internet You can surf the net at the *Río Bravo* restaurant north of the bridge.

Tourist information There's a useful website (Ⓦ www.mayaparadise.com) with good links and listings covering the Río Dulce region.

Accommodation

Casa Perico ☎ 7793 5666 or 5909 0721, Ⓦ www .casa-perico.de.vu. Swiss-owned place located in a little cove 1km northeast of the bridge, with dorm beds (❶), basic rooms (❷) and a private bungalow (❺) along with a lively atmosphere and great food. Call them for a free *lancha* pick-up.

Hacienda Tijax ☎ 7930 5505, Ⓦ www.tijax.com. 2min by water-taxi from the north side of the bridge, this place is a working teak and rubber farm with a pleasant lakeside plot and tasty, if slightly pricey, food. There's a great canopy jungle walk, hiking trails and horseriding, plus a swimming pool. Accommodation is not cheap, either in basic rooms (❹), cabins (❹) or bungalows (❽).

Hotel Backpackers ☎ 7930 5480/5168, Ⓦ www .hotelbackpackers.com) Right underneath the south side of the bridge, this place has both dorm beds and doubles. If staying in a dorm you have to pay Q4 for sheets and leave a deposit for towels. Owned by the nearby Casa Guatemala children's home, many of the young staff are former residents; it's also a good place to pick up information about the Río Dulce region. Dorms ❶, doubles ❷

Hotel Río Dulce ☎ 7930 5179/5180. Located on the north side of the bridge with clean, neat doubles with fans. ❸

Eating

For cheap grub, there's a strip of pretty undistinguished *comedores* on the main road close to the bus stop.

Bruno's South of the Río Bravo, *Bruno's* serves up international food (breakfasts from Q24) and offers North American news and sports coverage – it's very popular with the sailing fraternity – they have internet facilities here too.

Río Bravo On the north side of the bridge. Good place to meet other travellers, eat pizza or pasta and drink the night away – you can also surf the internet and make radio contact with most places around the river and lake from here.

Sun Dog Café Dutch-owned café on the other side of the street from *Río Bravo*, this is a great

place to relax and meet other backpackers. Good sandwiches and juices.

Moving on

By boat If you're heading for Lívingston via the Río Dulce gorge, the *lancha* boat captains will ambush you as soon as you step off a bus; boats (Q100 per person) leave when they have enough passengers until about 5pm.

By bus There are buses every 30min or so to Guatemala City and to Flores via Poptún until around 6pm. If you're heading towards Puerto Barrios, take the first bus or minibus to La Ruidosa junction (every 30min) and pick up a connection there. Heading to El Estor, there are buses around the lakeshore every 90min minutes (1hr 45min) between 6am and 4pm.

CASTILLO DE SAN FELIPE

Looking like a miniature medieval castle, the **CASTILLO DE SAN FELIPE** (daily 8am–5pm; Q20), 1km upstream from the Río Dulce bridge, marks the entrance to Lago de Izabal, and is a tribute to the audacity of English pirates, who used to sail up the Río Dulce to raid supplies and harass mule trains. The Spanish were so infuriated by this that they built the fortress to seal off the entrance to the lake, and a chain was strung across the river. Inside there's a maze of tiny rooms and staircases, plenty of cannons and panoramic views of the lake.

LAGO DE IZABAL

Guatemala's largest lake, the **LAGO DE IZABAL**, is most definitely worth a visit – not only does it boast great views of the highlands beyond its shores, but the west of the lake on the Bocas del Polichic is also home to incredible wildlife and plenty of untouched spots waiting to be explored. Some hotels in Río Dulce town, including *Hacienda Tijax* and *Hotel Backpackers*, organize tours around the lake or you can explore the north shore by bus along the road to El Estor. The **hot spring waterfall** (daily 7am–5pm; Q10) near the *Finca*

El Paraíso (see below), 25km from Río Dulce and 300m north of the road, is a truly remarkable phenomenon, with boiling water cascading into cooled pools, creating a steam-room environment in the midst of the jungle. There is also a series of caves above the waterfall, their interior of different shapes and colours (remember to bring a torch) – one of the employees at the ticket office can show you there. Buses and pickups travel in both directions until about 4.30pm.

Seven kilometres further west is the hidden **Boquerón canyon**, with near vertical cliffs rising more than 250m; villagers (including Hugo, a *campesino*-cum-boatman) will paddle you upstream in a canoe for a small fee.

> **TREAT YOURSELF**
>
> The Finca el Paraíso (☎7949 7131 or 7958 0013), two kilometres south of the hot waterfall on the lakeshore, is a perfect place to relax thanks to the delightfully peaceful location the hotel enjoys – read a book by the shore or go for a pleasant swim from the black-sand beach. The *finca* has large, comfortable but rarely occupied cabañas (⑦) that sleep up to four people, and a reasonable restaurant on the lakeside.

EL ESTOR

Supposedly given its name because of the English pirates who came up the Río Dulce to buy supplies at "the store", the tranquil lakeside town of **EL ESTOR** lies six kilometres further west of El Boquerón. In the 1970s, a subsidiary of a Canadian company obtained a forty-year nickel mining concession, but shortly ceased operations when the commodity price plummeted. Not only did the company's intrusive operations pose a serious threat to the Q'eqchi Maya community, but the resulting adverse health effects of the plant have

since been a cause of concern. Today, the town's ideal setting makes it a perfect place to explore the countryside nearby, which remains largely untouched. Locals are deservedly optimistic that the town can capitalize on the vast **ecotourism** potential of the lake and its surrounding areas, in particular of the Reserva Bocas del Polochic, harbouring numerous species of wildlife.

Arrival and information

By bus Buses arrive and depart from the Parque Central.

Bike rental You can rent bikes at 6 Av 4–26.

Tourist information *Café El Portal* (☎4181 6361), on the east side of the plaza, is probably your safest bet in terms of information. You can also organize tours from here, or try Hugo at *Hotel Ecológico*, or Oscar Paz, who runs the *Hotel Vista del Lago*. All can arrange boats and guides to explore the surrounding countryside, plus fishing trips on the lake.

Accommodation

Hotel Ecológico Cabañas del Lago ☎5597 6191 or 4037 6235. Located 1km east of the centre, in a prime, tranquil lakeside plot, the bungalows here are comfortable, spacious and attractive; the restaurant has stunning views and there is also a private beach– give Hugo or Sergia a ring and they will pick you up in town. Internet facilities available. ❸

Hotel Villela 6 Av 2–06 ☎5187 5043. A reasonable deal, with rooms, all with private shower, surrounding a courtyard. ❷

Hotel Vista del Lago ☎7949 7205. Probably the most atmospheric hotel in town, although fairly pricey, is set within a beautiful old wooden building by the dock, claimed by the owners to be the original "store" that gave the town its name; Che Guevara also once stayed here. It offers rather small, clean rooms with private bath – those on the second floor have commanding views of the lake. ❺

Posada Don Juan On the main square ☎7949 7296. Pleasant and clean excellent-value rooms with fan, right next to *Café Portal*. ❷

Restaurant Chaabil On the lakeside just east of the plaza. This place offers lovely, recently refurbished wooden rooms with hand-made beds and private bathrooms. ❸

Eating

Café El Portal On the main square, this little café serves top-notch Guatemalan food (Q15) and is popular with the locals.
Restaurant Chaabil Tasty food in a very pleasant setting right on the lakefront. Try the seafood (Q80) dish.
Restaurante del Lago On the square. This place also scores for *comida típica* (Q15).

Moving on

By boat There are no public boats to other destinations along the lake. You can hire a private *lancha*, although this will be fairly pricey.
By bus to: Río Dulce (hourly 6am–4.30pm; 1hr 45min). There are also buses to Cobán (6hr), and you can get to Lanquín via Cahabón – ask at *Café Portal* for the latest schedule.

RESERVA BOCAS DEL POLOCHIC

The **RESERVA BOCAS DEL POLOCHIC** is one of the richest wetland habitats in Guatemala, and shelters 275 species of birds and a large number of mammals, reptiles, amphibians and fish. The ecosystem is one of the few places in the country where you can find manatees and tapirs, and you're bound to spot (or certainly hear) howler monkeys.

A good place to stay is the village of **Selempím**, which is right on the edge of the reserve. Accommodation is in a large screened wooden house with bunk beds (❷) – this is organized through Defensores de la Naturaleza. You should also remember to bring bottled water as they do not sell any in the village. Locals organize treks into the foothills of the Sierra de las Minas or can take you kayaking around the river delta. To get to Selempím, catch a public *lancha* – these run on Mondays, Wednesdays and Fridays for Q25 one way; on other days, you'll have to get a private *lancha* which can amount to about Q500; obviously it's much cheaper if there's a big group. The reserve is managed by Defensores de la Naturaleza, 5 Av and 2 C, El Estor (☎7949 7130/7237, ⊛www.defensores.org.gt), who also organize excellent tours deep into the heart of the refuge (all of their proceeds go towards the conservation of the reserve). Hugo and Oscar in El Estor (see p.209) can also organize day-trip excursions to the zone nearest to El Estor.

The Verapaces

The twin departments of the **Verapaces** harbour some of the most spectacular mountain scenery in the country, yet attract only a trickle of tourists. **Alta Verapaz**, in particular, is astonishingly beautiful, with fertile limestone landscapes and mist-soaked hills. The mountains here are the wettest and greenest in Guatemala – ideal for the production of the cash crops of coffee, cardamom, flowers and ferns. To the south, **Baja Verapaz** could hardly be

---

VERAPACES HISTORY

The history of the Verapaces is quite distinct from the rest of Guatemala. The Maya here resisted the Spanish so fiercely that eventually the conquistadors gave up, and the Church, under the leadership of Fray Bartolomé de Las Casas, was given the role of winning the people's hearts and minds. By 1542 the invincible Achi Maya had been transformed into Spanish subjects, and the King of Spain renamed the province Verapaz (True Peace). Nonetheless, the Verapaces remain very much *indígena* country: Baja Verapaz has a small Achi outpost around the town of Rabinal, and in Alta Verapaz the Maya population is largely Poqomchi' and Q'eqchi'.

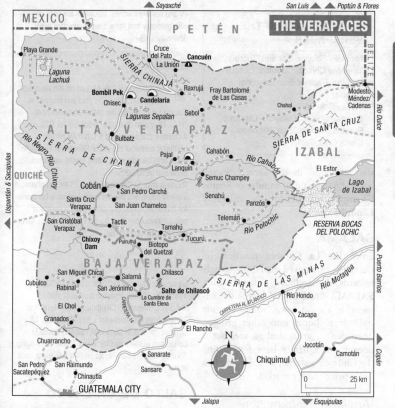

Sayaxché ▲ | San Luís ▲ ▲ Poptún & Flores

more different: a low-lying, sparsely populated area that gets very little rainfall.

Many travellers completely by-pass Baja Verapaz, whizzing through on Carretera 14 from Guatemala City to Cobán and the rest of Alta Verapaz. There are, however, a few sights worth stopping off for en-route. Clustered around the village of Pulrulhá are **sacred caves**, the **highest waterfall** in Central America and the **Biotopo del Quetzal**. To the west of the highway the **Salamá valley** drops dramatically away, leading to the sleepy department capital and beyond. To reach Salamá and the surrounding settlements you may need to change buses at **La Cumbre junction**, where a road plunges west from Carretera 14 into the valley. The junction is a popular interchange, with a handful of small *comedores* and snack vendors and a regular flow of public transport bound for Cobán, Guatemala City and towards Río Dulce.

North of La Cumbre and the quetzal reserve is the departmental border with Alta Verapaz, and shortly thereafter the city of **Cobán**, where you'll find great coffee, buzzing bars and a good range of budget accommodation. Heading further towards Petén, take time to check out some of the interesting community tourism projects that showcase Alta Verapaz's limestone landscape, as well as its living Maya heritage. Several of the sites here are part of the "Puerto al Mundo Maya", a government-sponsored programme promoting responsible tourism in the region (see p.221). The star attraction in the area, however, has to be the natural wonder of **Semuc Champey**, just outside the village of **Lanquín**.

SALAMÁ

From the La Cumbre junction on Carretera 14, a paved road drops steeply towards the secluded Salamá valley. **SALAMÁ** itself, capital of the department, is a quiet town, where you are unlikely to bump into other gringos. There isn't a great deal to see, but it does make a handy base for visiting the Chilascó waterfall and is home to a lively twice-weekly market.

Arrival and information

By bus Buses coming from CA-14 enter Salamá from the north. The town is strung out for some way before the central plaza. Stay on the bus until after it crosses the old bridge, from where it climbs a couple of blocks to the plaza. For orientation purposes, the Church is on the eastern side of the Plaza. Minibuses terminate and depart from the dusty car park off Avenida 6 one block west of the plaza.

Accommodation

Hospedaje Juarez 5 C & 10 Av ☎ 7940 1114. Undercutting the other accommodation by a mile, this place offers basic, bare rooms for bargain prices. Bathrooms are communal and clean. ❶
Hotel Real Legendario 8 Av 3–57 ☎ 7940 0501. Probably Salamá's nicest hotel, *Real Legendario* is smart and clean with comfortable beds, private hot-water bathrooms and cable TV. ❹
Posada Don Maco 3 C 8–26 ☎ 7940 0083. Friendly, family-run business offering the best deal in town. Rooms have private bath, cable

TV and homely touches; balconies are decked with greenery and there are pet squirrels kept downstairs. ❹

Eating

🍴 **Deli Donas** 5 C 6–61, just off the west side of the plaza. You'll be glad you stopped in Salamá when you try the coffee and cake here (15Q). They also do a good breakfast for Q20.
Antojitos Zacapanecos 6 C & 8 Av, on the northeast corner of the plaza. Simple cantina-style place with friendly staff. Filling tortilla with chicken, salsa and salad Q20.
Restaurante la Cascada 4 C & 10 Av. Set around a lovely courtyard, this restaurant offers a full menu for breakfast, lunch and dinner with a variety of popular favourites from burgers to grilled fish. Main dishes go for around Q50.

Moving on

By bus to: Chilascó (6:30am, 10am, 10:30am, 11am; 1hr 30min), from the northeast side of the plaza; Guatemala City (hourly 6am–4pm; 3hr 30min), from the southeast side of the plaza; La Cumbre (for connections with Pullman buses to Cobán and Guatemala City; every 15min 6am–6pm; 30min), from the parking lot on 6 Av one block west of the plaza.

SALTO DE CHILASCÓ

Just north of the La Cumbre junction, at Km 144.5, a track leads east from the highway, towards the dramatic scenery of the **Sierra de las Minas**. After 12km you reach the village of **Chilascó**, where the community administer the impressive **SALTO DE CHILASCÓ** (last entry 1pm; US$5; ⊛ www.chilasco.net.ms), the highest **waterfall** in Central America. Most transport will drop you at the information centre in Chilascó village, where you pay your entrance fee. From here it's a 3km walk, continuing along the track road past village houses and plantations, to the beginning of the trail that leads down to the foot of the falls. This trail begins as a steep, muddy mule-path heading down to a ridge flanked by broccoli plantations. Take the footpath to the left for much easier passage. After 1km the path plunges down into the forested valley. The well-maintained trail offers viewpoint picnic sites with views towards the Chilascó Falls, posted information on local flora and fauna, as well as midway down, a campsite with eco-toilet. Don't miss the **Saltito**, a delightful smaller waterfall halfway down, where you can bathe in the plunge pool and admire the stunning views. At the base of the main falls water cascades onto huge boulders and seemingly disappears into the cavernous valley beyond the trail's end. The walk back up to Chilascó village requires a moderate level of fitness (allow at least 2hr).

Microbuses from Salamá to Chilascó village pass the Chilasco junction of CA-14 at 7am, 11am, 11.30am and 1pm. Otherwise, walk 200m back towards La Cumbre, and you'll find the *Río Escondido Lodge*, where you may be able to arrange a lift for a fee ($10). Basic **accommodation** (❷) and food is available in Chilascó village. The last bus back to the highway leaves the village at 3pm.

BIOTOPO DEL QUETZAL

Back on CA-14 towards Alta Verapaz and Cobán, the road sweeps around endless tight curves below forested hillsides. Just before the village of **Purulhá** (Km 161) is the **BIOTOPO DEL QUETZAL** (daily 7am–4pm; US$3), an 11.5-square-kilometre nature reserve designed to protect the habitat of the endangered bird. The reserve comprises steep and dense rain- and cloudforest, pierced by waterfalls, natural pools and the Río Colorado. There are two **hiking** trails, one an easy one-hour circuit, and the other a half-day Stairmaster. Trail maps are sold at the information centre at the park entrance. There are picnic areas, but no food is allowed on the trails.

The best time to catch a glimpse of the quetzal is March–April at either dawn or dusk. Since the reserve is not open during these hours it's definitely worth spending the night to increase your viewing opportunities. You can stay near the reserve at the *Ranchitos del Quetzal* (☎5191 0042; ❸–❹), 100m north of the entrance. The owner here was cunning enough to nurture the habitat of the quetzal's favoured foods and nesting places, so it's now one of the prime places to view the plumed legend. There is also a simple *comedor* with meals for Q30.

THE RESPLENDENT QUETZAL

The quetzal, Guatemala's national symbol, has a distinguished past but an uncertain future. From the earliest of times, the bird's feathers have been sacred: to the Maya the quetzal was so revered that killing one was a capital offence, and the bird is also thought to have been the *nahual*, or spiritual protector, of the Maya chiefs. When Tecún Umán was slain by conquistador Alvarado, the quetzal is said to have landed on his chest, and consequently obtained its red breast from the Maya's blood.

Today the quetzal's image permeates the entire country: as well as lending its name to the nation's currency, citizens honoured by the president are awarded the Order of the Quetzal, and the bird is also considered a symbol of freedom, since caged quetzals die in confinement. Despite all this, the sweeping tide of deforestation threatens the existence of the bird.

The heads of males are crowned with a plume of brilliant green, while the chest and lower belly are a rich crimson and trailing behind are the unmistakable oversized, golden-green tail feathers, though these are only really evident in the mating season. The females, on the other hand, are an unremarkable brownish colour. Quetzals also can be quite easily identified by their strangely jerky, undulating flight.

Buses from Cobán pass the reserve entrance every thirty minutes. To the north of the Biotopo, just past Pulrulhá, are the sacred **Chicoy Caves** (daily 9am–5pm; US$3) where there are towering stalagmites of up to 20m.

INTO ALTA VERAPAZ

Beyond the quetzal sanctuary, Carretera 14 crosses into the department of Alta Verapaz. The first place of any size is **Tactic** – a small, mainly Poqomchi'-speaking town adjacent to the main road, which most buses pass straight through. The colonial **church** in the centre of the village, boasting a Baroque facade decorated with mermaids and jaguars, is worth a look, as is the Chi-Ixim chapel high above the town.

About 10km past Tactic is the turn-off for **San Cristóbal Verapaz**, a pretty town almost engulfed by fields of coffee and sugar cane, set on the banks of the Lago de Cristóbal. From here a mostly paved road continues to **Uspantán** in the western highlands.

COBÁN

Though not as immediately impressive as other Guatemalan tourist centres, once you get to know the welcoming mountain town of **COBÁN**, you may find yourself sticking around and making a few friends. When the weather is dry, Cobán has a perfect alpine climate, allowing for fantastic day-trips to surrounding forests, rivers, caves and natural swimming pools. It's thanks to this fresh mountain air (and a good deal of rain) that the town became an important coffee-growing centre; now the local coffee *fincas* offer tours and provide beans to the town's many excellent cafés. Ecotourism and cultural tourism are also bringing increasing business to Cobán.

What to see and do

Probably the nicest thing to do in Cobán is to simply slow down and enjoy the world-class coffee and local hospitality. However, there are also several interesting attractions. The town is centred on an elevated **plaza**, with the **Cathedral** gracing its eastern side. To the north and south the streets fall away steeply, whilst the main thoroughfare, **1 Calle**, stretches westwards to the mall of Plaza Magdalena, on the town's outskirts. The town's central area is divided into four zones, which are separated north–south by 1 Calle and east–west by 1 Avenida.

Finca Santa Margarita

For a closer look at Cobán's principal crop, take the guided tour offered by the **Finca Santa Margarita** (Mon-Fri 8am–12.30pm & 1.30–5pm, Sat 8am–noon; US$4), a coffee plantation just south of the centre of town at 3 C 4–12, Zona 2. The interesting tour (in English or Spanish) covers the history of the *finca*, examining all the stages of cultivation and production. You also get a chance to sample the crop and, of course, purchase some beans.

Museo El Príncipe Maya

Several blocks southeast of the central plaza you'll find an excellent collection of Maya artefacts and carvings inside the small **Museo El Príncipe Maya**, 6 Av 4–26, Zona 3 (Mon–Sat 9am–6pm; US$2), including shell necklaces, polychrome bowls and human figurines. Don't miss the eccentric flints or the main attraction: a stunning panel from a Cancuén altarpiece, embellished with 160 glyphs.

El Calvario

A short stroll north from the town centre is the church of **El Calvario**, one of Cobán's most attractive sights. Head west out of town on 1 Calle and turn right up 7 Avenida. You'll pass a number of tiny **Maya shrines** on the way up – crosses blackened by candle smoke and decorated with scattered offerings. There's a commanding view over the town from the whitewashed

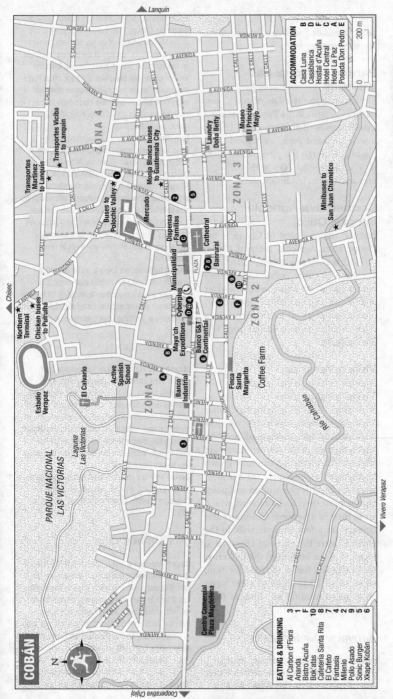

COBÁN

▲ Lanquín

◀ Chisec

▲ Cooperativa Chiol

▼ Vivero Verapaz

PARQUE NACIONAL
LAS VICTORIAS

Laguna
Las Victorias

Estadio
Verapaz

ZONA 1

ZONA 4

ZONA 3

ZONA 2

Coffee Farm

Río Cahabón

N

Northern ★
Terminal
Chicken buses ★
to Purulhá

Transportes ★
Martínez
to Lanquín

Transportes Viciba
to Lanquín ★

Buses to
Polochic Valley ❶

Mercado

Monja Blanca buses
to Guatemala City

Laundry
Doña Betty

Museo
El Príncipe
Mayo

Dispensa
Familias

Municipalidad

Cyberplus

Maya'ch
Expeditions

Banco G&T
Continental

Banco
Industrial

El Calvario

Active Spanish
School

Cathedral

Banrural

PLAZA

Finca
Santa
Margarita

Minibuses to
San Juan Chamelco ★

Centro Comercial
Plaza Magdalena

ACCOMMODATION
Casa Luna   B
Casablanca   D
Hostal d'Acuña   F
Hotel Central   C
Hotel La Paz   A
Posada Don Pedro   E

EATING & DRINKING
Al Carbon d'Flora   3
Ananda   1
Bistro Acuña   F
Bok xtas   10
Cafetería Santa Rita   8
El Cafeto   7
Fantasia   2
Milenio   9
Pollo Asado   5
Sonic Burger   5
Xkape Kobán   6

0   200 m

215

church, which has a distinctly pagan aura, often filled with candles and Maya worshippers.

Parque Nacional Las Victorias

On the northwest edge of town, just past El Calvario, is the **Parque Nacional Las Victorias** (daily 6am–5pm; US$1), a well-managed park, with good trails running through the pine forest. There is a campground (❶) with barbecue area and toilets, but no showers.

Cooperativa Agricola Integral Chijoj

Just ten minutes west of Cobán is the **Cooperativa Agricola Integral Chijoj** (US$10; ⓦ www.anacafe.org/coffeetour), a community-run coffee farm. Tours here include zip-lining across a river and a full explanation of the coffee-production process. To get here, take a micro heading west to **Chijoj** from 3 C, Zona 2 (Q2).

Vivero Verapaz

Another place worth a look is the **Vivero Verapaz** (Mon–Sat 9am–noon & 1–5pm; US$1.50), a former coffee *finca* just outside town that is now dedicated to the growing of **orchids**, which flourish in the sodden mountain climate. The plants are carefully grown in a shaded environment, and a farm worker will show you around and point out the most spectacular blooms, which are at their best between November and January. It's a forty-minute walk to the nursery: leave the plaza on Diagonal 4, turn left at the bottom of the hill, cross the bridge and follow the road for 3km; taxis charge US$2.50, or you can jump on a micro heading for **Tontem** from 3 Calle, Zona 2.

Arrival and information

By bus Unfortunately, almost all public transport arriving in Cobán drops you on the outskirts of town (with the exception of the Monja Blanca bus from Guatemala City, which drops you a block north of the plaza). Coming from points north you'll arrive at the Microbus terminal on the northern outskirts of town, and from Lanquin at the private terminals on the northeast side of town. Coming from the west or south, ask the driver to let you off at Plaza Magdalena, as the bus then heads off downhill away from town. From Plaza Magdalena or the northern terminals it's a 20min walk or Q15 taxi ride to the central plaza.

Tour operators Maya'ch Expeditions, 1 C 4–11, Zona 1 (ⓦ www.Mayachexpeditions.com), specializes in trips to Semuc Champey. ProyectoEco-Quetzal, 2 C 14–36, Zona 1 (Mon–Fri 9am–5pm; ⓦ www.ecoquetzal.org), arranges multi-day treks to the nearby Chicacnab cloudforest, where visitors stay with local Q'eqchi communities and provide a sustainable income for villagers, who also serve as guides. Many of Cobán's hotels also provide tour services, with shuttles and tours to nearby attractions.

Tourist information There is no Inguat office in town, but luckily the helpful staff at the *Casa Luna* (see below), more than adequately fill the information gap. An excellent map of Cobán and the Verapaces is available from Cyberplus on the plaza.

City transport

Microbuses For excursions just outside town (which most interesting attractions are), it's cheapest to flag down a micro. In fact, even If you have no desire to leave Cobán for the day, you will surely be offered a place onboard a passing micro. Many run east–west along calles 2 and 3 in Zona 2; you can flag them down or hang out on street corners with locals. You can also hop on for just a few blocks (fares Q1–3).

Taxis There is a constant pack of hopeful *taxistas* hanging out at the plaza. Agree fares before departure – within town these shouldn't exceed US$2.

Accommodation

Casa d'Acuña 4 C 3–11, Zona 2 ☎ 7951 0482, ⓔ casadeacuna@yahoo.com. Primarily a restaurant, this place also has a few decent dorms with two bunks in each and a couple of private rooms (all with shared bath). Many rooms face directly onto the restaurant courtyard, although things tend to close up early so this shouldn't cause too much disturbance. Dorms ❷, doubles ❸

🏃 **Casa Luna** 5 Av 2–28, Zona 1 ☎ 7951 3528, ⓔ casaluna@cobantravels.com. Steadily becoming Cobán's favourite backpacker haunt. Run by charming Lionel and his family, this small guesthouse is set around a pretty garden with sun-drenched hammocks. There is also a TV lounge, free breakfast, tour/shuttle service and free bike rental. All rooms have shared bath, but the water is piping hot! Dorms ❷, doubles ❷

Casablanca 1 C 3–25, Zona 1 ☎ 5931 7862. In a great location right on the plaza, this place offers cheap beds in basic, rather damp and dark rooms. There is a café and tour agency attached. Dorms ❶, doubles ❹

Hotel Central 1 C 1–79, Zona 4. ☎ 7952 1442, ℮ hotelcentraldecoban@yahoo.com. A good choice for couples looking for a comfortable private room. The rooms are bright, clean and come with TVs and private gas-fired hot-water bathrooms. Rooms are around a leafy courtyard, set back from the road. ❹

Hotel La Paz 6 Av 2–19, Zona 1 ☎ 7952 1358. This safe, pleasant budget hotel, run by a very vigilant *señora*, is probably the best deal in town. Rooms are basic but clean and face onto open corridor/ courtyard sitting areas. There is parking and a small *comedor* downstairs. ❷

Posada Don Pedro 3 C & 2 Av, Zona 2 ☎ 7951 0562. Friendly family-run place with simple rooms at simple prices. Most have shared baths, although one has a private shower and TV. Set around a cheerful courtyard. Laundry service offered. ❸–❹

Eating

Eating in Cobán comes down to a choice of some excellent European-style restaurants and very basic, cheap *comedores*. In the latter, look out for *kaq' ik*, a terrific turkey soup, but don't bother with the coffee. You'll find the cheapest food at the market, but as it's closed by dusk, head to the street stalls set up around the plaza.

Cafés

El Cafeto 2 C 1–36, Zona 2. Right on the plaza, this is another place to find a good cup of coffee (from the local Chijoj *finca*). There is a European-style snack/breakfast menu (Q15–25) and pleasant lazy-Sunday-morning ambience.

Fantasia 1 C 3–08, Zona 1. Down an alleyway off the north side of the plaza, this is a reasonable place for breakfast/lunch, with an extensive menu of sandwiches, burgers and tacos (Q10–30; also available with fries and a drink for Q30–40).

Xkape Kob'an Diagonal 4 5–13, Zona 2. The slogan here reads "Where culture and nature meet" – and for a community-oriented venture, sourcing local produce and recipes, they seem to have things about right. Though slightly more expensive than other cafés, the coffee here is the real deal, and the hot chocolate is hard to resist. The menu includes some interesting local specialities and unusual veggie options (mains Q20–60, snacks from Q15). Shake your maraca to order! Closed Sun.

Restaurants

Al Carbon d'Fiora 1 C 9–23, Zona 1. The meat dishes here justify an overnight stay in Cobán. Ingredients are imported and owner/chef Fiora lovingly prepares plates at his sizzling grill. Burgers (Q30–40) and steaks (Q70–90) are served with divine sautéed potatoes in a cheese and onion sauce, and garlic bread. The place is so popular with locals a new seating area is being opened upstairs. Open for dinner only (6.30–10pm).

Cafetería Santa Rita 2 C, on the plaza next door to *El Cafeto*. An archetypal *comedor* with friendly service and filling *comida típica*. Great prices – almost an entire menu is under Q20.

Pollo Asado 2 Av 3–04, Zona 2. A local canteen offering a cheaper alternative to the ubiquitous *Pollo Campero*. Grilled chicken, rice, salad, tortillas and drink for Q20.

Sonic Burger 1 C 3–50, Zona 3. The burgers here are the standard fast-food fare, but good value from Q10. Also nachos, sandwiches and salads, plus set meals from Q15.

TREAT YOURSELF

Bistro Acuña 4 C 3–17, Zona 2. This is the place to come for high quality and huge portions. The professional service complements the extensive menu, which includes Mexican and Italian favourites, as well as grilled meats and seafood (mains Q60–120). There is an enticing dessert cabinet, as well as freshly baked cake to take away. Eating breakfast here will keep you going for most of the day; the Spanish omelette (with chorizo, olives and pepper; Q45) comes with plantains, beans, cheese, cream, fresh bread, OJ and coffee.

Drinking and nightlife

Ananda 4 C 3–24, Zona 4. Interesting, alternative bar, popular with groups of students and run by an ultra-friendly young couple. There are always drink promotions, including tequila for Q5. It's a particularly good place for groups, as you can have your own private cushion-filled room for a minimum cover charge.

Bok'atas 4 C 2–34, Zona 2. Spanish-owned and themed bar/restaurant. Seating is outdoors but under cover and can be hard to come by at weekends, when locals flock here for tapas, draught beer and disco tunes. At Q20 the tapas isn't cheap, but portions are big and tasty – try the spicy roasted potatoes. Owner Rafael is renovating the large hall behind the bar and plans to host theatre, film showings, live music and more.

Milenio 3 Av & 1 C. Something of a local institution, this is the place young folk go for dancing and live music. There is a Q20 entrance fee and beers are Q20 a pop once inside.

Directory

Cinema Inside Plaza Magdalena (at the western end of C 1) is a three-screen cinema; each screen has two showings per day ($2).

Exchange Most banks and ATMs can be found on the plaza and along C 1. Banrural (on the southeast corner of the plaza) will change foreign currency and traveller's cheques. G&T Continental (1 C & 4 Av) will also change dollars.

Internet There are plenty of cybercafés around town. For fast connections and cheap prices head to Cyberplus (on the plaza), where they also have Skype (internet Q6/hr; Skype Q1.50/min to the US, Q2.50/min to Europe).

Language schools Cobán is becoming a popular place to pick up some Spanish. Recommended schools include: Active Spanish School, 3 C 6–12, Zona 1 (☎ 7941 7123, ✉ nirspanishschool @hotmail.com), and Muqb'ilb'e Spanish School, 6 Av 5–39, Zona 3 (☎ 7951 2459, ✉ muqbilbeav @yahoo.com), where they also offer Q'eqchi' lessons.

Laundry Doña Betty's Laundry, 2 C 6–10, Zona 3 (open 'till late daily). They provide wash and dry service in 2hr for Q30.

Post office 2 C & 2 Av (Mon–Fri 8.30am–5.30pm, Sat 9am–1pm).

Shopping The lively daily market is centred around the junction of 3 C & 1 Av at the meeting of zonas 1 & 3, and extends uphill to the streets behind the Cathedral, where you can find cheap street food. For supermarket shopping head to Dispensas Familias opposite the Cathedral, or Plaza Magdalena on the town's western outskirts, where you can also find a small selection of clothing stores. For souvenirs, Casa d'Acuña and Xkape Kob'an both have small shops selling local crafts and produce.

Telephones Teluga has its main office on the plaza. There are plenty of payphones here too.

Moving on

By bus to: El Estor (9.30am & 11am; 6hr), from 3 C A & 3 Av, Zona 4; Guatemala City (hourly 2am–4pm; 4hr 30min), from 2 C 3–77, Zona 4 (take these buses for the Biotopo del Quetzal, Chilascó and Salamá – change at La Cumbre); Lanquín (hourly 6am–6pm; 1hr 45min–2hr 15min; take these buses for Semuc Champey or Cahabón); Senahu (10.30am & noon; 5hr), from 3 C A & 3 Av, Zona 4.

By micro Micros for Chisec (1hr 30min), Fray Bartolomé de las Casas (3hr), Playa Grande (4hr), Raxrujá (2hr 30min) and Uspantán (3hr) depart the northern terminal at 3 Av, Zona 1, every 30min 5am–6pm. Micros for Sayaxché (daily 10am & 1.30pm; 4hr 30min) also depart the northern terminal; the 1.30pm departure continues to Flores (6hr 30min). For San Juan Chalmeco (10min) there are micros every 10min from the bridge at the bottom of 1 Av A, Zona 3.

AROUND COBÁN

The area surrounding Cobán is both craggy and lush, with limestone bedrock and a surface of patchwork fields. There are still some areas of forest, mainly to the southeast, but the Maya population of Alta Verapaz have turned most of the land over to the production of maize, coffee and ferns. It's worth venturing into this rural heartland of Guatemala to explore traditional market towns and their surrounding villages, as well as fresh-water swimming pools and stalagtite caves.

San Juan Chamelco

A few kilometres southeast of Cobán, easily reached by regular micros, **San Juan Chamelco** is the most important Q'eqchi' settlement in the area. It is claimed, in fact, that the village was never conquered by the Spanish, and certainly the community here remains largely indigenous. However, Chamelco's focal point is its hilltop **church**, a huge, open-plan space with timber frame roof and several Jesus effigies with bloody stigmata and massacred eyelashes. The best time to visit the village is the week preceding its annual **fiesta** (June 23), when celebrations include folk dancing in traditional dress and the arrival of numerous saints from neighbouring San Pedro Carcha, brought to greet the holy effigies from Chamelco's own church.

Just outside Chamelco are the **Grutas del Rey Marcos**, an extensive cave network (daily 7am–5pm; US$4, including the services of a guide, plus hard hat and boot rental). You can take a tour that explores up to 100m into the caverns, which are full of stalagmites that uncannily resemble various familiar objects. To reach the caves, catch a micro from the church in Chamelco headed for Santa Cecilia.

Micros congregate behind the church on the hilltop and head to Cobán and the surrounding Maya villages. To get to Chamelco from Cobán, head for the bridge at the southern end of 1 Avenida

in Zona 3, from where micros leave every ten minutes.

Swimming pools

On the road to Chisec, half an hour outside Cobán, is the **Ecocentro Sataña** (daily 9am–5pm; Q20), a bathing complex that includes both natural and man-made swimming pools in a jungle setting, with gardens and picnic areas as well as a restaurant at weekends. Take any micro headed to Chisec.

At the town of San Pedro Carcha, 5km east of Cobán, is the **Balneario las Islas**, another natural pool with a river tumbling into it. To get to Carcha there are regular departures from the lot opposite the Monja Blanca terminal in Cobán. The Balneario is about 15min east of town – locals should be able to direct you.

LANQUÍN

From Cobán a newly paved road heads east, almost as far as the village of **LANQUÍN** (the last 11km are painfully slow and bumpy). The journey is a stunningly beautiful one, in spite of the evident deforestation – sit on the right side of the bus for the best views. More and more backpackers are making the excursion in this direction to see the nearby natural wonder of Semuc Champey, and consequently some excellent accommodation and activity options have sprung up. Most visitors stay a minimum of two nights (either in Lanquín or around Semuc), with weekends and holidays being especially busy, as Guatemalans also flock to this national landmark.

The town of Lanquín itself is a sleepy, Q'eqchi' village superbly sheltered beneath towering green hills. As you enter the village from Cobán you pass the **Grutas de Lanquín** (daily 8am–6pm; US$4), from where the Río Lanquín emerges. The river is fairly feisty, but if you're up for it locals will rent you inner tubes and pick you up downstream. To view the caves you can enter without a guide, but for a closer look take the guided tour from *El Retiro* lodge (daily 4.30pm; Q55). At dusk every day thousands of bats fly out of the cave to feed – you can watch them for free from the entrance car park or anywhere along the river bank, but the tour also allows you the opportunity to stand in the cave entrance as they zip past you.

Arrival and Information

By bus If your bus terminates in Lanquín, you'll be dropped at the junction where the road splits east for Cahabón (and *El Retiro* lodge) and south for Semuc Champey (and the village centre, just up the hill). If heading for *El Retiro*, it's a 15min walk from the junction, so if your bus goes to Cahabón, stay aboard.

Exchange The village has a bank, in the centre of town on the road out towards Semuc Champey, but no ATM.

Tour operators Guatemala Rafting (℡ 7983 3056, ℮ info@guatemalarafting.com) is a Dutch-run outfit based next-door to *El Retiro* lodge in Lanquín. One-day rafting trip US$45, or two-day overnight expedition $135 (including food and equipment). Kayaks and two-person hotdog rafts also available.

Tourist information There's no official information outlet in town, but El Retiro can give information tailoured to backpackers' needs. The useful noticeboards here provide thorough information about onward transportation options.

Accommodation

Posada Ilobal Past the market and bank in the village centre ℡ 7983 0014. A small, cheerful posada, representing the best deal in Lanquín for a simple, clean and airy room. All rooms have shared bath and some have lovely views. **❷**

Rabin Itzam ℡ 7983 0076. Bright pink building right at the Cobán/Cahabón/Semuc junction. There is a selection of basic rooms here; the best are upstairs, opening onto the roof terrace with priceless views. **❷**

El Retiro ℡ 7983 0009. Something of a legendary travellers' hangout, this lodge consists of a series of bamboo cabins situated on the rolling green banks of the Río Lanquín, faced with patchwork views of the opposing side

of the valley. The accommodation ranges from camping (**❶**), to four-bed dorms and private two-bed lofts (**❶**), to private cabins and rooms with private bath (**❹**). The lodge also offers excellent tours to Semuc Champey and the Kan'ba Caves (US$20), and another to witness the bat exodus at the Grutas de Lanquín (US$8). Lockers, internet and book swap available. Reserve in advance, especially in high season.

Eating

Cafeteria Champey Halfway between *El Retiro* and the village, this place offers an alternative to those opting out of *Retiro*'s evening meal. They serve an interesting range of international dishes, including schnitzel and *shakshuka* (Q15–30).

El Retiro At the lodge. Definitely the place to be for hungry *mochileros* (backpackers). Hearty, family-style evening meals (Q40) and zingy happy-hour cocktails (Q10). Prices will start to add up, but it's hard to resist the banana and Nutella crêpes for breakfast (Q24) or falafel sandwich for lunch (Q22). You can eat here even if you're not staying, but it's a good idea to add your name to the dinner list in advance.

Moving on

By bus Buses for Cobán (1hr 45min–2hr 15min) depart the central junction (but also tour the village picking up potential passengers) in the morning from 5am hourly and in the afternoon at 2pm, 4pm and 5pm. Buses arriving from Cobán pass the central junction of Lanquin and continue to Semuc Champey or Cahabón (30–45min).

PARQUE NACIONAL SEMUC CHAMPEY AND THE KAN'BA CAVES

The big draws to Alta Verapaz are the extraordinary pools of **PARQUE NACIONAL SEMUC CHAMPEY** (daily 6am–6pm; US$6.50), southeast of Lanquín. Here the bulk of the Río Cahabón cuts underground, leaving a suspended limestone bridge. The top of the bridge is graced with a series of idyllic **pools** that descend in a natural staircase of turquoise waters, bordered by steep jungle gorge walls, while below the bridge is a raging torrent. A gruelling trail leads up to a viewpoint and another more leisurely to the pools themselves, where you can swim. Do not leave valuables unattended while you paddle. While you can visit on your own, most travellers choose to visit the national park as part of a tour, which avoids having to wait for infrequent public transport. In addition, coming with a tour (see p.220 for operators in Lanquín) can offer additional opportunities to explore: many allow you to descend underneath the bridge to reveal the raging river below. This is not for the faint of heart (it involves a rope ladder), but it does give a complete perspective on this outstanding geological feature.

To get to Semuc Champey without a tour you'll need to catch a **bus** from Cobán (5.45am, 11am, noon & 5pm; 1hr 30min–2hr) to Lanquín. Buses through Lanquin to Semuc are irregular, but it should be possible to flag down passing pick-ups as an alternative.

Another worthwhile adventure in the area is a visit to the privately owned **KAN'BA CAVES** (entrance by guided tour only 8am, 10am, 1pm & 3pm; US$6.50), on the riverbank directly opposite the national park entrance. Best for adrenaline junkies, tours here are run without hard hats and torches and instead feature stubby candles and the need to swim one-handed while holding them aloft. Sharp rocks and slippery surfaces add to this treacherous assault course, which will leave you

shivering and happy to emerge to the daylight.

Accommodation

Las Marias ☏7861 2209, ✉posadalasmarias @yahoo.com. About 1km before the national park and cave entrance. It's a rambling place with wooden walls partitioning dorms and private rooms. There are also larger group/family cabins for 8–11 people. *Marias* actually own the riverbank here and along as far as the national park, including the Kan'ba Caves, where guests receive discounted entry. There are rope swings and sunbathing decks, plus you can rent inner tubes. There is also a small restaurant here. Dorms ❶, doubles ❷–❹
El Portal ☏7983 0046/0043. Directly outside the national park entrance in a charming riverside location, this tasteful operation is threatening to break the monopoly long held by neighbouring *Las Marias*. A range of sleeping options are offered in pretty thatched cabins – the cheapest are dorms with mattresses or beds (both ❶) – and private doubles with or without bath (❷–❹). There is also a small restaurant and well-stocked bar. Electricity available 6–10pm.

Moving on

By bus There are irregular buses to Lanquín in the morning and early afternoon (30–45min). Alternatively, it may be possible to flag down a passing pick-up; make sure you pay for your ride.

EAST TO CAHABÓN

Beyond Lanquín the road continues 24km to the settlement of **CAHABÓN**. From here, a very rough road heads

---

PUERTA AL MUNDO MAYA

From Cobán a good road heads north towards Petén. On the way are a collection of sights worthy of exploration if you have the time. Administered by local communities, but promoted by the umbrella association **AGRETUCHI** (☏5978 1465, ✉Info@puertamundomaya.com ⓦwww.puertamundomaya.com), the attractions of the **Puerta al Mundo Maya** are monitored as low-impact, sustainable tourism sites which can benefit the local community. The Gateway to the Maya World is an innovative community tourism programme being developed with support from (among others) inguat, USAID and The National Geographic Society. Its attractions are dotted throughout northern Alta Verapaz and southern Petén. These include: two of the four Candelaria caves (see p.223), B'omb'il Pek Cave and the adjacent Río San Simon (see p.222), the Lagunas Sepalau (see p.222), Cancuén (see p.224), El Peru (see p.239) and El Mirador (see p.239).

south towards the village of **Panzós**, cutting high over the mountains through some of the finest, most verdant scenery in Guatemala. At the time of research there were no buses (only pick-ups) leaving Cahabón for the three-hour trip to El Estor in the Polochic Valley; check at *El Retiro* for the latest information. A more adventurous option is to cover this territory by **river**: the Río Cahabón is considered one of the best stretches of white-water in Central America. It's possible to arrange multi-day rafting trips out of Lanquín with Guatemala Rafting (see p.220), allowing you to connect with onward transport for Río Dulce and the Izabal area. High-water season is June to February, when rapids reach class IV/V; water levels may otherwise be too low.

CHISEC

CHISEC is a small town, bisected from north to south by CA-14. There's not much here – in fact, the huge plaza seems to account for half the town. However, there are a few hotels from which to base yourself for visiting nearby attractions.

What to see and do

Just outside Chisec are a couple of the attractions of the Puerta al Mundo Maya. These can be visited independently, although public transport is unreliable, so it may be worth contacting AGRETUCHI to help arrange a tour (see box, p.221).

B'omb'il Pek

2km north of town, with an office on the highway, is the entrance to the **B'omb'il Pek** caves. Tours (daily 8am–1pm; US$8) are community-run, and last between three and four hours. In the course of the tour you will be shown two caves. One is entered via a deep ravine, which you can rappel down to (for an extra US$3), or take a slippery

wooden staircase; the second cave boasts ancient paintings of monkeys. A pleasant addition to the tour involves inner tubing for thirty minutes (US$4) on the nearby **Río San Simón**, which cuts a tiny gorge through the rock. Regular micros pass the highway office, shuttling between Chisec and Raxrujá.

Lagunas Sepalau

Ten kilometres east of Chisec are the beautiful **Lagunas Sepalau** (daily 7am–5pm; US$8). Set among a protected forest reserve, these four turquoise pools are sourced by groundwater in the permeable limestone rock. Guides can escort you along a trail, pointing out wildlife and medicinal plants, and you can can swim or rent kayaks from several rocky beaches. Camping is permitted at the lakesides, as well as at the entrance, where there are showers and cooking facilities (❶). To get here from Chisec there is a 10am microbus and a few infrequent pickups that you can hitch a ride with (Q5). Stand on the track road heading east from the Municipalidad (on the Plaza), to flag one down. Returning, most transport passes the park in the afternoon; there is a 1pm micro and later pickups take the *Campesinos* back to town. Alternatively a taxi should cost Q50 each way.

Arrival and information

By micro Arriving from Cobán, you'll be dropped a block north of the plaza; otherwise, coming from the north it'll be the plaza itself (get off early if you want the *Hotel la Estancia*).

Tour operators AGRETUCHI (☎ 5978 1465, ✉ info@puertamundamaya.com) can provide information on community-based ecotourism activities around Chisec and beyond.

Accommodation

Hotel Elizabeth Opposite *La Estancia*. Rooms here are bare and rather cell-like, but among the cheapest in town. ❸
Hotel la Estancia ☎ 5514 7444. Sitting on the road north out of town, this multi-storey yellow

hotel is the best-quality place in town with its own, surprisingly decadent, swimming pool complex. Rooms have private bathroom and TV and come with or without a/c. ④–⑤

Hotel Nopales ☎ 5514 0624. On the plaza, this small hotel has basic rooms with bathroom, TV and fan. There is also a small *comedor* and an empty swimming pool. ③

Eating

Café la Huella On the main road, just off the north side of the plaza, this simple *comedor* offers cheap snacks and breakfasts for Q5–15.

Rancho el Potrillo A large thatched restaurant/bar northeast of the plaza. They serve breakfast (Q15–20), snacks (Q10–15) and main meals (Q25–30).

Restaurant Mi Casita One block north of the plaza, along from the microbuses heading north, this is a new, open-plan restaurant. A tasty plate of *comida típica* with beer will set you back Q35.

Directory

Exchange There are two banks on the plaza; the Agromercantil has an ATM.

Internet There are a couple of cafés on the main road heading north out of town.

Post office One block up from the eastern side of the plaza.

Moving on

By micro to: Cobán (1hr 30min) depart from the south side of the plaza, Raxrujá (1hr) and Playa Grande (2hr 30min) depart from one block north of the plaza. (Some northbound micros also continue on to Sayaxché or Fray Bartolomé de las Casas). Micros depart approximately every 30min.

RAXRUJÁ

The small town of **RAXRUJÁ** provides a handy base for visiting the nearby **Candelaria cave network** and the Maya ruins of **Cancuén**. The town itself, however, is little more than a 200m stretch of buildings along the roadside, centred at the junction where the paved road ends and rough tracks lead off to the village of La Unión to the north, or across a rickety bridge towards Fray Bartolomé de las Casas to the east.

Accommodation and eating

🏃 **Hotel Cancuén** ☎ 7983 0720. An excellent-value option at the western end of town. Rooms are with or without private bath and have cable TV and fan or a/c. The management are extremely friendly and run tours to their privately owned cave complex, as well as to the Cancuén ruins. There is a small *comedor* on site, plus internet access and cold drinks. ②–④

Hotel Gutierrez An alternative for budget rooms, *Hotel Gutierrez* has tiny cell-like rooms with fan and shared bath. It's near the centre of town opposite the football pitch. ②–③

Restaurant Steakhouse On the main road. Despite the name, this place serves the standard *comida típica*, though it is good value and tasty. Main dishes run 35–60Q and snacks, including a mountain of Mexican tacos, Q5–15.

Moving on

By micro to: Cobán (2hr 30min), Fray Bartolomé de las Casas (1hr) and Sayaxché (2hr) depart from the central junction every 30min between 6am and 5pm.

By bus to: Guatemala City (10hr). Departs *Hotel el Amigo* (on the main road) at 6pm daily.

AROUND RAXRUJÁ

The limestone hills around Raxrujá are riddled with cave networks and subterranean rivers. Also nearby is the rarely visted Mayan ruin of Cancuén (one of the sites promoted as part of the Puerta al Mundo Maya).

The Candelaria Caves

Candelaria Caves are a very accessible set of caves. Rather confusingly, there are four possible entrances: two are community-run (**Candelaria Camposanto** and **Mucbilha'1**; contact AGRETUCHI in Chisec, see p.221) and two are privately owned (**Cuevas de Candelaria** and **Candelaria los Nacimientos**) – the latter two are most easily accessible for independent travellers.

Hotel Cancuén in Raxrujá offers a full day tour (US$17) to Los Nacimientos, where you can visit the crystalline Cueva Blanca, as well as float for several hours through the creepy bat-filled caverns. Alternatively, to reach the Cuevas de Candelaria entrance, hop on a micro heading west from Raxrujá. After five minutes a path leads off the road, from the large "Cuevas de Candelaria" sign, towards a resort complex containing some overpriced rustic bungalows and a restaurant that offers probably the best food for miles around (mains from Q35). You don't have to be a guest to visit the caves here. A one-hour group tour on foot is US$4, or by inner-tube US$13.50. Usually you can tag onto a group if they have one visiting and simply pay per head. Otherwise, you need a minimum of three to obtain the above rates.

Cancuén

North of Raxrujá is the large Maya site of **Cancuén** (daily 8am–4pm; US$8), where a huge Classic-era palace has been unearthed. Uniquely, Cancuén seems to have lacked the usual religious and defensive structures characteristic of Maya cities, instead existing as an essentially secular trading city. The vast amounts of jade, pyrite, obsidian and fine ceramics found recently indicate that this was actually one of the greatest trading centres of the Maya world, with a paved plaza (which may have been a marketplace) covering two square kilometres. Cancuén is thought to have flourished because of its strategic position between the great cities of the lowlands, like Tikal and Calakmul, and the mineral-rich highlands of southern Guatemala. The site is administered by AGRETUCHI and there is a visitors' centre and toilets.

To **get to** Cancuén, pick-ups (approximately hourly) leave Raxrujá for the *aldea* of La Unión, 12km to the north, where boatmen will take you by *lancha* (Q30) for the thirty-minute ride along the Río Pasión to the site. It's also possible to travel via the village of La Isla, but connections here are not as good.

Fray Bartolomé de las Casas

One hour east of Raxrujá is the isolated settlement of **Fray Bartolomé de las Casas**, referred to as simply Fray (pronounced "Fry") by locals. The town has some basic accommodation and *comedores* plus ATMs and a thriving market. Otherwise, there isn't much of interest here. However, it is a main transport link between Alta Verapaz and other popular areas to the east and north. Regular transport leaves the market place bus terminal for Sebol/Raxrujá/Cobán and the village of Chahal (1hr), from where there are further micros heading east towards the highway junction of Modesto Mendes/Cadenas (2hr), where you can connect with passing transport to Poptún or Río Dulce. There is also a daily bus from Fray to Poptún (via San Luis). However, this is a painfully slow road and the bus departs at 3am, making the route via Chahal potentially quicker and certainly more convenient. In between Chahal and Modesto Mendes are the **natural pools** of Las Conchas and the nearby backpackers' hide-away of *Oasis Chiyu* (☎5839 4473, ⓦwww .naturetoursguatemala.com; ❹), where you can sleep in dorms and enjoy breakfast and dinner.

PARQUE NACIONAL LAGUNA LACHUÁ

In the far northwest corner of Alta Verapaz is the frontier town of Playa Grande and the nearby natural attraction of **PARQUE NACIONAL LAGUNA LACHUÁ** (daily 7am–4pm; US$5.50; ☎7861 0086), a great place to get off the beaten track for a day or two of tranquil, no-frills swimming and sunbathing. The lake is a near perfect disc of crystal water, ringed by tropical forest reserve, and the area is home to a host of wildlife, including jaguars, ocelots, otters and tapirs. The scrupulously maintained national park provides **camping** facilities (❶) as well as a lodge with mosquito-netted bunks (②). There are good cooking facilities and drinking water, but you need to bring your own food.

Microbuses from Cobán pass the park entrance hourly (4hr), or you can pick one up at the junction with the main road (2hr). You pay your entrance fee and accommodation costs at the **visitors' centre** on the road. It is also possible to leave your backpack here and take just a smaller bag on the sweaty 4km walk through the jungle to the lakeside lodge.

Petén

The low-lying northern department of **Petén**, once the Maya heartland, occupies about a third of Guatemala's territory but is home to just three percent of its population. Of late, though, there has been a wave of *ladino* immigration to the area, encouraged by the government in an attempt to bring this wild land into production. Vast swathes of rainforest have been cleared for ranching and commercial logging, despite the fact that forty percent of the department is officially protected by the **Maya Biosphere Reserve**. However, most sights of note are at least still shrouded in jungle, and you will doubtless witness some of Petén's remarkably vibrant wildlife.

El Petén also boasts an incredible number of **Maya sites** – several hundred ruined cities have been mapped in the region, though most are still buried beneath the jungle. The superstar attraction is **Tikal**, but other less visited highlights include atmospheric **Yaxhá**

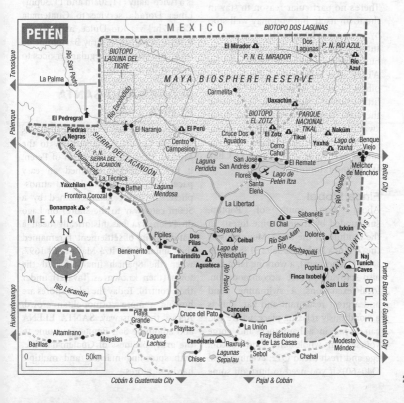

and the immense **El Mirador**. Of modern towns, the twin lakeside towns of **Flores** and **Santa Elena** form the hub of the department, and you'll find hotels and restaurants to suit all tastes. Halfway between Flores and Tikal is the tranquil alternative base of **El Remate**. The caves and scenery around **Poptún**, on the main highway south, also justify exploration, while down the other road south, **Sayaxché** is surrounded by yet more Maya sites.

POPTÚN AND AROUND

Heading north from the Río Dulce the smooth paved highway to Flores cuts through a degraded landscape of small *milpa* farms and cattle ranches that was jungle a decade or two ago. Many travellers choose to stop along the way at the sublime *Finca Ixobel* (see below) outside the small town of **POPTÚN**. There's no particular reason to stay in the town itself, but you may well stop by to use a cybercafé (try Servicio de Internet, next to the Fuente del Norte bus office) or banks (Bancafé has a Visa ATM). The area around Poptún also offers excellent opportunities to visit little-known attractions, including the Naj Tunich Caves, the delightful swimming pool of Las Cataratas waterfalls near the village of Mopán and the minor archeological sites of El Chal, Ixcún and Ixtontón.

Finca Ixobel

About 4km south of Poptún, surrounded by fragrant pine forests in the foothills of the Maya Mountains, is the 🏕 **Finca Ixobel** (☎5892 3188, ✉info @fincaixobel.com), a working farm that also provides guest accommodation, local excursions, a swimming pond and a great restaurant and bar. This is a wondrously relaxing place, where you can swing in a hammock and gorge yourself on wholesome food (bacon, egg and fresh bread Q12; evening meal Q40–60). If you need to burn off some

calories you can also hike, inner-tube or horse-ride and visit local caves, forests and swimming holes. Most people hang around longer than they'd originally planned, some staying to work as volunteers. The range of accommodation options includes: camping (①), dorms (①), treehouses (③), bungalows (⑤) and private rooms with or without bathroom (②–⑤).

To get to the *finca* ask the bus driver to drop you at the gate (marked by a large sign), from where it's a fifteen-minute walk through the pine trees; after dark, it's safest to head for the *Fonda Ixobel* restaurant in Poptún and they'll call a taxi to drop you off. When you leave, there are direct shuttle services to Flores and Río Dulce or alternatively back on the main road flag down a passing micro to Poptún town and arrange onward public transport. There is a twice-daily (11.30am and 11.30pm) Linea Dorada service to Guatemala City (7hr) via Río Dulce, as well as a 9.30am departure to Fray Bartolomé de las Casas (6hr) and regular services to Flores (2hr).

FLORES AND SANTA ELENA

Despite the legions of tourists that pass through **FLORES**, the gateway to the Mundo Maya and the capital of Petén, it has nonetheless retained an easy pace and a sedate, Old World atmosphere. This tiny island (joined by a 500m causeway to the shore) on Lago de Petén Itzá has historically been a natural point of settlement. It remained the capital of the Itzá Maya until 1697, when the Spanish finally forced the town (then known as Tayasal) under their control. Today the lake's shores are hosting a more cosmopolitan crowd. Across the causeway, **SANTA ELENA** and adjoining San Benito are home to the gritty business of Guatemalan life, with sprawling markets and multiple hardware stores.

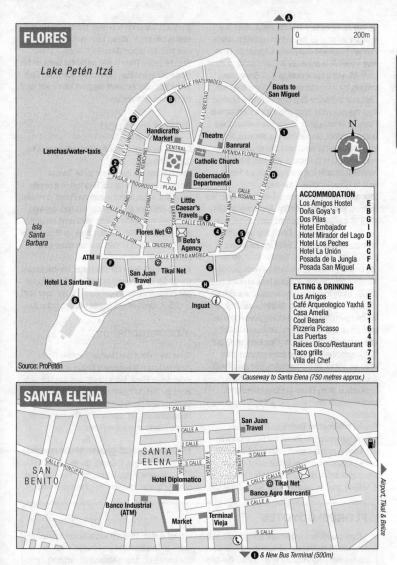

FLORES

0 — 200m

Lake Petén Itzá

CALLE FRATERNIDED

Boats to
San Miguel

AV. LA LIBERTAD

B

C

Handicrafts
Market

Theatre

Banrural

AVENIDA FLORES

Catholic Church

Gobernación
Departamental

Lanchas/water-taxis

CALLE LA UNIÓN

CALLEJON EL TENCINO

CENTRAL

PASAJE PROGROSO

CALLEJON PEDRITO

AV REFORMA

PLAZA

Little
Caesar's
Travels

CALLE
EL ROSARIO

CALLE 15 DESEPTIEMBRE

D

A

N

Isla
Santa
Barbara

CALLEJON DE JUNIO

AV BARRIOS

CALLE CENTRAL

Flores Net @

Beto's
Agency

AVENIDA SANTA ANA

4

5
6

ATM

F

EL CRUCERO

CALLE CENTRO AMÉRICA

@

Tikal Net

G

Hotel La Santana

San Juan
Travel

7

H

8

Inguat

i

Source: ProPetén

ACCOMMODATION

Los Amigos Hostel	E
Doña Goya's 1	B
Dos Pilas	G
Hotel Embajador	I
Hotel Mirador del Lago	D
Hotel Los Peches	H
Hotel La Unión	C
Posada de la Jungla	F
Posada San Miguel	A

EATING & DRINKING

Los Amigos	E
Café Arqueologico Yaxhá	5
Casa Amelia	3
Cool Beans	1
Pizzeria Picasso	6
Las Puertas	4
Raices Disco/Restaurant	8
Taco grills	7
Villa del Chef	2

▼ Causeway to Santa Elena (750 metres approx.)

SANTA ELENA

1 CALLE

San Juan
Travel

SANTA
ELENA

1 CALLE A

2 CALLE

4 AVENIDA

5 AVENIDA

6 AVENIDA

3 CALLE

SAN
BENITO

CALLE PRINCIPAL

3 CALLE

4 CALLE (CALLE PRINCIPAL)

Airport, Tikal & Belize

Hotel Diplomatico

@ Tikal Net

Banco Agro Mercantil

4 CALLE

Banco Industrial
(ATM)

Market

Terminal
Vieja

4 CALLE A

5 CALLE

C

▼ ① & New Bus Terminal (500m)

Flores boasts the lion's share of quality restaurants and decent budget accommodation, while Santa Elena is the region's transport hub and home to several banks and characterless expensive hotels. You will inevitably at least pass through Santa Elena on your way in and out of Flores, but there is no particular reason to visit here other than to check out the market, which chaotically surrounds the old (still partly used) bus terminal.

Arrival and information

By air The airport is in Santa Elena, 3km east of the causeway (a Q5 tuk-tuk or Q15 taxi ride into town). Returning to the airport, local buses leave from the Flores end of the causeway every 20min or so.

By bus All buses stop in Santa Elena. There is a new bus terminal on the northern outskirts, where Pullman buses and many micros terminate. From here a tuk-tuk to anywhere in Flores or Santa Elena costs Q5, and a taxi should be Q15. Some buses (notably the international services from Palenque, Chetumal and Belize City) drop you just a block up from the causeway, from where it's a short walk to Flores' accommodation. To confuse matters there is also a chaotic second (old) bus terminal, still in use for regional departures and arrivals. From here, you'll need to navigate your way through the market stalls onto C 4, from where it's a 10min walk to Flores (or Q5 in a tuk-tuk).

Tour operators These are ten-a-penny in Flores. You are most likely to deal with San Juan Travel (☎ 5847 4729, ✉ sanjuantravel@hotmail.com), on the Calle Sur (Flores) or 6 Av (Santa Elena). San Juan offers the most frequent return shuttle service to Tikal (Q60 return) and a popular "Sunrise Tour", allowing you flexibility in your return transport with several afternoon shuttles from the park back to Flores (Q300). Trying to muscle in on the sunrise action are Little Caesar (☎ 5418 4898, ✉ littlecaesarstravels @yahoo.com) and Beto, two local guides who have each set up agencies close to *Los Amigos* Hostel; Caesar speaks better English. Their tours are Q250/ Q240 respectively, including guide services, park entrance and return transportation. San Juan Travel also runs shuttles to domestic and international destinations. Many Flores-based agencies offer tours to remote Maya sites and will book flights and shuttles.

Tourist information There's no shortage of information sources in Flores, but be careful who you listen to as there are *coyotes* about (see box below). Inguat, the official tourist board, has an information booth at the airport (daily 7.30am–1pm & 4–6pm), another booth on Calle Sur in Flores (daily 7.30am–noon & 2–6pm; ☎ 5414 3594), as well as two larger offices, both on the main road east from the airport (Mon–Fri 7.30am–3.30pm; ☎ 5114 0109). There is also an Asistur booth on the causeway. In addition, *Los Amigos Hostel* and *Cafe Yaxhá* both offer excellent impartial advice and local information for travellers.

Island transport

Canoes Restaurant *Villa del Chef* rents canoes for Q20 per hour.

Lanchas You can hop across to the Tayasal Peninsula by *lancha* for Q5. They run on a regular basis until 11pm from the dock on Flores' northeast shores. Boatmen also offer day and half-day trips to explore the lake by *lancha*. Most hang out at the dock beside the *Villa del Chef*. Look for Miguel, who was born in Flores in 1925 and has some great stories.

Taxis and tuk-tuks For short hops, tuk-tuk drivers charge Q5 for anywhere in the Flores/Santa Elena/ San Benito area. For longer journeys, taxi fares start at Q15. To reach other lakeside villages, see p.231.

Accommodation

There are several good budget places in Flores itself, making it unnecessary to stay in noisier and dirtier Santa Elena. Many tour groups pass through, using the mid- to top-range accommodation, but there are also plenty of businesses tailored to the backpacker market. Unless otherwise marked, all places listed below are in Flores.

Hotels and guesthouses

Los Amigos C Central ☎ 7867 5975, ⓦ www.amigoshostel.com. The undisputed home of budget travellers in Flores, this is what

---

FLORES' COYOTES

Many travellers experience the hard sell on arrival in Flores from local ticket touts, known as *coyotes*. These guys know every trick in the book to persuade you to spend your money with them. Be especially aware on tourist shuttles arriving from Belize and Mexico, when you are likely to be travel-weary and green (ie, new to the country). Most *coyotes* speak excellent English and will bamboozle you with their seemingly exhaustive knowledge of your future travel options. Many susceptible backpackers are persuaded to book hotel rooms, tours and onward travel arrangements before even setting foot on Flores Island. In some cases *coyotes* have been found selling completely fake tickets; even if you do receive the service you've seemingly paid for, you will almost certainly have paid over the odds, as *coyotes* take a cut. Always buy tickets from a legitimate tour operator or hotel staff. Don't be in a hurry – if you shop around you're likely to get the best price and service.

all good hostels should be: cheap, clean, secure and with great services. Run by two Dutch guys and a posse of Guatemalan *chicas*, *Amigos* has a sociable, yet pleasantly mellow atmosphere. There are two large dorms (**①**), smaller four-person dorms (with private hot-water baths; **②**) and private doubles (without bath; **②**). Also provided are lockers, a bookswap, internet and extensive tourist information. There is also an excellent restaurant on site (see below).

Doña Goya's 1 C La Unión ☏ 7867 5513, ⓔ hospedajedonagoya@yahoo.com. Popular alternative to *Los Amigos* with dorm beds (**①**) and very pleasant private doubles (**③**). There is a great terrace upstairs for chilling, while downstairs is a small breakfast room with bookswap and internet facilities. A second branch of *Doña Goya's* is 20m around the corner.

Dos Pilas Alley off C Sur, ☏ 5064 3229. At the time of research this family-run business (formerly *Flores/Tikal Backpackers*), was going through a renovation to create a second dorm and several private rooms upstairs. The dorm mattresses are imaginatively housed in individual "tepees", each with their own fan and TV. The hostel's walls are testament to its popularity with graffiti scrawled in its praise from the international guests. Simple, economic food is served and there is a great lake view from the terrace upstairs. Tepee mattress **①**

Hotel Embajador Opposite the new bus terminal in Santa Elena ☏ no phone. If you're desperate to stay in Santa Elena for an early morning bus, this handy cheapie is a stone's throw from the terminal. It's basic but will suffice. **②**

Hotel Mirador del Lago C 15 Septiembre ☏ 7867 5409. Reasonable deal for private rooms on the lakeshore. Basic rooms have fan and bathroom but no view, while those facing the lake also have cable TV. There is internet, laundry service and a small restaurant. **②**–**④**

Hotel Los Peches C Sur ☏ 7867 5207, ⓔ hotelyrestaurantelospeches@gmail.com. Private rooms here are a bit shabby and overpriced, but there is also a huge lake-front dorm with its own bathroom and terrace. It could do with some finishing touches – despite the view, curtains would be nice – but is still a decent budget option. Dorms **①**, doubles **④**

Hotel La Unión C La Unión ☏ 7867 5531. On the western shore of the island with sunset views. For smart private rooms this place is excellent value – rooms are clean, bright and come with bathroom and fan. Those with direct lake view cost a bit extra. Downstairs is an internet café. **③**–**④**

Posada de la Jungla C Centroamerica ☏ 7867 5185, ⓔ info@travelpeten.com. This small but immaculate hotel is creeping into the mid-range budget, but still good value. Double rooms have fan, bathroom and cable TV. There are excellent views from the roof terrace. **④**

Posada San Miguel Across the lake in San Miguel village ☏ 7867 5312, ⓔ posadasanmiguel1 @gmail.com. A delightful family-run posada. For a private double it's better value than anywhere in Flores (even if you take into account the return *lancha* fare). Large lake-front rooms are best, with comfortable furnishings, private bathroom, TV and stunning views. There is a small beach directly out front and a simple *comedor* downstairs. **③**

Eating and drinking

There is a good selection of dining options in Flores, although due to the abundance of wealthy clientele prices are not necessarily low. For economical eats, head for the stalls on the plaza (7am–10pm) or on Calle Sur (5pm–1am). In Santa Elena there are numerous *comedores* where you can find the inevitable rice and beans for less than $2. Be aware that some local restaurants still serve wild game (such as *venado*, *pavo silvestre*, *coche de monte* or *tepesquintle*) – this is best avoided, as it is most likely to be poached from reserves. All restaurants and bars listed below are in Flores.

Restaurants and bars

Los Amigos C Central. It's hard to beat *Los Amigos* for value on portion size, and they have the best vegetarian selection in town (if not the entire country), including vegetable skewers or curry Q30. Also popular are the huge *licuados*; the banana, milk and cinnamon (Q12) is a meal in itself. Happy hour (7–8pm) means 2-for-1 beers and discounted cocktails.

🏃 **Cafe Arqueológico Yaxhá** C 15 Septiembre ☏ 5830 2060, ⓦ www.cafeyaxha.com. Good wholesome food. Most interesting is the pre-Hispanic menu of Maya specialities; the yucca, egg, tomato and herbs (Q30) is surprisingly tasty. The walls of the café are covered with posters and photos relating to local Maya sites, to which the German owners run excellent tours. They also offer excellent information about the immediate local area and run evening slide-shows.

Casa Amelia C La Unión. One of a string of attractively located restaurants on Flores' western shores, *Amelia* serves standard pastas (Q30) and pizzas (Q60) with a few veggie options (from Q25). The generous happy hour runs 5–9pm.

🏃 **Cool Beans** C 15 Septiembre. One of the most atmospheric places to eat and drink on the island, with a thatch-shaded seating area that runs down to a lakeshore garden where there are hammocks. The extensive menu features such favourites as granola, yogurt and fruit (Q18), brownies (Q5), nachos (Q20), club sandwiches (Q25) and refillable coffee (Q8). Open Mon & Wed–Sun till 9pm.

Pizzeria Picasso C 15 Septiembre. Deep-pan bases and generous toppings mean a regular pizza can feed two (unless your appetite is fuelled by a day's temple-climbing). Pizzas from Q35, pastas and burgers from Q25. Closed Mon.

Las Puertas C Central & Av Santa Ana. Worth it for the atmosphere, this bistro-style place is a bit pricey (beers Q20), but has a good menu with pastas and paninis for less than Q30 and some tempting desserts (tiramisu Q16). Opposite is a makeshift cinema, where you can watch a movie for Q20, including a free Cuba Libre.

Raices Disco/Restaurant Western end of C Sur. Head here for late-night cheap drinks and dancing. Beers and Cuba Libres go for Q10. The excellent restaurant downstairs specializes in grilled meats and packs in the tour groups. Closed Mon.

Villa del Chef C La Unión. Next door to *Casa Amelia*, this candle-lit pontoon offers good home-cooked plates. The fries are the closest you'll get to an English "chippy" on the island and the chicken skewers come recommended. Mains Q35–60. Happy hour 4.30–6pm.

Directory

Exchange Most banks and ATMs are in Santa Elena, around the central junction of 6 Av and 4 C, although there is now a temperamental ATM in Flores on C 30 Junio and one at the new bus terminal. Be alert on Sun when local thieves may take advantage of the lack of armed security at ATMs. There are currently a number of scams – check at *Los Amigos* for updates.

Internet There are several cybercafés along C Centroamerica. The cheapest is Beto's tour agency-cum-laundry-cum-internet café on Av Barrios (Q6/hr).

Language schools The only place in town offering Spanish classes was Academia de Español Dos Mundos (c/o *Cafe Yaxhá*), where 20 hours of one-to-one tuition costs US$100.

Laundry Cheapest is Beto's, just around the corner from *Los Amigos* on Av Barrios (wash and dry Q23). Since he runs sunrise tours to Tikal the shop is often closed until noon.

Post offices In Flores, on Av Barrios (Mon–Fri 8.30am–noon); in Santa Elena, C Principal, two blocks east of the Banco Agromercantil (Mon–Fri 8am–4.30pm).

Shopping As well as the plethora of tourist shops, there is a friendly handicraft market on the Parque Central (9am–9pm).

Moving on

By air to: Cancún (11.30am with TACA; 1hr 45min; US$220); Guatemala City (8.30am & 6.50pm with TACA, 4pm with TAG; 50min; from US$200 return). TACA information on ☎ 2470 8222, 🌐 www.taca .com; TAG information on ☎ 2380 9400. Demand is heavy for these flights, and over-booking is common. Reserve well in advance and arrive promptly for check-in. There is a Q20 departure tax charged on all flights. At the time of research, Tropic Air (for Belize City) had suspended flights.

By bus All services listed here depart from the new bus terminal in Santa Elena. Buses go to: Bethel (5am, with Fuente del Norte; 4hr); El Remate (6am & 7am, with Transportes Imperio Maya; 30–45min); Guatemala City (9pm & 11pm, with ADN; 3.30am, 4.30am, 7am, 7.45am, 8.30am, 9.45am, 10am, 11am, noon, 1.30pm, 2pm, 4.30pm, 6pm, 7.30pm, 8pm, 8.30pm, 9pm, 9.30pm, 10pm, 10.30pm, with Fuente del Norte; 8–9hr); Melchor de Menchos (2.30am, 5am, 6am, 4.30pm, 11pm, with Fuente del Norte; 2hr 30min); Río Dulce (6am, 10am, 2pm, with Maria Elena; 3hr); Sayaxché (6am, with Fuente del Norte; 2hr); San Salvador (6am, with Fuente del Norte; 15hr); Tikal (hourly 6am–1pm, with Transportes Imperio Maya; 1hr 30min); Uaxactún (1pm, with Transportes Imperio Maya; 2hr 30min). Many buses to Guatemala City stop in both Poptún and Río Dulce en route.

By microbus Local micros depart to Petén destinations from the Terminal Vieja (old terminal, buried within Santa Elena's market) usually 6am–5pm. Destinations include: Bethel (11.30am, noon, 3.30pm; 4hr); La Técnica, via Bethel (8am & 9am; 5hr); Melchor de Menchos, via El Remate (every 15min; 2hr 30min); Poptún (hourly; 2hr); Sayaxché (every 10min; 2hr); San José/San Andrés (every 15min; 1hr).

LAGO DE PETÉN ITZÁ

While the majority of visitors to Flores rightly prioritize a visit to Tikal, there are a string of other worthwhile day-trip excursions in the region surrounding **LAGO DE PETÉN ITZÁ**.

From Flores it's possible to visit a number of nearby attractions by *lancha*. These include: the tiny **Museo Santa Barbara** (8am–noon & 2–5pm; Q10), on an island just off Flores' western shores, which houses a collection of Maya pottery and a very old gramophone; **ARCAS**, an animal rescue NGO to the east of San Miguel village (9am–3pm; Q15), where you can volunteer (US$100 per week) or simply visit and see rescued parrots and monkeys; and beyond ARCAS, the **Petencito Zoo** (8am–5pm; Q20), which is home to (among others), crocodiles, tigers and some zippy waterslides. For the best *lancha* prices you'll need to get a group together and haggle fairly fiercely. Estimate about US$8 per hour.

Peninsula Tayasal

Incredibly, this attractive peninsula, just a five-minute *lancha* ride across the lake from Flores, is largely overlooked by the tourist dollars flooding into that town. The village of **San Miguel** and nearby **El Mirador** and **Playita el Chechenal** make for an easy off-the-beaten-track excursion. Regular *lanchas* leave from the northeast shores of Flores to San Miguel. To reach the Mirador it's a twenty-minute, fairly isolated walk. Follow the lakeshore west past the village, turn uphill after the last buildings, then follow the track up until it evens out to a shaded trail and take the left branch (keeping the lake to your left). Eventually you'll reach a clearing from where concrete steps lead up to the wooden lookout tower. There are fantastic views of the lake and its settlements. Back down at the clearing you can follow another trail for ten minutes, around the northern side of the peninsula (keeping the lake to your left), until you reach a signposted left turn for La Playita. You can see the turquoise water beckoning you and there is a quiet beach area with picnic benches and toilets (Q5). To return to San Miguel village, simply turn left at the end of the beach

LAGO DE PETÉN ITZÁ

road and follow the track for fifteen minutes to complete your circuit.

Actun-Kan Caves

Just north of Santa Elena, past the new bus terminal, is the entrance to the **Grutas Actun-Kan**, or serpent caves (8am–5pm; Q20). Bring your own flashlight and decent shoes, as the interior is dark and pretty slippery. The cave comprises a series of small passageways and some stalagtites apparently resembling well-known images. There are, however, no snakes. A tuk-tuk to the caves is Q5.

San Andrés and San José

Across the lake from Santa Elena and Flores are the quiet villages of **San Andrés** and **San José**. There is no longer a public boat service here as the road has been paved and regular micros now whiz past. The villages' roads slope steeply up from the shore, lined with colourful buildings. San José, in particular, has an impressive array of facilities (including a water park and music stadium). There is also a lovely public beach, a bank with planned ATM (under construction at the time of research) and several *comedores* serving *comida rápida*. The village is actually undergoing something of a cultural revival: Itzá, the pre-Conquest Maya tongue, is being taught in the large school.

Most visitors come this way to study or volunteer at one of the local language schools. Rates are around US$150–175 a week for twenty hours of one-to-one lessons, food and lodging with a local family – very few locals here speak English so you can progress quite quickly. Good schools include: Eco Escuela de Español (☎5940 1235, ⓦwww.ecoescuelaespanol .org), a community-run, long-established school in San Andrés; Escuela Nueva Juventud (☎5711 0040, ⓦwww .volunteerpeten.com), located in a 70-hectare medicinal plant reserve, just outside San Andrés; Escuela Bio Itzá

(☎7928 8056, ⓔescuelabioitza@hotmail .com), in San José, part of a project for the conservation of the Itzá biosphere and culture. Activities include volunteer work in the botanical garden and preparing natural medicines and cosmetics.

EL REMATE

The village of **EL REMATE** lies midway between Flores and Tikal on the northeastern corner of Lago de Petén Itzá. The lake is a beautiful turquoise blue here and many of the budget hotels offer swimming access – an extremely welcome idea after a sweaty morning climbing Tikal's jungle temples. As it is only a thirty-minute drive to Tikal from here, you also get to beat the crowds coming from Flores and arrive at an empty site to hear the jungle awake. All of El Remate's hotels offer door-to-door return shuttles to Tikal for Q50. All in all, it makes an excellent alternative to Flores for visits to the region.

What to see and do

On the north shore of the lake, fifteen minutes' walk from the centre of El Remate, the **Biotopo Cerro Cahuí** (daily 7am–4pm; US$3) is a 6.5-squarekilometre wildlife conservation area comprising lakeshore, ponds and some of the best examples of undisturbed tropical forest in Petén. There are hiking trails (4km and 6km), a couple of small ruins and two thatched *miradores* on the hill above the lake; pick up maps and information at the gate where you sign in. It's recommended to visit the park in the early morning as wildlife is most active and it is cooler at this time.

Arrival and information

By bus and microbus El Remate lies just north (15min walk) of the Puente Ixlú (sometimes known as El Cruce) junction. Many buses/micros taking the main road between Santa Elena and Melchor de Menchos on the Belize border will drop you here. Alternatively, some transport heading north of Puente Ixlú towards Tikal will pass through the village itself. The main bus stop is loacted in the village centre at the point where a minor road branches west (around the northern lakeshore) off the main Tikal road. However, you can ask your driver to drop you anywhere between the Puente Ixlú junction and the bus stop. For accommodation located on the northern lakeshore road you will need to walk.

Exchange There are no banks, but you can change dollars at *Hotel Casa Don David* in the village centre.

Tourist information There is an information booth on the left as you enter the village, but don't bank on it being open. Several hotels provide good tourist information and tours – try *Hotel Sun Breeze* and *Restaurant/Hotel Gardenias* for competitive prices to remote Maya sites such as Yaxhá.

Accommodation

El Remate has plenty of budget deals and a few mid-range options, too. You'll pay slightly more to have lake views or access, but the setting is so idyllic it's probably worth it. The following are listed in the order you reach them from Puente Ixlú.

Camping y Hotel El Paraíso One of the first places you come to on entering the village, on the right 50m off the main road. It's a simple place with rustic charm. Camping is available, and there are five basic rooms with bed and mosquito net. Camping ❶, rooms ❶

El Mirador del Duende High above the lake, reached by a stairway cut into the cliff ☎5300 1896. An incredible collection of igloo-like, white-washed stucco open bungalows/cabañas decorated with Maya glyphs. Though the views are unparalled, the rooms are basic and not especially secure. Great terrace overlooking the lake and cheap vegetarian food. ❶

Posada El Eden ☎7928 8043. Four very basic rooms with fan and mosquito nets on the lakeside, set in pretty gardens. The two rooms with views of the lake are preferable. Shared bathrooms are clean. ❷

Hostal Sak-Luk ☎5494 5925, ✉tikalsakluk @hotmail.com. Interestingly eccentric place owned by an artist who has used the hostel as his canvas. It is located on the hillside facing the lake and enjoys great views. There is a decent restaurant and a wood-burning stove for self catering. Dorms ❶, doubles ❷–❸

Hostal Hermano Pedro Just off the main road opposite the football pitch ☎5719 7394. A peaceful and relaxing house, with large homely rooms. Each has private bath and opens onto a communal

decked balcony area. A particularly good deal for solo travellers, as they charge per person, not per room. ❷

Hotel Sun Breeze Lakeside, in the centre of the village ☎7928 8044. This well-established family business offers immaculate rooms with private bath and veranda and more economical basic rooms without bath, but with glorious lake views. The friendly owners offer a laundry service as well as tours to local attractions. ❷–❹

Casa Roja 500m down the road to Cerro Cahuí on the right ☎5173 2593. Simple, well-constructed, stick-and-thatch cabañas. They rent beds dorm-style, and there is also one large two-bed room that makes a particularly good deal for a couple. There's also an inexpensive vegetarian restaurant and kayaks for rent. ❷

Casa de Doña Tonita 800m down the road to Cerro Cahuí on the right ☎5701 7114. Four basic clapboard rooms, built high above the lake, with great views, plus a six-bed dorm inside the thatched-roof of the restaurant next door. Dorms ❶, rooms ❷

🏃 **Mon Ami** 300m past *Dona Tonita's* ☎7928 8413, ✉hotelmonami@hotmail.com. Attractive rooms and bungalows with stylish, homely touches, set among wonderful gardens with views to the lake. There's also a superb in-house restaurant: try the chicken with lemon and herbs (Q35). Dorms ❶, rooms ❹–❺

Eating

Most restaurants are on the main road, though many hotels also have their own restaurants. *Casa Don David*, in the village centre, features a specials board tailored towards the palates of their international guests. Otherwise, wherever you go, don't expect anything flashy.

Restaurants

Restaurant Cahuí Opposite *Hostal Hermano Pedro*. This simple restaurant has a great lakeside setting and offers economical food, including burgers or spaghetti for Q20 and breakfast from Q16.

Restaurant Las Gardenias Back towards the village centre, this roadside *comedor* serves good-value meals from Q35 plus sandwiches from Q12. There is also a hotel and excellent information office.

Restaurant El Muelle Past the football pitch, south of *Restaurant Cahuí*. The menu here is a bit pricier – snacks (sandwiches, burgers and nachos Q15–25), mains (chicken, steak and fish Q45–70) – but you do get free use of the fantastic lakeside swimming pool if you eat here.

Moving on

By bus A few local buses and a swarm of minibuses ply the route to Flores (30–45min). You may have more luck walking to the Puente Ixlú junction and flagging one down there. For Belize (2hr), wait at Puente Ixlú for micros to Melchor de Menchos (every 15min). Alternatively, any hotel can book you a return shuttle.

TIKAL

Towering above the rainforest, **TIKAL** is possibly the most renowned of all Maya ruins (daily 6am–6pm; US$20). The site is dominated by five giant temples, steep-sided pyramids that rise up to 60m from the forest floor. In addition, literally thousands of other structures, many half-strangled by giant roots and still hidden beneath mounds of earth, demand exploration. The site itself is deep in the jungle of the **Parque Nacional Tikal**, and the forest is home to all sorts of wildlife, including howler and spider monkeys, toucans and parakeets. The sheer scale of the place is awe-inspiring, and its spirituality is spellbinding. Whether you can spare as little as an hour or as long as a week, it's always worth the trip.

What to see and do

The sheer scale of the ruins at Tikal can at first seem daunting. The **central area**, with its five main temples, forms by far the most impressive section; if you start to explore beyond this you can wander seemingly forever in the maze of smaller, unrestored structures and complexes. Whatever you do, Tikal is certain to exhaust you before you exhaust it. Rather too many visitors congregate to witness the sunrise when the forest canopy bursts into a frenzy of sound and activity. However, as the park officially opens at 6am, if you arrive independently at this hour, you can witness much the same atmosphere, yet without the

100-strong crowd of snap-happy tourists and their electronic digital camera soundtrack. There are two official park **museums**, the Museo Lítico (daily 9am–4pm; US$1.50) and the Museo Tikal (Mon–Fri 9am–5pm, Sat & Sun 9am–4pm; US$1.50) that house some of the artefacts found in the ruins, including jade jewellery, ceramics and obsidian flints, as well as numerous stelae.

From the entrance to the Great Plaza

From the site map at the entrance, a path branches right to **Complexes Q and R**. The first pyramid, with a line of eight stelae in front of it, is also known as the Temple of Nine Mayan Gods, where devotees can invoke the spirits with a simple ritual. Bearing left after Complex R, you approach the **East Plaza**; in its southeast corner stands an imposing temple, beneath which were found the remains of several severed heads, the victims of human sacrifice. From here a few short steps bring you to the **Great Plaza**, the heart of the ancient city. Surrounded by four massive structures, this was the focus of ceremonial and religious activity at Tikal for around a thousand years. Beneath the grass lie four layers of paving, the oldest of which dates from about 150 BC. **Temple 1** (or Jaguar Temple), towering 44m above the plaza, is the hallmark of Tikal. The skeleton of ruler Hasaw Chan K'awil (682–721 AD) was found in the tomb at the temple's core, surrounded by an assortment of jade, pearls, seashells and stingray spines. There's a reconstruction of the tomb (tumba 116) in the Museo Tikal. Standing opposite, like a squat version of Temple 1, is **Temple 2**, known as the Temple of the Masks for the two grotesque masks, now heavily eroded, that flank the central stairway. The **North Acropolis**, which fills the whole north side of the Great Plaza, is one of the most complex structures in the entire Maya world. In true Maya

THE RISE AND FALL OF TIKAL

900 BC First known settlement at Tikal.

500 BC Evidence of early stone buildings at the site.

c.10 AD Great Plaza begins to take shape and Tikal is an established major site with a large permanent population.

292 AD First recorded date on stelae at Tikal.

c.250 AD Continuous eruption of the Ilopango volcano causes huge devastation and disrupts trade routes, possibly leading to the decline and abandonment of El Mirador.

300 AD Tikal fills the subsequent power vacuum, allied with settlements at Kaminaljuyú and Teotihuacán.

550 AD Tikal hits its peak of dominance, having conquered neighbouring city-states and established an influence reaching as far as Copán in Honduras.

562 AD Caracol defeats Tikal. From the north, the city of Calakmul also emerges as a formidable rival.

c.700 AD As Calakmul's stranglehold begins to weaken, Tikal's legendary leader Lord Chocolate revives the city with a series of incredible victories deposing sequential kings of Calakmul.

869 AD Building ceases at Tikal.

899 AD Tikal abandoned.

1848 AD Ruins of Tikal officially rediscovered by a government expedition.

1956 AD Project to excavate and restore the buildings started.

1984 AD Most major restoration work completed.

style it was built and rebuilt on top of itself, and beneath the twelve temples that can be seen today are the remains of about a hundred other structures.

Central Acropolis and Temple 5

On the other side of the plaza is the **Central Acropolis**, a maze of tiny interconnecting rooms and stairways. The buildings here are usually referred to as palaces rather than temples, although their precise use remains a mystery. Behind the acropolis is the palace reservoir, which was fed with rainwater by a series of channels from all over the city.

Further behind the Central Acropolis is the 58-metre-high **Temple 5**. Some say you haven't really visited Tikal unless you've climbed the ladder at the side of Temple 5. You may not have realized that you suffered from vertigo until you try this; the view from the top is incomparable though.

From the West Plaza to Temple 4

Behind Temple 2 is the **West Plaza**, dominated by a large Late Classic temple on the north side, and scattered with various altars and stelae. From here the Tozzer Causeway leads west to **Temple 3** (55m), covered in jungle vegetation. Around the back of the temple is a huge palace complex, of which only the **Bat Palace** has been restored. At the end of the Tozzer Causeway is **Temple 4**, at 64m the tallest of all the Tikal structures, built in 741 AD. Twin ladders, one for the ascent, the other for the descent, are attached to the sides of the temple.

Mundo Perdido, Plaza of the Seven Temples and Temple of the Inscriptions

To the south of the Central Acropolis, reached by a trail from Temple 3, you'll find the **Plaza of the Seven Temples**, which forms part of a complex dating

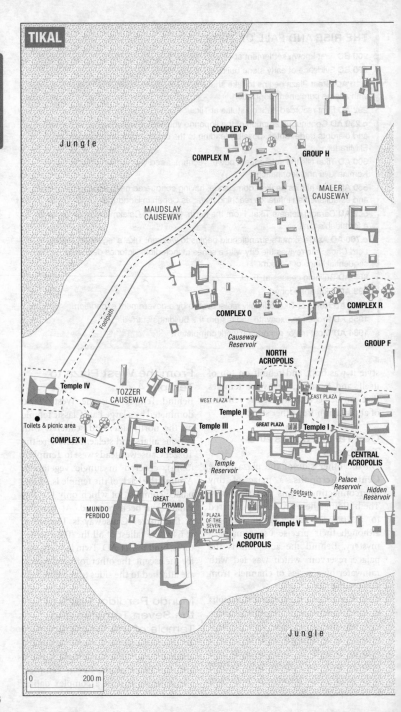

TIKAL

Jungle

COMPLEX P

COMPLEX M

GROUP H

COMPLEX N

GROUP H

MALER
CAUSEWAY

MAUDSLAY
CAUSEWAY

COMPLEX O

COMPLEX R

GROUP F

Causeway
Reservoir

NORTH
ACROPOLIS

Temple IV

TOZZER
CAUSEWAY

WEST PLAZA

EAST PLAZA

Toilets & picnic area

Temple II

GREAT PLAZA

Temple I

COMPLEX N

Temple III

Bat Palace

Temple
Reservoir

CENTRAL
ACROPOLIS

Palace
Reservoir

Hidden
Reservoir

Footpath

MUNDO
PERDIDO

GREAT
PYRAMID

PLAZA
OF THE
SEVEN
TEMPLES

Temple V

SOUTH
ACROPOLIS

Jungle

0   200 m

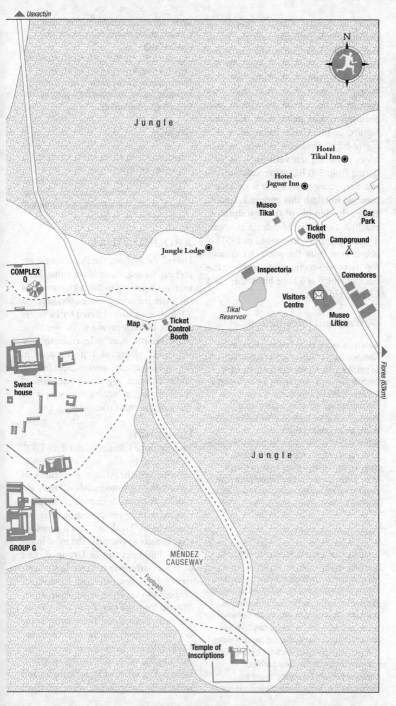

▲ *Uaxactún*

N

Jungle

Hotel
Tikal Inn ◉

Hotel
Jaguar Inn ◉

Museo
Tikal ■

Car
Park

Ticket
Booth

Campground
△

Comedores

Jungle Lodge ◉

Inspectoría ■

Visitors
Centre ■

▶ *Flores (63km)*

COMPLEX
Q

Tikal
Reservoir

Museo
Lítico ■

Map ■

Ticket
Control
Booth

Sweat
house

GROUP G

Jungle

MÉNDEZ
CAUSEWAY

Footpath

Temple of
Inscriptions

back to before Christ. There's an unusual triple ball court on the north side of the plaza, and to the east is the unexcavated South Acropolis. To the west, the **Mundo Perdido**, or Lost World, is another magical and very distinct section of the site with its own atmosphere and architecture. The main feature is the **Great Pyramid**, a 32-metre-high structure whose surface hides four earlier versions, the first dating from 500 BC. After accidents on the steep stone staircase, it is no longer possible to climb this pyramid. Finally, there's the **Temple of the Inscriptions**, reached along the Méndez Causeway. The temple (only discovered in 1951) is about 1km from the plaza. It's famous for its twelve-metre roof comb, at the back of which is a huge but rather faint hieroglyphic text.

Arrival and information

Arrival It's easy to get to Tikal from Flores and El Remate – see p.230 and p.232 for details. It should be possible to hitch a ride with one of the many shuttles, even if you don't have a pre-booked ticket.
Guides (US$60 for a 4hr tour). It is a worthwhile investment if you can afford it (get a group together). Ask at the ticket booth for services; many guides speak excellent English.
Visitors' centre Before the ticket booth and parking lot is a large visitors' centre. It houses toilets, souvenir stalls, an over-priced restaurant, a post office, a museum and, of greatest interest, a scale model of the site (a good place to orient yourself and overhear knowledgeable private guides).

Accommodation

There are three hotels at the ruins, all of them fairly expensive and not especially good value. There are good camping facilities, but most backpackers choose to visit Tikal as a day-trip. If you do decide to stay overnight, if you buy your park entrance ticket after 3pm, it will be valid for the following day as well. For food, if arriving before 9am, you should bring your own snacks and plenty of water. The best-value places for lunch are the small *comedores* opposite the visitor's centre.
Camping Between the parking lot and the *comedores*, a well-maintained campground has

toilets, showers and campfire facilities. There are also thatched shelters from which to hang hammocks. ❶
Jaguar Inn ☎ 7783 3647, ✉ contact@jaguartikal .com. The most economical of Tikal's hotels. Smart bungalows with bathroom, fan and porch hammock. You can also camp in the pretty garden. Camping ❶, bungalows ❻

Eating

Comedores Offering a limited menu of traditional Guatemalan specialities – eggs, beans, grilled meat and chicken (from Q25). For a more extensive menu, there's a decent restaurant at the *Jaguar Inn* (mains from Q40). Cold soft drinks and snacks are sold around the ruins by vendors.

AROUND TIKAL

Dotted throughout the Petén jungle are literally thousands of Maya ruins. With tourism booming in the region many of these are becoming more accessible via a selection of tours offered by Flores/El Remate-based operators. To see these more remote sites independently you will need plenty of time to account for sporadic transport schedules. In addition, some larger, still unexcavated sites require a local guide simply to navigate the ruins themselves.

Uaxactún

Twenty-three kilometres north of Tikal, strung out by the side of a disused airstrip, are the village and ruins of **Uaxactún** (pronounced "Wash-ak-toon"). The overall impact of the place may be a little disappointing after the grandeur of Tikal, but you'll probably have the site to yourself. The most interesting buildings are in **Group E**, east of the airstrip, where three low reconstructed temples, built side-by-side, are arranged to function as an observatory. Viewed from the top of a fourth temple, the sun rises behind the north temple on the longest day of the year and behind the southern one on the shortest day. On the other side of the airstrip is **Group A**, a series of larger temples and residential compounds, some of them reconstructed, a ball court and some impressive stelae.

If you end up **staying overnight** in Uaxactún you have two options: the welcoming *Campamento Ecológico El Chiclero* (T&F7926 1095; camping ❶, rooms ❹) offers clean rooms without bath, or you can camp or sling up a hammock. Owner Antonio Baldizón also organizes 4WD trips, and his wife Neria prepares excellent food. Otherwise, *Aldana's* is friendly but very basic with wooden rooms and camping (both ❶).

A **bus** leaves Flores at 1pm and passes through Tikal en route to Uaxactún. The return bus leaves Uaxactún at 7am, so if you want to explore the site independently you'll need to stay two nights (otherwise arrange a shuttle – cheapest done from El Remate).

Yax-há

Midway between El Remate and Melchor de Menchos, some 12km off the highway, is the restored site of **Yaxhá** (Wwww.visityaxha.com; US$10). The site is seldom visited, but is very well managed with an impressive collection of restored/reconstructed temples and palaces. Yaxhá's greatest attraction is its stunning location on the northern shores of the tranquil **Yaxhá Lagoon** (no doubt the site was originally chosen with this in mind). The best time to visit is to watch the sunset over the lake from the top of the **Temple of the Red Hands**. You ought to be lucky enough to see plenty of monkeys at this time too.

There is no **public transport** to the park entrance. However, on the main road, in the village of La Maquina, it should be possible to negotiate a price for a pickup (approx US$10). Ask at the *tienda* opposite the school. Alternatively, some El Remate hotels arrange return transportation, or you can take the excellent tour with *Cafe Yaxhá* in Flores, which also takes in the remote nearby site of La Blanca

and stops with a local village family for lunch (US$35).

El Zotz

Thirty kilometres west of Uaxactún, along a rough track passable by 4WD, is **El Zotz**, a large Maya site set in its own nature reserve. Totally unrestored and smothered by vegetation, El Zotz has been systematically looted, although there are guards on duty all year. Zotz means "bat" in Maya and each evening at dusk you'll see tens, perhaps hundreds of thousands of **bats** of several species emerge from a cave near the campsite – one of the most remarkable natural sights in Petén. From the tops of El Zotz's jungle-shrouded temples it's also possible to see the roof-combs of Tikal.

To get there you can rent vehicles, supplies and equipment in Uaxactún, or take a three-day tour from Flores (ask at *Los Amigos* to form a group). The tour involves approximately six hours of walking per day, two nights camping in the jungle and finishes at the ruins of Tikal.

El Perú

It's possible to reach the Maya ruins of **El Perú** independently but you'll need a tent, a good grasp of Spanish and plenty of initiative. A chicken bus leaves Santa Elena's Terminal Vieja at 10am for **Paso Caballos** (4hr), from where you can hike or take a boat to the site. The ruins are unexcavated and administered by the army, which has a base here. Bring plenty of food, and you'll probably be able to eat with the soldiers at their camp. It's best to take a guide to explore the site, as the ruins are completely isolated. Ask around in Paso Caballos.

El Mirador

Only accessible on foot or by mule, beyond the village of **Carmelita**, is the colossal Preclassic site of **El Mirador**. El Mirador is perhaps the most exotic and mysterious of all Petén's Maya sites.

Still buried in the forest, this massive city matches Tikal's scale, and may even surpass it. Rediscovered in 1926, it dates from an earlier period than Tikal, and was almost certainly the first great city in the Maya world.

The core of the site covers some sixteen square kilometres, stretching between two massive pyramids that face each other across the forest. The area around El Mirador is riddled with smaller Maya sites, and as you look out across the forest from the top of either of the main temples you can see others rising above the canopy on all sides – including the giant Calakmul in Mexico. Although much of the site is still buried, archaeologists are currently excavating and have already uncovered some fantastic Maya artwork inside some temples. It is likely that in the coming decades El Mirador will be opened up to mass tourism – there's even talk of a monorail through the jungle.

For the time being, however, getting to El Mirador is a substantial undertaking, with most backpackers opting to take a five-day tour from Flores (although during the rainy season this may not be possible). The tour involves up to eight hours of arduous jungle trekking per day. You'll need plenty of repellent (and alcohol) to kill off the mosies, ticks and other nasties. Tours provide horses/ mules to carry your food and equipment (which should also be provided). Tour prices start at US$160 per person for a group of six; ask at *Los Amigos* in Flores to get a group together.

SAYAXCHÉ

The small town of **SAYAXCHÉ**, on the banks of the Río Pasión, is a handy base for visiting the nearby archeological sites of Ceibal, Aguateca and Dos Pilas. The complex network of rivers and swamps that cuts through the surrounding area has been an important trade route since Maya times and there are several ruins in the area. Even

if you're not stopping, if you're travelling by road from Cobán to Flores, you'll pass through Sayaxché and find your bus boarding a ferry to shuttle across the river.

What to see and do

The Maya sites of Ceibal, Aguateca and Dos Pilas are seldom visited, and at the time of research had only limited administration and facilities. Access is also somewhat complicated by the isolated locations of these sites. However, whether you choose to arrive by boat or by trekking, the journey through the jungle gives these ruins a special "Heart of Darkness" aura. The town of Sayaxché makes a handy base from which to organise excursions. Ask for advice at the friendly *Restaurant Yaxkin*.

Ceibal

The most accessible and impressive of the sites near Sayaxché is **Ceibal**, reachable either by land or river. It's easy enough to make it there and back in an afternoon **by boat**; haggle with the boatmen at the waterfront and you can expect to pay around US$50 (for up to six people). The boat trip is followed by a short walk through towering rainforest. **By road**, Ceibal is just 17km from Sayaxché. Any transport heading south out of town passes El Paraiso from where an 8km track leads to the site through the jungle. Alternatively hire a pick-up for the full journey for $16 (ask at *Restaurant Yaxkin*, see p.242).

There is currently no entrance fee; although at the time of writing local authorities were hoping to develop facilities at the site. You can camp, but there are currently no toilets or drinking water.

Surrounded by forest and shaded by huge ceiba trees, **the ruins** are a mixture of cleared open plazas and untamed jungle. Though many of the largest temples lie buried under mounds, Ceibal does have some outstanding and well-preserved carving: the two main plazas are dotted with lovely **stelae**, centred around two low platforms. During the Classic period Ceibal was unimportant, but it grew rapidly between 830 and 930 AD, apparently after falling under the control of colonists from what is now Mexico. This is evident in the fantastic Mexican-influenced carving displayed at Ceibal.

Lago de Petexbatún: Aguateca and Dos Pilas

To the south of Sayaxché is **Lago de Petexbatún**, a spectacular expanse of water ringed by dense forest and containing plentiful supplies of snook, bass, alligator and freshwater turtle. The shores of the lake abound with birdlife and animals (including howler monkeys) and there are a number of Maya ruins. **Aguateca**, perched on a high outcrop at the southern tip of the lake, is the furthest away from Sayaxché but the most accessible, as a beautiful two- to three-hour boat-ride ($50) can get you to within twenty minutes' walk of the ruins. Alternatively you can head for the village of **Nacimientos** (no facilities apart from *tiendas*) from where it's a short walk to the site; a micro leaves Sayaxché at 2pm directly to Nacimientos, or from the highway junction of Las Pozas, south of Sayaxché, there are several chicken buses.

Extensive restoration work is still ongoing at this intriguing site, which is split in two by a natural chasm. The atmosphere is magical, surrounded by dense tropical forest and with superb views of the lake from two *miradores*.

INTO MEXICO

There are a number of possible routes into Mexico from Petén. The crossing via Bethel/La Técnica to Frontera Corozal is by far the most popular, due to much better public transport links. San Juan Travel in Flores (see p.238) offers a daily 5am shuttle ($30) directly to Palenque, the target for many backpackers. To do this route independently, you'll need to start early. There's a 5am bus from the main Santa Elena terminal to La Técnica (Q30). After four hours you reach the outskirts of Bethel, where you need to get your passport stamped (the bus should wait for you). Unfortunately this seems to be a bit of a sticky *migración* office for unofficial exit (and entry) taxes. Spanish may help you to talk your way around the officials and you can try asking for a receipt. Annoyingly, the easier option is to keep back a few dollars worth of quetzales to ease your passage out of Guatemala.

From Bethel you can arrange a *lancha* for the half-hour trip up the Río Usumacinta to Frontera Corozal. The *lancha* will cost Q200, so try to get a group together. A cheaper, but more arduous, option is to continue by bus (the same one) for another hour to La Técnica. Here regular *lanchas* zip across the river taking all of five minutes (Q15/M$20). Once on Mexican soil taxi drivers will take you to the minibus station and immigration office (no fare, they have a deal with the minibus companies!)

The northern *frontera*, reached from El Naranjo, is not recommended: it is a key trade route for narcotics.

There is also a border post at Pipiles, which can be reached by river from Sayaxché. There are however, no scheduled boat services. Ask at *Yaxkin Chel*, in Sayaxché, about the possibility of taking kayaks downstream. En route there are Maya communities who work in cooperatives to make handicrafts, promising for an interesting trip. From Pipiles you can arrange onward boat transport to the Mexican town of Benemerito, where there are basic hotels, restaurants and an immigration post. Buses leave Benemerito for Palenque (4hr) several times a day.

Currently there's no entrance charge, as the site is still not administered.

Within easy reach of Nacimientos village is **Dos Pilas**, where restoration is ongoing, buried in jungle west of the lake. Dos Pilas was the centre of a formidable empire in the early part of the eighth century, with a population of around ten thousand. Around the central plaza are some tremendous stelae, altars and four short **hieroglyphic stairways** decorated with glyphs and figures. To get to Dos Pilas from the lakeshore you have to trek 12km on foot (or by horse).

Arrival and Information

By boat/bus All transport arriving in Sayaxché will end up at the dock (on either bank of the Río Pasión). From Flores you'll arrive on the north bank and will need to catch a *lancha* (Q2) to the other side, where the bulk of Sayaxché stretches uphill and westwards along the riverbank. From the dock, the plaza is three blocks up and one to the left, where there is an ATM and an internet cafe.

Tourist information There is no official tourist information but the friendly owner at *Restaurant Yaxkin* (one block up from the dock, on the left), offers excellent free advice and has a big map of the area painted on the wall. Better still, if you're staying for a few days, head to the hotel *Yaxkin Chel*, where Don Rosendo Giron is a considerable authority on the area.

Accommodation

Hotel La Pasión ⊕ 4056 5044. Occupying the upper floors of this red-brick building (downstairs is a handy fried chicken takeaway), just 50m up from the dock. Rooms are spacious and surprisingly comfortable for the price. Each has cable TV, bathroom, fan and simple furnishings. Top-floor rooms, set back from the road, are best. There is also free coffee in the pleasant lounge area. ❸

Yaxkin Chel Paraiso In Barrio Esperanza, six blocks up and five across (southeast) from the dock ⊕ 4053 3484. Seven bungalows set in fantastic gardens, where the family grow cocoa, pepper and tropical flowers among other things. It's all fairly rustic, but the restaurant serves good food, and owner "Chendo" can arrange tours or transportation to help you explore the local area. ❷

Eating

El Botanero On the second-left street after the dock. Surprisingly stylish restaurant where they serve a selection of seasonal vegetables with the main plates of chicken (Q35), fish (Q70) and shrimp (Q90). There are also reasonably-priced cocktails (Q15)

Restaurant Yaxkin One block up from the dock, on the left (closes 8pm). Simple menu of mostly snack food. Sandwich and fries Q25. Very friendly with tourist information and smiling locals.

Moving on

By boat to: Mexico (see box, p.241).
By bus/micro to: Cobán (10am & 3pm; 4hr 30min); Flores (every 20min; 2hr); Raxrujá (every 20min; 2hr).

El Salvador

SANTA ANA:
El Salvador's second city,
home to the finest Parque
Central in the county ★

PERQUÍN:
see the horrors of the civil war
in the haunting Museo de la
Revolución Salvadoreña ★

BOSQUE
★ **EL IMPOSIBLE:**
this pristine mountain
forest is a haven
for native wildlife

SUCHITOTO: ★
widely considered the finest
colonial town in El Salvador

PACIFIC BEACHES:
try out the surf or
just bum around ★

ISLANDS OF THE
GOLFO DE FONSECA: ★
spend a quiet night on these tiny islands
sandwiched between El Salvador and Honduras

ROUGH COSTS

DAILY BUDGET Basic US$20/
occasional treat US$30

DRINK Coffee US$0.30, Pilsener beer
US$1

FOOD *Pupusa* US$0.35

HAMMOCK/HOSTEL/BUDGET HOTEL
US$3/US$8/US$15

TRAVEL San Salvador–Santa Ana by
bus (63km): 1hr 15min; US$0.80.

FACT FILE

POPULATION 6.9 million

AREA 21,040 sq km

LANGUAGE Spanish

CAPITAL San Salvador
(population: 1,570,000)

CURRENCY US dollar (US$)

INTERNATIONAL PHONE CODE
☏503

TIME ZONE GMT –6hr

Introduction

The smallest and most densely populated country in Central America, El Salvador is also the region's least visited nation. Known less for its world-class surf and stunning forest reserves than the vicious civil war it suffered through in the 1980s and gang violence that occurred in the 1990s, the country has long struggled to gain tourists' trust. Those that do make it here, however, are well rewarded by the hospitality of its proud inhabitants and the sheer physical beauty of the place. Almost every journey in El Salvador yields photogenic vistas: majestic cones of towering volcanoes, lush lowlands sweeping up through fertile hills, coffee plantations, rugged mountain chains – you'll see them all.

Pivotal **San Salvador** is one of Central America's nicest cities, boasting an emerging bohemian scene and student-heavy nightlife. Within easy reach is the glorious sweep of the **Pacific coast**, including surfers' favourite **Costa Balsámo**, dark beauties like **El Espino**, and white-sand fishing communities like **Los Cabanos**. Some of these beaches offer true seclusion, while others receive the best waves in all of Central America.

Further east are the undervisited mangrove swamps of the **Bahía de Jiquilisco** and the idyllic islands of the **Golfo de Fonseca**, while further inland the small city of **San Vicente** gives access to delightful artistic villages like floral **Alegría** and larger **San Miguel**, which hosts one of the biggest carnivals in Central America. The **Ruta de la Paz** climbs poor and rugged Morazán towards the moving war museum at **Perquín** and the town of **El Mozote**, the site of one of the civil war's worst atrocities – unmissable for anyone interested in El Salvador's recent history.

In the west, the laid-back grandeur of **Santa Ana** lies between the exquisite **cloudforests** of Montecristo and El Imposible. For climbers, the nearby **volcanic peaks** of Izalco and Cerro Verde provide good hiking, while at

their base is the spectacle of the deep blue crater lake of **Coatepeque**; for gastronomes, the **Ruta de las Flores** features **Juayúa**'s famous food festival, as well as other charming towns.

The north, though rough and wild, hosts the still unspoilt colonial gem of **Suchitoto**, above the glorious crater lake of Suchitlán, while **La Palma** is famous for its naïf crafts, producing wooden handicrafts, pottery and hammocks.

CHRONOLOGY

Pre-8000 BC Paleo-Indian cave-dwellers around Coritho are the first known inhabitants.

Pre-1200 BC Maya arrive from Guatemala.

900 AD Maya culture mysteriously collapses.

900–1400 AD Waves of Nahuat-speaking settlers, later dubbed "Pipils", migrate from Mexico, establishing seats of power at Cihuatán, Tehuacán and Cuscatlán.

1522 Conquistador Andrés Niño lands on Isla de Meanguera.

1524 Pedro de Alvarado crosses the Río Paz to conquer the area; he names the region "El Salvador".

1540 The Spanish secure dominion over the region under the Captainy General of Guatemala.

1600–1800 Hacienda feudalism creates a rich ruling elite and indentured labour force.

1811 Father José Delgado leads an unsuccessful revolution against the Spanish.

1821 Central American provinces, including El Salvador, break with Spain, but are annexed by Mexico.

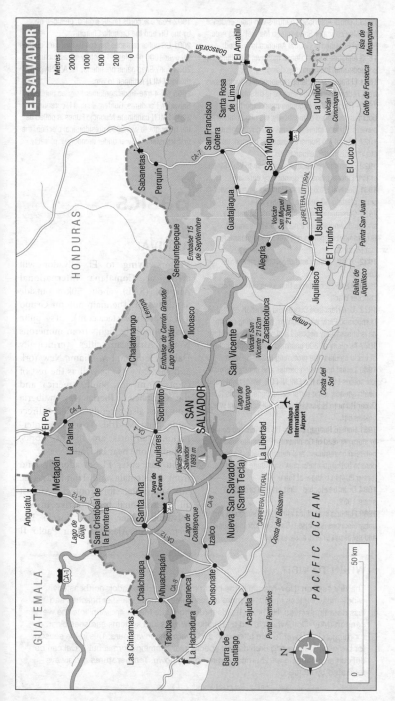

EL SALVADOR

Metres
2000
1000
500
200
0

GUATEMALA

HONDURAS

Anguiatú

CA-3

Las Chinamas

Metapán

Lago de Güija

La Palma

El Poy

CA-4

San Cristóbal de la Frontera

CA-12

Tacuba

La Hachadura

Apaneca

Ahuachapán

CA-8

Santa Ana

CA-1

Joya de Cerén

Aguilares

Suchitoto

Volcán San Salvador 1893 m

Lago de Coatepeque

Izalco

CA-8

Chalchuapa

Sonsonate

Acajutla

Barra de Santiago

Punta Remedios

CA-12

SAN SALVADOR

Nueva San Salvador (Santa Tecla)

Comalapa International Airport

La Libertad

CARRETERA LITORAL

Costa del Bálsamo

Chalatenango

Lempa

Embalse de Cerrón Grande/ Lago Suchitlán

Ilobasco

San Vicente

Volcán San Vicente 2182m

Zacatecoluca

Lago de Ilopango

Costa del Sol

Sensuntepeque

Embalse 15 de Septiembre

Guatajiagua

Alegría

El Triunfo

Lempa

Jiquilisco

Sabanetas

Perquín

CA-7

San Francisco Gotera

Santa Rosa de Lima

San Miguel

Volcán San Miguel 2130m

CARRETERA LITORAL

Usulután

Bahía de Jiquilisco

Punta San Juan

Gascorán

El Amatillo

La Unión

Volcán Conchagua

CA-1

El Cuco

Golfo de Fonseca

Isla de Meanguera

PACIFIC OCEAN

N

0   50 km

245

1823 Central American countries win independence from Mexico under Salvadoreño Manuel José Arce; Federal Republic of Central America is created.

1833 Anastasio Aquino leads massive, but ultimately unsuccessful, indigenous uprising.

1841 El Salvador declares independence, withdraws from Federal Republic; Republic is dissolved.

1840–1931 Coffee becomes main export crop; boom is controlled domestically, via oligarchic land-owners. Private interests dominate government.

1927 Liberal Pío Romero Bosque is elected, takes steps to dismantle oligarchies.

1929 Economy collapses in response to Wall Street crash; Liberal plans for democracy derailed.

1931 General Maximiliano Martínez seizes power in coup, starting 50 years of military rule.

1932 Communist-led rebellion against military and landowners sees thousands assassinated. Government response is a week-long massacre, "La Matanza".

1932–1980 Military and oligarchies jointly rule country.

1969 El Salvador attacks Honduras in the six-day "Soccer War".

1972 José Napoleon Duarte and Christian Democratic Party win elections, advocating reform; he is immediately deposed and exiled by the military.

1977 As many as 300 unarmed civilians shot in front of world media while protesting in San Salvador.

1980 Leftist opposition parties and guerrilla groups join forces to form the FMLN–FDR, while right-wing death squads wage terror campaigns. Archbishop Oscar Romero is assassinated; full-scale civil war breaks out.

1981 Ronald Reagan pumps US aid into the country to stem "spread of Communism", despite links between government and death squads. Salva-doreño battalion massacres the village of Mozote (see p.294) in a show of force.

1984 Duarte "elected" first civilian president since 1932.

1989 Fighting intensifies after FMLN's request to delay elections is refused; San Salvador is occupied, and six Jesuit priests assassinated.

1992 Peace accords finally signed, presided over by the UN and the Catholic Church.

2001 US dollar replaces the colón. Two earthquakes kill over 1000 people and destroy infrastructure.

2004 Tony Saca gains presidency for ARENA party, though FMLN is tipped to win.

2005 CA-4 free-trade agreement signed between El Salvador, Honduras, Guatemala and Nicaragua.

2008 FMLN candidate Mauricio Funes is polled as the favourite to win 2009 presidential election, the first transfer of power under democratic plurality.

Basics

ARRIVAL

Visitors **flying** to El Salvador will arrive at **Comalapa International Airport (SAL)**, about 50km outside San Salvador. The main hub for Grupo TACA (Ⓦ www.taca.com), it's quite busy, with daily flights from numerous North American cities (principally Dallas, Houston, LA, Miami, New York and Mexico City) as well as the rest of Central America, South America, and the Caribbean. Iberia (Ⓦ www.iberia .com) has also recently started a direct route from Madrid. Two more inter-national airports are in the works, including one near La Unión.

You can enter El Salvador by land from Guatemala and Honduras (see box opposite, for routes). Almost all international **buses** arrive in San Salvador, either at the Puerto Bus terminal on Alameda Juan Pablo II

WHEN TO VISIT

The dry season (Nov–March) is the best time to visit El Salvador: northeasterly winds make for less humid air, more accessible dirt roads, sandier beaches and less daunting waves. Humidity builds throughout late March and April into the wet season (May–Oct), which is fed by Pacific low-pressure systems and sees clear mornings cloud over to late afternoon and overnight downpours. This is the season for big waves, flowering orchids and spectacular lightning storms, but travel can be difficult and flooding and hurricanes are not unknown. Temperatures are always regulated by altitude.

LAND ROUTES TO EL SALVADOR

The main border crossings with Honduras are in the east at El Amatillo (see p.297), convenient for connections to Tegucigalpa, and at El Poy (see p.356) in the northwest.

The main border with Guatemala is at La Hachadura (see p.308) in the southwest, best for the Pacific beaches and used by international buses from Mexico. Another Guatemala crossing is at Las Chinamas (see p.314), just outside Ahuachapán, with regular connections to Guatemala City. The crossing at Anguiatú (see p.322), in the north near Metapán, is most convenient for Esquipulas. A smaller crossing at San Cristóbal (see p.319) is close to the city of Santa Ana.

or the Tica Bus terminal at the start of Calle Concepción. Many services from Guatemala also stop on Calle 27a Poniente in Santa Ana, and chicken buses run from border crossings to nearby towns in the daylight hours.

The only international **boat** runs from the Honduran and Nicaraguan islands in the Golfa de Fonseca to La Unión (see p.283). You must go through customs before travelling to the islands.

VISAS

Visas for El Salvador are not currently required for citizens of the US, Canada, Argentina, Australia, Brazil, Chile, Israel, New Zealand, Paraguay, Singapore, South Africa, most European countries, all Central American nations and many Caribbean islands; citizens of other countries need authorization from the immigration authorities. Under the CA-4 agreement (see p.48), there is now one tourist card for El Salvador, Guatemala, Honduras and Nicaragua; this is issued on entry – make sure you get a 90-day allowance rather than a 30-day one. Stays can be extended once by contacting the Dirección General de Migración y Extranjería, in the Galerias Escalón, Paseo Gen Escalón (☎2202-9650), in San Salvador, though you must be sponsored by a CA-4 national. Alternatively, you can pass out of the entire CA-4 zone and back in again – Belize is probably your best option. A US$10 border **entry fee** is levied at the airport, but only for nationals of Canada, China, Greece, Malaysia, Mexico, Portugal, Singapore and the US. See ⓦwww .elsalvador.org for details.

GETTING AROUND

El Salvador's **bus** network is without doubt the best way to travel. The size of the country, and the efficient road layout around the Carretera Interamericana, mean that budget travellers can get from one point to another within the country in less than a day.

By bus

Buses are subsidized and extremely cheap: a trip from San Salvador to Santa Ana (1hr 15min) costs just US$0.80. Centrally placed San Salvador, with its three busy bus terminals (see p.264), is the hub of all bus travel in the country. All other towns of any significant size have at least one bus terminal; in smaller urbanizations the corner of a block near the central square gets stacked up with buses picking up or dropping off. Services run in daylight hours, with rare exceptions going just after dusk, so plan your overnight stops carefully.

All routes are covered by the same "**chicken buses**" you'll see in other Central American countries – recycled and decorated US school buses. Occasionally you'll be issued a **ticket**, which will be inspected, so keep hold of it. Otherwise, always have change ready for your **fare**, as commission may be taken to change a note; you pay the driver if there is a turnstyle, and the guy yelling instructions and jumping on and off the bus if not. Most drivers will stop if hailed, and you can bang on the side of the bus or whistle to get off mid-trip. Big bags go in a heap at the back, and you'd be wise to follow them – but don't assume that other passengers are thieves. There are only three routes in the whole country served by the marginally more comfortable **coach-style buses**; these go to and from San Miguel, Santa Rosa de Lima and La Unión, cost US$2–2.50 and knock about an hour off the standard journey.

In terms of safety, hijackings are rare, but when they do occur, hold-ups generally take the form of an enforced collection; US$10 should suffice, as long as you're not flashing expensive stuff around. Maverick overtaking manoeuvres are a more common peril, and particularly bad in city **microbuses** – only take these if no chicken buses are around.

By car

Licensed **taxis** in El Salvador are yellow and black. They can be hailed or found in large towns and cities around the main squares, shopping centres or bus stations. There are no meters, so **fares** should be agreed before you set off. Expect to pay US$4–6 for most trips within San Salvador and US$3–5 in other cities, but you can bargain a bit if you are polite. As in most countries, avoid people offering lifts in other types of car.

It can be helpful to have a **car** if you want to explore some of the country's more remote areas, especially stretches of the Pacific coast (see box, p.272). Western companies **rent** at Western prices; local garages often charge a quarter of those rates (don't pay more than US$20). Check the yellow pages in San Salvador for rental agencies, or ask Lena at *Ximena's Guest House* (see p.265) or Manolo at Tacuba's *Hostel*

Mamá y Papá (see p.314) to help you out. In terms of driving, look out for abrupt coned-off lanes on the motorway – these are **police stops**, where you will be asked to present your passport, driving licence and car documents. If you need assistance, filling stations and mechanics are widespread along the road. At night, **cows** often wander onto main roads, including the Interamericana, so keep the speed down. Also, dirt roads can become impassable during the rainy season, even with a 4WD; ask locally about conditions before you set off. Armed hold-ups of private cars are very rare now, but keep US$20 or so aside just in case, and offer no resistance. It's good to rent an old-looking car, so as not to draw attention to yourself. In cities, thefts of cars, or items left in them, do occur, so it's wise to leave your car in a guarded or locked car park overnight.

Hitching is common off the highways. This said, hitching carries obvious risks, and we don't recommend it. If you do hitch, it's polite to offer payment – about the same as the bus fare – for the journey.

By bike

Bikes offer great freedom in rural areas, and you can take them on buses if you start to tire. Unfortunately, there are no formal rental places, but it is possible to do deals with locals and tour operators. Otherwise, a cheap mountain bike shouldn't cost more than US$30 to buy from a general store in any of the bigger towns.

By boat

Although only the islands of the Golfo de Fonseca and the islands of the Bahia de Jiquilísco require **boat** access, there are plenty of other opportunities to get out on the water. Scheduled services are always much cheaper (US$1–5), but *lancha* owners and fishermen need little

ADDRESSES IN EL SALVADOR

Navigating Salvadoreño cities is initially confusing but ultimately logical. As elsewhere, most cities are organized on the grid plan: streets running north–south are avenidas, those running east–west are calles. The main avenida and calle will have individual names (along with a few of the others) and the heart of any city is at their intersection – usually, though not always, at the Parque Central. North or south of this intersection avenidas are Norte (Nte) or Sur, while east or west calles are Oriente (Ote) or Poniente (Pte). Avenidas lying to the east of the main avenida are numbered evenly, increasing the further you go out; west of the avenida the numbers are odd. Similarly, calles have even numbers south of the main calle and odd numbers north. Addresses can be given either as the street name/number, followed by the building number, or as the intersection of two streets. So: "C 12 Pte #2330, Col Flor Blanca" is no. 2330, Calle 12 Poniente in the district (colonia) of Flor Blanca, while "10a Av Sur y C 3 Pte" is the intersection of 10a Avenida Sur and Calle 3 Poniente.

persuasion to provide private lifts and tours of the country's lakes and mangrove swamps. This is usually done as a set fee for the boat (usually about US$30, depending on duration), so getting into a sizeable group reduces the cost.

ACCOMMODATION

El Salvador's **accommodation** industry – long stagnant – is finally beginning to wake up to the traveller market: new places are appearing, and very few destinations have nowhere at all to stay. However, the number of **hostels** with dorm rooms is still less than ten nation-wide, with none in the east at all, so it's best to budget for cheap **hotels**. Unfortunately, thanks to dollarization, prices are pretty high: in San Salvador a clean, secure, double room comes to at least US$20 (❹), often more, while outside the capital you can expect to pay at least US$10–15, or US$20–25 for a/c (❷–❹). Lots of hotels rent multi-bed rooms (intended for Salvadoran families), where you can pack in like sardines – these can be a good way to cut costs if you're with a group. Discounts on longer stays are also often available. Rooms vary within an establishment, so look around. Hot water is a rare treat.

Camping possibilities are also expanding countrywide, with campsites now available at most lakes, national parks and several towns and beaches. Salvadoreños with spare land may be willing to let you pitch a tent – offer around US$3. Hammock-slinging is possible on some beaches (though steer clear of the more sketchy beaches around La Libertad, for safety reasons) and at some beach hotels (also for about US$3). The hotels will usually put your bag somewhere safe, if you ask.

Accommodation fills up around Santa Semana (the week before Easter), Christmas, the Fiestas Agostinas (the last week of July and first week of Aug) and/or at the time of local festivals; at these times it's worth **reserving** in advance.

FOOD AND DRINK

Eating well in El Salvador is far more about fresh ingredients than refined cooking. The main meal of the day is **lunch**, which most local people eat in a *comedor*, where *típicos* (local dishes of meat or fish, rice, vegetable or salad) and coffee go for around US$2–3, or a *pupusería*, where you can get **pupusas** (small tortillas served piping hot and filled with cheese (*queso*), beans (*frijoles*), pork crackling (*chicharrón*), or all three), for around US$0.35. *Pupusas* are normally made from cornmeal, and are served with hot sauce, tomato juice and/or *curtido*, a jar of pickled cabbage, beetroot and carrots. Many *comedores* serve evening *pupusas*, though most close early, between 7 and 8pm. The cleanliness and quality of establishments vary, but are rarely poisonous; if doubtful, choose one that's busy and cooks unfrozen meat.

A standard **breakfast** is composed of *frijoles*, *queso* and *huevos* (eggs, either fried or scrambled) along with coffee. This combination is tasty and energy-packed, which is lucky, as it is generally the only option. Although San Salvador's Western suburbs are the only place to find the full gamut of international cuisine, most towns have a handful of **restaurants**. Chinese, Italian and Tex-Mex, and Argentine meat-grilling restaurants are the most widespread, though their authenticity varies. **Vegetarians** will find dedicated restaurants only in the biggest cities, and should be prepared to eat a lot of beans and cheese. There are also US-style **fast-food chains** – whose pricing hilariously situates them as upmarket restaurants – throughout the country. Fried chicken is the *plat du jour*, and if you must have it, the *Pollo Campero* chain is best.

In addition to *pupusas*, other Salvadoreño **specialities** include *mariscada* (huge bowls filled with fish and crustaceans in a creamy soup), tamales (meat or chicken wrapped in maize dough and boiled in a leaf), *ceviche* (raw, marinated fish) and *sopa de frijoles* (black or red bean soup). On the coast, *conchas* (cockles or any other shellfish) are served raw with lemon juice, tomato, coriander and Worcestershire sauce. Try the *ostras* (oysters), especially in popular eateries by the sea; they are fresher here than in most Western restaurants.

Drink

Local **coffee** is very good, usually drunk black and strong at breakfast and mid-afternoon with tamales. In small villages it will be boiled up with sugar cane and called *lista*. El Salvador's tropical fruits make delicious **juices**. *Jugos* are pure juices – most commonly orange, papaya, pineapple and melon – mixed with ice. *Licuados* (sometimes called *batidos*) blend juice with sugar, ice and sometimes milk, while *frescos* are fruit-based sweet drinks made up in bulk and served with lunch or dinner. Unless you ask otherwise, sugar will be added to *jugos* and *licuados*. *Horchata* is a dense milk drink with a base of rice, sweetened with sugar and cinnamon.

The usual brands of **soft drinks** are available. **Water** is safe to drink in San Salvador only; elsewhere check that the water and ice used in drinks is purified. Bottled mineral water and bags of pure spring water are available almost everywhere, while most hotels provide drinking water. El Salvador produces five good **beers** – the most important decision you will have to make is between Pilsener and Golden Light. True lager followers will side for the excellent and textured former. Also well worth trying are Regia and the crisp Bahía; the costliest and worst is Suprema. **Aguardiente** is a sugar cane-based liquor, produced under government control and sold through outlets called *expendios*; Tic-Tac is a favourite label.

CULTURE AND ETIQUETTE

Salvadoreños are generally confident, principled, hard-working and keen to laugh; they will often vie to help travellers. This said, not many Westerners pass through the country, especially rural areas, so you may be regarded as something of an oddity, and children especially may stare and touch your hair. Over eighty percent of the population is **Catholic**, though Evangelism is on the rise.

You should be confident and **polite**: say "Buenos" (morning) or "Buenas" (evening) when you catch someone's eye or enter a room, shake hands when meeting and do not offend by being paranoid about your safety or belongings. Women should not react to macho male posturing, as this is seen as flirtatious; understand that if you dress to be noticed, you will be. Remember to wear sleeves and trousers and to remove hats when entering a church (women should cover their heads). Always ask permission before taking **photos** in indigenous areas, though you will generally find lots of eager posers.

Tipping at restaurants is not expected at the cheaper places, and may not be received well. More Western-style eateries may add around a ten-percent service charge, and you can increase this should you want to; tipping in bars in the capital goes down well too. Free guides should also be tipped. There is no need to tip anyone else, but if you are not awkward about it then they won't be offended. Gentle **bartering** is acceptable – sometimes it works, sometimes it doesn't.

SPORTS AND OUTDOOR ACTIVITIES

Fútbol (football, soccer) is by far the biggest spectator sport in El Salvador. There are two domestic seasons every year, the first (the *clausura*) runs every weekend from February to mid-May, the second (called *apertura*) goes from September to mid-December; both are followed by play-offs and finals. The big **teams** of the last few years are FAS from Santa Ana, Firpo from Usulután and Metapán. The quality of football is mixed but the crowds are awesome; don't bring anything valuable, and always sit with and cheer for the home side. See ⓦwww.laprensagrafica.com/futbol for fixtures and information. Great attention is paid to the international scene, too: the whole country has arranged itself behind two Spanish clubs, FC Barcelona and Real Madrid. **Baseball** is popular as well; San Salvador has a stadium, opposite the Artesan Market, with games on Sundays. Football, baseball and basketball games take place on widespread munipal facilities, in parks and on beaches across the country and if it is not a training session you will be more than welcome to join in.

In terms of outdoor activities, El Salvador's 320km of coastline is widely accepted to have the best **surfing** in Central America and is known for several world-famous breaks. The best areas are on the Costa del Bálsamo (see p.276) and the Eastern beaches around El Cuco (see p.281). See ⓦwww.surfingelsalvador .com for surf reports, beach reviews and general information. The best **hiking** is in the national parks. For good challenges try the Montecristo–El Trifinio Cloud Forest (see p.322), up the volcanoes of the Cerro Verde (see p.320) and through the dramatic, dry rainforest of Bosque El Imposible (see p.308). **Diving** here is not as good as in the Bay Islands or Belize, but there is the opportunity to see underwater thermal vents in a crater dive on Lago de Ilopango (see p.271), and the only Pacific coral diving in Central America is off Los Cóbanos (see p.307), along with a couple of good wreck dives. See ⓦwww.elsalvadordivers.com for more information.

COMMUNICATIONS

Mail (letters) from San Salvador generally take about one week to the US and nine or so days to Europe; there are parcel services available, but you should use a courier service if sending anything of value. The safest place to **receive letters** is at the *lista de correos* (Window 14) of the main post office in San Salvador (see p.268). **Post offices** across the country are generally open Monday to Friday 8am to 5pm and Saturday 8am to noon.

Telecom, the recently privatized telecommunications leader, has offices in every town (all daily 7am–6pm), from where you can make local, long-distance and international calls. For local calls, note that an eighth digit was added to all in-country numbers in 2005 – mobile numbers begin with a 7, land lines with a 2. Some signs and printed materials still list seven-digit numbers – just add a 2 to the start and you'll probably have the new one. **Public phones** – both the yellow Telecom booths (with instructions in both Spanish and English) or the lime-green Telefónica booths (instructions in Spanish only) in El Salvador are **cardphones**: all require prepaid cards, which can be purchased everywhere. You can make international calls from both types of cardphone (approximately US$1.50 per minute to Europe), but it's cheaper to go to a Telecom office. By far the cheapest option, however, is web-based calls; almost all internet places are now equipped with headsets. Alternatively, a pay-as-you-go **mobile phone** costs around US$15 and can make and receive international calls. There are two networks, Tigo and Claro; Tigo currently has better coverage. The telephone code for the whole of El Salvador is ⓣ503.

Internet of varying speeds is now available everywhere except a handful of beach communities. Rates range from US$0.60–1 per hour, often higher in hotels. In most large towns the government-funded **Infocentros** (daily 9am–6pm) have the fastest connections.

EL SALVADOR ON THE NET

ⓦwww.elsalvador.travel The newest official tourist site, with good information and a nascent directory of businesses.

ⓦwww.fotosdeelsalvador.com An appetite-whetting archive holding thousands of photos from across the country.

ⓦwww.lanic.utexas.edu/la/ca/salvador The most extensive list of relevant El Salvador links available.

ⓦwww.laprensagrafica.com & www.elsalvador.com The websites for the two big conservative daily papers (Spanish only).

ⓦwww.raices.com.sv A feisty and intelligent online magazine publishing excellent photography and regular opinion polls (Spanish only).

ⓦhttp://luterano.blogspot.com An excellent English-language blog, updated almost daily, summarizing current affairs and adding well-informed commentary.

CRIME AND SAFETY

El Salvador has a reputation for guns, gangs and danger, which, while not unfounded, is often perpetuated by travellers keen to enliven their tales. *Maras* (**gangs**) exist across the country, but really dangerous characters generally concern themselves with the more profitable fields of drugs, extortion and human trafficking; they don't look for tourists, nor will they be found in any of the neighbourhoods you are likely to visit. *Bollos* (**drunks**), the other main group of social outsiders, are generally too disconnected with reality to be any danger, but for the same reason should be avoided. For an excellent, realistic overview of crime in the region, see @www.unodc.org/documents/data-and-analysis/Central-america-study-en.pdf.

Generally, you should be okay if you stay confident (say "Buenos" to people), stay in groups and stay in busy areas. If you are being pestered don't show animosity and head for a busy café or restaurant. Try not to look rich and, if mugged, never fight back. It is worth keeping US$10–20 in one pocket while travelling, as this will be enough for most *banditos*. Be especially careful after nightfall in La Libertad, Sonsonate and San Salvador's centro; La Unión and San Miguel can also be dodgy. **Women travellers** should definitely stay in groups. Ignore the usual cat-calls and loud blown kisses, as attempts to scold will be seen as flirtatious; the less attention you pay, the less attention you will receive.

In the event of difficulties, the **National Civilian Police** (PCN) is one of the best forces in Central America, with little corruption and a good presence in cities, at least until nightfall. Additionally, an often English-speaking **tourist police** operates nationwide to guide treks, assist and advise, and can be reached on ☎2245-5448.

Statistically, the biggest threats to tourists in El Salvador are the **riptides**

> ### EMERGENCY NUMBERS
>
> **Cruz Roja** (ambulance) ☎2222-5155
> **Fire** ☎2271-2227/1244
> **Police** ☎911

on its beaches. It is best not to go out too far on your own and ask locally about the conditions. If you are unable to swim back, try not to panic, swim parallel to the shoreline and wait for the rip to die down. There is no coastguard, so call the police in an emergency, or better still find the nearest surfer.

MEDICAL CARE AND EMERGENCIES

Pharmacies are widespread, though stock varies; generally the Brasil Pharmacy chain is the best stocked. If you have stomach troubles and are not anti-medicine, almost every pharmacy has a one-day, three-pill miracle cure.

Two private **hospitals** in San Salvador – Hospital de Diagnóstico (C 21 Pte at 2a Diagonal ☎2226-8878) and Hospital Diagnóstico Escalón (C 3 Pte at 99a Av Norte ☎2264-4422) – provide the best medical services in the country. If you are in the east, San Miguel's Hospital Clínica Laboratorio San Francisco (5a Av Norte ☎2661-1991) is another good private hospital; otherwise, it's best to head to the capital. All three of these hospitals have 24hr emergency rooms. Have insurance documents or cash at the ready if you need treatment.

MONEY AND BANKS

El Salvador has officially used the **US dollar** (US$) since 2001. (Keep an eye on the news, though – this may change after the March 2009 presidential elections, when favourite Mauricio Funes may fulfil a long-standing FMLN promise to reintroduce the old currency, the *colón*.) All US dollar notes and coins are currently in free circulation, but try to stockpile US$1 and US$5 bills, as anything over US$10 is likely to send the shopkeeper running down the street in search of change.

ATMs are not universal, even in tourist destinations. Keep a stash of cash for Perquín, Tacuba, every beach outside of La Libertad, some parts of the Ruta de las Flores and the eastern craft towns. Elsewhere, the main **banks** – Banco Agrícola, HSBC, Scotiabank and Banco Cuscatlán – have ATMs (*cajeros*), which charge a handling fee of around US$1.70. Occasionally, they will inexplicably refuse your card (HSBC is the worst offender). Payment by **credit card** is unheard of at the budget level, but if you do encounter an establishment that will take your card there will be a commission charge of five percent. **Traveller's cheques** are becoming more widely recognized, but at present can only be changed in banks, for which opening hours are 8.30 or 9am until 4 or 5pm, though some of them close for an hour at lunch from 1 to 2pm. Some banks in the larger cities also open between 9am and midday on Saturday. There are **casas de cambio** (generally daily 9am–5pm) along Alameda Juan Pablo II in San Salvador, in Santa Ana and San Miguel and at the borders. Due to the foreign remittance industry there are Western Union and Moneygram outlets in almost every mid-size town, in case you get stuck.

INFORMATION AND MAPS

The national tourist board, **Corsatur** (W www.elsalvador.travel), has been bolstered by the Ministry of Tourism and its announced ten-year plan to increase tourism within the country. There is already tangible improvement in the form of an annual bilingual travellers' guide, *Guía de Viajero* – distributed only in the country, it's short on practicalities but a great travel teaser – as well as countrywide maps and a decent website. Corsatur has its main office in San Salvador at Alameda Doctor Araujo, Pasaje y Edificio Carbonel #2, Colonia Roma (Mon–Fri 8am–12.30pm & 1.30–5.30pm; T 2243-7835). The staff (who do not speak English) will help you out with enquiries if you persist. Three other, less helpful, outposts exist in Nahuizalco, Suchitoto and Puerto La Libertad, and there's a seldom-manned desk at the airport. Small towns like Apaneca and Perquín have kiosks that issue little more than pamphlets in Spanish, but often the best tips come directly from the hostel or hotel owners that have pioneered El Salvador's backpacker industry.

NATIONAL PARK INFORMATION

Officially, there is a permission-granting ritual that must be performed before you enter any of El Salvador's national parks; confusingly, parks are administered by three different agencies. All three also allow entry and have information about other, rarer, preserved areas as well.

The Instituto Salvadoreño de Turismo (ISTU), C Ruben Darío, 9a–11a Av Sur, San Salvador (Mon–Fri 8am–4pm, Sat 8am–noon; T 2222-8000, E istu@mh.gob .sv), manages Parque Nacional Walter T Deninger, and has information about all the country's national parks.

SalvaNatura, 33a Av Sur #640, Colonia Flor Blanca (Mon–Fri; 8am–12.30pm & 2–5.30pm; T 2279-1515, W www.salvanatura.org), covers the Bosque El Imposible and Parque Nacional Los Volcanes.

The snappily named Ministerio de Medio Ambiente y Recursos Naturales, C Las Mercedes, Km 5.5 Carretera a Santa Tecla (Mon–Fri, 7.30am–12.30pm & 1.30–3.30pm; T 2267-6276, F 2267-6259, W www.marn.gob.sv) issues permits to the Bosque Montecristo in person or by fax.

Maps of El Salvador are rare and terrible, except for those produced on the second floor of the Centro Nacional de Registros, 1a C Pte and 43 Av Nte #2310 (Mon–Fri, 8am–noon & 1–4pm; T 2261-8400, W www.cnr.gob.sv).

OPENING HOURS AND HOLIDAYS

Opening hours throughout the country tend to vary. The big cities and major towns generally get going quite early in the morning, with government offices working from 8am to 4pm and most businesses from 8.30/9am to 5/5.30pm, with some closing for an hour at lunch. Hotels in smaller places lock up for the night between 9 and 10pm, and you may be banging on the door for a while and paying extra if you don't warn them of your late arrival. On national holidays and public holidays everything will be shut, with some businesses also closing on the day of local fiestas. Museums and archeological sites all close on Mondays.

FESTIVALS

Ferías (festivals) in El Salvador, like the rest of the continent, are very important events in the calendar, and almost every town will have its own annual celebration, most often at the time of the day of the saint most connected to the place in question.

PUBLIC HOLIDAYS

Jan 1 New Year's Day
March/April Easter (Thursday–Easter Sunday)
May 1 Labour Day
Aug 1–6 El Salvador del Mundo
Sept 15 Independence Day
Oct 12 Columbus Day
Nov 1 Day of the Dead
Nov 2 All Saints' Day
Dec 24–25 Christmas
Dec 31 New Year's Eve

January Cristo Negro and Feria Gastronómica Internacional in Juayúa (Jan 8–15). Street fiesta with the best range and quality of food.
February Festival Internacional de Arte y Cultura in Suchitoto, a month-long celebration of classical music, opera, art, theatre.
March Santa Semana in Izalco, popularly known as the best place for the Easter processions and street paintings.
May Las Flores y Las Palmas in Panchimalco (2nd Sun) celebrates flower and palm-tree cultivation with music, dancing and fireworks.
July Fiesta al Divino Salvador del Mundo in San Salvador (July 25–Aug 6). Street party that shuts down the capital.
August Festival del Invierno in Perquín (Aug 1–6). Exciting, young and bohemian music and arts festival in the mountain town.
November Vírgen de la Paz celebrated in San Miguel (Nov 14–30). One of the biggest fiestas in Central America, with processions and multiple music floats, dancing and drinking.

San Salvador and around

Sprawling across the Valle de las Hamacas at the foot of the mighty Volcán San Salvador is the urban melee of **SAN SALVADOR**, El Salvador's mercurial capital. Founded in 1545, it remained a pretty minor place until 1785, when it was named the first *intendencia* within the Reino de Guatemala. Father José Delgado first made the call for independence here, and the city was the only capital of the Central American Federation, before being named capital of El Salvador when the federation dissolved in 1840. Not much remains of this illustrious history today, though: a series of earthquakes throughout the nineteenth and twentieth centuries, and bombings when the FMLN seized portions of the city in 1989, have levelled most of the centre. Little you can see predates the nineteenth century.

The atmosphere of the place is quite different, however; after two progressive mayorships and a more proactive chief of police, the city is going through something of a renaissance. Pleasant suburbs, great little parks, genuinely interesting museums, a bustling centre and thriving commercial zone make for an exciting place to explore, while a bohemian arts scene, good bars and safe clubs provide fun night-time distractions.

Northwest of the city, **Volcán San Salvador** looms over the valley and the suburb of **Santa Tecla**, while to the south the extensive **Parque Balboa** gives vistas the length of the coast. Tucked beneath the park, the village of **Panchimalco**'s splendid colonial church belies its predominantly indigenous populace. Fifteen kilometres east of San Salvador sits the country's largest crater lake, beautiful **Lago de Ilopango**, with views on a clear day across to the peaks of Volcán Chichontepec (see p.287). To the west are the natural gorge and pools of **Los Chorros**, a favourite weekend retreat for Salvadoreños from the city, and for those with an interest in archeology, the ruins of **Joya de Cerén**, which are of international importance for their remarkable state of preservation. The ruins at **San Andrés** nearby are rather more traditional in form, with pyramids and temples.

What to see and do

San Salvador's social and geographical landscape is fantastically linear. The eastern part of the city – industrial, poor, dangerous and not a recommended area for visitors – morphs into the crowded and pungent Centro Histórico, or **El Centro**, around the Terminal de Oriente bus station. The historic centre's churches and theatre are some of the country's best, though surrounded by chattering stall traders and street *comedores*. West of here the road creeps uphill to the more relaxed shops and services around the green acres of **Parque Cuscatlán**, and the heady commercialism of the Metrocentro. Continuing west, the climb continues to the trimmed hedges, fancy bars and cultural monoliths of the **Zona Rosa**, before finishing at the fine restaurants, exclusive nightclubs and guarded castles of **Colonia Escalón**. Floating above this east-to-west progression are the arty, studenty, liberal, traveller-friendly cafés, hostels and late-night bars north of **Boulevard los Héroes**.

Plaza Barrios

Though the heart of the raging *centro*, the rejuvenated **Plaza Barrios** is a good spot for a rest, with shaded benches and a good sampling of the local population present at any one time. Plaques on the central island commemorate the six Jesuit priests murdered at La UCA in 1989 (see p.263). On the plaza's western edge stands the **Palacio**

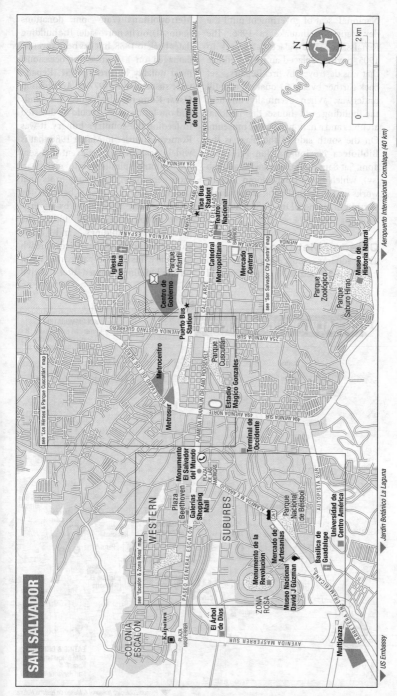

SAN SALVADOR

EL SALVADOR

SAN SALVADOR AND AROUND

N

0   2 km

▶ Aeropuerto Internacional Comalapa (40 km)

▶ Jardín Botánico La Laguna

▶ US Embassy

COLONIA ESCALON

Kalpataru

PLAZA MASFERRER

El Árbol de Dios

WESTERN

see 'Escalón & Zona Rosa' map

AVENIDA MASFERRER SUR

Plaza Beethoven

PASEO GENERAL ESCALON

Monumento de la Revolucion

Monumento El Salvador del Mundo

PLAZA DE LAS AMERICAS

Galerias Shopping Mall

SUBURBS

ALAMEDA M E ARAUJO

ZONA ROSA

Museo Nacional David J Guzman

Mercado de Artesanias

AUTOPISTA SUR

Parque Nacional de Béisbol

Basílica de Guadalupe

Universidad de Centro América

CARRETERA INTERAMERICANA

Multiplaza

▶ Jardín Botánico La Laguna

Terminal de Occidente

SOLVADOR DE LOS HEROES

see 'Los Héroes & Parque Cuscatlán' map

Metrosur

Metrocentro

AVENIDA GUSTAVO GUERRERO

ALAMEDA FRANKLIN DELANO ROOSEVELT

Estadio Magico Gonzales

49A AVENIDA NORTE

49A AVENIDA SUR

Parque Cuscatlan

Puerto Bus Station

CALLE ARCE

25A AVENIDA SUR

Centro de Gobierno

Iglesia Don Rua

AVENIDA ESPAÑA

Parque Infantil

ALAMEDA JUAN PABLO II

Tica Bus Station

CALLE DEL RIO

Teatro Nacional

Catedral Metropolitana

JUAN BARRIOS

Mercado Central

see 'San Salvador City Centre' map

AV INDEPENDENCIA

BLVD DEL EJERCITO NACIONAL

25A AVENIDA NORTE

Terminal de Oriente

Parque Saburo Hirao

Parque Zoológico

Museo de Historia Natural

AVENIDA

257

Nacional, seat of government until the devastating earthquake of 1986. The Renaissance-style palace dates back to 1905, having replaced an earlier edifice that was destroyed by fire. Repairs – set back further by a 2001 quake – are still underway. When eventually finished, the building will house the national archives and a national history museum. On the south side of the plaza is the **Biblioteca Nacional** (Mon–Fri 8am–4pm, Sat 8am–noon; ⓦ www.binaes.gob .sv), which houses Salvadoran literary works on the second floor, along with a portrait mapping all the presidents of El Salvador until 1994.

Catedral Metropolitana

The square's most imposing and notorious structure is the **Catedral** **Metropolitana** (7am–5pm; donations optional), on its north side. The building dates back to 1888, but has been severely damaged on a number of occasions, most notably by fire in 1951. Repairs were suspended in 1977 by **Archbishop Oscar Romero**, who argued that funds laid out for the work should be diverted to feeding the country's hungry. It was Romero's murder in March 1980 that is widely perceived as the event that sent the country spiralling into civil war: mourners carrying his body to its final resting place in a chapel beneath the cathedral were fired upon by government troops stationed on top of the surrounding buildings, and many were slaughtered as they tried to reach sanctuary inside the cathedral. Work on the building resumed after the civil

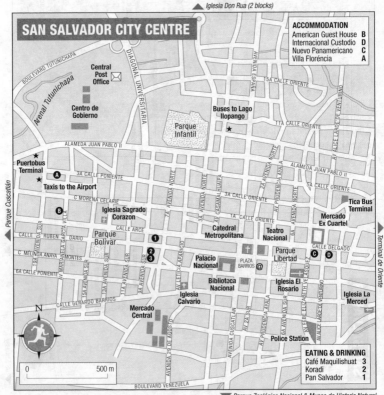

SAN SALVADOR CITY CENTRE

▲ Iglesia Don Rua (2 blocks)

ACCOMMODATION
American Guest House B
Internacional Custodio D
Nuevo Panamericano C
Villa Floréncia A

Central Post Office

Centro de Gobierno

Parque Infantil

Buses to Lago Ilopango

Puertobus Terminal

Taxis to the Airport

Iglesia Sagrado Corazon

Parque Bolívar

Parque Cuscatlán

Catedral Metropolitana

Teatro Nacional

Tica Bus Terminal

Mercado Ex Cuartel

Palacio Nacional

PLAZA BARRIOS

Parque Libertad

Terminal de Oriente

Biblioteca Nacional

Iglesia El Rosario

Iglesia Calvario

Iglesia La Merced

Mercado Central

Police Station

N

0   500 m

BOULEVARD VENEZUELA

EATING & DRINKING
Café Maquilishuat 3
Koradi 2
Pan Salvador 1

▼ Parque Zoológico Nacional & Museo de Historia Natural

war, and was finally completed in 1999. The colourful "naïf" murals around the main doors, by El Salvador's most famous artist, Fernando Llort, are worth admiring, and you can visit Romero's tomb in the eerie and expansive chapel below (Mon–Sat 9.30–11.30am & 2.30–4.30pm, Sun 8.30am–5pm; donations optional). Confession in the early-Christian, open confessionals of the side altars runs late morning and late afternoon every day.

Iglesia Calvario

One block south and two blocks west of the plaza, and in the jaws of the street market, is the dark, neo-Gothic and slightly derelict **Iglesia Calvario** (7am–5pm; donations optional), whose pretty blue and yellow roof is worth a look – the colours are the result of light passing through stained glass rather than paint.

Iglesia el Rosario

Two blocks east of Plaza Barrios is the wide and busy **Parque Libertad**, where the central statue of feather-winged Liberty stands watch over crowds that gather in the square. Dominating the east side, the smog-stained, concrete facade of the **Iglesia el Rosario** (6am–midday & 2–7pm; donations optional) looks like an industrial turbine. Do not, whatever you do, let this put you off, as the interior is the most spectacular and original in the country. Sunlight passing through stained glass set in the arc of the roof casts acid-bright colour dispersions across the brick walls, the contorted metal sculptures, the doll-like shrines and the chequered floor. Furthermore, the tomb of Father José Delgado, father of independence and the man who ended slavery in all of Central America, is beneath the church.

Plaza Morazán and the Teatro Nacional

One block north of El Rosario is the compact **Plaza Morazán**, bounded on its southern edge by the Renaissance-style **Teatro Nacional**. Built with the profits of the country's coffee plantations and reflecting the global vogue for French culture in the early twentieth century, the restored interior – all red plush, marble and decorative plasterwork – harks back to grander times. Regular musical and theatrical events are held here, including performances of the national orchestra most fortnights. Upcoming events can be found in the Friday edition or website of the national newspaper *Diario del Hoy* (Ⓦwww .elsalvador.com).

Parque Infantíl

Several blocks north of the Centro Histórico, near the intersection of Avenida España and Alameda Juan Pablo II, is the forested **Parque Infantíl** (Parque Campo Marte; daily 9am–5pm; US$0.57). Despite being a busy departure and arrival point for city buses, it is also popular with lunching workers from the nearby Centro de Gobierno and with local families, who picnic here on the weekends. There's a children's playground, forested tracks planted with native and medicinal species of trees, an open-air theatre and a monument to the heroes of 1890.

Iglesia Don Rua

Continue north past the eastern edge of the Parque Infantíl for five blocks and you come to perhaps the most commanding church in the city – and its largest functioning one – the **Iglesia Don Rua**. Built in the nineteenth century, the white bulk of the church towers above the surrounding houses and is particularly notable for its stunning stained-glass windows.

Parque Zoológicol and Museo de Historia Natural

A kilometre or so south of Plaza Barrios along Avenida Cuscatlán is the **Parque**

Zoológicol Nacional (Wed–Sun 9am–4pm; $0.60), with shaded paths, a good range of local birds and a great monkey island. In the park just south of the zoo, on the appropriately named Calle los Viveros ("plant/animal nurseries" road), the **Museo de Historia Natural** (Wed–Sun 9am–4.30pm; US$0.60) has some interesting exhibits on animals, plants, the country's geological development and a little botanical garden.

Parque Bolívar and Iglesia Sagrado Corazón

West along Calle Rubén Darío from Plaza Barrios is the recently refurbished **Parque Bolívar**, of little interest save for a horseback statue of the liberator himself. One block north, on Calle Arce, is the nineteenth-century **Iglesia Sagrado Corazón**, with impressive stained-glass windows and a wooden interior.

Parque Cuscatlán

Parque Cuscatlán, west of Parque Bolivar along Calle Rubén Dario, is a large expanse of shady walkways and grass lawns that not only offers respite from the heat and noise, but also is home to several interesting sights. The **Monumento a la Memoria y la Verdad** (Tues–Sun, 6am–6pm; free) lists the names of the thousands upon thousands who died or "disappeared" leading up to and during the civil conflict. Nearby, the **Sala Nacional de Exposiciones** (daily 9am–noon & 2–5pm; free) has interesting and high-quality rotating art exhibitions, while at the eastern end of the park, the **Tin Marín Children's Museum** (Tues–Fri 9am–1pm & 2–5pm, Sat & Sun 10am–1pm & 2–6pm; US$2; ✆www.tinmarin .org) may well be the best kids' museum ever, with attractions like painting a VW Beetle, sitting in a cockpit of a 727 and playing in a sloping house. A favourite is the grumpy little General Fintan who points and shakes his head when you

get near him. The only hitch is that if you are not a child, you will have to find one to accompany you in.

Boulevard de los Héroes

Eight blocks west of Parque Cuscatlán, Alameda Roosevelt crosses 49 Avenida Norte by **Estadio Mágico Gonzalez**, where international football matches are played. Three blocks north the avenida curls eastward and becomes **Boulevard de los Héroes**, dripping in American fast-food chains. Beyond these, at 27 Av Norte #1140, is the **Museo de la Palabra y la Imagen** (Mon–Fri 8am–noon & 2–5pm, Sat 8am–noon; US$2; ✆www.museo.com .sv), which holds exhibitions and installations focusing on the civil war (from a leftist viewpoint) and indigenous culture. The war photography regularly on display is moving, shocking and excellent. There's a recreation of **Radio Venceremos**, the clandestine guerrilla radio station that counterbalanced government media propaganda during the civil war, hidden at the back.

Colonia Centroamerica

Heading north of Boulevard los Héroes on Calle Centroamérica takes you into the arty and pleasant **Colonia Centro-américa**, the most traveller-friendly area of town. Straight up the hill on the calle, the **Parque Colonia Centro-américa** has two free flood-lit basketball courts, benches and gnarled trees to sit in; it's the only park you should consider being in after dark. At the northern end of the park, the **Museo de Arte Popular** (Tues–Fri 10am–5pm, Sat 10am–6pm; US$1; ✆2274-5154) has an interesting collection of folk art, in particular some fine examples of the miniature clay people made around Ilobasco and known as *sorpresas* (surprises) – see p.286 for more details about these. Call ahead for a free guide to the pieces, but only if you can speak Spanish, as their English is not good.

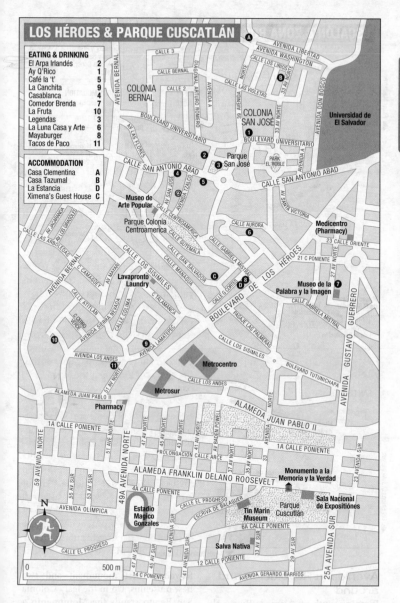

LOS HÉROES & PARQUE CUSCATLÁN

EATING & DRINKING

El Arpa Irlandés	2
Ay Q'Rico	1
Café la 't'	5
La Canchita	9
Casablanca	4
Comedor Brenda	7
La Fruta	10
Legendas	3
La Luna Casa y Arte	6
Mayaburger	8
Tacos de Paco	11

ACCOMMODATION

Casa Clementina	A
Casa Tazumal	B
La Estancia	D
Ximena's Guest House	C

Plaza de las Américas

Alameda Roosevelt continues west past Boulevard de los Héroes up to the rich but site-less suburbs of **Colonia Escalón**, on the slopes of Volcán San Salvador. Halfway along, the **Plaza de las Américas** contains a sculpture of the national symbol, **El Monumento El Salvador del Mundo**, which portrays Jesus standing on top of the globe. Curiously situated on the central island of a four-lane roundabout, you can just see it from a bus window.

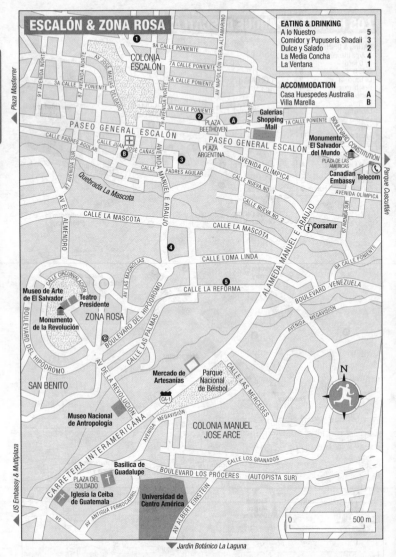

EATING & DRINKING

A lo Nuestro	5
Comidor y Pupusería Shadaii	3
Dulce y Salado	2
La Media Concha	4
La Ventana	1

ACCOMMODATION

Casa Huespedes Australia	A
Villa Marella	B

ESCALÓN & ZONA ROSA

COLONIA ESCALÓN

9A CALLE PONIENTE

7A CALLE PONIENTE

5A CALLE PONIENTE

3A CALLE PONIENTE

AV JOSE MATIAS DELGADO

91 AVENIDA NORTE

87 AVENIDA NORTE

3A AVENIDA NORTE

AV NAPOLEÓN VIERA ALTAMARINO

PASEO GENERAL ESCALÓN

CALLE PADRES AGUILAR

CALLE JUAN JOSE CAÑAS

PLAZA BEETHOVEN

Galerías Shopping Mall

1A CALLE PONIENTE

BOULEVARD CONSTITUCIÓN

Monumento El Salvador del Mundo

PLAZA DE LAS AMERICAS

PLAZA ARGENTINA

PASEO GENERAL ESCALÓN

AVENIDA OLÍMPICA

Canadian Embassy

Telecom

Parque Cuscatlán

Quebrada La Mascota

AV EL ALMENDRO

CALLE PADRES AGUILAR

CALLE NUEVA NO 1

CALLE NUEVA NO 2

Corsatur

AVENIDA OLÍMPICA

CALLE LA MASCOTA

CALLE LA MASCOTA

67 AVENIDA SUR

8A CALLE PONIENTE

ALAMEDA MANUEL E ARAUJO

AV JOSE MATIAS DELGADO

AVENIDA MANUEL E ARAUJO

CALLE LOMA LINDA

AV LAS MAGNOLIAS

CALLE LA REFORMA

BOULEVARD VENEZUELA

Museo de Arte de El Salvador

Teatro Presidente

ZONA ROSA

Monumento de la Revolución

BOULEVARD DEL HIPÓDROMO

CALLE LAS PALMAS

AVENIDA MEGAVISIÓN

SAN BENITO

BOULEVARD DEL HIPÓDROMO

AV DE LA REVOLUCIÓN

Mercado de Artesanías

Parque Nacional de Béisbol

CALLE LAS MERCEDES

CA-1

Museo Nacional de Antropología

CARRETERA INTERAMERICANA

AVENIDA MEGAVISIÓN

COLONIA MANUEL JOSE ARCE

CALLE LOS GRANADOS

Basílica de Guadalupe

PLAZA DEL SOLDADO

Iglesia la Ceiba de Guatemala

BOULEVARD LOS PRÓCERES (AUTOPISTA SUR)

AV ANTIGUA FERROCARRIL

N5

Universidad de Centro América

AV ALBERT EINSTEIN

N

0   500 m

Plaza Masferrer

US Embassy & Multiplaza

Jardín Botánico La Laguna

Avenida la Revolución and around

Running south off Alameda Roosevelt, 79a Avenida Sur crosses the river and turns into **Boulevard del Hipódromo**, the pumping central artery of the **Zona Rosa** evening playground. Running at right angles to the boulevard is **Avenida la Revolución**, home to San

Salvador's best monument and two best museums. Up in the leafy Colonia San Benito stands the **Monumento a la Revolución**, a vast, curved slab of concrete bearing a mosaic of a naked Goliath with head thrown back and arms uplifted. Built to commemorate the revolutionary movement of 1948, the monument's location – overlooking the bars and boutiques where the city's rich fritter their money away – is supremely ironic.

Behind the weeping Goliath, inside the Complejo Cultural, the **Museo de Arte de El Salvador** (Tues–Sun 10am–6pm; US$1.50; ⓦwww.marte.org.sv) has a great overview of modern Salvadoran art as well as temporary exhibitions, generally of works by Latin American artists. If you book two to four days in advance you can get a free English-speaking guide. Next door is the **Teatro Presidente**, less impressive than the Teatro Nacional but nonetheless featuring a packed schedule of opera, ballet, classical concerts and musicals.

The southern end of Avenida la Revolución holds the **Museo Nacional de Antropología "Dr David J. Guzmán"** (Tues–Sun 9am–5pm; US$3, or US$5 to use camera inside), named after an eminent Salvadoreño biologist and home to the nation's largest collection of cultural artefacts and anthropological displays, plus exhibits of modern Salvadoreño life and science. Perhaps the most important piece in the museum is the **Monolito del Jaguar**, a five-ton circular representation of a jaguar's head. It is worth phoning ahead to organize a free English-speaking guide, as the plaques are all in Spanish.

Carretera Interamericana

At the southern end of Avenida la Revolución is Alameda Araujo, which runs from Plaza de las Américas through the southwest quarters of the city to meet the Autopista del Sur. Here is possibly the most beautiful church in San Salvador, the **Basílica de Nuestra Señora de Guadalupe** (daily 7am–5pm; donations optional). Built after World War I and consecrated in 1953, the basilica is dedicated to the Virgen Morena, or Black Virgin, patroness of the Americas. Inside are lovely stained-glass windows and a 1950s mural of the Virgin and angels over the altar.

La UCA

Stretching behind the basilica is the campus of the fee-paying **Universidad de Centro América** ("La UCA"; also known as the Jesuit University), pleasantly laid out amid shady grounds. The moving **Centro Monseñor Romero** (Mon–Fri 8am–noon & 2–6pm, Sat 8am–11.30pm; free) at La UCA commemorates the assassinated Archbishop Romero, along with the six Jesuit priests, their housekeeper and her daughter, who were murdered here by the security forces in November 1989. Volunteer students act as guides to the small museum, which houses clothing, photographs and personal effects of Romero and the priests, along with those of other human-rights workers killed during the years of conflict. There are diagrams and explanations of the campus massacre, as well as eyewitness descriptions of other atrocities during the war, such as the massacres at Río Sumpul (May 1980) and Mozote (Dec 1981). Outside, a small rose garden has been planted in tribute; the circle of six bushes is for the six priests, the white rose in the centre is for Monseñor Romero.

Jardín Botánico la Laguna

A short distance south of the university, the tranquil **Jardín Botánico la Laguna** (Tues–Sun 9am–5.30pm; US$0.50) sits incongruously at the edge of an industrial park and at the foot of old volcanic cliffs. The garden contains plants from all over the world, set among shady trees and small streams, and is a good place to escape the city for an hour or two. Buses #101D and #44 will drop you off about five minutes' walk from the entrance.

Arrival and information

By air Comalapa International Airport (ⓦwww
.cepa.gob.sv) is a 45min drive southeast of the city
centre. Buses (#14, #15 and #29, among others)
stop by the highway turn-off to the airport; #29 then
stops in the city centre. If it is getting late take a

taxi; after 7pm taxis are the only way to get to the centre. Taxis Acacya (☎2271-4937) have a booth at the airport and charge US$25 day or night to the capital, regardless of numbers. They also run a *colectivo* service (9am, 1pm & 5.30pm from the airport; 6am, 7am, 10am and 2pm to the airport; US$3) leaving and arriving at their offices at 19a Av Nte & C 3 Pte #1107.

By bus International buses arrive at the Puertobus terminal by the Centro Gobierno (from Guatemala and Honduras), or at the Terminal de Occidente, Blvd Venezuela in the southwest of the city (from Guatemala). Tica Bus buses from Costa Rica, Nicaragua and Guatemala have their own terminal at C Concepción #121 in the Centro Histórico. Domestic buses from the north and east arrive at Terminal de Oriente, east of the centre, from where #9, #29 or #34 go to the centre and #29 and #54 go to Blvd los Héroes. Buses from the west and beaches west of La Libertad arrive at the Terminal de Occidente; bus #44 goes to Blvd los Héroes and #34 to the Terminal de Oriente via the Centro. Buses from the eastern coastal highway go to the Terminal de Sur, connected to the centre via #26 or #11B.

Tour operators Akwaterra (no office premises; ☎7888-8642, ⊛www.akwaterra.com) speak great English and run active ecotours on land and sea – everything from kayaking and surfing to horse-riding and mountain-biking. El Salvador Divers, C 3 Pte 5020-A at 99a Av Nte (☎2264-0961, ⊛www.elsalvadordivers.com), has diving trips along the Los Cóbanos/Los Remedios stretch of the Pacific coast and crater diving at Lake Coatepeque, plus PADI courses and equipment rental. Ríos Aventuras (☎2298-0335, Ⓔgrupotropic @navegante.com.sv) organizes rafting on the ríos Paz and Lempa for minimum groups of four people.

At most places tours start from around US$30 per person, more if the group is smaller.

Tourist information The offices of Mitur and Corsatur, both at Edificio Carbonel #1, Alameda Araujo (Mon–Fri 9am–5pm; ☎2243-7835 or 2241-3200, ⊛www.elsalvador.travel) give out quite basic maps and advertisement-laden "guides". If you are persistent they can answer any queries you have. ISTU, C Ruben Dario #619 (☎2222-8000, ⊛www.istu.gob.sv) provides information on national parks and *turicentros*, while the Ministerio de Trabajo, C Nuevo Dos #19 (☎2298-8739) run four centres providing free accommodation around the country (see box, p.270). For event listings, keep a lookout for *Ke Pasa*, a free weekly entertainment guide available in bars and restaurants. *The Revue*, Guatemala's English-language magazine, also includes an El Salvador section and is widely available throughout the city.

Travel agents The offices of most airlines with service to the country and many other travel agents can be found along the Alameda Roosevelt/Paseo Escalón, with TACA and AA offices in the Metrocentro (see p.267).

City transport

Buses The city bus network (schoolbuses and minibuses) runs from 6am until around 8pm and is comprehensive, frequent and cheap – it's US$0.25 to anywhere in the city. Pay the driver if there is a gate, or the roaming, shouting driver's assistant if not. Most stops are not marked, so look for large public buildings, shopping centres or groups of people waiting by the road; usually you can also hop on if they stop in traffic.

Taxis Yellow city taxis ply the streets and wait around bus terminals, markets and major shopping

---

USEFUL BUS ROUTES IN SAN SALVADOR

#29 From Terminal de Oriente to Metrocentro via Centro Histórico.

#30B Along Boulevard de los Héroes, up Alameda Roosevelt and part of Paseo Escalón, then turning west to run past the Zona Rosa.

#34 From Terminal de Oriente through Centro Histórico to Terminal de Occidente and out along the Carretera Interamericana, past the Mercado de Artesanías.

#44 Along Boulevard de los Héroes, onto 49a Av Sur close to the Terminal de Occidente, past the Universidad de Centroamérica and out past the US Embassy to Santa Elena.

#52 Along Alameda Juan Pablo I, past Metrosur and on to El Salvador del Mundo (opposite the Telecom office), then up Paseo Escalón past the Galerías shopping mall.

#101A/B/C/D From Centro Histórico up Alameda Roosevelt to Plaza de las Américas, then on to Santa Tecla.

areas. They cost US$4–6, which you should sort out before getting in. Take taxis after dark.

Accommodation

Accomodation in San Salvador can be defined by neighbourhood. The Centro Histórico is not generally conducive to peace of mind or a pleasant stay, and there is very little to do there at night but wait for a morning bus. The western suburbs are safe and there's plenty to see and do, but there are few genuinely budget options. North of Boulevard de los Héroes is middle ground, and much better for travellers: it's safe and with a good nightlife.

Centro Histórico

American Guest House 17a Av Nte 119, between C Arce & C 1 Pte ☎2222-8789, ©americanguesthouse@hotmail.com. Dimly-lit and rather gloomy rooms, but the service is friendly. Rooms, some oddly-shaped, come with a choice of private or shared bath, plus hot water and cable TV. International phone calls available and meals served at on-site café. ➋–➌

International Custodio 10a Av Sur 109 ☎2502-0678, ©peraltavictor62@hotmail.com. One of the centre's best options, with friendly service, great views from the roof, clean sheets and decent fans. Credit cards are accepted and the manager, who speaks good English, can give advice on the area. Reductions available on extended stays. ➋

Nuevo Panamerican 8a Av Sur, by the Mercado Ex-Cuartel ☎2221-1199 or 2222-2959, ©hayderiveracere@yahoo.es. Firm beds with ornate bedsteads, a choice of humming a/c or silent ceiling fans and en-suite showers all serve to make this a great choice in the centre. ➋

Villa Floréncia C 1 Pte 1023, between 17a & 19a Av Nte ☎2221-1706. One of several similar hotels in the area behind the Puerto bus terminal. With large, bright, airy en-suite rooms, cable TV and communal seating areas, this is perhaps the best of the bunch. ➌

Around Blvd de los Héroes

Casa Clementina Av Morazán 34 at C Washington, Col Libertad ☎2225-5962. Friendly, peaceful and secure with communal garden, TV and outdoor seating. Simply furnished but attractive cold-water en-suite rooms with fan. Rates include breakfast. Singles ➌, doubles ➎

Casa Tazumal 35a Av Nte 3 ☎2235-0156, ©casahuespedestazumal@hotmail.com. A good, homely hotel with plenty of perks – free daily internet access, airport or bus terminal pick-up, good food and laundry service (US$5) – supplementing their firm beds and clean rooms with cable TV. ➍

La Estancia Av Cortés 216 ☎2275-3381. A relaxed travellers' hostel with a large cable TV area, free kitchen use and coffee. The dorm bunks spill out into the corridor and the clean en-suite rooms are little, but are great value, especially the room with a private terrace. Dorms ➋, doubles ➌

Ximena's Guest House C San Salvador 202, Col Centro América ☎2260-2481, ©ximenas @navegante.com.sv. The original San Salvador hostel is not necessarily still the best. Beds are lumpy or saggy and the electric hot water (which you pay extra for) is shockingly inconsistent. It remains a travellers' favourite though, not least for the fruit breakfasts, helpful English-speaking owner and social evening atmosphere. Dorms ➋, doubles ➍

Colonia Escalón

Casa Huéspedes Australia 1a C Pte 3852 ☎2298-6035. Lacks the atmosphere of the Blvd de los Héroes hostels, but is certainly cleaner and more comfortable, offers free breakfast and internet and the showers are big and hot. It's incredible value for Escalón, but choose the cheapest rooms, as there is no massive difference in the more expensive – all rates are per person. ➌

TREAT YOURSELF

Villa Marella C Juan José Cañas and 83a Av Sur ☎2263-4931. The best deal of the upmarket Escalón hotels, with giant beds, powerful hot showers, complimentary mineral water, free internet, an indigo-coloured splash pool with accompanying loungers, great service and tasty, if equally costly, food. ➐

Eating

The best restaurants are concentrated in the western suburbs, catering to those with the money and time to indulge. There are *comedores* and *pupuserías* everywhere and, if they look hygienic or locals are eating at them you shouldn't be afraid to try. The Boulevard de los Héroes itself is dominated by local and inter-national fast-food chains, but there are good options off the main drag.

Centro Histórico

Café Maquilishuat C 4 Pte & 9a Av Sur. Sodas, great juices (US$0.80), and *típicos* (US$2–4) with a Mexican and American influence dished out on plastic trays in lively a/c surroundings.

Koradi 9a Av Sur 225, at C 4 Pte. One of the few places catering to vegetarians, with soya burgers (US$2.50), wholewheat pizzas and great juices. Open in the daytime only; closed Sun.

Pan Salvador C Arce, between 7a & 9a Av Sur. Popular with local workers, this busy *comedor* and bakery serves meat dishes for less than US$1, with combo deals for US$1.50 and coffee for US$0.35. The whole place is redolent with the scent of baking cakes.

Around Boulevard de los Héroes

Ay Q'Rico Blvd Universitario 217. Popular among the local students for its cheap daily menus (US$1.50–2) served with free beer. Also a wide selection of seafood and poultry dishes with a touch of Mexican flavour.

Café la 't' C San Antonio Abad 2233. Owner Anna has turned this into a great little arty café and bar offering a calendar of once-monthly live music and art exhibitions. The tiramisu (US$2.75) is rumoured to be the best in the country and the lemon, honey and vodka-filled "Café Ivanovic" cocktail (US$1.95) is excellent.

Casablanca C San Antonio Abad & Av San José. A well-prepared canteen menu (US$2–4), with large soup portions, is served in a cool and open room shielded from the traffic by climbing plants.

Comedor Brenda Next to the Museo de Palabra y Imagen. An outstanding *comedor* with *a la vista* (canteen) lunches for under US$2 and great snacks in the afternoon, including the best *yuca frita* (US$0.35) around. Open noon to 6pm.

La Fruta Av Maracaibo 519 ☎ 2260-1253. Come here for more than 200 juice combinations, as well as breakfasts and lunches made from all natural ingredients. Evening meals available if you call in advance. Mon–Sat 9am–6pm.

Mayaburger Behind the Esso station on C G Cortés. This trustworthy burger van outstrips the big franchises both on price (a two-burger sandwich, onions and salad are US$1.75) and taste – plus, it's open 24/7.

Tacos de Paco C Andes 2931. Tasty Mexican tacos (US$3–4) with a twist – they are served in a room that has original art on the walls and hosts poetry readings on Wed evenings. Open noon–3pm & 5–10pm.

Colonia Escalón and the Zona Rosa

Dulce y Salado 3 C Pte, by Plaza Beethoven. Although decorated like a little girl's bedroom, this little restaurant has good pancake, juice and coffee breakfasts (US$3) and great quiche (US$5.50).

Kalpataru Av Masferrer 147 ☎ 2263-1204. Imaginative vegetarian fare: try the *pupusas* (US$3) with unusual fillings like stir-fried broccoli and curried vegetables. There is a natural medicine counter and bookshop on site.

Comedor y Pupusería Shadaii 77a Av Sur, behind Super Selectos. The *comedor* and *pupusería* of choice for the area's workers, with *típicos* breakfasts (US$1.50) and lunches (US$1.80–2) that are the cheapest around.

Drinking and nightlife

San Salvador's clubs and bars are found mainly in the western suburbs, but there are also small pockets of expat and tourist nightlife, particularly in and around *Ximena's Guesthouse* and *La Estancia* in Colonia Centroamérica, behind Boulevard de los Héroes.

Around Blvd de los Héroes

El Arpa Irlandés Av A, on the west side of Parque San José. This shiny and polite bar is the place to come for a Guinness (US$3) or a Pilsener (US$1). There's a pool table, and rock bands on Sat nights, which draw a young crowd.

Café la 't' C San Antonio Abad 2233. Good cocktails (US$3) and a relaxed atmosphere make this a nice place to start off a night around Los Héroes. Open until 11pm or midnight on Fri–Sun.

La Canchita C Lamatepec, by C los Andes. This fun and feisty bar, which offers buckets of six bottles of beer for US$5 and has the best full-sized pool tables in town (US$1 per 30min), is the pick of several places in the area.

Legendas On the south side of Parque San José. This orange-walled late-night spot has darts, table-football, music that gets people dancing and neither charges entry nor inflates its beer prices. Rum & coke US$1.50.

La Luna Casa y Arte C Berlin 228 ⓦwww.lalunacasayarte.com. Hands down the best bar in San Salvador, with a film, live music and exhibition program every night. There is eclectic furnishing, the walls are decked in paintings and dripping in good taste. Brilliant cocktails (US$3) include ice cream and Baileys and White Russians. Check out the schedule online or nailed to the tree outside. Wed–Sun 7pm–2am. US$3–5 entry after 9pm.

Pueblo Viejo In the Metrosur on Blvd de los Héroes ☎2260-3551. The popular *Pueblo* has salsa dancing in a welcoming atmosphere Thurs–Sat 9pm–midnight. There are US$3 cover charges on Fri & Sat.

Colonia Escalón and the Zona Rosa

Envy 2nd floor, Multiplaza shopping mall, Antiguo Cuscatlán ☎2243-2576. The place to go for the rich San Salvador set. They all get dressed up, and you have to too (trousers, shirt, shoes). Music is dance, R&B and hip-hop. Entry US$5.

La Media Concha 79a Av Sur, by C La Mascota. Unlike the majority of Zona Rosa restaurant-cum-dancehalls, this bar, selling barbecue and beer giraffes (four-pint towers of beer; US$8.60) is brimming with personality and boasts a terrace to cool off when you become overwhelmed by the young Salvadoreños busting moves on dancefloor.

La Ventana Plaza Palestina, Col Escalón between 9a C Pe & 83 Av Nte. European-run restaurant and bar with an interesting selection of dishes (US$5–9) inspired by cuisines from around the world. Very popular at the weekends with expats, tourists and moneyed Salvadoreños. Daily until 1am.

Entertainment

Cinema There are a couple of multiscreen complexes – a Cinemark at the Metrocentro and an 11-screen Cinépolis at Galerías Escalón. Both show some original-language films and some dubbed (tickets US$2–3). Independent cinema can be found at La Luna (see above) on Wed–Sun, starting at around 7pm, or Café la 't' (see p.266) on Wed & Thurs around 8pm.

Dancing *Pueblo Viejo*, in the Metrosur (☎2260-3551), has salsa dancing on weekends (see above).

Theatre The Teatro Presidente (see p.263) and the Teatro Nacional (see p.259) host everything from ballet to musicals to opera at anything from US$3 to US$30, while the Teatro Luis Poma, just inside the main arched entrance to the Metrocentro, shows locally produced plays (US$5). Information can be found in the Friday edition and on the website of *El Diario de Hoy* (ⓦwww.elsalvador.com)

Shopping

Art The El Árbol de Dios art gallery, on Av Masferrer y C la Mascota (Mon–Sat 9am–6pm; free), is the shop of El Salvador's emblematic painter Fernando Llort. Everything from prints to cooking aprons in his naïf style can be purchased; most items are produced in the workshop in the back. Originals go for about half a million dollars.

Books The bookshop on the second level of the Metrocentro has a selection of English-language titles and some US magazines. Punto Literario, Blvd del Hipódromo 326, has English, French, German and Spanish literature, while *La Ventana* restaurant (see above) has a small selection of political and social texts (in English and Spanish) and US magazines and newspapers.

Malls Reputedly the largest shopping mall in Central America, the Metrocentro/Metrosur complex at the southern end of Blvd de los Héroes holds three storeys of expensive boutiques, sporting-goods

CRAFTS IN SAN SALVADOR

Artisan work is still highly valued in El Salvador, and many communities have defined themselves by a chosen craft. The most well-known types are the brightly painted, naïf-style wood and ceramics from La Palma, the hammocks from Concepción Quezaltepeque and the interesting ceramics at Ilobasco. These are far cheaper in their place of manufacture, but the Mercado Cuartel and the Mercado de Artesanías in San Salvador both have an extensive selection of goods from across the country at reasonable prices; a number of more expensive shops around town also carry smaller selections. Hammocks can usually be found for sale in the Parque Central in San Salvador.

outlets, pricey but well-stocked souvenir shops, a supermarket and a food court. Galerías Escalón, at Paseo Gen Escalón 3700, is the same but classier. Multiplaza, on the Carretera Panamericana to Santa Elena, with its flashy bars and restaurants, is the most upmarket.

Markets There are two good markets for artisan handicrafts: the central Mercado Ex Cuartel, three blocks east from the Teatro Nacional, and the higher-quality Mercado de Artesanías, opposite the baseball stadium on Alameda M E Araujo; see box, p.267, for more details. Southwest of Plaza Barrios are the ever-expanding street stalls of the Mercado Central, where anything and everything can be bought for about a dollar, even on a Sun.

Directory

Exchange Most banks ask for the original receipt when cashing traveller's cheques and give over-the-counter cash advances on Visa and MasterCard. Banco Hipotecario, at Av Cuscatlán between C 4 & 6 Ote, and other branches around the city, do not demand the receipt. American Express issues traveller's cheques from their office at 55 Av Sur, Edificio Credomatic, between Alameda Roosevelt & Av Olímpica (☎2245-3774). Banks and ATMs are ubiquitous around the western suburbs and Blvd de los Héroes.

Embassies Most embassies are located in or around the Paseo Escalón and Zona Rosa districts. The US embassy, the second most heavily fortified in the world, is on Blvd Santa Elena, Antiguo Cuscatlán ☎2501-2999/2004 (take bus #44). Canada is at Alameda Roosevelt y 63a Av Sur (☎2279-4655). British citizens should call the honorary consul on ☎2281-5555. Australians can contact the Canadian embassy.

Immigration Ministerio del Interior in the Centro de Gobierno, on Alameda Juan Pablo I (Mon–Fri 8am–4pm; ☎2221-2111), is the place to get stamps, tourist cards and visas extended.

Internet The Metrosur has two fast internet cafés; and Cyber Café Genus, on Av Izalco by the church, is also very friendly. Cyber snack, on the east side of Plaza Barrios, is fast enough. There are Infocentros on C Arce between 19a and 21a Av Sur, and in the Zona Rosa where Blvd del Hipódromo meets Av la Revolución. Expect to pay between US$0.60 and US$1.

Laundry Lavandería Lavapronto, C Los Sismiles 2944 (Mon–Sat 7am–7pm). An average load should cost US$2–3.

Libraries La UCA has a very good library, The Biblioteca Nacional is open to the public, but you have to show ID.

Medical care There's a 24hr pharmacy at Farmacia Internacional, Edificio Kent, Local 6, Alameda Juan Pablo II at Blvd de los Héroes. The Medicentro at 27a Av Nte and C 21 Pte has a number of doctors specializing in different fields.

Police The main station is in the Scottish castle-like building which occupies an entire block on 10a Av Sur at C 6 Ote (☎2271-4422).

Post office Behind the Centro de Gobierno on Blvd Centro de Gobierno; look for the large building with "UPAE" on the side. The *lista de correos* (Mon–Fri 8am–5pm, Sat 8am–noon) is at window 14 in the main section. There are smaller offices in the lower level of the Metrocentro mall.

Telephones Telecom, the French-owned former state phone company, has an enormous glass office at La Campana on Plaza de las Américas.

Moving on

San Salvador is El Salvador's bus hub, with the best land transport connections in the country. There are also flights, both domestic and international, out of the city's airport.

By air

You can get flights out of Comalapa airport with: TACA Airlines (ⓦwww.taca.com), to North, South and Central Americas and the Caribbean; American Airlines (ⓦwww.aa.com) and Continental Airlines (ⓦwww.continental.com), for the US; and Air Transat (ⓦwww.airtransat.com) to Canada.

By bus

San Salvador has three domestic terminals and two international terminals. Despite this, leaving the city is a remarkably easy exercise. Most international buses can also be caught on Blvd del Hipódromo as they leave the city, but these departures are very early in the morning, so check the day before and get a taxi. Bus route information is available in Spanish only from the Association of Salvadoran Bus Owners (AEAS; ☎2225-2661) at C 27 Pte 1132, Colonia Layco, or the tourist office.

Domestic bus terminals

Terminal de Occidente On Blvd Venezuela (reached by urban services #4, #27, #34 and #7C). Serves the south and west of the country.
Terminal de Oriente On Blvd del Ejército (reached by urban services #3, #5, #7, #8, #9, #28, #29, #34 and #42). Serves the east and north of the country.
Terminal del Sur On the Autopista a Comalapa (reached by urban services #11B, #21 and #26). The stop for buses along the eastern Carretera Litoral to Zacatecoluca and Usulután.

Domestic bus departures

Terminal de Occidente to: Ahuachapán (#202; frequent; 3hr 30min); Desvío Opico, via Joya de Cerén (#108; frequent; 1hr); La Libertad (#102; very frequent; 1hr); Metapán (#201A; twice hourly; 3hr 30min); Santa Ana, via San Andrés (#201; frequent; 1hr 20min–2hr); Sonsonate (#205; very frequent; 1hr 30 min).

Terminal de Oriente to: Chalatenango (#125; frequent; 2hr 30min); Ilobasco (#111; every 15min; 1hr 20min); La Palma/El Poy (#119; twice hourly; 4hr 30min); La Unión (#304; twice hourly; 3–4hr); San Francisco Gotera (#305 (direct); 3 daily; 3–4hr); San Miguel (#301; frequent; 3–4hr); San Vicente (#116; frequent; 1hr 30min); Suchitoto (#129; three hourly; 1hr 30min); Usulután (#302; 2 daily; 2hr 30min). Luxury services to San Miguel (every 40min; 2hr) and San Vicente (8 daily; 1hr) also depart this terminal.

Terminal del Sur to: Costa del Sol (#495; twice hourly; 2hr 30min); Puerto El Triunfo (#185; 6 daily; 2hr); Usulután (#302; frequent; 2hr 30min); Zacatecoluca (#133; frequent; 1hr 30min).

International bus terminals

Terminal Puertobus On Alameda Juan Pablo II (reached by urban service #52).

Terminal Tica Bus By the *Hotel San Carlos* on C Concepción (reached by urban services #29 and #34).

International bus departures

Terminal Puertobus to: Guatemala City (18 daily Mon–Sat, 4 daily Sun; 5hr); Managua, Nicaragua (daily; 11hr); San José, Costa Rica (daily; 18hr); San Pedro Sula, Honduras (2 daily; 6hr); Tapachula, Mexico (daily; 10hr); Tegucigalpa, Honduras (3 daily; 6hr 30min).

Terminal Tica Bus to: Tapachula, Mexico via Guatemala City (daily; 10hr/5hr); Panama City via San José, Costa Rica and Managua, Nicaragua (daily; 36hr/18hr/11hr).

AROUND SAN SALVADOR

San Salvador is an excellent transport hub, and within easy reach of the city are a number of destinations offering immediate relief from the heat and crowds. Head in any direction and in well under an hour you'll find lush, rolling countryside.

Los Chorros

West along the Carretera Interamericana from San Salvador light industrial and residential districts blend indiscernibly into **Santa Tecla**, briefly the capital in 1854 but now only of minor interest. Six kilometres farther along the highway, El Salvador's most popuar *turicentro*, **Los Chorros** (daily 7am–5pm; US$0.90), is a great spot for a swim. Small waterfalls cascade through mossy jungle slopes into a series of landscaped pools, suitable for bathing; there are public changing rooms and

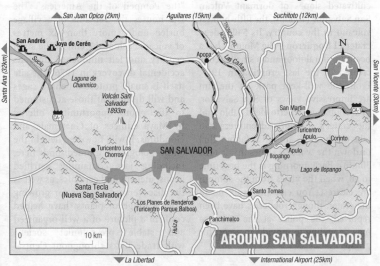

AROUND SAN SALVADOR

TURICENTROS AND CENTROS OBRAJO

Most large, urban settlements in El Salvador are within a stone's throw of one of the country's fourteen turicentros, public tourism centres designed to give city dwellers the opportunity to enjoy nature in comfortable surroundings. There are three in the vicinity of San Salvador – Los Chorros (see p.269), Apulo (p.271) and Parque Balboa (p.272) – but whichever city you're in, one is never far away. Most involve some kind of water-based diversion – swimming pools or natural lakes – along with ample provision of food and cabañas to escape the sun. Opening hours are between 9am and 5pm and there is an entry charge of something less than a dollar. Contact ISTU (see p.254) for more information.

For those who want full accommodation on the government, there are also four centros obrajo, or workers' centres, at El Tamarindo beach, Lago de Coatepeque, La Palma and Puerto la Libertad. Recently constructed and nicer than they sound, they are free of charge, provided you contact and visit the Ministerio de Trabajo (see p.264) with your passport beforehand. They are closed on Mondays and Tuesdays and, like the turicentros, get very busy on weekends and holidays.

showers – don't bring valuables – and a couple of *comedores* provide meals. If you're in a group and feel brave enough to ignore the warnings about robbers, the surrounding hills provide pleasant walks.

Take **bus #79** from 11a Avenida Sur and Calle Rubén Darío (every 15min; 30min), or any Santa Ana bus from the Terminal de Occidente, and ask to be dropped at the gate.

Volcán San Salvador

North of Santa Tecla lie the heavily cultivated slopes of dormant **Volcán San Salvador** (1960m), the fifth-highest volcano in the country. Its 540m-deep crater **El Boquerón** ("Big Mouth") has a beautiful floral floor and a smaller cone created in the last eruption in 1917. From the well-kept **park** on the rim are impressive views of San Salvador, Lake Ilopango, Puerto del Diablo and the crater's interior; adventurers can take on the walk around it (about 2hr) or down the wooded slopes inside (1hr 30min). Early morning is the best time to go, when the views from the summit are clearest. You can also walk up to the crater, though robberies have been reported; the police at the entrance may be willing to provide an escort for groups.

Bus #103 (hourly) and pick-ups run from 4a Avenida Sur and Calle Hernández in Santa Tecla (reached via the La Libertad, Santa Ana and Sonsonate buses from Terminal de Occidente), to Pueblo del Boquerón, 1km from the rim; the last bus down leaves mid-afternoon.

Joya de Cerén

Some 9km northwest of Los Chorros, the Maya and UNESCO World Heritage Site of **Joya de Cerén** (Tues– Sun 9am–4pm; US$2.85) may well be "the Pompeii of the Americas". The site houses the remains of a village buried under more than six metres of volcanic ash at the end of the sixth century and left untouched until its accidental discovery in 1976. The site itself is small, protected behind cages and will disappoint those accustomed to the photo opportunities offered by Maya edifices of Guatemala and Honduras. It will, however, delight the anthropologically minded: finds here, including jars containing petrified beans, utensils and ceramics, as well as the discovery of gardens for growing a wide range of plants, have helped confirm a picture of a well-organized and stable pre-colonial society, with trade links throughout Central

America. As yet, no human remains have been uncovered, which concurs with the hasty departure suggested by the number of artefacts discovered. A small, Spanish-language museum at the site details the development of the Maya culture and the excavation project itself.

Bus #108 from San Salvador's Terminal de Occidente runs right by the site – get off just after crossing the Río Sucio. If you wish to go to San Andrés (see below) in the same trip, start here and take #108 back towards San Salvador as far as the highway, where you can intercept a #201 (towards Santa Ana from the Terminal de Occidente) to San Andrés.

San Andrés

A few kilometres southwest of Joya de Céren over lush undulations of agricultural land lies the Maya ceremonial centre of **San Andrés** (Tues–Sun 9am–4.30pm; US$2.85). One of the largest pre-Columbian sites in El Salvador, originally supporting a population of about twelve thousand, the site reached its peak as the regional capital around 650–900 AD. Only sections of the ceremonial centre have been excavated – seven major structures including a temple, altar and indigo works – and sadly, they've been preserved using rather too liberal amounts of concrete. You can climb freely around the site, which is also a popular picnic spot at the weekends. A small, well-curated museum (Spanish only) includes a good model of what the site would have looked like in the late first millenium.

The #201 **bus** between Terminal de Occidente and Santa Ana will drop you by a black ruin on the highway a couple of hundred metres from the site – you will need to tell the driver to stop. It's possible to walk to Joya de Cerén in the same trip. A path leads across the fields behind San Andrés, coming out about 4km northeast at an abandoned railway station. From here take a left towards San Juan Opico; it is another 3km or so to Joya de Cerén. It is preferable to travel in a group.

Lago de Ilopango

Heading east from San Salvador, the Carretera Interamericana passes the city's dismal eastern slums and bends northwards. A few kilometres past the airport at Ilopango, a dirt road branches south and winds down through scrubby hillsides, offering stunning views across **Lago de Ilopango** to the peaks of Volcán San Vicente. The country's largest and deepest crater lake, resulting from one of the biggest eruptions in history in around 250 AD, Ilopango is a contrast of blue waters and tumbling, thickly vegetated cliffs. Further along the road, in the dusty hamlet of Apulo, the decent (but busy at weekends) **turicentro** (daily 8am–5pm; US$0.80) has a beach, swimming pools and fine *comedores*. Small boats tout for custom here (US$12/hr; reductions for groups), and drifting around the Isla de Amor or touring the rich lakeside communities is a pleasant way to spend a hot afternoon. The best **volcano diving** in the country also takes place under the surface of the lake, on the underwater volcanic cone La Caldera. This should be organized with El Salvador Divers (see p.264) in the capital beforehand.

Bus #15 runs from the corner of Calle 9 Pte and 1a Avenida Nte in San Salvador every half an hour or so.

Los Planes de Renderos

Overlooking the Valle de Hamacas from the brim of the valley's southern watershed, **Los Planes de Renderos** offers fresh air, good food and great views. The best panoramas of San Salvador are from the *Casa de Piedra* (Km 8.5), an open-fronted bar/restaurant serving seafood and *típicos* with weekend music or karaoke. Cheaper, though, is the *mirador* lookout point off the road just before the restaurant as you come up the hill. Another great restaurant is the barn-like *Pupusería Paty* (Km 10), which serves some of the best and biggest *pupusas* in the country. The best views of the coast are from the **Puerta del Diablo**, a split rock formation at the summit of the Cerro Chulo, a 40min walk from the road through the somewhat grubby **Parque Balboa** *turicentro* (Km 12; daily 8am–6pm; US$0.90). The rock's legendary origins – split by a bolt of lightning over three hundred years ago – have been eclipsed by its very real role in the civil war as a place of death squad interrogations, executions and body-dumping.

Bus #12 runs up the Carretera Los Planes, along which all kilometre markers are given, from Avenida 29 de Agosto. If you don't fancy walking to the Puerta del Diablo, you can take the bus to the last stop, at Km 14.

Panchimalco

Further south, the largely indigenous town of **Panchimalco** lies sleepily beneath the Puerta del Diablo. The area was once widely inhabited by the Panchos, descendants of the Pipils, and although a number still remain, traditional dress is rarely seen nowadays. The town's colonial **church**, built in 1725, is the oldest surviving church in the country and is also remarkable for its depiction of Jesus. There are indigenous **crafts** for sale too, including pre-Hispanic musical instruments, at the Casa de la Cultura. Usually a quiet place, things become livelier during the town's annual **festivals** (see p.255).

Bus #17 runs regularly to the town from Avenida 29 de Agosto in San Salvador.

The Pacific coast

El Salvador's **Pacific coast** is a 300-kilometre sweep of sandy tropical beaches, dramatic cliffs, mangrove swamps and romantic islands. While the tourist potential of many of the beaches is now being developed, most stretches of sand are still, blissfully, a far cry from international resorts. Indeed, the beauty of this part of the country lies in relaxing on clean, wide beaches, catching world-class waves or spending time in relatively untouched fishing villages.

Coming from San Salvador, the most accessible stretch of coast is the **Costa del Bálsamo**, extending around the small fishing town of **Puerto La Libertad**. This stretch boasts some of Central America's best surfing beaches, and El Salvador's biggest gringo community. Further down the coast are the green waterways and islands of the mangrove swamps of the **Bahía de Jiquilisco**, as well as what many consider to be the finest beach in the country, **Playa El Espino**. In the extreme east of the region you can catch early-morning *lanchas* to the tranquil islands of the **Golfo de Fonseca**, and away from faded **La Unión**.

The beaches west of Acajutla are best accessed via Sonsonate rather than along the coastal road, and are thus covered beginning on p.307.

PACIFIC COAST ROAD TRIP

Along with Ruta de las Flores (see p.309) and the climb to Perquín (see p.295), the Carretera Litoral, running the length of El Salvador's Pacific coast, is one of the country's best road trips. Public transport runs regularly to many places along the route. However, it's still worth renting a car for a few days to reach some of the more remote and beautiful beaches.

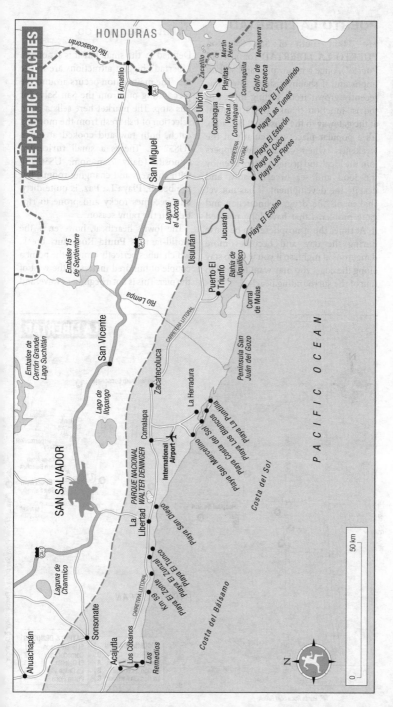

THE PACIFIC BEACHES

HONDURAS

Río Goascorán

El Amatillo

San Miguel

La Unión

Zacatillo

Martín Pérez

Playtas

Conchagua

Volcán Conchagua

Conchagüita

Golfo de Fonseca

Meanguera

Playa El Tamarindo

Playa Las Tunas

CARRETERA LITORAL

Playa El Esterón

Playa El Cuco

Playa Las Flores

Laguna el Jocotal

Jucuarán

Playa El Espino

Usulután

Puerto El Triunfo

Bahía de Jiquilisco

Corral de Mulas

Río Lempa

Embalse 15 de Septiembre

San Vicente

Península San Juan del Gozo

PACIFIC OCEAN

Embalse de Cerrón Grande/ Lago Suchitlán

Zacatecoluca

CARRETERA LITORAL

Lago de Ilopango

Comalapa

La Herradura

Playa La Puntilla

SAN SALVADOR

International Airport

Playa Los Blancos

Playa Costa del Sol

Playa San Marcelino

Costa del Sol

La Libertad

PARQUE NACIONAL WALTER DEININGER

Playa San Diego

Laguna de Chanmico

Sonsonate

Acajutla

Playa El Tunco

Playa El Zunzal

Km 59

CARRETERA LITORAL

Costa del Bálsamo

Los Cóbanos

Los Remedios

Ahuachapán

Laguna de Chanmico

N

0   50 km

PUERTO LA LIBERTAD

Just 34km south of San Salvador, **PUERTO LA LIBERTAD** (or just "El Puerto"), once a major port and still an important, if shabby, fishing town, has recently grown from surfing mecca to tourist junction thanks to its position at the gateway to the Costa del Bálsamo. It's a popular place, particularly at the weekends, when capital day-trippers join the local and gringo surfers to enjoy the food and sea breeze. Sadly, and despite the development, it has not yet shaken off the drug, delinquency and gang problems that have long plagued it. At times the atmosphere can be tense during the day, and becomes more dangerous at night, so if you want to stay along the coast you may want to head to one of the surrounding beaches.

What to see and do

Defined by the small bay it is set on, La Libertad's biggest attractions are in the sea. The main action occurs around the pier jutting out from the San Salvador bus stop. The **market** here sells a good selection of fish fresh from the morning catch, both raw and cooked at lunch (US$2–4). There's a small **turicentro** opposite (daily 7am–5pm; US$0.90), with showers and changing rooms, but the beach, **Playa La Paz**, is quite dirty, and becomes rocky and prone to rip-tides in the rainy season.

The town's heartbeat, however, is the world-famous **Punta Roca** surf break, which tubes perfectly around the point a couple of hundred metres to the west of the pier. This is not a beginner's wave, and

LA LIBERTAD

PACIFIC OCEAN

ACCOMMODATION	
Hotel Rick	D
Hotel Surf Club Inn	A
Mango's Lounge	B
La Posada Familiar	C

EATING & DRINKING	
El Buen Asado	1
Comedor Paty	2
El Delphin	5
La Dulce Vita	3
Punta Roca	4

Punta Roca Surf Break

> ### FISHY PRICING
>
> Restaurant **prices** on El Salvador's Pacific coast may seem inflated, but this is often due to the value of the ingredients. The unmissable coastal speciality, a creamy seafood soup called **mariscada**, contains crab, whole fish, langoustine and shrimp, is also one of the most expensive dishes – a good one is hard to find for under US$8, and should be closer to US$10. Oysters should cost around US$5, and a whole langoustine is hard to find for under US$10. It may seem like you're being overcharged, but the seafood is most likely very fresh, and you get what you pay for.

localism (local hostility to you sharing their great surf spot) does exist – confrontations are best avoided by hiring a local guide. Even if you don't surf, it is exciting just to go and watch experts take on the wave in the morning and evening, or at any of the regular surf events held here. **Surfboards** can be bought, sold, rented and repaired at the Hospital de Tablas, on the corner of 3 Avenida Sur and 2a Calle Pte (7am–4pm; US$12/day). If you need to work on your surf skills before hopping on a board, there are better beaches along the coast to the west (see p.276). For sunbathers, the small and busy **Flores beach** is a kilometre and a half east, reachable by bus #82.

Arrival and information

By bus Services from San Salvador arrive at 4a C Ote, by the pier. Buses to and from the eastern beaches go from 4 Av Norte, on the other side of the *turicentro*. Further up that road and left onto 1 C Ote is the stop for Sonsonate and the western beaches.

Accommodation

As a rule, the hotels on 5 Av Sur, on the west side of the bay, are in the safest part of town, but also the most expensive. You are perfectly safe in other areas, but it is riskier to go out at night. If you're hoping to get a room on a holiday weekend, it's best to book in advance.

Hotel Rick 5a Av Sur #30 ☎ 2335-3033. This traditional surfers' favourite is ideally located opposite Punta Roca. Rooms are all en-suite, with towels, toilet roll, cable TV and room for boards. There's a/c in some but a slightly musty smell in others. ❹

Hotel Surf Club Inn C 2 Pte #22 ☎ 2346-1104. Spacious en-suite rooms, with a/c options (US$8

more), cable TV, kitchenette, refrigerator and internet, and laundry available in the buiding. It's in the most dangerous area of the hotels listed, but the accommodation itself is probably the best deal. ❸

Mango's Lounge 4a C Pte between 1 & 3 Av Nte ☎ 2346-1626, ⓦ www.puntamango.com. A great cheap option. The basic rooms have TV, surf racks and optional a/c, and there are sofas and internet in the good communal lounge. They also provide competitive board rental, tours and lessons. ❹

La Posada Familiar 3a Av Sur at C 4 Pte ☎ 2335-3252. Very friendly and popular place with basic rooms, some with bath, all with outdoor hammocks. They are just about the cheapest in town, but certainly not the cleanest. A small *comedor* serves meals and you can see the sea from the roof veranda. ❷

Eating and drinking

The dining-out scene in La Libertad is quite pricey but varied, with an inevitable emphasis on seafood (see box above). The more expensive restaurants are gathered at the seafront at the western end of town, while savings can be made buying fish from the pier and supermarket lunches. The town gets unsafe at night, so any drinking is best done at *Punta Roca*.

El Buen Asado 3 Av Nte, by C El Calvario. The pick of the *pupuserías*, also serving good and sizeable bean, cheese and egg breakfasts (US$1.50).

Comedor Paty 2 Av Sur, by 2a C Ote. For huge juices (US$0.40) and *típicos*, this is your best choice in town.

El Delphin 5 Av Sur, opposite *Hotel Rick*. A good seafood joint closer to town, serving heaps of paella (US$9) for dinner and shrimp omelettes (US$4) for breakfast in nice surroundings on the western point.

Punta Roca 5 Av Sur ☎ 2335-4342, ⓦ www.puntaroca.com.sv. A local institution, after which the break itself is named. There is hearty food with a western nod (gringo fry US$7), and it is downright the best place for a Pilsener (US$1.25) in town. There used to, and there may yet again, be two good four-person rooms to rent above the restaurant – worth checking.

Directory

Exchange C Barrios, between 4 & 6 Av Nte. This is the only ATM along the Costa del Bálsamo, so stock up.

Internet Infocentro, 1a C Pte & 4 Av Nte (Mon–Sat 8am–6pm; US$1/hr), also has internet call capabilities.

Pharmacy Centro Médico Moises, C Barrios (Mon–Fri 7am–6pm, Sat 7am–noon; ☏2335-3531) is your best bet.

Post office 2a C Ote, between 2 & 4 Av Nte (Mon–Fri 8am–noon & 12.45–4pm, Sat 8am–noon).

Supermarket Supermercado de Todos, C Barrios, opposite the bank. It's the only supermarket along the Costa del Bálsamo, so stock up if you're camping.

Telephones Telecom (2a C Ote at 2 Av Sur) also has internet access.

Moving on

By bus to: La Perla, via all beaches including El Zonte and Km 59 (#192; twice hourly; 1hr 30min); Playa San Diego, via Playa Las Flores and Parque Walter Deininger (#80; twice hourly; 15min); Playa El Sunzal, via El Tunco (#80A/B; twice hourly; 40min); San Salvador, Terminal de Occidente (#102; very frequent; 1hr); Sonsonate, via all beaches to the west (#287; 7 daily; 2hr 30min); Zacatecoluca (#540; 7 daily; 1hr 20min) – change at Comalapa for the Costa del Sol.

COSTA DEL BÁLSAMO

Strung out on either side of Puerto La Libertad is the **COSTA DEL BÁLSAMO**, a favourite destination for surfers and day-trippers from the capital. The coast takes its name from the now-defunct trade in medicinal balsam that was once centred here,

before tourism took over as the main source of income. More and more expensive beach clubs are now popping up, as international tourists gain confidence in El Salvador, but reasonable accommodation and surfing communities still dominate. **West** of La Libertad, the Carretera Litoral ribbons through thickly wooded hills and tunnels to palm-fringed black beaches. To the **east** the beaches are more disappointing, infringed upon by the expansion of the town; the sole exception is the surfer-free **Playa San Diego**, a quick escape from the intensity of La Libertad. All kilometre distances given are for the Carretera Litoral, along which there are markers to help you out. La Libertad is the transport hub for the area – see above for details of moving on from that town.

Playa El Tunco

The beaches just west of La Libertad are crowded with people and resorts. Beyond these, at Km 42, **Playa El Tunco** has a much better atmosphere and the best nightlife on the stretch. The beach here is pebble-strewn, but the waves draw plenty of surfers and it is a good spot for the inexperienced to learn the sport. A single road leads down from the Carretera through the village to a fork; a right here leads to the beachfront, with an array of surf shops (expect to pay US$10 for a day's board rental and US$10 for an hour's lesson; bodyboards are also available for US$4/hr and US$8/day), and a left takes you parallel to the beach.

You won't have a problem finding a place to **eat**. On the beach, *Restaurante La Bocana* serves huge seafood platters and ice-cold beers, accompanied by sporadic live music. The next-door *comedor* has similar fare, and also shows DVDs. Go to ritzy *Hotel Roca Sunzal*, on the other side, only to eat *mariscada* (US$10); eating a meal here will allow you a few hours on their luxury poolside loungers.

Lining the estuary is a smattering of good **accommodation**: *Papayas* (❷) is the best value, with good communal space, including a treehouse-like roof terrace, a kitchen, DVDs and books. If that's full, *Mangle*, next door (❹), is similar in character though slightly more expensive. Spare a thought for the monkey on a chain in the back, however, and don't use the internet: it is fifty cents cheaper just across the road. For brand new, spotless rooms, a pool and huge showers, check out the *Tunco Lodge* (❹), opposite, while campers have a rare opportunity in *Roots*, along the road parallel to the beach (❶), which has its own tents to lend out and hosts renowned Saturday night beach parties. Remember not to stray too far from the party at these events, as muggings have occurred on the beach.

Playa El Sunzal

Wading across an ankle-deep estuary from El Tunco takes you to the long and wide black-sands of **Playa El Sunzal** (road access at Km 44.5). For surfing, this is the best learners' beach in the country, with long, uncrowded breaks. It's also good for sun-bathing, swimming and general playing on the beach. While this is all easily accessible from Tunco (and Tunco's surf shops are accessible from here), the atmosphere staying here offers a distinctly more laid-back alternative to its neighbour. Just off the Carretera on the beach, *Surfer's Inn* has well-shaded camping ❶) and basic, concrete en-suite rooms (❷) with access to a kitchen and fridge. Across the road, Ciber Fox (8am–8pm; US$1/hr) has the fastest internet around, and *San Patricio* (❸) has slightly more comfortable rooms with a splash pool. There is a string of *comedores* by the roadside. *El Sunzalito* does good breakfasts (US$1.25), and *Rancho Gladymar*, right on the beach, does a filling US$3 chicken, onion and tortilla meal and has US$1 beers.

Playa El Zonte

Down a track just beyond the bridge at Km 53, the small, surfer-dominated **Playa El Zonte** is a real gem, set apart by its stunning location between two high headlands and its friendly community vibe. Volcanic sands cover the beach in the dry season, but recede as the waves grow from March to October. The surf here is harder going for beginners than Sunzal and Tunco, better suiting those who are intermediate and above. However, this is no reason for non-surfers to avoid it, as anyone can enjoy the surroundings, swim and join evening games of football. **Hotel** and **restaurant** *Estancia Nativa*, situated on the right as you reach the beach (☏2302-6258; ❸), has pleasant rooms around a yard containing a pool, bar and pizza restaurant, as well as hammocks, plenty of reading material and a table football table. The owner, Alex, really knows his surfing and will organize rental (US$10/day) and surf lessons (US$10/hr).

The *comedor* opposite *Estancia Nativa* on the beach does good cheap burgers (US$2), but the best food is at *Costa Brava*, high on the cliffs at the western end of the beach. The owner is a cable TV chef and local celebrity, in view of which his big breakfasts (US$3)

> **TREAT YOURSELF**
>
> **El Dorado Surf Resort**
> Playa El Zonte ☏7226-6166, Ⓦwww.surfeldorado.com. There is a great atmosphere running through this top-notch surfer haven with spotless, comfortable rooms, starting with welcoming Quebecois owners Olly and Ben. Surfers (and non-surfers) will find everything they need – board hire, lessons, longboard skateboards, even a training pool – and the staff will even help guests plan the rest of their travels in the country. One of the country's best treats. ❼

and excellent seafood dishes (US$6) are great value. He will also organize trips to his turtle sanctuary in the dry season.

Playa San Diego

Five kilometres east from La Libertad, the beautiful **Playa San Diego**, with its clean, light and seemingly endless stretch of sand, is deserted during the week except for a few fishermen. A **turtle-nesting reserve** has recently been set up here to help protect these endangered species. Views to the sea from the road behind the beach are blocked by ranks of private homes behind locked gates, but if you get off the bus outside the *San Diego Beach* restaurant, there's a path just to the left of the nearby *Hotel Villa del Pacífico* that leads down to the sand. The cheap accommodation options are pretty poor; if you are set on staying the night, the *Hotel Villa del Pacífico* (☎2345 5681; ⑤) has a/c rooms with bath, plus a restaurant and a pool set in manicured gardens right by the beach. There are better eating options, including *La Fincita de Don Juan*, 1a C Pasaje #16, serving good-value chicken and steaks (US$3–5) as well as the obligatory fish dishes. The *Costa Brava* has similar prices and fare, and two swimming pools as well. *El Pijon*, at the eastern end of the beach road, is a good spot for a beer.

Parque Nacional Walter Deininger

A little further east along the Carretera Litoral, the **Parque Nacional Walter Deininger** makes a welcome alternative to beach pursuits. An extensive stretch of **dry forest**, it is home to a range of flora and fauna, including deer, falcons, racoons and the torogoz, the national bird. There's an 18km **trail** through the park, though shorter routes can be taken. Entry is US$0.80, but a guide must accompany you at a fee of US$11.50, so try to go in groups to reduce costs. Technically, you should also get permission from ISTU in San Salvador (see p.264) before coming out here, but pleading ignorance has been known to work.

ZACATECOLUCA

East of Playa San Diego, the Carretera Litoral swings inland to the small pre-Columbian, Nonualco city of **ZACATECOLUCA**, or Zacate, as it is known. Though it peacefully endured Spanish rule, it had a key role in 1833 in the indigenous revolt against El Salvador's newly independent rule, led by Anastasio Aquino from Santiago Nonualco. Supported both by local tribes and poor mestizos, and meeting with little effective resistance, Aquino at one point looked capable of marching on and taking the capital. Instead, his army contented itself with sacking

---

EL SALVADOR'S BEST HIDDEN BREAKS

Going west beyond El Zonte along the Carretera Litoral are three more great and often empty surfing spots. Km 59, a right-hand beach and point break, tubing when big (though poor at low tide), is often compared to Punta Roca, but without the crowds. Around the corner, Km 61 gives equally empty long breaks for longboarders. Further along, Playa Mizata at Km 87 is a wave machine, with point and beach breaks going right and left. All three can be reached on the #197 or #287 buses from La Libertad.

In the east of the country, Playa Las Flores (not to be confused with the Las Flores right next to La Libertad) has sandy right-hand point breaks, but far more special is Punta Mango, unreachable by car; boat trips here can be organized at *Mango's Lounge* in La Libertad (see p.275; ⓦwww.puntamango.com).

Zacatecoluca before moving on to San Vicente, giving government forces time to regroup. Today it is a pleasant place to lazily pass the time, though there is little to occupy go-getters here.

What to see and do

Apart from its big daily **market**, there's little of interest in Zacatecoluca except its proximity to the nearby beaches. The impressive, whitewashed Moorish **Catedral Santa Lucía** has good roof frescoes along with the usual doll-like statues. In front of the church stands a monument to the city's most famous son, **José Simeon Cañas**, the man responsible for the abolition of slavery across Central America. The cathedral is somewhat strangled by the jumble of market stalls around it, but if a priest is around he may let you climb the tower to see the marvellous **views** over the town and its volcano.

Arrival

By bus Buses arrive and depart from the bus station four blocks south of the Parque Central on Av J.V. Villacorte, except the Usulután bus, which stops only on the Carretera Litoral, two blocks further south.

Accommodation

Hotel Brolyn Av J.V. Villacorta #24 ☎2334-1084. A cheap option all round – the owner may proudly show you the switch that turns your cable into fuzzy pornography – but it's clean, en suite, has new mattresses and offers a/c. ❷

Primavera Av J.V. Villacorta #20 ☎2334-1346. Tidy rooms with good mattresses, bath, hammock and internet, plus a small pool, Jacuzzi and table tennis are all available here. ❸

Eating

Golden Gate 5a C Ote between Av J.M. Delgado & Av J.V. Villacorta. A decent and cheap Chinese restaurant by the bus station. Noodles US$1.
Sorbetería Estrella Polar Av N Monterrey and 5a C Ote. Home-made ice cream draws young Zacatecolucans here on dates, but there's also

decent vegetarian cooking on offer. Caramel boule US$0.35.
Verona's Pizza Off C Dr Molina. Freshly made crusty pizzas (US$5 regular size) in a very clean, white restaurant in an alley off the park. They're open 9am–8pm, if you want pizza for breakfast.

Moving on

By bus to: Costa del Sol, via all beaches to La Puntilla (#193; twice hourly; 1hr 30min); La Libertad (#540; 7 daily; 2hr); San Salvador, Terminal del Sur (#133; every 15min; 1hr); San Vicente (#177; every 15min; 1hr); Usulután (#302; twice hourly; 1hr 30min).

COSTA DEL SOL

Due south of Zacatecoluca lies El Salvador's premier beach playground, the **COSTA DEL SOL**, a fifteen-kilometre peninsula with a strip of palm-fringed beaches on the southern side. The clean expanses of sand here are good for swimming, but guarded by a wall of development built seemingly to force you through a pay-to-enter beach resort to gain access. This and the widespread artificial price inflation might lead you to believe that this is an area that does not wish to accommodate travellers on a budget, but there are some exceptions.

San Marcelino and Playa Costa del Sol

Behind **Playa San Marcelino**, the first beach along the strip, the rather plush *Costa del Sol Club* has swimming pools, sports facilities and a restaurant – try negotiating at the gate to be allowed in for the day. For an easier route to the water, continue some 3km east to **Playa Costa del Sol**, where a *turicentro* (daily 7am–6pm; US$0.90) rents cabañas for the day and has a couple of small restaurants.

Playa Los Blancos

A few kilometres further on, at Km 64, is **Playa Los Blancos** and the *Mini Hotel y Restaurante Mila* (☎2338-2074; ❸), the area's best deal, with small but comfortable rooms, a swimming pool and beach access. About 50m before it, *Hotel Haydee Mar* (☎ 2338-2046; ❸) has two pools and matches the price, but is haunted by a deadly sense of kitsch. The nameless *comedor* just past *Hotel Mila* (fifth along the row of eateries in the middle of the road) does good burgers and stays open until late for fair-priced beers.

La Puntilla

At the far eastern tip of the Costa del Sol, **La Puntilla** is an attractive array of thatch and bamboo beach settlements with a great view across the mouth of the **Estero de Jaltepeque**. A **boat trip** around the Estero is really the highlight of this section of coast. *Lancha* owners run trips from La Puntilla across to the **Isla de Tasajera**, around the mangrove swamps of the Estero and up the Río Lempa. You'll be approached by touts as soon as you step off the bus, but don't let yourself be led to a boat or you'll pay the "agent's" commission. It's better to go hunt a boat down yourself; it should cost about US$20, so try to get a group together to reduce costs.

There is cheap lodging here, but it is largely shockingly bad. *Rancho Playa Dorada*, at the end of the road (☎ 7141-8784; ❷), is the best of what's available: the good *comida* (US$4 *coctele*), kind service and new pool compensate for the prison-like rooms and seatless toilet. While at La Puntilla, it is well worth having seafood or oysters (US$5–8) while enjoying the views from the raised platform of *Raphael Antonio*, but check that they are in season. You can't miss the restaurant: it's the only two-storey platform there.

USULUTÁN

East of Zacatecoluca, the Carretera Litoral crosses the Río Lempa at San Marcos Lempa before running through lush, green coffee country to the city of **USULUTÁN**, on the southern slopes of

the volcano of the same name. Much like Zacatecoluca, it holds little interest except as a transit point on the route to the **Bahía de Jiquilisco**, or a stepping stone on the journey further east; even the Carretera Litoral seems to bypass it, branching off through the centre and reforming again at its extremities. At the eastern fork, market stalls invade the tarmac; buses arrive and depart from here. The westbound lane then takes the name Calle Grimaldi as it heads to the centre of town, passing through the neatly pruned Parque Central six blocks west.

Should you wish to **stay**, *La Posada del Viajero* (☎ 2662-0217; ❷), close to the centre on Calle 6 Ote between 2a and 4a Avenida Nte, is clean and friendly, with decent mattresses. *Tortas Lito's* on Calle Dr F Penado by 1 Avenida Nte has a good selection of big Mexican tacos and *enchiladas* and is open until 8pm.

Moving on, **buses** go from Usulután to: Playa El Espino (#351; 7 daily; 1hr 30min); Puerto El Triunfo (#363; frequent; 1hr); San Miguel (#373; frequent; 1hr 40min); San Salvador (#302; frequent; 2hr 30min); San Vicente (#417; 6 daily; 2hr); Santiago de Maria, for transfers to Alegría (#392C, #35, #348 or #349; very frequent; 45min).

THE EASTERN BEACHES

Wider and wilder than their western counterparts, the eastern beaches seem to be over-visited by Salvadoreños at the weekend but under-visited by travellers during the week. The exception is El Cuco, where the busy beachside community is supplemented by large annual doses of surfers during the wet season. The whole stretch, however, offers you the chance to stay in beautiful surroundings where you are unlikely to see another traveller for days on end.

Puerto El Triunfo

About 20km southwest of Usulután, down a road lined with sugar-cane fields, is **Puerto El Triunfo**, a sketchy port set on the north shore of the **Bahía de Jiquilisco**, separated from the ocean by the San Juan del Gozo peninsula. Formed by coastal mangrove swamps, the beautiful bay features 12km of waterways and a number of islands. A long, fine sandy beach forms the ocean side of the peninsula, while floating platforms can be swum to from the bay-side beach.

Passenger boats (US$2) cross to El Icaco on **Corral de Mulas** on the peninsula, leaving when full, which happens much more regularly in the early morning; if you miss these, renting a boat can be costly – expect to pay up to US$35. It is also a great place to walk and chat to locals. Other than the Islas de Golfo de Fonseca, Corral de Mulas offers the best opportunity to engage in real Salvadoran life; as well as camping you can ask to stay with a family when here. In both cases ask at the *alcaldía* and they will help you out. Otherwise, the small, grubby *El Jardín* (☎2663-6089; ❸) between the pier and the bus station in Puerto El Triunfo, is a decent plan B.

From Puerto El Triunfo, **bus** #363 makes the one-hour trip to Usulután every ten minutes. For San Salvador take the #185 (6 daily; 2hr) and for San Miguel go by the #377 (every 40min; 3hr).

Playa El Espino

At the far eastern end of the Bahía de Jiquilisco is one of El Salvador's finest beaches, **Playa El Espino**. The once-remote beach has been developed, with a 26km paved road from the Carretera Litoral opening it up to visitors. Sadly, some of this redevelopment has taken a distinctly garish aspect. The beach itself remains a singular beauty, however, and the water is bathtub-warm.

It is best to be in a group of four or five to **stay** cheaply on Espino: *Natali* (❼), to the right as you reach the beach, takes

five in their a/c and en-suite rooms – with use of a kitchen – including one in an indoor hammock; *Hotel Arcos del Espino* (☎2608-0785; ❼) has a/c, en-suite, spotless rooms and toilets, around a crystal-clear pool for four people. The solo traveller needn't fear, though, as *Rancho de Don Francisco*, on the other side of the beach, rents out hammocks (❷) to sleep under the stars. Book the hotels ahead at weekends.

A whole host of *comedores* and basic **restaurants** sell similar fare, though prices for seafood are high and the quality is mixed. Try *El Pacífico* on the eastern side of the beach for fried fish (US$3–8) and a beer on their relaxed and elevated terrace. On the western side, the wicker barn of *Restaurant y Bar Bambú* has cheaper food and karaoke, though it is only open Fridays to Sundays.

Two **buses** go to Usulután (#351 & #358B, changing at Jucurán to #358; 7 daily, last one back at 4pm).

Playa El Cuco

Thirty kilometres east of Usulután the Carretera Litoral turns south, winding up through glorious mountain views before descending again towards the east's most famous beach community, **Playa El Cuco**. The village itself is rather ugly and manic, with a beach-front crowded by tourism opportunists. The beaches to either side, however, are fantastic: the 300m breaks at **Las Flores** to the west and the wide and empty peace of **El Esterón** to the east.

Accommodation in the town is terrible, but there are good options to the east. The best by far are two flats for rent in El Esterón, at the end of the road running behind the beach. The smaller sleeps two in a simple room with bed, fan, window and bathroom next door (❸), but the spacious larger flat (❹), intended for four, has a fully equipped kitchen roof terrace with hammocks and chairs overlooking the beach. Reserve them with local surf godmother Joan (℡7789-6312), who has spare mattresses if needed. Closer to town along the stretch, the beach-fronted *Cucolindo* is the other decent budget option, with clean rooms (❹).

Joan also feeds weary surfers in a **restaurant** run from a summer house in her plant nursery in Esterón. The sign outside says *Federicos*, but it's known as *Rasta Pasta*, as she serves lasagnas, canellonis and pastas (US$8) to the sound of reggae (Fri–Sun only). The unnamed *comedor* at the end of the beach road and down the right-hand cul-de-sac has a tradition of excellent fish, bettered only by the fish fried (US$2) on the stall on the left as you approach the end of the beach road, known as *La Gimelos*. Fresh fish should be bought from the El Cuco co-operative, in El Cuco village, where there is also internet in the Centro de Internet on the main Plaza (US$1/hr).

Playa El Cuco is accessible by direct **bus** (#320; twice hourly; 1hr 30min) from the terminal in San Miguel. The ride is one of the finest bus journeys in the country, with spectacular views of the valleys and the ineffable Volcán San Miguel; sit on the right side of the bus on the way to El Cuco for the best view. For La Unión transfer at El Delirio.

Intipucá

Beyond El Cuco, the highway runs parallel to the coastline, passing a turn-off for the spotless little town of **Intipucá**. More Intipucans live in Washington, DC than in Intipucá, and remittances per head here are more than any other place in the country. This is evident: relaxed, safe and entirely paved, with phonebooths and moneywire companies encircling the plush Parque Central, it would be a perfect place to stay – if there was a hotel. It's worth having a look nonetheless, as the town is starting to awaken to tourism. There is a good Italian (spaghetti Bolognese US$5) and *típicos* **restaurant**,

Torentinos, overlooking the *parque* on the southwestern corner.

Buses run direct to La Unión (#339; 8 daily; 1hr 30min), passing beaches further east, and from the highway to San Miguel (#385; twice hourly; 1hr 30min), passing the turning to El Cuco. Buses and pick-ups also go direct to El Esterón (10min) or the highway (5min).

Playa Las Tunas and Playa El Tamarindo

Further east along the Carretera, past the featureless Playa El Icacal, another turn-off heads along a tooth-like peninsula pointing out across the mouth of the Golfo de Fonseca. **Playa Las Tunas** is the first beach that you encounter, with a fine dark sand beach and tides that wash right up into the village. It has a friendly atmosphere to it, and, budget-wise, it is your best option for accommodation on a beach between Cuco and La Unión. There's a small village here with several restaurants, the highlight of which is the *Rancho Las Tunas* (℡2526-5542), not only perched on a rock with water rushing around it at high tide, but also the best place for oysters (US$5) in the area. They also have two overpriced rooms (❺) on the beachside. Otherwise, *Hotel Restaurant Buenos Aires* (℡2681-5581; ❻), at the bend in the road a few yards past the village entrance, has basic, air-conditioned rooms and good grilled fish (US$3–5) served in the restaurant.

The final beach on the peninsula, **Playa El Tamarindo**, is a panorama-lover's dream. The huge golden arc of sand, backed by uninterrupted palm trees, curves around the mountainous bay; sitting beneath the Volcán de Conchagua, the islands of the Golfo de Fonseca loom large, and in the distance the mountainsides of Honduras are clearly visible. The only accommodation here, the *Tropitamarindo*

(☎2649-5082; ⑤), is too pricey for what are little more than standard mid-range rooms, but they will let you use the pool and loungers if you spend US$10, so it's a good spot for beers and food.

Buses to La Unión run along the peninsula, passing through Las Tunas as well (#383; three hourly); the last one back leaves at 5pm. For a much more interesting shortcut to El Tamarindo, take a boat from the pier at El Embarcadero (US$0.25) on the Carretera Litoral.

LA UNIÓN

The port town of **LA UNIÓN** sits in a stunning location on a bay on the edge of the Golfo de Fonseca. Faded since its glory days of colonial naval trade, La Unión's web of low white houses crumble a little further every day in the ferocious heat. The streets are rather depressing, and even the Parque Central, swamped by dilapidated market stalls selling cheap merchandise, lacks the character of other city squares. The new deep-sea port at **Puerto Cutuco**, the largest Pacific port in Central America, virtually contiguous with La Unión, has yet to bring the industry and prosperity it promises. Until it does – though there are no guarantees – the atmosphere around the town is unpleasant. As the beaches to the south and the border to the north are just as accessible from the cooler and less threatening San Miguel, the main reason for passing would be a visit to the isolated islands of the Golfo de Fonseca.

Arrival

By boat *Lanchas* from the islands of the Golfo de Fonseca arrive on the pier jutting out from the northern end of 3a Av Nte.
By bus The main bus terminal is on C 3 Pte, 4a–6a Av Nte, two blocks west and one north of the Parque Central. If you're travelling from the coastal highway, you will need the Terminal Los Cantones, two blocks south and one block west of the main terminal, on C San Carlos.

Accommodation

El Dorado C San Carlos & 2a Av Nte ☎2604-4724. The price and the pleasant, mango tree-filled courtyard will easily compensate for the soft mattresses and tatty en-suite bathrooms. There are fans and hammocks in the rooms and you can ask for extra beds to cram in economically. ②
Portobello 4a Av Nte at C 1 Pte ☎2604-4115. The best value a/c rooms in a very hot town are here, right in the thick of it. Large, clean rooms with partitioned baths in the rooms and good beds. ④
San Francisco C Menéndez between 9a & 11a Av Sur ☎2604-4159. Away from the hubbub, clean and spacious. Some rooms have balconies and all have en suite and cable. ③–⑤

Eating and drinking

Captain John's 3a Av Sur & C 4 Ote. The captain is proprietor of a pleasant outdoor terrace, where a wide choice of fish steaks, including marlin, sailfish and wahoo, are served in huge portions. Try the *tazón de sopa de pescado* (US$4).
Las Lunas 3a Av Nte by the pier. A good spot for a beer (US$1) by the water's edge. It has karaoke most nights and bands play on occasional Sat.
Maurita's C 3 Pte at Av Cabañas. The closest you'll come to a pavement café, with a large covered veranda from which to watch the street activity. The local favourite serves seafood, *ceviche* (US$3.50) and your typical *típicos*.
El Viajero C Menéndez, just off the Parque. A cavernous *comedor* next to the supermarket. Best for coffee, egg, cheese and bean cooked breakfasts (US$1.50).

Directory

Exchange Banco Agrícola, C 1 Pte & Av General Cabañas, or Scotiabank, 1a Av Nte on the Parque, both change money.
Immigration At Av Cabañas at 7 C Pte (☎2604-4375). Ask here about the party boat to Honduras (see box, p.284) and the planned ferry service to Nicaragua from the new port.
Internet Meg@byte, C 1 Pte between 2a & 4a Av Nte, is the cheapest and latest opening of the bunch around here (US$0.70–1/hr).
Supermarket The large Dispensa Familiar, on the southeast corner of the Parque, is open every day until 6 or 7pm.
Telephone Telecom is on C 1 Ote at 5a Av Nte, two blocks east of the Parque.

Moving on

By boat to: Isla Meanguera (once daily; 1hr 30min); Isla Zacatillo (once daily; 30min).

By bus Buses from the Terminal los Cantones go to: Conchagua (#382; 4 daily; 30min); El Tamarindo, via El Embarcada and Las Tunas (#383; every 20min; 1hr 30min); Intipucá (#339; 8 daily; 1hr 15min). Buses from main bus terminal go to: San Miguel (#324; very frequent; 1hr 30min); San Salvador (#304; twice hourly; 4hr); Santa Rosa de Lima (#342; every 15min; 1hr 30min) – change here for the Honduran border at El Amatillo. There are also luxury buses to: San Miguel (three between 5.45–6.45am & 4.15pm; 1hr) and San Salvador (4am, 6am & 12.30pm; 3hr).

AROUND LA UNIÓN

La Unión's surrounding attractions – namely, the islands of the **Golfo de Fonseca** – put its heat and anti-social hallmarks into quite some relief. If you visit the tranquil and rustic Isla Meanguera you will have to spend the night in one of its good hotels because of ferry times, but you will doubtless want to do that anyway.

Islas del Golfo de Fonseca

Four delightfully secluded **islands** – Conchagüita, Martín Pérez, Meanguera and Zacatillo – sit out in the **Golfo de Fonseca** under the stewardship of El Salvador. **Conchagüita** was sacked by English pirates in 1682 and the island remained deserted until the 1920s, when settlers finally began moving back. In its centre, on the Cerro del Pueblo Viejo, are the remains of a tiny pre-Columbian settlement; a path to the north of the ruins leads up to a large rock bearing engravings that some believe is a map of the gulf. Even now

you can see fairer, blue-eyed, pirate descendants throughout the islands' inhabitants, and rumour has it that Sir Francis Drake buried a stash of Spanish silver while at anchor on Meanguera. There are still plenty of secluded coves to explore, as well as good swimming and boundless scope for hiking. For fantastic views of the surroundings, climb Cerro de Evaristo, the highest peak on **Meanguera**. The best **beach** on the islands, El Majahual, is also on Meanguera. Wide, secluded and black sand, it can be reached on foot in 45 minutes by the road south of town and the track it turns into, or by boat in ten minutes if you can persuade a *lancha* owner. For bird lovers, the small outlying **Isla Meanguerita** can only be reached by *lancha*.

Island transport

Morning **ferries** leave from La Unión for Meanguera (US$2.50) and Zacatillo (US$2) between 10 and 11am. The only ferry back from Meanguera departs at 5am, so unless you plan to charter a private boat you will have to stay overnight. Local boatmen will rent out a *lancha* for the day at a non-negotiable US$70 per boatload, though you can commandeer one on the islands for a little less. Really quite alternatively, a **party boat** (☎2604-2222) leaves La Unión at 10am on Sat & Sun with plenty of beer, a karaoke machine and a fairly lame pool. It rarely stops at the islands, but you can enjoy the breathless gulf views from the devil-may-care atmosphere aboard.

Accommodation and eating

The smaller islands – Conchagüita, Zacatillo and Martín Pérez – have no **accommodation** options, but Meanguera is a terrific getaway spot. There are two good hotels here, with little difference between them: the pretty *El Mirador* (☎2648-0072; ❸) has spotless rooms with hard mattresses, en-suite

---

INTO HONDURAS BY PARTY BOAT

One Saturday a month the **party boat** sets off at 8.30am on a longer tour that stops at Amapala, on the Honduran island of El Tigre. From here, regular ferries make the trip back to **Coyolitos** on the mainland. To use this route, ask the tour company ahead (☎2604-2222), and visit the immigration office in La Unión on Av Cabañas at 7 C Pte (☎2604-4375).

baths, cable TV and perhaps a fractionally better view; *El Paraíso* (☎ 2648-0145; ❸) has older rooms, cable TV and en-suite baths with the elusive hot-water shower. They're close enough together to compare, and both have great seafood restaurants with shellfish under US$4. Otherwise, *comedores* in the village serve fresh seafood, delivered daily by a colourful fishing fleet that floats in the bay.

Conchagua

Looming to the south of La Unión is **Volcán Conchagua** (1243m), with beautiful views across the gulf to Nicaragua and Honduras. The friendly village of **Conchagua**, sitting on its northern slopes, was founded by the inhabitants of Conchagüita at the end of the seventeenth century. The climate is fresher here, a pleasant relief from the heat of La Unión, and walks around the village let you enjoy the scenery and possibly get chatting to the townsfolk. From Conchagua pick-ups will take you to the lookout point up the volcano, where there are short and long walking routes, camping (❶) and simple accommodation with shared bathrooms (❷) at a spectacular spot near the summit of the volcano. Take **bus** #382A from the Terminal los Cantones in La Unión; it leaves five times a day and takes fifteen minutes.

The east

The rough and wild terrain of **eastern El Salvador** remained relatively unexplored territory for the pre-Columbian Pipils, who did not venture far beyond the natural frontier of the Río Lempa into this land of lofty volcanoes, hot plains and mountain ranges. As a result, its Lenca inhabitants developed their society in isolation from the west, and it was only with some difficulty that the Spanish conquered this frontier. Today, coffee production around the region's major cities, the earthquake-damaged **San Vicente** and bustling **San Miguel** create a wealth that contrasts cruelly with the rural poverty found further north. Along the **Ruta de la Paz**, refugees from communities devastated by the civil war – this region saw the worst of the fighting – have in the last decade and a half returned to try and pick up the pieces in this wild and beautiful area, but their struggle with poverty is often painfully apparent.

Around San Vicente are several delightful villages, including the flower-filled mountain town of **Alegría** and the brilliant pottery centre of **Guatejiagua**. Buses head north along the mountainous **Ruta de la Paz** to the former guerrilla stronghold of **Perquín**, with its terrific war museum, and the haunting and unmissably sad village of **Mozote**, scene of a horrific massacre.

COJUTEPEQUE

Past Lago de Ilopango to the east, the Carretera Interamericana flies past the up-and-coming Sunday retreat of **COJUTEPEQUE**. There's little to see in the actual town, but half-an-hour's walk up the Cerro de las Pavas to the south is the shrine of the **Virgen de Fátima** of Portugal, a statue brought here in 1949 that attracts worshippers from across the region. For those who also worship food, a Sunday **food festival** to rival Juayúa's weekend festival (see p.310) has successfully been set up on the Cerro, under the backdrop of the summit's imperious views over Lago de Ilopango. There is also a **zoo** here with spider-monkeys and turkeys (the animal after which the town and hill are named); animal lovers may not want to visit the cramped cages, though. **Bus** #113 goes to San Salvador (frequent; 2hr) – get off on the highway for #301 to San Miguel or other services to towns further east.

ILOBASCO

Some 6km beyond Cojutepeque, a road branches north off the highway through beautiful rolling countryside to the small town of **ILOBASCO**, noted for its brightly painted earthenware decorated with animals and everyday scenes. The town's hallmark pieces are known as *sorpresas* (surprises) – detailed scenes of village life contained in small, clay shells like humble Fabergé eggs. The government arts organization **Cedart**, on Avenida Bonilla, has a small exhibition on the evolution of ceramic art in the town, and a collection of products in its shop; they'll direct you to a potter you like, or you can just stroll around and look in. Further down the avenida, *Italyan Pizza* cooks much better than it spells, with good Mexican fare as well as pizzas (US$4). If you have to stay, *Hotel Ilobasco*, 4a C Pte (☎2332-2563; ④) is friendly, though tatty and overpriced. **Bus** #111 (frequent; 1hr 30min) is the nominal service to San Salvador, but from the highway you can catch the quicker #301 to destinations along it in either direction.

SAN SEBASTIÁN

Between Ilobasco and San Vicente, a paved road leads off the Interamericana to the small village of **SAN SEBASTIÁN**, famous for its hammocks, patterned cloth sheets and bedspreads. The first place to start learning about the traditions and mind-bending patience involved in the town's chosen craft is the **Casa de la Cultura** on Calle Molina, though information and opening hours are limited. Several **weaving shops** around town will let you watch the goods being produced on simple wooden looms, though you will be pressured into buying. One of the oldest and best shops is Casa Durán, just off C Molina on 12a Av Nte. Soft **hammocks** are the prize item in town; compare prices and materials, then bargain before handing over any money. **Bus** #110 goes to San Salvador twice hourly and #176 goes to San Vicente four times a day.

SAN VICENTE

SAN VICENTE was founded in 1635 by fifty local Spanish families in accordance with the 1600 Law of the Indies, which prohibited the Spanish from living among the indigenous people. This division brought violence to the city in 1833, when the forces of Anastasio Aquino, leader of a Nonualco indigenous uprising, stormed the city. "Inebriated with alcohol and success", they removed the crown from the statue of San José in the Iglesia El Pilar and crowned Aquino "Emperor of the Nonualcos". The rebels then returned to Santiago Nonualco, some 30km away; here, Aquino was captured by government forces on April 23 and later sent back to San Vicente and hanged. Notwithstanding several guerrilla attacks in the 1980s, nowadays San Vicente is a calm, low-slung city with a rich agricultural area producing sugar cane, cotton and coffee. The town still has a conspicuous military presence – the town barracks are at the southwestern corner of the Parque Central – rivalled only by the number of American Peace Corps trainees, who come here to prepare for forthcoming missions.

What to see and do

The centrepiece of the Parque Central is the **Torre Kiosko**, an eye-catching open-fronted clock tower. Resembling a miniature Eiffel Tower, it was actually inspired by the Parisian monument. Although climbing atop it is no longer permitted (the 2001 earthquake rendered it rather lame), it is still ticking.

Two blocks south of the Parque on Avenida María de los Angeles is the **Iglesia El Pilar**, built in 1769 on the site where a miraculous shaking statue of the Virgin Mary persuaded one Manuela Arce not to stab her husband, or so it's told. Now restored after the earthquake damage, you can enter the building. The statue of San José, complete with crown, stands in a glass case behind the altar as you walk in.

An extensive **market** stretches over several streets to the west of the big green army barracks. In most respects pretty much like any other market, this one also sells the famous hammocks made in nearby towns such as San Sebastián, adding a notable splash of colour to the town.

Arrival

By bus The station is on C 8 Pte and 15a Av Sur, a long walk southwest of the centre, but all buses pass the Parque Central going in or out, so watch out for the tower of the Torre Kiosko and get off there.

Accommodation

There are not too many places to stay, but in the unlikely event that both the places listed here are full, there are also some basic guesthouses in the centre of town.

Casa de Huéspedes El Turista C 4 Pte 15 ☎2393-0323. The best option in town has simple rooms with fans around a leafy courtyard and below a good roof terrace. It's worth paying US$2 more for a private bathroom and cable TV, as the shared toilets aren't up to the same standard. ❷

Hotel Central Park On the west side of the Parque Central ☎2393-0383. Rooms are not tasteful, and en-suites can get a bit funky, though most have a/c and firm beds. There's a bar with pleasant communal balcony with views of the Parque and the restaurant serves well-priced *típicos* until 10pm.

Eating and drinking

San Vicente is quite responsive to evening activities and there are a number of bars around the park as well as good eating options around town. There's a nameless *pupusería* on Avenida C Miranda that does a range of good *pupusas* every night and also sells US$0.80 beers.

Casa Blanca 2 C Ote. Meat and fish dishes including *codorniz* (quail; US$7) served in a lovely shaded garden that doubles as a good place for an evening drink.

Dany's 4a C Pte just off Av C Miranda. Serves big portions of your typical Americanized cuisine

(hamburgers, tacos, pizzas; US$5) in a nice venue with wooden tables.

Pupusería Thea 1a Av Sur #68. A pretty place, with fairies on the walls, that is slightly marred by the greedy owner. Her best treats, though expensive, are worth it for their eccentricity: "golden nuggets" (US$8), and a steaming home-made brew, known as "gloín" (US$3.50).

Rivoly's On 1a Av Sur. A real treat of a *comedor a la vista* with big, fresh and tasty meat meals (chicken *con arosa* US$2.30) on spick-and-span orange tables. It also has good breakfasts, so no need to stray.

Directory

Exchange Banco Agrícola on the Parque, and a Scotiabank on the corner of 1a Av Nte and C Quiñonez de Osorio.

Internet Matrix on C 2 Ote by 2a Av Sur is fast with web-based call equipment (US$0.75/hr).

Pharmacy Santa Fé II, 4 C Ote (☎2393-6726), serves you after 9pm if you ring the bell.

Post office The office, with regular opening times, is on C 1 de Julio, one block south of the parque.

Telephones Telecom office is just off the corner of the Parque opposite the De Todo supermarket.

Moving on

By bus to: Carretera Interamericana, for #301 between San Salvador and San Miguel (#157; 10min; frequent); Costa del Sol (#193E; 4 daily; 2hr 30min); Ilobasco (#530; 3 daily; 1hr); San Salvador (#116; frequent; 1hr 30min); Usulután (#417; 6 daily; 2hr); Zacatecoluca (#177; 4 hourly; 50min).

AROUND SAN VICENTE

Near San Vicente is one of the most memorable-looking volcanoes in the country, the **Volcán Chichontepec**, which rises up into twin craters like the nostrils of a giant mole, while on the other side of town is the peaceful picnic spot of the **Laguna de Apastepeque**.

Volcán Chichontepec

San Vicente is dominated by the towering bulk of **Volcán Chichontepec** (also known as Volcán San Vicente) to the southwest. Meaning "Hill of Two Breasts" in Nahuatl, the twin peaks rise to 2181m, making it the second-highest volcano in the country. It's considered dormant, with cultivated lower slopes and the steep summit left to scrub and soil. A number of paths lead up the slopes from both the village of **San Antonio** on the east side and from **Guadelupe** on the northwest flank. It's a stiff walk of around three hours to the top from any of the trails, and good walking shoes, sun protection and lots of water are all essential. From the summit there are panoramic views north across the Jiboa valley, with San Vicente nestled at the bottom, and west across to Lago de Ilopango. **Buses** to San Antonio and Guadelupe leave every hour or so until mid-afternoon from San Vicente's market.

Laguna de Apastepeque

Laguna de Apastepeque, 3km northeast of the city (bus #156), is a small, well-maintained *turicentro* (daily 8am–6pm; US$0.90) set around a crater lake with clean blue water and shady banks. It is a great place to relax in the hammock you just bought, read and swim, though the good swimming makes this an extremely popular spot among families at weekends. If you don't get a picnic together there are unremarkable *comedores* around, and the *turicentro* has toilets and changing facilities.

ALEGRIÁ

At El Triunfo on the Carretera Interamericana a road leads south to Usulután, passing the pleasant town of Santiago de María, from where a steep road leads up the slopes of Volcán Tecapa to the floral haven of **ALEGRÍA**. The highest town in El Salvador, it offers predictably great views, and is also home to an extraordinary number of flower nurseries – it simply erupts with blossoms during orchid season. Paths lead up the volcano from town to the sulphurous **Laguna de Alegría**, a crater lake whose hot and cold waters will strip you of your dead skin if you can take the smell. It is an energetic walk of about one hour – try to get there at 4pm when the water is at its highest. The surrounding area is predominantly coffee-growing country, and occasionally beans are seen drying on the streets.

Arrival and information

By bus Buses stop on C Masferrer, a hundred metres or so to the west of the Parque Central.
Internet Café Casa Vieja, on 1 Av Nte at C Masferrer, is a quaint little café on the Parque that has fast internet for US$0.80.
Tourist information Alegriá has a real, live tourist kiosk at the southwestern corner of the Parque offering maps, accommodation, tours and flower information.

Accommodation

Casa Alegré Av C Campos ℡7201-8641. This hotel is the coolest place to stay, with firm beds in clean rooms with a shared bathroom below the studio of the artists that own it. ❷
Casa del Huésped la Palma On the east side of the Parque Central ℡2628-1012. The friendly old owners here have conveyed a great sense of past glory. Bed sizes and stiffness (in shared rooms) varies. A better deal for solo travellers, as rates are per person. ❷
Hostal Tecupa 3 C Ote ℡2628-1093. The good *comida* served in the flowery courtyard and its very clean toilet and shower make up for the quite shabby rooms. ❷

Eating and drinking

Café Expresso Southeast corner of the Parque. A classy place for a café (US$0.50). Nice breakfasts served until late morning.
Casa de Mi Abuelo 4a Av Nte & C M Aranjo. This streetside *comedor* and *tienda* serves ice cream, milkshakes and beers (US$1). Cool off or chill out on the shaded seating.
Christina's 4a Av Sur & Pasaje Grimaldi. The best *pupusería* in town, with a *chicharrón*-filled option (US$0.50) that is well above-average.
Merendero Mi Pueblito Opposite the *alcaldía* on C A Masferrer. The town's vogue restaurant, possibly because of the jaw-dropping views all the way to the northern border from its own *mirador*, but also perhaps the big portions (*pollo dorado* US$4) and veg options.

Moving on

By bus to: Santiago de María (#348; twice hourly; 15min). Change here for Usulután (#362; frequent; 45min) and the Carretera Interamericana (#362; frequent; 10min).

SAN MIGUEL

Some 135km from San Salvador, the bustling, hot and flat city of **SAN MIGUEL** is the country's main trade centre. Initially the least important of the Spanish cities, it grew wealthy, firstly through the profits of gold, and then on the coffee, cotton and *henequén* grown on the surrounding fertile land, leading to the nickname "The Pearl of the East". More recently it was a centre of arms trading during the civil war, though today the city's flat streets hum and rattle with more mundane forms of commerce and travellers will easily find the sort of facilities offered in the capital. But despite being the birthplace of several national heroes, the city is surprisingly short on sights and attractions, and the best time to visit is during the November **carnival**, supposedly the biggest in Central America. In any case it is the pivot of the east: a base for the beaches to the south or a stopover on journeys to Perquín and the Honduran border.

What to see and do

The city is laid out in the usual quasi-grid system, with the main avenida (Av Gerardo Barrios/Av José Simeón Cañas) and the main calle (C Chaparrastique/C Sirama) intersecting at **Parque Gerardo Barrios**, the Parque Central.

Parque David J. Guzmán

Although Parque Barrios is technically the central plaza, the heart of San Miguel – and a much better place to sit – is the shady **Parque David J. Guzmán**, a block away to the northeast. It was named after the eminent nineteenth-century Migueleño biologist and member of the French Academy of Science, whose name adorns the town, though his former residence on C 4 Pte lays derelict.

On the east side of the Parque Guzmán sits the **Cathedral**, built in the 1880s. Despite a modern make-over, it is still an impressive building, with a cast-iron statue of Christ bearing his crown of thorns standing between two red-roofed bell towers. Inside it is rather bare, with the famed statue of **Nuestra Señora de la Paz** (see box below) above the altar.

Just south of the cathedral is the **Antiguo Teatro Nacional**, a honey-coloured Renaissance-style building completed

---

NUESTRA SEÑORA DE LA PAZ

San Miguel's imposing cathedral, while rather disappointing inside, holds the cherished statue of Nuestra Señora de la Paz, the city's patroness. Though accounts differ as to how and when the statue arrived in the city, it is generally held that her true moment of glory came during the eruption of Volcán Chaparrastique on September 21, 1787. On seeing a glowing river of lava advancing on San Miguel, the terrified citizens, praying to the Virgin to save them, took the statue to the door of the cathedral and presented her to the volcano. The lava changed course and the city was saved. In honour of these events, San Miguel holds two months of fiesta, beginning with the Virgin "descending" the volcano on September 21 and culminating in a procession through the streets, attended by thousands, on November 21. A more recent coda to the fiesta is the annual carnival held on November 29, when live music, fireworks and street dancing dominate the whole town. Instituted in 1958, it has quickly grown to be the largest carnival in Central America (or so locals like to claim). If you're around during the festival look out for people wandering around holding large plastic iguanas aloft – the locals are nicknamed *garroberos* (iguana eaters) due to their penchant for the lizard's meat.

in 1909; performances occasionally take place here, particularly during fiesta time. Check the *Prensa Gráfica* on weekends for advertised shows. On the south side of the square, the colonnaded **Alcaldía**, dating from 1935, is in serious need of renovation.

Iglesia Capilla Medalla Milagrosa

Of the few other minor sights within town, the most appealing is the gothic **Iglesia Capilla Medalla Milagrosa**, located at the western end of Calle 4 Pte where it joins 7a Avenida Sur. Set in pretty gardens, the church was built by French nuns working in the hospital that once stood next door, and is known for its beautiful stained-glass windows, best seen on a clear evening

Arrival and information

By bus Buses arrive at the well-ordered main terminal on C 6 Ote between 8a & 10a Av Nte, four blocks (or 10min walk) east of the centre.
Tourist information There is no official tourist office, but staff at the Alcaldía (town hall) on the south side of Parque David J Guzmán will help you with quick questions.

Accommodation

The majority of accomodation choices cluster around the bus terminal, inevitably a rather sleazy area. There are great hotels away from this region, but you'll have to pay a bit more.

Caleta 3a Av Sur 601 between C 9 & 11 Pte ☎2661-3233. Clean and quiet hotel, popular with travelling businessmen during the week. There's a small courtyard with hammocks, and some rooms have private bath. Staff can also help arrange surf trips to secluded beaches. ❸

Hotel del Centro C 8 Ote 505 at 8a Av Nte ☎&☎2661-5473. This very friendly, helpful and spotlessly clean hotel is the best of the cheaper options around the bus terminal. The rooms are smallish but well arranged, with beds that are piled with cushions and have bedside lights; all rooms have bath and TV. There's free internet for guests and US$0.40 laundry washes. ❸

Hotel El Guanaco 8a Av Nte Pje Madrid ☎2661-8026, ☎2660-6403. A giant hotel that would be

great if it had more atmosphere, this place is only ever full during festival time. Nonetheless, it has big, airy and clean en-suite rooms all with a/c and cable TV. Meals are served in the restaurant opposite. It a better deal for groups, with an equally oversized six-man room for US$40. ❹

King Palace C 6 Ote ☎2661-1086. Good-value and professional hotel opposite the bus terminal. The clean rooms are en suite, some with balcony, cable TV, a/c and telephone. Facilities are list-worthy: secure parking, restaurant, fast internet, swimming pool and rooftop gym pool also available. ❺

Mir 4 C Ote 66 ☎7745-3348. Big and comfortable beds in clean enough en-suite rooms with fans, spotty cable and a fresh purple colour scheme. There are garden chairs to recline upon in the greenish courtyard and a stocked beer fridge. ❷

Monte Carlo 4 C Ote 610 ☎2660-2737. Another near-terminal budget option, this one has very firm beds (some with Doric bedsteads) that are quite thin in the rooms without a/c but big in the luxury rooms. Very clean toilets throughout and friendly owners. ❸

🏃 **Posada Real** 7a Av Nte at 2 C Pte ☎2661-7174. In by far the nicest area, and close to the nightlife, this two-storey spotless hotel has big rooms with great beds, clear cable and access to a patio on the second floor. They'll wash and iron clothes for US$0.30 an item. ❺

Eating

There are plenty of established places to eat in San Miguel, and new ones are popping up all the time, so it's worth gambling on unknowns. Local bakeries will also sell *tustacos*, a local speciality resembling a sweet tortilla.

Batyjugos Carlitos 1a Av Nte & C 4 Pte. Carlito serves excellent snacks and lunches in an intimate, colourful downstairs and roomier first floor. His speciality is a wide range of big *licuados* (US$0.70).

Café Cristy 5a Av Nte at 6 C Pte. A classy looking new canteen possessing an airy feel and bustling with patrons. The menu is standard *típicos*, but good at the price (*pollo con arosa* US$2).

Comedor Vicky 7a Av Nte. A small, friendly *comedor* that does an ice-cold, freshly squeezed orange juice (US$1) and cooked breakfast. The *Sopa Gallina India* (US$2) is fine for lunch too.

Conchadromo Esmerelda 6a Av Nte between C 4 & 6 Ote. Good, basic breakfasts and *comidas a la vista*. One of a clutch of similar places in a former parking lot. Closed Sun.

El Paraiso Parque Guzmán. Well-prepared *pupusas* and *comidas a la vista* (US$2.60) are dished out in an attractive colonial building in a conveniently

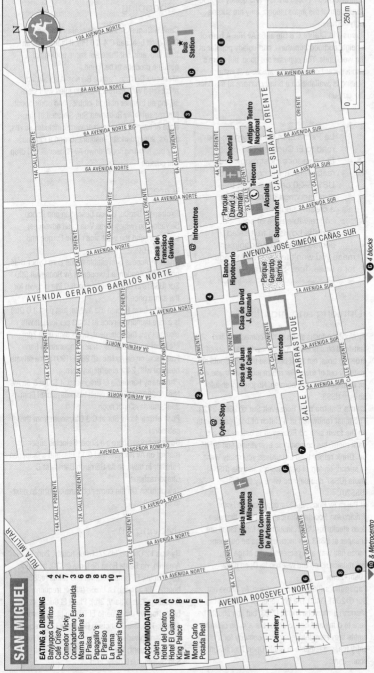

SAN MIGUEL

EATING & DRINKING

Batyjugos Carlitos	4
Café Cristy	2
Comedor Vicky	7
Conchadromo Esmeralda	3
Mama Gallina's	6
El Paisa	9
Papagallo's	8
El Paraíso	5
La Pema	10
Pupusería Chilita	1

ACCOMMODATION

Caleta	G
Hotel del Centro	A
Hotel El Guanaco	C
King Palace	B
Mir	E
Monte Carlo	D
Posada Real	F

central location. Prices are low and quality is good. Steer clear of the *jugos* though; they are surprisingly horrible.

Pupusería Chilita C 8 Ote at 6a Av Nte. A barn of a neighbourhood *pupusería*, particularly popular at the weekends. The *pupusas* are good, but there's also a decent selection of *comidas a la vista*. Seating is available on a breezy terrace at the back. Closed Sun.

> **TREAT YOURSELF**
>
> **La Pema** 5km from town on the road to El Cuco ☎2667-6055. El Salvador's most renowned restaurant. It will cost around US$15–20 per head, but the huge servings of *mariscada*, a creamy soup of every conceivable type of seafood, and the bowls of fruit salad served as an accompaniment mean you won't feel like eating again for a while. Tues–Sun 11am–5pm.

Drinking and nightlife

By night the focus shifts to the *comedores* and fast-food chains along Av Roosevelt. Think about ordering taxis, not least because the nightspots are quite far out of town. For return journeys, these can be arranged with the barmen. No journey should be over US$3.

Mama Gallina's Av Roosevelt Sur ☎2661-2123. The most renowned of a clutch of bar/restaurants on the town side on Roosevelt is ostensibly a big dark room, but company is everything and it fills up. Drink rather than eat unless you really want to spend; on top of beer there's sangria (US$4), shots (US$7 double) and wine by the bottle (US$20).

El Paisa Av Roosevelt Sur opposite the *Hotel Trópico Inn*. Popular Mexican food spot that also does steaks for US$7, though the large tacos are cheaper at US$3. It's more used as an outdoors booze hall with a big screen and a stage for live musicians on the weekends. Open daily 10am–2am.

Papagallo's Plaza Chaparrastique, Av Roosevelt Sur ☎2661-0400. The big venue of town has big Mexican dishes starting at US$3, but you should be here to drink and dance under the a/c. On certain nights they have live music and comedy for a US$5 entry fee, redeemable in drink. Open Thurs–Sun noon–2am.

Shopping

Centro Comercial de Artesanías Alameda Roosevelt between C 4 & 6 Pte. It is less artisan than souvenir, but there are some pockets of genuine produce to be found.

Mercado Central Parque Barrios. A sprawling affair lined with narrow warrens filled with stalls selling all manner of food, clothes and other goods.

Metrocentro Av Roosevelt Sur. Situated at the edge of town, this consumer vortex includes stores, banks, supermarkets, restaurants and a cinema; any bus heading south down Av Roosevelt will drop you outside.

Directory

Exchange BanCo, Banco Cuscatlán and Banco Salvadoreño (which gives Visa cash advances) cluster around the west side of the Parque and along C 4 Ote.

Internet Access is available at the Euro Cyber Café, part of the Academía Europea at Av Roosevelt 300 Sur (US$1/hr) or Infocentros on 6 C Pte in town for the same price.

Laundry Lava Rápido (6a Av Nte, just past 8 C Ote) is a rare laundry service at US$3 per load. It will also sell you the detergent. Open 8am until 7pm.

Medical care Hospital Clínica Laboratorio San Francisco, on 5a Av Nte (☎2661-1991), is a private hospital with 24hr emergency care.

Pharmacy Farmacia El Progresso, 4 C Ote & 6a Av Nte (☎2661-1098), is open weekdays until 6pm and Saturdays until noon.

Post office 4a Av Sur at C 3 Ote, south from the cathedral.

Supermarket There's a Super Selectos supermarket on Av Roosevelt at C 11 Pte, and a Dispensa Familiar in town on Av Gerrardo Barrios at C Chaparrastique.

Telephones On the corner of Parque Guzmán next to the Alcaldía.

Moving on

By bus to: Corinto (#327; twice hourly; 2hr); El Amatillo, via Santa Rosa de Lima (#330; frequent; 1hr 30min); El Tamarindo, via Las Tunas (#385; hourly; 1hr 30min); La Unión (#324; frequent; 1hr); Perquín (#332; 6 daily; 3hr); Playa El Cuco (#320; twice hourly; 1hr); Puerto El Triunfo (#377; every 40min; 1hr); San Francisco Gotera (#328; frequent; 1hr); San Salvador (#301; 4 hourly; 3hr); Usulután (#373; frequent; 1hr 15min). Luxury services go to San Salvador (10 daily; 2hr).

SAN FRANCISCO GOTERA

North of San Miguel, Highway CA-7 runs 25km to **SAN FRANCISCO GOTERA** (usually called "Gotera"). It's the least exciting of the towns along the Ruta de la Paz, but is a pivotal transport point for the more interesting destinations beyond. There's no real reason to stay here, as onward bus connections are good, but if you do get stuck, the *San Francisco*, on Av Morazán at C 3 Pte (☎2654-0066; ❸), a block away from the bus stop, is the best hotel in town, with a good range of rooms including en-suite doubles with cable TV and a/c. *Cocina de Chinchilla*, on C los Almendros, is good for pastas (US$4), vegetarian dishes (US$3.50) and burgers, but *Comedor Vanessa,* Barrio la Soledad #1, is where everyone in the know goes, with full meals costing US$2.25. If you have some time to kill, check out the panoramic view from the Parque Concordia.

Buses stop just after the dusty and ugly main square. Bus #332A runs regularly north to Perquín from the same place, and pick-ups do the route from the northern end of Avenida Morazán between 5am and 5.30pm. Bus number #328 makes the trip to San Miguel (every 10min; 1hr). Cacaopera can be reached by #337 (hourly; 1hr).

GUATAJIAGUA

Lying in the basin of an open valley between Gotera and the Interamericana, peaceful **GUATAJIAGUA** is a highlight of Salvadoran small town life. Like many other towns, Guatajiagua has a unified creative output – black clay pottery and sculpture – but the products are of far higher quality than the usual souvenirs. Moreover, the town is very approachable, and as yet untainted by tourism.

Calle Principal, running west of the parque, is the town's unofficial centre and the location of **Cedart** (Mon–Fri 8am–5pm, Sat 8am–midday), which provides a useful introduction to and an exhibition of local crafts (ask for directions to workshops if you see a piece you like). There are many **workshops** around town, including that of Sarbelio Vásquez Garcia, whose sculptures of a kneeling man you'll see imitated throughout town.

A **hotel** has finally opened in town, and it has not been done in half measures. The four-storey *Hotel Canales* (☎2634-5003; ❸) has spotless, light and airy rooms, with towels provided in the bathrooms and fans and TVs in the rooms. The best part is the views from the roof – you can see far past San Miguel in the next valley. There is also one excellent **bar** and **restaurant**, *Merendero de la Vista*, which is reached by heading right out of the hotel and left at the end of the road until you get to the Art Nouveau cross. You'll feel like you're in someone's living room as soon as you enter: there is a sofa and armchair and a little garden out back where you can play checkers with bottle caps. The owners offer good *hamburgesas* (US$1), *pupusas* (US$0.25) and cold beers for under a dollar (if you buy enough). Across the road from Cedart, an unnamed **internet** café provides connections for US$0.01 per minute.

Buses from San Francisco Gotera (#410; hourly; 1hr) stop by the market, as does the San Miguel bus (#326; hourly; 1hr 20min), which you can pick up at Chapeltique on the highway if you're coming from the west.

CACAOPERA

The small village of **CACAOPERA**, 11km north of Gotera, takes its name from the Ulúa language, and refers to the heavy cultivation of cacao in the area during colonial times. Indigenous culture and religion is still strongly adhered to in this region, and an excellent place to learn about it is the **Centro Maya Kakawira** (Mon–Fri 9am–3pm; US$1), which has fine exhibits on indigenous tradition and culture, as well as photos and arts and crafts. You can stay here, probably putting into practice what you have just learnt, as the bunk dorms (❶) have no electricity or water and buckets for toilets; you can self-cater on their fire. Another worthy stop is the colonial **church** dating back to 1660 (though heavily restored), with walls up to five metres thick. Adjacent is a bell tower with three huge bronze bells dating from 1772. The church is the focus of festivities on January 15–17, when the villagers dance in memory of the eight *caciques* (priests) and the indigenous warrior deities Tupaica and Tumaica. There are hourly **buses** (#337) here from Gotera.

CORINTO

From Cacaopera, a road heads a little further northeast to the town of **CORINTO**, an important commercial hub in the region and home to a **market** on Wednesday and Sunday that attracts vendors from neighbouring Honduras. There is the usual tack, but look for hand-rolled cigars and locally grown foods. The town's main claim to fame are the **Grutas del Espíritu Santo** (Tues–Sun 9am–4.30pm; US$2), a series of caves bearing pre-Columbian wall art located about fifteen minutes north of the village on foot through some pleasant scenery. Though faint, the art is said to date back some ten thousand years, and the whole area makes a very pleasant stroll. *Pollo Silvestre*, on 1 Calle Pte, does good *pollo dorado* (US$3), while *Café la Casona* on the parque has good pastries. There is a lack of recommendable **accommodation**; go to *Hotel Restaurante Familiar* (☎2898-2844; ❷) if you're stuck. Corinto can be reached as a day-trip from San Miguel (**bus** #327 from the main terminal), or #782 (hourly; 1hr) comes from Cacaopera.

MOZOTE

A few kilometres further on sits **MOZOTE**, the scene of the country's most atrocious wartime massacre (see box opposite). Today ruined Mozote is still virtually a ghost town, a situation that ensures a high volume of war tourism but obviously hinders the recovery progress. Families are slowly moving back, and a Claudia Bernard **mural** on the left side of the church describes the village's old agricultural life and hopes for the future.

Although the massacre's one survivor has now passed away, newer inhabitants are continuing the guide work she did, and are vital to understanding all the town's scars left from the war: you can see a bomb crater, the massacre's mass graves and the hole that the survivor hid in for five days (there's no charge, but tipping is expected). A moving **monument** to the victims features an iron sculpture of the silhouette of a family and a wall carrying the names of those killed. For a small fee (around US$4), local children will take you to the caves where the guerrillas were really hiding out, a pleasant walk of four or five kilometres through forest and brush, where wildlife abounds. The caves themselves are not overly spectacular, but it was from here that **Radio Venceremos** ("We Will Overcome") was first broadcast, and as you look out over the surrounding countryside it is easy to see why they were never discovered by the army.

Mozote can be reached by **foot** from Perquín (see below) or via a **pick-up** to Arambala, 3km down the CA-7, where you change to a Joateca bus that leaves at 8am every morning (the return bus leaves Mozote at 12.45pm).

PERQUÍN

At the Desvío de Arambala, the main paved section of road begins its final climb to **PERQUÍN**, a small and, given its history, surprisingly friendly mountain town set in the middle of glorious walking countryside. During the war the town was the FMLN headquarters, and in later years where they broadcast Radio Venceremos to the nation. Attempts by the army to dislodge the guerrillas mostly failed, leaving the town badly damaged and

deserted. Today, the "town that refused to die" has repaired most of its buildings, although the scars of war are still evident and nearly everyone has a horrendous tale to tell. Recently community action has been moving away from the retrospective outlook that war tourism has created, and instituted new schools, coffee production and a young and hip annual festival, the Festival del Invierno, which hosts live music and events in August.

What to see and do

The town itself is clumped around its pentagonal Parque Central, where there is a municipal basketball court. One block uphill is Calle de los Héroes, containing most of the town's attractions.

Museo de la Revolución

Perquín's main draw is the moving **Museo de la Revolución Salvadoreña** (Tues–Sun 8.30am–4.30pm; US$1.50), set up by former guerrillas in the wake of the 1992 Peace Accords. The curators travelled throughout the country collecting photographs and personal effects of "disappeared" guerrillas, a collection that is still growing and displayed in the first room. There is a succinct summary (in Spanish) of

LOS INOCENTES

In December 1981, the elite, US-trained Atlacatl army battalion entered the village of Mozote and rounded up its inhabitants on the suspicion that they had been harbouring FMLN guerrillas. Earlier, the villagers had been warned by guerrillas of the army's intent, but the mayor had been assured by the government that they would be safe staying put. This was not to be: under orders to set an example and obtain information, for three days the soldiers tortured and raped the inhabitants, before executing them all, including the children, who were shot in front of their parents. In all, some thousand people were killed, and their bodies subsequently burnt or buried in mass graves. The eyewitness testimonies to the events were ignored for years, and the bodies of the victims did not begin to be exhumed until 1992. Foreign groups are still working to uncover these mass-burial sites today; in some graves upwards of 85 percent of the bodies belong to children. On the right side of the church, a small garden for "the innocent ones" commemorates the utter tragedy of their lost lives.

the escalation to the armed struggle, now-disabled weaponry and examples of international propaganda aimed at bringing the events in El Salvador to the world's attention, but the most moving exhibits are perhaps the anonymous transcripts of witnesses of the Mozote massacre, and drawings by refugee schoolchildren, depicting the war's events as they saw them. A separate room contains the transmitting equipment and studio used by Radio Venceremos, whose clandestine broadcasts every afternoon throughout the war transmitted the guerrillas' view of events, as well as interviews and music. After the peace accords, the station received an FM licence, and is now a commercial music station based in San Salvador, a status viewed by some as a bit of a sell-out.

Outside the museum is the crater left by a 500lb bomb dropped on the village – next to which a disarmed one is on display, with "Made in the USA" stencilled on the side – and a mock-up of a guerrilla camp. Behind the museum lie the remains of the helicopter that was carrying Domingo Monterrosa (architect of the Mozote massacre) when it was shot down by the FMLN in 1984.

Cerro de Perquín

Opposite the museum, a track leads up from a parking lot to the panoramic views from the peak of the **Cerro de Perquín**. It is an easy 1km stroll to the top, where climbers can picnic and have their picture taken by a sign marking the summit. Consider taking a lot of pictures on the way up to make the climb seem longer when you come to tell the story.

Arrival and information

By bus Buses arrive on the south and west sides of the Parque Central, though it is easier to jump off before town for many of the accommodation options. Pick-ups from San Francisco Gotera stop one block south of the park on C San Sebastián.

Tourist information There's a small, but enthusiastic tourist office (Mon–Sat 8am–4pm; ☎2680-4086) on the west side of the Parque that can provide leaflets and maps and is the place to organize guided hikes.

Accommodation

There are quite a few places to camp in the hills around Perquín – it's worth asking at the tourist office for recommendations.

Hotel Perkin Lenca 1.5km south of town on CA-7 ☎2680-4046, ⓦwww .perkinlenca.com. The owner here, a former aid-worker called Ronald, built the entire site himself, including the huge barn where excellent meals are served (US$5–10) – worth a visit even if you don't stay here. Spotless, hot-water en-suites, firm beds, hammocks and tables on the porches, great views, table tennis, free internet and a laundry service and a pool (under construction at the time of writing) are worth every penny. Breakfast is included, and advance booking is recommended; he says he will give 20 percent discounts during the week if rooms are open – hold him to it. ⑤

Hotel y Restaurante La Posada Signed at Km 206 on CA-7, 500m south of town. This hotel used to be a saw-mill, evidenced by the lofty reception area, where simple *típicos* are served. The beds are firm and good, though the rooms quite dark, and the shared bathroom isn't en suite but there is toilet paper and seats. It stands alone for its pool table, in great condition, and gym facilities. ③

Perquín Real At the southern end of town on CA-7 ☎2680-4158, ⓔxiomvarela@yahoo.com. The best budget option in town has a row of spacious rooms with at least two double beds in each. The bathroom situation is a little sketchy (it's shared with the good restaurant in the courtyard, and still uses a bucket shower – quite abrasive in the cooler climate). ①

Turicentro Salto El Perol 4km east of town on the road to Marcala ☎2680-6071. These camping pitches, situated in one of three contiguous *turicentros* on the Río Guaco, have the best waterfall and fresh-water swimming pools, as well as *comedores*. The walk to town takes two hours. ①

Eating

Blanquita's Av los Próceres. This is the best *comedor* in town, with a small selection but popular *a la vista* and cakes. *Desayuno* US$1.50.

INTO HONDURAS: EL AMATILLO

Beyond Santa Rosa, the road connects with the Carretera Interamericana to run to the border over the Río Goascora at **El Amatillo**. The border crossing is easy and free but busy, and teeming with moneychangers – who generally do better rates than the bank here – and beggars. On the Honduran side, buses leave regularly until late afternoon for Tegucigalpa and Jícaro Galán, and there are also direct buses to Choluteca, for onward connection to the Nicaraguan border along the Carretera Interamericana.

Marisol Av los Próceres. If you fancy a drink or two, and good burgers and fries (US$2.50), this is your place, though it resembles a hospital in decor. It is open late (until 10pm at weekends)

La Muralla C de los Héroes, at the foot of the climb to the museum. The evening *pupusa* spot, frying on demand out front while the townsfolk watch dubbed America dramas on the cable inside. It costs around US$2 for five *pupusas*. Open until 9pm.

El Ocotal At Km 201 on CA-7 ☎ 2680-4190. As a hotel this is a paler version of *Perkin Lenca*; however, the restaurant is worth a trip, with good *sopas* (US$2.50) and a mean fried yucca on weekends. It is set in a pine forest, which curiously suits the 80s power ballads they favour on the stereo. Bring your swimsuit – you can use the pool once you've spent money.

Directory

Internet Access can be found on Calle de los Héroes for US$1/hr.
Pharmacy There's one next to the post office, with a fairly small stock.
Post office The post office is next door to the tourist office (Mon, Tues, Thurs & Fri, 8am–5pm).

Moving on

By bus to: San Miguel, via San Francisco Gotera (#332; 4 daily; 2hr); Mozote (#426; 2 daily; 20min).
By pick-up to: San Francisco Gotera (twice hourly; 1hr).

AROUND PERQUÍN

The area around Perquín makes very enjoyable **hiking**, the highlights of which are the route over **Cerro el Pericón** to Mozote, taking around three hours with a stop to swim in the middle, and a two-hour loop around **Cerro Gigante**. The tourist office (see p.296) can organize

guides a day in advance, some of which have reasonable English. Paying for a guide (around US$15 per group) is tremendously worthwhile, as they are mostly ex-guerrillas who will bring the history of the landscape to life.

SANTA ROSA DE LIMA

East of San Francisco Gotera, a road continues through hot, low hills to **SANTA ROSA DE LIMA**, a messy but thriving place with a large daily market, cheese industry and a well-maintained church. Besides the Wednesday **markets**, there's not much to do here, but it's a convenient stopover if you're crossing late from Honduras. The best of the few **places to stay** is *Hotel El Recreo*, on 4a Av Nte between C Giron and C 1 Ote (☎ 2664-2126; ❸), which has clean rooms with bath, though it does get a little noisy. The basic but adequate *El Tejano*, on C Giron between 6a and 8a Av Nte (☎ 2664-2459; ❷), is slightly cheaper, but has a 7am check-out. For **eating**, the very clean *Comedor Chayito*, at the corner of C Giron and C 1 Ote, does a good cheap *comida a la vista*. For something with a bit more kick, try *Taquería Tex Mex*, on Av G Arias between C 1 and 3 Ote. **Banks**, including Banco Cuscatlán, are clustered around the plaza at the centre of town. **Buses** arrive at the western end of 6 C Pte, and go to the border at El Amatillo (#346; every 20min; 1hr 30min), La Union (#304 or #342; frequent; 1hr 30min), San Miguel (#330; frequent; 1hr) and San Salvador (#306; twice hourly; 4hr).

The north

North of San Salvador, hilly pastures and agricultural land give way to the remote, rugged and sparsely populated Chalatenango and Cuscatlán provinces, a region of poverty and pride all but closed to outsiders until recently. The Spanish found few natural riches to attract them this far north, and successive generations of *campesinos* have vainly struggled to make a living. This harsh terrain created fertile ground for dissent and support for the FMLN, who controlled large parts of the department of Chalatenango for significant periods during the 1980s. Both army and guerrillas struggled to take control, leaving devastated communities in their wake and refugees fleeing across the border to Honduras. The legacy of the region's wartime status was not exclusively detrimental, however, and the effect of the subsequent repopulation has been the reinvention and modernization of its big towns. Each now has a very singular character and commitment: colonial **Suchitoto** is the darling of culture and tourism, **La Palma** is a mountainous escape with a legion of artisans and bustling **Chalatenango** is a centre of rural commerce.

SUCHITOTO

Cobbled and colonial **SUCHITOTO** perches like a crown on the ridge above the southern edge of Lago de Suchitlán. Regularly compared to Antigua in Guatemala, only "before it got so touristy", the left-leaning town was made a site of National Cultural Heritage in 1997, and culture is indeed the order of the day. There are food and arts festivals every weekend, and the month-long February festival of culture brings in the country's best painters, orchestras, performers and poets. This was not true during the 1980s, when the area was the scene of bitter fighting as the army struggled to dislodge FMLN guerrillas from their nearby mountain strongholds. Upwards of ninety percent of the inhabitants left the town, which was largely resettled by ex-guerrillas after the war. Today life here is generally quiet. The town offers great eating and drinking, and presents an antidote to rough travelling.

What to see and do

Suchitoto boasts some of the finest standing examples of colonial architecture in the country, so before getting stuck into the cafés and shops it is worth taking a stroll to admire the low red-tiled adobe houses stretching attractively along the town's streets.

The centre

Overlooking the Parque Central, the post-colonial **Iglesia Santa Lucía** has an impressive Neo-classical front and a particularly fine wooden altar and strange hollow wooden columns inside. The **Casa de Cultura** (Mon–Fri, 9am–5pm; free), a block north of the church, has displays on local history and information on local walks, while the shaded **Parque San Martín**, a couple of blocks west of the church, commands stunning and seemingly endless views across the blue waters of the lake. Group tours of the centre's architecture can be organized at the tourist office.

Museo de Alejandro Cotto

From the northeast of town, Avenida 15 de Septiembre leads down to the lakeshore, passing the **Museo de Alejandro Cotto** (Sat & Sun 2–6pm; US$4), a beautifully restored colonial house replete with a fine collection of local paintings, sculpture, indigenous artefacts and musical instruments. The owner, Cotto himself, is a famous Salvadoran writer and filmmaker, and is often here. The entrance price, while relatively steep, goes towards funding

Lago de Suchitlán, Museo de Alejandro Cotto & ❶ ▲

SUCHITOTO

ACCOMMODATION
2 Gardenias	A
Blanca Luna	E
Casa de Niña Rubia	F
El Cerrito	D
Villa Balanza	C
Vista del Lago	B

4 CALLE PONIENTE
2 CALLE PONIENTE
C. FRANCISCO MORAZÁN
AVENIDA 15 DE SEPTIEMBRE
3 AVENIDA NORTE
2 AVENIDA NORTE
1 AVENIDA NORTE

Centro Arte para la Paz
Parque San Martín
Teatro de las Ruinas
Galeria de Pascal
Police Station
Telecom
Alcadia
Parque Centenario
Casa de la Cultura
Pharmacy
Bus from San Salvador
Bus to Lago Suchitlán
Iglesia Santa Lucía

6 CALLE ORIENTE
4 CALLE ORIENTE
2 CALLE ORIENTE
4 C PTE

1 AVENIDA SUR
2 AVENIDA SUR
3 AVENIDA SUR
AVENIDA 6 DE NOVIEMBRE

N

0 — 100 m

EATING & DRINKING
Artex Café	10
Café Vistaconga	2
Casa del Escultor	5
La Fonda	1
El Necio	6
Noe's Disco	7
La Piedra	9
La Posada	4
Rinconcito del Gringo	8
El Tejado	3

▼ ❻ *& Los Tercios Waterfall*

the town's February arts and culture festival.

Lago de Suchitlán

It's a couple of kilometres to **Lago de Suchitlán**, but it's worth the trip as you can swim, and a couple of small lakeside bars are good for a relaxing drink. A small boat sometimes runs around the lake, or local fishermen may be persuaded to take you out onto the water. Trips to Isla de los Pájaros in the middle of the lake, the home of a range of fish-eating bird life, take about forty minutes (boat US$10–15). To get to the lake, walk north on Avenida 15 de Septiembre from the Parque Central and keep going, or take a mini-bus from the corner of that road and 4a Calle Pte (10min; US$0.30).

Los Tercios

You can also be dropped off at a trail on the lakeshore that leads to the **Los Tercios waterfall** (boat US$4–6), or walk to it by following the signposts south

out of town (30min). The waterfall is of note for the unusual hexagonal basaltic columns over which the water flows. It's interesting to see, but the water level can get low in the dry season.

Salto El Cubo

A better waterfall to swim in is **Salto El Cubo**, with its chilly twin pools. It is a pleasant one-hour walk west of town – go to the western end of Calle Morazán, then follow the sign down the track at the signpost.

Cerro Guazapa

A former guerrilla stronghold, the roads up and around **Cerro Guazapa** still bear witness to the crumbling remains of the trenches and dugouts used by both sides, now quietly submerged beneath green vegetation. Horseriding is popular in this area and hacks across the volcano can be organized through the tourist office (US$18 per person; 6hr). Check the condition of the horses before you go, as some aren't in great shape.

Arrival and information

By boat Ferries from San Francisco Lempa, across Lago de Suchitlán, arrive at the boat dock, 1.5km north of town along C al Lago. A microbus makes the journey up to the Parque Central for US$0.30.
By bus Buses stop at 1 C Pte, a block south of the tourist office.
Tour operators 4hr waterfall treks can be arranged at *Vistaconga* (see p.301) for just US$6 per person; they also do mountain-biking trips around the hills for US$7. If you wish to go further afield talk to Robert Broz at *Café El Gringo*.
Tourist information Possibly the best tourist office in the country is on C V Morazán & 2a Av Nte (Wed–Sun 8am–noon & 1–4pm; ☎2335-1782, Ⓦwww.suchitoto-el-salvador.com), with information on tours, sights and cultural events, also available through its bilingual website. If it is closed check *Café El Gringo* or *Artex Café* (see below), who are also mighty helpful.

Accommodation

More and more accommodation options are springing up as Suchitoto responds to increasing numbers of visitors. You can find pictures and information of most hotels, and restaurants, in town at Ⓦwww.gaesuchitoto.com. Book ahead on weekends, and for all of February.
2 Gardenias 3a Av Nte 48 ☎2335-1868, Ⓔhostal2gardenias@hotmail.com. The oldest backpacker spot in town has roooms that have become rather shabby, but a great mango-filled community space. There's internet access and a bar inside that serves reasonably priced food and drinks. ❷
Blanca Luna One block south of the Parque ☎2335-1661, Ⓔposadablancalunasuchitoto @hotmail.com. The newest addition to the cheap hotels in town has two or three double beds in the rooms, as well as fan, cable TV and en-suites, and there's a Jacuzzi-style pool in the back. The owners are jade-polishers. ❷
Casa de Niña Rubia Av 5 de Noviembre 29 ☎2335-1833. If the tourist-centric atmosphere gets to you, come here, where you literally stay with Ruby's family in her house. Two basic and clean rooms. ❶
El Cerrito On the track between 6 & 4 C Pte ☎2517-1665, Ⓔvmlc81@hotmail.com. It has just one room, with three hard double beds in it, although like a flat this leads to a sitting room with cable TV and a clean bathroom. Priced by the person, the room is rented like a dorm. ❶

Villa Balanza Parque San Martin ☎2335-1408, Ⓦwww.villabalanzarestaurante.com.sv. Two very good, wooden finished rooms behind the restaurant share a bathroom (with hot water!). There is an annexe with fine but not as nice en-suite rooms and a view of the lake. ❹
Vista del Lago At the end of 2a Av Nte ☎2335-1357. The rooms here are small and cubicle-esque, with passable beds and a shared bathroom, but the owners are relaxed, the cosy courtyard has a bar and food and the bench overlooking the lake is possibly the best spot in town for an evening drink. ❶

Eating

The selection of cuisine in Suchitoto is such that you only really expect from a large city, so it's worth staying on the cheap and splashing out on a nice meal.
Artex Café Plaza Central Ⓦwww.centroartex .org. Not only does this place have the best coffee in town (they'll sell you bags for US$4.50) but also fast internet (US$1/hr), excellent local cultural information (the café is run by a non-profit organization promoting the arts) and nice outdoor tables to have a beer (Pilsener US$1).
Casa del Escultor 6 C Ote & 3a Av Nte ☎2335-1711 or 7820-5092, Ⓦwww.miguelmartino.com. Not so much a restaurant as the art-filled house of an Argentine sculptor who cooks his country's famous giant grills every Sun lunch for a lucky few. Reserve ahead, or if you have a group of four or more call to arrange a day and time and he'll cook especially for you. It's worth it even at US$7–14.
La Piedra Opposite the church on Parque Central. It looks like a tourist trap, but there is good variety in the menu, including rabbit (US$7) and chorizo (US$4), and it does a great rum and coffee to pick you up mid-afternoon (US$1.50).
El Portal Parque Central. This is the most popular *comedor* in town, not only for its useful position. You can expect good versions of all the usuals and some interesting *pupusas* (spinach US$0.60).
Rinconcito del Gringo C V Morazán 27 ☎2327-2351. From the same gringo that runs the internet café and tours, this largely Mexican restaurant offers big, spicey portions that really should cost more (*quesadillas* US$4, half-litre mug of orange juice US$2). There's a good atmosphere when busy and occasionally it stays open later for drinkers. Closed Thurs.
El Tejado 3a Av Nte. Big meat and chicken dishes (US$6) are served in a pleasant garden with the requisite lake view. The best thing about this place is that it gives you access to the giant and clean

swimming pool to cool off on hot days. You may be asked for a US$3 supplement for this, but not always.

Villa Balanza At the *Villa Balanza* hotel. This tree-covered outdoor restaurant has a truly impressive war-themed decor. The food is good with breakfasts and lunches (chicken *suprema* US$6.50), both served by waitresses in "traditional" milk-maid outfits.

Vistaconga Final Cielito Lindo 8 ☎2335-1676. A friendly place with great lake views, live music or dance on Sat nights and tours arranged to surrounding attractions. There is a Mexican-inspired menu, and some reasonable cocktails (US$4). Closed Mon & Tues.

Drinking

Suchitoto is a good place to go out, both in terms of choice and safety, so take advantage. Nonetheless, if you're female and on your own in *El Necio* and *Noe's* you should expect the all-too-usual attention.

La Fonda Northern end of Av 15 de Septiembre ☎2335-1126. The largely expensive menu has some cheap and filling treats (seafood salad US$4), but it really comes into its own as a spot for evening drinks with great views of the lake.

El Necio 4 C Pte 9. The only out-and-out bar in town is a local favourite, serving regular priced beers (US$1) and spirits, amid guerrilla decor. Good for pre-*Noe's* warm up.

Noe's Disco 4 C Ote. Also known as *Disco Mowy*, this is the only place to dance in town and is cheap, cheeky and cheerful. The music is popular with obvious Latino influence, and the beers are normal price. Open weekends 8pm–2am.

Zukafé y Bar In *2 Gardenias* hostel. You can always expect travellers and good music here (occasionally live bands on Sat), there is art on the walls and although the food is average, you can't mess up a beer.

Shopping and entertainment

Arts and cultural venues are dotted around all Suchitoto's streets. It is well worth wandering around to find your own preferences.

La Galería de Pascal Av 15 de Septiembre. A rather large exhibition space that sells original paintings, which are naturally very expensive, but also local artisanal work.

Centro Arte para la Paz 4 C Pte & 6a Av Nte ⓦwww.centroartex.org. A venue for a range of arts events, including film, theatre, concerts and painting. It is linked with the *Artex Café* and that, along with its website, is where to find out what's going on.

Directory

Exchange There is, surprisingly, still no bank here, so bring plenty of cash if you want to settle in.

Internet *Café El Gringo*, 8a Av Nte 9, is a great internet café, not least because the gringo in question, Californian Robert Broz, is an authority on the town and area.

Laundry *Hotel El Obraje* on 2 C Ote, though dull accommodation, does loads for US$4–6.

Pharmacy Santa Lucía, on the corner of C V Morazán and Av 5 de Noviembre, is well stocked but closes between noon & 2pm, and at 6pm.

Police The tourist police force, who have a good presence in town, is open 24hr on the corner of Av 15 de Septiembre and 4 C Pte (☎2335-1141)

Moving on

By boat to: San Francisco Lempa (20min; 10 daily), from where buses travel to Chalatenango. Car ferries are cheaper than passenger ferries.

By bus to: Aguilares (#163; every 40min; 1hr) for transfer to Chalatenango (#125) & La Palma (#119); San Martin (#129; 10 daily; 1hr) for Cojutepeque (#119) or San Miguel (#301); San Salvador, Terminal de Oriente (#129; every 15min; 1hr 30min).

AGUILARES AND CIHUATÁN

Some 35km north of the capital on the border-bound CA-4, or the Troncal del Norte, lies the pleasant workaday town of **AGUILARES**, with nothing more to offer than a relaxing snack in the garden at *Río Bravo* on the Parque. Archeology buffs might want to pass through, however, as 4km to the north sit the ruins of **CIHUATÁN** (Tues–Sun 9am–4pm; US$3; ⓦwww.cihuatan.org), the most important Postclassic site in the country. Originally covering an area of around four square kilometres, Cihuatán (meaning "Place of Women" in Nahaut) was founded sometime after the first waves of Pipils (or Toltecs) began arriving in El Salvador in the tenth century and destroyed sometime around 1200 AD. The excavations, which includes stepped pyramids and a pelota court bearing a clear Mexican influence, were officially opened in November 2007, along with a very informative bilingual museum. To really get into it, it's worth reading the information on the website before going.

Take any **bus** from Aquilares or the capital to Chalatenango or La Palma and ask to be dropped at the gates – they're right on the highway.

CHALATENANGO

Further north along the Troncal del Norte is a major crossroads at the scrubby town of **Amayo**, the east branch of which leads through agricultural and pasture lands along the fringes of the lake to **CHALATENANGO**. An important centre of rural trade, Chalatenango has the rough-and-ready feel of a frontier settlement, an atmosphere enhanced by the raised wooden walkways fronting the buildings of the centre, which have now been declared a national monument. During the early 1980s this was under FMLN control, and though much of the town's physical damage has been repaired, a huge military garrison with bullet holes in its sides still looms over the central plaza, Its lawless reputation is now largely fictional though, and the town is busy, but very friendly.

What to see and do

Chalatenango lies in a beautiful setting – southeast of the La Peña Mountains, overlooking the distant Cerro Grande to the west and Lago de Suchitlán to the south – and a lot of its attraction lies in day-trips to what surrounds it (see p.303). However, the daily **market** that seals off Calle San Martín every morning from 5am to 1pm is full of fresh locally grown produce and cowboy attire, which is even more prevalent when the Friday horse fairs (auctions) come to town. Twenty minutes from the centre to the east is the **Agua Fría Turicentro** (daily 8am–5pm; US$0.90), with artificial pools, a water slide and a café in a nice park.

Arrival and information

By bus All buses arrive and depart from along 3a Av Sur. From here it's only a couple of blocks north to the Parque Central.
Exchange There are several banks with ATMs along 3a Av Sur.

Accommodation

Hotel La Ceiba Behind the garrison building on 1 C Pte ☎ 2301-1080. Friendly and with standard features for the price (cable, en-suite, a/c), this hotel has good views from its spot near the centre; the good and bad news is there is no longer a disco in the basement. ❸

Hotelito San José 3 C Pte ☎ 2301-0148. The thrifty choice, with firm beds, fans and occasional toilet seats in its rooms around a pleasant yard, but they aren't spotless and it's wise to arrive early and air the mildewy smell. ❷

La Posada del Jefe C el Instituto ☎ 2335-2450. The furthest option from the centre is spotless, with good beds and en-suites, and run by a lovely family, but at the price and at ten blocks uphill to the east of the centre, it's a bit steep. ❹

Eating and drinking

There is a nameless stall on the south side of the church on Calle San Martín. If you fancy an evening drink, this little stall does cheap beer as well as burgers, and stays open until 11pm.

Blanquita's on the corner of C Morazán & Av Libertad. The other good *comedor* in town, with, of course, much the same as well as good burgers and chips (US$2.30) though going to the toilet might put you off your food.

Columbia Café 4 C Pte. Its average US$1 sandwiches lack good ingredients, but not so their Irish coffee, which is topped with chantilly cream; they have an odd phone charger collection should you need more battery life.

Comedor Carmary 3a Av Sur on the other side of Pollo Campero. A popular *comedor* around lunchtime, serving the locally favoured *a la vista* (US$2–3), with vegetarian options too.

Don Mario's 3a Av Sur. No need to patronize the *Pollo Campero* next door – this Mexican-style grill does good big burritos for under US$4.

Otto's 6 C Pte at 1a Av Sur. Otto does pizzas as big as a car tyre (*especiale gigante* US$12) to feed more than one hungry traveller, with smaller options starting at US$2.

Sarito 1a Av Sur. The countrywide ice-cream shop has a branch here with plenty of different flavours to satisfy your needs on a hot day (US$1 a cone).

Moving on

By bus to: Concepción Quetzaltepeque (#300B; every 30min; 20min); La Palma – take the San Salvador bus and change at Amayo (#119; every

30min; 3hr); San Francisco Lempa (#542; 5 daily; 45min); San Salvador, Terminal de Oriente (#125; frequent; 2hr).

AROUND CHALATENANGO

The villages north of Chalatenango are spread across forested mountains and rarely visited. More adventurous travellers may want to explore beyond the artesan town of **Concepción Quetzaltepeque**, but if this is your goal, find information beforehand. By the lake, San Francisco Lempa is a great little stop before crossing the lake to Suchitoto.

Concepción Quetzaltenango

Twelve kilometres northwest of Chalatenango, the village of **Concepción Quetzaltepeque** is notable for its **hammock** industry. Workshops and homes around the village turn out colourful items in nylon and, less commonly, cotton and *mezcal* fibres for prices at about half those in San Salvador. If you are not very eager to look around the workshops that line the village's main street, most producers sell in the market at Chalatenango at roughly the same bargain rate. If you are a real hammock lover, however, try to catch the annual hammock festival, which takes place November 10–12.

San Francisco Lempa

The little, lakeside town of **San Francisco Lempa** is home to the pier for ferries to and from Suchitoto. The town itself is very pleasant for a dock community, but holds no real interest. In the vicinity, however, are an excellent restaurant and an excellent camping spot. *Tao Tao*, right next to the pier, is worth tripping to even if you're not getting a ferry. It serves tasty, big, predominantly seafood dishes (*camerones* soup US$4) on its lakeside veranda and will sort out boats or any kind of tourist information. Its best feature, though, is its booming jukebox, which carries Creedence, Jim Morrison, Cypress Hill, Michael Jackson and the Mighty Zep. Bring lots of quarters. The owners will either tell you how to walk to, or organize a boat to *Hacienda Grande*, 3km west along the shore (☏2375-1447). Probably the nicest camping (①; they have five tents available for those that need to borrow) in the country is here, next to their swimming pool and restaurant (*pollo dorado* US$4). They also have horses you can take out on your own around the surrounding countryside for US$4 per hour. Boats from San Francisco Lempa cost US$10, from Suchitoto US$20.

LA PALMA

Beyond Amayo, the Troncal del Norte winds up the Cordillera Metapán Alotepeque to the Honduran border through an abundance of vertiginous, pine-clad mountain views (for the best views sit on

the left-hand side of the bus on the way up). Eight kilometres short of the border lies the calm village of **LA PALMA**, supposedly named after the indigenous custom of building houses out of palms. The climate is cooler here and the peace is really only broken during the annual fiesta of **Dulce Nombre de María**, in the third week of February. But under the surface the village's plentiful *artesanías* are hives of industry, reproducing the brightly painted naïf-style representations of people, villages and farming life and religion made famous by Salvadoreño artist Fernando Llort in the 1970s on wooden and ceramic handicrafts and toys, which are now sold all over the world.

What to see and do

The **crafts industry** is the economic mainstay of the village, with **workshops**

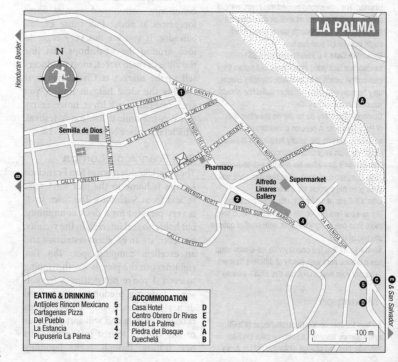

LA PALMA

Honduran Border

E & San Salvador

EATING & DRINKING	**ACCOMMODATION**
Antijoles Rincon Mexicano 5	Casa Hotel D
Cartagenas Pizza 1	Centro Obrero Dr Rivas E
Del Pueblo 3	Hotel La Palma C
La Estancia 4	Piedra del Bosque A
Pupuseria La Palma 2	Quechelá B

0 100 m

lining the main road. Most sell their goods on the spot and are pretty relaxed about visitors turning up to watch the work; prices are somewhat cheaper than in San Salvador and the items are hard to beat as presents for family and friends.

North of La Palma are several fine **hiking trails**, including El Salvador's highest mountain, **Cerro Pital** (2730m), 10km away on the Honduran border. A rough road branches east just before La Palma to run to Las Pilas on the lower slopes of the mountain; a dirt road also leads up from the village of **San Ignacio** (see p.306). Hiking to the summit is an adventure of two or three days, for which you will need to be fully equipped – the owners of the *Hotel La Palma* are a good source of information on shorter walks and guides.

Arrival and information

By bus There is no bus station as such. You can ask to get off at either end of town or in the centre; the bus goes along 2a Av Nte on the way up to the border, and C Delgado and Barrios on the way back down.

Tourist information There is a tourist office in the works. Until then, Oscar at *Piedra del Bosque* is a good source of local information.

Accommodation

There is plenty of good accommodation in La Palma at all price ranges – even free.

Casa Hotel Opposite *Hotel La Palma* ☎2335-9129. Cosy rooms with firm beds and good furnishings that include welcome bedside lights. The toilets have no seats. The owner offers a great one-month deal for US$35. **2**

Centro Obrero Dr Rivas 5km south of town on the Troncal del Norte. One of the four national workers' centres with free accommodation, this place offers simple but surprisingly clean cabins in a forested area with swimming pools.

Hotel La Palma Barrio el Tránsito ☎2335-9012. Supposedly the oldest functioning hotel in El Salvador, this reasonable place has clean, hot-water en-suites and huge Llortist murals. There's a pool and hammock area, but like its restaurant, it seems rather overpriced. **3**

Piedra del Bosque Across the river from C Independencia ☎2335-9067, ⓦwww .piedradelbosque.com. Owner Oscar built this entire ecological tree-house style complex, with cabins up the hill, a swimming pool fed by the river, clean toilets, a great restaurant, hammocks, space for camping, a rare stone museum, craft shop and bonfires in the evening. He, like his place, is charming and will talk you through everything here stone by stone. Camping **1**, doubles **3**

Quechelá 500m west of town by 1 C Pte ☎2305-9328, ⓔquechela@navigante.com. sv. This B&B is a little walk from town, but the tasteful bedrooms, amazing beds, hot-water baths, living room, bar, views of the mountains and friendly owners make it a good treat indeed. **6**

Eating

Antijoles Rincón Mexicano Next to *Casa Hotel*. American and Salvadoreño food with no pretence seved right on the street. It's cheap and hits the spot (hot dog US$1.25)

Cartagenas Pizza Av Delgado & 5a C Ote. Hearty grub like tacos and *enchiladas* as well as pizzas (US$2–12, depending on size). They do excellent banana and vanilla *licuados*, too (US$1).

Del Pueblo 2a Av Sur. A family-run establishment with bags of character, carved wooden chairs and candles, *Del Pueblo* serves a good-value menu featuring mostly meats and one of the best *típico* breakfasts around (US$3.25).

La Estancia C Barrios ☎2335-9049. Very busy with the locals, the menu here may seem pricey but it is also served in big portions; the US$3 Caesar salad is lighter and cheaper. The small-town bustle inside is overseen by colourful murals of rural life.

Pupusería La Palma C Barrios. The best *pupusería* in town is small and always busy with local residents, and serves soft and flavoursome *pupusas* (US$0.40), as well as *típicos* all day.

Shopping

Alfredo Linares Gallery C Barrios. A small gallery where the internationally established naïf artist exhibits with other local artists of his choice. The fine watercolour and pen-and-ink originals are a little steep, but there are also poster prints for US$8 and postcards for US$1.

Semilla de Dios 3 C Pte at 5a Av Nte ☎www .cooperativasemilladedios.com. An artistic production line built around Llort's iconic colourful naïf style. It is mostly exported, so that does mean there isn't a huge amount of hand-painted stuff for sale, but you can see how the work is done in the workshop.

Directory

Exchange Banco Cuscatlán on C Delgado exchanges currencies and has an ATM.
Internet Palma City Online, next to the supermarket on 2a Av Sur, has a fast connection, printing, photo-copying and web calls for just US$0.65/hr.
Pharmacy Farmacia San Rafael (Mon–Fri 8am–12.30pm & 1.30–6pm) on C Barrios has the usual stock of pills and toiletries.
Post office On 1 C Pte, with usual daytime opening hours.
Supermarket Super La Palma, on 2a Av Sur, is the saviour of self-caterers. It is open until 8pm every night.

Moving on

By bus to: El Poy (#119; twice hourly; 30min); San Ignacio (#119; twice hourly; 15min); San Salvador, Terminal de Oriente (#119; twice hourly; 3hr 30min).

SAN IGNACIO AND AROUND

The highway continues past La Palma to the Honduran border at El Poy, 11km away, a thirty-minute journey by bus. The village of **SAN IGNACIO**, 6km from La Palma and much quieter, also has a few craft workshops and two places to stay. In town, *La Posada de San Ignacio*, on the square (☎2352-9419; ❸),

has simple log cabins with shared bath, or rather better standard rooms with modern ceramic bathrooms. If you are a group of four to seven people, one of the three log cabins of *Cabañas Prashanti* (☎no phone; ❸), 500m north of town off the Troncal del Norte, will fit you all while providing a sitting room, self-catering and great views from the chairs on the porch. You can also camp at the *Parador de Compostella* (☎no phone; tents US$5), where there are good hikes and tours on horseback (US$12/hr). To get there you need to take an El Poy bus; look out for the big sign where the road to El Rosario turns off. Just short of El Poy, a road branching to the left crosses the Río Lempa and runs to the village of **Citalá**. From here a daily bus (5am) runs west through rugged wilderness and bandito country on the scenic mountain road to **Metapán**, over three to four hours. There's a basic *posada* (☎no phone; US$5) close to the centre of the village if you don't fancy the early morning walk.

The west

The rich landscape of western El Salvador in many ways offers a perfect advertisement for the country. Soft mountain chains edge back from valleys dominated by vibrant green expanses of coffee plantations. Spared from the most violent hardships of the conflict of the 1980s, the friendly towns and cities here have a relatively well-developed tourist infrastructure that makes travelling here easier than in other regions.

The joy of this part of the country consists largely of soaking up the atmosphere. The Carretera Interamericana runs between San Salvador and the main city of the west, **Santa Ana**, but the main access route to the southern part of the region leads through the sweaty town of **Sonsonate**, 65km west of the capital. From here, buses head off in several directions: down to the coast for the untouched beaches of **Los Cóbanos**, **Los Remedios** and **Barra de Santiago**; to the tranquil forest reserve at **Bosque El Imposible**; and northwest into the mountains. The mountain towns of **Apaneca** and **Juayúa**, and the nearby city of **Ahuachapán** are perfect for a few days' relaxation, and are conveniently situated near the border with Guatemala. The larger, centrally located Santa Ana is a mellow contrast to the capital, while the peaks of **Cerro Verde**, **Volcán Santa Ana** and **Volcán Izalco**, the sublime crater lake of **Lago de Coatepeque**, and the pre-Columbian site of **Tazumal** are all close by. In the north of the region, near the Guatemalan border, the accommodating little town of **Metapán** gives access to the **Bosque Montecristo**, where hiking trails weave through unspoilt cloudforest amid some of the most remote and perfectly preserved mountain scenery in this part of the world.

SONSONATE

SONSONATE, set in tobacco and cattle-ranching country, prickles with heat in the day and menace at night. It has a history of gang problems, and since there is nothing here to see, its best feature is the bus terminal, with connections to Los Cóbanos and Barra de Santiago to the south, and the Ruta de Flores to the north. There are good times to visit Sonsonate, chiefly the **Verbena de Sonsonate festival** at the

end of January, when there's a host of music and drama performances, and the town does a good **Semana Santa** celebration at Easter, when crowds flock to join the street processions and intricate pictures are drawn in coloured sawdust on the pavements.

With such good **accommodation** on the coast and up the Ruta de Flores, and plentiful bus connections until nightfall, you would have to be real idiot to get stuck here, but if it happens the ageing *Hotel Orbe* on Av F Mucci Sur and C 4 Ote (☎2451-1517; ❷), two blocks east of the Parque, has large, clean rooms with private bath, and cable TV and a/c for double that. If you want something nicer than the terminal *comedores*, *La Casona* on 3 C Pte is famed for its meaty *comida a la vista*, which will be around US$3. The bus terminal is 1.5km east of the centre – take bus #53C if you don't fancy walking.

Moving on

By bus to: Ahuachapán, via all towns on the Ruta de Flores (#249; every 15min; 2hr); Barra de Santiago (#285 direct/#259 getting off at the turning off the Carretera Litoral; 2 daily/frequent; 1hr 20min/1hr); Bosque El Imposible main entrance (#259; frequent; 1hr 20min); Los Cóbanos (#257; twice hourly; 40min); La Libertad, via the Costa Balsamo (#287; 2 daily; 2hr 45min); San Salvador (#205; frequent; 1hr 30min); Santa Ana (#216 via Los Naranjos/#209B via El Congo; 3 hourly/14 daily; 1hr 15min/1hr 45min).

LOS CÓBANOS AND LOS REMEDIOS

The idyllic white sand beach of **LOS CÓBANOS**, caressed by warm and gentle waves, is the place for sedate beach activities such as sunbathing and paddling, though it's also the only reef diving spot in the country. Just 25km due south of Sonsonate, via a fast highway, it is a favourite beach for Salvadoreño weekend breaks. At these times it is better to round the headland at the west end of the small bay to the quieter beach of **LOS REMEDIOS**. Although rather rocky, the pretty, gently curved beaches make a nice contrast to the dark palm-fringed expanses further down the coast.

There are two outstanding **accommodation** options at Los Remedios. The older *Los Cabanos Village Lodge* (T2420-5248, Wwww.loscabanos.com; ●) has thatched rooms with balconies onto the beach, fridges, coffee makers and great cleanliness. They also provide breakfast, use of the pool, and rent out snorkel gear and kayaks. A less expensive option is the unnamed beachhouse (●), right by the headland, just opened by the owners of Juayúa's *Hotel Anáhuac*. It offers two big and spotless rooms, a hot mosaic shower, a little pool and a kitchen to cook the morning catch. There are also plenty of hammocks and it backs right onto the beach. The best places to **eat** here are the fishermen's restaurants that line the shore. The delicious fish is all caught in the morning and cooked at lunch; the menu depends on what they caught. Pick any busy one – the one to the left of Tienda Angelito is excellent.

Bus #257 leaves Sonsonate twice every hour for Los Cóbanos until early evening, and there are also occasional direct buses from San Salvador (#207); the last bus leaves the beach at 5pm.

BARRA DE SANTIAGO

West of the rough and decaying port of Acajutla, the Carretera Litoral heads to the Guatemalan border at La Hachadura (see box below), with the slopes of the Cordillera Apaneca rising to the north and rolling pasturelands to the south. After 35km an unmarked track leads south to **PLAYA BARRA DE SANTIAGO**, a sandy strip of land separating the ocean from a protected estuary and mangrove reserve inland. The peninsula is well inhabited by a largely fishing community, but the expanse of beach is delightfully empty and the inhabitants still seem a little surprised to see visitors. The place to stay here is *Capricho Beach House*, on the left at the end of the road (T7932-2318/7931-4517), a side project from Lena at *Ximena's* in San Salvador. The rooms are nicer here, with firmer metal beds in the dorms (●) and doubles with fan (●) or a/c and en suite (●), and the outdoor kitchen is for public use. If you grow tired of the beach out front they will organize canoe trips into the nature reserve and probably the cheapest deep sea fishing around (US$27/hr). There are *tiendas* and *comedores* within walking distance.

Bus #259 from Sonsonate passes the turning from the Carretera, where pick-ups go the village or Lena can organize a lift. You can also wait for direct buses (#285) that go twice a day from Sonsonate.

BOSQUE EL IMPOSIBLE

Near the border along the Carretera Litoral is the sweaty and uninteresting town of Cara Sucia, from whose crossroads a road leads up to one of El Salvador's greatest hidden glories, the forest reserve of **BOSQUE EL IMPOSIBLE**, so-called because of the difficulty found in transporting coffee across its heights and gorges. Covering more than 31 square kilometres and

INTO GUATEMALA: LA HACHADURA

From Cara Sucia the highway continues the last few kilometres to La Hachadura, a 24hr border crossing used by international buses heading for Mexico and reached via bus #259 from Sonsonate. There's a small *hospedaje* on the Guatemalan side, and buses to Guatemala City (4hr, last bus 3pm), stopping at Esquintla along the way, leave from a kilometre down the road.

rising through three climatic zones across the Cordillera de Apaneca, the reserve contains more than four hundred species of trees and 1600 species of plants, some unique to the area. Birdwatchers may glimpse some of the more than three hundred species, including the emerald toucanet, trogons, hummingbirds and eagles, while the park provides a secure habitat for a diverse range of animals, including anteaters, the white-tailed deer and ocelot, plus over five hundred different species of butterfly.

Getting to El Imposible can be time consuming or expensive; there are no cheap options near the main entrance and most of the San Salvador operators listed on p.264 run expensive tours here. It is actually easier to approach from Tacuba in the north. Bus #259 stops at the crossroads in Cara Sucia on its way to the Guatemalan border – get off here and catch the 11am bus or 2pm pick-up to the park gate. There's a US$6 entry fee to enter the reserve, managed by a non-governmental organization, SalvaNatura (33 Av Sur 640, Col Flor Blanca, San Salvador; ☎2279-1515, ⓦwww.salvanatura.org) – you're meant to visit their office to pay and arrange a guide before, but you can usually do it by phone or just turn up and plead ignorance. The main entrance to the park is at the Desvío Ahuachapío turn-off from the Carretera Litoral, halfway between the Sonsonate–Acajutla road and Cara Sucia, and about 13.5km from the park itself. Inside the park

are *comedores* and a solar-powered visitors' centre which explains some animals found inside the park. Also nearby is the good, eco-neutral *Hostal El Imposible* (☎2411-5484; ⑤), with five comfortbale cabañas, a springwater pool and a very decent restaurant. SalvaNatura allows camping on three pitches, small campfires and rinsing (but not washing) in the river.

NAHUIZALCO

The population of the village of **NAHUIZALCO**, set on the southern edge of the range about 10km north of Sonsonate, is mostly descended from the region's indigenous peoples, although few wear traditional dress any longer. The town thrives on the manufacture of **wicker**, with workshops lining the main street. Some of the pieces are small enough to take home, and gentle bargaining is acceptable. As always, the Cedart on 3 C Pte is a helpful place to start and has a shop. The exciting-sounding candlelit night-markets are now largely lit by electricity, which scuppers the romantic notion that they were used out of necessity rather than choice. There are no hotels here, but *La Cocina de Doris* on 5a Av Nte is a large canteen serving tasty *típicos* (bean soup US$2.50). Bus #249, which runs the length of the Ruta de las Flores from Sonsonate to Ahuach-apán every fifteen minutes, stops at the highway turn-off, which is a 500m walk downhill to the centre.

JUAYÚA

Beyond Nahuizalco, the air freshens as the road winds its way up to the colourful and colonial **JUAYÚA** (pronounced "hwai-oo-a"). The settlement was tradi-tionally a coffee-producing town, but when coffee prices slumped in the early 1990s, Juayúans started the food festivals (*ferias gastrónomicas*) that dominate the centre every weekend. The town itself is safe at night, clean and attractive (new projects include murals by local painters in one block of C Mercedes), and the coffee-growing countryside around it offers plenty of activities to work off the weekend's indulgences.

What to see and do

On the west side of the main square stands the magnificent **Templo del Señor de Juayúa**. It was built in colonial style in 1957, and houses the Black Christ of Juayúa, carved by Quiro Cataño, sculptor of the Black Christ of Esquipulas in Guatemala (see p.199). Consequently, the town is something of a pilgrimage site, particularly during the January festival (Jan 8–15).

On Saturdays and Sundays the main square and roads leading onto it are replete with the **feria gastrónomica**'s food stalls; look out for iguana, paella, Chinese dishes, frogs, excellent seafood and chocolate-covered strawberries. Motorized trains (US$1; 30min) leave from in front of the church to the nearby coffee *co-operativa*, where a museum explains the processes involved in coffee production and sells the regional blend. There is a conga bus (US$5; 3hr) from the same place that tours the sights of the Ruta while a party atmosphere takes off on board.

Just 2km out of town, **Los Corros de la Callera** are the town's local swimming spot, with two pools artifi-cially created, the top one deep enough to jump in. You can walk it, or take a tuk-tuk at weekends. There is also

trekking, horseriding, geysers and further coffee tours to be had locally – organize trips with one of the tour operators listed below.

Arrival and information

By bus On weekdays, the Sonsonate-to-Ahuach-apán buses stop on the east side of the Parque Central, but at weekends they are pushed out to Pasaje San Juan, three bocks west along 4 C Pte.

Exchange Scotiabank, by the weekend bus stop on 4 C Pte, has an ATM.

Internet There is a café on 1a Av Nte, open until late, with internet calling capability for US$0.75.

Tour operators Juayatur (☎2469-2387) can provide guides to local attractions, including several nearby waterfalls. César at *Hotel Anáhuac* does similar tours, and speaks very good English; take a look at some of the options on the hotel's website (✇www.tikal.dk/elsalvador). Expect to pay up to US$6 per person for guides during the week, more on weekends.

Accommodation

It is largely quiet during the week, but at weekends you should book ahead.

Doña Mercedes 2a Av Sur & C 6 Ote ☎2452-2287. A cheerful place with comfortable rooms, hot water and cable TV. The shared bathrooms are very clean, or there are en suites for just US$2 more. ❹

Hotel Anáhuac 1 C Pte & 5a Av Nte ☎2469-2401, ✇www.tikal.dk/elsalvador. The clear choice in town and probably the best hostel in the country, run by the young and friendly couple César and Janne. Beds are comfortable, there are powerful hot-water showers, a lovely courtyard, art on the walls, free internet, a good DVD collection and tours organized (see above). Dorms ❷, doubles ❸

El Mirador 4 C Pte ☎2452-2432. A large hotel with hard mattresses in clean but gloomy en-suite rooms around a two-storey atrium. internet and laundry are available. ❸

Eating and drinking

Bar Jah By the eastern end of 2 C Ote. A truly brilliant little bar started up by a lovely English-speaking artist. The walls are lined with her paintings, collages and sculptures from recovered materials. With all the art around you may feel like being quite proper, but she prefers it when people go wild here. Pilsener US$1.

Café Festival On the south side of the Parque. This old *pastelería* overlooking the parque serves good coffee, traditional Spanish cakes and fine breakfasts.

El Mirador 4 C Pte. Go here to take breakfast on the third floor. They have pancakes (US$1.50) and fruit salads as well as the *típico* and the panoramic views, only slightly marred by the glass, are a good morning eye-opener.

Taquería Guadalupana 2 C Ote. Big portions of Mexican really good-value food on the menu here – daily meal deals for US$2.50. Tacos al pastor (US$2) is a favourite.

Restaurant RR C Mercedes, east of the church. One of the best restaurants around, *RR* reinvents Central American cuisine with a Western twist (red bean pasta US$8). A main course will cost around US$10, with vegeterian options slightly less. You won't get the chance to eat this well often.

Moving on

By bus to: Ahuachapán, stopping at Apaneca and Ataco (#249; twice hourly; 1hr 15min); Sonsonate, stopping at Nahuizalco (#249; twice hourly; 1hr).

APANECA

A short leg further along the road from Juayúa stands another quiet and charming mountain town – **APANECA**, founded by Pedro de Alvarado in the mid-sixteenth century. The town retains an air of friendly tranquillity, decorated by painted lampposts and tidy trimmed hedges, despite being both popular with weekend visitors and home to some fine dining and expensive accommodation. During the week, you're likely to have the place – and the wonderful surrounding mountain scenery – all to yourself.

What to see and do

There's little to do in Apaneca itself, but it's an enjoyable and not too strenuous

walk through woods and fincas to the **Laguna Verde**, a small green crater-lake 4km northeast of town. Fringed by reeds and surrounded by mist-clad pine slopes, the lake is a popular destination, and at the weekends you're likely to share the path with numerous families and groups of walkers. From the highway on the southern edge of town, follow the well-signed dirt road to the right of the garden centre, and keep going straight up. The hamlet just above the lake, reached after about ninety minutes, has sweeping views from Ahuachapán to Cerro Artillería on the Guatemalan border. The grassy slopes around the lake make a good spot for a picnic. Closer to town to the north, the smaller and less impressive **Laguna Las Ninfas** is an easy forest walk of about 45 minutes. Other outdoor options include horseriding tours; prospective guides usually gather around at 1a Avenida Nte at 4 Calle Ote, charging around US$5 per person. The town is also known for its *viveros*, or plant nurseries, and **Vivero Alexandro**, by the track up to Laguna Verde on the main road, will show you around, after which you can eat their strawberries in the cheaply priced on-site café.

Arrival and information

Exchange There is an ATM next to the Police station, two blocks north and one block east of the parque central.

Internet Turbonet on the far side of the parque from the tourist office (US$0.70/hr) lets you drink beers while doing your emails.

Tourist office It is literally an office, but there are some leaflets and a very helpful man at his desk. A kiosk, opposite, is manned at weekends.

Accommodation

Hostal Rural Las Orquídeas 4 C Pte between 1 Av Sur and Av Central ☏ 2433-0061. A well-signposted hostel at the north end of town with four clean, simple rooms and hot water. ③

Hostel Colonia 1a Av Sur by 6 C Pte ☏ 2433-0662. This pretty hotel does indeed have a colonial looking courtyard, but with sofas and hammocks in it. The rooms are good, with sturdy mattresses and en suite. ❸ – ❹

🏃 **Laguna Verde Guest House** Left at the school in the hamlet by Laguna Verde ☎7859-2865. In a magnificent position on the edge of the El Cuajusto Crater and a short walk from Laguna Verde, the "guest house" is in fact two delightfully remote structures: the white igloo with four bunks and a kitchenette is a good novelty, if a little damp-smelling, but the cabin is a better pick, with views down to Ahuachapán which are beautiful at night. No one lives on the site, so calling ahead is essential.

Eating

There is a nameless comedor next to the *tienda* on 1a C Pte. If you want your *típicos* cheap, this is the place to come. They do full cooked meals in the evening too.

🏃 **El Jardín de Celeste** Km 92.5 on the road to Ataco ☎2450-5647. Don't believe the hype: Ataco's renowned *La Cocina de mi Abuela* on 1a Av Nte is not what it once was and most now rate this hotel's restaurant to be the best around. It's not as expensive either, serving very well-prepared *típicos* like *pollo con arosa* as well as international dishes for under US$10, and with its own plant nursery on site, the surroundings are pretty good too.

Típicos Texizal 1a Av Nte. A brightly coloured and amiable restaurant, which has good daily meal offers for US$1.50 or bigger full meals for US$5 and tasty fried bananas for dessert.

Moving on

By bus to: Ahuachapán, stopping at Ataco (#249; twice hourly; 45min); Sonsonate, stopping at Nahuizalco (#249; twice hourly; 1hr 15min).

ATACO

Unlike its quiet neighbour, **ATACO** is full of vibrant life every day. Children play in the municipal basketball court on the square (they'll let you join in), older generations chat in the square and you'll see artisans at work throughout the town. Recently some good cheap accommodation and restaurants have emerged here, making it an up-and-coming destination.

What to see and do

Ataco is home to the artist "Axul", whose boldly coloured, manga-influenced painted illustrations of cats, moons and fish cover several buildings both here and in San Salvador. Her shop on the corner of 1a Avenida Nte and 1 Calle Pte sells canvases, masks, wooden figures and boxes painted in style for surprisingly little. She is also behind the Diconte Axul, on the corner of 2a Av Sur and C Centrale, which pools together the work of many local artists, along with general bric-á-brac. Tours of the surrounding area are available from the tourist booth at the entrance to town (see p.311) – the guides can take you to the swimming spots of the 50m Salto de Chacala as well as the upwelling of Chorros del Limo, the opposite of a waterfall, for around US$6 per person.

Arrival and information

By bus Buses come and go from beside the market on the corner of 2 C Pte & 4a Av Nte.
Tourist information There is a tourist kiosk, though it is only open on weekends from 7am until 7pm, at the entrance to town by the road out to Ahuachapán.

Accommodation

🏃 **Hostel Alepac** Southern end of 2a Av Sur ☎2450-5344. This new and exciting hostel is the town's first, with neat and comfortable dorms, as well as private rooms and camping, with tents provided. Amidst the eclectic decor is a very well-equipped kitchen, laundry and a TV with DVDs; the laid-back owner Alejandro wil sort tours for you too. Dorms ❷, doubles ❹
Posada Don Oli 1a Av Sur ☎2450-5155. Not bad at all for a second choice, this family-run hotel has swings in its pretty courtyard, hot water, and breakfast included. It's a better deal for four people who can all fit in one of the two rooms for $30. ❹

Eating

Doña Mercedes 2a Av Sur. A large, newly finished food hall with smart wooden tables that does an excellent range of *pupusas* for US$0.30 a piece and good *tortas* along with foreign beers.

Fonda y Vivero 1a Av Sur. A friendly and leafy restaurant that does good *típicos* in their open courtyard, including a great sausage and beans for $2.75.

El Portal Opposite the church. The ornate wooden doors and Maya artefacts seem to contrast sharply with the table-top cooker, but this is good quality *típicos* – the yucca fried in cinnamon is particularly good.

AHUACHAPÁN

From Apaneca the road tumbles down 13km or so to the city of **AHUACHAPÁN**. This area, and the lands further north, are some of the oldest inhabited regions of El Salvador, due in large part to the extremely fertile soil. Artefacts found in the region date back to 1200 BC and the early Maya. Ahuachapán is also one of the oldest Spanish settlements in the country, made a city in 1862, and like most towns in the area, its wealth grew from the coffee trade.

Today the city retains an air of peaceful charm, with tight streets and a quiet Parque Central. The main industry is geothermal electricity generation, at one time supplying seventy percent of the country's power, but the generator stations cannot be visited and like many of El Salvador's bigger cities, it is principally a springboard for surrounding attractions.

What to see and do

Confusingly, the **Parque Central** is not at the exact centre of town, but two blocks east of the intersection of the two main streets, Calle Gerardo Barrios and Avenida Francisco Menéndez. The latter and 2a Avenida Nte run parallel to each other from the bus terminal to the cathedral on the Parque.

The imposing white edifice of the **Iglesia Parroquia de Nuestra Señora de la Asunción**, on the Plaza Concordia, with good stained glass and a wooden ceiling, dominates the centre of the city and acts as the focus for the annual fiesta in the first week of February.

Some 5km east of town, near the hamlet of El Barro, are the **ausoles** (geysers) that form the basis of the local geothermal industry. The plumes of steam hang impressively over the lush green vegetation and red soil – particularly photogenic in the early-morning light. Access to the area is via the turn-off signed "Planta Geotérmica" on the road to Apaneca – get a pick-up or take the yellow school bus which leaves twice daily from the market. The plant itself is off-limits, but locals will allow you access to their land for a small fee, from where you can get a better view.

Arrival and information

By bus The terminal, a chaotic affair, is on Av Comercial, between C 10 and 12 Pte, eight blocks from the Plaza Concordia.

Tourist information There is no tourist office, but Tours & Aventuras (☎2422-0016) will tell you about things to do in the area while trying to sell you a tour.

Accommodation

Las Brisas del Mar On Laguna Espino ☎2443-0775. The local discoteca owner offers camping by the lake, with use of pool and hammocks. It is a pretty spot, and there is a restaurant on site too. ❷

La Casa Blanca 2a Av Nte at C Barrios ☎2443-1505, ⓦwww.casablancaahuachapan.com. A good value option, housed in a well-decorated colonial building with large, clean rooms, all with bath and TV. The restaurant is slightly overpriced but set around a relaxing courtyard. ❺

Hotel San José 6 C Ote ☎2443-0033. On the little plaza two blocks west from the bus station, this place has clean, recently refurbished en-suite rooms, though some are a little dark. ❹

Eating and drinking

Las Brisas del Mar On Laguna Espino ☎2443-0775. The best disco in town, which blares corny pop out over the lake, is actually 5km out of town, but call them and they will give you a free lift here, and back, from your hotel. It's really popular with the locals.

Casa Grande 4a Av Nte 2 There's plenty of character here, with loud music blaring and a standard menu featuring some game specialities including venison (*venado*) and rabbit (*conejo*) for under US$6.

La Estancia 1a Av Sur at C Barrios. Housed in a rather run-down former coffee mansion, this *comedor* has well-prepared *comida a la vista* at standard prices.

Mixta "S" 2a Av Sur by the Parque. A "mixta" is a flat bread stuffed with meat, cheese or vegetables, and that is what they do here for under US$2, as well as some fast food and a big selection of fruit juices.

Directory

Exchange Scotiabank is on the corner of C 4 Pte & Av Francisco Menéndez, with money exchange, traveller's cheque-cashing abilities and an ATM.

Internet Infocentros (US$1/hr), on C 3 Pte at 1a Av Nte, has a fast connection and headphones for web calls.

Pharmacy Farmacia Central, 2a Av Sur & C Barrios (☎2443-0158), will sort you out.

Post office There is a branch at C 1 Ote & 1a Av Sur (Mon–Fri 8am–5pm, Sat 8am–noon).

Supermarkets There are two supermarkets, De Todo and Despensa Familiar, by the bus terminal.

Telephones Telecom is at C 3 Pte & 2a Av Sur by the Parque.

Moving on

By bus to: Chalchuapa, for Tazumal (#210; frequent; 30min); Las Chinamas (#263; every 15min; 45min); Santa Ana (#202/#210; frequent; 1hr); San Salvador (#202; frequent; 3hr 30min); Sonsonate (#249; every 15min; 2hr 30min); Tacuba (#264/#15; three hourly; 40min).

AROUND AHUACHAPÁN

While the Ruta de Las Flores heads off to the east, there are also two great spots to the north and south. Tacuba, the southern one, is now the best point of entry to the dramatic Bosque El Imposible, and Tazumal, a short trip north, is one of the best Pipil sites in the country.

Tacuba

Fifteen kilometres west of Ahuachapán lies the quiet mountain village of **Tacuba**, reached via a winding and scenic road with grand views of coffee plantations and the Bosque El Imposible (see p.308). An important settlement existed here long before the Spaniards arrived, and the village retains strong folkloric traditions, although you'll only really notice these at fiesta time.

The town is small and welcoming, but the only thing to see is the ruins of the colonial church, which was much less ruined before the 2001 earthquake. Either the guard or Manolo of Imposible Tours (see box, p.315) will let you in to walk through and climb up the remaining structure. The real draw of Tacuba is, however, its back route into Bosque El Imposible and the outdoor activities it offers.

The mama and papa referred to at *Hostel Mamá y Papá*, 1 C 1 (☎2417-4268; dorms ❷, doubles ❸) are Mr and Mrs Gonzáles, parents of Manolo (see box opposite) and very good hosts. Hot showers, clean and comfortable rooms, coffees every morning and shady hammocks help, and the roof terrace is a nice place to watch the sunset with a beer. If this is full, *Miraflores* on 2a Av Nte (☎2417-4746; ❹) is bright and breezy and birds sing in the floral courtyard. Try to get an en-suite

INTO GUATEMALA: LAS CHINAMAS

From Ahuachapán, a reasonably good and very scenic road runs the 20km or so to the Guatemalan border, just past Las Chinamas. Local buses (#11AH) leave for the border every fifteen minutes, taking about an hour. International buses from Santa Ana also pass through at about 5.30am. There is no ticket office – stand on C 6 Pte more or less opposite the *Hotel San José* and flag them down. Buses run to Guatemala City from Valle Nuevo on the Guatemalan side.

IMPOSIBLE TOURS

Imposible Tours (ⓦ www.imposibletours.com), based in Tacuba, is without a doubt one of the best tour operations in the country, due in most part to good-humoured and charismatic leader Manolo Gonzáles, whose ceaseless enthusiasm for what he does comes from a genuine desire to get to know everyone he guides. Though the company's hallmark tour takes you along the back route to Bosque El Imposible along a series of occasionally staggering waterfalls, the set-up is flexible and you can work out what you want to do with him. Other ideas include mountain-biking along ridges to the coast, several day-treks and sitting in hot volcanic springs with a beer or two. Tours start from US$20 per person.

room – they are brighter and with two windows on the first floor. Rates include two meals. There is another good place to eat and drink opposite the hostel, as well as a few unextravagant *comedores* in town. Tacuba can be reached by bus (#264) or minibus (#15) every fifteen minutes from Ahuachapán, a journey of forty-five minutes.

Tazumal

Northeast from Ahuachapán, the road winds down onto a broad and scenic plain, and the town of **Chalchuapa**, whose main draw is the archeological site of **Tazumal** (Tues–Sun 9am–5pm; US$3) on the edge of town. The ruins over a period of 750 years, mostly during the Late Classic period (600–900 AD) are – by comparison with sites in Honduras and Guatemala – rather small, although they do have their own, impressive, beauty. Parts of the central and largest structure – a fourteen-stepped ceremonial pyramid, influenced by the style of Teotihuacán in Mexico and sadly rather sloppily restored – dating back to between 100–200 AD have been found beneath it. The Maya abandoned the city around the end of the ninth century, during the collapse of the Classic Maya culture, and, unusually, Pipils moved in and occupied the site, building a pyramid dating back to the Early Postclassic (900–1200 AD) and another pelota court, to the northwest corner of the site. Tazumal was finally abandoned around 1200 AD. A very

decent **museum** (same hours; Spanish only) displays artefacts discovered during excavations. The nearby ruins of El Trapiche and Casa Blanca are currently being excavated and aren't yet open to the public.

Bus #218 drops passengers off at a small plaza a few blocks from the centre of town; from here, walk uphill for about four blocks and follow the sign.

SANTA ANA

Self-possessed **SANTA ANA**, El Salvador's second city, lies in a superb location in the Cihautehuacán valley. Surrounded by green peaks, with the slope of Volcán Santa Ana rising to the southwest, the gently decaying colonial streets exude a certain bourgeois complacency and restrained, provincial calm that is generally only ruptured during the July fiesta, when a host of events bring the streets to life. It's a good place to relax, see the classiest Parque Central around and have a couple of nights out, though the natural attractions of Lago de Coatepeque, the forest reserve of Cerro Verde, and the Santa Ana and Izalco volcanoes all beckon.

What to see and do

Santa Ana's **town centre** is arguably the finest Parque Central in the country. The plaza itself is neatly laid out with a small bandstand, where people gather to sit and chat in the early evening, surrounded by eye-catching architecture.

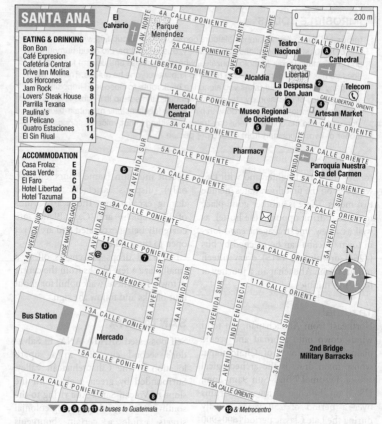

SANTA ANA

EATING & DRINKING	
Bon Bon	3
Café Expresion	7
Cafetéria Central	5
Drive Inn Molína	12
Los Horcones	2
Jam Rock	9
Lovers' Steak House	8
Parrilla Texana	1
Paulina's	6
El Pelicano	10
Quatro Estaciones	11
El Sin Riual	4

ACCOMMODATION	
Casa Frolaz	E
Casa Verde	B
El Faro	C
Hotel Libertad	A
Hotel Tazumal	D

0   200 m

El Calvario
Parque Menéndez
Teatro Nacional
Cathedral
Alcaldía
Parque Libertad
La Despensa de Don Juan
Telecom
Mercado Central
Museo Regional de Occidente
Artesan Market
Pharmacy
Parroquía Nuestra Sra del Carmen
Bus Station
Mercado
2nd Bridge Military Barracks
N

4A CALLE PONIENTE
2A CALLE PONIENTE
CALLE LIBERTAD PONIENTE
1A CALLE PONIENTE
3A CALLE PONIENTE
5A CALLE PONIENTE
7A CALLE PONIENTE
9A CALLE PONIENTE
11A CALLE PONIENTE
CALLE MÉNDEZ
13A CALLE PONIENTE
15A CALLE PONIENTE
17A CALLE PONIENTE

4A CALLE ORIENTE
CALLE LIBERTAD ORIENTE
1A CALLE ORIENTE
3A CALLE ORIENTE
5A CALLE ORIENTE
7A CALLE ORIENTE
9A CALLE ORIENTE
11A CALLE ORIENTE
15A CALLE ORIENTE

10A AV NORTE
2A AVENIDA NORTE
4A AVENIDA NORTE
2A AVENIDA NORTE
1A AVENIDA NORTE
3A AVENIDA NORTE
5A AVENIDA SUR

14A AVENIDA SUR
AV JOSE MATIAS DELGADO
10A AVENIDA SUR
8A AVENIDA SUR
11A CALLE PONIENTE
6A AVENIDA SUR
4A AVENIDA SUR
2A AVENIDA SUR
AVENIDA INDEPENDENCIA
3A AVENIDA SUR

▼ Ⓔ, Ⓨ, ⑩, ⑪ & buses to Guatemala   ▼ ⑫ & Metrocentro

Cathedral de Santa Ana

On the eastern edge of the Parque is the magnificent **Cathedral de Santa Ana**, an imposing neo-Gothic edifice completed in 1905. It's the second cathedral to occupy this site: a Spanish settlement was initially founded here in July 1569, when Bishop Bernardino de Villapando arrived en route from Guatemala. Commenting on the beauty and fertility of the area, he ordered work to begin on a church dedicated to Nuestra Señora de Santa Ana, the saint of the day of his arrival. Completed seven years later, this occupied the site of the present cathedral until it was destroyed in the early twentieth century to make way for the new building.

Inside the cathedral, the high naves, rather unsympathetically painted in pink and grey, soar upwards, and images – some dating back four hundred years – line the walls to the altar. Inset into the walls are plaques from local worshippers giving thanks to various saints for miracles performed.

Teatro Nacional

On the northern edge of the plaza, the **Teatro Nacional**, completed in Renaissance style in 1910, was funded by taxes on local dignitaries. Once the proud home of the country's leading theatre companies, the building became a movie theatre before falling into disuse. Now well-restored to something resembling its former glories, it once again hosts recitals and concerts, as well as exhibitions and plays. Check at the booth next to the entrance for upcoming dates.

Alcaldía

Facing the cathedral on the western edge of the plaza is the **Alcaldía**, another fine Renaissance-style piece of cream-coloured architecture – for writer Paul Theroux its facade possessed the "colonnaded opulence of a ducal palace." Although there is nothing to do in it, and for that matter nothing inherently ducal about it, the building is quite easy on the eyes.

Museo Regional del Occidente

On the second block down Avenida Independencia from the parque, the **Museo Regional del Occidente** (Tues–Sun 9am–noon & 1–5pm; US$0.35) provides a comprehensive introduction to the region's history and archeological sites, though the best bit is the room dedicated to the various evolving forms of legal tender in the country, right up to the dollar – it is a strangely exciting exhibit.

Arrival

By bus The main terminal is on 10a Av Sur between C 13 & 15 Pte. Buses for Metapán (#325) arrive and depart two blocks west of the main terminal, in front of the Despensa Familiar supermarket, and international buses to and from Guatemala arrive and depart from C 25 Pte between 6a & 8a Av Sur, just north of *Casa Frolaz*.

City transport

Buses Bus #51 runs between the centre and the bus terminal, and you can take any bus going up and down Av Independencia to get between the centre and the Metrocentro.
Taxis There are stands on the parque, outside the Metrocentro and on 10a Av Sur, by the market, or you can just hail one on the street. They should cost US$3–4, which you should politely agree beforehand.

Accommodation

The area around 8a and 10a Av Sur has the highest concentration of cheap and basic places to stay, codependent on the vice industry operating on the streets at night. Book ahead to get a spot in Casa Frolaz or Casa Verde.

Casa Frolaz 29 C Pte ☎2440-5302, ⓦwww.casafrolaz.com. One of the country's finest accommodation options is in the house of Javier Díaz, who by all accounts is descendant of one of the oldest families, a painter of international repute and certainly a perfect host. The lodging could be three times the price. Private kitchen, laundry, hot water and a fruit-filled garden. Camping ❶, dorms ❷, doubles ❸

Casa Verde 7 C Pte between 8a & 10a Av Sur ☎7860-7180. A new hotel and very good option close to the centre, and quite different from the standard of its neighbours. Spotless rooms on an open courtyard and really well-equipped kitchen. There are board games and a laundry machine and the young owners are keen and helpful. ❷

El Faro 14a Av Sur ☎2447-7787. Packets of sweet and savoury snacks await in these fairly clean rooms covered in bold murals. There is one good room with three double beds upstairs, hot water and a stained-glass balcony from where you can safely observe the vice below. The hotel is safe and secure, but you should not go out at night in the area alone. ❸

Hotel Libertad C 4 Ote at 1a Av Nte ☎2441-2358, ⓔjaval@navegante.com.sv. Great location right by the cathedral with gigantic, quite clean and basic rooms with TV, some with bathroom. There is free internet for guests. Bring your own padlock for the doors. ❸

Hotel Tazumal C 25 Pte & 10a Av Sur ☎2440-2830. Large rooms in an ageing building around a courtyard. Service is amiable and all rooms are en suite, some with cable TV, some with a/c. If both the *casas* are full, this is the next most pleasant in town. ❸

Eating

Santa Ana has a reasonable number of moderately priced places to eat. If you're desperate, there's fast food along Av Independencia, and in the Metrocentro.
Ban Ban Av Independencia Sur. The best bakery in town, with a second outlet in the Metrocentro, has sandwiches for lunch, and cake, pastries and coffee all day.

Café Expresión C 11 Pte between 6a and 8a Av Sur ⓦ www.expresion.com.sv. An arts and cultural centre, bookshop and internet café in bohemian surroundings. They do especially good sandwiches, as well as full meals (US$6–7) and desserts (US$2–3). Closed Sun.

Cafetéria Central 2a Av Sur between C 1 & 3 Pte. A good *comedor* for breakfast and cheap lunches. There's basic *comida a la vista* available, as well as excellent *pupusas* (US$1.50).

Lovers' Steak House 4a Av Sur & 17 C Pte ☎ 2440-5717. A huge meat grill and Santa Ana institution that serves huge portions of meat and seafood, accompanied by wine or beer, which will also be accompanied by a *bocadillo* (appetizer). Mains will cost around US$10, but you will surely be full when you leave.

Parrilla Texana C Libertad between 4a & 2a Av Sur. Meats served from the grill in a variety of combinations and forms in American diner-style decor. Though around the US$8 mark for a main course, the portions are large and the food good.

El Sin Rival C Libertad Ote. A cool place to chill out in the centre, this *sorbetería* serves small (US$0.50) and large (US$0.70) cones of sorbet – blueberry is the best of the original flavours. There are other branches in town.

> **TREAT YOURSELF**
>
> **Quatro Estaciones** 23 C Pte & 8a Av Sur ☎ 2440-3168. Unlike the other pricier options, this smart local favourite marks itself out by fine cooking rather than size of portion. It has an Italian influence with good bruschetta and spaghetti dishes accompanied by a fine wine menu and coffee selection. US$15–20 per head.

Drinking and nightlife

Much of Santa Ana's pretty decent nightlife is outside of the centre to the south, so get a taxi (US$3–4). Heading out, they're easily found on Av Independencia, on the way back, get the barman to arrange one.

Drive Inn Molina 25a Av Sur at Carretera Antigua ☎ 2447-5290. A little out of town and best accessed by taxi, this big and well-known nightspot has pool tables, live music and dancing. The best night to go is Thurs, but it's lively all weekend. Open from 11am until the early morning.

Los Horcones Next to the cathedral on Parque Libertad ☎ 2484-7511. The best views in the city, with seats on a rickety terrace facing the cathedral and plaza. There are drinks promotions on Sat, and things frequently kick off with some dancing by the tables.

Jam Rock Off the bypass south of town. This young and cool bar with regular and good live bands is *the* nightspot in Santa Ana at the moment. Beers are just US$1 and the atmosphere is very friendly.

Paulina's Av Independencia at C 7 Pte. Bar and restaurant with a variety of international meals for less than US$4 with a background of blaring music videos. Nicely furnished with log tables and chairs as well as a jukebox.

El Pelicano Av Moraga, 1km south of town ☎ 2449-0386. A small bar with good food, including over sixty appetizers (US$1.50–3), just three of which will fill you up. They play contemporary music and regularly host karaoke.

Entertainment

Cinema Cinemark, in the Metrocentro, shows dubbed or subtitled Hollywood blockbusters.

Theatre The beautifully restored Teatro Nacional (see p.259; ☎ 2447-6268) has a calendar of classical music, theatre and performance arts. Look out in the Friday *Prensa Gráfica* or stop by to find out times. Tickets should be under US$4 a show.

Directory

Exchange There is a clump of four or five banks around 2a Av Nte behind the Alcaldía, while Banco Cuscatlán is on the corner of C 3 Pte & Av Independencia.

Internet Time Out (open until 7 or 9pm; US$1/90min) is on 10a Av Sur by *Casa Frolaz*, while Infocentros, on Av Independencia between C 9 & 11 Ote, is near the centre (until 7pm; US$1/hr).

Market The Mercado Central is on 8a Av Sur between C 1 & 3 Pte, and the Mercado de Artesanías, with a range of national crafts, is on 1a Av Sur.

Post office The city's office is on Av Independencia between 7 & 9 C Pte (Mon–Fri 7.30am–5pm).

Supermarket La Despensa de Don Juan (8am–8pm), on the southeast corner of the park, has a good selection; there is also a bigger supermarket at the Metrocentro.

Telephones Telecom is on C Libertad at 5a Av Sur, just down from the Parque Central.

INTO GUATEMALA: SAN CRISTÓBAL LA FRONTERA

Crossing to Guatemala at San Cristóbal is quick and easy: open 24hr, it's free and there are frequent buses from Santa Ana (#36; 1hr) to the crossing. There are no official exchange facilities, but the touting moneychangers can offer reasonable rates. On the Guatemalan side, buses run to Asunción Mita, with connections to Guatemala City.

Moving on

By bus to: Ahuachapán (#210; frequent; 1hr); Chalchuapa (#218; frequent; 30min); Guatemala City, Guatemala (standard/first class; hourly/2 daily; 4hr/3hr 30min); Juayuá (#238; 6 daily; 1hr 30min); Lago de Coatepeque (#220; twice hourly; 1hr 30min); Metapán (#235; three hourly; 1hr 15min); Parque Nacional Los Volcanes (#248; 6 daily; 1hr 30min); San Cristóbal (#248; three hourly; 1hr); San Salvador (#201; frequent; 1hr 30min); Santa Elena, Belize via Flores, Guatemala (daily; 9hr); Sonsonate (#216/209; frequent; 1hr 15min/1hr 45min).

AROUND SANTA ANA

One of the best advantages to Santa Ana is its access to the volcano climbing and a crater lake as picturesque as you are ever likely to see to the southeast. As neither has particularly good accommodation, it's worth commuting for the day to each one.

Lago de Coatepeque

From El Congo junction, 14km southeast of Santa Ana, a winding branch road descends to the truly stunning crater-lake of **Lago de Coatepeque**. The views are so nice that it's worth getting off the bus at the *mirador*, 4km from the water's edge, so you can take your time soaking them in, and then walking down the rest of the way. As much of the shore is bounded by private houses, access to the water itself is difficult. **Boat rides** are available at *Turicentro Rancho Alegre* (in reality little more than a pier and a *comedor*), costing from US$3 per person for a thirty-minute trip to US$15 per person for a full circuit of the lake, with prices based on a group of four.

Accommodation on the lake is limited. If on a budget, there is a *Centro de Obreros* which is, of course, free so long as you have a permit from the Ministeros de Trabajo (see p.264). Bring a sleeping bag or sheets and mosquito repellent. The road leads on to the more comfortable *Hotel Torremolinos* (☎2441-6037, ✉hotel-torremolinos@gmail.com; ❹), with large, clean rooms, two pools and a small private beach. They also arrange boat trips, but rates are much higher than at Rancho Alegre. The *comedor* on the pier is pretty good, and nice and cheap; otherwise the restaurant in *Torremolinos* is the best around, and getting a meal could earn you the right to jump in the pool if you're not staying.

Buses #220 and #240 leave Santa Ana every thirty minutes for the lake, taking an hour and passing all points of interest mentioned. If you're heading back to San Salvador, take the Santa Ana bus as far as El Congo then walk down the slip road to the main highway and catch any bus running from Santa Ana to the capital.

PARQUE NACIONAL LOS VOLCANES

Around 14km southeast of Santa Ana on the Interamericana, a narrow road winds up from the El Congo junction through coffee plantations, maize fields and pine woods to the **PARQUE NACIONAL LOS VOLCANES** (daily 7am–5.30pm; US$1). Here the three volcanic peaks of Cerro Verde, Santa Ana and Izalco form a living example of geological evolution and offer great climbing and ecotourism opportunities.

What to see and do

The oldest volcano in the park, **Cerro Verde**, is now a softened, densely vegetated mountain harbouring a wealth of wildlife. **Santa Ana**, the highest volcano in the country at 2365m, has erupted out of its dormant state, whilst **Izalco**, one of the youngest volcanoes in the world, is an almost perfect, bare lava cone of unsurpassed natural beauty, and a very novel climb.

Volcán Cerro Verde

Dense forest fills the crater of the long-extinct **Volcán Cerro Verde**, inside of which a now-rare mix of Salvadoran flora and fauna combine, like a big bowl of nature soup. The numerous species of **plants**, include pinabetes and more than fifty species of orchid, are best viewed in season, while armadillos and white-tailed deer are shy and hard to see year-round. Agoutis, which look like tall guinea pigs, can be found rummaging in the forest floor, but it's the **birds** that are most regularly spotted. Hummingbirds and toucans are commonly seen, as is the shimmering green motmot (*torogoz* – El Salvador's national bird) identifiable by its pendulous tail. *Miradors* along the way overlook Volcán Santa Ana and, far below, Lago de Coatepeque.

From the car park (see below), go clockwise along the main trail, the *sendero natural*, for an enjoyable walk of around 45 minutes through the green calm of the forest. Smaller trails branch off through the trees if you want to explore. The trails are clear and very well managed, but can get busy at weekends.

Volcán Santa Ana

A path branches left from a signed turn ten minutes into the *sendero natural*, and leads eventually to the summit of **Volcán Santa Ana**, known also as "Ilamatepec" (Nahuat for "old lady mountain"). In October 2005 the old lady turned out to be a bit more vigorous than her name

suggests, erupting violently, killing two people in a a boiling mudslide that broke off down its side and spitting rocks, some the size of cars, in a one-mile radius. A second eruption was predicted, though has never materialized, and evacuated communities have long since moved back. Nonetheless, at the time of writing the trek to the top remained closed. If reopened, guided climbs will follow the same format as Volcán Izalco (see below); check with Corsatur (℡2243-7835) for an update. Some guides may offer to take you up through the woodlands and lava formation to the top, but as this involves hiding from the police, it is unadvisable.

Volcán Izalco

Sitting in contrast to the green slopes around it, the bleak, black volcanic pile of majestic **Volcán Izalco** began as a small hole in the ground in 1770. The volcano formed rapidly over the next two centuries, during which time its lava plume, known as the "lighthouse of the Pacific", was used by sailors to navigate. Then in 1966, just as a new hotel was built at its base, the plume dried up. Now guided tours leave daily at 11am from the car park for the steep climb to the top (3–4hr; US$1). The guides are compulsory, for your safety, set up in response to muggings. A marked trail leads from the lookout down for about thirty minutes to a saddle between Volcán Santa Ana and Volcán Izalco. From here it takes at least an hour to climb the barren moonscape of volcanic scree to the summit. Bring water and good shoes.

Arrival

Sonsonate-bound bus #248 runs directly to the car park (6 daily; 1hr 30min) from the Vencedora terminal in Santa Ana; catch the 8.30am departure if you want to catch the guides.

Accommodation

If you have your own tent, you can camp for free around the visitors' centre at the car park, though like most pitches in the country, there are no dedicated facilities, so bring food and water; ask a warden to tell you where to set up.

Moving on

The last bus from the car park leaves at 5pm and runs to El Congo only, from where you can pick up services to either Santa Ana or San Salvador.

METAPÁN

Forty kilometres north of Santa Ana, the small, friendly town of **METAPÁN** is scenically situated on the edge of the mountains of the Cordillera Metapán–Alotepeque, which run east along the border with Honduras. Metapán was one of only four communities that supported Delgado's first call for independence in 1811. With low-set, gently whitewashed buildings, it is one of the more pleasant of Salvadoran provincial towns, the market less unsightly than most and confined to the outskirts well away from the centre. The main reason for staying in Metapán, however, is for access to the international reserve of **Bosque Montecristo**, jointly administered by the governments of El Salvador, Honduras and Guatemala.

What to see and do

At the Parque Central, the **Iglesia de la Parroquia**, completed in 1743, is one of El Salvador's finest colonial churches, with a beautifully preserved facade. Inside, the main altar is flanked by small pieces worked in silver from a local mine while the ornately decorated cupola features paintings of San Gregorio, San Augustín, San Ambrosio and San Gerónimo. On the south side of the plaza, the colonnaded **Alcaldía** is an attractive building in its own right, watched over by two statues of jaguars symbolizing the strength and suffering of the indigenous people of the department. The west side, rather bizarrely, is formed by a concrete-grey football stadium, a hideous construction that somewhat ruins the ambience.

Arrival and information

By bus Buses arrive at the main terminal on the Carretera Internacional, five or six blocks from the centre down C 15 de Septiembre, which heads past the market and most of the hotels towards the centre.

Accommodation

Hotel California Carretera Internacional at 9 C Ote ☎2442-0561. Fans of new hotels will prefer to go a little further from the centre for these spotless en-suite rooms – arguably the best in town. ③
Hotel Central Av Isero Menendez ☎7535-6112. More basic, and cheaper, slightly creaky rooms are available here. It is not a bad choice though it is well cleaned and the beds are fine, but some may begrudge the lack of toilet seats. ②
Hotel Christina 4a Av Sur & C 15 de Septiembre ☎2442-0044. A nice hotel by the market which offers hot water, a/c and balconies over the street, supplies towels and has some lovely old furniture, although the beds are a little soft. ③–④

Eating

Antojitos La Nueva Esperanza Off the Parque on Av Benjamin Valiente. This lofty food hall in a colonial building is excellent, with seven dishes of *comida a la vista* a day (US$2–3). Open until 10pm at nights.
Casa de Teja Just off the north side of the Parque on Av 1a Nte. A new bar and restaurant with a well-procured collection of antique knick–knacks and well-prepared dishes like *mariscada* (US$6.50) and tacos (US$3). It's a good spot for a relaxed evening drink too.
Pastelería La Exquisita C 15 de Septiembre near *Hospedaje Central*. Best for breakfast, selling cakes and sweets as well as a small selection of lunches, all served by Osh-Kosh-wearing staff. Try a "Jennifer" – a cupcake that's so pretty you won't want to bite into it (US$1.50).

Directory

Exchange If you need to change money, there's a Banco Salvadoreño on the park and a Scotiabank at Av Ignacio Gomez and C 15 de Septiembre.
Internet Cyber Net, on the northeast corner of the park, is one of the best in the country, with a sofa and PlayStation as well as US$0.60 per hour connection.
Supermarket Near the bus terminal on Carretera Internacional is the Supermercado de Todo (7am–7pm).

Moving on

By bus to: Anguiatú and the Guatemalan border (#211A/#235; twice hourly; 30min); San Salvador (#201A; 6 daily; 2hr); Santa Ana (#235; three hourly; 1hr 30min).

AROUND METAPÁN

If you are not crossing the border yet, there is only one thing to see around Metapán: the beautiful Bosque Montecristo straddling the three countries of El Salvador, Honduras and Guatemala.

Bosque Montecristo

The brilliant **Bosque Montecristo** reserve rises through two climatic zones to the **Punto Trifinio**, the summit of Cerro Montecristo (2418m), where the borders of Honduras, Guatemala and El Salvador converge. The higher reaches of Montecristo, beginning at around 2100m, are home to an expanse of virgin **cloudforest**, with an annual rainfall of two metres and one hundred percent humidity. Orchids and pinabetes thrive in these climatic conditions, while huge oaks, pines and cypresses, some towering to over 20m, swathed in creepers, lichens and mosses, form a dense canopy preventing sunlight from reaching the forest floor. **Wildlife** abounds, with howler and spider monkeys the most visible mammals, and jaguars and other large mammals hiding out. **Birds** including hummingbirds, quetzals, toucans and the regional endemic bushy-crested jay are more easily seen. Walking straight to the summit is a truly rewarding climb of around four hours; the path from Los Planes leads through the cloudforest, however, and you can branch off in any direction – bring warm clothing and good footwear. Trails also lead from just below Los Planes to the peaks of Cerro el Brujo and Cerro Miramundo.

Arrival and information

The park entrance is 5km from Metapán. Pay the entrance fee (US$6 per person and US$1.50 per vehicle) here. After another 2km you come to the Hacienda San José, where the wardens are based and where you have to register. From here the road continues for another 14km before reaching Los Planes (1890m), where there is a small restaurant, camping area (no cost, but no equipment to rent; bring food and water), two new and simple cabañas sleeping up to eight each (US$35 per cabin) and an orchid garden.

Getting to Los Planes can be a little expensive, so try to get into a group of four and organize a taxi from around the Parque Central in Metapán (US$45 return). Alternatively, have a tour operator take you from San Salvador (US$30–50 per person; see p.264 for listings). Occasional pick-ups make the journey up for a negotiable fee; the best place to catch them is at the turning to the Bosque, by *Hotel San José* on the Carretera Internacional. You need to get permission to enter the Bosque in advance from the Ministerio de Medio Ambiente in San Salvador (☎2223-0444). Note that you're not allowed to enter on foot, and that the upper reaches of cloudforest are closed to visitors from May to October.

Honduras

BAY ISLANDS:
with a unique personality and world-famous diving,
these islands are the country's top destination
✪

COPÁN:
step back in time at
these spectacular
Mayan ruins
✪

LA MOSQUITIA:
an isolated and undisturbed
land, where nature still rules
✪

OLANCHO: ✪
tackle Honduras's most
stunning and challenging terrain

✪ **LAGO DE YOJOA:**
hide in caves, fly
over waterfalls, or just
enjoy the beautiful scenery

✪
GRACIAS:
one of the country's
oldest towns and the
gateway to the Parque
Nacional Celaque

ROUGH COSTS

DAILY BUDGET Basic US$30/
occasional treat US$45

DRINK Nacional beer US$1.50

FOOD *Almuerzo típico* US$2.75–5.25

CAMPING/HOSTEL/BUDGET HOTEL
US$2.75/US$4/US$5.25–11

TRAVEL Copán–San Pedro Sula
(140km) by bus: 3hr, US$5.25

FACT FILE

POPULATION 7.3 million

AREA 112,090 sq km

LANGUAGES Spanish, English in
the Bay Islands

CURRENCY Honduras Lempira (L)

CAPITAL Tegucigalpa (population:
1.7 million)

INTERNATIONAL PHONE CODE
☎504

TIME ZONE GMT –6

Introduction

All too often, Honduras receives short shrift on travellers' Central American itineraries: most visitors either race to see the Maya ruins at Copán or to the palm-fringed beaches of the Bay Islands, and skip the rest of the country entirely. And while these are two beautiful, worthy sights, there's much more to Honduras – from the wetlands of Mosquitia to the subtropical shore of the Golfo de Fonseca, this is a land of inspiring, often untouched natural beauty – and a longer visit will pay ample rewards.

Gradually, Honduras is waking up to its potential as an **ecotourism** destination – its network of national parks and preserves is extensive – and the potential benefits of an increased tourist infrastructure for the country's struggling economy (it's the second poorest country in Central America, with over of half of Hondurans living below the poverty line). The jewel in the crown Honduras's natural resources is the biosphere reserve of the **Río Plátano** in **Mosquitia**. Encompassing one of the finest remaining stretches of virgin tropical rainforest in Central America, the region is largely uninhabited and a trip here really does get you off the beaten track. On the Caribbean coast, **Tela** and **Trujillo** are good-sized towns with great beaches, while **La Ceiba**, a bit larger and with a thriving nightlife, is the departure point for the aforementioned **Bay Islands**, home to world-class diving and a rich cultural mix. Moving inland from the energetic city of **San Pedro**

Sula, the **Lago de Yojoa** region offers birdwatching, caves and a 43-metre waterfall, and the sparsely populated region of **Olancho** and the **Sierra de Agalta** national park has the most extensive stretch of virgin cloudforest in Central America. Meanwhile, colonial towns like **Santa Rosa de Copán** and **Gracias** offer fantastic restaurants, hot springs and access to indigenous villages. The capital, **Tegucigalpa**, is somewhat underwhelming, but is home to the best facilities and services in the country; while 100km south of the city lies the volcanic **Isla El Tigre**, a little visited but worthwhile getaway.

CHRONOLOGY

1000 BC Maya settlers move into the Río Copán valley.

100 AD Construction of the city of Copán begins.

426 AD Maya royal dynasty is founded. Copán, the civilization's centre for artistic and scientific development, controls area north to the Valle de Sula, east to Lago de Yojoa and west into present-day Guatemala.

WHEN TO VISIT

The climate in Honduras is generally dictated by altitude. In the central highlands, the weather is pleasantly warm in the daytime and cool at night. The hot Pacific and Caribbean coasts offer the relief of breezes and cooling rain showers, while San Pedro Sula and other lowland towns can be positively scorching in summer. Honduras's rainy season, "winter" (*invierno*), runs from May to November. In much of the country it rains for only a few hours in the afternoon, though along the northern coast and in Mosquitia rain is a constant feature year-round. October and November are the only months you might want to avoid in these parts: this is hurricane season.

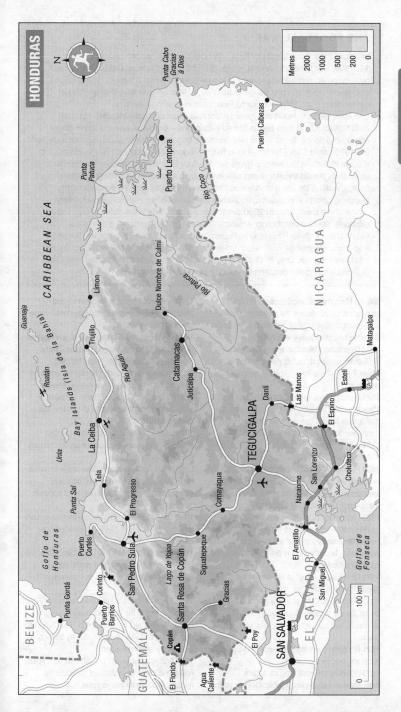

THE FOOTBALL WAR

In one of the more bizarre conflicts in modern Latin American history, on July 14, 1969, war broke out on the Honduras–El Salvador border. Ostensibly caused by a disputed result in a soccer match between the two countries, the conflict also stemmed from tensions generated by a steady rise in illegal migration of campesinos from El Salvador into Honduras in search of land.

In April 1969 the Honduran government had given settlers thirty days to return to El Salvador, and then begun forced expulsions – the result was the break-out of sporadic violence. In June, the two countries began a series of qualifying matches for the 1970 World Cup. The first game, held in Tegucigalpa, was won by Honduras, with a score of 1–0. At the second game (won 3–0 by El Salvador), held in San Salvador, spectators booed the Honduran national anthem and attacked visiting Honduran fans. The third, deciding match was then pre-empted by the El Salvadoran army bombing targets in Honduras, and advancing up to 40km into Honduran territory.

After three days, around 2000 deaths and a complete breakdown of diplomatic relations, the Organization of American States (OAS) negotiated a ceasefire, establishing a three-kilometre-wide demilitarized zone along the border. Tensions and minor skirmishes continued, however, until 1980, when a US-brokered peace treaty was signed. Only in 1992 did both sides finally accept an International Court of Justice ruling demarcating the border in its current location.

---

900 AD Maya civilization collapses, and Copán is abandoned. Lenca become the predominant indigenous group, settling in small, scattered communities and absorbing other indigenous cultures.

1502 Christopher Columbus arrives on the island of Guanaja, naming it "Isla de Pinos" (Island of Pines). First Catholic mass in Latin America is held on August 14.

1524 Hernán Cortés sends Cristóbal de Olid from Mexico to claim the isthmus in Cortes's name; the man arrives himself one year later, founds Puerto Cortés and Trujillo, then returns to Mexico.

1524–1571 Indigenous population declines from 400,000 to around 15,000.

1536 Pedro de Alvarado arrives from Guatemala to govern the territory. Lempira, a Lenca chieftain, amasses a 30,000-man force, which rebels against the Spanish. Comayagua is destroyed.

1539 Lempira is assassinated and the Spanish hold on Honduras is assured. Gold and silver are discovered in the country's interior and mining begins. The encomienda labour system is put in place, assuring social stratification.

1573 Comayagua, rebuilt, is designated the capital.

1800 With mines failing and droughts destroying agricultural harvests, the economy enters a crisis period. Society is deeply divided, and the country still has no national printing press, newspapers or university.

1821 Honduras gains independence from Spain, but is annexed by Mexico.

1823 Provinces of Central America declare themselves an independent republic. Civil war begins.

1830 Honduran Francisco Morazán elected president of Republic after defeating Conservative forces in Guatemala.

1839 Honduras and Nicaragua go to war against El Salvador. Morazán resigns, and the Central American Republic is essentially finished. Independence is not kind to Honduras' economy or infrastructure, and intense rivalry between Liberals and Conservatives keeps the country in an almost permament state of political and military conflict.

1876 Liberal Dr Marco Aurelio Soto is elected president. Improves infrastructure and encourages foreign investment.

Late 1800s Banana industry develops with arrival of US fruit companies, which gain control of national infrastructure; private interests dominate government.

1932 Tiburio Carías Andino elected president, rules as virtual dictator until 1948, but does balance economy.

1954 Banana Strike: 35,000 United and Standard Fruit workers stop work; as a result, labour unions are legitimized and labour protection laws drafted.

1956 A coup in October introduces the military as a new element in the country's hierarchy of power. Civilian government is reinstated in 1957, but a new constitution that year gives the military the right to disregard presidential orders.

1963 Another coup brings Colonel Oswaldo López Arellano to power as provisional president; he remains in power for twelve years.

1969 So-called "Football War" breaks out on the Honduras–El Salvador border (see box opposite).
1975 The "Bananagate" scandal (the payment of over $1 million to government officials by United Brand in return for reductions on export taxes) forces López to resign in April. Under his successors – all high-ranking military officials – the country becomes even more stratified.
1981 Honduras becomes focus for US-backed Contra war in Nicaragua; relationship between military and government grows closer; human-rights violations rise.
1989–1998 Following US withdrawal, economy collapses completely, but power is slowly wrested back from the military.
1998 Hurricane Mitch hits Honduras, killing over 7000. President Carlos Flores declares Honduras has been set back fifty years.
2001 Ricardo Maduro of the conservative National Party ends Liberal Party rule. He works to crack down on gang-related crime and encourage tourism post-Mitch.
2005 Manuel Zelaya of the Liberal Party of Honduras is elected.
2006 Honduras signs the Central America Border Control Agreement (CA-4), allowing tourists to travel freely between Honduras, Guatemala, El Salvador and Nicaragua for up to ninety days.

Basics

ARRIVAL

Visitors **flying** to Honduras have their choice of airports. The three most commonly used are: **Toncontín International (TGU)**, outside Tegucigalpa (allegedly one of the most dangerous airports in the world, for its difficult runway); **Ramón Villeda Morales International (SAP)**, southeast of San Pedro Sula; and **Juan Manuel Gálvez International (RTB)**, on Roatán. All three are served by direct flights from other Central American capitals, as well as North American (namely Miami, Houston and Atlanta) and South American destinations. Iberia also offers a direct flight from Madrid to San Pedro Sula.

You can enter Honduras by **land** from Guatemala, El Salvador and Nicaragua (see box below). International services such as Tica Bus (ⓦwww.ticabus.com) do long-haul trips from other Central American cities, but you can also travel via slower, cheaper local transport. If you do come by local bus, you'll have to disembark, cross the border on foot and change buses on the other side. The only water routes to Honduras are from Belize.

VISAS

Citizens of Australia, Canada, Japan, New Zealand, the UK, the US and most European countries do not need visas for stays in Honduras of up to ninety days. **Tourist cards**, given on entry, are good for stays of between thirty and ninety days. The card is a yellow slip of paper that needs to be returned when

LAND CROSSINGS AND SEA ROUTES TO BELIZE

Honduras has land borders with Guatemala, El Salvador and Nicaragua, and sea crossings with Belize.

For Guatemala, there are three crossings. The most frequently used is at El Florido for Copán Ruinas (see p.366); there is also a crossing at Agua Caliente (p.356) for Esquipulas and one at Corinto–Entre Ríos (see p.376), which connects Puerto Cortés and Puerto Barrios.

El Salvador has two crossings: El Amatillo (p.345) for eastern El Salvador, and El Poy for western El Salvador (p.356).

There are three crossings for Nicaragua. The easiest is Las Manos (see p.343), for Tegucigalpa; the others are at El Espino (see p.345) and Guasaule (see p.436).

For Belize, there are weekly skiffs from Puerto Cortés to both Placencia and Dangriga (see p.375).

you leave, or stamped if you extend your stay.

Honduras is part of the CA-4 border control agreement (see p.48), which means you can move freely within Honduras, Guatemala, El Salvador and Nicaragua without completing entry and exit formalities at immmigration checkpoints. Immigration officials at the first point of entry will determine the length of stay, which can be up to ninety days. If you wish to stay longer in any of the four countries you'll need to request a one-time extension of stay from local immigration authorities or travel outside the CA-4 countries and reapply for admission to the region.

GETTING AROUND

The primary means of transport for budget travellers in Honduras will be the buses, though to reach the popular Bay Islands you will need to invest in a flight or take a boat.

By bus

Bus services in Honduras are fairly well organized, with frequent departures from the main transport hubs of Tegucigalpa, San Pedro Sula and La Ceiba, as well as a network of local services. These local, or **"chicken" buses** (refurbished old American school buses) are the cheapest, and probably the most fun, but also get

packed and stop frequently, so can be quite slow. In addition to the local buses, on the longer intercity routes there's usually a choice of services, with an increasing number of luxurious air-conditioned **express buses** (*ejecutivos* or *lujos*) plus comfortable services with a few scheduled stops (*directos*). **Fares** are extremely low on most routes, at around US$0.80 an hour or less, though they can triple on some of the really smart services – travelling between Tegucigalpa and La Ceiba can cost as much as US$18. The express buses (for example, Hedman Alas and El Rey) need to have tickets bought in advance when possible; if you are getting on at smaller destinations the conductor will come through and collect the fare. The frequency of buses slows down considerably after lunch, so you should try to be at your final destination by 4pm when possible, to avoid getting stranded.

By car

If your budget will stretch, **renting a car** can open up the country's more isolated areas. Including insurance and emergency assistance, **rates** start at around US$58 a day for a small car, and US$90 for larger models and 4WDs. The highways connecting the main cities are well looked-after, but the numerous dirt roads in the highlands can be impassable at certain times of the year, so

ADDRESSES IN HONDURAS

As in most of the rest of Central America, Honduras's major cities are mainly laid out in a grid, with a park or plaza at the centre. Here calles run east–west, and avenidas north–south. In some towns, such as Santa Rosa de Copán, street names are followed by the designation "NO", "NE", "SO" or "SE" (northwest, northeast, southwest and southeast respectively), depending on their location around the central park. Note that smaller towns (including Copán) don't have street names, so addresses tend to be given in terms of landmarks. Exact street numbers tend not to exist anywhere; a city address written in the Guide as "C 16, Av 1–3", for example, means the place you're looking for is on Calle 16, between avenidas 1 and 3, while "Av 1, C 11–13" means it's on Avenida 1, between calles 11 and 13.

always seek local advice on conditions before starting out. Rental agencies can be found at the airports in San Pedro Sula, Tegucigalpa and Roatán as well as in San Pedro Sula and Tegucigalpa towns.

Taxis operate in all the main towns, tooting when they are available. Meters are nonexistent, so always agree on a price before getting in. Expect to pay US$1.75–2.25 for a city ride in Tegucigalpa or San Pedro, while in smaller towns the standard fare is around US$0.65. For safety, use taxis at night in the bigger towns.

Hitching is very common in rural areas, and generally safe. Keep an eye out for pick-up trucks with lots of people in the back, and stick out your thumb. You're expected to offer payment at the end of the ride, usually the same as the bus fare. Use common sense and don't hitch if alone.

By air

Internal **flights** in Honduras are very affordable. A small number of domestic airlines offer competitive fares, with frequent departures between Tegucigalpa and San Pedro Sula, La Ceiba and the Bay Islands. A one-way ticket between Tegucigalpa and San Pedro costs around US$45, while La Ceiba to Utila or Roatán is US$28 and La Ceiba–Palacios around US$40. There's a **departure tax** of US$3 for internal flights and US$27 for international flights.

By boat

Boats are the most budget-friendly option when it comes to reaching the Bay Islands. The *MV Galaxy 11* runs between La Ceiba and Roatán (1hr; US$16), while the *Utila Princess* runs to Utila (1hr; US$22). There are no scheduled services between the islands – you have to go via La Ceiba.

ACCOMMODATION

That Honduras is slowly waking up to tourism is reflected in the country's **accommodation** options. The larger cities – Tegucigalpa, San Pedro Sula – offer the widest range of places to stay, with something to suit all budgets. **Hostels** are beginning to spring up across the country, generally representing excellent value for money; Copán has two of the best budget hostels on the mainland. Of the Bay Islands, Utila is the cheapest and Roatán has a few places catering to backpackers, while Guanaja is aimed more at luxury tourists. On the mainland, US$5 (❶) gets you a basic room; US$10 (❷) and above will secure a well-furnished room, with extras such as TV, a/c and hot water. A twelve-percent tax is occasionally added to the bill. Usually the only time you need to **reserve** in advance is at Semana Santa or during a big local festival, such as the May Carnival in La Ceiba.

The only formal provisions for **camping** are at Omoa, Copán Ruinas and in some of the national parks. Elsewhere, pitching a tent is very much an *ad hoc* affair. If you intend to camp, make sure you ask permission from the landowner. Tempting though they may seem, the North Coast beaches are not safe to be on after dark and camping here is highly inadvisable.

See p.35 for an explanation of the accommodation price codes used in this Guide.

FOOD AND DRINK

Budget travellers can eat very well in Honduras. The best way to start the day is with a *licuado*, a sort of fruit smoothie. Many places mix them with bananas and cornflakes, so they're very filling. Most towns have **markets** where you can also pick up a huge amount of fresh produce. With an eye on your budget, you'll find that eating a big **lunch** is a better option than waiting for dinner. Market areas tend to be where you will find the cheapest *comedores*, where typical *almuerzos* of rice, beans, tortillas and meat can be had for around L50. The larger cities have a decently wide range of **restaurants**, including an increasing number of fast-food chains. On the whole, you'll pay L100 for a decent-sized lunch at a restaurant. The ever-popular Chinese eateries routinely have portions big enough for two. Most shops and facilities close from noon to 2pm so that families can enjoy lunch together

Honduran dishes to try include **anafre**, a fondue-like dish of cheese, beans or meat, or a mixture of all three, sometimes served as a bar snack, and **tapado**, a rich vegetable stew, often with meat or fish added. The north coast has a strong Caribbean influence with lots of seafood. **Guisado** (spicy chicken stew) and **sopa de caracol** (conch stew with coconut milk, spices, potatoes and vegetables) should both be sampled at least once. Probably the most common street snack, sold all over the country, is the **baleada**, a white-flour tortilla filled with beans, cheese and cream; two or three of these constitute a reasonable meal. Turtle eggs are widely sold on the coasts, but should obviously be avoided.

Drink

Licuados or **batidos** are a mix of fruit juice and milk. **Tap water** is unsafe to drink; bottled, purified water is sold everywhere and many hotels have water machines. The usual brands of **fizzy drink** are ubiquitous; the city of Copán also has its own *Copán Dry*, which comes in a few flavours.

In terms or alcohol, Honduras produces five brands of **beer**: Salvavida and Imperial are heavier lagers, Port Royal slightly lighter and Nacional and Polar very light and quite tasteless. **Rum** (*ron*) is also distilled in the country, as is the Latin American rotgut, **aguardiente**. Adventurous connoisseurs of alcohol might wish to try **guifiti**, an elixir of various plants soaked in rum, found in the Garífuna villages of the north coast.

CULTURE AND ETIQUETTE

Catholicism is the main **religion** in Honduras, and with it comes traditional values and roles. Family is very important, and children tend to grow up and settle close to their parents. (Increasingly, however, Honduran youngsters are going to the US in order to send back some money.) Anti-homosexual attitudes are prevalent, and while not illegal, public displays of affection are frowned upon.

Hondurans are very friendly, and, on the whole, are glad to have visitors in their country and keen to tell you about where they come from. Greeting shop assistants is polite, and in smaller towns a simple "buenos días" can win you new friends in no time. Of Honduras's population, 85–90 percent are *ladino* (a mix of Spanish and indigenous people). The rest of the country is a mixture of **ethnic minorities**. Prominent groups include the Maya Chorti in the department of Copán; the Lenca, with their traditional clothing, found along the *Ruta Lenca* in the area around Santa Rosa de Copán; and the Miskitos in La Mosquitia, many of who work as guides for the ever-increasing numbers of tourists.

A ten percent **tip** is the norm for waiters and tour guides, but is not expected in taxis.

HONDURAN EXPRESSIONS AND PHRASES

bola a dollar
jalón a pick-up

SPORTS AND OUTDOOR ACTIVITIES

The largest spectator sport in Honduras is **football**, and the Honduran national league (ⓦ www.lina.hn) and the major European leagues are all keenly followed. Olimpia and Motagua from Tegucigalpa, Marathón and Real España from San Pedro Sula and Victoria from La Ceiba are the biggest teams and usually pull in a fairly decent crowd. David Suazo, currently playing for Inter Milan, is one of the nation's favourite sons and you can't go very far without spotting him on a billboard or in a newspaper headline. **Tickets** never need to be bought in advance, as most games don't come anywhere near to being sold out.

With a number of national parks – most of which have accommodation and/or camping and well-marked trails – Honduras is a fantastic place to **hike**. Parque Nacional Celaque, with the highest peak in the country, is a great place to start. For water lovers, the Bay Islands offer some of the cheapest places in the world to take PADI **diving** certification courses; both the diving and the **snorkelling** are excellent. For the more sedentary, Lago de Yojoa (see p.349) has **fishing** and **birdwatching** trips.

COMMUNICATIONS

There are **post offices** in every town; letters generally take a week to the US and up to two weeks to Europe.

Opening hours are usually Monday to Friday 8am to noon and 2pm to 5pm, Saturday 8am to 1pm.

International **phone** calls can be made from Hondutel offices (there's a branch in every town), but are very expensive to Europe (around 44L/min) – you are much better off visiting an internet café with web-phone capabilities. Most Hondutel offices sell "Telecards", which have access codes on the back, and can also be used at any payphone. Local calls are very cheap, and can be made at payphones; regular local phone numbers have seven digits. If you are staying in Honduras for an extended period it is worth visiting an office of **mobile phone** provider Claro (the largest provider in Latin America) to see if your phone will accept a foreign SIM card; if your phone won't take one of their cards, new mobiles start at around L500.

Internet cafés can be found in most towns, and some hotels have internet available for guests; the average price is L20 per hour.

CRIME AND SAFETY

On the whole, Honduras is a safe place for tourists. Government crackdowns on "mara" (gang) culture have drastically reduced the amount of gang-related crime in recent years, and the installation of tourist police in towns like Tela has had a positive effect on crimes against tourists.

HONDURAS ON THE NET

ⓦ www.honduras.com The country's official website – unsurprisingly, one of the best general websites on Honduras.

ⓦ www.hondurastips.honduras.com The definitive guide to the country, also published as an irreplaceable monthly magazine (available free in hotels) detailing all the sights and latest developments of interest to tourists.

ⓦ www.letsgohonduras.com The website of the Instituto de Turismo offers a good introduction to the main attractions and numerous organized tour packages.

ⓦ www.marrder.com/htw The website of *Honduras This Week*, the country's only English-language newspaper.

ⓦ www.travel-to-honduras.com General site covering a range of subjects – everything from business and tourism to Spanish schools and volunteer work.

Travel in rural areas is generally an exercise in mutual trust and respect; in urban areas, however, **street crime** is a concern. Take the usual precautions, and try to avoid walking around at night. The Comayagüela district in Tegucigalpa, particularly around the market, and the streets south of the old railway line in San Pedro Sula are both considered highly dangerous after dark. Along the North Coast it's not advisable to walk alone on the beach at night. The regular **police**, though separate from the armed forces, are unlikely to be of much help if something does happen, but any incidents of theft should be reported for insurance purposes (see box below for contact numbers).

MEDICAL CARE AND EMERGENCIES

The Honduras Medical Centre, Av Juan Lindo in Tegucigalpa, is considered one of the best **hospitals** in the country; in San Pedro Sula head for the Hospital Centro Médico Betesda, Av 11a NO between C 11a & 12a NO. Facilities in rural areas tend to be much more limited, though most towns have at least one **pharmacy**, and staff tend to be very helpful. In general, it's worth trying to learn a little emergency Spanish, as English is not widely spoken. Pharmacists can issue prescriptions.

Honduras has one of the highest rates of AIDS in Central America, so it is especially important to take all the usual precautions when it comes to sex. Make sure, too, if you seek medical help that all instruments are sterilized.

EMERGENCY NUMBERS

☎ 195 Cruz Roja (Red Cross)
☎ 197 International operator
☎ 198 Fire
☎ 199 Police (☎ *199 from a mobile)

STUDENT AND YOUTH DISCOUNTS

ISIC cards qualify students for discounts at a handful of hotels and restaurants across Honduras. Check ⓦ www.isic.org for more information.

MONEY AND BANKS

Honduras's currency is the **lempira** (L), which consists of 100 centavos; at the time of writing, the exchange rate was 18.85L to US$1. Coins come as 1, 2, 5, 10, 20 and 50 centavos and notes as 1, 2, 5, 10, 20, 50, 100 and 500 lempiras. In heavily touristed areas – Copán, the Bay Islands – US dollars are widely accepted, but on the whole lempiras are the standard currency.

You will need **cash** for day-to-day expenses. Acceptance of foreign **debit cards** in ATMs can be a hit-and-miss affair. Make sure before you leave home that your PIN is four digits or less; your card will be rejected if it is longer. As a rule Visa is more widely accepted than other cards. Visa cardholders can also get cash advances in several banks, including Banco Atlántida; MasterCard is sometimes accepted but not to be relied upon.

Honduras has a number of national **banks**, of which the biggest are Banco Atlántida, Banco de Occidente and BAC/Credomatic. Most banks change **traveller's cheques** – American Express is the most widely accepted brand. When cashing traveller's cheques you will often be asked to show proof of purchase receipts and your passport. Banks in larger towns are generally open 8.30am–4.30pm and until noon on Saturdays, while those in smaller towns shut for an hour at lunch.

INFORMATION AND MAPS

The national tourist office, the **Instituto Hondureño de Turismo** (ⓦ www.letsgohonduras.com) is fairly helpful. The main office, in the Edificio Europa in Tegucigalpa (see p.338), can provide general **information** about where to go and what to see in the country. They also have booths at the Tegucigalpa and San Pedro Sula airports, and a free information service in the US (☏800/410-9608). Most towns you'll visit will have a municipality-run tourist office. These vary in helpfulness; the better ones sell maps, can arrange homestays and can tell you the cheapest places to stay. **National parks** and reserves are overseen by the government forestry agency, **COHDEFOR** (🌐www.cohdefor.hn). If you intend to spend much time in any of the parks, it's worth visiting one of their offices for detailed information on flora and fauna.

Honduras Tips, a free magazine found in the better hotels and tourist offices, has the most up-to-date information on hotel listings and bus routes – it is updated every few months. The magazine also has maps of most towns in the country.

The best **map** of Honduras is published by a German company, Reise Know-How (🌐www.reise-know-how.de), and can be purchased online or in any reputable booksellers; unfortunately, the chance of finding it in Honduras is unlikely.

OPENING HOURS AND PUBLIC HOLIDAYS

Business hours for **shops** are generally Monday to Friday 9am to noon and

PUBLIC HOLIDAYS

Jan 1 New Year's Day
March/April Semana Santa: Thursday, Friday and Saturday before Easter Sunday
April 14 Day of the Americas
May 1 Labour Day
Sept 15 Independence Day
Oct 3 Birth of Francisco Morazán
Oct 12 Discovery of America
Oct 21 Armed Forces Day
Dec 25 Christmas Day

2pm to 4.30 or 5pm, and Saturday from 9am to noon. **Museums** often stay open at lunch, but close for at least one day each week – this varies depending on the museum. On public holidays, almost everything closes.

FESTIVALS

Honduras's calendar is full of **festivals**, everything from small local events to major national parties. The following are just a few highlights.

February Pilgrims flock to Tegucigalpa to worship and celebrate the Virgen de Suyapa.
April Punta Gorda celebrates the arrival of the Garífuna (April 6–12).
May La Feria de San Isidro or Carnaval in La Ceiba, during the week leading up to the third Saturday. Festivities culminate in a street parade through the city centre, followed by live music until the early morning.
June San Pedro Sula holiday (June 29).

Tegucigalpa and around

Situated 1000m above sea level, deep in a mountain valley, the Honduran capital of **TEGUCIGALPA** is not, at least on first impression, the most welcoming city. The winding, narrow streets are thick with motorized traffic, and the sidewalks full to the gills with shoppers and loafers. This said, unlike other capital cities in the region, Tegucigalpa isn't totally without charms, and its colonial feel and cool climate actually make it an ideal starting point to allow you to get to grips with the Honduran pace of life.

Tegucigalpa's first mention in records is in the 1560s, when silver deposits ("tegucigalpa" means "silver mountain" in the Nahuatl language) were found in the hills to the east. It was given town status in 1768, and named a city in 1807. With wealth from the country's mines pouring in, the city's location at the centre of key trade routes became highly advantageous, and Tegucigalpa soon rivalled the then capital, Comayagua. In 1880, the Liberal President Soto officially shifted power to Tegucigalpa, and in 1932 Comayagüela became a part of the capital. Since then, the nation's economic focus has shifted to San Pedro Sula, but Tegucigalpa continues to function as the nation's political and governmental centre.

Surrounded by reminders of its past – crumbling colonial buildings and decaying nineteenth-century mansions – the city today is a vibrant, noisy place. A handful of churches and a fantastic new museum, as well as some smaller quirkier ones, will easily keep you entertained for a day or two. Given a little time, you'll see Tegucigalpa has a lot to offer.

What to see and do

The heart of Tegucigalpa's **old city** is the pleasant **Plaza Morazán**; a number of interesting churches and museums, plus many hotels, lie within easy walking distance of the square. East from the centre, two major roads, Avenida Jeréz (which becomes Avenida Juan Gutemberg and then Avenida La Paz) and Avenida Miguel Cervantes (changing its name to Avenida República de Chile), skirt the edges of **Colonia Palmira**, an upmarket district that is home to most of the capital's foreign embassies, luxury hotels, restaurants and wealthy residences. The **US embassy** lies along Avenida Juan Gutemberg about thirty minutes' walk from Plaza Morazán. Another landmark, the modern **Hotel Honduras Maya**, is on the Avenida República de Chile, just south of Colonia Palmira, fifteen minutes' walk east from the centre. A kilometre beyond the Hotel, an overpass gives access to eastward-bound **Boulevard Morazán**, Tegucigalpa's major commercial and entertainment artery. For some reason no city buses run along here, so you'll have to walk or take a taxi.

Running west from Plaza Morazán, the pedestrian-only **Calle Peatonal** is lined with shops, cafés and the fabulous new Museo para la Identidad Nacional (see p.338). Further west of the old centre, the character of the city rapidly becomes more menacing as you approach the banks of the Río Choluteca. Cross one of the bridges and you're in **Comayagüela**, always a poor barrio but now distinctly threatening after dark. Save for the **market**, the only reason to pass through is to change buses.

Plaza Morazán

Plaza Morazán is at the centre of life for most people who live and work in the capital. Shaded by a canopy of trees, and populated with shoe-shiners and other vendors, it's an atmospheric,

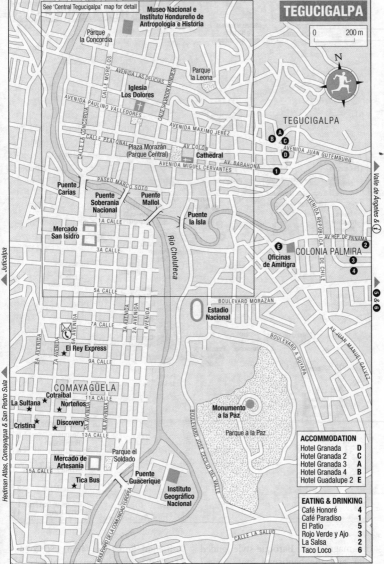

See 'Central Tegucigalpa' map for detail

Museo Nacional e
Instituto Hondureño de
Antropología e Historia

TEGUCIGALPA

0   200 m

N

Parque
la Concordia

AVENIDA LAS DELICIAS

Parque
la Leona

CALLE MORELOS

CALLE MORAZÁN

CALLE SALVADOR MENDIETA

Iglesia
Los Dolores

TEGUCIGALPA

AVENIDA PAULINO VALLEDORES

AVENIDA MAXIMO JEREZ

B A
C

AVENIDA JUAN GUTEMBURG

CALLE LA CONCORDIA

CALLE PEATONAL

AV COLON

D

Plaza Morazán
(Parque Central)

Cathedral

AVENIDA MIGUEL CERVANTES

AV. BARAHONA

1

Valle de Ángeles & ⓘ

PASEO MARCO SOTO

AVENIDA REPUBLICA

Puente
Carías

Puente
Soberanía
Nacional

Puente
Mallol

Puente
la Isla

1A CALLE

AV. REP. DE PANAMA

2

Mercado
San Isidro

Río Choluteca

3A CALLE

E

Oficinas
de Amitigra

COLONIA PALMIRA

DE CHILE

3

4

5 & 6

Juticalpa

5A CALLE

BOULEVARD MORAZÁN

Estadio
Nacional

7A CALLE

3A AVENIDA

2A AVENIDA

1 AVENIDA

BOULEVARD A SUYAPA

8A AVENIDA

7A AVENIDA

6A AVENIDA

El Rey Express

9A CALLE

AV. JUAN MANUEL GALVEZ

COMAYAGÜELA

Cotraibal

11A CALLE

Hedman Atlas, Comayagua & San Pedro Sula

La Sultana

Norteños

Cristina

Discovery

13A CALLE

5A AVENIDA

4A AVENIDA

Monumento
a la Paz

BOULEVARD JOSÉ CECILIO DEL VALLE

Mercado de
Artesanía

15A CALLE

Parque el
Soldado

Parque a la Paz

Tica Bus

Puente
Guacerique

Instituto
Geográfico
Nacional

BOULEVARD DE LA COMUNIDAD EUROPEA

CALLE LA SALUD

ACCOMMODATION
Hotel Granada   D
Hotel Granada 2   C
Hotel Granada 3   A
Hotel Granada 4   B
Hotel Guadalupe 2   E

EATING & DRINKING
Café Honoré   4
Café Paradiso   1
El Patio   5
Rojo Verde y Ajo   3
La Salsa   2
Taco Loco   6

HONDURAS

TEGUCIGALPA AND AROUND

if not particularly peaceful, place – definitely good for some people-watching. A **statue** at the centre of the square commemorates national hero Francisco Morazán, a soldier, Liberal and reformer who was elected president of the Central American Republic in 1830. On the east edge of the plaza, the recently refurbished facade of the **Catedral San Miguel**, completed in 1782, is one of the best preserved in Central America. Inside, look out for

335

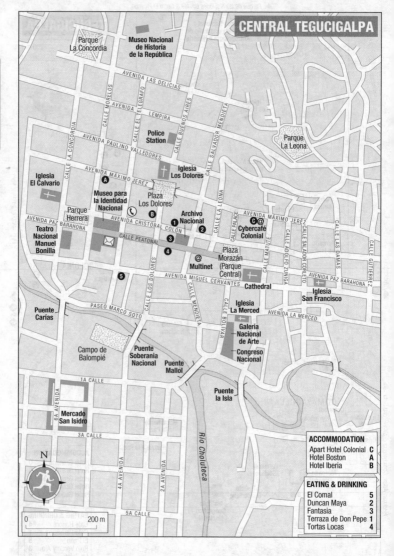

CENTRAL TEGUCIGALPA

ACCOMMODATION

Apart Hotel Colonial	C
Hotel Boston	A
Hotel Iberia	B

EATING & DRINKING

El Comal	5
Duncan Maya	2
Fantasia	3
Terraza de Don Pepe	1
Tortas Locas	4

the magnificent Baroque-style gilded altar and the baptismal font, carved in 1643 by indigenous artisans from a single block of stone.

Museo para la Identidad Nacional

The permanent exhibition at the excellent new **Museo para la Identidad Nacional**, on Calle Peatonal (Tues–Sat 9am–5pm, Sun 10am–4pm; L50; ☎238 7412/7395) focuses on the history of Honduras. Starting with the geographical formation of Central America, the displays move chronologically through the Maya civilization and colonial era to the various post-colonial presidents and their influence on the country. The museum's highlight is a 3D tour (Tues–Sat 10am, 11.30am, 2pm & 3.30pm,

Sun 11.30am & noon) of Copán that recreates how the Maya kingdom would have looked at the height of its power. Though all signage is in Spanish, there are English-speaking guides.

Iglesia San Francisco
Three blocks east of the museum, on Avenida Paz Barahona, the **Iglesia San Francisco** is the oldest church in the city, first built by the Franciscans in 1592, although much of the present building dates from 1740. No longer a functioning church, these days it houses a museum dedicated to the Honduran armed forces (Mon–Fri 8am–4pm; free). It's worth stepping into for a while if you're a fan of all things military, though the signage is all in Spanish.

Galería Nacional de Arte
Just south of the Parque Morazán and next to the Iglesia La Merced on Calle Bolívar, the **Galería Nacional de Arte** (Mon–Sat 9am–4pm & Sun 9am–1pm; L25) is home to an extensive and interesting collection of Central American art. Displays on the ground floor range from prehistoric petroglyphs and Maya stone carvings to religious art, while rooms upstairs house an ambitious selection of modern and contemporary Honduran art, including some works by Pablo Zelaya Sierra, one of the country's leading twentieth-century artists. Originally serving as a convent during the seventeenth century, and later as the national university, the building's Neoclassical facade sits rather uncomfortably alongside the stained concrete hulk of the **Congreso Nacional**, the country's seat of government next door.

Iglesia Los Dolores
A couple of blocks northwest from the central plaza, the pleasant, white, domed **Iglesia Los Dolores**, completed in 1732, sits next to the small **Plaza Los Dolores**. Its Baroque facade is decorated with a representation of the Passion of Christ,

featuring a crowing cock and the rising sun; inside, the elaborate gold altar dates from 1742. The plaza itself is crowded with cheap, shabby stalls.

Museo Nacional de Historia de la República
Two blocks west of Iglesia Los Dolores, a right turn onto Calle Morelos takes you on a fairly steep fifteen-minute walk to the Villa Roy, formerly a presidential mansion and now home to the **Museo Nacional de Historia de la República** (Mon–Sat, 8am–4pm; L20). The small but comprehensive exhibition within covers the political, economic and social development of the republic, alongside a display of less interesting presidential artefacts. Outside in the car park you can see five presidential limousines from various administrations: each one is progressively more luxurious. A block west off Calle la Concordia is a welcome patch of green, the **Parque La Concordia**, dotted with replicas of Maya sculptures.

Cerro El Picacho
To the north of Plaza Morazán, older suburbs – previously home to the wealthy middle classes and rich immigrants, now long gone – edge up the lower slopes of **Cerro El Picacho**. At the top, in the **Parque Naciones Unidas El Picacho**, stands the open-armed **Cristo del Picacho**, illuminated at night in a dazzle of coloured lights. Grab a picnic and escape to the park for fantastic views over the city. Take the El Hatillo bus from the corner of Calle Finlay and Calle Cristobal; it's a twenty-minute ride or L100 taxi fare.

Comayagüela
The brown waters of the polluted Río Choluteca form the border of Tegucigalpa's twin, **Comayagüela**, which sprawls away through down-at-heel business districts into industrial areas and poor barrios. There's little to see and the streets, invariably choked with

traffic, have a much less relaxed feel than those of Tegucigalpa proper. The stalls of **San Isidro**, the city's main **market**, jostle for space along the narrow alleys and pavements, sometimes spilling over into the streets themselves, and buses crawl through the crowds, often only inches from the vendors. The atmosphere is hot and frenetic, and often pungent with the scent of raw meat. Most stalls sell workaday produce, so there's not much to draw you here, but it is certainly a spectacle. Mind your possessions while walking around. For the market, cross at the Puente Carías bridge from Calle Morelos. An undeniably rough edge permeates the place at night, and even the inhabitants of Tegucigalpa prefer not to venture out here after dark.

Arrival and information

By air Toncontín International Airport is 7km south of the city. Taxis wait outside the terminal, but hailing one 50m down the highway will save you a couple of dollars. Bus #24 also passes the airport, running through Comayagüela and Tegucigalpa.
By bus There is no main bus station, with the result that each international or intercity bus line has its own terminal, most of them scattered around Comayagüela. For listings, see p.341. If travelling at night or alone it's best to take a taxi to your drop off point.
Tourist information The Instituto Hondureño de Turismo, in the Edificio Europa at Av Ramon Cruz and C República de México (Mon–Fri 8.30am–4.30pm; ☎ 222 2124 or toll-free in Honduras ☎ 800/222 8687, ✉ tourisminfo@iht.hn), provides maps of the country and major cities, as well as information in English on the country's main attractions. AMITIGRA, Edificio Italia at Av República de Panamá, Col Palmira (☎ 235 8494, ✉ amitgra @sigmanet.hn), provides access and entry information on the Parque Nacional La Tigra.
Travel agent Alhambra Travel (☎ 220 1700) in the *Hotel Honduras Maya*, Av República de Perú and C 3, is quick, friendly and efficient.

City transport

Buses Old US school buses run the urban routes, usually 6am–9pm. Route names and numbers are painted on the front and fares are L5 anywhere within the city. Pay your fare on the bus. Unfortunately, no buses pass close to Plaza Morazán or indeed Boulevard Morazán, but any bus signed "San Miguel" runs past the US Embassy.
Taxis Taxis are usually white with numbers painted on the side. A short ride within the city costs about L50 during the day, a little more at night. *Colectivo* taxis gather at predetermined stops (*puntos*); the most central one is on C Palace just north of Plaza Morazán. They generally leave when full with passengers going to a similar area of the city. Though you may have to wait around a bit, they are cheaper than standard taxis, costing around L10 per person.

Accommodation

As the national capital, Tegucigalpa's accommodation is pricier than other areas of Honduras. Although budget accommodation is available in Comayagüela, solo travellers are best off staying elsewhere, while others should stay in the area only as a last resort. If your budget will stretch, it is worth spending a little more for the extra comfort and safety.
Hotel Boston Av Máximo Jeréz 321, between C El Telégrafo and C Morelos ☎ 237 9411, ☎ 237 0186. Spotlessly clean en-suite rooms in a good location near Iglesia Los Dolores. The elegant communal TV area and inexhaustible supplies of hot water and free coffee make it a good deal. The large, old rooms at the front are nicer, despite the traffic noise. ④
Hotel Granada Av Juan Gutemberg at Av Cristóbal Colón ☎ 237 2381, ✉ hotelgranadategus@yahoo .com. Consistently popular budget option with basic but clean rooms, some with bath, plus hot water and a communal TV area. Better rooms have TV and en-suite bathroom. Ask for a room away from the street. ④
Hotel Granada 2 (☎ 222 0597, ☎ 237 0841) and **Hotel Granada 3** (☎ 238 4438, ☎ 237 0843), opposite each other on Subida Casa Martín, just off Av Juan Gutemberg. Similar to and just round the corner from the original *Hotel Granada*. All rooms at these hotels, including triples and quadruples, have private bath. Keep valuables locked away. ④.
Hotel Granada 4 Facing *Granada 3* ☎ no phone. The newest and nicest of all the *Granada* hotels. All rooms have TV and private bath, and internet is available in the entrance area (L20/hr). Rooms facing the street are a bit noisy. ⑤
Hotel Guadalupe 2 Av Juan Manuel Galvez 324 ☎ 238 5009/2958. Popular with Peace Corps volunteers, this hotel has 14 rooms all with

private hot-water baths. Communal areas have comfy sofas. ❹

Hotel Iberia Plaza los Dolores ☎ 237 9267. Rooms are basic but fine if you just need somewhere to crash at night. They're in a good location, and have nice communal areas, but no a/c and hot water is only available 6–8am. ❸

Eating

The centre boasts all the usual fast-food chains and cheap and cheerful café-style eateries, as well as a few good-value restaurants with meals under L100; nicer restaurants are to be found out in Colonia Palmira and along Blvd Morazán. Supermarket La Colonia, just south of the Parque, has a wide selection of canned and packaged goods for self-catering.

Cafés

Café Honore Av 1 B, off Av República de Panamá. Busy café where the young and trendy come to lunch on the best choice of sandwiches in town (half-baguette L115, whole L195). Continental ham-and-cheeses are on the menu as well as for sale at the on-site deli.

Café Paradiso Av Paz Barahona 1351. Great arty place to grab a quick snack – try the fantastic apple cake or a croissant – or lunch (set lunch L80). Open until 10pm, they also host film nights and live music on Fri.

El Comal On the corner of Av Miguel Cervantes and C Morelos. Small café with wooden tables and chairs selling breakfasts for L30, *almuerzos* for L36 and burritos for L23. Mon–Fri 7am–3pm.

Fantasia C Peatonal, halfway between Plaza Morazán and C Morelos. This bakery sells freshly made bread and a large selection of beautifully decorated cakes; filled rolls go for L19.

Taco Loco Blvd Morazán. Grab a handful of tacos (three plus drink L82) at this simple, open-kitchen Mexican snack bar. Delivery is also available. Open until 11pm.

Tortas Locas C Peatonal, halfway between Plaza Morazán and C Morelos. Booths line the walls of this Mexican fast-food restaurant serving up good-value lunches and breakfasts. Special combos for two from L30. Menu of the day under L100.

Restaurants

Duncan Maya Av Cristóbal Colón, two blocks west of Parque Central. Busy barn of a place, popular with the after-work crowd, who come for the large helpings of local food, burgers and snacks (all less than L100).

El Patio Far eastern end of Blvd Morazán. Typical Honduran restaurant offering traditional dishes in massive, good-value portions – try "El Conquistador", a breathtakingly enormous steak. This is a great place to introduce yourself to home-cooked Honduran cuisine (L200–300).

Rojo, Verde y Ajo Av 1 B, off Av República de Panamá. A reasonably priced restaurant with an international menu heavy on Mediterranean cuisine. The English-speaking staff is friendly and portions are large enough for you to feel that you've spent your money wisely. Most mains are under L300. Closed Sun.

La Salsa Av República de Panamá. Classy and civilized, this upmarket buffet-style lunchtime restaurant is a favourite with local VIPs. The terrace has views of the city and the Cristo de Picacho monument. Amazing salads, fresh juices (with refills) and cheesecake. Meat, rice and salad L120. Open for lunch only.

La Terraza de Don Pepe Av Cristóbal Colón 2062. On two floors above a fried-chicken shop, this restaurant is nice and airy. Serving up local dishes like chicken, beans and rice, the *menu del 3ra planta* is only L70. The top floor also hosts karaoke on Fri nights.

Drinking and nightlife

Most bars in the centre are fiercely local hangouts, so you're best off heading to Colonia Palmira and Boulevard Morazán. Clubs and bars here go in and out of fashion; for the most up-to-date tips ask at the tourist office and check *Honduras Tips*. Use taxis when going about at night.

Bars

Café Paradiso Av Paz Barahona 1351. Popular
with local artists, this is a great place to kick off the
evening (it's only open until 10pm), with film nights
mid-week and live music on Fri.

El Patio Blvd Morazán. Locals fill this place (not to
be confused with the restaurant of the same name)
for football games. Bar snacks are served with
drinks, but a full menu is also available. Live music
is often organized. Beers L35.

Sabor Cubano Opposite *Rojo, Verde y Ajo*. With
Cuban and Caribbean beats the music of choice,
this is the place to come for some Latin dancing.

Clubs

Bambu Blvd Morazán. The place to be on a Wed
night, *Bambu* draws in tourists, students and
volunteers with ridiculously cheap drinks. Open
Mon–Sat from 8pm. L120 entrance with ID; women
free on Wed.

La Grotta In the Colonia San Carlos. This upscale
disco is popular with the younger crowd. Full international bar and a selection of tropical cocktails.

Entertainment

Cinema The modern Multi Plaza complex (see
below) on Blvd Morazán has a cinema showing
subtitled Hollywood blockbusters for L60.

Sport The Estadio Nacional, at the western end
of Blvd Morazán, hosts international and domestic
football games.

Theatre The Teatro Nacional Manuel Bonilla
is 15min west of Parque Morazán along Calle
Peatonal; ask at the box office (☎ 222 4366) inside
for details of current shows.

Shopping

Books Metromedia, on Av San Carlos after
C Republica de Mexico, has a wide range of English-
language fiction, nonfiction and travel titles, as well
as used books and US newspapers and magazines.

Food and drink La Colonia supermarket, south of
the Plaza on C Bolívar, carries everything you need
to make lunches, as well as toiletries and alcohol.

Malls Multi Plaza, Av Juan Pablo 11, has everything
you could need, with international shops like Diesel,
Paul Frank and Mango; a huge food court with the
usual fast-food chains; and a cinema. Tigo and
Claro stores here also sell SIM cards and mobile
phones.

Markets San Isidro in Comayagüela sprawls
around Av 6 and C 1. Go in a group and keep an eye
on your things.

Directory

Exchange Virtually all banks will change dollars
and traveller's cheques. Banco Atlántida, on Plaza
Morazán (with 24hr ATM) and elsewhere, gives
advances on Visa cards, while Credomatic,
C Mendieta at Av Cervantes, gives both Visa and
MasterCard advances.

Embassies Belize, ground floor of *Hotel Honduras
Maya*, Av República de Perú and C 3 (Mon–Fri
9am–1pm; ☎ 238 4616); Canada, Edificio Finan-
ciero Banexpo 3, Col Payaqui, Blvd San Juan
Bosco (Mon–Fri 9am–3pm; ☎ 232 4551); Costa
Rica, Residencial El Triángulo, 1a Calle, Casa 3451
(Mon–Fri 8am–3pm; ☎ 232 1768); El Salvador,
Colonia Altos de Miramontes, Casa 2952, Diagonal
Aguan (Mon–Fri 8.30am–noon & 1–3pm; ☎ 232
4947); Guatemala, Colonia Lomas de Guijarro
(Mon–Fri 8.30am–3pm; ☎ 231 1543); Mexico,
Colonia Lomas del Guijarro, Av Eucalipto (Mon–Fri
8–11am; ☎ 232 0141); Nicaragua, C 11, Block M1,
Colonia Lomas del Tepeyac (Mon–Fri 8.30am–1pm;
☎ 232 1966); Panama, Edificio Palmira 200, Colonia
Palmira (Mon–Fri 8am–1pm; ☎ 239 5508); UK,
Centro Financiero Banexpo 3 piso, Colonia Payaqui
(Mon–Thurs 8am–noon & 1–4pm, Fri 8am–3pm;
☎ 232 0612); US, Av La Paz (Mon–Fri 8am–5pm;
☎ 236 9320).

Immigration Dirección General de Migracíon,
on Av La Paz, near the US Embassy (Mon–Fri
8.30am–4.30pm).

Internet Cybercafé Colonial, on Av Máximo Jeréz
behind the Parque (daily until 9pm; L18/hr);
Multinet, east end of C Peatonal (Mon–Fri 8.15am–
7.45pm, Sat 8.30am–7.30pm & Sun 9am–5.45pm;
L18/hr and calls L1/min to the US and L2–3 to
Europe).

Laundry Super Jet, Av Juan Gutemberg after
Parque Finlay, offers a reliable laundry service
and dry-cleaning charged by the item (Mon–Sat
8am–5pm).

Medical care Emergency departments (24hr) are
at Hospital Escuela, Blvd Suyapa (☎ 232 6234), and
Hospital General San Felipe, C La Paz by the Bolívar
monument.

Police Go to the FSP office on C Buenos Aires,
behind Los Dolores church, with any problems.

Post office C Peatonal at C El Telégrafo, 3 blocks
west of the main plaza (Mon–Fri 8am–7pm, Sat
8am–1pm). Window 1 on the ground floor deals
with the *lista de correos*.

Moving on

Travellers do leave Tegucigalpa via plane (mostly
for international destinations and the Bay Islands),

but buses are the most common way to reach other parts of the country.

By air

Flights to: La Ceiba (1 daily with Isleña); Roatán (via La Ceiba; 3 daily with Isleña); San Pedro Sula (2 daily with Isleña); Utila (via La Ceiba with Atlantic Airlines). All flights leave from Toncontín International Airport, 7km south of the centre.

By bus

Tegucigalpa does not have a central bus terminal. Instead, each bus company has its own office and bus stop – most are in Comayagüela. It's best to get a taxi if travelling from and to Comayagüela late at night.

Bus companies and stops

Cotraibal (C) Direct services to Trujillo depart from Av 7, C 11–12, Barrio Concepción. Information on ☏ 237 1666.

Cristina (CR) Direct services to La Ceiba depart from Av 8, C 12–13, Barrio Concepción. Information on ☏ 220 0117.

Discovery (D) Normal services to Juticalpa depart from Av 7, C 12–13. Information on ☏ 222 4256.

Discusa Litena (DL) Direct services to El Paraíso (for Nicaragua) depart from Contigo al Mercado Jacaleapa. Information on ☏ 230 2939.

El Rey (ER) Normal services to Comayagua, La Guama and San Pedro Sula depart from Av Centenario opposite Casa Jaar. Information on ☏ 237 1462.

El Rey Express (RE) Direct services to San Pedro Sula depart from Barrio Concepción. Information on ☏ 237 8561.

Hedman Alas (HA) Direct and luxury services to La Ceiba and San Pedro Sula depart from Av 11, C 13–14. Information on ☏ 237 7143.

King Quality (KQ) Luxury services to Guatemala City (Guatemala), Managua (Nicaragua) and San Salvador (El Salvador) depart from Blvd Comunidad Económica Europea, La Guanaja. Information on ☏ 225 5415.

La Sultana (LS) Normal services to Santa Rosa de Copán depart from Av 8, C 11–12. Information on ☏ 237 8101.

Mi Esperanza (ME) Luxury and normal services to Choluteca depart from C 23–24, Barrio Villa Adela. Information on ☏ 225 1502.

Norteños (N) Normal services to Comayagua, La Guama and San Pedro Sula depart from C 12, Av 6–7. Information on ☏ 237 0706.

Royeri (R) Normal services to Choluteca depart from C 23–24, Barrio Villa Adela. Information on ☏ 225 2863.

Tica Bus (TB) Luxury services to Guatemala City (Guatemala), Managua (Nicaragua), Panama City (Panama), San José (Costa Rica) and San Salvador (El Salvador) depart from C 16, Av 5–6, Barrio Villa Adela. Information on ☏ 220 0579.

Viana Clase Oro (V) Luxury services to La Ceiba and San Pedro Sula depart from Blvd Fuerzas Armadas. Information on ☏ 239 8288.

Domestic bus destinations

Choluteca With luxury ME (daily 6am, 10am, 2pm, 6pm); with normal ME (hourly 4am–6pm); with R (1–2 hourly 4am–5.45pm); 3hr 30min.

Comayagua With N (every 30min 6am–2.30pm); with ER (2 hourly 3am–7pm); 2hr.

Copán Ruinas Buses go via San Pedro Sula (see p.370).

Juticalpa With direct D (hourly 6.15am–4.15pm); with normal D (hourly 6.45am–5pm); 2hr 30min.

La Ceiba With CR (7 daily 5.45am–3.30pm); with HA (daily 5.45am, 10am, 1.30pm); with V (daily 6.45am & 2.30pm); 5hr 30min–7hr.

La Guama (for Lago de Yojoa) With N or ER, as per departures for San Pedro Sula.

San Pedro Sula With ER (1–2 hourly 3am–7pm); with HA (hourly 6.30am–5.30pm); with N (1–2 hourly 6am–2.30pm); with RE (1–2 hourly 6.30am-6.30pm); with V (Mon–Fri & Sun 6.30am, 1.30pm, 3.30pm, 6.15pm, Sat 6.30am, 9.30am, 1.30pm, 3.30pm); 3hr 30min. Take San Pedro Sula-bound buses for Lago de Yojoa (ask for La Guama), Copán Ruinas and Tela.

Santa Rosa de Copán With LS (daily 6am, 7.30am, 8.30am, 10am); 7hr.

Siguatepeque With N or ER, as per departures for San Pedro Sula; 2hr.

Tela Buses go via San Pedro Sula (see p.370)

Trujillo With C (daily 7.30am; 5hr 30min); 9hr.

International bus destinations

Guatemala City (Guatemala) With KQ (daily 6am & 1pm); with TB (daily 6am, with overnight in El Salvador).

Managua (Nicaragua) With KQ (daily 6am & 1pm); with TB (daily 9.15am; 8hr).

Panama City (Panama) With TB (daily 9.15am, with overnight in Managua and San José).

San José (Costa Rica) With TB (daily 9.15am, with overnight in Managua).

San Salvador (El Salvador) With KQ (daily 6am & 1pm); with TB (daily 5.30pm; 7hr).

AROUND TEGUCIGALPA

Though Tegucigalpa isn't as bad as it might be, chances are you'll want to escape the city pretty quickly – luckily, there are several places a short bus ride away where you can while away an afternoon or even a day or two. The famous Basílica de Suyapa takes only twenty minutes to reach, or for a really adventurous couple of days you can take yourself off to Valle de Ángeles for a morning before going on to the Parque Nacional La Tigra to hike amid the flora.

Basílica de Suyapa

Six or so kilometres east of Tegucigalpa's centre, the monolithic white bulk of the **Basílica de Suyapa** rises from the flat plains. Built in the 1950s, it is home to the **Virgen de Suyapa**, patron saint of Honduras. The statue of the Virgin was discovered by two *campesinos* in 1743. The story goes that after bedding down for the night, one of them noticed he was lying on something, but without looking to see what the offending object was, threw it to one side. Within a few minutes, however, the object had returned. The next day, the two carried the little statue down to Suyapa where, placed on a simple table adorned with flowers, the Virgin began to attract worshippers.

Today you can see the tiny statue (it's only 6cm tall) behind the wooden altar in **La Pequeña Iglesia**, the original eighteenth-century chapel behind the Basílica. According to legend, each time she is placed in the larger Basílica, the Virgin mysteriously returns to the simple chapel, built by Captain José de Zelaya y Midence in thanks for the recovery of his health. City **buses** to Suyapa run regularly from the Mercado San Isidro in Comayagüela (20min).

Valle de Ángeles

Continuing east, the road rises gently amid magnificent scenery, winding through forests of slender pine trees. Twenty-three kilometres from the capital is **Valle de Ángeles**, a former mining town now reincarnated as a handicraft centre and scenic getaway for *capitalanos*. Surrounded by forested mountains, the small town slumbers during the week, then explodes with activity on the weekends. If you're looking for souvenirs, the town is chiefly noted for its quality carved wooden goods. Numerous small shops around town sell crafts, and it's a nice place to while away a couple of hours. For **food**, *El Asado* opposite the municipality building is a quaint restaurant with a pleasant balcony where you can get a fantastic *almuerzo* for around L100.

Buses leave Tegucigalpa for Valle de Ángeles from an open lot near the San Felipe Hospital (every 45min until 6pm; 1hr) and terminate a couple of blocks from the town's Parque Central. Walk back down to the main road for return buses to Tegucigalpa; the last leaves at 5.30pm.

Parque Nacional La Tigra

The oldest reserve in Honduras, **Parque Nacional La Tigra** (daily 8am–2pm; US$10) was given protected status in 1952 and designated a national park in 1980. Only 22km from Tegucigalpa, its accessibility and good system of trails make it a popular destination; however, much of the original cloudforest has been destroyed through heavy logging, so what you see is generally secondary growth. Parts of the park still shelter oak trees, bromeliads, ferns, vines, orchids and other typical cloudforest flora, along with **wildlife** such as deer, white-faced monkeys and ocelots – though they tend to stick to parts of the park that are out of bounds to visitors. Though you can visit the park as a day-trip, if you want to see everything it's worth staying a couple of nights.

The park has two entrances. The western side is reached via the village of **Jutiapa**, 17km east of Tegucigalpa. Though slightly easier to reach from the capital, this entrance has few facilities.

INTO NICARAGUA: LAS MANOS

The Las Manos border crossing, some 120km from Tegucigalpa, is the most convenient place to enter Nicaragua from the capital. Buses run to the town of El Paraíso (Discusa Litena; hourly 6am–6pm; 2hr 15min), 12km from the border, from where minibuses and pick-ups shuttle to the border every thirty minutes or so. With an early enough start, it's possible to reach Managua (see p.416) the same day. Taxi drivers hawking for business may well tell you that no buses run to the border from El Paraíso, but this is not true. However, if you don't want to wait around for one of the buses, a taxi will cost you about US$2.75.

The border post itself is a collection of huts housing the immigration and customs officials. Both sides are open daily until 5pm and crossing is generally straightforward. There are no banks, but eager moneychangers accept dollars, lempiras and Nicaraguan córdobas. There's a US$0.50 exit tax to leave Honduras. On the Nicaraguan side, trucks leave every hour for Ocotal, from where you can pick up buses to Estelí and Managua.

Take the El Hatillo bus from the corner of Calle Finlay and Calle Cristóbal; it's a fifty-minute ride. The second entrance is best reached via the village of San Juancito, to which direct buses run from Mercado San Pablo, Barrio El Manchen (3 daily; 2hr) or from Valle de Ángeles (daily 7am, 11am, 3pm; pick-ups are also available). From San Juancito it is a steep 5km hike up the mountain to the visitors' centre; pick-ups are sometimes available to make the trip for around L250. The visitors' centre has accommodation for US$15 and the friendly warden is usually around to answer questions and provide trail maps. Guides (US$8.50 per day) are also available, though they only speak Spanish. The trails are well laid-out, and provide some easy hiking, either on a circular route from the visitors' centre or across the park between the two entrances.

Southern Honduras

Stark, sun-baked coastal plains stretch south from Tegucigalpa all the way to the Pacific Ocean. Though a world away from the clean air and gentle climate of the highlands, this region is nonetheless beautiful of its own accord, defined by a dazzling light and ferociously high temperatures. Traditionally a poor region, it's also a little-visited one, with the foreigners who do pass through usually in transit to Nicaragua or El Salvador. If you're really looking to get off the gringo trail, this is the place to do it.

The chief attraction in the area – and well worth a visit – is Isla El Tigre, a volcanic island set in the calm waters of the Golfo de Fonseca, while the colonial city of Choluteca offers a change of pace from the frenzy of the capital and makes a convenient stopover on the route to Nicaragua.

The main transport junction in this part of the country is the village of Jícaro Galán, at the intersection of Highway CA-5 and the Carretera Interamericana, some 70km south of Tegucigalpa. Buses stop here to exchange passengers before continuing west to the border with El Salvador at El Amatillo, 42km away (see box, p.345), or east to Nicaragua.

ISLA EL TIGRE

Boats depart the fishing village of Coyolito, on the coast of the Golfo de Fonseca, southwest of Jícaro Galán, for the volcanic ISLA EL TIGRE, whose conical peak rises sharply against the sky across the sparkling water. With good beaches, calm waters and constant sunshine, the island is an ideal spot to hide away for a couple of days.

What to see and do

The island's only town is **Amapala**, once the country's major Pacific port and now a decaying relic of the nineteenth century. Looking up from the dock, ageing wooden houses cluster along the hillside, while the newly restored church in the **Parque Central** shows signs of the island's desire to get on the tourist map. Nontheless, during the week there's every chance you'll be the only visitors on the island.

An 18-kilometre road runs all the way around the island, giving access to some glorious deserted **beaches**; it takes four or more hours to walk the whole thing, or you can take one of the moto taxis that hang around the end of the dock in Amapala (around L300 for a one-way trip around the island). A 45min walk east from the Parque Central takes you to **Playa del Burro**, where you can while away the afternoon people-watching – children and taxi drivers play football on the beach before cooling off in the sea. **Playa Negra**, ten minutes west of the plaza, is a pretty volcanic sand beach, while the popular **Playa Grande** is backed by rows of *comedores* serving freshly barbecued fish at the weekend.

From the southern side of the island there are stunning **views** across the gulf to Volcán Cosiguina in Nicaragua, and in some places to Isla Meanguera and mainland El Salvador. The island's peak can be climbed in a steep and very hot two- to three-hour **walk**; ask for directions to the start of the trail, about fifteen minutes' walk southwest of Amapala.

Arrival and information

By boat From Coyolito regular launches (1am–6pm; 15min) run to Amapala's dock, a small jetty with a new tourist office.

By bus Juanche buses from Tegucigalpa's Mercado Zonal Belen run directly to Coyolito, but departures are infrequent. Mi Esperanza runs a more reliable service to Choluteca, dropping you off at Jícaro Galán on the Carretera Interamericana, marked by a Dippsa fuel station. From here local buses wait on the highway to take the slow but beautiful road to Coyolito; the last stop is a few steps away from the dock.

Exchange There's no ATM on the island, but the Depósito, a large warehouse building on the road facing the pier, can change cash dollars.

Internet Available in a small building on the south side of the Parque Central (8am–noon & 2–5pm; L20/hr); it's dial-up and can be very slow.

Tourist information The helpful staff at the new tourist office on the pier (Mon–Fri 8am–noon, 2–5pm, Sat 8am–noon) offer maps and information, and can also organize homestays.

Accommodation

There is not a great deal of budget accommodation on the island. Your best bet is to contact the tourist office or Asociación de Casas Huéspedes (☎372 7137 or 895 8639) to arrange a homestay – homes all over the island offer rooms starting from L150 a night. Staying with a local family is a great way to experience real island life.

Mirador de Amapala East towards Playa del Burro, 5min from the Parque Central ☎795 8407/8592, ⓦwww.miradordeamapala.com. Clean en-suite rooms, a pool, restaurant, disco and well-equipped bar make a good option, particularly if you're in a group (there's a six-bed dorm available for L1600). A planned new extension should include a sun-bathing platform and ten more rooms, some of which will have beautiful views of the Golfo de Fonseca. ⑥

Playa Negra ☎220 1183, ⓔhotelplayanegra @hotmail.com. Set above Playa Negra, this is the biggest hotel on the island, with a pool, restaurant and comfortable rooms, all with private bath. The nightly rates are steep for the slightly worn appearance of the hotel and its grounds. ⑦

Eating

Dignita At the end of Playa Grande. This fish restaurant serves up seafood soup for L150, fried fish meals starting at L80 and freshly caught *langostines* for L230. During the week you can pretty much have the restaurant (and beach) to yourself.

Iris Facing the end of the pier, this two-storey house is both a café and a shop. It doesn't have a name, but Iris is in charge, and one of her sons is likely to be dishing out *licuados*, sandwiches (with chips

L40), burgers, enchiladas and tacos. It has a beach shack feel, with a room with wicker rocking chairs. You can buy basic toiletries, snacks and drinks in an attached, make-shift shop (daily 6am–10pm).

Veleros Playa del Burro. Palapa-roofed beach café. A great place to watch the locals coming and going on the launches. Sandwich and chips L35, seafood soup L160.

Moving on

By boat Launches (2am–6pm; 15min) leave regularly for Coyolito from Amapala's dock.
By bus From the Coyolito dock buses leave every 15min to the Jícaro Galán/Coyolito turn-off (1hr) for connections to Tegucigalpa or Choluteca.

CHOLUTECA

Honduras's fourth-largest city, with a population of around one hundred thousand, **CHOLUTECA**'s main attraction is its old colonial centre, one of the finest in the country. Most places of interest are grouped around the **Parque Central**, itself a pleasant place to enjoy the evening air. Dominating the square, the imposing seventeenth-century **cathedral** is worth a look for its elaborately constructed wooden ceiling. On the southwest corner of the square is the birthplace of **José Cecilio del Valle**, one of the authors of the Central American Act of Independence in 1821 and 1834 president-elect of the Federation, though he died in Guatemala before taking office. There are plans to turn this building into a municipal museum, though it has been closed to the public for some time. It is Valle's statue that stands in the middle of the square. Once you've seen the centre, there's not much reason to hang out in the heat, and most people move on fairly quickly.

Arrival and information

By bus The main terminal is ten blocks northeast of the Parque Central, a twenty-minute walk or L10 taxi ride. Mi Esperanza also has a stop down the street from the main terminal.
Exchange Banco Occidente, one block south of the Parque (Mon–Fri 8am–4pm, Sat 8am–noon), has a 24hr ATM.

Accommodation

Bonsai Av Valle ☏ 782 2648. The most basic rooms here are little more than a bed with fan and

---

INTO NICARAGUA OR EL SALVADOR: EL ESPINO, GUASAULE AND EL AMATILLO

Choluteca is a transport hub for most of the country's border crossings with Nicaragua and El Salvador.

For Nicaragua's El Espino border, buses run the 110km from Choluteca to San Marcos de Colón with El Rey Express (3 daily; 9am, 3pm & 7pm). From there frequent colectivo taxis (US$0.75) go to El Espino and the border 10km away. The border post itself (daily 8am–5pm) is quiet and straightforward, with moneychangers on both sides. On the Nicaraguan side, regular buses run to Somoto, 20km from the border. If you are crossing at Guasaule, white rapiditos leave every half hour from 6am until 5pm (40min) from Choluteca. There's regular transport from Guasaule on to Chinandega, León and Managua.

If you are heading for El Salvador, local buses run to El Amatillo (hourly 3.15am–5.45pm; 2hr 15min). This point of entry (open 6am–10pm) teems with border traffic, moneychangers and opportunistic beggars. Crossing, however, is straightforward. A bank on the El Salvadoran side changes dollars and lempiras, but you'll get slightly better rates from the moneychangers as long as you're careful. If coming from Tegucigalpa you don't need to go all the way to Choluteca – just change at Jícaro Galán onto the Choluteca–El Amatillo service. Over the border in El Salvador, buses leave for Santa Rosa de Lima – 18km away, and the closest place offering accommodation (see p.297) – and San Miguel (58km; see p.289) every ten minutes until around 6.30pm.

shared bathroom, but there are also a/c rooms with private bath. ❸

Santa Rosa On Av La Rosa between C Williams and C Paz Barahona ☎ 782 0355/0884. A good bet, with clean and simple rooms all with private bath and fan, and some with a/c and TV. Hammocks and wicker chairs surround the courtyard and a laundry service is available. There's a four-bed dorm room available for L3300. Doubles ❷–❹

Eating

Local *comedores* opposite the market have *almuerzos* for L40.

American Express Av 6 NO near C Williams. Serves great coffees and granitas, especially good if the heat gets to be too much.

Café Frosty C Williams near Av 6 NO. A diner-style eatery with dishes like burgers and chips (L59).

Moving on

By bus to: Tegucigalpa (4 daily with Mi Esperanza, 3hr; 12 daily with Royeri, 4hr). For buses to Nicaragua and El Salvador see box, p.345.

The central highlands

The only glimpse of Honduras's **central highlands** that most travellers see is the view from the bus window as they rush to see the ruins at Copán, or the border with Guatemala or onwards to the northern beaches. This would be a mistake, though, as the highlands have a little something for everyone. For adventure-seekers, especially, there's plenty to see and do – the region is one long expanse of rugged, pine-clad mountain ranges and fertile valleys peppered with natural hot springs, waterfalls and caves.

Moving north from Tegucigalpa on the **Carretera del Norte** (**CA-5**) highway, the first place of interest is the nation's former capital **Comayagua**, with its remnants of colonial architecture. Further along lies Honduras's biggest lake, the vast blue **Lago de Yojoa** – a bird-lover's paradise.

COMAYAGUA

Once the capital of Honduras, faded **COMAYAGUA** lies just 85km north of Tegucigalpa, at the northeast end of the fertile Comayagua Valley. Santa María de Comayagua, as it was first known, was built in 1539, and quickly gained prominence thanks to the discovery of **silver** nearby, becoming the administrative centre for the whole of Honduras. Following independence, however, the city's fortunes began to decline, particularly after Tegucigalpa was designated alternate capital of the new republic in 1824, and especially when President Soto permanently transferred the capital to Tegucigalpa in 1880. Although Comayagua is today a relatively rich and important provincial centre, its rivalry with Tegucigalpa has hardly waned over the centuries. The main reason to visit is the architectural legacy of the colonial period, in particular the dramatic cathedral overlooking the Parque Central.

What to see and do

Most sights of interest are within a few blocks of the large, tree-lined **Parque Central**, C 4–5 NO, Cero Av Norte–1 Av NO, which is graced by a pretty bandstand, a fountain and a handful of gun-wielding guards who protect the surrounding banks. It's a great place to watch city life, especially in the evenings, when music plays out of speakers. Few of the city streets are numbered, but the centre is relatively compact and orientation straightforward.

Iglesia de la Inmaculada Concepción

On the southeast corner of the Parque is the recently renovated **cathedral** (daily 7am–8pm), whose intricate facade consists of tiers of niches containing

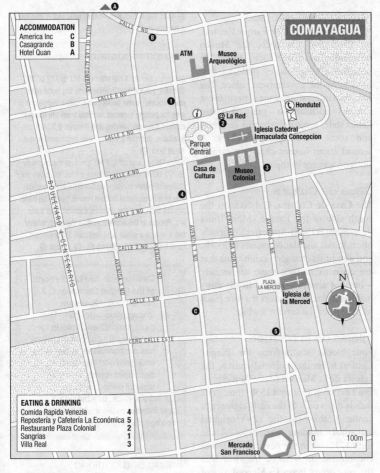

COMAYAGUA

ACCOMMODATION
America Inc	C
Casagrande	B
Hotel Quan	A

EATING & DRINKING
Comida Rapida Venezia	4
Repostería y Cafetería La Económica	5
Restaurante Plaza Colonial	2
Sangrias	1
Villa Real	3

Mercado
San Francisco

0   100m

statues of the saints. More properly known as **Iglesia de la Inmaculada Concepción**, it was the largest church of its kind in the country during the colonial period, housing sixteen altars, though only four of these survive today. The cathedral's bell tower, built between 1580 and 1708, is considered one of the outstanding examples of colonial Baroque architecture in Central America, and is home to the twelfth-century **Reloj Arabe**, one of the oldest clocks in the world. Originally made for the Alhambra in Granada, Spain, the timepiece was presented to the city in 1582 by King Philip II.

Museo Colonial

The small **Museo Colonial** (Tues–Sun 9am–noon & 2–4.45pm; L35), a block southeast of the Parque and housed in a few rooms of the Palacio Episcopal, is home to a collection of religious art, statues, chalices and documents – including the former president Francisco Morazán's marriage licence – from the city's churches. It also has some striking indigenous headdresses. The building was originally constructed for Comayagua's **university**, the first established in Central America, in 1678.

Museo Arqueológico

Two blocks north of the Parque Central, on Plaza San Francisco, the **Museo Arqueológico** (daily 8.30am–4pm; L20) occupies a single-storey building that used to be the government palace. The small but interesting range of permanent exhibits includes a pre-Columbian Lenca stele, some polychrome ceramics and some terrific jade jewellery. A second room houses changing exhibitions on a range of topics.

Casa de Cultura

The **Casa de Cultura**, C 4 NO, on the south side of the Parque (Mon–Thurs 9am–5pm, Fri 9am–9pm; free), officially offers music and dance lessons to locals, and also hosts changing exhibitions that are open to visitors; these are usually – but not always – related to the city's history. Its location makes it a nice place to hide from the sun for a while.

Iglesia de la Merced

Four blocks south from the Parque Central is another colonial church, the **Iglesia de la Merced** (daily 7am–8pm). Built between 1550 and 1558 (though its facade dates only to the early eighteenth century), this was the city's original cathedral, holding the Reloj Arabe until 1715, when the new cathedral was consecrated. In front of the church is the very pretty **Plaza La Merced**, site of a proposed souvenir market.

Arrival and information

By bus Buses drop passengers off on the highway at the top of "the Boulevard", which connects CA-5 to the centre; the stop is about 1km from the Parque Central – either a L15 taxi ride or 20min walk.
Exchange Banco Occidente on the Parque (Mon–Fri 8am–4pm, Sat 8–11.30am) changes dollars. Credomatic, on Av 1 NO just past C 6 NO, has an ATM that accepts MasterCard and Visa.
Internet La Red, on the Parque (Mon–Sat 8am–9pm, Sun 9am–8pm) charges L20/hr; computers have Skype.
Tourist information The tourist office on the north side of the Parque (Tues–Fri 8am–noon & 2–4pm, Sat & Sun 8am–noon) sells maps and has a helpful staff.

Accommodation

America Inc Av 1 NO after C 1 NO ☎772 0530, ✉hotel_americainc@yahoo.com. Big hotel with clean rooms; some twins come with a fridge and a sink for putting together lunches from the nearby market. Laundry service and internet (L30/hr) are available, and there's an on-site restaurant and a small pool. ❺
Hotel Quan Just off C 7 NO towards the highway ☎772 0070, ✉hquan@hondutel.hn. You have your choice of either modern motel-style accommodation or less pleasant budget rooms here – all have private bath, and the ones on the first floor have a/c. Rooms in the annexe across the road, where there is also a small pool and café for breakfast, have fridges. Main building ❹–❺, annex ❻

Casagrande Two blocks north of the Parque Central on C 7 NO ☎772 0512, ⊛www .casagrande-hotel.com. The most atmospheric hotel in town, this beautiful colonial mansion has a colonnaded, flower-filled courtyard and individually decorated rooms filled with tasteful period furniture. Laundry service, free breakfast and Internet make it well worth the splurge. ❼

Eating and drinking

An extensive general market four blocks south of the Parque Central sells meat and fish, while stalls around the main building have fresh fruit and vegetables. You can easily pick up an *almuerzo* for under L50 in the surrounding *comedores*.
Comida Rápida Venezia Av 1 NO, one block south of Parque. With canteen-style service this is a great, cheap place for lunch. Meats L23, pastas L22, salad L15. Closed evenings & Sun.
Repostería y Cafetería La Económica Av 1 NE. This bakery serves giant slabs of cake for L20 near Plaza La Merced. Grab a slice, sit and enjoy the plaza.
Restaurante Plaza Colonial Next to the cathedral, on the east side of the Parque Central ☎772 1836. This restaurant has two rooms inside and a courtyard, where you can either grab

a *comida rápida* (sandwiches L55, burgers L90; served until 5pm) or come for something a bit more special in the evening (pastas L120, meat dishes L150) and watch people congregate in the Parque.

Sangrias Just north of the Parque Central on Av 1 NO. This jazz and rock bar is housed in a 150-year-old building where giant handmade barrels serve as tables. It's the only place serving submarine-style sandwiches like you'd find at home (L100), as well as veggie burgers (L95) and beer (L25). It's also a nice spot for a few drinks in the evenings.

Tropical Juice Av 1 NO. *Licuados* and juices (L30) in every fruit mix imaginable – you can either drink them here or take away.

Villa Real A block southeast of the Parque on Av 1 NE. Set in a beautifully restored colonial home, this stylish restaurant has an extensive menu that includes pastas and grilled meat and fish dishes (L75–135). There's also a well-stocked bar with karaoke at weekends.

Moving on

By bus to: San Pedro Sula (with El Rey 1–2 hourly 3am–7pm; with Norteños 1–2 hourly 6.30am–2.30pm; with Rivera hourly 5am–4pm; 3hr 15min); Tegucigalpa (with El Rey 1–2 hourly 3am–7pm; with Norteños 1–2 hourly 6.30am–2.30pm; 1hr 30min). For Lago de Yojoa, catch any San Pedro Sula–bound bus and ask for La Guama.

LAGO DE YOJOA

Beyond Comayagua, the highway descends from the mountains and the air becomes appreciably warmer. Some 67km north of Comayagua sits the spectacular, sparkling blue **LAGO DE YOJOA**, a natural lake approximately 17km long and 9km wide. Its reed-fringed waters, sloping away to a gentle patchwork of woods, pastures and coffee plantations, are overlooked by the mountains of **Cerro Azul Meámbar** to the east and **Santa Bárbara** to the north and west. Both of these contain small but pristine stretches of **cloudforest** and are protected as national parks. The lake itself attracts over four hundred species of **birds**, one of the highest concentrations in the country.

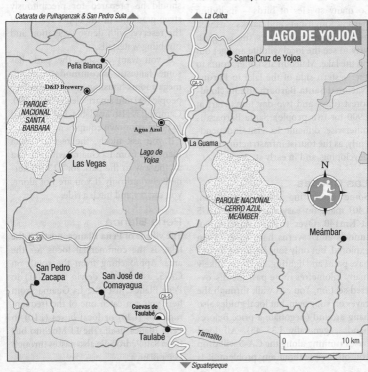

Catarata de Pulhapanzak & San Pedro Sula ▲   ▲ La Ceiba

LAGO DE YOJOA

Santa Cruz de Yojoa

Peña Blanca

D&D Brewery

PARQUE NACIONAL SANTA BARBARA

Agua Azul

La Guama

Lago de Yojoa

Las Vegas

PARQUE NACIONAL CERRO AZUL MEÁMBER

Meámbar

N

San Pedro Zacapa

San José de Comayagua

Cuevas de Taulabé

Taulabé

Tamalito

0   10 km

▼ Siguatepeque

During the week, the waters – and surrounding hotels – are virtually empty, making for a supremely relaxing place for a couple of days of rowing, birdwatching, sport-fishing and general outdoor exploring. However, at weekends the lake is a favourite with middle-class *hondureños*, and the peace can be shattered by the crowds and the buzz of jet-skis.

What to see and do

The area around Lago de Yojoa offers some of the most adventurous activities of the region: you can hike through the cloudforests of the national parks, get wet crawling behind a 43-metre waterfall and explore some dark and mysterious caves. If it's nature you're after, the very knowledgeable Malcolm, resident bird expert at *D&D Brewery* (see opposite), runs fantastic early morning tours on the lake (L600 for four people). With so many species of birds – including herons, kingfishers and hawks – as well as bats, iguanas and otters, this is a great way to see the local wildlife and get out on the lake. Malcolm also offers tours to the western side of the lake to **Parque Nacional Santa Bárbara** and its cloud-forest (one- and two-day tours start at L900 for two people). Santa Bárbara is otherwise difficult to visit independently, as the tourist infrastructure is still developing, and in early stages.

Las Cuevas

Some interesting **caves** (8am–4pm; L40) make an easy stop off the CA-5 at Km140. Over twelve kilometres of tunnels and caverns have so far been explored, but only four hundred metres have paths and lighting, and there's likely many kilometres more past the discovered section. You can walk through the caves on your own, but local guides also hang around (negotiate a price beforehand – generally L35–45). All local buses running along the CA-5 will drop you off here without any problem; it is also easy to catch a bus on to La Guama (L20 in a *rapidito*) for the lake or back to the junction at Siguatepeque (L15 in a *rapidito*) for connections to the west. Although very accessible, the caves can be slippery, so make sure you have decent shoes.

Parque Nacional Cerro Azul Meámbar

Continuing north, the highway divides at the small town of **La Guama**, from where a dirt road runs east for another 7km to the entrance to **Parque Nacional Cerro Azul Meámbar** (daily 8am–5pm; L30). Named after its highest peak, the blue-hued Cerro Azul Meámbar (2047m), this is one of the smaller and most accessible national parks, with a core of untouched cloudforest. The **visitors' centre** at the park's entrance has information on a number of short walking trails. Anyone planning to hike should be prepared for precipitously steep gradients in the upper reaches of the reserve, with dense vegetation and tumbling waterfalls.

If you want to stay, the park has some fantastic **accommodation** with mega rooms housing a minimum of 15 people (❷) and smart, clean triples (❻). Camping is also available, but you need to bring your own equipment.

If you ask nicely, the regular Santa Elena **bus** from La Guama will take you all the way to the park for L150. Alternatively, and only if you are not alone, you can try and hitch a ride.

Peña Blanca

The village of **Peña Blanca**, north of the lake, is the commercial focus for the area. Approaching from the south on CA-5, ask for the *desvío* (turn-off) to Peña Blanca, just after La Guama; from here you can catch one of the frequent *rapiditos* (L20) or local buses (L10) to Peña Blanca itself. The El Mochito bus from San Pedro Sula also passes through Peña Blanca.

Skynet cybercafé on the main road through Peña Blanca has **internet** at 15L an hour. Banco Occidente **changes dollars** and traveller's cheques, though there is no ATM. You can find **restaurants** in the village with lunches under L50, and there are also a couple of mini-supermarkets.

Catarata de Pulhapanzak

The absolute highlight of this region is the **Catarata de Pulhapanzak** (daily 8am–6pm; L30), a stunning, 43-metre-high cascade of churning white waters on the Río Lindo. Probably the prettiest waterfall in the country, the cascade is at its most dazzling in the early mornings, when rainbows form in the rising sun. It's easy enough to explore on your own – you can swim at the top of the waterfall, then climb down a set of steep, wet steps on the right-hand side past several viewpoints to the riverbank at the bottom of the falls. To really get the most out of your visit, though, take advantage of the fantastic **guided tours** run by the on-site staff (L100; wear sturdy shoes). They'll take you jumping or diving in and out of pools, ducking behind the falls – an experience not unlike being in a giant, powerful shower – and climbing in and out of the caves behind the curtain of water. It's not for the faint-hearted, but if you like adventure you'll be telling your friends about it for years to come. If heights aren't a problem then the canopy tour (L300) is another must: a network of five ziplines work their way down the river until you are flying through rainbows above the waterfall.

The falls are an easy fifteen-minute walk from the village of **San Buenaventura**, 8km north of Peña Blanca; buses between El Mochito and San Pedro Sula run hourly, passing through both Peña Blanca and San Buenaventura en route. The area immediately around the falls has been kitted out for its visitors. A football field just inside the entrance fills with locals at the weekend and a restaurant serves up cheap local fish and fried chicken and chips.

Accommodation

The accommodation options listed here also have dining facilities.

Agua Azul On the road between La Guama and Peña Blanca ☎ 991 7244, ✉ aboesch@hotmail.com. As popular with locals as it is with visiting Peace Corps volunteers. Rustic cabins enjoy a lovely setting among wooded grounds sloping down to the waterside, and the restaurant's veranda has fabulous views across the lake; there's also a pool, and the hotel rents boats (L200/hr) and kayaks (L150/hr). Buses between La Guama and Peña Blanca can drop you on the main road, from where it's a 10min walk to the hotel. Doubles ❹, 4-bed cabin ❻

D&D Brewery A little way outside Peña Blanca on the road to San Pedro Sula ☎ 994 9719, ⓦ www.dd-brew.com. This hotel and microbrewery has several varieties of beer and home-made sodas on offer for around L30 a mug. There are four private rooms (❸) and romantic cabins with a Jacuzzi (❺), as well as a very clean pool and restaurant. To get here take the El Mochito bus from Peña Blanca towards San Pedro Sula until you pass a bridge over a small creek. A signed dirt road heads off to the right past a stonewall to the premises (a 5min walk along this road).

The western highlands

The **western highlands** of Honduras are a picturesque landscape of pine forests, sparsely inhabited mountains and remote villages. The departments of **Lempira** and **Intibucá** contain the highest concentration of indigenous peoples in the country, and many of the towns in the region make up the so-called **Ruta Lenca**. Around the village of **La Esperanza** particularly, look out for Lenca women wearing traditional coloured headdresses while working in the fields.

The main road between La Esperanza and **Gracias**, the next settlement north, is unfortunately a slow and uncomfortable journey. The road is being improved, but slowly. However, if you're not in a rush it is a fun and beautiful journey and saves having to go north to San Pedro Sula and back south again. Once you finally get there, cobbled, colonial Gracias makes a relaxing base for hikes in the pristine cloudforest reserve of the **Parque Nacional Celaque**. An easy bus ride away is **Santa Rosa de Copán**, which is also a relaxing place to stay and still unspoilt, despite its growing popularity with tourists and its proximity to the **Copán ruins**.

LA ESPERANZA

Just north of the town of Siguatepeque, a good paved road heads west from CA-5 to the village of **LA ESPERANZA**, the centre of commerce for western Honduras and the capital of the department of Intibucá. During the week there's nothing much of interest here, but the town livens up considerably during the colourful **weekend market** (Sat & Sun), when Lenca farmers from surrounding villages pour into town.

It's likely that if you're heading to Gracias you'll need to **stay overnight** in La Esperanza due to the lack of buses. The centrally located *Hotel Urquia* (☎783 0435; ❷) is a reasonable bet. Some bathrooms only have a three-quarter wall and aren't the best if you need privacy, but newer rooms on the first floor are considerably nicer. For food, the local daily market sells a multitude of fresh fruit and vegetables, while *Opalaca's* restaurant has good-sized portions of international food (club sandwich and chips L68, burgers L55). For the more adventurous, barbecued meat dishes – including *huevos de toro* (bull's testicles; L110) – come to the table on a sizzling plate. La Esperanza has one ATM that takes Visa cards.

From the *desvío* (turn-off) to La Esperanza, just north of Siguatepeque, **buses** run to the town every couple of hours until mid-afternoon (68km; 2hr). Buses running between Tegucigalpa and San Pedro Sula can drop you off at the *desvío*.

SAN JUAN INTIBUCÁ

A bumpy 52km north of La Esperanza, the village of **SAN JUAN INTIBUCÁ** is slowly finding its way onto the tourist map thanks to a local *cooperativa* promoting the area's Lenca traditions. Information about available tours and demonstrations is available from *Hotel Guancascos* in Gracias (see p.353) or *La Casa de Gladis Nolasco*, a block from the Hondutel office on Calle Principal; options include participating in the roasting of coffee beans, hikes to nearby waterfalls and cloudforest, and observing the production of traditional handicrafts. There are three daily **pick-ups** from La Esperanza (10am–4pm; 1hr 30min) running to the town. If you're lucky, you can grab a *rapidito* back from San Juan to Gracias, although frequency is not all that reliable so a pick-up may be your only option.

GRACIAS

Founded in 1536 by Spanish conquistador Juán de Chavez, **GRACIAS** lies in the shadow of the nearby **Parque Nacional Celaque**. It's a hot and dusty cobbled town, but well located for day-trips to surrounding natural attractions, including the park and some natural **hot springs** (daily 7am–11pm; L30), about an hour's walk south or L100 return in a mototaxi. These are small pools purpose-built for bathing in the 36–39°C waters here; an on-site *comedor* serves basic meals. By foot, take the road back towards La Esperanza until you reach the right hand turn-off for the *Aguas Termales*.

Arrival and information

By bus The terminal is three blocks west of the Parque Central.

Exchange Banco Occidente, one block west of the Parque (Mon–Fri 8am–4pm, Sat 8–11.30am), changes dollars, cash and traveller's cheques, but doesn't have an ATM.

Internet Ecolcm, in front of *Guancascos* hotel, charges L20/hr.

Tourist information The office in the centre of the Parque (daily 8am–noon & 1–4.30pm) sells maps (L15) and offers good information.

Accommodation

Both *Erick* and *Josue* allow you to leave bags if hiking at the National Park. *El Jarron* café (Mon–Sat 7.30am–5pm, Sun 7.30am–noon) has tents to rent (L60/night).

Erick One block north of the Parque ☎656 1066. This favourite backpackers' hostel is hard to miss, in a green brick building. Rooms are clean but basic with pipes for showers. Some bathrooms are separated by a half wall, so not completely private. ❷

Hospedaje Josue Next to the market ☎940 6182. The well-kept courtyard and rooms with private bathrooms are much nicer than the shared-bathroom rooms. You can wash clothes here, too. ❷.

Eating

Guancascos Three blocks west and two blocks south of the Parque Central. This hotel and restaurant draws most diners in town with mains for L140 and beers for L30; you can enjoy them on a very pleasant terrace. The owner, Frony, is also an excellent source of local information.

El Jarrón This restaurant south of the Parque has typical breakfasts and lunches for L45.

Riconcito Graciano Two blocks west and south of the Parque. The menu here features dishes made solely from organic, local ingredients, with mains from around L60.

Moving on

By bus to: San Pedro Sula (1 daily direct with Gracianos, 5 daily with Congolón; 4hr); Santa Rosa de Copán (various buses from main terminal throughout the day; 1hr 15min). For Copán, take any San Pedro Sula-bound bus and change at La Entrada.

PARQUE NACIONAL CELAQUE

PARQUE NACIONAL CELAQUE (L50) protects one of the largest and most impressive expanses of virgin cloudforest in Honduras. Thousands of years of geographical isolation has resulted in several endemic species of flora. Locals also claim that the park is home to more quetzals than all of Guatemala, though you'll still have to keep a sharp eye out to see one. A bit more obvious, and the focus of the park, is the nation's highest peak, **Cerro Las Minas** (2849m), part of the Montaña de Celaque escarpment.

What to see and do

Rambles and hikes of all experience levels are possible in the park. The most exciting and scenic option is the six-kilometre marked **trail** up to the summit of Cerro Las Minas. In the upper reaches of the park much of the main trail consists of forty-degree slopes, so this is not a hike for the unfit. If the peak is your aim, you'll need to **camp** at one of the two designated camping spots – Campamento Don Tomás and Campamento Naranjo – along the way (L50). The cloudforest proper doesn't begin until after the latter, so if you can, try to make it this far. Guides aren't necessary for the main trail, but you'll need one if planning to undertake the more difficult treks on the southern slopes; these can be arranged through *Hotel Guancascos* (see above) in Gracias.

Arrival and information

Arrival The park is best approached from Gracias; the entrance is a hot and dusty 8km walk from town. Take the dirt road through the village of Mejicapa, from where a marked track leads uphill to the entrance. Pick-ups are sometimes available. Pay your entrance fee at the little *Comedor Villa Verde* opposite the school.

Information *Guancascos* in Gracias functions as an unofficial information centre for the park. As well as selling booklets and maps, they can arrange lifts up to the lodge, gear, guide and entrance (L450–550 per person per day).

Accommodation and eating

From the entrance, a track leads for another 2km or so through the pine forest to the basic lodge, where there are bunkrooms and showers (). If planning an overnight stay bring your own food supplies, or *Doña Alejandra*, just outside the lodge entrance, serves dinners for L35 until 7pm. Sleeping bags, decent boots and a change of warm clothing are essential.

SANTA ROSA DE COPÁN

It's an easy ninety-minute bus ride 45km northwest from Gracias to **SANTA ROSA DE COPÁN**, a colourful colonial relic built on the proceeds of the tobacco industry. Unusual for a town of this size, the majority of its streets are still cobbled, preserving an authentic feel in spite of the town's unashamedly commercial outlook. While fresh in the mornings and evenings, Santa Rosa de Copán heats up during the day.

What to see and do

Chosen in 1765 as the headquarters of the Royal Tobacco Factory, the golden weed continues to play a role in the local economy. The **Flor de Copán Cigar Company** maintains offices in the town centre – in the original Royal Tobacco building on Calle Centenario – but their **factory** is located 2km northwest of the town centre, about 300m after turning right out of the bus station. Around thirty thousand hand-rolled cigars are produced daily, and **tours** in Spanish and English are available at 10am and 2pm (US$2). In **Colonia San Martín**, a short taxi ride away, is another mainstay in the local economy, the **Beneficio Maya** (www.cafecopan.com) coffee finca. A family-run business, they offer tours (US$2) during the coffee season (Nov–Feb) but welcome visitors year

Boulevard Jorge Bueso Arias, Copán, Gracias & San Pedro Sula ▲

ACCOMMODATION

Alondras	C
Blanca Nieves	A
El Rosario	B

EATING & DRINKING

Antojitos Mita's	1
Cristy	4
Cuartes	7
Pizza Pizza	5
El Rodeo	6
Ten Napel Café	2
Weekends Pizza	3

SANTA ROSA DE COPÁN

0   100 m

round. Tours at both factories should be organized through the tourist office at least a day ahead.

Back in the centre of town is the delightful, shady **Parque Contreras**, also called the Parque Central, with a beautiful cathedral on its eastern side. **Calle Centenario**, lined with shops and restaurants, runs along the southern edge of the Parque, past the town's central **market** a couple of blocks east.

Arrival and information

By bus Buses arrive at a terminal just off the highway, 2km northwest of the centre. Taxis (L12) and the yellow buses marked "urbanos" (L5) run regularly to the Parque Contreras.
Tour operators Lenca Land Trails (ⓔ lencatours @gmail.com; based in the *Hotel Elvir*) offers a number of excellent tours, including trips to Parque Nacional Celaque, indigenous villages and hot springs, all for around US$40. Max Elvir, a local guide, is very flexible so chat with him about what you want to see and he will try to arrange it.
Tourist information ⓦ www.visitsantarosadecopan .org. The tourist office in the centre of the Parque has city maps (L15) and internet (L15/hr) and a friendly and helpful staff (Mon–Sat 8am–noon & 1.30pm–6pm).

Accommodation

A great option in Santa Rosa de Copán is to organize a homestay through the tourist office. They start at about L120 per night, and offer a nice insight into everyday family life.
Alondras Av 2 SO ☎ 662 1194/3583. Opt for one of the upstairs bedrooms for a bit more light. The open communal area has lots of seating, and coffee, juice and pastries are available at breakfast. ❹–❺
Blanca Nieves Av 3 NE ☎ 662 1312. A decent budget option with friendly owners. Access is through a small shop, but rooms are neat and comfortable; the en-suite ones are larger and better value than those with shared bathrooms. ❶–❷
El Rosario Av 3 NE ☎ 662 0211. Next door to *Blanca Nieves*, and with a similar choice of rooms, both en-suite and with shared bath. Rooms are clean, but some are a little dark and cell-like, and those with bathrooms are little more than a room portioned off with a shower curtain. ❷

Eating

Santa Rosa's great number of visitors has resulted in something of a glut of eating establishments. Cheap *comedores* line the bus station and upstairs in the Mercado Central, where filling *almuerzos* can be had for L25–35. In the evenings street vendors sell *tamales* and tortillas around the Mercado Central and Parque. Most restaurants offer specials, giving options that won't upset your budget.

Restaurants

Antojitos Mita's C Centenario. Sweet little place that sells breakfast in a cup (banana and cornflake *licuado*) L20! Lunches, burgers and sandwiches, too, all for under L35.
Cristy C Centenario. Really popular with locals, this canteen-style cafeteria is great for a quick lunch – you can get different meats, potato, salad, rice, mash, noodles and vegetables. One meat, two sides and a drink L53, three sides L62. Open for breakfast and lunch only.
Pizza Pizza Five blocks east of the Parque along C Centenario. This was western Honduras's first pizza restaurant and is justifiably popular among the travelling community. An "almuerzo combo" of pizza, garlic bread and drink costs about L67. Closed Wed.
El Rodeo Av 1 SE, one and a half blocks south of the Parque. The best steaks in town, with huge slabs of meat served at very reasonable rates. Burgers, tacos and sandwiches are all under L50, and most mains are under L135; they also offer a "cocina económica" menu with meals for L73. Open until late with live music at the weekends.
Ten Napel Café C Centenario, Av 3–4 SO. Sells locally produced soft drink Copán Dry (L10) as well as a good selection of coffees (L18–25) and cakes (from L18). wi-fi and souvenirs available.
Weekends Pizza Av 4 NO & C 2 SO. New pizza restaurant in a brightly coloured space with a few tables in a shaded courtyard. Great place if you're in a group. Pizzas start at L105.

Drinking

Cuartes C 1 SE, Av 4–5 SE. A Mexican bar and restaurant with karaoke at the weekends. Cocktails are L55 and main meals under L155. The kitchen is open until 11pm, and the bar until 2am.
El Rodeo Av 1 SE, one and a half blocks south of the Parque. Has music at the weekends and a great atmosphere. Most cocktails run L30–40, and they sell spirits by the bottle, which can be a great deal if you have a group.

Directory

Exchange Banco Occidente, south of the Parque, has a 24hr Visa/Plus ATM and also changes cash dollars and traveller's cheques. A second ATM (Mon–Fri 9am–4pm, Sat 9am–noon) is opposite Manzanitas supermarket.

Internet The cheapest rates are available at the tourist office (L15/hr), but access is also available at the Copán Virtual Centre in Casa Arias, C Centenario (Mon–Sat 8am–10pm).

Post office On the west side of the Parque (Mon–Fri 8am–noon & 2pm–5pm, Sat 8am–noon).

Shopping Supermarket Manzanitas, C Real Centenario and Av 2 NE (Mon–Sat 8am–7.30pm, Sun 8am–2pm) has the usual cans and packets and a wide choice of bottled spirits. The Mercado Santa Teresa has fresh fruit and vegetables.

Telephones Hondutel, on the west side of the Parque (daily 7am–9pm). You can also make calls to the US (L1/min) and Europe (L5/min) at the Copán Virtual Centre.

Moving on

Regular urbanos (city buses) run between the Parque and the main bus terminal (L5).

By bus to: Copán (take any San Pedro Sula-bound bus and change at La Entrada, or go direct to La Entrada); La Entrada (local service every 30min; 1hr); Nueva Ocotepeque (hourly 8.45am–8.30pm with La Sultana de Occidente; 2hr); San Pedro Sula (direct with La Sultana de Occidente hourly 4am–1pm, 2hr 30min; local services every 30min, 3hr 30min); Tegucigalpa (direct with La Sultana de Occidente hourly 4am–1pm; 7hr 30min).

COPÁN RUINAS

A charming town of steep cobbled streets and red-tiled roofs set among green hills, **COPÁN RUINAS** has more to offer than just its proximity to the infamous archeological site of Copán. Despite the weekly influx of visitors, which contributes a large part of the town's income, Copán Ruinas has managed to remain largely unspoilt and genuinely friendly. Many travellers are seduced by the delightfully relaxed atmosphere, clean air and rural setting, and end up spending longer than planned, studying Spanish, eating and drinking well or exploring the region's other minor sites, hot springs and the beautiful countryside.

What to see and do

Half a day is enough to take in virtually all the in-town attractions. The **Parque Central** – lined with banks, municipal structures and a simple, whitewashed

---

INTO EL SALVADOR AND GUATEMALA: EL POY AND AGUA CALIENTE

Buses to both El Salvador and Guatemala pass through Nueva Ocotepeque (hourly from Santa Rosa de Copán with Sultana; 2hr). It's a dirty, busy town, and most people change buses and move on quickly, but if you get stuck, the *Hotel Turístico*, up from the bus stop (☎653 3639; ❷), is a good option. The Banco de Occidente, near the bus stop, changes currencies and traveller's cheques, but you'll get better rates for Guatemalan quetzales at the border.

For El Poy (El Salvador), *rapiditos* run the 7km from Nueva Ocotepeque every 15min 6am–6pm (10min). El Poy itself is drab and dusty, but the crossing is straightforward, as the immigration windows are next to each other in the same building just a short walk from where the bus drops you. Banpaís (Mon–Fri 8am–noon & 1pm–5pm) will change currencies. For most nationalities, there's no fee to enter El Salvador, though residents of Canada, Greece, Portugal and the US will be charged US$10 for a tourist card. Buses to La Palma, the nearest town over the border, and San Salvador leave every thirty minutes until 4.30pm.

For Agua Caliente (Guatemala), yellow local buses make the thirty-minute trip from Nueva Ocotepeque every thirty minutes until 6.30pm (L20). There are no banking or accommodation facilities on the Honduran side. Over in Guatemala, minibuses leave every twenty minutes for Esquipulas (see p.198) until 6pm.

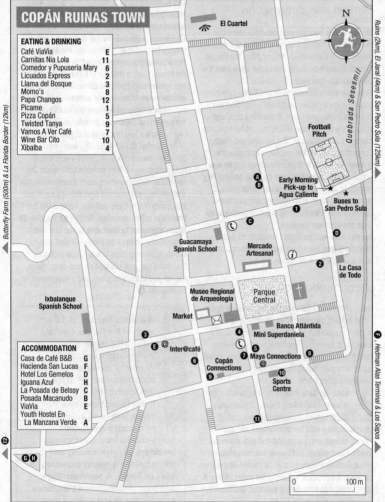

COPÁN RUINAS TOWN

Bird Park (3km), Finca El Cisne & Hot Springs (22.5km) ▲

Ruins (2km), El Jaral (4km) & San Pedro Sula (125km) ▶

Butterfly Farm (500m) & La Florida Border (12km) ◀

◀ Hedman Alas Terminal & Los Sapos ▶

EATING & DRINKING

Café ViaVia	E
Carnitas Nia Lola	11
Comedor y Pupusería Mary	6
Licuados Express	2
Llama del Bosque	3
Momo's	8
Papa Changos	12
Picame	1
Pizza Copán	5
Twisted Tanya	9
Vamos A Ver Café	7
Wine Bar Cito	10
Xibalba	4

ACCOMMODATION

Casa de Café B&B	G
Hacienda San Lucas	F
Hotel Los Gemelos	D
Iguana Azul	H
La Posada de Belssy	C
Posada Macanudo	B
ViaVia	E
Youth Hostel En La Manzana Verde	A

El Cuartel

Football Pitch

Early Morning Pick-up to Agua Caliente

Buses to San Pedro Sula

Guacamaya Spanish School

Mercado Artesanal

La Casa de Todo

Ixbalanque Spanish School

Museo Regional de Arqueología

Parque Central

Market

Banco Atlántida
Mini Superdaniela

Inter@café

Copán Connections

Maya Connections

Sports Centre

0   100 m

Baroque-style church – has a series of sweeping pillars and arches on its north side and remains a popular place to kill time.

On the west side of the plaza is the **Museo Regional de Arqueología** (daily 9am–5pm; US$3), housing some impressive Maya carvings from the Copán region, including glyph-covered Altars T and U and **Stela 7**, discovered just 100 metres from the Parque Central

in town. There are also two remarkable **tombs**, one of which contains the remains of a female shaman, complete with jade jewellery, an entire puma skeleton, the skull of a deer, and two human sacrificial victims.

One block west of the Parque is the food market, while the Mercado Artesanal, selling classic tourist fare like T-shirts and handicrafts, is one block south of the Parque.

Arrival and information

By bus Buses from the east generally terminate by a small football field at the entrance to town, though some continue up the low hill to the Parque Central. Buses from Guatemala enter town from the west and stop just before the Parque.

Tour operators Basecamp, in the *ViaVia* café (see opposite), does "rural adventures", including tours to a local coffee plantation, horseriding trips and visits to the hot springs. Hiking, motorbike trips and travel to La Moskitia can also be arranged. Copán Connections, under *Twisted Tanya* (see opposite), is a one-stop source of information on Copán and popular destinations like Lago de Yojoa and the Bay Islands. In addition to information on hot springs, indigenous villages and canopy tours, Jennifer of Copán Connections can help organize post-activity yoga and massage sessions.

Tourist information Copán Connections and Basecamp (see below) are excellent sources of local and national information.

Accommodation

Some of the best hostels in this region are in Copán – and indeed, it's probably worth staying at one of them, so you can save up for the area's other attractions. Beware of unofficial hotel representatives trying to shepherd you into hotels upon arrival (some may even board buses armed with a highly developed sales pitch).

🏃 **Casa de Café B&B** At the southwest edge of town, overlooking the Río Copán valley ☎651 4620, ⓦwww.casadecafecopan.com. A charming place with ten comfortable and airy rooms, all with wood panelling and nice individual touches, and private bathrooms with steaming hot water. Outside there's a fabulous garden where you can lie in a hammock and enjoy the views all day. A huge vegetarian breakfast is included, and there's free coffee, a library and TV. ❻

Iguana Azul Next to the *Casa de Café B&B* ☎651 4620, ⓦwww.iguanaazulcopan.com. The definitive budget choice, with three private rooms and two very pleasant dorms with shared bath and decent mattresses. Amenities include a pretty garden, communal area and laundry facilities, plus great travel information. Dorms ❶, doubles ❸

La Posada de Belssy One block north of the Parque Central ☎651 4680, ⓔlaposadadebelssy @gmail.com. With a small pool, hot-water bathrooms and use of a kitchen, this popular choice for those who want to have the flexibility to cook without having to share a dorm. Laundry service also available. ❸

Los Gemelos Close to the bus stop ☎651 4077. Friendly backpacker stronghold with basic but spotless rooms with fans, all with shared bath. This is one of the best budget options in town with reliable hot water, so it fills up quickly. ❷

Posada Macanudo One and a half blocks north of the Parque Central ☎651 4771. Rooms are clean and simple, each furnished differently and with fan and hot water. All except one room has a private bathroom. A lovely terrace with hammocks overlooks the outskirts of Copán and the surrounding hills. ❹

🏃 **ViaVia** Two blocks west of the Parque Central ☎651 4652. This hotel-cum-café-cum-tourist office has great-value, simple but spotless rooms with en-suite bathrooms. The hospitable Belgian owners speak excellent English, and will help you organize trips through the onsite Basecamp office. Salsa and film nights bring the crowds in at the weekends. Singles ❸, doubles ❸

Youth Hostel en la Manzana Verde One and a half blocks north of the Parque Central. Under the same ownership as *ViaVia* (☎same phone), this hostel has well-planned six-bed dorm rooms, kitchen and laundry facilities, and a noticeboard for information. ❶

Hacienda San Lucas 1.8 km south of the Parque Central ☎651 4106, ⓦwww .haciendasanlucas.com. Wonderful converted farmhouse accommodation set in the hills south of town, with breathtaking views over the valley. There's an attached restaurant with excellent home-cooked food (rates include breakfast), plus horseriding and hiking trails to a nearby archeological site Los Sapos. A new meditation and yoga platform offers the chance for reflection as you look out over Copán, and massages can also be arranged by Copán Connections or the *Hacienda*'s owner, Flavia. Your time at the *Hacienda* really comes into its own in the evening, though, when hundreds of candles are lit all over the grounds and you can watch the night unfold over the ruins. ❾

Eating

Copán's wide range of places to eat mostly cater specifically to the town's foreign visitors. Standards are usually very high, with generous portions and good service. Virtually all restaurants stop serving at 10pm.

Cafés

Café ViaVia Two blocks west of the Parque. Belgian-owned establishment with a streetside terrace and leafy garden. In addition to an array of sandwiches and good breakfasts – including pancakes and omelettes – there is a very reasonably priced fixed menu with vegetarian options, where nothing costs more than L100.

Licuados Express One block east of the Parque. Open by 6.30am, this little juice bar serves delicious *licuados* (L25), juices and breakfasts to the town's early birds. Try the amazing pineapple-and-coconut *licuado* or a peanut butter-and-jam bagel (L45).

Picame One block northeast of the Parque. A new café perfect for breakfast. Its chalk-board menus list more than 12 types of *baleadas* (L20–40) and baguettes (L50–85), as well as Mexican nachos, tacos and burritos (L80). Closed Tues.

Vamos a Ver Café One block south of the Parque. Busy Dutch-owned garden café, popular with travellers thanks to affordable and delicious homemade soups, sandwiches and snacks. Sandwiches and burgers under L80, mains under L100.

Xibalba Inside hotel *Camino Maya*, at the southeast corner of the Parque. Opens at 6.30am with traditional full English breakfasts accompanied by a drink and a mountain of fruit is on the menu for L100. Hiking specials available include a big breakfast and a packed lunch.

Restaurants

Carnitas Nia Lola Two blocks south of the Parque. This popular restaurant/bar serves large portions of delicious grilled and barbecued meats (L95–265), plus vegetarian dishes. It's equally frequented as a drinking venue, with 2-for-1 cocktails between 6.30 and 8.30pm. *Anafre* (a kind of Honduran fondue) is included with a food order. Good veggie options; sandwiches and burgers are L100–130.

Comedor y Pupusería Mary One block southwest of the Parque. This great local restaurant has *pupusas* with various fillings for L10–15. Two to three will keep you going for a while.

Llama del Bosque Two blocks west of the Parque. Slightly old-fashioned restaurant with a reasonably priced menu including local breakfasts, meat and chicken dishes, *baleadas* and snacks (most dishes L40–100).

Momo's One block south of the Parque. For huge, bargain-priced meat dishes, this atmospheric log restaurant has an open-air barbecue. Massive main and a drink L100.

Pizza Copán Half a block south of the Parque. Both locals and tourists come here to indulge in delicious pizza and pasta (L130–230). Take-away available – lucky, as they're generous with both portions and toppings. One pizza can easily be shared between two or taken home for later.

Twisted Tanya One block south of the plaza. The best food in Copán, with mozzarella and melon salads, salmon pasta and filet mignon. Three courses will set you back US$18, but Tanya has a backpacker's special until 6pm for just US$6 and 2-for-1 cocktails galore. Watch out for the potent but delicious "Jamaicanmecrazy". Closed Sun.

Drinking

Papa Changos Five blocks south of the Parque Central. Best late-night venue in town, if not for the only fact that it is open the latest. Things don't really get going much before 10pm, when they start playing a mix of rock and reggae. New laws have come in that mean it closes at midnight on weekdays and 2am weekends. Open Thurs–Sun.

Wine Bar Cito One block south of the Parque. Cushioned bottle crates for seats and low lighting make this little bar a cosy spot for a drink. Open until late.

Café ViaVia Wed is salsa night with lesson and a free *cuba libre*, Sat has a DJ and Sun is Oscar night, with films shown. Closes at midnight.

Shopping

Books Exchange available at La Casa de Todo, on the next corner from the *Hotel Los Gemelos*. Just up the hill Colibrí Bookshop (closed Tues) sells English and Spanish books and DVDs as well as magazines, guidebooks and maps.

Crafts and souvenirs At Arte Acción (Mon-Fri 8am–5pm; ⊛www.arteaccionhonduras.org) 100% of profits go towards art projects and organized cultural activities for children in Copán. The shop sells items made by the children during these projects. Libélula, opposite *ViaVia*, is a fair-trade shop selling beautiful local jewellery, clothes and souvenirs. Proceeds go towards a health and education program for local Maya villages. Casa Villamil, north of the Parque, has upscale gifts like beautiful Jade jewellery, while La Casa de Todo has every souvenir imaginable.

Directory

Exchange Banco Atlántida, on the Parque Central, will change traveller's cheques and cash dollars (Mon–Fri 9am–4pm, Sat 8.30–11.30am). Banco

Atlántida's ATM (24hr) accepts Visa and MasterCard, and a door down a second ATM accepts Visa.

Immigration The *migración* is on the west side of the Parque next to the museum (Mon–Fri 7am–4pm).

Internet There are several internet cafés in town, including Maya Connections, just south of the plaza (L20/hr) and La Casa de Todo (daily 7am–9pm; L20/hr), but cheapest is Inter@Café, next door to ViaVia (L15/hr).

Language schools Guacamaya (☎651 4360, Ⓦwww.guacamaya.com), one block north of the plaza, is the older of the two schools and more expensive. Ixbalanque (☎651 4432, Ⓦwww.Ixbalanque.com), a block and a half west of the plaza, is also worth considering. Four hours of classes plus full family-based accommodation with meals costs US$210 (Ixbalanque) and $225 (Guacamaya) a week (US$140 without accommodation).

Laundry La Casa de Todo has a one-day service (L10/pound, minimum charge L50).

Post office Behind the Museo Regional de Arqueología (Mon–Fri 8am–noon & 2–5pm, Sat 8am–noon).

Telephones There's a Hondutel office next to the post office (daily 7am–9pm; L2/min to the US and L44/min to Europe).

Moving on from Copán

By bus to: El Florido (local minibuses run throughout the day from the Parque); Guatemala City (2 daily direct shuttles, 5.30am from outside Copán Connections and noon outside ViaVia); La Entrada, for connections to Santa Rosa de Copán and Gracias (local buses every 30min; 1hr); San Pedro Sula (4 daily with Hedman Alas 5.15am, 10.30am, 2.30pm, 5pm, 2hr 45min; with local bus from the football pitch regularly, 3hr). For Tegucigalpa, Tela and La Ceiba, you must go via San Pedro Sula.

AROUND COPÁN RUINAS

While the main draw for travellers to Copán is the nearby ruins, there's a lot more on offer to help while away a few days. Nature parks give visitors the chance to walk amongst beautiful butterflies and exotic birds, while lesser-known archeological sites like Las Sepultras can be void of fellow tourists and a local family-run farm can show you how your morning cup of coffee came into existence.

Enchanted Wings Butterfly House

A twenty-minute walk west from the plaza, along the road to Guatemala, stands the **Enchanted Wings Butterfly House and Nature Centre** (daily 8am–4.30pm; L115), owned by an American enthusiast and his Honduran wife. On entry you will be shown and talked through any butterflies they are currently breeding before walking into a large enclosure where you're surrounded by fluttering wings. The delicate creatures won't hesitate to pause and catch their breath while resting on your head. Types to look out for include the speckled brown "giant owl" and the scarlet-and-yellow "helicopter". Butterflies hatch in the morning hours, so time your visit accordingly. In a further enclosure over two hundred orchids, around a third of Honduras's native species, are on display. For your best chance to see flowering orchids visit between February and April or July and August.

Macaw Mountain Bird Park

On the other side of town, 3km north of the plaza, the **Macaw Mountain Bird Park** (daily 9am–5pm; US$10) is home to parrots, macaws and toucans rescued from captivity. Worth the hefty entrance fee, your ticket gives you entrance for three days – with walk-through aviaries, an interaction zone, a stunning forest location, nature trail and a natural pool for swimming, you'll want to take advantage of all three. The restaurant, where they also roast and sell locally grown coffee, offers great seafood from the Bay Islands.

Las Sepultras

Two kilometres east of Copán along the highway is the smaller archeological site of **Las Sepultras** (daily 8am–4pm; entrance with the same ticket as for Copán, see p.361), the focus of much interest in recent years because of the information it provides on daily domestic life in Maya times. Eighteen of the forty-odd residential compounds at the site have been excavated, yielding one hundred buildings that would have been inhabited. Smaller compounds on the edge of the site are thought to have housed young princes, as well as concubines and servants. It was customary to bury the nobility close to their residences, and more than 250 tombs have been excavated around the compounds – given the number of women found in the tombs it seems likely that the local Maya practiced polygamy. One of the most interesting finds – the tomb of a priest or shaman, dating from around 450 AD – is on display in the museum in Copán Ruinas town.

Luna Jaguar hot springs

Twenty-two kilometres north of Copán and set in lush highland scenery dotted with coffee *fincas* and tracts of pine, the newly built **Luna Jaguar spa resort** is a great place to relax. Here thermal waters pour into the cold-water river,

creating natural pools and showers. L40 will get you into the man-made pools, but across the river, with another L200 entrance fee, you enter a world fit for a Maya king. Pools and footbaths pop up everywhere, and a Maya temple next to a natural steam bath offers massages.

To get to the *aguas termales*, speak to one of Copán's tour operators for buses (see p.358), or plan on hitching a ride on a passing pick-up. The latter is reasonably easy to do from outside the *Hotel Paty* in Copán or near the bird park; expect to pay around US$1 for the ride, which takes about fifty minutes. Don't leave the springs any later than 3.30pm if you're planning to hitch back to Copán.

COPÁN

Set in serene, rolling hills 45km (as the crow flies) from Santa Rosa de Copán, **COPÁN** (daily 8am–4pm; ruins US$15 (includes entrance to Las Sepultras), entrance and tunnels US$30, everything US$37) is one of the most impressive of all Maya sites. Its pre-eminence is not due to size – in scale it's far less impressive than sites such as Tikal or Chichén Itzá – but to the overwhelming legacy of artistic craftsmanship that has survived over so many centuries. Thanks to years of promotion from the Honduran government and tour operators, Copán now ranks as the second most visited spot in the country after the Bay Islands.

Museum of Mayan Sculpture

Opposite the visitors' centre at the ruins (see p.366) is the terrific **Museum of Mayan Sculpture** (daily 8am–4pm; US$7), arguably the finest in the entire Maya region, with a tremendous collection of stelae, altars, panels and well-labelled explanations in English. Entrance is through an impressive doorway made to look like the jaws of a serpent; you then pass through a tunnel signifying the passage into *xibalba*, or the underworld.

> **TREAT YOURSELF**
>
> If you want to get a real insight into the local way of life, take a day-trip or stay overnight at the agri-turism centre at Finca El Cisne (☎651 4695, ⓦwww .fincaelcisne.com) 23km north of Copán. Owner Carlos's family has worked the land here since 1885, and they now invite guests to explore their working farm, which is involved in the production of cardamom, coffee and cattle. Day-long tours (from US$59) include transport to and from the *finca*, fantastic scenic horseriding, swimming in the Río Blanco and a trip (entrance included) to the Luna Jaguar hot springs. Tours of more than one day (from US$77) include accommodation, dinners and breakfasts. Visits can be arranged through the Basecamp office in Copán Ruinas.

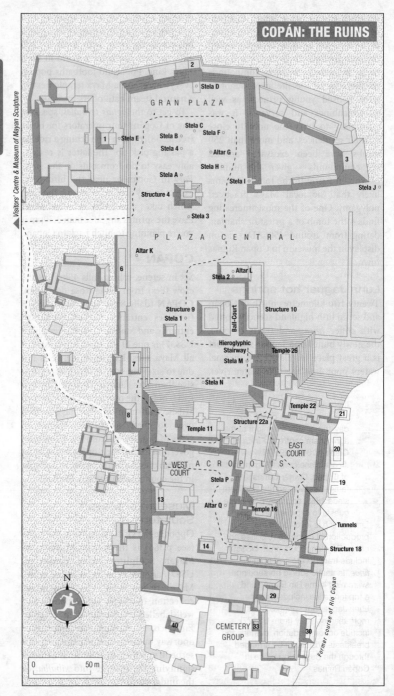

COPÁN: THE RUINS

Visitors' Centre & Museum of Mayan Sculpture

GRAN PLAZA

Stela D

2

1 ○ Stela E

Stela C

Stela B ○   ○ Stela F

Stela 4 ○   ○ Altar G

Stela H ○

Stela I ○

3

Stela J ○

Stela A ○

Structure 4

Stela 3 ○

PLAZA CENTRAL

Altar K ○

Altar L ○

Stela 2 ○

6

Structure 9   Structure 10

Stela 1 ○

Ball-Court

Hieroglyphic
Stairway   Temple 26

7   Stela M ○

Stela N ○

8

Temple 22

Structure 22a   21

Temple 11

20

EAST
COURT

WEST
COURT   A C R O P O L I S   19

Stela P ○

13   Tunnels

Altar Q ○   Temple 16

14   Structure 18

N

29

40   CEMETERY   33   30
        GROUP

0 ──── 50 m

Former course of Río Copán

Once out of the tunnel you are greeted by a dominating, full-scale, flamboyantly painted replica of the magnificent **Rosalila Temple**, built by Moon Jaguar in 571 AD and discovered intact under Temple 16. A vast crimson and jade coloured mask of the Sun God, depicted with wings outstretched, forms the main facade. Other exhibits concentrate on aspects of Maya beliefs and cosmology, while the upper floor houses many of the finest original sculptures from the Copán valley, comprehensively displaying the skill of the Maya craftsmen.

Plaza Central and Gran Plaza

Straight through the avenue of trees from the warden's gate lie the **Plaza Central** and **Gran Plaza**, large, rectangular arenas strewn with the magnificently carved and exceptionally well-preserved stelae that are Copán's outstanding features. The northern end of the Great Plaza was once a public place, the stepped sides bordered by a densely populated residential area, **Structure 4** in the centre of the two plazas is a modestly sized pyramid–temple.

Dotted all around are Copán's famed **stelae** and altars, made from local andesite. Most of the stelae represent **Eighteen Rabbit**, Copán's "King of the Arts" (stelae A, B, C, D, F, H and 4). Stele A (731 AD) has 52 glyphs along its sides including the emblem glyphs of the four great cities of Copán, Palenque, Tikal and Calakmul – a text designed to show that Eighteen Rabbit saw his city as a pivotal power in the Maya world. The original is now in the museum. Stele B (731 AD) depicts Eighteen Rabbit bearing a turban-like headdress intertwined with twin macaws, while his hands support a bar motif, a symbol designed to show the ruler holding up the sky. Stele C (730 AD) is one of the earliest stones to have faces on both sides. Two rulers are represented here:

facing the turtle shaped altar (a symbol of longevity) is Eighteen Rabbit's father Smoke Jaguar, while on the other side is Eighteen Rabbit himself. **Stele H** (730 AD), perhaps the most impressively executed of all the sculptures, shows Eighteen Rabbit wearing the latticed skirt of the Maize God, his wrists weighed down with jewellery, while his face is crowned with a stunning headdress.

Ball-court

South of Structure 4, towards the Acropolis, is the I-shaped **ball-court** (738 AD), one of the largest and most elaborate of the Classic period, and one of the few Maya courts still to have a paved floor. Dedicated to the great macaw deity, both sloping sides of the court are lined with three sculptured macaw heads. The rooms overlooking the playing area are thought to be where priests and the elite watched the game.

Hieroglyphic Stairway

Protected by a vast canvas cover just south of the ball-court is the famed **Hieroglyphic Stairway**, perhaps Copán's most astonishing monument. The stairway comprises the entire western face of the Temple 26 pyramid, and is made up of some 72 stone steps; every block forms part of the glyphic sequence – around 2200 glyph blocks in all, forming the longest-known Maya hieroglyphic text. Since their discovery at the end of the nineteenth century and a well-meaning reconstruction in the 1930s, the blocks have become so jumbled their true meaning is unlikely ever to be revealed. It is known that the stairway was initiated to record the dynastic history of the city; some of the lower steps were placed by Eighteen Rabbit in 710 AD, while Smoke Shell rearranged and completed most of the sequences in an effort to reassert the city's dignity and strength in 755 AD. At the base of the stairway the badly

COPÁN RUINS HISTORY

Once the most important city-state on the southern fringes of the Maya world, Copán was largely cut off from all other Maya cities except Quiriguá, 64km to the north in Guatemala (see p.200). Archeologists now believe that settlers began moving into the Río Copán valley from around 1400 BC, taking advantage of the area's rich agricultural potential, although construction of the city is not thought to have begun until around 100 AD. For those interested in finding out more, *Vision del Pasado Maya* by Fash and Fasquelle, available from the museums, is an excellent historical account of the site's history in Spanish.

426 AD Yax K'uk Mo' (Great Sun First Quetzal Macaw), a warrior–shaman, establishes the basic layout of the city. Yax K'uk Mo's son Popol Hol creates a cult of veneration for Yax K'uk Mo' which continues for over fifteen generations.

553 AD Golden era of Copán begins with the accession of Moon Jaguar, and the construction of his magnificent Rosalila temple.

578–628 AD Reign of Smoke Serpent.

628–695 AD Reign of Smoke Jaguar.

695–738 AD Eighteen Rabbit reigns and oversees the construction of the Gran Plaza, the final version of the ball-court and Temple 22 in the East Court, creating much of the stonework for which Copán is now famous.

Following Eighteen Rabbit's capture and decapitation by Quiriguá's Cauac Sky, construction at Copán comes to a halt for seventeen years.

749–763 AD Smoke Shell reigns and completes the construction of the Hieroglyphic Stairway.

760 AD Copán's population booms at around 28,000, the highest urban density in the entire Maya region.

763–820 AD Yax Pasaj, Smoke Shell's son, commissions Altar Q, which illustrates the entire dynasty from its beginning.

776 AD Yax Pasaj completes the final version of Temple 16.

822 AD Ukit Took' assumes the throne; the only monument to his reign, Altar L, was never completed. Skeletal remains indicate the decline of the city was provoked by inadequate food resources created by population pressures.

1576 Don Diego de Palacios, a Spanish court official, mentions the ruins of a magnificent city "constructed with such skill that it seems that they could never have been made by people as coarse as the inhabitants of this province" in a letter.

1834 Explorer Juan Galindo writes an account of the ruins.

1839 John Stephens, the US ambassador to Honduras, buys the ruins. Accompanied by Frederick Catherwood, a British architect and artist, they clear the site and map the buildings. *Incidents of Travel in Central America, Chiapas and Yucatán* is published by Stephens and Catherwood, and Copán becomes a magnet for archeologists.

1891 British archeologist Alfred Maudsley begins a full-scale mapping, excavation and reconstruction of the site sponsored by Harvard University's Peabody Museum.

1935 Washington Carnegie Institute diverts the Río Copán to prevent it carving into the site.

1959–60 Archeologists Heinrich Berlin and Tatiana Proskouriakoff begin to decipher the site's hieroglyphs, leading to the realization that they record the history of the cities and the dynasties.

1977 Instituto Hondureño de Antropología e Historia starts running a series of projects, including the tunnelling, with the help of archeologists from around the world.

1989 Rosalila Temple, buried beneath Temple 16, is discovered.

1993 Papagayo Temple, built by Popol Hol and dedicated to his father Yax K'uk Mo', is discovered.

1998 Yax K'uk Mo's tomb is discovered.

weathered **Stele M** depicts Smoke Shell and records a solar eclipse in 756 AD.

Temple 11

Adjacent to the Hieroglyphic Stairway, and towering over the extreme southern end of the plaza, are the vertiginous steps of **Temple 11** (Temple of the Inscriptions). At its base, **Stele N** (761 AD) represents Smoke Shell. The depth of the relief has protected the nooks and crannies, and in some of these you can still see flakes of paint – originally the carvings and buildings would have been painted in a whole range of bright colours, but only the red has survived.

Acropolis

South of the Hieroglyphic Stairway monumental temples rise to form the **Acropolis**. This lofty inner sanctum was the reserve of royalty, nobles and priests where religious rituals were enacted, sacrifices performed and rulers entombed. For over four hundred years, the temples grew higher and higher as new structures were built over the remains of earlier buildings. A warren of excavated tunnels, some open to the public, bore through the vast bulk of the Acropolis to the Rosalila Temple and several tombs.

Popol-Na

A few metres east of Temple 11 are the **Popol-Na** (Structure 22A), a governmental building with interlocking weave-like brick patterns, and **Temple 22**, which boasts some superbly intricate stonework around the door frames and was the site of religious blood-letting ceremonies. The decoration here is unique in the southern Maya region, with only the Yucatán sites such as Kabáh and Chicanna having carvings of comparable quality.

East Court

Below Temple 22 are the stepped sides of the **East Court**, a graceful plaza with life-sized jaguar heads – the hollow eyes would have once held jade or polished obsidian. Dominating the Acropolis, **Temple 16** built on top of the **Rosalila Temple** is the tallest structure in Copán, a thirty-metre pyramid completed by the city's sixteenth ruler, Yax Pasaj, in 776 AD. It was Maya custom to ritually deface or destroy obsolete temples and stelae. Yax Pasaj's extraordinary care to preserve the Rosalila Temple beneath illustrates the importance of the previous centre of worship during a period that marked the apogee of the city's political, social and artistic growth. The discovery of the Rosalila Temple has been one of the most exciting finds of recent years.

You can now view the brilliant original facade of the buried temple by entering through a short **tunnel** – an unforgettable, if costly (US$12), experience, as it may be sealed again in future years. The admission price also includes access to two further tunnels, which extend below the East Court and past some early cosmological stucco carvings – including a huge macaw mask – along with more buried temple facades and crypts including the Galindo tomb.

At the southern end of the East Court is **Structure 18**, a small square building with four carved panels, and the burial place of Yax Pasaj, who died in AD 821. The diminutive scale of the structure reveals how quickly decline set in. The tomb, empty when excavated by archeologists, is thought to have been looted on a number of occasions. South of Structure 18, the **Cemetery Group** was formerly thought of as a burial site, though it's now known to have been a residential complex for the ruling elite.

West Court

The second plaza of the Acropolis, the **West Court**, is confined by the south side of Temple 11 and Temple 16. At the base of Temple 16 and carved in 776 AD, **Altar Q** celebrates Yax Pasaj's accession to the throne on July 2, 763 AD. Six

The Guatemalan border is just twelve kilometres west of Copán, and crossing at the El Florido border post – usually busy with travellers coming to and from the ruins – is pretty straightforward, though it can be slow. Minibuses and pick-ups leave for El Florido from just west of the Parque about every thirty minutes until around 4pm. Copán Connections and Basecamp in Copán Ruinas (see p.358) have direct shuttles to Antigua and Guatemala City daily at 5.30am and noon for US$12 with connections to Río Dulce. There's no bank, but the ever-present moneychangers handle dollars, lempiras and quetzales at fairly good rates.

From the border, buses leave every thirty minutes (the last is at 4pm) for Chiquimula (1hr 15min; see p.197), 57km away down a smooth, newly paved road.

hieroglyphic blocks decorate the top of the altar, while the sides are decorated with sixteen cross-legged figures who represent previous rulers of Copán. All point towards a portrait of Yax Pasaj, which shows him receiving a ceremonial staff from the city's first ruler, Yax K'uk Mo', thereby endorsing Yax Pasaj's right to rule.

Arrival and information

From Copán Ruinas centre the ruins are an easy 15min walk along a shaded pavement following the highway; you can also grab a mototaxi from the Parque Central (5min; L10). On entrance you'll see to your right the cafeteria and souvenir shop; in front of you is the Museum of Mayan Sculpture; and to your left is the visitors' centre, where you pay your entrance fee. From here it's a 200m walk east to the warden's gate, where your ticket will be checked and you'll be greeted by squabbling macaws. Guides are available and are well worth the fee – they do an excellent job bringing the ruins to life; get together with other visitors to spread the cost (around US$35 for 2hr).

LA ENTRADA

Northeast from Copán the CA-11 winds its scenic way through lightly wooded mountains and fertile pasture to **LA ENTRADA**, a distinctly unpleasant junction town 55km northeast of Copán. It's only useful for its bus connections to San Pedro Sula, Santa Rosa and Copán Ruinas. If you get stuck here, *Hotel San Carlos* (☎898 5228; ❹), at the junction of CA-11 and CA-4, is the best of the available **accommodation**, where rooms

are at least comfortable and secure with en-suite bathroom and TV.

Olancho

Stretching east of Tegucigalpa to the Nicaraguan border and north into the emptiness of La Mosquitia, the sparsely populated uplands of **Olancho** are widely regarded as the "Wild East" of Honduras: an untamed frontier region with a not-entirely undeserved reputation for lawlessness. Over time, everyone from the first Spanish settlers to the Honduran government has had trouble imposing law and order here, and in many respects today is no different: the region's profitable cattle-ranching industry (which has encroached into national parks and other protected areas) and the logging of its massive forests (much of which is done illegally) have led to the creation of a powerful local oligarchy supported by military and police connivance. As a result, environmental issues have been sidelined, and activisits have been threatened and even killed. These territorial issues should not pose a problem to travellers, but obviously steer clear of any situations that seem dangerous.

Despite Olancho's size – it makes up a fifth of Honduras's total territory – tourist attractions in this region are few, and its high, forested mountain ranges interspersed with broad valleys make getting from place to place difficult and slow. However, these same ranges harbour some of the country's last untouched expanses of tropical and **cloudforest**: the national parks of **El Boquerón** and **Sierra de Agalta** are awe-inspiring. Along the valleys, now given over to pastureland for cattle, are scattered villages and towns. Both **Juticalpa**, the department capital, and **Catacamas**, at the eastern end of the paved road, are good bases for exploring the region.

Olancho's **climate** is generally pleasant, with the towns at lower altitudes hot during the day and comfortably cool at night; up in the mountains it can get extremely cold after dark. Once off the main highway, **travelling** becomes arduous, with the dirt roads connecting villages served by infrequent and invariably slow public transport.

JUTICALPA

Situated towards the southern end of the Valle de Catacamas, about 170km from Tegucigalpa, **JUTICALPA** is a thriving, pleasant little provincial city, where the streets are busy night and day with bustle and commerce. With a reasonable number of hotels and restaurants, it can be a refreshing place to spend a few days. The city's focal point is the leafy **Parque Banderas**, which includes a small pool of rather disgruntled-looking turtles – one suspects this is largely due to the lack of water. The majority of hotels, restaurants, banks, internet cafés and other facilities are on the streets around here. The general **market** stretches for a few blocks to the west, along Calle Perulapan. When the town's attractions have worn thin, the **cinema** at C 1, Av 2–3 shows subtitled US releases.

Arrival and information

By bus Juticalpa's two bus terminals are just off the highway on 1 Av SE, which leads straight to the centre, a 15min walk north. Local buses run from the terminal on the right side of the road (facing town); while direct buses to Tegucigalpa and the north coast use the other side.

Exchange Several banks dot the perimeter of Parque Banderas.

Internet The best access can be found at Ciber Café on C 1 NO, one block from *Hotel Honduras*. They also provide international phone services for L20 per minute.

Tourist information The local COHDEFOR office (daily 8am–4pm; ☎885 2253) is in a green house at the bottom of Av 7 between C 14 and 13, about two blocks west of the bus terminal.

Accommodation

Don't expect too much in the way of cosseted luxury in town, or indeed anywhere in Olancho.

Hotel Honduras C1 NO ☎785 1580. Rooms here are lifeless but clean, and all have overhead fan, TV and en-suite bathroom. ❸

Hotel Reyes C1 NO, on the same street as Ciber Café ☎785 2232. Charming, family-run hotel with clean, well-ventilated rooms (though they could use a lick of paint). The same can be said for the shared bathroom. ❶

Eating

Juticalpa's range of restaurants is also pretty modest, though there's a healthy profusion of inexpensive *comedores* and street-food stalls around Parque Banderas.

🏃 **Fresh Juice and Fruit** Next to *Hotel Honduras*. This friendly little café serves up great breakfast and a range of different fruit juices. Fresh fruit juice L30.

Restaurante Tai Ka Lock On the Parque. Cheap and cheerful Honduran-style Chinese dishes. Mains L50.

Moving on

By bus to: Catacamas (23 daily; 40min); La Ceiba (2 daily; 9hr); Tegucigalpa (20 daily; 2–3hr); Trujillo (daily 4am; 7hr).

MONUMENTO NACIONAL EL BOQUERÓN

Twenty kilometres east of Juticalpa, **MONUMENTO NACIONAL EL BOQUERÓN**, one of the last remaining tracks of **dry tropical forest** in

Honduras, is home to a wide variety of wildlife, including more than 250 species of bird.

What to see and do

To see the forest properly, you'll want to hike the moderately strenuous main **trail** through the reserve. The trail runs from where the bus drops you off near the Puente Boquerón bridge to a point a few kilometres west of the main entrance; the walk is manageable in one day if you get an early start.

Follow the track starting on the left-hand side of the Río Olancho – though it crosses over several times, so be prepared to wade – and after about a kilometre the path enters the gorge, eventually emerging onto the flood-plain at the other side. From here it is around two more easy hours through level pastureland to the village of **La Avispa**. Beyond the village, the path loops steeply uphill and through the cloudforest section of the park; you have a pretty good chance of seeing some of the country's elusive bird and animal life here, including mixed flocks of brightly coloured trogons and quetzals that feed together at fruiting trees. The reserve is also the only known Honduran location of the white-eared ground sparrow, fairly easily seen in the undergrowth. Beyond the cloudforest the walk is downhill all the way, with the path finally emerging a few kilometres later on the highway at Tempisque, west of the main entrance.

Arrival and information

Arrival Monumento Nacional El Boquerón is about halfway between Juticalpa and Catacamas. Any bus going between the two towns can drop you near the start of the main trail, by the Boquerón bridge. After you're done trekking, you can easily flag down buses to either place on the main highway.

Information The reserve is easily accessible as a day-trip from Juticalpa, though there are facili-ties should you want to camp (free, unless you have a guide with you). It is advisable to visit the COHDEFOR office in Juticalpa before setting out (see p.367), as the trail can be hard to follow, especially after heavy rainfall, and there are no rangers or information facilities once you reach the park. You need to bring all your own food and water.

CATACAMAS

CATACAMAS, midway along the Valle de Catacamas beneath the southern flanks of the Sierra de Agalta, is a smaller version of Juticalpa. Even fewer tourists visit here than come to that city – Catacamas is at the end of one of the paved roads through the region – which no doubt contributes to the affable, small-town charm of the place. It does, however, have a more spectacular setting than its larger neighbour: a short walk up to the **Mirador de la Cruz**, fifteen minutes from the centre on the northern side of town, gives superb views over the town and valley.

What to see and do

The main reason for coming out this far is to visit the **Cuevas de Talgua** (daily 9am–4pm; US$5). Located six kilometres north of town on the banks of the Río Talgua, the caves are one of the country's foremost historical sites, thanks to the discovery made here of a **prehistoric burial ground** featuring hundreds of skeletons arranged in chambers deep underground. Though the burial ground itself is out of bounds to visitors, the rest of the site has been developed for tourists, with a museum telling the tale of the finds and trails leading through the caves. To get here, take the local **bus** from Catacamas to Talgua, leaving town at 6am and 11am. The last return departs Talgua at 1pm.

Arrival

By bus Buses terminate four blocks south of Catacamas's Parque Central; the Parque itself, dominated by a giant ceiba tree, is a short walk away up a slight hill.

Accommodation

Accommodation in Catacamas is very limited. Those places that do exist are all located around the Parque Central.

Colina Av SW, just off the corner of the Parque ☎799 4488. *Colina* is the best hotel in town, with reasonably comfortable rooms set round a courtyard, all with bath, TV and fans. ②

Oriental ☎799 4038. Almost next door to *Colina*, *Oriental* is slightly cheaper and has a selection of basic but orderly rooms, some with private bath. ②

Eating

Restaurante Jardín Oriental This is the better of the two Chinese restaurants that stand side by side on the Parque. Mains L60.

Directory

Exchange There are a few banks situated around the park and in the streets just to the north.
Internet Access is available at a few places in town, the best being the one right on the Parque Central.
Post office Is located just north of the Parque Central.

Moving on

By bus to: Catacamas (23 daily; 40min); Tegucigalpa (22 daily; 3–4hr).

PARQUE NACIONAL SIERRA DE AGALTA

Draped across the sweeping ranges of the Sierra de Agalta, the vast **PARQUE NACIONAL SIERRA DE AGALTA** shelters the most extensive stretch of **virgin cloudforest** remaining in Central America. Though the area has been designated a protected area since 1987, large stands of pine and oak in the lower parts of the park have nonetheless still been logged, and much of the land cleared for cattle pasture. The higher reaches of the mountains, however (including Honduras's fourth highest peak, La Picucha), are so remote that both vegetation and wildlife have remained virtually untouched. Here a typical cloudforest of oaks, liquidambar and cedar, draped in vines and ferns, cover the slopes up to about 2000m, where they give way to a dwarf forest.

In addition to the flora, the park's isolation ensures a protected, secure environment for a biologically diverse range of **mammals** and **birds**, many of them extremely rare. Tapirs, jaguars, ocelots, opossums and three types of monkey are among the species of mammal recorded. More evident are the birds, of which more than four hundred species have been sighted. Along with longer **hikes**, which require the assistance of a guide (see below), easier jaunts are available in the environs of the park, allowing you to hunt for all these animals.

Arrival and information

Arrival The easiest points of entry for the park are along the northern edge of the Sierra, via the small towns of Gualaco and San Esteban, which you can reach off Highway C-39 between Juticalpa and Trujillo. The daily bus from Juticalpa (4am) passes by both – just ask the driver to stop so you can hop off; additional pick-ups from the market in Juticalpa also make the trip.
Information There's no accommodation in the park other than official camping spots, for which you'll need to bring all equipment and supplies. Hiring a guide is pretty much essential for hiking the difficult trails: ask at the COHDEFOR offices in Gualaco, San Esteban or Juticalpa (see p.367).

The north coast

Honduras's **north coast** stretches for some 300km along the azure fringes of the Caribbean. A magnet for Hondurans and foreign tourists alike, the region provides sun, sea and entertainment in abundance, especially in the coastal towns of **Tela**, **La Ceiba** and **Trujillo**, with their broad expanses of beach, clean warm waters, plentiful restaurants and buzzing nightlife. **San Pedro Sula**, the region's major inland city and transport hub, provides amenities of a strictly urban kind. Dotted along the north coast between these main towns are a number of laid-back **villages** blessed with unspoilt **beaches**. Populated by the **Garífuna** people (decendants of African slaves and Carib people; see p.103), these villages are often very much removed from the rest of Honduran culture and society, and can feel like visiting an entirely different country.

When beach life loses its appeal, there are several **natural reserves** to visit in the region. The national parks of **Cusuco**, **Pico Bonito** and **Capiro y Calentura**, whose virgin cloudforest shelters rare wildlife, offer hiking for all levels; the wetland and mangrove swamps at **Punta Sal** and **Cuero y Salado** require less exertion to explore. The region's two **dry seasons** – December to April, and August to September – are the best times to visit the north coast. Temperatures rarely drop below 25–28°C, but the heat is usually tempered by ocean breezes. **Transport** is reasonably good, with frequent buses along the fast, paved highway that links the main coastal towns; as usual, reaching the remoter villages and national parks requires some forward planning.

SAN PEDRO SULA

The country's second city and driving economic force, **SAN PEDRO SULA** sprawls across the fertile Valle de Sula ("Valley of the Birds" in Usula dialect) at the foot of the Merendón mountain chain, just an hour from the coast. Flat and uninspiring to look at, and for most of the year uncomfortably hot and humid, this is a city for getting business done, rather than sightseeing. It's also the **transport hub** for northern and western Honduras, meaning a visit here is usually unavoidable, even if only to pass through. On a more positive note, San

Pedro's **facilities** rate alongside Tegucigalpa, with an international airport, foreign consulates and a wide range of hotels, restaurants and shopping outlets – indeed, thanks to its practical location and better transportation links, travellers who stick to the north of the country (as so many do) rarely need to make a visit south to the capital.

What to see and do

San Pedro's reputation – it is more dangerous than the rest of the country, and its attractions are few and far between – generally precedes it, causing most tourists to get in and out as quickly as possible. While that may be wise, those who stick around often shed their preconceptions very quickly, provided they use a bit of common sense when taking in the few sights to hand.

San Pedro's centre is in the southwest sector of the city. Running west from the **Parque Barahona**, Calle 1 is also known as Boulevard Morazán for the twelve blocks before it meets the **Avenida Circunvalación** ring road, which separates the city centre from San Pedro's wealthier residential districts. Most of what you'll want to see in the city is within walking distance of the centre; the city's main general **market** is towards the southeastern edge of this area. The streets south of the market and over the old railway track can get rough, and although foreigners are unlikely to be targeted, neither are really places to be wandering around after dark.

Parque Barahona

San Pedro's central plaza, the large **Parque Barahona**, is the city centre's focus, teeming with vendors, shoeshine boys and moneychangers. The Parque's centrepiece is a large fountain with bridges and bronze statues of washerwomen beating their clothes on the rocks. On its eastern edge, the colonial-style **Catedral Municipal**, completed

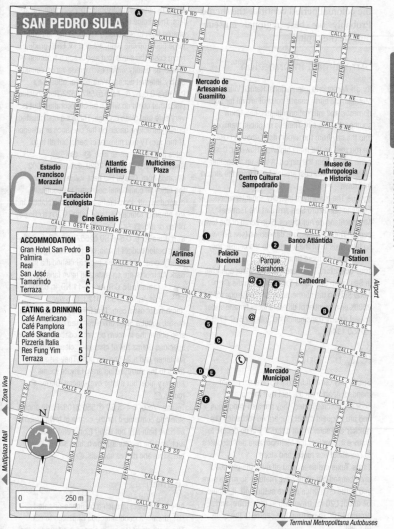

ACCOMMODATION

Gran Hotel San Pedro	B
Palmira	D
Real	F
San José	E
Tamarindo	A
Terraza	C

EATING & DRINKING

Café Americano	3
Café Pamplona	4
Café Skandia	2
Pizzería Italia	1
Res Fung Yim	5
Terraza	C

Terminal Metropolitana Autobuses

in the mid-1950s, is open to the public, but there's nothing of partiular interest inside. Facing it across the Parque is the unremarkable **Palacio Municipal**, home to the city administration.

Museo de Antropología e Historia

The **Museo de Antropología e Historia** (Mon & Wed–Sat 9am–4.30pm, Sun 9am–3pm; US\$2; ☎557 1496), a few blocks north of the Parque at Av 3, C 4 NO, is well worth a visit. The museum's collection of meticulously displayed and well looked after pre-Columbian sculptures, ceramics and other artefacts, the majority recovered from the Sula valley, outlines the development of civilization in the region from 1500 BC onwards; weaponry and paintings from the colonial period continue the theme. Probably the best regional museum outside the capital.

Arrival and information

By air Aeropuerto Internacional Ramón Villeda Morales, the north coast's point of arrival for both domestic and international flights, lies 12km southeast of the city. There is no public transport into the city from the airport itself, though buses do run past on the main highway. However, this is quite a hike from the airport. A taxi, an altogether better option, will cost around L150 from the airport into town.

By bus The majority of intercity and international buses to San Pedro Sula arrive at the Terminal Metropolitana de Autobuses, 5km south of the town centre. The city buses are dangerous (see below), so take taxis from the terminal to the centre; they should cost no more than L50.

Tour operators There are numerous tour agencies in San Pedro Sula; Sula Tours, based in the *Gran Hotel Sula* on the northern side of the Parque (☎ 545 2600), do a number of different tours far and wide.

Travel agent Transmundo de Sula, Av 5, C 4 NO (☎ 550 1140).

City transport

Buses City buses (L5) exist but are not recommended. Apart from the fact that they are hopelessly complicated, they are also dangerous and are frequent targets for armed robberies. It's quicker and safer to get a taxi. If you do decide to chance it, check at the Metropolitana de Autobuses to see about bus routes and stops.

Taxis Taxis cruise around all over the place. All are licensed but none have meters, so make sure you settle on a price before setting off. It should be about L20 for travel within the centre, and around L100 to go from the centre to the edge of town.

Accommodation

San Pedro is the second largest city in Honduras and one of the fastest growing in Latin America. As a result, there is a good array of safe budget options, most of which are towards the southern side of town along Avenida 6. It's not advisable to be tempted by any of the super cheap hotels – most aren't secure and can be dangerous.

Gran Hotel San Pedro C 3, Av 1–2 SO ☎ 550 1655, ⓔ hotelsanpedro@hotelsanpedrosa.com. A large, rambling establishment popular with travellers. The choice of rooms ranges from basic with shared bath to reasonably spacious options with large beds, private bath, a/c and TV. Each grade of room costs the same, but ask to see a selection of rooms, as quality within each grade varies considerably. Internet access available for guests. ❹

Palmira C 6, Av 6–7 SO ☎ 557 6522. Ramshackle place that could do with a bit of decoration, but is very safe and clean enough. There's a complicated pricing structure based on the presence or absence of fan, a/c, TV and number of beds, but all in all rates are on the cheap side. ❷–❹

Real Av 6, C 6–7 ☎ 550 7929, ⓔ hotelreal2002 @yahoo.com. One of the best-value options in the city. The communal courtyard is beautifully decorated with local crafts and climbing plants, and the en-suite rooms are large, with TV and a choice of fan or a/c. ❹

San José Av 6, C 5–6 SO ☎ 557 1208. One of the city's better budget hotels, offering clean, good-sized rooms, which are simply furnished if a little dark. All rooms are en suite and have fans. ❷

Tamarindo C 9, Av 10–11 NO, in Barrio Los Andes ☎ 557 0123, ⓦ www .tamarindohostel.com. This friendly Honduran-run hostel, about a 5min drive from the centre, is a step above the in-town accommodation, with spacious dorms full of character, clean bathrooms, a kitchen and a swimming pool. They also run tours to the surrounding area. Private rooms are very nice, but a little over-priced. Dorms ❸, rooms ❻

Terraza Av 6, C 4–5 SO ☎ 550 3108. Fairly priced, safe and convenient for the centre of town. Rooms all have bath and hot water (some also have a/c), and the restaurant downstairs serves good breakfast and dinner specials. ❸

Eating

As you'd expect in such a business-oriented city, there's a good selection of places to eat. The more down-to-earth places are found in the centre, while the stretch of Avenida Circunvalación south of Calle 1 – the so-called "Zona Viva" – is the place to go if you want to treat yourself to a splurge.

Café Americano On the western corner of the Parque Central on C 2 SO. Modern *Starbucks*-style coffee house with good mochas, cappuccinos and even frappuccinos to recharge your batteries. Coffee L20.

Café Pamplona On the Parque Barahona. Always crowded with locals, this place has kitsch 1970s decor, an extensive menu (mains L60) and decent coffee. The conch soup is a delicious house speciality. Open 'til 8pm.

Café Skandia In the *Gran Hotel Sula* on the northern side of the Parque Central. A/c and open 24hr, the *Skandia* is something of a San Pedro institution, offering tasty sandwiches, light meals and snacks, all for around L80. A great place for lunch.

Pizzería Italia C 1, Av 7 NO. Cosy little place serving good pizza (around L80) and a small selection of pasta dishes (around L100).

Res Fung Yim Av 6, C 4–5 SO. San Pedro Sula has an abundance of Chinese restaurants, and this is one of the best, not least for its convenient location near a lot of the budget hotels. The huge portions will set you back no more than L120.

Terraza In the *Terraza* hotel. The location – in a hotel – shouldn't put you off. The menu includes a range of Honduran and western cuisine; the dinner special is usually very good and never more than L100.

Drinking and nightlife

Like most big cities San Pedro Sula has a range of evening entertainment. All of the action is out in the Zona Viva, where a group of bars and clubs around Avenida 16 get very lively after dark. Take taxis out there. In general, the clubs are safer than the bars, which can get very dangerous. Some are fine, but none are particularly special.

Amnesia On the corner of Av 15 and C 7. The most European-style club in the city, with the music almost always a mix of Euro and Latin beats, and the crowd made up of rich locals. Things get going every night around 10pm and keep on till the early morning.

Confetti's Av Circunvalación, C 14–15 NO. Friendly *discoteca* that plays a combination of Latino pop and Euro dance music almost every evening.

Karaoki Club C 11, Av 14–15. One of the more popular hang-outs for the younger crowd, playing a large selection of Latin and European songs every night.

Entertainment

Centro Cultural Sampedrano C 3, Av 3–4 NO ☎553 3911. This cultural centre regularly hosts concerts and plays; the building also houses the public library.

Cinema There are two modern multi-screen cinemas in town: Multicines Plaza, at Av 10 & C 4 NO, and Cine Géminis, at C 1 & Av 12 NO – both are within easy walking distance of the centre and show new Hollywood films and the occasional Latin American offering.

Shopping

Books The cigar shop in the *Gran Hotel Sula* has a small assortment of English-language fiction, books on Honduras and US magazines and newspapers.

Markets The Mercado Guamilito, Av 9, C 6–7 NO, is an indoor market with numerous stalls selling hammocks, ceramics, leatherwork and wooden goods; gentle bargaining should get you better prices. A couple of shops on the Calle Peatonal, just off the Parque Central, sell similar stuff, though prices are higher and the range not as wide. The Mercado Municipal, centred between Av 4–5 SO and C 5–6 SO and along the old rail track, has stalls spilling onto the streets for several blocks. You can find a bit of everything here. For more targeted shopping options, numerous malls are dotted around the city centre.

Directory

Airlines Atlantic, at Av 10, C 3–4 NO (☎552 7270) or at the airport (☎668 7310); Isleña/TACA, at Parque Benito Juárez (☎558 1604) or at the airport (☎668 3292); Sosa, at C 1, Av 7–8 SO (☎550 6545) or at the airport (☎668 3223). American (☎553 3526), Continental (☎557 4141) and Delta (☎550 8188) are all at the airport.

Car rental Molinari, in the *Gran Hotel Sula* on the northern side of the Parque Central (☎533 2639); Omega, Av 3, C 3–4 NO (☎552 7626).

Consulates Belize, on the road to Puerto Cortés (☎551 6247); El Salvador, Av 11, 5–6 NO (☎557 5591); Germany C 1, 8–9 SO (☎553 1244); Mexico, C 2, Av 20–21 SO (☎552-3672); Netherlands, Av 15, C 7–8 (☎557 1815); Nicaragua, Av 5, Av 4–5 SO (☎550 0813); Spain, Av 2, C 3–4 NE (☎553 2480); UK, C 2, Av 18–19 NO (☎550 2337); US, in the Banco Atlántida building on the northern side of the Parque (☎558 1580).

Exchange Banco Atlántida has a number of branches downtown, including one on the Parque Central with an ATM; there are several other banks along C 2 between Av 5 and 6.

Internet There are countless internet cafés in town. Just off the Parque next to *Café Americano* is Diosita.net, which has good, cheap connections and decent international phone rates. Llamadas, on Av 4, C 3–4 SO, one floor up from street level, also has a quick connection.

Medical care Hospital Centro Médico Betesda, Av 11, C 11–12 NO.

Post office C 9, Av 3 SO (Mon–Fri 7.30am–8pm, Sat 7.30am–12.30pm).

Telephones Hondutel, on the corner of C 5 and Av 5, is open 24hr.

Moving on

By air to: Belize City (with Atlantic & TACA; 55min); Guanaja (with Atlantic & Sosa; 2hr 50min); Guatemala City (with TACA; 1hr 10min); La Ceiba (with Atlantic, Isleña/TACA & Sosa; 30min); Managua (with Atlantic & TACA; 2hr 25min); Panama City, via San Salvador (with TACA; 5hr 55min); Roatán (with Atlantic & Sosa; 2hr 35min); San José (with TACA; 2hr 15min); San Salvador (with TACA; 50min); Tegucigalpa (with Atlantic, Isleña/TACA & Sosa; 45min); Utila (with Atlantic & Sosa; 2hr 15min).

By bus to: Comayagüela (14 daily; 3–4hr); Copán Ruinas (11 daily; 3hr); Gracias (1 daily; 5hr); Guatemala City (2 daily; 8hr); La Ceiba (22 daily; 3hr); La Entrada (25 daily; 1–2hr); Managua (1 daily; 12hr); Ocotopeque (5 daily; 5hr); Puerto Cortés (70 daily; 1hr); Pulhapanzak and Lago de Yojoa (14 daily; 1hr 30min); San Salvador (2 daily; 6hr); Santa Rosa de Copán (6 daily; 3hr); Siguatepeque (14 daily; 3hr); Tela (18 daily; 1hr 30min); Tegucigalpa (30 daily; 4hr); Trujillo (18 daily; 5–6hr). All services listed here leave from the main Terminal Metropolitana Autobuses, south of town.

PARQUE NACIONAL EL CUSUCO

If the charms of San Pedro Sula rub off quickly, as they may well do, a short journey out of the city to one of the country's best national parks can transport you into an entirely different world. Some 20km west of San Pedro in the Sierra del Merendón, the stunning **PARQUE NACIONAL EL CUSUCO** (daily 8am–4.30pm; US$15) supports an abundant range of animal and plant life, quite a bit of which is rare or threatened.

What to see and do

The lower reaches of the park have long been settled by humans and were heavily logged during the 1950s; the mixed pine and broadleaf forest you see today is secondary growth. At around 1800m the **cloudforest** begins, its dense oaks and liquidambars – which tower to 40m in some places – stacked over avocados and palms, and supporting mosses, vines, orchids and numerous species of heliconias, recognizable by the red or orange brackets holding the blossoms. Studies carried out in the park in the 1990s revealed the existence of at least seventeen species of plants not previously recorded in Honduras.

To see as much as possible, the best plan is to arrive in the afternoon, camp overnight and walk the park's good **trails** early in the morning. Four trails, ranging between 1km and 2.5km, have been laid out among the lower sections of cloudforest (there is no access to the highest, steepest sections of the reserve), taking you through a hushed world of dense, dripping, multilayered vegetation. If you're incredibly lucky, you might spot the reserve's namesake *cusuco* (armadillo), as well as monkeys and possibly even a jaguar. The dazzling range of birdlife includes quetzals, best spotted from April to June, along with trogons, kites and woodpeckers.

Arrival and information

Arrival The park is not too hard to reach from San Pedro, through the trip is time-consuming. Take a westbound bus to the small town of Cofradía (buses to and from La Entrada or Santa Rosa pass through), the main point of access, 18km southwest of San Pedro off Highway CA-4. You'll have to wait here for onward transport (in the form of a pick-up) to the village of Buenos Aires, 5km beyond which you'll find the park's visitors' centre. Another option is to rent a car in San Pedro (see p.373 for listings) – a 4WD can make the whole journey in about two hours, depending on the state of the road.

Information Cusuco is managed by the Fundación Ecologista, which has offices in San Pedro Sula at 12 Av NO, C 1–2 (☎ 557 6598, ✉ fundeco@netsys .hn). Information leaflets are usually available, and they can also advise on getting to the reserve. The park's visitors' centre has displays on the park's wildlife and trail maps.

Accommodation

The visitors' centre has a designated campsite, but it's only a place to pitch a tent – there are no services. Alternatively, there is a small house for rent with kitchen facilities (reserve at the Fundación Ecologista office in San Pedro Sula, US$10 per person with a minimum of four).

PUERTO CORTÉS

North of San Pedro Sula, Highway CA-5 runs through the flat agricultural lands and lush tropical scenery of the Sula valley. After 60km the four-lane highway reaches the coast at **PUERTO CORTÉS**, Honduras's main port. There's nothing here to entice, and you'll likely pass through only to change buses en route to Omoa or to hop aboard a boat for Belize.

Arrival

By bus Three companies run buses between San Pedro Sula and Puerto Cortés, including the reliable Citul, who run the hour-long trip every 30min between 6am and 6pm. The Citul terminal in Puerto Cortés is a block north of the main plaza at Av 4 and C 4.

Accommodation

If you do stay here, be prepared to pay for it – real budget accommodation is non-existent.
Hotel Mr. Ggeerr ☎ 665 4333. C 9, Av 1–2. The hotel with the strangest name in Honduras, is your best bet. Rooms all have a/c and en-suite bathroom. ❹

Eating

There is also little choice in terms of places to eat.
Repostería Plata Av 3 and C 2. Popular with locals for their buffet meals, this place has the added advantage of being open on Sun, when all other restaurants are closed. Mains from L60.

Moving on

By boat There are ferries to Big Creek and Placencia in Belize (see box below).

By bus to: Corinto, for Guatemala (30 daily; 4hr); Omoa (42 daily; 1hr). Buses leave from the Transportes Citral terminal, which is on C 4 around the corner from the Citul terminal.

OMOA

Spreading inland from a deep bay at the point where the mountains of the Sierra de Omoa meet the Caribbean, the fishing village of **OMOA** has become increasingly popular in recent years, with travellers coming here for total rest and relaxation. Once a strategically important location in the defence of the Spanish colonies against marauding British pirates, today the village dozes lethargically under the heat of the Caribbean sun.

What to see and do

Omoa's one outstanding sight, the restored **Fortaleza de San Fernando de Omoa** (Mon–Fri 8am–4pm, Sat & Sun 9am–5pm; US$2), stands amid tropical greenery in mute witness to the village's colourful history. Now isolated a kilometre from the coast, having been beached as the sea has receded over the centuries, the triangular fort was originally intended to protect the port of Puerto Barrios in Guatemala. Work began in 1759 but was never fully completed due to a combination of inefficiency and a labour shortage. The steadily weakening Spanish authorities then suffered the ignominy of witnessing the fortress be temporarily occupied by British and Miskito military forces in October 1779. A small museum on site tells the story of the fort and

---

INTO BELIZE BY FERRY

In theory, two companies (Express and Water Taxi) run **boats** between **Belize** and Honduras, although in reality the timetables are inconsistent and boats rarely leave on time. When running, both companies' boats leave from Barra La Laguna, about 3km southeast of Puerto Cortés (take any bus going to Omoa and ask to be dropped). The Express boat is scheduled to leave Monday at 11:30am, and the Water Taxi on Monday and Tuesday at noon. Both go to Big Creek and Placencia (US$50 one way; 3hr).

displays a selection of military paraphernalia including cannons and period weaponry.

The narrow village **beach**, lined with colourful fishing boats, offers stunning views west across the curve of the bay and the mountain backdrop. At weekends hordes of day-trippers turn up and it's often too crowded for comfort. Better swimming can be had by walking five minutes or so out of the village in either direction, while fifteen minutes around the headland to the east lies a much wider and usually empty expanse of beach.

Arrival and information

By bus The buses between Puerto Cortés and Corinto pass the southern end of the village at a crossroads. From here a road runs 2km to the beach (walking is pretty much the only method of transport), where you'll find most of the action. Most services can be found on this main road.
Exchange Banco de Occidente can advance cash on your cards but has no ATM.
Internet Alta Velocidad, next door to Banco de Occidente, has the town's best connection and charges about L20.

Accommodation

Rising numbers of foreign tourists have led to the opening of a handful of reasonably comfortable places to stay, but the range is still far behind more notable towns along the north coast.
Fisherman Along the beach road ☎658 9224. Another good budget option right on the beach. The quality of rooms varies: some have had recent decoration and some don't see much light at all, so make sure you view a few before deciding. ❷
Roli's Place Along the main road about 200m from the sea ☎658 9082. An excellent budget place with comfortable rooms as well as camping, hammocks (both US$3 per person) and dorms; they also have kayaks and bikes, a kitchen and laundry facilities. Dorms ❶, rooms ❸

Eating

The best places for meals are the *champas* (restaurants) that sit right along the seafront. They all serve up the same kind of fare, a mix of Honduran and European dishes. All are informal and you should expect to never pay more than L80 for an average meal.
Champa Johnson The best of the *champas* along the beach, with a pleasant setting and great service. The seafood is recommended but wildly expensive. Regular mains from L60. Seafood from L200.
Tatiana Half hotel, half restaurant, on the beach. This place serves up a range of meat dishes, including some very tasty pork chops. Mains from L80.

Moving on

By bus to: Corinto, for Guatemala (42 daily; 1hr); Puerto Cortés (42 daily; 1hr).

TELA

Sitting midway around the Bahía de Tela, surrounded by sweeping beaches, **TELA** has a near-perfect setting. In the past, the town has suffered from a reputation for unpredictability and violence, but a pilot force of bilingual tourist police (now being imitated throughout the country) is substantially cleaning up the town's image, although things can still get rowdy at weekends. Whether you choose to partake in the nightlife or not, the wealth of fantastic **natural reserves** – including Punta Sal – within minutes of the town makes Tela well worth a visit. Be aware that Tela is one of the

---

INTO GUATEMALA: CORINTO

Moving on from Omoa to Guatemala is an excruciatingly slow journey along the notoriously bumpy road leading southwest to Corinto, 2km from the border (buses every 20min 8am–4pm). Corinto has its own *migración* (daily 8am–5.30pm). Pick-ups shuttle to and from the border, from where you can catch a minibus (every 30min) into Guatemala; there's usually an exit fee of US$1–2 charged. Minibuses pass though the village of Entre Ríos, for Guatemalan *migración*, to Puerto Barrios, an hour from the Honduran border.

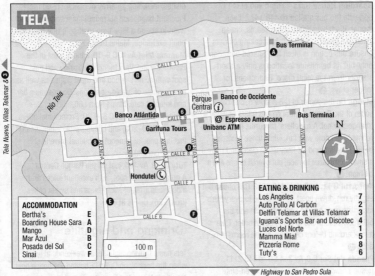

TELA

Tela Nueva, Villas Telamar &

Río Tela

Bus Terminal

CALLE 11

CALLE 10

Parque Central

Banco de Occidente

Banco Atlántida

Espresso Americano

Bus Terminal

Garífuna Tours

Unibanc ATM

CALLE 9

CALLE 8

AVENIDA 2

AVENIDA 3

AVENIDA 4

AVENIDA 5

AVENIDA 6

AVENIDA 7

AVENIDA 8

AVENIDA 9

N

Hondutel

CALLE 7

ACCOMMODATION

Bertha's	E
Boarding House Sara	A
Mango	D
Mar Azul	B
Posada del Sol	C
Sinai	F

CALLE 6

0   100 m

EATING & DRINKING

Los Angeles	7
Auto Pollo Al Carbón	2
Delfin Telamar at Villas Telamar	3
Iguana's Sports Bar and Discotec	4
Luces del Norte	1
Mamma Mia!	5
Pizzería Rome	8
Tuty's	6

▼ Highway to San Pedro Sula

main destinations for Hondurans during Semana Santa (Easter Holy Week) and booking several weeks, if not months, ahead is advisable for that period.

What to see and do

Today's Tela is a product of the banana industry. In the late nineteenth century United Fruit built a company town – **Tela Nueva** – here, on the west bank of the Río Tela; the old town became known as **Tela Vieja**. These distinctions still stand. The old town, which lies about 2km north of the highway and two blocks from the beach on the east bank of the river, encompasses the **Parque Central** and main shopping area. Five blocks west from the Parque Central is the Río Tela, and on the other side of the river, Tela Nueva. A fifteen-minute stroll covers practically everything there is to see (not a lot). However, it's the **beaches** that most people come for; those in Tela Vieja, though wide, are more crowded than the stretch of pale sand in front of the hotel *Villas Telamar* in Tela Nueva. Even better beaches can be found along the bay outside town – if you walk far enough

in either direction you should be able to have one entirely to yourself.

Arrival and information

By bus Most local bus services, including the half-hourly buses to and from La Ceiba, use the terminal on the corner of Av 9 and C 9 NE. Buses to the surrounding villages use the terminal two blocks north at C 11 and Av 8 NE.

Tour operators Garífuna Tours, C 9, Av 4–5 SO (☎ 448 2904, ⊛ www.garifunatours.com), run trips to Punta Sal and Punta Izopo (US$18 per person) as well as the "EcoPass" tour, which encompasses visits to both places plus Pico Bonito for US$58.

Tourist information The tourist office is in the municipal building off the southeast corner of the Parque Central (Mon–Fri 8am–6pm, Sat 8am–noon; ⊛ www.tela-honduras.com).

Accommodation

Many of Tela's older hotels are quite run-down. There are, however, a number of newer, better-value places opening up as the town becomes more of a fixture on the backpacker trail. Many of these tend to get busy at weekends, when it pays to book ahead.

Bertha's Av 2, C 6–7 ☎ 448 1009. Rooms are spotlessly clean and most have en-suite bathrooms. A good option if elsewhere is full. ❸

Boarding House Sara Eastern end of C 11 opposite the bus station ☎ 448 1477. Even though it's falling apart at the seams, cheap rates and welcoming English-speaking owners ensure this option is often full. Shared bathrooms only, but its beachside location is only a short stagger from the local disco. Reductions for longer stays. ❶

Mango On the corner of C 8 and Av 5, one block south of the Parque Central ☎ 448 0338, ⓦ www.mangocafe.net. A travellers' favourite, the cheaper rooms here come with fan, while those a notch better have a/c and TV. Rooms are clean and there's a small communal terrace, but overall prices are a bit high. ❸

Mar Azul C 11, Av 3–4 ☎ 448 2313 This cheap but slightly run-down hotel might not be to everyone's taste: the beds can be uncomfortable and the bathrooms are prone to being out of order. Take a look around before deciding, as the rooms vary a lot. ❶

Posada del Sol C 8, Av 3–4 SO ☎ 448 2111. Rustic *posada* with pleasant, if basic, en-suite rooms. There's an outdoor seating area in a nice garden, making this one of the better budget options in town. ❶

Sinai At the southern end of Av 5 ☎ 448 1486. Friendly, well-run place with tasteful en-suite rooms as well as rooms with shared bathrooms. It's a bit of a walk from the beach, but it's well worth it. ❷–❸

Eating

Tela has an interesting mix of places to eat, with foreign-run restaurants that cater to the steady flow of European and North American visitors competing with locally owned seafood places. One staple that shouldn't be missed is the delicious *pan de coco* (coconut bread) sold by Garífuna women and children on the beach and around town.

Auto Pollo Al Carbón At the western end of C 11, by the bridge. Informal place on the doorstep of the Caribbean Sea. They serve chicken and not much else, but in terms of value for money, you can't do much better. Mains from L40.

Los Angeles C 9, Av 1–2. Four blocks west of the Parque Central. The huge servings of Chinese food here are easily big enough to serve three people. If you're looking to convert your money into as much food as possible, this is the place to come. Mains from L60.

Luces del Norte On the corner of C 11 and Av 5. Popular with foreign tourists, *Luces del Norte* offers a good range of seafood dishes, including an array of conch-based meals. Pleasant beachside surroundings mean you might want to spend a little time reading a title from the book exchange. Mains from L80.

Mamma Mia! Av 4, C 9–10, a block west of the Parque Central. Very friendly Italian-owned pasta spot with some seafood and meat dishes as well as a wide range of breakfast options. Doubles as a bar and internet café. Mains from L60.

Pizzería Rome Av 2, C 8–9 SO. Promotional offers on pizza (L80–200) and cheap pasta dishes mean this is a popular hangout for budget travellers. Mains from L80.

Tuty's C 9, Av 4–5, just off the Parque Central. A great breakfast spot, with excellent juices and a delicious array of sticky buns and sweet cakes (from L20). Opens at 6am.

Drinking and nightlife

Tela has a thriving nightlife, at weekends at least, when the bars along Calle 11 behind the beach host crowds listening to salsa, reggae and mainstream dance music. Some of these places on this strip don't have names (and some change names every few months), so you'll just have to take a stroll and see what's going on.

Delfín Telamar at Villas Telamar 1km west of town, in Tela Nueva. This is the place to go for a tranquil drink whilst enjoying the Caribbean sea breezes. It's also home to the *Guarumas Disco Bar*, which is a lively spot open most nights till 11pm.

Iguana's Sports Bar & Discotec Av 2, C 10–11, up by the bridge in the northwest of town. This lively disco really gets going at weekends and is a popular hangout for locals and travellers alike.

Mango (see above). The hotel organizes regular evenings of Garífuna music and dancing on the grounds.

Directory

Exchange There is a Unibanc ATM on the southern side of the park. Banco de Occidente, on the eastern side of the Parque, does cash advances, while Banco Atlántida, on the corner of Av 4 and C 9, can change traveller's cheques.

Internet Espresso Americano, on the southeastern corner of the Parque, has a good, cheap connection (L10).

Post office At Av 4, C 7–8 SO, two blocks south of the Parque Central.

Telephones The Hondutel office is next to the post office.

Moving on

By bus to: La Ceiba (42 daily; 2hr 30min); San Pedro Sula (8 daily; 2hr). To get to San Pedro Sula you can also get a taxi out to the highway south of town and flag down one of the buses coming from La Ceiba.

AROUND TELA

Even if you're quickly bored with Tela itself, there is an abundance of places to visit in the nearby area. These include the **Garífuna villages** along the bay on pristine beaches on either side of town, the **Punta Sal** wildlife reserve, and **Lancetilla**, 5km south of town and probably the finest botanical reserve in Latin America. To get to any of these places, you can take taxis or rely on local buses, but renting a bike is probably the most enjoyable way to get around; ask at Garífuna Tours (see p.377) for rental information.

Garífuna villages

The **Garífuna communities** of the north coast have an entirely different history and culture from the Mestizo people who represent the majority of Hondurans. The villages, located on quiet and expansive stretches of beach, are an interesting getaway for a few hours. Weekends are the best time to visit them, when people congregate to perform the traditional, haunting and melodic drum-driven rhythms of Garífuna music.

Heading west from Tela, a dirt road edges the bay between the seafront and the **Laguna de los Micos**, which forms the eastern edge of Punta Sal (see below). Seven kilometres along this road is the sleepy village of **Tornabé**, and, beyond that, **Miami**, which is set on a fabulous stretch of beach at the mouth of the lagoon. Though Tornabé has a few brick-built houses, Miami consists of nothing but traditional palm-thatched huts.

Buses run to Tornabé from the eastern end of Calle 10 in Tela every hour on the hour, from 6am to 5pm. From Tornabé pick-ups run to Miami at 6.30am and 12.30pm Monday to Saturday, with returns at 8am and 2pm. **Accommodation** in both towns is limited. Local families may rent out extremely basic rooms if you ask around, or you're left with expensive, resort-style hotels.

Parque Nacional Jeanette Kawas (Punta Sal)

The **Parque Nacional Jeanette Kawas** (daily 6am–4pm; US$3), commonly known as **Punta Sal**, is a wonderfully diverse **reserve** encompassing mangrove swamps, coastal lagoons, wetlands, coral reef and tropical forest, which together provide habitats for an extraordinary range of animal, bird and plant life. Jeanette Kawas, for whom the reserve is named, was instrumental in obtaining protected status for the land, in the face of intense local opposition; her murder, in February 1995, has never been solved.

Lying to the west of Tela, curving along the bay to the headland of Punta Sal (176m), the reserve covers three lagoons: **Laguna de los Micos**, on the park's eastern side; **Laguna Tisnachí**, in the centre; and the oceanfront **Laguna El Diamante**, on the western side of the headland. More than one hundred species of bird are present, including herons and storks, with seasonal migratory visitors bumping up the numbers; animals found in the reserve include howler and white-faced monkeys, wild pigs, jaguars and, in the marine sections, manatees and marine turtles. Boat trips along the Río Ulúa and the canals running through the reserve offer a superb opportunity to view the wildlife at close quarters. Where the headland curves up to the north, the land rises slightly to Punta Sal; a **trail** over the point leads to small, pristine **beaches** at either side.

It's possible to visit parts of Punta Sal independently – you can rent a **boat** in Miami (see above) to explore the Laguna de los Micos and surrounding area – though most people opt to join the trips organized by Garífuna Tours (see p.377). You could also **hike** the scenic eight kilometres from Miami to the headland along the beach.

Jardín Botánico de Lancetilla

The extensive grounds of the **Jardín Botánico de Lancetilla** (Mon–Fri 7.30am–3pm, Sat & Sun 8am–3pm; US$6), 5km south of Tela, started life in 1925 as a United Fruit species research and testing station, and over time has grown into one of the largest collections of fruit and flowering trees, palms, hardwoods and tropical plants in the world. There are also 365 recorded species of bird. Guided **tours** of the arboretum and birdwatching tours are available, and visitors are also free to wander at will along the marked **trails**; maps are available at the **visitors' centre** at the entrance to the park. A small swimming hole in the Lancetilla River is at the end of one of the trails, and can make for a refreshing break.

To get to Lancetilla, take a San Pedro Sula-bound **bus** from Tela for a couple of kilometres to the signposted turn-off; ask the driver to drop you. From here, the park is a further 3km. There's a *comedor* and a small **hostel** (❸–❹) at the visitors' centre; beds should be reserved on ☎448 1740.

LA CEIBA

Some 190km east along the coast from San Pedro Sula, steamy **LA CEIBA**, the lively capital of the department of Atlántida, is the gateway to the Bay Islands. Though the town is completely bereft of architectural interest and its sandy beaches are strewn with garbage, it does at least enjoy a remarkable setting at the steep slopes of the Cordillera Nombre de Dios. Bustling and self-assured by day, La Ceiba is also home

to a cosmopolitan mix of inhabitants, including a large Garífuna community, but it's the night that's really celebrated here, with visitors and locals gathering every night to take part in the city's vibrant dance scene.

Ceiba, as it's generally known, owes its existence to the banana industry: the Vaccaro Brothers (later Standard Fruit and now Dole) first laid plantations in the area in 1899 and set up their company headquarters in town in 1905. Although fruit is no longer shipped out through La Ceiba, the plantations are still important to the local economy, with crops of pineapple and African palm now as significant as bananas.

What to see and do

Most things of interest to visitors lie within a relatively small area of the city, around the shady and pleasant **Parque Central**, with its busts of Honduran historical heroes. The unremarkable whitewashed and powder-blue **Cathedral** sits on the Parque's southeast corner. Running north from the Parque almost to the seafront, Avenida San Isidro, Avenida Atlántida and Avenida 14 de Julio frame the main commercial district, with shops, banks, a couple of supermarkets and the main municipal market. For an interesting five-minute diversion, stroll a block west of the Parque to the **Oficinas del Ferrocarril Nacional**, planted with tropical vegetation and dotted with museum-piece train carriages, many dating from the days of the peak of the banana trade.

All the **beaches** within the city limits are, sadly, too polluted and dirty for even the most desperate. Better by far is to head east to the much cleaner beaches a few kilometres out of town (see p.384). Calle 1, in the northwest end of town near the seafront, extends east from the old dock and over the river estuary into **Barrio La Isla**, a quieter residential district, mainly home to Garífuna.

▲ Dock for ferries to Bay Islands

LA CEIBA

CARIBBEAN SEA

Old Dock

BARRIO LA ISLA

BARRIO INGLÉS

Immigration

La Moskitia
Ecoadventuras

Garifuna
Tours

Parque
Bonilla

Market

Banco Credomatic

Oficinas
de Ferrocarril
Nacional

Molinari

Parque
Central

Transmundo

Aerolíneas Sosa

Banks

Bank

Cathedral

Atlantic
Airlines

Centro
Internacional
de Idiomas

Lavandería

Stadium

AVENIDA MANUEL BONILLA

AVENIDA DIONISIO DE HERRERA

AVENIDA PEDRO NUÑO

AVENIDA MIGUEL PAZ BARAHONA

AVENIDA 14 DE JULIO

AVENIDA ATLÁNTIDA

AVENIDA SAN ISIDRO

AVENIDA REPÚBLICA

AVENIDA SAN ISIDRO

AVENIDA 15 DE SEPTIEMBRE

CALLE 4
CALLE 5
CALLE 6
CALLE 7
CALLE 8
CALLE 9
CALLE 10

CALLE 2
CALLE 3

CALLE 4
CALLE 5
CALLE 6
CALLE 7
CALLE 8
CALLE 9

CALLE 11
CALLE 12
CALLE 13

▼ Airport, San Pedro Sula, Butterfly & Insect Museum

▼ Megaplaza Mall

▼ Hospital

▼ Post Office

Bus Station

0   200 m

N

EATING & DRINKING
La Casa de Barbacoa	10
La Casona	7
Chef Guity	1
Coconut	4
Expatriate's Bar & Grill	11
Flipper	6
El Guapo's	2
Mango Tango	5
Masapán	8
La Palapa	3
Super Baleada	9

ACCOMMODATION
Amsterdam 2001	A
Banana Republic	F
Caribe	C
Los Guacamayos	E
Rotterdam Beach	B
San Carlos	D

Museum of Butterflies and Insects

About a kilometre south of the plaza is the private **Museum of Butterflies and Insects** (Mon–Sat 8am–noon & 1–4pm; Etapa 2, Casa G-12, C Escuela Internacional, Colonia El Sauce; US$1.35; ⓦ www.hondurasbutterfly.com), where over twelve thousand specimens from 68 countries are on view, though almost three-quarters are native species. Displays explain trapping techniques, and there are videos in English and Spanish.

Arrival and information

By air Aeropuerto Internacional Golosón is 9km from the centre, off the main highway west to San Pedro Sula. There's no local transport into town from the airport, but a taxi into the centre should cost no more than L100.

By boat The ferries to and from Roatán and Utila in the Bay Islands use the Muralla de Cabotaje municipal dock, about 5km east of the city. A shared taxi should usually cost L120 per taxi (4 people) to the pier and L40 per person from it.

By bus Long-distance and local buses arrive at the main terminal, 2km west of the centre; taxis to downtown, usually shared, charge L15 per person. Local buses also run into town and will cost about L5.

Tour operators Several companies offer tours to the surrounding area and further afield. Recommended are Garífuna Tours, at the northern end of Av San Isidro (ⓣ 440 3252, ⓦ www.garifunatours .com); La Moskitia Ecoaventuras, C 1, Av 14 de Julio–Av Atlántida (ⓣ 440 2124, ⓦ www.honduras .com/moskitia); and Jungle River Tours, based at the *Banana Republic Guesthouse*, Av República, C 12–13 (ⓣ 440 1268).

Tourist information There is a rather lacklustre tourist office on C 8 one block east of the Parque Central.

Travel agent Transmundo, at Av San Isidro, C 9–10.

Accommodation

Given La Ceiba's status as both a provincial and a party centre, it comes as no surprise that there's a range of budget places to stay. The only problem will be in deciding whether you want to be near the centre or closer to the nightlife along Calle 1. Prices inevitably tend to rise around Carnaval time in May, when reserving ahead becomes essential.

Amsterdam 2001 1 C, Av Barahona, Barrio La Isla ⓣ 442 2292. Dutch-run hotel, just up from the beach. Dorms are dilapidated but rooms are adequate, some with bathroom. It's run down, but cheap enough for a brief stay. Dorms ❶, rooms ❷

Banana Republic Av República, C 12–13 ⓣ 441 9404. Once the heart of the backpacker scene in La Ceiba, *Banana Republic* is now starting to show its age but is still a decent option. The rooms are much better than the dorms; the less said about the shared bathroom the better. Dorms ❶, rooms ❹

Caribe C 5, Av San Isidro–Atlántida ⓣ 443 1857. *Caribe* is perfectly acceptable if other places in town are full. There are both dorms and private rooms; the dorms are very basic, with little ventilation or light, and the shared bathroom doesn't stay clean for long. Dorms ❶, rooms ❷

🏃 **Las Guacamayas** Av Colon, C 11–12 ⓣ 406 8198. Extremely clean and full of character, this hostel offers homely dorms, a patio overlooking the street, TV area, kitchen, laundry service and free internet. It's a real bargain. There are no private rooms, only dorms. ❷

Rotterdam Beach C 1, Av Barahona, Barrio La Isla ⓣ 440 0321. Next door to *Amsterdam 2001*, and certainly preferable. The rooms all have a certain smell (not bad, just a bit different) to them, so take a look around before deciding. Good location though, right in the heart of Zona Viva. ❷

San Carlos Av San Isidro, C 5–6 ⓣ 443 0330. Well-run and popular travellers' stronghold set in the heart of town, with a selection of simple but clean and safe rooms, all with fans. Located above a bakery, so you'll be woken by the scent of freshly baked bread. ❷

CARNAVAL IN LA CEIBA

The most exciting time to be in La Ceiba is during Carnaval, a weeklong bash held every May to celebrate the city's patron saint, San Isidro. Dances and street events in various barrios around town culminate in an afternoon parade on the third Saturday of the month. The 200,000 or so partygoers who attend Carnaval every year flock between the street events and the clubs on Calle 1 in the Zona Viva, where the dancing continues until dawn. Book accommodation well ahead for Carnaval time.

Eating

The range of restaurants in La Ceiba is disappointing for such a big city, with most of the central choices being cheap *comedores* serving similar unhealthy menus of largely fried foods. Heading out to the beach things improve slightly, although prices are predictably higher.

La Casa De La Barbacoa C 12, two blocks east of Av 14 de Julio. Great barbecue place run out of a local Honduran–American's home, with tables and chairs out on the street. Huge dishes of meat will set you back no more than L60.

Chef Guity C 1, just across the river in Barrio La Isla. Very good Garífuna restaurant in the Zona Viva, close enough to the coast to feel the sea breeze. Try the "King Fish" for only L60.

Coconut On the same road as *Amsterdam 2001* and *Rotterdam Beach* hotels. You can sit upstairs on their wooden stools and watch city life go by while listening to the waves lap onto the beach and munching on typical Honduran and Mexican dishes (from L100). Transforms into a popular bar after dark.

Expatriate's Bar and Grill C 12, two blocks east of Av San Isidro. Airy, North American-owned thatched bar/restaurant with excellent vegetarian dishes, grilled chicken and fish and barbecued ribs. Welcoming atmosphere and popular with resident foreigners, so it's also a good source of local information. Closed Sun. Mains from L100.

Flipper On the corner of Av Atlántida and C 5. Good burgers, steak sandwiches and *minutas* as well as *comida a la vista* and *licuados*. Breakfasts available. Mains from L40.

Masapán C 7, Av La República–Av San Isidro. Consistently popular self-service cafeteria with a cheap buffet of Honduran and American-style food. Not to be confused with the fast-food joint of the same name on the corner. Mains from L40. Open 24hr.

Super Baleada On the corner of Av Colón and C 12. The cheapest meal you're likely to have in La Ceiba and surely one of the best. The *baleadas* (wheat flour tortillas, often quite thick, folded in half and filled with mashed fried beans) are delicious, and come in all different varieties – with meats, fish, cheese, etc. Try the "super baleada" (L50) if you're up for the challenge, but be warned that not many finish it. Mains L10–60.

Drinking and nightlife

Not for nothing does La Ceiba have a reputation as the place to party. A hedonistic local crowd, plus a steady trickle of tourists and a growing number of resident expats have helped to create a buoyant atmosphere. Night action takes place along C 1, which runs parallel to the seafront. Nicknamed the "Zona Viva" due to its preponderance of bars and clubs, the area hums most nights of the week, though weekends are really explosive, with a profusion of places to drink and get down. Just have a stroll down the street to see what's going on and where the crowds are. Outside of the Zona Viva, *Expatriate's Bar and Grill* is a good place for an evening drink.

La Casona On the corner of C 4 and Av Pedro Nuño. The hippest disco in town, *La Casona* attracts a much younger crowd than elsewhere. Reggaeton and merengue are permanently on the playlist. Cover L100.

El Guapo's Bar C 1. Hugely popular on Fri and Sat nights, this place has a fantastic atmosphere, especially when the karaoke takes over.

Mango Tango On the corner of C 1 and Av Barahona. Tropical-style bar with live music on weekends and a selection of Honduran bar food. Singers and bands are encouraged to perform.

La Palapa C 1. Very popular spot in the Zona Viva known for its large dancefloor and great restaurant. Sat nights are especially exciting: live bands appear perform a mix of merengue, reggae and rock cover songs. Open Tues–Sun from 6pm.

Directory

Airlines Atlantic, at the corner of Av 15 de Septiembre and Av República (☎440 2343); Isleña/Taca (☎441 3190), at the Megaplaza Mall; Sosa (☎443 1399), on the eastern side of the Parque.

Car rental Molinari, in the *Gran Hotel Paris* on the northern side of the Parque (☎443 0055).

Cinema The Megaplaza mall has two screens that show subtitled Hollywood movies every night for US$2.50.

Exchange Most of the banks are on C 8 and Av 14 de Julio one block east of the Parque. Ban Red 24 has an ATM, while Banco Ficohsa will change traveller's cheques. The Megaplaza mall also has several banks.

Immigration C 1, Av Atlántida–14 de Julio.

Internet Multi Net, on the corner of Av San Isidro and C 6, has the best connection (L20) and also offers international calls.

Language school Centro Internacional de Idiomas, Av San Isidro, C 12–13 (☎440 1557, ⓦwww .hondurasspanish.com), is a good Spanish school with a/c classrooms. Rates are US$190 weekly for four hours of one-to-one tuition and homestay, including all meals.

Laundry Lavandería Express, opposite *Expatriate's Bar and Grill* (7.30am–5.30pm).

Medical care Hospital D'Antoni, at the southern end of Av Morazán.

Post Office Av Morazán, C 13–14.

Shopping The main general market is on Av Atlántida, C 5–7. The Megaplaza mall is in the southern outskirts of town past the hospital.

Telephones Hondutel, at Av Ramón Rosa, C 5–6 (7.30am–5.50pm).

Moving on

By air to: Belize City (with Atlantic; 2hr 25min); Brus Laguna (with Sosa; 45min); Guanaja (with Atlantic, Isleña/Taca, Sosa; 20min); Managua (with Atlantic; 2hr); Puerto Lempira (with Atlantic, Sosa; 1hr 10min); Roatán (with Atlantic, Isleña/Taca, Sosa; 20min); San Pedro Sula (with Atlantic, Isleña/Taca, Sosa; 30min); Tegucigalpa (with Atlantic, Isleña/Taca, Sosa; 40min); Utila (with Atlantic, Sosa; 15min).

By boat to: Roatán (on the *Galaxy Wave*; 2 daily; 2hr); Utila (on the *Utila Princess II*; 2 daily; 45min).

By bus to: Copán Ruinas (2 daily; 6hr); Guatemala City (2 daily; 11hr); Olanchito (for Juticalpa; 12 daily; 3hr); San Pedro Sula (21 daily; 3hr 30min); Tegucigalpa (10 daily; 6hr 30min); Tela (27 daily; 2hr); Trujillo (22 daily; 3hr–4hr 30min).

AROUND LA CEIBA

The broad sandy beaches and clean water at **Playa de Perú** and the village of **Sambo Creek** are easy day-trip destinations east of La Ceiba. A trip to explore the cloudforest within the **Parque Nacional Pico Bonito** requires more planning, although the eastern edge of the reserve, formed by the **Río Cangrejal**, is still easily accessible, and also offers opportunities for swimming and white-water rafting. Meanwhile, a trip to the serene islands of the **Cayos Cochinos** is thoroughly worth the small effort it takes getting out there.

Playa de Perú

Ten kilometres east of the city, **Playa de Perú** is a wide sweep of clean sand that's popular at weekends. Any local **bus** running east up the coast will drop you at the highway-side turn-off, from where it's a fifteen-minute walk to the beach. About 2km past the turning for Playa de Perú, on the Río María, there's a series of **waterfalls** and **natural pools** set in lush, shady forest. A path leads from Río María village on the highway, winding through the hills along the left bank of the river; it takes around thirty minutes to walk to the first cascade and pool, with some muddy sections and a bit of scrambling during the wet season.

Sambo Creek

There are further deserted expanses of white sand at the friendly Garífuna village of **Sambo Creek**, 8km beyond Río María. You can eat excellent fresh fish at a couple of good **restaurants** in the village, including the expat-owned *Sambo Creek* – it's the only place in town that serves ice cream and a must-stop on really hot days. Olanchito or Juticalpa **buses** from La Ceiba will drop you at the turn-off to Sambo Creek on the highway, a couple of kilometres from the village; slower buses run all the way to the village centre from La Ceiba's terminal every 45 minutes.

Parque Nacional Pico Bonito

Directly south of La Ceiba, the Cordillera Nombre de Dios shelters the **Parque Nacional Pico Bonito** (daily 6am–4pm; US$6), a remote expanse of tropical broadleaf forest, cloudforest and – in its southern reaches, above the Río Aguan valley – pine forest. Taking its name from the awe-inspiring bulk of Pico Bonito (2435m), the park is the source of twenty **rivers**, including the Zacate, Bonito and Cangrejal, which cascade majestically down the mountains' steep, thickly tree-covered slopes. The park also provides sanctuary for an abundance of wildlife, including armadillos, howler and spider monkeys, pumas and ocelots. The lower fringes are the most easily accessible, with a small number of **trails** laid out through the dense greenery.

The easiest way to get into the park is to enter via the *Lodge at Pico Bonito* (☎440 0389, ⊛www.picobonito.com), a world-class **jungle lodge** with bungalow accommodation, gourmet cuisine, a pool and a sublime setting in the foothills of the forest reserve. Trails from the lodge snake up through the tree cover to a lookout from where Utila is visible, and down to beautiful river bathing pools. You don't have to be a guest at the lodge to access the park and trails, but you will have to pay a US$17 fee. To get there head for the village of **Los Pinos**, 12km from La Ceiba on the Tela highway, from where the hotel is signposted, 3km away up a dirt side-road. Alternatively, tour companies in La Ceiba operate day- and overnight trips to Pico Bonito for around US$30 per person (see p.382 for recommended operators).

Río Cangrejal

The **Río Cangrejal**, which forms the eastern boundary of the Parque Nacional Pico Bonita, boasts some of the best class III and IV rapids in Central America; **white-water rafting** and **kayaking** trips are organized by some of the tour companies listed on p.382. There are also some magnificent swimming spots, backed by gorgeous mountain scenery, along the river valley. It's tricky to get to the river under your own steam, but *Jungle River Lodge* (☎440 1268, ⊛www .jungleriverlodge.com), managed by the same people as the *Banana Republic Guesthouse* (see p.382) offers an array of packages from US$35. They can arrange your transport, and also have a river lodge in the park with a bar, a restaurant and a choice of private and dorm accommodation.

Refugio de Vida Silvestre Cuero y Salado

Thirty kilometres west from La Ceiba, the **Refugio de Vida Silvestre Cuero y Salado** (daily 7am–4pm; US$10; ☎440 1990) is one of the last substantial remnants of wetlands and mangrove swamps along the north coast. The reserve is home to a large number of endangered animals and bird species, including manatees, jaguars, howler and white-faced monkeys, sea turtles and hawks, along with seasonal influxes of migratory birds.

To get to the reserve independently, catch an hourly **bus** (6.20am–3.30pm) from La Ceiba's terminal to the village of **La Unión**, 20km or so west. From here, you can either make your way on foot through the fruit plantations – it takes around an hour and a half to walk the 8km – or travel by *burra*, a flat, poled railcar (locals charge between US$5–15, depending on numbers, to shunt you along the tracks). A visitors' centre sits at the end of the track; canoe tours can be arranged here, and there is also some accommodation, in the form of a small dorm (US$7).

Cayos Cochinos

Lying 17km offshore, the **Cayos Cochinos** (**Hog Islands**) comprise eleven privately owned cayes and two thickly wooded islands – **Cochino Mayor** and **Cochino Menor**. Fringed by a reef, the whole area has been designated a **marine reserve**, with anchoring on the reef and commercial fishing both strictly prohibited. The small amount of effort it takes to get to the islands is well worth it for a few days' utter tranquillity.

Organized **accommodation** on the two islands is limited to overpriced resort-style places. However, do not despair, as cheaper accommodation does exist, in the traditional Garífuna fishing village of **Chachauate** on **Lower Monitor Caye**. The villagers have allocated a hut for visitors to sling their hammocks in and they will also cook meals for you. There's no fixed cost, but a stay never costs that much. Basic groceries are available in the village, but there is no running water or electricity and toilets are latrines.

You will have to pay a bit to travel to the islands, especially if you're on your own. The only feasible way to get there is with the fishermen who sail from the Garífuna villages of **Sambo Creek** or **Nueva Armenia** (around US$25 per person return). **Buses** from La Ceiba run every 35 minutes to Sambo Creek (45min), and six buses make the trip to Nueva Armenia (2hr). Alternatively, several tour companies in La Ceiba offer day-trips and overnight stays, starting from around US$35 per person (see p.382). There is a US$5 fee for visiting the Cayos Cochinos independently, and a US$10 fee if you are with a tour group. Ask when arranging anything whether the price you are quoted includes the entrance fee.

TRUJILLO

Perched above the sparkling waters of the palm-fringed Bahía de Trujillo, backed by the beautiful green Cordillera Nombre de Dios, **TRUJILLO** immediately seduces the small number of tourists who make the 90km trip from La Ceiba. The city has a very different feel from its big north coast neighbours, La Ceiba and Tela – it's beautifully relaxed. This sleepy demeanour, combined with fantastic beaches and affable inhabitants, make it a relaxing stop, or even a destination in its own right.

The area around present-day Trujillo was populated by a mixture of Pech and Tolupan groups when Columbus first disembarked here on August 14, 1502; the city itself was founded by Cortés's lieutenant, Juan de Medina, in May 1525, though it was frequently abandoned due to attacks by European pirates. Not until the late eighteenth century did repopulation begin in earnest, aided by the arrival, via Roatán, of several hundred Garífuna. In 1860, a new threat appeared in the shape of US filibuster and adventurer William Walker, who in June of that year briefly took control of the town. Executed by firing squad in September of that year by the Honduran authorities, he is buried in Trujillo's cemetery.

What to see and do

Much of Trujillo's charm lies in meandering through its rather crumbly streets, where the heat of the sun is alleviated by a constant breeze. The town proper stretches back five or so blocks south of the **Parque Central**, which is just fifty metres from cliffs overlooking the sea. On the north side of the square is a bust of Juan de Medina, who founded the town on May 18, 1525. Southwest from the centre, a couple of blocks past the market, is the **Cementerio Viejo**, where Walker's grave lies overgrown with weeds.

The town's most outstanding attractions by far, though, are its **beaches**, which have long stretches of almost pristine sand. The glorious sweep of the **Bahía de Trujillo** is as yet unaffected by excessive tourist development, and its calm, blue waters are perfect for effortless swimming. The beaches below town, lined with *champas*, are clean enough, but the stretches to the east, beyond the disused airstrip, are emptier. It's also possible to walk east along the beach to the reserve of **Laguna de Guaimoreto** or west to the Garífuna village of **Santa Fe**.

Fortaleza de Santa Bárbara

Just along from the Parque is the town's main attraction, the sixteenth-century **Fortaleza de Santa Bárbara** (daily 8am–noon & 1–4pm; L60), site of William Walker's execution. Recently restored to incorporate a new museum, the low-lying fort hangs gloomily on the edge of the bluffs, overlooking the coastline that it singularly failed to protect against pirates. The museum charts the town's often-colourful history, and has an exhibition room on Garífuna culture.

TRUJILLO

N

Bahía de Trujillo

Fortaleza de
Santa Bárbara

Banco Atlántida

Parque
Central

Ciber Café

SunJam Language School

Hondutel

Market

Cementerio
Viejo

Barrio Cristales, 3 & C

Museo y Piscinas & Riveras De Pedregal

B, Bus Terminal & Laguna de Guaimoreto

ACCOMMODATION	
Casa Alemania	A
Casa Kiwi	B
Cocopando	C
Emperador	D
Plaza Centro	E
Villas Brinkley	F

EATING & DRINKING	
Black and White	3
El Bucanero	4
Chicken Express	5
Lempira Villas Brinkley	F
Playa Dorado	1
Rogue's Galeria	2
La Truxillo	6

0   200 m

F & Parque Nacional Capiro y Calentura

Museo y Piscinas Riveras del Pedregal

Turn right past the Cementerio Viejo and a ten-minute stroll brings you to the privately run **Museo y Piscinas Riveras del Pedregal** (daily 7am–5pm; US$2.60), an eccentric collection of rusty junk. Almost all of the original pre-Columbian ceramics once held by the museum have been sold off, though the replacement replicas are pretty convincing. Outside, the wheels of an American jumbo jet that crashed in the area in 1985 can be seen without having to part with the entrance fee. Behind the building are a couple of small, naturally fed swimming pools.

Barrio Cristales

Back at the Parque Central, walk west for ten minutes and you'll reach the **Barrio Cristales**, the site of the country's first mainland **Garífuna settlement**, founded in 1797. There are two Garífuna shops here, the Souvenir Artesma Garífuna and Gari Arte. Both sell authentic Garífuna art and pottery.

Parque Nacional Capiro y Calentura

Directly above the town lies the dark green swathe of **Parque Nacional Capiro y Calentura** (daily 6am–5pm; free). The reserve's huge cedars and pines tower amid a thick canopy of ferns and flowering plants and vines, many of them used for medicinal purposes. As a result of the devastation wrought by Hurricane Fifi in 1974, much of the cover is secondary growth, but it still provides a secure habitat for howler monkeys, reptiles and a colourful range of birdlife and butterflies. You can walk into the reserve by following the dirt road past the *Villas Brinkley* – it winds, increasingly steeply, up the slope of Cerro Calentura to the radio towers just below its summit; a ten-kilometre walk, this is best done in the relative cool of early morning. Alternatively, you could negotiate with a taxi driver to take you to the top and then walk down. There are lots of other trails as well – the whole park is great for hiking, though unfortunately there don't seem to be any trail maps to be had, so you'll have to do a bit of exploring.

Arrival and information

By boat The infrequent boats from Guanaja dock at the pier at the eastern end of the beach.

By bus The bus terminal is to the east of town, at the bottom of the hill leading into the centre. From here infrequent urban buses head up the hill to the Parque Central, or you can take a taxi (L20).

Tourist information There's a small tourist office on the eastern side of the Parque, next door to the Fortaleza de Santa Bárbara office. Its opening hours are sporadic; don't be surprised if it's closed for most of the day.

Accommodation

There's not much in the way of budget accommodation in town. That said, there are a couple of excellent places in glorious settings just outside the centre.

Casa Alemania 1km east of town ☎ 434 4466. This German-run hotel offers a dorm and some private rooms. The dorm is spotlessly clean and includes a kitchen and bathroom but only has 6 beds. They have a restaurant that serves breakfast, lunch and dinner. Dorms ②, rooms ④

Casa Kiwi 7km east of town ☎ 434 3050, ⓦ www.casakiwi.com. Undoubtedly one of the best hostels on the north coast. Dorms are standard, clean and include a hot-water shower; there's a restaurant on site that serves a range of dishes, including some vegetarian meals; and the bar will stay open as long as you like. It's a great place for meeting people heading out to La Mosquitia, and the staff have good information on the best ways of travelling there. Dorms ①

Cocopando 1km west of centre in Barrio Cristales ☎ 434 4748. Barrio Cristales's best-value budget hotel, with a beachside setting, simple, clean rooms and a great *comedor* downstairs. Gets noisy at weekends when the neighbouring dance hall fires up. ②

Emperador By the market ☎ 434 4446. The town's best budget hotel, run by an extremely friendly family. Rooms are clean and warm, have en-suite bathroom, TV and fan. All rooms face out to a small courtyard and the family runs the restaurant next door. ②

Plaza Centro By the market opposite *Emperador* ☎ 434 3006. Clean but dark rooms, en-suite bathrooms and ceiling fan set around an inside courtyard. Seriously lacking character, but one of the few decent budget options in town. ③

Villas Brinkley 1km south of town ☎ 434 4444, ⓔ brinkley @hondutel.hn. One of the most pleasing hotels in Honduras, with a relaxed, welcoming ambience and superb views from the terrace over the whole stretch of the bay and its glistening waters. There's a range of tastefully furnished rooms, all with bath and some with a/c and kitchen. The hotel also has a pool, and the restaurant is a good place to come for a meal even if you're not staying here. ④

Eating

The best places to eat in Trujillo are the informal *champas* (bar/restaurants) on the beach, where you can dine in the warm evening air, listening to the waves. The main cluster is on the beach below town – follow the ramp from the northwest corner of the Parque.

El Bucanero In the *Hotel Colonial*, just off the Parque Central. The decent menu here includes some good, cheap seafood options. At night the place morphs into a bar with happy-hour drink offers and a youthful ambience. They are open for breakfast. Mains from L80.

Chicken Express Half a block north of the market. This friendly informal place serves up a range of hearty fried- or roast-chicken dishes. Films and soccer games are shown at night on their large projector. Mains L60–100.

Lempira Villas Brinkley At *Villas Brinkley*. Feast on well-cooked European and Honduran dishes while admiring the fabulous views, then walk it all off on the stroll back to town. Moderately expensive, but worth every lempira for the quality and setting. Mains from L120.

Playa Dorada On the beach below town. The most popular of the beach *champas*, largely due to it being a fair bit cheaper than most of its undistinguishable neighbours. The menu, with mains from L60, consists of the typical mix of Honduran, Mexican and American-style dishes.

Rogue's Galeria On the beach below town. Commonly referred to as "*Jerry's*", this engaging American-owned bar/restaurant features superb seafood and has plenty of hammocks for daytime chilling. Also has a book exchange. Mains from L60.

Drinking and nightlife

Black and White On the beach in Barrio Cristales. *Black and White* attracts a mainly Garífuna crowd, with reggaeton blasting till the early hours.

La Truxillo Up the hill towards the western side of town. Certainly the most popular place on the weekends, when it heaves to Latin American rhythms and the bar fills up with a young crowd.

Directory

Exchange Banco Atlántida, on the Parque, gives Visa cash advances.

Internet Try Ciber Café, on the eastern end of the main road running through town (9am–10pm; L20).

Language school SunJam School (☎ 434 3935, ✉ trujillosunjam@hotmail.com) offers 20 hours of lessons a week for US$100, not including accommodation.

Post office Three blocks south from the southeast corner of the Parque.

Telephones The Hondutel office is next to the post office.

Moving on

By bus to: La Ceiba (18 daily; 3hr); Puerto Castilla (7 daily; 45min); San Pedro Sula (18 daily; 5–6hr); Tegucigalpa, via Juticalpa (1 daily, 5am; 12hr); Tegucigalpa, via La Ceiba (2 daily, 1am and 4.45am; 10hr); Tocoa (24 daily; 2hr 30min).

By boat Island Tours (☎ 434 3421) runs twice-weekly boats to Guanaja (Thurs & Sun 3pm; 2hr) in the Bay Islands, departing from the dock on eastern end of the beach.

AROUND TRUJILLO

Expanses of white-sand **beach** stretch for miles around the bay from Trujillo. All beaches are clean, wide and perfect for swimming; don't take anything valuable with you, though, and don't venture onto them after dark.

Aguas Calientes

Taking a hot bath in the heat of the Caribbean may not strike everyone as an appealing thought, but a soak in the clean and very hot mineral waters of the **Aguas Calientes** springs (daily 7am–9pm; US$3), 7km inland from Trujillo, feels delightfully decadent. The

experience can be topped off with a drink at the bar of the rather slick *Agua Caliente* hotel in the grounds. Any bus heading to Tocoa will drop you off at the entrance to the springs; return buses stop running at around 5.30pm.

La Mosquitia

Occupying the northeast corner of Honduras is the remote and undeveloped expanse of **La Mosquitia** (often spelt "Moskitia"). Bounded to the west by the mountain ranges of the Río Plátano and Colón, with the Río Coco forming the border with Nicaragua to the south, this vast region comprises almost a fifth of Honduras's territory. With just two peripheral roads and a tiny population divided among a few far-flung towns and villages, entering the Mosquitia really does mean leaving the beaten track. There are few phones in the region, and all accommodation is extremely basic, often without electricity and with latrine-style toilets. Getting around requires a spirit of adventure and the willingness to lose track of time, but the effort is well rewarded. In terms of practicalities, available food is usually limited to rice, beans and the catch of the day, so if you're making an independent trek, bring enough food with you for your party and guides.

To the surprise of many who come here expecting to have to hack their way through jungle, much of La Mosquitia is composed of marshy coastal wetlands and flat savanna – likened by some to the landscape of parts of the southern US. The small communities of **Palacios** and **Brus Laguna** are access points for the **Río Plátano Biosphere Reserve**, the most famous of five separate reserves in the area, set up to protect one of the finest remaining stretches of virgin tropical

MOSQUITIA HISTORY AND POLITICS

Before the Spanish arrived, the Mosquitia belonged to the Pech and Sumu. Initial contact with Europeans was comparatively benign, as the Spanish showed only a slight interest in the area, preferring to concentrate instead on the mineral-rich lands of the interior. Relations with Europeans intensified when the British began seeking a foothold on the mainland in the seventeenth century, establishing settlements on the coast at Black River (now Palacios) and Brewer's Lagoon (Brus Laguna), whose inhabitants – the so-called "shoremen" – engaged in logging, trading, smuggling and fighting the Spanish.

Britain's claim to Mosquitia, made nominally to protect the shoremen, though really intended to ensure a transit route from the Atlantic to the Pacific, supposedly ended in 1786, when all Central American territories except Belize were ceded to the Spanish. In the 1820s, however, taking advantage of post-independence chaos, Britain again encouraged settlement on the Mosquito Coast and by 1844 had all but formally announced a protectorate in the area. Not until 1859 and the British–American Treaty of Cruz Wyke did Britain formally end all claims to the region.

The initial impact of mestizo Honduran culture on Mosquitia was slight. Since the creation of the administrative department of Gracias a Dios in 1959, however, indigenous cultures have become gradually diluted: Spanish is now the main language, and the government encourages mestizo settlers to migrate here in search of land. Pech, Miskito and Garífuna communities have become more vocal in recent years in demanding respect for their cultural differences and in calling for an expansion of health, education and transport infrastructures.

rainforest in Central America. **Puerto Lempira**, to the east, is the regional capital.

The largest ethnic group inhabiting the Mosquitia are the **Miskitos**, numbering around thirty thousand, who spoke a unique form of English until as recently as a few generations ago (see box above). There are much smaller communities of **Pech**, who number around 2500, and **Tawahka** (Sumu), of whom there are under a thousand, living around the Río Patuca.

PALACIOS

Sited on what was once the British settlement of Black River, **PALACIOS** lies just west of one of the Río Plátano Biosphere Reserve's three coastal lagoons, Laguna Ibans. Served by regular flights to and from La Ceiba, this is frequently the starting point for organized trips to the Río Plátano Biosphere Reserve, and, for independent travellers, a logical place from which to begin exploration of the region.

What to see and do

Dotted along the Caribbean shoreline around Palacios is a cluster of interesting **Garífuna villages**, including **Batalla**, just to the west of town across the Palacios lagoon, and **Plaplaya**, about 8km to the east, where a **turtle project** has been established. Highly endangered giant leatherbacks, the largest species in the world (reaching up to 3m in length and 900kg in weight), nest in the beaches around the village between April and June. There's a resident Peace Corps worker stationed here to oversee the project, and volunteers are welcome.

Accommodation

Hotel Moskitia ☎978 7397. This is the most modern and comfortable hotel in town, complete with a bar and restaurant on site. ④

Rio Tinto Adequate rooms can be had at this hotel run by local Don Felix Marmol, who is also the Isleña/Taca agent. ②

RÍO PLÁTANO BIOSPHERE RESERVE

The **RÍO PLATANO BIOSPHERE RESERVE** is the most significant nature reserve in Honduras, sheltering an estimated eighty percent of all the country's animal species. Visitors usually come to experience the rare tropical rainforest, but the reserve's boundaries – which stretch from the Caribbean in the north to the Montañas de Punta Piedra in the west and the Río Patuca in the south – also encompass huge expanses of coastal wetlands and flat savanna grasslands. Sadly, even international recognition of the importance of this diverse ecosystem, signalled by its World Heritage status, hasn't prevented extensive destruction at the hands of settlers: up to sixty percent of forest cover on the outer edges of the reserve has disappeared in the last three decades.

To get the most out of the park you'll want to hire a **guide** in Las Marías (see below). The local guides have organized themselves into a rotation system, so that everyone gets some work. One pleasant, if rather wet, trip you can make is by *pipante* (pole-propelled canoe), five hours upstream to rock **petroglyphs** at Walpulbansirpi, carved by an unknown people – these are more or less at the heart of the reserve. The journey itself is the main attraction, along channels too shallow for motorized boats to pass; in sections you'll be required to leave the boat and make your way through the undergrowth. *Pipantes* require three guides each, but carry only two passengers and cost US$25 (not including guides).

Arrival and information

Arrival Getting to the heart of the Río Plátano reserve requires travelling up the Río Plátano from Palacios to the small village of Las Marías a Pech and Miskito settlement about seven hours inland, upstream from the coast.

LA MOSQUITIA TRAVEL

A number of companies in La Ceiba, San Pedro and Tegucigalpa offer a variety of tours to the Mosquitia. The advantages of an organized tour are that all the planning is done for you and you can count on being accompanied by knowledgeable guides. Travelling independently is by no means impossible, though, as long as you're prepared to go with the flow.

Transport to and within La Mosquitia is mainly by air or water: the main centres of Puerto Lempira, Palacios and Brus Laguna are connected to La Ceiba by regular flights, while launches ply the waterways connecting the scattered villages. Bear in mind that all schedules, especially those of the boats, are subject to change and delay; transport on the rivers and channels is determined by how much rain has fallen.

Flights to La Mosquitia depart from La Ceiba only (see p.382). Aerolineas Sosa (La Ceiba ☎443 1894; Puerto Lempira ☎433 6432; Brus Laguna ☎443 8042) and Atlantic Airlines (La Ceiba ☎440 2343) both have regular services. Ground transport to the region, in the form of one bus, does exist, but progress by road is extremely slow and indirect. It is, however, the cheapest way to get to La Mosquitia. Take the bus from Trujillo to Tocoa (a long and bumpy ride), from where pick-ups run to Limón and Iriona; you can carry on to Palacios from these two destinations. The *Casa Kiwi* hostel in Trujillo (see p.388) is a good place for information on entering by road and meeting others who are preparing to make the trip.

Once in the Mosquitia, boat fares are relatively high (because of fuel costs). Hiring a boat to get from the coast to Las Marías (see above) will cost at least US$120, even after bargaining hard, and not including food for the guides. Another alternative is to charter a boat from Trujillo or La Ceiba to Palacios, though you'll need to be part of a group.

Information For general information about the reserve, ask around in San Juan del Sur or La Ceiba – there are no dedicated information facilities in Mosquitia. There are some basic *hospedajes* in the village, *Hospedaje Doña Justa* and *Hospedaje Doña Rutilia*. Each serves meals, and plenty of prospective guides are available to help you explore the river and surrounding jungle for US$8–10 a day.

BRUS LAGUNA

Thirty kilometres east along the coast from Palacios, on the southeastern edge of the Laguna de Brus, is the friendly Miskito town of **BRUS LAGUNA**. *La Estancia*, on the main street (☎433 8043; ❸), has 12 basic rooms with en-suite bathroom. The town is mostly seen by visitors as they are coming or going – regular **flights** connect the town with La Ceiba, and guides and boats can be hired for multi-day trips, travelling up the Río Sigre into the southern reaches of the Río Plátano reserve.

PUERTO LEMPIRA

Capital of the department of Gracias a Dios, **PUERTO LEMPIRA** is the largest town in La Mosquitia, with a population of eleven thousand. Set on the southeastern edge of the biggest of the coastal lagoons, Laguna de Caratasca, some 110km east of Brus Laguna, the town survives on government administration and small-scale fishing and shrimping. Like Brus Laguna, Puerto Lempira is mostly used by travellers as a transit hub – flights connect it with the rest of Honduras, and it's close to the border with Nicaragua. The best of the available **accommodation** is at the *Gran Hotel Flores* (☎433 6421; ❸) in the centre of town, where the small rooms all have a/c and bath; the *Hospedaje Santa Teresita*, opposite (☎433 6008; ❸), is clean but basic. Banco Atlántida, next to *Hotel Flores*, will change traveller's cheques and gives Visa cash advances. Mopawi (☎433 8659, ✉mopawi@optinet.hn), the Mosquitia **development organization**, has its headquarters in the town, three blocks south of the main dock.

The Bay Islands

Strung in a gentle curve 60km off the north coast, the **Islas de la Bahía**, with their clear waters and abundant marine life, are the country's main tourist attraction. Fringed by a coral reef, the islands are a perfect destination for cheap water-based activities – diving, sailing and fishing top the list – or just relaxing. Composed of three main islands and some 65 smaller cayes, the chain lies on the **Bonacca Ridge**, an underwater extension of the Sierra de Omoa mountain range. **Roatán** is the largest and most developed of the islands, while **Guanaja**, to the east, is a bit more upmarket (though still affordable). **Utila**, the closest to the mainland, is a target for budget travellers from all over the world.

The Bay Islands' history of conquest, pirate raids and constant immigration has resulted in an unusual society. The islands' original inhabitants were recorded by Columbus in 1502, but the indigenous population declined rapidly as a result of enslavement and forced labour. Following a series of pirate attacks, the Spanish evacuated the islands in 1650. Roatán was left deserted until the arrival of the Garífuna in 1797. These three hundred people, forcibly expelled from the British-controlled island of St Vincent following a rebellion, were persuaded by the Spanish to settle in Trujillo on the mainland, leaving a small settlement at Punta Gorda on Roatán's north coast. Further waves of settlers came after the abolition of slavery in 1830, when white Cayman Islanders and freed slaves arrived first on Utila, and later spread to Roatán and Guanaja.

Today, the islands retain their **cultural separation** from the mainland, although the presence of Spanish-speaking Hondurans and North

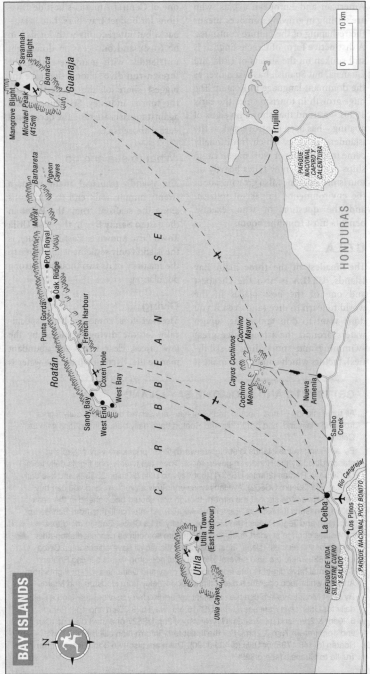

BAY ISLANDS

N

0   10 km

Mangrove Blight
Savannah
Bonacca Blight
Michael Peak (415m) ▲
Guanaja

Barbareta
Pigeon Cayes
Morat
Port Royal
Oak Ridge
Punta Gorda
French Harbour
Roatán
Sandy Bay
West End
West Bay
Coxen Hole

Trujillo

PARQUE NACIONAL CAPIRO Y CALENTURA

C A R I B B E A N   S E A

Cayos Cochinos
Cochino Mayor
Cochino Menor

HONDURAS

Nueva Armenia

Sambo Creek

Río Cangrejal

La Ceiba

Los Pinos

PARQUE NACIONAL PICO BONITO

Utila
Utila Town (East Harbour)

Utila Cayes

REFUGIO DE VIDA SILVESTRE CUERO Y SALADO

American and European expats, who are settling in growing numbers, means the reshaping of the culture continues. A distinctive form of Creole English is still spoken on the streets of Utila and Guanaja, but Spanish has taken over as the dominant language in Roatán. The huge growth in tourism since the early 1990s – a trend that shows no signs of abating – has been controversial, as the islanders' income, which traditionally came from fishing or working on cargo ships or oil rigs, now relies heavily on tourism. Concern is also growing about the environmental impact of tourism and the question of who, exactly, benefits most from the boom.

UTILA

The smallest of the three main Bay Islands, **UTILA** is also the cheapest and one of the best places in the world to learn to dive (and even if you don't want to don tanks, the superb waters around the island offer great swimming and snorkelling possibilities), factors which combine to make it one of Central America's best destinations for budget travellers. Life is laid-back, but interactions with locals can be frosty and on occasion downright unfriendly, with many resenting the foreign-run dive schools that take the biggest share of the proceeds from the tourist industry. So while crimes against tourists are rare, the occasional verbal abuse isn't.

What to see and do

The island's principal **main road**, a twenty-minute walk end to end, runs along the seafront from **The Point** in the east to **Sandy Bay** in the west. **Utila Town** (also known as East Harbour), is the island's only settlement and home to the majority of its two thousand-strong population.

Diving

Most visitors come to Utila specifically for the **diving**, attracted by the low prices, clear water and abundant marine life. Even in winter, the water is

---

GETTING TO AND FROM THE BAY ISLANDS

All three islands – Utila, Roatán and Guanaja – are served by several daily flights from the mainland, and both Utila and Roatán have daily boat connections with La Ceiba.

By air Flying to the islands is straightforward; ticket prices are very cheap and standardized by the Honduran government. There are twenty-one flights daily from La Ceiba to Roatán (20min; US$37), four daily to Utila (20min; US$32), and five daily to Guanaja (30min; US$52). Availability is very rarely a problem, and you can buy your tickets on the spot at the airport, though you should book ahead in the peak holiday seasons (Christmas, Easter and August). All internal flights from San Pedro Sula (1hr) and Tegucigalpa (1hr) stopover briefly in La Ceiba. Bear in mind that schedules change at short notice and flights are sometimes cancelled altogether. The domestic airlines, Isleña/Taca, Sosa and Atlantic all have offices in La Ceiba (see p.383). There are also several international non-stop flights serving Roatán: Continental have direct flights from Houston daily and Delta have direct flights from Atlanta, while Taca operate a direct flight once weekly from Houston and Miami.

By boat Most travellers use the excellent scheduled ferry services leaving La Ceiba daily for Utila (*Utila Princess II*; 1hr; US$16 one way) at 9.30am and 4pm (return 6.20am & 2pm) and for Roatán (*Galaxy Wave*; 2hr; US$27 one way) daily at 10am and 4pm (return 7am & 2pm). For the latest ferry information call the offices in Roatán (☎445 1795) or Utila (☎425 3390). There are also two boats weekly from Trujillo to Guanaja (see p.389).

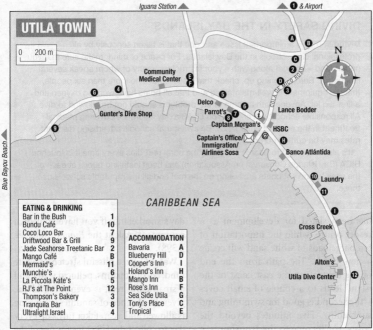

UTILA TOWN

0 — 200 m

Iguana Station ▲

▲ ❶ & Airport

N

Community Medical Center

Gunter's Dive Shop

Delco

Parrot's

Captain Morgan's

Captain's Office/Immigration/Airlines Sosa

Lance Bodder

HSBC

Banco Atlántida

Laundry

Cross Creek

Alton's

Utila Dive Center

Blue Bayou Beach ◄

CARIBBEAN SEA

EATING & DRINKING

Bar in the Bush	1
Bundu Café	10
Coco Loco Bar	7
Driftwood Bar & Grill	9
Jade Seahorse Treetanic Bar	2
Mango Café	B
Mermaid's	11
Munchie's	6
La Piccola Kate's	5
RJ's at The Point	12
Thompson's Bakery	3
Tranquila Bar	8
Ultralight Israel	4

ACCOMMODATION

Bavaria	A
Blueberry Hill	D
Cooper's Inn	I
Holand's Inn	H
Mango Inn	B
Rose's Inn	F
Sea Side Utila	G
Tony's Place	C
Tropical	E

Airport & Beach ▼

generally calm and common sightings include nurse and hammerhead sharks, turtles, parrotfish, stingrays, porcupine fish and an increasing number of dolphins. **Whale sharks** also continue to be a major attraction – the island is one of the few places in the world where whale sharks will frequently pass close to shore.

On the north coast of the island, **Blackish Point** and **Duppy Waters** are both good sites; on the south coast the best spots are **Black Coral Wall** and **Pretty Bush**. The good schools (see box, p.397, for suggestions) will be happy to spend time talking to you about the merits of the various sites.

Rather than signing up with the first dive school representative who approaches you, it's worth spending a morning walking around checking out all the schools. You want to feel comfortable with your decision, as diving can be dangerous – it is imperative that you get along with your instructor (see box,

p.396). Price is not really a consideration, with the dozen or so dive shops all charging around US$225 for a three- to five-day PADI course; advanced and divemaster courses are also on offer, as are fun dives, from US$25.

Swimming and snorkelling

The best **swimming** near town is at the **Blue Bayou**, a twenty-minute walk west of the centre, where you can bathe in chest-deep water and snorkel further out; there's a US$1.50 charge to use the area, which also boasts a small sandy beach, food stand and a rickety wooden pier where you can sunbathe in peace away from the sandflies. Hammocks are slung in the shade of coconut trees and there's snorkelling gear available for rent (US$1.50 per hour). East of town, **Airport Beach**, at the end of the old dirt airstrip, offers good snorkelling just offshore (though access is more difficult), as does the little reef beyond the **lighthouse**. The old airstrip area has been slated for development as a resort centre, while the importation of ten bargeloads of white sand will create a new beach. The path from the end of the airstrip up the east coast of the island leads to a couple of small coves – the second is good for swimming and sunbathing. Five minutes beyond the coves, you'll come to the **Ironshores**, a mile-long stretch of low volcanic cliffs with lava tunnels cutting down to the water.

Utila Iguana Station

The **Utila Iguana Station** (Mon, Wed & Fri 2–5pm; US$2.20), signposted from the road five minutes west of the dock, is a breeding centre for the endangered Utila spiny-tailed iguana, found only on the island and facing extinction. Guided tours explain the life cycle of the species. It's worth a visit, especially if you need a break from all the diving.

Utila Cayes

The **Utila Cayes** – eleven tiny outcrops strung along the southwestern edge of the island – were designated a wildlife refuge in 1992. **Suc Suc** (or Jewel) **Caye** and **Pigeon Caye**, connected by a narrow causeway, are both inhabited, and the pace of life is even slower than on Utila. Small launches regularly shuttle between Suc Suc and Utila (US$8), or can be rented to take you across for a

day's snorkelling, if you have your own equipment. Ask at the *Bundu Café* (see p.398).

Water Caye, a blissful stretch of white sand, coconut palms, pellucid water and a small coral reef, is even more idyllic given its absence of sandflies. Camping is allowed and a caretaker turns up every day to collect the US$2 fee for use of the island. To stay you'll need a tent, food, equipment for a fire and water. Water Caye is also the venue for the SunJam festival (see p.398).

Arrival and information

By air The airport is 3km north of Utila Town at the end of the island's second main road, Cola de Mico Road, which heads inland from the dock. Taxis wait for arriving flights, so you shouldn't have trouble finding one to take you into town. The old dirt airstrip at The Point is no longer used for commercial flights.

By boat All boats dock in the centre of Utila Town.

Tourist information Captain Morgan's Travel (☎ 425 3349), at the dock, can help you with ferry and flight tickets. They can also look after your bag while you search for a place to stay.

Island transport

ATVs and scooters Motorized transport can be rented at Bodden, behind the HSBC by the dock.
Bikes Bikes can be rented from Delco, next to Henderson's grocery store west of the dock, and other places around town – rates start at around US$5 a day.

Accommodation

Utila has more than enough affordable guesthouses and hotels, and a profusion of rooms for rent. With the exception of Semana Santa and parts of the high season, there's always somewhere available. Most of the dive schools have links with a hostel, and enrolling in a dive course may get you a few free or discounted nights' accommodation. Everywhere is within walking distance of the dock; the accommodation listed below is in the order that you come to it from the dock. There are no designated places to camp except on the cayes.

East of the dock

Holand's Inn 2min from the dock ☎ 425 3206. Rooms here are pretty standard, with clean private bathroom and fan. Decent option if a little over-priced. ❸

Cooper's Inn 5min from the dock ☎ 425 3184. One of the best budget places on the island, with orderly, basic rooms (all with fans) and very friendly management. There is use of a shared kitchen, shared bathrooms and restaurant. ❷

Cola de Mico Road

Blueberry Hill On the left side of the road right before the *Jade Seahorse* ☎ 425 2199. Locally owned, no-frills hotel renting out rooms and apartments. The only difference between the two is that with the apartment you get a private bathroom, which for one extra dollar is well worth it. Rooms ❶, apartments ❷

Tony's Place Opposite *Mango Inn* ☎ 425 3376. The simple but spotless rooms (with fan) are amongst the best value on the island. The shared bathrooms are squeaky clean and the owner is friendly and informative. Hummingbird feeders attract birds, including the rare Canivet's Emerald. ❷

Mango Inn 5min from the dock ☎ 425 3335, ⓦ www.mango-inn.com. A beautiful, well-run place, timber-built in Caribbean style and set in shady gardens. The range of rooms stretches from thatched, a/c bungalows to pleasant dorms. There's a book exchange and laundry service, and the attached *Mango Café* is a popular spot for an evening drink (see p.398). Rates drop by at least half if you're diving with the Utila Dive Centre. ❷, rooms ❻

Bavaria Up on the hill just past the *Mango Inn* ☎ 425 3809. Removed from a lot of the hustle and bustle of the main street. All rooms come with private bathroom and there is a balcony to sit out on and enjoy the tranquil setting. ❷

West of the dock

Rose's Inn 4min from the dock ☎ 425 3127. Rooms are on the small side, but this well-kept hotel is still a fine option. Communal kitchen and hot-water bathrooms are also a bonus. ❷

Tropical 4min from the dock, next door to *Rose's Inn* ☎ 425 3568. Very popular backpackers' stronghold. The small functional rooms all have fans and there's a communal kitchen. ❶

Sea Side Utila 8min from the dock, opposite Gunter's Dive Shop ☎ 425 3450. Certainly the best budget accommodation on the island: the shared rooms fit three people and each includes a spotlessly clean bathroom. Communal kitchen and internet access is available. There is also a balcony which overlooks the street below and is perfect for a Caribbean sunset. ❶

DIVE SCHOOLS IN UTILA

As soon as you get off the boat you'll be met by **dive school** representatives laden with maps and information. Many schools offer free accommodation during their courses, but it's worth checking out the various options before signing up. Recommended schools include:

Alton's Two minutes' walk west of the airstrip ☎ 425 3704, ⓦ www.altonsdiveshop.com.

Captain Morgan's On the corner opposite the dock ☎ 425 3349, ⓦ www.divingutila.com.

Cross Creek Five minutes' walk east of the dock ☎ 425 3397, ⓦ www.crosscreekutila.com.

Gunter's Eight minutes' walk west of the dock ☎ 425 3350, ⓔ ecomarine@gmail.com. They also rent sea kayaks (US$5 per day).

Parrots Two minutes' walk west of the dock ⓦ http://tiny.cc/Yb1fB. Utila's only locally owned dive school.

Utila Dive Centre Near the end of the road west of the dock, close to the bridge ☎ 425 3326, ⓦ www.utiladivecentre.com.

Eating

Lobster and fish are staples on the islands, along with the usual rice, beans and chicken. With the tourists, however, have also come European and American foods – pasta, pizza, burgers, pancakes and granola. Since most things have to be brought in by boat, prices are higher than on the mainland: main courses start at around US$4, and beers cost at least US$1. For eating on the cheap, head for the evening stalls on the road by the dock, which do a thriving trade in *baleadas*. Note that many restaurants stop serving at around 10pm.

East of the dock

Bundu Café 1min from the dock. A very popular travellers' hang-out serving European-style breakfasts and lunches along with *lassi*-style milkshakes. Curry night on Thurs and live music on Sat. Mains from US$4.

Mermaid's 2min from the dock. Fast-food buffet with pizza, Chinese food and pasta at reasonable rates served under a breezy canvas roof. Mains from US$3.

RJ's at The Point Beside the bridge. Popular with dive crews and students, with a gregarious atmosphere and excellent meat and fish barbecues. Get there early if you want a table, as it fills up quickly. Open Wed, Fri and Sun 5.30–10.00pm only. Mains from US$5.

Cola de Mico Road

Thompson's Bakery A great place to read, drink coffee and meet other travellers while sampling the good-value breakfast (omelettes US$2) or the range of daily baked goods including delicious johnny cakes.

West of the dock

Munchies 1min from the dock. The best breakfast on the island, with a range of cooked food and fresh fruit, smoothies and *licuados*. Check out the Iguana Garden at the rear, a steep wall inhabited by a group of spiny-tailed iguanas. Try the lunch special (US$4).

La Piccola Kate's 1min from the dock. The island's only Italian restaurant boasts a wide selection of pasta, salads and daily specials including a free starter. Bread is home-made and many of the dishes are more imaginative than the standard Bolognese pastas that are sold elsewhere. Try the grilled aubergine and pesto starter. Mains from US$6.

Ultralight Israel 7min from the dock. Excellent Middle Eastern cuisine: falafel, fresh pita bread, *sabich* and numerous hummus dishes feature on this menu and make it one of Utila's best. Mains from US$4.

Driftwood Bar and Grill West of the dock, right and the end of the path. The menu could be criticized for being a bit generic – it's the usual mix of Honduran, Mexican and American-style dishes – but it's a nice place, sitting out on a wooden jetty with friendly staff and a relaxed atmosphere. Mains from US$4.

Drinking and nightlife

Despite its tiny population, Utila is a fearsomely hedonistic party island, especially in the first week of August when the annual SunJam Festival takes place (see below).

Bar in the Bush Along the Cola de Mico Rd towards the new airport. This huge open-air bar is the only late-night venue on the island, open until 3am, and often with live DJs. Open Fri until 3am.

Coco Loco Bar Just west of the dock. This is the hottest place in town for travellers. It draws a lively bunch with its extended happy hour and regular house, techno and reggae parties. Happy hour from 4–7pm.

Jade Seahorse Treetanic Bar A short walk up the Cola de Mico Road. Unquestionably the most eccentric place on the island. Run by an American artist and designed in his own unique style, this hotel/restaurant/bar is a maze of colour and reflection that really comes alive by night.

Mango Café At the *Mango Inn*. A popular spot for cheap beer and a quiet drink.

Tranquila Bar Next to *Coco Loco Bar*. This bar is a lively venue, popular with locals and tourists. A little more laid-back than frantic *Coco Loco*.

SUNJAM FESTIVAL

The SunJam Festival (www.sunjamutila.com), held every year in the first week of August, is a two-day rave, with European house and techno DJs. It takes place on Water Caye, the largest and most picturesque of the tiny cayes to the southwest of the island. SunJam is a secretive affair and information is released on very short notice, usually just a few weeks before it's due to take place, so if you're going to be in the area, keep your ear to the ground.

Directory

Airlines Tickets for Sosa can be purchased in the captain's office by the dock. Isleña/Taca has an office 2min west of the dock.
Books The *Bundu Café*, on the main street, east of the dock, has a book exchange.
Exchange Banco Atlántida and HSBC, both close to the dock, change money and offer cash advances on Visa cards.
Immigration At the captain's office (Mon–Fri 9am–noon & 2–4.30pm).
Internet Numerous internet cafés have sprung up along the coastal road, but shop around as some still charge as much as US$5 an hour for connections that are no better or worse than those at the average rate of US$2. There is one café just east of the dock on the corner.
Laundry Services available in a nameless building about 2min east of the dock.
Medical care The Community Medical Center is 2min west of the dock (Mon–Fri 8am–noon).
Post office In the large building at the main dock (Mon–Fri 9am–noon & 2–4.30pm, Sat 9–11.30am).
Telephones Many of the internet cafés offer web calls at good rates. Avoid the Hondutel office, next to the *migración*, as rates are extortionate.

ROATÁN

Some 50km from La Ceiba, **ROATÁN** is the largest of the Bay Islands, a curving ridged hump almost 50km long and 5km across at its widest point. Unfortunately, Roatán can be a hard place to enjoy if you're on a budget. Unless you restrict yourself to the very cheapest places, you should expect your spending to go way above average. The island's accommodation, geared towards more upmarket tourists, mostly comes in the form of all-inclusive luxury resort packages, although there are a few good deals to be found, especially in **West End**. Like Utila, though, Roatán is a superb **diving** destination, but also offers some great hiking, as well as the chance to do nothing except laze on a beach. **Coxen Hole** is the island's commercial centre.

What to see and do

Roatán's abundance of great diving and superb beaches often take away from the charm of some of the island's smaller towns and villages. It's worth taking time out to explore the less travelled parts of the island where you can really get a sense of what it would have been like before the tourists arrived.

Coxen Hole

Coxen Hole (also known as Roatán Town) is uninteresting and run down; most visitors come here only to change money or shop. All of the town's practical facilities and most of its shops are on a hundred-metre stretch of **Main Street**, near where the buses stop.

Sandy Bay

Midway between Coxen Hole and West End, **Sandy Bay** is an unassuming community with a number of interesting

ROATÁN: WEST END

ACCOMMODATION
Burke's Place	A
Chillie's	C
Georphi's Tropical	G
Mariposa Lodge	F
Posada Arco Iris	B
Sea Breeze Inn	D
Valerie's	E

Roatán Institute for Deep Sea Exploration

Half Moon Bay

Native Sons

ATM
Coconut Tree Divers

ATM

Captain Van's Rentals

Roatán Rentals
Ocean Connections

West End Divers

Coxen Hole

Laundry

Barefoot Charlie's

EATING & DRINKING
Argentinian Grill	1
Bakery #2	3
Le Bistro	7
Blue Channel	6
Cannibal Café	4
Foster's	10
Lighthouse Restaurant	5
Rotisserie Chicken	8
Rudy's Coffee Shop	9
Sundowners	2

0   200 m

West Bay

attractions. The **Institute for Marine Sciences** (Sun–Tues & Thurs–Sat 8am–4.30pm; US$3), based at *Antony's Key Resort*, has exhibitions on the marine life and geology of the islands and a museum with useful information on local history and archeology. There are also bottle-nosed **dolphin shows** (4pm; US$3, closed Wed), and you can dive or snorkel with the dolphins (US$112 and US$84 respectively). Across the road from the institute, several short nature trails weave through the jungle at the **Carambola Botanical Gardens** (daily 8am–5pm; US$3), a riot of beautiful flowers, lush ferns and tropical trees.

West End

With its calm waters and incredible sandy beaches, **West End**, 14km from Coxen Hole, makes the most of its ideal setting at the southwest corner of the island. From the beautifully sheltered, palm-fringed **Half Moon Bay** at the northern end of town, a sandy track runs a kilometre or so along the water's edge through the heart of the West End, past a plethora of guesthouses, bars and restaurants, geared towards independent travellers of all budgets. Thanks to the

presence of a year-round community of sun worshippers and a rash of dive shops, the village retains a laid-back charm during the day whilst adopting a vibrant, party feel after dark. Nowhere else on Roatán will you get such an eclectic mix of people, attracted not only by the relaxed nature of the town, but also the unrivalled potential for watersports.

West Bay

Two kilometres southwest of West End, towards the extreme western tip of Roatán, is the stunning white-sand beach of **West Bay**, fringed by coconut palms and washed by crystal-clear waters. The beach's tranquillity has been mildly disrupted by a rash of cabaña and hotel construction, but it's still a sublime place to relax and enjoy the Caribbean. There's decent snorkelling at the southern end of the beach too, though the once pristine reef has suffered in recent years from increasing river run-off and the close attentions of unsupervized day-trippers.

From West End, it's a pleasant 45-minute stroll south along the beach and over a few rock outcrops; alternatively you can take one of the small launches that

---

WATER SPORTS IN AND AROUND WEST END

Dive courses for all levels are available in West End. Prices are officially standardized, with a four-day PADI open-water course costing around US$250, but it's worth asking around as some schools include basic accommodation, and sporadic price wars have been known to break out. Fun dives are set at US$35 a dive, though again substantial discounts are often on offer, with ten-dive packages set at around US$250. Recommended West End–based schools include West End Divers (@www.westendivers.com), Ocean Connections (@www.ocean-connections .com), Coconut Tree Divers (@ www.coconuttreedivers.com) and Native Sons (@www.nativesonsroatan.com).

The reef lying just offshore provides superb snorkelling, with the best spots being at the mouth of Half Moon Bay and at the Blue Channel, which can be accessed from the beach 100m south of *Foster's* bar. You can also rent sea kayaks from the *Sea Breeze Inn*, close to the entrance road; expect to pay around US$12 for a half-day or US$20 for a full day. Underwater Paradise, based in the *Half Moon Bay Resort*, runs popular, hour-long glass-bottomed boat tours from US$18 per person. For something completely different, visit the Roatán Institute for Deep Sea Exploration (@www.stanleysubmarines.com). Run by an American who built his own submarine, in which he takes intrepid tourists to depths of 2000ft, it's located on the northern side of Half Moon Bay.

leave regularly from West End Divers. A dirt road also runs here: from West End, head up the road to Coxen Hole and take the first turning on the right.

French Harbour

Leaving Coxen Hole, the paved road runs northeast past the small secluded cove of Brick Bay to **French Harbour**, a busy fishing port and the island's second largest town. Less run-down than Coxen Hole, it's a lively and interesting place to spend the day. Should you have time, stop by the town's private **Iguana Reserve** (daily 9am–5pm; US$1), home to more than 2800 specimens of four species; all the proceeds of the entry fee go towards the care of the animals. To get there, follow the signs to the *Fantasy Island Resort* until you see signs leading to the centre.

Oak Ridge

From French Harbour the road cuts inland along a central ridge to give superb views of both the north and south coasts of the island. After about 14km the road reaches **Oak Ridge**, an attractive fishing port with wooden houses strung along its harbour. There are some nice unspoiled beaches to the east of town, accessible by launches from the main dock, and other nearby communities can be reached by boat cruises through the mangroves.

Punta Gorda

About 5km from Oak Ridge on the northern coast of the island is the village of **Punta Gorda**, the oldest Garífuna community in Honduras. The best time to visit is for the anniversary of the founding of the settlement on April 12, when Garífuna from all over the country attend the celebrations. At other times it's a quiet and slightly dilapidated little port with no buildings of note. From the end of the paved road at Punta Gorda, it's possible to continue driving along the dirt track which runs east along the island, passing the turn-off for the

secluded **Playa Beach** after around 1.5km. A further 5km or so along is **Camp Bay Beach**, an idyllic stretch of white sand and coconut palms.

Port Royal

The road ends at the village of **Port Royal**, on the southern edge of the island, where the faint remains of a fort built by the English can be seen on a caye offshore. The village lies in the **Port Royal Park and Wildlife Reserve**, the largest refuge on the island, set up in 1978 in an attempt to protect endangered species such as the yellow-naped parrot.

The eastern tip of Roatán is made up of mangrove swamps, with a small island, **Morat**, just offshore. Beyond is **Barbareta** caye, which has retained much of its virgin forest cover. The reef around Barbareta and the nearby **Pigeon Cayes** offers good snorkelling; launches can be hired to reach these islands from Oak Ridge for around US$35 for a return trip.

Arrival and information

By air Regular domestic and international flights land at Roatán's only international airport, on the road to French Harbour, 3km east of Coxen Hole – the main town on the south side of the island. There are information and hotel reservation desks, car rental agencies and a bank at the airport.
By boat Roatán's harbour, known as Brick Bay, sits directly between the towns of Coxen Hole and French Harbour.
Tourist information There is an official tourist office just north of the road running into Coxen Hole.

Island transport

Bikes and cars Captain Van's, at the southern end of Half Moon Bay, rents out bicycles (US$9), mopeds (US$39) and motorbikes (US$45). Opposite, you can rent cars from Roatán Rentals.
Minibuses There are two minibus routes covering all of the island's main settlements. Bus #1 (every 30min) goes from Coxen Hole to French Harbour, stopping in Oak Ridge. Bus #2 (every 15min) goes from Coxen Hole to Sandy Bay, stopping in West End. The price depends on how far you're going, and travel times depend largely on the driver.

Taxis It's never hard finding a taxi in Roatán, though as with everything else, it is often a lot more expensive than on the mainland. From the airport or harbour to West End expect to pay US$5 in a shared ride and up to US$15 on your own.

Accommodation

Most of the accommodation in West End is charmingly individualistic but not easy on the pocket: you won't find anywhere near the same value for money that you do on the mainland. Heavy discounts are available during low season (April–July & Sept to mid-Dec), particularly for longer stays.

West End

Burkes's Place At the northern end of the main beach road ☎445 1252. One of West End's best deals, this family-run hotel has cared-for rooms, all equipped with hot-water bathrooms and fan. There is also a fantastic kitchen which has all the tools necessary to cook up a real feast. ❹

Chillie's Half Moon Bay ☎445 4062, ⊛www.nativesonsroatan.com/chillies. Well set-up backpackers' choice, with the option of rooms with shared bath or private cabins. Communal kitchen also available. Also home to Native Sons Divers. ❹–❺

Georphi's Tropical Towards the southern end of the main beach road ☎445 1794, ⊛www.roatangeorphis.com. One of the better deals on the island, with a mix of budget-style rooms and more upmarket cabins. The rooms are fairly basic, but well looked after and all have private bathroom. ❹

Mariposa Lodge On a side-street halfway down the main beach road ☎445 4450. A good-value, quiet lodge with two apartments – complete with sundecks, kitchen and cable TV – and a small cabin with three private rooms, all sharing a large kitchen and bathroom. ❺–❻

Sea Breeze Inn Just south of Half Moon Bay behind the *Cannibal Café*. ☎445 4026, ⊛www.seabreezeroatan.com. A mix of rooms, studios and apartments. The rooms are reasonable but very small and include a fridge and hot showers. The studios are more expensive but altogether much better value with a large kitchen and aesthetic decor. Recommended if you're staying for any length of time in West End. ❹–❺

Valerie's About 300m down the main beach road, then up a signposted dirt track ☎no phone, ⊛www.roatanonline.com/valeries. A love-it-or-hate-it bohemian hostel. Set up with a profusion of quirky accommodation, including two trailer-style rooms, two apartments, a small house, one large gloomy dorm and another smaller, more inviting one. Guests are free to use the kitchen and bathrooms, at their own risk. If you're prepared to deal with its faults, *Valerie's* is the kind of place where your first impressions aren't always correct. Dorms ❶ Rooms from ❷

Coxen Hole

Unless you've got an early ferry or flight, it's unlikely you'll want to stay in town.

Hotel Cay View About 10min north from the dock ☎445 0269. Fairly decent rooms with TV and hot showers. ❹

TREAT YOURSELF

Posada Arco Iris Half Moon Bay ☎445 4264, ⊛www.roatanposada.com. Set in attractive gardens just off the beach, with excellent, imaginatively furnished and spacious rooms, studios and tastefully decorated apartments, all with fridge and hammocks, and some with a/c. ❺–❼

Eating

There's a more than adequate range of places to eat in West End, with fish, seafood and pasta featuring heavily on many menus, though prices are on the high side.

West End

Argentinian Grill Half Moon Bay. Argentine-run restaurant with authentic *churrascos*, grilled meats and seafood at reasonable (by Roatán standards) prices (from US$10). Portions are huge and service efficient.

Bakery#2 Half Moon Bay, on the left-hand side of the road. Good place for breakfast (French toast US$2) and one of the few places open early in the morning. Seating is outside on a narrow veranda overlooking the beach.

Le Bistro Halfway down the main beach road, above West End Divers. This bijou Thai–Vietnamese restaurant serves up the best food in the whole of Roatán. It's great value (mains from US$6) and phenomenally popular – get there early if you want a table.

Cannibal Café Just south of Half Moon Bay, in front of the *Sea Breeze Inn*, serving typical Mexican fare at very reasonable prices. If you're craving some spice, you can have your entire meal covered in green chilli for no extra cost. They also have a "burritos challenge": eat three large burritos and get them for free. Mains from US$5.

Lighthouse Restaurant Close to the seafront between West End and Half Moon Bay. Big portions of reasonably priced Caribbean food served up in friendly, diner-like surroundings. Mains from $8.

Rotisserie Chicken Towards the southern end of the main beach road. If you're looking for the most food you can get for as little money possible, then this is the place. A mix of Honduran and Mexican cuisine is served alongside some large side dishes that can be added to the main meal for very little extra. The *quesadillas* are particularly good. Always busy, so get there early. Mains from $4.

Rudy's Coffee Stop Towards the southern end of the main beach road. *Rudy's* serves legendary breakfasts, including banana pancakes (US$3.50), omelettes, fresh coffee and juices. Opens at 6.30am, so it's ideal for an early meal and a quick getaway. Closed Sun.

Sandy Bay

Rick's American Café If you're looking to eat in Sandy Bay *Rick's* is well worth the climb to the top of the hill above the road. This café serves possibly the largest burgers in the Bay Islands. Mains from US$8.

Drinking and nightlife

Drinking can drain your pocket fast, so seek out the half-price happy hours featured at many of the restaurants and bars in town, some lasting until 10pm.

West End

Blue Channel About 250m down the main beach road. This restaurant-cum-bar-cum-cinema shows movies and sporting events most nights on their large projector. They also host local bands. Admission is free if you're eating, otherwise it's US$2.75.

Foster's At the second of the big piers to the south of town. A West End institution. Fri nights get rowdy when Foster's hosts a weekly reggae jump-up.

Sundowners Opposite Native Sons, Half Moon Bay. This tiny bar often kicks the night off with happy hour from 4–7pm.

Directory

Exchange West End has an ATM in the lobby of the *Dolphin Hotel*, and another one outside the Coconut Tree supermarket, both in Half Moon Bay. In Coxen

Hole Banco Atlántida has an ATM, and to change traveller's cheques you could try the HSBC.

Internet Though widely available, internet connections in West End are slow and overpriced; Barefoot Charlie's towards the southern end of West End charges US$7/hr and also has a book exchange. Paradise Computers in Half Moon Bay charge US$10/hr. In Coxen Hole rates are lower than the rest of the island, though still expensive; try Martínez Cyber beside the HSBC bank on the main street.

Immigration The *migración* is near the small square on Main Street in Coxen Hole.

Laundry Bamboo Hut Laundry, at the southern end of West End, will wash five pounds for US$4.

Post office Near the *migración* and the small square on Main Street in Coxen Hole.

Supermarket HB Warren is the largest supermarket on the island, and there's a small and not too impressive general market just behind Main Street in Coxen Hole.

GUANAJA

GUANAJA, some 25km long and only four kilometres wide at its largest point, is divided into two unequal parts by a narrow canal – the only way to get between the two sections of the island is by water-taxi, which adds both to the atmosphere and to the cost of living. The island is very thinly populated – most of Guanaja's twelve thousand inhabitants live in **Bonacca** (also known as **Guanaja Town**), a crowded settlement on a small caye a few hundred metres offshore. It's here that you'll find the island's shops, as well as the bulk of the less unreasonably priced accommodation. The only other settlements of any substance are **Savannah Bight** (on the east coast) and **Mangrove Bight** (on the north coast). Note that sandflies and mosquitoes are endemic throughout the island, so arrive prepared to deal with them.

What to see and do

Wandering around Bonacca's warren of tight streets, walkways and canal bridges makes for an interesting half-hour or so – though government plans to eliminate the town's tiny waterways for new roads means the town may

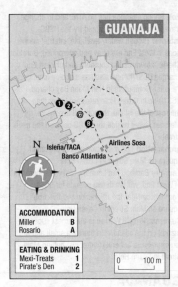

GUANAJA

N Isleña/TACA   Airlines Sosa
    Banco Atlántida

ACCOMMODATION
Miller   B
Rosario   A

EATING & DRINKING
Mexi-Treats   1
Pirate's Den   2

0   100 m

The **Mestizo Dive Site** was opened in 2002 to mark the 500th anniversary of Christopher Columbus's visit, with sunken statues of the explorer and national hero Lempira on a reef surrounded by genuine Spanish colonial artefacts, including a cannon.

Arrival and information

By air The Guanaja airstrip is on the larger, northern section of the island, next to the canal. Aside from a couple of dirt tracks there are no roads, and the main form of transport is small launches. You can hire a water-taxi, though high fuel costs are reflected by the fares. If you have pre-booked a resort on the island you will be met at the airport.
By boat Island Tours (☎ 371 0373) runs twice-weekly boats to Trujillo (Tues and Fri 9am; 2hr).
Tour operators To get to some of the underwater sites you'll have to contact one of the hotel-based dive schools: the *Island House Resort* (☎ 9991 0391) usually has the best rates at around US$70 for two dives including equipment.

Accommodation

Miller Halfway along the main causeway, Bonacca ☎ 453 4327. Housed in a slightly run-down building, though the rooms are in reasonable condition; most have hot water and, for a little extra, a/c and cable TV. ⑤
Rosario In a green building, opposite the main causeway, Bonacca ☎ 453 4240. Clean, well-ventilated rooms all with hot-water bathrooms. A good option if *Miller*, across the street is full. ⑤

Eating and drinking

Mexi-Treats Just past *Pirate's Den*. This Mexican restaurant is the best in town, serving up some surprisingly tasty dishes. Mains from L80.
Pirate's Den Towards the western end of the main causeway. Good for fresh seafood, daily lunch specials and Fri barbecues. Mains from L100.

Directory

Airlines Sosa has an office opposite the Bank. Isleña/Taca has an office at the main dock.
Exchange You can change dollars and get cash advances at Banco Atlántida, to the right of the dock.
Internet Can be found on the main causeway for under L20.

not be the Honduran Venice for much longer. Virtually all the houses in town are built on stilts – vestiges of early settlement by Cayman islanders – with the main causeway running for about 500m east–west along the caye.

Though Guanaja's Caribbean pine forests were flattened by Hurricane Mitch, there's still some decent hiking to be found. A wonderful trail leads from Mangrove Bight up to **Michael's Peak**, the highest point in the Bay Islands (412m) and down to Sandy Bay on the south coast, affording stunning views of Guanaja, Bonacca and the surrounding reef. Fit walkers can do the trail in a day, or you can camp on the summit, provided you bring your own provisions.

Some of the island's finest white-sand beaches lie around the rocky headland of **Michael's Rock**, near the *Island House Resort* on the north coast, with good snorkelling close to the shore. **Diving** is excellent all around the main island, but particularly off the small cayes to the east, and at **Black Rocks**, off the northern tip of the main island, where there's an underwater coral canyon.

Nicaragua

THE CORN ISLANDS:
picturesque and relaxed little Caribbean islands

GRANADA:
one of the oldest Spanish-founded cities in Latin America

LEÓN:
be reminded of the country's revolutionary past

ISLA DE OMETEPE:
hike the island's mysterious twin volcanoes in the middle of Lago de Nicaragua

SAN JUAN DEL SUR:
the most popular surf and beach holiday town in the country

RÍO SAN JUAN:
explore pristine tropical forest and the ruins of El Castillo

ROUGH COSTS

DAILY BUDGET Basic US$16–25/ occasional treat US$45–65

DRINK Beer US$1

FOOD *Comida típica* US$2–4

CAMPING/HOSTEL/BUDGET HOTEL US$1.50–4/US$5–10/US$15–30

TRAVEL Managua–San Juan del Sur by bus (roughly 135km): 2hr 30min–3hr 30min, US$7.50.

FACT FILE

POPULATION 5.5 million

AREA 130,000 sq km

LANGUAGES Spanish, Creole English on the Atlantic Coast

CURRENCY Nicaragua córdoba (C$)

CAPITAL Managua (population: 1.5 million)

INTERNATIONAL PHONE CODE ☎505

TIME ZONE GMT –6hr

Introduction

Wedge-shaped Nicaragua may be the largest nation in Central America, but it is also one of the least visited. Still, many travellers who spend any time here find that Nicaragua is their favourite country in the isthmus – one simply can't remain immune to the country's extraordinary landscape of volcanoes (seventeen in all), lakes, mountains and vast plains of rainforest. In comparison with the Maya ruins of Guatemala or the national parks of Costa Rica, the country offers few traditional tourist attractions – almost no ancient structures remain, and years of revolution, civil war and natural disasters have laid waste to museums, galleries and theatres – and a chronic lack of funding, high inflation and unemployment have impoverished the country's infrastructure. It's these same qualities, though, that make Nicaragua an incorrigibly vibrant and individualistic country, with plenty to offer travellers prepared to brave the superficial obstacles of economic chaos, cracked pavements and crammed public transport.

Virtually every traveller passes through the capital, **Managua**, if only to catch a bus; there's little to detain visitors in the capital, however, and many quickly head for **Granada**, with its splendid lakeside setting and wonderful colonial architecture. A smattering of **beaches** along the Pacific coast, from **San Juan del Sur** to **Jiquilillo**, continues to attract the **surfing** and backpacking crowds, while the beautiful – and as yet unspoilt – **Corn Islands**, just off the coast of **Bluefields**, offer idyllic white sand beaches framed by wind-swept palm trees and the azure Caribbean Sea. Culture and the arts are very much alive in Nicaragua; visit **Masaya**'s Mercado Nacional de Artesanía to find some fantastic-value high-quality crafts, or stay on the **Solentiname Archipelago** and learn about the primitive painting traditions that have flourished there. **León**, the birthplace of poet Rubén Darío, is often considered the country's cultural capital – look for the famous **murals** depicting Nicaragua's turbulent political history. Ecotourism, volcano-viewing and hiking are the attractions of the **Isla de Ometepe**, with its thrilling twin peaks rising out of the freshwater lake. In the central region, where much

WHEN TO GO

Nicaragua has two distinct seasons, the dry and the wet. The rainy season, or *invierno* (winter), runs roughly from May to November. *Verano* (summer December–April) is extremely hot and often uncomfortably dry. Fewer travellers come in the rainy season – which alone could be a reason for choosing to put up with the daily downpour. On the Pacific Coast, rain often falls in the afternoons from May to November, although the mornings are dry. The central mountain region has a cooler climate with sporadic rainfall all year, while the Atlantic Coast is very wet, hot and humid year-round, with September and October being the height of the tropical storm season.

of the country's export-grade coffee is grown, the climate is refreshingly cool; hiking and birdwatching are the main activities near the mountain town of **Matagalpa**. More than anything, though, the pleasures and rewards of travelling in Nicaragua come from interacting with the inhabitants of the country's complex society – Nicaraguans tend to be engagingly witty and exceptionally hospitable. The best thing you can do to enjoy Nicaragua is to arrive with an open mind.

CHRONOLOGY

1000 AD Aztec migrate south after the fall of Teotihuacán (Mexico), following a prophecy that they would settle where they found a lake with two volcanoes rising from it – Isla de Ometepe.

1522 The Spanish arrive and name the region "Nicaragua", after the indigenous groups living there.

1524 Spanish establish the settlements of Granada and León.

1821 Nicaragua gains independence from Spain as part of the Central American Federation.

1838 Nicaragua becomes an independent nation (save the Atlantic coast, which is claimed as British territory).

1855 American adventurer William Walker takes control of the government.

1857 Walker is overthrown by joint efforts of Nicaragua, Costa Rica, Guatemala and the US. He is later executed in Honduras.

1857–1893 "The Thirty Years": a period of relative prosperity. US companies come to dominate Nicaraguan government.

1893 General José Zelaya seizes control, establishing a dictatorship.

1909 Civil war breaks out. 400 US marines land on the Caribbean coast. Zelaya resigns.

1912–1925 US military bases are established.

1927 Augusto Sandino leads a guerrilla campaign in protest at the US military presence. US takes over Nicaraguan military and develops Nicaraguan National Guard.

1934 Under orders of National Guard commander General Anastasio Somoza, Sandino is assassinated.

1937 Somoza "elected" president, commencing forty-year dictatorship.

Somoza is assassinated by Rigoberto López ~rez. One of Somoza's sons, Luis, becomes interim president, and another, Anastasio, head of the National Guard.

1961 Frente Sandinista Liberación Nacional (FSLN), or Sandinista National Liberation Front, is founded.

1967 Luis Somoza dies; his brother Anastasio becomes president.

1972 Massive earthquake flattens Managua, killing some 10,000.

1978 Opposition leader Pedro Chamorro is assassinated by National Guard; demonstrations and fighting spread across the country.

1979 Sandinistas gain control of the country, and Somoza is forced to flee. Revolution is officially won on July 19. Liberal Sandinistas are in control of government.

1981 Unhappy with Nicaragua's left-wing policies and communist ties, the US funds Contra troops in an anti-Sandinista campaign.

1984 FSLN's Daniel Ortega wins presidential election.

1988 FSLN and Contras sign a ceasefire.

1990 Violeta Chamorro defeats Daniel Ortega to become Latin America's first female president. US cuts off aid to Contras.

1996–2001 Right-wing Arnoldo Alemán, former mayor of Managua, serves as president.

1998 Hurricane Mitch devastates region.

2001 Alemán's vice president, Enrique Bolaños, is elected.

2002–03 Alemán is jailed on charges of embezzlement and money laundering.

2004–05 The World Bank and Russia clear much of the country's debts, as part of the Heavily Indebted Poor Countries Initiative.

2006 Former president Ortega wins the November elections and returns to power.

Basics

ARRIVAL

If arriving on an international flight, you'll land at **Augusto C. Sandino International Airport (MGA)** in Managua. As well as flights from neighbouring capitals such as San José and San Salvador (served mainly by COPA and TACA), Managua receives direct flights from major US hubs Atlanta,

Miami and Houston. Spirit Airlines (Ⓦwww.spiritair.com) has the best budget flights from North America; Continental, American Airlines and Delta also fly North American routes.

You can enter Nicaragua by land from Honduras and Costa Rica (see box below). International **buses** all pull into Managua, often via Granada and Rivas (if coming from the south). Crossings will be facilitated on international services such as Tica Bus; it's also possible to take local services to and from the border.

There is a **water** crossing from the border at Los Chiles, Costa Rica (see box, p.573), to San Carlos; from here it is a 10–12hr bus ride or 1hr plane ride on to Managua.

VISAS

American, Australian, British, Canadian and most EU nationals do not currently require **visas**. There is a US$5 **entry fee**, which you pay upon arrival. You will also receive a **tourist card** at this time, which allows for stays of thirty to ninety days depending on your nationality. The permitted length of your visit will be hand-written on the entry stamp in your passport. While all tourist cards allow for thirty days entry, it is only the number written in your passport that

---

LAND AND SEA ROUTES TO NICARAGUA

Nicaragua shares borders with Costa Rica and Honduras. The busiest Nicaraguan land entry/exit point is at Peñas Blancas (see p.458), on the southern border with Costa Rica. Los Chiles in Costa Rica provides a water crossing further east, to San Carlos on the Río San Juan. The two main border crossings with Honduras in the north, meanwhile, are at Guasaule (see p.436) and Las Manos (see p.439), with the latter providing easiest access to Tegucigalpa.

ADDRESSES IN NICARAGUA

Nicaraguan towns are usually set up in a vague grid system, with a commercial build-up around the parque central and main streets, and residential neighbourhoods sprawling outwards from the centre. Only main streets are labelled with signs, and even the cities (except Granada) lack names for most of their streets. Smaller towns do not have any street names at all, depending instead on their direction from the main square: calles go east–west and avenidas north–south, with a central calle and avenida acting as the grid's axis. Calles and avenidas northeast of the main park are generally designated *noreste* (NE), those northwest are *noroeste* (NO), southeast are *sureste* (SE) and southwest *suroeste* (SO). There is no set numbering system for streets in Nicaraguan towns, and this, combined with the lack of street names, result in addresses that refer to locations' proximity to local landmarks, such as churches, rotundas or traffic circles, malls, banks, restaurants and gas stations. This is especially the case in Managua, whose confusing orientation makes it worthy of a box unto itself (see p.419).

counts. Check with your airline to see if the country's US$35 departure tax has been included; otherwise this can be paid in the airport before departure. As part of the CA-4 agreement (see p.48), visitors are granted ninety days of travel within Nicaragua, Honduras, Guatemala and El Salvador. Thirty-day extensions can be granted for a fee, and travellers who overstay the limit may face a fine.

GETTING AROUND

Finding your way around Nicaragua is half the fun of travelling in the country. Public transport, especially buses, is geared toward the domestic population, and is very cheap; bus stops, however, are not usually marked and so you will likely have to rely on a local's assistance to find your destination.

By bus

The standard local **buses** in Nicaragua are the usual old North American school buses, though an increasing number of express minivans and minibuses also serve the more popular routes – only a few córdobas more, they are less crowded, stop less frequently and occasionally even have air-conditioning. Most **intercity buses** begin running between 4am and 7am, departing about

every thirty minutes, or when the bus is full, with last buses leaving by 5 or 6pm. **Bus stops** (never marked) are usually at the local market, and fares are very cheap – generally US$0.75–3. If you are carrying luggage and want to keep it with you, you may be charged half-fare – or even full fare – for the space it occupies (otherwise it goes on the roof). Any luggage stored on the roof rack should be free of valuables, or locked; inside the buses pick-pocketing is common, so be sure to keep bags and small packs in sight.

By car

Taxis – many on their last legs – are most often seen in cities, but they also make long-distance journeys; a good deal, especially if in a group, since drivers charge by the distance travelled. In Managua, most taxi fares are C$20–50 during the day, and C$40–80 at night. Outside the capital, in-town fares vary, but are usually around C$10–20. Always negotiate the fare before getting into the cab.

Renting a car in Nicaragua is probably the best way to explore the country's many beaches. Rental is most reliable in Managua. You need a valid licence, passport and a credit card. Make sure you take out full-cover

insurance, as the number of road accidents in Nicaragua is increasing. Throughout the country road signage is quite poor, and you'll need to ask directions frequently. As with other Central American countries, don't drive at night – it's less a question of crime than the lack of lighting disguising potholes, sudden deviations in the road or even the road disappearing altogether, as well as cattle straying onto the highway. Rates average US$35 a day for the cheapest models. A 4WD is necessary outside of the capital.

Nicaraguans are a little surprised to see foreigners **hitching**, although it's common for locals to do so. Women only hitch when accompanied by men, and it's wise to follow this rule as a traveller. You will be expected to pay for your lift, but usually no more than US$1.50–2, even for trips of a couple of hours.

By boat

Boats provide vital links around Nicaragua's numerous waterways and two large lakes. You can get part of the way from Managua and the Pacific lowlands to the Atlantic Coast by water; once on the eastern side of the country, nearly all travel runs along the complex network of rivers and lagoons of Mosquitia. Journeys are unscheduled, long and unpredictable. Travellers most commonly take boats between El Rama and Bluefields; Rivas or Granada and Ometepe; and Granada or Ometepe and San Carlos – this route is a notoriously long and rough voyage. San Carlos can also be accessed by boat from the border crossing at Los Chiles.

By air

Nicaragua has two private domestic airlines, La Costeña (Ⓦwww.tacaregional.com/costena) and Atlantic Airlines (Ⓦwww.atlanticairlinesint.com), though at the time of writing Atlantic had ceased operations indefinitely in the country (though not in Honduras, the airline's home country) – check with the airline for the latest information before booking flights. La Costeña operates reliable (and very scenic) **flights** between Managua and key destinations around the country, including Bluefields, the Corn Islands and Puerto Cabezas, all of which are otherwise difficult to reach. They also cover the Managua–San Carlos route (US$75 or US$116 return).

ACCOMMODATION

Most budget travellers to Nicaragua at some point find themselves in a Nicaraguan **hospedaje** – a small, pension-type hotel, most often family-owned and run. Most are basic, though some, especially those in old Spanish colonial-style houses, are truly characterful. As a rule, simple *hospedajes* charge around US$4–10 (❶–❷); most require payment in cash, often in córdobas. This covers a bed and fan; in many places you'll have to share a bathroom, and breakfast is not normally included in the price. There are about five **hostels** in the country – generally *hospedajes* take their place. **Hotels** (US$20 and up; ❹) tend to be more "luxurious", with air-conditioning, cable TV and services like tours and car rental; you are less likely to see these in very small towns. Throughout the country **camping** is problematic, although not impossible; sandflies, mosquitoes, rain and theft are only a few of the deterrents to setting up a tent. If you're determined, the most promising areas in which to camp are beach spots around San Juan del Sur, Isla Ometepe and the Corn Islands. See p.35 for an explanation of the accommodation price codes used in this Guide.

FOOD AND DRINK

Central markets in Nicaraguan towns are guaranteed to have snack spots, with at least several small **comedores** or **cafetines** offering cheap **comida corriente** ("running/fast food"), a set plate of meat, rice and salad, for around US$2.50. Throughout Nicaragua **street-side kiosks** sell hot meals, usually at lunch time. You'll soon become familiar with their plastic tablecloths, paper plates and huge bowls of cabbage salad; the food is cheap, generally well prepared and safe to eat. **Restaurants** are more expensive, and generally open for lunch and dinner. As in the rest of Central America, **lunch** is the main meal.

Nicaraguan **food** is based around the ubiquitous **beans**, **rice** and **meat**. Everything is cooked with oil – even the rice is fried. Meals usually include **chicken**, **beef** or **pork**, most deliciously cooked *a la plancha*, on a grill or griddle, and served with **gallo pinto** (beans and rice), plantain, and shredded cabbage salad. There's little difference between breakfast, lunch and dinner, though breakfast will most likely involve an egg instead of meat. Roast chicken, pizza and Chinese restaurants also crop up in most towns. On the Atlantic Coast the cuisine becomes markedly more **Caribbean**. Here rice is often cooked in mild coconut milk, and the staple fresh **coconut bread** is delicious. **Ron don** ("run down"; in local parlance "to cook") is a stew of yucca, chayote and other vegetables, usually with meat added, which is traditionally eaten at weekends. Weekends are also the time to eat **nacatamales**, parcels of corn dough filled with either vegetables, pork, beef or chicken, which are wrapped in a banana leaf and boiled for a couple of hours.

On the sweeter side, tropical **fruit** is abundant, cheap and delicious. Throughout the country you'll see **ice-cream** sellers pushing their Eskimo carts. The quality isn't great, but the company produces an extraordinary range of flavours, including many local fruits and nuts.

Drink

Given Nicaragua's heat, it's just as well that there's a huge range of cold drinks, or **refrescos** (usually shortened to *frescos*), available. These are made from grains, seeds and fruits, which are liquidized with milk, water and ice. Some unusual ones to look for include *cebada en grano*, a combination of ground barley and barley grains mixed with milk, coloured pink and flavoured with cinnamon and lots of sugar; *pinolillo*, a spiced maize and cacao drink; and *semilla de Jicaroa* (or "Hickory seed"), which looks and tastes like chocolate. Just about every fruit imaginable is made into a *fresco*, including watermelon, granadilla (a passion fruit variety), papaya, pithaya (dragon fruit) and rock melon. During the rainy months, keep your eye out for *pitahaya* juice. Made from the fruit of a cactus, it's a virulent purple in colour and incredibly tasty.

Tap water is generally not friendly to tourist stomachs, but bottled water is found everywhere, as well as soft drinks. Nicaragua has two local brands of **beer**, Victoria and Toña, both lagers. For spirits, local Flor de Caña **rum** comes in dark and white, gold, old, dry and light, and is an excellent buy at just US$5–10 per bottle. It's usually brought to the table with a large bucket of ice and some lemons, but you can mix it with soft drinks for something a little less potent. A national **cocktail**, the *Macuá* – a potent combination of white rum and fruit juices (usually lemon and guava) – has recently emerged.

CULTURE AND ETIQUETTE

Nicaraguans are generally courteous and appreciate this trait in visitors. It is considered polite to address strangers with "Usted" rather than "Tú", though eventually, familiarity usually allows the use of "Tú" or even "Vos". You will often hear the term *Adiós* (literally, "to God")

411

NICARAGUAN EXPRESSIONS AND PHRASES

Adiós (pronounced a-dee-oss) Used as a greeting in passing.

Dale pues (pronounced dah-lay pway) Literally, "give it, then", it's used to say "ok", "go on", "fine", "it's on", etc.

Por fa (pronounced as is) A shortening of *por favor (*please).

used as a greeting – hardly surprising in a country where ninety percent of the population follows a Christian denomination. The older generations in particular are often religiously conservative in appearance and manner. Accordingly, *machista* attitudes are still prevalent, noticeably more so than in neighbouring Costa Rica. Female travellers may be harassed by cat-calls from local (usually young) men; this is best ignored, and occurs much less frequently if moving around within a group or when accompanied by a man.

With regard to **tipping**, most restaurants, particularly in the capital, will add a ten- to fifteen-percent service charge onto the bill; always check if this is included. Elsewhere, tips are not expected.

SPORTS AND OUTDOOR ACTIVITIES

Rather surprisingly for a Latin American country, Nicaragua's national sport is **baseball**, and every town has a field and numerous, active leagues. Ask your local taxi driver about league games, for which most of the town will turn out in support. **Football** may be played by children in the street, but lacks the popularity here that it has in other Latin countries.

Visiting **surfers** are drawn to the country's Pacific coast, where there seems to be an endless run of deserted beaches with great breaks; the most

popular area (with good tourist amenities) is around **San Juan del Sur**, near the Costa Rican border (see p.456) – you'll find the most surf camps, teachers, and board sales or rentals in this area. The country's landscape also provides a good selection of areas for **hiking**, from stunning volcanoes (like those on **Isla de Ometepe**; see p.460) to the mountainous **Selva Negra** forests around Matagalpa (see p.441). On the Atlantic coast, **diving** and **snorkelling** are a must, particularly on the **Corn Islands** (see p.475), where you can reach wrecks and reefs from right off the beach. Much of the coral is in good condition, and the abundance of undersea wildlife makes for spectacular viewing. Nicaragua is also the only country in the world currently offering **ashboarding** – essentially using a snowboard to ride the ashes on the **Cerro Negro** volcano near León (see p.432).

COMMUNICATIONS

Most towns in Nicaragua have post offices (except on the Atlantic coast, where they are few and far between), but the **mail** service is best in Managua. Rates in the capital are also the lowest (a postcard to the US is C$10, C$13 to Europe). Theft from letters is an increasing problem, especially with mail sent into the country, so it's wise not to trust cash or anything valuable to the postal service. To locate or contact a post office (generally open 8am–5pm), see Ⓦ www.correosdenicaragua.com.

Nicaraguan **telephone** company **Enitel** has an office in every town of any size throughout the country; in smaller towns their offices also serve as a "post office". There are virtually no coin-operated phones in Nicaragua; Publitel **calling cards** (in denominations of US$5, US$10 and US$20) are available from Enitel offices and work by punching in a designated code. They can be useful for both **domestic** and **international** calls, but only for the

NICARAGUA ON THE NET

ⓦ www.hotelesdenicaragua.net This INTUR-supported site has excellent tourist information, with listings including hotels, medical facilities and transportation services.

ⓦ www.nicaliving.com Expat forum with some useful tips on travel and news in Nicaragua.

ⓦ www.vianica.com Useful website with contributions from business owners and expats, good for general information on sights and travel.

ⓦ www.visit-nicaragua.com INTUR's tourism promotions site, with general information on tourist attractions, cultural activities and amenities.

latter in larger towns such as Managua, Granada and León, so it's often easier and cheaper to use phone services at a **cybercafé** if you want to call home. **Mobile phones** can be purchased cheaply (from US$12) and used for making local calls, but the fierce competition between the two major companies, Claro and Movistar, means that cross-network calls are extremely expensive. Local phone numbers generally have seven digits, formatted as one group of three then a group of four. Calling Nicaragua from abroad, the **country code** is ☎505.

The proliferation of **internet** cafés in Nicaragua – you'll find at least one in even the smallest towns – means that the internet is the easiest and cheapest method of communication. Rates – generally C$10–20 – often rise in smaller or more remote towns, where connections can be also painfully slow, so be patient.

CRIME AND SAFETY

High rates of poverty and unemployment in Nicaragua have contributed to a rising crime rate, most often manifested to visitors in the form of **petty theft**, especially on buses. Nicaraguans suffer from this as well as tourists; locals don't carry anything valuable in outside pockets, and spread money over several pockets or purses – you should do the same. The only place where you really need to worry about **assault** is Managua. It's best not to walk around the capital at night – especially around the Tica Bus station – or to go out alone to bars, and always be alert when leaving banks or *casas de cambio*. It's a good idea to take a taxi after changing money. Larger hotels will have safes where you can leave valuables. Wherever you are, **women** should be wary of going out alone at night, though the chief threat is being harassed by groups of drunken men.

The **police** in Nicaragua are generally reliable, except perhaps the traffic police (*policía de tránsito*), who are infamous for targeting foreigners and who will take any chance to give you a fine (*multa*). To **report a crime** you must go to the nearest police station. If you need a police report for an insurance claim, the police will ask you to fill out a *denuncia* – a full report of the incident. If the police station does not have the *denuncia* forms, ask for a *constancia*, a simpler form, signed and stamped by the police. This should be sufficient for an insurance claim.

Visitors to Nicaragua should carry their **passport** on them at all times, though a photocopy is acceptable; police checks still exist, though are not as common as they used to be.

MEDICAL CARE AND EMERGENCIES

Serious medical situations should be attended to at a **hospital**; most towns and cities have one. Failing this, find a Red Cross (Cruz Roja) post, medical centre or pharmacy for advice on treatment. Head for the capital in the case of a serious medical emergency. **Pharmacies** are generally open between 8am and 5pm, although many stay open later. Farmacia Medco (☎1-800-2224) has several branches in Managua, including one at Plaza España and one at Rotonda Bello Horizonte.

MONEY AND BANKS

Nicaragua's **currency** is the **córdoba** (C$), which is divided into 100 centavos; at the time of writing, the exchange rate was C$19 to US$1. Notes come in denominations of 10, 20, 50, 100 and 500 córdobas; coins come in denominations of 1 and 5 córdobas, and 25 and 50 centavos. Get rid of C$100 and C$500 notes when you can – in most places they're about as welcome as a stack of Russian rubles, and no one ever has change. US dollars are very useful across Nicaragua, although US$100 bills can usually only be changed at a bank.

Banks are usually open from 8am to 4pm and may close for an hour or so over lunch (12.30–1.30pm); many are also open on Saturday mornings until noon. Most will change US dollars, but no other currency. Currency-exchange houses, called **casas de cambio** (mostly found only in Managua), are another option for changing dollars and also traveller's cheques, but you will not get the best exchange rates. **Moneychangers** (*coyotes*) operate in the street, usually at the town market, though it's easy to get ripped off here.

One of the main hassles of Nicaragua is the refusal of many banks to acknowledge the existence of **traveller's cheques**;

only the **Banco de América Central (BAC)** will change them, although at much poorer rates than cash. **Credit cards** such as Visa and MasterCard are generally accepted in more expensive hotels and restaurants and can also be used to pay for car rental, flights and tours. All branches of Bancentro and BAC advance cash on major cards. BAC, Bancentro, Banco ProCredit and Banpro's **ATM** machines all accept foreign-issue cards, and in most reasonable-sized towns you will find at least one of these. That said, you can't rely on ATMs alone and, especially out of the major centres, you'll have little alternative but to carry a decent amount of cash. There are currently no ATMs in the Río San Juan area or on Little Corn Island.

INFORMATION AND MAPS

The national tourist board, **INTUR** (Ⓦwww.intur.gob.ni), has **information** offices throughout the country, with the largest in Managua, and although the staff are usually friendly and well intentioned, they generally only speak Spanish and can't offer much practical help; you're unlikely to come away with much more than a bunch of colourful leaflets. Ask for a copy of the quarterly *Between the Waves* magazine (free), a useful English-language publication geared towards expats and travellers. It's packed with articles on history, business, tourist activities and destinations within Nicaragua, often including up-to-date transport schedules. If INTUR doesn't have it, you should be able to pick it up in selected restaurants, travel agencies, embassies and bigger hotels.

You can pick up a useful **map** of Managua in the city's INTUR office, although paper maps of other cities (save perhaps Granada and León) are usually very hard to come by. Handy downloadable maps are available at Ⓦwww.ineter.gob.ni under *"mapas"*,

> ## PUBLIC HOLIDAYS
>
> **January 1** New Year's Day
>
> **Easter week** Semana Santa
>
> **May 1** Labour Day
>
> **July 19** Anniversary of the Revolution
>
> **September 14** Battle of San Jacinto
>
> **September 15** Independence Day
>
> **November 2** All Souls' Day (Día de los Muertos)
>
> **December 7 & 8** Inmaculada Concepción
>
> **December 25** Christmas Day

and ⓦwww.eaai.com.ni has two useful free maps.

OPENING HOURS AND PUBLIC HOLIDAYS

Shops and **services** in Nicaragua still observe Sunday closing: otherwise you'll find most things open from 8am to 4pm. Many **businesses**, **museums** and **sites** close for lunch, normally shutting their doors between noon and 2pm, before reopening again until 4 or 5pm. Supermarkets, smaller grocery shops and the small neighbourhood shops called *pulperías* or *ventas* generally stay open until 8pm. **Bars** and **restaurants** tend to close around 11pm or midnight, except for nightclubs and dance clubs – most of which are in Managua – which stay open until 2am or later. Public holidays (see box above) see almost everything shut down, so don't plan on visiting tourist attractions over those dates.

FESTIVALS

Nicaragua's calendar includes plenty of festivals, everything from local events to nationally celebrated fiestas. In addition, each town in Nicaragua has its own patron saint whose saint's day is observed with processions and celebrations called Toro Guaco, during which you might catch a glimpse of old customs inherited from the Aztecs mixed with mestizo figures like the masked *viejitos* (old ones – masks of old men and women worn by young and old alike). In all cases, Nicaraguans love to dance, and you will probably see folkloric dances in the streets, usually performed by children. The calendar below only lists as few highlights of the nation's celebrations.

March–April At Easter the whole country packs up and goes to the beach: buses are packed, hotel rooms are at a premium, and flights to the Corn Islands are fully booked. Semana Santa (Holy Week) processions, in which crowds follow *pasos* (depictions of Christ and the Virgin), are the biggest in Granada.

May The Atlantic coastal town of Bluefields celebrates Palo de Mayo, an adapted May Day fiesta flavoured with the Caribbean rhythms of reggae and soca – a fusion of dance and folklore.

July The holiday marking the Revolution (July 19), is still celebrated ardently by Sandinistas and is usually accompanied by parades and marches; in Managua, the Plaza de la Revolución fills with Sandinista supporters, who gather in memory of the historical events.

December–January Throughout much of the country, New Year's Eve is mainly celebrated in the home, although San Juan del Sur is known for drawing a crowd of young revellers. Bear in mind you'll find most things closed on January 1.

Managua and around

Hotter than an oven and crisscrossed by anonymous highways, there can't be a more visitor-unfriendly capital than **MANAGUA**. Less a city in the conventional sense than a conglomeration of neighbourhoods and commercial districts, Managua offers few sights and cultural experiences – in fact, most visitors are so disturbed by the lack of street names and any real centre that they get out as fast as they can.

Not even the city's setting on the southern shore of **Lago de Managua** is particularly pleasant: the area is low-lying, swampy and flat, relieved only by a few eroded volcanoes. It also, unfortunately, sits on top of an astounding eleven **seismic faults**, which have shaken the city severely over time. The result has been a cycle of ruin and rebuilding, which has created a bizarre and postmodern mixture of crumbling ruins inhabited by squatters, hastily constructed concrete structures and gleaming new shopping malls and hotels. The old city centre, damaged further in the **Revolution** of 1978–79 and never thoroughly repaired, remains eerily abandoned.

All this said, there *are* things to enjoy here, although being a tourist in Managua does require a good degree of tenacity. Also, as Nicaragua's largest city and home to a quarter of its population, the city occupies a key position in the nation's economy and psyche, and offers more practical services than anywhere else in the country.

What to see and do

For the visitor, sprawling Managua can thankfully be divided into a few distinct areas. The **old ruined centre** on the lakeshore, finally undergoing redevlopment, is the site of the city's tourist attractions, including the few impressive colonial-style buildings that have survived all the earthquakes. **Lago de Managua**, which forms such a pretty backdrop to this part of the city, is, unfortunately, severely **polluted** from sewage and regular dumpings of garbage and chemical waste.

Just to the south, but visible from everywhere, is the city's main landmark, the **Crowne Plaza**, formerly the **Hotel InterContinental** (not to be confused with the new *InterContinental Metrocentro* hotel in the south of the city), whose white form, reminiscent of a Maya pyramid, sails above the city. Walking just west of the *Crowne Plaza* and twelve or so blocks south of the old ruined city centre brings you to the backpacker-frequented barrio **Marta Quezada**. Here, rock-bottom prices and proximity to international bus connections somewhat make up for the area's notorious reputation as dangerous, crime-ridden barrio. A further 2km south, around **Plaza España**, you'll find many of the city's banks, airline offices and

---

SAFETY IN MANAGUA

While the country of Nicaragua remains one of the safest destinations in Central America, gang warfare is a problem, and certain parts of Managua (Villa Revolución, for example) are stamping grounds for pandillas, young thugs who won't think twice about robbing you or locals. While it's unlikely you'd be hanging around these areas anyway, tourists have also recently been robbed in broad daylight in barrio Marta Quezada, so it's to your benefit to be on guard wherever you are in the city. If you're alone it's advisable to take a taxi after dark instead of getting around on foot, even for short distances.

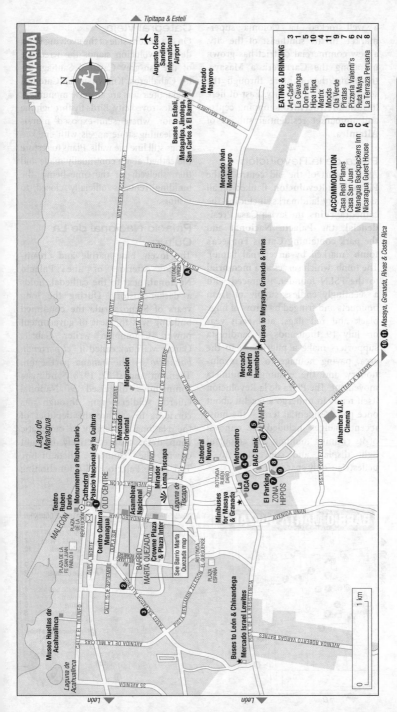

MANAGUA

MANAGUA AND AROUND

NICARAGUA

▲ Tipitapa & Estelí

Lago de Managua

Laguna de Acahualinca

León ▼

León ▼

▼ ⑩, ⑪ Masaya, Granada, Rivas & Costa Rica

EATING & DRINKING
Art-Café   3
La Cavanga   1
Don Pan   5
Hipa Hipa   10
Matrix   4
Moods   11
Ola Verde   9
Piratas   7
Pizzeria Valenti's   6
Ruta Maya   2
La Terraza Peruana   8

ACCOMMODATION
Casa Real Planes   B
Casa San Juan   D
Managua Backpackers Inn   C
Nicaragua Guest House   A

Augusto César Sandino International Airport

Mercado Mayoreo

Buses to Estelí, Matagalpa, Jinotega, San Carlos & El Rama

Mercado Iván Montenegro

Mercado Roberto Huembes

Buses to Maysaya, Granada & Rivas

Alhambra V.I.P. Cinema

Mercado Oriental

Migración

Catedral Nueva

Metrocentro

BAC Bank

ALTAMIRA

El Parking

ZONA HIPPOS

La UCA

Mirador Loma Tiscapa

Laguna de Tiscapa

Asamblea Nacional

Minibuses for Masaya & Granada

Teatro Ruben Dario

Cathedral

Monumento a Ruben Dario

Palacio Nacional de la Cultura

OLD CENTRE

Centro Cultural Managua

Crowne Plaza & Plaza Inter

BARRIO MARTA QUEZADA

See Barrio Marta Quezada map

Museo Huellas de Acahualinca

Buses to León & Chinandega

Mercado Israel Lewites

MALECON

PLAZA DE LA REVOLUCION

PLAZA DE LA FE SAN JUAN PABLO II

PLAZA ESPAÑA

1 km

417

a well-stocked La Colonia super-market. In the southeast of the city, a new commercial district has grown up along the **Carretera a Masaya**, the main thoroughfare through the southern part of the city. East of here lies the **Metrocentro** shopping centre and upmarket residential suburb of **Altamira**.

Plaza de la Revolución

At the heart of the old centre is the **Plaza de la Revolución**, flanked on all sides by city landmarks, including the cathedral **ruins**, the lavish **Casa Presidencial**, the **Palacio Nacional** and the park containing **Carlos Fonseca's tomb** (marked by an eternal flame). The tomb, which serves as a **memorial** to the FSLN founder, is graced with a seemingly endless supply of fresh bouquets and fringed by a row of huge black and red flags, and each year on July 19 thousands of Sandinista supporters make a pilgrimage to the area, paying homage to the revolutionary and the ensuing Sandinista movement. The Plaza de la Revolución itself tends to undergo a facelift about once per presidential term – the most recent changes included the removal of its running fountain and colourful light display, and conversion to a pedestrian-only space.

Catedral Vieja

On the eastern side of the evolving Plaza de la Revolución stands the wreckage of the ash-grey Catedral Santiago de los Caballeros. Known as the **Catedral Vieja**, the ruins are an eerie monument to a destroyed city. Birds fly through the interior, where semi-exposed murals and leaning stone angels with cracked wings still line the walls. Plans to restore the cathedral are continually made and then shelved; for the time being, the building remains officially closed to visitors.

Palacio Nacional de La Cultura

The lovely blue-marble and cream-stucco exterior of the **Palacio Nacional**, next to the cathedral, holds a darker history. During the long years of Somoza rule the columned building was the seat of government power: Colombian writer Gabriel García Márquez called it "*el partenón bananero*" – the banana parthenon. Then, on August 22, 1978, Sandinista commandos disguised as National Guard soldiers ran through its corridors to capture the deputies of the National Assembly, a cinematic coup d'état that effectively brought down the Somoza dictatorship. Today, the Palacio, still a functioning

BARRIO MARTA QUEZADA

ACCOMMODATION	
Apartamentos Los Cisneros	D
Casa Castillo	A
Casa Gabrinma	F
Euro	B
Los Felipe	E
Hospedaje Santos	C

EATING & DRINKING	
Ananda	1
Bar Shannon	9
Buffet La Vista	6
Café Tonallí	10
La Casa de los Mejía Godoy	7
Las Cazuelas	2
Cocinarte	11
Comida Sarah's	4
Mirna's	8
Norma	5
Tipico Doña Pilar	3

Old Centre

Montoya Statue &

CALLE 27 DE MAYO

Cine Dorado (closed)

CALLE 8A

CALLE 9A

AVENIDA WILLIAMS ROMERO

AVENIDA 10A

AVENIDA 9A

AVENIDA 8A

AVENIDA 7A

AVENIDA 5A

AVENIDA 4A

AVENIDA 3A

AVENIDA 2A

AVENIDA BOLIVAR

Tica Bus Terminal

CALLE 10A

Crowne Plaza Hotel

N

INTUR

0   300 m

NAVIGATING MANAGUA

In a city where nobody uses street names (if they actually exist) or addresses, it's helpful to have your destination given to you in terms of neighbourhood and distance from a landmark – taxi drivers will most easily find places in relation to a well-known city fixture. For destinations around barrio Marta Quezada, use the *Crowne Plaza*, Tica Bus terminal, Cine Dorado (now closed), or Montoya statue as a reference point; the Metrocentro shopping centre is a useful landmark around Zona Hippos and Los Robles.

Distances are measured in metres as much as in blocks – in local parlance, 100m is a city block, or cuadra. Sometimes an archaic measure, the vara, is also used: one *vara* (a yard) is interpreted as roughly equivalent to a metre. To confuse the issue still further, many Managuans do not use the cardinal points in their usual form: in Managua north becomes *al lago* – towards the lake; *al sur* is south; *arriba* – literally, "up", is to the east; and *abajo*, "down", is to the west. So, "del Hotel InterContinental (now the *Crowne Plaza*, although many people still use its old name) una cuadra arriba y dos cuadras al lago" means one block east and two blocks north of the *Crowne Plaza*.

government building, also houses the national library and archives, and a **museum and art gallery** (Mon–Fri 8am–noon & 2–5pm, US$2; Sat 8am–noon, Sun 9am–4pm, free). There's a good display of Nicaraguan handicrafts, colourful murals and large sculptures, plus a few pre-Columbian artefacts. The museum frequently holds cultural and artistic events of dance, poetry and *artesanía*; ask at reception about upcoming events.

Casa Presidencial

The plaza's north side is home to a salmon-and-mustard eyesore, the **Casa Presidencial**, completed in 2000. Constructed against the advice of seismologists, the building is an unflattering monument to the style and substance of Arnoldo Alemán's corrupt presidency and a pale imitation of the far more arresting Palacio Nacional opposite, whose style it apes but fails to match. The Ortega administration has seen the building renamed La Casa de Los Pueblos ("the house of the villages"), to demonstrate his government's empathy with its people. Housing Ortega's offices, the building is off-limits to the general public.

Centro Cultural Managua

Immediately southwest of the Palacio National is a distinctive green building housing the **Centro Cultural Managua** (☎222-2068). The former home of the *Gran Hotel*, the exterior of the low-slung, mock-colonial structure gives you a bit of an idea of how pre-earthquake Managua looked. Inside, the downstairs area hosts sporadic exhibitions and seminars, including the **Sábado de Artesanía**, a crafts fair held on the first Saturday of each month. Prices are higher than in the outdoor Mercado Roberto Huembes (see p.426), but lower than in the *galerías* and art shops. The centre's upper floors house many of the country's arts organizations; it's worth going upstairs just to see the **historic photographs** lining the corridor. Some show Managua before the 1972 earthquake – it was an attractive city of palm trees and some colonial architecture – while others, taken immediately following the quake, show crumpled buildings, crushed cars and gaping holes in the road.

Teatro Nacional Rubén Darío

Perched like a huge white futurist bird north of the Plaza de la Revolución is the

Teatro Nacional Rubén Darío (Mon–Fri 9am–6pm, Sat–Sun 10am–3pm; ☎222-7426, ⓦwww.tnrubendario.gob.ni), Managua's main cultural venue. Foreign orchestras and dance troupes on tour perform here, along with Nicaraguan theatre groups. It's worth going inside the building just to see the massive chandeliers, marble floors and stirring view out to the lake from the enormous second-floor windows. South of the theatre is the **Monumento a Rubén Darío**, a striking sculpted memorial to the iconic poet (see p.431), restored in 1997.

Malecón

North of the theatre, a determined attempt has been made to spruce up the previously seedy lakeshore boardwalk, or **malecón**, with bars and food kiosks, plus a couple of fairground rides. A statue of Latin American liberator **Simón Bolívar** sits in the middle of the nearby roundabout, guarding the shorefront's entrance. The area gets quite lively at weekends, though it's fairly deserted during the week except for stray kissing teenage couples. There are pleasant views to the north from the malecón, where **Volcán Mombotombo** and little **Mombotombito** sit side by side against the horizon on the far shore of the lake, 50km away.

Plaza de la Fe San Juan Pablo II

Just south of (or opposite) the malecón is the vast **Plaza de la Fe Juan Pablo II**, a square whose central obelisk commemorates Pope John Paul II's two visits to Nicaragua. You'll also find here the Concha Acústica or "acoustic shell" statue (resembling a large white wave), which serves as a stage for public concerts and shows. Like the malecón, the plaza is rarely busy (unless there is an event, perhaps three or four times a year), and is also one of the fiercest suntraps in the city,

though it looks better at night when floodlighting adds some definition to its vast expanse.

Museo Huellas de Acahualinca

Volcán Mombotombo's capacity for destruction is evoked in the **Museo Huellas de Acahualinca** (Mon–Fri 8am–5pm, Sat 9am–4pm; US$2), just west of the malecón in barrio Acahualinca (take a taxi or bus #112), a rudimentary and under-funded affair but still worth a look for a glimpse into the area's history. On display are animal and human footprints from prehistoric nomads – preserved in volcanic ash, the footprints date back between 6000 and 10,000 years.

Loma de Tiscapa

Directly behind the landmark *Crowne Plaza*, a path winds upwards (about a 30min walk or brief taxi ride) to the **Loma de Tiscapa**, or Tiscapa Historical National Park, which overlooks the small and unremarkable **Laguna Tiscapa** in the centre of the city. Here you'll find the bunker-like remains of El Chipote, formerly Somoza's presidential palace and prison, where many Sandinistas were held and tortured during the regime. Above the prison sits a silhouetted statue of **Sandino**, marking the spot of the revolutionary leader's assassination; nearby lie a tank and statue donated to Somoza by Mussolini, relics of the former regime.

The **views** of the city from here are excellent, stretching north to Lago de Nicaragua and the distant volcanoes and south beyond the new cathedral towards Masaya. They can be enjoyed by **canopy tour**, if you're feeling adventurous (Tue–Sun 9am–5pm; US$15; ☎886-2836 or 872-2555). Three cables cover over a kilometre, allowing you to glide high above the city and lagoon. Note that the whole area is closed to the public on Mondays.

Carretera a Masaya and the Metrocentro

About 1km south of the laguna is Managua's biggest concentration of residential and commercial neighbourhoods. The main thoroughfare through this part of the city is the **Carretera a Masaya**, hemmed in to the east by the embassy neighbourhood of Altamira and to the west by La UCA, or the Universidad Centroamericana. It's on this road, just south of Pista Juan Pablo II, where you'll find the **Metrocentro** shopping centre, which boasts shops, a food court, banks, a cinema and the *InterContinental Metrocentro* hotel.

Catedral Nueva

A short walk from the Metrocentro shopping centre, in the middle of a field, is the Catedral Metropolitana de la Purísima Concepción, known simply as the **Catedral Nueva**, a remarkably unorthodox piece of architecture whose roof resembles a collection of large concrete hand grenades. The interior (open for worship daily 6am–10pm) is rather stark, with a bleeding figure of Christ encased in glass being the only interesting feature, while the gift shop outside sells an amazing variety of religious paraphernalia, including literature and ornaments.

Arrival and information

By air The Augusto César Sandino International Airport is 11km east of Managua; on arrival, you'll have to pay a US$5 entry fee. Designated airport taxis wait just outside the terminal doors; reportedly safer and always air-conditioned, these cost US$12–15 for journeys to most parts of the city. The drivers are all registered and wear white uniforms. If you cross the street from the airport you can catch a normal taxi (at your own risk), which shouldn't cost more than C$100. There are several ATMs here, and the Banco de la Producción has a window where you can change dollars but not traveller's cheques. You'll also find car rental agencies in the arrivals hall at the northern end of the airport.

By bus Most international services come into barrio Marta Quezada in central Managua (see p.427 for international terminals). Domestic buses arrive at one of the several crowded, noisy and generally chaotic urban marketplaces that also serve as bus terminals: from Masaya, Granada, Rivas or other southern destinations, you'll come into the Mercado Roberto Huembes near the Carretera a Masaya on the southeastern edge of the city; buses from the north and east – including Estelí, Matagalpa, Jinotega, San Carlos and El Rama – arrive at the terminal in the Mercado Mayoreo in barrio Concepción, near the airport; buses from the northwest towns of León and Chinandega use the busy Mercado Israel Lewites in the southwest of the capital. Regular express minivans from Masaya and Granada pull into a small unmarked terminal on the highway opposite La UCA, near the Metrocentro. Taxis crowd the arriving buses, so moving on from the markets should not be a problem.

TOUR OPERATORS IN MANAGUA

Given the largely erratic schedules of Nicaraguan transport, if you're short of time it's worth considering an organized tour – particularly to remote or difficult to reach areas like the Solentiname Archipelago or the Río San Juan.

Careli Tours Opposite El Colegio Pedagógico, Planes de Altamira ☎278-6919, ⓦwww.carelitours.com. Good for best-of-Nicaragua type packages as well as trips combining Nicaragua and Costa Rica, both lasting around a week.

Nicaragua Tours ☎449-9333 or 777/798-1591 (US toll-free), ⓦwww .nicaraguatours.org. Well-organized company with half-day tours from US$45 – explore Masaya market and volcano, or the Pueblos Blancos. Prices include pick-up and drop-off at all hotels in Managua.

Tourist information There is an under-stocked INTUR desk at the airport. The INTUR headquarters are in central Managua, one block south and one block west of the *Crowne Plaza* (Mon–Fri 8.30am–12.30pm & 1.30–5pm; ☎254-5191, ⍟www.intur.gob.ni). The staff are well-intentioned and some speak English, but don't have much in the way of hand-outs; however, it's worth buying the excellent city map of Managua (US$5) from them, if available. You should also be able to pick up a copy of the free quarterly English-language magazine *Between The Waves* (also available in embassies and at selected hotels, restaurants, tourist offices, travel agencies and airports throughout Nicaragua), which has well-written features on travel, history, business and tourist activities as well as news, mini-guides for various towns and cities, and selected transport schedules.

City transport

Buses Buses, generally labelled with a route number, cover the main city routes (see box below, for useful passages). The fares are dirt-cheap (about C$2–5), but pick-pocketing is common and aided by the crush of bodies on these routes, so be alert. Fares are paid in cash, on board – change is scarce for larger notes so use coins and smaller bills whenever possible. If unsure of your destination, ask the driver to point out stops, which are unmarked. Services start at 5am and continue until 10pm, becoming less frequent from about 6pm onwards.

Taxis Taxis are cheap and plentiful in Managua, with most trips costing around C$20–50 (always agree on a price before setting off). Drivers always like to have more than one passenger at a time, and will stop to pick up and drop off people en-route (if travelling alone, it's recommended that you sit up front next to the driver). Legitimate taxis have red licence plates and are officially registered; locals will tell you that these are safer and more reliable. Generally cheap, and with friendly, talkative drivers, they are always in good supply – as a tourist, taxis will honk at you as a matter of course, whether you want one or not.

Accommodation

Barrio Marta Quezada, the site of most international bus terminals, is the place for cheap, *hospedaje*-type accommodation; most places are scattered in a two-block radius on either side of the Tica Bus terminal. Arriving at the station, you will be met by touts, usually children, offering to take you to a *hospedaje*; they receive a fee from hotel owners for bringing people off the buses. There's no harm in going with them, since you're under no obligation to stay if you don't like the *hospedaje* they take you to. Do not pay the tout directly, as they may inflate the room price to cover their fee. Elsewhere in the city, you'll likely find neighbourhoods more secure and friendly than Marta Quezada, although taxis and buses will be necessary for transport.

USEFUL MANAGUA BUS ROUTES

The following routes are some of the useful stops and connections on public transport:

#108 Reparto Schick–Primavera Carretera Norte, Mercado Oriental, Nueva Rotunda Santo Domingo, Máximo Jeréz, Altamira D'Este, Mercado Huembes.

#109 Hospital Lenin Fonseca–Reparto Schick Malecón, Teatro Nacional Rubén Darío, Centro Cultural, Palacio Nacional, Plaza Inter, Hospital Bautista, Mercado Huembes.

#110 Seminario Nacional–Mercado Mayoreo Las Piedrecitas, Mercado Israel Lewites, La UCA, Rotonda Rubén Darío, Rotonda Santo Domingo, Altamira, Centro Comercial Managua, Mercado Huembes, Mercado Iván Montenegro.

#112 Centro Cívico–Villa Libertad Mercado Israel Lewites, Museo Huellas de Acahualinca, Malecón, Teatro Nacional Rubén Darío, Carretera Norte, Mercado Iván Montenegro.

#113 Ciudad Sandino–Mercado Oriental Las Piedrecitas, American Embassy, Montoya Statue, Marta Quezada, Plaza Inter.

#119 Refinería–Villa San Jacinto Las Brisas, Rotonda Güegüense/Plaza España, UCA, Metrocentro, Los Robles, Altamira, Rotonda Centroamérica, Colonia Centro América, Mercado Huembes.

Barrio Marta Quezada and around

Apartamentos Los Cisneros One block north and one and a half blocks west of the Tica Bus terminal ☎222-3535/7273, ⓦwww.hotelloscisneros.com. The sole "upmarket" option in the heart of Marta Quezada, offering self-contained two-person apartments with fridge, cooker, breakfast bar and optional fan or a/c. Singles ❹–❻, doubles ❺–❼

Casa Castillo One block west and one and a half blocks north of Tica Bus ☎222-2265. Hospitable, family-run *hospedaje* with basic (if rather dowdy) rooms with private bath; the ones right at the back and upstairs are larger and quieter. Singles ❷, doubles ❸

Casa Gabrinma One block south and half a block east of Tica Bus ☎222-6650. Welcoming and friendly guesthouse where the tidy rooms – all with ceiling fans – are set around a leafy inner courtyard. ❷

Euro One block west and half a block south of Plaza Inter shopping centre ☎222-4045, ⓦwww.hoteleuronic.com. A newer hotel, with lots of varnished wood and gleaming tiles indoors despite the concrete, bunker-like exterior. Cable TV, a/c and hot water come standard, though the upstairs rooms are actually brighter and better value. There's also a sunny swimming pool out back. Singles ❹–❺, doubles ❻–❼

Los Felipe One and a half blocks west of Tica Bus ☎222-6501/7050, ✉losfelipe@ideay.net.ni. This friendly hotel has 27 clean if slightly cheerless rooms nestled amid an urban jungle of tropical foliage. All come with private bath and TV, and there are internet and laundry services available as well as a swimming pool and restaurant. Singles ❸–❹, doubles ❹–❺

Hospedaje Santos One block north and one and a half blocks west of Tica Bus ☎222-3713. Sprawling, ramshackle *hospedaje* popular among travellers, with tons of atmosphere, funky art on the walls and an indoor patio with cable TV. Rooms, however, are dark and none too clean – try to get one upstairs, where ventilation is better. All have ceiling fan, and some come with private bath. Singles ❷, doubles ❸

Elsewhere in the city

Casa San Juan C Esperanza 560, behind La UCA ☎278-3220, ⓦwww.hotelcasasanjuan.com. Welcoming mid-range guesthouse in a quiet neighbourhood. The spacious and spotless rooms come with a/c, cable TV and well-equipped modern, private bathrooms. Breakfast is included and other meals are available with advance notice. The hotel is popular, so reserve in advance. Singles ❻, doubles ❻, triple ❼

Managua Backpackers Inn 75 varas south of *Chamán* nightclub, Los Robles ☎267-0006 or 414-4114, ⓦwww.managuahostel.com. A well-located, friendly and perennially busy hostel with tidy dorms and private rooms, some with en-suite bathroom. There's a courtyard garden with a pool, shaded by a mango tree and surrounded by deck chairs and hammocks, large communal kitchen and TV room, free internet and laundry services. Dorms ❷, singles ❹, doubles ❹–❺

Nicaragua Guest House Two blocks south and two and a half blocks west of Rotonda La Virgen ☎249-8963, ⓦwww.3dp.ch/nicaragua. A small guesthouse with basic rooms, all en-suite with TV and a fan or a/c, and a cool courtyard garden. Don't miss the strict 11pm curfew. Singles ❸–❺, doubles ❹–❺

Eating

Wherever you walk in Managua – on the street, at the bus stop or even under a shady tree – you will find someone selling a drink or a *comida corriente*. Good, cheap food on the hoof is also easy to get in any of Managua's major markets – look out for *pupusas*, actually a Salvadoran concoction of cheese, tortillas, sauce and meat. You can also fill up on greasy, delicious food from any of the eateries down on Managua's malecón. Hygienically speaking, the food is safe to eat, and you can get a decent meal for as little as two dollars. Managua also has a surprisingly cosmopolitan selection of restaurants: Chinese, Spanish, Mexican, Japanese, Italian, Peruvian, North American – even vegetarian. Cafés are thin on the ground, though, and the ones that do exist tend to be frequented by expats and wealthier Managuans.

Barrio Marta Quezada and around

Ananda Next to the Montoya statue: from the Cine Dorado, walk two blocks towards the lake then eight blocks west. An excellent vegetarian restaurant set around a covered patio and garden, this place is a veritable oasis amid Managua's concrete chaos. There's a varied menu including a good-value *plato del día*, nice bread and superb milkshakes (C$20) – try the papaya. A meal plus drink will cost around C$60–80. Closed Sun.

Buffet La Vista One and a half blocks west of the Tica Bus station. One of many eateries of the plastic chairs-outside-a-house variety, serving a largely local clientele, *La Vista* offers tasty and good-value plates with open-grilled meat, rice, beans and salad (C$45).

Café Tonalli Two blocks east and half a block south of Tica Bus. Principally a bakery selling whole-wheat and specialist breads, there are also a few tables in a leafy garden where you can enjoy healthy dishes like veggie lasagna and pesto. Good breakfasts served, too: muesli, fruit and yogurt (C$25), fresh coffee (C$6) and croissants baked on the premises. Mon–Sat 7am–3pm.

Las Cazuelas One block east of *Hospedaje Santos*. A small restaurant with a nice atmosphere, red-checked tablecloths and a huge menu of local and international cuisine in the heart of barrio Marta Quezada. A meal will set you back around C$80–100.

Cocinarte One block south of the INTUR office. A large, open-air restaurant under a thatched palm roof, offering yummy international vegetarian dishes such as chickpea masala (C$80), cauliflower cheese (C$80) and falafel with pita and hummus (C$70). Closed Sun.

Comida Sarah's Opposite *Hospedaje Santos*. Despite the dilapidated exterior, lack of menu and busy, roadside location, *Sarah's* is great for huge, cheap (C$40–80) servings of simple, filling food like veggie soups, pasta and chicken dishes.

Mirna's One block west and south of the Tica Bus terminal. This small, family-run place has become something of an institution. They're open from 6.30am (7am on Sun) for *típica* or gringo breakfasts and you can tuck into the *comida casera* buffet (C$60) from noon until 3pm.

Norma Half a block south of *Hospedaje Santos*. A simple branch of a bakery chain, where you can pick up a coffee and cake for C$20.

Tipico Doña Pilar One block east of *Hospedaje Santos*. Another good neighbourhood eatery with simple plastic chairs and a large grill set on the sidewalk. A plate of *comida típica* (try the grilled chicken) will set you back C$50 (drink included).

Metrocentro and around

Don Pan One and a half blocks south of Monte de Los Olivos. The most renowned bakery in town, with a modern café in front where you can enjoy their mouth-watering selection of croissants, pastries and other sweet treats as well as fresh coffee (C$14–40), sandwiches, bagels & cream cheese (C$25) and salads (C$70). There's also a branch at Km 4 Carretera Norte.

Ola Verde Planes de Altamira, 2 blocks west and half a block north of Pharoah's Casino. A fantastic vegetarian-friendly restaurant with on-site organic shop selling Nicaraguan fair-trade products. Most main dishes will set you back about C$100–160, but the locally-sourced produce is fresh and the menu is inventive and delicious; try a Maya nut speciality or the goat's cheese lasagna, C$140. Closed Mon.

Pizzeria Valenti's One block east of *Domino's Pizza*, house no. 6 ☎278-7474. An outside patio, ice-cold mug of draught beer and one of *Valenti's* thin-crust pizzas; filling and good value considering the area, a pizza and a beer will cost about C$100.

La Terraza Peruana Planes de Altamira No. 14, 150m south of *Ola Verde*. In a pretty setting with outdoor terraced seating, *La Terraza* offers typical Peruvian dishes such as *ceviche* and *tiradito* (C$150) or *aji de gallina* (C$110), as well as *chica morada* (a purple corn drink; C$20). Beautifully prepared and mouth-wateringly delicious, it's worth the slight splurge. Closed Mon.

Drinking and nightlife

Managua's nightlife has been given a shot in the arm in the last decade or so with the return of some of the "Miami Boys" – businessmen and influential families who had fled revolutionary Nicaragua to settle in Miami – who have helped drive the demand for upmarket bars and discos. The city offers a good choice of venues for drinking and dancing for those on a budget as well as the plusher options, as most places only charge a few dollars cover and drinks are either included in the cover charge, or cost around US$1–3 (C$20–60). Musically, you can expect to hear the strains of merengue, salsa, reggaeton, pop, electronic music and even Nica *rancho* music (not unlike American country).

Bars

Art-Café Opposite the Las Palmas park ☎607-5104. A café/bar/cultural space, with a yummy Mexican menu on Sun (US$2–5), and live music shows where you'll hear everything from trova to reggae. Cover US$2–4.

Bar Shannon Two blocks east of *Los Felipe*. Established Irish-owned bar in the heart of barrio Marta Quezada. The clientele is a good mix of locals and travellers, and though you can't always bank on getting a Guinness they do sell London Pride (C$35). The owner can direct you to the popular late-night drinking and dancing spots on the fast-changing Managuan scene. Toña (local beer) C$18.

La Casa de Los Mejía Godoy Colonia Los Robles, opposite the *Crowne Plaza* ☎222-6610, ⓦlosmejia godoy.zonaxp.com. The brainchild of Nicaraguan guitar-playing and song-writing brothers Luis Enrique and Carlos Mejía Godoy, this is a cultural centre and bar rolled into one. There's an art gallery, CD and bookstore to browse as well as a café/bar selling *comida típica*. On Tues there's a tango class, on Thurs young local musicians jam here, and the brothers themselves normally perform on Fri & Sat. Cover C$200. Closed Sun and Mon.

La Cavanga In the northeast corner of the Centro Cultural Managua. A microcosm of Nicaraguan culture, this little bar plays traditional Nicaraguan music (Thurs–Sat) and is decorated with black and white photos of Old Managua and a few paintings by Ernesto Cardenal. It's one of the best bars in Managua, packed in the early evening with government workers and students. Toña (local beer) C$18.

El Parking Half a block north of *La Terraza*, Planes de Altamira. Massively busy on the weekends, this loud and crowded bar has a large outdoor patio and great cocktails (C$50–90).

Piratas C Principal, Zona Hippos. A pirate-themed bar with two rooms (head for the comfy bamboo seating near the front) and a crowded outdoor terrace. Well-priced drinks (beer for C$12 and cocktails for C$50) and an interesting soundtrack of everything from reggaeton to 90s grunge.

Clubs

Chamán Half a block east of the *Hotel Real Inter-Continental Metrocentro* hotel. Caters to a younger crowd, with an emphasis on rock and alternative sounds as well as a bit of reggae and salsa. There's

regular live music and the occasional rock-centric talent contests are worth a look. Thurs is ladies' night (free entry), while cover charge is usually US$3–4.

Hipa Hipa Plaza Coconut Grove, half a block west and two blocks south of Distribuidora Vicky. Trendy club with three dance floors. Regularly packed on weekends with a young, hedonistic crowd – including a good few gringos – grooving to salsa, merengue, reggaeton, hip hop and techno. Cover charge is US$5–10, often including at least one drink; on Wed (ladies' night) women enter free.

Matrix On the Carretera a Masaya, opposite the *Hilton* hotel. A busy nightclub popular with a younger, largely local crowd, where everybody dances into the small hours. Cover is usually C$100–200 for men and C$50–100 for women, with free drinks at happy hour (10pm–midnight). Beer C$18.

Moods Second floor of the Galerias Santo Domingo. One of the swankiest nightspots in town, *Moods* stands out for its excellent DJs spinning electronic music, fancy cocktails (C$40–80) and hip crowd. Cover C$100–300.

Ruta Maya 150m east from the Montoya statue ☎268-0698. Another cultural centre/bar which plays host to a diverse cross-section of the city's musical and artistic talent (Thurs, Fri & Sat) and tends to attract an older, more sophisticated crowd. Seating is outdoors under a big marquee and traditional Nica food is also available (C$60). Gig tickets are between US$4–7.

Entertainment

Cinema Cinemark Metrocentro (☎271-9402/9037), Cinemas Inter in Plaza Inter (☎222-5122), Cinemas Galerias in Galerias Santo Domingo (☎276-5065).

Theatre Teatro Nacional Rubén Darío (see p.420), is recognized as one of the best theatres in Central America with a main auditorium seating 1200 people, an exhibition space on the second floor, and an experimental theatre in the basement. Events are scheduled there most weekends and it's easy to get to, with bus #109 stopping right in front. Check the website or listings in *La Prensa* for details of performances.

Shopping

Books Hispamer (from UCA: one block east, one block south and then one block east again) has the largest selection of academic, fiction and nonfiction books (in Spanish) in Nicaragua. There's a small shelf of classic and modern English-language fiction and Oxford editions, the latter handy if you're

Alhambra V.I.P. Centro Commercial, Camino de Oriente (☎270-3846). The tickets at this cinema might seem steep (C$110 a show), but once you're inside you'll see what the fuss is all about. Each person gets a leather seat, which reclines completely and comes equipped with a call button for summoning a waiter and ordering food. The menu offers movie snacks like popcorn (C$30), nachos and cheese (C$40), sandwiches, and drinks (beer C$30), which will be discreetly delivered to your side through the darkness. The overly powerful a/c is perhaps the only downside; be sure to bring a sweater with you.

hard up for something to read. Also sells a selection of mainly classical CDs and stationery.

Food and drink Well-stocked chains La Colonia and La Unión sell a large selection of local and imported food including organic produce. You can also buy a lot of the basics at local *pulperías*, small shops set up in people's houses. Fruits and vegetables are cheapest at the weekend markets, when the growers come into town to sell their produce.

Markets Mercado Mayoreo, in barrio La Concepción, near the airport, is divided into separate areas for different types of produce. You can also get a cheap meal at the market café while waiting for northbound buses. Mercado Oriental, a few blocks southeast of the old centre, is a small, lawless city-within-a-city where you can buy just about anything, but need to keep a close eye on your pockets and an even closer eye on your back – Nicaraguans will tell you that this is one of the most dangerous places in the country. If you must go, take someone with you. In the streets around the entrance to the market are many shops selling furniture and electrical goods. If you can manage it, it's worth buying a rocking chair here: beautifully made, they cost around C$500, and can be bought disassembled for carrying onto the plane. Mercado Roberto Huembes, near the Carretera a Masaya in the south of the city, is somewhat safer to wander around than the Oriental and has an excellent crafts section. You can find rocking chairs here, too, and some of the best hammocks in the world – everything from a simple net one (C$120) to a luxury, two-person, woven cotton one with wooden separators and beautiful tassels (from C$800). Products made of leather

and skins are in abundance, but choose carefully as many of the species used are endangered. Traditional clothing is cheap, finely embroidered and perfect for the tropics. Paintings in the style of the artists' colony on the Solentiname Islands are available here, along with many fine pen-and-ink drawings and abstract works. You can buy Nicaraguan cigars as well as wicker products (*mimbre*) such as baskets, mats, chairs and wall hangings.

Directory

Exchange Central banks that exchange foreign currency include Banpro and Bancentro, both on the Carretera a Masaya near the *Hotel Princess*, and BAC (Banco de América Central), Plaza España. Both Bancentro and BAC offer advances on credit cards; BAC will change traveller's cheques. ATMs accepting foreign cards (Visa, MasterCard and Cirrus) can be found by both the aforementioned banks and in most malls, as well as in many Shell and Texaco garages and at the airport.

Embassies and consulates Canada, C El Nogal, no. 25, one block east of la Casa Nazareth (☎268-0433); US, Cancillería, Km 5.5, Carretera Sur (☎252-7100).

Immigration Departamento de Migración y Extranjeria, two blocks north of Los Semáforos de la Colonia Tenderí (Mon–Fri 8am–noon & 2–4pm; ☎244-3989). There is also a branch within Metrocentro shopping centre. Which deals with visitors who have entered by air only.

Internet Internet Pioneer, Level 3, Plaza Inter (C$25/hr); Cyber C@fe, one and a half blocks south of the *Crowne Plaza* (C$20/hr); Cyber@Center, Av Williams Romero, one block north of Cine Dorado (C$20/hr); Kafe@Internet, Av Willams Romero, one block north of the Cine Dorado (C$20/hr).

Medical facilities Hospital Bautista, in barrio Largaespada (☎249-7070/1005, ⓦwww .hospitalbautistanicaragua.com), or Hospital Metropolitano Vivian Pellas, Km 9 ¾, Carretera a Masaya, 250m west (☎255-6900, ⓦwww.metropolitano .com.ni); both are good private hospitals with 24hr emergency departments, where treatments run from US$25. Dr Enrique Sánchez Delgado, in Bosques de Altamira, Casa #417, two blocks east and half a block north of the Cine Altamira (☎278-1031), speaks English and German and charges around C$600 for a consultation.

Pharmacies Medco is one of the larger chains, with branches at Bello Horizonte or Plaza España (☎251-4438). Alternatively, try the 24hr pharmacy at the Hospital Bautista.

Post office Palacio de Correos (Mon–Fri 8am–5pm, Sat 8am–noon), half a block west of Palacio Nacional.

Telephones The Enitel office is three blocks west of the Catedral Vieja (daily 7am–9pm). Cyber@ Center, on Av Williams Romero, has good (and cheap) internet phone facilities, with a number of private, convenient booths.

Moving on

Even if you don't particularly want to go to Managua, as the transport hub of the country it's virtually impossible to avoid. From here you can get virtually anywhere by bus, and even several hard-to-reach destinations (such as Bilwi, the Corn Islands and San Carlos) by air from the Augusto C. Sandino airport.

By air

Flights depart from Managua's Augusto C. Sandino Airport. Copa have direct, daily **international flights** between Managua and San José, as well as flights to and from Panamá. Taca also has flights connecting Managua with both San José and San Salvador. When leaving, note that all international departures are subject to a US$32 departure tax that must be paid (in dollars or córdobas) at check-in. If you do leave the country by air, note also that you won't receive an exit stamp in your passport. Domestic airline La Costeña (☎ 263-2142/2144) runs frequent and reliable scheduled services to and from the Atlantic Coast, including San Carlos (US$75 or US$116/return). There are daily services to Puerto Cabezas, Waspán and Minas on the northern Atlantic Coast (US$100–150 return); flights run to Bluefields (US$82 or US$127/return) several times a day, with connecting flights to the Corn Islands (US$64 or US$99/return), and there's also a direct Managua–Corn Island flight with La Costeña (US$107 or US$165/return) departing twice daily. Advance reservations are essential; the airline has an office at the airport and agencies across the city. Tickets can be reserved and changed over the phone – always reconfirm on the day of your flight, as the system is very casual in Nicaragua and your seat may easily be given away; if you are "bumped", you should be offered a seat on the next available plane.

By bus

The busiest domestic bus routes are those between the capital and the provincial cities, particularly León in the northwest and Granada in the south. Other main routes run to Matagalpa, Estelí, Masaya and Rivas, the last for connections to the Costa Rican border and the beach town of San Juan del Sur.

Domestic bus stops

Domestic buses depart from one of several markets in Managua (see p.426), with the exception of Granada and Masaya minibuses, which can be hailed on the Carretera a Masaya by the Hotel *InterContinental Metrocentro*, or around the corner at La UCA.

Domestic destinations

Note that buses listed as having regular departures (hourly or more frequent) run from 5am–6pm, unless otherwise stated.

Bluefields Express departure from Mercado Iván Montenegro daily 9pm.
Chinandega Second-class departures from Mercado Israel Lewites every 30min; 2hr.
Estelí Second-class departures from Mercado de Mayoreo every 30min; 3hr 30min.
Granada Second-class departures from Mercado Huembes every 15min; 1hr. Express departures from La UCA every 15–20min; 1hr.
León Second-class departures from Mercado Israel Lewites every 15–30min; 1hr 30min.
Masaya Second-class departures from Mercado Huembes every 30 min; 45min. Express services from La UCA every 15–20min; 1hr,
Matagalpa Second-class departures from Mercado de Mayoreo every 30min; 3hr.
El Rama Five daily second-class departures from Mercado de Mayoreo; 10hr. Express departure from Mercado Iván Montenegro daily 9pm.
Rivas Second-class departures from Mercado Huembes every 25min; 2hr 25min.
San Carlos Five daily second-class departures from Mercado de Mayoreo; 10–12hr.

International bus stops

Three major companies serve the international bus routes between Central America's capitals. The Tica Bus (☎ 222-6094, ⊛ www.Ticabus.com) station sits two blocks east and one block south of the old Cine Dorado, while the King Quality (☎ 228-1454, ⊛ www.kingqualityca.com) station is nearby on Calle 27 de Mayo, opposite Plaza Inter. Transnica (☎ 270-3133, ⊛ www.transnica.com) buses depart from 300m north and 50m east of the Rotonda Metrocentro.

International destinations

Guatemala City Departures with: King Quality (daily 2.30am & 3.30am; 15–17hr); Tica Bus (daily 5am, with overnight in San Salvador; 15hr).
San José Departures with: King Quality (daily 1.30am; 9hr); Tica Bus (daily 6am, 7am & noon; 9hr); Transnica (daily 5.30am, 7am, 10am & 3pm; 9hr).

San Salvador Departures with: King Quality (daily 3.30am, 5.30am & 11.30am; 11hr); Tica Bus (daily 4.45am; 12hr); Transnica (daily 5am & 12.30pm; 10hr).

Tegucigalpa Departures with King Quality (daily 3.30am & 11.30am; 9–10hr); Tica Bus (daily 5am; 8hr); Transnica (daily 2pm; 6hr).

AROUND MANAGUA

The **beaches** around Managua don't have the white sand and clear water of places like the Corn Islands or San Juan del Sur and La Flor, but the water is warmer and they're easy to reach. Managuans visit on day-trips, particularly on national holidays, when the beaches – and public transport – get amazingly crowded, especially at Easter and Christmas: watch your belongings wherever you go.

Pochomíl and Masachapa

The closest beaches to the city are **Pochomíl** and the nearby town of **Masachapa**, 3km beyond, around an hour and a half by hourly **bus** from the Mercado Israel Lewites. If you come by car there's a small fee (C$20) to enter Pochomíl, but once here you can settle in for the day, as there are restaurants all along the sand, and motorbikes and horses for rent. There are various accommodation options here if you fancy staying, although the cheaper options aren't exactly enticing. There are also several very basic *hospedajes* in Masachapa, though it's more of a fishing village and its beach is not as clean as Pochomíl.

La Boquita

Southwest along the coast from Masachapa is the town of **La Boquita**, an area developed for tourism (C$60 entry) and offering plenty of places to relax and eat. The beach here can be dangerous, with large rocks hidden in the shallows, but the river mouth opening onto the beach provides a safe place to swim. **Minibuses** depart from the stop at La UCA, while regular buses leave from the Mercado Israel Lewites for Diriamba, where you can change for a Boquita-bound bus.

El Velero

The hilly coast around **El Velero** (C$35 entry), some 40km northwest of Managua towards León, is wilder than the beaches further south, punctuated by cliffs and peninsulas. A holiday village of sorts, El Velero is less frequented by day-trippers than Pochomíl or La Boquita, and consequently far more relaxed. Shady huts line the beachfront, along with showers, changing rooms and a number of food stands. The beach itself is excellent for swimming, and children can play safely in a rock pool at low tide. You can **stay**

TREAT YOURSELF

Hotel Vista Mar (☏265-8099 or 855-6889, ⊛www .vistamarhotel.com), a beach resort just outside Pochomíl, offers mock-colonial, wooden bungalows in immaculately landscaped grounds complete with extravagant swimming pools, fountains and even a wind-powered well pump. Rates include three meals a day, snacks and drinks. You'll also have access to the on-site bar and restaurant. ❾

Montelimar (☏269-6752, ⊛www.barcelo.com), a short distance north of Pochomíl, is the number-one resort in all of Nicaragua. Once the beach house of Somoza, it was turned into a resort by the Sandinistas and is now run by a Spanish company. One of Nicaragua's few five-star hotels, *Montelimar* has a relaxed atmosphere with a lovely private beach, four restaurants, four swimming pools, a small zoo and casino, and planned activities such as dance classes, horseriding, tennis, windsurfing and volleyball. Most people come on a package, but you can book once you've arrived in Nicaragua. ❾ here at the beach-side cabinas (℡809-7800 or 688-0463; ⓖ), originally set up for government workers, and still run by the Instituto Nicaragüense de Seguridad Social (℡222-6300/6301) Rooms have air-conditioning, a fridge and private bath, and there's a restaurant and bar in the grounds. To get to El Velero, take a **bus** from Mercado Israel Lewites (C$25), or head to León, alight at Puerto Sandino and take a *camioneta*. All in all, it's a three-hour journey from Managua.

The north

Nicaragua's **north** is really two regions, divided by geography and climate. The **northwest** is hot and dry with grassy plains, perfect for cattle ranching, punctuated by dramatic volcanoes. The largest city in the northwest, and once the capital of Nicaragua, is **León**, birthplace of the Sandinistas. In the **northeast**, the landscape is altogether different, with mountainous hillsides covered in bright green coffee plants and cows grazing in cool alpine pastures. Set within a circle of mountains, the northeast has a more temperate climate and very productive soil, with plenty of tobacco plantations and an economy based on coffee, grains, vegetables, fruit and dairy farming. The 150km journey north from Managua to **Estelí**, the northeast's largest city, is one of the most inspiring in the country, as the Carretera Interamericana winds through the grassy Pacific plains, skirting the southern edge of Lago de Managua before climbing slowly into a ribbon of blue mountains.

Many travellers coming from the south notice a distinct difference in the north's inhabitants as well as its geography. In both the Sandinista Revolution years and during the Contra–Sandinista struggles of the 1980s, this region suffered considerably. Many scars still have not healed; northerners are poorer and more battle-hardened, and can sometimes seem less forthcoming than Nicaraguans in other areas.

LEÓN

The capital of Nicaragua until 1857, **LEÓN**, 90km northwest of Managua, is now a provincial city, albeit an energetic, architecturally arresting one. A significant element in the city's healthy buzz is the presence of the **National University** (the country's premier academic institution) and its large student population, swelled by the ranks of young people studying at León's various other colleges and universities.

For all its present peace and prosperity, León has a violent history. The original León was founded by Hernández de Córdoba in 1524 at the foot of Volcán Momotombo, where its ruins – now known as **León Viejo** (see p.435) – still lie. The city was subsequently moved northwest to its present-day location soon after León Viejo's destruction by an earthquake and volcanic eruption in 1609. In 1956, the first President Somoza was gunned down in León by the martyr-poet Rigoberto López Pérez. During the Revolution in the 1970s, the town's streets were the scenes of several decisive battles between the Sandinistas and Somoza's forces, and many key figures in the Revolution either came from León or had their political start here. Although many years have passed since then, and most of the Sandinista graffiti has been painted over, the city continues to wear its FSLN heart on its sleeve: the street signs read "León: ciudad heroica – primera capital de la revolución", and there are still a few fine examples of the city's famous murals.

What to see and do

León's heartbeat is the **Parque Central**, which is shadowed by the largest cathedral in Central America. **Calle**

Map: LEÓN

ACCOMMODATION
El Albergue	B
Avenida	A
Big Foot	D
Casa Ivana	G
La Casona	I
Clínica	H
Guest House La Calle de los Poetas	F
Lazybones	C
Vía Vía	E

Map labels: 6A CALLE NORTE · 5A CALLE NOROESTE · 4A CALLE NOROESTE · 3A CALLE NOROESTE · 2A CALLE NOROESTE · 1A CALLE NOROESTE · CALLE CENTRAL RUBÉN DARÍO · 1A CALLE SUROESTE · 2A CALLE SUROESTE · 4A CALLE SUROESTE · 5A CALLE NOROESTE · 5A AV NOROESTE · 4A AV NOROESTE · 3A AV NOROESTE · 2A AV NOROESTE · AV NOROESTE · AV JOSÉ DE LA CRUZ MENA · AV CENTRAL · 1A AV NORESTE · AV NORESTE · AV SANTIAGO · ARGUELLO · AV COMANDANTE PEDRO ARÁUZ · OTILIO DE LEÓN · 3A CALLE NORESTE · 2A CALLE NORESTE · 1A CALLE NORESTE · CALLE CENTRAL RUBÉN DARÍO · 1A CALLE SURESTE · 2A CALLE SURESTE · 3A CALLE SURESTE · 4A CALLE SURESTE · AV SURESTE · 1A AV SURESTE · 2A AV SURESTE · 3A AV SURESTE · 4A AV SURESTE · AV CENTRAL · 2A AV SUROESTE · 3A AV SUROESTE

Map points: Bus Terminal · Subtiava & Las Peñitas · Parque San Juan · Iglesia de San Juan · INTUR · UNAN · Iglesia de la Recolección · Quetzaltrekkers · La Unión supermercado · Casa Rigoberto López Pérez · La Merced · Bank · Centro de Arte Fundación Ortiz-Guardia · Galería Héroes y Mártires · Bank · Mausoleo Héroes y Mártires · Museo Rubén Darío · Parque Rubén Darío · Entitel · Parque Central · Cathedral · Mercado · Asociación de Combatientes Históricos Héroes de Veracruz · Museo de Leyendas y Tradiciones · Managua & Discoteca Dilectus · N · 0 400 m

EATING & DRINKING
Ben Linder Café	4
Café El Sesteo	6
CocinArte	8
Dave's Shark Pitt	1
Don Señor	5
Guadalajara	3
Taquezal	7
Vía Vía	E
White House Pizza	2

Central Rubén Darío runs directly north of the Parque cutting the city in two from east to west, while **Avenida Central** runs between the Parque and Cathedral north to south. Unlike other cities in Nicaragua, in practice León has street signs, though in reality people will still give you directions in relation to a landmark.

Parque Central

The **Parque Central**, at the intersection of Calle Central Rubén Darío and Avenida Central, is centred on a statue of General Máximo Jeréz guarded by four lions. It's a good place to take the city's pulse, visited as it is by a constant stream of locals, street vendors and tourists. If you value your hearing, avoid the Parque at 7am and noon, when a ludicrously loud air-raid siren wails

across the city – a throwback to the days when workers flocked in to León's booming cotton factories.

Cathedral

The city's most obvious attraction is its colossal **Cathedral** (open from sunrise to late evening), a cream-coloured structure of epic proportions towering over León from the heart of the city. Begun in 1747, it took nearly a hundred years to complete. Despite its massive and lofty exterior, the only items of interest inside are the statues of the Twelve Apostles and the tomb of local hero **Rubén Darío**, Nicaragua's most famous writer and poet, which is guarded by a statue of a weeping lion. Mass is held daily at about 5pm and are worth attending, if only to people-watch.

Asociación de Combatientes Históricos Héroes de Veracruz

On the western side of town is one of the city's Sandinista strongholds, the decaying **Asociación de Combatientes Históricos Héroes de Veracruz** building, now functioning as a museum highlighting the Revolution's effects on León (daily 8am–noon, 2–6pm & 8–10pm; donations requested). FSLN combat veteran and guide Dionísio Meza Romero supplies enthusiastic and knowledgeable explanations on the extensive collection of photos, articles and news clippings documenting the Revolution, its historical antecedents and its aftermath.

Mausoleo Héroes y Mártires

The northeast corner of the Parque is home to the **Mausoleo Héroes y Mártires**, a star-shaped monument dedicated to those who died fighting for freedom during the civil war, surrounded by a large mural colourfully detailing Nicaragua's history from pre-Columbian times to the ending of the civil war. Another famous **mural**, opposite, depicts a hat-wearing Sandino squashing a whey-faced Uncle Sam underfoot.

La Recolección

Two blocks northeast of the Parque is one of Nicaragua's finest colonial churches, **La Recolección**, with a beautiful Mexican Baroque facade dating from 1786, and some fine mahogany woodwork inside.

Parque Rubén Darío

Followers of Nicaragua's other religion, poetry, might want to head for the **Parque Rubén Darío**, a block west of the Parque Central, which is home to a statue of the rather sombre-looking poet dressed in suit and bow tie.

Centro de Arte Fundación Ortiz-Guardián

Sitting on Calle Central Rubén Darío a little to the west of Parque Rubén Darío is the **Centro de Arte Fundación Ortiz-Guardián** (Tues–Sat 10.30am–6.30pm, Sun 11am–7pm; US$0.80), an expansive art gallery in two renovated colonial houses. The collection features an engrossing cross-section of Latin American art, including pre-Hispanic and modern ceramics and some great black and white photos of Nicaraguan rural religious festivals.

Museo Archivo Rubén Darío

A few blocks further west is the **Museo Archivo Rubén Darío** (Mon–Sat 9am–noon & 2–5pm, Sun 9am–noon; donations requested) housed in a substantial León residence that was the home of the poet's aunt, Bernarda. Inside, the lovingly kept rooms and courtyard garden are home to wonderfully frank plaques narrating the story of Darío's tempestuous personal life and diplomatic and poetic careers, along with personal possessions and commemorative items, such as Rubén Darío lottery tickets.

Casa Rigoberto López Pérez

Two blocks west and a block north of the Parque Central, a dowdy FSLN office

RUBÉN DARÍO

Born in 1867 in a village outside Matagalpa, the writer Rubén Darío is little-known beyond Latin America, but is one of Nicaragua's most famous sons. *Azul …*, published in 1888, became particularly influential and is often cited as a cornerstone for the birth of Spanish language modernism. Nearly a century after his death in 1916, he remains one of the region's most influential poets.

bears a plaque commemorating the spot where the young poet and revolutionary **Rigoberto López Pérez** assassinated the dictator General Somoza on September 21, 1956, before he himself was shot some fifty times by the National Guard. The plaque is the only thing to see; the building was named after López Pérez in the wake of the event.

Galería Héroes y Mártires

Continuing in a revolutionary vein, the **Galería Héroes y Mártires** (Mon–Sat 9am–5.30pm; donations requested), a block north and half a block west of the Parque Central, houses wall after wall of simple, moving black and white photos of Nicaraguans (men and women, young and old) killed fighting for the Sandinista cause during the civil war. There's also a small crafts shop attached, the proceeds of which go towards the gallery's upkeep.

La Veinte Uno

Three blocks south of the cathedral lie the ruins of **La Veinte Uno**, the National Guard's 21st garrison and scene of heavy fighting in April 1979. The garrison now houses two very different, seemingly unconnected museums, which together oddly go by the long-winded title of **Museo de Leyendas y Tradiciones General Joaquín de Arrechada Antigua Cárcel de la Veinte Uno** (Tues–Sat 8am–noon & 2–5pm, Sun 8am–3pm; C$7). One half of the building houses a bizarre collection of ghoulish figures from Nicaraguan folklore, including a chariot-riding grim reaper, while the other half focuses on the garrison's ugly past, with a small collection of revealing black-and-white photos taken during and after the Somoza era. Captions in Spanish document the torture that went on inside the garrison. You can also peer into the eerily empty cells at the rear of the building.

Subtiava

Four kilometres west of the city centre is the barrio of **Subtiava**, which long predates León and is still home to many of the city's indigenous population. It is also the site of one of the oldest **churches** in the country. Recently renovated, the small adobe building is not always open, but worth a visit if you're catching a bus to or from the beach at Las Peñitas (see p.434).

Arrival and information

By bus Buses arrive at the anarchic, traffic-clogged terminal northeast of the centre, from where you can hop in a taxi (standard fare anywhere in town is C$20) or walk the eight blocks west into town.

Tour operators Big Foot Adventure, at the *Big Foot Hostel* (see p.433; www.bigfootadventure .com), run volcano scree-boarding trips to nearby Cerro Negro. Quetzaltrekkers, C 2, Av 2–3 NE (311-6695, www.quetzaltrekkers.com), is an ethical tour company offering volcano treks around the country, including trips to Mombacho (US$50), Cerro Negro (US$20), Cosigüina (US$60) and Telica (US$37), as well as the Asososca Lagoon (US$30); prices include all transport, food, water, entry fees and guide. If your timing is right, you can even join a full-moon lava hike up Volcán Telica (US$30). All profits go towards supporting street children in León. FSLN combat veteran Dionísio Meza Romero offers "Historical Revolutionary" tours of León

THE GIGANTONA OF SUBTIAVA

In November and December, the one sight in León not to be missed is that of posses of young boys hammering away at snare drums while a huge Gigantona (a *papier-mâché*, Rio Carnaval–style figure of an elegant colonial-era lady, directed from underneath by a slightly older teenager) weaves among them. Traditionally, the boys are given a few córdobas for a recital of poetry, typically that of national bard Rubén Darío. The *gigantonas* are judged during the festivities of La Purísima (a festival celebrating the Virgin Mary's conception) on December 7, with the best winning a prize.

(Mon–Sat 9am & 3pm; C$70) from the Asociación de Combatientes Históricos Héroes de Veracruz (see p.431).

Tourist information INTUR, on Av José de la Cruz Mena, C 2–3 NO (Mon–Fri 8am–noon & 2–5pm; ☎311-3782), and has a few leaflets and maps and general tour information. Much better is the tourist office at the *Vía Vía* hostel, Av 2 NE, C 1–2 (☎311-6142).

Accommodation

Budget accommodation in León has really taken off in the last few years, and there is now an abundance of good-value hostels.

Hotels and guesthouses

El Albergue C 3 NE, Av 3–4 ☎478-6497. One of the more peaceful places in town, set around a narrow courtyard with high walls that drown out much of the street noise. The dorms are clean, well-ventilated and secure, and the private rooms are large but basic. There's also a small kitchen and bar. Sizeable discounts for volunteer workers. Dorms ❶, doubles ❸

Avenida Av Comandante Pedro Aráuz, C 5–6 NE ☎311-2068. Popular budget option with basic but clean and bright rooms set around a small leafy courtyard, some with private bath and all with ceiling fan. ❷

Big Foot Av 2 NE, C 1–2 no phone, ⓦwww .bigfootadventure.com. Located right opposite *Vía Vía*, this is very much the social gathering spot for the younger backpacker crowd. The huge dorms are kept fairly clean, but watch your belongings, as there's easy access from the bar out front. A large kitchen is available, as is a small foot-shaped pool. Dorms ❶

Casa Ivana C 2 SO, Av 2–3 ☎311-4423. Spartan, spacious rooms (private bath optional) in an atmospheric old house. The leafy courtyard and communal area with lived-in rocking chairs is an added draw. ❷

La Casona Av 1 SO, C 3–4 ☎311-5282, Ⓔhostelcasona@yahoo.es. Friendly hostel with six basic rooms, some gloomier than others. Positive attributes are a sociable, comfortable living area, kitchen, friendly management, laundry facilities and hammocks. ❷

Clínica Av 1 SO, C 2–3 ☎311-2031. Possibly the only hostel-cum-dental clinic in existence, this friendly, family-run place offers decent rooms (some with private bath) around a tiny courtyard. The upstairs rooms (with foliage-shaded balcony) are the most desirable, but negotiating the precipitous staircase after a few beers might present a problem. ❶

Guest House La Calle de los Poetas C Central Rubén Darío, Av 4–5 SO ☎311-3306, Ⓔrsampson@ibw.com.ni. Undoubtedly one of the best deals in the city, with four cool, quiet, tastefully furnished rooms (with fan and private bath) set around a pretty colonial courtyard and bordered by a large, rambling garden. The owner, a knowledge-able host, also runs an informal tour agency. ❸

Lazybones Av José De La Cruz Mena, C 2–3 SO ☎311-3472, ⓦwww .lazyboneseleon.com. Certainly the best hostel in León, this place is a real treat. The dorms are clean and comfortable, and the three showers mean you should never have to wait in line for too long. Large pool and pool table, free coffee and tea, internet with wi-fi and a 10min international phone call. Dorms ❷, rooms ❹

Vía Vía Av 2 NE, C 1–2 ☎311-6142, ⓦwww.viaviacafe.com. Opposite *Big Foot*, and just as popular. The lively on-site bar and restaurant (with pool table and live music) are probably *Vía Vía*'s biggest draws, although there are hammocks ($2 per night), book exchange and even salsa-dancing and Spanish classes. Accommoda-tion consists of a crumbling colonial dorm and a few basic rooms with fan and shared bath. Dorms ❶, rooms ❷

Eating

León boasts a cosmopolitan and ever-increasing range of places to eat and drink, from the ubiqui-tous pizza joints and stalwart seafood restaurants to chic café-bars and bohemian hangouts. Most of the restaurants and pizza places close around 10pm, while the trendier places stay open until the small hours, especially at weekends.

Restaurants

Ben Linder Café On the corner of Av 1 NO and C 2. Named after an American volunteer who worked tirelessly for the local community but was murdered by the Contras in 1989, this nonprofit fair-trade cafe is a great place to come for a light lunch, with toasted sandwiches and salads on the menu. Mains from C$40.

Café El Sesteo C Central Rubén Darío, on the corner of the Parque Central. The town's main café and the only one with alfresco tables, *El Sesteo* looks out over the Parque Central and Cathedral, making it a great place to people-watch and take in the atmosphere. Food is expensive, so it's best to stick to drinks: try their "famous" *cacao con leche* (C$30).

CocinArte On the corner of Av 4 SO and C 4. Colourful restaurant towards the southern end of town serving a large vegetarian menu as well as local specialities. Fri is couples evening and Sun features chess tournaments, attended by locals and tourists. There is a tourist info centre under the same roof. Mains from C$50.

Dave's Shark Pitt Av 1 NE, C 2–3. A popular hangout for local university students, largely due to the fact that it regularly hosts live music. The menu consists of truly huge portions of Mexican and Honduran food: one plate is easily enough for two people. Mains from C$40.

Guadalajara On the corner of Av 1 NE and C 2. Delicious, good-value and well-presented Mexican food with bench-style tables. Try the *quesadillas*, a steal at C$35.

Taquezal C 1A SO, Av 1–2. Rustic, slightly fraying but very stylish and atmospheric café/bar with candle-lit tables and a good menu featuring decent vegetarian pasta dishes, Chinese food, wonderful iced tea with lemon and a fine selection of espresso drinks. Mains from C$80. Closed Sun.

Vía Vía Av 2 NE, C 1–2 ☎311-6142. The restaurant at the hostel is regularly full, especially when live music or Monday night trivia is on the menu (phone ahead if you want a table). Its selling point is its lively atmosphere, but they also do great Honduran cuisine, as well as Mexican and European dishes. Mains from C$60. Closed Wed.

White House Pizza Av 1A NE, C 2–3 ☎311-7010. With the tastiest and most professional pizza in town (a medium margarita will set you back about C$80), this chain does a roaring trade most nights. They'll also deliver to your hotel.

Drinking and nightlife

León is Nicaragua's party town (by national standards), thanks in large part to its many students, and Friday and Saturday nights are always lively. People tend to converge on one or two places – look around and see what's going on.

Discoteca Dilectus On the highway to Managua on the south side of the city. This is about as close as you're going to come to a European-style nightclub. Things get going around 10pm and the playlist is the usual blend of salsa, merengue, reggaeton, techno and hip-hop. Cover US$1.

Don Señor C 1, Av 1–2 NO. With tables downstairs overlooking La Merced church, a dance floor upstairs and *El Álamo* bar right next door, this compact setting is ever-popular with locals and tourists.

Directory

Exchange There's a cluster of banks on the corner of C1 NE and Av 1, all with ATMs that accept Visa.

Internet Cyber Flash (.com), next to *Big Foot Hostel* has the fastest connection (US$1/hr). They also do photocopies and burn pictures from your camera to disk.

Post office Av 3 NO, C 3–4.

Telephones The Enitel office (Mon–Sat 7am–8pm, Sun 7am–5pm) is on the west side of the Parque.

Moving on

By bus to: Chinandega (55 daily; 1hr 30min); Estelí (4 daily; 2hr 30min); Las Peñitas (14 daily; 45min); Managua (40 daily; 1hr 15min–2hr 15min); Matagalpa (3 daily; 3hr); San Isidro (for Matagalpa and Estelí; 24 daily; 2hr).

AROUND LEÓN

Worthwhile day-trip destinations from León include the Pacific beach of **Las Peñitas**, west of the city and easily accessible by bus, and the UNESCO World Heritage site of **León Viejo**, best reached in a car or taxi – a trip on public transport entails some fancy footwork to make the connections, and even then leaves you with a bit of a walk.

Las Peñitas and Poneloya

For monster Pacific waves, **Las Peñitas**, 20km west of León, is the most impressive beach in the country. The water here is notoriously rough, due to a combination of powerful waves and riptides, so much so that it was recently the location for Nicaragua's first ever surf competition. Despite this, you can actually swim here reasonably safely. **Poneloya**, 2km north, is a different story: ask locals about riptides (*corrientes peligrosos*) before venturing into the water here, and never swim alone.

Most travellers come to Las Peñitas as a day-trip from León. **Accommodation** in town is limited. Options include *Playa Roca* (☎428-8903, ⊛www .hotelplayaroca.com; dorms ❷, rooms ❹), a thatched–roof cabaña right on the beach. Dorms are pretty basic, but the on–site restaurant cooks up rather good seafood. Right at the end of the road where the Pacific curves round into an idyllic little bay is the *Barco de Oro* (☎317-0275, ⊛www.barcadeoro.com; ❸–❹). Formerly a nightclub frequented by Somoza, it's now a tranquil traveller's haven. The pleasant rooms have rustic wooden beds, en–suite bathrooms and a lovely upstairs balcony for sunset–watching. The French owner (who also speaks good English) works closely with the local community and can hook you up with one of the fishermen for a trip to the nearby **Isla Juan Venado**, a nature reserve and turtle-nesting site.

Buses to Las Peñitas (45min) leave León from the Terminal Poneloya on C Darío, near the Subtiava church (see p.432) every 55 minutes (until 6pm). The last bus back to León leaves at 6.45pm.

León Viejo

Founded in 1524, **León Viejo** (daily 7am–6pm; US$2, including guided tour), 32km east of the modern city and now designated a UNESCO World Heritage site, was the original site of **León**, before it was destroyed by an earthquake and volcanic eruption on December 31, 1609. Among the ruins excavated since the site's discovery in 1967 are a cathedral, monastery and church. In November 2000, the graves of Nicaragua's first three bishops were uncovered; their remains are now interred in large coffins carved by Nicaraguan sculptor Federico Matus. The headless remains of Nicaragua's founder, **Francisco Fernández de Córdoba** were also discovered here, amid the ruins of La Merced church. The site's setting is nearly as impressive as its archeological import, within sight of the lake and under the looming shadow of Momotombo. The best view of the surroundings is to be had from the old fort, located east of the main ruins.

The site is accessible from **La Paz Centro**, a village about 60km north of Managua, which you can reach via the frequent León–Managua service – just ask them to drop you. It's best to get an early start, as the last bus returns to León from La Paz at 2pm. There's a local bus from La Paz Centro to and from the site.

CHINANDEGA

CHINANDEGA, 35km northwest of León, is primarily a working city and forms one of the many cogs in the Nicaraguan economy. Set on a plain behind the looming form of Volcán San Cristóbal, the area's dry, kiln-like climate is ideal for growing cotton, the area's main economic activity, along with Flor de Caña **rum**, Nicaragua's export-grade tipple, produced in a distillery on the outskirts of town. Almost always overlooked by travellers – and not without reason – Chinandega is really best visited as a stop-off on the way to the Honduran border.

Arrival and information

By bus Buses arrive at the market southwest of the centre, known as the Mercado Bisne – *bisne* being short for "business".

Exchange You can change dollars and traveller's cheques at Bancentro, which also has an ATM, on the opposite corner from the Shell garage.

Tourist information There's an INTUR office four blocks east from the Parque, where you can get info on climbing the nearby volcanoes.

Accommodation

Don Mario Two blocks north of the Parque ☎341-4054. There is not much by way of accommodation in Chinandega, but if you do stay, *Don Mario* is your best bet, with welcoming rooms, clean private bathroom, and cable TV. ❸

Eating

Res Kingdom Pizza One block north of the bank ☎341-8911. Does a range of tasty pizzas, and delivers to your hotel.

Moving on

By bus to: Guasaule (every 20min; 1hr); León (55 daily; 1hr 30min) Managua (22 daily; 2–3hr).

Crossing into Honduras via Guasaule is relatively hassle-free and shouldn't take more than half an hour in total. The exit tax is currently US$2; the official line is that this fee must be paid in US dollars, but if you don't have them it's fairly common to be allowed to pay in córdobas, although your exchange rate will take a beating. The border post is open 24 hours, but if you cross between noon and 2pm or after 5pm, you'll have to pay an extra US$2. It's about 1km between the Nicaraguan border post and the Honduran side, across an impressive bridge. You can either walk or take one of the bicycle taxis from Guasaule bus station. The entrance fee for Honduras (post open 24hr) is currently US$3. From the border there's a direct bus to Tegucigalpa every two hours.

ESTELÍ

Though the largest town in the north, at first sight ESTELÍ can seem downtrodden and poor. However, while it does have its poverty–stricken barrios, it's also an engaging place and a hotbed of political activity. Notorious for this staunchly leftist character and legendary tenacity, Estelí saw heavy fighting and serious bloodshed during the Revolution. Somoza bore a particular grudge against the town's inhabitants, and waged brutal offensives on the city. The scars have not really healed, either on the bombed–out buildings that still dot the streets or in people's minds, and the region remains a centre of undiminished Sandinista support – walk around a bit and you can glimpse something of the liberal vision that inspired so many people during the 1980s.

Estelí's relatively rural setting also means there are some attractive options for day-trips. El Salto de la Estanzuela – a secluded waterfall within walking distance of the centre – makes for a great day out, while the wonderful Miraflor nature reserve is just under 30km away.

What to see and do

Although Estelí lacks the stunning mountain views of Matagalpa, the centre of town is well kept and pleasant to wander around, and the climate is refreshingly cool. Much of the pleasure lies in soaking up the atmosphere, particularly along Avenida Central, where shops' wares spill out onto the street and the windows display cowboy boots and the local farmers' favourite Western-style hats.

The town's Parque Central isn't as nice as some others in the country, but is nonetheless busy from dawn until dusk. The cathedral on the eastern side of the Parque has a rather austere facade, making it one of the least interesting in the country. The south side of the Parque is dominated by the Centro Recreativo Las Segovias, which puts on regular music and sporting events, particularly basketball games. The Casa de Cultura, another cultural venue a block to the south, hosts local art exhibitions, dancing and music events. Across the street, the Artesanía Nicaragüense has a reasonable selection of crafts, pottery and cigars.

Galería de Héroes y Mártires

Just south of the Parque Central is the tiny Galería de Héroes y Mártires (daily 9am–4pm; donations requested) a simple yet moving museum devoted to the Revolution and to the many residents of Estelí who died fighting in it. The women who work at the Galería are, for the most part, mothers and widows of soldiers who were killed. Donations are very much appreciated.

Arrival and information

By bus Estelí has two bus terminals: the shiny and surprisingly orderly Cotran Sur R.L. station, at the southern entrance to town, serves all destinations south of Estelí, while the older station, 5min north, serves all destinations north of Estelí, plus express buses to Managua, Masaya and León.

Tour operator UCA Miraflor, Av 4 NE, C 2–3 (☎713-2971, ⓦwww.miraflor.org), runs tours to the reserve and can also give you general information on getting there independently.

Tourist information INTUR, Av Central, C Transversal–1 NE (Mon–Fri 8am–noon & 1.30–5pm; ☎713-6799, Ⓔesteli@intur.gob.ni), has up-to-date bus timetables and details on visiting Miraflor nature reserve and the El Salto de la Estanzuela waterfall.

Accommodation

Estelí has never featured on the backpacker trail in the same way that León does, and as a result budget accommodation leaves a lot to be desired. Like León, Estelí also has an early-morning air-raid siren wake-up call, so if you're a light sleeper you should consider a room as far from the centre as possible.

Hospedaje Chepito Av Central SO, C 8–9 ☎713-3784. Small, simple and dirt-cheap family-run *hospedaje* with camp beds and clean concrete floors. Very popular with Nicaraguans. ①

Hospedaje San Francisco Av Central SO, C 7–8 ☎713-3787. Almost the cheapest accommodation in town, but it shows. Rooms are extremely basic and can start to feel like prison cells if you stay indoors for any length of time. ①

Hospedaje San Ramón Av Central SO, C 7–8 ☎714-0970. Family-run place behind a general store. Rooms are fairly basic and allow for very little ventilation, but the owners are friendly and the shared bathroom is clean. ①

Miraflor Av 1 NO, C 3–4 ☎713-2003. Small hotel with homely rooms, overhead fan and decent bathroom. There's also a restaurant and bar on site. It's a good deal, especially if you're travelling with someone else (and don't mind sharing a bed). ②

Nicarao Av Central, C Transversal–1 SE ☎713-2490. Small hotel popular with gringos, possibly thanks to its covered patio where you can relax and dine on the lunch specials (US$3). Keep an eye out for the number of flightless birds housed here. You have a choice of budget or more attractive, comfortable rooms, all good value. ❷

Sacuanjoche Av 1 SE, C 2–3 ☎713-2482. Bright, fresh rooms with comfy beds, tiled floors, clean bathroom and varnished wooden ceilings, all set around a pretty patio. Good-value restaurant on site. ❶

Eating

Estelí's restaurants depend little on tourists, and as a result most are fairly low-key. Although there are no stand-outs, all the restaurants are great value.

Restaurants

Coffe Café C Transversal, Av Central–1. Simple coffee shop serving up omelettes, waffles and sandwiches as well as a range of other light snacks. One of the best places in town for breakfast (plate of fresh fruit C$40).

Fuji Hipa Rincón Chino Av Central, C 9–10. This restaurant does good-value Chinese food as well as some local dishes. An average meal will set you back no more than C$80.

La Gran Vía Av 1 SE, C Transversal–1. Busy restaurant specializing in good, fairly expensive Chinese food (the C$40 lunch specials – served 11am–4pm – are much better value), although there's a small selection of decent pasta dishes. Also does delicious flan and cheesecakes. Closed Sun.

Licuados Ananda C Transversal, Av Central–1. The Estelí branch of this Managua restaurant has tranquil outdoor tables next to a strangely disused swimming pool. Great for breakfast and snacks with a range of cheap, healthy vegetarian fare including yogurt, muesli, *licuados*, tacos and *repochetas*. Mains C$60.

El Rincón Pinareño Av 1 SE, C Transversal–1 ☎713-4369. Phenomenally popular, the *Pinareño* specializes in cheap, mouth-watering Nicaraguan fare with a Cuban bias. There's also a good range of tortillas (even a Mexican chorizo version) and daily specials. Mains C$60.

Tacos Mexicanos Beverly On the corner of C 2 NE and Av 2. Small place across from the cathedral serving up your usual Mexican fare, including excellent *quesadillas*. Mains C$60.

Vuela Vuela On the corner of C 3 NE and Av 1. Smart café/bar that's an NGO initiative with profits going to help disadvantaged youths back into the job market. The menu features a tasty, authentic range of Spanish tapas. Treats like gazpacho and *papas bravas* make this place a must, as does the healthy breakfast menu. Mains C$80.

Drinking and nightlife

There are few real bars in Estelí. Cllubbers are better catered for, but most of the healthy selection of discos are located far from town.

Bars

La Confianza Av Central, C Transversal–1 NE. Although *La Confianza* seems to be kept in perpetual darkness, this lively place is one of the few bars in the centre of town. They also serve decent-sized plates of tapas. Beers cost about C$15.

Rincón Legal On the corner of Av 1 SE and C 9. This absorbing Sandinista bar has occasional live music and is always busy late in the evening. Posters, news clippings and murals fill the walls, and if you're interested there's always someone around to explain their relevance. Beers around C$15.

Directory

Exchange There's a bank on every corner of C Transversal and Av 1 SO. Banco de América Central (Mon–Fri 8.30am–5pm, Sat 8.30am–noon), on the southwestern corner, is the only one that changes traveller's cheques.

Internet Esteli@net and Compucenter, both on C Transversal, Av Central–1 SO, have similar connection speeds and near identical prices at about US$1/hr.

Language schools Horizonte, a well-respected school, on Av 1 SE, Cal 9–10 (☎713-4117 ✉horizonte@ibw.com.ni), does courses for US$150 per week that include accommodation with a local family. The Galería de los Héroes y Mártires also runs informal language classes based on learning about the area and the effects of the civil war.

Telephones The Enitel office (Mon–Fri 8am–8pm, Sat 9am–5pm) is on C Transversal, Av 1–2 NE.

Moving on

By bus to: León (4 daily; 2–2hr 30min; alternatively, get on any bus to Matagalpa and get off at the San Isidro junction); Managua (29 daily; 2–3hr); Matagalpa (24 daily; 1hr–2hr); Masaya (2 daily; 3hr); Ocotal (12 daily; 2hr).

AROUND ESTELÍ

Estelí is blessed with beautiful natural surroundings. **Miraflor** to the north provides numerous opportunities for wildlife-spotting, while the waterfall of **El Salto de la Estanzuela** makes for a refreshing day-trip.

Miraflor nature reserve

The wonderful **Miraflor nature reserve**, 28km northeast of Estelí, is one of the country's least known but most worthwhile attractions. It covers 206 square kilometres of forest, part of which is farmed by a group of agricultural co-ops – over five thousand locals currently produce coffee, potatoes, milk, cheese and exotic flowers in and around the protected area. One of the project's main aims is to find sustainable ways in which farming and environmental protection can co-exist; the emphasis is firmly upon community-centred tourism.

The reserve itself comprises several different **ecosystems**, ranging from savannah to tropical dry forest and humid cloudforest. To best appreciate this diversity it's advisable to stay for at least two or three days, either walking or horseriding between the zones and staying with different families each night. Guides can also take you to the reserve's waterfalls and caves, once inhabited by the ancient Yeluca and Cebollal mountain peoples. In terms of flora and fauna, Miraflor is one of the richest reserves in the country, with over three hundred species of bird including quetzals, *guardabarrancos* (the national bird of Nicaragua) and *urracas*, a local type of magpie, as well as howler monkeys and reclusive mountain lions. There are also over two hundred species of orchid.

To get to the reserve take one of the **buses** from the northern bus terminal in Estelí. Several different buses run to different parts of the reserve. UCA Miraflor in Estelí (see p.437), is the place to get any advice if setting out independently, though they also run tours into the reserve and can arrange accommodation for you.

El Salto de la Estanzuela

Another very rewarding trip from Estelí is to **El Salto de la Estanzuela**, one of the few waterfalls in Nicaragua easily accessible on foot from a major centre of population. Located in the **Reserva Natural Tisey-Estanzuela**, it's a lovely two-hour walk through green, gently rolling hills – although it's also possible to drive right to the foot of the falls. The path begins just past the hospital at the southern entrance to town, by the *Kiosko Europeo*; follow the path for 4km or so until you see a sign for "Comunidad Estanzuela"; go through the gate on the right-hand side and follow the path for another 1km. The falls themselves – 35m or so in height – are located at the bottom of a steep flight of steps and are fairly spectacular, cascading into a deep pool perfect for swimming in. The only downside is the litter carelessly strewn around the rocks in front of the falls. As always, be careful not to go directly underneath the falling water as rocks do occasionally fall down, especially after heavy rainfall. Nearby is **El Mirador**, one of the most spectacular viewpoints in all Nicaragua; on a clear day it's possible to see volcanoes as far away as El Salvador.

INTO HONDURAS: LAS MANOS

Though not quite as busy as the crossing at Guasaule, the Las Manos border crossing for Honduras is nonetheless relatively trouble-free. The exit fee is US$2, although this fee doubles if you arrive at lunchtime (noon–2pm), at weekends or on public holidays. The official line is that it must be paid in US dollars, but it's fairly common to be allowed to pay in córdobas. The post is open 24 hours, but vehicles can only cross between 8am and 5pm. Continuing on, there are regular buses from Las Manos to the nearest town, El Paraíso, while two direct buses a day leave for Tegucigalpa (usually at about 9am and 2pm).

OCOTAL

A dusty highway leads north from Estelí to **OCOTAL**, a pleasant, cool place located in a bowl of green mountains, and a useful stopover on the way to or from the Las Manos border post and Honduras. The best place to stay is the *Hotel Frontera* (☎732-2668, ✉hofrosa@ ibw.com.ni; ❹), 1km north of town by the Shell station. All rooms have TV, air-conditioning and bath with hot water, and there's also a bar, restaurant and swimming pool.

Buses run between Ocotal and Estelí roughly every hour until 6pm (there are also frequent express buses from Ocotal to Managua until 3.30pm). Buses for Los Manos leave every half hour until 4.40pm. The bus terminal is on the highway 1km south of town.

MATAGALPA

Known as "La Perla del Septentrión" – "Pearl of the North" – **MATAGALPA** is spoken well of by virtually everyone

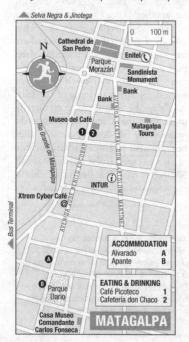

▲ Selva Negra & Jinotega

0   100 m

Cathedral de San Pedro
Parque Morazán
Enitel
Sandinista Monument
Bank
Bank
Museo del Café ❶ ❷
Matagalpa Tours
Río Grande de Matagalpa
AVENIDA CENTRAL
JOSE BENITO ESCOBAR
CUBA
BARTOLOME MARTINEZ
❶ INTUR
Xtrem Cyber Café @
Bus Terminal
Ⓐ
Ⓑ Parque Darío

ACCOMMODATION
Alvarado　　　A
Apante　　　　B

EATING & DRINKING
Café Picoteco　　1
Cafetería don Chaco　2

MATAGALPA

Casa Museo Comandante Carlos Fonseca

in Nicaragua, principally, perhaps, because of its relatively cool climate: at about 21–25°C, it's considered *tierra fría* in this land of 30°C-plus temperatures. Located 130km northeast of the capital on the Carretera Interamericana, Matagalpa is a small, quiet town set among blue-green mountains covered in coffee plantations. Most visitors come here to visit the **Selva Negra**, to the north of the city and one of the country's premier tourist attractions.

What to see and do

Matagalpa's services, hotels and restaurants are spread out between the seven blocks that divide the town's two principal parques: **Parque Morazán** to the north and the slightly smaller **Parque Darío** seven blocks to the south. The town's two main thoroughfares, **Avenida José Benito Escobar** and **Avenida Central**, link the two squares.

The town

At the northern end of town, sunny **Parque Morazán** fronts the **Catedral de San Pedro**, dating from 1874. Unusually, the cathedral was constructed side-on, with its bell towers and entrance facing away from the Parque. A large **Sandinista monument**, consisting of three men firing guns, stands on the eastern side. The smaller, shady **Parque Darío** is the site of several *hospedajes* and restaurants.

The **Casa Museo Comandante Carlos Fonseca** (Mon–Fri 2–4pm; donations requested), 100m southeast of the Parque Darío, documents the life of martyred local hero Carlos Fonseca (co-founder of the Sandinista National Liberation Front), gunned down by Somoza's National Guard in 1976.

One and a half blocks south of Parque Morazán, the **Museo del Café** (Mon–Fri 8am–noon & 2–5pm, Sat 8am–noon; free) houses some interesting old photos of Matagalpa life and explanations of the coffee-growing process. The museum sells quality coffee and is also behind Matagalpa's new **Feria Nacional del Café** (held in Nov), a festival celebrating the town's coffee expertise, with seminars, talks and performances of local music.

Arrival and information

By bus Matagalpa's bus terminal is southwest of the city centre; it's about a 10min walk from the terminal to Parque Darío.
Tour operators Matagalpa Tours, one block southeast of Parque Morazán (☎772-0108, ⓦwww.matagalpatours.com), offers excursions to the surrounding area, including tours of local coffee plantations.
Tourist information INTUR (Mon–Fri 8am–12.30pm & 2–5pm) is four blocks south of Parque Morazán on Av Central. The friendly and well-informed staff offers details about visiting coffee estates in the region, a trip known as the Ruta del Café.

Accommodation

The choice of accommodation In Matagalpa isn't great, but has improved significantly in recent years; nonetheless, many tourists still head out of town to stay at the *Hotel Selva Negra* (see p.442).
Hotel Alvarado Just north of Parque Darío on Av José Benito Escobar ☎772-2830. Certainly the most charming place in town, this family-run hotel above a pharmacy has cute, wood-panelled rooms, the most desirable being on the top floor. All rooms have en-suite bathrooms and fans. ❷
Hotel Apante On the east side of Parque Darío ☎772-6890. Offers tasteful, immaculate rooms with TV, colourfully tiled, hot-water bathroom and modern, comfortable beds. Some rooms are a lot bigger than others, so ask to see a few before choosing. ❷

Eating

Café Picoteo Next door to the Museo del Café. Great place for breakfast and a fresh cup of Matagalpan coffee. Mains C$20.
Cafeteria don Chaco Two blocks south of Parque Morazán on Av José Benito Escobar. Intimate little restaurant serving up a range of Honduran and Mexican dishes. With a popular bar to the back, this place can get very busy in the evenings, only adding to its already great atmosphere. Mains C$50.

Directory

Exchange A number of banks sit on Av Central just south of Parque Morazán: Bancentro will change dollars and traveller's cheques.
Internet Xtrem Cyber Café, halfway along Av José Benito Escobar, is the cheapest place in town for internet access (around US$1/hr) and international phone calls.
Telephones Enitel, a block east of the Cathedral (Mon–Fri 8am–7pm, Sat 9am–1pm).

Moving on

By bus to: Estelí (24 daily; 1hr 45min); Jinotega (26 daily; 1hr 30min); León (1 daily; 3hr; alternatively get on any bus to Estelí and get off at the San Isidro junction); Managua (29 daily; 3hr); Masaya (2 daily; 3hr 30min).

AROUND MATAGALPA

Although Matagalpa has an exceptional natural setting, most of the area is inaccessible to the independent traveller. The best place to get a feel for it is in the grounds of the *Selva Negra* hotel, where footpaths weave through the thick tropical forest.

Selva Negra

North of Matagalpa, the **Selva Negra** is an area of dark blue, pine-clad mountains named by the area's German immigrants in the nineteenth century after their homeland's Black Forest, which it strangely resembles. Due to its high altitude (around 1570m), the area has a spring-like climate and a refreshing average temperature of 18°C. An amazing variety of **wildlife** flourishes in these pristine and sparsely populated tropical forests, including over eighty varieties of orchid, many birds (including the elusive quetzal), sloths, ocelots, margay, mountain lion, deer and howler monkeys – all of which are more likely to be spotted here than anywhere else in the country.

Unfortunately, you can't just head off into the mountains: much of the terrain is farmed or under coffee cultivation, and trails are virtually non-existent. Because it offers an accessible route to the forest and mountains, nearly everyone who comes to the area stays in the **hotel** *Selva Negra*, 10km from Matagalpa on the road to Jinotega (☏612-3883, Ⓦwww.selvanegra.com; dorms ❷, rooms ❺). An establishment of national repute, the hotel has individually designed cabañas set in beautifully landscaped grounds, and dorms. There's a pricey restaurant on site serving traditional German fare as well as local options and a hearty breakfast buffet (Sun only). The **trails** are fairly short and it's perfectly feasible to come up from Matagalpa early in the morning and pack most of them into a day's hiking; all you'll have to pay is the entrance fee of US$1.60 (which can be spent at the hotel restaurant if you don't want to stay). The hotel's owners have grown coffee here since 1891, and the *finca* still produces some of the best export-grade coffee in the country; the estate employs 250 workers, most of whom live nearby, with a school and health clinic on site. Worthwhile **tours** of the operation are run daily at 9am and 3pm (US$5 for guests, US$7 for visitors).

Jinotega

Set amid cool, lush mountains 34km north of Matagalpa is the pleasantly nondescript town of **Jinotega**, famous for the coffee grown nearby. It's worth coming up here for the ride, as the journey between here and Matagalpa is one of the most magnificent in the country, winding slowly though misty green mountains. The climate is significantly cooler than much of Nicaragua, with low cloud and drizzle not uncommon; bring a sweater or light jacket.

Most travellers only stop here on day-trips from Matagalpa, but if you miss the last bus, the best-value **accommodation** option is *Hotel Bosawas* (☏782-3311; ❶), on Av Central three and a half blocks north of the Parque. Rooms are attractive – if unusually sterile – and have an option of shared or private bathroom. The hotel also has family rooms, which are good value if you're in a group. For **eating**, *Restaurante Soda El Tico* (☏782-2059), a block south of the cathedral, serves up your standard buffet-style fare (mains from US$3) and is always popular with locals for its good service.

Buses run every thirty minutes to nearby Matagalpa, taking just over an hour, while ten buses daily make the trip to the capital, Managua.

The southwest

The majority of Nicaragua's population lives in the fertile plain that makes up the **southwest** of the country. Bordered by Lago de Nicaragua to the east and the Pacific to the west, and studded by volcanoes – Volcán Masaya, Volcán Mombacho and the twin cones of Ometepe's Concepción and Maderas – the southwest is otherwise a flat, low, grassy plain, ideally suited to cattle (indeed, most of what is left of Nicaragua's beef industry is concentrated here), while coffee plantations can be found at higher altitudes.

Masaya, 29km south of Managua, and **Granada**, 26km further south, are the region's only two cities of any size; Masaya's enormous crafts market attracts virtually everyone who comes to Nicaragua, while the nearby **Parque Nacional Volcán Masaya** offers the most accessible volcano-viewing in the country. The picturesque "**Pueblos Blancos**", or White Towns, lie on the road connecting Managua, Masaya and Granada; the latter, with its fading classical-colonial architecture and lakeside setting, is undeniably Nicaragua's most beautiful and popular city, and also makes a good base for exploring such nearby outdoor attractions as the **Isletas de Granada** and **Volcán Mombacho**. Some 75km south of Granada, **Rivas**, the gateway to Costa Rica, is of little interest in itself, though many travellers pass through on their way south or en route to the popular beach town **San Juan del Sur**.

MASAYA

Set midway between Managua and Granada and shadowed by the hulking form of Volcán Masaya, **MASAYA**'s stirring geography would make it an attractive town to visit even if it weren't also the centre of Nicaragua's **artesanía production** and home to two colourful

crafts markets. These are of quite recent provenance – only during the Sandinista years did Masaya develop its crafts tradition into a marketable commodity – but the city is now by far the best place in the country to buy hammocks, rocking chairs, traditional clothing, shoes and other souvenirs. Many of the crafts on sale come from designs that originated in the indigenous barrio of **Monimbó**, and the district continues to churn out a sizeable proportion of the region's handicrafts. Most visitors come here on day-trips from Managua or Granada – a sensible plan, since Masaya doesn't have a large range of hotels but the bus services are fast and efficient.

▲ El Coyotepe Fort & Managua

MASAYA

ACCOMMODATION		EATING & DRINKING	
Don Pepe	E	Comedor La Criolla	1
Hostal Santamaria	F	Fruti Fruti	2
Hotel Central	B	La Jarochita	3
Hotel Montecarlo	D	Panaderia y	
Hotel Regis	C	Reposteria Norma	5
Madera's Inn	A	Restaurante Che-Gris	6
		La Ronda	7
		Tele Pizza	4

Volcán Masaya

Laguna de Masaya

San Jerónimo

CALLE PALO BLANCO

Cablenet Café

CALLE EL POCHOTILLO

AVENIDA SAN JERONIMO

AVENIDA SERGIO DELGADILLO

AVENIDA EL PROGRESO

Estadio

CALLE EL CALVARIO

CALLE EL ESTADIO

CALLE LA REFORMA

Parroquia La Asunción

BAC & ATM

CALLE CENTRAL

Enitel
Bancentro

Parque Central

Police

Mercado Nacional de Artesanía

Mercado Ernesto Fernández & Bus Terminal

CALLE SIMPSON

Banpro & ATM

CALLE SAN MIGUEL

INTUR

Minibuses to/from Managua

Iglesia San Miguel

Red Cross

0   300 m

▼ Church of San Sebastian & Monimbó

443

What to see and do

Masaya is an attractive place to explore on foot: there's fairly little traffic in the streets, the heat is bearable and all the sights are within walking distance of each other.

Parque Central

What little action there is in downtown Masaya takes place in the local hangout, the **Parque Central**, where – with the help of Spanish finance – **La Parroquia de la Asunción** church has been renovated. It boasts images of various Central American saints inside, swathed in coloured satin and wilting gold lamé.

Iglesia de San Jerónimo

Rather more plain in its decor is the **Iglesia de San Jerónimo**, 600m north, the best example of colonial architecture in Masaya, despite its run-down condition. The statue of San Jerónimo on the altar depicts an old man wearing a loincloth and a straw hat, with a rock in his hand and blood on his chest, evidence of self-mortification. Both churches are open to the public daily 6am to 8pm.

Mercado Nacional de Artesanía

Two blocks east of the Parque Central sits the Mercado Viejo, or Old Market (daily 8am–6.30pm), which has been converted into the grandly named **Centro Cultural (Antiguo Mercado de Masaya) – Mercado Nacional de Artesanía**. Behind the large, fortress-style grey walls lies a complex network of stalls selling paintings, many in the naïf-art tradition of the Solentiname archipelago, as well as large, excellent-quality hammocks, carved wooden bowls and utensils, simple wood-and-bead jewellery, cotton shirts, straw hats and leather footwear, bags and purses. Bargaining is accepted, and although prices are generally quoted in córdobas, traders will accept US dollars (small bills are best), though you may get change in córdobas. There are also a few cafés and restaurants in the grounds, which are the site of the weekly **Jueves de Verbena** party night (see box below, for details). Check out the giant wall map of the country, which shows the places in Nicaragua where crafts are produced. If your Spanish is up to it, ask about visiting artisans at work in their homes and workshops.

Laguna de Masaya

The **Laguna de Masaya** beckons on the western side of town, seven blocks from the Parque Central. Despite its crystalline and inviting appearance, the *laguna* is actually highly polluted with sewage effluent from the town. It's still worth the walk to see it, however, as the waterfront has stunning views of the smoking cone of Volcán Masaya (see p.446).

FESTIVITIES IN MASAYA

The most exciting time to visit Masaya is on Sundays between mid-September and mid-December, when the town indulges in a ninety-day period of revelry known as the Fiesta de San Jerónimo. The beginning of the fiesta sees one of the most fascinating processions in Nicaragua, the Torovenado, when Monimbó's large gay population comes out in style, indulging in a spot of cross-dressing and pastiche. A more recent invention is the popular Jueves de Verbena festival, held every Thursday evening throughout the year in the renovated Mercado Nacional de Artesanía. The evenings are a spirited celebration of indigenous culture, music and gastronomy, with locals and tourists dancing, singing, eating and drinking the night away.

Arrival and information

By bus Buses from Managua and Granada arrive at the huge, dusty terminal next to Masaya's main market, to the east of town; it's a longish walk to the centre from here, so ask to be let off earlier, at the Iglesia San Jerónimo.

By minibus Minibuses from Managua arrive at and depart from (every 15min) the street in front of the small Parque San Miguel, three blocks east of the Parque Central.

Tourist information The INTUR office (☏ 522-7615), half a block south of the police station and the Mercado Nacional, can provide some information on local hotels and volcano tours.

Accommodation

Masaya isn't really the place to bed down for the night; the market aside, there's not a huge amount to do and most people visit Masaya on a day-trip from Granada or Managua. That said, there are several reasonable budget options for lodging, most of them clustered a few blocks north of the Mercado Nacional.

Don Pepe A block and a half north of La Asunción ☏ 614-4119. A family-run hotel and restaurant in a converted house, *Don Pepe* has a large dining area and lovely garden area, while the four large rooms feature polished wooden floors and huge, comfy beds. The tasty *comida típica* goes for about C$100 a plate. Singles (with shared bath) ❹, doubles (en suite) ❺

Hostal Santamaria Half a block southeast of the Mercado Nacional ☏ 522-2411, ⓦ www.hostalsantamarianic.com. The 22 tidy rooms here, all en suite with cable TV, are quiet and cool and just a stone's throw from the old market. Singles ❸, doubles ❹–❺

Hotel Central Next door to *Hotel Regis* ☏ 522-2867. There's not much difference in ambience between *Central* and *Regis*, its next-door neighbour, but the rooms are brighter (with private bath optional) and the breakfasts cheaper. ❷

Hotel Montecarlo 50m south of *Fruti Fruti* ☏ 522-2927. Though the downstairs rooms are small and dark, there's a lovely, big, wooden-floored room upstairs with balcony; ask if it's free. ❷

Hotel Regis One block east and half a block south of Iglesia San Jerónimo ☏ 522-2300. A spotlessly clean bargain, despite cell-like, wood-panelled rooms with thin partition walls. ❶

Madera's Inn One block north of *Hotel Central* ☏ 533-5825, ⓦ www.hotelmaderasinn.com. Probably the best of the lot in Masaya, with 13 bright and cosy rooms, including a dorm, spread over a tidy and welcoming family house. Rooms come with shared or private bath and either fan or a/c, and breakfast is included. Dorms ❶, doubles ❷

Eating and drinking

Comedor La Criolla A block north of *Madera's Inn*. Offers a popular buffet with filling *comida típica* plus rarities like cannelloni for C$60 (including a soft drink).

Fruiti Fruiti Opposite *Hotel Regis*. A healthy choice for breakfast (C$30–40) or lunch, with a large selection of exotically flavoured smoothies (C$30–40) and decent coffee (C$8).

La Jarochita On Av Sergio Delgadillo, north of La Asunción ☏ 522-4831. A charming Mexican restaurant where the waitresses are kitted out in traditional dress, and you can dine on authentic burritos (C$70), *quesadillas* (C$60) and *mole* (C$160), and wash it down with tequila or a cold beer (C$20).

Panaderia y Reposteria Norma Across from the police station, just north of the Mercado Nacional. Another branch of the cheap and delicious bakery, with an overwhelming menu of cakes (C$4–9), pastries (C$5–10) and other baked delights, as well as cheap coffee (C$4).

Restaurante Che-Gris On the southeast corner of the Mercado Nacional. Perfectly situated for a quick snack, this place is renowned for its delicious *brochettas* (meat on skewers; C$100–180).

La Ronda An airy bar and restaurant overlooking La Asunción and the Parque Central, *La Ronda* draws a local crowd with cheap beer (C$16, or C$28 for a litre).

Tele Pizza Half a block north of La Asunción, this place has decent-sized pizzas from C$60–80, as well as pastas (C$60) and salads (C$60–80).

Directory

Exchange Banks and ATMs are plentiful in Masaya; there's a handy Banpro machine in the old market, and a branch of BAC opposite the police station where you can change dollars and traveller's cheques.

Internet Access available at Mi PC a Colores, next door to *Hotel Regis* (C$20/hr); they also have dirt-cheap international calling rates. Alternatively, try USB Cyber Connection (C$20/hr) next to the INTUR office, or the Cablenet Café beside *Fruti Fruti*.

Post office There's a tiny office one block north of the Mercado Nacional next to the BAC (Mon–Fri 8am–noon & 1–4.30pm, Sat 8–11.30am).

Moving on

By bus to: Granada (daily 4.30am–6pm; 45min); Jinotepe (daily 5am–6pm; 1hr 25min); Managua (daily 4.10am–6pm; 1hr 10min). Buses leave from the station next to the municipal market, four blocks north of the artisans' market, all departing roughly every fifteen minutes.

AROUND MASAYA

Attractions around Masaya include the natural sites of Masaya's namesake **volcano** and a crater-lake, **Laguna de Apoyo**, which can be explored on foot and with a guide. The nearby **Pueblos Blancos** are famous for various forms of artisanal crafts, including pottery, which is made in the small workshops throughout the villages. The historical site of **Coyotepe,** meanwhile, is a must for anyone interested in the nation's political history.

Coyotepe

Three kilometres out of town on the road to Managua is the old fort of **Coyotepe**. Built on a hilltop by the Somoza regime to house political prisoners, the abandoned and decaying structure commands stunning views of Masaya, Laguna de Apoyo and the volcanoes of Masaya and Mombacho, and also offers an eerie reminder of the atrocities carried out here by Somoza's National Guard: when Sandinistas stormed the fort during the Revolution, the National Guard responded by slaughtering all those inside. Bring a torch and you can poke around in the darkened and eerie dungeons. From Masaya, take any Managua-bound **bus** and ask to be let off at the entrance, from where a winding path leads up to the untended fort. On your return, simply flag any Masaya-bound bus down from the roadside.

Parque Nacional Volcán Masaya

Just outside Masaya, the **Parque Nacional Volcán Masaya** (daily 9am–4.45pm; C$75; ☎522-5415) offers you the chance to peer into the smoking cone of a volcano, as well as some more typical – but still stunning – long-distance views. Gazing warily down into the crater's precipitous, sulphurous depths, you can well imagine why the Spaniards considered this to be the mouth of hell itself – the large white cross above the crater marks the spot where a Spanish friar placed a cross in the sixteenth century, an attempt to exorcise the volcano's demonic presence. This is still one of the most active volcanoes in the world; the last eruption occurred in 2001, but plumes have been spotted since then.

The **park entrance** lies between Km 22 and Km 23 on the Managua–Granada highway, about 4km north of Masaya. You can get off any **bus** (except the express) between Managua and Masaya or Granada at the entrance. Alternatively, you could hire a taxi from Masaya. About 1.5km before the park entrance, along the approach road, is the **Centro de Interpretación Ambiental** (daily 9am–4pm), home to an exhibition outlining the area's geology, agriculture and pre-Columbian history, along with an interesting three-dimensional display of the country's chain of volcanoes. You can organize a **guide** for excursions into the park, use the toilet facilities and stock up on cold drinks and water here before the climb.

From the park entrance you can either **hike** the fairly steep five-kilometre paved road up to the crater and back again or organize transport with a park ranger (C$40); ask at the centre detailed above. You must have a **guide** to do the hike; the ranger service also offers guided **tours** on two other trails, Sendero Los Coyotes and Sendero de Las Pencas, as well as short trips to the extinct cone of Comelito and the subterranean Cueva Tzinancanostoc, where you'll see bizarre lava formations and a bat colony. Look out for the stunted bromeliads common to high-altitude volcanic areas, and the famous *chocoyos del cráter*, small green parrots that have thrived in an atmosphere that should be poisonous.

Pueblos Blancos

Scattered within a fifteen-kilometre radius of Masaya are the "**Pueblos Blancos**" or White Towns: **Nindiri**, **Niquinohomo**, **Masatepe**, **Catarina**, **Diria** and **Diriomo**. The name comes from the traditional whitewash used on the villages' houses – called *carburo*, it is made from water, lime and salt – as well as a past tradition of practising white (good, not-evil) magic in the area. The white buildings are pretty, but there's not much more to see: although each town has its own specific artisan traditions and fiestas, and local identity is fiercely asserted, they seem remarkably similar, sleepy towns with a few hangers-out around nearly identical central squares. **Catarina** is the prettiest, the main draw being **El Mirador**, a lookout point at the top of the village that stares right down into the blue waters of the collapsed crater lake of **Laguna de Apoyo**, with Volcán Masaya looming behind it. Restaurants, cafés and *artesanía* stalls have sprung up around the viewpoint.

A regular local **bus** runs roughly every thirty minutes from Masaya's main bus terminal to Catarina. From Granada, buses to Niquinohomo pass through the town, or alternatively you can take any Masaya or Managua bus and ask to be let off at the Catarina turning, from where you'll need to take another short bus ride to the edge of the village.

Laguna de Apoyo

Now a natural reserve, the volcanic lake known as the **Laguna de Apoyo** draws tourists with its mineral-rich waters, tropical rainforest and stunning views. Nature-lovers will be entranced by the rare **flora and fauna**, with animals including howler monkeys, armadillos and toucans making their home here. *Crater's Edge Hospedaje* (☏895-3202, ⓦwww.craters-edge.com; dorms ❷,

doubles ❹–❺) has pretty rooms set in a stunning garden with panoramic lake views and a lakeside bar. The open-air dorms have the best view, while private rooms are more expensive and attractively presented.

From Managua, catch an express **minibus** to Granada and ask to be let off at the Laguna entrance; from here, it's a fifteen-minute taxi ride (C$10) or a ninety-minute hike. Masaya has direct buses to the Laguna departing at 10am and 4pm. Transfers to and from *Crater's Edge* can also be arranged through partner *Hostel Oasis* in Granada (see p.451).

GRANADA

Set on the western shore of Lago de Nicaragua, some 50km southeast of Managua, **GRANADA** was once the jewel of Central America. The oldest Spanish-built city in the isthmus, it was founded in 1524 by Francisco Fernández de Córdoba, who named it after his hometown in Spain. During the colonial period Granada became fabulously rich, its wealth built upon exploitation: sited only 20km from the Pacific, the city was a transit point for shipments of gold and other minerals mined throughout the Spanish empire.

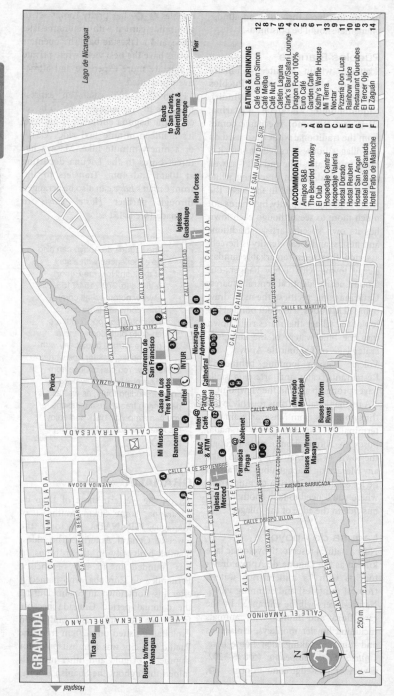

GRANADA

Lago de Nicaragua

Pier

Boats to San Carlos, Solentiname & Ometepe

Hospital

Tica Bus

Buses to/from Managua

CALLE INMACULADA

CALLE AMELIA BENARD

AVENIDA BOOAN

AVENIDA ELENA ARELLANO

CALLE LA LIBERTAD

CALLE LA CONSULADO

CALLE 14 DE SEPTIEMBRE

Iglesia La Merced

CALLE EL REAL XALTEVA

CALLE ESTRADA

AVENIDA BARRICADA

CALLE LA CONCEPCION

CALLE OBISPO ULLOA

LA HOYADA

CALLE EL TAMARINDO

CALLE LA CEIBA

CALLE NUEVA

Police

AVENIDA GUZMÁN

CALLE SANTA LUCIA

CALLE EL CISNE

Convento de San Francisco

Casa de Los Tres Mundos

Enitel

INTUR

Mi Museo

Bancentro

Inter@ Café

BAC & ATM

Farmacia Praga

Kablenet

CALLE ATRAVESADA

Nicaragua Adventures

Cathedral

Parque Central

CALLE VEGA

Mercado Municipal

Buses to/from Rivas

Buses to/from Masaya

CALLE EL ARSENAL

CALLE CORRAL

CALLE LA LIBERTAD

Iglesia Guadalupe

Red Cross

CALLE LA CALZADA

CALLE EL CAIMITO

CALLE CUISCOMA

CALLE SAN JUAN DEL SUR

CALLE EL MARTIRIO

N

0   250 m

ACCOMMODATION

Amigos B&B	J
The Bearded Monkey	A
El Club	B
Hospedaje Central	D
Hospedaje Valeria	C
Hostal Dorado	E
Hostal Reuben	H
Hostal San Angel	G
Hostel Oasis Granada	I
Hotel Patio de Malinche	F

EATING & DRINKING

Café de Don Simon	12
Café Melba	8
Café Nuit	7
Cafetín Laguna	15
Clark's Bar/Safari Lounge	4
Dragon Food 100%	2
Euro Café	5
Garden Café	6
Kathy's Waffle House	1
Mi Tierra	13
Nectar	9
Pizzeria Don Luca	11
Rainbow Juice	10
Restaurant Querubes	16
El Tercer Ojo	3
El Zaguán	14

In the mid-nineteenth century Granada fell to American adventurer William Walker, who gained control of the city – and, by default, the entire country for a brief time. Granada paid dearly for the eventual overthrow of Walker; as he retreated in the face of international resistance, he ordered for the city to be burned to the ground. Small scars from this fire remain visible in several parts of the city.

Today Granada is central to the Nicaraguan government's tourism ambitions. The city's popularity with foreign visitors has led to a large-scale restoration of the old **colonial buildings**, many of them newly repainted in pastel shades, and a burgeoning network of foreign-owned bars, restaurants and hostels have sprung up. The city also makes a good base from which to explore the lake, volcanoes, the Zapatera archipelago and Isla de Ometepe, while more adventurous travellers might head on from here to the Solentiname Islands and San Carlos (see p.465).

What to see and do

There are few "must see" attractions in the city itself, but most of the pleasure is simply in strolling the streets and absorbing the colonial atmosphere – be sure to take a peek through the open front doors of the private houses along Calle La Calzada to see the magnificent interior courtyards which adorn some of the houses.

Parque Central

At the centre of town sits the attractive, palm-lined **Parque Central**, where you could spend hours just sitting under shaded trees. A few small kiosks sell snacks, and an ice-cream seller wanders around ringing his handbell in search of trade. On the east side of the Parque is the large **cathedral** (open daily to the public as a house of worship), built in 1712 and damaged in the 1850s during William

Walker's ordered burning. Neglected for many years, the cathedral was much improved by a facelift in 2006.

As well as the cathedral, many of the city's most captivating historic houses line the square. The palatial red house with white trim on the corner of Calle La Calzada, across from the cathedral, is the **Bishop's Residence**, with a columned upstairs veranda typical of the former homes of wealthy Granadino burghers.

Casa de Los Tres Mundos

About 50m north of the cathedral on the Plaza de la Independencia is the stately **Casa de Los Tres Mundos** (daily 7.30am–6pm; C$19; Ⓦ www.c3mundos .org). Built in 1724, it has been restored and turned into a centre of culture and music, with art exhibitions and informal rehearsals. Visitors can wander among its covered and open courtyards and maze-like corridors – the wooden panelling and staircases found within are rare in this concrete-and-adobe country.

Convento de San Francisco

Originally dating from the sixteenth century but rebuilt in 1867 after Walker's attack, the historic **Convento de San Francisco** (Mon–Fri 8.30am–5.30pm, Sat 9am–4.30pm; C$40) is two blocks northeast of the cathedral. The cultural centre next to the convent has been converted into one of Nicaragua's best pre-Columbian museums, housing many of the **petroglyphs** recovered from Isla Zapatera. Hewn from black volcanic basalt in about 1000 AD, these petroglyphs depict anthropomorphic creatures – half man, half lizard, turtle or jaguar – which probably had ritual significance for the indigenous peoples who inhabited the islands. It was also from the confines of this convent that in 1535 **Frey Bartolomé de las Casas**, apostle of the indigenous peoples of Central America, wrote his historic letter to the Spanish Court, condemning the Indians' mistreatment at the hands of the Spanish. The Convento also houses the city **library**: many of Walker's filibusters are buried in the catacombs in its basement.

Mi Museo

Set in a stunning converted colonial house one block northwest of the Parque Central on the Calle Atravesada, **Mi Museo** (Mon–Sat 8am–5pm, Sun 8am–noon; free) is a gallery showing a private collection of over five thousand pieces of pre-Columbian ceramics, the oldest of which dates back to 500 BC. Animal forms, depicted on jars, plates and urns of various sizes, include birds, crocodiles and toads.

Torre de Nuestra Señora de Los Angeles

For panoramic views of Granada's rooftops, as well as the lake and volcano, climb the tower (open daily; C$20 – pay the attendant in the stairwell) at **La Iglesia de Nuestra Señora de Las Mercedes** (The Church of Our Lady of Mercy), also know as La Merced, which sits two blocks west of the cathedral on Calle 14 de Septiembre; yet to receive a lick of new paint, it has a shabby-chic charm of its own. The tower is accessed at the front of the church on the left. If you suffer from vertigo, you may be put off by the tiny winding staircase with low railings that leads you upstairs. Once up top, there's a wrap-around balcony for taking photos or simply soaking up the view.

Lago de Nicaragua

The shoreline of **Lago de Nicaragua** is about 1km east of the Parque Central; head down the wide boulevard of Calle La Calzada and the huge vista of the lake stretches across the horizon. The lakefront itself is pretty quiet, unless you happen to arrive as the boat from San Carlos or Ometepe is docking, when you can watch Granadinos meeting friends and family and see queasy passengers disembark as bananas, chickens and livestock are unloaded along the narrow dock. To the south a small park lines the lake, a few hundred metres beyond which is the entrance to the town's **Central Turístico Inturismo** (8am–6pm, free after 6pm; C$10; ☎879-9068), a group of lakeside bars and cheap eateries, a narrow little beach and usually packed grassy areas – look for the strange little castle that marks the entrance. It's popular at weekends, but take care here after dark.

Arrival and information

By boat Boats from both San Carlos (2 weekly) and Altagracia (2 weekly) dock at the pier at the bottom of C La Calzada.

TOUR OPERATORS IN GRANADA

Momobotour On C Atravesada next to the BDF bank ☎552-4548, ⓦwww .mombotour.com. Deals with the area's original canopy tour (US$35), as well as kayaking and mountain-biking excursions (US$25 and up).

Nahual Tours Next to *Hospedaje Central*, C La Calzada ☎475-9825 or 955-2602, ⓦwww.nahualtours.es.tl. A friendly, Nica-run operator with well-priced tours (from US$17 per person). There's also a small souvenir shop at the office selling handmade jewellery, postcards and T-shirts.

Nicaragua Adventures Just before Tierra Tour on C La Calzada ☎552-8461, ⓦwww.nica-adventures.com. The best place in Granada to plan onward travel. Helpful owner Pierre speaks English, French and German (as well as Spanish) and can help book La Costeña flights as well as organize tours around the country.

Tierra Tour On C La Calzada two blocks east of the cathedral ☎552-8273 or 862-9580, ⓦwww.tierratour.com. Offers tours of the Isletas (US$18 per person), as well as city and volcano tours; groups of more than two receive a discount.

By bus Buses from Managua come into the terminal west of town, 700m from the Parque Central, from where you can walk or grab a taxi into the centre (expect to pay around C$20). Arriving from Rivas and points south, buses pull up at the *mercado*, a short walk southwest of the centre. Express minivans from Managua arrive at the small terminal half a block south of the Parque Central, though most will let you off at the plaza. If you're travelling from Costa Rica, the Tica Bus for Managua will stop and let you off at its Granada office.

Tourist information Granada's INTUR office (Mon–Fri 8am–noon & 2–5pm; ℡ 552-6858) is on C El Arsenal, diagonal to the Convento San Francisco, and stocks information on climbing local volcanoes and other attractions.

City transport

Taxis Line up in front of the *Hotel Alhambra* on the Parque Central. Any trip in Granada should cost C$10–20.

Accommodation

The range of places to stay in Granada has improved immeasurably over the past five years and renovation work continues apace. The city now boasts a comprehensive variety of budget accommodation options.

Amigos B&B C Estrada near C Atravesada, just before *Hostel Oasis Granada* ℡ 552-2085. A sweet family-run B&B with dorms, as well as private rooms. Guests have use of the communal kitchen and internet, and laundry services are also available (US$4–6). Dorms ❷, doubles ❸

The Bearded Monkey C 14 de Septiembre near C Corral ℡ 552-4028, ⓦ www.thebeardedmonkey .com. Busy backpacker hangout. The renovated colonial house, set around a large, verdant courtyard, has hammocks, internet access, TV and a strictly monitored book exchange. You can crash in a hammock, in one of the large, impersonal dorms or in a variety of private rooms. Snacks and meals also available on site. Hammock ❶, dorms ❷, rooms ❸–❹

El Club Corner of C la Libertad and Av Barricada ℡ 552-4245, ⓦ www.elclub-nicaragua.com. Chic, friendly, bar/restaurant with original, luxurious, great-value rooms – ask for one at the back on the funky mezzanine level. Singles ❼, doubles ❼

Hospedaje Central C La Calzada ℡ 552-5900. The sprawling accommodation here consists of dorm beds, and very basic, screened rooms with either shared or private bath. There's also a popular bar and restaurant serving "gringo" food. Dorms ❶, rooms ❷

Hospedaje Valeria C El Martirio, tw[...] blocks east and half a block north of [...] ℡ 454-1325. A newly converted colo[...] large rooms all boasting TV, en-suite [...] water. Guests have free bike and inte[...]

Hostal Dorado C Real Xalteva near C[...] one and a half blocks west of the cathedral. A maze of hammocks, courtyards and rooms, some of which are a claustrophobe's nightmare, are set in another lovely converted house. The dorms are some of the cheapest in town and there's also free internet and laundry services. Dorms ❶, rooms ❸

Hostal Reuben Av Guzmán next door to *Hostal San Angel* ℡ 552-4591. A central, popular traveller hangout with large rooms set around a courtyard garden. Accomodation consists of basic private rooms and musty dorms. Dorms ❶, rooms ❸

Hostal San Angel Av Guzmán, half a block south of the cathedral ℡ 552-6373, ⓔ mariacampos118@hotmail.com. This welcoming, family-run hostel offers one of the best deals in town; the quiet and tidy rooms are all en suite with good mattresses and a fan, and breakfast is included. ❹

Hostel Oasis Granada C Estrada near C Atravesada, 100m north of Masaya bus terminal ℡ 552-8006, ⓦ www.nicaraguahostel.com. A self-proclaimed "backpackers' paradise", this imaginatively conceived hostel offers comfortable dorm beds and private rooms in a restored colonial house. Also free internet, laundry, bar and even a tiny swimming pool. ❷

TREAT YOURSELF

El Patio de Malinche C Caimito near C El Cisne ℡ 552-2235, ⓦ www .patiodelmalinche.com. An immaculate colonial conversion set around a tropical courtyard (with pool). The rooms feature cool tiled floors, high ceilings and original wood beams, a/c and wireless internet, and those upstairs have fantastic views of the Mombacho volcano. Full breakfast included. ❽

Eating

Granada offers an increasingly cosmopolitan variety of places to eat, with Italian and Spanish food featured prominently. Budget travellers can grab a quick but basic bite at the town market, and in the early evening a couple of small food stands open

⌐n the Parque Central, selling cheap and filling .meat and rice dishes.

Restaurants

Café de Don Simón On the Parque Central. Urbane little coffee shop with rustic alfresco tables and an endless choice of coffees (from C$15), popular with gringos. Daily from 6.30am.

Café Melba Opposite *Hospedaje Valeria*. The only strictly vegetarian spot in town serves options of green salads (C$50–90) and sandwiches, and has occasional free movie screenings in the evenings.

Cafetin Laguna C Estrada, opposite *Amigos B&B*. A simple local eatery with hearty breakfasts (C$50–60) and Nica-style fast food like potato omelette and grilled *guapote* (C$40–95).

Dragon Food 100% C El Arsenal, half a block south of the Convento San Francisco. Authentic Chinese food with a great "chop suey popular" for C$50. You can also request off-menu items and order take-away.

Euro Café Northwest corner of the Parque Central. A quiet and comfy café with great coffees (C$14–40), paninis (C$35), salads (C$50–55), ice cream (C$19) and assorted pastries (C$14–35). There's free ping-pong for customers and the building also encompasses a bookstore/exchange and Seeing Hands, a nonprofit which trains blind people as masseuses.

Garden Café east of Entitel on C La Libertad and C El Cisne. A cool and quiet haven from the hot and bustling streets, set around a leafy courtyard complete with tinkling fountain, is tucked inside yet another colonial conversion. There's an extensive breakfast menu (C$20–80) as well as tasty soups (C$45), salads and sandwiches, and free wi-fi. Closed Sun.

Kathy's Waffle House Opposite the San Francisco convent on C El Arsenal. A breakfast institution in Granada with huge waffles (C$75–90), pancakes (C$65–95) and omelettes (C$75) served on a breezy patio terrace looking across to the convent.

Pizzeria Don Luca C La Calzada, opposite *Hospedaje Cocibolca*. Popular and unpretentious, with pleasingly authentic Italian food; the home-made bread is delicious and the fiendishly hot *arrabiata* comes recommended. Pizza C$45–75, pastas C$75–95. Closed Mon.

Rainbow Juice Two blocks east of the cathedral on C La Calzada. While the menu is limited to juice, it's quite the selection, with exotic Nicaraguan fruits that don't exist elsewhere, like *nispero* and *jocote*. Smoothies, some of which include healthy ginger and other natural additives, are C$20–45, and you can also have breakfast (C$30–50).

Restaurant Querubes Half a block north of the market on C Atravesada. A *buffet típica*, where hefty portions of rice, beans, plantain, salad and meat come to C$65. "Gringo-style" fast food like burgers and tacos also come cheap (C$30–40).

TREAT YOURSELF

El Zaguán C Cervantes, directly behind the cathedral. Tucked down a little side-street just off C La Calzada, this grill-house has one of the best reputations in town. The restaurant is set in a converted house with a large, open-air courtyard and the mouth-watering menu includes top quality steak and fish – try the melt-in-your-mouth sirloin (C$240) or fresh *guapote* (C$140). Closed Sun.

Drinking and nightlife

Most travellers in search of alcohol and company tend to head either to C La Calzada or the buzzing bars at the *Hospedaje Central* and *The Bearded Monkey*. There are also some great venues for a night out in Granada, with music ranging from acoustic Nicaraguan folk to the ever-present strains of reggaeton.

Bars and clubs

Café Nuit 50m east of *El Club*. A chic, verdant garden-bar with live music daily; it's one of the few places in town where you'll hear typical Nicaraguan music, as well as hip-hop, reggaeton, salsa and pop. Beer C$22, cocktails from C$45. Closed Tues.

César Discoteca On the lakefront in the Complejo Turístico. Granada's largest and most popular club has a party setting, under an open-air *rancho*. Latin and disco rhthyms prevail, and the beer is cheap at C$15 a bottle.

Clark's Bar & Safari Lounge Corner of C la Libertad and C Atravesada. A disco/bar with wonderfully eccentric decor and a tiny dancefloor upstairs with booming speakers. *Safari Lounge* (bottom floor) is a good spot for people-watching with a beer (C$18).

El Club Corner of C de la Libertad and Av Barricada at El Club hotel. One of the hippest bars in the city with good music, great food and friendly hosts. Beer C$20–35.

Mi Tierra On the corner of C Atravesada and C Real Xalteva. An upstairs balcony-bar with booming speakers, usually crammed with a merry crowd of locals. Below the bar are several eateries, open late for post-boozing munchies. Beer C$18.

Nectar C La Calzada. A funky, organic cocktail bar with promo cocktails (C$40–70) and yummy fruit juice for the non-drinkers (C$25). Trying to nab a table outside on the sidewalk is a mission, but it's better than sweating inside. Closed Mon.

El Tercer Ojo C El Arsenal, opposite the Convento de San Francisco. Deliciously different, vaguely bohemian tapas bar and deli rolled into one; the wine-fuelled happy hour (5–7pm) is a particularly good time.

Directory

Bike rental Try Nahual Tours (see p.450; US$4–7 for either half or a full day) or *Hotel Joluva* on C Cuiscoma, (US$5/day).

Exchange All banks in town change dollars, and the Banco de América Central (BAC), on the corner of C La Calzada and La Libertad, will change traveller's cheques, and also has one of many ATMs in the city.

Internet Cafés have sprung up all over around town; most popular is Kablenet on C Real Xalteva (daily 8am–10pm; C$16/hr).

Laundry Several spots offer services for dirty travellers; try Mapache on the corner of C La Calzada and C El Cisne (☎611-3501). Prices start at C$55; the company also offers free pick-up and delivery, as well as bike rentals (C$8/day).

Pharmacy The Praga pharmacy on C Real Xalteva is well-stocked (daily 7am–10pm).

Post office On C El Arsenal (Mon–Fri 8am–noon & 1–5pm, Sat 8am–noon).

Telephones The Enitel office is a block north of the cathedral (Mon–Fri 8am–6pm, Sat 8am–1pm).

Moving on

By boat to: Altagracia (Mon & Thurs 3pm; 4hr) and San Carlos (Mon & Thurs 3pm; 14hr) depart from Granada's main dock. Tickets (C$30–60 to Altagracia, C$40–80 to San Carlos) are available on the day of travel between noon and one thirty, from the dock office at the bottom of C La Calzada.

By bus Express minibuses to Managua (frequent; 50min) leave from a terminal half a block south of the Parque Central, while normal buses (frequent; 1hr 20min) leave from Av Elena Arellano. Buses for Rivas (10 daily; 1hr 15min) and Nandaime (frequent; 1hr) use the small terminal in the market at the southern end of C Atravesada. Masaya-bound buses (both express and normal; frequent; 45min) depart from the even smaller terminal next to the Palí on C 14 de Septiembre.

AROUND GRANADA

Although Granada is a convenient jumping-off point for trips to Ometepe and Solentiname (see p.467), there are a couple of worthwhile day-trips closer to hand.

Isla Zapatera

About 20km south of Granada, in Lago de Nicaragua, **Isla Zapatera** is one of over three hundred and fifty islands scattered about the lake, all believed to have been formed from the exploded top of Volcán Mombacho. At 52 square kilometres, Zapatera is the largest of the islands, skirted by attractive bays and topped by the much-eroded form of an extinct volcano. Many of the pre-Columbian artefacts and treasures you find in museums throughout the country came from this group of islands, which must have been of religious significance for the Chorotega-descended people who flourished here before the Conquest. Guides should be able to show you **El Muerto** (The Dead), a site chock-full of the remains of tombs, several **petroglyphs** and the scant remains – a few grassy mounds and stones – of **Sozafe**, a site sacred to the Chorotegas. These remains apart, there's really very little to see, bar lovely views of the lake.

The only way to go is with a **travel agency**, such as Nahual or Tierra Tour in Granada (see p.450), which offer informed but costly archeological excursions to the island (from US$40), or via the Sonzapote project (run by the island's community). *Albergue de Sonzapote* (☎899-2927 or 941-2584) offers basic, solar-powered **accommodation** (❶) and inexpensive meals, allowing you to explore the island at leisure. Sonzapote's boat makes a ration run three times a week (Mon, Wed & Sun; US$5), simultaneously transporting guests to and from the island, picking passengers up at the dock in the Complejo Turístico.

Isletas de Granada

The alternative to a tour of Isla Zapatera is a *lancha* ride round the **Isletas de Granada**. Every tour operator in Granada (including Nahual and Tierra Tours) runs boat tours for C$300–400 per person. These generally last two or three hours and include a stop and drink at *Restaurant Anis*, on one of the islands. Boats depart from Puerto Cabaña Amarilla, within the Complejo Turístico, a fifteen-minute walk beyond the entrance. Take a hat and plenty of sunscreen – the sun out on the water is punishing.

Volcán Mombacho

Created in 1983, the **Reserva Nacional Volcán Mombacho** (Tues & Wed 8am–5pm for groups of ten or more, Thurs–Sun for the general public; US$10) was set up to protect and study the unique ecology of Volcán Mombacho, whose slopes are home to one of only two **cloudforests** (the other is at Volcán Maderas on Isla Ometepe) in Nicaragua's Pacific region. The reserve is run by the **Fundación Cocibolca** (⊛www .mombacho.org), whose interesting **research station and visitors' centre** at the volcano's summit acts as the centre for the study and protection of the reserve's flora and fauna – which includes three species of monkey, 22 species of reptile, 87 species of orchid, 175 species of bird and some fifty thousand species of insect. There's also an "eco-albergue" with simple **rooms** where you can bunk down (☎248-8234/8235; ❺, dinner, breakfast & transport included). There are four **trails** around the four craters at the top of the volcano with signs explaining some of the reserve's unique flora and fauna; El Puma is a 4km "difficult" hike and requires a guide. At the furthest point of the trail the views open out to provide a magnificent panoramic vista of Lago de Nicaragua, Granada, Las Isletas, Masaya and Laguna de Apoyo.

To get to the volcano take any **bus** from Granada bound for Rivas or Nandaime and ask to be let off at the turn-off for the park (at Intersection El Guanacaste). From the turn-off it's a 2.5km walk to the entrance, from where it takes two hours to walk to the top. Alternatively, you can take the "Eco-truck" to the summit – it leaves from the reserve entrance at 8.30am, 10am, 1pm and 3pm.

RIVAS

Most travellers experience **RIVAS** as a dusty bus stop on the way to or from Costa Rica, San Juan del Sur or Ometepe, unaware of the important role the unprepossessing town has played in Nicaraguan history. Founded in 1736, it became an important stop on the route of Cornelius Vanderbilt's Accessory Transit Company, which ferried goods and passengers between the Caribbean and the Pacific via Lago de Nicaragua – the town's heyday came during the California Gold Rush, when its languid streets were full of prospectors travelling with the Transit Company on their way to the goldfields of the western US. Modern-day Rivas isn't anything special, but it's actually not such a bad place to get stuck for a day.

What to see and do

The colonial church near the Parque Central, **La Parroquia San Pedro**, is worth a visit, primarily for a fresco featuring a maritime-themed depiction of Catholicism triumphing over the Godless communists. Also worth seeking out is the **Museo de Antropología e Historia de Rivas** (daily 8am–noon, 2–5pm; C$20), five blocks west of the Parque. Among the museum's highlights are recently unearthed artefacts of the local Nahua Nicarao people dating from the fourteenth to sixteenth centuries, prehistoric animal bones (thought to be from a mammoth), stuffed animals and even some dusty Latin 78rpm records from the early twentieth century.

Arrival

By bus Buses pull into the station in the market. From here it's a quick taxi (C$20) or *papano* (bicycle taxi; C$10–20) ride to anywhere in town.

Accommodation

Hospedaje Coco Next to *Hospedaje Primavera* ☎563-3298. Slightly cheerier and cleaner than the surrounding hostels, *Coco* offers simple rooms with a fan and shared bathroom. ❷–❸

Hospedaje Hilmor Behind La Parroquia San Pedro, one block east of the Parque ☎830-8157. Starkly simple rooms (many dark and windowless) with shared bath. ❷

Hospedaje Primavera Next to Tica Bus and the Shell station ✉salvador_taylor@yahoo.es. Dark, slightly damp rooms at rock-bottom prices. ❶

🚶 **Hotel Gauri** One block north of the market, ☎600-7292. A spotless family-run hotel where the en-suite rooms all have a fan and (optional) TV; there's also an on-site budget restaurant and secure parking provided. ❷

Principe No 4 Next to *Hotel Gauri* ☎937-1883. Clean, good-sized rooms (with en suite and fan). The attached restaurant has decent sandwiches (C$35–45) and chicken dishes (C$50–60). ❷

Eating

A quick, cheap meal can be picked up at any of the *comedores* in the market, where you'll find good chicken, pork or beef and rice dishes, and tamales. There are also some decent restaurants serving pizzas, Chinese and Mexican options.

Restaurants

Chop Suey At the southwest corner of the Parque Central. A mixed Nica/Chinese menu offering good chicken fried rice (C$95) and special "chow mein" (C$100) as well as *típico* plates.

Comedor Emanuel Opposite *Hospedaje Primavera*. This local buffet restaurant is a good budget option,

serving large plates of *comida típica* for C$45 (drink included).

Pizza Hot At the northeast corner of the Parque Central. Slightly greasy pizzas (from C$65) and burgers (C$40–45) are an alternative to the usual fare of beans and rice.

Repostería Don Marcos 50m east of *Pizza Hot*. Excellent for breakfast or stocking up for a long bus ride; a pineapple pastry goes for C$3, or a cheese croissant for C$6.

🚶 **Rincón Mexicano** Half a block north of the Parque Central. Offers a good selection of enchiladas and *chimichangas* (C$70), and a set lunch for C$55. Sit upstairs on the small, breezy balcony.

Vila's Rosti-Pizza On the Parque Central next to *Chop Suey*. Serves North American-style steaks, salads, burgers and pizzas (C$30–150).

Directory

Exchange BAC (Mon–Fri 8.30am–4.30pm, Sat 8.30am–noon), next to the police station, will change traveller's cheques and dollars and there are several ATMs around the Parque Central.

Internet Cafés are all over Rivas; try Cyber Yesca (C$10/hr or C$13/hr on Sun), one block south of *Chop Suey*, or Cyber Latino, two and a half blocks west of the Parque, and next to the *correo*.

Medical care The Farmacia Meridional, three blocks west and two blocks south of the Parque, is well-stocked and offers on-site medical consultations (closed Sun).

Telephones For cheap international calls, the Fono Center on the southwest corner of the Parque is open daily, with calls from C$2/min.

Moving on

By bus to: Granada (frequent 6am–3pm; 1hr 30min); Managua (frequent 4.30am–5.30pm; 2hr 30min); Peñas Blancas (9.20am, 9.30am, 10.30am, 10.40am, 11am, 11.30am, noon, 1pm, 1.30pm, 2.30pm, 4.30pm & 5.30pm; 45min); San Juan del Sur (frequent 7.30am–5.30pm; 45min–1hr). All these services depart from the ragged market and bus terminal three blocks south

---

ONWARD TRAVEL: ISLA DE OMETEPE

One of the three routes out to **Isla de Ometepe** (see p.460), in Lago de Nicaragua, is via **San Jorge**, which is just east of Rivas on the lakeshore. San Jorge is reachable by both bus and taxi from Rivas; you can get boats from here out to the island. See p.461 for more information about travel to Ometepe.

and two blocks west of the Parque Central. As well, both Transnica and Tica Bus pass through Rivas (by the Texaco station) en-route to Central American capitals.

By taxi This is the best way to get to San Jorge (for Ometepe); rides cost US$1–2.

SAN JUAN DEL SUR

You would never suspect it, but in the mid-1800s the sleepy fishing village of **SAN JUAN DEL SUR** was a crucial transit point on Cornelius Vanderbilt's transisthmian steamboat line, on which people and goods were transported to Gold Rush–era California. A second age of glory arrived in the 1980s, as hordes of *internacionalistas* visited, making the town a well-known **holiday spot**. Today San Juan del Sur is the most popular beach town in Nicaragua, at least with foreign travellers – European backpackers and American surfers together make up the biggest contingent. Located in a lush valley with a river running down to the town's beach, the setting is beautiful; the beach

itself is a long wide stretch of fine dark sand running between two cliffs. With excellent seafood restaurants and an increasing number of good places to stay, San Juan is the kind of town where you could easily spend a few days.

What to see and do

The lack of conventional sights in San Juan del Sur means that most people are engaged either in sunning themselves on the beach or undertaking something more energetic in the surrounding azure seas. The water here is generally calm and shallow, although in town, it's also somewhat polluted – swim at your own risk – so hostels and hotels all offer trips to the stunning and fairly deserted beaches just along the coast.

Surfing, sailing, diving and fishing

Surfing is the most popular sport in town, and you can easily rent boards and arrange transport to some of the more

SAN JUAN DEL SUR

N

EATING & DRINKING

Big Wave Dave's	5
Chicken Lady	8
El Gato Negro	6
Iguana Bar	2
Jerry's Pizza	9
Marie's Bar	4
Pelican Eyes	11
Soda Margarita	7
Soda Mariel	10
Sunset Discoteca	1
Tsunami Bar	2

Mercado

Cyber Leo

Bus stop

Biblioteca Movil

Banco Pro Credit & ATM

Cyber Call

Parque Central

Andrea's Laundry

ACCOMMODATION

Casa 28	A
La Casa Feliz	D
Casa Oro	E
Hotel Estrella	B
Joxi Hotel	C
Rebecca's Inn	F

0   100 m

REFUGIO DE VIDA SILVESTRE LA FLOR

The Refugio de Vida Silvestre La Flor, 19km south of San Juan del Su[...] entrance fee; ☎248-8234/8235, ⊛www.mombacho.org), is an excellen[...] spot to spend a night. It has good surf, a beautiful white sandy beach [...] of shady trees, and there are more great empty beaches within walkin[...] a guarded reserve dedicated to protecting the sea turtles, primarily the Olive Ridley species, that nest here in large numbers between July and January. Mosquitoes and voracious sandflies are abundant – take repellent. To reach La Flor you'll either need to arrange private transport (taxis cost US$25 one way) or catch the once-daily bus that leaves San Juan del Sur in the mid-afternoon. There are a couple of tents at La Flor rented out on a first-come, first-served basis. Camping costs C$500 per night (for unlimited numbers); otherwise, be prepared to string up a hammock. Contact the park managers for further information.

remote beaches around town. San Juan del Sur is also a good spot for **sailing**. All-day cruises sailing south to Brasilito Beach can be arranged – ask at *Casa Oro* or *Marie's Bar* – while water-taxis to playas Maderas and Majagual (12km to the north), leave from the area in front of *Hotel Estrella* at 10 or 11am daily, returning at 4 or 5pm (40min; C$160 return). You can also travel there by taxi (C$200 one way). **Deep-sea fishing** is very good in this area and a number of companies organize trips; try *Casa Oro* for their backpacker-oriented fishing tours. **Scuba diving** can be organized at the scuba shack 50m north of *Tsunami* bar (⊛www.scubashack-nicaragua.com; two-tank dive US$92).

Arrival

By bus Public buses (C$35) reach San Juan del Sur about 45min after leaving Rivas, pulling up outside the market. The direct express bus from Mercado Huembes in Managua (daily 4pm, arriving 6.30–7pm) arrives at the same place.

Accommodation

Like Granada, San Juan del Sur is witnessing a considerable expansion of tourist accommodation. There's everything from well-appointed hotels to surfers' dens. Bear in mind that many places instigate price hikes in high season (Christmas and Easter) and on weekends, during which time you're advised to reserve in advance. Campers have several grounds to choose from, though none are in

town; try playas Maderas or Majagual, both north of the centre, for basic facilities (C$30/hammock, C$40/tent, C$60/rent-a-tent); ask at any surf shop in town for directions.

Casa 28 Half a block south of *El Gato Negro* ☎568-2441 or 680-1902. A reasonable budget option offering basic rooms with a fan and shared bath. Quad bikes (US$13/hr) and motorbikes (US$8/hr) are available to rent here. ②

La Casa Feliz One block east of the *mercado* ☎689-7906, ⊛www.lacasafeliz .com. A friendly, Canadian-run surfer haven with cosy TV room, kitchen and outdoor bamboo shower, as well as groovy low-rider bikes for rent. Surf rentals, trips and lessons can be arranged here. Dorms ②, doubles ③

Casa Oro One block west of the Parque Central ☎568-2415, ⊛www.casaeloro.com. Friendly hostel offering dorms as well as comfortable rooms with choice of a/c. Boasts a funky garden patio with hammocks and great kitchen facilities. Beach, sailing and surf trips can be arranged here. Prices double at Easter, Christmas and New Years. Dorms ②, rooms ④

Hotel Estrella On the beachfront, half a block west of *Joxi Hotel* ☎568-2210 or 955-1288. With sweet private balconies affording great beach views, and nice rooms with shared bath, this hotel is one of the best deals in town. There's no communal kitchen or living room but meals are available for about US$2–4. ①

Joxi Hotel Next to Cyber Call ☎568-2157. The charm of this manically busy hotel lies in the large, hammock-bedecked balcony. Simple rooms with a/c, TV and en-suite. ③

Rebecca's Inn Just off the northwestern edge of the Parque ☎675-1048. A family-run inn with colourful, clean, wood-panelled rooms (fan and shared bath) and friendly service. ③

Pelican Eyes A block and a half east of the Parque Central in San Juan del Sur, *Pelican Eyes* is the one of the plushest hotels in the area, but you don't have to shell out for the rooms (US$125–370) to benefit from the amenities on offer. There's a great happy hour (5–8pm) on Wed and Fri nights, when two Toña beers will set you back C$25, and cocktails like a mojito or macuá are two for C$50. You can also pay US$5 to use the infinity pools (with staggering views of Bahía San Juan) here during the day.

Eating

Seafood is king in San Juan del Sur, and a whole baked fish, big enough for two, costs only about C$130, while fresh lobster starts at around C$200. There are plenty of bars and restaurants serving seafood along the beachfront, though the same dishes are considerably cheaper and often equally tasty at the *comedores* inside the market (C$45 for a big plate). For those not into seafood there are a number of decent alternatives.

Big Wave Dave's Half a block east of *Iguana Bar*. *Dave's* has a tasty menu featuring hearty North American dishes such as massive, quality burgers (C$90–150), good salads (C$50–115) and delicious "Big Arse Breakfasts" (C$45–100).

"Chicken Lady" *Asados Juanita*, at the central market. A word-of-mouth traveller's favourite, this street-side BBQ serves great chicken plates for C$45. Evenings only.

El Gato Negro A block east of *Marie's Bar*. A funky, colourful bookstore with a tasty menu, although the FAQs are pretentiously longer than the food list (sandwiches C$35–100, great coffees C$20–55).

Jerry's Pizza Opposite the central market. *Jerry's* has decent pizzas (C$70–125), lasagna (C$90) and breakfast (C$25–80) during the day, then turns into a popular bar in the evenings (beer C$18).

Soda Margerita Across from the market on the northwest side. Sells good *comida típica* at C$80 per plate in a simple setting with few tables. Closed Mon.

Soda Mariel A block west of *Jerry's*. Offers cheap breakfasts (C$15–40), veggie plates (C$25–50) and yummy *refrescos* (C$12–20).

Drinking and nightlife

The seafront bars are perfectly located for soaking up the sunset with a cold beer. As well as *Sunset*, several clubs and bars are open as late as three or four in the morning – all cater to an interesting mix of locals, tourists and resident surfers.

Iguana Bar Opposite *Marie's Bar*. This place is booming at night, when locals and tourists crowd the huge bamboo balcony overlooking the beach and bay. Beer C$20–35, cocktails C$35 and up.

Marie's Bar Across from *Iguana Bar*. *Marie's* is a long-running gringo drinking hole, with cold beer (C$20), German snacks and eclectic music.

Sunset Discoteca One block north of *Iguana Bar*. The local late-night place of choice to "shake it" to the sound of reggaeton, salsa and tropical rhythms. Cover C$50, beer C$20.

Tsunami Bar 50m north of *Marie's*. Hugely popular with a young, surfer crowd, *Tsunami's* heaving

INTO COSTA RICA: PEÑAS BLANCAS

Crossing the border at **Peñas Blancas** can be a time-consuming process; don't be surprised if it takes up two hours. Local buses from Rivas go all the way to the border; if you're leaving from San Juan del Sur, take the Rivas bus only as far as the highway and then catch a connecting bus – there's no need to go all the way back to Rivas. If you're travelling on to a Central American capital, you can also head back to Rivas and catch a Transnica or Tica Bus as it passes through (see p.459 for details). These buses have priority at border crossings, which may speed up your journey.

The crossing is open for travellers 8am–8pm. Officials on hand at the gate may divest you of a US$1 municipal fee to supply you with the relevant forms. Fill them in and take these to the customs building, where you'll be charged an exit tax varying between US$2–4 (US dollars only) according to the time of day. To enter Costa Rica, you'll have to buy a tourist card (US$6) in the Nicaraguan *migración*. It's a 500m walk to the Costa Rican *migración* where you'll be charged a US$3 municipal fee and from where there is regular onward transport to San José.

dancefloor blares salsa, reggaeton and Latin beats. Beer C$20.

Directory

Exchange Banks have popped up all over town, and there are four ATM machines. Bancentro, next to *Big Wave Dave's*, and Banco Pro Credit, one block east of *Hotel Estrella* (both Mon–Fri 8am–noon & 1–4.30pm, Sat 8am–noon), will change US dollars but not traveller's cheques.
Bike rental Bikes can be rented at many hotels, including *La Casa Feliz* and *Hospedaje Elizabeth*, for US$6–8/day.
Internet and telephones You can make cheap international calls at both Cyber Leo (opposite *Casa 28*) and Cyber Call (next to *Joxi Hotel*); both charge an hourly rate of C$20 for internet usage.
Laundry Easy to do; several hostels have DIY facilities (washboards, not machines) and there are several independent laundries charging about US$3–5 per load; try Andrea's, half a block south of *Casa Oro* or Gaby's, opposite *Jerry's Pizza*.
Medical care Issues can be addressed at the 24hr clinic just east of the Texaco gas station.

Moving on

By bus Public buses leave San Juan del Sur from outside the market and pull up next to Rivas' marketplace about 45min later. There is a "direct" express bus – also departing from outside the market – to Mercado Huembes in Managua (daily 5 & 7am, arriving 8.30 & 10.30am). Make sure to keep your receipt; if you switch buses in Rivas, you will need this to show that you have paid your fare. There are also 8 daily buses – again via Rivas – leaving for Granada (2hr 45min; C$55).

Lago de Nicaragua

Standing on the shore and looking out into vast **Lago de Nicaragua**, it's not hard to imagine the surprise of the Spanish navigators who, in 1522, nearly certain they were heading towards the Pacific, found the lake's expanse instead. In all likelihood, they weren't too far off – merely a few thousand years – as both it and Lago de Managua were probably once part of the Pacific, until seismic activity created the plain that now separates the lake from the ocean. Several millennia later, by the time the Spanish had arrived, the Lago de Nicaragua was the largest **freshwater sea** in the Americas after the Great Lakes: fed by freshwater rivers, the lake water gradually lost its salinity,

while the fish trapped in it evolved into some of the most unusual types of fish found anywhere on earth, including freshwater shark and swordfish. Locally, the lake is still known by its indigenous name, Cocibolca ("sweet sea").

It's easy to be captivated by the natural beauty and unique cultures of the **islands** that dot the southwest sector of the lake, including twin-volcanoed **Isla de Ometepe** and the scattering of small islands known as the **Solentiname Archipelago**. On its eastern edge the lake is fed by the 170-kilometre **Río San Juan**, which you can boat down to the remote **El Castillo**, an old Spanish fort surrounded on all sides by pristine jungle. The Río San Juan and El Castillo are reached via the largest town on the east side of the lake, **San Carlos**, a muddy, bug-ridden settlement, mainly used by travellers as a transit point.

Making your way around the lake can be quite an undertaking: Lago de Nicaragua is affected by what locals call a "short-wave phenomenon" – short, high, choppy waves – caused by the meeting of the Papagayo wind from the west and the Caribbean-generated trade winds from the east. Crossing can be hell for those prone to seasickness. You'll need to be prepared for the conditions and patient with erratic boat schedules.

ISLA DE OMETEPE

Almost everyone who travels through Nicaragua comes to **ISLA DE OMETEPE**, Lago de Nicaragua's largest island, to experience its lush scenery and tranquil atmosphere. Ometepe's name comes from the Nahuatl language of the Chorotegans, the original inhabitants of Nicaragua, who called it Ome Tepetl – "the place of two hills" – for its two volcanoes. The island has probably been inhabited since the first migration of indigenous groups from Mexico arrived in this area, and a few stone sculptures and **petroglyphs** attest to their presence on the island. Even from the mainland, taking in the sight of its two cones, you can tell it's a special place.

The higher and more symmetrical of the two is **Volcán Concepción**

ISLA DE OMETEPE

Dock for boats to Granada & San Carlos
Boats to Granada & San Carlos
Puerto de Gracia
Altagracia
La Sabana
Boats to San Jorge
Moyogalpa
Volcán Concepción 1610m
Ojo de Agua
Playa Santo Domingo
Puesta del Sol
Esquipulas
San José del Sur
Istmo de Istián
Santa Cruz
Petroglyphs
Balgüe
Finca Magdalena
Laguna Charco Verde
El Quiste
Lago de Nicaragua
Merida
Volcán Maderas 1345m
La Palma
Isla el Congo
San Pedro
San Ramón
0   10 km
N

TRAVEL TO AND FROM ISLA DE OMETEPE

The only way to travel between Isla de Ometepe and the mainland is by boat.

Getting to Ometepe

The majority of travellers come by ferry (C$40–60) or *lancha* (C$30) from San Jorge, northeast of Rivas (see p.455). There are ten daily departures from San Jorge, though itineraries change regularly, especially between the rainy and dry seasons, so it's best to check before travelling; call Exploring Ometepe (see p.463) or enquire at the INTUR office in Granada (see p.451). *Lanchas* and ferries from San Jorge arrive in Moyogalpa, at the dock at the bottom of the main street, a steep and narrow avenue lined with shops and the bulk of the town's accommodation.

There are also currently two boats a week from both Granada (Mon & Thurs, arriving at 7pm; C$35–60) and San Carlos (Tues & Fri, arriving at midnight; C$50–85), which dock on the north coast, near Altagracia.

Moving on from Ometepe

At the time of writing, returning to San Jorge from Moyogalpa's dock there were *lanchas* at 9am, 12.30pm, 1.30pm and 3.30pm, as well as six daily ferries. Check ⓦwww.transportelacustre.com for current sailing times, though note that ever-changing schedules mean it is best to double-check times with your hotel owner or a local tour company (such as Ibesa) the day before you plan to leave. You'll need to take an early-morning crossing if you want to travel on to Peñas Blancas and the Costa Rican border, though if you take the 1.30pm crossing you should still be able to get on to a Granada or Managua-bound bus.

You can also return to Granada on the ferry, (Wed & Sat 12.30am), or head south to San Carlos (Mon & Thurs 7.30pm) from the docks outside Altagracia.

(1610m), Nicaragua's second highest volcano. Much of the island's 30,000-strong population live around the foot of Volcán Concepción, where you'll find the main towns of **Moyogalpa** and **Altagracia**. Smaller, extinct **Volcán Maderas** (1394m) is less perfectly conical in shape, but clothed with precious **cloudforest**, where you're likely to spot such **wildlife** as white-faced (*carablanca*) and howler (*mono congo*) monkeys, green parrots (*loro verde*) and blue-tailed birds called *urracas*. Almost all activities on the island are based in the outdoors: **walking**, **hiking**, **volcano-viewing**, **volunteering** and **horseriding** are among the most popular.

What to see and do

Ometepe's sights are a haven for nature-lovers. In addition to its volcanoes, beaches – particularly **Playa Santo Domingo** – and waterfalls, another popular spot to visit is the **Ojo de Agua**,

a series of concrete reinforced pools fed by natural springs.

Moyogalpa

Moyogalpa, the largest town on the island, sits on the northwest side of Volcán Concepción. There really isn't much to see or do in town – even the tiny archeological **museum**-cum-internet café, with a few pieces of pre-Columbian pottery, is only worth a visit if you've got some time to kill before heading back to the mainland – and most travellers stay either because they've arrived on a late ferry or they're catching an early one in the morning. If you're looking for a base from which to explore the island, tiny Playa Santo Domingo or *fincas* such as Magdalena and Merída are more inviting options.

Altagracia

While there's also very little to detain travellers in **Altagracia**, a sleepy town set slightly inland on Ometepe's northeastern side, it is quieter and less touristed than Moyogalpa. The **Parque Central** is ringed by several pre-Columbian statues found on the island, while the **Museo de Ometepe** (daily 8am–5pm; C$20), off the west side of the park, houses a few more local archeological finds.

Volcán Concepción

The **hike** (8hr return) up **Volcán Concepción** starts from just outside Altagracia. Much of the climb is extremely steep and it's compulsory to hire a **guide** – see p.463 for suggestions. Note that of the various **trails** leading to the volcano, La Sabana – often cited as the best access route – is actually one of the most daunting, with a lack of tree cover that can lead to heat exhaustion. La Concha is probably the best trail, cooler with more foliage. The hike is quite an exercise, but the dramatic views from the top, encompassing neighburing Volcán Maderas and the expanse of surrounding Lake Nicaragua, are breathtaking.

Playa Santo Domingo

Stretching for more than a kilometre on the east side of the narrow isthmus separating the two volcanoes is the grey-sand **Playa Santo Domingo**. This is the most swimming-friendly beach on the island (though the lake can be surprisingly rough at times), and many volcano-climbers and hikers spend a day soaking up some sun here. The beach is accessed from the main

road circling Concepción (see above), although the first kilometre or so of the road that forks off to Santo Domingo is in exceptionally bad condition (4WD is essential).

Volcán Maderas

The **hike** (7hr return) up the verdant slopes of dormant **Volcán Maderas** is less arduous than the steep climb up and down Concepción, though it can nonetheless be a wet, muddy and slippery walk. The final stretch down into the crater is not for the faint of heart; the rocks are almost sheer and you'll have to use a rope. Birds and howler monkeys can be heard (if not seen) all the way up, and the summit gives stunning views of Concepción and the lake. The crater itself is eerily silent and still, its lip covered by a mixture of dense, rainforest-like vegetation and a few bromeliad-encrusted conifers. Mandatory **guides** can be hired through a tour agency or from the *Finca Magdalena* for around C$200–400 per person – see p.463 and p.464 for details. Make sure you take plenty of water, sunscreen and perhaps a bathing suit; the clear water in the crater lagoon is good for a (chilly) swim.

The rest of the island

If you have time, it's worth exploring the towns dotted around the lower slopes of Maderas. **Petroglyphs** are scattered over this part of the island: one group of them is located between the hamlets

---

SAN DIEGO DE ALCALÁ

Every year during the third week of November, Altagracia celebrates the week-long fiesta of San Diego de Alcalá, in honour of the village's patron saint. If you're passing through on November 17 you may be lucky enough to see one of the highlights of the festival, the Baile del Zompopo ("dance of the leaf-cutter ant"). The locals set out from the church in a traditional procession through the streets, parading aloft an image of San Diego. Participants act out the distinctive dance with tree branches held aloft – representing the indigenous leaf-cutter ant – while moving to traditional drum rhythms.

of Santa Cruz and La Palma – ask at the *Finca Magdalena* for a guide (C$90), as you'll need someone to show you where they are. Petroglyphs can also been seen at the tiny archeological **museums** in Moyogalpa (see p.461) and Altagracia (see p.462). Another easy one-hour hike from the *Finca Magdalena* will take you to the pleasant, but extremely cold, **San Ramón waterfalls**; guides are available from tour agencies. There's also accommodation at the biological station here (from C$200/night); ask at *Hacienda Mérida* (see p.464) for details. The naturally fed pools at **Ojo de Agua**, or "eye of the water", a twenty-minute hike from Villa Paraíso near Playa Santo Domingo, also merit a visit. If you've just hiked a volcano, there's nothing more refreshing than climbing on the rope swing and diving in to one of the rainforest-shaded pools.

Information

Tourist Information There's no INTUR office on Ometepe, but the island's tour agencies (see below) also serve as tourist info centres.

Tour operators Exploring Ometepe (T647-5179, E ometepeisland@hotmail.com), in Moyogalpa just up from the dock on the left, runs good-value excursions to the San Ramón waterfalls and guided hikes up both volcanoes (C$200–400 per person, with a minimum of three persons in the group). Ibesa Tours, 100m east of the main dock (T614-1499 or 831-2121, E ibesatourservice @yahoo.es) can provide car, motorbike and bicycle rentals, and will help you plan your route using their handy free maps. Ibesa also arranges guided volcano hikes (C$200–400 per person) and offers information on all tourist activities and accommodation.

Island transport

A dirt and gravel road circles Volcán Concepción, though in the rainy season one stretch between Moyogalpa and Altagracia can become impassable, while another very rough road (4WD only) goes around Volcán Maderas. Navigating the island's roads is an adventure in itself.

Bikes and mopeds Ometepe is actually one of the best places in Nicaragua to do some cycling,

even if the state of the roads takes a little bit of getting used to. For bicycles, try *Hotel Bahia* (US$8/day), Ibesa Tours (US$6/day) or *Hacienda Mérida* (US$15/unlimited use); mopeds or scooters (US$40/24hr) can be hired from *Robinson's Place* (T691-5044), and motorbikes from Ibesa Tours (US$40/day).

Buses A dilapidated bus with an erratic schedule shuttles between the Moyogalpa docks and Altagracia (usually 3–5 times daily Mon–Sat 6.10am–6pm, Sun 8am–6pm; 1hr 30min), along some pretty bad roads. Some of these buses go on to Playa Santo Domingo, Mérida (southern Maderas) or Balgüe, on the northern side of Maderas, the jumping-off point for *Finca Magdalena* and Volcán Maderas, although schedules fluctuate.

Taxis Minibus taxis vie for tourist trade, charging about C$500 for a trip from Mérida to Moyogalpa – a good option if travelling in a group. You can also hire these drivers/minibuses for the day; beware, however, of drivers telling you that the last bus has already left in order to get your custom. Try Victor Velasquez (T857-3659) for taxi services as well as volcano camping trips (C$500 per person, two persons minimum) and ecological walks.

Accommodation

Ometepe's accommodation is pretty basic, which means there are plenty of budget options. In town, rooms are simple, concrete and dry-wall cubicles, while those at the various *fincas* and haciendas can be charmingly rustic, with lots of polished wood and hammocked balconies.

In Moyogalpa

Hospedaje Central Three blocks east and one south of the dock T459-4262, E ometepehc @yahoo.com. A good hostel with an on-site bar and restaurant (mains C$40–120), offering spacious doubles with optional a/c and bath, as well as dorms, a relaxing, hammock-bedecked courtyard and a friendly rescued deer living in the garden. Hammocks ①, dorms ①, rooms ②

Hotel Aly 100m up the main street from the docks T941-0096, E hotelitoaly@yahoo.com. Within stumbling distance of the docks (for early departures) *Aly* offers good-sized, simple rooms (all en-suite); a/c costs a bit more. Basic meals are also served (C$40–100). ②

Hotel Casa Familiar Three blocks east (uphill) and half a block south of the dock T469-4240, E islacasafamiliar@hotmail.com. Friendly option where rooms have private baths and a choice of a/c or fan; the knowledgeable owner can provide guides and organize tours. Singles ①, triples ③

PUESTA DEL SOL HOMESTAY

For an authentic Ometepe experience, consider arranging a homestay with a local family: this is easily done through the Puesta del Sol collective. For US$15 per night (plus the cost of three meals), one of fifteen families within the female-led collective will take you in (offering rooms for up to four people) and share their home with you. The collective has small plots of land growing organic herbs, fruits and other plants; you can learn about the cultivation and uses of these plants, as well as experience life with a typical Nica family. Contact the collective's president, Cruz Ponce (☎695-7768), for further details.

In Altagracia

Hotel Castillo 100m south and 50m west of the Parque Central ☎552-8744, ⊛www.elhotelcastillo .com. Basic but spotlessly clean rooms, some with private bath, as well as a good restaurant, large hammocks and the only cybercafé in town. Singles ❶–❸, doubles ❸–❺

Hotel Central Two blocks north of the Parque Central ☎552-8770. Probably the best choice in town, with excellent-value rooms, some with a balcony and private bath, and sweet little cabanitas. There's also a restaurant and bicycle rental (C$120; 8am–6pm). Rooms ❷, cabanitas ❷

Posada Cabrera On the north side of Parque Central ☎820-4499. Six simple, tidy rooms – with rather saggy mattresses – in a friendly family home. You'll also find a basic cafeteria and pharmacy on site. ❶

The rest of the island

Finca Magdalena ☎855-1403, ⊛www .fincamagdalena.com. This supremely welcoming old hacienda, converted by the Sandinistas into an organic coffee co-operative (still going strong), has bags of character and stunning views across the lake. Accommodation consists of hammocks or camping (❶), large dorm rooms (❷), partitioned private rooms (❷), or a private en-suite hut (❻). A restaurant on the veranda serves hearty meals and organic coffee, which you can also buy and take with you. To get here, take the bus from Altagracia to Balgüe, from where it's a 20min walk up a signposted path.

Hotel Finca Santo Domingo At Playa Domingo ☎820-2247, ⊛www.hotelfincasantodomingo .com. Beach-front rooms here (which accommodate between one and four people) are clean and large, with fans or a/c, shared or private bath, lots of varnished wood and a windswept patio. They also offer small rustic cabinas, which are across the road from the beach, and the restaurant serves up buffet plates of *comida típica* (C$40–100). Rooms ❺, cabinas ❻

Hacienda Mérida On the south side of Maderas ☎868-8973, ⊛www.hmerida .com. Excellent-value rooms in a sprawling, ex-Somozan "holiday home". The private rooms (❹) with balconies have great views, comfy beds and hammocks, while the dorms (within the original staff-house; ❶) are charmingly cosy. Friendly, English-speaking owner Alvaro can organize all sorts of trips and tours, and has also set up various volunteering opportunities, from an English exchange to work at the local pre-school. Laundry services, Spanish classes, bike/kayak rentals are available, as well as delicious meals using local products (US$2–6). To get here, take a Mérida-bound bus (roughly three daily) or a private taxi (US$30; can be arranged by the *Hacienda*).

Monkey Island Hotel A 15min walk east of *Hacienda Mérida* ☎844-1529 or 659-8961, ⊛www.freewebs.com/monkeysisland. While the buildings and grounds lack the historical charm of *Finca Magdalena* or *Hacienda Mérida*, this hotel offers some excellent budget accommodation with camping (❶), dorms (❶) and basic private rooms (❶). Meals are also served on request for US$2–3.

El Zopilote In the village of El Madroñal, exactly halfway between Balgüe and Playa Santo Domingo ⊛www.ometepezopilote.com. An eccentric, Italian-owned *finca ecológica* offering hammocks (❶) and camping space (❶), as well as dorms (❶) and private rooms (❷) in rustic thatched huts. The *finca* hosts occasional full-moon dance parties, and voluntary work opportunities are available. To get here, head for Santa Cruz on Mérida- or Balgüe-bound buses.

Eating

Moyogalpa has the largest number of places to dine on the island. There are also many unmarked homes (usually with a barbecue grill out front) where typical meals are prepared from C$45. If you're staying outside of town, most of the *fincas* and haciendas have excellent on-site restaurants.

Restaurants

The American A block east of the main dock in Moyogalpa. Café serving gringo-style food like waffles (C$45–50), chili con carne (C$100), peanut butter and jelly sandwiches (C$35), key lime pie (C$45) and great coffees (C$10–20). There is also a book exchange on the premises.

Chido's Pizza Two blocks east and half a block west of the dock in Moyogalpa. A local hangout with a small patio balcony. Decent pizzas start at C$70 and cold beer is only C$15.

Comedor Nicarao West side of the park in Altagracia. A busy little restaurant with large helpings of *comida típica* for breakfast (C$30), lunch and dinner (C$45–50). Closed Sun.

Restaurante Ranchitos Opposite *Casa Familiar* in Moyogalpa. A Nica-style menu of meat and seafood plates (C$80–100), served under a bamboo-clad *rancho*; there are also a few simple rooms with a fan and en-suite bath (❶–❷).

Soda Yaras 100m east of the main dock in Moyogalpa. Serves plates of *comida corriente* (such as fried chicken or steak with rice, beans and salad) for C$40.

Drinking and nightlife

Aside from the occasional full-moon parties at *El Zopilote*, there's not a huge party scene on Ometepe; Moyogalpa has the busiest bars and "nightlife'"on the island.

Bars

Johnny's Place Dock-side in Moyogalpa. *Johnny's* caters to a local crowd, playing all kinds of Latin rhythms – salsa, reggaeton, *rancho*. Open on weekdays as a bar and at weekends as a discoteca.

Timbo al Tambo Opposite *Hotel Aly* in Moyogalpa. A funky little café/bar playing Latin rhythms to a lively local crowd. Beer C$17.

Yogi's Bar Three blocks east and one and a half blocks south of the main dock in Moyogalpa. A sports bar and restaurant with cold, cheap beer (C$15), excellent breakfasts (C$45–65), sandwiches (C$50–70), burgers (C$60–90) and fresh-baked desserts (C$10–30). There's also a movie room with free daily screenings of films and international sports matches, and a laundry service.

Directory

Moyogalpa is home to most of Ometepe's services. **Exchange** Banco ProCredit, three blocks east of the dock on the main street, changes dollars and has an ATM.

Internet In Moyogalpa, try Cyber @rcia, next to the bank on the main street (C$20/hr), or Cyber Ometepe, opposite the bank (C$15/hr). Altagracia's only option is Cyber Vajoma, in the *Hotel Castillo* (C$30/hr). Most of the *fincas* and haciendas also offer internet access.

Laundry Services are provided by many hotels on the island; alternatively, *Yogi's Bar* does loads from C$35.

Medical care Emergencies can be attended to at the Héroes y Mártirez Hospital on the road from Moyogalpa to Altagracia.

Post office Mail can be sent from the *correo*, half a block north of the central park (Mon–Fri 8am–12.30pm & 1–5pm, Sat 8am–noon).

Telephones Make calls from Enitel (Mon–Sat 8am–5pm), half a block north of *Yogi's Bar*, or try Cyber Ometepe (see above).

SAN CARLOS

Sleepy, bedraggled **SAN CARLOS**, at the southern end of the lake and the head of the Río San Juan, has to be one of the most unprepossessing towns in the whole country. Despite its position as one of the main transit towns for the lake area, an air of apathy pervades its ramshackle buildings and muddy streets. This could certainly be the fault of the fire that destroyed most of the town in 1984, or the climate – baking heat alternates with torrential downpours – but there also appears to be a general lack of civic pride. The people are friendly enough, but you'll want to plan your connections so you won't have to spend the night here – travellers generally pass through from Los Chiles in Costa Rica in order to make the lake trip to Granada, or to go to the **Solentiname Archipelago**. Increasingly, more determined ecotourists are also coming through to pick up a boat to **El Castillo** and points further south along the **Río San Juan**.

Arrival and information

By air La Costeña flies from Managua to San Carlos (US$116 return) twice daily (8.30am & 1.30pm; 45min), landing at the tiny, muddy field of an airstrip just north of town. It's not quite within walking distance from town, but a taxi (5min) should cost about C$20.

By boat Boats depart Granada for San Carlos on Mon and Thurs at 2pm, arriving in San Carlos around 4am the next day at the eastern dock by the Petronic station; from here it's a 10min walk or 2min taxi ride to any of the town's accommodation. You can either strike out to find a hotel, or wait around (for about an hour) for boats on to El Castillo. The ferry from Solentiname arrives at the *muelle municipal*, or municipal dock, opposite the town's main strip.

By bus Buses (erratic in the rainy season) currently depart Managua's Mercado Mayoreo bus terminal at 6am, 7am, 10am and 1pm, taking 9–12 hours to reach San Carlos; these arrive at an unmarked stop opposite the eastern dock and Petronic station.

By car If you plan on doing the heroic 300-kilometre drive yourself, get your hands on a sturdy 4WD with high clearance.

Tourist information There's a small INTUR office in San Carlos, one block east of the main square (Mon–Fri 8am–noon & 2–5pm; Sat 8am–noon; ☎853-0301), where you can get up-to-date info on Solentiname and points south on the Río San Juan. The CANTUR office (Mon–Fri 8am–5pm), situated at the main dock in a small hectagonal building also provides touristic information, along with a free map of town.

Tour operators Viajes Turísticos, on the main street opposite the *muelle municipal* and CANTUR tourist booth (☎583-0039), runs local boat trips (from US$120; 8-person maximum) and is a wealth of information, a handy alternative if the tourist offices are closed.

Accommodation

San Carlos has a lot of transient traffic, which is reflected in the spartan decor and indifferent management style of its hotels. There's little to choose between the few vaguely acceptable and not overly bug-ridden, sinister or noisy places in town.

Hospedaje Peña Just north of *Restaurante Kaoma* ☎283-0298. Cramped and run down, with skimpy mattresses and an experience of a shared bathroom, though at least there are good views of the lake from the upstairs rooms. ❶

Hotel Cabinas Leyko Two blocks west of the Parque ☎583-0354. Decent, if slightly damp wooden rooms with wall fan or a/c, screened windows (a must here) and shared or private bath. There's also a balcony with rocking chairs and lake views. ❸–❻

Hotel San Carlos In front of the market ☎583-0256. The place of choice for the itinerant crowd, with damp, musty, insalubrious and noisy rooms; the sole saving grace is the wooden porch right on the water. ❷

Eating

🍴 Restaurante El Granadino Overlooking the Malecón, 100m north of the CANTUR office. The best restaurant in town, set on a huge wooden balcony overlooking the main square and dock. Try a yummy soup (C$60) or their good-value half-portion plates (C$65).

Restaurante Kaoma Just behind *Soda Fortaleza*. Dishes up good, filling seafood and vegetarian (on request) plates for C$80–200.

Restaurante El Mirador Inside the ruins of San Carlos' old fort, this restaurant overlooks the southwestern end of the dock area. You can dine on chicken and seafood dishes in the C$60–90 range.

Soda La Amistad Three doors down from *Soda Fortaleza* on the Malecón, and similar in menu, although *La Amistad* does better barbecued meats (C$30–50).

Soda Fortaleza On the Malecón. A super budget snack spot, with coffee (C$4) and breakfasts (from C$25), as well as lunch and dinner plates, like roast chicken, from C$30.

Variedades Iris Opposite *Restaurante Kaoma*. Serving "gringo-style" fast food, such as hot dogs (C$20–35), burgers (C$20), submarine sandwiches (C$40–50) and salads (C$50) – a change from beans and rice.

Directory

Exchange The Banco de Finanzas, one block east of the Parque Central, will change dollars but there's no ATM, so arrive with plenty of cash.

Internet Access can be found at Cyber Café Infinito, half a block north of the bank (C$20/hr), although the (frequently) slow connections require a saint's patience.

Post office One block further east from the bank (Mon–Fri 8am–noon & 1pm–5pm, Sat 8am–1pm). Don't expect mail sent from here to get anywhere quickly.

Telephones Make calls from the Enitel office next to the post office (Mon–Sat 8am–5pm, Sun 9am–5pm).

Moving on

By air There are currently two daily flights (9.25am & 2.25pm) from the tiny airport at San Carlos to Managua.

By boat Boats departing for Solentiname leave from the main dock in San Carlos, while those for Granada, El Castillo, Sabalos, San Juan del Norte, Ometepe and Los Chiles leave from the dock on the east side, by the Petronic station. The current return schedule for Altagracia/Granada is Tues and Fri at 3pm.

By bus The gruelling bus to Managua (6am & 8am; 10–15hr) departs from opposite the Petronic Station.

SOLENTINAME ARCHIPELAGO

Lying in the southeast corner of Lago de Nicaragua, the **SOLENTINAME ARCHIPELAGO** is made up of 36 islands of varying size. For a long time it was the islands' colony of naïf-art **painters** that brought it fame – priest and poet Ernesto Cardenal lived here for many years before becoming the Sandinistas' Minister of the Interior in the 1980s, and it was his promotion of the archipelago's primitive art and artisan skills that led to the government declaring Solentiname a national monument in 1990 – but today the islands are better known for their unspoilt natural beauty and remarkable wildlife. The archipelago's **isolation** keeps all but the most determined independent travellers away, so it's a nice departure from the backpacker trail.

What to see and do

The archipelago's largest islands are also the most densely inhabited: **Mancarrón**, **La Venada**, **San Fernando** (also referred to as Isla Elvis Chavarría) and **Mancarroncito**. Most people stay on Mancarrón and make trips to San Fernando and other nearby islands. It's worth paying a visit to the small MUAS **museum** on San Fernando (US$2), where you'll find information on the local wildlife, petroglyphs, medicinal plants and, of course, the local artisanal process – you'll also have the opportunity to purchase artwork here. Make sure you bring plenty of córdobas with you – there's nowhere to change money on the islands. Other than that, there's absolutely nothing to do in Solentiname, except hunt out some of the

pintores primitivos, if your Spanish is up to it. Much of the **wildlife** in the area corresponds to that of northern Costa Rica, just over the border, and the dense jungles stretching from the eastern shore of Lago de Nicaragua to the Caribbean.

Arrival

By boat A "ferry" goes to Mancarrón (also calling at La Venada and San Fernando) from San Carlos twice a week (Tues & Fri noon; 3hr; C$80), although it's always best to check departure times at the dock. Unless you come on a tour, this is currently the only way to get here by scheduled transport, although unscheduled private *pangas* make the same trip, leaving constantly – ask around at the San Carlos docks. For group travel, you might want to use the high-speed services of the Ortíz family. These services are also available from ferry-owner José Pineda (☏ 466-4712), who also offers Solentiname tours from US$15.

Accommodation

There are currently no restaurants, as such, in Solentiname, although the rise in tourism may prompt locals to open eateries in the future. Currently, almost all accommodation options offer inclusive meals; failing that, owners will point you to the nearest hotel that has a dining room.

On Mancarrón

Buen Amigo ☏ 869-6619. A clean, basic and friendly *hospedaje* located up the hill past the *Hotel Mancarrón*. You can also buy meals for C$60 –140. ②

Cabañas Villa Esperanza Opposite *Buen Amigo* ☏ 583-9020. Three sweet little *cabinitas*, all painted green. Rates include three meals per day. ④

On San Fernando

Celentiname ☏ 893-1977, ⓦ www .solentiname.com. A 15min walk left of the main dock, the pretty wooden cabinas and terrazas here are set in a luscious garden and have superb views. Rates are all-inclusive. ⑤

Hotel Cabañas Paraíso Opposite *Mire Estrellas*, ☏ 894-7331 or 278-3998. The most modern accommodation on San Fernando, with large and airy rooms and a terraza dining room overlooking the lake (which serves as the island's bar and restaurant). ⑥

Mire Estrellas Beside the dock ☎894-7331. Cheap, simple rooms with a hammocked balcony on the lake. ②

Moving on

By boat Returning to San Carlos, boats depart from Mancarrón at 4.30am on Tues and Fri.

RÍO SAN JUAN

At one hundred and seventy kilometres in length, the mighty **RÍO SAN JUAN** is one of the most important rivers in Central America. In colonial times it was the route by which the nascent cities of Granada and León were supplied by Spain and emptied of their treasure by pirates, though nowadays the river area has staked its economic hopes on **ecotourism**. Relatively pristine, it's also very quiet and somewhat wild – the only settlements nearby are remote and sleepy villages whose inhabitants make their living by fishing and farming. If you don't mind being hundreds of miles from civilization of any kind, then a boat ride on the Río San Juan is the trip for you.

You do have to be prepared to do battle with the **elements**. Make sure you have a mosquito net, raincoat, plastic bags, sunglasses, mosquito repellent, sunscreen, a torch, good boots (available to borrow from guides and river lodges), matches, candles, bottled water, a first-aid kit and, if possible, a snakebite kit. The nearest medical assistance is available on the Costa Rican side, in Los Chiles and in Ciudad Quesada, so you should be prepared for any emergency.

What to see and do

Most travellers see the Río San Juan from a boat between **San Carlos** on the eastern shore of Lago de Nicaragua and the old Spanish fort of **El Castillo**, the only real tourist attraction in the area. **Wildlife** is abundant along the river, and travellers who venture up- or downstream will certainly spot sloths, howler monkeys, parrots and macaws, bats, storks, caimans and perhaps even a tapir.

El Castillo

The full name of the Río San Juan's historic fort is La Fortaleza de la Limpia y Inmaculada Concepción, though everyone refers to it simply as **El Castillo**. Lying on a hillock beside a narrow stretch of the Río San Juan, the fort was built by the Spanish as a defensive measure against the pirates who continually sacked Granada in the seventeenth century. It was more or less effective for a hundred years, until the British finally took it in 1780, after which it was abandoned for nearly two centuries. The Nicaraguan Ministry of Tourism, with the help of funds from various overseas governments, has now renovated and restored the low stone structure. There's a **library** (closed at weekends) inside the walls with over a thousand books on the history of the castle and the Río San Juan area, plus a small **museum** (daily 8am–noon & 2–5pm; US$2) with dusty armaments of the period, information on the area's history and a few random artefacts found during the restoration of the castle. There's also a small **tourism office** just up from the dock (Mon–Sat 8–11am & 2–5pm), run by the Asociación Municipal de Ecoturismo El Castillo (☎583-0185). They offer canoe trips (US$35; 3–4hr) and walking tours in the nearby biological reserve. Local guide Miguel Su (☎432-8441, ⓔcastillokayak@yahoo.es) leads kayak and canoe river tours from El Castillo (in Spanish & English; US$25 for 5hr).

Reserva Biológica Indio Maíz

Downstream from El Castillo, heading out towards the Caribbean, the northern bank of the Río San Juan forms part of the 3000-square-kilometre **Reserva Biológica Indio Maíz**, the largest nature reserve in Nicaragua. The climate here is very wet and hot, with the vast expanses of dense rainforest sheltering many species, including the elusive manatee, jaguars, tapirs, scarlet macaws, parrots and toucans. The pristine Indio Maíz vegetation stands in sharp contrast with the Costa Rican side, where agriculture and logging have eroded the forest. The only real tourist infrastructure in the area is **Refugio Bartola** (☎880-8754), a scientific research station offering eleven rudimentary but comfortable wooden rooms (7), all with private bath and full board.

While you'll have to hire a private boat from El Castillo (at least US$40 one way) to get to the research station, it is possible to travel all the way from San Carlos down to **San Juan del Norte** on the Caribbean by cheap scheduled transport (Tues & Fri 6am; 9hr; C$180). From there you just might be able to hitch a lift on a boat going up the coast. For such an adventure, however, you'll need a lot of time and even more cash; the scarcity of public transport beyond San Juan del Norte means that boat owners can pretty much name their price.

River transport

Boats Boats leave San Carlos (from next to the Petronic station) for El Castillo at 8am, noon and 3pm (2hr 30min; C$77–120); the last returns at 2pm. During the week there may be several more daytime departures. You can also rent a *panga* (motorized dugout boat, holding up to eight people) in San Carlos for about US$180. Ask around at the docks and compare prices.

Accommodation

The trip to and from El Castillo can be completed in a day, but if you want to hang around, the small and friendly village around the fort offers several accommodation options and is a charming place to rest up for a few days, especially if you've been travelling hard and fast via San Carlos. Just over halfway between San Carlos and El Castillo, the small riverside town of Sabalos also offers much better accomodation than you'll find in San Carlos. Sabalos can be reached on *lanchas* travelling between San Carlos and El Castillo, or by private *panga*.

El Castillo

Albergue El Castillo On the hill by the entrance to the ruins ☎939-4477. Offers simple but comfortable rooms with mosquito nets and fans in a huge, wooden cabin-style hotel with balcony and great river views. Breakfast is included. (3)

Casa de Huésped Chinandegano 5min from the dock, on the left ☎583-0191. A hotel and restaurant with small, colourful and spotlessly tidy rooms (plus great mattresses). The *comida típica*, served on the large, riverfront balcony, is great value (C$40–80). Singles (2), doubles (3)

Hospedaje Melany 5min from the dock, on the right ☎404-8777 or 621-7298. A pretty, riverside house with fantastic upstairs balcony. The rates for the large, comfortable rooms (mostly en-suite) include breakfast. Tours (including kayaking: US$35/per person, 5hr) can be arranged here. (3)

Hospedaje Universal ☎666-3264. Just left of the dock, this is a basic, family-run hostel, with small, wood partition rooms and shared modern bath along with a newly built wooden balcony (with hammocks) right on the river. (1)

Sábalos

Hotel Sábalos ☎894-9377, ⓦwww.hotelsabalos.com.ni. A great budget hotel just up the river from *Sábalos Lodge*. The en-suite rooms are rather plain, but immaculately tidy, all accessed by a large, wooden porch overlooking the river. A variety of tours can be arranged here. Singles (3), doubles (5)

Sábalos Lodge ☎850-7623 or 278-1405 (Managua office), ⓦwww.sabaloslodge.com. A rustic-chic "eco-lodge" with en-suite cabinas in wild jungle grounds inhabited by howler monkeys

TREAT YOURSELF

The **Monte Cristo River Resort** (☎583-0197 or 649-9012, ⓦwww.montecristoriver.com), 6km west of El Castillo (the boat from San Carlos to El Castillo usually stops here), has luxury wooden cabins with TV, fridge and kitchen. Further upscale comforts include a hot tub and swimming pool as well as water-skiing facilities and sport-fishing trips. (6)–(9)

INTO COSTA RICA: LOS CHILES

There are currently three boats per day (10.30am, 1.30pm, 4pm; C$300) leaving from the east *muelle* (dock) in San Carlos for **Los Chiles** in Costa Rica; note, however, that in common with most boats in this region, they'll only leave if and when full. You'll have to get your **exit stamp** from the customs office at the dock before departure and you'll pay US$4–6 depending on the time of day, payable in either dollars or córdobas. Coming the other way the charge is US$8–10 depending on the time of day. The actual border post is 3km before you reach Los Chiles; you get an entry stamp to Costa Rica at the Los Chiles *muelle*. Be aware that Costa Rican officials are rigorous in their checks on Nicaraguans in this area and there's always a chance that your boat will be sent back if you're travelling with Nicaraguans whose paperwork isn't satisfactory.

and hummingbirds; stay in one of the larger, river-front thatched huts for a real Tarzan experience. Meals are available on request from the restaurant (US$5–10). Cabins ⑤–⑦

Eating

El Castillo

Restaurante Cafalito Right on the dock, this is the most convenient place in town. The tables are upstairs on a lovely wooden open-air deck where you can dine on a whole fried fish for C$140 or shrimp in garlic sauce for a hefty C$200.

Restaurante Vanessa A few hundred metres along from the dock on the left. A couple of dollars will get you a large plate of *comida típica* (C$90–150), a drink and even a serving of Vanessa's wonderful ice cream.

Soda la Conchita Opposite *Restaurante Cafalito*. Perfectly located for a quick, cheap lunch (C$40) before catching the 2pm boat; dine upstairs for inspiring views and cooling breezes.

Soda la Orquidea Opposite *Hospedaje Aurora*. Has a sweet little upstairs balcony for morning coffees (C$6) and good-value meals (C$35–45).

The Atlantic Coast

Nicaragua's low-lying **Atlantic Coast** makes up more than half the country's total landmass. However, it's mostly made up of impenetrable mangrove swamps and jungle, and as such only a few places in the region attract visitors in any number: **Bluefields**, a raffish and rain-lashed port town, and the **Corn Islands**, two small islands with sandy beaches, swaying palm trees and a distinctly Caribbean atmosphere. Outside these areas, the coast remains a largely unknown tangle of waterways and rainforests, and should be approached with caution and negotiated only with the aid of experienced locals. Indeed, there is only one town of size in the northern half of the coast – **Puerto Cabezas** (officially named Bilwi). Although few travellers make the trip up here (flying is the only real transport option), the town is actually more approachable than Bluefields, with pretty cliffs and beaches within walking distance as well as various worthwhile excursions in the surrounding area.

The possibilities for ecotourism in this vast coastal region are obvious, though a scarcity of resources and a lack of cooperation between central and local government have so far stymied all progress, while the long-discussed road linking Managua and Bluefields has similarly failed to leave the drawing board. Meanwhile, the region's extreme **isolation** and distance from the market economy mean that you can't count on getting food, water and consumer goods in most places outside of Puerto Cabezas and Bluefields. If you're intending to travel outside these areas, or to spend any length of time in the region, it's a good idea to stock up on **consumer** goods – both for yourself and for trade – in one of Managua's markets.

EL RAMA

Poor and downtrodden, **EL RAMA** is a major transit point to the Atlantic Coast – this is the last town on the coast accessible by road, from here on you'll have to travel by boat or plane – though most travellers only stop long enough to change from the Managua bus to a boat for Bluefields, or vice versa. The town is nevertheless a pleasant enough place to spend the night if you don't manage to make a connection, though water shortages are a common problem.

Accommodation

Hospedaje El Viajero ☎ no phone. Just up from the dock on the left, this place has basic, good-value upper rooms with balcony. ❷

Eco-Hotel El Vivero ☎ 517-0340. Just outside of town on the road from Managua, this is another good option, with tidy rooms in a large wooden building, set in the jungle. ❻

Eating and drinking

Bar Y Restaurante Caribbean Two blocks north and three blocks east of the dock. This Dutch-owned restaurant/bar does seafood for around C\$140 and decent *comida corriente* for C\$60. The wood-panelled upstairs bar doubles as a disco at weekends.

Moving on

By boat The public ferry service (5–7hr; C\$140) along the Río Escondido between El Rama and Bluefields goes out of service from time to time. When running, it leaves El Rama at 1pm. A better bet is the high-speed *panga* (2hr; C\$170) that runs daily from 5.30am until about 1pm, although with sufficient demand another may leave later in the afternoon. An easier alternative is provided by the

---

HISTORY AND POLITICS ON THE ATLANTIC COAST

Unsurprisingly, the Atlantic coast never appealed to the Spanish conquistadors, and, further repelled by disease, endless jungle, dangerous snakes and persistent biting insects, the Spanish quickly made tracks for the more hospitable Pacific zone. As a result, Spanish influence was never as great along this seaboard as elsewhere, and other nations stepped in to the region. English, French and Dutch buccaneers had been plying the coast since the late 1500s, and it was they who first made contact with the Miskito, Sumu and Rama peoples who populated the area. Today the ethnicity of the region is complex. The indigenous peoples mixed with slaves brought from Africa and Jamaica to work in the region's fruit plantations, and while many inhabitants are Afro-American in appearance, others have Amerindian features, and some combine both with European traits. Creole English is still widely spoken.

During the years of the Revolution and the Sandinista government, the FSLN met with suspicion on the Caribbean Coast. In part this was due to the area's traditional mistrust of the government in Managua, and also to a lack of sympathy with the Sandinistas' values. Nearly half the Miskito population went into exile in Honduras, while a much smaller number made their way to Costa Rica. In 1985 the Sandinistas tried to repair relations by granting the region political and administrative autonomy, creating the territories RAAN (Región Autonomista Atlántico Norte) and RAAS (Región Autonomista Atlántico Sur), though this only served to stir up further discontent, being widely seen as an attempt to split the Atlantic Coast as a political force. In 2002, the Indigenous Council of Elders announced the creation of an independent "Communitarian Nation of Moskitia", with its own parliament and laws. Little seems to have come of this development, with more weight given to the belated codification, in 2003, of the 1987 autonomy law. Recently, tensions have arisen in the wake of Hurricane Felix, which struck RAAN in late 2007; Ortega's government has postponed general elections due to the weakened infrastructure of the region, which has resulted in ongoing unrest.

Vargas Peña (in Managua ☎ 280-4561, in Bluefields ☎ 572-1510), which offers a combined bus-and-*panga* service from Managua (Mercado Iván Montenegro) to Bluefields, costing around C$380 and leaving daily at 9pm and arriving in Bluefields the following morning at around 8am.

By bus There are eight buses daily to Managua, all of which depart in the early morning.

BLUEFIELDS

Despite its romantic name, there are no fields, blue or otherwise, near steamy **BLUEFIELDS**, the only town of any size on the country's southern Atlantic Coast. In fact, it acquired its name from a Dutch pirate, Abraham Blaauwveld, who holed up here regularly in the seventeenth century. It still has something of the fugitive charm of a pirate town, perched on the side of a lagoon at the mouth of the Río Escondido, though this is about the only allure it holds. Most travellers only spend a night or two here, on the way to or from the Corn Islands.

Except in May, when there's a short dry season, it **rains** torrentially. During these downpours the town can look somewhat forlorn, an impression compounded by the unlikely and unceasing soundtrack of mournful American country music blaring from the bars, restaurants and houses. The foul climate only adds to a definite sense of small-town suffocation and on weekends and at nights especially, the streets never feel like an especially safe place to be. Tourists are occasionally targeted for petty theft so watch your back and (at night) don't stray from the centre of town. This shouldn't be too difficult, as most of the hotels are centrally located.

The few streets in Bluefields are named. Calle Central is the main drag and runs north–south alongside the bay. The three streets running east–west are Avenida Reyes, Avenida Cabezas and Avenida Aberdeen. However, no one uses these names at all, resorting to the usual method of directing from landmarks: the Moravian Church, the Mercado at the end of Avenida Aberdeen and the Parque to the west of town are the most popular ones.

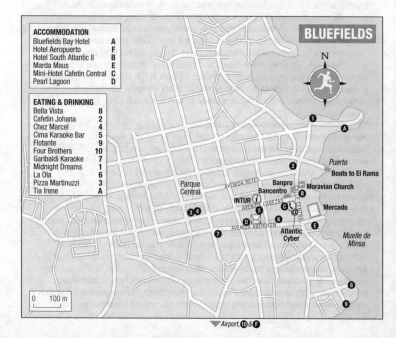

ACCOMMODATION

Bluefields Bay Hotel	A
Hotel Aeropuerto	F
Hotel South Atlantic II	B
Marda Maus	E
Mini-Hotel Cafetin Central	C
Pearl Lagoon	D

EATING & DRINKING

Bella Vista	8
Cafetin Johana	2
Chez Marcel	4
Cima Karaoke Bar	5
Flotante	9
Four Brothers	10
Garibaldi Karaoke	7
Midnight Dreams	1
La Ola	6
Pizza Martinuzzi	3
Tia Irene	A

BLUEFIELDS

N

Puerto
Boats to El Rama

Parque Central

AVENIDA REYES

Banpro
Bancentro
Moravian Church

INTUR

AVENIDA CABEZAS

Mercado

AVENIDA ABERDEEN

Atlantic Cyber

Muelle de Minsa

0   100 m

▼ *Airport,* ⑩ & Ⓕ

¡MAYO YA! FESTIVAL

During the month of May, particularly in the last week, the streets of Bluefields are taken over by ¡Mayo Ya! or Palo de Mayo, one of the most exciting fiestas in the country. Derived from the traditional May Day celebrations of the British Isles and celebrating the arrival of spring, ¡Mayo Ya! features a mixture of reggae, folklore and indigenous dance that young Blufileños pair ingeniously with the latest moves from Jamaica. The celebrations wrap up with the election of the Mayaya Goddess, the queen of the festivities.

The town is occasionally plagued by electricity and water **shortages** – a good reason to bring a torch and batteries, as well as a few candles, and to stock up on bottled water when you can.

Arrival and information

By air La Costeña flights from Managua land at the airstrip 3km south of the town centre; remember to confirm your return flight as soon as you arrive. Taxis will take you into town for about C$15.

By boat The public ferry from El Rama arrives at the dock about 150m north of the town's Moravian Church. From the dock you can walk to all accommodation in Bluefields' "centre" – a three-block by three-block area where all the hotels, restaurants and services are concentrated.

Tourist information The small INTUR office, in the barrio Central opposite Salon Siu (Mon–Fri 8am–noon & 2–5pm; ☏ 572-0221), has friendly staff who will try to answer any queries you might have, although a lack of maps and tourist info make the office somewhat redundant.

Accommodation

Lodging in Bluefields is underwhelming, with gloomy, noisy, overpriced rooms the norm. The cheaper, more basic establishments attract a raffish local clientele – one reason why some places have a curfew.

Bluefields Bay Hotel In barrio Pointeen ☏ 572-2143. Probably the best choice in town, with comfortable rooms boasting private bath, a/c and hot water. Breakfast at on-site restuarant *Tia Irene* is included. ❺

Hotel Aeropuerto Right by the airport ☏ 572-2862. Perfectly located for travellers flying out the next day, the rooms here are all large. However, some are dark and musty while some have wood panelling and windows leading onto a balcony with great views of the lagoon, so ask to see a selection. ❸

Hotel South Atlantic II Adjacent to the Moravian Church ☏ 822-2265. The priciest place in the centre, with private bath, a/c, TV and a gleaming upstairs "Sports Bar" with American football on TV and an extensive menu. ❺

Marda Maus ☏ 572-2429. This place by the central market has a selection of simple, slightly shabby rooms (many windowless); those upstairs are cleaner and more spacious. ❸

Mini-Hotel Cafetin Central Opposite Bancentro ☏ 572-2362. Offers one of the best deals in the centre. Rooms are clean and compact (if maddeningly noisy) with private bath and a choice of fan or a/c, varying in quality but not price; ask to see a selection before choosing. ❹

Pearl Lagoon Next to the *correo* ☏ 572-2411. A dirt-cheap *hospedaje* with extremely basic rooms, all with fan and double bed. ❶

Eating

Except for seafood, which is as plentiful and fresh as anywhere in Nicaragua, Bluefields doesn't offer a great deal of choice on the eating front. There are some international choices, but these tend to vary in quality and rise in price. The cheapest eats are, naturally, found in the market.

Restaurants

Bella Vista Five blocks south and one block east of the Moravian Church. Set in an atmospheric wooden building with great views, right on the lagoon, *Bella Vista* serves tasty and relatively inexpensive seafood; fish (C$60–80), lobster (C$140–160) and shrimp (C$130) dishes all served with salad and sides, and they also do some basic Chinese dishes such as chop suey (C$65).

Cafetin Johana 100m north of the Moravian Church. Serves *comida corriente* – everything from grilled pork (C$80) to burgers (C$40) – as well as large breakfasts (C$50) and great tropical fruit *batidos* (C$15). There are also a few basic rooms for rent as well (with fan, double bed and shared bath; C$150/night).

MOSQUITOES AND NO SEE 'UMS

Bluefields can feel like the mosquito capital of the world, at least at dawn or dusk, when clouds of the creatures descend on any inch of exposed flesh. You need to take precautions: use plenty of repellent and wear long sleeves and trousers (along with socks). Malaria is present in the region – see p.43 for precautionary details – and coils, a mosquito net and a sleeping bag offer useful protection as well. If desperate, try rubbing a lime or lemon into your skin (as the smell puts off most mosquitos), although be careful; doing so during the day will make *ceviche* of your skin.

As if that weren't enough, the sandflies that populate the coast are even more virulent than the mosquitoes. Known throughout English-speaking Central America as "no see 'ums", sandflies are seemingly immune to every repellent known to man except, bizarrely, Avon's Skin-So-Soft body oil. This is not sold in Bluefields, but is available at Francy's Beauty Supplies in Managua's Metrocentro (see p.421); otherwise, ask around, as locals in the know may have procured a supply.

Chez Marcel One block south of the Parque. The tablecloths and plastic flowers here indicate that this restaurant is one of the fanciest places in town, but there are some cheap options, like the Caesar salad (C$45) or delicious orange chicken (C$100), which won't break the bank.

La Ola 100m east of the *correo*. A good, mixed menu of *comida corriente* (C$25–65), seafood (C$130) and Chinese dishes (C$80) served on a breezy balcony overlooking the main street in town.

Pizza Martinuzzi Next to *Chez Marcel*. Has good pizza (from C$40) and roast chicken combos (C$35–75), served in a small, fiercely ventilated little restaurant.

Tia Irene in the *Bluefields Bay Hotel*. A popular local choice, this tropical, bamboo-clad *rancho* sits on the water and is packed to the rafters on the weekends, when the small dancefloor comes alive. There are daily specials of Creole cuisine including *rondon* (C$65), plates of *comida típica*, and good cocktails from C$45.

Drinking and nightlife

Whatever else it is, Bluefields is certainly not short on nocturnal excitement. Country and western strains dominate dancefloors, as well as the Caribbean-flavours of soca and reggae. It's a fairly safe town for walking although you should travel in groups, especially at night.

Bars

Cima Karaoke Bar 50m west of Bancentro. You'll probably hear this popular bar, a reggae and soca stronghold with speakers blasting into the street, before you see it. The upstairs club is open daily, while the downstairs karaoke runs

Thurs–Sun. Cover charges (C$20–30) only apply on weekends.

Flotante Five blocks south of the Moravian Church. Another waterfront building on stilts holding an indoor dancefloor. With beer from C$15, this is a popular spot on the weekends.

Four Brothers On the southwestern side of town (a short taxi ride), this is the granddaddy of the Caribbean music scene in Bluefields, and commands a loyal, largely Creole crowd.

Garibaldi Karaoke Three blocks west of Bancentro. A karaoke outlet for frustrated singers. There's a cover charge of C$20–30 on weekends.

Midnight Dreams Three blocks north of the Moravian Church. A waterfront watering hole with a dancefloor playing country, soca, reggae and Latin rhythms. Beer C$17.

Directory

Exchange There are several ATMs in town; one at Bancentro, opposite *Hotel Central*, and another at Banpro opposite the Moravian church. Both banks can change dollars but not traveller's cheques.

Internet Access is available at Atlantic Cyber, 50m south of the Moravian Church, or at the Cine Crismar, opposite *Chez Marcel* (C$10/hr).

Post office There's a correo on the main street, one block east of *La Ola* (Mon–Fri 8am–noon & 1–4.45pm, Sat 8am–noon), although sending mail from this coast is notoriously slow.

Telephones Calls can be made from the cyber cafes or the Enitel office (Mon–Fri 8am–5.40pm, Sat 8am–1pm), next to *Hotel Central*.

Moving on

By air There are several daily flights to Managua with La Costeña, as well as flights to Big Corn Island. All flights depart from the airport south of town.

By boat The erratic ferry to El Rama departs from the northern dock in Bluefields on Mon, Tues, Sat and Sun at 5am.

THE CORN ISLANDS

Lying 70km off the country's Atlantic coast, the **CORN ISLANDS** offer white beaches, warm, clear water and even a bit of dreadlocked Rastafarian culture. The islands are the epitome of relaxation and the kind of place you come to intending to stay for a couple of days and end up hanging around for a week or more. Like many parts of the Caribbean coast, during the nineteenth century both the larger **Corn Island** and the tiny **Little Corn** (or La Islita) were a haven for **buccaneers**, who used them as a base for raiding other ships in the area or attacking the inland towns on Lago de Nicaragua. These days it's drugrunners who use the islands, unfortuntaely, as part of the transportation route for US- and Europe-bound cocaine. The islands' other notable trade is in turtle flesh – officially legal, though conducted in a rather clandestine manner. Despite these somewhat shady activities, the islands are safe to visit and the beaches are lovely.

What to see and do

Most visitors pass through the larger Corn Island, home to all the services and with a decent selection of hotels and restaurants, on the way to idyllic Little Corn; it's best to try them both out, as each island has plenty to offer. Easily reached by *panga* from the bigger island, Little Corn is extremely quiet, with **rustic** tourist amenities – bring sunscreen, mosquito repellent, a flashlight and an emergency roll of toilet paper. Set on just three largely undeveloped square kilometres, with a po[...] one thousand, the is[...] palm trees and beau[...] **beaches**, great snorkell[...] good swimming, and a[...] of peace and quiet – wit[...] island, traffic consists a[...] bikes, dogs and wheelbar[...]ws.

Corn Island

It's possible to walk round the entire island in about three hours. **Brig Bay** (just south of the fish-processing plant) is very tranquil. **Long Bay**, across the airstrip heading east, is quieter and less populated and there are plenty of places to swim in either direction. The southwest bay, **Picnic Centre**, is a fine stretch of sand near a loading dock – it's the site of a huge party during Semana Santa, when crowds of people come over from Bluefields and the locals set up stalls to sell food and drink. Further around the island is **South End**, where there's some coral reef good for snorkelling.

About 1.5km offshore to the southeast, in about twenty metres of clear water, is the wreck of a Spanish galleon, while the beach in front of *Hotel Paraíso* boasts three newer wrecks, lacking the historical excitement of the galleon but boasting excellent marine life within wading distance of the shore.

Little Corn Island

If you're going to work up the energy to do anything at all here, it's likely to be **diving** or **snorkelling**; the island has around nine square kilometres of glorious, healthy reef to explore. Little Corn is even easier to navigate than its larger neighbour; everyone will visit Pelican Beach, as all *pangas* arrive and depart here, and most backpackers stay on **Cocal Beach** on the east side of the island. The north end, great for snorkelling, is even more remote and quieter than the rest of the island, and therefore best suited to couples or families.

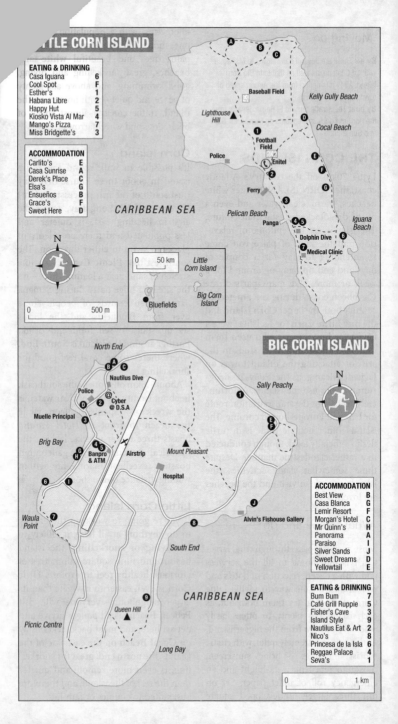

LITTLE CORN ISLAND

EATING & DRINKING
Casa Iguana	6
Cool Spot	F
Esther's	1
Habana Libre	2
Happy Hut	5
Kiosko Vista Al Mar	4
Mango's Pizza	7
Miss Bridgette's	3

ACCOMMODATION
Carlito's	E
Casa Sunrise	A
Derek's Place	C
Elsa's	G
Ensueños	B
Grace's	F
Sweet Here	D

Baseball Field
Kelly Gully Beach
Lighthouse Hill
Cocal Beach
Football Field
Police
Enitel
Ferry
CARIBBEAN SEA
Pelican Beach
Panga
Iguana Beach
Dolphin Dive
Medical Clinic

N

0   50 km
Little Corn Island
Bluefields
Big Corn Island

0   500 m

BIG CORN ISLAND

North End
Nautilus Dive
Police
Cyber @ D.S.A
Muelle Principal
Brig Bay
Banpro & ATM
Airstrip
Sally Peachy
Mount Pleasant
Hospital
Waula Point
South End
Alvin's Fishouse Gallery

N

ACCOMMODATION
Best View	B
Casa Blanca	G
Lemir Resort	F
Morgan's Hotel	C
Mr Quinn's	H
Panorama	A
Paraiso	I
Silver Sands	J
Sweet Dreams	D
Yellowtail	E

EATING & DRINKING
Bum Bum	7
Café Grill Ruppie	5
Fisher's Cave	3
Island Style	9
Nautilus Eat & Art	2
Nico's	8
Princesa de la Isla	6
Reggae Palace	4
Seva's	1

CARIBBEAN SEA
Queen Hill
Picnic Centre
Long Bay

0   1 km

Arrival and information

Corn Island

By air The better option, at least for those prone to seasickness, is to take a plane, not least because the flight from Managua (1hr) gives an astounding view of the country. La Costeña (☎263-2142/2144) operates two flights daily from Managua to Corn Island (US$130 return). It's important to confirm your return flight once you arrive, particularly around Easter, when things get very busy.

By boat Cargo boats and freight ferries are now the only options for water-based travel to the island. Currently, the *Rio Escondido* (☎572-2668; C$150; 5–7hr) departs Bluefields on Wed at 9am (returning Thurs at 9am), and the *Captian D* (C$300) leaves on Wed at 10am (returning at midnight on Fri) – phone ☎850-2767 to check the schedule. All boats arrive at the main (and only) dock, the Muelle Principal, on the west side of the island, opposite *Habana Libre* restaurant.

Tour operators You can arrange snorkelling trips through the *Hotel Paraíso* (see p.478) or Nautilus Dive (☎575-5077, ⊛www.divebigcorn.com), who also offer dives with boat, guide and complete equipment for US$35 per person, fishing trips and snorkel tours (US$15). Another option for an organized snorkelling trip is Dorsey Campbell (☎659-3634), who lives in the relaxed hamlet of Sally Peachy; US$12 will get you equipment for as long as you want, plus Dorsey's formidable expertise and knowledge of the local coral and marine life. If you can't get him on the phone, you'll probably find him in the vicinity of the *Pulpería Victoria*.

Tourist information There's a small INTUR desk, under construction at the time of going to press, with maps and information immediately outside of Big Corn airport.

Little Corn Island

By boat A regular *panga* leaves the small jetty at the northern end of Brig Bay on Corn Island at 10am and 4.30pm daily, returning from Little Corn at 7am and 2pm (25min; C$120). A harbour tax of C$3 must be paid at the harbour entrance on Big Corn. The boat drops you off on Little Corn's western side, amid the island's only real cluster of population and facilities, limited as they are. A concrete causeway serves as the main thoroughfare.

Tour operators There are two marine-sports outfits, both of which run PADI-certifying courses: Dolphin Dive (☎690-0225, ⊛www.cornislandsscubadiving .com), run from the fancy *Hotel Delfines*, charges marginally less at US$35 for a one-tank dive and

US$15 for guided snorkel tours. If dives here are full, try the equally friendly PADI-affiliated Dive Little Corn, ⊛www.divelittlecorn.com, just south of *Miss Bridgette's*.

Island transport

Corn Island

Buses Two local minibuses circle the island in opposite directions every forty minutes or so, commencing at 7am (C$5). They pass the airport before heading into town or out to the southwest bay where the ferry comes in.

Golf carts These can be hired from *Arenas Hotel* on Picnic Beach (US$40/3hr), or enquire at the *Paraíso Club* (see p.478).

Taxis Await incoming flights at the airport and can take you to your hotel; trips cost C$15, or C$20 after 8pm.

Accommodation

Corn Island has some decent *hospedajes* and hotels, which are extremely busy during the Christmas/New Year period, as well as throughout Semana Santa. Most of the *hospedajes* are scattered around the village and along Brig Bay. If you decide to opt for one of the places towards Southwest Bay, be aware that many taxis refuse to drive on this road due to its poor condition (set to be improved, but this may take years), especially if the weather is less than optimal.

There's a fair selection of accommodation on Little Corn considering its size, much of it lacking permanent electricity and running water, but compensating with stunning vistas and first-rate tranquillity.

Corn Island

Best View Tucked behind *Panorama*, just north of Brig Bay ☎575-5118. Great-value, immaculate rooms with good, firm beds and clean en-suite bathrooms; those at the back have amazing ocean views. ④

Casa Blanca 100m south along the rough beach track skirting Brig Bay. A windswept, isolated *hospedaje* with clean, atmospheric, but tiny wooden rooms. Fans and mosquito nets supplied. There are also pleasant verandas with hammocks. ③

Lemir Resort Next to *Yellowtail* ☎575-5059. A bargain for those travelling in groups, with large, cool cabins set across the road from the sea. ④

Mr Quinn's Just before *Casa Blanca* ☎451-7213. A new green-and-purple casita on the beach with five simple rooms, all en-suite with fan. One of the best deals on the island. ❸

Morgan's Hotel Towards North End ☎575-5052. Although this place offers bright, pleasant rooms with TV, fan and choice of shared bath, its real attraction lies in the great-value, newly built two-storey apartments. The upstairs rooms are nicest: bright and fresh with a balcony, great views and sea breezes. ❻

Panorama 20m north of the Nautilus Dive Shop ☎575-5065. A pretty bungalow offering several new, spotless rooms; the pricier rooms with a/c also come with hammocked porches and wicker rocking chairs. ❹

Silver Sands Near *Casa Canada* on the east side of the island ☎948-1436. Rustic wooden cabinas, just off a fabulous, empty beach, set in a large hammock-filled garden. Friendly owner Ira also offers camping (US$8/tent), food on request at the bar/restaurant, snorkel equipment hire and fishing tours. ❹–❻

Sweet Dreams Just next to the harbour ☎575-5195. The location makes this perfect for those heading off to Little Corn. The hotel has simple, tidy rooms, mostly en-suite, and a restaurant attached. ❸–❺

🏃 **Yellowtail** In Sally Peachy by the *Pulpería Victoria* ☎659-3634. Run by the amiable Dorsey Campbell, these two brightly painted, little cabinas (en-suite with double bed) are a great deal. ❸

Little Corn Island

🏃 **Carlito's** On Cocal Beach ☎657-0806. A friendly, beachfront backpacker hangout with individual en-suite cabinas (❸–❹), as well as basic rooms (❸). Meals also available for around C$100.

Casa Sunrise On the north end of the island ✉heikorah@hotmail.com. Thatched cabinas and a house that can be rented as a whole (US$40/night), or each room individually. ❹–❻

Elsa'a Next to *Grace's* on Cocal Beach ☎690-0215. An island institution, with double cabinas (❹) and small double rooms (❷) in thatched huts on the beach. You can also hire snorkel gear by the day and eat in the on-site restaurant (C$90–200).

Grace's Rasta-coloured bamboo huts are wedged between *Carlito's* and *Elsa's* ☎853-8179. Extremely popular, as it's the only *hospedaje* on the island with a communal kitchen, and the busiest night-time bar on the east side. Singles ❷–❹, doubles ❸–❹

Sweet Here 200m north of *Carlito's*. Three small, simple cabinas on the beach (accommodating 1–3 people), with shared bath. ❷

Derek's Place North Little Corn ☎665-7688, ⊛www .dereksplacelittlecorn.com. Rustic-chic, wood and bamboo cabinas on stilts, on a beautiful and quiet beach. Set away from the bustle of the village and backpacker-hotspot Cocal Beach, Derrick's is a treat for couples seeking relaxed privacy. ❺

Ensueños On Little Corn left of *Derrick's* ⊛www.ensuenos -littlecornisland.com. A collection of thatched-hut, candle-lit cabinas and houses made of driftwood and other "organic" materials, all beautifully and individually designed. The outdoor bathroom is something straight out of Swiss Family Robinson. Cabinas ❹–❺, houses ❻–❾

Hotel Paraíso Club At the southern end of Brig Bay ☎575-5111, ⊛www.paraisoclub.com. Attractive thatched cabins with patio/hammocks set amid palm and banana trees, right on the beach. There's also internet access, snorkelling equipment for hire, horseriding tours, a laundry service and a pleasant restaurant under a large *rancho*. The friendly owners can provide help and advice on just about anything island-related, and offer discounts for stays of over a week. Singles ❻, doubles ❼

Eating

Seafood lovers are in for a treat on the islands as it's easy to get a good feed of fish, prawns or lobster for reasonable prices (C$100–200). Unfortunately, Big Corn Island is also home to some of the slowest, most dithering service in Nicaragua; all part of the island's laid-back charm, but be prepared for a long wait. For inexpensive meals, there are several nameless *comedores* in town just opposite the dock (like the green house), which serve large plates of *comida típica* for C$50 (drink included). For good deals on Little Corn, *Elsa's*, *Grace's* and *Carlito's* places, on the east side, all serve up cold beers and plates for C$100–180.

Corn Island

Café Ruppie Next to *Reggae Palace* disco. A super cheap snack-stop: dine on tacos (C$20) and sandwiches (C$50) on your way to the harbour. Six simple rooms are also available (US$10).

Fisher's Cave Beside the harbour entrance, and also known as *Lidia's Place*. Seafood specialists, with large "natural aquariums"' from which you can select your dinner. Try the lobster brochettes (C$180); the portions are large enough to share.

🏃 **Nautilus Eat & Art** 5min north of the harbour. This place has a charming balcony decked in fishing lanterns, with a creative, international (and vegetarian-friendly) menu making the most of the local ingredients. Try the Caribbean curry (C$120), pizza (C$110), large salads (C$85–100) or "Nautilus breakfast" with smoothie, coco bread and homemade guava jam (C$70).

Seva's In Sally Peachy near *Yellowtail*. Locally reknowned restaurant facing the sea, serving tasty grilled fish (C$120) and oddities like shrimp chop suey (C$100), as well as sandwiches (C$30–60).

Little Corn Island

Hotel Casa Iguana On the lower-east side of the island. A busy little bar/restaurant (with meals ordered in advance, US$14 lunch & dinner or US$5 for breakfast, per person) serving excellent mojitos (C$65) made with organic mint from the garden. Fourteen luxury cabinas (US$45–85) are also available.

🏃 **Esther's** *Pan de Coco*, or coco bread (C$15/loaf), is famous on the island and comes out of the oven here at about 2.15pm. Find her on the path from the school to the baseball field, cooking out of a small, signed shack.

Habana Libre Located at the dock, this is the most touristy spot on the island – mainly due to the prices. Try the seafood in Cuban sauces, C$160–180.

Kiosko Vista al Mar Just north of Dolphin Dive. This is a nondescript little eatery/bar with great food, service and cocktails; the piña coladas (C$65; served in fresh coconuts) are reputedly the best on the island, and the snacks are tasty (sandwiches from C$60).

Mango's Pizza At the bottle house, offers a welcome change from rice, beans, and all things coconut; the cheesy pizzas (C$150–200) and calzones (C$100–150) are also available for delivery or take-away!

Miss Bridgette's Opposite the dock. Renowned for having good seafood at the best prices on the island, *Miss Bridgette's* is always busy; lobster and *rondon* go for C$150 (the later requires advance notice).

Drinking and nightlife

Corn Island

Bum Bum On the beach, south of *Princesa de la Isla*. A new bar (with camping facilities, US$10) with a large dancefloor under a thatched *rancho*. Beer C$20.

Island Style On Long Bay. Opens on the weekends, serving cold beer (C$20) in a thatched hut on the beach.

Nico's The most popular nightspot on the island, with a small waterfront balcony and heaving dancefloor where you join locals in "sexy dancing" to reggaeton and Caribbean rhythms, or swaying to country music. Beer C$20.

Reggae Palace The biggest disco in town, centrally located and spinning reggae, soca and Garífuna music on weekends. The lack of ventilation, coupled with frantically swinging hips makes this place an extremely sweaty venue.

Sweet Corn Dance Hall If it's more of a local vibe you're after, try this place, at the back of the Sweet Corn Minimarket towards the South End area of the island.

Little Corn Island

The Happy Hut The place to dance to reggae on a weekend; it's located in the "village" behind *Kiosko Vista al Mar*. Beer C$20.

Directory

Exchange On Big Corn Island, the Banpro, south of the centre on the road from the airport, has an ATM but won't change traveller's cheques. It's best to come armed with plenty of dollars or córdobas.

Internet Access on Big Corn Island is provided by the DSA Cyber Café just beyond *Nautilus Eat &Art*

THE RAAN: NORTHERN NICARAGUA

The northern coast of Nicaraguan Mosquitia is one of the most impenetrable and underdeveloped areas of the Americas. No roads connect the area with the rest of the country, and the many snaking, difficult-to-navigate rivers and lagoons, separated by thick slabs of jungle, prevent the casual traveller – or any non-local, for that matter – from visiting the area. Bordered at its northern extent by the Río Coco, Nicaragua's frontier with Honduras, Mosquitia is dotted by small settlements of the indigenous Miskito peoples. The area was highly sensitive during the war years of the 1980s, when Contra bases in Honduras continually sent guerrilla parties over the long river border to attack Sandinista army posts and civilian communities in Mosquitia and beyond. The Sandinistas forcibly evacuated many Miskitos from their homes, ostensibly to protect them from Contra attacks, but also to prevent them from going over to the other side.

Few travellers come to Puerto Cabezas, the only town of any size and importance in the area: getting around in these parts is difficult and as it's a region where people have very little money but a lot of guns, it's important to know what you are doing if you venture outside the port town. There are still isolated violent incidents in the region, most recently concerning the 2008 elections. More than anywhere else in Nicaragua, services are poor, consumer goods nearly nonexistent, and food hard to come by. Make sure you bring plenty of córdobas and perhaps a few dollars too.

(Mon–Fri, 8am–8pm, Sat 5.30–9pm), C$30/hr. On Little Corn, *Hotel Los Delphines* offers the only service, charging a monopolistic C$200/hr.

Medical care Assistance can be found at the Hospital on Big Corn, or the Red Cross on Little Corn.

Post office and telephones On Big Corn you can make international calls (but not send mail; for this you need the *farmacia*-cum-*correo* opposite the airport, open 7am–9pm) at the Enitel office just round the corner from the *Fisher's Cave* restaurant (Mon–Sat 8am–noon & 1.30–4pm).

Shopping On Big Corn, Nautilus Art & Gift Shop sells hand-made recycled artwork (featuring shells and coconuts) and postcards, while Alvin's Fishhouse Gallery near *Silver Sands* features watercolours of island scenes by artist Rainy Burnf.

PUERTO CABEZAS

Small and scruffy **PUERTO CABEZAS** or **BILWI**, as it's been officially named in defiance of central governmental control (the name means "snake leaf" in the Mayangna-Sumo indigenous tongue), is the most important town north of Bluefields and south of La Ceiba in Honduras. Everyone seems to have come to this town of thirty thousand people in order to do some kind of business, whether it be a Miskito fisherman walking the streets with a day's catch of fish dangling from his hand, a lumber merchant selling planks to foreign mills, or the government surveyors working on the all-season paved road through the jungle that may one day link the town with Managua. Nevertheless, there is real potential for tourism here and there's at least one organization (AMICA) in town organizing trips to the isolated communities and beauty spots located largely to the south. Given the friendly, and in general, welcoming nature of the inhabitants, it's a potential that will hopefully be realised one day, finance notwithstanding.

What to see and do

The town's amenities are all scattered within a few blocks of the Parque Central, a few hundred metres west of the seafront. The water at the local **beach** below the hotels can be clear and blue if the wind is blowing from the northeast, although the towns-people usually head to Bocana beach a few kilometres away; taxis can take you here for about C$15.

As well as being the base for AMICA's trips to nearby communities, Puerto Cabezas also serves as the headquarters for YATAMA (Yapti Tasba Masraka Nanih Aslatakanka, which translates roughly as "Children of the Mother Earth"), a political party which fights for the rights of the indigenous Atlantic Coast peoples, and which is fiercely opposed to central government, whether Conservative, Liberal or Sandinista.

Arrival and information

By air For security reasons, most travellers arrive by plane. La Costeña flights from Managua touch down at the airstrip 2km north of the town centre. Taxis will cost no more than C$10–15 per person.

Drivers wait at the airport when flights are due to arrive.

Tour operators AMICA (☎282-2219, ✉asociacionamica@yahoo.es), four blocks south of the main square, runs trips to the lagoon-side fishing village of Haulover, the long black-sand beach at Wawa Bar and the small community of Karata, most of whose members were displaced in Honduras and Costa Rica during the war but many of whom have now returned.

Tourist information The INTUR office (Mon–Fri 8am–noon and 1–5pm), behind the market, 100m west of *Hotel Perez*, can provide information about local hotels and restaurants.

Accommodation

Hospedaje Bilwi 50m south of *Miramar* on the waterfront. A sprawling guesthouse with cheap but

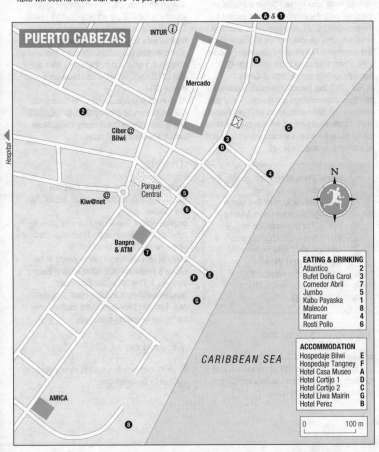

PUERTO CABEZAS

INTUR ⓘ

Mercado

Ciber @ Bilwi

Parque Central

Kiw@net

Banpro & ATM

Hospital

CARIBBEAN SEA

AMICA

N

EATING & DRINKING
Atlantico	2
Bufet Doña Carol	3
Comedor Abril	7
Jumbo	5
Kabu Payaska	1
Malecón	8
Miramar	4
Rosti Pollo	6

ACCOMMODATION
Hospedaje Bilwi	E
Hospedaje Tangney	F
Hotel Casa Museo	A
Hotel Cortijo 1	D
Hotel Cortijo 2	C
Hotel Liwa Mairin	G
Hotel Perez	B

0   100 m

poky rooms; those with a/c are more expensive but equally small and dark, ask to see a selection. ❹

Hospedaje Tangney Next to *Hospedaje Bilwi* ☏697 3518. Another ramshackle, colourful guesthouse with simple and slightly shabby rooms and the choice of fan or a/c. ❷

Hotel Casa Museo 400m north and 100m east of the INTUR office ☏792-2225. One of the prettier options in town, offering bright rooms with high ceilings and a choice of fan or a/c. Singles ❸, doubles ❹–❺

Hotel Cortijo 1 100m north of the Parque ☏792-2340. Intimate, cool and comfortable wooden rooms (all with fan and private bath) strung along a delightful balcony, itself wrapped around a lush garden with resident parrots. They also have a laundry service and do decent breakfasts with real coffee. ❹–❺

Hotel Cortijo 2 The charming and highly recommended sister hotel to *Hotel Cortijo 1*, located on the street behind main street (running parallel to the sea) ☏282-2223. Also great value, providing large, seductive wooden rooms with private balcony and hammocks. There's also a convenient wooden jetty running right down to the beach. ❹–❺

Hotel Perez Fifty metres north of *Cortijo 1* ☏792-2362. This friendly, ageing place boasts the novelty of carpeted floors and European-style glass windows; the best rooms, which you'll pay more for, are out back around the old wooden balcony. Meals (C$40–80) and refrescos are also available, as well as internet access (C$15/hr). ❸

TREAT YOURSELF

Hotel Liwa Mair 50m south of *Hospedaje Tangney* ☏792-2225. Under the same management as *Casa Museo*, this is the best choice in town; the huge rooms have high ceilings and enormous windows, and those upstairs have wonderful private balconies with hammocks. ❺–❻

Eating and drinking

Atlantico 100m west of Cyber Bilwi, is a large bar (and disco on the weekends) where you can grab a cold beer (C$15) and groove to Soca and Calypso as well as local Miskita rhythms.

Bufet de Doña Carol Opposite the market next to *Hotel Perez*, is a simle local eatery serving bargain plates of *comida típica* for C$60.

Comedor Abril Opposite Banpro is another cheap, home-style restaurant with *comida corriente* from C$50–70 and lobster dishes from C$70.

Disco Bar y Restaurante Miramar One block north and 75m east of the Catholic church, also has a small balcony with sea views, but it's not in the same league as Kabu Payaska even if the beer is cheaper (C$15). There're also a few decent Chinese options on the menu, including chop suey (C$80).

Jumbo On the main street leading northeast from the Parque. Offers a cheaper alternative of comida típica from C$65, also making its living from dancing; reggae, soca, salsa and calypso can be heard every night except Mon.

Kabu Payaska Situated on a bluff 2km north of town, is an unforgettable place to enjoy fresh fish (C$200) and bowls of seafood soup for around C$120; it's pricey but the glorious Caribbean views make for a memorable meal.

Restaurante Malecoón 300m south of *Liwa Mairin*. Another beach-front restaurant specialising in seafood; lobster and shrimp dishes are a reasonable C$120–140, while the cold beers are a good deal at C$14.

Rosti Pollo Opposite *Jumbo's*. The place to eat chicken in town, be it fried (C$65), grilled (C$75) or *a la jalita picante* (in hot sauce, C$65). Meals include a refresco or soft drink.

Directory

Exchange The Banpro opposite the Enitel office has an ATM, and will change dollars but not travellers cheques.

Internet Access is available at several cafes; try Cyber Bilwi 100m east of the Atlantico or Kiw@net, off the Parque Central, both C$15/hr.

Medical care Assistance can be sought at the Clinica & Farmacia Sukia, 100m south of Banpro (Mon–Fri, 1.30–6.30pm, Sat 8am–noon).

Telephones There's an Enitel office (Mon–Fri 8am–6pm, Sat 8am–1pm) at the southern edge of the Parque for making calls.

Moving on

By air As with arrivals, travellers usually depart by plane on La Costeña flights.

Costa Rica

HIGHLIGHTS

LIBERIA:
this welcoming cowboy city
cranks up during its fiestas,
with rodeos, bullfights
and roving marimba bands

TORTUGUERO:
see green sea turtles tumble ashore
at this important nesting site

MONTEVERDE:
walk the trails of these
ancient, brooding cloudforests

**PUERTO VIEJO
DE TALAMANCA:**
surf the Salsa Brava and sway
to reggae in this lively little surf town

PARQUE NACIONAL CORCOVADO:
Costa Rica's last great wilderness –
steamy rainforest teeming with wildlife
and ringed by pristine beaches

ROUGH COSTS

DAILY BUDGET Basic US$25–30/
occasional treat US$70

DRINK Beer US$1.75

FOOD *Casado* US$3–5

CAMPING/HOSTEL/BUDGET HOTEL
US$2–6/US$8–15/US$19–34

TRAVEL San José–Puerto Viejo
(210km) by bus: 4hr 30min, US$8

POPULATION 4.1 million

FACT FILE

AREA 51,000 sq km

LANGUAGES Spanish (official),
Creole (Mekatelyu) on the
Caribbean coast

CURRENCY Costa Rica colón
(CRC; c)

CAPITAL San José (population:
350,000)

INTERNATIONAL PHONE CODE
☎506

TIME ZONE GMT -6hr

Introduction

In sharp contrast to the turbulence experienced by so many of its neighbours, Costa Rica has become synonymous with stability and prosperity – Costa Ricans, or Ticos, enjoy the highest rate of literacy, health care, education and life expectancy in the isthmus. The country has a long democratic tradition of free and open elections, no standing army (it was abolished in 1948) and even a Nobel Peace Prize to its name, won by current president Oscar Arias. Indeed, Costa Rica's past and present are so quiet, comparatively, that it's often said that the nation lacks a history or identity. This is far from the truth: Costa Rica's character is rooted in its distinct local cultures, from the Afro-Caribbean province of Limón, with its Creole cuisine and Caribbean English, to the traditional ladino values embodied by the *sabanero* (cowboy) of Guanacaste.

For travellers, Costa Rica is regarded as the prime **ecotourism** destination in Central America. Each year many thousands of visitors come to experience the extreme biodiversity offered by its 161 parks and reserves, from **Monteverde** to **Corcovado** to **Tortuguero**; hiking, rafting and zip-line canopy tours are the most popular activities for exploring the enormous array of exotic flora and fauna. There's also the country's incredibly varied landscape: active volcanoes, such as **Arenal** and **Rincón de la Vieja**, punctuate its mountainous spine, while the beaches on both coasts – **Jacó**, **Tamarindo** and **Puerto Viejo de Talamanca**, among others – provide excellent surfing. The potent combination of sights and activities, accessibility and the country's relative safety do mean that Costa Rica can on occasion be expensive and crowded, but no trip to Central America would be complete without a trip here.

WHEN TO VISIT

Costa Rican weather can be unpredictable – and varied – but you can count on some general trends. The main rainy season runs from May to November, peaking in September and October (on the Caribbean coast, rain falls April–Aug and Nov–Dec). These months are less crowded and generally cheaper, as hotels, tours and activities lower their prices to attract the smaller numbers of tourists. Peak season (Dec, Jan and at Easter) is the most expensive time to visit – accommodation and transportation require advanced bookings during these times.

CHRONOLOGY

1000 BC Several autonomous tribes inhabit Costa Rica, the Chorotegas being the most numerous. Foundations are laid at the Guayabo settlement, which is later abandoned around 1400 AD.

1502 AD Christopher Columbus lands on the Caribbean coast.

1506 Diego de Nicuesa is dispatched by Spain's King Fernando to govern the region; expedition fails.

1522 A third Spanish expedition sails from Panama to settle the region, which they name Costa Rica (Rich Coast). The indigenous people begin a campaign of resistance.

1540 The land is named part of the area of New Spain. Settlement is slow, mainly taking place in the centre of the country. After it's discovered that there is no gold in the region, Spain largely ignores its colony for the next several hundred years.

1723 Volcán Irazú erupts, nearly destroying the capital at Cartago.

1821 Costa Rica wins its independence from Spain.

1823 Civil war breaks out, resulting in San José being named the federal capital. Costa Rica becomes a state in the Federal Republic of Central America.

1824 Juan Mora Fernandez becomes the nation's first elected head of state. He encourages coffee cultivation with land grants, thereby creating an elite class of coffee barons.

1838 Costa Rica withdraws from the Federal Republic, and declares itself a sovereign state.

1843 Coffee becomes the nation's major export crop after British merchant William Le Lacheur establishes a direct trade route between Costa Rica and England.

1856 American adventurer William Walker invades Costa Rica with dreams of annexing Central America to the US, but is defeated by Costa Rican troops, including national hero Juan Santamaría.

1870 General Tom Guardia seizes power, ruling as dictator for 12 years. In contrast to his ascent, his policies include curbing military power and taxation on coffee earnings to fund public works.

1948 President Rafael Calderón Guardia refuses to relinquish power after losing election to Otilio Ulate. Civil war erupts; "Don Pepe" Figueres defeats Calderón, becomes interim president, then returns power to Ulate. Later elected to two terms as president, Figueres abolishes the armed forces, establishes citizenship rights for blacks and institutes the female vote.

1981 Economic crisis – Costa Rica defaults on loan interest payments, accruing one of world's highest per capita debts – and instability, caused by civil war in Nicaragua.

1987 Costa Rican President Oscar Arias Sánchez is awarded the Nobel Peace Prize for his efforts in ending the Nicaraguan civil war.

2007 Costa Rica signs controversial CAFTA (a free-trade agreement with the US and Central American neighbours) into law after several years of fiery debate.

Basics

ARRIVAL

Visitors flying to Costa Rica usually arrive at **Juan Santamaría International Airport (SJO)** in Alajuela (30min from San José). Iberia and KLM are the

LAND ROUTES TO COSTA RICA

Costa Rica has several land borders with its neighbours, Nicaragua and Panama. The main border crossing with Nicaragua is at Peñas Blancas (see p.568). Further east, there is another crossing at Los Chiles (see p.573), though it also involves a boat trip.

The main crossing for Panama is at Paso Canoas (see p.584). Sixaola (see p.533), on the Caribbean coast, is a smaller crossing, as is Río Sereno in the southern highlands.

only airlines to offer direct flights from Europe (Madrid and Amsterdam); alternatively, connecting flights can be taken from numerous North American cities, including Chicago, Houston, Los Angeles, New York and Toronto. Flights from North America also arrive at **Liberia International Airport** in Guanacaste, on airlines that include Delta, United and Continental, from Atlanta, Miami, Newark and Vancouver.

The majority of travellers entering Costa Rica by **land** arrive with Tica Bus (☎2221-0006/8954, ⓦwww .ticabus.com), which provides services from neighbouring Central American countries. There are overland border crossings with Nicaragua in the west, and Panama in the east (see box above, for routes).

VISAS

Costa Rica does not require a **visa** for North American and European nationals for visits of less than thirty days, though Irish, Australian and Bulgarian citizens require visas for stays of thirty to ninety days. A passport valid for at least six months and return ticket are required for everyone entering the country. **Tourist cards** are issued upon arrival or may be given to you in advance by your airline. When entering

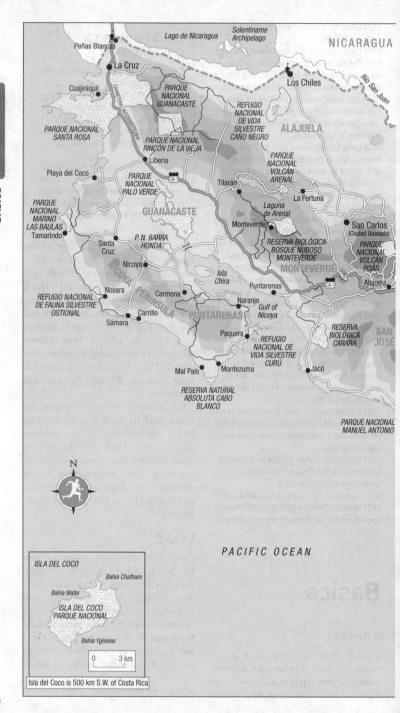

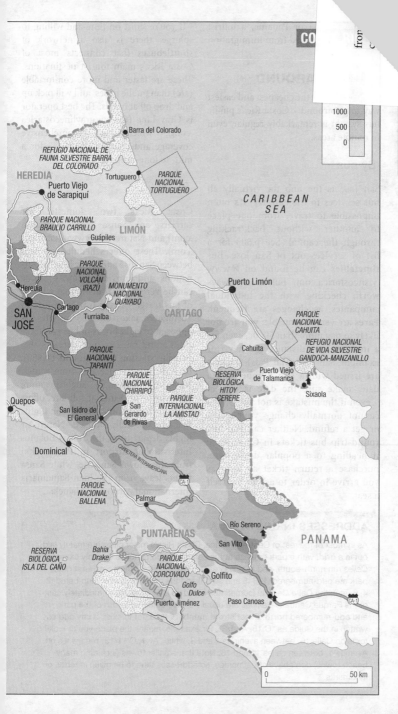

Nicaragua or Panama, a tourist
...d can be obtained from immigration
(US$6).

GETTING AROUND

Buses are by far the cheapest and easiest
way to get around – Costa Rica's public
bus system is remarkably regular, even
in remote areas.

By bus

San José is the hub for virtually all
bus services in the country; it's often
impossible to travel from one place
to another without backtracking
through the capital. See p.505 for a
list of services out of San José. Bus
timetables can be found on ⓦwww
.visitcostarica.com, but it is always
worth checking with the individual
companies, as changes are frequent.
Fares are very reasonable: you are not
likely to pay more than 5000c, even for
a mid- to long-distance journey (for
example, San José–Mal País). **Tickets**
are issued with a seat number and a
date; make sure the date is correct
– even if the mistake is not yours, you
cannot normally change your ticket
or get a refund. Neither can you buy
round-trip bus tickets in Costa Rica;
if heading to a popular destination,
purchase a return ticket as soon as
you arrive in order to assure yourself
a seat.

If you're short on time and willing to
splurge, there is also a network of
shuttlebuses that connects most of
Costa Rica's main tourist destinations.
These are faster and more comfortable
(a/c) than public buses, and will pick up
and drop off at hotels. The best operator
is Gray Line (ⓦwww.graylinecostarica
.com), which has comprehensive
coverage and charges US$25–43 for a
mid- to long-range journey.

By air

Costa Rica's two domestic **air**
carriers are Sansa (ⓦwww.flysansa
.com) and NatureAir (ⓦwww.natureair
.com). These offer scheduled services
between San José and many beach destinations and provincial towns. These
can be very handy, saving many hours
of bus travel – flying from San José to
Tortuguero takes only 55 minutes, as
opposed to eight hours of bus and ferry
rides – and rates are not unreasonable
(usually starting from around US$50).
Both airlines service the same routes;
NatureAir, although slightly more
expensive than Sansa at full fare, offers
"*loco*" prices (from US$15) for flights
that are not fully booked. NatureAir
flights depart from the Tobias Bolaños
International Airport in Pavas, 6km
from downtown San José, while Sansa
flights leave from the Juan Santamaría
International Airport in Alajuela.

ADDRESSES IN COSTA RICA

As in most of the rest of Central America, Costa Rica's major cities are mainly laid
out in a grid, with a park or plaza at the centre (Puerto Limón is the only exception).
Calles run north–south, and *avenidas* east–west. Generally the *calles* east of the
park are odd-numbered (1, 3, 5 and so on) and the ones west even-numbered (2,
4, 6, etc); the Calle Central (sometimes noted as C 0) is usually immediately east
of the Parque Central. *Avenidas* are usually even-numbered south of the park,
and odd-numbered north. Exact street numbers tend not to exist; a city address
written in the Guide as "C 16, Av 1/3", for example, means the place you're looking
for is on Calle 16, between avenidas 1 and 3, while "Av 1, C 11/13" means it's on
Avenida 1, between calles 11 and 13. Note that smaller towns (including many
beach towns) don't have street names, so addresses tend to be given in terms of
landmarks.

By car

Car rental and gas in Costa Rica are expensive, and road conditions can be poor, especially in more rural areas. However, having your own transport can be useful for visiting some of the country's more exciting sights, such as the Central Valley's volcanoes and the Osa Peninsula; there are few public buses that serve these routes, and the timetables of those that do exist often leave you with little time for exploration. Rentals vary from around US$200 per week for a regular vehicle, and from US$325 for 4WD (both including insurance), and you can expect to pay roughly US$60 a tank on a mid-sized vehicle. To rent, you will need a credit card with sufficient credit for a security deposit or the entire cost of the rental. Exercise caution in choosing a rental company – some here have been known to claim for "damage" they insist you inflicted on their vehicle. Full insurance should cover you, and is recommended. While the majority of companies are based in San José, many also have offices in Liberia, Tamarindo and Jacó.

Taxis are plentiful in urban areas – look for maroon-coloured vehicles with yellow triangles containing the license number marked on the front passenger door, and a taxi sign on the roof. Intra-city trips should set you back about US$1–4, while long-distance, inter-city trips cost upwards of US$25 – more expensive than a shuttle or regular bus.

By bicycle

Cycling is a cheap and popular way to get around Costa Rica, and it is not uncommon to spot people pedalling along the dusty roads. The poor condition of the country's roads is really the only deterrent to this mode of transport; helmets are a must. Most beach towns will have at least one bicycle rental outlet, with prices from US$3–15 a day. With the quality of bicycle varying from shiny and new to creaking and rust-encrusted, it is worth checking the equipment before you pay.

ACCOMMODATION

Although Costa Rica is considered one of the most expensive countries in Central America, there is still a good amount of affordable lodging. Most towns have some range of places to stay, and even the smallest settlements have a basic **pensión** or **hospedaje**. US$5–15 (2500–7500c) a night will cover a dorm or room in a hostel, while for around US$25–35 (12,500–17,500c) a night you'll get a comfortable en-suite room, with a fan and possibly even a TV and phone, in a bed and breakfast environment. There are four HI hostels in Costa Rica (see Ⓦwww.hihostels.com); card-holders can save about US$2 a night. When looking at prices, be sure to ask if the national **hotel tax** (which stands at 16.39 percent, including a three percent "tourist tax") has been added to the published price. For an explanation of the accommodation **price codes** used in the Guide, see p.35. Book in advance if you can; reservations are a necessity in the high season (Dec–April).

Camping is fairly widespread. In the beach towns especially, you will usually find at least one well-equipped private campsite. Alternatively, you might be able to find a hotelier (usually in an establishment at the lower end of the price scale) willing to let you pitch your tent in the grounds. Though not all national parks have campsites, the ones that do are generally good, with at least some basic facilities, and cost around US$3 per person per day. You may also be able to bunk at the ranger station in some national parks.

FOOD AND DRINK

The cheapest places to eat in Costa Rica are **sodas**, which are a sort of cross between North American diners and

British greasy spoons. *Sodas*, serving breakfast and lunch options, offer set *platos del día* (daily specials) for about US$4. **Restaurants**, particularly those serving international fare, can be pricey – expect to pay from US$10 for a main course in the capital, and almost double that in coastal towns. A town's central **market** is usually a safe bet for a quick feed, and if you tire of rice and beans or roast chicken, most towns will have a budget-friendly pizza parlour or Chinese restaurant. In general, eateries here **open** early, around 7am, and most are empty or closed by 10 or 10.30pm.

Tican cuisine can be economical and filling, with staples such as **gallo pinto** ("painted rooster"), a breakfast dish of rice and beans, often served with meat or eggs, and **casados** ("married"), combinations of rice, beans, salad, plantain and some kind of meat of fish that are frequently large enough for two to share. Fried/roast chicken is a national favourite, with cheap and cheerful chains such as *Rosti Pollos* found everywhere. **Bocas** ("mouth" snacks) are great for keeping hunger at bay, and are commonly offered at bars where there's no formal menu. Fresh **fruit** is cheap and plentiful – try some less familiar fruits, like *mamones chinos* (a kind of lychee), *maracuya* (passion fruit) and *marañón*, whose seed is the cashew nut. With so much fresh produce, vegetarians generally do quite well in Costa Rica; most menus will have a meat-free option. You will also find excellent fresh **fish** here, including *pargo* (red snapper) and *corvina* (sea bass), with Tican-style *ceviche* as a speciality.

Drink

Costa Rica is famous for its **coffee**, and it is not hard to locate a decent *café negro*. Another highlight of Costa Rica are its **juices** or *refrescos naturales*, combining fresh tropical fruit, ice and either milk (*leche*) or water (*agua*). You'll find **herb teas** throughout the country; those

served in Limón are especially good. In Guanacaste you can get the distinctive corn-based drinks **horchata** and **pinolillo**.

Costa Rica has several local brands of lager **beer** (all brewed by the same company). Most popular, and cheapest, is Imperial, but Bavaria Gold is the best of the bunch. Pilsen and Rock Ice (beer with lemon flavour) are also worth a try. Imported beers are available in bars, restaurants and hotels as pricier options.

For an after-dinner drink, try creamy, Baileys-style coffee **liqueurs** such as the famous Café Rica. For those with a stronger stomach, there is an indigenous sugarcane-based spirit, **guaro**, of which Cacique is the most popular brand. The **drinking age** in Costa Rica is 18, and many clubs and bars will only admit those with ID, so carry a photocopy of your passport.

CULTURE AND ETIQUETTE

Costa Rica is a friendly country. Although many Ticos speak English, an effort to **communicate** in Spanish is much appreciated; a greeting – usually "Buenas", a shortening of "good day/afternoon/evening" – is always well received. Though officially a **Catholic** nation, the degrees of orthodoxy are hugely varied and many denominations of Christianity are observed.

Macho attitudes still exist. Gay and lesbian travellers should be discreet, but an increasing number of gay-friendly hotels and nightclubs, particularly in the capital, tells of a gradual shift in mentality. Solo **women** can travel alone with relative confidence. While gringa-enticement is a rather competitive and popular way to pass the time – particularly in beach towns – and such focused attention can be intimidating, it is usually harmless and can be easily ignored. Women wanting to visit a church will need to make sure their shoulders are covered and that they have something to cover their heads.

Friendly **bartering** is worth a try at craft and artisan markets, but you are unlikely to get discounts anywhere else. In regard to **tipping**, most restaurants include a ten percent service charge in the bill. In fancier establishments, a small tip is expected. It is also polite to offer a token amount when photographing locals or performers (especially in a touristy setting).

SPORTS AND OUTDOOR ACTIVITIES

With a national team that has qualified for the last three World Cups, **fútbol** (or soccer) is Costa Rica's most popular spectator sport. There's a fiercely competitive national league, and you'll find some kind of pitch in every town. Check Ⓦwww.futboltico.com for current information on the national teams, tickets and schedules.

The nation's **surf** – some of the best in Central America – is one of its biggest draws. Over fifty well-known breaks dot the Pacific and Southern Caribbean coasts, and all beach communities offer a selection of teachers and board rental companies; Jacó, Mal País and Puerto Viejo are among the most popular beach locations. The teeming oceans (and rivers) also bring in masses of sport-fishing and scuba-diving fanatics, although prices are generally steep. **Snorkelling** is the most economical way to get up close to the marine life. The best areas for exploring brilliant corals are Cahuita and Manzanillo, where equipment rental is available from local tour offices and may even be provided by your hotel or *cabina*. **Kayaking** is growing in popularity as a good, green way to explore the country's many lagoons, rivers and beaches. **Whitewater rafting** is a more exciting way to do the same. Organized tours are readily available.

There's also a vast array of land-based sights on offer, and many activities with which to enjoy them. Zip-line **canopy tours** make the most of the country's ancient rainforests, while **hiking** is the best way to visit the nation's many volcanic sites; **horseriding** is also frequently offered for volcano tours but check the condition of the horses before you pay, as animal neglect or mistreatment is not unknown.

COMMUNICATIONS

The most reliable place from which to send **mail** is San José's Correo Central, or main post office (see p.505), which is also the best place to collect post. Most towns here have a *correo* where stamps can be purchased and letters sent, but those along the coasts (particularly the Caribbean) can be extremely slow at shifting post. **Opening hours** for nearly all Costa Rica's post offices are Monday to Friday from 7.30am to 6pm. Those in San José and Liberia also have limited Saturday hours (8am–noon).

Public **phones** require phonecards (*tarjetas telefónica*), which are available from most grocery stores, street kiosks and pharmacies. The cards can be used at any public payphone, or (with permission) on hotel and residential phone lines. ☎199 cards are for international calls, ☎197 cards for domestic/local calls; international cards come in two denominations: 3000c (17min talk time to the US, 12min to Europe) and 10,000c. Many payphones also accept credit cards. Dial ☏09 or 116 to get an English-speaking operator and make a collect call overseas; dial ☏110 for internal collect calls. There are no area codes and all phone numbers have eight digits. As of March 2008, ☏2 precedes all landline numbers, while mobile phone numbers are prefixed with an ☏8. Visitors cannot purchase local, pre-paid SIM cards for **mobile phones** (you must be a resident to do so); however, some of the more upmarket hotels and car-rental agencies may be able to arrange mobile phone rentals. While tri-band European cell phones are more likely to get a signal than those from the US, roaming charges will be very high in both cases.

Internet rates are low in major towns – usually US$1–1.50 per hour – and rise up to US$3 per hour in smaller towns and more remote areas; you'll find an internet café in almost every town in Costa Rica. Many hostels and hotels, particularly in the capital, will provide free internet.

CRIME AND SAFETY

Costa Rica is a relatively safe country and the crime that does exist tends to be **opportunistic** rather than violent. Pick-pocketing and luggage theft are the greatest threats facing most travellers; it is never safe to leave possessions unattended, especially on the beach. If you have anything stolen you will need to report it immediately at the nearest police station (*estación de policía*, or *guardia rural* in rural areas), where you can file a report. Tourist-related crime, such as overcharging, can be addressed to the ICT in San José (see p.500).

Car-related crime, particularly that which involves rental vehicles, is on the rise, so park vehicles securely (never on the street), especially at night. A common scam is to pre-puncture rental-car tires, follow the car and pull over to "offer assistance"; beware of good Samaritans on the roadside. Drivers with a puncture are recommended to keep driving to the nearest service station or public area to change tires.

MEDICAL CARE AND EMERGENCIES

The **medical care** in the Valle Central (where ☏911 is fully functional) is much better than in neighbouring countries,

EMERGENCY NUMBERS

All emergencies ☏911
Police ☏117
Fire ☏118
Red Cross ☏128
Traffic police ☏2222-9330/9245
Private ambulance Emergencias 2000, Guanacaste and Puntarenas ☏2380-4125

but the coastal areas and more remote corners of the country are lacking in doctors and facilities. **Pharmacies**, found in almost every town and generally open from 8am to 4.30pm, might be able to suggest a local with medical experience in case of emergency; otherwise, head to a hospital in the nearest large city.

INFORMATION AND MAPS

The best source of **information** about Costa Rica is the Instituto Costarricense de Turismo, or ICT (@www.visitcostarica.com). The main office (☎2299-5800) is in San José, somewhat inconveniently located on the Juan Pablo II Bridge along the General Cañas highway; a smaller San José branch (☎2222-1090) sits in a bunker underneath the Plaza de la Cultura. The staff can provide up-to-date maps, museum details and bus schedules. There are small ICT booths at the main entry points to the country – Peñas Blancas on the Nicaraguan border and San José's Santamaría International Airport – and in Papagayo, Guanacaste. Aside from these, there are no other official tourist offices, and you'll have to rely on locally run initiatives, hotels and tourist agencies for information.

For **maps**, @www.maptak.com has handy, downloadable plans of the provinces and their capitals, as does the Costa Rica Guide (see "Costa Rica on the Net" box opposite). Many places will have an informative town map on a billboard; these are usually centrally located.

MONEY AND BANKS

The official currency of Costa Rica is the **colón** ("c"; plural *colones*), colloquially referred to as "pesos". There are two types of **coin** in circulation: the old silver ones (denominations of 5, 10 and 20) and newer gold ones (denominations of 5, 10, 25, 50, 100 and 500). There are also four bank **notes** (1000,

2000, 5000 and 10,000 colones). Many establishments will not accept torn notes; these can be exchanged at banks. US dollars (US$) are accepted at hotels and tourist sights across the nation, but *colones* are generally necessary for local transport and food.

Banking hours tend to be Monday to Friday, 9am to 4pm. Banco Nacional de Costa Rica (@www.bncr.fi.cr) is the country's most popular bank, with branches nation-wide. **Debit cards** are extremely useful, with most cities and towns boasting at least one ATM machine, or *cajero automático* (though there are none in Tortuguero). **Credit cards** are generally handy for making deposits or even obtaining cash advances; Visa is more widely accepted than MasterCard. **Traveller's cheques** should be bought in US dollars only – Costa Rican bank staff will stare blankly at other currencies. Bring plenty of cash when visiting smaller towns and beaches, as banking facilities can be scarce.

SPANISH LANGUAGE

"Pura vida" or "pure life", pronounced "poo-ra vee-da", is a phrase you are bound to hear. It is used to mean "cool", "all right", "all good" and so on.

OPENING HOURS AND PUBLIC HOLIDAYS

Shops and businesses are usually open weekdays from 9am to 6pm (**malls** open about 10am–9pm), with shorter hours on Saturdays. Most businesses are closed on Sundays, while many museums shut on Mondays. The main public holidays, when all banks, post offices, museums and government offices close, are listed in the box below.

FESTIVALS

Costa Rica celebrates many **festivals**, or *feriados*, throughout the calendar year. The dates below only touch on the highlights – Ticos love a party and find many excuses for celebration.

January Palmares Civic Fiesta is celebrated over two weeks with concerts, carnival rides and bullfights.

March Celebrations held throughout the country in honour of San José Day (March 19).

PUBLIC HOLIDAYS

January 1 New Year's Day

March/April Holy Thursday, Good Friday, Holy Saturday, Easter Monday

May 1 Labour Day

July 25 Guanacaste Day (Guanacaste Province only)

August 15 Mother's Day/Assumption Day

September 15 Independence Day

December 25 Christmas Day

April Fiesta honouring Juan Santamaría on April 11 marks the death of Costa Rica's national hero.

August The Nation's Patron Saint, La Negrita, is honoured with a pilgrimage to Cartago (Aug 2).

October The whole country, but particularly Límon Province, where there are Carnival festivities, celebrates its day of discovery, Columbus Day (Oct 12).

December The last week of the month is a non-stop street party in Zapotee, with music, bullfights, rides and games as part of the celebrations.

San José

Sprawling smack in the middle of the fertile Valle Central, **SAN JOSÉ** has a spectacular setting, ringed by soaring mountains and volcanoes on all sides. That's where the compliments end, however, and you'll be hard pressed to find anyone, even a native *Josefino*, who has much good to say about the city's potholed streets and car-dealership architecture – not to mention the choking diesel fumes, kamikaze drivers and chaotically unplanned expansion. In general, travellers talk about San José as they do about bank lines and immigration offices: a pain, but unavoidable. This said, if you've been travelling through the region, you'll find that compared to, say, Managua or Guatemala City, San José has some vibrant and cosmopolitan offerings. Most people end up spending a few days here – the city is a major transportation hub, and many journeys across the country involve backtracking through the capital – and find they can enjoy it.

What to see and do

Few travellers come to San José for the sights, and it is certainly not a place that exudes immediate appeal. It does have its diversions, however, including some nice museums and galleries. It's also a manageable city, with all the attractions close together. The **Parque** Central lies at the centre of the city, but the **Plaza de la Cultura** is considered San José's social core. The area around it is subdivided into little neighbourhoods (**barrios**) that flow seamlessly into one another. Barrios Amón and Otoya, in the north, are the prettiest, while those to the east – La California, Escalante and Los Yoses – are home to comfortable houses and the odd embassy. Further east lies the studenty municipality of **San Pedro**, home to the University of Costa Rica (UCR).

Museo de Oro Precolombino

The Plaza de la Cultura cleverly conceals one of San José's treasures, the **Museo de Oro Precolombino**, or pre-Columbian Gold Museum (daily 9.30am–5pm; 3900c; ☎2243-4216, ⓦ www.museosdelbancocentral.org). The bunker-like underground space is a touch gloomy, but the gold on display is truly impressive and includes the largest array of animal-shaped gold ornaments and figurines in Central America. The exhibition also has dioramas, photos and a short video which explain the animal-influences and uses of gold in Costa Rica's ancient indigenous cultures.

Teatro Nacional

San José's heavily columned, grey-brown **Teatro Nacional** (Mon–Sat 9am–4pm, with complimentary tours every hour; 2800c; ☎2221-5341,

---

SAFETY IN SAN JOSÉ

San José is a relatively safe city, but there is still some degree of danger, mainly in mugging, purse-snatching or jewellery-grabbing. Keep a tight grip on your belongings, especially around the Coca-Cola bus terminal and the area east of the station – roughly from C 20 to 0, between Av 0 and 9 – which encompasses the *zona roja*, or red light area. Other dodgy areas, day and night, include Merced (C 4/12, Av 4/10) just southwest of the centre. If driving in the centre of the city, keep windows rolled up so no one can reach in and snatch your bag.

Also, watch out when crossing the street, anywhere in the city: drivers can be aggressive and accidents involving pedestrians are common.

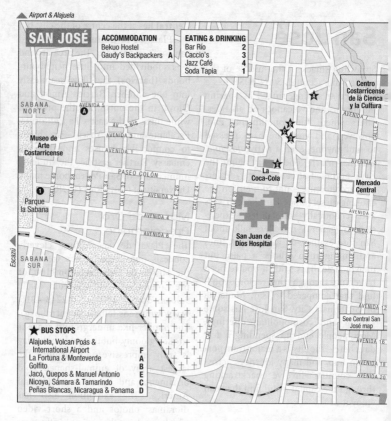

SAN JOSÉ

ACCOMMODATION	
Bekuo Hostel	B
Gaudy's Backpackers	A

EATING & DRINKING	
Bar Río	2
Caccio's	3
Jazz Café	4
Soda Tapia	1

Airport & Alajuela

AVENIDA 7

SABANA NORTE

AVENIDA 5

Centro Costarricense de la Cienca y la Cultura

AVENIDA 7

AV 3-BIS

AVENIDA 3

Museo de Arte Costarricense

AVENIDA 1

AVENIDA 3

PASEO COLÓN

La Coca-Cola

Mercado Central

Parque la Sabana

AVENIDA 26

AVENIDA 2

AVENIDA 4

AVENIDA 6

San Juan de Díos Hospital

AVENIDA 2

AVENIDA 4

SABANA SUR

Escazú

See Central San José map

AVENIDA 12

AVENIDA 16

AVENIDA 18

AVENIDA 20

★ BUS STOPS	
Alajuela, Volcan Poás & International Airport	F
La Fortuna & Monteverde	A
Golfito	B
Jacó, Quepos & Manuel Antonio	E
Nicoya, Sámara & Tamarindo	C
Peñas Blancas, Nicaragua & Panama	D

www.teatronacional.go.cr) sits on the corner of C 5 and Av 2, behind the Plaza de la Cultura. The theatre's marbled stairways, gilt cherubs and red-velvet carpets would look more at home in Old Europe than in Central America, and remain in remarkably good condition, despite the dual onslaught of the climate and a succession of earthquakes. During the day you can wander around the post-Baroque splendour, even if you're not coming to see a performance (see p.504 for details). In the gallery (Mon–Sat 9am–4pm; free), ever-changing exhibits are open to the public; check the website for details. The elegant attached café (Mon–Fri 9am–5pm, Sat 9am–4pm) serves pricey coffees and European-style cakes.

Museo del Jade

Three blocks northeast of the Plaza de la Cultura, at Av 7, C 9/11, on the north side of Parque España, rises the INS, or Institute of Social Security, building. On its eleventh floor, this uninspiring edifice houses one of the city's finest museums, the **Museo del Jade** (Mon–Fri 8.30am–3.30pm, Sat 9am–1pm; 1100c; ☎2287-6034, ⓦportal .ins-cr.com/Social/MuseoJade), which is home to the world's largest collection of American jade. The displays are subtly backlit to show off the multi-coloured and multitextured pieces to full effect. You'll see a lot of **axe-gods** – anthropomorphic bird/human forms shaped like an axe and worn as a pendant – as well as various ornate (and rather heavy-looking) necklaces

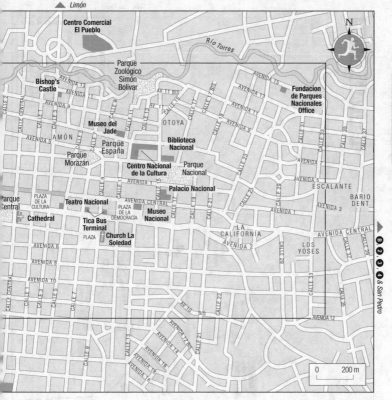

and fertility symbols. Incidentally, the **view** from the museum windows is one of the best in the city, taking in the sweep of San José from the centre to the south and then west to the mountains.

Museo de Arte y Diseño Contemporáneo

Sprawling across the entire eastern border of the Parque España, the former National Liquor Factory, dating from 1887, today houses the Centro Nacional de Cultura, home to the cutting-edge **Museo de Arte y Diseño Contemporáneo** (Mon–Sat 10.30am–5.30pm; 1100c (free Mon); ☎2257-7202, ❅www .madc.ac.cr). The cosmopolitan, multimedia displays features pieces by domestic artists as well as works from across Latin America. Exhibits change frequently, but the museum is definitely worth a visit to see what's going on in the arts in the Americas. There's also a theatre in the complex – a wander around during the day may offer interesting glimpses of dancers and musicians rehearsing. Unfortunately, performances are not open to the public.

Museo Nacional

Heading two blocks south from the Centro Nacional de Cultura along C 11 brings you to the concrete Plaza de la Democracia, a rather soulless square. A mess of terraced concrete slopes up towards the fortress-like edifice of the **Museo Nacional**

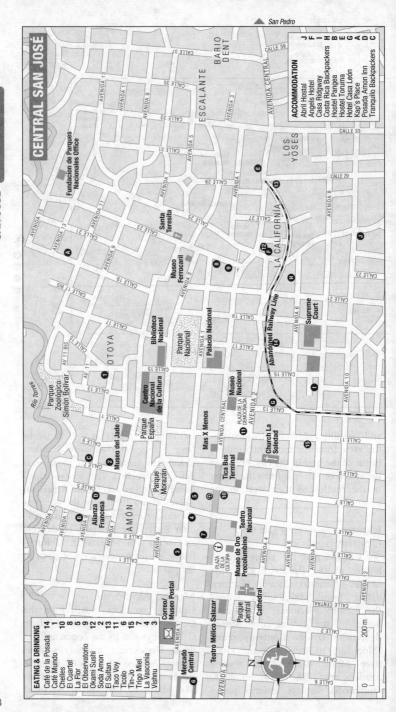

CENTRAL SAN JOSÉ

EATING & DRINKING
Café de la Posada   14
Café Mundo   10
Chelles   8
El Cuartel   5
La Flor   9
El Observatorio   12
Okami Sushi   2
Soda Amon   13
El Sultan   11
Taco Voy   6
Ticolo   15
Tin-Jo   7
Trigo Miel   4
La Vasconia   3

ACCOMMODATION
Abril Hostal   J
Angels Hotel   F
Casa Ridgway   I
Costa Rica Backpackers   H
Hostel Pangea   B
Hotel Casa León   E
Hotel Toruma   G
Kap's Place   A
Posada Amon Inn   D
Tranquilo Backpackers   C

San Pedro

(Tues–Sat 8.30am–4.30pm, Sun 9am–4.30pm; 2200c; ☎2257-1433, ⓦwww.museocostarica.go.cr), home to the country's most important archeological exhibits. Highlights include petroglyphs, pre-Columbian stonework, wonderful anthropomorphic gold figures (in the Sala Arqueológica) and an open courtyard offering great views of the city.

Mercado Central

Northwest of the Parque Central and the commercial centre in the block between Av 0/1 and C 6/8 is San José's **Mercado Central** (Mon–Sat 6am–6pm), or central market. Entering its labyrinthine interior you're confronted by colourful arrangements of fruits and vegetables, dangling sides of beef and elaborate, silvery ranks of fish. Shopping for fruits, vegetables and coffee here is less expensive than in a supermarket, and the glut of *sodas* inside means it's the best place in town to get a cheap bite – not only that, but the view from a counter stool is fascinating, as traders and their customers jostle for *chayotes*, *mamones*, *piñas* and *cas*. Watch your belongings, or better yet bring nothing, as the bustling crowds and diverting sounds and sights make this a great spot for you to be pick-pocketed or have your bag stolen.

Parque la Sabana

Stretching west from the market is the Paseo Colón, a wide boulevard of shops, restaurants and car dealerships. At the very end of the *paseo*, the solid expanse of green known as **Parque la Sabana** was San José's airport until the 1940s, and is now home to the country's key art museum. Housed in a converted air terminal, the attractive **Museo de Arte Costarricense**, Av 0, C 42 (Tues–Fri 9am–5pm, Sat–Sun 10am–4pm; 2800c, free Sun; ☎2222-7155, ⓦwww.musarco.go.cr) has a good collection of contemporary

Costa Rican art, as well as the Jardín de Esculturas (sculpture garden) and Salón Dorado (golden room) which contains a huge mural, painted by French artist Louis Ferón in 1940.

On the southwest corner of Parque la Sabana, forming part of the University La Salle, is the quirky natural science museum, the **Museo de Ciencias Naturales** (Mon–Sat 7.30am–4pm, Sun 9am–5pm; 825c; ☎2232-1306). Walk right in, and after about 400m you'll see the painted wall announcing the museum; the entrance is at the back. Displays range from pickled fish and snakes to some rather forlorn taxidermy exhibits – age and humidity have taken their toll.

San Pedro

First impressions of the student district of **San Pedro**, which begins when you pass the traffic circle at the San Pedro mall (you'll know it for its Flintstones-style jutting boulders), can be off-putting: the Avenida Central (also known here as Paseo de los Estudiantes) is lined with gas stations and dull malls as it passes through the area. Walk just a block away from the *paseo*, however, and you'll find a lively combination of university-student ghettos and elegant residential houses. The area also claims some of the city's best bars, restaurants and nightlife, especially along the **Calle de la Amargura**.

You'll most likely arrive here in a taxi or on one of the buses from downtown San José. Buses stop opposite the small **Parque Central**, centred on a monument to John F. Kennedy. Walking north from the square, through three blocks of *sodas*, bars, restaurants and abandoned railway tracks, you come to the cool, leafy campus of the **University of Costa Rica (UCR)**, one of the finest universities in Central America.

Arrival and information

By air Costa Rica's main airport, Juan Santamaría International (☎2443-0840), is 17km northwest of San José and 3km southeast of Alajuela. Taxis line up just beyond the airport exit and should cost around 8300c to the city centre. Buses to downtown San José depart from the airport bus stop just outside the terminal.

By bus Most international buses from Nicaragua, Honduras, Guatemala and Panama pull into the Tica Bus station, Av 4, C 9/11 (☎2221-8954), next to the yellow Soledad church. The city has no central domestic bus terminal; the nearest thing to it is La Coca-Cola (named after an old bottling plant that used to stand on the site), five blocks west of the Mercado Central at Av 1/3, C 16/18 (the main entrance is on C 16); most buses from the Pacific coast arrive here. There are also a multitude of independent bus company stops in the blocks around La Coca-Cola. The Terminal del Caribe, Av 13, C Central, deals with transport to and from Limón. Arrivals from Monteverde and La Fortuna will pull into the Terminal Atlántico Norte at C 12, Av 7/9, and buses travelling between Golfito, Nosara, Tamarindo and San José use the Alfaro-Tracopa Terminal at C 14, Av 3/5. The quickest (and, in the case of those leaving from Coca-Cola area, safest) way to get to and from the bus stations is by taxi, which should cost around 2800c.

Tourist information San José's central ICT office (Mon–Fri 9am–5pm; ☎2229-1090, ⊛www .visitcostarica.com), underneath the Plaza de la Cultura and next to the gold museum at C 5, Av 0/2, has free maps, tour brochures and booklets detailing the (ever-changing) national bus schedule. They also hand out *San Jose Volando* (⊛www .sanjosevolando.com), a free monthly culture guide. For information on all the nation's parks, head to the central office for the FPN, or Fundación de Parques Nacionales, at Av 15, C 23/33 (☎2257-2239, ⊛www.fpncostarica.org).

City transport

Buses The bus network, connecting central San José with virtually all of the city's suburbs, generally runs daily 5am–10pm. Bus stops in the city centre seem to change every year; currently, most buses to San Pedro, Tres Ríos and other points east leave from Av Central, C 9/15, and buses for Paseo Colón and Parque la Sabana (labelled "Sabana-Cementerio") from the bus shelters on Av 2, C 5/7. All buses have their routes clearly marked on their windshields, and usually the fare, too. Fares are payable either to the driver or conductor when you board and are usually about 150c, though the faster, more comfortable *busetas de lujo* (luxury buses) to the suburbs cost upwards of 300c. Bus drivers or conductors always have lots of change.

TOUR OPERATORS IN SAN JOSÉ

As Costa Rica's main city, San José is home to scores of tour and activity operators. Those listed here are experienced and reliable, and are all licensed (and regulated) by the ICT. Be wary of fly-by-night operations, of which there are plenty. You often see, for instance, posters advertising "packages" to Tortuguero or Monteverde for US$80–100 – less than half the price of a regular package. These are not really packages at all, and never worth the price: you may find yourself responsible for your own transport or accommodation, and no tours, orientation or guidance will be given.

Costa Rica Expeditions C 0, Av 3 ☎2257-0766, ⊛www.costaricaexpeditions .com. This US-based firm is the most established and experienced of the major tour operators. They offer white-water rafting day-trips from US$75 per person.

Ecole Travel C 7, Av 0/1 ☎2256-0295, ⊛www.ecoletravel.com. Small agency popular with backpackers offering two-night tours to Tortuguero (US$249) and 3-day tours to Corcovado as well as day-trips for US$50–100.

Expediciones Tropicales C 3b, Av 11/13 ☎2257-4171, ⊛www.costaricainfo.com. Another backpackers' favourite with knowledgeable guides, running the popular "Four-in-One" day-tour of Volcán Poás and nearby sights (US$87; 11hr), as well as a host of other trips from San José.

Specops ☎+1/941/346-2603, ⊛www.specops.com. Adventure education group, comprising US Special Forces veterans and expert Costa Rican guides, specializing in white-knuckle thrills, jungle-survival courses and adventure film and photography.

Cars You won't want – or need – a car in the city, but one can be useful for heading out on day-trips within the Central Valley, where public transport can be inconveniently scheduled. See p.504 for agency listings.

Taxis Cheap and plentiful, even at odd hours of the night and early morning. Licensed vehicles are red with a yellow triangle on the side, and have "SJP" ("San José Publico") license plates. A ride anywhere within the city will cost 1100–2200c, and about double that out to the suburbs. The starter fare (450c) is shown on the red digital display; make sure the meter is on before you start (ask the driver to *toca la maría, por favor*) or agree on the fare in advance. Taxis usually line up along the Parque Central, but licensed vehicles are also safe to hail on the street.

Accommodation

The budget-to-moderate accommodation choices in San José are fairly good value, with plenty of hostels, guesthouses and family-run hotels. The very cheapest rooms are in the insalubrious area around La Coca-Cola; while there are a couple of decent budget places here, the area is best avoided. Be prepared to reserve in advance in high season (Dec–May) and at holidays.

Hostels

Abril Hostal Av 10, Contra 204 (which becomes C 25) ☎2234-1310, ✉sabrinavargas@ice.co.cr. Budget option with bright, spacious rooms (dorms only), a large garden and a small roof terrace. Day-trips can be arranged at a discount. 10.30pm curfew. Dorms ③

Bekuo Hostel Av 8, C 41/43 ☎2234-1091, Ⓦwww.hostelbekuo.com. Spotless rooms, most with private baths, located in Los Yoses, a 10min walk from downtown and bordering San Pedro. ⑤

Casa Ridgway C 15, Av 6 bis (Av 6/8) ☎2233-6168 or 2222-1400, Ⓦwww.amigosparalapaz .org. Clean and secure Quaker-run guesthouse with cheap, single-sex dorms plus a few private singles and doubles. Free breakfast. Alcohol is banned and it's "quiet time" from 10pm. Dorms ②, singles ③, doubles ④

Costa Rica Backpackers Av 6, C 21/23 ☎2221-6191 or 2223-2406, Ⓦwww.costaricabackpackers .com. Popular budget guesthouse where facilities include a restaurant, garden with outdoor kitchen and swimming pool and tour services. Their separate guesthouse across the road has more expensive private doubles. Dorms ③, doubles ⑤

Gaudy's Backpackers Av 5, C 36/38 ☎2258-2937 or 2248-0086, Ⓦwww.backpacker.co.cr.

A cheap and cheerful hostel near Parque La Sabana – rooms are a bit cramped but the house has a cosy atmosphere and friendly staff. Dorms ③, doubles ④–⑤

Hostel Pangea Av 7, C 3/3b ☎2221-1992, Ⓦwww.hostelpangea.com. San José's party hostel boasts a pool, rooftop restaurant, bar and dancefloor. There is no communal "living room" or kitchen, however, and all rooms, both dorms and private, share bathroom facilities. Dorms ③, doubles ⑤

Hostel Toruma Av Central, C 29/31 ☎2234-8186 or 2224-4805, Ⓦwww.hosteltoruma .com. Set back from Av Central, this hostel aims to be upscale, with a Neoclassical exterior, high ceilings and polished wood floors. There's a pool and internet access, but no kitchen. Dorms ③, doubles ⑥–⑦

🏃 **Tranquilo Backpackers** C 7, Av 9/11 ☎2223-3189, Ⓦwww.tranquilobackpackers .com. The most laid-back hostel in town, *Tranquilo* attracts a mix of travellers with its funky painted walls, lazy hammocks, ambient music and DIY breakfast pancakes. Downstairs rooms can get noisy (reception provides earplugs) – upstairs private rooms are larger and quieter. Dorms ③, doubles ⑤

Hotels, inns and B&Bs

Angels Hotel C 25, Av 0/2 ☎2258-8273, Ⓦwww .angelshotel.com. Family-run *casa de huéspedes* of seven large and immaculate rooms, with shared and private baths. There's laundry service, assistance with travel and tours, a garden and a great little *soda* on site. ⑥

Hotel Casa León Av 6 bis, C 13/15 ☎2221-1651, Ⓦwww.hotelcasaleon.com/English.htm. Along the city's abandoned railroad tracks, this small, quiet guesthouse has basic private rooms with shared or private baths and also arranges tours and car rental. It can be hard to find: tell your taxi driver it's a *calle sin salida* (dead-end road). ⑤

Kap's Place C 19, Av 11/13 ☎2221-1169, Ⓦwww.kapsplace.com. Run by Karla Arias (a bottomless source of information), the hotel has 22 rooms of varying size and price, a fully equipped communal kitchen and a large apartment. Quiet time 8pm–8am, and smoking permitted only out front. Tours arranged on request. Singles ④–⑥, doubles ⑤, triple ⑦

Posada Amon Inn C 5, Av 9 ☎2222-6700/1350, Ⓦwww.costaricarrangements.com. Sweet little converted guesthouse with large, simply furnished rooms accommodating between one and six people, as well as a laundry service, free internet and breakfast. Singles ④, doubles ⑤–⑥

Eating

For a Central American city of its size, San José has a surprising variety of restaurants, but the 23 percent tax on restaurant food can easily wreck a budget; it's cheapest to eat in the centre, at the *sodas* and snack bars, where the tax doesn't apply. A sit-down breakfast or lunch at a soda will rarely set you back more than 2800c. Cafés and bakeries also abound: some have old-world European aspirations; others are resolutely Costa Rican, with *Josefinos* piling in to order birthday cakes or grab a coffee.

Cafés and bakeries

Café 1930 In the *Gran Hotel Costa Rica*, Av 2, C 3/5. The closest thing in San José to a European street café. The food's not cheap (coffee 750c), but this is a good place to sit and watch the buskers and street performers in the Plaza de la Cultura. Open 24hr.

Café de la Posada C 17, Av 2/4 ☎ 2258-1027. This café (attached to the pretty *Posada de Museo Hotel*, ⑥ – ⑨) offers cakes and coffees (700c), all-day Continental breakfasts (2150c) and lunch options that include tasty quiches (2000c) and empanadas.

Trigo Miel C 3, Av 0/1 ☎ 2221-8995. The best-stocked branch of a national bakery chain. There's a mouth-watering selection of cakes, breads and pastries – try a delicious *cangrejo* (croissant) with *dulce de leche*. Eat in (they also offer a daily lunch plate), take away or order delivery. Pastries 150–500c, *plato del día* 2500c.

Sodas

Amon C 7, Av 7/9. A tiny neighbourhood *soda* with cheap breakfasts of *gallo pinto*; the few tables are always packed so you may have to wait for a seat. Breakfast from 1100c, *casado* 1700c.

Tapia C 24, Av 2 ☎ 2222-6734. Retro-style diner with a huge menu – everything from fruit salads (850–2000c) to burgers and sandwiches (1000–4000c). Open 24hr.

La Vasconia Av 1, C 3/5 ☎ 2223-4857. Features an enormous stack of cheap breakfasts and lunch specials, including *casados* (1400c) and *ceviche*. Photos of the national football team (some dating back to 1905) adorn the walls.

Vishnu Av 1, C 1/3 ☎ 2256-6063. Cheery vegetarian *soda* serving healthy *platos del día* with brown rice and soup for around 1500c, and tasty sandwiches from 1200c.

Restaurants

Café Mundo Av 9, C 15 ☎ 2222-6190. This Italian-influenced restaurant may seem like a splurge, but the half-size portions (from 2000c) are a bargain and leftovers can be wrapped up for takeaway. There's a variety of balcony and courtyard seating, and a busy bar (attracting a largely gay clientele). Mains 4000–8000c.

La Flor Av 1, C 5/7 ☎ 2257-1561. Somewhat lacking in atmosphere but popular with working *Josefinos*, this downtown eatery offers good-value lunch meals (*casado*, juice and dessert 1900c).

Okami Sushi Av 0, C 23/25 ☎ 2221-0725. A slightly pricier alternative to the surrounding *sodas* and restaurants, *Okami* has a decent Japanese menu; the katsu and teriyaki plates come with rice, vegetables and miso soup for 4000–6000c. Rolls 1500–3500c.

Taco Voy Av 2, C 13 ☎ 2257-8280. Cheap and easy Mexican snacks, including quesadillas, tacos, burritos and *huaraches*. Portions 1200–3000c.

Ticolo Branches at the Mall San Pedro & Mercado Central. Tican fast food – mostly sandwiches, burgers and *casados* – with large platters and meal deals. The market (Av 0, C 6) is great for people-watching. *Casado* or sandwich plus side dish and drink 1200–2500c.

Tin-Jo C 11, Av 6/8 ☎ 2221-7605. Popular and fairly formal pan-Asian restaurant, with decent vegetarian options. The soups and coconut curries are particularly good. On a budget, skip the alcohol and share a (good-sized) portion. Soups 1500–3500c, curries 4000–6000c.

Drinking and nightlife

San José's nightlife is gratifyingly varied, with scores of bars. Stay away from the centre of town (see box, p.503), and head instead to Los Yoses, where Av Central features a trail of sports and soft-rock bars, or San Pedro, which is geared towards the university population. Bars often change character on weekends, when they host live music acts. If you want to dance, check out one of the city's many discos, but do not confuse these with the erotically associated "nightclubs" (see box opposite). Cover charges run about 2800c and often include a free drink; many establishments allow women to enter for free if business is slow. The **Centro Commercial El Pueblo**, just north of the cty centre, is home to a maze of discos, bars and snack joints, and provides an expensive but easy night out; expect to spend upwards of 5500c on drinks. Taxis back to the centre from El Pueblo charge a base rate of US$4. With the exception of the university bars in San Pedro, most places close by 2 or 3am, earlier on Sun.

PROSTITUTION AND SEX TOURISM IN SAN JOSÉ

Prostitution is legal in Costa Rica and, in San José, very mainstream. Sex tourism is somewhat of a problem here, and you'll find that many of the "bars" downtown – especially in the *zona roja* (or red light district) between La Coca-Cola and the Calle Central – are, in reality, little more than pick-up joints for professional transactions. The term "nightclub" generally implies some form of erotic entertainment, while a *discoteca* will be somewhere to dance (with your clothes on) – be aware of this distinction.

Bars

Bar Río On Blvd Los Yoses, the continuation of Av Central. A busy sports bar with a big terrace at the front and a large dance area (occasionally staging live music) at the back. Beer 1000c.

Caccio's C de la Amargura, San Pedro. Insanely popular student hangout with cheap pizza and cold beer (600c).

Chelles Av 0, C 9. A simple, brightly lit bar with football on the television, cheap beers (770c) and 24hr service.

El Cuartel Av 1, C 21/23. A San José institution, popular with a young crowd. The restaurant is open for lunch and dinner (plates from 2500c). Mon and Wed nights there's live music; cover 3000c. Beer 1000c.

Jazz Café Av Central, San Pedro ☎2253-8933, ⓦwww.jazzcafecostarica.com. The best place in San José to hear live jazz and Latin rhythms, with an intimate atmosphere and consistently good acts. The *bocas* are tasty but not cheap, so stick to beer (1000–1500c). Doors open at 9pm, music 10pm–2am. Cover 2000–4500c (depending on the act).

El Observatorio C 23, Av 0/1. A funky, warehouse-style bar that often showcases independent films and music. Beer 1000c, cocktails 2500c.

El Sultan Av 0, C 29. Middle Eastern-themed pub, with good falafel and pita (2200c) and cheap beer (600c) pulling in a young crowd. Tues and Thurs are busiest.

Discos

Bongos El Pueblo. A small club offering numerous drink promotions. The packed dancefloor is dominated by Latin beats and live music most weekends. Cover 1000–3000c; ladies free before 10pm.

Castro's C 22, Av 13. This popular spot attracts local crowds of all ages; you can have a bite and watch the crowds, or hit the dancefloor to tropical rhythms (salsa, cumbia and merengue) and reggaeton.

Déjà Vu C 2, Av 14/16. One of the hottest gay clubs (drag night on Sat) in town, housing two large dancefloors of banging electronic music, as well as the more intimate *Sinners* bar. The neighbourhood is pretty scary, so take a taxi. Cover 1600–2200c.

Ebony 56 El Pueblo. A young crowd fills the large dancefloors playing salsa, pop and reggaeton; ladies' night on Thurs is buzzing. Cover 1000–3000c.

Infinito El Pueblo. One of the busiest clubs in town, with three large dancefloors playing mix of international music.

Terra U C de la Amargura, San Pedro ⓦwww.terrau.com. Hugely popular student disco, with three open-air levels and a heaving dancefloor where Latin and tropical rhythms predominate.

Vertigo Edificio Colón Paseo Colón, Av 38/40 ⓦwww.vertigocr.com. A swanky Euro-style club with electronic music – from local and international DJs – on the main floor, and a hip-hop/chill-out lounge upstairs. Cover 1000–12,000c, depending on the lineup.

Entertainment

Josefinos love the theatre, and there's a healthy range of affordable venues, although you often need a strong grasp of Spanish to follow the rapid, colloquial dialogue. All performances are listed in the *Cartelera* section of the *Tiempo Libre* supplement in *La Nación* on Thurs, and the *Tico Times*. Going to the cinema in San José is a bargain, with tickets costing around 1600–2800c. Cinemas generally show subtitled versions of the latest American movies; the few that are dubbed will have the phrase "hablado en Español" in the newspaper listings or on the posters. Most of the large, multi-screen cinemas are in suburban malls, including the Multiplaza Escazú and Real Cariari, and require a taxi ride.

Theatre

Mélico Salazar Av 2, C 0 ☎2221-4925, ⓦwww.teatromelicosalazar.go.cr. Draws great musical talents from Costa Rica and further abroad. Tickets US$2–20.

Teatro Laurence Olivier Av 2, C 28 ☎2223-1960. A small venue favouring experimental performances, with a gallery and popular *Shakespeare* bar downstairs. Shows cost around 3000c per ticket.

Teatro Nacional Av 2, C 3/5 ☎ 2221-1329, ⓦ www.teatronacional.go.cr. The most important theatre in the country, with productions ranging from Shakespeare to Chinese acrobatics. Ticket prices start at about 2800c, depending on the act.

Cinema

CCM Mall San Pedro (see below) ☎ 2283-5716. A huge complex of screens playing international films. The a/c can get pretty chilly, so bring a sweater.

Cine Magaly C 23, Av 0/1 ☎ 2223-0085. Across the road from some of the city's hottest bars, this cinema plays new releases, mostly in English.

Sala Garbo Av 2, C 28 ☎ 2222-1034. A small venue with two screens showing foreign-language art-house movies.

Shopping

Avenida Central (C 3/6) is good for fairly cheap shoes and clothing, although you'll also find more expensive shops, including a Levi's store and upmarket surf/skate chain Arenas. San José's souvenir and crafts shops are well stocked and in general pretty pricey; it's best to buy from shops run by regulated crafts co-operatives – more of the money filters back to the artisans. There are several markets that are good for browsing. Malls are very popular, springing up all over the capital's suburbs and housing European stores like Mango and Zara, as well as US chain stores, restaurants and entertainment venues.

Books

7th Street Books C 7, Av 0/1 ☎ 2256-8251. Both new and used books; it's good on English literature and also has a wide selection of books and maps on Costa Rica in English and Spanish. Mon–Sat 9am–6pm, Sun 10am–5pm.

Chispas C 7, Av 0/1 ☎ 2223-2240 or 2256-8251. Sells new and secondhand books, and has the best selection of English-language fiction in town. It also carries a good array of guides and books about Costa Rica (in English and Spanish), plus several English-language magazines and newspapers. Mon–Sat 9am–6pm.

Librería Internacional Branches at Av 0, C 0/1 (☎ 2257-6563; Mon–Sat 9am–7pm) and in the Multiplaza Escazú (☎ 2201-8320; daily 10am–10pm). The biggest selection of stock in town, with books in Spanish, English and German.

Mora Books Av 1, C 3/5, in the Omni building ☎ 2383-8385. A good selection of secondhand English-language books, CDs, guide books, magazines and comics. Mon–Sat 11am–7pm.

Food and drink

Supermarkets The cheapest is Mas x Menos (Av 0, C 9/11; daily 8am–9pm), which stocks mainly Costa Rican brands of just about everything. There are several branches in San José and one in San Pedro on Av 0, 300m north of the church. Branches of the Automercado, Perimercado and the Am-Pm supermarkets are springing up all over the place.

Malls

Mall San Pedro Av 0, C 47, at the Fuente de La Hispanidad. A large complex with a multitude of clothing stores, a multi-screen cinema complex, nightclub and food court with a breezy, outdoor balcony.

Multiplaza Escazú On the highway outside the city. Another enormous complex with international chains, bars and restaurants, and a huge cinema.

Markets

La Casona C 0, Av 0/1. Two-floor marketplace with stalls selling ethnic Latin American products such as Guatemalan knapsacks and bedspreads and Panamanian *molas*. Quality at some stalls is pretty poor. Mon–Sat 9.30am–6.30pm, Sun 9.30am–5.30pm.

Mercado Nacional de Artesanía y Pintura C 22, Av 2 bis. Touristy street market in the Plaza de la Democracia featuring all the usual items: hats, T-shirts, Sarchí ox-carts, jewellery, woodwork, hammocks and fabrics. Daily 8am–6pm.

Plaza Esmerelda Pavas, in the city suburbs. A huge craft co-operative where you can watch cigars being rolled, necklaces set and Sarchí ox-carts painted. Closed Sun.

Directory

Car rental Alamo, Paseo Colón ☎ 2242-7733, ⓦ www.alamocostarica.com; Avanti, at the airport and Paseo Colón, C 30/32 ☎ 2430-4647, ⓦ www.avantirentacar.com; Payless, C 10, Av 13/15 ☎ 2257-0026, ⓦ www.paylesscr.com; Tricolor, at the airport ☎ 2440-3333, ⓦ www.tricolorcarrental.com.

Embassies and consulates Canada, Calle del Golf and Autopista 7 ☎ 2242-4400; UK, 11th floor, Edificio Centro Colón, Paseo Colón, C 38/40 ☎ 2258-2025; US, opposite the Centro Comercial in Pavas, or Av 0, C 120 (☎ 2519-2000) – take the bus to Pavas from Av 1, C 18.

Exchange State-owned banks include the
Banco de Costa Rica, Av 0/2, C 4/6 (Mon–Fri
8am–4pm; Visa only) and Banco Nacional, Av
1/3, C 4 (Mon–Fri 8.30am–3.30pm; Visa only).
Private banks include ScotiaBank, C 5, Av 0/2
(Mon–Fri 8.30am–6.30pm, Sat 9am–1pm; Visa &
MasterCard). There's an American Express office
in the Oficentro (Edificio 1), Sabana Sur (Mon–Fri
8.30am–5pm; ☎2242-8585). All currency
exchange in San José is done at banks.

Immigration *Migración* (Mon–Fri 8am–4pm;
☎2299-8100) is in Uruca, on the airport highway
opposite the Hospital México; take an Alajuela bus
and get off at the stop underneath the overhead
walkway. Get there early if you want visa extensions
or exit visas. Larger travel agencies listed on p.500
can take care of the paperwork for you for a fee
(roughly US$10–25).

Internet Free at most hotels and guesthouses,
but there are also plenty of cafés; expect to pay
around 300c/30min. Try Café Digital, Av 0, C 5/7,
which also has a *soda*; Internet Club, C 7, Av 0/2;
or CyberCafe Las Arcadas, Av 2, C 1/3, with a laundry
on site.

Laundry Offered by many hotels and guesthouses.
Otherwise, try Lava Sol C 5, Av 9/11 or Sixaola (one
of a chain), Av 2, C 7/9.

Medical care The public hospital is San Juan de
Dios, Paseo Colón, C 14–16 (☎2257-6282). The
private hospital is Clínica Biblica, Av 14/16,
C 0/1 (☎2522-1000, emergencies ☎2522-
1030); basic consultation and treatment starts at
about US$100.

Pharmacies Clínica Biblica, Av 14, C 0/1 (☎2522-
1000), is open 24hr. Farmacia Fischel has branches
at Av 3, C 2 (Mon–Sat 7am–7pm, Sun 9am–5pm)
and Av 2, C 5/7 (Mon–Fri 7am–8pm, Sat 8am–7pm,
Sun 8am–6pm).

Post office The Correo Central (ⓦwww.correos
.go.cr; Mon–Fri 7am–5pm, Sat 7am–noon) is at
C 2, Av 1/3.

Moving on

By air

The nation's domestic airlines, Sansa and Nature
Air, have several daily flights to Liberia, Jacó and
Tambor from Juan Santamaría airport.

By bus

San José is the transport hub of Costa Rica, and
eventually, all roads lead to it. A bewildering
number of bus companies use the city as their
base; although many services depart from the
Coca-Cola terminal (C 16, Av 1/3), many

others leave from independent stops in the
streets around, or from the Terminal Caribe
(C 0, Av 13).

Bus companies and stops

ATC Departs for La Fortuna/Arénal from C 12, Av
7/9. Information on ☎2255-0567/4318/4300.

Deldú Departs for Peñas Blancas from C 14,
Av 3/5. Information on ☎2256-9072 or
2677-0091.

Empresa Alfaro Departs for Nicoya, Nosara, Playa
Sámara & Tamarindo from Av 5, C 14/16. Information on ☎2222-2666.

Empresarios Unidos Departs for Puntarenas from
C 16, Av 12. Information on ☎2222-8231, 2222-
9840 or 2661-3138.

Hermanos Rodriguez Departs for Mal País from
La Coca-Cola. Information on ☎2642-0219.

King Quality Departs for El Salvador and
Nicaragua from C 12, Av 3/5. Information on
☎2258-8834.

Lumaca Departs for Cartago from C 5, Av 10.
Information on ☎2537-2320.

Mepe Departs for Cahuita, Manzanillo, Puerto Viejo
de Talamanca and Sixaola from Terminal Caribe.
Information on ☎2257-8129 or 2758-1572.

Metropoli Departs for Volcán Irázu from Av 2,
C 1/3. Information on ☎2536-6052.

Microbuses Rapiditos Heredianos (MRA)
Departs for Heredia from C 1, Av 7/9. Information on
☎2233-8392.

Nica Expreso Departs for Managua from C 16,
Av 3/5. Information on ☎2256-3191.

Panaline Departs for Panama City from C 16,
Av 3/5. Information on ☎2256-8721, ⓦwww
.panalinecr.com.

Pulmitan de Liberia Departs for Liberia and Playa
del Coco from C 24, Av 5/7. Information on ☎2222-
1650 or 2666-3818.

Station Wagon Departs for Alajuela from Av 4,
C 12/14. Information on ☎2441-1181.

Tica Bus Departs for Guatemala, Nicaragua,
Panama, El Salvador and Honduras from C 26,
Av 3. Information on ☎2221-0006, ⓦwww
.ticabus.com.

Tilarán Departs for Santa Elena/Monteverde from
C 12, Av 7/9. Information on ☎2222-3854.

Tracopa (domestic) Departs for Paso Canoas
and Golfito from Av 5, C 18/20. Information on
☎2771-4214.

Tracopa (international) Departs for Panama from
Av 5, C 14/16. Information on ☎2222-2666 or
2223-7685.

Transnica Departs for Nicaragua from C 22,
Av 3/5. Information on ☎2223-4242, ⓦwww
.transnica.com.

Transportes Blancos Departs for Puerto Jiménez from C 14, Av 9/11. Information on ☎ 2257-4121 or 2735-5189.

Transportes Caribeños Departs for Puerto Limón from Terminal Caribe. Information on ☎ 2221-2596 or 2222-0610.

Transportes Morales Departs for Dominical, Jacó and Quepos/Manuel Antonio from La Coca-Cola. Information on ☎ 2223-1109 or 2643-3135.

Tuasa Departs for Alajuela and Volcán Poás from Av 2, C 12/14. Information on ☎ 2222-5325 or 2442-6900.

Domestic bus destinations

Alajuela With Station Wagon or Tuasa. Departures every 10min 4.30am–11pm, then every 30min; 35min.

Cahuita With Mepe. Departures daily 6am, 10am, 2pm, 4pm; 4hr.

Cariari (From the Terminal del Caribe, for Tortuguero): departures daily 6.30am, 9am, 10.30am, 1pm, 3pm, 4.30pm, 6pm, 7pm, 10.30pm; 1hr 30min.

Cartago With Lumaca. Departures every 10min 5.05am–midnight; 45min.

Dominical With Transportes Morales. Departures daily 6am, 3pm; 7hr.

Golfito With Tracopa. Departures daily 7am, Sun also 3.30pm; 8hr.

Heredia With MRA. Departures every 10min 5am–3am; 30min.

Jacó With Transportes Morales. Departures daily 6am, 7am, 9am, 11am, 1pm, 3pm, 5pm, 7pm; 2hr 30min.

La Fortuna/Arénal With ATC. Departures daily 6.15am, 8.40am, 11.30am; 4hr 30min.

Liberia With Pulmitan. Departures daily 6am, 7am noon, 3pm, 5pm, 6pm, 7pm (Fri only), 8pm; 4hr 30min.

Mal País With Hnos Rodriguez. Departures daily 7am, 3.30pm; 5hr 15min.

Manzanillo With Mepe. Departures daily noon; 4hr 30min.

Monteverde/Santa Elena With Tilarán. Departures daily 6.30am, 2.30pm; 5hr.

Montezuma (From La Coca-Cola; ☎ 2642-0219): departures daily at 7.30am & 3pm; 5hr.

Nicoya With Empresa Alfaro. Departures daily 5.30am, 7.30am, 10am, noon, 1pm, 3pm, 5pm, 6.30pm; 5hr.

Nosara With Empresa Alfaro. Departures daily 5.30am; 6hr.

Paso Canoas With Tracopa. Departures daily 5am, 7.30am, 6.30pm, also Sun 11am; 6hr.

Peñas Blancas With Deldú. Departures hourly 3am–7pm; 6hr.

Playa del Coco With Pulmitan. Departures daily 8am, 2pm, 4pm; 5hr.

Playa Sámara With Empresa Alfaro. Departures daily noon & 6.30pm; 5hr.

Puerto Jiménez With Transportes Blancos. Departures daily noon; 8hr.

Puerto Limón With Transportes Caribeños. Departures hourly 5am–7pm; 2hr 30min.

Puerto Viejo de Sarapiqui (From Terminal del Caribe; ☎ 2222-0610): departures daily 6.30am, 7.30am, 10am, 11.30am, 1.30pm, 2.30pm, 3.30pm, 4.30pm, 5.30pm, 6.30pm; 2hr.

Puerto Viejo de Talamanca With Mepe. Departures daily 6am, 10am, 2pm, 4pm; 4hr 30min.

Puntarenas With Empresarios Unidos. Departures hourly 6am–7pm; 2hr 20min.

Quepos/Manuel Antonio With Transportes Morales. Express departures daily 6am, noon, 6pm, 7.30pm, also Mon–Sat 9am, 2.30pm; local departures daily 7am, 10am, 2pm, 3pm, 4pm, also Mon–Fri 5pm; 3hr 45min–4hr 30min.

Sarchí (From C 18, Av 5/7; ☎ 2258-2004): departures Mon–Fri 12.15pm, Sat noon; 1hr 30min.

Sixaola With Mepe. Departures daily 6am, 10am, 2pm, 4pm; 6hr.

Tamarindo With Empresa Alfaro. Departures daily 8.30am & 3.30pm (via Liberia); 5hr 30min.

Volcán Irazú With Metropoli. Departures daily 8am (returning 12.30pm); 2hr.

Volcán Poás With Tuasa. Departures daily 8.30am; 1hr 30min.

International bus destinations

El Salvador With King Quality (departures daily); Tica Bus (departures daily).

Guatemala With Tica Bus (departures daily).

Honduras With Tica Bus (departures daily).

Nicaragua With King Quality (departures daily); Nica Expreso (departures daily); Tica Bus (departures daily); Transnica (departures daily).

Panama With Panaline (departures daily); Tica Bus (departures daily); Tracopa (daily 7.30am).

The Valle Central and the Highlands

Despite its name – which translates literally as "Central Valley" – Costa Rica's **Valle Central** is actually an intermontane plateau poised at an elevation of between 3000 and 4000m. The area supports roughly two thirds of Costa Rica's population, as well as its four most important cities – San José and the provincial capitals of **Alajuela**, **Heredia** and **Cartago**. Other than that, it's a largely agricultural region, with green coffee terraces shadowed by the summits of the surrounding mountains, many of which are volcanoes. These volcanoes, especially **Irazú** and **Poás** and the surrounding national parks, are the chief attractions for visitors, but there's also good **whitewater rafting**,

and the **Monumento Nacional Guayabo**, the country's most important archeological site.

Most people use San José as a base for forays into the Valle Central: with the exception of Alajuela the provincial capitals have little to entice you to linger. If you do want to get out of the city and stay in the Valle Central, the nicest places are the lodges and inns scattered throughout the countryside.

ALAJUELA

With a population of just 45,000, **ALAJUELA** is Costa Rica's second largest city; it's also only thirty minutes from downtown San José. There's not much to specifically see here – most travellers use Alajuela as a jumping-off point for departure and arrival into the rest of the country, as well as a base for visiting the surrounding sights. The city's few attractions, such as they are, are all less than a minute's walk from the Parque Central.

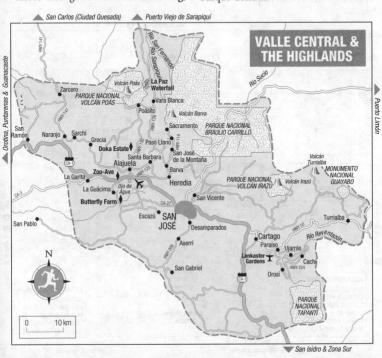

VALLE CENTRAL & THE HIGHLANDS

What to see and do

The most impressive sight in Alajuela is the sturdy-looking whitewashed former jail, Av 3, C 0/2, which houses the **Juan Santamaría Cultural-Historical Museum** (Tues–Sun 10am–6pm; free; ☎2441-4775). Dedicated to Alajuela's most cherished historical figure – drummer-boy-cum-martyr Juan Santamaría, who sacrificed his life to save the country from American adventurer William Walker in 1856 – the museum's curiously monastic atmosphere is almost more interesting than the small collection itself, which runs the gamut from mid-nineteenth-century maps of Costa Rica to crumbly portraits of figures involved in the battle of 1856. One block south of the museum is a small **plaza** also named for Santamaría, on the north side of which you'll find the recently renovated **municipal theatre** (☎2436-2362). The restored, Art Deco-inspired facade houses an auditorium, gallery and café, although these spaces are only open to the public when there are performances or events (call for information).

Arrival and information

By air Juan Santamaría International Airport is less than 3km from the city. Many hotels and hostels will arrange a free pick-up with prior notice; otherwise take a yellow or red bus marked "Alajuela" from outside the airport.

By bus Tuasa buses (red and black) from San José arrive at the Tuasa station, C 8/10, Av 0/1, three blocks west of the Parque Central; the daily bus to Poás also passes through this stop. Station Wagon buses (beige and orange) from San José drop you off on Av 4, C 2/4, 50m southwest of Parque Juan Santamaría.

By car Take the *pista* towards the airport (General Cañas Highway), then the turn-off to Alajuela, 17km from San José – don't use the underpass or you'll end up at the airport.

Tourist information There's no official information source in town. Goodlight Books, Av 3, C 1/3, is the best place to go with questions, though their help is limited.

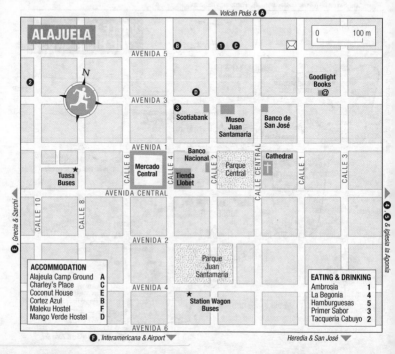

ALAJUELA

▲ Volcán Poás & Ⓐ

0   100 m

AVENIDA 5

Ⓑ   ❶ Ⓒ   ✉

Goodlight
Books
@

Ⓔ, Grecia & Sarchí ◀

❷

N

AVENIDA 3

Ⓓ

❸
Scotiabank

Museo
Juan
Santamaría

Banco de
San José

AVENIDA 1

Banco
Nacional

CALLE 6   Mercado Central   CALLE 4   Tienda Llobet   CALLE 2   Parque Central   CALLE CENTRAL   Cathedral ✝   CALLE 1   CALLE 3

Tuasa
Buses ★

AVENIDA CENTRAL

CALLE 10   CALLE 8

AVENIDA 2

Ⓕ, Interamericana & Airport ▼

Parque
Juan
Santamaría

Heredia & San José ▼

Ⓐ Ⓔ & Iglesia la Agonía ▶

AVENIDA 4

Station Wagon
Buses ★

AVENIDA 6

ACCOMMODATION
Alajeula Camp Ground	A
Charley's Place	C
Coconut House	E
Cortez Azul	B
Maleku Hostel	F
Mango Verde Hostel	D

EATING & DRINKING
Ambrosia	1
La Begonia	4
Hamburguesas	5
Primer Sabor	3
Tacqueria Cabuyo	2

Accommodation

Alajuela Camp Ground Next to *Quinta San Angel* on the road to Tuetal (north of Alajuela) ☏2398-9024, ⓦwww.alajuelacampground.com. Excellent accommodation with camping facilities, basic dorms and private rooms. There's also a huge garden with fruit trees and soccer pitch. Camping ❷, dorms ❷, doubles ❹

Charly's Place Av 5, C 0/2 ☏2441-0115 or 8385-9891, ⓦwww.charlysplacehotel.com. Clean and basic rooms of varying capacity, all en suite with cable TV and breakfast included, plus use of a kitchen and internet access. Group discounts available. Singles ❺, double ❽

Coconut House Across from Parque Loma, 10m south and 350m west of La Trinidad supermarket ☏2441-1249, ⓦwww.coconuthouse.info. Great hotel with cosy rooms (all en suite) and good included buffet breakfast. Tours and car rental can be organized. ❺

Cortez Azul Av 5, C 2/4 ☏2443-6145, ⓔhotelcortezazul@gmail.com. This artist-run establishment has simple rooms (including two dorms) with lovely wooden floors, sculptures and mosaics. Dorms ❷, doubles ❺

Maleku Hostel 50m west of the main entrance of the new hospital ☏2430-4304, ⓦwww.malekuhostel.com. The best budget option in town, this is a small and cheerful family home with immaculate rooms and great advice on local travel and activities, plus free airport transfers. Dorms ❷, doubles ❺

Mango Verde Hostel Av 3, C 2/4 ☏2441-6330, ⓔmirafloresbb@hotmail.com. Another good budget choice, with simple en-suite rooms and an attractive blue-walled courtyard. ❸

Eating

Ambrosia Av 5, C 2. Economic Tican cuisine with some Italian-style options, including a hearty lasagna. *Casado* 1700c, lasagna 1800c.

La Begonia C Ancha (C 9), Av 6 ☏2442-9846. Serves coffee (800c) from the nearby Doka estate (which you can buy in bulk), as well as pastries, cakes and empanadas.

Hamburguesas C Ancha (C 9), Av 0/2. A basic eatery with cheap fast food and popular ice creams (350c).

Primer Sabor Av 3, C 2/4. A good choice of cheap dishes from a large Chinese menu (2000–3500c); try the chop suey and other Cantonese specials. Closed Tues.

Tacqueria Cabuyo C 10, Av 3/5. A tiny taco stand, hugely popular with a local crowd for the cheap and filling snacks on offer. Tacos 300c.

Directory

Exchange Banco Nacional, C 2, Av 0/1; Banco de San José, C 0, Av 3; and Scotiabank, C 2, Av 3, can all change dollars and traveller's cheques.

Internet Goodlight Books, Av 3, C 1/3 (daily 9am–6pm), has internet access, as well as a good selection of secondhand books and maps, coffee and cakes.

Post office The *correo* (Mon–Fri 8am–5.30pm, Sat 7.30am–noon) is at Av 5, C 1.

Moving on

By bus Buses moving on from San José (towards the Pacific) pass through Alajuela, but only stop depending on vacancy. Hotels should be able to pre-arrange for a bus to stop and pick you up. Services to Jacó (3 daily; 3hr 30min), La Fortuna/Arénal (3 daily; 3hr 30 min), Monteverde (2 daily; 3hr), Liberia (frequent; 4hr 30min) and Puntarenas (frequent; 2hr 30min) all depart from La Radial bus stop, 75m south of the Shell gas station (or *bomba*) at C 4, C Ancha (Av 10). Services to Grecia (frequent; 1hr) and Sarchí (frequent; 1hr 15min) depart from C 8, Av 0/1. Services to nearby attractions – La Guácima Butterfly Farm (3 daily; 2hr), Zoo-Ave (frequent; 15min) and Sabanilla (for Doka Coffee Farm; frequent; 40min) – depart from the El Pacífico station, half a block south of the Tuasa terminal at C 8/10, Av 0/2,

AROUND ALAJUELA

Heading **north** from Alajuela, the road begins to climb, the terrain becomes noticeably greener and the air considerably cooler. Along this ascent you'll find numerous *cabinas* and chalets in rural settings with nice views and access to the nearby volcano, as well as several bars and restaurants that offer excellent views of the Valle Central. Travelling **south** to nearby destinations such as the Butterfly Farm, you'll pass rural stretches of land and forest; if you carry on south you'll eventually hit the urban sprawl of San José.

Doka Estate Coffee Farm

Some 15km north of Alajuela, between the towns of San Isidro and Sabanilla, you'll find the **Doka Estate Coffee Farm** (tours daily 9am, 10am, 11am, 1.30pm,

2.30pm, also Mon–Fri 3.30pm; US$16; ☎2449-5152, ⓦwww.dokaestate.com), which produces Café Tres Generaciones. Knowledgeable and enthusiastic guides lead tours of the farm, explaining the entire coffee-making process, from germinated seed to sun-dried bean (try to catch the 11am tour, when a cart ride takes you deep into the estate). Once you've toured the plantation, roasting factory and drying patios, there's a free tasting and the inevitable stop in the gift shop; they can pack and mail coffee to the US and Canada. To see the coffee-pickers in action, come at harvest time (Nov–Feb).

Many tour companies in San José (including Expediciones Tropicales, see p.500) include the farm on their itineraries. To arrive **independently**, take a bus from Alajuela to Sabanilla Parque and find a local taxi or car (about 1000c) to the estate. At the end of the tour, try to hitch a lift back to Alajuela with returning tour groups; alternatively, the farm can arrange a taxi pick-up.

La Guácima Butterfly Farm

Twelve kilometres southwest of Alajuela, **La Guácima Butterfly Farm** (daily 8.30am–5pm, last tour 3pm; US$15; ⓦwww.butterflyfarm.co.cr) breeds valuable pupae for export to zoos and botanical gardens all over the world. The farm also has beautiful views over the Valle Central. In the wet season you should aim to get here early, as the rain forces the butterflies to hide, and the clouds obscure the view; on a sunny day, however, when the butterflies are active, it's a glorious sight; there are thousands of them fluttering about like colourful tornados.

From Alajuela, **buses** (marked "La Guácima Abajo") leave from the area southwest of the main bus terminal; the Butterfly Farm is practically the last stop. Buses from San José (2hr) leave from Av 4–6, C 10, at 7am, 8am, 11am

and 2pm. Buses returning to Alajuela are frequent; for San José, enquire upon arrival for return times.

Zoo-Ave

The largest aviary in Central America, **Zoo-Ave** (daily 9am–5pm; US$15; ⓦwww.zooave.org), at Dulce Nombre, 5km northeast of La Garita, a small town near Alajulea, is just about the best place in the country to see the fabulous and many-coloured birds – especially macaws – that inhabit Costa Rica.

The La Garita **bus** from Alajuela (15min) passes right by, leaving from the area southwest of the main terminal; on your return, you can flag down an Alajuela bus on the main road where you arrived.

SARCHÍ

Touted as the centre of Costa Rican arts and crafts, the village of **SARCHÍ**, 30km northwest of Alajuela, is a commercialized place – firmly on the tourist trail but without much charm. Its setting in the hills is pretty enough, but don't come expecting to see picturesque scenes of craftsmen sitting in small historic shops: the work is done in factories. The most famous item produced here is the **Sarchí ox-cart**, a kaleidoscopically painted square cart of Moorish origin; other crafts include tables, bedsteads and leather rocking chairs (about US$90).

Large *fábricas* (workshops) line the main road from **Sarchí Sur**, leading up to the residential area of **Sarchí Norte**. The best local **hotel** is the *Hotel Daniel Zamora* (☎2454-4596; ⑥), on a side street opposite the football pitch in Sarchí Norte, which has clean rooms and hot water. For **food**, try *Restaurante Helechos* at the Plaza de Artesanía, which serves plates of Mexican and Tican fare (3000c), or *La Cafeteria*, next to the I.C.E in Sarchí Norte, which serves good *gallos* (filled tortillas), *pupusas* (700c) and *casados* (1600c).

Local **buses** from Alajuela run approximately every thirty minutes from 5am to 10pm. Buses back (via Grecia) can be hailed on the main road. From **San José** an express service (1hr–1hr 30min) runs from La Coca-Cola every hour from 6am to 8pm. **Taxis** between Sarchí Sur and Sarchí Norte, or to Alajeula or Zarcero, can be called on ☏2454-4028. The Banco Nacional on the main road beyond the church (in Sarchí Norte) **changes dollars and cheques**, as does a smaller branch in the Mercado de Artesanía, Sarchí Sur.

PARQUE NACIONAL VOLCÁN POÁS

PARQUE NACIONAL VOLCÁN POÁS (daily 8am–4pm; US$10), just 55km from San José and 37km north of Alajuela, is one of the most easily accessible active volcanoes in the world. Its history of eruptions goes back some eleven million years – the last gigantic blowout was on January 25, 1910, when it dumped 640,000 tonnes of ash on the surrounding area – but at the moment it is comparatively quiet. The weather is make-or-break for viewing the volcano, as mists arise from nowhere and can cover the crater within minutes; getting there early means you have a better chance of actually seeing the sights.

What to see and do

You need to get to the volcano before the clouds roll in, which they inevitably do, sometimes as early as 10am, even in the dry season (Dec–April). Poás has blasted out three craters in its lifetime, and due to more or less constant activity, the appearance of the **main crater** is subject to change – it's 1500m wide and filled with milky turquoise water from which sulphurous gases waft and broil. Although it's an impressive sight,

you only need about fifteen minutes for viewing and picture-snapping – if you are lucky enough to see the view before the mist rolls in.

Walks

The park features a few well-maintained, short and unchallenging **trails**, which take you through a strange, otherworldly landscape, dotted with smoking fumaroles (steam vents) and tough ferns and trees trying valiantly to hold up against regular sulphurous scaldings. Advice and a general map can be found at the **visitors' centre**, next to the car park/bus stop, and all the trails are clearly marked.

The **Crater Overlook** trail (750m; 15min) winds its way from the visitors' centre to the main crater, along a paved road. Side-trail **Sandero Botos** (1.4km; 30min) heads up through the forest to the pretty, emerald Botos Lake, which fills an extinct crater and makes a good spot for a picnic. Named for the pagoda-like tree commonly seen along its way, the **Escalonia** trail (about 1km; 30min) starts at the picnic area (follow the signs), then takes you through the forest, where the ground cover is less stunted compared to that at the crater.

Wildlife-watching

A wide variety of **birds** ply this temperate forest, among them the ostentatiously colourful quetzal, the robin and several species of hummingbird. Although a number of large mammals live in the park, including coyotes and wildcats such as the margay, you're unlikely to spot them. One animal you probably will come across, however, is the small, green-yellow **Poás squirrel**, which is endemic to the area.

Poás is also home to a rare version of cloudforest called dwarf or **stunted cloudforest**, a combination of pine-needle-like ferns, miniature bonsai-type trees and bromeliad-encrusted cover, all of which has been stunted by an onslaught of cold (temperatures up here can drop to below freezing), continual cloud cover and acid rain from the mouth of the volcano.

Arrival and information

By bus A Tuasa bus leaves daily at 8.30am from Av 2, C 12/14, in San José, travelling via Alajuela (1hr 30min).

By car If you want to reach Poás before both buses and clouds, either drive or take a taxi from Alajuela (roughly US$40) or San José (US$50–60) – reasonably affordable if split between a group of people.

Tourist information The park's visitors' centre, next to the car park at the entrance, has a souvenir shop, bathroom facilities and an expensive cafeteria.

Tours Most visitors get to the volcano on prearranged tours from San José – (approximately US$45 per person for a 4–5hr trip; see p.500 for details of tour operators). The "Four-in-One" tour organized by Expediciones Tropicales (℡2257-4171, ⓦwww.costaricainfo.com) is very popular, and also takes in the La Paz Waterfall Gardens, Parque Nacional Braulio Carrillo and a boat ride on Río Sarapiquí (US$87 per person, including breakfast, lunch and guide; 11hr).

Accommodation

There are plenty of places to stay in the vicinity of the volcano, including a couple of comfortable mountain lodges on working dairy farms (you'll need a car to get to them) and other, more simple and inexpensive places that can be reached on the daily bus to Poás. There is no camping allowed in the park.

Lodges

Lo Que tu Quieras 4km before the park entrance ℡2482-2092 or 8814-9150, ⓔlomasdeperseverancia@yahoo.com. A good budget option for the area, comprising three simple wooden cabins (one with a fireplace for the chilly mountain nights) with en-suite bathrooms. The on-site restaurant has huge picture windows that show off the stunning views and serves local dishes and tasty drinks – try the home-brewed cardamom or raspberry cocktails. Camping is also permitted (❷). Rooms ❺

Mirador Quetzal Just before *Lo Que tu Quieras* ℡2482-2090, ⓔrestmiradorquetzal@latinmail .com. This simple spot is the cheapest in the area,

with basic en-suite double rooms. The attached restaurant (8am–9pm daily) serves typical food at very reasonable prices; breakfast is included in your room price. ❺

LA PAZ WATERFALL GARDENS

A fifteen-kilometre drive east of Poás is one of Costa Rica's most popular attractions, the **LA PAZ WATERFALL GARDENS** (daily 8am–5pm; US$32; ⓦwww.waterfallgardens.com), an immaculate series of riverside trails linking five waterfalls on the Río La Paz. The trails are all set in a large colourful garden, and there's also a butterfly observatory, aviary, trout lake, frog exhibit and serpentarium. From the reception centre, visitors can take one of several self-guided tours, which wind prettily through the site and along the river. Viewing platforms at various points along the trails mean allow you to get both above and underneath the waterfalls, the highest of which, **Magia Blanca**, crashes deafeningly down some 40m. The marked trails conclude at the top of the **La Paz Waterfall**, Costa Rica's most photographed cascade (it can also be seen from the public highway below).

There's no public transport to the gardens, and most people visit them as part of a tour from San José (see p.500 for operators). If you're **driving**, take a right at the junction in Poásito towards Vara Blanca; on reaching the village, take a left at the gas station and follow the well-marked signs for 5km.

HEREDIA

Just 11km northeast of San José is the lively town of **HEREDIA**, boosted by the student population of the Universidad Nacional (UNA) at the eastern end of town. The town centre is prettier than most, with a few historical buildings, though it is a bit run-down. Lacking any major tourist draws, however, Heredia is used by travellers mainly as a base for trips to Volcán Barva and Braulio Carillo national park.

What to see and do

Heredia's layout conforms to the usual grid system, centred on the quiet **Parque Central**, draped with huge mango trees and overlooked by the plain **Basílica de la Inmaculada Concepción**, whose unexcitingly squat design – "seismic Baroque" – has kept it standing since 1797, despite several earthquakes. North of the plaza, the old colonial tower of **El Fortín**, "the Fortress", features odd gun slats which fan out and widen from the inside to the exterior, giving it a medieval look; you cannot enter or climb it.

East of the tower on Avenida Central, the **Casa de la Cultura**, an old colonial house with a large breezy veranda, displays local artwork, including sculpture and painting by local schoolchildren (generally open Mon–Fri 10am–5pm, occasionally on weekends). The **Mercado Central**, Av 6/8, C 2/4 (daily 5am–6pm), has the usual mess of aisles lined with rows of fruit and veg, dangling sausages and plump prawns.

Arrival and information

By bus Buses arrive along Av 6, C 3.
Exchange Banco Nacional, C 2, Av 2/4, and Scotiabank, Av 2, C 0 (also open Sat 8am–4pm) can change dollars and traveller's cheques.

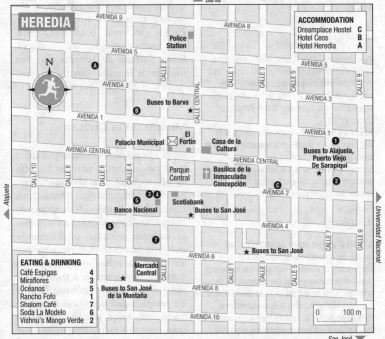

Post office The *correo* (Mon–Fri 8am–5.30pm, Sat 7.30am–noon) is on the northwest corner of the Parque Central.

Taxis Available taxis line up on the east side of the Mercado Central, between Av 6 and 8, and on the southern side of the Parque Central.

Accommodation

Accommodation in downtown Heredia is pretty sparse, though it's unlikely you'll need to stay in town, since San José is within easy reach and there are also several more interesting hotels in the country nearby.

Dreamplace Hostel Av 2, C 3/5 ☎ 2506-1111, ⓦ www.costaricatravel.ch. A good budget hostel with bright rooms and a small garden terrace. Dorms ❸, rooms ❹–❻

Hotel Ceos C 4, Av 1 ☎ 2262-2628, ⓦ www .hotelamericacr.com. A small hotel with ten simple rooms all with private bath, hot water and cable TV. There's also a restaurant serving local cuisine. You can't miss the Canadian flags outside. Singles ❹, doubles ❺, triple ❻

Hotel Heredia C 6, Av 3/5 ☎ 2238-0880, ⓦ www .hotelamericacr.com. Another good option, with twelve basic rooms offering en-suite bathrooms, hot water and cable TV. Singles ❸, doubles ❹, triple ❺

Eating

Café Espigas C 2, Av 2, southwest corner of the Parque Central. Though serving meal combos that include casados, burgers and sandwiches, this café specializes in Britt Finca coffee, with good cappuccinos and espressos. Coffee 600c, meal combo 2650c.

Soda La Modelo C 6, Av 4. A busy central soda with good budget staples, from *casados* (1800c) to cakes (500c). Open 24hr.

Shalom Café C 2, Av 6/4. A fine alternative to *gallo pinto* and *casados*, this small eatery serves great pita and falafel combos for 2200c.

Drinking

Nightlife is student-driven, restricted to a few local spots – the crowds head to the capital to party. If you're young or studently inclined, head to the four blocks immediately west of the university for the best bars. Keep an eye out for Tican chains *Vishnu* and *Trigo Miel*, which also have branches here.

Miraflores Av 2, C 2, upstairs from *Café Espigas*. This bar/disco is a popular night spot, especially Mon, Tues and Thurs, when there's live music; otherwise, Latin and reggae beats dominate the dancefloor.

Océanos C 4, Av 2/4. Nautically themed bar decorated with an assortment of fishing parapher-nalia and surfboards. It's popular with students for its cheap drinks and good *bocas*. Beer 650c.

Rancho Fofo C 7, Av 0. Just blocks from the university campus, this bar and seafood restaurant is massively popular with local students – there's lots of banging music and happy hour drink promo-tions. Beer 800c, bar snacks 1500c.

Moving on

By bus to: San José (C 6, Av 3; frequent; 45min). Services to Paso Llano and Sacramento, for Volcán Barva and PN Braulio Carrillo (frequent; 1hr), will drop you within 5km of the park's entrance. The town has no central bus terminal, but a variety of well-signed stops are scattered across town, mainly around the Mercado Central, from where most local buses leave.

AROUND HEREDIA

North and east of Heredia the terrain climbs to higher altitudes, reaching its highest point at **Volcán Barva**, at the western entrance of wild and rugged **Parque Nacional Braulio Carrillo**. The towns around here – **Barva, Santa Barbara de Heredia** and **San Joaquín de Heredia** – are the favoured residences of expats, but there's little to detain the visitor.

Museo de la Cultura Popular

Set in a large house in landscaped coffee fields two kilometres north of Heredia, the **Museo de la Cultura Popular** (Mon–Fri 9am–4pm, Sat–Sun 10am–5pm; US$2; ☎ 2260-1619, ⓦ www.ilam.org .cr/museoculturapopoular) tries to give an authentic portrayal of nineteenth- and early twentieth-century campesino life. The kitchen has been preserved as it would have been on a coffee finca, and you can sample authentic food of the period, including *torta de arroz, pan casero* and *gallos picadillos*, although apart from this there's little to do other than to wander around the house and the carefully kept gardens. Frequent buses depart Heredia from Av 1, C 1/3, and can be flagged down on the road for the return journey.

Parque Nacional Braulio Carrillo and Volcán Barva

The **PARQUE NACIONAL BRAULIO CARRILLO** (8am–4pm; US$10 advance purchase, US$15 on site), 35km northeast of San José, covers 325 square kilometres of virgin rain- and cloud-forest. The growth here gives you a good idea of what much of Costa Rica used to look like fifty years ago, when approximately three-quarters of the country's total terrain was virgin rainforest.

The park has five staffed **ranger stations**, or *puestos*. There are picnic facilities and several marked trails leading from the *puestos* into the forest. If you want to **stay** near the volcano, basic huts and **camping** facilities are available at the Barva *puesto* (☎2261-2619); this is the most commonly used entry point, and also marks the entry point for trails up the dormant **Volcán Barva** (separate entry US$7). The **main trail** (3km; about 1hr) up Barva's slopes begins at the western edge of Braulio Carrillo, and ascends through dense deciduous cover before reaching the cloudforest at the top. Along the way you'll get panoramic views over the Valle Central. Many travellers wander off the trails and get lost; take a compass, water and food, a sweater and rain gear, just in case. **Security** has become a growing problem in the park; leave nothing in parked vehicles, and try to find a guide for longer hikes. Try to get to the park early in the morning to enjoy the clearest views at the top, and be prepared for serious mud in the rainy season.

You can get to the village of Sacramento, 3km from the entrance, by bus from Heredia, but there's no public transport beyond here. If driving you'll have to cope with a bad stretch of road just before the volcano – a 4WD is necessary.

CARTAGO

CARTAGO, meaning "Carthage", was Costa Rica's capital for three hundred years before the centre of power was moved to San José in 1823. Founded in 1563 by Juan Vázquez de Coronado, the city, like its ancient namesake, has been razed a number of times, although in

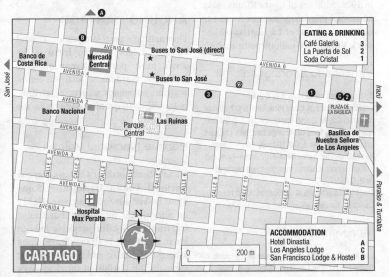

EATING & DRINKING
Café Galeria — 3
La Puerta de Sol — 2
Soda Cristal — 1

Banco de Costa Rica

Mercado Central

Buses to San José (direct)

Buses to San José

Banco Nacional

Parque Central

Las Ruinas

Plaza de la Basílica

Basílica de Nuestra Señora de Los Angeles

Hospital Max Peralta

ACCOMMODATION
Hotel Dinastia — A
Los Angeles Lodge — C
San Francisco Lodge & Hostel — B

San José

Irazú

Paraíso & Turrialba

CARTAGO

0   200 m

this case by **earthquakes** rather than Romans – two, in 1823 and 1910, practically demolished the place. Most travellers don't actually stay here, but pass through the town to visit the basilica and ruins on trips to Volcán Irazú.

What to see and do

Cartago's highlight is the **Iglesia de la Parroquía** (known as "Las Ruinas"), which sits on the eastern end of the concrete Parque Central. Originally built in 1575, the church was repeatedly destroyed by earthquakes, but stubbornly rebuilt by the Cartagoans each time, until the giant earthquake of 1910 finally vanquished it. Only the elegantly tumbling walls remain, enclosing pretty subtropical gardens. The ruins are not open to the public, but a view of them can be enjoyed from the central park across the road.

From the ruins it's five minutes' walk east to Cartago's only other attraction: the cathedral, properly called the **Basílica de Nuestra Señora de Los Angeles**, at C 16 and Av 2, which was rebuilt in a decorative Byzantine style after the original was destroyed in an earthquake in 1926. Millions of Costa Ricans make an annual pilgrimage here in August to honour the statue of **La Negrita** (or the Black Virgin), the nation's patron saint.

Arrival and information

By bus Buses arrive at Av 4/6, C 2/4.
Exchange Banco de Costa Rica, Av 4, C 5/7; Banco Nacional, C 3, Av 2; and Scotiabank, Av 2, C 2/4 (all open Sat 9am–1pm) will change traveller's cheques.
Internet Café at Av 4, C 8/10 (daily 10am–10pm).
Post office The *correo* (Mon–Fri 7.30am–6pm, Sat 7.30am–noon) is 10min from the town centre at Av 2, C 15/17.
Taxis There is a rank at Las Ruinas. A trip to nearby Lankaster Gardens should cost about US$25.

Accommodation

Los Angeles Lodge On the square by the Basilica ☎2551-0957. The *Lodge* offers simple en-suite

rooms and breakfast, as well as the *Puerta del Sol* restaurant downstairs. Ask at the bar if there's no one in reception. ⑥
Hotel Dinastia C 3, Av 6/8 ☎2551-7057. A basic hotel with spartan rooms (some en suite) but friendly service and a good central location, 75m north of the central market. ④
San Francisco Lodge & Hostel C 3, Av 6/8, next to *Hotel Dinastia* ☎2574-2359, ⓔhotelsanfranciscolodge@costariccense.com. The only truly budget hostel in town, with plain dorms and free breakfast. Rooms are booked as a whole, so groups will do better here. ③

Eating

Café Galeria Av 4, C 6/8. Good coffee and cakes, as well as breakfast and lunch, are served here in a small space decorated with local artwork. Coffee 600c, *gallo pinto* 1200c.
La Puerta Del Sol Av 4, C 18, across from the basilica. The usual assortment of *casados* and burgers, at restaurant prices. This is one of the most popular places in town (especially on Sun), so service can be slow. Plates 2000–4000c.
Soda Cristal Av 4, C 16. This cheap and central *soda* offers decent *comida t'pica* and cold beer. Beer 750c, *casado* 1700c.

Moving on

By bus to: San José (every 10min 5am–midnight, then every hour), leave from Av 4/6, C 2/4.

AROUND CARTAGO

Dominating the landscape around Cartago, mighty **Volcán Irazú** is the area's most popular excursion. The **Lankaster Gardens**, a botanical centre with an enormous variety of orchids, is the other frequented day-trip in the area.

Parque Nacional Volcán Irazú

Some 32km north of Cartago, **Parque Nacional Volcán Irazú** (daily 8am–4pm; US$10 advance purchase, US$15 on site) makes for a long, but scenic, trip from the city. The park's blasted-out lunar landscape is dramatic, reaching a height of 3432m and giving fantastic views to the Caribbean on clear days, while the inactive Diego de la Haya crater is creepily impressive, its deep depression filled with a strange green lake. Two marked **trails** lead from the entrance, where you'll find the ranger's booth, to the crater.

Only one public **bus** runs to the park, originating from the *Gran Hotel Costa Rica* in San José (daily 8am) – be there early in high season to get a seat. It picks up passengers at Las Ruinas in Cartago at 8.45am, then returns to San José around noon. The bus pulls in at the crater parking area, where there are toilets and a **visitors' centre** offering information on the park and containing a snack bar (open on weekends).

If you want to spend more time than the bus allows, the Ricardo Jimenez Oreamuno recreational area southwest of the volcano has several trails and **camping** facilities; contact the ranger station (☎2551-9398) for info. Five kilometres before the park entrance *Nochebuena* offers further lodging (☎2530-8013/8023) and a volcano museum (US$4) consisting of a short video, and detailed accounts of volcano history and the flora and fauna that survive in the harsh climate. The simple cabin for rent has three bedrooms and a sweet fireplace (☎).

Lankaster Gardens

Orchids are the main attraction at **Lankaster Gardens** (daily 8.30am–4.30pm; US$5; ☎2552-3247), a tropical garden and research station 6km southeast of Cartago. The dry months of March and April are the best time to see the blooms.

To get to the gardens take a Paraíso bus from Cartago, getting off when you see the *Casa Vieja* restaurant, about ten minutes out of town. Take the road to your right, signposted to the gardens, then turn right again at the fork – it's about a ten-minute walk. Alternatively, a taxi from Cartago costs US$25.

TURRIALBA

The pleasant agricultural town of **TURRIALBA**, 45km east of Cartago on the eastern slopes of the Cordillera Central, has sweeping views over the rugged eastern Talamancas, though there's little to keep visitors here – most are likely to see it as part of a trip to the **Monumento Nacional Guayabo** or en route to a **whitewater rafting** or **kayaking** trip on the Reventazón or Pacuaré rivers. Costa Rica Expeditions and Expediciones Tropicales (see p.500) offer rafting day-trips for US$75–100, and many of the mountain-lodge-type hotels in the area have guided walks or horseback rides up dormant **Volcán Turrialba**. San José–Turrialba buses leave every hour between 5am and 10pm from C 13, Av 6/8.

Monumento Nacional Guayabo

The most important archeological site in Costa Rica, the **Monumento Nacional Guayabo** (daily 8am–4pm; US$7; ☎2559-0099 or 2556-9057) lies 19km northeast of Turrialba. Though interesting, in truth there's not a great deal to see (really just some stone heaps), as the site's importance has more to do with the dearth of any other surviving contemporary structures in Costa Rica. Guayabo belongs to the archeological-cultural area known as **Intermedio**, which begins roughly in the province of Alajuela and extends to Venezuela, Colombia and parts of Ecuador. Archeologists believe that Guayabo was inhabited from about 1000 BC to 1400 AD; most of the heaps of stones and basic structures now exposed were erected between 300 and 700 AD.

Daily **buses** run to Guayabo from Turrialba from 100m south of the main bus terminal (Mon–Sat 11am & 5.15pm, returning 12.30pm & 5.30pm; Sun 9am, returning 5pm), though the inconvenient timetable means you either have not enough or too much time at the site. **Driving** from Turrialba takes about thirty minutes; the last 4km is on a bad gravel road – passable with a regular car, but watch your clearance. **Taxis** charge around US$30 from Turrialba.

Limón Province and the Caribbean coast

Sparsely populated **Limón Province** sweeps south in an arc from Nicaragua down to Panama. Hemmed in to the north by dense jungles and swampy waterways, to the west by the mighty Cordillera Central and to the south by the even wider girth of the Cordillera Talamanca, the region has a lost, end-of-the-world feel.

Limón holds much appeal for ecotourists, having the highest proportion of protected land in the country. At **Tortuguero** you can watch giant sea turtles lay their eggs, while at **Cahuita** and **Manzanillo** you can snorkel coral reefs and surf at **Puerto Viejo**. In addition, more than anywhere else in Costa Rica, the Caribbean coast exudes a sense of **cultural diversity**. The largest

city, **Puerto Limón**, is a port town with a large (mostly Jamaican-descended) Afro-Caribbean population; Caribbean **English** or patois is spoken widely along the coast. Near the Panamanian border you'll find communities of indigenous peoples from the **Bribrí** and **Cabécar** groups.

Getting around Limón Province can require patience. From San José to Puerto Limón there are just two roads, and from Puerto Limón to the Panama border at Sixaola there is one narrow and badly maintained route. North of Puerto Limón there is no public land transport at all: instead, private *lanchas* ply the coastal canals connecting Moín, 8km north of Puerto Limón, to Tortuguero and Río Colorado near the Nicaraguan border. There are also scheduled flights from San José to Tortuguero. It's worth nothing that travel in northern Limón province is not as cheap as in other parts of the country due to a scarcity of options; even cheaper boat routes add up when you take connecting bus/taxi trips into account.

PUERTO LIMÓN

PUERTO LIMÓN, 165km east of San José, is Costa Rica's main port, with a somewhat neglected air and a reputation as Central America's prime drug-trafficking gateway. The place does have some rough edges, and while the stories Highland Ticos tell of the place are a bit exaggerated, it's worth watching your back – much of the town is not safe for

---

CARNAVAL IN LIMÓN

Though in the rest of the Americas Carnaval is usually associated with the days before Lent, Limón takes Columbus's arrival in the New World – October 12 – as its point of celebration. El Día de la Raza (Columbus Day) is basically an excuse to party.

The carnival features a variety of events, from Afro-Caribbean dance to Calypso music, bull-running, children's theatre, colourful *desfiles* (parades) and firework displays. Most spectacular is the Gran Desfile, usually held on the Saturday before October 12, when revellers in Afro-Caribbean costumes parade through the streets. This is the most popular time of year to visit Limón. so book rooms well in advance.

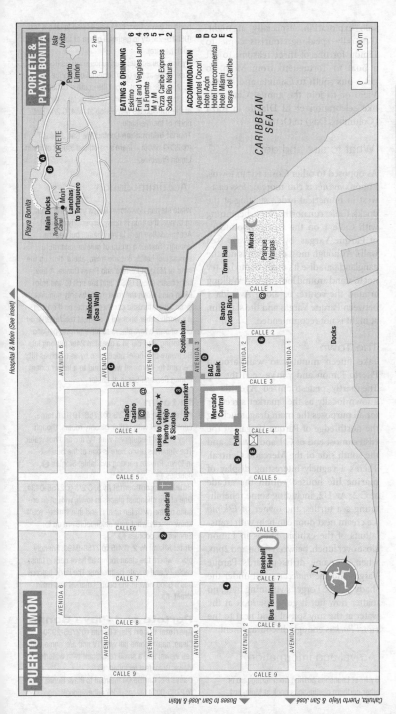

PUERTO LIMÓN

Hospital & Moín (See inset) ▲

PORTETE & PLAYA BONITA

Isla Uvita

Playa Bonita

Main Docks

Tortuguero Canal • Moín
Lanchas to Tortuguero

PORTETE

Puerto Limón

0   2 km

EATING & DRINKING
Eskimo   6
Fruit and Veggies Land   4
La Fuente   3
M y M   5
Pizza Caribe Express   1
Soda Bio Natura   2

ACCOMMODATION
Apartotel Cocori   B
Hotel Acón   D
Hotel Intercontinental   C
Hotel Miami   E
Oasys del Caribe   A

CARIBBEAN SEA

0   100 m

AVENIDA 6
AVENIDA 5
AVENIDA 4
AVENIDA 3
AVENIDA 2
AVENIDA 1

CALLE 1
CALLE 2
CALLE 3
CALLE 4
CALLE 5
CALLE 6
CALLE 7
CALLE 8
CALLE 9

Malecón (Sea Wall)

Town Hall

Parque Vargas

Mural

Scotiabank

Banco Costa Rica

BAC Bank

Radio Casino

Buses to Cahuita, Puerto Viejo & Sikaola ★

Supermarket

Mercado Central

Police

Cathedral

Baseball Field

Bus Terminal

Docks

N

◀ Cahuita, Puerto Viejo & San José   Buses to San José & Main ▲   Buses to San José & Moín ▼

solo exploration, especially at night. Generally speaking, tourists come to Limón for one of three reasons: to get a **boat** to Tortuguero from Moín, to get a **bus** south to Cahuita and Puerto Viejo or to join the annual Carnaval-like celebration of **El Día de la Raza** (Columbus Day) in October.

What to see and do

As opposed to other Costa Rican towns, Limón's *avenidas* run more or less east–west in numerical order, starting at the docks. *Calles* run north–south, beginning with **Calle 1** on the western boundary of **Parque Vargas**, by the *malecón* (sea wall). Although most of Limón is not the gangland paradise it's made out to be, try not to stand around looking lost. Walking around the centre, or along Avenida 1 between Parque Vargas and the stadium, at night is not recommended.

The Town

Take fifteen minutes to walk around Puerto Limón and you've seen the lot. The partly pedestrianized **Avenida 2**, known locally as the "market street", is for all purposes the main drag, touching the north edge of Parque Vargas, at the easternmost end of C 1 and Av 1/2, and the south side of the **Mercado Central**. There's a vaguely interesting display of **marine life** housed within the arcade at C 2, Av 1/2, including some rehabilitating sea turtles; the owner of *Eskimo* ice cream next door can help with translations of the exhibit. Shops in Limón close over lunch, between noon and 2pm, when everyone drifts towards Parque Vargas and the *malecón* to sit under the shady palms. Forget swimming here, no matter how hot it gets; one look at the water at the tiny spit of sand next to the *Hotel Park* is enough discouragement.

Arrival and information

By boat Launches arriving from Tortuguero or other northern destinations dock at Moín, just north of town; from here you'll need to take a taxi (US$15–25, try to gather a group at the dock to split the fare).

By bus Transportes Caribeños services from San José arrive at the Gran Terminal del Caribe at Av 2, C 7/8. Arrivals from the south – Cahuita, Puerto Viejo and Panama (via Sixaola) – terminate at the Transportes Mepe stop at Av 4, C 2/4, just north of the Mercado.

Tourist information Contact the San José ICT (℡ 2299-5800) – there's no official tourist office in Limón Province.

Accommodation

While staying downtown keeps you in the thick of things, the area is noisy, especially at night. Accomodation here is very basic, but secure enough. There's a group of quieter (and more expensive) hotels outside town, about 4km up the road to Moín at Portete and Playa Bonita. A taxi here costs about US$2, and the bus to and from Moín runs along the road every twenty minutes or so. Opportunistic car theft is rife, so if driving, it's worth either booking a room at the *Hotel Acón*, one of only a few places to have private parking, or storing your car in a guarded 24hr parking lot. Be aware that hotel prices rise by as much as fifty percent for Carnaval week, and to a lesser extent during Semana Santa at Easter.

In town

Hotel Acón Av 3, C 2/3 ℡ 2758-1010. A large, central hotel with rather gloomy rooms, though they are well-equipped with TV, a/c and hot water. The *Aquarius* disco here is one of the busiest in town. Private parking available. Singles ⑤, doubles ⑥

Hotel Intercontinental Av 5, C 2/3 ℡ 2758-0434. One of the cheapest places in town, with plain en-suite rooms (with fan or a/c) and thin walls – you'll know exactly what your neighbours are up to. Singles ②, doubles ③

Hotel Miami Av 2, C 4/5 ℡ 2758-0490. Friendly place where the clean rooms all have ceiling fans, cable TV and private bathrooms. The large balcony has a good view of the central market and main street. ④

Portete and Playa Bonita

Apartotel Cocori Playa Bonita ℡ 2795-2930. Clean, basic rooms (all with TV and a/c, some with sea views) and a small restaurant with waterfront views. Breakfast included. ⑥

Oasys del Caribe On the road to Playa Bonita ℡ 2795-0024, ✉ oasysdelcaribe@googlepages.com.

Clean rooms with fan or a/c, set in lush gardens with a pool and on-site restaurant. ⑤–⑥

Eating and drinking

Limón has pretty good, varied food. The town's speciality is Creole cooking – rice and beans cooked in coconut milk, jerk chicken and spicy meat stews – though many restaurants serve Chinese options, as well as *comida t'pica*. There's a host of decent *sodas* inside the Mercado Central. Most locals hang out with a beer in the evenings, but gringos, especially women, should avoid bars, particularly those that have large placards blocking views of the interior. Don't drink the tap water in Limón.

Restaurants and bars

Eskimo In the arcade at C 2, Av 1/2. Ice cream (350c), excellent coffees (300c) and pastries and basic dishes served in a clean and breezy passageway. Abraham, the friendly owner, speaks English and is a good source of information on the area.

Fruit and Veggies Land C 7, Av 2/3. The place to detox, with a huge display of fresh local produce, delicious *batidos* and fruit salads. Juices 600c, salads from 900c.

La Fuente C 3, Av 3/4. Large bar/restaurant with kitsch decor and friendly service. The menu ranges from filling burgers (1200c) to chop suey (1500c), and the bar is always crowded.

M y M Av 2, C 4/5. A barn-like eatery with a tacky, 1980s Christmas interior and huge menu offering seafood, Chinese and Tican dishes at bargain prices. Cheeseburger 900c, chow mein 2500c.

Pizza Caribe Express Av 4, C 2. Cheap and slightly greasy pizzeria also serving spaghetti (1500c) and sandwiches (700c). Small pizza 2000c.

Soda Bio Natura C 6, Av 4. A healthy option with good breakfast choices (around 1600c). Try a thirst-quenching fruit *batido* (550c) or some avocado toast (700c).

Directory

Exchange Banco de Costa Rica, Av 2, C 1 (Mon–Fri 8am–4pm), and Scotiabank, Av 3, C 2 (Mon–Fri 8.30am–4.30pm, Sat 8.30am–3.30pm), will change dollars.

Internet At Cyber Internet, Av 4, C 3 (daily 9am–8pm) or in La Casona souvenir shop, C 1, Av 2 (Mon–Sat 8am–5pm), across from Parque Vargas.

Medical care Hospital Dr Tony Facio Castro (☏ 2758-0580), at the north end of the malecón, or the 24hr Red Cross centre (☏ 2758-0125) on Av 1, one block south of the market.

Post office The *correo* (Mon–Fri 8am–5.30pm, Sat 8.30am–noon) is at Av 2, C 4, though the mail service from Limón is dreadful.

Moving on

By boat *Lanchas* (US$50 per person; 3–5hr) make the trip to Tortuguero from the docks at Moín, just outside of town to the north. Arrive early (7–9am), although you may be able to find boatmen until 2pm. If you are travelling alone or in a couple, try to get a group together at the docks.

By bus From the Gran Terminal del Caribe terminal: Transportes Caribeños services run to San José (hourly 5am–7pm), and Trasaca (☏ 2797-2036, ⓦ www.trasaca.com) services run to Guápiles, Moín (Mon–Fri hourly 5.30am–6.30pm) and Siquirres. From the Transportes Mepe office (☏ 2758-1572/0618) at C 3, Av 4 buses (hourly 5am–6pm) to: Bribrí (3–4hr); Cahuita (1hr); Puerto Viejo (1hr 30min–2hr); Sixaola (3–4 hr). Buses also run to Manzanillo (5 weekly, 4 Sat–Sun; 2–3hr).

By taxi Taxis line up outside the main bus terminal, and will do trips to Moín (US$3–5), Cahuita and Puerto Viejo (US$40–50).

TORTUGUERO

The peaceful village of **TORTU-GUERO** lies on a thin spit of land between the sea and the Tortuguero Canal, at the corner of one of Costa Rica's great natural attractions – **Parque Nacional Tortuguero**. Despite its isolation – 254km from San José, and 83km northwest of Limón – the area is extremely popular with visitors, mainly because of its spectacular biodiversity. It can rain up to 300 days a year here, and the soggy environment hosts a wide abundance of species: fifty kinds of **fish**, over 100 **reptiles**, over 300 species of **birds** and 60 species of **mammals**, several under the threat of extinction. Most notably, the beach here is one of the world's main nesting sites for **green sea turtles**.

What to see and do

It's the **turtles** that draw the crowds. Though the most popular – and expensive – way to see them is on one of hundreds of **packages** that use the

GETTING TO TORTUGUERO

Getting to Tortuguero independently can be tricky – you can either do a combination bus/boat route, or you can fly.

By bus In San José, buses depart for the town of Cariari from the Gran Terminal del Caribe (C 0, Av 13) – catch one at 6.30am, 9am or 10.30am to make the onward connections from Cariari to Tortuguero. Purchase tickets in advance from the Guápiles counter (℡2222-0610) in the terminal. Upon arrival in Cariari, you have a few options, all of which involve a bus-to-boat transfer. Coopertraca (℡2767-7590 or 8368-1275) has a ticket office at the arrival terminal, with onward bus connections to La Pavona (1hr 30min; US$2), from where the boats launch, at 6am, 9.30am, 11.30am and 3pm. Clic Clic (℡2709-8155 or 8844-0463) also does the trip (6am and noon). Buses leave from the old station in Cariari, about five blocks north of the arrival terminal. If your bus gets in to Cariari at 3pm, just missing the last bus connection, you can still get to the docks before the last boats leave at 4.30pm – you'll have to take a taxi (US$20–30).

By boat Coopertraca has boats (US$3) departing from La Pavona (7.30am, 10.30am, 1.30pm & 4.30pm), as does Clic Clic (6am, 8.30am, 11.30am, 1.30pm, 3.30pm & 4.30pm). Ruben Bananero (℡2709-8005) has more expensive services: buses with onward boat connections (via the Geest plantation) from San José and Cariari, as well as two daily boats (10am and 3pm) from Moín. From Moín you can also find *lanchas* willing to take you up the canal anytime from 6am until 2pm.

By air Sansa (℡2223-4179) and NatureAir (℡2299-6000) offer daily flights from San José to Tortuguero (departing 6–7am; 40–50min).

all-inclusive "jungle lodges" in the canals near the village, you can also visit Tortuguero and the park **independently**, staying in *cabinas* in the village and arrange trips with local guides.

The Town

Covered in wisteria, oleander and bougainvillea, Tortuguero village looks like a dilapidated tropical garden. It is centred on the main **dock**, or *muelle*, where all the *lanchas* arrive. The main signpost here has a village map to help you orient yourself. Two dirt paths run north–south through the village – the "main street" and "Avenida 2", or secondary street – from which narrow paths go off to the sea and the canal. At the north end of the village there's a **Natural History Museum** (daily 10am–5.30pm; US$1) run by the Caribbean Conservation Corporation (www.cccturtle.org), which houses a small but informative exhibition explaining the life cycle of sea turtles and a video

explaining the history of turtle conservation in the area.

Parque Nacional Tortuguero

Entrance to the park (8am–4pm; US$10; ℡2710-2929) is at the **Cuatro Esquinas Station**, just south of the village and reached by the main path (right from the main dock). During the day you can walk the generally well-maintained, self-guided **El Gavilán trail** (1km), which starts at the entrance and skirts a small swamp, covering the width of the land from lagoon to sea. You can also amble for up to 30km south along the **beach**, enjoying a bit of crab-spotting or birdwatching as you go, as well as looking for turtle tracks, which resemble the two thick parallel lines trucks leave in their wakes. Check with local information sources before swimming, though – currents can be strong, and sharks present.

Turtle tours

You can watch the turtles lay their eggs by taking part in a **turtle tour**. These trips, led by certified guides, leave nightly at 8pm and 10pm from the village. There are more than a hundred certified guides in Tortuguero; they charge US$15–20 for a tour, and tend to hang around the main dock in search of custom. You'll also need to buy a ticket (US$10) from rangers at the park entrance, east of the main dock. No more than two hundred people are allowed on the beach at any one time, visitors must wear dark clothing, refrain from smoking and are not allowed to bring cameras (still or video) or flash-lights. Everyone must be off the beach by midnight.

Boat tours

Almost as popular as the turtle tours in Tortuguero are the **boat tours** through the area's canals and *caños*, or lagoons, to spot animals including monkeys, caiman and Jesus Christ lizards, and birds including herons, cranes and kingfishers. Fishing trips and boat rentals (US$10–15/hr) are offered by most tour operators.

Cerro Tortuguero

It's possible to scale **Cerro Tortuguero**, an ancient volcanic deposit looming above the flat coastal plain 6km north of the village. A climb up the gently sloping side, on either the **La Ceiba** or **La Bomba trails** (90min return), leads you to the "peak", from where there are good views of flat jungle and inland waterways. It is possible to do this hike alone, but paying a guide means you are more likely to actually see snakes (before stepping on them) and other camouflaged wildlife along the way; many local operators offer guided hikes from US$20.

Arrival and information

By air Flights land at the airstrip some 4km north of the village; if you are staying at a lodge, they will come and pick you up; otherwise you'll have to walk.
By boat All *lanchas* pull into the dock, or *muelle*, in the centre of Tortuguero town. Guides wait here to scavenge independent travellers.
Tourist information See ⓦ www.tortuguerovillage .com for local maps, tour information and a comprehensive business listing. In the village, handy maps and advice can be found from the Pura Vida Tours "office" at *El Muellecito* restaurant.

Accommodation

Staying in Tortuguero on a budget entails bedding down in one of the independent cabinas in the village. Camping on the beach is not allowed, but you can pitch your tent by the park entrance for US$3 a day.
Cabinas Aracari South of the football pitch ☎2709-8006. Clean, comfortable cabinas, all with private bath, cold water and fan, set in a beautiful tree-filled garden. ④
Cabinas Balcon del Mar On the beachfront, just south of *Cabinas Icaco* ☎2709-8124 or 8870-6247. These six rooms are the cheapest lodging in town; those upstairs in the main house have a balcony, while the separate cabinas are en suite. ②

TURTLE TIME

Every year Tortuguero is overrun with visitors who come for one reason – to see marine turtles lay their eggs (an event called the desove). Although Tortuguero is by no means the only place in Costa Rica to see marine turtles nesting, three of the largest kinds of endangered sea turtles regularly nest here in large numbers. Along with the green (verde) turtle, named for the colour of soup made from its flesh, you might see the hawksbill (carey), with its distinctive hooked beak, and the ridged leatherback (baula), the largest turtle in the world, which can easily weigh 300kg – some are as heavy as 400kg and reach 3m in length. The green turtles and hawksbills nest in the greatest numbers from July to October (Aug is the peak month); the leatherbacks come ashore from March to May.

TOUR OPERATORS IN TORTUGUERO

There are many tour operators in Tortuguero offering competitively priced excursions; Caiman and Tunan have some of the cheapest available. Most cabinas will be able to organize tours for you, as well.

Caiman/Pura Vida Tours At *El Muellecito* restaurant (☎2814-7403 or 2709-8104, ✉abeldiaz1978@hotmail.com). Organizes turtle and canoe tours, as well as *lancha* trips to Moín, Puerto Viejo and Cahuita. Brothers Alfonso and Abel, who run the trips, speak some English.

Caribeño Fishing Tours Next to *Miss Junie's* (☎2709-8026). Offers rod fishing, as well as all the other tours, although at US$65/hr, they are not cheap.

Tunan Tours At the *Dorling Bakery* (☎2709-8132 or 8876-2263). Organizes all sorts of tour and *lancha* trips; English-speaking guides are available.

Cabinas Caribbean Sunrise On the left, past the *Taberna Punta de Encuentro* ☎2709-8167, ✉sunrisetortuguero@yahoo.com. Large, cool rooms (all with en suite, cable TV and fans, and some with kitchens) run by American surfer Gary. ❹

Cabinas Icaco On the beachfront, 100m south of *Miss Miriam II* ☎2709-8044, ✉elicaco1 @yahoo.es. A large green building with 14 rooms, all en suite with hot water and fan. There's a good communal kitchen and relaxing hammock area; camping facilities also available. Camping ❶, rooms ❸

Cabinas Meriscar South of *Cabinas Aracari*, 100m before the beach ☎2709-8202. Two cabins with private bathrooms, plus some cabinas with shared bathroom – they're slightly gloomy, but large and clean. Camping available in the garden. Camping ❶, rooms ❷

Cabinas Princesa del Rio On the main street, between the dock and park entrance ☎2709-8131. The best of the three *Princesa* locations in town, with cabinas right on the riverside. Basic rooms are for one to three people; the nicest ones at the end look out onto the lagoon. ❷

Cabinas Tortuguero Across from the *Taberna* ☎2709-8114 or 8839-1200, ✉cabinas _tortuguero@yahoo.com. Rooms (all en suite with fans) are set in a lovely garden and food is available at the restaurant, with an hour's notice (6am–6.30pm). ❹

Eating

Tortuguero village offers good homely food, typically Caribbean, with wonderful fresh fish. The only disadvantage is that prices tend to be high: expect to pay up to twice as much for a meal as you'd pay in other parts of Costa Rica.

Buddha Café Next to the I.C.E. building. A swanky riverfront café with an overpriced Italian-style menu, but good coffee (café latte 1600c) and a lovely outdoor garden facing the river. Closed Wed.

Dorling Bakery Across from The Jungle souvenir shop. A great spot for breakfast or a snack, with delicious cakes, cookies, pies and ice cream – try the banana bread (600c) or guava pie. Seating available in the riverside garden, which has a pretty view. Coffee 600c.

La Lapa Verde Just past *Cabinas Aracari*. A cheery *soda*, decorated in pastels and plastic flowers, with large *casados* (2500c) and good *refrescos* (500c). Doña Florentina, who runs the kitchen, makes a mean rice and beans (3500c).

Miss Miriam's II On the beachfront, next to the Adventist church. Cheerful and immaculate restaurant serving Caribbean fare. Rooms available, too (❹). Meals 2800–5600c.

El Muellecito Next to the Super Nicarao. Tortuguero's best budget option, with a filling, *soda*-style menu. Breakfasts 1100–1600c, grilled fish with sides 2200c.

Soda Culebra At the main dock. Cheap fried chicken, *casados* and coffee (600c); it's the best spot for a quick caffeine injection before setting off.

Drinking and nightlife

La Culebra Next to the main dock. This is the town's most popular watering-hole: the riverfront bar is loud and the dancefloor fills up with locals at night. Beer 750c.

Restaurante Princesa On the beachfront, behind Souvenir Pura Vida. Though the mainly seafood menu is expensive, the beachside location and booming tropical rhythms make it a good spot to grab a beer (1000c).

Taberna Punto de Encuentro Riverside, 100m east of the main dock. An alternative to *La Culebra*, with pool tables and a large dancefloor looking out onto the river – great for sunset views, although the music volume can detract from the surroundings. Cheap dishes are served from the kitchen and *Cabinas Tropical* also have rooms (**2**). Beer 1000c.

Directory

Exchange There is no bank in Tortuguero, but in the high season supermarkets will offer cash advances for a fee.
Internet At the café across from the Paraíso Tropical dock (open May–Oct 11am–8pm; US$4/hr).
Medical care Ebais, across from the main dock, serves as a clinic, but the doctor only visits once a week.
Post office The *correo* is in the middle of the village.
Telephones At *Miss Junie's* restaurant, the central Super Morpho supermarket, across from the I.C.E. and outside *Cabinas Aracari*.

Moving on

By air Nature Air and Sansa both have daily flights back to San José.

By boat Coopertraca (4 boats daily) and Clic Clic (5 boats daily) offer transport to La Pavona, and onwards to Cariari and San José, while Ruben Bananero offers daily boats to Moín. Many local tour operators also arrange *lancha* trips south to Moín (from US$25 per person) – try Caiman/Pura Vida tours across from the main dock.

CAHUITA

The tiny coastal village of **CAHUITA**, 43km southeast of Limón, comprises just two puddle-dotted, gravel-and-sand streets running parallel to the sea, intersected by a few cross-streets. Few locals drive (bicycles are popular), so most of the vehicles you see kicking up the dust belong to visitors. Though the principal daylight activity in Cahuita is taking a boat trip out to **Parque Nacional Cahuita**'s coral reef to **snorkel** (see p.528), the fairly empty stretches of sand along the water make the beaches here perfect for relaxing and sun-bathing as well.

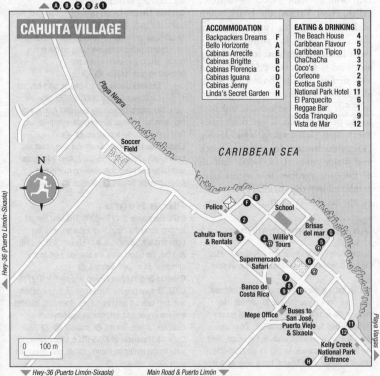

CAHUITA VILLAGE

▲ **A**, **B**, **C**, **D** &**1**

ACCOMMODATION	
Backpackers Dreams	F
Bello Horizonte	A
Cabinas Arrecife	E
Cabinas Brigitte	B
Cabinas Florencia	C
Cabinas Iguana	D
Cabinas Jenny	G
Linda's Secret Garden	H

EATING & DRINKING	
The Beach House	4
Caribbean Flavour	5
Caribbean Tipico	10
ChaChaCha	3
Coco's	7
Corleone	2
Exotica Sushi	8
National Park Hotel	11
El Parquecito	6
Reggae Bar	1
Soda Tranquilo	9
Vista de Mar	12

Playa Negra

Soccer Field

CARIBBEAN SEA

N

Hwy-36 (Puerto Limón-Sixaola)

Police

School

Brisas del mar

Cahuita Tours & Rentals

Willie's Tours

Supermercado Safari

Banco de Costa Rica

Mepe Office

Buses to San José, Puerto Viejo & Sixaola

Kelly Creek National Park Entrance

Playa Vargas

0   100 m

What to see and do

Cahuita's main street runs from the national park entrance at **Kelly Creek** to the northern end of the village, marked more or less by the football pitch. Beyond here it continues two or three kilometres north along Black-Sand Beach. The small **park** at the central crossroads downtown is the focal point of the village, where locals wait for buses and catch up on recent gossip.

The beaches

It's possible to swim on either of the village's two **beaches**, although neither is fantastic: the first 400m or so of the narrow white-sand beach just south of town is dangerous on account of riptides, while **Black-Sand Beach (Playa Negra)**, northwest of town, is littered with driftwood, although you can swim in some places. Sometimes called **Playa Vargas**, the beach south of Punta Cahuita in Parque Nacional Cahuita is better for swimming than those in the village; however, it's slightly awkward to get to (see p.528). You can also **surf** at Cahuita; boards are available to rent from the Info Boutique next to Super Safari supermarket, and next to the police station. If you don't fancy snorkelling, *Cabinas Brigitte* and Mr Big J's organize **horse rides** along the beach and jungle hikes (US$25–35), and all of the tour agencies in Cahuita offer combined Jeep trips to local villages and nearby beaches (US$40).

Arrival and information

By bus Buses stop outside *Bar y Restaurante Vaz*. Current timetables are posted at the Mepe office there.

Tourist information The *Costa Rican Caribbean Info Guide* (free, if you can find it), unfolds into maps of the local area and a directory of accommodation and businesses in Cahuita. Otherwise, the only sources of information in the village itself are the tour companies: Mr Big J's (☎2755-0353), across from the main square, has a book exchange

and laundry facilities; Turística Cahuita (☎2755-0071) sells the *Tico Times*. Both agencies, as well as Cahuita Tours and El Parquecito, offer local trips and national park and snorkelling tours (from US$15 per person).

Accommodation

Cahuita is popular with budget travellers, but it's not rock-bottom cheap. Groups get the best deal, as most cabinas charge per room and have space for at least three or four people. The centre of the village has scores of options, and there's also accommodation along the long (3km or so) road that runs along Playa Negra, though this area is reputedly dodgy; solo women travellers may feel more comfortable staying in town. Several camping options can be found in the vicinity, including the jungle grounds at the Puerto Vargas ranger station in the national park (along the trail and around the point from the Kelly Creek station; see p.528).

In the village

Backpackers Dreams Across from *Miss Edith's* ☎2755-0174. A crumbling, ramshackle house with the most basic rooms in town. ③

Cabinas Arrecife On the seafront, just north of the police station ☎2775-0081 or 8835-2940, ⓦcabinasarrecife.com. A relaxed, backpacker-style atmosphere with hammocks slung on the porch, cheap, simply furnished rooms and snorkelling gear for hire. ④–⑤

Cabinas Jenny On the beach, 50m beyond *Caribbean Flavour* ☎2755-0256 ⓦwww.geocities.com/cabinasjenny. Beautiful rooms with high wooden ceilings, sturdy beds, mosquito nets, fans and wonderful sea views. ④–⑤

Linda's Secret Garden Down the side street just before Kelly Creek ☎2755-0327. A no-frills option with large and basic non-smoking rooms and a jungle garden. Singles ②, doubles ③

Playa Negra

Bello Horizonte ☎2755-0206. The best budget lodging along the Playa Negra stretch, with ten large and simple cabinas with kitchen, fridge, bath and fan; the nicest ones are seaside, next to the upmarket *Blue Spirit Cabinas*. ④

Cabinas Brigitte Just behind *Reggae Bar* ☎2755-0053, ⓦwww.brigittecahuita.com. A cosy location with two cabinas and two rooms. Breakfast, internet and laundry on site, and horses and bicycles available for hire. Rooms ④, cabinas ⑤–⑥

Cabinas Florencia ☎2755-0124. Large, basic en-suite rooms rented by friendly locals, and an on-site *soda*. Clean and safe. ④

Cabinas Iguana Past *Cabinas Brigitte* ☎2755-0005, ⊛www.cabinas-iguana.com. Lovely wood-panelled cabinas on stilts, set back from the beach, and a main lodge with a big screened veranda, plus laundry service, book exchange and small pool. Groups get better deals. ❹

Eating

Cahuita has plenty of places to eat fresh local food, with a surprisingly cosmopolitan selection. As with accommodation, prices are not low – an evening meal starts at around 2800c – and service tends to be laid-back: leave yourself lots of time to eat.

Restaurants

The Beach House 50m east of Dr. Bike's. This brightly painted bakery has yummy breakfasts (2200c), including waffles and home-made bread, although the portions are not overly generous.
Caribbean Flavour Next to *El Parquecito*. Cheap eats in a central location, with friendly, laid-back service. The reggae bar here also sells alcohol to take away. Breakfast 1600c, cheeseburger 1600c, *casado* 2200c.
ChaChaCha Diagonal to *Corleone*. Fantastic gourmet cuisine – exotic salads and seafood – at manageable prices, served in a pretty setting with fresh flowers and fairy lights. Cocktails 2200c, mains 3600–6600c.
El Parquecito Behind the village park. A good place for breakfast (2200–3600c), with fresh juices, pancakes and French toast, and the best iced coffee (1600c) along the coast.
🏃 **Exotica Sushi** Next to *Soda Tranquilo*. A tiny eatery covered in twinkling lights, *Exotica* serves incredibly eclectic but beautifully prepared dishes: think both sushi and gourmet pitas. The promotion platters are huge and filling. Roll 4400c, pita meal 3800c, platter 5500c.
Soda Tranquilo Diagonally across from the bus station. One of the cheaper options in town; the location makes it a good spot to grab a *boca* while waiting for the bus. *Bocas* 1600c, *casados* 2200c.
Vista de Mar By the park entrance at Kelly Creek. Known to locals as "El Chines", this barn-sized restaurant has a vast menu featuring several inexpensive rice-and-bean combos and Chinese dishes. Mains 2800–5500c.

Drinking and nightlife

Caribbean Tipico Across from *Coco's*. The less popular of the two main bar/discos in town (although it actually has the nicer balcony), with equally loud music and erratic opening hours.

Coco's At the main junction in the town centre. This unavoidable bar and disco is *the* night-spot in Cahuita, with frequent live music, cheap beer and a strong rum punch. Beer 1100c, punch 2800c.
National Park Hotel By the park entrance at Kelly Creek. A rocking nightly disco in the high season. Beer 1100c.
Reggae Bar Attached to the *Reggae Cabinas*, Playa Negra. The restaurant's beachside location makes it a good place to grab a cold beer and enjoy the sea breeze. Beer US$2.50, cocktail from US$5.

Directory

Bicycle rental Bikes and scooters are available to rent from several places; try friendly Dr Bike's (8am–6pm daily), diagonal to *Coco's*, for the cheapest rates (bikes US$2.50/day, scooters US$35/day).
Exchange Banco de Costa Rica (Mon–Fri 8am–4pm), one block from the bus station in the Centro Comercial White Sand, has an ATM.
Internet At the CyberNet Café in *Cabinas Palmar*, Willie's Tours (☎2843-4700), or at *Cabinas Brigitte* in Playa Negra.
Medical care Ebais medical clinic, across from the Centro Comercial Safari, south of the bus stop (closed Tues, Sat & Sun).
Police The *guardía rural* is on the last beach-bound road at the north end of the village.
Post office Next door to the police station, the *correo* (technically Mon–Fri 7.30am–5pm) keeps erratic hours.

Moving on

By bus to: Limón (15 daily); San José (4 daily; 4hr). A local bus runs from Cahuita to Puerto Viejo (15 daily 6am–7pm; 40min) and continues on to Bribrí, Sixaola and the Panamanian border. There is also a Limón–Manzanillo route that stops in Cahuita, with 4–5 daily buses.

PARQUE NACIONAL CAHUITA

PARQUE NACIONAL CAHUITA (daily 8am–5pm; "pay what you want" if entering at Kelly Creek, US$10–15 at the Puerto Vargas entrance) is one of the smallest protected areas in the country, covering the wedge-shaped piece of land from Punta Cahuita back to the main highway and, crucially, the **coral reef** about 500m offshore. Every tour operator in the area offers exploratory snorkelling trips – with guided assistance you will see the best of the reef and the animals that live here. On land, Cahuita shelters the litoral, or coastal, rainforest, a lowland habitat of semi-mangroves and tall canopy cover which backs the white-sand beaches of Playa Vargas and Playa Cahuita. **Birds**, including ibis and kingfishers, are in residence, along with white-faced (*carablanca*) and howler monkeys, coati, raccoons, sloths and snakes.

The park has two **entrances**, one at Kelly Creek, at the southern end of Cahuita village, and the other at Puerto Vargas, 4km south of Cahuita. The park's one **trail** (7km), skirting the beach, is a very easy walk, with a path so wide it feels like a road. The Río Perezoso, about 2km from the Kelly Creek entrance, or 5km from the Puerto Vargas trailhead, is not always fordable. Similarly, at high tide the beach, Playa Vargas, is impassable in places: ask at the ranger station about *marea*, or tide, schedules. Many **snorkellers** swim the 200 to 500m from Puerto Vargas out to the reef; again, ask about currents before diving in. **Camping** (❶) is allowed near the Puerto Vargas *puesto*; you must enter through this section of the park to camp here.

PUERTO VIEJO DE TALAMANCA

It's **surfing** that really pulls the crowds to the languorous hamlet of **PUERTO VIEJO DE TALAMANCA**, offering some of the most challenging waves in the country, the famous "**Salsa Brava**". The **village** itself lies between the thick forested hills of the Talamanca mountains and the sea, where locals bathe and kids frolic with surfboards in the waves. The main drag through the centre, potholed and rough, is crisscrossed by a few dirt streets and an offshoot road that follows the shore. As in Cahuita, many expats have been drawn to Puerto Viejo and have set

PUERTO VIEJO DE TALAMANCA

ACCOMMODATION	
Cabinas Lika	G
Cabinas Oro	E
Casa de Rolando	F
Corazon Caribe	C
Hotel Puerto Viejo	D
Kaya's Place	H
Las Olas	A
Rocking J's	B

N

CARIBBEAN SEA

Buses to Cahuita
Limón, Sixaola,
Manzanillo &
San José

Playa Negra

Cahuita & Bribrí

up their own businesses (you'll find places offering health foods and New Age remedies); and like Cahuita, most locals are of Afro-Caribbean descent. In recent years, Puerto Viejo's backpacker and surf-party culture has created a small **drugs scene**; as a result theft has increased, but these robberies are always opportunistic, not violent.

What to see and do

In a town where surfboards dominate both the roads and the beaches, it is hard to spend time here without hitting the waves; the best **surf** is from December to March and July to August. There are plenty of places to **rent boards** and book lessons (see p.530) and the surf ranges from beginner waves on Playa Negra to the advanced, reef-side break of Salsa Brava; group lessons are the cheapest way to go. The surf crowds ensure a hot, young nightlife, which seems to be the focus of many backpackers here.

While there are no malls in the vicinity, and shopping here consists mainly of expensive, touristy boutiques, the run of **market stalls** along El Parquecito Cove offers jewellery and handmade crafts – well worth a browse.

Arrival and information

By bus Buses from San José (via Limón and Cahuita) arrive across from *Bar Maritza* in the centre. Beware: the coast road around Puerto Viejo is unpaved and very bumpy.
Tourist information No official source, but the village's tour operators can give you advice and maps. The most helpful are Puerto Viejo Adventures & Tours and ATEC (see box, p.530).

Accommodation

Accommodation in the village consists of a range of hotels and cabinas, the cheapest of which have cold showers and no internet access.
Cabinas Lika On the street behind the bank ☏ 2750-0209. A simple, hammock-strewn option with a garden kitchen and secure parking. Discounts for groups and in low season. **4**
Cabinas Oro 75m south of *Baba Yaga* ☏ 2750-0469. *Oro* offers some of the cheapest lodging in town, with four basic rooms (en suite with fan). **2**
Casa de Rolando 75m south of *Soda Miss Sam's* ☏ 2750-0339. Spotless, family-run *cabinas* and mini-apartments set in lovely gardens. **4**
Hotel Puerto Viejo Next to *Baba Yaga* ☏ 2750-0620. Long-running hostel with plain wooden cabinas, most with shared bath, and a large communal kitchen. Always full of surfers and young people; owner Kurt speaks English and rents out surfboards. **2**
Kaya's Place Playa Negra, 200m north of town ☏ 2750-0690, ⊛ www.kayasplace.com. A laid-back hotel on the beach, with a variety of rustic-chic rooms. **5–8**

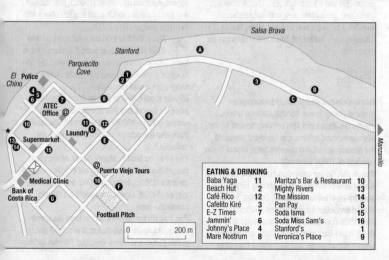

EATING & DRINKING			
Baba Yaga	11	Maritza's Bar & Restaurant	10
Beach Hut	2	Mighty Rivers	13
Café Rico	12	The Mission	14
Cafelito Kiré	3	Pan Pay	5
E-Z Times	7	Soda Isma	15
Jammin'	6	Soda Miss Sam's	16
Johnny's Place	4	Stanford's	1
Mare Nostrum	8	Veronica's Place	9

Las Olas On the main road, past the *Salsa Brava* restaurant or before Cut Bak ☎2750-0424, Ⓔlasolascr@gmail.com. No-frills beachfront rooms with bath and fan, and a *soda* on site. Camping facilities also available. Camping ❶, doubles ❸

Rocking J's On the main road, 100m past Tuanis Bikes ☎2750-0657, Ⓦwww.rockingjs .com. A maze of facilities including hammocks (❶), camping (❶), shared cabinas (❷), private rooms (❹) and a treehouse (❺). The beachside compound, perennially busy with backpackers, includes a large garden, chill-out areas, and (a not-so-cheap) restaurant. Tours and rentals can be organized.

Eating

Puerto Viejo has a surprisingly cosmopolitan range of places to eat. Good, traditional Creole, vegetarian, Italian and Thai cooking, as well as the obvious seafood options, can be found alongside the cheaper *sodas* and bakeries here; expect to pay upwards of 1600c for meals.

Beach Hut On the main road just before *Stanford's*. A road-and-beachside shack, serving English-style fry-up breakfasts (2200c), burgers, and good stuffed baguettes for lunch (from 1600c).

Café Rico Opposite *Cabinas Casa Verde* ☎2750-0510. A laid-back café serving the best coffee in town – import grade, and thus pricier than other

locations – as well as tasty sandwiches, crepes and breakfast. Rooms (❹), bike rental and laundry service also available.

Cafelito Kiré On the main road, 100m before Tuanis Bikes. A German bakery with good breakfast, including fresh croissants (600c). Coffee 400c, breakfast plate 1500c.

Jammin 100m east of the bus stop. A central "Juice and Jerk Joint" decked out in Rasta colours, serving excellent smoothies (1100c), jerk chicken and johnny cakes (350c); good veggie options also available (veggie curry 3300c)

Mare Nostrum On the main road, next to *Chile Rojo*. The best budget seafood spot in town, with an overwhelmingly large menu; the fish in sauce (from 3900c), seafood paella (4400c) and sangria are house specialities.

Mighty Rivers Next to *Sunset Sports Bar*. The place for snacks and treats, with home-made waffles (2200c–3300c) and ice cream; the locally cultivated macadamia milkshakes (1100c) are delicious.

The Mission Next to *Mighty Rivers*. An excellent budget choice. The Caribbean buffet features good *casados* (2200c), burgers (1100c) and speciality curries (4400c). Ocean-front seating available across the road.

Pan Pay On the seafront across from the police station. A popular breakfast spot with well-priced coffee (300c) and cakes, delicious Spanish tortillas and tasty take-away sandwiches. Baguette 2200c, breakfast 2200c.

Soda Miss Sam's Three blocks back from the seafront, past *Baba Yaga*. Caribbean dishes at reasonable prices, especially the rice and bean combos (1600c). What the place lacks in ambience, it makes up for in price and quality (though the service is not speedy).

Soda Isma On the main road, 150m east of the bank. Cheerful Caribbean home-cooking served on a small wooden porch in the centre of town. Rice and beans 2200c.

Veronica's Place Behind Aventuras Bravas. The only strictly vegetarian place in town, offering reasonably priced macrobiotic dishes (lunch 2800c). Three bright en-suite rooms and two single rooms (females only) also available (singles ❷, doubles ❸).

Drinking and nightlife

Puerto Viejo has the best backpacker nightlife on the east coast, particularly in the high season. Essentially, there's a designated popular hangout for each night of the week.

Bars and clubs

Baba Yaga 50m north of *Hotel Puerto Viejo*. A Rastafied joint with a simple (cheap) bar offering plenty of drink promotions and a massive sound system. On reggae night (Sun) and ladies' night (Tues), the crowds spill out onto the street.

E-Z Times One block south of the police station. A chilled-out bar and pizzeria; not the cheapest, but the treehouse setting and ambient music make it good value. There's a good selection of beer, rum and cocktails, and games to play if the weather's acting up. Beer 1100–1600c.

Johnny's Place Next to *Pan Pay*. The best place for late-night dancing in town, with a large waterfront seating area and massive indoor dancefloor; the

blaring music runs from reggae to dancehall to funk. Beer 1100c.

Maritza's Bar & Restaurant 50m east of the bus stop. Across from the beach, with indoor and outdoor seating, this place has a DJ or live music on most nights. Beer 1100c.

Stanford's Just east of the main street. Restaurant and bar with a large disco – you can dance to the sound of reggae and waves crashing against the shore. The food in the upstairs restaurant is a bit of a splurge, but the pool table and great sea views make it a worthy spot for a cold beer, while the club downstairs favours salsa and reggae beats. Beer 1100c, *bocas* 1100–2200c.

Directory

Bicycle rental Several rental shops are in town – try Tuanis Bicycles on the road to Manzanillo, just before *Rocking J's* (7.30am–6pm daily; US$4/24hr). Hotels and *cabinas* also rent out bikes (US$3–6/day).

Exchange Bank of Costa Rica (Mon–Fri 8am–4pm; Visa only), across from the *Super Puerto Viejo*, has an office and ATM. Mastercard users can obtain cash advances at *Cabinas Los Almendros* (opposite *Jammin*) for a small fee.

Internet At the ATEC office on the main road (see opposite), and in the *Jungle Café*, next to *Pizzeria Boruca* and behind *Café Viejo*.

Medical care Two clinics in the area: Sunimedica (☎52750-0079), next to the *correo*, and the larger Hone Creek Clinic (☎2756-8022), 5km north of town at El Cruce. Treatment can also be sought at the Farmacia Amiga, located in the small commercial centre next to the post office and Sunimedica clinic.

Post office The *correo* (Mon–Fri 8am–noon & 1–5.30pm) is in the small commercial centre two blocks back from the seafront.

ATEC AND THE KÉKÖLDI RESERVE

Skirted by the Kéköldi Reserve (🌐www.kekoldi.org), inhabited by about two hundred Bribrí and Cabécar peoples, Puerto Viejo retains strong links with indigenous culture. The Asociación Talamanqueña de Ecoturismo y Conservación, or ATEC, is a grassroots organization set up by members of the local community. As well as being able to tell you where to buy locally made products, the group arranges some of the most interesting tours in Costa Rica. Day-trips to the reserve cost US$18–35, and include a guided hike and lunch; these can also be extended (at a cost) for overnight stays. Other activities include a Caribbean cooking class (US$20/2hr) and tour of an organic chocolate farm (US$35/4hr with snack and lunch). If you're spending a few days in the region, an ATEC-arranged trip is a must – contact the Puerto Viejo office (☎2750-0191; on the main street, 100m west of *Chile Rojo*) at least one day in advance.

Moving on

By bus to: Cahuita (15 daily; 40min); Manzanillo (5 daily; 45min); Puerto Limón (15 daily; 2hr 30min–3hr), San José (4 daily; 4hr 30min–5hr).

SOUTH TO MANZANILLO

The 12km of coast between Puerto Viejo and **MANZANILLO** village – dotted by the tiny hamlets of **Playa Cocles**, **Playa Chiquita**, **Punta Uva** and **Punta Mona** – is one of the most beautiful stretches in the country. Though not spectacular for swimming, the **beaches** are nonetheless exceedingly picturesque. If you don't want to pay to stay in the area, the whole stretch can be reached by bicycle from Puerto Viejo (1–2hr); a cycle tour of the beaches can easily be done as a day-trip. The little-visited but fascinating **Refugio Nacional de Vida Silvestre Gandoca-Manzanillo**, bordering the Río Sixaola and the international frontier with Panama, incorporates the small hamlets of Gandoca and Manzanillo and covers fifty square kilometres of land and a similar area of sea. It was established to protect some of Costa Rica's last few **coral reefs**, of which **Punta Uva** is the most accessible. You can **snorkel** here, or **dive** (see p.530 for tour operator information). **Playa Manzanillo** also has a large shelf of coral reef just offshore, which teems with marine life and offers some of the best snorkelling in Costa Rica. The village itself is small and charming, with stunning beaches, laid-back locals and a couple of great places to eat and hang out.

Arrival and information

By bus Manzanillo can only be accessed on the road from Puerto Viejo. There are five daily buses that run from Puerto Limón, via Cahuita and Puerto Viejo. Cycling is also an option, and will take about an hour and a half; the road runs alongside the beaches.
Internet Available at Inet in Manzanillo's mini-centre (Mon–Sat 9am–4pm).
Tour operators Aquamor, opposite the *Soda Rinconcito Alegre* (℡ 2759-9012, ⌨ www .greencoast.com/aquamor.htm), offers diving, snorkelling and kayaking trips, PADI courses and equipment rental, (kayak US$6/hr, boogie board US$4/hr, snorkelling gear US$3/hr).
The Talamanca Dolphin Foundation (℡ 2759-9115, ⌨ www.dolphinlink.org) offers boat tours as part of their research and protection programmes (US$35 per person; minimum two people).

Accommodation

Prices in this area are higher than in Puerto Viejo, but couples and loners might enjoy the tranquillity and the opportunity to splash out on accommodation for a few days.
Cabinas Bucus Manzanillo ℡ 2759-9143, ✉ meltema1981@yahoo.de. Four pristine double rooms with wooden shutters and balconies, backing on to jungle. Run by local guide Omar and his German wife Melte, who lead informative jungle tours (in Spanish and English) and rent snorkelling equipment and rubber boots. ❺
Cabinas Faya Lobi Manzanillo ℡ 2759-9167, ⌨ www.cabinasfayalobi.com. Four rooms in a large, stucco house that looks out on the jungle. There's a shared kitchen, porches and hammocks. ❹
Cabinas Manzanillo Manzanillo ℡ 2759-9033 or 8839-8386. New, concrete cabinas with eight rooms, all with fan, en-suite bath and cable TV; the upstairs rooms have better jungle views. Laundry service, bike rental and tours also organized. ❺
Miraflores Playa Chiquita ℡ 2750-0038, ⌨ www .mirafloreslodge.com. Rustic, comfortable lodge opposite the beach. The upstairs rooms are brighter – with high bamboo ceilings – and there's an outside breakfast area. The owner has excellent contacts with local Kéköldi Bribrí communities and runs imaginative tours. ❺–❼
Pangea Manzanillo ℡ 2759-9204, ✉ pangea @racsa.co.cr. Three beautifully decorated rooms with private bath and breakfast included, set in a tropical garden. ❻

Eating and drinking

Batik Café Next to MINAE (the office of the Ministry of the Environment and Energy), Manzanillo. A funky little café, selling local arts and crafts and offering a simple menu (1100–4400c). Camping facilities also available (℡ 2759-9151; ❶).
Maxi's Manzanillo. Large upstairs restaurant with great views over the beach and renowned grilled seafood. The portions are expensive but enormous, so good for sharing, or the *soda* downstairs is a bit cheaper. Mains 3300–11,000c. *Cabinas* also available (❺–❼).

Soda La Playa Next to *Maxi's*, Manzanillo. A typical *soda* serving good-value breakfasts (1600c), sandwiches (1100c) and *casados* (2200c).

Soda El Rinconcito Alegre Diagonal to Aquamor, Manzanillo. The cheapest food in town, with a handy takeaway service for beach trips. Sandwiches from 830c, pancakes 1100c, spaghetti 1600c.

Vida Sana Across from *Playa Chiquita Lodge*. Halfway along the road between Puerto Viejo and Manzanillo, this is a great spot for a filling breakfast or tasty ice cream (1100–3900c).

Moving on

By bus to: Puerto Limón (daily 5am, 7am, 8.30am, 10.30am, 12.45pm, 5.15pm; 1hr 40min),: San José (daily 7am; 4hr 30min).

BRIBRÍ

From a few kilometres north of Puerto Viejo the paved road (Hwy-36) continues inland to **BRIBRÍ**, about 10km southwest, arching over the Talamancan foothills with views of the green valleys stretching ahead to Panama. This is banana country, with little to see even in Bribrí itself, which is largely devoted to administering the affairs of indigenous reserves in the Talamanca mountains. Bribrí does, however, have a Banco Nacional (Mon–Fri 8.30am–4pm), which has an ATM and changes money and traveller's cheques. Carrying on south from here will lead you to the Sixaola–Guabito border crossing, 34km along a stretch of pot-holed road.

The Central Pacific

From cool, undulating forests to rolling waves and scorching sands, the physcial attributes of the **Central Pacific** region are some of the most varied and highly regarded in the country. Every year thousands of travellers make the rugged, 170km trek northwest from San José to the **Monteverde** and **Santa Elena** reserves, to meander on foot through some of the Americas' last remaining pristine cloudforest or to take part in a high-adrenaline canopy tour, for which the area is famous. Meanwhile, only a hundred or so kilometres away, facing out onto the Pacific, **Jacó** is perhaps the most popular **surf destination** in Costa Rica. With consistent, mid-sized waves, it's a great place for beginners and anyone looking to brush up on their technique. Further south, still on the coast, the **Parque Nacional Manuel Antonio** draws visitors eager to walk its trails in search of monkeys and rare birds, and discover the park's exceptional secluded beaches.

Buses to the region from San José are reliable and cheap, and, with a bit of organization, it is easy to travel without doubling back to the capital. Be prepared, though, for some "roads" of startlingly poor quality. In particular, the final 35km stretch to Monteverde will astound, although as much for the scenery as the off-roading. Even in the dry season anything but a 4WD will struggle if you're driving.

SANTA ELENA

The hub of the Monteverde region, and the base for most trips and tours into the surrounding cloudforest, **SANTA ELENA** is one of the most visited settlements in Costa Rica, with all the practical facilities a weary traveller could hope for. Once sleepy, the little community is growing rapidly, despite the best efforts of the local community, and you may be staggered by the noise created by the construction sites and work vehicles, which chug through town towards Monteverde.

What to see and do

You'll soon have Santa Elena staked out: the centre of town is basically three streets in a triangle, amongst which sit a plethora of hostels, cafés and tour agencies. The real action is outside the town, in the form of forest tours, wildlife adventures and the Reserva Santa Elena itself.

Orchid Gardens

The **Orchid Gardens** (daily 9am–5pm; US$8), in the centre of Santa Elena,

boast more than four hundred different species of the flower, including the world's smallest. February is the best month to go to see them in bloom; otherwise, it's probably only worth the money for real enthusiasts.

Reserva Santa Elena

The **Reserva Santa Elena** (daily 7am–4pm; US$12; ☏ 2645-5390, ⓦ www.monteverdeinfo.com/reserve), 6km northeast of the village of Santa Elena, is an area of exceptional natural beauty, and offers a true glimpse of the rich biodiversity of the cloudforest. Established in 1992, the park strives to be self-funding, assisted by donations and revenue from entrance fees, and gives a percentage of its profits to local schools. Much of the maintenance and building projects depend on volunteers, usually foreign students. The trails within are highly rewarding for the keen-sighted walker, especially early in the morning, before visitors really start to pile in. You can hike with or without a guide, though the guided nature walks (7.30am, 11.30am & 7pm, from the visitors' centre; US$15) are highly recommended. There are boots for rent and information about the trails at the **visitors' centre** at the entrance to the park.

Canopy tours

Although the reserves of Monteverde and Santa Elena still pull in the region's biggest crowds, many people now visit the region purely to experience one of its adrenaline-inducing **canopy tours**. Several agencies in town can organize tours (see box, p.536), taking adrenalin-junkies into the parks to swing from zip lines hundreds of feet in the air, amid the canopy layers. These are thrilling, but know that if you've come to appreciate the area's wonderful wildlife, your best options are still the guided walks and trails within the parks.

TRAVEL TIPS: MONTEVERDE REGION

Getting to the Santa Elena/ Monteverde region independently from San José, especially in the dry season, entails some pre-planning. Demand for the two daily buses is high, and you may need to buy your ticket a few days in advance. Once you arrive, buy your return ticket immediately. There's less demand for bus seats travelling from Puntarenas, and you should be able to get away with not booking.

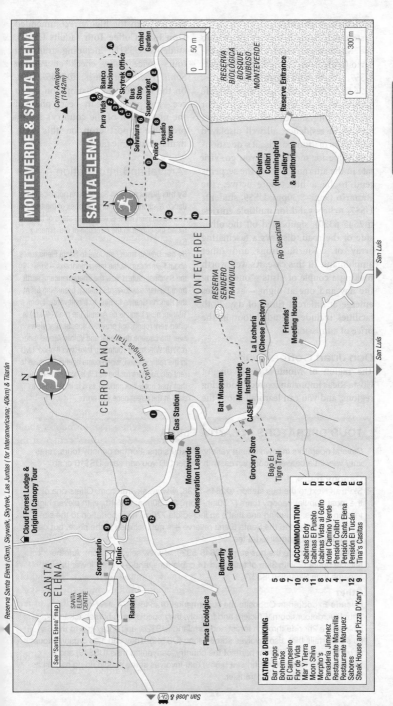

MONTEVERDE & SANTA ELENA

Reserva Santa Elena (5km), Skywalk, Skytrek, Las Juntas (for Interamericana; 40km) & Tilarán

Cerro Amigos (1842m)

SANTA ELENA

0 | 50 m

Orchid Garden

Pura Vida @
Banco Nacional
Skytrek Office
Bus Stop
Supermarket
Selvatura
Desafio Tours
Police

COSTA RICA

THE CENTRAL PACIFIC

*RESERVA
BIOLÓGICA
BOSQUE
NUBOSO
MONTEVERDE*

0 | 300 m

Reserve Entrance

Galería
Colibrí
(Hummingbird
Gallery
& auditorium)

CERRO PLANO

MONTEVERDE

Río Guacimal

*RESERVA
SENDERO
TRANQUILO*

San Luis ▶

San Luis ▶

Cerro Amigos Trail

Cloud Forest Lodge &
Original Canopy Tour

SANTA
ELENA

SANTA
ELENA
CENTRE

See 'Santa Elena' map

Serpentario

Clinic

Ranario

Finca Ecológica

Butterfly
Garden

Bajo El
Tigre Trail

Grocery Store

Monteverde
Conservation League

CASEM

Monteverde
Institute

Bat Museum

Gas Station

La Lechería (Cheese Factory)

Friends'
Meeting House

ACCOMMODATION

Cabinas Eddy	F
Cabinas El Pueblo	D
Cabinas Vista al Golfo	H
Hotel Camino Verde	C
Pensión Colibrí	A
Pensión Santa Elena	B
Pensión El Tucán	E
Tina's Casitas	G

EATING & DRINKING

Bar Amigos	5
Bohemios	6
El Campesino	7
Flor de Vida	10
Mar Y Tierra	3
Moon Shiva	11
Morpho's	8
Panadería Jiménez	2
Restaurante Maravilla	4
Restaurante Marquez	1
Sabores	12
Steak House and Pizza D'Kary	9

San José & ◀ (☎)

535

Wildlife exhibits

Just outside Santa Elena, on the road to the Monteverde reserve, the **Serpentario** (daily 9am–10pm; US$9, students US$7, tickets valid for multiple entries; ☎2645-5238) is one of many wildlife showcases in the region, with a number of unnerving snakes and a few other reptiles in residence, all well displayed with information panels. It's questionable value for money – if you go, visit late in the afternoon, when the serpents tend to be a little more active. The **Ranario** (9am–8.30pm; US$9, students US$7, tickets valid for multiple entries; ☎2645-6320), signposted off the other side of the road, displays a fascinating array of colourful frogs and other amphibians. In this case, it's well worth making a couple of visits – one during the day and one at night – as species emerge at different times of day. Both facilities include a guided tour in the price of admission.

Don Juan Coffee Tour

The region of Monteverde is one of Costa Rica's important coffee-producing regions, and you can learn all about the process with the highly recommended **Don Juan Coffee Tour** (adults US$25, students US$18, including transfers; tours twice daily, check at *Pensión Santa Elena* for times; ☎2645-7100), on the road out to Tilarán. You get to see – and participate in – each phase of the production of the country's highly profitable export crop on this well-managed organic farm.

Arrival and information

By bus Buses arrive in Santa Elena opposite the Banco Nacional at the northern apex of the triangle. The bus station itself is within five steps of the stop, round the corner in the direction of the Jiménez Bakery.

By car Driving from San José to Santa Elena takes about four hours via the Interamericana – this, the Sardinal route, takes the Interamericana north from Puntarenas towards Liberia, branching off at the Rancho Grande turning to Monteverde. From Tilarán, near Laguna de Arenal, the road (40km) is often very rough, but provides spectacular views over the Laguna de Arenal and Volcán Arenal (see p.570) in the rainy season, when some agencies refuse to rent regular cars for the trip. It is worth checking that your hotel has parking as it is impossible to park in the street once you arrive.

TOUR OPERATORS IN SANTA ELENA

Several operators in town offer a variety of excursions. For the canopy tours, rates vary very little between companies; with student ID you can save US$10 or so.

Canopy tours

Skytrek Next to the bus station ☎2645-5238, ⊛www.skytrek.com. Offers one of the most popular canopy tours (7.30am–3pm; 2hr 30min; US$40), with eleven high-tension cables, including one that's an incredible 770m. Transportation to the site – 3km up the road to the Santa Elena reserve – is not included in the price, but can be arranged for a small extra fee.

Selvatura Opposite the bus stop ☎2645-5929, ⊛www.selvatura.com. Another reliable operator with 3km of trails and 14 cable runs, and a slightly lower pricing scheme than Skytrek (US$37).

Other

Desafío Expeditions Opposite the supermarket ☎2645-5874, ⊛www
.monteverdetours.com. Efficient and friendly, they specialize in horseback tours, including a 2hr ride through forest and farmland (US$20) and a day-trip to the San Luís waterfalls that also involves some hiking (US$49). They can also organize tours of up to a week in different parts of the country, canyoning trips (US$49) and a transfer to La Fortuna (4–5hr; see p.569) that involves some scenic riding as well as the usual vehicle and boat transfer.

Tourist information Although there are plenty of tour operators in town (see box opposite), it is definitely worth visiting the staff at the *Pensión Santa Elena*, next to the Banco Nacional, who offer excellent impartial tourist information to everyone, not just guests, and may even be able to help you save a few dollars by booking things through them. Camera de Empresarios Turisticos y Afines, on the corner as you enter Santa Elena (☎ 2645-5027 ✉ turismomv@rasca.co.cr), also has a friendly, well-informed staff that can provide you with information on all activities in the area.

Accommodation

All the region's cheapest accommodation is in Santa Elena. Almost all places offer tourist information, and most can book tours (for which they will receive commission). In the dry months you should book a room in advance; in the wet season you can just turn up. Prices are soaring all the time – be warned that they may already have increased since the time of writing.

Cabinas Eddy Along the main road into town from San Jose, just before the town entrance ☎ 2645-6635, ⓦ www.cabinas-eddy.com. Although this hostel has taken a rather aggressive marketing approach – stationing pushy girls at the bus stop – it is a reasonable option. Both dorms and private rooms are cheap, bright and clean, with all mod-cons, including free internet. The only downside is the walk along the main highway to get there, and the view of a rather unattractive concrete lot from the front rooms. ❷

Cabinas Vista al Golfo A 15min walk from the town centre, up the hill behind the supermarket ☎ 2645-6321/9917, ⓦ www.cabinasvistaalgolfo .com. This hotel offers the best value in the area. The atmosphere is relaxed, with hammocks and a well-equipped kitchen, and the bedrooms bright and clean. The upstairs terrace boasts stunning views of the Gulf of Nicoya. Book in advance in the dry season. ❷–❹

Cabinas El Pueblo Down a dirt track behind the supermarket ☎ 2645-5273/6192, ⓦ www .cabinaselpueblo.com. Attractive little hostel just far enough from the centre to miss traffic noise. Reasonably priced rooms are pleasant and light if a bit basic, and rates include breakfast and hammocks. Very good tourist info on offer, but like many places *El Pueblo* takes a commission for booking tours. ❸

Hotel Camino Verde Opposite the bus station ☎ 2645-6296, ⓦ www.exploringmonteverde .com. Remarkably cheap, basic rooms (both dorms and private, with shared or private bath) in a little wooden hotel at the back of a centrally located internet café. The rooms facing the back are quieter than those at the front; almost all lead off a bright kitchen area. ❶–❸

Pensión Colibrí 50m back from the main road behind *Pensión Santa Elena* ☎ 2645-5682. A charming Tico family hand-constructed this pretty and rather chintzy little hostel. Rooms are clean and well maintained, and the building's location helps dull the noise of the relentless motorbikes. Watch your step on the staircase. ❹

Pensión Santa Elena Next to the Banco Nacional ☎ 2645-5051, ⓦ www.pension santaelena.com. All types of rooms – from shared dorm to private en suite – at excellent rates, along with a communal kitchen, free internet and the most knowledgable employees in town. Booking in advance is a must. Check here before you book any tours – they can do it for you, often for significantly cheaper than the tour offices. Camping ❶, dorms ❷, doubles ❹

Pensión El Tucán At the bottom of the triangle on the way to Cerro Plano ☎ 2645-5017. One of Santa Elena's longest-standing budget hostels, *El Tucán* definitely has a certain charm, though beware the traffic noise. Very small but cosy wooden rooms and shared hot-water baths; classier rooms are in cabins with private bath and balcony. ❷

Tina's Casitas Along the dirt road behind the supermarket ☎ 2645-5641 or 8820-4821, ⓦ www .tinascasitas.de. These simple cabinas are a good budget option. Surrounding a shared kitchen and with views of the gulf of Nicoya, all rooms make fine use of attractive natural woods, and some have private hot-water baths. Note that the rooms away from the office are of distinctly worse quality, so check where your room is. ❷–❹

Eating

El Campesino Down the hill from Desafio Tours towards Cerro Plano ☎ 2645-6883. Homely little place run by an expansive Tico and his young son. The decor is engagingly quirky, with nautical murals and stuffed toys hanging from the ceiling. Flavoursome and filling mains (mostly steaks and seafood) run 3500–6000c, so go with an appetite.

Mar Y Tierra Opposite the bus station. The attractive view of the square and the tasty food (the seafood linguine is excellent) at *Mar Y Tierra* are just about enough to compensate for the staff's superior attitude. A decent selection of mains fall between 3000c and 5000c.

Morpho's Opposite the Supermontro supermarket. Serving easily the best food in Santa Elena, *Morpho's* offers such dishes as *corvina al aguacate* (sea bass in avocado sauce), flavoursome steaks and sumptuous desserts. It's very atmospheric in the evening, though you will wait for a table. Beware the rising prices (mains 3500–6000c).

Panadería Jiménez Opposite the bus station, they offer a mouthwatering selection of sandwiches and high-calorie pastries (250–2000c) ideal for picnics or in the event you just can't face more rice and beans.

Restaurante Maravilla Next to *Panadería Jiménez* ☎ 2645-6623. The perfect spot for an early breakfast, this little soda offers *gallo pinto* for 1500c. For dinner, traditional *casados* and *arroz con* whatever (6000–10,000c) are served alongside fish dishes, burgers, spaghetti and delicious *naturales*.

Restaurante Marquez At the northern point of the triangle, next to Pura Vida Internet ☎ 2645-5918. This pretty seafood restaurant is welcoming and fairly priced, with some very tasty dishes (mains 4000–6000c). The staff is as charming as the views out the big open window at the back. Closed in the afternoon between lunch and dinner.

Drinking and nightlife

Bar Amigos Behind the *Camino Verde* hotel. This typical Tico nightclub, complete with disco balls, thudding basslines and a huge dancefloor, could be described as "so bad it's good". The drunken brawls that frequently occur at the end of the night just add to the flavour. National beers 830c.

Bohemios In the Tree House complex opposite the bus station ☎ 2645-5750. When will you ever see another bar built around a living tree? Good pizza (3000–4500c) and live music, although the beer's a bit pricey.

Directory

Exchange Banco Nacional, at the northern apex of the triangle, has a Cirrus/MC/Visa/Plus ATM.

Internet At Pura Vida, opposite the bank, for US$3/hr.

Laundry At Pura Vida, opposite the bank – US$7 for as much as you can stuff into a huge plastic bag.

Moving on

By bus to: Monteverde (5 daily; 30min); Puntarenas (3 daily; 3hr); San Jose (2 daily; 5hr); Tilarán (2 daily; 3hr). Travelling to all other destinations is difficult – you get a bus to the Interamericana and hitch from there. From Tilarán there are buses to La

Fortuna and Arénal (although a much quicker and more pleasant option is the boat-jeep-boat transfer – see box, p.572). It is quicker and easier to travel into Nicoya and Guanacaste from Puntarenas.

By shuttle A *colectivo* makes the return trip from Santa Elena to Monteverde (30min) at 6.45am, 7.45am, 11am, noon, 2pm & 4pm. Schedules are likely to change, however, so check at the *Pensión Santa Elena* for current times.

By taxi Taxis are easy to get hold of en route or through your hotel. Trips from Santa Elena to Monteverde should cost in the region of US$6.

CERRO PLANO

The **CERRO PLANO** effectively encompasses the five-kilometre stretch between Santa Elena and Monteverde. Leaving Santa Elena, the road twists and turns all the way to the Monteverde reserve entrance, offering some unforgettable views en route, as well as some natural diversions and excellent restaurants. Although the distance is easily walkable, the quantity of traffic can result in a mudbath or dustbath depending on the season, and the road's steep incline can be off-putting year-round. Hitching on the road is easy, and the frequent buses to and from Santa Elena and the reserve are an easy way to save your legs.

What to see and do

The Monteverde region offers an impressive array of activities. The five kilometres between Santa Elena and Monteverde towns alone are home to a butterfly garden, another smaller forest reserve and a surprisingly interesting museum devoted to bats.

Butterfly Garden

The **Butterfly Garden** (daily 9.30am–4pm; US$8, students US$6, kids US$3; ☎ 2645-5512) provides a fine opportunity to walk among the butterfly species from Costa Rica's varying climatic regions. It's best to arrive between 10am and 2pm, as the butterflies are most active at these hours. This said, the four butterfly farms and unimpressive natural history museum will likely only inspire the most devoted butterfly fans. It's a short taxi ride (roughly 10min) off the main road.

Children's Eternal Rain Forest

A small private reserve, the **Children's Eternal Rain Forest**, or **Bosque Eterño de los Niños** (℡2645-5554, ⓦwww .acmcr.org/reserve_rainforest.htm), close to the Monteverde settlement, offers a smaller-scale opportunity to see the landscape for which the region is famous. During the day, visitors are only permitted along the **Bajo El Tigre trail** (daily from 8am, last entrance at 4.30pm, reserve closes at dusk; US$5), which is physically separated from the rest of the reserve. It is a short, easy trek at lower elevations than in the cloudforest reserves with great views out to the Golfo de Nicoya: sunsets from here can be spectacular.

For a slightly different experience, you can take one of the reserve's **twilight walks** (daily 5.30pm; 2hr; US$22, including transfers). Although the route never strays too far from civilization, the informative guided tour gives you a good chance of seeing a variety of nocturnal animals, including porcupines, tarantulas, armadillos, agoutis, sloths and a marvellous variety of insects and roosting birds. The trail begins just before the cheese factory (see p.540).

The Bat Museum

The **Bat Museum** (daily 8.30am–9.30pm; US$8, students US$6, children under 6 free; ℡2645 6566, ⓔpaseodestella @gmail.com), situated next to *Stella's* bakery fifteen minutes from Santa Elena along the road to Monteverde, is well known for its interesting natural exhibits, multimedia presentations, and for reversing day and night in the viewing gallery so that the nocturnal beings are up and about for day-time visitors. It also houses the excellent *Café Caburé*, serving typical Tican and Argentine lunches (2500–4000c).

Eating

The following restaurants are listed in order of distance from Santa Elena along the main road. Bear in the mind that you will definitely have deserved your delicious meal if you choose to walk – although not a great distance, the road is an impressive uphill climb.

Flor de Vida 5min from Santa Elena, via taxi. A relaxed vegetarian café and restaurant with smart decor offering both snacks and more substantial, international fare (try the delicious vegetable stir-fry, 3000c). Nice forest views through the windows.

Moon Shiva 7min from Santa Elena, via taxi ℡2645-6270, ⓦwww.moonshiva.com. Restaurant renowned as much for its nightly live music as for its delicious Israeli/Mediterranean menu (mains 4000–5000c). The owner has just opened a bar downstairs boasting an international beer menu and good cocktails (US$4), with the kind of trendy interior design you might find in Marrakech or SoHo.

Steak House and Pizza D'Kary 10min from Santa Elena, via taxi ℡2645-6774. Cerro Plano's best pizza joint, and the steak isn't bad either, though it will cost you more than you would like (pizza from 5000c, steak from 6000c). However, both are delicious, and the authentic steakhouse atmosphere is worth experiencing.

Sabores Just off the main road, along the turn-off to the Butterfly Garden ℡2645-6174. Come here for the ice cream to end all ice cream. *Sabores* is an institution in the area, and its sundaes (1000c) and iced coffees shouldn't be missed.

MONTEVERDE

The mountainous, tropical **MONTE-VERDE** region is one of the most visited parts of Costa Rica, thanks to its astounding natural beauty. Home to several private nature reserves, including the famous **Reserva Biológica Bosque Nuboso Monteverde**, the district's terrain – from semi-dwarf stunted forest to thick, bearded cloudforest – rarely fails to impress. Meanwhile, the area is of cultural interest as well – its namesake villge, the settlement of Monteverde, is a small Quaker community established in the 1950s. Although integrated into

Costa Rican society, many of the Quakers still make a living from dairy farming, producing the region's distinctive **cheese**.

What to see and do

Roaming Monteverde's cloudforest is the highlight for most visitors, though there are a handful of other attractions in the area as well, including some smaller forest reserves, a cheese factory, a bat museum and, of course, canopy tours (see p.536 for suggested operators).

Reserva Biológica Bosque Nuboso Monteverde

The world-renowned **Reserva Biológica Bosque Nuboso Monteverde**, or Monteverde Cloudforest Reserve (daily 7am–4pm; US$12, students US$6; ☏2645-5122, ⓦwww.cct.or.cr), protects the last sizeable pockets of primary cloudforest in Mesoamerica. Stretching over 105 square kilometres, it supports six different **ecocommunities**, hosting an estimated 2500 plant species, more than 100 species of mammals, some 490 butterfly species and over 400 species of birds, among them the resplendent **quetzal**. Though the cloudforest cover – dense, low-lit and heavy – can make it difficult to see the animals, the park

is nonetheless a mecca for nature-lovers and an essential stop during any trip to Costa Rica.

The reserve runs excellent **guided walks** (7.30am sharp, or 7.30am and 8am if demand is high; 10-person max per time – try to arrange in advance through *Pensión Santa Elena* (see p.537); 2–3hr; US$15, plus the US$12 entrance fee). Seemingly rather pricey, the guides are actually good value for money, and the experience educational. You can also walk the trails without a guide – they are clearly marked, and you can get maps and interpretive booklets at the reserve office – though you're almost certain to see less. **Temperatures** are cool (15° or 16°C). Be sure to carry an umbrella, light rain gear, binoculars and insect repellent. It's just about possible to get away without **rubber boots** in the dry season, but you will most definitely need them in the wet. The reserve office rents both boots and binoculars (US$1.50), as do some hotels.

In an attempt to limit human impact and conga-line hiking a number of **rules** govern entrance to Monteverde, including a quota of 160 visitors at any one time. Consider booking a ticket a day in advance – either *Pensión Santa Elena* will do this for you, or you can call yourself. Bookings aren't available

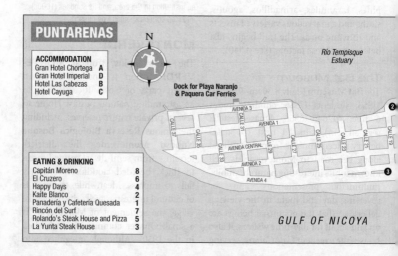

PUNTARENAS   N

ACCOMMODATION
Gran Hotel Chortega   A
Gran Hotel Imperial   D
Hotel Las Cabezas   B
Hotel Cayuga   C

Río Tempisque Estuary

Dock for Playa Naranjo & Paquera Car Ferries

AVENIDA 3
AVENIDA 1
AVENIDA CENTRAL
AVENIDA 2
AVENIDA 4

CALLE 37 · CALLE 35 · CALLE 33 · CALLE 31 · CALLE 29 · CALLE 27 · CALLE 25 · CALLE 23 · CALLE 21 · CALLE 19

EATING & DRINKING
Capitán Moreno   8
El Cruzero   6
Happy Days   4
Kaite Blanco   2
Panadería y Cafetería Quesada   1
Rincón del Surf   7
Rolando's Steak House and Pizza   5
La Yunta Steak House   3

GULF OF NICOYA

more than 24 hours in advance. Things get noisy and crowded between 8 and 11am, when the tour groups arrive.

Reserva Sendero Tranquilo

The **Reserva Sendero Tranquilo**, a private reserve in the grounds of a local farm behind the cheese factory in Monteverde, offers informative guided tours (book on ☏2645-5010; US$20) through primary- and secondary-growth forest. It's relatively unknown, and so offers a much more tranquil walking experience, although the number of animals you might spot is relative to its size.

La Lechería

Still using the traditional methods undertaken by their forefathers, the cheese-makers at **La Lechería**, or the Quaker Cheese Factory (tours 9am & 2pm; US$8; ☏2546-7090, ⓦwww.crstudytours.com) offer informative tours on the process used to make the unique cheese of the region, plus an interesting slideshow of the history of the region.

Arrival

By shuttle Shuttles from Santa Elena drop off right outside the Monteverde reserve after passing through Cerro Plano.

Accommodation

Budget travellers will unfortunately find little in the way of cheap accommodation in this area, but this should not cause too many problems, given the ease with which one can get to and from Santa Elena (see p.538).

In the reserve, three shelter facilities cater for overnight and long-distance hikers. These outposts, the closest of which is a two-hour hike from the reserve entrance, cost US$5 per person per night, plus the entrance fee for each day you're in the reserve. Water and simple cooking facilities are available, but you need to take your own food and sleeping bag. Book in advance.

Moving on

By shuttle The *colectivo* makes the return trip (30min) from Santa Elena to Monteverde at 7.15am, 8.15am, 11.30am, 12.30pm, 2.30pm & 4.30pm. For travel beyond Santa Elena, see p.538.

PUNTARENAS

Built on a sand spit only a few blocks wide, heat-stunned **PUNTARENAS**, 110km west of San José, has the look of raffish abandonment that haunts so many tropical port cities. Decidedly from an older era, the town's cracked, potholed streets are shaded by mop-headed mango trees and lined with wooden buildings painted in

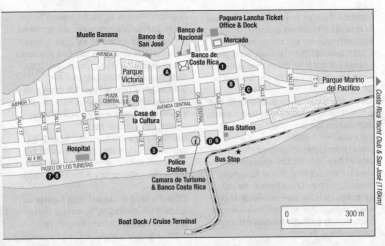

sun-bleached tutti-frutti colours. There's little for visitors to see or do – the town is of most use for its transport connections between the southern Nicoya Peninsula and the mainland. Despite being almost entirely surrounded by water, there is no surf and the water is not really considered clean enough to swim in. Don't be put off, though, as Puntarenas has something of a rustic charm by day, and you can spend a very relaxing few hours here soaking up the sun and local atmosphere, admiring the quaint little church (Av Central, C 5/7) and wandering through the vibrant food market (in the northeast corner of town, off Av 3). Note, however, that at night the town adopts a rather seedier feel, so avoid wandering about alone after dark.

Arrival and information

By boat The dock for the main *lanchas* from Paqueras and Naranjo, on the Nicoya Peninsula, is on the northwestern point of town. The smaller passenger ferry from Paqueras comes in further east along the coast behind the Mercado Central on Av 3.

By bus The main bus station is a large blue block on the corner of C 2 and Paseo de los Turistas, near the old train tracks and the old dock that juts out into the gulf. Services from Manuel Antonio and Quepos arrive at the gas station two blocks north.

Exchange There are three banks with ATMs along Av 3; all also offer currency exchange.

Internet Possibly the best internet café (daily 8.30am–5pm; US$1.50/hr) in Costa Rica is under a canopy just east of the church in the pedestrian centre. The owner will lock up your backpack all day for a very small fee.

Taxis Available taxis line up along the beach road in front of the Banco Costa Rica by the bus station. Journeys from here to anywhere in town should cost a maximum of US$5.

Tourist information The Cámara de Turismo (Mon–Fri 8am–5pm, Sat 8am–noon) is in an office above the Banco de Costa Rica on Paseo de los Turistas opposite the Cruise Terminal; the staff can provide maps and travel information. At the time of writing, a regional tourist office was under construction by the Port Administration Office on the other side of the road.

Accommodation

There are several reasonable cheap hotels in the area, although the exponential increase in prices has affected Puntarenas as much as anywhere else. Wherever you stay, make sure your room has a working fan. All places have cold-water showers unless otherwise stated.

Gran Hotel Chortega C 1, Av 1/3 ☎2661-0998. With decidedly retro decor, this well-located hotel offers good security and relative value for its clean, if rather sterile rooms. ④–⑤

Gran Hotel Imperial Paseo de los Turistas, C 0/2 ☎2661-0579. Extremely handy for the bus station, this hotel is in a characterful, if rather faded, wooden building, with turquoise walls and an interior garden. Rooms are spacious, dark and basic; some have an attractive wooden balcony looking out into the courtyard. Safe location, as the police station is across the road. ④–⑤

Hotel Cabezas Av 1, C 2/4 ☎2661-1045. The best budget option in town, this bright and sunny hotel offers pretty pink and cream rooms, a private car park and excellent security. The *dueña* is quite the matriarch, but it adds to the familial ambience. ③–④

Hotel Cayuga C 4, Av 0/1 ☎2661-0244/0344, ✉cayuga@racsa.co.cr. *Cayuga's* plain, dark reception area doesn't do justice to its clean, spacious rooms (although the retro decor is an acquired taste). They have a laundry service, and the attached restaurant is good for *gallo pinto* (1600c) and tasty evening meals. ④

Eating

El Cruzero Paseo de los Turistas, opposite the bus station. Cheerful little open-walled *soda* decked out in vibrant greens and yellows and boasting views of the sea (and the bus station). Laid-back staff serves tasty *gallo pinto* from 1500c, *casados* from 2000c.

Kaite Blanco Av 1, C 17/19 ☎2661-4842. Delicious typical Tican and fresh fish dishes (from US$4) and a dynamic atmosphere (especially at the weekends, when there's live music). Also an excellent bar for cocktail lovers.

Panadería y Cafetería Quesada C 2, Av 1/3. In a good location if you're staying near the market, this is a real local joint – it's always full of families and Tico couples. *Gallo pinto* for less than 1500c, *casados* from 2000c.

Rolando's Steak House and Pizza Paseo de los Turistas & C 3. Always lively thanks to its position on the waterfront by the dock, *Rolando's* can't match *La Yunta* for quality of food, but it is cheaper

ONWARD TRANSPORT: NICOYA PENINSULA

Ferries from Puntarenas go to two destinations on the Nicoya Peninsula: Paquera and Naranjo. There is absolutely *nothing* in Naranjo, apart from a *soda* by the ferry dock and *Hotel El Ancla*, which will cost in the region of US$60 a night. Buses run to Nicoya from here four times daily (7:30am, 12:15pm, 3:45pm and 8:50pm), although it is advisable to check these times before you set off from Puntarenas. Buses to the beaches along the southern tip only run from Paquera. Be warned that Paquera can be downright threatening at night. If you have to stop over, *Cabinas Ginana* (☎2641-0119; ②) is secure, has clean, inexpensive rooms and a vast restaurant. Buses depart daily from Paquera (7am, 8am, 10am, noon, 2pm and 4pm) to Montezuma, via Cóbano.

and a great place for a beer and a pizza. Mains 2000–5000c.

La Yunta Steak House Paseo de los Turistas, C 19/21 ☎2661-3216. Recommended for its welcoming atmosphere and juicy steaks. The views of the sea really remind you that you're on holiday. Mains 3000–7000c.

Drinking and nightlife

The nightlife along the Paseo de los Turistas really takes off at the weekends. The bars do have a good-natured party atmosphere, but be sure to get a taxi back to your hotel, as the area gets dodgy later on.

Capitán Moreno Right on the beach, this open-walled bar/club has a massive dancefloor and is hugely popular with Ticos, who come to show off their karaoke talents and Latino moves. Cheap beers and live music.

Happy Days Paseo de los Turistas & C 9. With a new upstairs balcony level and a massive Elvis figurine, it's easy to work out this bar's musical orientation.

Rincón del Surf Next to *Capitán Moreno*, *Rincón del Surf* is on a smaller scale, with a similar drinks list, Including a few cocktails, and lively local atmosphere, but just as loud.

Moving on

By boat to: Naranjo (from the Northwestern Dock; for links to Nicoya and the western peninsula): daily 6am, 10am, 2.20pm, 7pm; Paquera (from the Northwestern Dock; for links to Montezuma, Santa Teresa and Mal País): 10 daily 4.30am–10.30pm; Paquera (from behind the Mercado Central): Mon–Sat 7.30am, 11.30am, 2pm, 4pm.

By bus to: Jacó and Quepos (6am, 9am, noon, 4.30pm; 1hr 30min and 2hr 30min); Liberia (4.30am, 5.30am, 7am, 8.30am, 9.30am, 11.30am, 2.30pm, 3pm, 8:30pm; 3hr); San José (hourly 4am–7pm; 2hr); Santa Elena/Monteverde (7.50am, 1.15pm, 2.15pm; 3hr 30min).

JACÓ

The thriving resort of **JACÓ** can make no claim to either class or exclusivity: stretching three kilometres along a main road parallel to the **beach**, it's little more than a brash strip of souvenir shops, bars, restaurants and hotels. As the closest beach to the capital, it's long been a very popular weekend destination for *Josefinos* during the summer months, and now foreign investment is allowing for almost unrestrained development. This said, the long sandy beach remains reasonably clean and spacious, and the **surf** is good year-round – indeed, surfing is pretty much the only thing to do here, and the town is built around the industry. Dozens of places rent **boards** and give lessons (see p.544). If playing in the big waves isn't your thing, there's also some nice snorkelling around **Isla Tortuga**, off the coast of the Nicoya Peninsula. A number of operators in town can arrange trips (see p.544).

SAFETY IN JACÓ
Jacó has a reputation for being unsafe, and a hive of prostitution and illegal drugs. Make sure that your hostel has good security, and avoid wandering around by yourself at night. Don't take taxis that aren't the typical yellow and black, as they are unlikely to be unlicensed. However, privately booked taxis may be all black: it's worth checking when you call. The beach is notoriously dangerous at night – stay away.

Arrival and information

By bus Buses from Quepos drop off in front of the Banco Nacional in the centre of town, and those from San José at the bus station at the Pizza Hut complex at the northern end of town. The walk into town from the bus station will take roughly 10min, but there are plenty of taxis circling the complex.

A & San José ▲

JACÓ

0   100 m

PACIFIC OCEAN

BOULEVARD
BOULEVARD

Bus Station

Chuck's WOW Surf

CALLE ANCHA

CALLE ANITA

B

1
2

CALLE LAS PALMERAS

CALLE LAS OLAS

CALLE ANCHA

3

4 Laundry

CALLE DE BOHÍO

C

5

COCAL

D

6

@ Banco Nacional

7

Mas x Menos Supermarket

★ Bus to Quepos

★ Bus to Puntarenas

CALLE LA CENTRAL

E

CALLE EL HICACO

F **8**

Aquamatic Coin Laundry

The Red Cross

AV PASTOR DÍAZ

CALLE LAS BRISAS

G, **9**, **10**, Manuel Antonio, ▼ Condor Biker & Quepos

ACCOMMODATION		EATING & DRINKING	
Cabinas Antonio	A	Barco de Mariscos	6
Cabinas Rutan	B	Bohío Grill	5
Camping El Hicaco	F	Marea Alta	10
Hotel Cometa	D	Monkey Bar	3
Hotel de Haan	C	Pachi's Pan	7
Hotel Kangaroo	G	Los Sabores Ticos	9
Nathon's Hostel	E	Soda Rustica	8
		Sunrise	1
		Toucan Jam	4
		Wahoos	2

Tour operators King Tours (☎2643-2441, ⊛www .kingtours.com) offer a good range of quality land- and water-based activities, including kayaking and snorkelling (both US$60), canopy tours (US$75) and day-trips to Isla Tortuga (US$100). It seems a lot of money to fork out, but the prices are the same across the board in Jacó, and similar throughout this part of the country. For surfboard rental, try: Chuck's WOW Surf, Av Pastor Díaz at C Ancha (☎2643-3844; US$65 for 3hr), or with Gustavo Castillo (☎2643-3574 or 8829-4697), an experienced local surfer and teacher based on the beach in front of Bohío Grill.

Local transport

Bikes Condor Biker rents mountain bikes for US$10 a day, but widespread bike theft has left them insisting on a US$100 deposit and copy of passport. Some people rent mopeds (about US$35 a day from Condor Bikes) and head out onto the Costañera Sur highway to explore Playa Hermosa (see p.546). **Taxis** Karen Ruz (☎8835-9385 or 2643-2323/5353) provides excellent, reliable service at any time of day, as well as sound advice and information on the area. 24-hour taxis also available on ☎2643-2020/1919.

Accommodation

Though there are numerous hotels and cabinas, it's wise to reserve in advance during the high season (Dec–April), especially at weekends. Most places are right on or nearby the main strip.
Cabinas Antonio ☎2643-3043. Friendly, peaceful place north of the Pizza Hut and bus station. Although a bit more expensive than the hostels, it boasts a lovely pool area, neat little rooms with hot water and private parking. There is a laundry next door and you're a few yards from the beach. **4**
Cabinas Rutan On C Anita ☎2643-3328 or 8858-5029, ⊛www.cabinasrutan.com. This unpretentious little place offers rather dark but clean, well-ventilated dorm rooms and cold-water showers. Free internet and a 10% discount at Chuck's WOW Surf for all guests; boards available to rent for US$3/hr. Dorms **2**
Camping El Hicaco On C Hicaco. Big, attractive campsite (bring your own tent), with showers, lockers and parking available for a small fee. Good central location, though it is next to a high-rise hotel. **1**
Hotel Cometa Av Pastor Díaz just along from the Banco de San José ☎2643-3615. Central hotel on the main road, with bright and quiet rooms. Prices vary a good deal depending on the amenities, but

the cheaper options are clean and good value. Discounts are available for long stays, and the trilingual owner is affable and laid-back. ⑤–⑦

Hotel de Haan On C El Bohío ☎2643-1795, ⓦwww.hoteldehaan.com. Just off the main strip, and fairly quiet. Cavernous dorms are wooden and very rustic, with shared hot-water bath and kitchen; private rooms are essentially the same – you're just paying more for privacy. Great pool area and a friendly vibe. Free internet for guests. Dorms ③, doubles ⑤

Hotel Kangaroo ☎2643-3351, ⓦwww.hotel-kangaroo.com. About a kilometre south of the main strip (take a taxi home at night), this hostel is superficially attractive if you're looking to escape the bustle of town. They offer board rental and there is a nice pool area, but the security is a bit lax and the staff are rather stand-offish. Dorms ③, rooms ④

Nathon's Hostel On C Hicaco, just beyond *Camping Hicaco* ⓦwww.nathonshotel.com, ⓔnathonsplace@aol.com. Despite a very basic entrance, this Texan-owned, no-frills surfer hostel is kitted out with a/c and clean hot showers, good security, laundry service and a great central location. Board rental US$10. Dorms ③, rooms ⑤

Eating

Barco de Mariscos Av Pastor Díaz. This happening, friendly, nautical-themed seafood and pizza restaurant is a little pricey, but if you "build your own pizza" you'll get a good deal and a delicious meal for 2500c. Other mains 3500–6000c.

Marea Alta Just south of the Red Cross. Open 24hr for end-of-the-night munchies, but by no means a fast-food joint. Tasty breakfasts and *casados* 1500–3000c.

Pachi's Pan Opposite Banco Nacional. Fantastic bakery and café with everything you need for picnics and Continental breakfasts. Most items cost 250–4000c.

Los Sabores Ticos At the southernmost end of town. Also known as *Tico Flavours*, *Sabores Ticos* is a bit "plastic tablecloth", but offers large plates of tasty and filling typical fare for heart-warming prices (*gallo pinto* for less than 1000c, empanadas 250c).

Soda Rustica On C Hicaco. This is a very popular *soda*. An enormous plate of steaming local cuisine and a juice will run you 2000c.

Sunrise Av Díaz, on the left just before Chuck's. Opens at 6.30am for huge, delicious breakfasts (2500–4000c). The larger-than-life owner's motto is "no one leaves hungry", even late at night – pizza is served till 2.30am.

Drinking and nightlife

Jacó's nightlife is hedonistic and sleazy, with young holidaymakers jostling for bar space with prostitutes and their clientele.

Bohío Grill On C de Bohío. This trendy spot on the beach strikes the perfect balance between swanky cocktail bar and friendly hang-out, with a warm atmosphere and live music almost every night. Try the *caipirioskas*, which taste especially good at 2-for-1.

Monkey Bar Av Pastor Díaz, opposite C las Palmeras. Entices the population with 2-for-1 offers and ladies' nights, but is more often than not just a hang-out for cigar-smoking expats and their lady friends.

Toucan Jam Av Pastor Díaz, between C Las Olas and C El Bohío. Kitted out with balloons and pool tables, *Toucan Jam* boasts a long cocktail list for the thirsty weekend crowd. A hearty food menu is on offer during the day, but it's definitely more popular as a night spot.

Wahoos Av Pastor Díaz, just before Chuck's and *Sunrise*. A lively mix of café and bar, but mostly bar, offering big breakfasts washed down with a Bloody Mary for last night's hangover. Good nachos to accompany your beer and friendly relaxed atmosphere.

Directory

Books Books and Stuff, on the main drag just opposite C El Bohío, sells postcards and stamps, and has a wide selection of secondhand books on sale.

Exchange There are several banks along the main strip. Banco Nacional (Mon–Fri 8.30am–3.45pm, Sat 9am–noon) has an ATM and currency exchange.

Internet Café Internet, next to Mas X Menos, charges US$2/hr for quick connection and webcams. For cheaper international calls try Mexican Joe's, further north along the main road.

Laundry Aquamatic, just north of the *Toucan Jam* on the main drag, charges US$8 for every 5kg you drop off. If you want to do your own washing, it'll cost you US$6.

Medical care The Red Cross (☎2643-3090) maintains a clinic on the southern end of the strip between C El Hicaco and C Las Brisas.

Moving on

By bus to: Puntarenas (from outside the Banco Nacional; 6am, 9am, noon, 4.30pm; 1hr 30min); Quepos (from outside the Banco Nacional; 6.30am, 9.30am, 12.30pm, 4pm, 6pm; 2hr); San José (from the Pizza Hut complex; 5am, 11am, 3pm, 5pm; 2hr 30min).

PLAYA HERMOSA

If lively Jacó has worn you out, the peaceful community of **PLAYA HERMOSA** is only 7km away. Offering a long stretch of darkish sand that has a challenging, often fierce, break, the beach town is, on the whole, pricier than Jacó, but makes a nice break from the crowds. *Cabinas Las Arenas* (Ⓦwww .cabinaslasarenas.com; ⑥) is an ideal place to stay for surfers with its familial atmosphere, hot showers and rustic wooden cabins, and *Jammin'*, a relaxed rasta restaurant, serves generous portions of surfer-friendly fare (main US$6–8). The bus from Jacó to Quepos runs through here – ask the driver for the right stop – or you can take a taxis (US$8).

QUEPOS

Arriving in **QUEPOS** from points north, it's immediately apparent that you've crossed into the lush, wetter southern Pacific region: the vegetation is much thicker and greener. The town itself, backed against a hill and fronted by a muddy beach, can look pretty ramshackle, but it's a friendly place, with plenty of hotels, bars and restaurants. You'll notice the proliferation of **sport-fishing** imagery – of all the sport-fishing grounds in Costa Rica, the Quepos area has the most variety, and many small tour agencies cater more or less exclusively to sport-fishers. There are also opportunities for all sorts of other **outdoor activities**, from horseriding on the beach to rafting and kayaking to dolphin-watching. For most visitors, however, it is town's proximity to Parque Nacional Manuel Antonio and its beaches, 7km south, that draws them to Quepos.

Arrival and information

By bus All buses, including the Quepos–Manuel Antonio shuttle, arrive at and depart from the bus station in the centre of town. A taxi rank is conveniently located opposite. The bus station is one of the best places in town to get your backpack stolen, so keep your eyes open.

Tour operators Lynch Tours (see above) offers horseriding trips on the beach and up into the mountains, sea kaying (US$60) and canopy tours to the Rainmaker Conservation Project (US$65), among other activities. Equus Stables, on the road to Manuel Antonio (☎2777-0001, Ⓔhavefun @racsa.co.cr), also organizes horseriding. Iguana Tours (☎2777-1262, Ⓦwww.iguanatours.com) run a variety of jungle tours and transfers from their office by the soccer pitch. Rafting outfitters Los Amigos del Río (☎2777-0082) have an office between Quepos and Manuel Antonio (look for a large orange building on the left with inflatable rafts outside). Sunset cruises around the Manuel Antonio beaches are recommended; contact Sunset Sails (☎2777-1170), who also offer dolphin-watching excursions for US$65.

Tourist information Lynch Tours, one block west of the northern side of the shopping centre (☎2777-1170, Ⓦwww.lynchtravel.com), offers friendly, bilingual, impartial advice on the area, providing some tours themselves and recommending other local establishments for others.

Accommodation

Cabinas Helen A block south of the Mercado and two east of the soccer pitch ☎2777-0504. Clean, secure cabinas in the back of a family home, with private bath, fridge, fans, small patio, parking and laundry service. ⑤

Cabinas Estefan At the beginning of the road to Manuel Antonio ☎2777-4452. These little cabins are popular with national tourists. Despite the somewhat unfinished exterior, all rooms have hot water, and there's a pool. Location is everything, with a bus stop to Manuel Antonio 20 seconds up the hill, and a supermarket on the corner. ④

Wide Mouth Frog Backpackers Two blocks west of the bus station ☎2777-2798/0093. Behind the high-security gate you'll find a veritable oasis. Clean, cheery rooms – both dorms and private rooms – form a quad around the pool area. The staff are delightful, and have a mountain of information on tours, as well as slow (but free) internet. A/c available for US$10. Dorms ②, rooms ④–⑤

Eating and drinking

Bar los Pescadores Next door to *Wanda's*, this similarly themed fisherman's bar has a "2 beers for

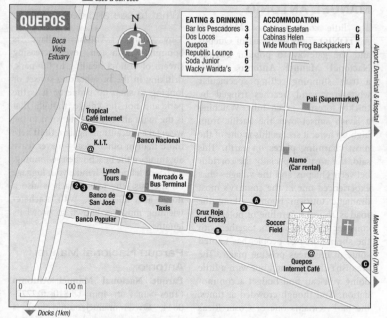

QUEPOS

Jacó & San José

N

Boca Vieja Estuary

EATING & DRINKING
Bar los Pescadores 3
Dos Locos 4
Quepoa 5
Republic Lounce 1
Soda Junior 6
Wacky Wanda's 2

ACCOMMODATION
Cabinas Estefan C
Cabinas Helen B
Wide Mouth Frog Backpackers A

Airport, Dominical & Hospital

Pali (Supermarket)

Tropical Café Internet @ **1**

K.I.T. @

Banco Nacional

Lynch Tours

Mercado & Bus Terminal

Alamo (Car rental)

2 3

Banco de San José

4 5

Taxis

Banco Popular

Cruz Roja (Red Cross)

6

A

Soccer Field

B

@ Quepos Internet Café

C

Manuel Antonio (7km)

0 — 100 m

Docks (1km)

2 bucks" deal on Sun, and serves up burgers and sandwiches from 2000c.

Dos Locos 50m west of the taxi rank. Good-quality Mexican food is served by an attentive staff at this smart little restaurant. Lunch 2500–4000c.

Quepoa Opposite the bus station. The veranda of this restaurant is the only place you'll want a table, as the main section is reminiscent of a barn. Open 24hr for *comida t'pica* and burgers, things also heat up on Wed and the weekends when the karaoke DJ comes to town.

Republic Lounge On the road parallel north of *Wanda's*. A swanky new addition to the Quepos scene, with a powerful cocktail list (2000–3000c), and a chic retro decor that would feel more appropriate in London. The *mojitos* are spot on.

Soda Junior This tiny, Tico-run *soda* just north of the bus station is the best place in town for fried chicken and lip-smacking cheap *casados*. *Gallo pinto* 1500c, *arroz con* whatever you want 1500–2500c.

Wacky Wandas A rowdy, all-American bar 100m west of taxi rank serving cheap beer and US$5 cocktails. No food, although for a special occasion (there are plenty) Wanda and her gang will head to the kitchen to rustle up a fine

spread of free burgers and salads for their friends.

Directory

Exchange The Banco Nacional just northwest of the bus terminal does currency exchange. They will change traveller's cheques, as will Lynch Tours.

Internet K.I.T Internet café, on the 2nd floor of the commercial centre, is definitely one of the best, with lightning-fast connections (US$2/hr) and CD-burning capabilities.

Medical care Hospital Dr Max Teran (☎2777-0200), near the airport, has an excellent reputation.

Post office The post office (Mon–Fri 8am–5pm) is at the eastern end of town.

Moving on

By bus to: Jacó (4.30am, 7.30am, 10.30am, 12.30pm, 3pm; 2hr); Puntarenas (4.30am, 7.30am, 10.30am, 12.30pm, 3pm; 3hr); San Isidro, via Dominical (6.30am, 7.30am, 2.45pm, 3.30pm; 3hr); San José (6am, 9.30am, noon, 3pm (Sun only), 5pm; 3hr).

MANUEL ANTONIO

The little community of **MANUEL ANTONIO**, 7km southeast of Quepos and the gateway to popular **Parque Nacional Manuel Antonio**, enjoys a truly stunning setting: spectacular white-grey sand beaches fringed by thickly forested green hills. Watching a lavish sunset over the Pacific from high up here, it seems this is one of the most charming places on earth. This said, the area – especially the corridor between Quepos and the village – has experienced one of the country's most dramatic tourism booms. Along the road is an unbroken line of hotels and construction sites, which, together with the sheer influx of people, has tainted some of the area's pristine magic. The area isn't cheap, either, but with a little doing you can find budget accommodation. And though crowded at times, the park remains one of Costa Rica's loveliest destinations.

What to see and do

Tiny Manuel Antonio village is booming, with an ever-increasing stream of visitors heading to the park, drinking in the breathtaking sunset or looking to snap up property. It is the park and not the village, though, that is the main attraction. One word to the wise: take precautions against **theft** here more than in other areas – never leave anything on the beach when swimming, and don't let people handle your luggage on the bus. The town beach is also a no-go area after dark, with machete-wielding muggers known to prowl its lengths.

Parque Nacional Manuel Antonio

Parque Nacional Manuel Antonio (Tues–Sun 7am–4pm; US$10; ☎2777-0644, ⓦwww.manuelantonio.com) is the second most popular national park

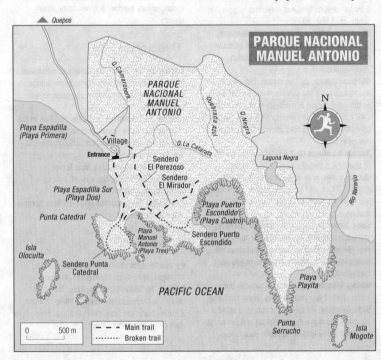

in the country, despite being the smallest in area. It preserves lovely **beaches, mangroves** and humid tropical **forest**. You can also see the unique *tómbolo* of **Punta Catedral**: a rare geophysical formation, a *tómbolo* is created when an island becomes slowly joined to the mainland through accumulated sand deposits. **Wildlife** – including sloths, snakes, green kingfishers, laughing falcons and capuchin monkeys – is in abundance. The **climate** is humid and hot, averaging 27¼C, and although drier in the rainy season than other parts of the country, showers are nonetheless a constant threat.

A complex **trail** network allows visitors to explore deep into the park. You can swim at **Playa Espadilla Sur** (or Playa Dos), which is long and usually very calm, or at **Playa Manuel Antonio** (also called Playa Tres or Playa Blanca), which is immediately south of Punta Catedral and more sheltered than the other beaches. Dangerous riptides plague otherwise beautiful **Playa Espadilla** (Playa Primera), so only swim here with extreme caution. **Guides** are available for hire at the park (US$20), and can be quite helpful, as untrained eyes may find it difficult to pick out wildlife among the dense foliage (this is one of those places where snakes could be mistaken for vines). Ring the park office to reserve a guide.

Arrival and information

By bus Services from Quepos (every 20min) travel through Manuel Antonio proper and drop passengers off 200m before the park entrance at the mini roundabout. There are stops in both directions all along the 7km route and the buses run in a continuous loop all day. Buses from San José arrive into Quepos bus station and from here the frequent local buses take you on to Manuel Antonio.

By taxi You can take a taxi from Quepos (about US$4), but many will pick up a maximum of four lone passengers together, generally only for trips the whole distance from Quepos to Manuel Antonio.

Internet Available next to the *Marlin Restaurant* along the boulevard, although the connection is so slow it's almost faster to bus to Quepos and use one of the high-speed connections there.

Tour operators Apache Tours, in front of *Las Gemelas* bar on the boulevard (☎8868-7468), offers a full range of activities (most US$55–95), including dolphin-watching, horseriding, jet-skiing, whitewater rafting and ATV hire. Ask for Christi, who is bilingual and knowledgeable about the area. Kayaks del Amor, on the beach in front of *Marlin Restaurant* (☎2777-5125), have been around for a while with great-value snorkel and kayak rental (US$10/hr, US$20 with guide).

Accommodation

The budget accommodation in Manuel Antonio is of decidedly variable quality. Be sure to book in advance or you'll have to settle for one of the not-so-good places. Staying in the park over night is forbidden, and wardens come round in the evenings to make sure no one has been left behind.

Manuel Antonio village

Almendros ☎2777-0225. Further along from *Costa Linda*, this great place on the edge of the park offers a lovely tiled pool area, parking, spotless cabins, hot water and a good restaurant that serves breakfast (US$2–4). ❼

Backpackers Costa Linda ☎2777-0304, Ⓔ costalindamicha@yahoo.de. Up the hill away from the beach, this lively little place offers cheery dorms and private rooms, as well as beers in the restaurant/reception area. People come from far and wide for the incredible 1500c breakfast (fresh fruit, pancakes and *gallo pinto*). Book in advance. Dorms ❷, rooms ❹–❺

Cabinas El Gordo At the top of the right-angled road to the beach ☎2777-5333. The little blue cabins here are a bit dilapidated, but you are surrounded by Tico families and right on the edge of the park. ❸

Cabinas Ramirez ☎2777-5333. Just at the entrance to the village, the cabins here are rather dark and pokey, but always full. The camping area is essentially excellent, with electricity and good servicios, but thieves are known to walk the beach in front, and the security isn't watertight. Best to stay here if you're in a group. ❷

Tico Lodge 200m up the road up from the beach ☎2777-5085. Though the rooms are a bit bland for the prices, the pretty red cabins do hold a certain charm. Excellent security, good tour advice, laundry service and private car park all available. ❻–❼

The road from Manuel Antonio to Quepos

Backpackers Manuel Antonio On the main road, halfway between Quepos and Manuel Antonio ☎8820-4621, ⓦwww.backpackersmanuelantonio .com. This hostel boasts hot-water showers, spotless dorms, private rooms and communal areas and a good location (handy for the bus, *Angel* restaurant, the supermarket and laundry). Camping may be possible, too. Dorms ❷, rooms ❺

Cabinas Picis ☎2777-0046, ⓦwww .cabinaspicis.com. A 10min walk from Manuel Antonio back towards Quepos, the cabinas here are fantastic, with private beach access and breakfast available (US$5). ❹–❺

> **TREAT YOURSELF**
>
> **Casa Buena Vista B&B** Off the main road, 2km from Manuel Antonio ☎2777-1002, ⓦwww.casabuenavista .net. Perhaps a bit pricey, but a stay at this haven of calm is a must. The cabins are set in the forest leading down to the beach, offering simple but spotless and comfortable rooms, and marvellous views of the palm-fringed coastline. The owner is very friendly, and has lots of information about the region. Rates include breakfast. ❼

Eating and drinking

Eating in Manuel Antonio village can get expensive. Perhaps more than elsewhere, prices should be taken as a rough guide (no pun intended), as they will have inevitably increased. There's no real nightlife scene, so evenings are pretty quiet.

Restaurants and bars

Angel 3km from Quepos ☎2777-2282. Unquestionably the best place in town for relaxed Tico hospitality and cuisine, with great *casados* for 7000c and 3000c beers. It's quite hard to spot to find – it's tucked away between the laundry and the football pitch.

Las Gemelas ☎2777-5278. Right on the main strip, cheerful *Las Gemelas* is reminiscent of a cheap Ibiza beach bar with thumping music and white sombreros. The happy hour (4–6.30pm) cocktails (4000c) are tasty, the staff friendly and the *casados* delicious. Perfect for a drink while enjoying the sunset.

Marlin Restaurant This long-running institution in Manuel Antonio bustles all day, offering an extensive menu of both typical and American food. Another great spot to watch the sunset and drink in the atmosphere over a beer. Breakfast from 1500c, lunch from 3000c.

Vela Bar In Manuel Antonio village, up the road from the beach ☎2777-0413. The swankiest food in the village, with dishes (from around 3500c) that feature good grilled fish, plus some vegetarian choices and paella.

Moving on

By bus Moving on from Manuel Antonio requires heading back to Quepos on one of the shuttle buses that depart every 20min. From Quepos, buses run along the Pacific Coast and to San José (see p.547).

The Nicoya Peninsula

The Nicoya Peninsula is probably the most popular tourist destination in Costa Rica. Most people come for the beaches: although places like surf-crazy Tamarindo have long been popular with foreigners, quieter spaces like playas Nosara and Sámara offer more space for contemplation of the beautiful coastline. Some of the beaches in the northern section of the peninsula (officially Guanacaste province) can be a bit difficult to reach on public transport, but the rewards are great for those who brave the challenge. Meanwhile, much of the southern peninsula (officially Puntarenas province) has been cleared for farming, cattle-grazing or, in the case of some areas, **upmarket golf courses**. Friendly **Cóbano**, 6km inland, is the largest (although still minute) town in the southwest of the peninsula, with good amenities including a gas station, *correo*, supermarket, *guardia rural* and a few bars. There's also a Banco Nacional, with

EL PUENTE LA AMISTAD

Opened in 2003, El Puente la Amistad (the Friendship Bridge) joins the mainland to the Nicoya Peninsula across the Río Tempisque near Puerto Moreno. Though at the time of the bridge's opening there was an understandable degree of concern about its impact on the region – especially the amount of human traffic – for the present the general consensus seems to be that since travelling from the mainland to the peninsula via the bridge is both cheaper and faster (it saves either taking a costly ferry ride or routing from the capital north to Liberia and back south again), it is generally a boon to the community and the tourism industry.

a Cirrus/MC/Visa ATM – the only reliable one in the area. There is little else of interest for travellers here, and most pass right through on the way to **Montezuma** or Santa Teresa, two of the most popular beach hang-outs in the country, both only accessible by rough and rugged dirt roads lined with steep pasture on both sides.

MONTEZUMA

The colourful beach resort of **MONTE-ZUMA** lies near the southwestern tip of the Nicoya Peninsula, about 40km south of Paquera, where the ferry from Puntarenas arrives. Some three decades ago a handful of foreigners fell in love with the place – it is astoundingly beautiful – and settled here. Then it was just a fishing village, largely cut off from the rest of the country; nowadays it's totally devoted to tourism, with virtually every building offering gringo-friendly food, accommodation or tours. This said, there's somehow been little large-scale development – Montzuma remains basically a village, and the coastline itself relatively unspoilt. Heading in either direction are some of the loveliest beaches in the country: grey-white sands, dotted with jutting rocks and leaning palms and backed by lush greenery, including rare Pacific lowland tropical forest.

What to see and do

Other than hanging out and sipping smoothies, there's not much to do in the village itself: the single most popular activity around town is probably an excursion south to the **Cabo Blanco** reserve (see p.553). Despite the inviting coastline, **swimming** isn't very good on the beaches immediately north of Montezuma – there are lots of rocky outcroppings, the waves are rough and the currents strong. Should you fancy a dip, it's better to continue north towards Playa Grande along an attractive, winding **nature trail** (1.5km; 30min), which dips in and out of several coves. There's reasonable swimming here, and decent surfing, as well as a small water-fall at its eastern edge; you may see some people sunbathing nude, though this isn't particularly appreciated by locals.

Montezuma's environs are laced with a number of **waterfalls**, the closest of which is about a one-kilometre walk towards Cabo Blanco, and then another 800m on a path through dense growth (signed). Always take care with water-falls, especially in the wet season, on account of **flash floods**, and under no circumstances try to climb them. It is possible to take a **horse ride** (roughly US$35) to places that are otherwise difficult to reach on foot; contact Zuma Tours (see p.552) in town.

You can also visit **Isla Tortuga** from here – it is far cheaper a trip than from Jacó (see p.544). It's a popular place to **snorkel** or swim in calm, warm and shallow waters, and sunbathe. A full day, including lunch, guide and transport, costs about US$45, less than half what you'll pay from the mainland. **Diving** is

MONTEZUMA

Cóbano & Paquera ▲

Playa Grande ▲

Librería Topsy

Abastecedor
Montezuma

Bus
Stop

Sun Trails
Internet
@

Laundry

Mini-market

Chico's Shop

Zuma Tours

PACIFIC OCEAN

N

0   100 m

EATING & DRINKING	
Bakery Café	1
Chico's	5
Cocolores	4
Montesol	6
Organico	2
Soda Naranja	3

ACCOMMODATION	
Hotel Aurora	B
Hotel Lys	E
Hotel El Parque	C
The Mochila Inn	A
Pensión Arenas	D
Pensión Lucy	F

▼ Cabo Blanco, Cabuya & Mal País

also a popular, if rather more expensive, attraction (two-tank dive and full-day snorkelling US$180).

Arrival and information

By bus Services arrive and depart from outside the supermarket in the centre of town.

Books Librería Topsy, along the beach road with a small library service, sells foreign newspapers and books and maps of the area, and will post stamped mail for you. The charming American owner can offer advice on the area.

Internet Sun Trails central tour office, along the beach road towards Librería Topsy, houses an internet café (daily 8am–9pm; US$2/hr).

Tour operators Zuma Tours, next to the super-market on the road towards the beach (☎ 2642-0024, ⓦ www.zumatours.net), is the most reputable tour operator in town, kitted out with all the necessary qualifications for snorkelling (US$45), canopy tours (US$35), etc. For anything they don't offer, they can point you in the direction of good neighbouring operators.

Accommodation

There are a a fair number of places to stay in Montezuma, but it's a popular destination and things can fill up, so you might consider reserving in advance. Camping on the beach isn't illegal, but isn't recommended for safety reasons.

Hotel Lys Just south of the centre ☎ 2642-0642. Popular with budget travellers who spend more time on the beach than indoors. However, the rooms are scrubbed clean daily, and the price is a winner, particularly considering it's right on the beach. Breakfast available for 1000c. ❷

Hotel El Parque Just north of *Pensión Arenas*. The least exciting of the three beach hotels. Rooms are a bit musty and the mattresses particularly foamy, but with the beach on the doorstep who needs to be indoors? ❷

The Mochila Inn 150m down the road to Cóbano ☎ 2642-0030. This secluded hostel, with all sorts of accommodation options, is a sanctuary for wildlife, especially monkeys, who come by for lunch. Reggae plays gently through the communal area, and the mood is supremely relaxed. Cabins

Hotel Aurora In the centre of the village, at the intersection of the road to Cóbano and the road to the beach ☎2642-0051, Ⓦwww.playamontezuma .net/aurora.htm. This charming and delightfully peaceful all-wooden hotel features sea views through the trees and 16 varied rooms – the older budget rooms are especially good value, with communal fridge, orthopedic mattresses and hot water in the shared bathrooms. Hammocks swing in a communal balcony area, which is complete with a bubbling fountain. The German owners will bend over backwards to make you feel welcome, and the fully equipped kitchen and dining area gives you the chance to save the extra you're spending on the room by cooking your own meals. ❻

are very basic and back-to-nature – there is an al fresco lavatory. Camping ❶, dorms ❷, rooms ❹, cabins ❹–❺

Pensión Arenas Just north of *Hotel Lys* ☎2642-0306. The second of three hotels lined up along the beach, *Arenas* is pretty run-down but has a certain faded charm, with pink and white decor and cosy (to say the least) rooms with shared baths. The beach garden is pretty inviting. ❷

Pensión Lucy 500m south of the centre ☎2642-0273. A Montezuma stalwart containing clean and basic rooms with cold-water showers and a nice seaside veranda upstairs. There are also a couple of rooms with private bath. It's one of the village's best cheapie options, if a little quirky. The owner also offers a reasonable laundry service and runs an inexpensive eatery next door. ❸

Eating and drinking

Bakery Café Directly opposite Librería Topsy. Pretty murals lend a relaxed beach vibe to this open-walled café. The smoothie list has answers for even the heaviest of night-befores, though the food is a little pricey (organic sandwiches starting at 2500c).

Chico's At the bottom of the road down to the beach, *Chico's* attracts a mix of local kids, who arrive packed in the back of pick-ups, and tourists, all guzzling from a surprisingly well stocked bar and

shouting above the music. It closes at 2am, after which people tend to adjourn to the beach for some al fresco drinking.

Cocolores An excellent restaurant in a garden by the beach. The varied international menu includes a couple of vegetarian options as well as a toothsome coconut fish curry (US$6) and tasty Lebanese salad (US$4). Fine value for the quality on offer. Closed Mon.

Montesol Next door to the supermarket. Run by a bubbly group of local ladies who specialize in classic Tican dishes – big, hearty *pintos* for 1500c and all the other usuals for similarly good value. You can't go wrong with anything on the menu.

Organico Next to *Soda Naranjo*, before the *Bakery*. Lives up to its name by offering up great organic treats, including falafels, salads, sandwiches and some local cuisine. The smoothies are fantastic. As at home, you pay more to eat healthy – expect lunch to be around 3500c.

Soda Naranja Hidden behind a wall of leafy foliage, this popular *soda* serves up delicious *casados* and fresh fish dishes at some of the best prices in town (starting at 1500c). Check out the daily specials.

Moving on

By boat to: Jet-boats to Jacó (US$30) can be arranged by Zuma Tours (see p.552).

By bus to: Cabo Blanco (departs from the *Parqueo* on the road towards Mal País; 5 daily; times change frequently); Cóbano (3 daily; times change frequently); Mal País (3 daily; times change frequently); Paquera: (6 daily; times change frequently, but the latest is usually around 4pm); San José (5.45am (Mon–Fri only), 8.15am, 3.30pm.

RESERVA NATURAL ABSOLUTA CABO BLANCO

Seven kilometres southwest of Montezuma, up a particularly rocky track, the **RESERVA NATURAL ABSOLUTA CABO BLANCO** (Wed–Sun 8am–4pm; US$8; ☎2642-0093, Ⓦwww .caboblancopark.com) is Costa Rica's oldest protected piece of land, covering the entire southwest tip of the peninsula. The natural beauty of the area is complemented by the array of wildlife found here, including howler monkeys, sloths and snakes.

Hiking and wildlife-watching are the main activities, and visitors can enjoy stunning, if rather strenuous, **trails** through the evergreen forest while soaking up the sounds of the jungle. The pristine white beaches within the reserve's boundaries offer a great chance to spot an array of sea birds, including the brown booby, which favours the islands dotted off the coastline as nesting places. One particularly attractive trail (5km; 2hr) leads from the ranger centre through the forest to **Playa Cabo Blanco** and **Playa Balsitas** – two very lovely, deserted (depending on the season) spots, though they're not great for swimming. The ranger hut, where you pay your entrance fee, also has a supply of trail maps.

Tours are readily available, but the reserve is easy enough to reach by public transport. An old **bus** rattles back and forth between Montezuma and Cabo Blanco five times daily, leaving from the side of Montezuma's *parqueo*, although it may not run in the rainy season. **Jeep-taxis** also make the trip from Montezuma to Cabo Blanco, for US$10 per person. If you like **mountain biking**, you could ride the 9km down to Cabo Blanco, walk the trails and bike back in a day. Mind the height of the two creeks en route, though, as you might not get through them at high tide. You can't stay in the park, so have return transport planned. Check that you've got enough sunblock and water: the sun is stronger than you might think.

MAL PAÍS AND PLAYA SANTA TERESA

The long beach of **PLAYA SANTA TERESA**, at the tip of the peninsula on the Pacific side, is luring in increasing numbers of travellers for its picturesque setting and excellent surf. By contrast, the tranquil muddle of houses, restaurants and breathtaking coastline that make up neighbouring **MAL PAÍS**

remain virtually untouched. Despite the development in the area as a whole – a surf community is fast establishing itself in these parts – the atmosphere is still chilled out and very friendly. Everything from daytime activities to nightlife revolves around the beach: try to time your stay for one of the full-moon parties.

Arrival and information

By bus Services from Cóbano arrive three times daily to Playa Carmen (the intersection at which the right fork takes you to Santa Teresa, and the left to Mal País). The early morning bus then goes on to Mal País and the two afternoon ones to Santa Teresa. Santa Teresa is all of one (very) dusty track; a good landmark is *El Pulpo* restaurant, on the right-hand side about 1km from Playa Carmen – it marks the beginning of the village centre. Mal País is far less developed so ask the bus driver to drop you off at your destination.

By taxi Taxis from Cóbano will cost in the region of US$22. There is no taxi rank as such in Santa Teresa (and nothing of the sort in Mal País), but hotels are happy to book for you.

Exchange Playa Carmen (at the intersection of the roads from Cóbano, Mal País and Santa Teresa) is home to a Banco Nacional with a temperamental ATM.

Tour operators Tropical Tours, opposite the Banco Nacional in Playa Carmen (℗ 2640-1900, ⓦ www .caboblancopark.com/tropicaltours), offers everything from canopy tours to horseriding. The office has a slow internet connection (US$3/hr). Surf schools are everywhere: most hostels offer lessons and board rental, but Pura Vida (℗ 2640-0118), on the beach 200m north of Playa Carmen intersection, is a reputable independent store that offers both lessons and boards.

Accommodation

Cabinas Mar Azul Mal País ℗ 2640-0075. A sign on the side of the road invites you down a dirt track to one of the most idyllic spots on the coast. The cabins are pretty rustic but, considering the stunning beach location, excellent value. The attached restaurant and bar get fairly rowdy on a Fri. Camping ❶ (bring your own tent), rooms ❸

Cuesta Arriba 300m north of the football pitch in Santa Teresa ℗ 2640-0607. Seems like more of a luxury villa than a hostel, with whitewashed walls, attractive arches and spacious communal areas. Dorms are equipped with sturdy bunks and proper mattresses, and there are plenty of hammocks. A peaceful spot. ❸

🏄 **Wave Trotter Surf Hostel** Up the hill behind *El Pulpo* in Santa Teresa ☎2640-0805, ⓦwww.wavetrotterhostel.com. This Italian-run hostel is a surfer's paradise, complete with boards lining the walls and chilled beats echoing through the communal area. The only thing topping the hot-water showers and clean, comfortable dorms is the feeling that you're being welcomed into a family. Book ahead. ❸

Eating and drinking

🏄 **Baraka Café** Santa Teresa. Experience possibly the best breakfast ever in this laid-back artisanal café. They serve lattes in huge comforting mugs and fabulous tostadas with real raspberry jam (1500c). Even the pinto (2500c) tastes like a delicacy.

Burger Rancho Santa Teresa. Burgers (2000–4000c) that prove it's actually possible to get a real one in Costa Rica without paying a fortune for the privilege.

El Pulpo Santa Teresa ☎2640-0685. Friendly restaurant serving up some truly excellent pizzas (2500–4000c) and empanadas (500c), well worth the slightly elevated prices. If you're too relaxed to leave your hammock to go for dinner, they'll deliver.

Moving on

By bus to: Montezuma (8:30am & 3:30pm; 45min, Cóbano (three daily; times change frequently; 45min). You can transfer in Cóbano for services to San José (6:15am (Mon–Fri only), 8:45am & 4pm).

NICOYA

Busy and rather unattractive, **NICOYA** is one of the largest settlements on the peninsula. Though it has little to offer the traveller, it is a perfectly good place to spend the night if you are waiting for a bus transfer between the southern areas of the peninsula and Playa Tamarindo. The **Parque Central**, centring on a ramshackle but beautiful white adobe church, is nice to meander through, but beyond this you probably won't feel the need to stay long.

Arrival and information

By bus Buses from Liberia and all other destinations arrive at the sizeable bus station at Nicoya's southernmost point, just before the road bridge leading out of town.

Exchange Banco Costa Rica, around the park, has an ATM, as does the Banco Nacional.

Internet Available directly opposite *Hotel Jenny* (daily 9am–8pm; US$ 1/hr).

Post office The *correo* is on the southwestern point of the Parque Central.

Accommodation

Hotel Jenny 100m northwest of the bus station ☎2685-5050. Friendly and secure, with old, basic rooms with a/c, TV and phone. Its location is perfect for all the things you might need during a stop-over. ❹

Eating

Cafetería Daniela 100m east of the parque. A popular choice for breakfast (1000–1500c) and lunch (1500–2000c). You can peruse the local art on the walls while you eat.

Soda Yadira 200m north and 25m east of Hotel Jenny. Another bustling local favourite – you may have to wait for a table. Breakfast here will set you back roughly US$1.50, with *casados* and *arroz con* anything for US$3–4.

Moving on

By bus to: Liberia (every 30min 3.50am–8.20pm; 2hr); Sámara (5am, 6am, 8am, 10am, 11am, noon, 1pm, 2pm, 3pm, 4.30pm, 6.30pm, 9.45pm; 1hr); San José (10 daily 3am–5pm; 4hr).

PLAYA SÁMARA

SÁMARA, one of the most peaceful, though increasingly upmarket, beach resorts on the Nicoya Peninsula, lies 30km southwest of Nicoya at the end of a (very) rough dirt road. Compared to other Pacific beach towns, it's quite remote and relatively inaccessible, which makes for a nice and relaxing atmosphere. The long, clean beach here is one of the nation's calmest for swimming – there's a reef about a kilometre out that takes the brunt of the Pacific's power.

The moderate waves make Sámara a great place to learn to surf.

Arrival and information

By bus Buses arrive in Sámara along the main road to the beach, stopping almost at the shore by the football pitch.

Exchange There is a Banco Nacional with ATM and the facilities to exchange dollars on the road to the church.

Internet A café on the main street next to the Artisanal gallery charges US$1.50/hr for high-speed connections.

Tour operators Sámara Adventures, on the beachfront road just south of the centre (☎ 2656-1054, ✉ samaradventures@ice.co.cr), runs a variety of fishing and watersports excursions. The employees at Tío Tigre (follow the beachfront road towards *Hotel Casa del Mar*, and take first left; ☎ 2656-0098) will instruct you in sea-kayaking and also run dolphin-watching cruises. Matteo Caretti at the Marea Surf Shop (☎ 8887-3059, ✉ mareasurf@ hotmail.com) is a kind, reassuring and professional instructor.

Accommodation

Staying in Sámara is getting pricier all the time, although during the low season most hotels can offer better rates than the ones listed here. On high-season weekends you should have a reservation no matter how much you're looking to spend.

El Ancla On the beachfront road 200m south of the centre ☎ 2656-0284. Simply furnished rooms right on the beach, with cold-water bathroom and fan. Try to get an upstairs room – the downstairs ones feel dark. Friendly *dueña* and good beachfront seafood restaurant (see below). ❷

Camping Coco ☎ 2656-0496. In a fabulous palm-dotted beach location, this campsite offers basic *servicios* and provides electricity until 10pm. Keep a good eye on your stuff, though – the beaches are notorious for pickpockets at night. Camping ❶

🏃 **Hotel Casa del Mar** On the beach road, on the left-hand side if coming from the football pitch ☎ 2656-0264, ⓦ www.casadelmarsamara .net. Small hotel set around a compact pool has spotless rooms (some with beach views), a delightful staff, good beds, fans, private hot-water baths and private beach access. Book in advance, they're usually packed to the rafters. ❻

Hotel Playa Sámara Behind the football pitch ☎ 2656-0190. One of the cheaper option in towns, with basic, electric-green rooms. Note that the

music from the club next door pounds late into the night. ❷

Posada Matilori Take the first left along the beach road, then the first right. ☎ 2656-0291 or 8817-8042, ✉ posadamatilori@racsa.co.cr. The prices at this laid-back hotel have increased, but it is still an appealing option, with clean, homely rooms with orthopedic mattresses, laundry service and boogie boards. ❼

Eating

El Ancla At *El Ancla* hotel. With a long menu of fish dishes (4000–6000c) and a pretty setting close to the water, this spot attracts plenty of holidaying Ticos, who know good seafood when they smell it.

🏃 **El Dorado** 150m past the Banco Nacional. For outstanding Italian food (2500–7500c), wine and hospitality, look no further. In true Mediterranean style, the Italian owners run things exactly as they would back home. This is one of the finest restaurants in the region.

Jardín Marino On C Principal opposite the football pitch. You'll find reasonably priced food at this popular restaurant, although the staff can only be described as surly. The burgers are incredible (2000c).

Pizza and Pasta a Go-go Serving rather pricey but filling pizzas (from 4000c) with a mind-boggling list of toppings, this restaurant underneath *Hotel Guiada* is a good spot to come when you're craving some gringo food.

Soda Sheriff Rustic On the beach at the bottom C Principal. One of the few real *sodas* left in town, with wooden tables for al fresco dining under the shade of a huge *nigueron* tree. Breakfast 1500c, lunch 1500–2500c.

Drinking and nightlife

La Vela Latina South of the centre on the beach. Sit in rocking chairs as the friendly staff here mix you one of their cracking daiquiris (US$4).

Shake Joe's On the beach, 25m south of C Principal. This stunning beach spot is better for a sunset beer or cocktail than the rather expensive food on the menu (breakfast US$6).

Tutti Frutti On the beach. Packed with Ticos and tourists alike at the weekend; the volume, if perhaps not the quality, of the music keeps the party going until 3am. Entry US$2.

Moving on

By bus to: Nicoya (5:30am, 7am, 10:30am, 1pm, 3:30pm; 2hr); San José (5am, 8:30am; 5hr).

By car The road to Nosara from Sámara is more of a jungle expedition, including two river crossings, so be sure you're in a 4WD and your Indiana Jones hat.

PLAYAS NOSARA

The stimulating 25km drive from Sámara north to the **PLAYAS NOSARA** runs along shady, secluded dirt and gravel roads punctuated by a few creeks – a 4WD is essential during all seasons. Generally referred to collectively, there three rugged beaches in the area – Nosara, Guiones and Pelada – of which **Playa Guiones** is the most impressive, and most popular with surfers. All three, however, are great places for beach-combing, and the vegetation, even in the dry season, is greener than further north. The beach settlement itself is spread over a large area; the main village of Nosara sits some 3km inland, and is home to an airstrip and the only (seriously primitive) "gas station" in the area. Some attempts have been made to limit development in the area – a good deal of the land around the Río Nosara has been designated a wildlife refuge – and the vast majority of people who come to Nosara are North Americans and Europeans in search of quiet and natural surroundings. Unfortunately, accommodation for backpackers is increasingly hard to find.

Arrival and information

By bus Buses arrive at the Abastecedor general store in Nosara proper, via the settlement next to Playa Guiones.

Internet Available at the Nosara Office Center (US$3/hr).

Post office The *correo* (Mon–Fri 7.30am–6pm) is next to the airstrip in Nosara.

Tourist information A useful listings website is ⓦ www.nosara.com. Also, the Nosara Office Center, by the airstrip in Nosara, offers helpful information.

Accommodation

Accommodation around the Playas Nosara is of high quality, but there's not a lot to keep the budget traveller happy.

Cabinas Dilan Nosara village ☎ 2682-0371. Basic, new little cabins with good mattresses and private bathrooms. You can stumble to the *soda* next door for breakfast. ❸

Kaya Sol Back from Playa Guiones ☎ 2682-0080, ⓦ www.kayasol.com. This is a popular and relaxed spot designed with surfers in mind. Accommodation comes in bungalows equipped with fan and fridge, and some with small kitchen. There's a restaurant serving gringo favourites to the sounds of Bob Marley. Dorms ❷, cabins ❻–❼

Solo Bueno On the road to Playa Guiones ☎ no phone, ⓦ www.solobuenohostel.com. The owners of this place are surf addicts, and it shows in the ambience and decor – dorms are basic and the reception area packed with hammocks. You can camp on the grounds (tents for rent); they've recently installed *servicios*. Camping ❶, dorms ❷

Tucan Cabins On the beach road in Playa Guiones, 100m from Banco Costa Rica. It might be expensive, but this place has everything: hot-water showers, a relaxing pool area, ping-pong tables and an in-house bar and restaurant, all in a lush garden just a stone's throw from the beach. Worth it if you're in a group. ❽

Eating and drinking

The Nosara area has experienced a mini-explosion of restaurants in the past few years. Many of them are very good, and prices are not as high as you might expect, given the area's relative isolation. There are a number of places in Nosara village, most of them around the soccer field or on the road into town, though most of the better restaurants are huddled together near Playa Guiones, which is where the majority of tourists eat. The Super Nosara supermarket, in Nosara proper to the south of the soccer field, is a good place to stock up if you're self-catering.

Restaurants

La Casona At the entrance to Nosara proper, this is a great spot for a tasty and relaxed evening meal, and, although it can look pricey, all the traditional *casados*, etc are in the US$5–8 price range.

Gilded Iguana Behind Playa Guiones. Upmarket gringo bar with Mexican food, and well-priced lunch specials, including filet of *dorado* (2500c) and fish and chips (4000c). Closed Sun–Tues.

Rancho Tico On the corner before you enter Nosara proper. The welcoming *dueña* serves up an appetizing collection of traditional dishes, with *casados* around 2500c, and *arroz con* anything between 1500–3000c.

Robin's Café 50m beyond Banco Costa Rica. Enjoy delicious organic sandwiches (2000–2500c), crepes and ice creams in the little garden in front of this café.

Soda Vanessa In Nosara village. A typical *soda* with filling and well-prepared *casados* for under 1500c, as well as other snack-style fare.

Moving on

By bus to: Nicoya (5am, 8am, 1pm, 3pm; 2hr); San José (5 daily; times change frequently; 5hr). For Sámara take the bus to Nicoya and stop at Bomba de Sámara (ask the driver). From here you can jump on buses passing through to Sámara from Nicoya.

REFUGIO NACIONAL DE FAUNA SILVESTRE OSTIONAL

Eight kilometres northwest of Nosara, Ostional and its chocolate-sand beach make up the **REFUGIO NACIONAL DE FAUNA SILVESTRE OSTIONAL**, one of the most important nesting grounds in the country for **Olive Ridley turtles**, which come ashore here to lay their eggs between May and November. If you're in town during the first few days of the *arribadas* – the mass arrivals of turtles to lay eggs – you'll see local villagers carefully stuffing bags full of eggs and slinging them over their shoulders. This is quite legal: villagers of Ostional and Nosara are allowed to harvest eggs, for sale or consumption, during the first three days of the season only. You can't swim here, though, since the water's too rough and is frequented by sharks.

It takes about fifteen minutes to drive the gravel-and-stone road from Nosara to the refuge; alternatively you can bike it or take a taxi (around US$3). No buses run from Nosara, although hitching from the village is reportedly easy.

PLAYA TAMARINDO

Stretching for a couple of kilometres over a series of rocky headlands, **PLAYA TAMARINDO** is one of the most popular Pacific coast beaches, though it couldn't be any less Costa Rican in character – locals and expats are completely outnumbered by tourists, and developers encroach a bit further every day. Nonetheless, the sprawling beach **village** boasts a decent selection of restaurants, a lively beach culture and a great party vibe, at least during high season.

There are loads of things to do outside in Tamarindo. It's the perfect beach for beginner surfers: gentle waves push against the grey-white sands on a daily basis, all year round. Legions of places **rent surfboards** – typical prices are US$10 for a day's rental of a longboard, or US$60 for a week. Another excellent surf beach, Playa Langosta, lies a few kilometres south of town. Other exceptional activities based in town are river estuary tours through the mangroves of Parque Nacional Las Baulas (see p.560) and moonlight turtle tours to the same park (Nov to mid-Feb only), as well as windsurfing and snorkelling.

Arrival and information

By bus There is no bus terminal to speak of, but all buses arrive by the village loop at the southern tip of the high street. You're right in the thick of things here.

Tour operators Some of the best operations in town for surfing are: Iguana Surf, 500m along the road to Playa Langosta (☎ 2653-0148, ⓦ www .iguanasurf.net), which will almost certainly have you standing on a board by the end of your first class (around US$45, including board rental); Chica

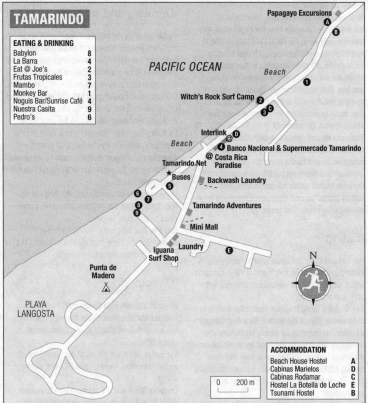

TAMARINDO

EATING & DRINKING

Babylon	8
La Barra	4
Eat @ Joe's	2
Frutas Tropicales	3
Mambo	7
Monkey Bar	1
Noguis Bar/Sunrise Café	4
Nuestra Casita	9
Pedro's	6

PACIFIC OCEAN

Beach

Papagayo Excursions

Witch's Rock Surf Camp

Interlink

Banco Nacional & Supermercado Tamarindo

Tamarindo.Net

Costa Rica Paradise

Buses

Backwash Laundry

Tamarindo Adventures

Mini Mall

Iguana Surf Shop

Laundry

Punta de Madero

PLAYA LANGOSTA

Beach

N

0   200 m

ACCOMMODATION

Beach House Hostel	A
Cabinas Marielos	D
Cabinas Rodamar	C
Hostel La Botella de Leche	E
Tsunami Hostel	B

Surf (☎ 8827-7884, ✉ chicasurfschoolcr@hotmail
.com), an all-girls surf school and shop just off
the loop in the centre of town; and local institution
Tamarindo Adventures (☎ 2653-0108, ⓦ www
.tamarindoadventures.net). For river estuary and
turtle tours, Papagayo Excursions (☎ 2653-0254
ⓦ papagayoexcursions.com; estuary tour US$35,
turtle tour US$40), a friendly and very professional
outfit based 1km north of the town centre on the
road to Liberia, offers the best rates.

Accommodation

Expect to shell out for accommodation in
Tamarindo: even the budget stuff here is more than
virtually everywhere else.

Beach House Hostel On the road towards
Liberia, roughly 1km from the centre
☎ 2653-0938, ⓦ www.tamarindoecoadventure
.com. Staying at this laid-back hostel is a bit like

having your very own beach villa – there's an
amazing communal terrace, a/c, proper mattresses
and wonderful beach views. Totally chilled surf vibe
– so peaceful, in fact, that monkeys swing by in the
mornings. Dorms ❸, rooms ❺

Cabinas Marielos On the main road
☎ & ☎ 2653-0141. Light and clean basic rooms
with fan, cold water and the use of a small
kitchen in pleasant and colourful grounds set
back from the main road. The owner is professional with a wealth of knowledge, and runs turtle
tours in season. A/c costs a bit more. ❺

Cabinas Rodamar Opposite Witches Rock
Surf Camp ☎ 2653-0109. Basic backpackers'
hangout, with dark *cabinas* in an institutional-style
compound set back from the main road. That said,
rooms are a cheerful blue colour, and have big
beds, quirky cold-water showers and aren't bad for
the price. The atmosphere is friendly, and you can
use the kitchen. ❸

Hostel La Botella de Leche ☎2653-0944, ⓦwww.labotelladeleche.com. Take the road towards Playa Langosta from the beach road, then take the left fork at the Playa Langosta turning to reach this excellent backpacker hostel offering comfortable, a/c dorm accommodation and a sociable environment, with a communal kitchen and free high-speed internet. Designed with surfers in mind, you can rent and repair boards here, as well as arrange classes. Very popular – reserve ahead. Dorms ❷, rooms ❹

Tsunami Hostel Opposite *Beach House Hostel* ☎2653-0280. Although there is better accommodation around for the price, the rooms here are clean and nicely set back from the main road; the ones further up the hill are smarter, and cost slightly more. The well-equipped kitchen and large parking area are definite perks. ❹

Eating

You can self-cater at Supermercado Tamarindo, located just before the turn towards Playa Langosta, which also has a good selection of toiletries and after-sun products.

Eat @ Joe's Along the main road, 50m from the town centre. Part of the Witch's Rock Surf Camp, a hostel/surf shop/bar for mainly North American teenagers, this friendly hang-out serves up rather expensive sushi as well as some truly excellent nachos (US$3), if you just want an enormous snack. The regular live music in the evenings is wildly entertaining.

Frutas Tropicales One of the few genuinely cheap places in Tamarindo. As the name suggests, there's plenty of tropical fruit in this little snack bar – try a *refresco*. Otherwise the menu is the usual *soda* fare, with *casados* (1750c) and hamburgers (1500c) both good bets.

Noguis Bar/Sunrise Café On the Tamarindo loop. Casual café serving excellent breakfasts (US$4), good breads, pastries and coffees – which you can either eat at the breezy seaside tables or take away – and fine meals such as fish tacos and fresh fillets in the US$6–12 range. Stop by at sunset to enjoy a cold beer.

Nuestra Casita Tucked away beyond *Pedro's* and *Babylon*, this adorable Tico spot dishes up a brilliant typical breakfast for US$2.50, and *casados* for US$3 in a secluded area away from the mad buzz of town. Well worth the time it takes to find it.

Pedro's Just along the beach from *Noguis*, this restaurant is effectively a gazebo with trestle tables. They'll fix you up good local grub in the US$4–6 range while you play with the sand between your toes.

Drinking and nightlife

People generally congregate in one chosen bar or club each evening. Hang about on the beach for a few hours and you'll hear the evening's hot nightspot.

Babylon Off the main road behind the loop. Usually the hottest spot in town, complete with cheap beers (1000c) and the latest chart hits. The music goes on till around 4am. Get a taxi at the end of the night to avoid any unwanted attention on the walk home.

La Barra This funky little bar/club is most popular with Ticos, although they're happy to share the dancefloor. Merengue and salsa carry on till around 1am, when the DJ begins to mix the latest pop hits. Good fun all round.

Mambo On the Tamarindo loop. Blasting out hip-hop classics from the mid-90s, *Mambo* is a good place to start your evening.

Monkey Bar Said to be "good on a Friday", *Monkey Bar* is otherwise fairly unmemorable, but has 2-for-1 offers and a ladies' night.

Directory

Internet Interlink High Speed café, 10m from *Cabinas Marielos* towards the turning circle, has quick connections (US$2/hr) and international phone calls.

Exchange ATMs are dotted all over town, notably on the main road. There's an HSBC here, among others.

Laundry Wash and dry at Lavandería Backwash (US$1.50/kg), left as you turn up towards Playa Langosta from the main beach road.

Moving on

By bus to: Liberia (5.30am, 9am, 11.30am, 1pm, 5pm; 2hr); San José (Mon–Sat 3.30am & 5.45am; 5hr 30min, Sun 5.45am & 12.30pm; 6hr); Santa Cruz, for points south (5 daily; times change frequently; 1hr 45min).

PARQUE NACIONAL MARINO LAS BAULAS

On the Río Matapalo estuary between Conchal and Tamarindo, **PARQUE NACIONAL MARINO LAS BAULAS** (9am–4pm, open for guided night tours in season; US$16, including tour; ☎2653-0470) is less than a national park than a reserve, created to protect the nesting grounds of endangered **leatherback**

turtles. These ancient creatures, which come ashore to nest from October to February, have laid their eggs at **Playa Grande** for possibly millions of years, and it's now one of the few remaining such nesting sites in the world. This said, someone seems to have given developers carte blanche in the area, the effects of which remain to be seen. The beach itself offers a beautiful sweep of light-coloured sand, and outside laying season you can surf, though swimming is rough.

Around 200m from the park entrance, the impressive **El Mundo de la Tortuga** exhibition (2–6pm, or later when turtles are nesting; US$5) includes an audio-guided tour in English and some stunning turtle photographs. You'll learn about the leatherback's habitats and reproductive cycles, along with the threats they face and current conservation efforts. There's also a souvenir shop and a small café.

There are two official entrances to Playa Grande, though **tickets** can only be bought at the southern entrance, where the road enters the park near the *Villa Baulas*. Booking your tickets in advance (on the park number) is highly recommended, as numbers are strictly limited. There is no public transport to the park. Most people visit by **boat** from Tamarindo, a service that usually comes as part of tour packages, or can be booked when you call to reserve your entrance ticket.

PLAYA DEL COCO

Thirty-five kilometres west of Liberia, **PLAYA DEL COCO** was the first Pacific beach to hit the big time with weekending Costa Ricans from the Valle Central. It's turned out to be something

PLAYA DEL COCO

0   50 m

Buses

Football Pitch

Coco Palms Hotel

@

Coco Medical

EATING & DRINKING
Coco Coffee Company	6
Coco Mar	1
Jardín Tropical	3
Lizard Lounge	5
Papagayo Seafood	7
Soda Papagayo	8
Soda Teresita	2
Zouk Santana	4

ACCOMMODATION
Cabinas Coco Alegre	D
Cabinas Jivao	F
Cabinas "Rooms to Rent"	C
Cabinas Ruby	A
Cabinas Tony	E
Mar y Mar	B

Banco Nacional & Supermercado Luperon

of a nightmare: a cross between an upmarket resort, filled with imposing hotels, casinos and restaurants, and a hot-spot for budget travellers in search of Jaegermeister and a dancefloor. Indeed, its main appeal is its status as the only place on this part of the coast with reasonable budget accommodation – surfers use it as a jumping-off point for Witch's Rock, up the coast, and for playas Hermosa and Panamá. It's fine for a couple of days, with the aforementioned nightlife and some good diving operators, but how long it remains interesting is all down to personal taste.

What to see and do

There isn't a huge amount to see *or* do. The main track down to the beach is a noisy, dirty melange of roaring 4WDs and souvenir markets, while the area nearer the beach is a little quieter, with the football pitch, the budget accommodation and some funky cocktail bars that get packed out most nights with visiting surfers and Ticos from the surrounding villages. Due to the high numbers of boats in the bay the water is rather polluted, and not very appealing for swimming. Diving, however, is a popular activity in the region, although there is no beach diving – dive centres take you to the islands off the coast, such as **Isla Santa Catalina**, 20km offshore.

Arrival and information

By bus Buses stop at the Parque at the bottom of the main road, virtually on the beach. Although this is the official bus stop, you will not find any bus information here – ask in the *sodas* on the beach if you need to check schedules.

Tour operators Rich Coast Diving, on the main road about 300m from the beach (℡2670-0176, Ⓦwww.richcoastdiving.com), organizes snorkelling and scuba trips, and rents out mountain bikes; the staff speaks English. Summer Salt Dive Centre, next to *Jardín Tropical* (℡2670-0308, Ⓦwww.summer-salt.com), offers custom diving packages (about US$70 for two dives), PADI courses and whale-watching excursions.

Accommodation

Coco has lots of fairly basic cabinas. In the high season you should make sure to reserve for weekends, but you can probably get away with turning up on spec mid-week, when rooms may also be a bit cheaper. Bargains also abound in the low season.

Cabinas Coco Alegre Following the road leading left in front of the football pitch, double back round to the left beyond the *Coco Palms Hotel* ℡2670-1994. Run by a wonderful Tico family, the rooms here, each with two double beds, are admittedly boiling hot, but come with sturdy fan, fridge and private cold-water shower. ❹

Cabinas Jivao Within the same little annexe of town as *Coco Alegre* ℡2670-0769. Similar standard to *Coco Alegre*, with clean rooms with bunks and private cold-water baths. Definitely book in advance, particularly at weekends. ❷

Cabinas "Rooms to Rent" On the road to the left in front of the football pitch, directly opposite *Coco Palms Hotel* ℡8887-3192. So new they didn't have a name at the time of writing, these cabins are great. Some rooms are more basic than others, but the highlight is a lovely communal balcony and kitchen with pool table. ❺

Cabinas Tony Opposite *Cabinas Jivao*. ℡2670-0528. Another secure set of cabinas in the secluded strip. The price is unquestionably the main selling point (the rooms aren't much to look at) and it's away from the rowdy town centre. ❷

Mar Y Mar On the beach just south of the football pitch ℡2670-1212. Clean rooms with private bathrooms around a rather run-down inner courtyard. The beach location is beautiful by day, but far from safe at night: do not walk back alone from the town centre after dark. ❸

Eating

Coco Coffee Company This smart coffee bar under *Papagayo Seafood* sells cappuccinos and good but overpriced sandwiches (2500c).

Jardín Tropical The best breakfast in town is served overlooking the *Parque* at the far end of town. *Gallo pinto* 2000–2500c.

Papagayo Seafood On the main road, on the second floor opposite the casino. A rather upmarket seafood restaurant decked out in nautical artefacts and fairy lights. The seafood-orientated menu is quite expensive but very good value – the fish dishes are superbly fresh, and you definitely won't leave hungry. Prices range between US$9–12.

Soda Papagayo On the main drag, opposite the casino hotel. A colourful *soda* that plays chilled beats throughout the day in the centre of the strip. Sandwiches for 1500c, and *casados* for 2000c.

Soda Teresita Opposite the *Parque* at the bottom of the main road. Pretty pink *soda* with some tables outside overlooking the beach. Good typical breakfasts and *casados* for 1500–2000c.

Drinking and nightlife

Coco Mar Right on the beach to the right of the *Parque*, this is where it all kicks off after the bars closed, with cocktails aplenty and a young, enthusiastic crowd.

Lizard Lounge At the corner of the right turn to *Cabinas Ruby* and Mapache. The most popular bar on the strip serves great cocktails (US$4) to the beat of well-mixed electronic and pop classics.

Zouk Santana On the main drag, below *Lizard Lounge*. Gringo bar that does well off the back of the *Lizard Lounge*. Drinks are more expensive, but there's a happy hour 5–7pm, and lively themed nights.

Directory

Exchange Banco Nacional (Mon–Fri 8.30am–3.45pm), 500m up the main road from the beach next to the supermarket Luperón, will exchange dollars and has an ATM.

Internet Try Café Pillis (daily 8am–9pm; US$1.50/hr), on the second floor above the souvenir shop, opposite the football pitch on main road.

Medical care The Coco Medical Centre (☎2670-1557, ⓦ www.crsalud.com) is in the Centro Comercial El Pueblito, signposted from *Lizard Lounge* on the road to *Cabinas Ruby*.

Post office The *correo* (Mon–Fri 7.30am–5pm) is in front of the bus station, opposite the *parque* at the bottom of the main road.

Moving on

By bus to: Liberia (5am, 6:30am, 8:30am, 10am, 12:45pm, 3pm, 5pm, 6pm; 45min); San José (5am, 11am, 3pm, 5pm; 5hr).

PLAYA PANAMÁ AND PLAYA HERMOSA

Sheltered from the full force of the Pacific, the clear blue waters and volcanic sands at **PLAYA PANAMÁ** and **PLAYA HERMOSA**, just up the road to the north of Playa del Coco, provide the perfect environment for a couple of days' relaxation, or even as a day-trip from Coco. Diving is the highlight of the area; jet-skis and horseriding tours are also available, but for far higher prices than in other parts of the country. Diving Safaris de Costa Rica, in Playa Hermosa just beyond the supermarket on the main road to the beach (☎2672-1259, ⓦ www .costaricadiving.net), is the diving authority in the region. They can provide everything from snorkel hire (US$5/2hr) to PADI courses (one-day dives from US$75).

Unfortunately, budget **accommodation** at Playa Panamá is non-existent, and is restricted to only a few options at Playa Hermosa. *Hotel Las Iguanas* (☎2672-0065; ❺), 25m from the beach on the left side of the main road, is easily the best budget option in town, offering basic but well-ventilated rooms overlooking a lovely swimming pool and a secluded garden. *Ecotel*, on the beach 500m north of the main road (☎2672-0175, ⓕ2672-0146; ❹), also has a lovely relaxed atmosphere, though you should be prepared for virtually no privacy – the rustic, back-to-nature hostel has enormous shared floors.

Buses run from Liberia to Playa Hermosa three times a day (times are always changing) and cost US$0.50. A **taxi** will cost you around US$5 from Playa del Coco.

Guanacaste

Guanacaste Province, bordered to the north by Nicaragua and the Pacific Ocean to the west, is distinctly different from the rest of Costa Rica. Though these days little remains of the **sabanero** (cowboy) culture, music and folklore for which the region is famous, there is undeniably something special about the place. The **landscape** is certainly beautiful, even though much of it has come about essentially through the slaughter of tropical dry forest: the wide rolling plains and the brooding humps of volcanoes are washed in muted earthy tones. Its **history**, too, is distinct: if not for a very close vote in 1824, Guanacaste might have been part of Nicaragua. While it is the province's beaches (roughly two-thirds of the Nicoya Peninsula is in Guanacaste) that attract the most visitors, the mud pots and stewing sulphur waters of **Parque Nacional Rincón de la Vieja**, and the tropical dry forest cover of **Parque Nacional Santa Rosa**, draw scores of nature aficionados to the interior every year.

LIBERIA

Despite the busloads of visitors arriving via the nearby international airport every day, the provincial capital of **LIBERIA** happily remains unchanged: it's still the epitome of dignified (if somewhat static) rural life. At present most travellers use the town simply as a jumping-off point for the national parks of **Rincón de la Vieja** and **Santa Rosa**, an overnight stop to or from the **beaches** of the Nicoya Peninsula (see p.550) or a break on the way to Nicaragua. It would be no hardship, however, to while away a little longer in the "**ciudad blanca**" (white city, on account of its white-washed houses). Everything you might need for a relaxing stay of a day or two is here – limited but well-priced accommodation, and a couple of nice places to eat and drink.

Liberia also boasts several lively local **festivals**, one of which is in early March, when there's ten days of parades, bands, fireworks and bull-running. On July 25, **El Día de la Independencia** celebrates Guanacaste's independence from Nicaragua with parades, rodeos, fiestas and roving marimba bands.

EATING & DRINKING

Bar Lib	5
Los Comales	1
Rancho Dulce	4
Rincón del Pollo	3
Las Tinajas	2

ACCOMMODATION

Cabinas El Tucán Blanco	D
Hotel La Casona	C
Hotel Liberia	A
Hotel Posada del Tope	B
Hotel La Siesta	E

San José

What to see and do

The town is arranged around its large **Parque Central**, properly called Parque Mario Cañas Ruiz. It's dedicated to *el mes del anexión*, the month of the annexation (July), celebrating the all-important fact that Guanacaste is not in Nicaragua. This is one of the loveliest central plazas in the whole country, ringed by benches and tall palms that shade gossiping locals. Its **church** is startlingly modern – somewhat out of place in this very traditional town.

About 600m away at the very eastern end of town, the colonial **Iglesia de la Agonía** is more arresting, with a mottled yellow facade. On the verge of perpetual collapse – it has had a hard time with earthquakes – it's almost never open, but you could try shoving the heavy wooden door and hope the place doesn't collapse around you. The town's most interesting street is **Calle Real** (marked as Calle Central on some maps). In the nineteenth century this was the entrance to Liberia, and practically the entire thoroughfare has now been restored to its original – and strikingly beautiful – colonial simplicity.

Arrival and information

By air Liberia's international airport is 12km west of the town. Flights arrive largely from North America, although flights from Europe have been introduced since a recent overhaul of the airport drastically increased its size. From here a taxi into Liberia will cost US$15, or there are frequent shuttle buses from outside the airport that cost US$0.50.

By bus All buses except those arriving from and leaving to San José and Peñas Blancas will arrive at the Terminal Liberia, at the northwestern edge of town. The Pulmitan Terminal, for San José and Peñas Blancas services, is one block southeast of Terminal Liberia.

By car From the northbound Interamericana, turn right into town at the major intersection (large enough for traffic lights). This will bring you to the town centre and the park. Make note of the gas station on the corner too – it is often used as a landmark. The left-forking road at this intersection takes you to the beaches.

Tourist information The main tourist office has closed, but the owner of the *Hotel Liberia* (T 2666-0161) can answer any questions about the area, and provides information and a shuttle service to Rincón de la Vieja.

Accommodation

Cabinas El Tucán Blanco Av 4, C 4/6 T 2666-7740, E tucanblanco@yahoo.com. Off the main road with parking in front, the large rooms here boast a/c, clean bathrooms and kitchenettes and cable TV. Not much to look at, but the owners are lovely and the security top-notch. ⑤

Hotel La Casona Av 6, C 0 T 2666-2971. This sleepy hotel is rather dark, but has quite a dignified air owing to the colonial reception area. Rooms are basic and a bit gloomy, but good value, including a/c and private cold shower. Reserve in advance. ⑤

Hotel Liberia C 0, 75m south of the Parque Central T 2666-0161, E hotelliberia@hotmail.com. Well-established, friendly, hostel-like hotel in a historic house – look for the orange exterior. Bare and basic rooms with shared cold-water bath are set around a sunny courtyard. The hotel staff can organize transport to Rincón de la Vieja. Visa accepted; reservation and deposit required in high season. Dorms ②, rooms ④

Hotel Posada del Tope C 0, 150m south of the *gobernación* T &F 2666-3876. Popular, cheap option in a beautiful old house. Six basic rooms with fan and shared showers in the old part are clean but stuffy; rooms across the street in a new annexe with cable TV cost only slightly more and are set around a charming courtyard. The manager runs transport to Rincón de la Vieja. Visa and MasterCard accepted. Old wing ②, new wing ④

Hotel La Siesta C 6, Av 4/6. T 2666-2950/3505, E lasiestaliberia@hotmail.com. This pretty hotel centres around an inner courtyard complete with fountain and swimming pool. Friendly Tico owners keep things simple, and offer free internet and a laundry service; the rooms all have a/c and cable TV. ⑦

Eating

Liberia has several restaurants that are particularly good for breakfast and lunch. Local treats include *natilla* (sour cream) eaten with eggs or *gallo pinto* and tortillas. For a real feast, try the various *desayunos guanacastecos* (Guanacastecan breakfasts). For rock-bottom cheap lunches, head for the stalls in the bus terminal, *Las Tinajas* or the town's various fried-chicken places.

Restaurants

Los Comales C Real, Av 3/5. A typical *soda*, very popular with locals for its generous portions of tasty rustic food. *Gallo pinto* 1500c, *casados* 2000–3000c.

Rancho Dulce C Real, Av 0/2. Small and lovable *soda* serving *casados* (1500c), sandwiches, empanadas and *refrescos*: great for a cheap lunch. You can sit at the tiny outdoor stools (if you have a small bottom) or tables. A reliable choice at any time of day.

Rincón del Pollo Av Central, 50m west of the Parque Central. A simple, open place where only 1500c will get you half a roast chicken, tortillas and salad.

Drinking and nightlife

Bars

Bar Lib On the Interamericana, in the Plaza Santa Rosa Centro Comercial. The newest and swankiest bar in town, *Bar Lib* boasts classic but over-priced cocktails (US$5) and deafening music till 2am at the weekends.

🏃 **Las Tinajas** On the west side of the Parque Central. The tables on the veranda of this old house are good for watching the goings-on in the parque while enjoying a *refresco* or cold beer. Basic *casados* and excellent hamburgers (2000c) are also served. There's regular live music; the place is basically the town's best bar.

Clubs

Kurú The town's main disco, a couple of hundred metres west of the Interamericana down the road to the beaches, gets lively with salsa and merengue, especially on weekends and holidays.

Tsunami Across the road from *Kurú* and down a side street. Another, smaller disco which is dead apart from Sat nights, is great fun when it's busy, serving international beers for US$2.50.

Entertainment

Liberia's main Saturday evening activities involve the locals parading around the Parque Central in their finery, having an ice cream and maybe going to the cinema at the Cine Liberia, in the shopping mall a kilometre south of the main Interamericana intersection.

Directory

Exchange Av Central is littered with banks, including Banco Nacional and Banco Costa Rica,

both across from the Parque Central. Both have ATMs and will exchange traveller's cheques.

Internet Cybermania (daily 8am–10pm), in a small business centre on the north side of the Parque Central, is a/c and cheap, as is the handy Planet Internet, on C Real just off the Parque Central (daily 8am–10pm, Sun 9am–9pm). Both cost about US$2/hr.

Post office The *correo* (Mon–Fri 7.30am–6pm, Sat 7.30am–noon) is between Av 3 and Av 5 in the white house across from the empty square field bordered by mango trees.

Moving on

By air Both Sansa and Nature Air run several flights daily from Liberia airport to the main international airport near Alajuela.

By bus to La Cruz/Peñas Blancas and Nicaragua (5.30am, 8.30am, 9am, noon, 1pm, 3pm, 5pm, 6.30pm; 2hr; US$1.25); Nicoya (every 30min 4.30am–8.20pm; 1hr 40min; US$1.25); Playa Panamá via Playa Hermosa (4.45am, 7.30am, 11.30am, 1pm, 3.30pm, 5.30pm; 1hr 15min; US$0.90); Playa Tamarindo (3.50am, 6.10am, 8.10am, 10am, 11.10am, 12.45pm, 4.30pm, 6pm; 2hr; US$1.25); Playa del Coco (5.30am, 7am, 9.30am, 11am, 12.15pm, 2.30pm, 4.30pm, 6.30pm; 1hr; US$0.75); Puntarenas (5am, then hourly 8.30am–3.30pm; 3hr; US$1.50); San José (hourly 4am–8pm; 4hr 30min; US$5); Santa Rosa (take the bus for the Nicaraguan border and ask to be dropped at the park; 40min).

PARQUE NACIONAL RINCÓN DE LA VIEJA

The earth around **PARQUE NACIONAL RINCÓN DE LA VIEJA** (daily 8am–4pm; US$6; ☏2661-8139) northeast of Liberia, is actually alive and breathing: **Volcán Rincón de la Vieja**, the park's namesake, is still active. Though it last erupted in 1991, rivers of lava continue to boil beneath the thin epidermis of ground, while **mud pots** (*pilas de barro*) bubble and puffs of steam rise out of lush foliage, signalling sulphurous subterranean springs. The dramatically dry surrounding landscape, meanwhile, varies from rock-strewn savanna to patches of tropical dry forest and deciduous trees, culminating in the blasted-out vistas of the volcano crater itself. This is great terrain for **camping**, **riding** and **hiking**, with a comfortable, fairly dry heat – although it can get damp and cloudy at the higher elevations around the crater. **Birders**, too, will enjoy Rincón de la Vieja, as there are more than two hundred species in residence.

What to see and do

The park has **hiking trails** for all enegry levels, which begin from one of the two *puestos* (ranger stations) – Santa María to the east, and Las Pailas to the west. Most start from Las Pailas, although the main one – the demanding uphill track to the volcano's **crater**, which can be tackled on foot, horseback or a combination of the two – can be embarked on from both. This is considered one of the best hikes, if not *the* best hike, in the country. A variety of elevations and habitats reveals hot springs, sulphur pools, bubbling mud pots and fields of purple orchids, plus of course the great smoking volcano at the top. It is possible to hike without a guide, but should you wish to organize a guided trek ask at Las Pailas (☎2661-8139). Alternatively, most hotels offer treks. Ring ahead before you start out, as the trail is often closed due to low visibility or high winds.

If you don't fancy the climb, there are more **gentle walks** in the Las Pailas sector, and one in the Santa Maria sector, that take you to fumaroles and mud pots, and you can also hike to two waterfalls, the *cataratas escondidas*. From the Las Pailas entrance, there's also another very satisfying walk: a 6km circular trail that takes you around some highly unusual natural features, with bubbling mud pots and a mini-volcano as well as steaming sulphurous vents that make for a highly atmospheric experience. The *puesto* Santa María is an old colonial house, rumoured to once be the country retreat of US President Lyndon Johnson, and has some rustic sleeping arrangements (see below).

Arrival and information

There is no public transport to either park entrance, although taxis (easily obtainable via your hotel) run from Liberia for roughly US$20.

For Sector Pailas Travel through the hamlet of Curubandé, 6km north of Liberia along the Interamericana. The 20km road (1000c to pass through a private section) is a dirt track and the signpost modest, so keep your eyes peeled. Hitching is said to be feasible along this road; if you're driving, a 4WD is recommended year-round, and compulsory in the wet season. Transfers from *Hotel Posada del Tope* and *Hotel Liberia* (see p.565) are available (US$15), but priority goes to hotel guests.

For Santa María Go through Liberia's Barrio La Victoria in the northeast of the town (ask for the *estadio* – the football stadium – from where it's a signed 24km drive to the park). The *Rinconcito Lodge* is near the park along this stretch. Transfers are available from the hotels, and also the *Rinconcito Lodge*.

Accommodation

Most budget travellers stay in Liberia: there is not much reasonably priced accommodation around the park, and there are no restaurants, so you must depend on the hotels there for food. However, there are a couple of decent options.

Camping There are sites (US$2 per person) at both ranger stations – Santa María is better equipped – with pit toilets, showers and grills, but you must bring your own food and drinking water. Be prepared for cold nights, strong winds and fog.

Santa María Lodge ☎2661-8139. You can stay in the very rustic bunk rooms within the *puesto* (ring the office at Santa María in advance).

Rinconcito Lodge On the road to Santa María ☎2666-2764, ✉rinconcito@racsa.co.cr. The cheapest option close to the park, this ecofarm has plain but good-value cabinas with hot-water shared or private bath. All-day horseriding and trekking tours on offer (US$35–45), and the owners are a good source of local advice. Meals and box lunches available. You can camp for free in the grounds if you buy food from the hotel, or for US$5 per person if you self-cater. ⑤

PARQUE NACIONAL SANTA ROSA

Established in 1971, **PARQUE NACIONAL SANTA ROSA** (daily 8am–4pm; US$15; ☎2666-5051), 35km north of Liberia, is one of the most popular in the country, thanks to its good trails, great surfing (though poor swimming) and prolific turtle-spotting opportunities.

Santa Rosa has an amazingly diverse topography for its size, ranging from mangrove swamp to rare tropical dry forest and savanna. With a staggering biodiversity of mammals, birds, amphibians and reptiles, Santa Rosa is also of prime interest to anyone keen to do some wildlife-spotting. Jaguars and pumas prowl the park, but you're unlikely to see them. Coati, coyotes and peccaries, on the other hand, are often found snuffling around watering holes. Between July and November (peaking in Sept–Oct), the sight of hundreds of **Olive Ridley turtles** (*lloras*) nesting on Playa Nancite puts all other animal sightings into obscurity; a maximum of twenty visitors are allowed access to the nesting area each day (call ahead to reserve your place). Though too rough for swimming, the picturesque **beaches** of Naranjo and Nancite, about 12km down a bad road from the administration centre, are popular with serious **surfers**.

Arrival and information

By bus Buses from Liberia (use the Peñas Blancas/La Cruz service) run past the entrance. Tell

the driver well in advance that you want to stop at the park. The entrance hut is signed from the Interamericana; it is a 7km walk from here to the campsite and administration/visitors' centre.
By car Driving is easy; go north from Liberia on the Interamericana roughly 35km.
Visitors' centre This is effectively the main reception (T 2666-5051, F 2666-5020), where you pay your entrance fee and pick up information.
Camping The camping facilities (US$2 per person, pay at administration centre) are some of the best in the country. There are two sites: La Casona campground has bathrooms and grill pits; Playa Naranjo, on the beach (and only open outside the turtle-nesting season), has picnic tables and grill pits, a ranger's hut with outhouses and showers and apparently, a boa constrictor in the roof. Watch your fires (the area is a tinderbox in the dry season), take plastic bags for your food, do not leave anything edible in your tent (it will be stolen by scavenging coati) and carry plenty of water.
Food Acquire food before entering the park. Drinks are sold at the visitors' centre, but little else.

Zona Norte

Costa Rica's **Zona Norte** ("northern zone") spans the hundred-odd kilometres from the base of the Cordillera Central to just short of the mauve-blue mountains of southern Nicaragua. Cut off from the rest of the country by a lack of roads, the Zona Norte has developed a unique character, with independent-minded farmers and Nicaraguan refugees making up large segments of the population. Many people from the north hold a special allegiance to, and pride in, their area. The landscape is special, too: less obviously picturesque than many parts of the country, the entire region nonetheless has a distinctive appeal, with lazy rivers snaking across steaming plains and flop-eared cattle languishing beneath the riverside trees.

Most travellers only venture up here to see the perpetually active **Volcán Arenal**. To the east is the humid **Sarapiquí** area, with its tropical forest **ecolodges** and research stations of **La Selva** and **Rara Avis**. Further north, the remote flatlands are home to the increasingly accessible **Refugio Nacional de Vida Silvestre Caño Negro**, which harbours an extraordinary amount of birdlife. There's a serviceable **bus** network, though if you're travelling outside the La Fortuna or Sarapiquí areas, you should consider renting a car. The area around Árenal is best equipped for

visitors; between Boca de Arenal and Los Chiles in the far north, on the other hand, there is a real shortage of accommodation, though fuel and food are in good supply.

LA FORTUNA

That the north attracts the numbers of visitors it does is mainly due to majestic **Volcán Arenal**, one of the most active volcanoes in the Western hemisphere. Just 6km away, **LA FORTUNA DE SAN CARLOS**, or **La Fortuna**, as it is more often called, was until recently a simple agricultural town but has boomed beyond recognition due to its perfect location as a jumping-off point for volcano-based activities. There's not much to do in the town town itself except book tours, eat, sleep and look at views of the volcano – when you can see it; the summit can be shrouded in clouds for days at a time, and from town glimpses of rolling lava are often scarce. Practically speaking, La Fortuna has excellent bus connections, and is something of a transport hub for the whole region.

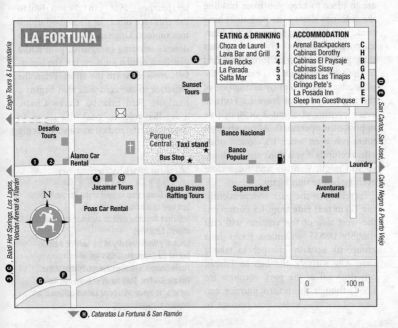

LA FORTUNA

Eagle Tours & Lavandaria

EATING & DRINKING
Choza de Laurel — 1
Lava Bar and Grill — 2
Lava Rocks — 4
La Parada — 5
Salta Mar — 3

ACCOMMODATION
Arenal Backpackers — C
Cabinas Dorothy — H
Cabinas El Paysaje — B
Cabinas Sissy — G
Cabinas Las Tinajas — A
Gringo Pete's — D
La Posada Inn — E
Sleep Inn Guesthouse — F

Sunset Tours

Desafio Tours

Álamo Car Rental

Parque Central — Taxi stand
Bus Stop

Banco Nacional

Banco Popular

Laundry

Jacamar Tours

Aguas Bravas Rafting Tours

Supermarket

Aventuras Arenal

Poas Car Rental

N

San Carlos, San José
Caño Negro & Puerto Viejo

Baldi Hot Springs, Los Lagos, Volcán Arenal & Tilarán

0 — 100 m

Cataratas La Fortuna & San Ramón

As with other high-traffic areas, beware of opportunistic **theft** in La Fortuna: you're not likely to experience anything too malicious, but don't walk around alone late at night, and avoid "guides" offering their services on the street.

What to see and do

The natural wonders of the region lend themselves to both active and relaxing pursuits; from tough hikes to relaxing bathing opportunities, there is something for everyone.

Volcán Arenal

Volcán Arenal is spectacular from afar, whether admired from La Fortuna, where its slopes are still a lush green, or from the barren and desolate western face, where the foliage has been gradually scorched by the ash and lava that tumble down the side every day. You can get a bit closer to the action by heading to the **Parque Nacional Volcán Arenal** (daily 8am–4pm; US$10); though fences are in place to keep you from tackling the volcano's slopes, the park does have some good **trails**, including the four-kilometre "Tucanes" trail that passes through the section of forest flattened by the 1968 eruption. You can't visit the park after dark except by taking one of the **night tours** that leave La Fortuna every evening at about 3 or 4pm (see opposite for operators). Although most tours run even when it's cloudy, none offers refunds if you don't see anything, so you might want to wait for a clear evening before signing up.

Travelling to the park independently, the 12km **taxi ride** from La Fortuna to the west side of the volcano will cost roughly US$35, so unless you're in a group, it's actually cheaper to take a tour. Alternatively, the **bus** to Tilarán can drop off at the park entrance for US$1, though the return journey can be a bit tricky – unless you manage to connect with the infrequent return bus, your only option is to hitch back with other park visitors.

Hot springs

There are three lodges, all approximately 13km west of La Fortuna, offering visitors the opportunity to watch the volcano's pyrotechnics while soaking in **hot springs** – but you may pay through the nose for the privilege. Of the three, **El Tabacón** (daily 10am–10pm; US$60, US$40 after 7pm; ☎2391-1900, ⓦwww.tabacon.com) is the most expensive. **Baldi Hot Springs** is slightly less pretentious (daily 10am–10pm; US$25; ⓔbaldihotsprings@arenal.net). Unofficially, you can book for this one through the Aventuras Arenal (see opposite) for roughly US$6 less.

Cataratas La Fortuna

You can make an excursion to La Fortuna's stunning **waterfalls** (*cataratas La Fortuna*), which sit amidst some beautiful jungle terrain just 6km from the south side of the church in town. A taxi journey (US$8) can take you right to the entrance office, or it's a good uphill trek on foot. Once in, it is a steep climb down a winding overgrown path and a gruelling return journey, but the waterfalls are well worth the effort. From the entrance to the *cataratas* also begins a hardcore 5km hike up **Cerro Chato**, a smaller volcanic peak tha clings to Arenal's skirts, and offers views of its big brother.

Arrival and information

By bus Buses stop in front of the Parque Central, just east of the church.
Internet Available next to Jacamar, opposite the church (US$1/hr).
Laundry Wash and dry at the service a block before *La Choza Inn* (US$3/kg).
Taxis There's a rank on the south side of the Parque Central. They rarely (if ever) use their meters, so agree on a price before getting in and beware of overcharging.

TOUR AND ACTIVITY OPERATORS IN LA FORTUNA

Price competition between tour agencies in La Fortuna is fierce. You may save a few dollars by going with the cheapest agency, but you could end up on a badly organized tour with under-qualified guides, or no lunch – get as many details as you can before you put down your cash. In general, go with an established tour operator, and not one of the freelance "guides" who may approach you, some of whom have been involved in serious incidents over the years.

Aventuras Arenal 150m east of the soccer pitch (☎2479-9133, ⓦwww .arenaladventures.com). Professionally run trips by this reliable operator, plus transport arrangements to just about anywhere in this country.

Desafío Tours West of the church ☎2479-9464, ⓦwww.desafiocostarica .com. Friendly, efficient, community-aware rafting specialists who run tours (US$65) on the Río Toro, kayak trips on the Río Arenal (US$55) and demanding guided hikes up Cerro Chato (US$45). Their Monteverde transfer includes a lakeside horse ride (US$65), and they can sort out flights, tours and accommodation anywhere in the country.

Eagle Tours In the reception area of *La Choza Inn* ☎2479-9091, ⓦwww.eagletours .net. Highly recommended tours with well-qualified guides. Volcano tours (US$45) include the entrance fee to the hot spring of your choice, and they have a good day-trip to Caño Negro (see p.573; US$45), as well as jeep-boat-jeep transfers to Monteverde (see p.572; US$22). Discounts available for hotel guests.

Jacamar Next to *Lava Rocks* restaurant ☎2479-9767, ⓦwww.arenaltours.com. Operator running an Arenal night tour (US$25), trips to Caño Negro (see p.573; US$50) and rafting excursions on the Río Peñas Blancas. Their boat-and-taxi transfer to Monteverde costs US$23 and takes two and a half to three hours.

Accommodation

Budget accommodation is everywhere in La Fortuna, though the lodges around the periphery are, without exception, for the moneyed traveller.

Arenal Backpackers 500m west of the town centre ☎2479-7000, ⓦwww .arenalbackpackersresort.com. Dorms and rooms are spacious, clean and bright with firm mattresses, there's free internet and a pool area, and it's got its own in-house tour operators. Potentially the best hostel in the country. Dorms ❸, rooms ❼

Cabinas Dorothy 500m south of the town centre, just past the bullring ☎2479-8068. A little far out of town and a bit tatty-looking, but these *cabinas* are friendly, secure and very comfortable. ❷

Cabinas El Paysaje 100m north of the church ☎2479-9007. Lovely owner with very basic accommodation, but solo travellers get private rooms and hot-water bath without paying extra. Well located in a quiet but central part of town. ❸

Cabinas Sissy 100m south and 125m west of the central park ☎2479-9256, Ⓔhotelreyarenal @hotmail.com. Basic budget travellers' hangout – friendly and clean, with a variety of rooms with fan and private or shared hot-water bath; some have cable TV. There's also a simple shared kitchen. You can camp, too. Camping ❶, doubles ❹

Cabinas Las Tinajas 100m north and 25m west of the central park ☎2479-9308, Ⓔcbtinajas@gmail .com. Small complex of four clean, well-furnished, airy cabinas equipped with cable TV, fan and good hot-water bath. There are rocking chairs on the terrace, and the owners are very friendly: it adds up to a good value. ❺

Gringo Pete's 3000m southeast of the central park ☎2479-8521, Ⓔgringopetes2003@yahoo.com. Another fantastically cheap option with comfortable dorms and private rooms, and sociable communal areas. Dorms ❶, doubles ❷

La Choza Inn 300m west of the church ☎2479-9091. In a quiet pocket of the town, the little wooden dorms and private rooms in these cabinas are clean and well maintained. Internet is free and there is a full communal kitchen. Guests get a discount at Eagle Tours, which is run out of the reception area. Dorms ❸, rooms ❹

La Posada Inn 300m east of the central park ☎2479-9793, Ⓔlavaroja@hotmail.com. Incredibly cheap rooms owned by a charming and hospitable family. Communal garden, private parking and an attractive garden. Dorms ❸, doubles ❹

Sleep Inn Guesthouse 350m southwest of the central park ☎2394-7033, Ⓔcarlossleepinn @hotmail.com. Renowned for larger-than-life owner Carlos, aka "Mr Lava-Lava". He offers volcano tours for the best price in town, and you can't help feel like part of the family as soon as you arrive, even if the living quarters are rather basic. ❷

Eating and drinking

Choza de Laurel 200m west of the Parque Central on the main road. A lively, atmospheric place to enjoy high-quality, albeit expensive, meals (most mains US$8 plus). The food is delicious, and you won't leave hungry.

Lava Bar and Grill On the main road 50m before the church. By day a restaurant with well-prepared and reasonably priced wraps, salads and light meals (US$5–7), this is also a trendy evening spot.

Lava Rocks Opposite the church. Not to be confused with *Lava Bar and Grill*, this admittedly rather bland-looking place is one of the best in town for delicious, well-priced meals (*casados* from US$5) and heartbreakingly nice staff.

La Parada Opposite the bus stop on the central park. Perfect for an early breakfast, this popular *soda* is a fine spot to sit and watch the world. The *casados* are hardly inspiring, but they are big, filling and only US$4.

Salta Mar Opposite *Arenal Backpackers*. Dinner might be a touch over budget, but the breakfasts are uplifting (US$3–4) and the fresh-fruit smoothies win first prize for both taste and presentation.

Moving on

By bus to: Monteverde (take the 8am bus to Tilarán, changing there for the 12.30pm bus to Monteverde; 6–8hr; US$3); Puerto Viejo de Sarapiquí (take the bus to San Carlos/Ciudad Quesada (1hr 30min; US$1.20) at 5am, 8am, noon, 3pm; change there for Sarapiquí (3hr; US$2.20) at 4.40am (Fri only), 6am, 9.15am (Sun only), 10am, noon, 3pm, 4.30pm, 5.30pm, 6.30pm); San José (12.30pm, 2.30pm; 4hr; US$3), via San Carlos (1hr 30min); Tilarán (8am, 4.30pm; 3hr 30min; US$1.40).

LOS CHILES

Few tourists make it to **LOS CHILES**, a border settlement just 3km from Nicaragua. There are really only two reasons to come: to try to rent a boat or horse to go to **Caño Negro**, 25km downstream on the Río Frío (see opposite), or to cross the Nicaraguan border, although the majority of travellers still cross at Peñas Blancas (see p.568). Two luxury **buses** per day run to Los Chiles from C 12, Av 7/9, in San José (5.30am & 3.30pm; 5hr), stopping at the small bus station. Also pulling in here are the almost hourly buses from San Carlos (Ciudad Quesada). Return buses to San José leave Los Chiles at 5am and 3pm.

Although Los Chiles has no official **tourist information**, everyone in town knows the current bus schedules and the times of the river-boat to the Nicaraguan border, though you'll need Spanish to ask around. Servicios Turísticos Caño Negro (☎2471-1438), based at the *Cabinas Jabirú*, a block west and north of the bus station, can give some general tourist information and runs a variety of trips. You can **change dollars** and traveller's cheques at the Banco Nacional on the north side of the soccer pitch (Mon–Fri 8am–3.30pm); it also has an ATM accepting Visa/Plus/Cirrus/MasterCard.

LA FORTUNA TO MONTEVERDE: JEEP-BOAT-JEEP TRANSFERS

By far the most interesting way to travel between two of the country's major attractions, La Fortuna and Monteverde (see p.539), is by a "jeep–boat–jeep" transfer, a time-saving and spectacularly pretty connection. The trip takes two to three hours depending on road conditions, and shows off both the breathtaking mountain pastures of Monteverde, and your first (or last, depending on the direction) glimpse of majestic Volcán Arenal. Prices depend entirely on where you book the journey, so shop around – many hotels and tour operators can arrange them. The least expensive trip available at the time of writing was at *Arenal Backpackers* in La Fortuna (see p.571; US$18). If you are travelling the other way, *Pensión Santa Elena* (see p.537) can book it for cheapest.

REFUGIO NACIONAL DE VIDA SILVESTRE CAÑO NEGRO

The largely pristine **REFUGIO NACIONAL DE VIDA SILVESTRE CAÑO NEGRO** (daily 8am–4pm; US$10, included in tour prices; ☎2471-1309), 25km west of Los Chiles, is one of the best places in the Americas to view huge concentrations of both migratory and indigenous birds, along with mammalian and reptilian river wildlife. Until recently its isolation – it's 192km from San José – kept it well off the beaten track, though nowadays more and more tours are visiting the area (you can visit on an excursion from La Fortuna – see p.571 for operators – or any of the larger hotels in the Zona Norte); getting there independently is still fairly complicated.

Arrival and information

By boat It's possible to rent a boat for travel down the Río Frío from Los Chiles (US$75–100).
By bus Buses officially leave from Los Chiles at 5am & 2pm (1hr), but it is worth confirming hours back as times are typically liable to change. The ranger station will have information on this, and has the facilities to book a taxi for you.
Accommodation It's possible to stay in the Ranger Station (☎2471-1309; US$6). Camping (US$5, payable to the ranger) is permitted, but no formal facilities are provided. There is some very basic accommodation available in the village of Caño Negro also.

Entrance US$10, payable at the Ranger Station. They have information on the refuge and can advise on transport (☎2471-1309)
Guides Hiring an experienced guide to the area is well worth the money. If you are travelling independently, ring the ranger station in advance to arrange this.

PUERTO VIEJO DE SARAPIQUÍ

Steamy, tropical and carpeted with fruit plantations, the eastern part of the Zona Norte bears more resemblance to the hot and dense Caribbean lowlands than the plains of the north and, despite the toll of deforestation, still shelters some of the best-preserved premontane rainforest in the country. The largest settlement, **PUERTO VIEJO DE SARAPIQUÍ**, is principally a river transport hub and a place for the region's banana, coconut, and pineapple plantation workers to stock up on supplies and have a beer or two. You will find most, if not all, of the area's budget accommodation here, as well as some excellent river-based activities and impressive hiking trails.

There are two options when it comes to getting here from the Valle Central. The western route, which takes a little more than three hours, goes via Varablanca and the La Paz waterfall, passing the hump of Volcán Barva. This route offers great views of velvety green hills clad with coffee plantations, which turn, eventually, into rainforest. It's faster (1hr–1hr 30min), but marginally less scenic, to travel via the **Guápiles Highway**. The region receives a lot of **rain** – as much as 4500mm annually – so wet-weather gear is essential.

Arrival and information

By bus The bus station is in the centre of town on the main road by the football pitch.

Exchange Banco Nacional (Mon–Fri 8.30am–3pm), at the far northern end of C Principal, exchanges traveller's cheques and dollars.

Internet Internet La Viña (US$0.80/hr), in the bookstore adjacent to La Viña supermarket, whose sign is visible across the football pitch from the bus station.

Tour operators Souvenir Río Sarapiquí is opposite the Banco Nacional on the main road (℡2766-6727 ✉luisalbertosm@racsa.co.cr). The owner is a reliable source of information on all that the region has to offer. They offer good rates on rafting, kayaking, hiking and, naturally, canopy tours. Aguas Bravas (℡2292-2072 or 2776-6524, ⊛www.aguas-bravas.co.cr) is a great company for rafting trips. Their offices are 100m down from Banco Nacional towards the river.

Accommodation

B&B Andrea Cristina 1km west of town on the road to Chilamate ℡2766-6265, ⊛www.andreacristina.com. A veritable tropical haven, with lovely, quirky cabins amongst the jungle plants. The hospitable owner has a wealth of information on conservation projects, and offers river and trekking tours. ❻

Hotel Bambú Above the bus station opposite the football pitch ℡2766-6005. This centrally located hotel has a wonderful pool, a reasonable restaurant and clean rooms with private hot showers. However, the noise from the main road can be overpowering, and for a similar price you can stay at one of the luxury lodges on the road to San Miguel. ❽

Mi Lindo Sarapiquí On the corner of the football pitch as you enter town ℡2766-6281/6074. A good budget option, with clean, spacious rooms, private hot showers and a friendly atmosphere. The restaurant attached is very popular, and also houses an internet café (US$0.80/hr). It is worth noting that if you arrive before 10am you will not be able to get in. ❺

Eating

Nearly all hotels have restaurants open to guests and general public, but *Soda Llyxi*, on the road into town 10m before the football pitch, really stands out. Clean and bright open-fronted *soda* complete with wooden benches and a TV and dishing up delicious *gallo pinto* for US$2 and rocket fuel coffee for US$0.40.

Moving on

By bus to: San Carlos/Ciudad Quesada, for buses to La Fortuna, Monteverde and points west (5.30am, 8.30am, 10.30am, 12.15pm, 2.30pm, 4pm, 6pm, 6.30pm, 7pm; 3hr); San José, Terminal del Caribe (5.30am, 7am, 8am, 11am, 1.30pm, 3.30pm, 5.30pm; 1hr 30min–2hr).

AROUND PUERTO VIEJO DE SARAPIQUÍ

The lush Caribbean climate and vegetation in the area around Sarapiquí make for a striking environment, so it makes sense that the activities on offer are of an outdoor nature.

Rara Avis

The incredible and completely isolated private rainforest reserve of **Rara Avis** (℡2253-0844 or 2764-3131, ⊛www.rara-avis.com), 17km south of Puerto Viejo, also acts as an expensive tourist lodge and a **research station**, accommodating student groups and volunteers from around the world whose aim is to develop rainforest products – orchids, palms and so forth – as crops for the use of local communities. It offers one of the most thrilling and authentic eco-experiences in Costa Rica, featuring both primary rainforest and some secondary cover. The rich array of **wildlife**, both flora and fauna, can't fail to impress, and you could meander the excellent trail network for days.

Visiting the park is usually a pre-meditated venture, requiring at least one night's stay in one of the lodges, and recommended perhaps only to the true nature enthusiast, or someone with deep pockets. Most people organize their trip here before arriving in Costa Rica as it takes a great deal of planning: the route alone up to Rara Avis involves getting to the village Las Horquetes, either by taxi or bus from Puerto Viejo, where you will meet a pre-booked **tractor** that will take you the rest of the 15km journey. Both students and visitors are required to book in advance, as space is limited and very costly: lodges in the park (the only option) cost in the region of US$50 per person per night, minimum (rates include all meals, transport to and from Las Horquetas, and guided walks).

Estación Biológica La Selva

A fully equipped research station, **Estación Biológica La Selva**, 93km northeast of San José and 4km southwest of Puerto Viejo de Sarapiquí (☎2766-6565, in San José ☎2240-6696, ⓦwww.ots.ac.cr), is probably the best place to visit in the Sarapiquí region, especially if you are a botany student or have a special interest in the scientific life of a rainforest. Like Rara Avis, it is also a superb birder's spot, with more than four hundred species of indigenous and migratory **birds**.

While the research students and scientists who come here receive heavily subsidized accommodation and meals,

the regular visitor does not, and you will find yourself paying roughly US$90 a night for very basic living quarters. However, visiting on half-day guided **treks** (US$30) through the extensive trails is a worthy option if you can't afford the fees. Call or reserve online in advance.

Río Sarapiquí

The roaring **Río Sarapiquí** used to be the most important trade route in northern Costa Rica, ferrying coffee and bananas between Nicaragua, southern Costa Rica and overseas. Its main job nowadays is to satisfy the adrenaline-fuelled desires of even the most adventurous visitors, as a prime location for some of the most invigorating **white-water rafting** and **kayaking** in the country. Visit Souvenir Río Sarapiquí (see p.574) or Aguas Bravas (see p.574) to see about arranging trips.

The Zona Sur

Costa Rica's **Zona Sur** ("southern zone") is the country's least-known region, both for Ticos and for international travellers, although tourism has begun to increase in recent years. Geographically, it's a diverse area, ranging from the agricultural heartland of the Valle de El General to the high peaks of the Cordillera de Talamanca. South of Cerro el Chirripó, one of the highest peaks in Central America, the cordillera falls away into the lowlands of the Valle de Diquis and the coffee-growing Valle de Coto Brus, near the border with Panama. Climatically, the Osa Peninsula, Golfito and Golfo Dulce experience rain even during the dry season, and during the wettest part of the year (Oct–Dec), spectacular thunderstorms canter in from the Pacific.

The region's chief draw is the **Osa Peninsula**, home to **Parque Nacional Corcovado**, one of the country's prime

THE ZONA SUR & OSA PENINSULA

rainforest hiking destinations, and the remote and picturesque **Bahía Drake**. More accessible, the **Playa Dominical** area of the Pacific coast is a surfing destination of tremendous tropical beauty. **Golfito**, the only town of any size, isn't particularly exciting, though it has improved since being made a tax-free zone for goods from Panama.

DOMINICAL

DOMINICAL, 44km south of Quepos (see p.546), probably represents the face of things to come along this stretch of the Pacific coast. Previously a secluded

fishing village, it has of late begun to expand dramatically. The coastal areas to the south, still largely unspoilt stretches of beach and rainforest, are rapidly being bought up by hungry property developers and hotel chains. The fear, expressed by many locals, that the area is destined to become the country's next Manuel Antonio – a once pristine area, now massively overdeveloped – seems about to be realized. Despite its recent growth, though, the town remains relatively small-scale, with just a few dirt track roads. **Surfing** is the big draw; thousands of (mainly American) visitors flock in every year to ride the beach break during the day before heading to the town's numerous beachfront bars. Swimming is ill advised in the area due to strong riptides.

Arrival and information

By bus Buses travel the length of the strip before turning at the end and coming back the same way in order to leave town. The bus stop is opposite the telecommunications building at the southern end of town.

Internet Access at the *Arena y Sol* hotel and restaurant on the main street (US$2/hr).

Tour operators You can rent or buy surfboards at Jungle Jive Surf Camp (℡2316-0651, Ⓦwww .junglejivesurfcamp.com; US$40/2hr), which runs from Blowfish, a shop about halfway along the main road. They sell beach clothing, too. Dominical Surf and Adventures (℡8839-8542, Ⓦwww .dominicalsurfadventures.com) also rents boards and has information on a number of tours in the area, including rapelling, paragliding and rafting.

Tourist information Southern Expeditions (℡2787-0110, Ⓦwww.southernexpeditionscr .com), at the northern end of town, gives good impartial advice on the area as a whole.

Accommodation

Dominical is full of hotels, but those geared towards the budget traveller and surfer are not of a high standard. It is worth spending a few extra pennies if you can.

Arena y Sol Along the main drag just before the right turn down to the beach ℡2787-0140, Ⓔinfo@arenaysol.com. Very clean, modern rooms – sleeping up to five – with a/c and cable TV. Internet is free for guests, and breakfast is included. The pool provides blessed relief from the heat. ❼

Camping Antorchas Just off the beach road towards *Dominical Backpackers* Ⓦwww .campingantorchas.com. This campsite has a kitchen, free parking and surfboard rental. ❶

Dominical Backpackers At the northern end of the beach strip ℡2787-0026. This place is popular with die-hard surfers looking for nothing more than a place to rest when it's too dark to surf. It's well situated and one of the cheapest options in town, but the little rooms are dark and of pretty poor quality. Security isn't brilliant but you can lock up your bag in reception. Dorms ❷

Piramys ℡2787-0196. Feels like a hippy commune, with a jumble of attractive but basic rooms, airy

mezzanines and an al fresco kitchen. Some rooms have hot water. A minor downside: while very peaceful, its bucolic location makes it prone to uncomfortably large spiders. Dorms ❷, doubles ❹

San Climente Inn On the main road just before the right turn down to the beach ℡2787-0026. Wooden cabins are simple, clean and secure. You pay more for hot water, a/c and sea views. ❺

Tortilla Flats On the beach ℡2787-0033, Ⓔtortflat@racsa.co.cr. Popular surfers' hotel with brightly decorated en-suite rooms and a beachfront bar where crowds gather every evening to watch the sunset. ❺

Eating and drinking

The Back Porch In a little cluster of huts at the entrance to the village ℡2322-1968. This café serves up real cappuccino (1000c), with soy milk if you're that way inclined, and delicious bagels (1500–2500c). The lovely American owner will make you feel right at home.

Maracatú Funky little restaurant roughly in the middle of the drag opposite the *San Climente Inn* offering a mouth-watering selection of vegetarian and fish dishes in the 3000–6000c range. Wed is Reggae Night, and on Tues it hosts an open jam session.

Soda Nanyoya At this breezy, open-walled barn-cum-resto tucked away behind the town's fruit stand you may have to queue for a table to get the freshest orange juice you'll ever taste and yummiest breakfast in town. Blissfully low prices (*gallo pinto* 1000c).

Tortilla Flats At the *Tortilla Flats* hotel. The best spot in town to watch the sun set while nursing a cool beer (happy hour 4–6pm). A tasty menu offers typical and American food from 1500c.

Moving on

By bus to: Quepos (7.30am, 8am, 10.30am, 1.45pm, 4pm, 5pm; 2hr); Palmar (4:30am, 10.30am; 2hr) buses run from here to Bahía Drake and Puerto Jiménez; San Isidro (6.45am, 7.15am, 2.30pm, 3.30pm; 1hr); Buses depart from San Isidro to San José twice daily. Times change frequently so check with one of the hotels for up-to-date schedules.

BAHÍA DRAKE

The **BAHÍA DRAKE** (pronounced "Dra-kay") is one of the most stunning – and remote – areas in Costa Rica, with the blue wedge of **Isla del Caño**, a prime snorkelling destination, floating just off the coast and fiery-orange Pacific sunsets. The tiny hamlet of **Agujitas**, on the bay 10km south of Bahía Drake town, makes a wonderful base for the majority of travellers that come to the area to explore **Parque Nacional Corcovado**, which sits on the southwest corner of the Osa Peninsula – the park's San Pedrillo entrance is within walking distance, and hikers can combine serious trekking with serious comfort at either end of their trip by staying at one of the upscale rainforest ecolodges that have sprung up around the park in recent years

Brave is the person who tackles the buses in this area; they run very infrequently and without any real schedule, so it's probably worth coming by car if you want to explore around here. This said, the roads are frightful and littered with river crossings, so be careful and ask local advice, especially if there's been a lot of rain.

Arrrival and information

By bus Two buses a day pass through Bahía Drake from Rincón. There may be one passing as late as

7pm, but it is unwise to be travelling that late as you could well end up stranded in Rincón, essentially a hostel-free intersection. If you can afford it, a taxi to Sierpe from San Isidro costs US$15 and from there you can take a river taxi (2hr) to Bahía Drake for US$30. From the south, there is a bus from La Palma to Drake (1hr 30min) at 11.30am and another at 1.30pm. Rumour has it there is also one that leaves at 5pm. There is also a *colectivo* (a sort of open-back truck-taxi) that runs to La Palma from Puerto Jiménez, starting at 6am, last one at roughly 4pm.

Tourist information The tourist office, set back from the beach just next to the Corcovado Foundation (☎8818-9962, ✉info@corcovadoexpeditions .net), has information on a range of tours, including trips to Isla del Caño, mangroves and canopy tours and entry into Corcovado. It also has unreliable internet access. The Fondación Corcovado (☎2297-3013, ⊛www.corcovadofoundation .org), a volunteer organization set up to maintain the park, improve local amenities and rally against encroaching developers, maintains a beachfront office that doubles as an unofficial tourist information and has a wealth of information about park etiquette and practicalities.

Accommodation

Nearly all the accommodation listed here offers tours, from snorkelling to horseriding, in the region

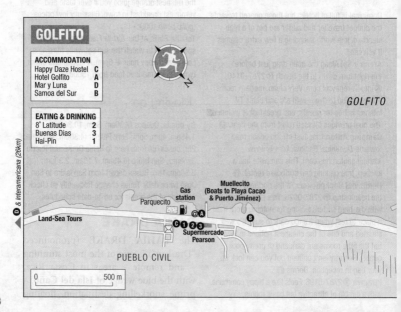

GOLFITO

ACCOMMODATION
Happy Daze Hostel **C**
Hotel Golfito **A**
Mar y Luna **D**
Samoa del Sur **B**

EATING & DRINKING
8° Latitude **2**
Buenas Dias **3**
Hai-Pin **1**

GOLFITO

D & Interamericana (26km)

Land-Sea Tours

Parquecito

Gas station

Muellecito (Boats to Playa Cacao & Puerto Jiménez)

Supermercado Pearson

PUEBLO CIVIL

0   500 m

of US$75. All have cold water unless otherwise stated. Camping on the beach is frowned upon, though many people do it; don't leave any litter if you do. Unless otherwise specified, all the places listed here are in the settlement of Agujitas.

Cabinas Jade Mar 200m up from the beach ☎2384-6681, Ⓦwww.jademarcr.com. This pretty hostel boasts lovely sea views through the jungle, hammocks and a nice communal deck. Dorms ❸–❹, doubles ❹

Cabinas Manolo At the bottom of the last hill coming into Agujitas ☎2885-9114, Ⓦwww .cabinasmanolo.com. Rooms at this friendly Tico-run hostel are small and a bit musty, although clean and brightly coloured, and most have a little balcony with hammock. Tours on offer for US$75. ❷–❸

Jardin Corcovado In Bahía Drake. Opened so close to printing that it didn't have a phone line, this family-run hostel just up from the beach offers spotless rooms with tiled floors and high ceilings. ❸

Eating

Mar y Bosque In Agujitas. Specializing in delicious fruit juices and pancakes as well as *pinto* (US$3), this beautiful open-air *soda* overlooks a butterfly-filled garden and the sea through the trees. Esteban, the son of the owner, offers a reliable and very informative trip into the Corcovado reserve (☎2311-7402).

Restaurante Jade Mar In Agujitas ☎2822-8595. The only real restaurant outside of the lodges, this open-sided strip-lit place is always busy with locals and visitors. The big menu offers everything from lobster (US$20) to lasagna (US$4).

Moving on

By bus Leaving the village of Agujitas, there are buses at 4:30am and 12:30pm to Rincón, where connections run to San Isidro and San José. The Rincón service also goes onto La Palma, where you can pick up connections to Puerto Jiménez.

GOLFITO

The former banana port of **GOLFITO**, just 33km north of the Panamanian border, stretches along the water at the cusp of the glorious Golfo Dulce. The shadow of the Osa Peninsula shimmers in the distance, and everywhere the vegetation has the soft muted look of the tropics. The town's history is inextricably intertwined with the giant **United Brands** company, which first set up here in 1938. When it pulled out in a hurry in 1985, it created a social vacuum, and Golfito became known as one of the most unsavoury towns in

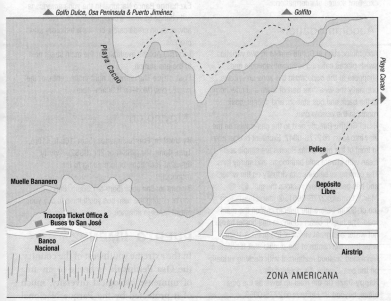

▲ Golfo Dulce, Osa Peninsula & Puerto Jiménez ▲ Golfito

Playa Cacao

Playa Cacao

Police

Depósito Libre

Muelle Bananero

Tracopa Ticket Office & Buses to San José

Banco Nacional

Airstrip

ZONA AMERICANA

all Costa Rica. These days the area is steadily improving, thanks primarily to a government incentive that established Golfito as a tax-free zone (*depósito libre*) for imports from Panama. South of the *depósito libre*, and the more affluent part of town, is the **pueblo civil**, where you'll find good-value hotels and *sodas*, as well as the *lancha* (ferry) across the Golfo Dulce to Puerto Jiménez and the Osa Peninsula. There isn't a huge amount to do in Golfito, but it is a pleasant enough place to stay if you need somewhere to stop for the night if you're waiting to cross to Puerto Jiménez, or to cross the border into Panama.

Arrival and information

By boat A *lancha* arrives six times daily (5am–4.30pm) from Puerto Jiménez to the tiny *muellecito* (little dock) behind *Hotel Golfito*. Check in the hotel for up-to-date schedules.

By bus Services stop by the Banco Nacional. Buy your return ticket as soon as you disembark.

Tour operators Land-Sea Tours (ⓣ&ⓕ 2775-1614, ⓔ landsea@racsa.co.cr), on the waterfront at the southern end of the *pueblo civil*, organizes a wide range of tours, has a book exchange and is an excellent source of information.

Accommodation

Accommodation in Golfito comes in two varieties: swish places catering to businesspeople and shoppers at the *depósito* in the *zona americana*, originally the wealthier part of town and now home to the bank and bus station, and decent, basic rooms in the *pueblo civil*.

Hotel Golfito Directly next to the gas station on the way into town ⓣ 2775-0047. Excellent budget hotel in front of the *muellecito*. Rooms are simple and clean with private cold bathrooms and sturdy fans. The communal balcony sits virtually on the water, and has beautiful views across the gulf. ③–⑥

Mar Y Luna ⓣ 2775-0901, ⓔ maryluna@racsa .co.cr. 500m before the *pueblo civil* on the main road. The bright, clean cabins in this hostel have hot water and great views of the *golfo*. A 10min walk from the centre of the *pueblo civil*, it boasts a renowned seafood restaurant with decking virtually on the sea. Singles ④, doubles ⑤

Happy Daze On the road up towards the post office, beyond *8° Latitude* ⓣ 2775-0058,

ⓦ www.happydazecostarica.com. The Californian owner has allowed his surfer attitude to flow into this little hostel with shared kitchen and TV room, and welcoming, albeit rather shambolic, dorms. He offers waterfall and fishing trips, and surf lessons for US$20. Discounts for long stays and in the low season. ②

Samoa del Sur On the main road between the *zona americana* and the *pueblo civil* ⓣ 2775-0233, ⓕ 2775-0573, ⓔ samoasur@racsa.co.cr. Fourteen spacious, though slightly gloomy, rooms on the water, with a large and rather raucous bar/restaurant, a favourite for US marines on leave. ⑤

Eating and drinking

Buenos Dias In front of the gas station ⓣ 2775-1124. This cheerful café dishes up *gallo pinto* for US$3 amidst real American diner decor with Disney paraphernalia on the walls.

Hai Pin ⓣ 2775-0032. All-out Chinese restaurant up behind *Buenos Dias* that entices locals and tourists. Typical Chinese fare for US$3–5.

8° Latitude Run by an eccentric and charming American couple, this is a perfect place for a weary traveller to enjoy a cold beer in friendly surroundings. If you're around during the Super Bowl, owner Sally cooks up a feast for drinkers.

Directory

Exchange Banco Nacional In the *zona americana* will change traveller's cheques and give cash advances on credit cards, but it's a tediously slow process.

Internet Access available on the main street next to the gas station.

Post office The *correo* is right in the centre of the *pueblo civil* (Mon–Fri 8.30am–4pm).

Moving on

By boat to: Puerto Jiménez (5am, 10am, 11am, 1pm, 4pm; 1hr (US$4) or 2hr (US$2) – verify times at your hotel before going to the *muellecito*.

By bus to: San José (5am & 1.30pm; 8hr) – if you're getting the 5am bus you'll have to buy your return ticket in advance.

PUERTO JIMÉNEZ

In the extreme southwest of the country, the **Osa Peninsula** is home to an area of immense biological diversity, much of it protected by the Parque Nacional

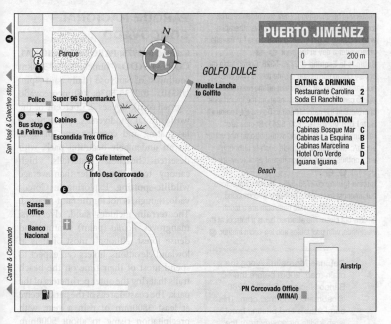

Corcovado. Most visitors to the area base themselves in the tiny, friendly town of **PUERTO JIMÉNEZ**. From here, you could feasibly "do" the whole peninsula in four days, but this would be rushing it, especially if you want to spend time walking the trails and wildlife-spotting at Corcovado – better to allot five to seven days or more.

You can pick up the *colectivo* from here to Carate, 43km southwest, or to Bahía Drake, from where you can enter Corcovado (see p.582). If you're driving yourself, don't try coming in anything but a 4WD at any time of year. Though the roads have been "improved" in recent years, it's still a horrendously bumpy ride. Note too that Puerto Jiménez is home to the only gas station on the entire peninsula, so be sure to fill up before you head out.

Arrival and information

By bus There's only one daily bus from San José Transporte Blanco terminal; it arrives into the bus station on the western side of town; if you don't want to arrive in the dark you could take the early bus to Golfito and the *lancha* from there to Puerto Jiménez to arrive in time for the sunset.

Exchange Banco Nacional (Mon–Fri 8.30am–3.45pm), on the main road two blocks north of the centre, has an ATM and currency exchange.

Internet Café Internet Osa Corcovado (Mon–Fri 8am–8pm, Sat 10am–6pm, Sun 10am–4pm; US$2/hr; ☎2735-5230, ⊛osacorcovado.com). The owner gives information as well.

Tour operators Escondida Trex (☎2735-5210, ⊛www.escondidatrex.com) offers simple and excellent-value kayak and dolphin-watching trips (US$35), and snorkelling and mangrove tours, all by very knowledgeable guides.

Tourist information Corcovado Information Centre (MINAI; ☎2735-5036, ✉pncorcovado@gmail.com) is the government body in charge of Corcovado National Park, and is manned by friendly rangers. You must come here to reserve your time in the park (max 5 days/4 nights) if you want to trek independently.

Accommodation

Jiménez's hotels are reasonably priced, clean and basic, and are fast growing in number. Though it's best to reserve in the dry season, this may not always be possible, as phone lines sometimes go down.

Cabinas Bosque Mar ☎2735-5385. By the time they finish renovating the TV room and kitchen this hostel will be enormous. They can organize area tours, and the owner is a trained physiotherapist who hopes to begin offering massages for travellers weary after a day in the park. ❹–❺

Cabinas la Esquina ☏2735-5328. Comfortable mix of very cheap dorms and private rooms with shared hot baths on a quiet corner just off the main road. The *dueña* can ramble on for hours about the importance of protecting the natural habitat. Dorms ❷, rooms ❷

Hotel Oro Verde ☏2735-5241. Rooms are reasonable, if a little dark, with optional hot water and a/c. In-house tour guide Josh is bubbling with enthusiasm for the national park (day-trips US$45). ❷–❸

Iguana Iguana ☏2735-5258. Nine cabins spread out amongst trees and a leaf-strewn compound, these cabinas with private bathroom are a touch gloomy but clean. The attached bar is a hotspot at the weekends, with pool tables and log-cabin interior. ❷

Eating and drinking

Restaurante Carolina A hub of activity throughout the day, this restaurant bang in the centre of town serves up local dishes for US$3–5.

Soda Paco Around the corner from the supermarket. A tiny, familiar spot with delicious *pinto* for 1500c and fresh juices.

Soda El Ranchito Overlooking the football pitch, this *soda* also has a welcoming ambience and good hearty breakfasts (1000c).

Moving on

By bus to: San Isidro (5am & 1pm; 6hr); San José (5am; 8hr).

By colectivo to: Carate (6am & 1pm; 1hr 30min).

PARQUE NACIONAL CORCOVADO

Created in 1975, **PARQUE NACIONAL CORCOVADO** ("hunchback"), 368km southwest of San José (daily 8am–4pm; US$10; ☏2735-5036, ✉pncorcovado @gmail.com), houses 2.5 percent of the world's total biodiversity, protecting a fascinating and complex area of land. It's an undeniably beautiful park, with deserted beaches, waterfalls, high canopy trees and better-than-average **wildlife-spotting**. Exploring in Corcovado, though, is not for the faint-hearted. The **terrain** includes sand, riverways, mangroves, *holillo* (palm) swamps and dense forest, although most of it is at lowland elevations; hikers can expect to spend most of their time on the beach trails that ring the outer perimeters of the park. The coastal areas of the park receive at least 3800mm of **rain** a year, with precipitation rising to about 5000mm in the higher elevations of the interior. There's a dry season (Dec–March), however, and the inland lowland areas, especially those around the lagoon, can be amazingly **hot**.

What to see and do

The *pulpería* in the village of **Carate**, about 43km from Jiménez, sells basic foodstuffs; you can also camp here for a nominal fee. From here it's a nearly two-hour walk along the beach to the park entrance at **La Leona** *puesto*, although you can stop off for refreshment en route at the Corcovado and La Leona tent camps. It's then a sixteen-kilometre hike – allow six hours, as you have to wind along the beach, where it's slow going – to **Sirena**, the biggest *puesto* in the park, where you can stay in the simple lodge, exploring the local trails around the Río Sirena. If you're walking from Bahía Drake, you'll enter the park at **San Pedrillo** *puesto* and walk the 25km to Sirena from there.

The small hamlet of La Palma, 24km north of Puerto Jiménez, is the starting point for the walk to the Los Patos *puesto*, a twelve-kilometre hike, much of it through hot lowland terrain. You need to arrive at Los Patos soon after dawn; if you want to stay in La Palma and get up early, *Cabinas Corcovado* (no phone; ➋) is a good bet. The relatively new El Tigre *puesto*, at the eastern inland entrance to the park, is a good place to have breakfast or lunch with the ranger(s) before setting off on the local trails. To get there from Jiménez, drive 10km north and take the second left, a dirt track, signed to El Tigre and Dos Brazos. Taxis cost in the region of US$10.

The **El Tigre** area, at the eastern inland entrance to the park, is gradually becoming more developed, with short walking trails being laid out around the *puesto*. These provide an introduction to Corcovado without making you slog it out on the marathon trails, and it can easily be covered in a morning or afternoon.

The trails

The sixteen-kilometre trail from **La Leona to Sirena** runs just inland from the beach, which at least makes it easy to keep your bearings. If you can avoid anything untoward, you should be able to do the walk in five to six hours, taking time to look out for birds. En route, if you're lucky, you may be able to spot a flock of **scarlet macaws**, who roost in the coastal trees, and perhaps **monkeys** as well, particularly white-faced capuchins, which are the most confident and inquisitive of the park's four breeds of monkey. Take lots of sunscreen, a big hat and at least five litres of water per person – the trail gets very hot, despite sea breezes.

The really heroic walk in Corcovado, all 25km of it, is from **Sirena to San Pedrillo** – the stretch along which you'll see the most impressive trees.

It's a two-day trek, so you need a tent, sleeping bag and mosquito net, and you must be able to set up camp in the jungle. Fording the **Río Sirena**, just 1km beyond the Sirena *puesto*, is the biggest obstacle. The deepest of all the rivers on the peninsula, it has to be crossed with care and at low tide only: not only does it have the strongest out-tow current, but sharks come in and out in search of food at high tide. Get the latest information from the Sirena rangers before you set out.

The trail across the peninsula from **Los Patos to Sirena** is 20km long. You may want to rest at the entrance, as this is an immediately demanding walk, continuing uphill for about 6–8km and taking you into high, wet and dense rainforest – and after that you've still got 14km or so of incredibly hot lowland walking to go. This is a trail for experienced rainforest hikers and hopeful **mammal**-spotters: taking you through the interior, it gives you a reasonable chance of coming across, for example, a margay, peccaries, or the tracks of tapirs and jaguars. It's a gruelling trek, especially with the hot inland temperatures (at least 26°C, with 100-percent humidity) and the lack of sea breezes.

Arrival and information

Accommodation It costs US$2 per night to camp in the *puestos*, or US$6 to sleep in the accommodation block at Sirena (plus US$2 reservation fee). You should bring your own tent, mosquito net, sleeping bag, food and water.

Eating You can either take meals with the rangers (breakfast US$3, lunch and dinner US$6; pay in colones at the *puesto*) or bring your own utensils and use their stove.

Tours To increase your chances of seeing some of the park's wildlife, it's well worth investing in the services of a guide: a twelve-hour trek should cost about US$45.

Visitor information You have to reserve a space in Corcovado in advance – this will include meals and either camping space or lodging at the puesto of your choice. To reserve, fax the park's Puerto Jiménez office (ⓕ 2735-5276), or, if you're already in the country, visit the Fundación de Parques Nacionales office in San José (see p.500), who will fax or telephone Corcovado on your behalf. Within the park, **all puestos** have camping areas, drinking water, information, toilets and telephone or radio. Wherever you enter, jot down the details of the **marea** (tide tables), which are posted in prominent positions. You'll need to cross most of the rivers at low tide; to do otherwise is dangerous. Rangers can advise on conditions. Plan to hike early – though not before dawn, due to snakes – and shelter during the hottest part of the day. Rangers at each *puesto* always know how many people are on a given trail, and how long those hikers are expected to be. If you are late getting back, they'll go looking for you. It's especially important to brush up on your **Spanish** before coming to Corcovado. You'll need to ask the rangers for a lot of information, and few, if any, speak English. If you're not fluent, bring a phrase book. If you hike with a guide, all these details will be dealt with for you. All reputable tour operators use bilingual tour guides.

PASO CANOAS

The only reason to come to **PASO CANOAS** is to cross the border into Panama; you will not want to stay here longer than you have to. As you arrive, either driving or on the Tracopa or international Tica Bus service, you'll pass the Costa Rican customs checkpoint, where everybody gets a going-over. Foreigners don't attract much interest, however; customs officials are far more concerned with nabbing Ticos coming back over the border with unauthorized amounts of cheap consumer goods. The border is open 24 hours, but if you're waiting overnight for an early bus, *Cabinas Romy*, along the road past the station for buses to Neily, is an acceptable place to bed down for the night with vibrantly decorated clean little rooms (❷). There is a Banco Nacional on the Costa Rican side open between 8:30am and 4pm which has an **ATM** and currency exchange.

Panama

Introduction

A narrow frontier that divides oceans and continents, Panama has long been one of the world's greatest crossroads – even since before the construction of its famous canal. Though its historical ties to the US have led to an exaggerated perception of the country as a de facto American colony, Spanish, African, West Indian, Chinese, Indian, European, and some of the least assimilated indigenous communities in the region have all played a role in the creation of the most sophisticated, open-minded and outward-looking society in Central America. The comparatively high level of economic development and use of the US dollar also make it one of the more expensive countries in the region, but the wildlife-viewing and adventure travel options are excellent, and the still relatively undiscovered nightlife of Panama City is a diamond in the rough. The S-shaped isthmus remains a vital thoroughfare of international commerce as well as a growing destination for international tourism and investment.

Cosmopolitan and contradictory, **Panama City** is the most exciting capital city in Central America, its multiple personalities reflected in the frenzied energy of its international banking centre, the laid-back street life of its old colonial quarter and the antiseptic order of the US-built Canal Zone. Located in the centre of the country, it is also a natural base from which to explore many of Panama's most popular destinations, including its best-known attraction, the monumental **Panama Canal**. The colonial ruins and Caribbean coastline of **Colón province** are also within reach of the capital. East of

Panama City stretches **Darién**, the wild, rainforest-covered frontier between Central and South America, while to the north, along the Caribbean coastline, **Kuna Yala** is the autonomous homeland of the Kuna, who live in beautiful isolation on the coral atolls of the **San Blas Archipelago**. West of Panama City, the Carretera Interamericana runs through the Pacific coastal plain, Panama's agricultural heartland. This region lures travellers intrigued by the folkloric traditions and nature reserves of the **Azuero Peninsula** and the protected cloudforests of the **Chiriquí Highlands** on the Costa Rican border. The mostly

WHEN TO VISIT

Panama is well within the tropics, with temperatures hovering at 25–32°C throughout the year, and varying only with altitude (the Chiriquí Highlands generally run 15–26°C). Visiting Panama during the dry season (mid-Dec to April; known as *verano*, or summer) maximizes your chance of finding sunny days. However, seasonal climatic variation is really only evident on the Pacific side of the country's mountainous spine. The average annual rainfall here is about 1500mm; on the Caribbean, about 2500mm fall and are spread more evenly throughout the year. From May to December, the storms of the Pacific's winter (*invierno*) rainy season are intense but rarely extended.

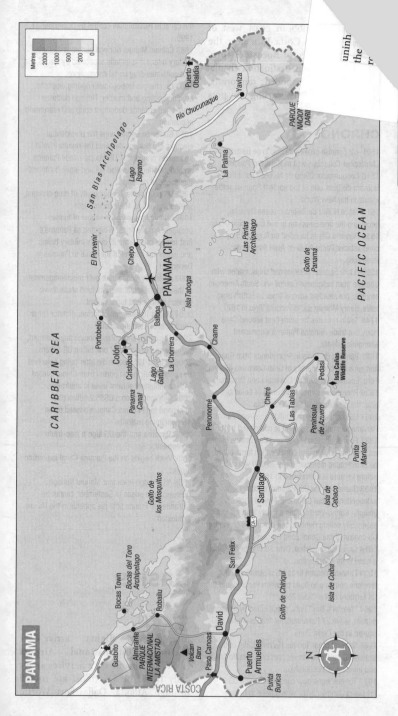

...bited Caribbean coast west of ...Canal meets Costa Rica near the ...mote archipelago of **Bocas del Toro**, a popular vacation destination thanks to its largely unspoiled rainforests, beaches, coral reefs, surfing hotspots and easygoing vibe.

CHRONOLOGY

1501–02 Spanish explorers Rodrigo de Bastidas and Christopher Columbus visit modern-day Panama.

1510 Conquistador Diego de Nicuesa establishes Nombre de Dios, one of the earliest Spanish settlements in the New World.

1513 Vasco Núñez de Balboa crosses Panama, becoming the first European to see the Pacific Ocean.

1519 Panama City is founded on August 15 by conquistador Pedro Arias de Ávila (known as Pedrarias).

1596–1739 Spanish colonies and ships, loaded with treasure from indigenous Central and South American empires, are attacked several times by British privateers. Henry Morgan sacks Panamá Viejo in 1671.

1746 Spain reroutes treasure fleet around Cape Horn, but trade remains Panama's dominant economic activity.

1821 Panama declares independence from Spain, and joins the confederacy of Gran Colombia (Bolivia, Peru, Ecuador, Venezuela, Colombia and Panama).

1830 Panama becomes a province of Colombia after the dissolution of Gran Colombia.

1851 US company begins building railroad across Panamanian isthmus; project is completed in 1855.

1881 French architect Ferdinand de Lesseps begins excavations for Panama Canal, which turns out to be unmitigated disaster. Some 20,000 workers die before venture is abandoned in 1889.

1903 Backed by the US, Panama declares independence from Colombia. French engineer Philippe Bunau-Varilla signs a treaty with the US, essentially selling rights to the canal, and giving the US control of the Canal Zone "in perpetuity".

1914 Canal is completed. Over 75,000 people have a hand in its construction.

1939 Panama ceases to be US protectorate, but tensions continue to build between Panama and the US territory of the Canal Zone.

1964 "Martyr's Day" riots, precipitated by a student protest, leave 27 Panamanians dead and over 500 injured in the Canal Zone.

1968 General Omar Torrijos Herrera, Chief of the National Guard, overthrows president Arnulfo Arias and imposes a dictatorship.

1977 Torrijos signs new canal treaty with US President Jimmy Carter, who agrees to transfer the canal to Panamanian control by December 31, 1999.

1983 Colonel Manuel Noriega becomes de facto military ruler. He is initially supported by the US, but also cultivates drug cartel connections.

1988 US charges Noriega with rigging elections, drug smuggling and murder; Noriega declares state of emergency, dodging a coup and repressing opposition.

1989 Guillermo Endara wins the presidential election, but Noriega declares the results invalid and seizes presidency. US troops invade Panama and oust Noriega, but also kill and leave homeless thousands of civilians.

1992 US court finds Noriega guilty of drug charges, sentencing him to 40 years in prison.

1999 Mireya Moscoso, the widow of former president Arnulfo Arias, is elected as Panama's first female president. US closes military bases and hands full control of the canal to Panama in December.

2003 A country-wide strike over mismanagement of the nation's social security fund shuts down public services and turns violent.

2004 Martin Torrijos, son of former dictator Omar Torrijos, is elected president.

2004 The canal, under Panamanian management, earns record revenues of one billion US dollars.

2006 At least 125 people die after being poisoned by cough medicine, imported from China, tainted with an industrial solvent used in antifreeze.

2006 Referendum on a US$5.2 billion plan to expand the Panama Canal is passed by an overwhelming majority.

2006 Panama and the US sign a free-trade agreement.

2007 Work begins on the Panama Canal expansion project.

2008 A US judge rules that Manuel Noriega, released from prison in September, cannot be extradited to France until his appeals in the US are exhausted.

Basics

ARRIVAL

International **flights** arrive at **Tocumen International Airport (PTY)** in Panama City. Services arrive daily from the US (most are routed through Atlanta, Dallas/Fort Worth,

LAND AND SEA ROUTES TO PANAMA

Panama has two land routes to Costa Rica: the main border crossing along the Carretera Interamericana at Paso Canoas (see p.584), and the less-frequented border outpost at Guabito on the Caribbean coast (see box, p.665), which allows for access to the Bocas archipelago.

We don't currently recommend crossing by land from Colombia. While there are no official sea crossings to this country, in Colón it is possible to book passage on private yachts heading for Colombia, sometimes stopping in the San Blas region on the way (see box, p.625).

Houston or Miami) and other Central and South American cities; KLM and Iberia fly from Amsterdam and Madrid, respectively. Flights from San José, in neighbouring Costa Rica, often stop in David before continuing on to Bocas del Toro or Panama City.

It is possible to enter Panama by **land** from Costa Rica and Colombia (see box above), though due to security concerns we don't recommend crossing from Colombia. Though you can take local transport and switch **buses** at the border, the slightly costlier fares on international services run by Tica Bus (@www.ticabus.com) and Panaline (@www.panaline.cr.com) give you a better shot at an efficient and hassle-free passage. To avoid undue trouble, keep your documents, stamps, and tourist visas in order. In addition to official documents, travellers at the border crossing will often be asked to show an onward or return ticket to provide proof of eventual departure from Panama. If travelling on a one-way ticket, *migración* is likely to require advance purchase of bus fare back to San José.

There are no regular **boat** services between Panama and its neighbours, but a growing number of backpackers are booking passage on private yachts from Colombia (see box, p.625).

VISAS

Travellers from Australia, Canada, Ireland, New Zealand, the UK and the US can do not require **visas** to enter Panama. Visitors from Ireland and the UK can also enter Panama without a **tourist card**; those from Australia, Canada, New Zealand and the US must pay for a US$5 tourist card upon arrival. Significant price increases for the cards were being discussed at time of writing, so check @www.panaconsul.com before you leave. Immigration generally stamps passports for ninety-day visits, but determining the length of a pass is entirely at the discretion of immigration authorities; extending your stay can be costly and time consuming.

GETTING AROUND

Ease of travel within Panama varies according to geography. Although the Canal corridor and the western Pacific region are covered by a comprehensive road network served by regular public transport, both eastern Panama and Bocas del Toro are linked to the rest of the country by just a single road.

By bus

Where there are roads, **buses** are the cheapest and most popular way to travel. Panama City is the hub of the network, with regular buses to Colón, Metetí in Darién, Almirante (for Bocas del Toro) and all the western cities and towns. Buses vary in comfort and size, from modern, air-conditioned Pullmans to smaller "coaster" buses and old US school buses. Smaller towns and villages in rural areas tend to be served by less frequent minibuses, pick-up trucks

As in most of the rest of Central America, Panama's towns are mainly laid out in a grid pattern. *Calles* run north–south, and *avenidas* east–west. Both *calles* and *avenidas* are generally numbered in order, calles north to south and avenidas west to east. In larger cities, Panama City in particular, roads, especially major throroughfares, usually have two or more names. Outside larger cities, exact street numbers tend not to exist. Smaller towns often don't even have street names, so addresses are frequently given in terms of landmarks.

and flat-bed trucks known as *chivas* or *chivitas*, converted to carry passengers, while Colón and David are also served by express buses, which are more expensive, more comfortable and faster.

Most buses are individually owned, and even when services are frequent, **schedules** are variable. Cities and larger towns have bus terminals; otherwise, buses leave from the main street or square. You can usually flag down through-buses from the roadside, though they may not stop if they are full or going a long way. In general, you can just turn up shortly before departure and you should be able to get a seat, though the express buses to and from David as well as international buses to Costa Rica are definitely worth **booking** in advance. **Fares**, as elsewhere in Central America, are good value: the most you'll have to pay is US$23 for the overnight, ten-hour ride from Panama City to Almirante. Long-distance fares are set out in advance, with tickets bought in a terminal and a receipt printed – nearly all such bus rides are very structured. *Colectivos* are generally a bit looser about pricing and ticketing, but they are less used here than in other countries in Central and South America.

By car

At around US$40 a day or US$200 a week (more for 4WD), **car rental** is reasonably priced but not cheap. However, having your own transport is a good way of seeing the country, especially the Canal corridor, areas close to Panama City and the Azuero Peninsula. All of the main rental companies are based in Panama City airport, but some also have offices at the regional airports and in David. **Driving** in Panama is pretty straightforward, though even the paved roads in the canal corridor and the west can be badly maintained. The main roads on the Azuero Peninsula are in good condition, however, as are the secondary roads to Cerro Punta, Boquete, El Valle and Almirante. **4WD** is rarely necessary except during the rainy season and in more remote rural areas, particularly Darién. Police **checkpoints** appear throughout the country, mainly on provincial borders, and normally you are only required to slow down. If the police ask you to stop, in most cases they will just want to know your destination and see your license.

Hitching is possible, but carries all the obvious risks. Private cars are unlikely to stop for you on main roads, though in more remote areas, hitching is often the only motor transport available, and there is little distinction between private vehicles and public transport – drivers will pick you up, but you should expect to pay the same kind of fares you would for the bus.

In larger cities, like Panama City and David, taxis are plentiful and inexpensive, with fares based on a zone system: US$1.25 plus US$0.25 for each zone boundary crossed and US$0.25 for each additional passenger. Most intra-city rides will cost less than US$2 and none should cost more than US$3. There are many unlicensed cab drivers patrolling the streets who are willing to negotiate on prices, but who may engage in unscrupulous practices. Even licensed cab drivers won't hesitate to exploit an obviously unsavvy, lost or needy tourist. Specifically, be wary of price gouging on the Panama City Causeway.

By boat

Scheduled **ferries** run from Panama City to Isla Taboga as well as between Bocas del Toro and Almirante and Changuinola. Motorized **water-taxis** and **dugout canoes** are an important means of transport in Bocas, Darién and Kuna Yala, though the only scheduled small boat services are the water-taxis in Darién (between Puerto Quimba and La Palma). Otherwise, you'll have to either wait for somebody going your way, or hire a boat. The latter can be expensive, but becomes increasingly economical the more people there are to share the boat. Hiring a dugout canoe also opens up possibilities for wilderness adventure – up jungle rivers to isolated villages or out to uninhabited islands.

By air

Cities and larger towns are served by regular **flights** through Aeroperlas (☎315 7500, ⊛www.aeroperlas.com), the principal domestic carrier, which also has regular flights to parts of Darién and Kuna Yala, and Air Panama (☎315 0439, ⊛www.flyairpanama.com), which also flies to parts of Darién as well as the Las Perlas islands. With the exception of these more isolated areas, though, most destinations are so close to Panama City that it's scarcely worth flying, especially because flight prices are on the rise (return flights between Panama City and Bocas cost around US$180 during high season at the time of writing).

By bike

Cycling is a popular way to get around in western Panama, where roads are generally paved and traffic scarce (away from the Carretera Interamericana and other major routes), and towns usually have a shop offering parts and simple repairs. The stretch from the continental divide to Chiriquí Grande on the road from David to Almirante, in particular, is a cyclist's dream – some 40km downhill on a well-surfaced, less-driven main road through rainforest-covered mountains. Other good roads for cycling include all those on the Azuero Peninsula and the roads to Cerro Punta and El Valle off the Interamericana.

By rail

The **transisthmian railway** (⊛www .panarail.com; US$22, children US$11), which runs alongside the canal between Panama City and Colón, offers an excellent way of seeing the canal and the surrounding rainforest.

ACCOMMODATION

Most areas of Panama offer a wide choice of places to stay. In general, the cheapest **hotel** rooms, normally doubles with private baths and air-conditioning, may cost US$20–25 (④) a night, although **hostels** – most common in well-travelled spots like Bocas Town, Boquete, David, Isla Taboga and Panama City – will often put you up for under US$12 (③). In **Panama City**, where many hotels target business travellers, prices tend to be slightly higher, while at the very low end of the market some hotels cater largely to Panamanian couples – with hourly rates. Outside of Panama City and Bocas del Toro, you don't usually need to **book in advance**, except at weekends and during public holidays, fiestas and Carnaval. During these times prices can double in certain hotels. The ten percent **tourist tax** charged on hotel accommodation is usually included in the quoted price and has been factored into our accommodation price codes. See p.35 for an explanation of the price codes used in this book.

There are no official **campsites** in Panama, but it is possible to camp in remote rural areas and national parks if you ask permission. This said, other than on uninhabited islands in Kuna Yala or deep in the wilderness, camping is never really necessary – even in the smallest villages there's almost always somewhere you can bed down for the night. If you do camp, either a **mosquito net** or mosquito coils (known as *mechitas*) are essential in some places. Almost all the national parks have ANAM (see p.596) **refuges** where you can spend the night for US$5–10, though this fee is not always charged. They are usually pretty basic, with bunk beds, cooking facilities and running water.

FOOD AND DRINK

Street vendors are less common in Panama than elsewhere in Central America. The cheapest places to eat are the ubiquitous canteen-like **self-service restaurants** (sometimes called *sodas* or *cafeterias*), which serve a limited, but filling, range of Panamanian meals for a few dollars; these usually open for lunch and stay open late. Larger towns usually have some more **upmarket restaurants** with waiter service, where a main dish may cost US$5–10, as well as US-style fast-food places. There is often a five percent **tax** to pay on meals. Large **supermarkets** in the major cities offer a good range of cold and hot snacks to either eat in or take out.

Known as *comida típica*, traditional Panamanian cooking is similar to what you find elsewhere in Central America. Rice and beans or lentils served with a little chicken, meat or fish form the mainstay, and *yuca* (cassava) and plantains are often served as sides. The national dish is **sancocho**, a chicken soup with *yuca*, plantains and other root vegetables flavoured with coriander. **Seafood** is plentiful, excellent and generally cheap, particularly *corvina* (sea bass), *pargo rojo* (red snapper),

lobster and prawns; there is an excellent fresh fish market on the outskirts of Panama City. Fresh tropical **fruit** is also abundant, but rarely on the menu at restaurants – you're better off buying it in local markets. Popular **snacks** include *carimañolas* or *enyucados* (fried balls of manioc dough filled with meat), *empanadas*, *tamales* and *patacones* (fried, mashed and refried plantains).

The diverse **cultural influences** that have passed through Panama have left their marks on its cuisine, especially in Panama City, where there are scores of Greek, Italian, Chinese, Lebanese and American restaurants. Almost every town has at least one Chinese restaurant, often the best option for **vegetarians**. Perhaps the strongest outside influence on Panamanian food, though, is the distinctive **Caribbean** culture of the West Indian populations of Panama City, Colón province and Bocas del Toro. This usually involves seafood and rice cooked in lime juice and coconut milk.

Drink

Coffee is excellent where grown locally (in the Chiriquí Highlands) and generally good throughout Panama, made espresso-style and served black or with milk as *café americano*. The **drinking water** of Panama City is so good that it is known as the "Champagne of the Chagres". Iced water, served free in restaurants, along with tap water in all towns and cities except Bocas del Toro and remote areas, is perfectly safe. **Chichas**, delicious blends of ice, water and tropical-fruit juices, are served in restaurants and by street vendors everywhere (except in Kuna Yala, where *chicha* is a ceremonial drink made from fermented sugar-cane juice flavoured with coffee or cacao). **Batidos**, delicious when prepared with fresh fruit, are thick milkshakes. Also popular are **pipas**, sweet water from green coconuts served either ice cold or freshly hacked from the palm tree. Said to cleanse the system, these can also have diuretic properties when consumed in large quantities.

Beer is extremely popular in Panama. Locally brewed brands include Panama, Atlas, Soberana and Balboa; imported beers such as Budweiser, Heineken and Guinness are available in Panama City. For a quicker buzz, many Panamanians turn to locally produced **rum** – Seco Herrerano (known as *seco*), Carta Vieja and Abuelo are the most common brands – though imported whiskies and other spirits are widely available. You can get **wine**, mainly from Chile and California, in most towns, with the best selections found in the large supermarkets.

CULTURE AND ETIQUETTE

Panama, like much of the rest of Latin America, is **socially conservative**, with a vast majority of the population reported as Roman Catholic. Thanks to the country's rather international history more religions are present than in other parts of the region, but the combination of a largely Catholic cultural identity, economic stratification and other ingrained colonial legacies has produced a country and people that appreciate rules and accept established social castes. This is not to say, however, that Panamanian society is stagnant. The history of the US presence, widespread access to global media and entertainment and relatively diverse demographics as well as recent economic expansion have all contributed to making Panama a country familiar with change.

A **macho** attitude is nonetheless prevalent throughout Panama. Objectification of the female body is common, though generally not blatant outside of Panama City. For women travelling in Panama, unsolicited attention in the form of whistles and cat-calls is almost inevitable, though usually easily ignored. In personalized settings, more

PANAMANIAN EXPRESSIONS

Spanish
Chuleta used when someone is very surprised, in order not to say "chucha"
En serio? "For real?", "No way!", "Seriously?"
Esa vaina "that thing"
Un pelao a young boy (from *pelado*)
Priti "pretty"

West Indian from the Caribbean
Buay "boy"
Wha'happ'nin' buay "How are you doing?"

respect is typically accorded, though intimate advances are often very direct. Overall, the Caribbean and indigenous areas of Panama hold more relaxed and less macho attitudes, though revealing clothing is not tolerated (except on the beach) in Bocas del Toro, where even men are required, by law, to wear shirts in public. Attitudes toward homosexuality are, by and large, intolerant.

Tipping is only expected in more expensive places, where a tip is sometimes included on the final bill, or where service has been particularly good.

SPORTS AND OUTDOOR ACTIVITIES

With every important match being televised and broadcast on radio, both European and Latin American **football** leagues have a broad fan base and are closely followed in Panama, but **baseball** (*beisbol*) is Panama's official national sport. The baseball season in Panama is short, starting up in January and continuing through the northern hemisphere's winter months (Panama's dry season). There are ten teams in the national league, each representing one of Panama's provinces, and home teams are sacred to their impassioned fans, making the experience of attending a game lively and culturally rich. The baseball stadium in Panama City, Estadio Rod Carew, is named after Major League Baseball Hall-of-Fame player and Panamanian native Rod Carew. It's a large, modern complex that holds 26,000 and is nestled in the hillside of Cerro Patacon between Avenida de la Paz and Autopista Panamá–Colón, just north of the city. You can get tickets to a game for less than US$5, and, other than during the play-offs, the stadium is never full. **Boxing** is also popular in Panama, with Panamanian Roberto Durán arguably one of the best competitors the sport has ever seen.

There is a wealth of outdoor activities available to you in Panama. **Hiking**, **rafting**, **surfing** and **diving** are probably the most common and easily accessible. Boquete, in the Chiriquí Highlands, provides an ideal departure point for **hikes** up the Volcán Barú (see p.658), Panama's highest point, as well as for **rafting** trips down the formidable Río Chiriquí and Río Chiriquí Viejo (see p.661). Bocas del Toro is a world-renowned **dive** site (see p.662) with trips ranging from all-day snorkel tours to underwater exploration of shipwrecks and spectacular reef walls. Even experienced divers should make an effort to dive in the Panama Canal, where huge amounts of machinery and entire villages submerged by the rising waters of Lago Gatún make for an unusual underwater attraction. Bocas also can have excellent **surf**, though it is seasonal and less consistent than on the Pacific coast. Ancon Expeditions (see p.606) is a good place to start for information on arranging trips, and websites like ⓦwww.wannasurf.com will give a listing of the best breaks.

COMMUNICATIONS

Other than in remote areas, Panama's **communications** network is good. **Letters** posted with the Correo Nacional (COTEL) cost US$0.35 to both the US and Europe, and should reach their destination within a week or two. Even though most small towns have a **post office** (*correo*), it's best to post mail in Panama City. Most offices have an *Entrega General* (**Poste Restante** or General Delivery) where you can receive mail; in Panama City your correspondent must specify the post office zone: the most central is Zone 5, on Av Central/Via España. Post office **opening hours** are generally Monday to Friday from 8am to 5pm, Saturday 8am to noon.

Panama's privatized telephone company is owned by Cable & Wireless.

PANAMA ON THE NET

ⓦ**www.ancon.org** National Conservation Association website. Panama's most influential environmental group has general information (in Spanish) on national parks, ecology, voluntary work and endangered species, as well as scientific papers.

ⓦ**www.focuspublicationsint.com/New_Site/index.html** Website of *El Visitante/ The Visitor*, a dual-language, bi-monthly publication.

ⓦ**www.thepanamareport.com** A comprehensive site providing information for tourists and those interested in living or working in Panama.

ⓦ**www.thepanamanews.com** Panama's frequently updated online newspaper is a good place to keep up with the latest events.

ⓦ**www.pancanal.com** The official site of the Panama Canal Authority, offering plenty of information and news, a history of the canal and photographs, as well as live webcams at two locks.

ⓦ**www.visitpanama.com** Panamanian Tourist Institute site, with information on attractions and links to hotels, airlines, tour agencies and other related sites.

Local calls are cheap, and there's a wide network of payphones that take phonecards sold in shops and street stalls in denominations of $3, $5, $10 and $20. Local numbers should have seven digits, local mobile numbers eight digits. You can make **international collect calls** from these payphones via the international operator (☎106), and both AT&T (☎109) and MCI (☎108) can place collect or credit-card calls to the US. Panama's **country code** is ☎507. **Mobile phone** coverage is growing, but is still best in cities and larger towns. It shouldn't be a problem to buy a local SIM card in Panama City and replace the card in your own phone with it. Mobile phone codes begin with a "6" or a "5".

You should be able to find an **internet** café almost anywhere you go; rates are normally US$1 per hour, but can go up to US$2 per hour in more remote towns. Note that the "@" symbol is achieved by simultaneously depressing the Alt, 6 and 4 keys or the Alt and Q keys depending on the keyboard. Many internet cafés also provide international phone calls for about US$1.50 for the first minute and US$0.25 per minute thereafter. Wireless internet, or wi-fi, is becoming more common, especially in Panama City.

CRIME AND SAFETY

Panama has something of an unjust reputation as a dangerous place to travel. Although **violent crime** does occasionally occur, Panama is far safer than most other countries in Central America. Nonetheless, you should take special care in **Colón**, as well as in the El Chorillo and Santa Ana districts of **Panama City**. Late at night or when carrying luggage, take a taxi. Outside these two cities, the only other area where there is any particular danger is near the **Colombian border** in Darién and Kuna Yala. This frontier has long been frequented by guerrillas, bandits and cocaine traffickers, and several travellers attempting to cross overland

to Colombia have been kidnapped or killed – or have simply disappeared. It is possible to visit some areas of Darién in relative safety, including parts of the national park, but we recommend that you only travel here as part of an organized tour group specializing in the region or after having taken expert advice – see p.631 for more information about the region. Note, too, that many of the boats that ply the coast are involved in smuggling.

If you become the victim of a crime, report it immediately to the local **police** station, particularly if you will later be making an insurance claim. If treated respectfully, Panamanian police are generally honest and helpful, though it is not uncommon for travellers to be asked to present identification when walking in the city at night. In Panama City the **tourist police** (*policia de turismo*) are better prepared to deal with foreign travellers and more likely to speak English – they wear white armbands and are often mounted on bicycles or mopeds.

Although by law you are required to carry your **passport** at all times, you will rarely be asked to present it except when in transit; in fact, when walking around the towns and cities it may be better to carry a copy of your passport (including the entry stamp) – indeed, this is what the tourist police recommend. When caught without identification, a "fine" may be levied on the spot, usually about US$20, or you could be taken to the immigration office, *migración*, and held until your identity is verified.

MEDICAL CARE AND EMERGENCIES

Medical care in Panama is best sought in the two largest cities: Panama City and David. Panama City has a handful of top-notch **hospitals** with many US and European trained doctors and English speaking staff; see p.611 for listings. As most doctors and hospitals expect payment up front, frequently in cash, check the travel coverage clauses in your health insurance plan or purchase supplementary traveller's insurance before you leave home. The best plans cover doctor's visits, and emergency evacuation from remote areas or to your home country, if necessary, for more serious medical issues.

Pharmacies (*farmacias*) are numerous; Farmacias Arrocha is the largest national chain, and its stores stay open until 11pm. Pharmacies in Supermercado Rey grocery stores are open 24 hours. Hospitals and occasionally health clinics have pharmacies onsite, and many types of medicines are available over the counter, without a prescription.

MONEY AND BANKS

Panama adopted **US dollars** (referred to interchangeably as *dólares* or *balboas*) as its currency in 1904, and has not printed any paper currency since. The country does, however, mint its own coinage: 1, 5, 10, 25 and 50 **centavo** pieces, which are used alongside US coins. Both US$100 and US$50 bills are often difficult to spend, so try to have US$20 as the largest bills you carry. It is difficult to **change foreign currency** in Panama – change any cash into US dollars as soon as you can. In Panama City there are Banco Nacional branches at the airport and on Via España in the El Cangrejo district, or you could try Panacambios, a *casa de cambio* also on Via España. Foreign banks will generally change their own currencies.

Traveller's cheques are the safest way to carry your money and are easy

to change so long as they are issued by major companies (Amex, Visa and MasterCard) and are in US dollars. The three major **banks** in Panama – Banco Nacional, Banistmo and Banco General – will all change these, as will some of the international banks in Panama City. Most banks are open from 8am to 3pm Monday to Friday, and from 9am to noon on Saturday; almost all branches have **ATMs**, as do many large supermarkets. Major **credit cards** are accepted in most hotels and restaurants in Panama City and the larger provincial towns, though hardly anywhere in Bocas del Toro. Visa is the most widely accepted, followed by MasterCard.

INFORMATION AND MAPS

Good, impartial information about Panama is hard to come by once you're in the country. The best internal source of information is the Panamanian Tourist Institute, **IPAT** (🌐www .visitpanama.com), which has its main office in Panama City (see p.605) and many provincial branches. You can get some useful information at the Panama City office – advice, free maps, leaflets – but unless you go there with some fairly specific questions you may end up with little more than glossy brochures. The provincial offices vary, but even in the most rudimentary you should be able to find someone who speaks English. *The Visitor/El Visitante*, a free, twice-monthly **tourist promotion magazine** in English and Spanish, is available at IPAT offices, hotels and restaurants throughout Panama, and lists attractions and upcoming events. Several **tour operators** based in Panama City (see p.606) can give you advice on the rest of the country, though they will naturally do so in the hope of selling you a tour.

Panama's **national parks** and other protected areas are administered by the National Environment Agency, **ANAM** (🌐www.anam.gob.pa). The main office in Panama City (see p.606) is, in theory, keen to promote ecotourism, though they offer almost no information. The ANAM regional offices are generally more helpful (though still unaccustomed to the idea of travellers visiting the parks independently), and are an essential stop before visiting areas where permission is needed or if you want to spend the night in a refuge.

The best **map** of Panama (1:480,000; available online at Ⓦwww.itmb.com and Ⓦwww.amazon.com) is produced by International Travel Maps. In country, large-scale maps are available at the Instituto Geográfico Nacional Tommy Guardia (Mon–Fri 8.30am–4pm) on Via Simon Bolívar, opposite the entrance to the university in Panama City. Good-quality maps of Panama City are available at petrol stations, tour agencies and shops throughout the city for US$5–10.

OPENING HOURS AND PUBLIC HOLIDAYS

Opening hours vary from establishment to establishment, but generally businesses and government **offices** are open Monday to Saturday from 8 or 9am to 4 or 5pm. **Museums** generally open the same hours from Tuesday to Saturday, with some also opening on Sunday morning and some closing for the lunch hour at around 12.30 or 1pm. **Shops** are usually open from Monday to Saturday from 9am to 6pm.

Panama has several national **public holidays** (see box), during which most government offices, businesses and shops close. Panama City and Colón also each have their own public holiday, and there is one public holiday for government employees only. When the public holidays fall near a weekend many Panamanians take a long weekend (known as a *puente*) and head to the beach or the countryside, so it can be difficult to find hotel rooms during these times. Several of these public holidays also coincide with **national fiestas** that continue for several days.

PUBLIC HOLIDAYS

Jan 1 New Year's Day
Jan 9 Martyrs' Day (in remembrance of those killed by US troops in the 1964 riots)
Feb/March (date varies) Carnival
March/April (date varies) Good Friday
May 1 Labour Day
Aug 15 Foundation of Panama City (Panama City only)
Nov 2 All Souls' Day
Nov 3 Independence Day (from Colombia, 1903)
Nov 4 Flag Day (government holiday only)
Nov 5 National Day (Colón only)
Nov 10 First Cry of Independence
Nov 28 Emancipation Day (independence from Spain)
Dec 8 Mother's Day
Dec 25 Christmas Day

FESTIVALS

January Feria de las Flores y del Café in Boquete (date varies).
February Comarca de Kuna Yala (Feb 25) celebrates the Kuna Revolution of 1925, their independence day; Carnaval (date varies Feb–March) celebrated all over the country, but especially in Las Tablas and Panama City.
March Semana Santa (date varies March–April) celebrated everywhere, but most colourfully in La Villa de Los Santos, Pesé and Guararé, on the Azuero Peninsula.
April Feria de las Orquideas in Boquete (date varies); Feria International del Azuero in La Villa de Los Santos (date varies).
June Corpus Christi (date varies) in La Villa de Los Santos.
July Nuestra Señora del Carmen (July 16) on Isla Taboga; Patronales de La Santa Librada and Festival de la Pollera in Las Tablas (July 20–22).
August Festival del Manito Ocueno (date varies) in Ocu.
October Festival of Nogagope (Oct 10–12) on Isla Tigre, Comarca de Kuna Yala; Feria Kuna (Oct 13–16) on Isla Tigre; Festival de la Mejorana (Oct 21) in Guararé; Fiesta de Cristo Negro (Oct 21) in Portobelo.
November The "First Cry of Independence" (Nov 10), Independence Day, celebrated as part of "El Mes de la Patria".

Panama City

Few cities in Latin America can match the diversity and cosmopolitanism of **PANAMA CITY**: polyglot and postmodern before its time, its atmosphere is surprisingly more similar to the mighty trading cities of Asia than to anywhere else in the region. The city has always thrived on commerce; its unique position on the world's trade routes and the economic opportunity this presents has attracted immigrants and businesses from all over the globe. With nearly a third of the country's population living in the urbanized corridor between Panama City and Colón, the capital's metropolitan melting pot is a study in contrasts. East and West, ancient and modern, wealth and poverty: they all have a place in Panama City.

Panama City's layout, too, encompasses some startling incongruities. On a small peninsula at the southwest end of the Bay of Panama stands the old city centre of **San Felipe**, a breezy jumble of ruins and restored colonial buildings; 4km or so to the northeast rise the shimmering skyscrapers of **El Cangrejo**, the modern banking and commercial district. West of San Felipe, the former US Canal Zone town of **Balboa** retains a distinctly North American character, while eastward from El Cangrejo, amid sprawling suburban slums, stand the ruins of **Panamá Viejo**, the first European city on the Pacific coast of the Americas. Isles of tranquillity far from the frenetic squalor of the city include **Isla Taboga**, the "Island of Flowers" some 20km off the coast; the islets of the Amador Causeway alongside the Pacific entrance to the canal; and the **Parque Nacional Metropolitano**, an island of tropical rainforest within the capital. Panama City is also a good base for day-trips to the canal and the Caribbean coast as far as Portobelo.

What to see and do

The old city centre of **San Felipe** (also known as Casco Viejo or Casco Antiguo) is the most picturesque and historically interesting part of Panama City and houses many of its most important buildings and several museums. Declared a UNESCO World Heritage site in 1997, it is gradually being restored to its former glory after decades of neglect, though it can still be a dangerous neighbourhood at night, as it is surrounded by slums. The bougainvillea-shaded **Paseo Las Bóvedas**, running some 400m along the top of the old city's defensive wall between the Plaza de Francia and the corner of Calle 1 and Avenida A, affords views of the modern city and ships waiting to transit the canal.

To the west, the **Amador Causeway** marks the entrance to the canal and the Canal Zone, comprised of the Causeway, Fort Amador and the town of Balboa. East along the bay from San Felipe, the pulsing and chaotic commercial heart of the capital lies in the neighbouring districts of **Bella Vista**, **El Cangrejo** and **Punta Paitilla**, where the majority of banks, hotels, restaurants, shops and luxurious private residences can be found.

ORIENTATION IN PANAMA CITY

Getting around Panama City can be disconcerting, so it's often best to take a taxi to your accommodation. Confusingly, many streets in Panama City have at least two names: Avenida Cuba, for instance, is also Avenida 2 Sur, and the road commonly known as Calle 50 is also Avenida 4 Sur or Avenida Nicanor de Obarrio. We have used the most common names throughout this account.

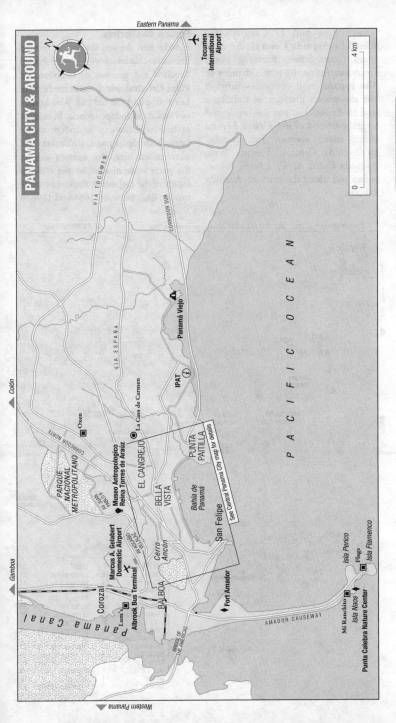

San Felipe and El Cangrejo are joined by **Avenida Central**, the city's main thoroughfare. Running north from San Felipe, its name changes to **Via España** as it continues through the downtown districts of Calidonia and La Exposición and the residential neighbourhood of Bella Vista. Several other main avenues run parallel to Avenida Central: Avenida Perú, Avenida Cuba, Avenida Justo Arosemena and, along the seafront, Avenida Balboa.

Plaza Catedral

Elderly men dressed sharply in pressed linen suits chat amiably among the shaded benches and gazebos of cobblestoned **Plaza Catedral**, which sits at the heart of San Felipe and the old city. Also known as Plaza de la Independencia, in honour of the proclamations of independence from both Spain and Colombia that were issued here, the western side of the plaza is dominated by the classical facade of the **cathedral**, flanked by white towers. Built between 1688 and 1796, it

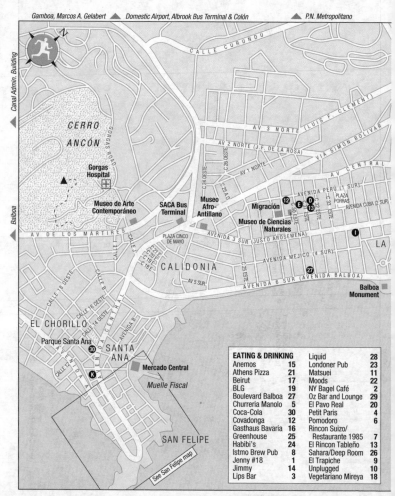

Gamboa, Marcos A. Gelabert ▲   Domestic Airport, Albrook Bus Terminal & Colón   ▲ P.N. Metropolitano

EATING & DRINKING		Liquid	28
Anemos	15	Londoner Pub	23
Athens Pizza	21	Matsuei	11
Beirut	17	Moods	22
BLG	19	NY Bagel Café	2
Boulevard Balboa	27	Oz Bar and Lounge	29
Churreria Manolo	5	El Pavo Real	20
Coca-Cola	30	Petit Paris	4
Covadonga	12	Pomodoro	6
Gasthaus Bavaria	16	Rincon Suizo/	
Greenhouse	25	Restaurante 1985	7
Habibi's	24	El Rincon Tableño	13
Istmo Brew Pub	8	Sahara/Deep Room	26
Jenny #18	1	El Trapiche	9
Jimmy	14	Unplugged	10
Lips Bar	3	Vegetariano Mireya	18

was constructed using stones from the ruined cathedral of Panamá Viejo (see p.612). Three of its bells were also recovered from its predecessor; reputedly, they owe their distinctive tone to a ring thrown by Empress Isabella of Spain into the molten metal from which they were cast. They ring throughout the day to announce Mass.

Across the square from the cathedral is the bare concrete skeleton of the **Hotel Central**, built to replace the *Grand Hotel*, which was, in its time, the plushest hotel

in Central America. It was here that jubilant crowds gathered in 1903 to celebrate Panamanian independence by pouring champagne over the head of General Huertas, the defecting garrison commander, for over an hour. In 2004 the hotel closed for restoration, and at the time of writing the work was still years from completion.

Southeast of the cathedral is the Neoclassical Palacio Municipal, whose small **Museo de Historia Panameña** (Mon–Fri 8.30am–3.30pm; US$1) offers

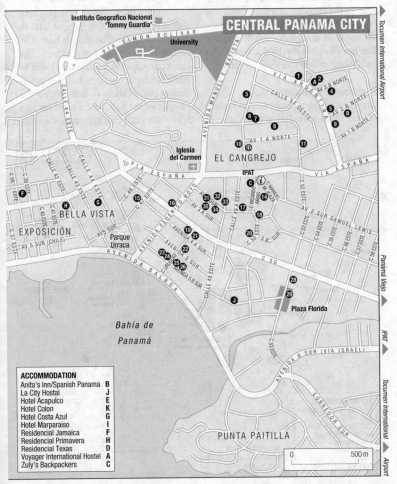

CENTRAL PANAMA CITY

ACCOMMODATION

Anita's Inn/Spanish Panama	B
La City Hostal	J
Hotel Acapulco	E
Hotel Colon	K
Hotel Costa Azul	G
Hotel Marparaiso	I
Residencial Jamaica	F
Residencial Primavera	H
Residencial Texas	D
Voyager International Hostel	A
Zuly's Backpackers	C

Map labels: Instituto Geografico Nacional 'Tommy Guardia'; University; VIA SIMÓN BOLÍVAR; VIA ARGENTINA; VIA ESPAÑA; EL CANGREJO; Iglesia del Carmen; BELLA VISTA; EXPOSICIÓN; IPAT; Parque Urraca; AVENIDA BALBOA; Bahía de Panamá; Plaza Florida; PUNTA PAITILLA; CORREDOR SUR; AVENIDA B SUR (VIA ISRAEL); 0 500 m

Right margin: Tocumen International Airport; Panamá Viejo; IPAT; Tocumen International Airport a cursory introduction to Panamanian history.

Museo del Canal Interoceánico

The excellent **Museo del Canal Interoceánico** (Tues–Sun 9am–5.30pm; US$2; ⓦwww.museodelcanal.com), on the south side of the Plaza Catedral, explains in great detail the history of the country's transisthmian waterway. Photographs, video footage and historic exhibits – including the original Canal treaties – document everything from the first Spanish attempt to find a passage to Asia to the contemporary management of the canal. All displays are in Spanish, but most of the guides speak English. The museum has disabled access and a small shop selling Canal memorabilia.

Palacio Presidencial

On the seafront two blocks north of the Plaza Catedral along Calle 6,
the **Palacio Presidencial**, originally built in 1673, was home to several successive colonial and Colombian governors. In 1922 it was rebuilt in grandiose neo-Moorish style under the orders of President Belisario Porras, who also introduced white Darién herons to the grounds, giving the palace the nickname of "Palacio de las Garzas". The birds and their descendants have lived freely around the patio fountain ever since, although rumour has it that when US President Jimmy Carter visited the palace in 1977 for the signing of the new canal treaty his security team sprayed the building with a disinfectant that proved fatal to the herons, and replacements had to be rushed in under cover of darkness. The streets around the palace are closed to traffic and pedestrians, but the presidential guards allow visitors to view the exterior of the palace between 7am and 5pm daily via a checkpoint on Calle 4.

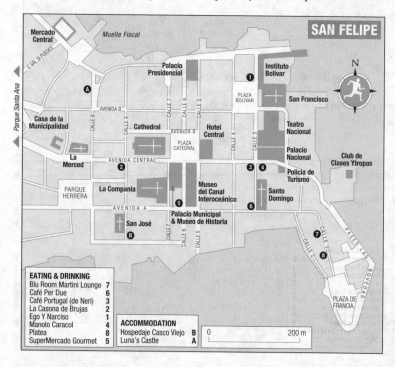

EATING & DRINKING	
Blu Room Martini Lounge	7
Café Per Due	6
Café Portugal (de Neri)	3
La Casona de Brujas	2
Ego Y Narciso	1
Manolo Caracol	4
Platea	8
SuperMercado Gourmet	5

ACCOMMODATION	
Hospedaje Casco Viejo	B
Luna's Castle	A

Plaza Bolívar

A block back down Calle 6 and two blocks east along Avenida B is **Plaza Bolívar**, an elegant square dedicated in 1883 to Simón Bolívar, whose statue, crowned by a condor, stands in its centre. Bolívar came here in 1826 for the first Panamerican Congress, held in the chapter-room of the old **monastery** on the northeast corner of the square. The building has been beautifully restored and the courtyard has a magnificent translucent roof. Unfortunately, the building now houses government offices, and non-official visitors are not permitted. Next door stands the church and monastery of **San Francisco**, built in the seventeenth century but extensively modified since. The church is usually closed, but if you ask in the parish office on Avenida B someone may be willing to open it up and show you around. Other than the carved wooden confessional dating to 1736 the interior is unspectacular, but the tower offers fine views across the city.

Teatro Nacional

Just south of Plaza Bolívar on Avenida B is the **Teatro Nacional**, designed by Genaro Ruggieri, the Italian architect responsible for La Scala in Milan. Extensively restored in the early 1970s and built to the most exacting acoustic standards, the splendid Neoclassical interior is richly furnished and decorated in red and gold, with French crystal chandeliers, busts of famous dramatists and a vaulted ceiling painted with scenes depicting the birth of the nation by Panamanian artist Roberto Lewis. When the theatre is open to the public (see p.610) there is usually a docent on hand to give tours of the building.

Club de Clases y Tropas

From the parking lot at the end of Avenida B it's a two hundred-metre walk south along the seafront to the corner of Avenida A and Calle 1. This stretch passes some immaculately restored nineteenth-century houses to the west and, overlooking the sea to the east, the ruined shell of the **Club de Clases y Tropas**. This recreation centre for Noriega's national guard was destroyed during the US invasion. More recently, a formal ball scene for *Quantum of Solace*, the twenty-second movie in the James Bond series, was filmed here in 2008. Though a bombed-out ruin, with its position on the waterfront it is still a dominating feature of the old quarter, and an integral piece of Panamanian history.

Plaza de Francia

A hundred metres south along Calle 1 lies the **Plaza de Francia**. Enclosed on three sides by seaward defensive walls, it's the site of a **monument** dedicated to the thousands of workers who died during the disastrous French attempt to build the canal (see p.617). The Neoclassical **French Embassy** building, fronted by a statue of Pablo Arosemena, stands on the north side of the square. The elegant building to the east was formerly the Palace of Justice; it was badly damaged during the US invasion in 1989 and is now home to the **National Cultural Institute**. During the colonial period the square was a military centre, the vaults under the seaward walls serving as the city's jail; built below sea level, they would sometimes flood at high tide, drowning the unfortunate prisoners within. Known as **Las Bóvedas**, some of the vaults have been restored: one houses a French restaurant that shares the same name, and another a small art gallery.

Church and Convent of Santo Domingo

Two blocks west along Avenida A from the corner with Calle 1 stands the ruined Church and Convent of **Santo Domingo**, completed in 1678 and famous for the **Arco Chato** (flat arch).

Only 10.6m high but spanning some 15m with no external support, the Arco Chato was reputedly cited as evidence of Panamá's seismic stability when the US Senate was debating where to build an interoceanic canal. Unfortunately, the arch collapsed just after the centenary celebrations of Panamá's independence in 2003. Although the reason for the collapse is unclear, some say it was due to the estimated twenty thousand people who descended on San Felipe for the celebrations.

Church of San José and Plaza Herrera

West along Avenida A at the corner with Calle 8 is the **Church of San José**. Built in 1673 and since remodelled, the church is exceptional only as the home of the legendary Baroque Golden Altar, one of the few treasures to survive Henry Morgan's ransacking of Panamá Viejo in 1671 – it was apparently painted or covered in mud to disguise its real value.

One block west of San José, Avenida A emerges onto **Plaza Herrera**, a pleasant square lined with nineteenth-century houses. This was originally the Plaza de Triunfo, where bullfights were held, but was renamed in 1922 in honour of General Tomás Herrera, whose statue stands at its centre. Herrera was the military leader of the short-lived independence attempt in 1840; he went on to be elected president of Colombia, but was assassinated in 1854. The area can be dodgy at night, so is best avoided after dark.

Avenida Central

Avenida Central runs all the way from the waterfront in San Felipe north through the poorer barrios of Santa Ana and El Chorillo towards the more modern portion of the city. The pedestrianized, ten-block stretch between **Parque Santa Ana**, a small park and busy transport hub, and

Plaza Cinco de Mayo is the liveliest and most popular **shopping** district in the city. Blasts of air-conditioning and loud music pour from the huge superstores that line the avenue, while hawkers with megaphones attempt to entice shoppers inside with deals on clothing, electronics and household goods. Nowhere is the diversity and vitality of the city more evident. Because the avenue runs through some of the poorer areas of town, it's best not to venture down any side streets.

Plaza Cinco de Mayo

As Avenida Central emerges onto **Plaza Cinco de Mayo**, the pedestrianized section ends and the maelstrom of traffic takes over again. The plaza is actually two squares rolled into one. The first has a small monument to the volunteer firemen killed while fighting an exploded gunpowder magazine in 1914; *bomberos* occupy a revered position in a city that has so often been devastated by fire. The second square, Plaza Cinco de Mayo proper, borders the legislative palace compound and has a black, monolithic monument emblazoned with the nationalist slogan: "Ni limosnas, ni millones, queremos justicia" ("Neither alms, nor millions, we want justice"). Heading north from here, Avenida Central splits, with the north fork called Avenida Central and the south called Avenida Justo Arosemena (Av 3 Sur).

Museo Afro-Antillano

At the corner of Avenida Justo Arosemena and Calle 24, an unmarked, wooden former church houses the **Museo Afro-Antillano** (Tues–Sun 9am–4pm; US$1), dedicated to preserving the history and culture of Panama's large West Indian population. It is very small, but its exhibits – featuring photographs, tools and furniture – give a good idea of the working and living conditions of black canal workers. There are also

THE AFRO-ANTILLANOS

Some five percent of Panama's population are Afro-Antillanos – descendants of the black workers from the English- and French-speaking West Indies who began migrating to Panama in the mid-nineteenth century to help build the railroad and canal. Widely considered second-class citizens or undesirable aliens, Afro-Antillanos worked and lived in appalling conditions under French and American control. Most of the twenty thousand workers who died during the French canal attempt were West Indians, and the mortality rate was four times higher among black workers than white during US construction.

Unfortunately, Panamanian treatment of Afro-Antillanos during the first half of the twentieth century was little better than French or American. Consequently, though they are somewhat less discriminated against than other black populations in Central America, Afro-Antillanos remain among the most marginalized segments of the population.

In spite of these obstacles, more than a century after their arrival in Panama, the Afro-Antillanos maintain a vibrant and distinct culture whose influence is widely felt in contemporary Panamanian society. Many second- and third-generation Afro-Antillanos still speak the melodic patois of the West Indies, and the street Spanish of Panama City and Colón is peppered with Jamaican slang. Unique Protestant beliefs imported from the West Indies continue to thrive, heavily spiced Caribbean dishes permeate Panamanian cuisine, and the music, from jazz in the 1950s to "reggaespañol" in the 1990s, has made an indelible mark on the region.

a small library and occasional events, including Afro-Antillano cookery courses and jazz festivals.

Museo de Ciencias Naturales

Northeast of Plaza Cinco de Mayo, Avenida Central remains the city's main thoroughfare and a busy shopping street as it runs through the barrios of Calidonia and La Exposición. Two blocks east of Avenida Central on Avenida Cuba between Calle 29 and Calle 30, the **Museo de Ciencias Naturales** (Tues–Sat 9am–4pm; US$1) offers a basic introduction to Panama's geology and ecology, with many stuffed animals – look out for the pickled fer-de-lance, the venomous snake that killed the director of Panama's old zoo in 1931.

Balboa Monument

A short walk south down Calle 30 from the science museum brings you to waterside Avenida Balboa, and, several blocks to the north in a small, shady park, the glorious **Balboa Monument**. Erected in 1913 with Spanish help, the likeness of Vasco Núñez de Balboa, the sixteenth-century explorer, stands atop a globe with a sword in one hand and a flag in the other, looking out in perpetual triumph on the southern ocean he "discovered".

Arrival and information

By air International flights arrive at Tocumen International Airport (☏ 238 4322), about 26km northeast of Panama City. Domestic flights arrive at Marcos A. Gelabert Airport (☏ 315 0241), better known as Albrook. Cabs from the airport to the city cost about US$15 per person, with prices dropping depending on the number of people with whom you share.

By bus International buses from Costa Rica and domestic buses from almost everywhere in the interior of Panama arrive at and depart from the Albrook terminal, very close to the domestic airport.

Tour operators ANCON Expeditions, Edificio El Dorado, C Elvira Mendez (☏ 269 9415, ⊛ www.anconexpeditions.com), the commercial arm of the National Conservation Association, provides Panama's best ecotours. Scuba Panamá, Av 6 Norte at C 62A (☏ 261 3841, ⊛ www.scubapanama.com), offers countrywide diving excursions, equipment sale and rental and diving instruction.

Tourist information The main IPAT office (Mon–Fri 8.30am–4.30pm; ☎ 226 7000, ⓦ www .visitpanama.com) is on the north side of the Atlapa Convention Centre on Av Israel, in the suburbs east of El Cangrejo. For simple queries, ask at the IPAT booth on the corner of Via España and C Ricardo Arias in El Cangrejo, or at the international or domestic airport. Panama's national parks and other protected natural areas are managed by the National Environment Agency (ANAM; ☎ 315 0855, ⓦ www.anam.gob.pa), in Edificio 804 at the former US military base of Albrook.

City transport

Bikes The safest place to ride a bicycle in Panama City is on Amador Causeway, where you can rent bikes at either end. Near the future site of the Museo de la Biodiversidad (see p.614) are Bicicletas Moses (Sat & Sun during daylight hours) and Tony's Bike Rentals (Tues–Sun 10am–6pm during the high season). Both outfits charge US$2–3 per hour. Rali-Carretero, Via España at Av Argentina (☎ 263 4136, ⓦ www.rali-carretero.com), has a good range of spare parts and a maintenance centre.

Buses Panama City's public buses – known as diablos rojos, or red devils – are the cheapest way to get around. They cost just US$0.25 per ride, payable on exit, and operate 6am–midnight. There are no fixed routes or schedules: destinations are painted on the windscreen. Buses head almost everywhere in the city from Plaza Santa Ana and Albrook bus terminal.

Taxis Taxis are plentiful and inexpensive, with fares based on a zone system: US$1.25 plus US$0.25 for each zone boundary crossed and US$0.25 for each additional passenger. Most intra-city rides will cost less than US$2 and none should cost more than US$3.

Accommodation

There are three main areas to stay in Panama City. A growing number of budget travellers opt for San Felipe, the city's old colonial centre. The restoration of many of the area's historic buildings makes it a pleasant retreat from the congestion and the pollution of the rest of the city. A number of lively bars and restaurants as well as some new backpacker-friendly hostels have also made it a popular nightlife destination. Between San Felipe and the banking district of El Cangrejo there's not much of interest, but the Calidonia/La Exposición area offers a wide selection of unexceptional but affordable modern hotels and *pensiones*. The safer and somewhat quieter districts of Bella Vista and El Cangrejo, the hub of the city's nightlife and commercial activity, have the densest concentration of hostels in addition to a few mid-range options. These hostels are generally where you will find the best information on the city and boat trips to Colombia. With Panama's booming tourist economy it is a good idea to book in advance no matter where you're staying. It's also best to exercise caution in most of Panama City's neighbourhoods after dark. Hot water is standard, and most places have a/c and cable TV.

San Felipe and Amador

Hospedaje Casco Viejo C 8a, nos. 8–31 ☎ 211 2127, ⓦ www.hospedajecascoviejo .com. A brightly painted VW van marks the entrance to this well-kept and surprisingly spacious hostel just off Av A and around the corner from the Iglesia de San José. Shared kitchen, free wi-fi and rooftop access. Dorms ②, doubles ④

Hotel Colon C 12 Oeste at Av B ☎ 228 2506. This old, run-down property is the picture of wasted potential. Beautiful tilework in the lobbies, wide staircases, old-fashioned lifts and a great view from the third-floor balcony are its redeeming features, though they don't make up for the dark rooms and uncomfortable mattresses. ③–④

Luna's Castle C 9a Este between Av B & Av Alfaro ☎ 262 1540, ⓦ www.lunascastle.com. Currently only with dorms open, Luna's will inevitably become a hotspot in San Felipe thanks to its huge property, experienced owners and creative and hard-working staff. wi-fi, shared kitchen, solar hot water, laundry, balconies and an on-site bar. Dorms ②

Calidonia and La Exposición

Hotel Acapulco C 30 between Av Cuba and Perú ☎ 225 3832, ⓔ hotelacapulco@hotmail.com. A travellers' favourite for its solid value and friendly service. With all the standard amenities plus small balconies on some upper-level rooms, it has a touch more charm than many of the hotels in the area. ④

Hotel Marparaiso C 34 at Av Justo Arosemena ☎ 227 6767, ⓦ www.marparaisopma.com. Booking two nights' stay upon arrival will get you free transport from the airport. Guests enjoy discounted breakfasts in the restaurant downstairs, and there's free wi-fi throughout. The rooms are a bit rundown and the street noise can be bothersome, but it's not much different from other accommodation you'll find in the area. ④

Residencial Jamaica Av Cuba at C 38 Este ☎ 225 9870. A good deal for the price, Jamaica's rooms are bright and clean and include TV, a/c and hot water. ④

Residencial Texas C 31 between Av Cuba and Av Perú ☎ 224 1467. This basic option has TV, a/c, hot water, large bathrooms and rock-hard mattresses. It's a good deal, but not the most charming place in this charmless neighbourhood. ④

Bella Vista and El Cangrejo

Anita's Inn C G at Via Argentina ☎ 213 3121, ⓦ www.hostelspanama.com. Half a block off Via Argentina, *Anita's* is clean, quiet and competently run by the kind owner. Due to its partnership with the on-site language school Spanish Panama (see p.611), rooms are often reserved for students and are generally rented on a longer-term basis. ④

Hostal La Casa de Carmen C 1, no. 32 ☎ 263 4366, ⓦ www.lacasadecarmen.net. Strongly recommended by travellers and therefore usually full, so book ahead. *Carmen* attracts a wide age range and the serene and colourful surroundings and long list of free services (breakfast, internet, shared kitchen, laundry, hot water and sitting area with barbeque) could occupy you for your entire stay. Dorms ③, doubles ⑤

Hotel Costa Azul C 44 Este at Av Justo Arosemena ☎ 225 4703, ⓔ hotelcostaazul@cwpanama.net. A small hotel with friendly service, internet, bar and parking. The bright, clean and spacious rooms have hot water, a/c and cable TV. ⑤

Residencial Primavera Av Cuba at C 42 ☎ 225 1195. The friendly service and location in a residential area on the edge of Bella Vista make this a pleasant place to stay and a great deal. Rooms have fans and basic bathrooms. ④

Voyager International Hostel Edificio Emilsani, 2nd Floor, C Felipe Motta at Via Argentina ☎ 260 5913, ⓦ www.geocities.com/voyagerih. Near Einstein's Head, the locally famous giant bust of the brilliant physicist, this is a typical hostel. Well-worn and not overly concerned with cleanliness, *Voyager* has dormitories – some with a/c – and private rooms. There's also a communal kitchen, laundry service, living room, bag storage and internet. It's a good place to meet other travellers and get information, and has established relationships with yacht captains who make trips to San Blas and Colombia. Dorms ③, doubles ⑤

Zuly's Backpackers C Ricardo Arias ☎ 269 2665, ⓦ www.zulysbackpackers .com. As far as hostels in Panama City go, this one's an institution. Though small, and only offering dorms, it has a shared kitchen, living room (where there's always a football match on), balcony, a rotating cast of international travellers and a wealth of information on the city and boat trips to Colombia. Dorms ②

La City Hostel Coral Plaza, Apt 1B, Edificio Marbella Building ☎ 6497 5672, ⓦ www .miradoradventures.com. This urban venture by the owner of the well-known *Hostel Nomba* in Boquete is spotlessly clean, spacious and well laid out. There's a huge kitchen, internet, laundry facilities, indoor and outdoor lounge areas, and private rooms that can accommodate up to four. Best of all, you couldn't be any closer to the hip nightspots on Calle Uruguay. Dorms ③, rooms ⑤–⑦

Eating

Panama City's cosmopolitan nature is reflected in its restaurants: anything from US fast food to Greek, Italian, Chinese, Japanese and French can easily be found, and excellent seafood is widely available. Cheap takeout meals are available from the Rey supermarket (open 24hr) on Via España, including half a rotisserie chicken (US$3), potato salad and fruit salad (US$1 each).

San Felipe and Amador

Café Per Due Av A at C 3a. Italian-owned and operated, this little gem serves the best pizza in the city. On a basic pie the thin, oven-crisped crust is crowned with fresh tomato, basil, cheese and garlic; even with your most creative set of toppings, the prices can't be beat (salads US$4–6, pizzas US$5–9).

Café Portugal (de Neri) Av Central at C 3a. This little café will take you back a hundred years or so with its rough-hewn wood tables along a cobbled street, though the free wi-fi and a/c will quickly return you to the present. US$3–5 will get you an appetizer, and staples like chicken fingers, pizzas and salads are all under US$10. The coffee is great, and an afternoon beer here is a good way to escape the heat.

Lum's Carretera Diablo, Building 340, Ancon. Near the canal in Ancon, this enormous building is popular for its bar-like atmosphere, complete with billiards, foosball and good beer selection, and filling American-style meals. US$5–10 for appetizers and entrees.

Mi Ranchito Calzador de Amador, near the Nature Center (see p.614), this place is extremely popular with locals for its cocktails, seafood and sunset city views. The round-trip taxi fare can make a visit here a bit pricey. Mains US$8–12.

SuperMercado Gourmet Av A at C 6. A small corner market serving good sandwiches and excellent set lunches for US$2–5. Also has a decent selection of hard-to-find gourmet and imported goods.

Calidonia and Santa Ana

Boulevard Balboa Av Balboa at C 31 Este. The spartan 1970s interior here is livened up by a smart lunch-time crowd of local politicians and office workers. Although specialising in toasted sandwiches (US$3), the lengthy menu also includes a number of filling Panamanian dishes (from US$5), such as a chicken and rice platter (*pollo y arroz*) or *ceviche de corvina*.

Coca-Cola On Plaza Santa Ana, C 12 at Av Central. The self-proclaimed "oldest restaurant in Panama" and something of an institution among the city's older residents, who gather to drink coffee, read the paper and discuss the news. Filling Panamanian staples (*ceviche*, chicken with rice, soups) for about US$3, and generously portioned breakfasts cooked to order.

Covadonga C 29 at Av Perú. A 24hr restaurant in the bottom floor of a hotel by the same name, *Covadonga* has reasonably priced (US$5–10) Panamanian and international dishes. Hints of Colombian, Greek and Spanish influences abound, from the Colombian flag on the wall to the Greek salads and flan.

El Rincón Tableño Av Cuba at C 31. Another example of the city's ubiquitous, huge, cafeteria-style eateries, *Tableño* serves up *comida típica* with relish and at economical prices, under US$5. Try the *sancocho* here.

Bella Vista and El Cangrejo

Athens Pizza (Pano's Kretan House) C 48 Este at C 50, behind the Delta petrol station. Near the popular nightspots on C Uruguay, this joint serves up a tasty and filling meal for around US$5. The Greek dishes are abundant and the pizza is the best comfort food you'll find in Panama. Closed Wed. There's another branch on C 57 (closed Tues).

Beirut C 49 A Este at Av 3 Sur, opposite the *Marriott*. A nice range of tasty Lebanese food (from US$4), with a large combo platter for two going for US$10. Popular with wealthy locals for its good service, hookah rental and occasional belly-dancing on weekends.

Churrería Manolo Via Argentina no. 12 and the Times Square Plaza in the Obarrio District. A reasonably priced, 24hr, cafeteria-style restaurant serving up several delicious styles of its namesake, the sweet and delectable *churro*. They also serve a wide variety of medium-priced (US$8–15) entrees to a business crowd.

Jenny #18 Via Argentina at C Felipe Motta. The number reveals that this is part of a franchise of cafeteria-style restaurants serving *comida típica* for under US$5.

Jimmy C Manuel M. Icaza, just off Via España. Extremely popular 24hr restaurant-cafeteria in the heart of El Cangrejo, with a wide choice of Panamanian food ranging from grilled meat and fish to sandwiches, pizza and strong coffee. Most of the large and varied menu can be had for under US$5. Takeout available.

Matsuei C Eusebio A. Morales, near *Hotel El Parador*. A Japanese restaurant with friendly service and a large menu that offers sushi, tempura, curries and teriyaki. Prices range from US$9 to US$30 for a large sushi tray (which can be shared). Closed Sun lunch.

NY Bagel Café On Plaza de Einstein, C Felipe Motta at Via Argentina. A popular hangout for travellers, expats and wealthy locals, this is one of the few bagel joints in Panama, serving a wide variety of their namesake plus fruit smoothies, good coffee and more. Most items are under US$5; free wi-fi for customers.

Petit Paris Off Via Argentina. A speciality bakery heralded by European travellers as the real deal.

The pastries and sweets are handmade and delicious, and there's free wi-fi for customers. The well-crafted treats are a bit more expensive, around US$2–6, but well worth it.

Pomodoro C 49B Oeste in *ApartHotel Las Vegas*. Extremely popular Italian place with good atmosphere, including outdoor seating in an enclosed tropical garden. The excellent pizzas and pastas starts at US$5.

El Trapiche Via Argentina. Slightly upmarket, but still affordable, traditional Panamanian cuisine in a lively atmosphere, with three-course set lunches, tasty meat and fish dishes and filling breakfasts. A favourite in the city, the prices will run US$7–12 for most entrees.

Vegetariano Mireya C 50 Este, a block south of Via España. Small, inexpensive, self-service vegetarian restaurant with a menu of hot dishes that change daily, as well as a salad bar. Large, filling meals can be had for under US$5.

Drinking and nightlife

Panama City is very much a 24hr metropolis, and its residents like nothing better than to drink and dance into the early hours. At one end of the great range of places to go are the cantinas and bars around Avenida Central: hard-drinking dives where women are rarely seen. Most of the upmarket places are around El Cangrejo, Amador and Casco Viejo. Once in a particular neighbourhood, it's easy and relatively safe to walk between venues at night.

Cover charges are more often levied on weekends and tend to be high, but often include several free drinks. Most clubs are closed Mondays and Tuesdays. The website ⓦwww.panama1.com gives a comprehensive list of clubs and bars in the city.

San Felipe, Amador and Santa Ana

Blu Room Martini Lounge C 1. A popular first stop for people making a night of it in San Felipe. Latin music dominates and the club can be selective over its clientele, so dress smart.

La Casona de las Brujas Av 8a. Artsy, laid-back and hip, the "witches' lair" provides a casual venue for live music and art displays and has beer and cocktails for under US$5.

Ego y Narciso Plaza Bolívar ☎262 2045. There are plenty of places to go for tapas and a drink, but these Peruvian and Italian sister restaurants, a world away on the relaxed and picturesque Plaza Bolívar, will give you a glimpse of colonial-era Panama City. There are tables in the square to appreciate twilight in an historic city.

Flags Calzador de Amador. A vast, modern, open-fronted complex with four restaurants, a bar area and great views of Panama City across the bay. It's particularly popular on weekends, when the central stage plays host to live music, including salsa bands.

Party Bus Panama ☎301 0010, ⓦwww.partybuspanama.com. If you haven't yet had your fill of bus trips, this self-contained, moving party is an easy, gimmicky night out. Call or email for reservations; the basic 2hr tour costs US$25 per person and includes an open bar.

Platea C 1, in front of the old *Club Union* ☎ 228 4011. Upscale jazz bar underneath the pricey *Scena* restaurant – if you crave jazz, this is the place to go.

Bella Vista and El Cangrejo

Anemos C 47. This chatty club gets going late, so early in the night there are all kinds of drink specials and no cover charge, though there's not much of a crowd before midnight.

BLG C Uruguay between C 50 and Av 4a Sur. *BLG* serves the gay community and everyone else unlimited drinks with the US$25 cover charge. It's quickly becoming a well-known party spot, and the frequency of excellent DJs spinning seriously good groves will only make it more popular.

Gasthaus Bavaria C 50, Building 25. As the name implies, this hip yet bare-bones dive is fashioned after a German alehouse. Paulaner and Warsteiner are both on tap for US$2, and Spaten comes in a bottle.

Greenhouse With two locations in the trendiest parts of town (one on C Uruguay near C 48, another on Via Argentina near Plaza de Einstein), the *Greenhouse* franchise is a popular though somewhat pricey spot to get the night started.

Habibi's Off C Uruguay. Right in the thick of things, *Habibi's* has seemingly limitless indoor and outdoor seating where club-goers gather to enjoy hookahs and cocktails, each for around US$5.

Istmo Brew Pub Av Eusebio A. Morales. If you're craving something other than the standard local *cerveza*, *Istmo* is sure to refresh your tired palate – all of the beer is brewed on site in beautiful copper kegs – and entertain with its open-air atmosphere, pool table and televised football matches. The food's on the pricey side, but cocktails are US$4 and beer runs US$2–6, ranging from bottles to pints to litre-sized steins.

Lips Bar and Dance Club Av Manuel Espinoza Batista. A relative newcomer to the gay scene, *Lips Dance Club* is an upscale joint filled with sharply dressed office types.

Liquid Discothèque C 50 at C Jose de la Cruz. *Liquid* plays a range of music, from Europop to house, for a well-dressed, over-25 crowd spinning on the huge dance floor. In keeping with the chic image, the cover charge can get pricey on weekends.

Londoner Pub C Uruguay. A slightly over-modernized take on the British pub, the *Londoner* has several beers on tap, darts, a small stage and flat-screen TVs showing football matches. It's missing the warm woods and cosy corners of a true pub, but its location draws a crowd on busy nights (Thurs–Sat).

Moods C Uruguay. This popular spot brings in a slightly older clientele on weekdays, when there's no cover, but its prime location and live reggae draws all kinds on the weekends (cover around US$8).

Next Av Balboa, Marbella. A giant discotheque, enormous and pulsing with house beats and human energy. If this is what you're looking for, you won't even have to go inside to know you've found it. Drink specials early in the night.

Oxen Tumba Muerto, in front of Plaza Edison. Well away from the city centre along Av Ricardo J. Alfaro, this lively club is ready and waiting for you to dance the night away. If you've busted one too many moves, take a break to watch the drag show on weekend nights.

Oz Bar and Lounge C 53 Este, Marbella. Upscale and loungey, *Oz* spins chill-out electronic noise for a scenester crowd and offers all kinds of ladies' specials. Karaoke on Tues.

El Pavo Real C 51 Este at C 50. Made famous by the novel *The Tailor of Panama*, this "English" pub is popular with expats and wealthy Panamanians.

There are darts, pool tables and frequent live music from 11pm, as well as expensive drinks and food, including the inevitable fish and chips ($7).

Sahara/Deep Room C Uruguay. A popular after-hours gathering spot for a diverse crowd, *Sahara* is an oasis of energy in the wee hours. Cover charges (around US$5) are selectively enforced and mixed drinks can get expensive.

Unplugged Via Veneto, beneath *Restaurante Don Lee*. Recently moved from its old location on the C Uruguay circuit, *Unplugged* is a hotspot for hipsters and folks looking for a music-focused bar. Drinks and cocktails (US$3–8) are nothing fancy.

Entertainment

There are all sorts of things to see and do that don't involve drinking or dancing (at least to electronic music). Check the papers as well as Ⓦ www.thepanamanews.com and Ⓦ www.prensa.com for entertainment listings, including live music and theatre.

Cinema There are lots of cinemas in the city showing current, subtitled Hollywood blockbusters. Prices range from $3 to $6; Ⓦ www.cinespanama.com and Ⓦ www.prensa.com list current showtimes. Try the Alhambra, on Via España in El Cangrejo; the Cinemark, in the Albrook Mall, across from the bus terminal, which shows a wide selection of current movies; or Extreme Planet and Kinomaxx, which are within 100m of each other on Av Balboa, near Av Israel and Via Italia in Punta Paitilla.

Cockfighting This exceptionally bloody betting game and spectacle is immensely popular throughout the country. If you've the stomach for it, it can be seen at Club Gallístico, Via España at Via Cincuentenario (Mon, Sat & Sun; US$1; ☎ 221 5652).

Theatre Most theatre productions are in Spanish, and can be found advertised outside theatre buildings and in local papers like *La Prensa*. The Teatro Balboa, Stevens' Circle, Balboa (☎ 228 0327), hosts jazz, folk dancing and theatre productions sponsored by the National Cultural Institute. The Teatro Nacional, Av B, Plaza Bolívar (☎ 262 3525) hosts theatre and ballet productions.

Traditional Panamanian dancing Venues include: Las Brisas de Amador, Calzador de Amador; Las Tinajas, C 51 Este at Av Federico Boyd (Tues & Thurs–Sat from 9pm; reservations recommended; US$5 cover charge; ☎ 269 3840); and Mi Pueblito, Av 4 de Julio, Amador (Fri & Sat evenings).

Shopping

Books Exedra Book, on Via Brazil at Via España, is a large, modern bookstore with café and internet

(Mon–Sat 9.30am–9.30pm, Sun 11am–8.30pm). Librería Argosy, on Via Argentina at Via España, sells mostly used books, with a wide collection of titles in Spanish and English. Gran Morrison, on Via España in El Cangrejo, is a department store selling a good range of English-language books on Panama.

Crafts and souvenirs Mercado de Buhonerías y Artesanías is on Plaza Cinco de Mayo behind the old railway building, and Mercado Nacional de Artesanías is next to the ruins of Panamá Viejo but is slated to move down the street to the new government museum complex when that is completed – currently the shopping area is split into stalls and you can get a good representation of the country's different ethnic groups and their wares. There is also Gran Morrison on Via España in El Cangrejo, Mi Pueblito on Av 4 de Julio on the way out to Amador and several souvenir shops lining Via Veneto, the centre of the banking district in El Cangrejo. A handful of shops catering to tourists are also clustered along C 1 in San Felipe, at the foot of the peninsula near Plaza de Francia.

Malls Albrook Mall in the Albrook bus terminal; El Dorado on Av Ricardo J. Alfaro; Isla Flamenco on Calzador de Amador; Multicentro on Av Balboa at Av Israel. Additionally, Av Central, the pedestrian zone running between Plaza Cinco de Mayo and San Felipe, is the place to go for low prices on any type of goods.

Directory

Car rental Most major rental companies have desks at the airport.

Exchange Branches of Banco Nacional de Panamá (BNP; Mon–Fri 8am–3pm, Sat 9am–noon) and Banistmo (Mon–Fri 8am–3.30pm, Sat 9am–noon) across the city change traveller's cheques and allow cash withdrawals on credit cards; most have ATMs. Foreign currency is more difficult to change – foreign banks will generally change foreign currencies, especially their own, and there is a licensed exchange house, Panacambios (Mon–Fri 8am–4pm; ☎ 223 1800), in the Plaza Regency Building on Via España, opposite the Rey supermarket. American Express is in Torre BBVA, 9th Floor, Av Balboa (Mon–Fri 9am–noon; ☎ 225 5858).

Embassies Australia (in Mexico; ☎ 52/55 1101 2200); Canada, World Trade Center, 1st Floor, Commercial Gallery, C 53E, Marbella (Mon–Fri 8.30am–1pm; ☎ 264 9731, after-hours ☎ 613 996 8885); Costa Rica, Av Samuel Lewis (☎ 264 2980); Mexico, C 58 at Av Samuel Lewis (☎ 263 4900); UK, MMG Tower, 4th Floor, C 53E, Marbella (Mon–Thurs 7.30am–3.30pm, Fri 7.30am–12.30pm; ☎ 269 0866); US American Citizens Service, PAS Building

783, Demetrio Basilio, Lakas Ave, Clayton (Mon–Fri 8am–5pm; ☎ 207 7000).

Immigration Av Cuba at C 29. Come here (Mon–Fri 8am–3pm) to extend your visa or to get permission to leave the country if you have been in Panama for over three months – for the latter you will also have to visit the office of Paz y Salvo (Mon–Fri 8.30am–4pm) in the Ministerio de Hacienda y Tesoro on Av Cuba at C 35. At both offices it's best to arrive early; take a ticket and be prepared to wait.

Internet There's a large number of internet cafés throughout the city, especially in El Cangrejo on Via Veneto, C 49B Oeste, a block up from Via España. Rates typically run around US$0.50/hr.

Language schools Berlitz, C 47, Edificio Marbella ☎ 265 4800, ⓦ www.berlitz.com; ILERI, Via La Amistad, El Dorado ☎ 260 4424; Spanish Panama, off Via Argentina, El Cangrejo ☎ 213 3121, ⓦ www .spanishpanama.com.

Medical care Hospital Nacional, Av Cuba, C 38/39 (☎ 207-8100/8102; emergencies ☎ 207-8110); Centro Médico Paitilla, C 53 and Av Balboa (☎ 265-8800); Clínica Hospital San Fernando, Via España (☎ 278-6305/6364; emergencies ☎ 278-6300); and Hospital Punta Pacífica, C 53 in Bella Vista (☎ 263-5287).

Pharmacies Farmacias are found all over the city and often include a big green sign with a medical cross; Farmacia Arrocha is popular – the largest branch is on Via España in front of *El Panama* hotel, and there are others on Via Argentina and one in Punta Paitilla. El Rey supermarket (24hr) will also fill prescriptions at their pharmacy counter.

Police Emergencies ☎ 104; tourist police ☎ 270 2467.

Post office The most central post office is on Av Central at C 34, opposite the Don Bosco church; there's another in El Cangrejo in the Plaza de la Concordia shopping centre on Via España. Both Mon–Fri 7am–6pm, Sat 7am–5pm.

Telephones Public phone booths throughout the city take US$5, US$10 and US$20 phone-cards; some take coins. The main Cable & Wireless office (Mon–Fri 7.15am–6.30pm, Sat 7.30am–2pm) is in the Banco Nacional building on Via España. Calls cost US$0.10, US$0.25 and US$0.35/min for local, long distance and mobile calls, respectively. Most internet cafés offer cheap international calls for about $0.25/min ($1.50 for first minute).

Moving on

There are lots of daily flights to destinations all around the country, but buses are cheaper and go to nearly all the same places.

By air

All domestic flights leave from Marcos A. Gelabert domestic airport in Albrook. The only operators are Aeroperlas (☎ 315 7500, ⓦ www.aeroperlas.com) and Air Panama (☎ 316 9000, ⓦ www.flyairpanama .com). All internal flights have a maximum luggage weight limit of 25lb, which sometimes includes carry-ons; excess is charged at US$0.30–0.50 per pound.

Air destinations

Bocas del Toro With Aeroperlas and Air Panama (4–5 daily; 1hr).

Chitré With Air Panama (3 daily; 40min).

Contadora With Aeroperlas and Air Panama (2 daily; 20min).

David With Aeroperlas and Air Panama (6 daily; 1hr).

El Real With Aeroperlas (3 weekly; 1hr).

Kuna Yala Daily flights on Aeroperlas and Air Panama (30min–1hr 15min) to: Achutupo, Ailigandi, Cartí, Corazón de Jesús, El Porvenir, Mulatupo, Playon Chico, Puerto Obaldia, Río Sidra, Tupile and Ustupo.

Jaqué With Aeroperlas (3 weekly; 1hr 10min).

La Palma With Aeroperlas (3 weekly; 1hr 25min).

By bus

All domestic buses – with the exception of those to Ancon, Balboa, Gamboa, Paraiso and the Canal Zone (all of which are served by several city buses daily from the terminal at Plaza Cinco de Mayo) – depart from the modern Terminal de Buses in Albrook. International services with Tica Bus depart from their terminal, also in Albrook.

Domestic bus destinations

Almirante and Changuinola Two departures daily; 10hr.

Chitré Hourly departures; 4hr.

Colón Local departures every 20min (2hr); express departures every 20min (1hr).

David Local departures hourly (7hr); two express departures daily (5hr).

El Valle Departures every 30min; 2hr 30min.

Gamboa Eight departures daily; 45min.

Las Tablas Departures every 2hr; 4hr 30min.

Meteti Seven departures daily; 7–8hr.

Ocú Eight departures daily; 4hr.

Paso Canoas Nine local departures daily (9hr); 2 express departures daily (7hr).

Penonomé Departures every 30min; 2hr 30min.

Santiago Departures every 30min; 4hr.

Sona (St Catalina) Departures every 20min; 5hr.

International bus destinations

San José (Costa Rica) With Tica Bus (☎ 314 6385, ⓦ www.ticabus.com). Two departures daily: 11am (executive class; 14–15hr) & 11pm (economy class; 16–17hr).

AROUND PANAMA CITY

Panama City's sites showcase the breadth of the city and will take you to its every corner. From the ruins of Panamá Viejo, to the Amador Causeway, to the urban jungle of the Metropolitan National Park, you will see man-made and natural, old and new, and everything in between.

Panamá Viejo

On the coast about 6km east of El Cangrejo stand the ruins of **Panamá Viejo**, the original colonial city founded by Pedro Arias de Ávila in 1519. Abandoned in 1671 after being sacked by Henry Morgan and his band of pirates, many of its buildings were later dismantled to provide stones for the construction of San Felipe, and in recent decades much of the site has been built over as the modern city has spread eastward. Despite this encroachment, a surprising number of the original buildings still stand.

The best place to start a visit is the museum (Tues–Sun 9am–5pm; US$3, US$6 with entrance to ruins; ☎ 224 2155, ⓦ www.panamaviejo.org) on Via Cincuentenario near the ruins, where exhibits explain to visitors the changes that have taken place since this was a tiny Indian village around 500 BC. Only one section of the ruins, the former **Plaza Mayor**, requires an entry fee. The major draw here is the three-storey square stone tower of the cathedral, built between 1619 and 1629, that has a modern stairway with a lookout at the top and is flanked by the square **cabildo** (town hall) to the right and the bishop's house to the left. Nearby and free to the public is the site of La Merced, the church and monastery where Francisco Pizarro took communion before embarking on the conquest of Peru in 1531. La Merced was once considered

Panama City's most beautiful church, and survived Morgan's burning of the city by his use of it as a headquarters.

To **get to** Panamá Viejo, either take a taxi (US$3–4) or catch any bus marked "Panamá Viejo" or "Via Cincuentenario". If you're short on time and leaving Panama by air, you can see quite a lot of the ruins by asking your taxi driver to take the slow route to the airport via Panamá Viejo.

Balboa

To the southwest of Calidonia and El Chorillo, Panama City encompasses the former Canal Zone town of **Balboa**, administered by the US as de facto sovereign territory from 1903 to 1979. Balboa retains many of the characteristics of a US provincial town: clean and well ordered, it stands in stark contrast to the chaotic vitality of the rest of the city. However, it conceals a troubled past.

Along the border of the former Canal Zone runs **Avenida de Los Mártires**. An extension of Avenida 4 de Julio and often called by the same name, Avenida de Los Mártires was named in honour of the 21 Panamanians killed by the US military during the riots of 1964 (see p.588). A sculpture by González Palomino, depicting three people climbing a flagpole, was erected here in 2004 as a tribute to the fallen; above it rises **Cerro Ancón**, crowned by a huge Panamanian flag that is visible throughout the city.

Just off the entrance to Cerro Ancón from Avenida de Los Mártires is **Mi Pueblito** (Tues–Sun 9am–9pm; US$1, free on holidays), a theme-park–style replica of the traditional villages of four of Panama's ethnic groups. Although aimed primarily at Panamanian tourists, it's worth visiting if you are not going to see the real thing. Folk dances are performed on Friday and Saturday evenings and restaurants serve traditional food.

Museo de Arte Contemporáneo

Some 200m east of the entrance to Cerro Ancón, on Avenida de los Mártires, is a turnoff that leads to Gorgas Road. This winds around the side of Cerro Ancón to the Canal Authority Building in Balboa Heights (see below), about twenty minutes away on foot. Just off Gorgas Road to the right, the **Museo de Arte Contemporáneo** (Tues–Sun 9am–5pm; free; ☎262 3380, ⌨www .macpanama.org), housed in a former Masonic temple, has a small collection of modern paintings and engravings by Panamanian and Latin American artists and temporary international exhibitions.

Canal Authority Administration Building

Continuing around Cerro Ancón, passing the Palace of Justice and several beautiful estates on Heights Road, Gorgas Road reappears to the right (heading left will take you to the summit of Cerro Ancón) and winds down to the three-storey **Panama Canal Authority Administration Building** (daily 8am–11pm; free), built during the canal construction and still home to the principal administration offices. Inside, four dramatic murals by US artist William Van Ingen depict the story of the canal construction under a domed ceiling supported by marble pillars.

At the rear of the building, where a Panamanian flag now flutters, a broad stairway runs down to the **Goethals monument**, a white megalith with stepped fountains that represent the canal's different locks, erected in honour of George Goethals, chief engineer from 1907 to 1914 and first governor of the Canal Zone. Beside the monument is **Balboa High School**, whose ordinary appearance belies the dramatic events it has witnessed. It was here in 1964 that Zonians attacked students attempting to raise the Panamanian flag, triggering the **flag riots** that left 21 Panamanians dead. During the 1989 invasion, the school was used as a detention camp for Panamanian prisoners, some of whom were allegedly executed by US soldiers.

Fort Amador

From Balboa, Calle Amador runs towards the Causeway through **Fort Amador**, a former US military base that was returned to Panama in 1996 and is now being redeveloped as the centrepiece of the country's plans to promote tourism in the former Canal Zone. The complex will include luxury hotels and a marina as well as the **Museo de la Biodiversidad** (ⓦ www .biomuseopanama.com), a "biodiversity exhibition centre" designed by architect Frank Gehry. Construction of the centre started in February 2004, and was scheduled for completion in 2006, but was still underway in 2008.

Amador Causeway

The **Amador Causeway** (**Calzada de Amador**) runs 6km out into the bay, linking the mainland with the tiny islands of **Naos**, **Perico** and **Flamenco**. The Causeway is a popular weekend escape for the city's residents, who come here to jog, swim, stroll, rollerblade or cycle (you can rent bicycles at the entrance at Bicicletas Moses and just before the bridge to Perico at Tony's Bike Rentals; see p.606) and to enjoy the sea air and the views of the city and the canal.

On Punta Culebra, accessible from the end of Naos, 4km along the Causeway, the **Punta Culebra Nature Center** (Tues–Thurs & Sun 10am–6pm, Fri & Sat 10am–8pm; US$2; ⓦ www.stri.org), run by the Smithsonian Institute, offers an introduction to Panama's marine ecology, including an aquarium where you can stroke sea urchins, starfish and sea cucumbers. There is a small **beach** and **swimming pool** (daily 10am–5pm; $5) just outside the entrance. On the

opposite side of Punta Culebra is the departure point for passenger ferries to Isla Taboga and for some ships embarking on canal transit tours. The second island, tiny Perico, hosts **Las Brisas de Amador**, a strip mall almost entirely made up of restaurants where city-folk frequently enjoy cocktails and appetizers before a night out. Finally, Flamenco is home to a marina and shopping centre (ⓦ www.fuerteamador .com) and is also a popular nocturnal hangout thanks to its abundant bars and restaurants.

Parque Natural Metropolitano and Museo Antropólogico Reina Torres de Araúz

A couple of kilometres north of central Panama City, the 2.65-square-kilometre **Parque Natural Metropolitano** (open 6am–6pm) is an unspoilt tract of tropical rainforest that is home to more than two hundred species of birds and mammals, such as titi monkeys, white-tailed deer, sloths and agoutis. In a slice of the former Canal Zone that reverted to Panamanian control in 1983, the park provides an excellent introduction to the rainforest environment. It's possible to complete all of the main trails in just a few hours; the best of these is the combined La Cienaguita and MonoTiti trail (3km), which leads to a *mirador* with fantastic views across the forest to the city. As elsewhere, the best time to see wildlife, particularly birds, is early in the morning – there is nothing to stop you from coming in earlier than the official opening time to take advantage of this. The **park office** (Mon–Fri 8am–4pm, Sat 8am–1pm; US$2 – you need only pay if entering the park during official hours) and main entrance is on Avenida Juan Pablo II; some buses can drop you nearby, and a taxi from El Cangrejo should cost about US$2. There is a small exhibition centre and library here, and three-hour guided tours can be arranged (US$2 per person; book in advance).

Nearby, the **Museo Antropólogico Reina Torres de Araúz** (Tues–Sun 10am–4pm; US$2) is a worthy stop, with displays including the Salón de Oro, an exhibit of pre-Columbian gold objects, as well as carved stone statues from the ancient Barriles culture of Chiriquí.

Isla Taboga

Twenty kilometres off the coast and about an hour away by boat, tiny **Isla Taboga** is one of the most popular retreats for Panama City residents, who come here to enjoy the island's clear waters, peaceful atmosphere and verdant beauty. Known as the "Island of Flowers" for the innumerable fragrant blooms that decorate its village and forested slopes, Taboga gets very busy on weekends, particularly during the summer, but is usually quiet during the week. Passenger ferries (Mon, Wed & Fri 8.30am & 3pm, Tues & Thurs 8.30am, Sat & Sun 8am, 10.30am, 4pm; US$6, students US$3.50) leave for the island from the Flamenco Marina at the end of the Amador Causeway.

Taboga's one **fishing village** is very picturesque, with narrow streets, white-washed houses and dozens of gardens filled with bougainvillea and hibiscus. Most visitors head straight for one of the sections of **beach**, either right in front of the village or in front of the defunct *Hotel Taboga*, to the right of the pier as you disembark. The water is calmer here and the view of Panama City is magnificent, though the trash on the beach is distressing.

Behind the village, forested slopes rise to the 300-metre peak of **Cerro Vigia**, where a viewing platform on top of an old US military bunker offers spectacular 360-degree views. It's about an hour's climb through the forest to the *mirador* – follow the path some 100m up behind the church until you find a sign marked Sendero de los Tres Cruces, beyond which the trail is easy to follow. The other side of the island is home to one of the biggest brown pelican breeding colonies in the world and, together with the neighbouring island of Uraba, forms a protected wildlife refuge.

Thanks to the abundance of marine life, particularly around El Morro, a rocky island off the coast, accessible by a sandbar at low tide, snorkelling and diving are popular activities on Taboga. The *Kool Hostel* (℡690 2545) rents equipment – there's usually someone hanging around the pier – though for diving you're better off organizing a trip with one of the dive companies in Panama City.

Two hotels have restaurants: the *Chu* serves reasonable Chinese dishes and good seafood on a broad wooden balcony over the beach, while *Vereda Tropical Hotel* offers more varied and expensive international and Panamanian cuisine in a breezy, Caribbean-coloured and Spanish-tiled hillside location. Opposite the church, standalone *Aquario* serves good seafood dishes (US$3–8).

The Panama Canal and Colón Province

Stretching eighty kilometres, from Panama City in the south to Colón in the north, the **Panama Canal** is a work of mesmerizing engineering brilliance. One of the largest and most ambitious endeavours ever undertaken by man, the waterway allows massive vessels – which otherwise would have to travel all the way south around Cape Horn – to traverse the isthmus in less than one day. East of the Canal spreads the rainforest of **Parque Nacional Soberanía**, the greatest possible contrast to its mechanical might. Delve into the park's

THE PANAMA CANAL AND COLÓN PROVINCE

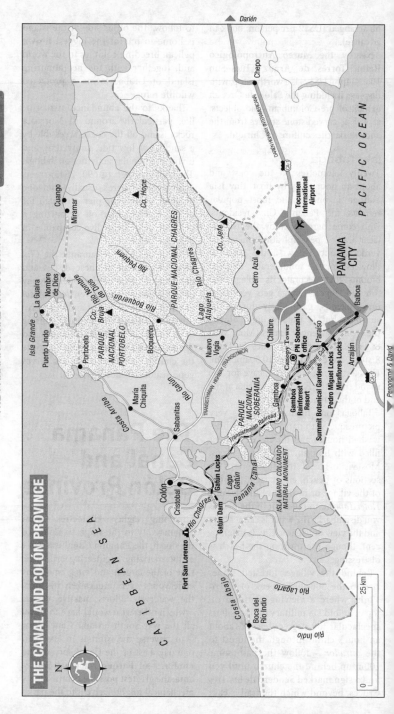

THE CANAL AND COLÓN PROVINCE

CARIBBEAN SEA

PACIFIC OCEAN

Darién

Chepo

DARIÉN HIGHWAY INTERAMERICANA

Tocumen International Airport

PANAMA CITY

Balboa

Arraiján

Peñonomé & David

Cerro Azul

Chilibre

Canopy Tower

PN Soberania office

Paraíso

Gaillard Cut

Pedro Miguel Locks

Miraflores Locks

Gamboa

Gamboa Rainforest Resort

Summit Botanical Gardens

PARQUE NACIONAL SOBERANÍA

Transisthmian Railroad

ISLA BARRO COLORADO NATURAL MONUMENT

Lago Gatún

Panama Canal

Gatún Dam

Gatún Locks

Colón

Cristóbal

Fort San Lorenzo

Río Chagres

Sabanitas

Nuevo Vigía

Boquerón

PARQUE NACIONAL PORTOBELO

Portobelo

Puerto Lindo

Isla Grande

La Guaira

Nombre de Dios

Cuango

Miramar

María Chiquita

Costa Arriba

Co. Bruja

Río Nombre de Dios

Río Boquerón

PARQUE NACIONAL CHAGRES

Río Pequení

Co. Hope

Co. Jefe

Lago Alajuela

Río Chagres

TRANSISTHMIAN HIGHWAY (TRANSISTMICA)

Río Gatún

Costa Abajo

Río Lagarto

Boca del Río Indio

Río Indio

0   25 km

N

humming, humid atmosphere on one of its many accessible pathways, and you'll discover unparalleled biodiversity. **Colón**, at the Atlantic entrance to the Canal, and only a boat or train or bus ride away from Panama City, seems like a different world from the capital – a brief tour of the poverty-stricken city from the safety of a taxi leaves no doubt as to the canal's socioeconomic importance. Forty-five kilometres north-east of Colón lies another port – **Portobelo** – whose glory days are even more distant. Its riches once proved irresistible to such pirates as Sir Francis Drake and Henry Morgan, and its once-mighty fortifications are now atmospheric ruins.

THE CANAL AND THE CANAL ZONE

The **PANAMA CANAL** really is amazing, both physically and in concept. The basis of the country's modern economy, it's also the key to much of its history: were it not for the US government's determination to build the waterway, Panama might never have come into existence as an independent republic. Construction on the project began in the late nineteenth century, initiated by the French, but their efforts were abandoned in 1893, having taken the lives of nearly twenty-two thousand workers through disease. The US took up the construction ten years later, aided by more powerful machinery than the French had been using and improved understanding of malaria and yellow fever control. The job was finally finished in 1914, the isthmus having been breached by the 77 kilometre-long canal, with vessels raised from and lowered to sea level by three sets of locks totalling 5km in length.

From 1903 to 1977, the strip of land that extends five miles on either side of the canal was de facto US territory, an area known as the **Canal Zone**. After more than ninety years the waterway was finally handed over to Panamanian jurisdiction at midnight on December 31, 1999, to be managed thereafter by the Autoridad del Canal de Panamá (ACP). In 2006 a proposal for a $5 billion expansion of the canal, due to be completed in 2015, was approved first by President Torrijos and then by an overwhelming majority in public referendum. The ACP claims that the expansion will directly benefit Panama's people, though critics contend that the country will be crippled by debt – the project will be paid for by increased tolls, supplemented by $2.3 billion in loans – and that only the elite of society will benefit.

CANAL GEOGRAPHY

From the Bahía de Panamá on the country's Pacific coast, the canal runs at sea level approximately six kilometres inland to the Miraflores Locks, where ships are raised some 16.5m to Lago de Miraflores. About two kilometres further on, ships are raised another 10m to the canal's maximum elevation of 26.5m above sea level, after which they enter the Gaillard Cut. This fourteen-kilometre slice through the shifting shale of the continental divide was the deepest and most difficult section of the canal construction and was plagued by devastating landslides.

The canal channel then continues for 38km across the broad expanse of Lago Gatún, once the largest artificial lake in the world. Covering 420 square kilometres, it is tranquil and stunningly beautiful; until you see an ocean-going ship appear from behind one of the densely forested headlands, it's difficult to believe that this is part of one of the busiest waterways in the world. At the lake's far end ships are brought back down to sea level in three stages by the Gatún Locks, after which they run 3km through a narrow cut into the calm Caribbean waters of Bahía Limón.

What to see and do

A striking mix of man's mastery of nature and nature magnificently untamed, the canal region has an eclectic range of attractions. A day-trip from Panama City could see you scanning the rainforest canopy for harpy eagles from the top of a former radar station, taking in the engineering masterpiece of the Miraflores **Locks**, or visiting an indigenous Emberá community in **Parque Nacional Chagres**. If you are in the mood for hiking, try out the celebrated routes of Camino de Cruces and the Pipeline Road in **Parque Nacional Soberanía**. The first takes you along the crumbling cobblestones laid by the Spanish to transport treasure across the isthmus, while the latter is a pathway legendary among globetrotters for its abundance of birdlife. A cool and comfortable early morning train ride on the **Transisthmian Railway** to **Colón** gives wonderful panoramic views of the canal and the

---

EXPLORING THE CANAL AND CANAL ZONE

The nicest and most interesting way to explore the Canal and its surroundings is by boat, though this can be pricey, as vessels are charged around US$17,000 to make the trip. More economically, buses also serve the roads along the Canal, or you can take a ride on one of Central America's only passenger trains.

By boat Canal & Bay Tours in Panama City (℡209 2009 or 2010, ⊛www .canalandbaytours.com) offers half-day partial transit (Sat only) of the canal through Miraflores and Pedro Miguel locks and into the Gaillard Cut (US$115). Full transit, including Lago Gatún and Gatún Locks, is offered once a month (US$165). Alternatively, ANCON Expeditions (see p.606) runs the excellent Panama Canal Rainforest Boat Adventure (US$115 including lunch), which transports you to Gamboa by bus and then winds among the huge cargo ships transiting Lago Gatún, seeking the wildlife that inhabits the canal's islands. It runs daily (minimum two people). A much more affordable option is to get taken on as a linehandler aboard one of the private yachts that transit the canal. Law requires four linehandlers on each boat. It's a straightforward role, but be aware that it carries genuine responsibility. You will not be paid, although food and drink are usually supplied. Your best chance of getting linehandling work is either to ask the staff at the Panama City hostels or the Colon yacht club if they can advise you as to the current favoured hang-out for the yacht owners.

By bus A road served eight times daily by buses from the Panama City terminal near Plaza Cinco de Mayo (see p.604) runs 26km along the side of the canal, past the Miraflores and Pedro Miguel locks (15–20min to either), to the town of Gamboa near Lago Gatún (1hr). It passes the Parque Nacional Soberanía office (p.620) and the entrances to Summit Botanical Gardens and Zoo (see opposite) and the *Canopy Tower* (p.621). If time is short, you can easily find a taxi in Panama City to take you to Miraflores, wait for an hour or so and take you back for US$20–25. The Gatún Locks, on the Caribbean side, can be visited via Colón (see p.621).

By rail The Transisthmian Railway (7.15am from Corozal, 5.15pm from Colón; US$22 one-way; ℡317 6070, ⊛www.panarail.com) runs along the east side of the canal. Primarily for moving freight, once a day a passenger train makes the one-hour journey from Panama City to Colón and back. An observation carriage with oversized windows gives a widescreen version of whatever the view is offering – canal, rainforest or lake – and there are open-sided sections between carriages throughout the train. A taxi to the train station at Corozal, 2km north of Albrook bus terminal (see p.605), costs US$4–6 (agree in advance on the price), or you could take a bus to the terminal and a shorter taxi ride from there. Arrive at the terminal thirty minutes in advance to secure a ticket.

rainforest, and from that infamous city it is a hot and bumpy bus ride northeast along the coast to **Portobelo**. Note that if you take the bus from Panama City towards the Atlantic coast you can cut Colón out entirely by leaving the bus at Sabanitas, and waiting there for a Portobelo-bound bus coming from Colón.

Miraflores Locks

Heading north out of Panama City along the Canal, the first sight of note are the **Miraflores Locks**. The first lock gates here are the biggest in the whole canal system. Even so, they open in just two minutes, guiding ships through by electric locomotives known as mules. The **visitor complex** (daily 9am–5pm; US$5–8; ☎276 8325, ⓦwww.pancanal .com) is a ten-minute walk from the point on the main road where any Gamboa-bound **bus** from Panama City can drop you off – just indicate to the driver where you are going. The US$5 ticket allows access to the observation decks only; for US$8 you can also check out the exhibitions and watch a short movie about the canal, but they don't merit parting with the extra cash. The best time to see ships passing through is 8am to 10.30am, when they come up from the Pacific side, and after 3pm, when they complete their descent from the Atlantic side. There is an overpriced café (*empanadas* US$1.60, soda US$1.40) here, as well as an expensive restaurant and a souvenir shop.

Summit Botanical Gardens

At a fork in the road roughly nine kilometres on from the Miraflores Locks is the office for Parque Nacional Soberanía (see p.620). The left fork, heading towards Gamboa, brings you to **Summit Botanical Gardens and Zoo** (daily 9am–6pm; US$1; ☎232 4854, ⓦwww.summitpanama.org). Any Gamboa-bound **bus** from Panama City can drop you off at the entrance.

Established by the US in 1923, the gardens house more than fifteen thousand plant species spread throughout the landscaped grounds, as well as a popular zoo. The wonderful harpy eagles, patriarchs of the rainforest canopy food chain, perch high in their huge enclosure and peer down disdainfully at visitors, while a nearby crocodile in a murky pond and a group of tapirs – granted a more spacious enclosure than many of the other animals – are also highlights.

Gamboa

Eight kilometres north of the botanical gardens lies the curious town of **Gamboa**, built by the US in the 1930s. With its wooden buildings, "No Necking" sign at the half-empty swimming pool and McGrath Field, a grassy expanse with a baseball diamond

> **TREAT YOURSELF**
>
> Just outside Gamboa, the Gamboa Rainforest Resort (☎314 5000, ⓦwww .gamboaresort.com) lies among the rainforest overlooking the convergence of Río Chagres and Lago Gatún. Though the rooms here are extremely pricey (even as a treat), consider splurging on one of the tours or activities on offer, perhaps topped off with a drink and fantastic views from the bar. Tours include a boat ride on the Chagres (30–40min; US$15), a birding trip along Pipeline Road (see p.620; 3hr, departs 6.45am; US$35 plus US$3.50 park fee) and the popular aerial tram (2–3hr; 9.15am, 10.30am, 1.30pm & 3pm; US$50), which is rather like a tropical ski-lift and offers a unique view of the forest ecosystem. At the summit an observation tower gives a spectacular panorama over the canal, the lake and the Río Chagres, and the ticket price also includes guided tours of a butterfly house, an orchid nursery, a serpentarium and an aquarium with freshwater fish and reptiles.

and wooden bleachers, it feels like an abandoned small American town. The Smithsonian Tropical Research Institute occupies a number of properties in the town, and their small dock is the jumping-off point for trips to Isla Barro Colorado (BCI), the principal site for their research. Several hundred metres north of Gamboa is the entrance to Pipeline Road (Camino del Oleoducto), a 24-kilometre trail through the Parque Nacional Soberanía and one of the world's premier birding sites. There's a small grocery shop (daily 8am–7pm) in town, a snack van, an HSBC ATM and a post office (Mon–Fri 8am–3pm). To get here take one of the eight **buses** that run daily from Panama City.

Isla Barro Colorado

As the waters of Lago Gatún began to rise after the damming of the Chagres in 1913, much of the wildlife in the surrounding forest was forced to take refuge on points of high ground, which eventually became islands. One of these, **Isla Barro Colorado** (BCI), administered by the Smithsonian Tropical Research Institute, is among the most intensively studied areas of tropical rainforest in the world. Though the primary aims of the reserve are conservation and research, you can arrange visits through the STRI (one tour daily Tues, Wed & Fri–Sun; US$70, students US$40; ⓣ212 8951/8026, ⓦwww.stri.org) – contact them well in advance. The tour lasts between four and six hours and most guides speak English (double-check when booking). The experience does not come cheap, although the expense is worth it if you want a truly insightful introduction to tropical rainforest ecology – these are some of the world's top experts on the subject – and the chance to see birds, monkeys and tapirs. The cost covers the boat from Gamboa pier, the tour and lunch at the island.

Parque Nacional Soberanía

Stretching along the eastern flank of the canal, the 220-square-kilometre **Parque Nacional Soberanía** (daily 6am–5pm; US$5; ⓦwww.anam.gob.pa) provides essential protection for the rainforest-covered watershed that is vital for the canal's continued operation. Just thirty minutes from Panama City by road, Soberanía is the most easily accessible national park in Panama and is popular with both locals and visitors. Most spend just a few hours exploring one of the trails, all of which are well marked and pass over rugged terrain cloaked in pristine rainforest, offering reasonable odds of seeing monkeys, innumerable birds and, if you're really lucky, large mammals such as deer or tapir.

You can collect **trail** information and pay the US$3.50 park entrance fee at the **park office** (Mon–Fri 7.30am–4pm; ⓣ232 4192), where the road to Gamboa branches off the main road from Panama City. Indicate to the bus driver that you want to go to the park office. There may be rangers on hand at the trailheads who you can pay if you don't make it to the office.

All the trails have something to recommend them, but a few stand out. **Plantation Road**, which begins at a right-hand turn-off 1.5km past the Summit Botanical Gardens and Zoo, runs some 4km to an intersection with Camino de las Cruces. Plantation Road itself follows a stream (Río Chico Masambi) and offers great birdwatching. Camino de las Cruces is a remnant of the cobbled track that the Spanish colonizers used to transport their goods and treasures to Portobelo on the Caribbean coast. To get to the Plantation Road turn-off (which is also the turn-off for *Canopy Tower* [see opposite], so you could check both out) either walk the 1.5km from the zoo if you are there or take the Gamboa-bound bus directly there from Panama City, indicating to the driver that you want to go to *Canopy Tower*. It is possible to **camp** in the park – pay US$5 at the park office – but bear in mind how intense the rainforest can be.

Parque Nacional Chagres

East of the highway that connects Panama City with Colón – the Transistmica – lies **Parque Nacional Chagres**, 1290 square kilometres of mountainous rainforest comprising four different life zones that are home to more than three hundred bird species and several Emberá communities displaced by the flooding of Lago Bayano, further east.

The park is a bit tricky to get to independently, but *La Casa de Carmen* in Panama City (see p.607) offers a trip to visit an **Emberá-Drúa** community in the park (US$75 per person; often cheaper with larger groups). The price includes transportation, a traditional meal and the opportunity to purchase handicrafts direct from their creators.

COLÓN

COLÓN, situated at the Atlantic entrance to the Panama Canal, is all rubble and colour. The city is dangerously poor, with a bad record of violent crime, but the majority of its residents – mostly descendants of West Indians who came here to build the canal – present a strong case for Colón as a warm and welcoming place. It often feels like all 150,000 or so of them are out of doors and on the streets, milling around as taxis and buses relentlessly strong-arm each other around the grid. Nonetheless, for some Colón's edginess will not appeal in the slightest, and will only be a necessary evil in finding linehandling work and visiting the nearby Gatún Locks, Fort San Lorenzo or the Costa Arriba (although in this case the city could be avoided entirely by changing buses at Sabanitas). Indeed, most visitors to Colón come solely to shop at the Colón Free Zone, a walled enclave where goods from all over the world can be bought at very low prices, and assiduously avoid the rest of the city. However, the combination of a luxurious railroad trip from Panama City followed by a taxi tour of this unique and decaying town is fascinating, and can give powerful insights into what the canal has meant physically and economically to the country.

The city's history is a study in contrasts. Founded in 1852 as the Caribbean terminal of the transisthmian railway, conceived to speed up the journey of US gold prospectors whose preferred route to the west exploited the narrowness of the isthmus, it initially enjoyed a degree of prosperity. In 1869, however, the completion of the transcontinental railway in the US reduced traffic across the isthmus, and the town began to

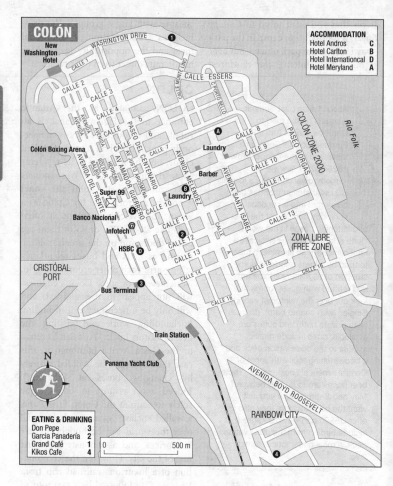

COLÓN

New Washington Hotel

WASHINGTON DRIVE

CALLE 1

CALLE 2

CALLE 3

CALLE 4

CALLE MONTE LIRIO

CALLE ESSERS

C PORTO BELLO

5

6

Colón Boxing Arena

AVENIDA AVENIDA AVENIDA HERRERA BALBOA BOLÍVAR

AVENIDA DEL FRENTE

PASEO DEL CENTENARIO

AV. AMADOR GUERRERO

AV. JUSTO AROSEMENA

Super 99

Banco Nacional

Infotech

HSBC

Laundry

Barber

Laundry

AVENIDA MELÉNDEZ

CALLE 10

CALLE 11

CALLE 12

CALLE 13

CALLE 8

CALLE 9

CALLE 10

CALLE 11

AVENIDA SANTA ISABEL

CALLE 13

CALLE 15

CALLE 16

COLÓN ZONE 2000

PASEO GORGAS

Río Folk

ZONA LIBRE (FREE ZONE)

CRISTÓBAL PORT

Bus Terminal

CALLE 14

CALLE 16

Train Station

Panama Yacht Club

AVENIDA BOYD ROOSEVELT

RAINBOW CITY

N

ACCOMMODATION
Hotel Andros   C
Hotel Carlton   B
Hotel International   D
Hotel Meryland   A

EATING & DRINKING
Don Pepe   3
Garcia Panadería   2
Grand Café   1
Kikos Cafe   4

0   500 m

slip into decline. Its fortunes revived somewhat with the early stages of the French canal construction in 1879, though it suffered another setback in 1885, when Pedro Prestan, a Haitian rebel, burned it to the ground. Rebuilt by the French, it prospered again when the US took up the canal construction effort. By the 1950s, Colón was Panama's main port. Despite this, and the success of the Free Zone (founded in 1949), the rest of the city was slowly eroding – the employment that had vanished when the canal was completed in 1914 profoundly undermined the city. The

situation today remains much the same: although the port and Free Zone continue to thrive, little of the money they generate stays in Colón – indeed many of the workers in these areas live in Panama City. In the face of extreme poverty and unemployment levels, the crime rate – particularly drug-related crime – has rocketed.

What to see and do

From the bus terminal, a left turn takes you north up **Avenida del Frente**. Running along the waterfront of Bahía Limón,

SAFETY IN COLÓN

Although sometimes exaggerated, Colón's reputation throughout the rest of the country for **violent crime** is not undeserved, and if you come here you should exercise extreme caution – mugging, even on the main streets in broad daylight, does happen. Don't carry anything you can't afford to lose, try to stay in sight of the police on the main streets and take **taxis** whenever possible. Many drivers will give tours of the city (about US$10/hr); consider hiring one out if you want to have a look around the city.

it was once the city's main commercial road but is now crumbling. Just off it on Calle 6, the **Colón Boxing Arena** was built in the 1970s to nurture the mass of local talent, including "Panama Al" Brown, one of the greatest boxers of all time, but today there's little to see other than a wallful of photographs. The **New Washington Hotel** (☎441 7133, ⓦwww .newwashingtonhotel.com), at the north-ernmost end of Av del Frente, was built in 1913 and has clung onto its chandeliers and marble stairs, doing its best to live in the past. Famous guests have included Bob Hope, who entertained troops here during World War II, and former British Prime Minister David Lloyd George. Its rooms are vastly overpriced but you could always come for a drink on the seafront veranda and watch the ships in the bay.

Cristóbal

Behind the bus terminal is the port enclave of **Cristóbal**, formerly part of the Canal Zone and still one of Latin America's busiest ports, handling more than two million tons of cargo a year. Apart from the yacht club (see p.624) there's not much of interest here and most of the port is off-limits to visitors anyway.

Colón Free Zone

The southeast corner of Colón is occupied by the **Zona Libre**, or Free Zone (ⓦwww .colonfreezone.com). Covering more than a square kilometre, this is the second biggest duty-free zone in the world after Hong Kong, with an annual turnover

of more than US$10 billion. Colón's residents are not allowed in unless they work there, but you and your wallet are free to enter if you present your passport at the gate. Once inside you'll find that the streets (as potholed as everywhere else in Colón) are lined with nothing but shops, big and small, and brand names of all shapes and sizes clinging to every patch of grimy wall. Most of the trade is in bulk orders, but you can sometimes buy individual items at low prices – shop around. You may be approached by someone asking what you are here to buy – they aim to act as your personal haggler but it is better to go it alone. Officially, goods bought here must be sent to the international airport for you to pick up as you leave the country. Although the shop workers and checkpoint guards will not always enforce this, be prepared for it to happen.

Near the Free Zone, an enclave known as **Colón Zone 2000** has been set up in the hopes of luring passengers from the many cruise ships that pass through the canal, but it has little to offer besides souvenir shops and a fairly hopeless IPAT office.

Arrival and information

By boat Yachts coming through the canal dock outside the Panama Canal Yacht Club in Cristóbal, behind the bus station, and you can usually pick up taxis in the vicinity.

By bus The bus terminal is on the corner of Av del Frente & C 13. Buses arrive from Panama City every 20–30min, 4am–10pm. Don't linger – jump into one of the many taxis that cluster in the nearby streets.

Tourist information There's an IPAT in Colón Zone 2000 (Mon–Fri 8.30am–4.30pm; ☏ 475 2301, Ⓦ www.ipat.gob.pa or Ⓦ www.visitpanama.com), but it is not overburdened with useful information.

City transport

Taxis Most trips in the city will cost US$1. You can also hire drivers for around US$10/hr, plus a bit more for stopping and starting, to take you around the city. A couple of drivers worth seeking out for their friendliness and street smarts are Teddy Luna (☏ 6584 3780) and Ruperto McClean (☏ 6471 6081 or 441 8428). Both speak fluent English.

Accommodation

If you are going to stay overnight, it's worth splashing out on a more expensive hotel with armed security and a restaurant so you won't have to go out at night.

Hotel Andros Av Herrera ☏ 441 0477, Ⓦ www .hotelandros.com. Very clean but a little cramped-feeling. Rooms have cable TV, private bathrooms and a/c. There's internet, too, and a restaurant (fried chicken and rice $4) – two fewer reasons to go wandering round the city. ⑥

Hotel Carlton Av Mélendez and C 10 ☏ 447 0111/0349, Ⓔ oscalo85@hotmail.com. A weary but proud place, with photographs of the canal, a display of flags and an impressive central staircase in the lobby. The rooms (en suite, a/c) are a bit shabby considering the price but they have a good selection of in-house services, including a restaurant (mains US$6–8), laundry and pharmacy. ⑤

Hotel Internacional Av Bolívar ☏ 445 2930 or 441 8879. Threadbare rooms with a/c, private bath and TV. The restaurant downstairs does sandwiches (US$2–3), breakfast (US$2–3) and standard mains (US$4–7). ⑤

Hotel Meryland C 7, opposite Parque Sucre ☏ 441 7055/7127, Ⓦ www.hotelmeryland.com. Little atmosphere, but it's tucked away in a leafy and relatively safe patch of the city and a cut above all other options. Smart, tiled, spacious and professionally staffed, with beds fit for coin bouncing. The restaurant serves soups (US$2.50) and a good selection of mains (US$7). ⑥

Eating

Though Colón's kitchens are known for their Caribbean influence and heavy reliance on seafood, spices and coconut milk, the most authentic places are too riskily situated to visit safely. If you can find a willing cab driver, ask to be escorted to the little

red streetside grill opposite *Hotel Carlton*. Its fresh and cheap pepper-stuffed fish (US$2) is a favourite and comes with *patacones*. *Garcia Panadería*, a bakery at the corner of Paseo del Centenario and C 12, is also worth a visit, but again, only by taxi.

Café Maritano's Next to the IPAT office in Colón Zone 2000 (see opposite). This place lies in wait for cruise-ship passengers missing their fancy coffee drinks; grab a latte for US$2.50.

Don Pepe In the bus terminal. A tiny kiosk to one side of the food counter's seating area, it has a green sign with yellow writing and sells excellent sticky buns (US$0.60) for your journey.

Grand Café At the northeast end of town near Washington Drive ☏ 433 2092. Smoke a hookah and enjoy the view of the boats bobbing off shore. Buzzy atmosphere but professional attitude; the menu includes pizza (medium US$4–6), falafel (US$5), meat and fish dishes (US$8–12) and more.

Kikos Café A US$2 taxi ride to the Arco Iris neighbourhood (also known as Rainbow City) will bring you to this cosy little restaurant. The area is much calmer than Colón proper and the owner keeps a watchful eye so that you can relax and enjoy stuffed fish (US$5), *bacalao* (US$5) or smoked pork chops (US$5) out on the shady terrace. All dishes come with coconut rice and *patacones*.

Directory

Exchange There is a branch of Banco Nacional in the Free Zone on C 14 and another on Av Bolívar near C 10 (Mon–Fri 8am–3pm).

Internet Infotech (daily 8am–pm; US$1/hr) is on Av Herrera near C 10.

Laundry On the corner of Av Santa Isabel & C 9, in a relatively safe part of town.

Pharmacy In the Super 99 supermarket on Av Bolívar.

Post office On C 9 near Av Balboa (Mon–Fri 7am–6pm, Sat 7am–5pm).

Telephones There are public phones in Colón Zone 2000.

Moving on

By boat To enquire about linehandling opportunities along the canal go to the Panama Canal Yacht Club, behind the bus station, and speak to the yacht owners. Though theoretically possible, the chances of getting a ride from one of the freight ships that leave Colón for Kuna Yala and Colombia are extremely slim; this is also not a particularly safe way to travel, as it's impossible to tell what ships are drug-running.

By bus to: Gatún Locks (every 20min until 5pm; 15min); La Guaira (6 daily; 2hr–2hr 30min); Miramar (6 daily; 3hr); Nombre de Dios (6 daily; 2hr–2hr 30min); Portobelo (every 30min until 9.45pm; 1hr 30min); Panama City (local every 30min until 10pm, 2hr 30min; express every 45min until 8.30pm, 2hr).

By taxi A cab to Fort San Lorenzo (no bus service) runs US$30–40 return plus waiting time.

AROUND COLÓN

If you don't fancy a taxi tour of Colón, then get straight onto a bus to the mighty Gatún Locks or splash out on a cab to the beautiful and atmospheric Fort San Lorenzo.

Gatún Locks

From Colón, a road runs 10km southwest to the Gatún Locks (daily 8am–3.45pm), where ships transit between Lago Gatún and Bahía Limón. The nearly two-kilometre-long locks, which raise and lower ships the 26.5m between the lake and sea level in three stages, are among the canal's most monumental engineering features. The observation platform at the visitors' centre is so close to the canal that you could speak quite easily to anyone on deck of the ships – your best chance of having a chat is between 9am and 11am, and after 3pm.

Buses from Colón terminal (see above) will drop you just before a swing bridge by a road branching off to the left; the visitors' centre and entrance to the observation deck is a five- to ten-minute walk down this road. You will see an HSBC ATM and a gift shop (daily 8am–3.45pm) where you buy your US$5 entrance ticket. A taxi from Colón costs about US$5 each way, plus more for waiting time.

Fort San Lorenzo

With a spectacular setting on a promontory above the Caribbean and overlooking the mouth of the Río Chagres, Fort San Lorenzo is the most impressive Spanish fortification still standing in Panama. Until the construction of the railway, the Chagres was the main cargo route across the isthmus to Panama City, and thus of enormous strategic importance to Spain. The first fortifications to protect the entrance to the river were built here in 1595, but the fort was taken by Francis Drake in 1596 and, though heavily reinforced, fell again to Henry Morgan's pirates in December 1670. Morgan then proceeded up the Chagres and across the isthmus to ransack Panama City. The fortifications that remain today were built in the mid-eighteenth century. The site as a whole is imposing, with a moat surrounding stout stone walls and great cannons looking out from the embrasures, all of it kept in isolation by the dense rainforest all around.

Fort San Lorenzo can only be reached by taxi. With waiting time it is a US$30–40 return trip from Colón, one hour each way, passing through rainforest and the former US training base of Fort Sherman, which until 1999 was home to the 17,000-acre US Army Jungle Warfare Training Center. If a vessel is passing through Gatún Locks you may be stuck on either side for around an hour.

PORTOBELO

The Costa Arriba, stretching northeast of Colón, features lovely beaches, excellent diving and snorkelling and the historic towns of Nombre de Dios and **PORTOBELO** ("beautiful harbour"). After the former was destroyed by Francis Drake in 1597, Portobelo was founded to replace it as the Atlantic terminus of the Camino Real – the route across the isthmus along which the Spanish hauled their plundered treasures. Its setting on a deep-water bay was supposed to make it easier to defend from the ravages of pirates, and for 150 years it played host to the famous *ferias*, the grand trading events held when the Spanish treasure fleet came to collect the riches that arrived on mule trains from Panama City. Unsurprisingly, the pirates who scoured the Spanish Main – most famously Henry Morgan – could not resist the wealth concentrated in the royal warehouses here. Eventually the Spanish decided enough was enough: the treasure fleet was rerouted around Cape Horn and Portobelo's star began to fade. Even though the town today has a somewhat depressed atmosphere,

the remnants and ruins of its former glories retain an evocative power. More powerful still – at least to the thousands of pilgrims who come to gaze on it – is the agonized face of the small Black Christ statue in the Church of San Felipe. As an outsider to the traditions, it is fascinating to consider what enormous significance can be projected onto one small object.

What to see and do

Most of the town is pretty down-at-heel, with the **ruins** being the main attraction. Walking into Portobelo along the road from Colón brings you to the well-preserved **Santiago Battery**, which still features fourteen rusting but menacing cannons. The road then leads to the main tree-shaded plaza, just off which stands the **Casa Real de la Aduana** (daily 8am–4pm; US$1), the royal customs house, which has been restored with Spanish help and now houses a small museum. It was the biggest civil building in colonial Panama and stored the Camino Real treasure awaiting transport to Spain. As well as a brief exhibition outlining the history of Portobelo, the museum has a display of the purple robes donated each year to the revered Black Christ (see below). The icon itself can be found in the large, white **Church of San Felipe**, on the square a further one hundred metres

THE BLACK CHRIST OF PORTOBELO

Without question the most revered religious figure in Panama, the Black Christ of Portobelo draws tens of thousands of pilgrims to the town every October. A small figure carved from black cocobolo wood with an agonized face and eyes raised to heaven, the Black Christ is reputed to possess miraculous powers. The origins of the icon still remain something of a mystery. Some say that it was found floating in the sea during a cholera epidemic, which ended after the Christ was brought into the town; others maintain it was on a ship bound for Colombia that stopped at Portobelo for supplies and was repeatedly prevented from leaving the bay by bad weather, sailing successfully only when the statue was left ashore. Every year on October 21 up to fifty thousand devotees, known as Nazarenos and dressed in purple robes, come to Portobelo for a huge procession that is followed by festivities throughout the night.

If you plan to visit Portobelo or points further east, be aware that there are **no ATMs** past Colón and – make sure to take money out in one of those two towns before making your way to the coast.

along the road. Looking out onto the bay behind the church is the **San Geronimo Battery** – creep to its outermost edge and peep out through the arrow slats.

Arrival and information

By bus Buses for Portobelo leave from Colón; if you're coming from Panama City and want to avoid Colón, change at the Rey supermarket in Sabanitas, 14km before Colón. Buses from Colón arrive every 30min and stop near the Church of San Felipe in the centre of town, within a few minutes' walk from all the town's main sights and accommodation.
Internet Internet Enilda, on the square near the church, has two computers (Mon–Fri 9am–5pm; US$1/hr), a scanner, printer and photocopier.
Telephones There's a public phone next to *Restaurante Yaci* on the square near the church.
Tour operator Panama Divers (℡314 0817 or 6613 4405, ⊛www.panamadivers.com/portobelo .htm) works with *Coco Plum* (see below) and offers a package for US$125 that includes transportation from your Panama City accommodation, two day-dives in Portobelo (with a Divemaster) and tours of the ruins there.
Tourist information IPAT have a CEFATI office (Mon–Fri 8.30am–4.30pm; ℡448 2200) – a more visitor-friendly version of their regular offices, with information displayed visually – at the fork in the road as it enters town.

Accommodation

Bar-Disco La Aduana On the main plaza by the Casa Real de la Aduana ℡6529 6322 or 448 2925 (ask for Odalis). There are basic en-suite rooms above this bar. Don't stay here on a weekend if you want to get any sleep. ❸
🏃 **Coco Plum** On the road towards Colón ℡264 1338, ⊛www.cocoplum-panama .com. This place, a few minutes' drive from the town centre, has luxurious cabins (with TV and a/c) that sleep up to four people as well as two simpler backpacker rooms. The cute wooden pier has a little dining area and the bar looks out onto the ocean. If heading here from central Portobelo

take one of the rare taxis (US$2) or jump on a bus bound for Colón or Sabanitas; if coming from Colón, ask the bus driver to drop you on the way into town. Rooms ❹, cabins ❼
Hospedaje Sangui On the road to Nombre de Dios/Isla Grande ℡448 2204 or 6651 8972. The helpful English-speaking owner offers basic, clean rooms with fan and shared bath. Prices are often negotiable. ❹

Eating

Las Anglas At the *Coco Plum* ℡264 1338. Specializes in fish dishes (US$8–12), with alternatives including burgers (US$5) and breakfast ($3).
Restaurante Ida On the square near the church. Offers meat stews and fried fish dishes (US$3–4), and can rustle up a veggie-friendly plate of rice, beans and plantain for US$2.
Restaurante Yaci On the square near the church. Expect good, simple Caribbean-influenced food, like rice, salad and spicy octopus in coconut milk (US$4).

Moving on

By bus to: Colón (every 30min until 6pm; 1hr 30min); La Guaira (6 daily; 30min–1hr); Miramar (6 daily; 1hr 30min–2hr); Nombre de Dios (6 daily; 30min–1hr).

AROUND PORTOBELO

Exploring this area means exploring the coast. Isla Grande is a well-established getaway for Panamanians and tourists alike, while a more adventurous trip may be possible from the village of Miramar, where you might catch a ride on a trading boat all the way to Kuna Yala.

Parque Nacional Portobelo

The rugged coast around Portobelo is officially part of the **Parque Nacional Portobelo**, and although the area receives little protection or responsible management – you don't need permission from ANAM to enter – it does have good **beaches** and some of the best diving and snorkelling on the Caribbean coast, including coral reefs, shipwrecks and, somewhere in front of Isla de Drake, the as-yet-undiscovered grave of Francis Drake, buried at sea in a lead coffin after he died of dysentery in 1596. Most of this area can be reached only by sea; you can either hire a boatman in town or join an excursion with PADI-certified *Panama Divers* (see p.627).

Miramar

Around six buses daily go from Colón all the way to **Miramar**, passing through Portobelo on the way. The second-to-last stop along this stretch of coastline, the town is mainly of use as a possible jumping-off point for Kuna Yala, the frontier of which is about 25km further east along the coast. **Kuna trading boats** travel between Miramar and the *comarca* – you may be able to catch a lift with one of these. You will need to be at the village's dock no later than 10am. Expect to pay around US$10–15, though this may

be negotiable. The journey can take anywhere from four to seven hours: the boats head first to El Porvenir and then on to other points on the coast. Note that between January and April the seas are often too rough for this journey. Check with Serge, the owner of *Hotel Restaurant Paraíso* in Miramar (☎6689 4943 ⒺE sergelaverre@hotmail.com, ⓦwww .paraisomiramar.blogspot.com; ❹–❺), before making the trip to town. The hotel has a swimming pool and serves high-quality cooking; camping may also be permitted.

ISLA GRANDE

Some 12km northeast along the coast from Portobelo, a side road branches off the badly potholed pavement and runs a few kilometres to the tiny village of **La Guaira**, from where launches provide transport to **ISLA GRANDE**, a hugely popular weekend resort for residents of Colón and Panama City.

Though undeniably beautiful, friendly and relaxed, with some good beaches, Isla Grande is no more spectacular than other parts of Costa Arriba. It does, however, have better facilities. The best **swimming beach**, known as "La Punta", is around the island to the right (southwest) as you face the mainland; the beach round the other side is good for **surfing**. For snorkellers, there's plenty to see around the Christ statue in front of the village, though beware of the current beyond the reef and of passing boats. Sundays, in particular, can be extremely crowded, but if you are in the mood for drinking and socializing then weekends here could well be for you. The island is much quieter during the week.

Arrival and information

By boat Launches (US$2) to Isla Grande leave from La Guaira. There are around six buses daily from Colón to La Guaira, via Portobelo. The last one back to Colón, via Portobelo, leaves at 1pm (Mon–Sat) or 4pm (Sun). Check with locals that this timetable holds.

Accommodation

During the summer and at weekends it's worth booking ahead.

Hotel Sister Moon ☎6661 6740. In a great elevated position in the northeast of the island with fine views of the ocean, the single rooms here are basic, and rather musty. There are also a few "backpacker" bunk beds, but these are sometimes only offered on weekdays, so book ahead. Bring a towel and a sheet or sleeping bag. Dorms ❷, singles ❹

Super Cabañas Jackson On the seafront main path ☎448 2311. The rooms are a little threadbare and uninteresting, but this place is about as cheap as it gets on the island. Their rates tend to vary a little, so do ring ahead to check prices and book. ❹

Eating

Candy Rose This place is strong on seafood dishes, often with the spiciness that is popular along this coastline (US$7 and upwards).

Villa Ensueño Near the Christ statue. Offers a similar deal to *Candy Rose* and does great fried fish and *patacones* for around $6.

Moving on

By boat Launches to La Guaira cost US$2.

Darién

The sparsely populated 17,000 square kilometres that make up **Darién** is one of the last great, untamed **wildernesses** in America. The beginning of an immense forest that continues almost unbroken across the border into the Chocó region of Colombia and down the Pacific coast to Ecuador, this was the first region on the American mainland to be settled by the Spanish. Although they extracted great wealth from **gold mines** deep in the forest at Cana, they were never able to establish effective control over the region, hampered by the almost impassable terrain, the fierce resistance put up by its inhabitants and European pirates and bands of renegade African slaves known as *cimarrones*.

The **Interamericana** is the only road that takes the plunge and enters the region, but it goes no farther than the settlement of **Yaviza**, 276km east of Panama City. Along the border with Colombia, the **Parque Nacional Darién**, the largest and most important protected area in Panama, safeguards

---

THE PEOPLE OF DARIÉN

Darién's population is made up of three main groups: black, indigenous and colonist.

Other than a few Kuna communities, the indigenous population of Darién is composed of two closely related but distinct peoples, the Wounaan and the more numerous Emberá, both semi-nomadic South American rainforest societies. Recognizable by the black geometric designs with which they decorate their bodies, the Emberá-Wounaan, as they are collectively known, have been migrating across the border from Colombia for the past two centuries. Only since the 1960s have they begun to settle in permanent villages and establish official recognition of their territorial rights in the form of a *comarca*, divided into two districts: the Comarca Emberá Cemaco, in the north, and the Comarca Emberá Sambú, in the southwest.

The black people of Darién, descended from *cimarrones* and released slaves, are known as Dariénitas or libres (the free) and are culturally distinct from the Afro-Antillano populations of Colón and Panama City (see p.605).

The colonists, meanwhile, are the most recent arrivals, poor peasants driven off their lands in western Panama by expanding cattle ranches and encouraged to settle in Darién during the construction of the Darién Highway. Many colonists still wear their distinctive straw sombreros as a badge of identity and maintain the folk traditions of the regions they abandoned.

vast swathes of forest that support one of the most pristine and biologically diverse ecosystems in the world, as well as a large indigenous population.

In recent times, the combination of drug trafficking and the decades-long Colombian **civil war** spilling over into Panama has made the border area utterly treacherous. The Marxist guerrillas of the Colombian Revolutionary Armed Forces (FARC) have long maintained bases close to the border in Darién, but right-wing paramilitary groups backed by powerful landowners and drug traffickers have taken to pursuing them, terrorizing isolated Panamanian communities they accuse of harbouring the guerrillas. Given the **security**

concerns affecting the border area, including parts of the national park and the Comarca Emberá Cemaco, a visit to southwestern Darién is the safest way to experience the ecology and culture of the region independently. Currently it is not advisable to go further south than the mouth of the Sambú River. Once in Darién, check whenever you can for news of recent incidents or developments.

THE DARIÉN HIGHWAY

East of Panama City the **DARIÉN HIGHWAY** (the Interamericana) is well paved as far as Lago Bayano, after which the pace slows down considerably and the road becomes gravelly

DARIÉN PRACTICALITIES

Most people who travel to Darién go with a tour. However, taking everything into your own hands and going independently is entirely feasible (see box, p.632, for travel information to and within the region). This course of action does require a certain leap of faith – you cannot plan every last detail before you leave – and some knowledge of Spanish, but the very fact that it is not a simple undertaking is what makes it so special. Before making the journey to Darién it is a good idea to check with ANAM in Panama City and the Darién National Park office at El Real (☎299 6965) regarding the current safety situation in the region. The office in Panama City will likely be more discouraging than the staff at the El Real office, who are more in tune with the day-to-day developments.

Supplies
Whether you go with a tour operator or on your own, there are a few items you should take with you.

Clothing You will want long pants and long-sleeved shirts, partly to keep the huge variety of insect life at bay, but also because it can get quite cool during the night. Do not take or wear anything that resembles army fatigues or has a camouflage pattern.

Equipment You will be able to pick up basic provisions (including bottled water), but it is advisable to pack a small supply of food even so, a ration of bottled water, and water-purifying tablets. If you are sleeping on a floor in a village you will need something to sleep on, in or under, and a mosquito net. Bring a cover for your pack for boat travel and damp conditions. A large stash of US$1 bills is recommended.

Medication You should start taking anti-malaria medication well before you arrive. Be aware that chloroquine is not sufficient in Darién – check the exact requirements with your doctor before your trip.

Tour operators
There are several operators in Panama City that run trips to Darién, ranging from short stays to two-week, trans-Darién treks.

Advantage Panama ⊛www.advantagepanama.com/darienadventure. Runs a good-value "Darién Adventure" tour (US$197), setting off from Tortí, which is located on the Interamericana around 50km beyond Lago Bayano. This company is also involved in important conservation work.

Ancon Expeditions ⊛www.anconexpeditions.com. Roundly praised but very expensive tours – their three-day "Coastal Darién Explorer" package is US$625.

Exotics Adventures ☎223 9283 or 6673 5381, ⊛www.panamaexoticsadventures .com. A French-owned outfit that offers slightly more affordable packages (US$500–600 for a three-day, two-night tour) and also owns some beautiful lodges for those willing to splash out even more.

Panamaniac ☎6718 2826, ⊛www.panamaniac.net. Director Vincent Westmaas is an excellent source of information regarding travel in the region and is happy to give advice, whether or not you take one of his tours.

for long stretches. Just before the lake, the highway passes through the quiet village of El Llano, where a side road leads up towards **Kuna Yala** (see p.637). From the lake the highway rolls on for 196km through a desolate, deforested landscape, passing Emberá-Wounaan hamlets, with their characteristic open-walled houses raised on stilts, and half-hearted roadside settlements. The results of illegal logging on either side of the highway – leaving behind low-grade cattle pasture – are plain to see. The highway ends on the banks of the Río Chucunaque at **Yaviza**, the start of the Darién Gap, though most buses only go as far as **Metetí**, fifty kilometres before Yaviza and 25km beyond **Santa Fe**.

DARIÉN TRAVEL

To get to Darién independently, you can either fly or take the bus. Once you've arrived, boats are the best way to get around.

Getting there

By air Both Aeroperlas (☎315 7500, ⊛www.aeroperlas.com) and Air Panama (☎316 9000, ⊛www.flyairpanama.com) offer flights to Darién (US$100 return). Aeroperlas currently flies to Bahía Piña only, in the far south of the region – not a particularly useful starting-point. Air Panama flies to La Palma, Sambú and Garachine, all of which lie near the Gulf of Panama coast and are good jumping-off points for boat-based exploration of the more accessible – and much safer – parts of Darién.

By bus Buses run from Panama City to Metetí (hourly 4am–6am, every 1hr 30min 7.15am–4.15pm; 6hr 30min) and to Yaviza (4am & 5am; 8hr 30min). Both of these small towns lie to the north of – and make good gateways to – the parts of the region that are accessible to (and usually safe for) visitors.

Getting around

By boat The inhabitants of Darién use *piraguas* – motorized dug-out canoes – as well as slightly more modern boats. It is difficult to estimate costs of boat travel, particularly as fuel prices were rising steadily at the time of writing. In general, you will find trips far cheaper if you can latch onto someone who is already heading in the direction you want to go (trading or fishing boats), so you are simply hitching a ride, rather than chartering a boat and crew. A ride from La Palma to Mogué, for instance, could be as little as US$5 if you find someone who is already going there, or upwards of US$100 (return) if you have to hire someone's services.

Santa Fe

You can hop off the bus at **Santa Fe**, around 25km before Metetí, and pay a visit to the indigenous Wounaan village of **Puerto Lara** (also known as Boca de Lara). Call Neldo Pisario (only Spanish spoken; ☎6702 0434), the tourism committee president, to arrange your visit and accommodation, should you wish to stay the night. The road to the village is being steadily improved and he will be able to tell you if *chivas* are currently running along it. If not, you will need to take one from Santa Fe to the port in La Cantera (20min), from where Neldo will make sure there's a boat to the village. The cost of the boat ride varies, so ask ahead – it can be as much as US$45 with return. In terms of **accommodation**, you will stay in one of two purpose-built tourist houses (❸). Meals are US$2.50 and guided trail tours and fishing trips are around US$15. When you're ready to

move on, one option is to hire a boat from here for the approximately two-hour ride to La Palma (see p.634).

Metetí

Fifty kilometres before Yaviza the highway passes through **Metetí**, a small roadside settlement that has grown in importance as an administrative and commercial centre in recent years. For most buses, the town's miniature **Terminal de Transporte de Darién** is the end of the road, though you can wait here for the one *chiva* (6am–5pm; 20min) that shuttles back and forth between Metetí and **Puerto Quimba**, for **water-taxis** (7.30am–5.30pm; 30min; US$3) to La Palma. The Puerto Quimba dock area is nothing more than a dirt road with space for vehicles to park, a pier, a police hut (where you can register your details and movements again, for safety's sake) and a tiny bar.

If you miss your onward connection in Metetí, there are payphones and a small **restaurant** at the bus terminal, and you can **stay** at the very basic *Hotel Felicidad* (☎299 6188/6544; ❷–❸).

Yaviza

Yaviza marks the end of the Interamericana and the beginning of the Darién Gap. If the police on the highway deem that it is safe to visit, then the town can be used as a gateway into the **Parque Nacional Darién**. The two daily buses from Panama City that come this far pull in beside the dock at the entrance to the town. From here, the only real street runs down to a small square. If police are present, it is advisable to check in with them so that a record of your movements exists in case of emergency. To get to the park, head down to the port in the morning, when there are likely to be lots of motorized dugout canoes (*piraguas*) trading goods. You can usually hire one of these to take you to **El Real** (US$5), where the Parque Nacional Darién office is (daily 8am–4pm; ☎299 6965). You'll need to pay the park fee here (US$5) before entering the park. Buses return from Yaviza to Panama City at 4am and 7am (8hr 30min).

PARQUE NACIONAL DARIÉN

Covering almost 5800 square kilometres of pristine rainforest along the border with Colombia, **PARQUE NACIONAL DARIÉN** is possibly the most biologically diverse region on earth – over five hundred bird species have been reported here. Inhabited by scattered indigenous communities, the park contains the largest expanse of forest in Central America that has not been affected by logging and provides a home for countless rare and endangered species, including jaguars, harpy eagles and several types of macaw. Parts of the park are normally safe to visit, but the security situation can change rapidly, so it's a good idea to phone the park office in El Real (see below), the starting point for trips into the park, or the ANAM office in Panama City (see p.606) in order to check on the current status before you arrive.

To **enter** the park you need permission from the **ANAM Parque Nacional Darién office** (daily 8am–4pm; ☎299 6965) in El Real. (Note that most of the rangers speak only Spanish.) The fee for park access is US$5 per day. Check here, too, about the relative safety and accessibility of the park's

INTO COLOMBIA: THE DARIÉN GAP

The Darién Gap is a band of dense and entirely untamed rainforest, just 100km or so in length, that keeps the northern strand of the Interamericana (Panamerican Highway) from joining up with the southern strand, thus rendering land travel from Panama to Colombia truly hazardous. Because of this, crossing the Gap has always been one of the most celebrated adventures in Latin America. However, given the present security situation we do not recommend you attempt this trip. Even if you can find guides willing to take you (no easy task in itself, given that many of the villages in the region have been attacked or overrun by bandits and the inhabitants have fled), chances are high that you will be robbed or kidnapped; many travellers have disappeared or been killed attempting this trip in recent years. It's also worth remembering that there is a war raging across the border in Colombia.

Currently the Panamanian authorities are not allowing civilians to travel east of Boca de Cupe. Should the security situation in Darién improve, however, then before crossing you must first get permission from ANAM (see p.606) as well as the Colombian consulate in Panama City. (If you have been in Panama for more than three months, make sure you have your exit permission from *migración*.) In Colombia you must register on arrival with DAS, the immigration agency.

ranger stations, all of which have basic lodges (④). One such outpost, **Pirre Station** in the Rancho Frío area of the park, is a three-hour walk through the forest from El Real and is normally safe to visit; the park office can provide a guide (US$15–20) to take you there. There are plenty of trails into the forest from Rancho Frío, including one through cloudforest to the peak of Cerro Pirre (1200m).

Necessary **supplies** include food, mosquito repellent and nets or coils, bedding and a water bottle and purifiers, even if you plan on staying at one of the ranger stations. Gifts for the park guards (such as food, drink, batteries and newspapers) are much appreciated.

LA PALMA

LA PALMA's spectacular setting, overlooking the broad mouth of the Río Tiura, surrounded by densely forested mountains and with ruined colonial forts for neighbours, makes it a worthy capital of Darién Province, however small it may be. The town clings to a steep slope that runs down to the seafront; the only **street**, a narrow strip of concrete, is the focus of all the town's pent-up energy – on weekend evenings it feels like a miniature city. Indeed, soaking up the atmosphere while you negotiate the next leg of your Darién travels is about all there is to do. Although you can easily work out how much transportation *to* La Palma will cost it is far less easy to estimate what any onward travel is likely to set you back – it will have to be by boat, and the price of fuel is steadily rising. The opportunities to come into contact with indigenous communities are greater in the Sambú area, but to get there you need to fly (although a one-way boat ride from La Palma would be around the US$150 mark), which cranks up the expense of your Darién trip from the outset. Whilst you are here it's worth telling the **police** in town where you are going next, even if it is back on yourself, and checking on any developments or incidents in the region.

Arrival and information

By air Air Panama (ⓦ www.flyairpanama.com) flights arrive from Panama City twice a week (Mon & Fri) at the airstrip, a 20min taxi ride (US$20) outside of town.

By boat Water-taxis from Puerto Quimba arrive at the dock below the main street, virtually opposite Mini Mercado La Virgen del Carmen.

Exchange There is a branch of Banco Nacional (Mon–Fri 8am–3pm) with a 24hr ATM at the far end of town if you take a right from the taxi dock.

Tourist information IPAT employee Clementino Berugate (☎ 299 6337 or 6770 8890, ⓔ cberrugate@ipat.gob.pa), whom you'll find in the MICI office (Ministerio de Comercio e Industrias; Mon–Fri 8.30am–4.30pm) opposite the Banco Nacional, can help you arrange boat travel. Also ask at the booth that sells tickets for the boat to Puerto Quimba, next to the water-taxi dock.

Accommodation

Hotel Biaquiru Bagara ☎ 299 6224. This family-run place is dashingly handsome. Rooms are wood-panelled with bamboo ceilings, and there's a large terrace upstairs with hammocks and views of the water; there's also an open-sided bar at the front looking out on the street. The owner, Profesora Lesbia Alarcon, can help you arrange boat trips but speaks only a little English. Come out of the taxi dock, turn left, keep going past the commercial dock and it is on the left in a green-painted building that says, confusingly, "Casa Ramada". ②–④

Hotel Tuiro Left from the water-taxi dock ☎ 299 6316. This blue building, just before the commercial dock, is very noisy when the bar next door gets going. Rooms are clean enough, though the doubles with a/c are significantly nicer, with firm beds; towels and soap are provided. ④

Eating

A nameless **food stand** opposite *Hotel Biaquiru Bagara* does delicious *hojaldres*, deep-fried to order, for US$0.20.

Restaurante Aqui Me Quiedo On the main street opposite *Hotel Tuiro*. The steak here is a little tough, but the sheer size of the *patacones* makes up for it; they, plus a nice salad, can be yours for US$2.50.

If you want a beer they will grab one from the bar across the road.

Moving on

By air Air Panama flights depart twice a week (Mon & Fri) from the airstrip.
By boat to: Puerto Quimba (5.30am–4.30pm; 30min). These water-taxis are met by the *chiva* back up to Metetí (see p.632). Get to the dock at least half an hour before the first boat or the last boat leaves; buy tickets from the booth next to the dock.

AROUND LA PALMA

Exploring La Palma's **surroundings** requires a bit of prep work and can be accomplished in a couple of different ways. Sometimes a cargo boat delivering and collecting goods in Darién's villages will be heading in a convenient direction, in which case you may be able to jump aboard for a fee of US$5–10. You might also pay someone to take you to your destination directly, though this would likely mean adding a zero to the price above. While taking a boat to Sambú could be costlier than flying from Panama City, you won't break the bank paying for a ride to the nearby islands of Boca Grande and Boca Chica, where you can see fortifications built by colonial Spaniards to protect the gold mine at Cana from pirates. Ask at the MICI office (see p.634) for boat travel information.

Mogué

You may be able to find a boat from La Palma headed towards **Mogue**. The trip is a fantastic two hours through the Golfo de San Miguel, past forested islands and a wild coastline fringed with mangroves and deserted beaches, and up the Río Mogué to the small Emberá community here. If you don't mind sleeping on a floor with your own sleeping gear you can **stay** the night for US$15, plus a little more for meals. To arrange your visit, contact Garcilazo, the president of the tourism committee, by calling the village's public phone (☎ 333 2513). He can arrange a short **hike** to a harpy eagle nesting site, as well as a boat from La Palma. If you find a boat that is heading this way you may only pay US$6, but if you hire one just for you it will be as much as US$100.

THE SETTLING OF NEW EDINBURGH

In the late 1600s, the Scots gambled half the country's wealth on a colony in Darién in the hopes of transforming Scotland into a trading power to rival England. A fleet of five ships and 1200 men set sail in July 1698 and, arriving in the Caribbean, attempted to trade goods and restock the ships, though their wigs, shoes, stockings, thick cloth and Bibles found few takers in the tropics. The fleet finally anchored in Caledonia Bay, and for five months the Scots worked hard to build New Edinburgh, hindered by low rations and disease. The only help they received came from the local Kuna. When, after ten months, the promised supply ships failed to materialize, the Scots set sail for home. Only one ship, the *Caledonia*, made it back to Scotland. A second fleet, however, set sail just two months after this first group abandoned the settlement, but shortly after their arrival in 1700 they drew the attention of the Spanish based in Portobelo. Small battles soon broke out – with the Kuna lending their military muscle to the Scots – but within six months the Scots finally surrendered to the Spanish. They were allowed to evacuate with full military honours, but none of the ships made it back to Scotland. The venture crippled Scotland financially, leaving the kingdom at the mercy of rival England. Several years later, in 1707, England agreed to compensate all those who had subscribed to the venture in return for the creation of a joint kingdom of England and Scotland.

SAMBÚ

The small town of **SAMBÚ** is the best place to base yourself for affordable exploration in Darién. Although there's little to do in the town itself, a day spent among the locals lends valuable insight into the simple and tough livelihoods of those inhabiting this culturally diverse and isolated community. Small cargo boats frequently stop here, and you can watch the locals unload their cargo of building supplies and petrol and then load the vessels with hardwood and empty soda bottles, as well as sacks of plantains and oranges brought downriver in small dugout canoes from the more isolated **Emberá** communities deep in the rainforest. Many of these communities welcome visitors, and making a trip along the Río Sambu to them is really the highlight of the area.

What to see and do

Exploring the area around Sambú is most rewarding if you are not restrictive about where you want to go. It is possible to hire the services of boatmen (usually two, working as a team) to take you to spend a night or two in some of the **communties** along the river where you will pay around US$5–10 for accommodation, most likely on a family's floor, plus a few dollars more for meals. You will also pay for your boatmen's accommodation and meals. As wise as it is to be courteous and affable, it's equally important to be on the ball regarding **costs** when you arrange such river trips. Agree on everything very clearly before you accept – this is where having some Spanish is very important. Transport prices are determined based on the predicted amount of gasoline required and the services of the boatmen. If you inform yourself of the current cost of gasoline, you'll be less likely to be hoodwinked – but you should remain wary of extra costs slipping in. If there is

a **police** presence in town, sign in with them; you may also be approached for payment of a **fee** (around US$10) for entry into the Sambú river area.

Arrival and information

By air Air Panama (@ www.flyairpanama.com) flights arrive from Panama City three times a week (Mon, Wed & Fri) at the airstrip just outside of the town.

Tourist information Keep an eye out for Ricardo Cabrera (@ 6687 2271, @ ricardosambu@yahoo .com), a great source of information regarding river transport. He speaks good English and has a small hotel in Sambú that offers relatively luxurious rooms (④). If you can't reach him on his cell phone try the community phone at @ 333 2512.

Accommodation and eating

You can ask the people who live in Sambú if anyone there could put you up for the night – this will almost certainly be possible. You will normally be asked for US$5–10 per night for **lodging** and a little more for food. The owners of *Sambú Hause* (see box below) can arrange for you to stay in sleeping quarters in the village owned by Juancito, a local who works with the owners in arranging trips for the *Sambú Hause* guests. He charges around US25 per night, not including meals.

TREAT YOURSELF

If you feel like laying your head somewhere homely after a day's exploration, heave your trembling river legs to Sambú Hause (@ 6766 5102, @ www .sambuhausedarienpanama .com), about 500m from the Sambú airstrip. Rooms are clean and comfortable and there's a sitting room, kitchen and porch with an outdoor grill. Maria, one of the owners, can show you around the village and arrange river trips (US$35/hr) and jungle treks to interior villages (US$15/hr). The owners can also help with arranging lodging in the village (see above). This is one of the few affordable upscale accommodation options in Darien. Rates include meals. ⑨

There's a restaurant next to the small dock in Sambú, plus a number of small shops selling a range of supplies, including pots and pans, tinned foods and instant noodles.

Moving on

By air Air Panama flights depart three times a week for Panama City (Mon, Wed & Fri) from the airstrip. You should confirm your flight at least an hour before your scheduled departure at the hut behind the main drag in town.

Kuna Yala

Stretching nearly four hundred kilometres, **Kuna Yala** – the autonomous *comarca* (territory) of the Kuna people – takes in the narrow band of mainland Panama north of the Serranía de San Blas and the sweep of nearly four hundred tropical islands that is the **San Blas Archipelago**. The Kuna like to say that there is one island for every day of the year. However, only around forty of the islands are inhabited, some straining to contain towns, others little more than sandbanks that a lone family has made their home, and you're unlikely to visit more than a handful.

The Kuna have gradually made their way here over the centuries, migrating first from Colombia to the Darién region sometime in the sixteenth century. Abandoning that area after years of struggles with the Spanish and the Emberá tribe, they settled afresh along the coast and on the San Blas islands in the nineteenth century, but it took what they call "the Revolution" in 1925 to have the territory recognized as theirs alone. To this day, no non-Kuna may live in the *comarca*; it's a privilege just to enter it and an even greater one to hop among the islands, soaking their beauty, and to spend the night in the midst of the community, perhaps sleeping in the same room as a Kuna family. Learning a little about their cultural heritage and how it informs their personal worldview (particularly amongst the younger Kuna) and observing the fascinating ins and outs of island life are excellent reasons to come here – even if you can't stand beautiful beaches.

KUNA CULTURE

Kuna society is regulated by a system of highly participative democracy: every community has a *casa de congreso* where the *onmakket*, or congress, meets regularly. Each community also elects a *sahila*, usually a respected elder, who attends the Kuna General Congress twice a year. The General Congress is the supreme political authority in Kuna Yala, and in turn appoints three *cacique* to represent the Kuna in the national government.

Colonial missionaries struggled in vain to Christianize the Kuna, who cling to their own religious beliefs, based above all on the sanctity of Nan Dummad, the Great Mother, and on respect for the environment they inhabit. Though Kuna men wear standard Western clothes, Kuna women wear gold rings in their ears and noses and blue vertical lines painted on their foreheads; they don headscarves and bright bolts of trade cloth round their waists, their forearms and calves are bound in coloured beads and their blouses are sewn with beautiful reverse-appliqué designs known as molas.

Given that no non-Kuna is permitted to live on the islands and that tourism is a prickly issue here, your status as an outsider is symbolic and your behaviour will likely be scrutinized. Cover up unless it is clearly fine to do otherwise, and cut out public displays of affection. You must ask permission to visit the islands – ask advice of people you meet to find a contact – and to take photographs.

What to see and do

If you are coming to Kuna Yala as part of a tour, you will most likely be booked into accommodation on either Cartí Yantupu or Cartí Sugtupu. Most package rates include three meals per day and one day-trip **excursion**. These are almost always to pretty, uninhabited or nearly uninhabited islands, where you'll be dropped off in the morning and picked up in the afternoon. Of the most regularly visited day-trip destinations, tiny **Dog Island** (Achutupu/Isla Perro) is one of the most enjoyable – a cargo ship was wrecked here in the 1940s, making for great snorkelling. Other trips are sometimes made to **Kuna cemeteries** on the mainland; ask at your accommodation for the rundown of possible destinations. All the islands are owned by someone, and when your hotel drops you off for your afternoon of sun-drenched laziness you will most likely be approached for your payment of a "visitor tax", usually US$1. Be aware also that anything surplus to your package will cost twice what you'd expect to pay on the mainland. When you go out on your excursion, make sure to bring **water** and something to do, whether it's a book or snorkelling gear.

If you're heading here on your own, most lodgings accept independent bookings and will pick you up from the airstrip. Often there will be no charge for this – confirm in advance – although if you are heading to Isla Tigre you will have to pay for transfer from the Corazón de Jesus airstrip (see p.640). For individual accommodation **listings**, see the island accounts that follow. Unless otherwise stated, accommodation prices – both packages and independently arranged – include three meals and one excursion. Your first night's accommodation on San Blas will have a **surcharge** of US$2 – a tax for entry into the *comarca*. Bring a flashlight, as electricity is usually switched off around 10pm, if there is any at all.

El Porvenir

El Porvenir is the administrative capital of Kuna Yala and home to the airport

KUNA YALA

SAN BLAS

Wichudup

Masargandup

Ukuptupu ✈ El Porvenir

Wichub Wala
Nalunega

Achutupu (Dog Island)

Isla Corbisky

Isla Yerba (Kagantupu)

Ogobsibudup (Coco Blanco)

Isla Aguja (Needle Island/Icodub)

Isla Robinson

GOLFO DE SAN BLAS

Narranjos Grandes

Cartí Yantupu

Cartí Sugtupu

✈ Cartí

N

Río Sidra

✈ Río Sidra

for the nearby islands of Wichub Wala, Nalunega and Ukuptupu, whose hotels send boats to await the flights. If you haven't reserved a place to stay the boatmen should be able to sort you out on their cellphones. If not, you could try for a bed here at *Hotel Porvenir* (☏221 1397 or 6692 3542, ⓦwww .hotelporvenir.com; ⓪). This is the only one of these four islands that you can swim at – at the others the toilets flush straight into the sea – but it's better to push on if possible, as there's really nothing of interest here.

Nalunega

Hotel San Blas (☏6749 9667, ⓔhotel sanblas@hotmail.com; ⓪–⓪), on **Nalunega**, is the biggest and oldest hotel on the islands. Fenced off from the village with its own stretch of beach, it offers a choice of basic rooms (with gaps between the top of the walls and the ceiling) in a modern concrete building, or cooler sand-floored cabins on the pleasant beach in front (no swimming). Bathrooms are shared. The owner, Luis Burgos, and several of the staff speak some English.

Wichub Wala

Kuna Niskua (☏259 9136 or 6709 4484; ⓪) on **Wichub Wala** offers smart cabañas with private cold-water bathrooms, a communal dining area and an elevated terrace slung with hammocks. There's a nice village feel here and you can wander around and pick up some good-value handicrafts (US$5–20). There's a telephone here and a flag flying above the island, red and gold with a reverse swastika, symbolizing the Kuna revolution.

Ukuptupu

Cabañas Ukuptupu (☏6514 2788 or 293 8709, ⓦwww.ukuptupu.com; ⓪), on **Ukuptupu**, occupies a former Smithsonian marine research station built on a tiny, semi-submerged coral outcrop. Cool, well-built rooms connect via walkways over the sea, and a bar and pool table and a small beach area with hammocks (no swimming) make up for the lack of a Kuna community here. The family takes pride in its business, serving up excellent food with daily menu changes and a stock of veggie-friendly

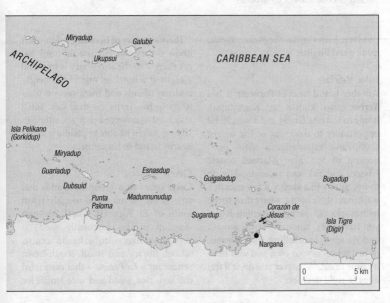

Budget-wise, the best way to experience the San Blas Archipelago is to book a package visit through one of the Panama City hostels (see p.606). However, it is also possible to visit independently.

With a tour

Tours to the region usually comprise transport by 4WD to the Cartí River (US$20–25 each way), pick-up from here by the owners of the accommodation you have been booked into (usually on Cartí Sugtupu or Cartí Yantupu) and transport to the islands. A night's stay as part of a package will cost US$25–35; this usually includes three meals and a day-trip to a more picturesque island.

On your own

By air Aeroperlas (☎ 315 7500, ⓦ www.aeroperlas.com) and Air Panama (☎ 316 9000, ⓦ www.flyairpanama.com) together service the islands daily. Flights (US$50–55) leave from Marcos A. Gelabert domestic airport in Albrook. In the Archipelago, the principal airstrip for visitors is on El Porvenir, though you should fly to the airstrip on the island of Corazón de Jesús if visiting Isla Tigre. Flights are frequently delayed or cancelled, but there are sometimes flights not listed on the website, so phone in advance. Luggage exceeding 12kg incurs a surcharge of $0.50 per kilogram. Flying between the islands is more difficult – see the Aeroperlas website for the few connection possibilities.

By boat Though by no means the easiest option, it is possible to get a ride from Miramar, on the Costa Arriba, aboard a boat bringing supplies to the islands. Boats travel to El Porvenir and sometimes further east. Boat transfer to the islands is usually an additional fee if you are booking your own transport.

By road In good conditions, a 4WD can whisk you from Panama City to the Cartí River in 3–4hr. From the drop-off it's a short boat transfer to the islands. In wet conditions, though, the time can easily double. This is the preferred package-tour mode of transport, but you can also book your own ride for US$20 each way by calling Rigoberto González (☎ 6527 3367), his partner Boyd (☎ 6719 9889) or Alexis Lam (☎ 6634 9384 or 6528 5862).

---

produce. Juan Garcia, the owner, speaks quite good English.

Isla Yerba

Another island near El Porvenir is **Isla Yerba** (also known as Kagantupu), home to just one family and a wonderful opportunity to duck out of the tourist traffic and experience a slow, quiet version of San Blas. Married couple Ulysses and Yaki can accommodate up to five guests in a shelter a few minutes' walk from their house, where they string hammocks (❸; bring a sleeping bag if you have one). You can borrow a mask and do some snorkelling with Ulysses, or just relax on your own and wait until it's time to eat. Whatever you do, it'll feel like the right decision.

There's no way of **booking** – you won't know if they can put you up until you get there – so the surest way is to spend a night at a hotel on one of the neighbouring islands and mention you want to go to Isla Yerba the next day. You'll also need to arrange a pick-up, although Ulysses might be able to paddle you to a nearby island in his canoe.

Cartí

Cartí refers to a group of islands and an area on the mainland roughly 10km south of El Porvenir. **Cartí Sugtupu** (Sugdup is also frequently used) is very town-like, with a health centre, school, library and small, rough-hewn restaurant – *La Pampa* – that does fried chicken, rice, salad and nice lentils for

US$3. You can observe the community meetings that take place every evening, and from February 1 to 25 there's a daily dramatization of the 1925 revolution, when a number of the islanders dress, disconcertingly, as policemen.

Overall the island is a little drab, with the exception of its small but excellent **museum** (US$2). Fascinatingly cluttered, it's covered floor-to-ceiling with drawings and paintings in various styles – some by children – representing different aspects of Kuna culture, myth and history. The curator and guide takes pains that you grasp the significance of the displays, speaking in Spanish with bits of English thrown in.

Backpacker San Blas (ⓔsanblas adventures@yahoo.com; ⑤) on **Cartí Sugtupu**, run by two brothers, is offered as an opportunity to "come and stay with a friendly family!" *Cabañas Cartí* (☎6740 7535, ⓔcabanascarti @hotmail.com; ⑤), on neighbouring **Cartí Yantupu**, offers a similar deal. Visitors sleep in houses provided by families, who move elsewhere for the duration of the visit, and enjoy leisurely, sociable meals in the clearing between the abodes. After dinner the chairs and tables are pushed back and some of the islanders perform a traditional dance, at the end of which tips are encouraged.

Another **accommodation** option on Cartí Yantupu is the home of a man named Yeyo (☎6716 0658). The house can usually hold six guests (four beds and two hammocks), but if demand is high some family members will spend the night at a relative's. The base rate is US$10 per night for lodging and US$2 per meal, but you may have to wrestle to get that, and will pay more for any transportation. Yeyo may also be able to arrange a better rate for you on Isla Aguja.

Isla Aguja

On nearby **Isla Aguja** (Needle Island/ Icodub), *Hotel Icodub* (☎6654 6277; ⑤) has a lovely, spacious beach. There are two cabins, each sleeping seven people in hammocks, and two for the family that lives here. Luis Barnett is the owner and promises big breakfasts and fish, lobster and octopus for dinner.

Isla Tigre

Despite its substantial population, **Isla Tigre** (also known as Digir) is spacious, relaxed and far less tourist-weary than the islands further west. An old airstrip occupies its western end, with ⚑ *Cabañas Tigretupu* tucked away to one side of it, isolated from the village and filled with the constant chatter of the ocean. The seven, very basic,

INTO COLOMBIA: PUERTO OBALDÍA

You can enter Colombia by land via Puerto Obaldía, a remote border outpost at the far southeastern edge of Kuna Yala, served by light aircraft from Panama City, though this trip is not recommended due to the aforementioned security concerns. Aeroperlas runs one flight Wednesday through Sunday (US$53 one-way). After going through customs and providing the Colombian consulate with proof of onward travel, you can take a boat (about US$10) to Capurganá, a small fishing village and holiday resort on the Colombian coast, where DAS (☎00574 824 3838, ⓦwww.das.gov.co) will stamp your passport. From Capurganá, ADA (☎00574 444 42 32, ⓦwww.ada-aero.com) flies to Medellín and other destinations in Colombia. There are also boats from Capurganá across the Gulf of Urabá to Turbo. From Turbo you can catch one of the regular light aircraft flights to Medellín and Cartagena, or continue your journey by bus. There are places to change money around the border, but they charge around twenty percent commission, so it is best to change only a small amount and wait until you reach a town with an ATM.

sand-floor cabañas (❷; meals not included) sleep between one and three people. The **restaurant** serves excellent food: octopus, king prawns and peppers in a Chinese-style sauce with fried rice, washed down with a cold beer, is a mere US$5.50. Trips to other islands run US$15–20 and a visit to a Kuna cemetery costs US$10. Call ☎333 2006/2005 if you wish to reserve a cabaña, although these numbers are for the two public phones on the island so you may need to let it ring for a while before someone picks up.

To get here you really need to fly to **Corazón de Jésus**; a boat from the Cartí area (nearly 30km away) would cost nearly US$60 if you managed to find one at all. Transport to and from Corazón de Jésus airstrip is US$18 each way.

Central Panama

Central Panama is a strikingly diverse region that rewards exploration. Head west from Panama City and your bus will barely have hit top speed before you can hop off and spend some time sprawled on one of the abundant beaches just south of the Interamericana. It's worth spending a night in the relative cool of **El Valle**, a popular weekend getaway for Panama City residents before heading down into the **Península de Azuero**. Here you can visit some of the towns founded by the colonial Spanish and explore two islands – Isla Iguana and Isla Cañas – that are both wonderful, but in very different ways.

INTERAMERICANA BEACHES

West of Panama City, the **Interamericana Highway** runs along a narrow plain squeezed between the Pacific and the slopes of the Cordillera Central. At the border of Coclé Province, 193km from Panama City, the road forks at **Divisa**: the Interamericana continues west to Santiago, the capital of Veraguas Province, while the Carretera Nacional turns south into the Península de Azuero.

For 50km beyond the village of Bejuco (around 60km west of Panama City and 120km east of Divisa), the coast is lined with some of the most beautiful and popular **Pacific beaches** in Panama, all just a few kilometres from the highway and accessible by taxi or local bus.

Playa Gorgona

Playa Gorgona is best visited as a day-trip – there are cabañas but they're aimed at groups and start at US$45. You can grab a bite to eat at *Arena Mar*, a decent, slightly overpriced beachside restaurant that'll serve your fried fish and *patacones* (US$5) before they stop sizzling.

To **get here**, take any westbound bus from Panama City along the Interamericana and inform the conductor of your destination. After about one hour, you'll be dropped off on the highway near the turn-off for the beach. Ask the bus conductor to point out the road you need; you can either walk the 3km straight down to the beach or take a taxi (US$2–3). Getting back, a taxi may be hanging around near the beach but you should be prepared to walk the 3km to the highway.

Playa Coronado

Roughly 3km west of Playa Gorgona you come to the turn-off for **Playa Coronado**, near the huge Rey super-market sign. You can catch a local bus down to the beach, where you can stay at *Sea Sol Beach Coronado Guest House* (☎6689 1262, ⓦwww.seasolbeach.com; dorms ❸, doubles ❻), which has shared bathrooms and a communal kitchen – buy food at the supermarket before heading down here – and rents kite-surfing equipment. You can rent **surfboards** from the nearby surf school; if the oily-looking water off the beach here doesn't entice you, there's clearer surf in the direction of the fancy hotels. If you're not staying in Playa Coronado you're technically not allowed to use the beach, but you can take a shot at charming the checkpoint guard.

Playa Santa Clara

Thirty kilometres east of Penonomé (see p.645), **Playa Santa Clara** is probably the area's loveliest beach, with white, dust-fine sand as far as the eye can see.

The four split-level, eye-catching cabañas here are part of *Cabañas Las Veraneras* (☎993 3313, ⓦwww .lasveraneras.com.pa; ●), referred to as "Las Parranderas". Each basic cabin sleeps three and has a private bathroom; one has ocean views. This is a very atmospheric, not to mention well-run and friendly, place. If you're here just for the day, you can use the *rancho* (small thatched sun-shade) on the beach and the lodging's toilets and showers (US$1). There is also a **restaurant** that does hamburgers (US$3.50) and a veggie omelette (US$4) but specializes in tasty fish dishes ($7.50–11). Nearby bar and restaurant *El Balneario* (☎993 2123) allows camping for US$3, which also buys you use of their bathroom, shower and changing rooms. The restaurant closes at 6pm, so get there early for their fresh fish and plantain dishes (US$7–9).

Take a **taxi** from the highway (US$2); there's usually one hanging around by the beach to take you back. Moving on from Santa Clara, **Penonomé** (see p.645) is a thirty- to forty-minute bus ride west.

EL VALLE

Ninety-six kilometres west of Panama City, a twisty road climbs up into the cordillera to **EL VALLE**, a small village in a fertile valley that was once the crater of a volcano. At 600m above sea level, El Valle is comparatively cool, and the surrounding countryside is good for walking or horseriding. Renowned for its flowers – particularly its orchids, which appreciate the slightly lower temperatures – the area is a popular retreat for Panama City residents on weekends.

What to see and do

Most of the village's amenities can be found on **Avenida Central**, along with signposts pointing the way to all local attractions, most of which are located on the outskirts of the village. In the centre, the **daily market** draws the biggest crowds, especially on Sundays, when locals pour in to sell their fruit, flowers and crafts (including carved soapstone, traditional earthenware pottery and woven baskets). A small **museum** (Sun 10am–2pm; US$0.50), run by nuns, houses exhibits on local history and folklore and stands next to the church of San José. Beyond the church by the Río Anton, a side road leads to the enjoyably quirky **thermal baths** (daily 8am–noon & 1–5pm; US$1). They are reputed to have medicinal powers.

El Chorro Macho is a 35-metre waterfall in a private reserve (daily 6am–5pm; US$3.50), with ziplines (US$12 or US$45) fitted around it. To get here, take a local bus headed for La Mesa from Av Central, or walk in half an hour (take the right-hand fork at the western end of town). You can wander around the site, criss-crossing the rope bridges, checking out the waterfall and swimming in the pool, accessed through a gate just before the shack where you pay. As far as the **zipline** goes, the less expensive, abridged version is not worth the money – it's over in a matter of seconds. If you're intent on doing it, splash out on the more expensive ride, which passes amongst the platforms and over the waterfall.

Head 1km up a signposted side road off Av Principal to visit the **El Nispero zoo**

and orchid nursery (daily 7am–5pm; US$2). Though most of the animals look miserable, seeing Panama's endangered golden frogs is certainly a treat. Further afield, innumerable trails climb up into the **cloudforests** of the surrounding mountains, including one to the peak of **La India Dormida**, the mountain ridge that looms over the valley to the west and whose silhouette quite strikingly resembles a woman lying on her back, supposedly a sleeping Indian princess.

Arrival and information

By bus Buses pull in at the covered market on Av Principal. Direct buses from Panama City arrive 7.30am–6.30pm.

Exchange Banco Nacional has an ATM on Av Principal, near the turn-off for El Nispero.

Internet There are around 20 computers in the public library (Mon–Sat 8.30am–3.30pm; US$1/hr).

Tourist information There's a small IPAT office in a kiosk next to the market, but Pepe Galarza, the owner of *Hotel Don Pepe* – often to be found in his souvenir shop next door – is a good source of local information.

Accommodation

Accommodation prices in El Valle reflect its popularity among Panamanians, who flock here for Carnaval, public holidays and weekends. You might also ask around (try the market or *Hotel Residencial El Valle*) for Abrahan Ali, a local politician who sometimes rents a house in the middle of town for as little as US$30 per night.

Cabañas Potosi ☎ 983 6181, ⓦ www .cabinsinpanama.com. Comfortable, good-looking rooms in a series of smart concrete cabañas. Offers camping for US$10 (bring your own tent) plus an extra US$1 to use the facilities, including an outdoor grill. Continue west 150m past the church, take the road to the right, then the fork to the left and continue for 1.5km. ⑥

Hospedaje y Restaurante Niña Delia Av Central ☎ 983 6110 or 6509 2189. The rooms here are a little threadbare, but the shady, thatched area adjoining creates a pleasant, peaceful atmosphere. Definitely browse the rooms here (all en suite) – of the six, one is far nicer than the others. There's also a restaurant (see opposite). Singles ③, doubles ④

Hotel Don Pepe Av Central ☎ 983 6425, ⓕ 983 6835, ⓦ www.hoteldonpepe.com.pa. A very smart place where rooms have cool, tiled floors and are so big the beds look lonely. They rent out bikes (US$2/hr, US$12/day) and there's a restaurant downstairs (see below). If they're not full try haggling for a better price. Singles ⑤, doubles ⑥

Hotel Residencial El Valle Av Central ☎ 983 6536 or 6615 9616, ⓦ www.residenciaelvalle.com. Clean, tidy and rather handsome, this is altogether a nice place to rest your head. All rooms are en suite with TV (some with cable) and hot water. The large communal area, which includes a fridge, is slung with hammocks. Internet use is free and there's a small souvenir shop downstairs. The owners can arrange horse rental. ⑥

Santa Librada Av Central ☎ no phone. These rooms (en suite) are quite shabby but they are kept clean. Plus, you'll be able to sit yourself down in the restaurant and order your *hojaldres* before you've even finished rubbing the sleep out of your eyes. ③–④

Eating

Two stalls on Av Central open in the early evening and sell good fried chicken; another nearby sells very fine *batidos* (ask them to hold the sugar). The *abarroteria* next to the library deals in lovely little ice-cream cones (try the *guanabana*) for US$0.30. Opposite is a *panadería* whose breadstuffs are fresh and delicious.

🏃 **Anton Valley Hotel** Av Central ☎ 983 6097 or 6484 5978, ⓦ www.antonvalleyhotel .com. The breakfast here, open to the public, is naughtily good. Choose from walnut-and-cinnamon waffles, platters of fresh fruit or proper Panamanian breakfasts – eggs, *salchicha*, tortilla, *hojaldres* (fried dough), *carimañolas* (fried balls of manioc dough filled with meat), and farmer's cheese – all for US$3.

Hospedaje y Restaurante Niña Delia Av Central ☎ 983 6110 or 6509 2189. The food is basic but you can enjoy your ham omelette (US$2) or spaghetti Bolognese (US$3) in the nice, thatched outdoor seating area. There's a pool table, too.

Pollos Ricos del Valle Av Central. Come for the fast food you know you want – a whole chicken is US$5 or a hamburger US$1.25.

Restaurante Bruschetta Av Central. Small but in demand among locals, this place serves vegetable bruschetta (US$4), Caesar salads (US$4), *churrasco argentino* (US$6) and more. Closed Tues.

Restaurante Don Pepe Av Central ☎ 983 6425, ⓦ www.hoteldonpepe.com.pa. Neat and airy with pink tablecloths and a mountain view from the window seats. The chef, professionally trained, is the town's culinary champion. Try the shrimp in creole sauce (US$7), *ceviche de corvina* (US$4) or pancakes (US$2.50).

Restaurante Santa Librada Av Central. This is a warm-feeling place with porcelain plaques of suns, butterflies and cockerels swarming all over the walls. The menu includes *batidos* (US$2), ham and eggs (US$3), *corvina* in garlic sauce (US$7) and *pollo guisado con patacones* (US$4).

Moving on

By bus You can either take a direct bus to Panama City (around 2hr; last bus at 6pm) or a minibus to San Carlos (morning and evening), where you can flag down buses heading in either direction along the Interamericana.

PENONOMÉ

Founded in 1581 as a *reducción de Indios* – a place where conquered indigenous groups were forcibly resettled so as to be available for labour service – and briefly the capital of the isthmus after the destruction of Panamá Viejo, **PENONOMÉ** was named after Nomé, a local chieftain cruelly betrayed and executed here by the Spaniards after years of successful resistance. Now the capital of Coclé Province, Penonomé doesn't have much to see apart from a small museum, though it makes a good enough base for exploring the surrounding area.

What to see and do

From the makeshift bus terminal – really just the point on the Interamericana where buses pick up and drop off – Penonomé's busy commercial **main street**, referred to as either Via Central or Avenida J.D. Arosemena, runs a few hundred metres to the **Plaza 8 de Diciembre**. Featuring a statue of Simón Bolívar and the inevitable bandstand, the square is flanked by several government buildings and an unspectacular cathedral. From here, head two blocks down Calle Damián Carles, take a right and continue for two blocks and you'll arrive at the **Museo de Penonomé** (Tues–Sat 9am–5pm; US$1), near

Parque Ruben Dario Carles. Here you'll find pre-Columbian ceramics decorated with abstract designs and colonial religious art. Upstairs in a creaking attic are artefacts arranged to evoke what a local residence may have looked like in the past.

The streets around the **market**, up towards the town plaza, are packed with *campesinos* from local villages selling produce and buses pushing through to the terminal. At night, when the stalls are abandoned and the few little bars are full and blaring out music, the street is full of crushed fruit and woefully drunken men.

Arrival

By bus Buses that travel the Interamericana pick up and drop off opposite the *Hotel Dos Continentes* at the intersection of Av J.D. Arosemena (Via Central) and the Interamericana. Buses from Panama City arrive every 30min.

Accommodation

Estrella Roja ☎ no phone. Outward appearances can be deceiving – the rooms aren't terrible, and the neighbourhood is residential, and does not feel threatening. They don't take reservations by phone, so you'll just have to take your chances. To get here, head northwest from the bus terminal along Via Central; at *Bar Mingo*, take a left up Av Cincuentenario. The hotel is at the very end of this road, at the T-junction with C Damián Carles. ❷

Hotel Dos Continentes Av J.D. Arosemena (Via Central), right opposite the bus terminal ☎ 997 9325/9326. This is a big place with a/c rooms with private baths. The staff are really helpful. Room no. 605 is decked out with a leopard-print duvet cover. ❹

Eating

Hotel Dos Continentes Av J.D. Arosemena (Via Central), right opposite the Interamericana bus terminal ☎ 997 9325/9326. The restaurant at the town's main hotel, but very popular in its own right. The food will keep you focused on your plate, and not on the lack of view: try the shrimp omelette and *patacones* (US$4) and steak and fish dishes (US$4–8). They also serve *bollo* – plantain mashed and then compacted into chunks (weirder sounding than it tastes).

Restaurante Gran China C Hector Conte Bermudez, just west of the Interamericana bus terminal. Tasty Chinese food in huge portions, served up by extremely friendly staff in a cool airy dining room. Wonton soup goes for US$2 and a meal of garlic shrimp, fried rice and salad costs US$5.

Las Tinajas On the Interamericana around 100m west of *Hotel Dos Continentes*, this place has basic strip-lit canteen serving stations with a circular, thatched seating area to the side. The food is not as fresh as it might be, but judging by the length of the line, it's popular among locals. Try the *sopa de carne* (US$1.50) or pork fried rice (US$1).

Directory

Exchange There is a Banco Nacional on Av J.D. Arosemena/Via Central (Mon–Fri 8am–3pm & Sat 9am–noon).
Internet Internet Cybernetic is up some stairs to the side of Banco Cuscatlán on Av J.D. Arosemena/Via Central (daily 9.30am–11pm; $0.60/hr).
Pharmacy There are three pharmacies in the immediate vicinity of *Hotel Dos Continentes*.
Post office Near Plaza 8 de Diciembre.

Moving on

By bus Services to Chitré (every 30min; 1hr 30min) leave from the Shell station, as do buses to Panama City (every 30min; approx 2hr).

AROUND PENONOMÉ

From the market area in Penonomé, *chivas* and *busitos* (minibuses) head off to villages scattered in the folds of the cool, forested mountains that rise to the north.

Chiguirí Arriba

Of the potential destinations in the mountains, **Chiguirí Arriba**, 29km to the northeast, makes an easy day-trip with plenty of good hiking trails, spectacular views, succulent-looking red chickens running about and a thirty-metre waterfall nearby – local children may guide you there for a small tip. There's a shop and local hang-out that sells coffee, multicoloured popcorn,

Quaker Oats and a curiously wide range of artist's materials.

The first **bus** to Chiguirí Arriba from Penonomé is at 6am, the next at 9am and then approximately every hour to hour and a half until late afternoon; arrive at least fifteen minutes before the bus leaves. The last bus back to Penonomé from Chiguirí Arriba leaves at 3.30pm from in front of the shop.

CHITRÉ

Some 2km before Chiguirí Arriba is La Posada Ecológica Cerro La Vieja (☎983 8900/8905, ⓦwww .posadalavieja.com; ⓑ), a small but luxurious eco-resort set amid beautiful gardens and a private forest reserve. The rooms have balconies that look out over the valley so you can swing in the hammock and watch nature showing off – it's like taking one enormously deep and relaxing breath. Spa services are pricey (50min massage US$35) but the guided walks are good value – you can take a tour even if you're not a guest. A five-hour guided walk along the Sendero La Iguana costs US$15, including a packed lunch. The restaurant serves Panamanian dishes such as fish in garlic sauce (US$7) and – particularly good – beef in Creole sauce ($8). If arriving by bus, confirm with your driver that you can disembark here; if not, a taxi should cost around US$30 from Penonomé.

The capital of Herrera Province and the largest town on the Azuero Peninsula, **CHITRÉ** is a slow-paced market centre studded with colourful discount stores. The gleaming white cathedral at its heart only accentuates the shabby state of the streets around it. Other than the market there's not much to see here, but Chitré is the peninsula's main transport hub and as such it is a good base for exploration. Ten minutes north of Chitré, the village of **La Arena** is famous for its pottery, sold on the roadside by the potters.

What to see and do

Chitré centres on the bandstand, trees and benches of **Parque Unión**. The square is flanked on one side by the **cathedral**, with its impressive vaulted wooden roof and extensive wooden panelling decorated with gold. The seemingly immovable glass windows are hinged at the centre so that they may swivel, allowing breezes into the cathedral – a pleasingly curious sight. The cathedral faces down Avenida Herrera – walk down a block and turn left on Calle Manuel Correa and you'll reach the **Museo de Herrera** (Tues–Sat 8am–noon & 1–4pm, Sun 8–11am; US$1), three blocks away. Set in an elegant colonial mansion, the museum has a collection of pre-Columbian pottery from the surrounding area and a good display on local folklore and customs, featuring traditional masks, costumes and musical instruments.

Arrival and information

By bus Buses from Panama City pull in at the terminal on the southern outskirts of town. Local buses do run to the town centre from the terminal but if you miss one it is only a 10min walk.
Tourist information There is an IPAT office in Los Santos (☎ 995 2339) and one in La Arena (☎ 995 2339), but none in Chitré proper.

Accommodation

Book accommodation in advance around Carnaval.
Hotel Bali Av Herrera, north of the cathedral ☎ 996 4620, ⊛ www.hotelbalipanama.com. Nicely renovated, with free internet, an Indonesian restaurant downstairs, and 28 rooms with hot water, cable TV and a/c. ❹
Hotel Rex On the north side of Parque Unión ☎ 996 4310. The rooms are basic but comfortable and well looked after, and include TV and hot-water bathroom. The balcony affords a nice view of

Parque Unión. ❹
Hotel Versalles Paseo Enrique Geenzier ☎ 996 4422/3133, ⊛ www.hotelversalles.com. There's a pool and even a conference room here, which sounds flash, but the rooms (en suite, a/c) are plain, and it's a bit far from the centre. ❺
Pensión Central Av Herrera, north of the cathedral ☎ 996 0059. A bit musty, but clean and good value. Rooms come with balcony, a/c and private bathroom. ❹

Eating

El Anzuelo Paseo Enrique Geenzier. Beyond *Hotel Versalles*, with a rambling outdoor eating area, this place is full of contented diners and plates empty but for fish heads. Fish dishes (including croaker, dorado and mahi, not just the ubiquitous *corvina*) US$5.50–9.
Café Chiquito Av Herrera. Taxi driver-approved, this spot serves simple rice-with-meat or rice-with-fish dishes (US$3–4).
Restaurante El Mesón Parque Unión. In *Hotel Rex*, this restaurant has a longstanding reputation for good eats, such as grilled *brochetas de langostinos* (US$9.50) and pizza (US$5–7).
Tulas Restaurante C Meliton Martin. People crowd round the small canteen counter at lunchtime, guessing at the relative tastiness of the hotpots on offer. It doesn't often disappoint. The selection changes daily, the prices scrawled on a blackboard. A full meal including rice, stew and *patacones* won't exceed US$2–3.

Directory

Exchange There's a branch of HSBC (Mon–Fri 9am–1pm) on Av Herrera near Sanchi Computers, and a branch of Banco Nacional (Mon–Sat 9am–1pm) on Paseo Enrique Geenzier, northwest of the town centre.
Internet J.C. Evolution Internet is on C Manuel Maria Correa, off Av Herrera, north of the cathedral; Internet Sanchi Computers is on Av Herrera. Both charge US$1 per hour.
Pharmacy On Av Herrera near the cathedral.

Moving on

By bus Services to Panama City (hourly; 4hr), Santiago (every 30min; 1hr 20min), Las Tablas (every 15min; 45min) and villages in the interior of the peninsula leave from the terminal (see above). You can catch a bus to the terminal from the stop next to the fountain by the museum.

LAS TABLAS

LAS TABLAS, south along the Peninsula's coast from Chitré, was founded in the seventeenth century by refugees fleeing by sea from Panamá Viejo after Henry Morgan and his band of pirates sacked it. The settlers dismantled their ships to build the first houses, hence the town's name, which means "the planks".

Though you wouldn't believe it if you turned up at any other time of year, this quiet, colonial market town hosts the wildest **Carnaval** celebrations in Panama (see box below). For five days in February the place is overwhelmed by visitors from all over the country, who come here to join in the festivities. The town divides into two halves – **Calle Arriba** and **Calle Abajo** – to fight a pitched battle with water, paint and soot on streets awash with *seco*, Panama's vicious firewater. Less raucous but just as colourful is the fiesta of **Santa Librada** in July, which includes the **pollera fiesta**, celebrating the peninsula's embroidered, colonial-style dresses. Produced in the town, they are something of a national symbol.

The only real sight in Las Tablas – and it's a good one – is the church, **Iglesia Santa Librada**. With the doors on both sides usually kept wide open, the town's balconies and bright colours seem to crowd in from outside. Locals wander in one side and out the other, too, almost as if the church were just part of the street furniture. Don't miss the pulpit and what looks like a lid suspended above it – a kind of sermon extinguisher.

RELIGIOUS FESTIVALS IN THE PENÍNSULA DE AZUERO

Jutting out into the Pacific Ocean, the Península de Azuero was one of the first regions of Panama to be settled by Spanish colonists. The towns and villages you come across – the main recommended bases include Chitré, Las Tablas and Pedasí – in this dry, scrubby landscape hum with their colonial heritage, visually manifested in the traditional handicrafts and folk costumes of the region, but the real giveaway is the gusto with which the people throw themselves into their religious fiestas. Usually honouring a particular patron saint, many of these date back almost unchanged to the days of the early settlers. Religious processions are accompanied by traditional music, fireworks and costumed folk dances which are as pagan as they are Catholic. Listed below are just a few of the major events; every village and hamlet has its own fiesta, and there's almost always one going on somewhere – IPAT in Los Santos has good information on all these.

Jan 6 Fiesta de los Reyes and Encuentro del Canajagua in Macarcas.

Jan 19–22 Fiesta de San Sebastián in Ocú.

Feb (date varies) Carnaval in Las Tablas (and everywhere else in the country).

March/April (date varies) Semana Santa, celebrated most colourfully in La Villa de Los Santos, Pesé and Guararé.

Late April Feria International del Azuero in La Villa de Los Santos.

June (date varies) Corpus Christi in La Villa de Los Santos.

June 24 Patronales de San Juan in Chitré.

June 29–30 Patronales de San Pedro y San Pablo in La Arena.

July 20–22 Patronales de La Santa Librada and Festival de la Pollera in Las Tablas.

Aug 15 Festival del Manito in Ocú.

Sept 24 Festival de la Mejorana in Guararé.

Oct 19 Foundation of the District of Chitré, in Chitré.

Nov 10 The "First Cry of Independence" in La Villa de Los Santos.

Arrival and information

By bus Buses from Panama City pull up on Av Laureano Lopez, at the terminal near the Shell station a few blocks from the square, while those from Chitré arrive at Parque Porras.

Tourist information There is an IPAT office in Los Santos (☎ 995 2339) but none in Las Tablas proper.

Accommodation

If you want to come for Carnaval, you're better off seeking a room in Chitré, though even there accommodation is booked up well in advance.

Hotel Manolo Av Belisario Porras ☎ 994 6372. Also known as *Hotel Piamonte*. If you don't like one room, ask to see – or smell – another, as the quality is not consistent. There's internet for US$1/hr. ❺

Pensión Mariela Opposite *Hotel Manolo* ☎ 994 6473. Cheaper than its neighbour, with generally nicer rooms. Doubles with private bath, TV and a/c are twice the price of the three most basic rooms. ❷

Eating and drinking

Bar Cinquentenario Parque Porras. An entire wall of the upstairs pool room opens to the outdoors, helping you keep a cool head while you get hustled.

El Mesón Parque Porras. Frequently clogged with people hungry for their pizzas (US$3–4) and deliciously good-value chicken or beef stews (US$1.50).

Los Portales Av Belisario Porras. This place has a small terrace for dining right on the sidewalk, offering fine people-watching, though you'll be asking for trouble come Carnaval. A little overpriced but it's good-quality cooking. King prawns in oyster sauce $8.

Portofino Parque Porras, next door to *El Mesón*. The menu's uncannily similar to its neighbour's, but it's your guess which one's the copycat. *Portofino* does a fine line in *batidos* (guanabana, papaya, etc), though, all for around US$1.

Restaurante El Caserón Off Av Belisario Porras. On its own down a dusty, gravelly side road (with *Pensión Mariela* on your left, take the second road on the left), but its checked tablecloths and pink server uniforms brighten things up. Their pizzas (US$3–4) and mixed meat grills (US$6–7) are the house speciality, and highly recommended.

Restaurante Manolo In *Hotel Manolo*. Specialist in killer breakfast combinations, like ham, eggs and *derretidos* – grilled cheese toasties – for $2.50.

Directory

Exchange Banco Nacional is near the bus station on Av Laureano Lopez (Mon–Fri 8am–3pm & Sat 9am–noon).

Laundry With *Pensión Mariela* on your left, take the second road on the right (Mon–Sat 8am–6pm & Sun 8am–noon).

Pharmacy There are two on Parque Porras.

Post office Down the side road opposite the Banco Nacional on Av Laureano Lopez (Mon–Fri 7am–6pm, Sat 7am–5pm).

Moving on

By bus to: Chitré (every 20min 6am–7pm; 45min), from Banco Nacional de Panamá on Av Laureano Lopez; Panama City (hourly 6am–8pm, Fri & Sun until 5.30pm; 4hr 30min) from the terminal (see above); Pedasí (hourly 6am–7pm; 45min) from outside the supermarket on Av Belisario Porras; Tonosí (hourly; 1hr 30min), from outside the same supermarket. To go west from Las Tablas, take a Panama City bus and get off at Divisa. Cross over the highway to catch west-bound buses for either Santiago (30min from Divisa), the main way-point between here and David, or David itself.

PEDASÍ

It's 42km south through cattle country from Las Tablas to **PEDASÍ**, a friendly, uneventful little village best known as the hometown of ex-President Mireya Moscoso (1999–2004) and as the jumping-off point for Isla Iguana, Isla Cañas and the beaches in the surrounding area.

What to see and do

Other than the **church** on the town square, which features chandeliers and a cheerful blue-sky-and-green-fields mural behind the altar, most activites in Pedasí involve day-trips to the **islands**. Dive-N-Fish Pedasí (daily 7–11am & 1–5pm; ☎ 995 2405, ⓦ www.dive-n-fishpanama.com), near the Accel gas station at the north end of town, offers a range of good-value activities in the area, including trips to Isla Iguana (US$45, plus US$3.50 park fee); ask about camping. Night trips to try and catch a glimpse of turtles laying their eggs on the beach at Isla Cañas (US$45) leave at 10pm and return at 4am. Whale-watching trips, typically most successful between April and November, combined with snorkelling or an Isla Iguana visit, go for US$45. Divemaster-led scuba-diving tours (US$75 for two tanks) are also on offer; groups leave at about 9am (weather permitting).

Arrival and information

By bus Buses pull up on the one main street through the town.

Exchange The Caja de Ahorros bank (Mon–Fri 8am–3pm, Sat 9am–noon), on the main street, has an ATM.

Telephones There's a payphone outside *Residencial Moscoso*.

Tourist information The IPAT office (Mon–Fri 9am–noon & 1–5pm; ☏ 995 2339) is on the left as you enter the village from the north, near Dive-N-Fish Pedasí. Though it does have official opening hours, it is staffed irregularly, in which case the staff at Dive-N-Fish Pedasí are happy to help with queries.

Accommodation

🏃 **Dim's Hostel** ☏ 995 2303. This longstanding option has pretty, cosy rooms with dainty curtains on the windows and comfortable beds. There's a hammock-slung patio in the lush garden out back with a large, palm-thatched roof anchored to the trunk of a mango tree – a very nice place for a beer and a snooze. Prices include breakfast, a/c, private bathroom (cold water) and TV. Singles & doubles ❺

Residencial Moscoso ☏ 995 2203. Well acquainted with backpackers, the *Moscoso* is clean and friendly – the reception is in the owner's living room. Dorm rooms have fans and shared bathrooms (with bracingly cold showers), and there's internet for US$1/hr. Dorms ❷, doubles ❹

Eating

Aside from the options listed below, there's a seemingly unnamed and slightly untamed-looking restaurant near Dive-N-Fish Pedasí that does fried *corvina*, rice and *patacones* for US$2.25, and chicken with spaghetti for US$1.75.

Angela On the main street. Sit and eat on the front porch – the one car that passes every couple of minutes is unlikely to have you wheezing all over your lunch. The food is simple, freshly-cooked and tasty, with fish soup for US$1.50 and delicious breaded chicken pieces (*deditos*) with beans, rice and salad for US$2.75.

Dulceria Yely Opposite *Residencial Moscoso*. With a cabinet full of delicious cakes at just US$0.60 a slice, you could get through a whole one yourself very quickly.

Tiesto On the square behind the main road. An airy place with a high roof and a stone arch that does good-quality brick-oven pizzas for around US$4.

Moving on

By bus Services for Tonosí or Cañas (1hr 15min/45min) leave from the main street in town, as do buses back to Chitré (hourly 6am–5pm; 45min).

AROUND PEDASÍ

Pedasi is a great base for exploration of this area's fascinating marine identity. You can set off in search of whales, iguanas and sea turtles safe in the knowledge that you can come back here and lay your head somewhere cosy.

Playa El Arenal

Playa El Arenal, a very long, very empty and very flat beach, is a thirty-minute walk from Pedasí or a few dollars in a taxi. It's roundly recommended by locals for its tranquil waters. Keeping a low profile on the edge of the beach is *Coco's*, a restaurant owned by a local co-operative. When local fishermen bring in their catch, the restaurant gets first pick at rock-bottom prices, which they pass on to customers. The fried fish (US$3.50 with *patacones*) is truly delicious, which must be down to its freshness – not to mention the view, the beer and the calm.

Isla Iguana

Some 7km off the coast of Pedasí lies **Isla Iguana**, an uninhabited wildlife reserve managed by the state and surrounded by the most extensive **coral reefs** in the Bahía de Panamá, making it one of the best sites for **snorkelling** and **diving** in the country. The island has white-sand beaches, crystalline waters and a colony of magnificent frigate birds, and between April and November you may see **whales**. Despite the island's name, iguanas have bee[...] to the locals' fondness [...] Since the island was decla[...] park, however, their number[...] creeping back up.

You can **hire a boat** to take [...] from **Playa El Arenal** (see [...]ve). Fishermen charge about US$40 for a return trip (20min each way); on weekends you may find other visitors to share the cost. Take all the food and drink you need. To **camp** on the island, arrange a pick-up time with your boatman.

ISLA CAÑAS WILDLIFE RESERVE

Archeological evidence suggests that people have been coming to the area now designated as the **ISLA CAÑAS WILDLIFE RESERVE** to hunt turtles and harvest their eggs for many centuries, although the island was only settled in the 1960s. Since 1988, the hunting of turtles here has been prohibited and a co-operative has been established to control the harvest. Members watch over the beaches at night and collect the eggs as soon as they are laid, keeping eighty percent for sale and consumption and moving the rest to a nursery where the turtles can hatch and return to the sea in safety. A night-time **turtle walk**, at least half an hour in each direction along the beach, will set you back about US$10. Flash-light use is stringently rationed, as the

---

THE ISLA CAÑAS ARRIBADA

Isla Cañas has one of the few beaches in the world that sees the phenomenon known as the arribada, when thousands of female sea turtles simultaneously come ashore to lay their eggs. It's still not entirely understood what triggers this mass exodus from the sea at one particular moment, though smaller numbers emerge at other times, too, within a roughly ten-day period on either side of a full moon (when tides are highest, allowing the turtles to lay their eggs further up the beach). Whether or not your visit coincides with an arribada (usually Aug–Nov), if you come between May and January you'll almost certainly see green, hawksbill or Olive Ridley turtles laying their eggs at night. From December to March there's a good chance of seeing leviathan-like leatherbacks, which can weigh over 800kg.

ISLA CAÑAS TRAVEL

Getting to and from Isla Cañas is not as straightforward as you might hope. To reach the island, you'll need to start out from Pedasí. Here, flag down a bus on the main road heading for Tonosí, or wait outside *Angela* restaurant (see p.650). The buses (hourly 7am–4pm) look like vans and should display their destination inside on the windscreen; tell the driver you want to go to the jumping-off point for the island (the "dock"). You could also take a taxi for around US$25, but make sure the driver takes you past Cañas town to the jumping-off point, which they're often loath to do because of the poor road. When you arrive at the dock – essentially the point where the road ends and the mangrove swamp begins – there will often be boats waiting. If there are none smack loudly on the metal wheel rim that is hung up in a tree near the edge of the swamp. This will alert people on the island (it is very close) and someone will come to get you presently.

For moving on, one scheduled boat leaves the island daily at 7am to make the 7.30am bus to Las Tablas. One bus leaves the dock daily at 7.30am for Las Tablas, and another at 8am for Tonosí (35min), from where you can connect for Las Tablas (Mon–Thurs & Sat hourly 6am–4pm, Fri 6am–5pm, Sun 7.30am–4pm; 1hr 30min). There are no taxis in Cañas town; you'll have to arrange pick-up by a Pedasí-based driver.

turtles are frightened by them. The long, near-silent walk along soft sand, the lapping water and the incredible number of stars may just lull you into dreamland on your feet. If you find yourself with sand in your mouth and don't know why, blame the turtles.

Accommodation and eating

The functional but unmemorable **main village** on Isla Cañas is prepared for visitors, as are the mosquitoes and sandflies. The co-operative that manages the turtles has set aside a building where seven people can **stay** (US$15 each); the larger of the two rooms has air-conditioning. Don't expect much for your money. Window-less cabañas cost US$5, but if you go this route be prepared for serious battle with mosquitoes. There's a small **restaurant** near the dock where you can eat for just US$2, although the food does not seem especially fresh. Another accommodation option is to arrange a **homestay** with the lovely Enie. Room is around US$5, not including board, though she's a fine cook.

Chiriquí Province

Striking out west along the Interamericana from the Península de Azuero will bring you into the rich agricultural province of **Chiriquí** and ultimately to **David**, Panama's second city and a crossroads for travellers heading through Central America. Until you enter the region the 120km or so from Divisa (where you can switch to a westbound bus on leaving the Península de Azuero) is pretty dull. But soon you'll be gazing at the beautiful **Chiriquí Highlands** away to the north, and at the roadside you'll occasionally see stalls set up by the Ngobe-Buglé to display their wares, such as traditional dresses and necklaces. By the time the bus reaches the Tabasará river, hills are crowding all around you. David is surprisingly calm for such an important city and you'll find lots of other travellers recharging their batteries here. The real treat of this westward slog, however, is the opportunity to visit the beautiful, chilly highlands where you can sniff orchids, drink amazing coffee and lay your head in some great accommodation. If you are want to break the long journey west and see some sea before heading upwards then a visit to **Isla Boca Brava** is highly recommended.

ISLA BOCA BRAVA

At opposite ends of **ISLA BOCA BRAVA**, a mere fifteen minute-walk apart, are two accommodation options that offer wildly different experiences. One – *Hotel Y Restaurante Boca Brava* – offers eye-wateringly strong cocktails and raucous dancing while the other – *Tucan Lodge* – offers total peace and quiet. Both do what they do very well. To reach Boca Brava, you'll need to get off the bus at the Horconcitos turn-off, a six- to seven-hour journey from Panama City, or three- to four-hour journey from Divisa. During the day there are always taxis waiting here to take people down to the village of Boca Chica (40min; $15), which is the jumping-off point for the island. If you arrive after hours and no taxis are present, try Rodney (☎6561 4470) or Jovane (☎6655 8723), but try to inform them of your approximate arrival time in advance. You'll be dropped at the dock near *Wahoo Willy's*, a bar, restaurant and hotel. The boat ride across to Boca Brava is US$1 if going to *Hotel Y Restaurante Boca Brava*, or US$5 if going to *Tucán Lodge*. The island has two beaches – both are quite plain – and is criss-crossed by paths that are nice to ramble around on. The island's small

size ensures that you are not in any danger of getting lost.

Accommodation

Hotel Y Restaurante Boca Brava ☎700 0017, ✉hotelbocabrava@hotmail.com). This place is fun if you're after incredibly strong cocktails and dancing; the accommodation – everything from hammocks (❶) to doubles (❺) – is ok but a little shabby. Kayaks can be hired (US$15 for 4hr), and trips to nearby beaches arranged (US$4–7).

DAVID

Three Spanish settlements were founded in this area in 1602; **DAVID** was the only one to survive repeated attacks from indigenous groups. It developed slowly as a marginal and remote outpost

of the Spanish Empire, but in 1732 it was overrun and destroyed by British-backed Miskito groups raiding from Nicaragua. As settlement of Chiriquí increased in the nineteenth century, David began to thrive again, this time as a market and transportation centre. Today, despite being a busy commercial city – the third largest in Panama after Panama City and Colón – and the focus of Chiriquí's strong regional identity, it retains a sedate provincial atmosphere. Hot and dusty, its unexceptional modern architecture spreads out on a grid (the only surviving feature of the original colonial settlement). There's not a lot going on here, but plenty of travellers drop in en route from Panama City to Costa Rica, Bocas del Toro or the Chiriquí Highlands. At Carnaval, of course, things spice up considerably, and David also has a festival all its own:

the **Feria de San José** thunders its way through ten raucous days every March.

What to see and do

David centres on **Parque Cervantes**, a fine, tree-shaded place to relax with a cup of freshly squeezed sugarcane juice (*caña*) perked up with tropical lemon, or a dose of coconut water (*agua de pipa*). Three blocks southeast of the park, down Calle A Norte on the corner with Avenida 8 Este, the **Museo de Historia y Arte José de Obaldía** (Mon–Sat 8.30am–4.30pm; US$1) has a small but intriguing collection focusing on local history and culture, ranging from pre-Columbian artefacts and colonial religious art to relics from the Coto War with Costa Rica and photographs of David in the early twentieth century. The building is a beautiful colonial mansion that was home to successive generations of the distinguished Obaldía family – José was the founder of the province of Chiriquí, and later generations included presidents of both Colombia and Panama.

A decidedly less highbrow diversion is the **Balneario Río Nueva Barranca**, an outdoor swimming pool (US$2) ten to fifteen minutes out of the city by bus. Take any bus marked "Frontera/Concepción/Armuelles/San Andres" from the terminal or outside the Super 99 supermarket near the *The Purple House* (see below). Tell the conductor where you want to be let off.

Arrival and information

By air Flights from Panama City and Bocas del Toro arrive at the airport, about 5km out of town and a US$3 taxi ride away.

By bus Buses from Panama City, Almirante, Boquete, Cerro Punta and Paso Canoas, as well as TRACOPA international buses from San José, all pull in at the terminal on Paseo Estudiante.

Tourist information There is an IPAT office (Mon–Fri 8am–4pm; ☎775 4120/2839) opposite Importadores Ropa Americana on Av 6 Este, near C Central. The *Purple House* (see below) posts details of other cultural events in the city, publicity written by locals for locals, that would probably not come to your attention otherwise.

Accommodation

Bambú Hostel In the San Mateo Abajo neighbourhood, C de la Virgencita ☎730 2961, ⓦwww.bambuhostel.com. Southwest of the

---

DAVID ORIENTATION

Getting around David can be somewhat confusing, despite the grid layout. Be aware that although most people refer to the streets in the town by using their alphabetical or numerical designation – Calle B Sur, Avenida 3 Oeste, etc – many streets have another name (often honouring a famous person or date) and this designation frequently appears on the street sign.

---

centre, a five-minute taxi ride from the bus station, this place has a variety of accommodation options (camping, dorms and private rooms) as well as a kitchen, a large backyard with fruit trees, a swimming pool and free internet. Camping ❶, dorms ❷, doubles ❺

Pensión Costa Rica Av 6 Este ☎775 1241. Though in a handsome building with a nice reception area – it features a grandfather clock and a set of encyclopedias – many of the rooms are musty and with walls that do not reach right up to the ceiling. Even so, they're not bad. ❸

Hotel Occidental Parque Cervantes ☎775 4068. Good-value and spacious a/c rooms – those at the front of the building are brighter and share a balcony overlooking the square. ❸–❹

Pensión Fanita C B Norte ☎6660 5383. This large, ramshackle, but very atmospheric wooden house has been owned by the same Chinese immigrant family for many years. The more expensive rooms have an unsafe-feeling balcony. internet is US$0.50/hr, and Ernesto, the manager, speaks perfect English. ❶–❷

🏃 **The Purple House Hostel** C C Sur at Av 6 Oeste ☎774 4059, ⓦwww.purplehousehostel.com. An excellent base for plotting your next move. You can pick the brains of others recharging at this backpacker outpost and consult the folders stuffed full of information on David and the rest of the country. There are seventeen dorm beds and two private rooms, all clean and comfortable. internet (one computer), wi-fi and limitless coffee are all on the house, though a/c costs extra. Definitely try to book ahead, and be aware that there's limited availability in Oct. Dorms ❷, doubles ❹

Eating

Calle F Sur has a collection of street food stalls known as Mercados de Fritura. They open up around 6pm and keep on frying tasty bits and pieces (such as *hojaldres*, stuffed yucca, beef and pork) until the early hours.

Café Java Juice C F Sur. Delicious *batidos* and a general feeling of relative healthiness. A banana split is US$2, a quality burger US$1. There's another branch on Av Francisco Clark at Plaza Florencia.

Casa Vegetariana C Central. A buzzing little veggie takeout where you can see everything being freshly prepared and pick and mix portions of various creations for US$0.30 each. On the sweeter side, both fruit juice and fruit salads are US$1.

🏃 **El Fogón** Av 2 Oeste ☎775 7091. Big and popular, with warm earthy colours and a good atmosphere. Try the *filete de pescado a la* *parmesana* (US$7) or the spaghetti Bolognese (US$4).

MultiCafe In the same building as *Hotel Occidental*, Parque Cervantes. A huge and deservedly popular canteen serving tasty standards such as lasagna for US$1.50 and a range of Mexican-influenced dishes such as *quesadillas* for US$0.65.

Restaurante Charlie C B Norte. Housed in the museum-like *Pensión Fanita*, the restaurant isn't so cheery but the okay Chinese food is cheap, though as basic as can be: rice and meat dishes are $1.50, meat soup is $0.60.

El Rincón Libanés C F Sur. Looks as benevolently on veggies as it does on meat-eaters, serving up hummus, moussaka and *kibbe*, among other treats. Falafel and pitta will set you back US$4.50, as will a refreshing Lebanese salad. A selection of *mezze* for one is US$13.50 – not cheap, but a welcome change from the usual Panamanian fare.

Drinking and nightlife

As far as **nightlife** goes, the scene is constantly changing so ask around on arrival, or just listen for music playing – open-air public parties sometimes take place. Around five nightclubs operate at any one time, but usually only one or two are popular. Wednesdays are generally Ladies' Nights. There are no established gay nights in the city.

Opium Next to the Crown Casino, opposite the Super 99 on C F Sur. This place is currently in favour with the kids in David. Men need to dress smartly. It doesn't usually get going until around 11pm and the preferred style of music is a Panamanian brand of reggae. Entry around US$5.

Top Place With three locations – one on C F Sur, opposite Super 99 supermarket, one on C Central and Av Cincuentenario and one on Av Obaldía, near the bus terminal – these are consistently good spots for a beer and a game of pool.

Tsunami In the Chiriquí Mall. Very similar to *Opium*, though this one will cost you a US$2–2.50 taxi ride too.

Directory

Car rental Budget (☎721 0845) and Thrifty (☎721 2477), both at the airport.

Cinema The screen at the *Gran Hotel Nacional* (C Central) shows all the new stuff.

Consulate Costa Rica, Calle C Norte (☎774 1923).

Exchange Banco Nacional (Mon–Fri 8am–3pm, Sat 9am–noon) is on Parque Cervantes; Banistmo (Mon–Fri 8am–3.30pm, Sat 9am–noon) is a block away from Parque Cervantes on C C Norte. The casinos may break notes for you.

Immigration C C Sur ☎775 4515. For visa extensions or permission to leave the country. Mon–Fri 8am–3pm.

Internet There are internet cafés all over the city. One is opposite the *McDonald's* on C F Sur (24hr; US$0.75/hr).

Laundry Plenty throughout the city, but there's one on C Central at Av 6 Este. Daily 7.30am–7pm.

Hospital There are two well-regarded hospitals – Hospital Chiriquí on C Central at Av 3 Oeste and Mae Lewis Hospital, which is on the Interamericana.

Pharmacy The Romero supermarket on C F Sur has a 24hr pharmacy; Farmacia Revilla is on Parque Cervantes.

Post office A block away from Parque Cervantes on C C Norte (Mon–Fri 7am–6pm, Sat 7am–5pm).

Moving on

By air Flights to Panama City and Bocas del Toro leave from the airport, which is about 5km out of town and a US$3 taxi ride away. Both Aeroperlas (☎315 7500, ⊛www.aeroperlas.com) and Air Panama (☎316 9000, ⊛www.flyairpanama.com) run flights every day from David to Panama City. Aeroperlas has one flight a day Mon–Fri to Bocas del Toro from David.

By bus to: Almirante (see Changuinola); Boquete (every 30min 5.15am–9.45pm; 1hr); Cerro Punta (every 15min 5am–8pm; 2hr); Changuinola (every 30min until 7pm; 4hr 30min); Panama City

INTO COSTA RICA: PASO CANOAS

You can cross the border into **Costa Rica** at the Paso Canoas crossing, 56km west of David along the Interamericana. After passing through *migración* (24hr) and customs (a formality unless you have anything to declare), you simply walk across the border, though queues for both can be long if international buses are passing through. The banks in David can be reluctant to change dollars to colones so it is best to change them at the border. There are banks (Banco Nacional de Panama and Banco Nacional de Costa Rica) on both sides of the border that will usually change currency, as well as individuals who provide a money-changing service.

THE CHIRIQUÍ HIGHLANDS

North of David, you can escape the flat heat of the city and take refuge up in the cool of the Chiriquí Highlands, a region of cloudforests, fertile valleys and charming settlements. There are riches here, all so different, and yet all sharing the same basic characteristics of head-clearing air, cold nights and a deep, relentless green. The small town of Cerro Punta is a charming – and often chilly – place to spend a night and acts as a fine base for trips to Guadalupe, Parque Internacional La Amistad and along the Quetzal Trail. The more substantial town of Boquete has its own attractions, particularly coffee-related, but is also a great base for activities from rafting to hot spring near-scalding.

(roughly hourly 6.30am–8.15pm; 7–8hr; express at 10.45pm, midnight & 3am; 6hr); Paso Canoas (every 10min 4.30am–9.30pm; 1hr 20min).

CERRO PUNTA

Almost 2000m above sea level in a bowl-shaped valley surrounded by densely forested mountains, **CERRO PUNTA** is the highest village in Panama. In the eighty or so years since it was settled, the town's fertile soil has produced some eighty percent of all the vegetables consumed in Panama – there are little patches of cultivated land everywhere you look – although this agricultural boom has not done the surrounding forests any good. The town's altitude gives it a very special atmosphere – it seems incredibly crisp, and the taste of the food and the smell of the orchids seem all the better for it.

What to see and do

Everything in tiny Cerro Punta is spread out along the main road from David and a side road leading towards Parque Internacional La Amistad (see p.658). Nothing much at all happens here, although groups of men hang around as if something might. Instead it's the scenery, together with the cool, crisp mountain air (it even gets cold at night – a rare luxury in Panama), that makes Cerro Punta a perfect base for **hiking** – the pristine cloudforests of Parque Internacional La Amistad and Parque Nacional Volcán Barú are both within easy reach. These parks are perhaps the best places in all of Central America to catch a glimpse of the elusive resplendent quetzal, particularly in the dry season between January and April.

The nearby village of **Guadalupe**, famous for its jam, orchids and neat little gardens, is also worth a visit. The jam is made from the strawberries that grow in the area, small enough that you'll find some whole ones as you spread it on your bread. Buy it in the local shop or at the stalls that are sometimes set up in the road. Take a local bus from the centre of Cerro Punta. You can enjoy orchids at **Finca Dracula Orchid Farm** (daily 8am–5pm; US$3; ☎771 2070, ✉fdracula@cwpanama.net), a ten- to fifteen-minute walk from *Los Quetzales Lodge and Spa* (see below). With the lodge on your left, head up the road until the wooden "Dracula" sign pointing left; the farm is a further five minutes in this direction.

Arrival and information

By bus Services from David stop on the one main street running through the town.

Accommodation

Hotel Cerro Punta On the main street ☎771 2020. Chalet-style lodging whose appealing rooms have pretty curtains and ivy growing past the windows. Those windows, however, face out the back and not towards the mountains and fantastic views. ⑤

Hotel Los Quetzales Lodge and Spa In Guadalupe ☎771 2182/2291, ⓦwww .losquetzales.com. This hotel accommodates backpackers, honeymooners, families and retirees, and makes it look easy. Budget travellers will find only the camping and the dorm beds – chunky wood, quality bedding – affordable, though there are also rooms, suites and cabins on offer. There are several activities to partake in, including bike and horseriding, and lots of long or short walks through the surrounding cloudforest. In the restaurant, pizza and pasta go for around US$5. Camping ❸, dorms ❸, doubles ❼

Pensión Eterna Primavera On the road towards La Amistad ☎ no phone. Here's your chance to stay with the eccentric Panamanian grandmother you didn't know you had. The rooms are actually funny: think single cigarette butt in a cupboard, *Muppet Show* linens and an ornament of a lizard holding a gun to its head. Awfully, terribly brilliant. ❸

Eating

La Fresa In Guadalupe, down the side road by the bus stop. The good chicken stew here (US$1.50) will warm you up in the cool of the mountains.

Hotel Cerro Punta On the main road, this excellent restaurant has floor-to-ceiling windows showing off the view as you munch on carefully prepared meals. The flavourful grilled fish with home-made french fries and broccoli salad (US$7) is worth every cent. A breakfast of pancakes, local strawberries, syrup and a big mug of coffee is only US$4.

Restaurante Anthony On the road to La Amistad. Clean and friendly, this place deals in your basic but nicely done *comidas corrientes* such as US$2 portions of *arroz de guandú* (Panamanian dish of rice and beans) with chicken, pork or beef.

Moving on

By bus Local buses run regularly throughout the day to Guadalupe. Buses to David (every 15min 5am–6pm; 2hr) leave from the main street.

PARQUE INTERNACIONAL LA AMISTAD

PARQUE INTERNACIONAL LA AMISTAD covers four thousand square kilometres of rugged, forested mountains teeming with wildlife (including five cat species), on either side of the border with Costa Rica. Although most of Panama's share technically falls in Bocas del Toro, the sliver that is in Chiriquí, and easily reached from Cerro Punta, is best prepared for visitors. Here there are three well-marked **trails**, including a four-kilometre round-trip to a 55-metre waterfall.

To **get to the park** from Cerro Punta, take a local bus to Las Nubes. There's a permanently staffed **park office** here, where you must pay the US$3 admission charge; they also have a refuge (US$5 per night) – bring your own food, warm clothes and, ideally, a sleeping bag, as it gets cold at night.

PARQUE NACIONAL VOLCÁN BARÚ

The Sendero Los Quetzales, or **Quetzal Trail**, is the most popular of the trails in this one hundred and forty square kilometre **PARQUE NACIONAL VOLCÁN BARÚ**, which also serves as home to **Volcán Barú**, Panama's highest peak. It runs from Cerro Punta across the northern flank of Volcán Barú to Boquete. In this direction the trail is downhill. You'll pass through various life zones as you descend, and on reaching Boquete you'll have the satisfaction of having travelled on foot between the Highlands' two principal towns, a journey which otherwise would require a bus down from the mountains to David and back up again.

Sendero Los Quetzales

To reach the trailhead, take a **taxi** from Cerro Punta to the El Respingo ranger station (US$10–15) and pay your US$3.50 park entry fee. From here – the start of the trail – to the Alto Chiquero ranger station near Boquete – the end – should take you between four and six hours. From **Alto Chiquero** it's another 8km to Boquete but the walk is enjoyable, continuing along the Río Caldera and affording direct access to a pretty little waterfall and a scenic hike through coffee *fincas* and rural communities. You might also be able to hitch a ride or catch a taxi into town for a few dollars.

To avoid lugging all your gear along with you on the trail, consider staying in David, leaving the bulk of your luggage at your lodging and taking an early-morning bus to Cerro Punta. Upon arrival in Boquete, catch a bus back to David – this journey can also be broken with an overnight at Cerro Punta, Boquete or indeed both. Note that walking the trail in the other direction, from Boquete to Cerro Punta, involves some steep climbs.

Volcán Barú

Boquete's most majestic attraction is **Volcán Barú**, Panama's tallest mountain (3475m) and an extinct volcano that dares all visitors to take it on. A 22-kilometre road winds up to the cloud-shrouded peak through spectacular scenery. From the top, the cloud cover breaks every so often to reveal the sight of at least one of the oceans. Outside of the mid-December-to-April dry season, your best chance of enjoying the view is to be on the peak at dawn. To manage this, you'll need to camp out or walk all night. Boquete Outdoor Adventures (see p.661) offers a US$90 tour that leaves either early morning or late evening. In the latter case you will not camp but walk throughout the night with a break at the summit at sunrise. Boquete Mountains Safari Tours (see p.661) offers a US$80 tour leaving in the morning. Both operators provide food and water and transportation to the end of the paved road.

To go it alone you will need to take a *transporte urbana* minibus or a taxi (US$5–6 during the day, up to US$20 at night) from Boquete. This will bring you 6km to the end of the paved road, after which it becomes a rough track passable only with a customized 4WD. Beyond this point it's a steep and strenuous four- to eight-hour hike and another six hours or so back to Boquete. Take waterproof clothing, dress in layers and wear good hiking shoes. You will also

need plenty of **food and water.** If you wish to camp (US$5), there is an area near the ANAM ranger station (☎no phone) close to the summit where you can set up your tent. If there is room in the station you may also be able to spend the night there for $5.

BOQUETE

BOQUETE is set in the tranquil Caldera Valley, 1000m above sea level. Thirty-seven kilometres north of David, it is the biggest town in the Chiriquí Highlands. The slopes surrounding the town are dotted with coffee plantations, flower gardens and orange groves and rise to rugged peaks that are usually obscured by thick clouds. When those clouds clear, however – most often in the morning – you can see the imperious peak of Volcán Barú, which dominates the town to the northwest. Foreign investment has flooded the area in recent years, seeing

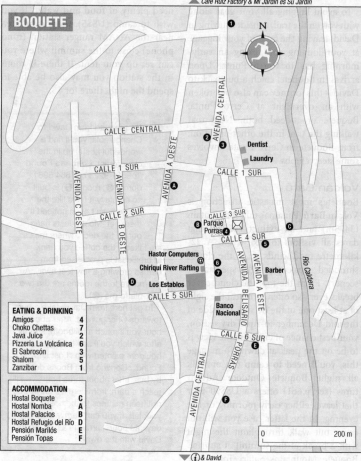

BOQUETE

N

EATING & DRINKING

Amigos	4
Choko Chettas	7
Java Juice	2
Pizzeria La Volcánica	6
El Sabrosón	3
Shalom	5
Zanzibar	1

ACCOMMODATION

Hostal Boquete	C
Hostal Nomba	A
Hostal Palacios	B
Hostal Refugio del Río	D
Pensión Marilós	E
Pensión Topas	F

CALLE CENTRAL
AVENIDA CENTRAL
AVENIDA A OESTE
AVENIDA C OESTE
AVENIDA B OESTE
CALLE 1 SUR
CALLE 2 SUR
CALLE 3 SUR
CALLE 4 SUR
CALLE 5 SUR
CALLE 6 SUR
AVENIDA A ESTE
AVENIDA BELISARIO PORRAS
AVENIDA CENTRAL
Dentist
Laundry
Parque Porras
Hastor Computers
Chiriquí River Rafting
Los Establos
Barber
Banco Nacional
Río Caldera

0   200 m

CHIRIQUÍ PROVINCE

PANAMA

the construction of an all-inclusive luxury condo, targeting retirees from the US, and the clearing of cloudforest to make way for golf courses.

What to see and do

The big attraction of Boquete is the opportunities it affords for exploring the surrounding **countryside**. As well as the climb to the summit of the volcano – a strenuous day's walk or a couple of hours' drive – there are plenty of less demanding walks you can make along the narrow country lanes.

Café Ruiz

One of these walks, heading out of town to the north towards the hamlet of Alto Lino, takes you past the **Café Ruiz factory** (☎720 1000, ⓦwww.caferuiz .com), which offers tours (Mon–Sat 9am & 1pm; 3hr; US$25) that explore every step of the coffee-making process, from the farm to the roasting plant. A 45-minute tour (Mon–Sat 8am; US$7) visits only the roasting plant.

Mi Jardín es Su Jardín

Mi Jardín es su Jardín (9am–6pm) is a bountiful, landscaped garden with a slender metal tower that affords nice views as well as access to a mysterious slide that goes directly into a flowerbed. It's worth wandering up here, particularly if you're visiting the nearby Café Ruiz factory, which is just before it.

Los Pozos de Caldera

At the hot springs known as **Los Pozos de Caldera** you can alternate between dips in the scalding hot water and heart-alarming splashes in the frigid river. Boquete Mountains Safari Tours (see below for details) runs half-day tours (US$45, without horses US$35) to the springs, which include an optional hour's horseriding. They are based on Avenida Central, south of the main square.

Water sports

Over thirty-five rivers in Chiriquí Province are used for **kayaking** and **rafting**, including the Río Caldera, Río Gariché, Río Chiriquí and Río Chiriquí Viejo, with whitewater of every classification. Tour operators in town (see below) can arrange day-trips and courses for all experience levels, for around US$60–80.

Piscina La Estancia (US$1), 3.5km from the town centre, is a fun outdoor swimming pool with two slides: one straight, fast and undulating, the other bendy, leisurely and tubular. It's a US$2 taxi ride from town. Up in the hills and with some great views just outside the entrance, it's a nice place to spend an hour or two.

Arrival and information

By bus Buses from David arrive at the main square (Parque Porras), and minibuses head up to the surrounding hamlets from the streets around this same square – taking one of these and then walking back to town is a good way to see the nearby countryside.

Tour operators Boquete Mountains Safari Tours (☎6627 8829 or 6742 6614, ⓦwww.boquetesafari .com) runs trips to the Pozos de Caldera. The founder of Boquete Outdoor Adventures, in the Los Establos complex (☎720 2284 or 6474 0274, ⓦwww.boqueteoutdooradventures.com), has been running white-water trips since 1997. Chiriquí River Rafting, on Av Central (☎720 1505/1506, ⓦwww.panama-rafting.com), also offers rafting trips. There's also the Boquete Tree Trek (Mon–Sat 7.30am–12.15pm & 1.15–4.30pm; ☎720 1635, ⓦwww.aventurist.com), a zipline tour through the canopy of the forest near Volcán Barú at the Los Establos complex on the corner of Av Central and C 5 Sur.

Tourist office IPAT has a tourist information centre (daily 9.30am–6pm) overlooking the town at Alto Boquete on the road towards David. Although few staff members speak English, they are reasonably helpful, offering maps and basic information on walks in the countryside around Boquete. The view is nice from up here, but you can get better advice from the hotels in Boquete.

Accommodation

Accommodation prices often increase on weekends and holidays, so check ahead of time.
Hostal Boquete Near the Río Caldera ☎720 2573, ⓦwww.hostalboquete.com. Run by a young American man, four of the nine rooms here have balconies overlooking the fast-flowing river at the back, but if you don't get one of those he has installed decking out there too – a great place for

FESTIVAL DE LAS FLORES

January's Festival de las Flores y del Café sees Boquete's otherwise tasteful and discreet appreciation of coffee and flowers give way to lusty rejoicing. Throughout the ten-day celebrations the local fairgrounds explode with flower fireworks – you'll never see so many orchids – to coincide with the coffee harvest that ensures the next money-spinning batch of the region's most famous export. The locals adjust their own gardens accordingly, and stalls spring up selling food, handicrafts and plentiful coffee to the thousands of visitors wandering around, followed everywhere by loud, live music. In the evenings the rum is cracked open and people dance around the fairgrounds until the break of day. Book accommodation far in advance.

cold beers in the even colder night. Bathrooms have hot water. ④–⑤

Hostal Nomba Av A Oeste ☎6401 6278, ⓦwww .miradoradventures.com. Very popular with backpackers, this place has two kitchens and the staff speak English. They can help you arrange a camping trip on the mountain or near the hot springs and have equipment for hire. Dorms ②, doubles ④

Hostal Palacios Av Central ☎720 2040. *Palacios* has a friendly owner and a buzzingly central location. There are posters and photos everywhere and not a lot of space in the communal kitchen, adding to this place's intense atmosphere. Dorms ②, rooms ③

Hostal Refugio del Río Av B Oeste ☎720 2088 or 6613 1179, ⓦwww.refugiodelrio.com. This place is so handsome you'll think there must have been some mistake as they lead you to the dormitory. But there isn't, and even the bedding, seemingly of crushed velvet, exceeds expectations. There's also space for camping, a flash kitchen and lovely gazebo with a barbecue pit. Dorms ②, doubles ④

Pensión Marilós Av A Este at C 6 Sur ☎720 1380, ⓔmarilos66@hotmail.com. This place feels like a home, with a nice dining area, intriguing paintings on the walls and tiled corridors. Rooms are airy and sheets are crisp. The owner is helpful and speaks English. Bathrooms are shared. ③

Pensión Topas Av B. Porras ☎720 1005, ⓦwww .pension-topas.com. There are two nice rooms here with the backpacker in mind; the shared bathroom is solar-powered. Camping in the garden is permitted for a small fee, and you can hire bikes too. The owner speaks English. ③

Eating and drinking

Amigos South side of main square. Owned by a Canadian, tourists feed here while waiting for their morning tours. With live music during the week, there's a fair bit of drinking here, too. Big ol' breakfast US$4–5.

Choko Chettas Av Central, next to *Pizzeria La Volcánica*. Bright and glossily colourful, as if the ice cream desserts weren't fun enough. Marshmallow and strawberry kebab US$2.

Java Juice Av Central. A café that gives some thought to vegetarians as well as greasy burger-eaters. Burgers US$3–4, *batidos* US$1.50.

Pizzeria La Volcánica Av Central. Small restaurant, popular with locals, dishing up good-value pizza (mediums US$6–7).

El Sabrosón Av Central. Plain and airy canteen with good Panamanian food and fish cooked to order. Rice, beans, salad and something meaty US$2.50–3.

Shalom C 4a Sur. A rare purveyor of the bagel and other savouries. Small pizza-like snack US$1.

Zanzibar Av Central. A bar with plenty of comfy seats, dimly lit for seduction or naps. It has the feel of a hangout for young locals and travellers who haven't got round to leaving town yet. Occasionally gets going on weekends.

Directory

Bike rental You can rent bikes (US$15/day or US$3/hr) at the Boquete Tree Trek office in the Los Establos complex.

Books There's an English-language bookstore (Mon–Fri 9am–6pm) in the Los Establos complex.

Exchange There is a Banco Nacional (Mon–Fri 8am–3pm, Sat 9am–noon) on the main road a block south of the main square, which changes traveller's cheques. There's also a Banco General ATM in the Los Establos complex.

Internet Hastor Computers Internet Café (daily 8am–11pm; US$1/hr), on the second floor of the building opposite *Pizza La Volcánica* on Av Central.

Post office On the main square (Mon–Fri 7am–6pm, Sat 7am–5pm).

Moving on

By bus Buses back to David (every 30min 5.30am–7pm) leave from the main square (Parque Porras).

Bocas del Toro

Isolated on the Costa Rican border between the Caribbean and the forested slopes of the Cordillera Talamanca, **Bocas del Toro** ("mouths of the bull") is one of the most beautiful areas in Panama. It's also one of the most remote – the mainland portion of the province is connected to the rest of Panama by a single road, and the island chain offshore requires a ferry ride to reach.

Christopher Columbus first explored the coast of Bocas del Toro in 1502 in the search for a route to Asia; later, during the colonial era, European pirates often sheltered in the calm waters of the archipelago. By the nineteenth century, English ships from Jamaica were visiting

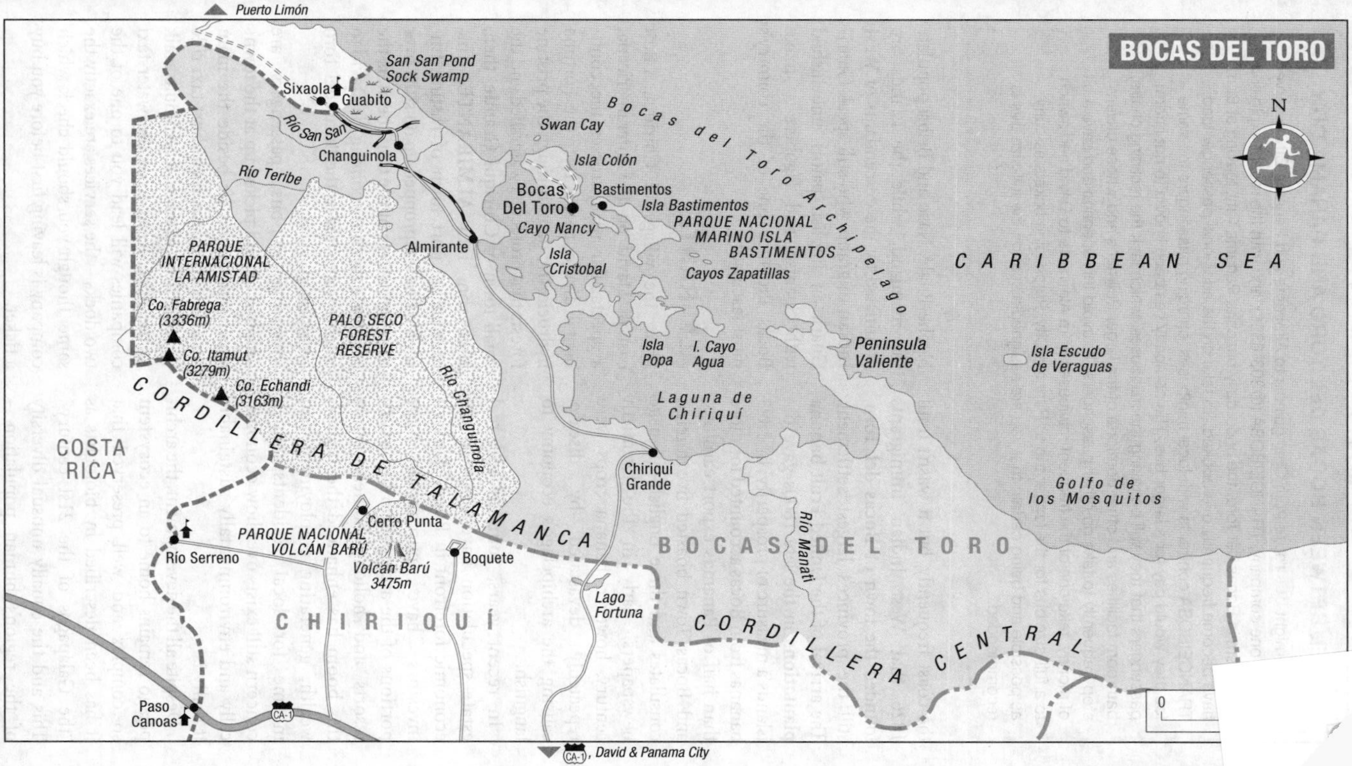
BOCAS DEL TORO
N
Puerto Limón
San San Pond
Sock Swamp
Sixaola
Guabito
Río San San
Changuinola
Río Teribe
Swan Cay
Isla Colón
Bocas del Toro Archipelago
Bocas
Del Toro
Bastimentos
Isla Bastimentos
PARQUE NACIONAL
MARINO ISLA
BASTIMENTOS
Cayo Nancy
Almirante
Isla
Cristobal
Cayos Zapatillas
CARIBBEAN SEA
PARQUE
INTERNACIONAL
LA AMISTAD
Co. Fabrega
(3336m)
Co. Itamut
(3279m)
Co. Echandi
(3163m)
PALO SECO
FOREST
RESERVE
Río Changuinola
Isla
Popa
I. Cayo
Agua
Peninsula
Valiente
Isla Escudo
de Veraguas
Laguna de
Chiriquí
CORDILLERA DE TALAMANCA
COSTA
RICA
Chiriquí
Grande
Golfo de
los Mosquitos
Cerro Punta
PARQUE NACIONAL
VOLCÁN BARÚ
Boquete
Río Serreno
Volcán Barú
3475m
BOCAS DEL TORO
Río Manatí
Lago
Fortuna
CHIRIQUÍ
CORDILLERA CENTRAL
Paso
Canoas
CA-1
0
CA-1, David & Panama City

the coast frequently, but it wasn't until 1826 that West Indian immigrants founded the town of **Bocas del Toro**, still the province's largest settlement. The arrival of the United Fruit **banana plantations** in the late 1800s gave the islands a measure of prosperity; by 1895 bananas from Bocas accounted for more than half of Panama's export earnings, and Bocas Town boasted five foreign consulates and three English-language newspapers. Early in the twentieth century, however, banana crops were repeatedly devastated by disease, causing the archipelago's economy to languish.

In recent years, **tourism** and real estate speculation have come to the economic forefront in Bocas. Foreign investors have purchased huge portions of the archipelago for luxury resorts and holiday homes. While this boom has enhanced the region's wealth, generating employment and income for local residents, much concern still exists over how economically and environmentally sustainable it really is.

Despite all the development, the archipelago remains home to an **ecosystem** so complex and well preserved that it has been described by biologists as "the Galapagos of the 21st century". This and the equally unusual diversity of the region's human population –

Ngobe-Buglé, Naso and Bribrí populate the mainland, while the islands are dominated by the descendants of **West Indian** migrants who still speak Guari-Guari, an English patois embellished with Spanish and Ngobere – make Bocas Province one of the country's most fascinating.

ALMIRANTE

From the village of Chiriquí, 14km east of David on the Interamericana, a spectacular road crosses the continental divide, passes over the Fortuna hydroelectric dam, through the pristine forests that protect its watershed and the small town of **Chiriquí Grande**, then, 50km on, into **ALMIRANTE**. This ramshackle port town of rusting tin-roofed houses, propped up on stilts over the calm waters of the Caribbean, is the best place for those coming via David to catch a water-taxi to the Bocas del Toro archipelago.

Arriving by bus, passengers are dropped off and picked up at the town's small bus station or beside the main road; in either case, it's a short taxi ride (US$0.50) or about a ten-minute walk to the port. Touts from the water-taxi companies will lead you to one of the two docks – the services are exactly the same, though you should check which company is leaving first before you buy a ticket.

Water-taxis to Bocas (US$4) leave every thirty minutes until about 6.30pm; the trip takes half an hour. The *Palanga*, or **car ferry**, runs to the islands four days a week and takes two hours (US$15). **Buses** for Changuinola (US$1), where you can get connections to the border, are frequent. There are frequent buses and *colectivos*, or mini-buses, between Almirante and David (4hr; $7) and you can catch the "express" bus to Panama City three times daily (8am, 7pm, 8pm; 10hr; US$23).

CHANGUINOLA

Sixteen kilometres from the border and 29km west of Almirante through seemingly endless banana plantations, **CHANGUINOLA** is a typically hot and uninteresting banana town where almost everyone works for the Chiriquí Land Company ("the Company", successor to United Fruit). **Buses** from Almirante and the border at Guabito arrive at the town terminal. **Water-taxis** to Bocas del Toro (US$4; 45min) leave every 45 minutes until 5:30pm from the dock near Finca 60, on the outskirts of town. Buses to Guabito and the border (20min) leave every thirty minutes. You can also catch a through bus to San José from Changuinola (10am; 8hr).

BOCAS TOWN

On the southeastern tip of Isla Colón, the provincial capital of **BOCAS DEL TORO,** otherwise known as Bocas Town, is the easiest base from which to explore the islands, beaches and reefs of the archipelago. The town, connected to the rest of the island by a narrow causeway, is busy and bustling, especially during the high season from December through April, when it explodes with tourists and backpackers. Rickety wooden buildings painted in faded pastels and a friendly and laid-back, mostly English-speaking population welcome you to the island's casual mêlée. The fact that there's nothing much to see is hardly a problem for those who like to dance and drink the night away after a hard day in the sea and sun.

What to see and do

Snorkelling is one of the main activities around Bocas Town. The tour operators listed on p.667 offer a variety of snorkel tours catering to backpackers and costing US$20–30, depending on destinations and gear rental. Endless possibilities exist for **boat excursions** further afield as well: east around the Península Valiente to the Isla Escudo de Veraguas, which aficionados consider one of the best diving spots in the whole Caribbean, or up one of the rivers into the rainforests of the mainland to visit isolated Ngobe-Buglé communities. Alternatively, you can head to Dolphin Bay, where you have a good chance of seeing the rather shy **bottle-nosed dolphins** that live here year-round. Be aware that bad weather may result in a change of itinerary or even cancellation and that beyond the main islands the sea can get very rough.

INTO COSTA RICA: GUABITO

From Changuinola the road runs 16km to the border with Costa Rica at Guabito–Sixaola, where there's little more than a few shops selling consumer goods to Costa Rican day-trippers. It's a short walk from the *migración* (daily 8am–6pm, closed for 1hr at lunch) across a bridge to Costa Rica, where you can change currency in the town of Sixaola (see p.533). Note that time changes (shifting 1hr back) when you cross the border to Costa Rica. You can also catch a through bus to San José from the border (9am, 11am, 4pm; 7hrs; US$10) or, if you just don't want to leave that Caribbean vibe behind, stop for a while in Puerto Viejo in northeastern Costa Rica (see p.573) (buses hourly, 6am–5pm; 4–5hr; US$3).

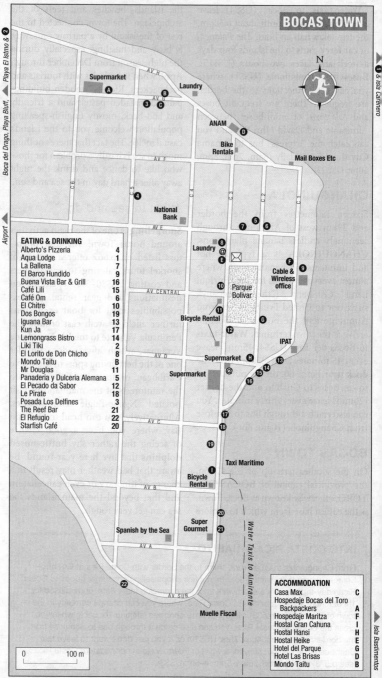

BOCAS TOWN

N

▲ 1 & Isla Carenero

◄ Playa El Istmo & 2

◄ Boca del Drago, Playa Bluff,

◄ Airport

Supermarket Ⓐ

AV H

Laundry

AV G

③ ③Ⓑ
Ⓒ

ANAM Ⓓ

Bike Rentals

Mail Boxes Etc

AV F

C6 C5 C4 C3 C2 C1

National Bank

AV E

④

⑤
⑦ ⑥

Ⓕ

⑧ⓔ
@

Laundry

✉

Parque Bolívar

Cable & Wireless office ⑨

AV CENTRAL

⑩

Ⓖ

Bicycle Rental

⑪

⑫

IPAT

⑬

AV D

Supermarket Ⓗ

⑭
⑮

Supermarket

@

⑯

AV C

⑰

⑱

⑲

Taxi Marítimo

AV B

Bicycle Rental Ⓘ

Water Taxis to Almirante

AV A

Spanish by the Sea

Super Gourmet

⑳
㉑

㉒

Muelle Fiscal

AV SUR

0 — 100 m

EATING & DRINKING
Alberto's Pizzeria	4
Aqua Lodge	1
La Ballena	7
El Barco Hundido	9
Buena Vista Bar & Grill	16
Café Lili	15
Café Om	6
El Chitre	10
Dos Bongos	19
Iguana Bar	13
Kun Ja	17
Lemongrass Bistro	14
Liki Tiki	2
El Lorito de Don Chicho	8
Mondo Taitu	B
Mr Douglas	11
Panadería y Dulcería Alemana	5
El Pecado da Sabor	12
Le Pirate	18
Posada Los Delfines	3
The Reef Bar	21
El Refugio	22
Starfish Café	20

ACCOMMODATION
Casa Max	C
Hospedaje Bocas del Toro Backpackers	A
Hospedaje Maritza	F
Hostal Gran Cahuna	I
Hostal Hansi	H
Hostal Heike	E
Hotel del Parque	G
Hotel Las Brisas	D
Mondo Taitu	B

► Isla Bastimentos

▼ Changuinola & Bocasdel Drago

Arrival and information

By air All flights arrive at the Bocas Airport, a small but modern building and airstrip four blocks from the main street. Aeroperlas (℡757 9341) and Air Panama (℡757 9841) both offer multiple daily flights from Panama City and David.

By boat Ferries from Almirante dock near the southern end of the main street, while scheduled water-taxis arrive and depart from the Taxi Maritimo dock next door – unscheduled water-taxis to the various islands and beaches also dock here, or they can be hailed from anywhere on the seafront.

Tourist information The IPAT office (Mon–Fri 8.30am–4.30pm, Sat & Sun 9am–4pm; ℡757 9642; Ⓔipatbocas@cw.net.pa) provides information, toilet facilities, internet and an exhibit on the history and ecology of the archipelago. ANAM's local office, C 3 & Av H (℡757 9442), gives permission to camp within the Isla Bastimentos Marine Park and can organize a visit to see turtles laying their eggs (May–Sept). Detailed maps of the area are available from most shops for US$2, and Ⓦwww.bocas.com is a good resource for hotel and tour operator information.

City transport

Bikes Bicycles are available for rent at Bocas Bikes, Av G at C 3 (US$2/hr or US$10/day), and mopeds at Bicicletas Lau, C 3 at Parque Bolívar (US$15/hr or US$90/day, with US$50 deposit).

Taxis Though everything in town is within easy walking distance, taxis are readily available (US$0.50 per person).

Accommodation

There's a good range of accommodation in Bocas, though it can be difficult to find a room during the high season and nearly impossible for groups of two or more without reservations. Things also fill up quickly on weekends and holidays, so it's a good idea to book in advance. However, several budget accommodations don't accept reservations, so it's best to arrive mid-morning. Hot water is not usually provided.

Casa Max Av G between C 4 & C 5 ℡757 9120, Ⓔcasa1max@hotmail.com. The clean, cheerfully painted rooms with balconies and comfortable beds give this place a homey feel, though the international cast of characters adds a bit of excitement. There's a pleasant patio area, a restaurant and good advice from the Dutch owners. ❹

Hospedaje Bocas Del Toro Backpackers Av G ℡757 9211. An incredibly cheap, if basic, option with dorms and a helpful manager. There's a shared kitchen, hammocks and a sand-floored TV lounge, but the shared bathrooms are less than sanitary. Dorms ❷

Hospedaje Maritza C 1 between Av Central and Av E ℡ 6654 3771. Across from the *Barco Hundido*,

---

TOUR OPERATORS IN BOCAS TOWN

There are loads of tour operators in town – below is just a small selection of what's available.

ANCON Expeditions at *Bocas Inn*, Av G at C 3 ℡757 9600, Ⓦwww.anconexpeditions.com. Excursions into the marine park and the forests on the mainland. Slightly more expensive than other operators but the most organized, with good boats. The only tour company in town with experienced naturalist guides.

Bocas Water Sports C 3 at Av A (℡757 9541, Ⓦwww.bocaswatersports.com). Professional and well-established US-run outfit offering diving, kayaking and snorkelling outings as well as equipment rental.

La Buga Dive Av Sur next to *El Refugio* (℡6781 0755, Ⓦwww.labugapanama.com). Offers mainly scuba packages.

Catamaran Snorkeling Tours Av Sur (℡757 9710, Ⓔmovida@cwp.net.pa).

J&J and Transparente Tours C 3 (℡757 9915, Ⓔtransparentetours@hotmail.com). Run by experienced locals, this long-established company gives regular trips into the marine park and more. They also rent out snorkel gear.

Starfleet C 1 (℡757 9630, Ⓦwww.starfleetscuba.com). Canadian company with a friendly, professional team focusing on diving excursions and full PADI open-water diving courses (about US$225).

this small and pleasant inn has a few clean, basic rooms and apartments at a good price. There's hot water but no a/c, and the only drawback to staying here is the disco across the way that thumps well into the night. ④

Hostal Gran Cahuna C 3 at Av B. Just needing a few finishing touches at the time of writing, this promises to be a solid budget option on the main island, with dormitory-style housing. No a/c, but the traditional, open-shuttered and large-windowed rooms allow ocean breezes to trundle in unfettered. Dorms ②

Hostal Hansi C 2 at Av D ☎757 9932. A relaxed, comfortable and economical place that caters to couples and more mature single travellers. Named after the large and friendly feline who's really the one in charge, it has a shared kitchen and simple, immaculate double and single rooms with private and shared baths, respectively. Singles ②, doubles ④

Hostal Heike C 3 between Av Central & Av E ☎757 9708, ⓦ www.bocas.com/heike.htm. The friendly sister hostel to *Mondo Taitu* (see below), *Heike* offers dorms with fans (one with a/c) that share clean, hot-water bathrooms. There's also a communal kitchen, a balcony overlooking the main street and free wi-fi. Dorms ②

Hotel Las Brisas C 3 at Av H ☎757 9248, ⓔ brisasbocas@cwb.net.pa. On the water, *Las Brisas* has a range of rooms, from water-view and well-kept with a/c to ramshackle and run-down with fan. ④–⑥

Mondo Taitu Av G between C 4 & C 5 ☎757 9425, ⓦ www.mondotaitu.com. The most original surfer hostel/party bar on Bocas, *Mondo Taitu* is full of youthful exuberance. It has a rainwater filtration system that provides fresh drinking water and is also working to promote awareness of an underutilized recycling centre on Bocas. All rooms and dormitory accommodation share hot-water bathrooms, plus there's a communal kitchen and a small cocktail bar. Dorms ②, doubles ④

Eating

Bocas has an excellent range of restaurants, with several international and budget options. Lobster, conch, octopus and other locally caught specialities taste particularly delicious in local coconut milk and Caribbean spice preparations. Be aware that restaurant opening hours can be erratic. Tap water is not drinkable, so don't expect free iced water. A large range of groceries is available at supermarkets, though prices are higher than on the mainland.

Cafés

Café Lili C 1 at Av D. The Caribbean fare here includes delicious home-made bread and good breakfasts (US$4–6). The waterfront location is priceless.

Café Om Av E at C 2. The Canadian–Indian owner draws from traditional family recipes, dishing out excellent curries with rice, naan and homemade chutney (US$6), as well as juices and wraps (US$4). Open Mon, Tues & Thurs–Sun for breakfast and dinner.

Panaderia y Dulceria Alemana Av E at C 2. The place to go for a European-style bakery breakfast. The combination of a Nutella-filled croissant and delicious cup of coffee will make your mouth water (US$2.50).

Starfish Café C 3. A good stop if you just can't live without that speciality coffee drink, *Starfish* also serves sandwiches and other snacks from US$3.

Restaurants

Alberto's Pizzeria C 5 Av E–F. This spacious, open-fronted restaurant serves good pizza and spaghetti dishes (US$4–10). Open Mon–Sat 5–11pm.

La Ballena Av E at C 3. An Italian restaurant serving great seafood, pizza and meat dishes (about US$8); the tables outside and impressive wine list are an added bonus.

Buena Vista Bar & Grill C 1 at Av D. This seafront eatery draws visiting Americans with US sports on satellite TV and US-style burgers, sandwiches and salads (from US$5). In the evening larger meals are served, including ribs. Closed Tues.

El Chitre C 3 & Av Central. Locals trust this eatery serving solid *comida típica* at low prices (from US$2), and so should you.

Dos Bongos C 3 at Av C. *Bongo*'s is an open-air eatery on the main drag serving *comida típica* and other offerings to a mixed clientele for just slightly inflated prices. US$5–10 for entrees.

Kun Ja C 3 at Av C. This Chinese restaurant, with indoor and waterfront seating, is one of the friendliest budget spots in town. It serves large portions of tasty meat and seafood dishes with either fried rice, chow mein or chop suey (US$4). Takeout is available. Closed Tues.

El Lorito de Don Chicho C 3 at Av E, across from Parque Bolívar. *Lorito* serves tasty, inexpensive, self-service Panamanian food – locals seldom eat anywhere else. *Don Chicho's* conglomerate also includes an internet café and a laundry next door; there's an accurate bus schedule to Boca del Drago out front. Breakfast and lunch for under US$5.

Mr Douglas C 3 at Av Central, across from Parque Bolívar. Apparently inspired by well-known US fast-food chains, *Mr Douglas* has just about every kind of deliciously greasy food you can imagine at money-saving prices. Let's face it – we all need comfort food sometimes. Burger and fries for US$5.

El Pecado da Sabor C 3. Not to be missed, the chef here cooks a combination of delicious Thai, Lebanese and Mexican dishes made with the finest local and imported ingredients (US$3–10). The best tables are on the rickety balcony overlooking the main street. Closed Sun & Mon.

Posada Los Delfines C 5 at Av G. This patio diner, in front of the hotel of the same name, has a daily US$5 breakfast buffet and reputedly the best rice and beans on the island. You can also pick up free wi-fi here.

El Refugio Av Sur. The building is rather flimsy, but it houses the only restaurant in town where you can watch the sun set over the mainland from the water's edge. The quiet atmosphere and good seafood and meat dishes cost a few extra dollars, from US$7.

Drinking and nightlife

Several restaurants double as music and drinking venues in the evening, plus there are a few good bars where you can relax with a cold Balboa Ice or cocktail. On weekends, many locals head to *Discoteca El Encanto* on seafront Calle 3 to dance the night away to pounding reggae beats.

Bars

La Iguana C 1. The *Iguana's* happy-hour drink specials make it one of the most popular places to kick the night off.

Mondo Taitu Av G. With all kinds of creative cocktails and drink specials, there's a frat-house–style theme party here most nights of the week, and these guys take their dress-up almost as seriously as their commitment to sustainable travel.

Le Pirate C 3. Seafront restaurant serving unremarkable fish and seafood – it's more popular as a bar, especially for sundowners.

The Reef Bar C 3. At the southern tip of the street, come here for a true local experience, with cheap drinks and dancing on weekends.

Clubs

Aqua Lodge Isla Carenero. Just across the water, a US$1 boat ride away, *Aqua Lodge* really gets going on ladies' nights (Wed & Sat) with free drinks until midnight for the girls, a big, starlit dancefloor and a water trampoline and diving board on which to cool your heels.

El Barco Hundido C 1, beside the Cable & Wireless office. Locally known as the "Wreck Deck", this spot is the most popular hangout for locals, tourists and surfers, who come here to drink cold beer (US$2) until the early hours. A DJ performs most nights, playing a mix of modern R&B, '80s pop and the ubiquitous Bob Marley. Opens at 7pm and gets lively after 9pm.

Liki Tiki Playa El Istmito, Feria del Mar. Large, American-run beachfront bar and restaurant with volleyball court that's about a 20min walk out of town from the main street. Closed Mon and Tues.

Directory

Exchange At Banco National, C 4 (Mon–Fri 8am–2pm, Sat 9am–noon), you can change traveller's cheques and use the 24hr ATM. *Hotel Estrella De Bocas*, C 1, is the only place in town that exchanges euros.

Internet Bocas@internet, C 3 (7am–10pm; US$2/hr); Don Chicho Internet, C 3 (7am–11pm; US$2/hr); Cable & Wireless, C 1 (Mon–Fri 8am–noon & 1–4pm).

Language schools Spanish by the Sea, Av A at C 4 (☎ 757 9518, ⓦ www.spanishbythesea.com), is one of three lively and relaxed schools for travellers run by a hip Dutch/Tico family. Offers affordable lesson plans for extended vacationers as well as a 6hr crash course for US$60.

SURFER'S PARADISE

In the past few years, Bocas has been gaining more attention as an international surfing destination. The best waves come between December and March, and there are many excellent and varied surfing spots in the area. Although none are within walking distance of Bocas, the town is nonetheless the best base. The main hotspots include Carenero, off the northeastern tip of Isla Carenero; Dumpers, just north of Boca del Drago; Paunch, on the northeastern tip of Isla Colón; Red Frog Beach, on Bastimentos; and Silverbacks, between Bastimentos and Carenero. The first three break over a reef, so wear booties.

Laundry The best place in town is behind *Don Chicho's* – a slim alley behind the internet spot leads you back to the laundry (US$5/bag).

Medical care There is one hospital on the island at Av G & C 10 (☎757 9201). It has 24hr emergency services.

Pharmacies Chen Pharmacy and Rosa Blanca Pharmacy are both on C 3 near Av A. They're open on island time, generally Mon–Sat 9am–5pm.

Post office The main post office is on Av E (Mon–Fri 8am–4pm, Sat 8am–noon). There's also Mail Boxes Etc, Av F (Mon–Fri 8am–5pm, Sat & Sun noon–5pm; ☎757 9660, @mbebocasv98 @yahoo.com).

Supermarkets Isla Supermercado, Av 3, is the main grocery. Super Gourmet, Av A and C 3, carries hard-to-find items and is a good option for vegetarians; also has a decent lunch counter. Supermercado Hawaii, Av G, has a small selection but cheaper prices for basic items.

Surfboard rental Surfboards generally rent for US$15–20/day, but prices vary with size, quality and availability. One option is Tropix, C 3 (closed Sun); there's also Flow, Av E, and *Hostal Heike/ Mondo* Taitu, C 3 at Av G.

Telephones See Internet, p.669.

Moving on

By air to: Changuinola (4–5 daily; 15min); David (Mon–Fri 2 daily; 30min); Panama City (4–5 daily; 1hr); Puerto Limón (1 daily; 30min); San José (via David: Mon, Wed, Fri, Sun 2 daily; direct: 1 daily; 1hr 30min). All flights leave from the airport on Av E, a few blocks from town. The operators are Aeroperlas (☎757 9341, @www.aeroperlas.com), Air Panama (☎ 757 9841, www.flyairpanama.com), and Nature Air (☎800 433 7300). All flights have maximum weight limits of 25lb, which sometimes includes carry-on luggage; excess is charged at US$0.30–0.50 per pound.

By boat to: Almirante (every 30min; 30min); Changuinola (8 daily; 1hr).

AROUND BOCAS TOWN

The islands, cayes and mainland waterways surrounding Bocas Town offer wide-ranging opportunities for relaxing on pristine beaches, visiting Ngobe-Buglé villages and diving near unspoilt coral reefs. A quick bus or cab ride away are the beaches of the rest of **Isla Colón**, while nearby *islas* Carenero and Bastimentos are favoured by visiting surfers. Most visitors make a point of exploring the **Parque Nacional Marina Isla Bastimentos**, a renowned marine park that stretches across a series of islands in the archipelago.

Boca del Drago

Boca del Drago is a small fishing community set on one of Isla Colón's broad horseshoe bays, whose palm-fringed beach and calm, coral-filled waters are perfect for swimming. A great budget option for groups seeking a paradise well outside the city limits is *Cabañas Estefani-ECOTEC* (☎6624 9246; camping ❶, rooms ❸). Students with the Institute for Tropical Ecology and Conservation (@www.itec-edu .org) stay here while doing fieldwork. Next door, *Yarisnori* serves simple, delicious seafood (closed Tues). A **bus** (1hr) runs to Boca del Drago from the square in Bocas Town several times daily; end-of-day services back to Bocas can get crowded. Alternatively, you can hire a **taxi** in Bocas to take you to either Boca del Drago (US$25) or **Playa Bluff** (US$20) and arrange to be picked up later. Otherwise, the best way to get around the island is to rent a bicycle in Bocas Town.

Isla Carenero

Just 200m across the water from Bocas Town, tiny **Isla Carenero** is beginning to receive more visitors thanks to a new backpackers' hostel and bar/disco, *Aqua Lodge* (☎6734 2550; dorms ❷), and the most accessible and consistent surf break in the archipelago at Punta Carenero. On the westward side of the island, a narrow concrete path goes as far as the small marina; the island is rather dingy here, and wooden houses on stilts stand over the partially water-logged and heavily littered ground. The eastern side is accessed by a sandy path with small bridges over the many drainage channels and, though more pleasant than the west side of the island, it's hardly pristine.

To get to the island, catch a **water-taxi** (US$1) from Bocas. For great seafood, head to *The Pickled Parrot* or *Dona Mara*.

Bastimentos

Outside the national marine park on the western tip of Isla Bastimentos, the small fishing community of **Basti-mentos** is not really set up for mass tourism, making it a great place to stay if you're seeking more relaxation than Bocas Town offers. Be sure to bring cash, though, as there's no bank or ATM on the island. Regular **boats** run from the water-taxi terminal in Bocas Town (US$2.50 per person).

An undulating concrete path acts as the community's main thoroughfare, snaking its way between the coastline and a steep, green hillside dotted with wooden stilt houses. A jungle path, occasionally impassable after heavy rains, leads to several pristine beaches twenty minutes away on the other side of the island.

Unfortunately, major developers have plans to mar this unspoilt natural habitat with enormous luxury resorts. One major project has been hampered by angry local and expat communities, but another developer is expected to buy the land and continue the project.

Accommodation

Beverly's Hill ☎757 9923. A gem on the hillside behind the main path, this place offers rooms in cabañas set in a garden that's home to the elusive red frog. For a few extra dollars, try the top room with "the best view on the island". ❹

Hostal Bastimentos ☎757 9053. This sprawling maze of a backpackers' hostel gives a choice of accommodation, from dorms to posh bedrooms with a/c and hot water. There's a communal kitchen and vibe here, and it's just a 20min jungle hike to a pristine, undeveloped beach. Dorms ❸, doubles ❹

Hospedaje El Jaguar ☎757 9383, ✉hosp _jaguar@hotmail.es. This purple, hammock-strewn spot over the water is clean, comfortable and run by the Archibalds, one of the best-known families on the island. ❹

Tio Toms ☎757 9831, ⊛www.tio-tom.com. A thatched-roof inn built over water, with five simple rooms and great breakfasts cooked by the German owners. An avid naturalist, the man of the house also offers customized tours exploring the islands' natural wonders. ❹

Eating

Pelicanos ☎757 9830. At the east end of town, with a bar and a terrace over the water and a friendly owner who can arrange tours, this popular place serves home-made Italian dishes at fair prices (US$5–10). It's known for its pizzas.

Restaurante Ali Katy Another Archibald institution, *Ali Katy* has the best hot pepper sauce in the archipelago and the coldest beer on the island. Local dishes US$3–10.

Restaurante Sweet Amy *Sweet Amy* makes a delicious and filling pancake breakfast for under US$5. Lunches and dinners run up to US$15.

The Rooster ☎6788 9186. Over the water and next door to *Roots*, there are plenty of good vegetarian options here at economical prices (US$3–6). Try the stir-fry. Closed Mon.

Roots The most popular eatery in town, *Roots* serves up dynamite *comida típica*, which in this context means fresh seafood and coconut rice dishes (US$3–10). Closed Tues.

Up in the Hill ✉upinthehill_shop@yahoo .com. The couple who own this organic snack shop have nurtured a holistic farm/retreat. The lemonade is squeezed fresh, the brownies are delectable and the organic products are numerous and varied (US$3–5). In addition to all this, they occasionally take on volunteers. From town, follow the path near the police station and continue through the jungle, keeping watch for markers along the way.

Parque Nacional Marina Isla Bastimentos

Most visitors to Bocas come to explore the pristine beauty of **Parque Nacional Marina Isla Bastimentos**, a 130-square-kilometre reserve encompassing several virtually undisturbed ecosystems that include rainforest, mangrove and coral reef supporting an immense diversity of marine life, including dolphins, sea turtles and a kaleidoscopic variety of fish.

Some of the best **beaches** in the archipelago are also in the park, on the eastern side of the island facing the open sea. Due to their powerful surf and currents, however, swimming here is dangerous, but they are huge, uncrowded and undeveloped. The most popular is **Red Frog Beach**, an idyllic stretch of sand that takes its name from the tiny bright-red poison-dart frogs (don't touch!) that inhabit the forest behind the beach and are found nowhere else in the world.

Much further east, the fourteen-kilometre stretch of **Playa Larga** is an important nesting site for sea turtles between May and September. There's an ANAM ranger station here, where you may be charged a $10 park entrance fee,

and a basic refuge where you can camp for another $10; you'll need to stay overnight if you want to see the turtles lay their eggs. Request permission from the ANAM office in Bocas Town (see p.667) to come here.

Southeast of Isla Bastimentos, but still within the park, are the **Cayos Zapatillas**. Two dreamy, coral-fringed islands, the Zapatillas are excellent for snorkelling but you must pay the park admission fee at the ANAM station on the southern island. On the prettier northern island, camping is also possible with permission from ANAM in Bocas Town.

The easiest way to visit the marine park and other spots around Bocas Town is with one of the area's **tour companies** (see box, p.667). A number of agencies offer day-trips to beaches and snorkelling spots in and around the park, typically costing US$15–30 per person and including a stop at a restaurant for lunch (US$6–10). The more expensive tours often provide free cold drinks and snorkelling equipment. Alternatively, you can hire a **boat** in Bocas Town or Bastimentos: with a group of four or more people this could be cheaper than an agency tour and lets you decide exactly where you want to go. A typical day's excursion might include a visit to the Cayos Zapatillas in the morning, lunch and snorkelling at Crawl Cay and an afternoon on Red Frog Beach.

Language

Language

There's a bewildering collection of languages across the Central American isthmus, numbering well above thirty in all; fortunately for the traveller, there are two that dominate – English, primarily in Belize, the Bay Islands of Honduras, and the Atlantic coast and Corn Islands of Nicaragua, but spoken to some extent all along the Caribbean coast; and Spanish everywhere else.

ENGLISH

Belizean English may sound familiar from a distance and, if you listen to a few words, you may think that its meaning is clear. Listen a little further, however, and you'll realize that complete comprehension is just out of reach. What you're hearing is, in fact, **Creole**, a beautifully warm and relaxed language, typically Caribbean and loosely based on English, with elements of Spanish and indigenous languages. A similar dialect, Guari Guari, is spoken in the Panamanian province of Bocas del Toro. Written Creole, which you'll come across in Belizean newspapers, is a little easier to get to grips with. There's an active movement in Belize to formalize the language and a dictionary is currently in production. Luckily, almost anyone who can speak Creole can also speak English.

In the Bay Islands of Honduras things are much simpler. English is English rather than Creole, and immediately understandable, albeit spoken with a unique, broad accent. Influenced by Caribbean, English and Scots migrants over the years, local inflexions turn even the most commonplace of remarks into an attractive statement. English, however, is slowly being supplanted by Spanish as the language heard on the street, as growing numbers of mainlanders make the islands their home.

SPANISH

Those new to the region can take heart – **Spanish**, as spoken across Latin America, is one of the easier languages there is to learn and even the most faltering of attempts to speak it is greatly appreciated. Apart from the major tourist areas in Guatemala, Costa Rica and in some parts of Panama and Honduras, English is not widely spoken; taking the trouble to get to know at least the basics of Spanish will both make your travels considerably easier and reap countless rewards in terms of reception, appreciation and understanding of people and places.

Overall, Latin American Spanish is clearer and slower than that of Spain – gone are the lisps and bewilderingly rapid, slurred, soft consonants of the old country. There are, however, quite strong variations in accent across Central America: Guatemalan Spanish has the reputation of being clear, precise and eminently understandable even to the worst of linguists, whilst the language as spoken in Honduras – thick and fast – can initially bewilder even those who believed themselves to be reasonably fluent. Nicaraguans in particular take great pleasure in fooling around with language, creating new words, pronouncing certain letters differently and employing different grammar. There are enough Nicaraguanismos – words and sayings particular to Nicaragua – to fill a 275-page dictionary. As far as pronunciation goes, the "s" is often dropped from word endings and the "v" and "b" sounds are fairly interchangeable.

Pronunciation

For the most part, the rules of **pronunciation** are straightforward and strictly observed. Unless there's an accent, words ending in d, l, r and z are **stressed** on the last syllable, all others on the second last. All **vowels** are pure and short.

A somewhere between the "A" sound of back and that of father

E as in get

I as in police

O as in hot

U as in rule

C is soft before E and I, otherwise hard; cerca is pronounced "serka".

G works the same way – a guttural "H" sound (like the ch in loch) before E or I, a hard G elsewhere; gigante is pronounced "higante".

H is always silent.

J is the same sound as a guttural G; jamón is pronounced "hamon".

LL sounds like an English Y; tortilla is pronounced torteeya. In some areas it is pronounced like an English J.

N is as in English, unless there is a tilde (accent) over it, when it becomes like the N in "onion"; mañana is pronounced "manyana".

QU is pronounced like an English K.

R is rolled, **RR** doubly so.

V sounds like a cross with B, vino becoming beano.

X is slightly softer than in English, sometimes almost like SH, so that Xela becomes "sheyla"; between vowels in place names it has an H sound – México is pronounced "May-hee-ko".

Z is the same as a soft C; cerveza is pronounced "servesa".

Formal and informal address

For English speakers one of the most difficult things to get to grips with is the distinction between formal and informal address – when to use it and to whom and how to avoid causing offence. Generally speaking, the third-person "**usted**" indicates respect and/or a non-familiar relationship and is used in business, for people you don't know and for those older than you. Second-person "**tú**" is for children, friends and contemporaries in less formal settings. (Remember also that in Latin America the second-person **plural** – "vosotros" – is never used, so "you" plural will always be "ustedes"). In day-to-day exchanges, genuine mistakes on the part of an obviously non-native

speaker will be well received and corrected with good humour.

One idiosyncrasy is the widespread use of "**vos**" in Central America. Now archaic in Spain, it is frequently used in place of *tú*, as an intimate form of address between friends of the same age. In most tenses, conjugation is exactly the same as for *tú*. In the present indicative, however, the last syllable is stressed with an accent (*tú comes/vos comés*); in "-ir" verbs in this tense, the final "i" is kept instead of changing to an "e" (*tú escribes/vos escribís*). In commands, the vos form drops the final "r" of the infinitive, replacing it with an accented vowel (*tú come/vos comé*). Take your lead from those around you – if you are addressed in the "*vos*" form it is a sign of friendship and should be reciprocated; on the other hand it is sometimes seen as patronizing to use it with someone you don't know well.

Nicknames and turns of speech

Nicknames are very common in Central America, used in both speech and writing and for any situation from addressing a casual acquaintance to referring to political candidates. Often they centre on obvious physical characteristics – *flaco/a* (thin), *gordo/a* (fat), *rubio/a* (blond).

Often, these nicknames will be further softened by **diminution** – the addition of the suffix *-ito* or *-ita* at the end of nouns and adjectives, a trend used sometimes with a passion in everyday speech. You are quite likely to hear someone talk about their *hermanito* for example, which translates as "little brother" regardless of respective ages, whilst *mi hijita* ("my little daughter") can as easily mean a grown woman as a child.

Also very common are **casual street addresses**, used lightly in brief encounters and to soothe transactions. Heard in virtually every country are *(mi) amor* – used in much the same way as "love" in England and also between friends

– as is *jóven* or *jovencito/a*, young one. More specific to each country (often but not always between men) are terms used to make casual questions or remarks less intrusive. *Papa* (literally "father") is used daily in Honduras, for example as in "*¿Qué hora tiene, papa?*" (What time is it?), whilst the Nicaraguans use *primo* (cousin). Panamanian men regularly address each other as *compadre*, often abbreviated to *compa*. In Nicaragua, the local term (a fond one) for foreigners is *chele/a*.

Politesse

Verbal courtesy is an integral part of speech in Spanish and one that – once you're accustomed to the pace and flow of life in Central America – should become instinctive. Saying *buenos días/buenas tardes* and waiting for the appropriate response is usual when asking for something at a shop or ticket office for example, as is adding *señor* or *señora* (in this instance similar to the US "sir" or "ma'am"). The response when thanking someone for a service is more likely to be *para servirle* (literally "here to serve you") rather than the casual *de nada* ("you're welcome"). The *tss tss* sound is commonly employed to attract attention, particularly in restaurants. In this very polite culture shouting is frowned upon.

On meeting, or being introduced to someone, Central Americans will say *con mucho gusto*, "it's a pleasure", and you should do the same. On departure you will more often than not be told *¡que le vaya bien!* ("may all go well"), a simple phrase that nonetheless invariably sounds sincere and rounds off transactions nicely. In rural areas, especially, it is usual to leave even complete strangers met on the path with *!Adiós, que le vaya bien!* Note that the Castilian term **coger** (to take/grab) has a very different meaning in Central and South America, where the verb **tomar** is commonly used. Make sure you therefore say "tomar un autobus" (get the bus), instead of the Castilian "coger un autobus"!

WORDS AND PHRASES

Basic words

a lot	mucho
afternoon	tarde
and	y
bad	mal(o)/a
big	gran(de)
boy	chico
closed	cerrado/a
cold	frío/a
day	día
entrance	entrada
exit	salida
girl	chica
good	bien/buen(o)/a
he	él
her	ella
here	aquí
his	suyo
hot	calor/caliente
how much	cuánto
if	si
information	información
later	más tarde/después
less	menos
ma'am/missus	señora
man	señor/hombre
miss	señorita
more	más
morning	mañana
night	noche
no	no
now	ahora
open	abierto/a
or	o
please	por favor
she	ella
small	pequeño/a
sir/mister	señor
thank you	gracias
that	eso/a
their	suyo/de ellos
there	allí
they	ellos
this	este/a
today	hoy
tomorrow	mañana
what	qué
where	dónde
when	cuándo
with	con
without	sin
woman	mujer/hembra

yes	sí
yesterday	ayer

Basic phrases

Hello	¡Hola!
Goodbye	Adiós
See you later	Hasta luego
Good morning	Buenos días
Good afternoon	Buenas tardes
Good night	Buenas noches
Sorry	Lo siento/Discúlpeme
Excuse me	Con permiso/perdón
How are you?	¿Cómo está (usted)?/ ¿Qué tal?
Nice to meet you	Mucho gusto
Not at all/ You're welcome	De nada
I (don't) understand	(No) Entiendo
Do you speak English?	¿Habla (usted) inglés?
I (don't) speak Spanish	(No) Hablo español
What (did you say)?	¿Mande?/¿Cómo?
Could you ..., please?	¿Podría ... por favor?
... repeat that	... repetirlo
... speak slowly	... hablar más despacio
... write that down	... escribirlo
My name is ...	Me llamo ...
What's your name?	¿Cómo se llama usted?
I'm from	Soy de ...
... America	... Estados Unidos
... Australia	... Australia
... Canada	... Canadá
... England	... Inglaterra
... Ireland	... Irlanda
... New Zealand	... Nueva Zelanda
... Scotland	... Escocia
... South Africa	... Sudáfrica
... Wales	... Gales
Where are you from?	De dónde es usted?
How old are you?	¿Cuántos años tiene? (usted)
I am ... years old	Tengo ... años.
I don't know	No sé
Do you know ...?	¿Sabe ...?
I want	Quiero
I'd like ...	Quisiera ... por favor
What's that?	¿Qué es eso?
What is this called in Spanish?	¿Cómo se llama este en español?
There is (is there)?	Hay (?)
Do you have ...?	¿Tiene ...?
What time is it?	¿Qué hora es?
May I take a photograph?	¿Puedo sacar una foto?

Basic needs, services and places

ATM	cajero automático
bank	banco
bathroom/toilet	baño/sanitario
beach	playa
bookstore	librería
border crossing	frontera
cheap hotel	un hotel barato
church	iglesia
embassy	embajada
highway	carretera
immigration office	inmigración
internet café	cibercafé
lake	lago
library	biblioteca
laundry	lavandería
map	mapa
market	mercado
museum	museo
national park	parque nacional
pharmacy	farmacia
(main) post office	el correo (central)
restaurant	restaurante
supermarket	supermercado
telephones	teléfonos
telephone office	cabina de teléfono
tourist office	oficina de turismo

Numbers, months and days and colours

Numbers (números)

1	un/uno/una
2	dos
3	tres
4	cuatro
5	cinco
6	seis
7	siete
8	ocho
9	nueve
10	diez
11	once
12	doce
13	trece
14	catorce
15	quince
16	dieciséis
17	diecisiete
18	dieciocho
19	diecinueve
20	veinte

677

21	veintiuno
22	veintidos
30	treinta
40	cuarenta
50	cincuenta
60	sesenta
70	setenta
80	ochenta
90	noventa
100	cien
101	ciento uno
200	doscientos
201	doscientosuno
500	quinientos
1000	mil
1999	mil novecientos noventa y nueve
2000	dos mil
100,000	cien mil
1,000,000	un millón

first	primero/a
second	segundo/a
third	tercero/a
fifth	quinto/a
tenth	décimo/a

Months (meses)
January	enero
February	febrero
March	marzo
April	abril
May	mayo
June	junio
July	julio
August	agosto
September	septiembre
October	octubre
November	noviembre
December	diciembre

Days (días)
Monday	lunes
Tuesday	martes
Wednesday	miércoles
Thursday	jueves
Friday	viernes
Saturday	sábado
Sunday	domingo

Colours (colores)
red	rojo/a
orange	naranja
yellow	amarillo/a
green	verde
blue	azul
indigo	índigo/a
violet/purple	violeta
white	blanco/a
black	negro/a
brown	marrón
grey	gris

Getting around

Transportation
bus	autobús/camión
bus station	estación de autobuses
bus stop	parada de autobús
boat	barco/lancha
ferry	transbordador
dock/pier	muelle
airplane	avión
airport	aeropuerto
car	carro
4WD	tracción integral
taxi	taxi
truck	camión
pick-up	camioneta
hitchhike	autostop (hacer autostop: to hitchhike)
train	tren
train station	estación de trenes
bicycle	bicicleta (abb. bici)
motorcycle	moto
ticket	billete
ticket office	taquilla
I'd like a ticket to …	(Necesito) un billete para …
How much is a … ticket to …?	¿Cuanto cuesta un billete de … a?
… first-class	… primera clase
… second-class	… segunda clase
… one-way	… sólo ida
… return/round-trip	… ida y vuelta
I would like to rent a …	Me gustaría alquilar un/una …
Where does … to … leave from?	¿De dónde sale …para …?
What time does the … leave for …?	¿A qué hora sale …para …?
What time does the … arrive in …?	¿A qué hora llega … en …?

Directions
Where is …?	¿Dónde está …?
How do I get to …?	¿Por dónde se va a …?
I'm looking for …	Estoy buscando …
Is this the way to …?	¿Es esta la carretera hacia …?
I'm lost	Estoy perdido/a
Is it far?	¿Está lejos?

left	izquierda
right	derecha
straight ahead	derecho/recto
north	norte
south	sur
east	este
west	oeste
street	calle
avenue	avenida
block	manzana

Money (dinero) and shopping

How much is it?	¿Cuánto es/cuesta?
It's too expensive	Es demasiado caro
Do you have anything cheaper?	¿No tiene algo más barato?
Do you accept …?	Aceptan …?
… credit cards	… tarjetas de crédito
…travellers' cheques	… cheques de viajero
… US dollars	… dólares americanos
I would like to change some dollars.	Me gustaría/tengo que cambiar unos dólares
Can you change dollars?	¿Pueden cambiar dólares?
What is the exchange rate?	¿Cuál es el tipo de cambio?

Shopping

I would like to buy …	Me gustaría comprar …
… a bag	… un bolso
… a book	… un libro
… clothes	… ropa
… film	… una película
… a hammock	… una hamaca
… a hat	… un sombrero
… a jacket	… una chaqueta
… a mobile phone	… un móvil
… a painting	… un cuadro
… a shirt	… una camisa
… shoes	… unos zapatos
… a skirt	… una falda
… a sleeping bag	… un saco de dormir
… socks	… unos calcetines
… a tent	… una carpa
… trousers	… un pantalón
… underwear	… ropa interior
I'm just looking	Estoy mirando
Could I look at it/that?	¿Puedo ver eso/aquello?
Please give me …	Deme …, por favor
… one like that	… uno asi

Accommodation

Is there a … nearby?	¿Hay … aquí cerca?
… guesthouse	… casa de huéspedes
… hotel	… un hotel
… hostel	… albergue de juventud (also hostal)
… campground	camping
Do you have …?	¿Tiene …?
… a room	… un cuarto
… with two beds	… con dos camas
… a double bed	… con cama matrimonial
… a dorm room	… cuarto colectivo
… a tent	… una carpa
… a cabin	… una cabina
It's for	Es para
… one person	… una persona
… two people	… dos personas
… for one night	… una noche
… one week	… una semana
Does it have …	¿Tiene …?
… a shared bath	… baño compartido
… a private bath	… baño privado
… hot water	… agua caliente
Can one …?	¿Se puede …?
… camp (near) here?	¿… acampar aquí (cerca)?
… sling a hammock here?	¿ … poner una hamaca aquí?
… swim here?	¿… nadar aquí?
How much is it …?	¿Cuánto es/cuesta …?
… per night	… por noche
… per person	… por persona
… per room	… por cuarto
Does the price include breakfast?	¿El precio incluye el desayuno?
May I see a room?	¿Puedo ver un cuarto?
May I see another room?	¿Puedo ver otro cuarto?
Yes, it's fine.	Sí, está bien.
I'd like to reserve a …	Me gustaría reservar un/una …

Health and safety

I'm sick.	Estoy enfermo/a
He/she is sick.	Él/Ella está enfermo/a.
I'm allergic to …	Soy alérgica a …
He/she is allergic to …	Él/Ella es alérgica a …
I need to see a doctor	Tengo que ver un doctor.
He/she needs to see a doctor	Él/ella tiene que ver un doctor.

I need to go to …	Tengo que ir …
… the hospital	… al hospital
… a health clinic	… a una clínica
… a pharmacy	… a una farmacia
He/she needs to go to…	Él/ella tiene que ir a …
I have a …	Me duele …
… headache	… la cabeza
… stomach ache	… el estómago
I have a fever	Tengo fiebre
I have hurt my…	Me dice daño …
… arm	… al brazo
… back	… a la espalda
… foot	… al pie
… head	… a la cabeza
… hand	… a la mano
… knee	… a la rodilla
… leg	… a la pierna
… neck	… al cuello
He/she has hurt	Él/ella se hizo daño …
I was bitten/ scratched by …	Me mordió/arañó …
… a dog	… un perro
… a cat	… un gato
… a snake	… una serpiente
… a mosquito	… un mosquito
… a spider	… una araña
… a jellyfish	… una medusa
He/she was bitten/ scratched by …	Le mordió/arañó un/una …
I am dehydrated	Estoy deshidratado/a
medicine	medicina
dose/dosage	dosis
sunscreen/sunblock	crema solar/filtro solar
bug repellent	repelente para insectos
antibiotics	antibióticos
It's an emergency	Es una emergencia
police	policía
policeman	un policía
police station	comisaría
tourist police	policía turística
ambulance	ambulancia
fire brigade	bomberos
Red Cross	Cruz Roja
Help!	¡Ayuda!
Fire!	¡Fuego!
Go away!	¡Váyase!
Leave me alone!	¡Déjeme en paz!
I've been robbed	Me han robado
He/she has been robbed	Le han robado
I need to fill out an insurance report	Tengo que rellenar una reclamación de seguro
I need help	Necesito/preciso ayuda
Please can you help me?	¿Me podría ayudar por favor?

MENU READER

While menus vary by country and region, these words and terms will help negotiate most menus.

Basic dining vocabulary

almuerzo	lunch
carta (la)	menu
cena	dinner
cocina	kitchen
comida corriente	cheap set menu, usually served at lunch time
comida típica	typical cuisine
cuchara	spoon
cuchillo	knife
desayuno	breakfast
merienda	afternoon tea
mesa	table
plato	plate
plato del día	dish of the day
plato fuerte	main course
plato vegetariano	vegetarian dish
servilleta	napkin
silla	chair
taza	mug/cup
tenedor	fork
vaso	glass
La cuenta, por favor	The bill, please
¿Contiene …?	Does this contain …? (for food allergies, vegetarians, etc)
Soy vegetariano/a	I'm a vegetarian
No como carne.	I don't eat meat

Basic food vocabulary

arroz	rice
aceite	oil
ajo	garlic
ajillo	garlic butter
arroz	rice
azúcar	sugar
chile	chilli
galletas	biscuits
hielo	ice
huevos	eggs
mantequilla	butter
mermelada	jam
miel	honey
mixto	mixed seafood/meats
mostaza	mustard
pan (integral)	bread (wholemeal)
pan de coco	coconut bread
pimienta	pepper
queso	cheese

sal	salt
salsa de tomate	tomato sauce

Frutas (fruit)

cereza	cherry
chirimoya	custard apple
ciruela	plum
coco	coconut
durazno	peach
frutilla	strawberry
guayaba	guava
higo	fig
lima	lime
limón	lemon
manzana	apple
maracuyá	passion fruit
melón	melon
mora	blackberry
naranja	orange
papaya	papaya
pera	pear
piña	pineapple
pitaya	cactus fruit
plátano	banana
sandía	watermelon
tomate de arbol	tree tomato
tamarindo	tamarind
toronja	grapefruit
uva	grapes

Legumbres/verduras (vegetables)

aguacate	avocado
alcachofa	artichoke
apio	celery
arvejas	peas
berenjena	aubergine/eggplant
brécol	broccoli
calabaza	pumpkin
calabazín	courgette/zucchini
cebolla	onion
champiñón	mushroom
coliflor	cauliflower
curtida	pickled cabbage, beetroot and carrots
ensalada	salad
espinaca	spinach
frijoles	beans
frijoles volteados	refried beans
gallo pinto	mixed rice and beans
hongo	mushroom
lechuga	lettuce
lentejas	lentils
maíz	sweet corn/maize
menestra	bean/lentil stew

palmito	palm heart
papa	potato
papas fritas	French fries
pepinillo	gherkin
pepino	cucumber
tomate	tomato
zanahoria	carrot

Carne (meat) and aves (poultry)

bistec	steak
búfalo	buffalo
carne	beef
carne de chancho	pork
cerdo	pork
chicharrones	pork scratchings, crackling
chuleta	pork chop
chumpipe	turkey
conejo	rabbit
cordero	lamb
filete	steak
gallina	hen
jamón	ham
lechón	suckling pig
lomo	steak
pato	duck
pollo	chicken
res	beef
ternera	val
tocino	bacon
venado	venison

Menudos (offal)

corazón	heart
chunchules	intestines
guatita	tripe
hígado	liver
lengua	tongue
patas	trotters

Mariscos (seafood) and pescado (fish)

almejas	clams
anchoa	anchovy
atún	tuna
bacalao	cod
calamares	squid
camarón	shrimp
cangrejo	crab
ceviche	raw seafood marinated in lime juice with onions
corvina	sea bass
erizo	sea urchin
gambas	prawns
langosta	lobster/crayfish

langostina	king prawn
lenguado	sole
mejillónes	mussels
ostra	oyster
pargo rojo	red snapper
pulpo	octopus
trucha	trout

Soups (sopas)

caldo	broth
caldo de gallina	chicken broth
crema de espárragos	cream of asparagus
sopa de caracol	spicy conch stew
sopa de frijoles	bean soup
sopa del día	soup of the day
tapado	a seafood soup, served on the Caribbean coast of several countries in the isthmus

Bocados (snacks)

bocadillo	sandwich
casado	meal of rice, beans, salad and meat or fish (phrase mainly seen in Costa Rica, translating to "married")
chuchito	corn-dough parcels made with beans and eggs (sometimes also pork), popular in Guatemala and El Salvador
empanada	cheese/meat pastry
hamburguesa	hamburger
nacatamales	corn-dough parcels filled with vegetables, pork, beef or chicken
patacones	fried green plantains
pupusa	small, thick tortilla filled with cheese, beans or pork and topped with salad
salchichas	sausages
tamale	ground maize with meat/cheese wrapped in leaf
tortilla	toasted maize pancake
tortilla de huevos	omelette
tostada	toast

Postres (desserts)

ensalada de frutas	fruit salad
flan	crème caramel
helado	ice cream
pastel	cake
piñonate	candied papaya
torta	tart
tres leches	cake made with three varieties of milk

Bebidas (drinks)

agua (mineral)	mineral water
… con gas	… sparkling
… sin gas	… still
… con/sin hielo	… with/without ice
… con limón	… with lemon
aguardiente	raw alcohol made from sugar cane
aromática	herbal tea
hierba luisa	lemon verbena
manzanilla	camomile
menta	mint
café	coffee
café con leche	milk with a little coffee
cerveza	beer
gaseosa	fizzy drink
horchata	milky, cereal-based drink sweetened with cinnamon
jugo	juice
leche	milk
licuado	fresh fruit milkshake
limonada	fresh lemonade
raspados	ice shavings with sweet topping
refresco	generic term for cold soft drinks
ron	rum
licor	spirits
té	tea
vino blanco	white wine
vino tinto	red wine

Cooking terms

a la parrilla	barbecued
a la plancha	grilled
ahumado	smoked
al ajillo	in garlic sauce
al horno	oven-baked
al vapor	steamed
apanado	breaded
asado	roast
asado al palo	spit roast
crudo	raw
duro	hard boiled
encebollado	cooked with onions
encocado	in coconut sauce
frito	fried
picante	spicy hot
puré	mashed
revuelto	scrambled
saltado	sautéed
secado	dried

USEFUL VOCABULARY

abastecedor a general store that keeps a stock of groceries and basic toiletries

aguacero downpour

ahorita right now (any time within the coming hour)

alcalde mayor

aldea village

algodón cotton

almohada pillow

antorcha torch

artesanía craft

ayuntamiento town hall/government

bahía bay

balneario resort or spa

barranca steep-sided ravine

barrio neighbourhood, or area within a town or city; suburb

biotopo protected area of national ecological importance, usually with limited tourist access

bomba pump at a gas station

cabaña literally a cabin, but can mean anything from a palm-thatched beach hut to a US-style motel room; usually applies to tourist accommodation

caballo horse

cabina cubicle/booth/cabin

cacique chief (originally a colonial term, now used for elected leaders/figureheads of indigenous *comarcas* in Panama)

cafeteria café

calzada road/carriageway

cama bed

camioneta small truck or van (in Guatemala, a chicken bus)

campesino peasant farmer, smallholder, cowboy

campo countryside

cantina local, hard-drinking bar, usually men-only

carro car, equivalent of the Castilian *coche*

casa de cambio currency exchange bureau

cascada waterfall

caseta telefónica phone booth

catedral cathedral

cepillo de dientes toothbrush

chabola shack

chapín slang term for someone from Guatemala

chicle sapodilla tree sap from which chewing gum is made (also means chewing gum)

chiquillos kids; also *chiquititos*

chorreador sack-and-metal coffee-filter contraption, still widely used

Churrigueresque highly elaborate, decorative form of Baroque architecture (usually found in churches)

cigarrillo cigarette

ciudad city

Clásico period during which ancient Maya civilization was at its height, usually given as 300–900 AD

colchón mattress

colectivo shared taxi/minibus, usually following fixed route (can also be applied to a boat – *lancho colectivo*)

colina hill (also *el cerro*)

colonia city suburb or neighbourhood, often seen in addresses as "Col"

comedor basic restaurant, usually with just one or two things on the menu, always the cheapest place to eat; literally "dining room"

conquistador "one who conquers": member of early Spanish expeditions to the Americas in the sixteenth century

convento convent or monastery

cordillera mountain range

correo aéreo air mail

corriente second-class bus (also *camioneta*)

cuadra street block

cuevas caves

descompuesto out of order

Dios God

discoteca club/disco

Don/Doña courtesy titles (sir/madam), mostly used in letters, for professional people or for a boss

dolor pain/ache

edificio building

efectivo cash

ejido communal farmland

encendedor lighter (for cigarettes)

encomienda package/parcel

entrada entry/entry fee

estatua statue

extranjero foreigner

fecha date

feria fair (market); also a town fête

fiesta party

finca ranch, farm or plantation

finquero coffee grower

fósforos matches

gambas buttresses; the giant above-ground roots that some rainforest trees put out

gasolina petrol

gasolinera gas station

golfo gulf

gringo/gringa any white-skinned foreigner, particularly a North American; not necessarily a term of abuse, it does nonetheless have a slightly pessimistic connotation

gruta cave

guaca pre-Columbian burial ground or tomb

hacienda big farm, ranch or estate, or big house on it

henequén fibre from the *agave* (sisal) plant, used to make rope

hospedaje very basic pensión or small hotel

huipil Maya woman's traditional dress or blouse, usually woven or embroidered

huracán hurricane

I.V.A. sales tax

indígena an indigenous person; preferred term among indigenous groups, rather than the more racially offensive *índio*

invierno winter (May–Oct)

isla island

jardín garden

jornaleros day labourers, usually landless peasants who are paid by the day, for instance to pick coffee in season

juego de pelota ball-game/ball-court

ladino a vague term – applied to people it means Spanish-influenced as opposed to indigenous, and at its most specific defines someone of mixed Spanish and indigenous blood; it's more commonly used simply to describe a person of "Western" culture, or one who dresses in "Western" style, be they of indigenous or mixed blood

lavabo sink

lista de correos general delivery

litera bunk bed

llave key

malecón seafront promenade

manzana street block, also called *cuadra*

mar sea

mestizo person of mixed indigenous and Spanish blood, though like the term *ladino* it has more cultural than racial significance

metate Pre-Columbian stone table used for grinding corn

milpa maize field, usually cleared by slash-and-burn farming

mirador look-out point

mochila backpack

mochilero backpacker

moneda coins

montar a caballo to go horse-riding

natural an indigenous person

neotrópicos "neotropics": tropics of the New World

noreste northeast; often seen in addresses as "NE"

noroeste northwest

nublado cloudy

occidente west

oriente east; often seen in addresses as "Ote"

otoño autumn

paisaje landscape

palacio mansion, but not necessarily royal

palacio de gobierno headquarters of state/federal authorities

palacio municipal headquarters of local government

palapa palm thatch (used to describe any thatched/palm-roofed hut)

panadería bakery

parque park

paseo a broad avenue; also a walk, especially the traditional evening walk around the plaza

pasta de dientes toothpaste

pelota ball, or ball-court

pensión simple hotel

peón farm labourer, usually landless

personaje someone of importance, a VIP, although usually used pejoratively to indicate someone who is putting on airs

piscina swimming pool

planta baja ground floor – abbreviated PB in elevators

plaza square

Plateresque elaborately decorative Renaissance architectural style.

poniente west; often seen in addresses as "Pte"

Postclásico period between the decline of Maya civilization and the arrival of the Spanish, 900–1530 AD

Preclásico archeological era preceding the blooming of Maya civilization, usually given as 1500 BC–300 AD

primavera spring

propina tip

pueblo town/village

puente bridge

puerta door

Pullman fast and comfortable bus, usually an old Greyhound

pulpería general store or corner store; also sometimes serves cooked food and drinks

quetzal quetzal (bird), and also the currency of Guatemala

recibo receipt

rancho palm-thatched roof; can also mean a smallholding

redondel de toros bullring, used for local rodeos

río river

ruinas ruins

sábana sheet

sabanero cowboy

sacbé Maya road, or ceremonial causeway

saco de dormir sleeping bag

santo saint

seda silk

sendero path

sierra mountain range

soda Costa Rican cafeteria or diner; in the rest of Central America it's usually called a comedor

sol sun

stela freestanding carved monument; most are of Maya origin

sincretismo syncretism, the attempted amalgamation of different religions, cultures or schools of thought; mainly applied to religion and in Central America usually refers to the merging of Maya and Catholic beliefs

sótano basement

sudeste southeast (also sureste)

sudoeste southwest (also suroeste)

temporada season: *la temporada de lluvia* is the rainy season

terremoto earthquake

terreno land; small farm

tiempo weather (can also mean time)

tienda shop

tierra land/earth

típico/típica literally "typical"; used to describe food or, in Guatemala, the multi-coloured textiles geared to Western customers

traje traditional costume (also means suit)

vela candle/sail (of a boat)

ventana window

verano summer (Dec–April)

vista view

volcán volcano

Travel
store

NOTES

Small print and

Index

A Rough Guide to Rough Guides

Published in 1982, the first Rough Guide – to Greece – was a student scheme that became a publishing phenomenon. Mark Ellingham, a recent graduate in English from Bristol University, had been travelling in Greece the previous summer and couldn't find the right guidebook. With a small group of friends he wrote his own guide, combining a highly contemporary, journalistic style with a thoroughly practical approach to travellers' needs.

The immediate success of the book spawned a series that rapidly covered dozens of destinations. And, in addition to impecunious backpackers, Rough Guides soon acquired a much broader and older readership that relished the guides' wit and inquisitiveness as much as their enthusiastic, critical approach and value-for-money ethos.

These days, Rough Guides include recommendations from shoestring to luxury and cover more than 200 destinations around the globe, including almost every country in the Americas and Europe, more than half of Africa and most of Asia and Australasia. Our ever-growing team of authors and photographers is spread all over the world, particularly in Europe, the USA and Australia.

In the early 1990s, Rough Guides branched out of travel, with the publication of Rough Guides to World Music, Classical Music and the Internet. All three have become benchmark titles in their fields, spearheading the publication of a wide range of books under the Rough Guide name.

Including the travel series, Rough Guides now number more than 350 titles, covering phrasebooks, waterproof maps, music guides from Opera to Heavy Metal, reference works as diverse as Conspiracy Theories and Shakespeare, and popular culture books from iPods to Poker. Rough Guides also produce a series of more than 120 World Music CDs in partnership with World Music Network.

Visit www.roughguides.com to see our latest publications.

Rough Guide travel images are available for commercial licensing at www.roughguidespictures.com

Rough Guide credits

Text editor: Ella Steim, Mani Ramaswamy
Layout: Dan May, Pradeep Thapliyal
Cartography: Katie Lloyd-Jones
Picture editor: Sarah Cummins
Production: Rebecca Short
Proofreader: Stuart Wild
Cover design: Chloë Roberts
Editorial: **London** Ruth Blackmore, Andy Turner, Keith Drew, Edward Aves, Alice Park, Lucy White, Jo Kirby, James Smart, Natasha Foges, Róisín Cameron, Emma Traynor, James Rice, Emma Gibbs, Kathryn Lane, Christina Valhouli, Monica Woods, Alison Roberts, Joe Staines, Peter Buckley, Matthew Milton, Tracy Hopkins, Ruth Tidball; **New York** Andrew Rosenberg, Steven Horak, AnneLise Sorensen, Anna Owens, Sean Mahoney, Paula Neudorf; **Delhi** Madhavi Singh, Karen D'Souza, Lubna Shaheen
Design & Pictures: **London** Scott Stickland, Diana Jarvis, Mark Thomas, Chloë Roberts, Nicole Newman, Emily Taylor; **Delhi** Umesh Aggarwal, Ajay Verma, Jessica Subramanian, Ankur Guha, Sachin Tanwar, Anita Singh, Nikhil Agarwal
Production: Vicky Baldwin

Cartography: **London** Maxine Repath, Ed Wright; **Delhi** Rajesh Chhibber, Ashutosh Bharti, Rajesh Mishra, Animesh Pathak, Jasbir Sandhu, Karobi Gogoi, Alakananda Bhattacharya, Swati Handoo, Deshpal Dabas
Online: **London** George Atwell, Faye Hellon, Jeanette Angell, Fergus Day, Justine Bright, Clare Bryson, Áine Fearon, Adrian Low, Ezgi Celebi, Amber Bloomfield; **Delhi** Amit Verma, Rahul Kumar, Narender Kumar, Ravi Yadav, Debojit Borah, Rakesh Kumar, Ganesh Sharma, Shisir Basumatari
Marketing & Publicity: **London** Liz Statham, Niki Hanmer, Louise Maher, Jess Carter, Vanessa Godden, Vivienne Watton, Anna Paynton, Rachel Sprackett, Libby Jellie, Holly Dudley; **New York** Geoff Colquitt, Nancy Lambert, Katy Ball; **Delhi** Ragini Govind
Manager India: Punita Singh
Reference Director: Andrew Lockett
Operations Manager: Helen Phillips
PA to Publishing Director: Nicola Henderson
Publishing Director: Martin Dunford
Commercial Manager: Gino Magnotta
Managing Director: John Duhigg

Publishing information

This first edition published February 2009 by
Rough Guides Ltd,
80 Strand, London WC2R 0RL
345 Hudson St, 4th Floor,
New York, NY 10014, USA
14 Local Shopping Centre, Panchsheel Park,
New Delhi 110017, India
Distributed by the Penguin Group
Penguin Books Ltd,
80 Strand, London WC2R 0RL
Penguin Group (USA)
375 Hudson Street, NY 10014, USA
Penguin Group (Australia)
250 Camberwell Road, Camberwell,
Victoria 3124, Australia
Penguin Group (Canada)
195 Harry Walker Parkway N, Newmarket, ON,
L3Y 7B3 Canada
Penguin Group (NZ)
67 Apollo Drive, Mairangi Bay, Auckland 1310,
New Zealand
Cover concept by Peter Dyer.

Typeset in Bembo and Helvetica to an original design by Henry Iles.

Printed and bound in China.

© Rough Guides

No part of this book may be reproduced in any form without permission from the publisher except for the quotation of brief passages in reviews.

704pp includes index

A catalogue record for this book is available from the British Library.

ISBN: 978-1-85828-804-8

The publishers and authors have done their best to ensure the accuracy and currency of all the information in **The Rough Guide to Central America on a Budget**, however, they can accept no responsibility for any loss, injury, or inconvenience sustained by any traveller as a result of information or advice contained in the guide.

1 3 5 7 9 8 6 4 2

Help us update

We've gone to a lot of effort to ensure that the first edition of **The Rough Guide to Central America on a Budget** is accurate and up to date. However, things change – places get "discovered", opening hours are notoriously fickle, restaurants and rooms raise prices or lower standards. If you feel we've got it wrong or left something out, we'd like to know, and if you can remember the address, the price, the hours, the phone number, so much the better.

Please send your comments with the subject line "**Rough Guide to Central America on a Budget Update**" to ©mail@roughguides.com. We'll credit all contributions and send a copy of the next edition (or any other Rough Guide if you prefer) for the very best emails.

Have your questions answered and tell others about your trip at
Ⓦcommunity.roughguides.com

Acknowledgements

Thanks to all the writers who updated this edition: Jamey Bergman (Panama & introduction), Flo Chick (Basics & Guatemala), Sarah Cummins (Honduras), Kiki Deere (Guatemala & Language), Amber Dobrzensky (Costa Rica & Nicaragua), Donald Eastwood (El Salvador), Ingrid Gustafson (Belize), Neil McQuillan (Panama),

Charlotte Melville (Costa Rica) and Alex Trillo (Nicaragua & Honduras).

Thanks also to Joseph Petta for editing the Panama chapter, Greg Ward for a fine index, Diana Jarvis, Katie Lloyd-Jones, Dan May, Mani Ramaswamy, Andrew Rosenberg and Ella Steim.

Photo credits

All photos © Rough Guides except the following:

Introduction

Horseback riding in the Arenal region of Costa Rica © Nik Wheeler/Danita Delimont/Drr.net

Musician by a mural in Juayúa, El Salvador © Donald Eastwood

Festivals and events

Todos Santos Cuchumatán, Guatemala © Jorge Uzon/Corbis

Carnaval, Panama City © Alberto Lowe/Reuters/Corbis

Garífuna Settlement Day, Dangriga, Belize © Danita Delimont/Alamy

Day of the Dead, Santiago Sacatepéquez, Guatemala © J Marshall-Tribaleye Images/Alamy

Semana Santa, Antigua, Guatemala © Michel Friang/Alamy

History and culture

Kuna woman smoking a pipe, San Blas Archipelago, Panama © James Brunker/magicalandes.com

War Memorial in El Mozote, El Salvador © Donald Eastwood

Cathedral of León, Nicaragua © G Richardson/Drr.net

Outdoor activities

Tourists rafting the Chiriquí River, Panama © TS Corrigan/Alamy

Hiking in the Selva Negra, Nicaragua © Nik Wheeler/Corbis

Diving in Roatán, Honduras © WaterFrame/Alamy

Surfing at Punta Mango, El Salvador © Roberto Escobar/epa/Corbis

Index

Map entries are in colour

G

H

I

J

K

L

NOTES

Map symbols

maps are listed in the full index using coloured text

International boundary	Border crossing
Chapter division boundary	Place of interest
Carretera Interamericana	Gardens
Major road	Statue
Minor road	Transport stop
Unpaved road	Internet access
Pedestrianised street	Information centre
Steps	Post office
Path	Phone office
Railway	Hospital
Ferry route	Fuel station
River	Toilets
Mountain range	Accommodation
Mountain peak	Restaurant
Volcano	Sports field
Waterfall	Stadium
Cave	Building
Viewpoint	Church
Ruin	Market
Lighthouse	Park
Airport	Marshland/swamp
Airstrip	Beach
Monument	Cemetery